www.wadsworth.com

www.wadsworth.com is the World Wide Web site for Wadsworth and is your direct source to dozens of online resources.

At *www.wadsworth.com* you can find out about supplements, demonstration software, and student resources. You can also send email to many of our authors and preview new publications and exciting new technologies.

www.wadsworth.com
Changing the way the world learns®

VOICES OF WISDOM
A Multicultural Philosophy Reader
Fifth Edition

Gary E. Kessler
California State University, Bakersfield

THOMSON

WADSWORTH

Australia • Canada • Mexico • Singapore • Spain • United Kingdom • United States

THOMSON
WADSWORTH

Publisher: Holly J. Allen
Philosophy Editor: Steve Wainwright
Assistant Editors: Lee McCracken, Anna Lustig
Editorial Assistant: Melanie Cheng
Marketing Manager: Worth Hawes
Marketing Assistant: Kristi Bostock
Advertising Project Manager: Bryan Vann
Print/Media Buyer: Rebecca Cross
Permissions Editor: Sarah Harkrader
Production Service: Ruth Cottrell

Text Designers: John Edeen/Lisa Delgado
Copy Editor: Ruth Cottrell
Cover Designer: Laurie Anderson
Cover Image: Wearing Blanket, c. 1870; Navajo. Gift of the Descendants of Helen Weeks Winchester and Captain Harrison Samuel Weeks. Photograph © 1988 The Detroit Institute of the Arts
Compositor: G&S Typesetters, Inc.
Cover and Text Printer: Maple-Vail

For more information about
our products, contact us at:
Thomson Learning Academic Resource Center
1-800-423-0563
For permission to use material from
this text, contact us by:
Phone: 1-800-730-2214
Fax: 1-800-730-2215
Web: http://www.thomsonrights.com

Library of Congress Control Number: 2003104974
ISBN 0-534-60570-2

Wadsworth/Thomson Learning
10 Davis Drive
Belmont, CA 94002-3098
USA

Asia
Thomson Learning
5 Shenton Way #01-01
UIC Building
Singapore 068808

Australia/New Zealand
Thomson Learning
102 Dodds Street
Southbank, Victoria 3006
Australia

Canada
Nelson
1120 Birchmount Road
Toronto, Ontario M1K 5G4
Canada

Europe/Middle East/Africa
Thomson Learning
High Holborn House
50/51 Bedford Row
London WC1R 4LR
United Kingdom

Latin America
Thomson Learning
Seneca, 53
Colonia Polanco
11560 Mexico D.F.
Mexico

Spain/Portugal
Paraninfo
Calle/Magallanes, 25
28015 Madrid, Spain

To Peacemakers

Contents

Preface

Since the publication of the first edition of *Voices of Wisdom*, I am gratified to note that more introductory textbooks now incorporate a multicultural perspective—a perspective that was unique to this introductory reader when it was first published in 1992. At that time the introductory readers that were available treated philosophy as if it were entirely an Anglo-European male phenomenon. Little or no attention was given to Hindu, Buddhist, Chinese, African, Native American, Latin American, and feminist philosophy. *Voices of Wisdom* helped to change that situation, offering to those who wished it the possibility of assigning significant readings that represent the global nature of philosophizing. This fifth edition continues to offer a multicultural perspective and has benefited from the teaching and learning experiences of the many instructors and students who used the previous editions. Readers have learned that ideas from other cultures are worth careful consideration and that these ideas make important contributions to human understanding.

Philosophy in a Multicultural Perspective

Although I wish to stress the universal nature of philosophizing, I am well aware of the dangers of anachronism. A text of this sort faces not only the problems associated with anachronism in the historical sense but also what we might term "cultural" anachronism. The writings of ancient philosophers mingle with modern texts, and thinkers from different cultures are brought together. The student may get the impression that Plato, Buddha, Nietzsche, Confucius, Descartes, and Aristotle are all contemporaries discussing the same issues with the same concepts in English! There are similarities. But there are also vast differences. Where appropriate, the important similarities and differences are stressed in my introductory remarks.

My selection of issues betrays my own Anglo-European perspective. Whereas many of the topics are fundamental and universal (How should one live? Is knowledge possible? What is really real?), their importance and centrality differ from tradition to tradition. The mind–body problem, the puzzle of freedom and determinism, the problem of moral skepticism—these problems are not necessarily the central ones that gripped the minds of Chinese or Indian philosophers. Just as Anglo-European philosophers have not had much to say about Karma, Buddhist thinkers have not been overly concerned with proving the existence of God.

However, I do believe this Western way of organizing the material is justified in this instance. Even though the significance of the problems and the way they are formulated differ from culture to culture, many of the underlying issues are the same. One cannot reflect for long on Karma and reincarnation without addressing issues relating to freedom and human identity. Furthermore, I think it best, for introductory and practical purposes, to organize the material around traditional Anglo-European philosophical themes. Many students already have some concern with these issues (for example, the existence of God). In addition, most introductory courses deal with these themes, and this book allows instructors to continue that practice, but some new and different voices are emphasized thereby enriching philosophical thinking.

It should be noted that there exists no culturally neutral set of categories for organizing the material. If I had used the dominant concerns of, let us say, the Indian tradition (concerns such as release from suffering, duty and the stages of life, and the nature of bondage) to organize the selections, I would not have thereby escaped a cultural perspective. Perhaps, as a multicultural approach becomes more commonplace in introductory courses and as Western philosophy becomes more open and diverse, new categories will emerge. However, until that day, the sources need to be organized in some fashion. What is important is that we are aware of the limitations of our categories and that we continually remind ourselves of the diverse and subtle ways that long-held biases influence the way we select and organize materials.

Historical and cultural comparisons are inevitable, and I encourage them. However, I wish to stress that this reader is not meant to be primarily an exercise in comparative philosophy. It is meant to serve a course that introduces students to *doing* philosophy by drawing on *multicultural* resources. The students who read this text should be impressed with the rich diversity that comprises global philosophizing and should learn the art of philosophizing in a broader and more inclusive context than is usual.

I do wish to stress that it is *global* philosophizing with which I am concerned. Some associate the word "multicultural" almost exclusively with "multiethnic" and "minorities." Those who do so may expect more African American, Latin American, Native American, and feminist philosophers than I have included. These voices also need to be heard, and I have included many. However, my primary concern has been to provide sources that promote an *international* perspective. I believe it is important to educate students for the current century in which an understanding of the interconnectedness of all peoples will be increasingly important in determining the policies and practices of nations.

Topics

Voices of Wisdom includes much philosophical material that has come to be regarded as classic in the West. This material is included for two reasons. First, most students take an introductory philosophy course in conjunction with general education and, as part of that experience, it is important for them to read philosophical writings that are significant to the Western cultural tradition. Second, this writing is good philosophy (that is why it has become classic), and students should experience the ideas of profound philosophical minds. However, profound philosophical minds exist all over the world and, whereas other styles of thinking and other traditions may be very different, they are no less important.

Although the topics in this new edition remain largely unchanged, there are twenty-one new or revised selections. The revisions not only reflect recent events but also add different perspectives and fresh material.

Part I deals with introductory matters. In Chapter 1, I discuss the nature of philosophy, the meaning of rationality, and the value of studying philosophy, and I offer some practical advice on how to read philosophical texts. A new selection, written for this volume by Professor Joseph Prabhu, illustrates the value of studying philosophy from a multicultural viewpoint. Chapter 2 from the previous edition has been eliminated, but some of the material has been incorporated in Section 1.5.

Part II, "Ethics," begins by exploring the questions "How Should One Live?" (Chapter 2) and "How Can I Know What Is Right?" (Chapter 3). These are significant questions that have received much global attention in one form or another. Further, these are questions with which students can connect personally, and therefore I have found it useful to place them early in the text. Chapter 2 incorporates the material from Chapter 3 of the Fourth Edition. Chapter 3 includes most of the material from Chapter 4 of the Fourth Edition, but there are two new selections (Section 3.5, "Care versus Rights," and Section 3.6, "Moral Relativism").

I have included two chapters on political and social philosophy in Part II, "Ethics," because both deal with issues relating to justice. Chapter 4, "What Makes a Society Just?", contains material formerly found in Chapter 5. Chapter 6, "Is Justice for All Possible?", incorporates some of the material formerly found in Chapter 6 but adds three significant new selections. Section 5.4 deals with the issues surrounding globalization and justice, and Section 5.5 discusses terrorism. Dealing with these issues makes the text more responsive to current events of great moment. Section 5.6, "Justice and the Land," is also new and another issue of great importance as the earth becomes steadily more polluted at the hands of an ever-growing human population.

Part III, "Epistemology," introduces students to the topics "Is Knowledge Possible?" (Chapter 6) and "Does Science Tell Us the Whole Truth and Nothing but the Truth?" (Chapter 7). Both of these chapters incorporate much of the material formerly found in Chapters 7 and 8. There is a new selection in Chapter 7 from the writings of Karl Popper (Section 7.2).

Part IV, "Metaphysics," is divided into five chapters: Chapter 8, "What Is Really Real?"; Chapter 9, "Are We Free or Determined?"; Chapter 10, "What Am I?"; Chapter 11, "Who Am I?"; and Chapter 12, "Is There a God?" Chapter 8 is a virtually unchanged version of what was Chapter 9 in the previous volume. One new selection by Laura Ekstrom (Section 9.2) appears in Chapter 9. Chapter 11 of the Fourth Edition has been divided into two chapters, one of which (Chapter 10) focuses on issues relating to the mind–body problem along with problems involved in understanding the nature of the mind. A revised version of the selection from Descartes' Meditation VI along with two new essays (Sections 10.4 by Bruce Hinrichs and 10.5 by John Searle) constitute the changes in Chapter 10. Chapter 11 is a new chapter that focuses on problems of personal identity. There are three new essays: Section 11.3, "Divided Minds and the Nature of Persons" by Derek Parfit; Section 11.4, "Brainstorms" by Daniel Dennett; and Section 11.6, "Crossing" by Deirdre McCloskey. Chapter 12 has been extensively revised with the addition of new material on "Arguments for God's Existence" (Section 12.2), "Hinduism and Science," (Section 12.3), "The Mystery of Evil," (Section 12.5), and "Are All Religions True?" (Section 12.7). These revisions reflect a broader range of issues characteristic of the philosophy of religion than the previous focus on God's existence and nature.

In order to include all this new material, I have had to leave out some selections from the last edition. To compensate for this loss, I have created a companion Web site for *Voices of Wisdom* at http://philosophy.wadsworth.com that contains links to much additional material. I have also moved my suggestions for further readings and videos to the Web site, thereby creating more space in the text for additional material.

In making these revisions I have tried to be responsive to reviewer's suggestions, thereby, I trust, making *Voices of Wisdom* more useful for introductory courses.

Pedagogical Features

I agree with John Dewey's notion that we learn by doing. In my experience, the more I can get my students to do for themselves, the more they learn. Thus, rather than providing summaries of the selections—a practice that can discourage careful reading by students—I provide the background information they need to understand the selections, and I supply questions that are designed to guide the students' reading *prior* to the selections. This approach encourages students to read the selections for themselves and to formulate their own questions about the material. It also gives instructors an opportunity to require students to answer the questions in a philosophical journal before class meetings. The questions and the students' responses can then be used as the basis for class discussion. Students are thereby encouraged to become actively engaged in the process of figuring out what a text means.

In most chapters the material is arranged chronologically. Sometimes, however, another sort of arrangement is more pedagogically useful, and so I have not restricted myself to the chronological pattern in all cases.

I have put technical terms in bold type on their first occurrence and provided brief definitions. A glossary (Appendix I) provides a convenient reference for those terms and their definitions.

Appendix II provides a brief pronunciation guide to Chinese, Sanskrit, and Arabic words. Foreign words can be daunting to readers and this pronunciation guide should alleviate some of the unease they may feel.

The companion Web site for this text is an important pedagogical feature. The Internet contains much information about philosophical topics as well as classic philosophical texts from around the world. Searching the Web is second nature to most students, and directing them to this companion site will help them understand more of the material and lead them further on their journey into the exciting realm of philosophical thought. The supplemental material found on the Web site will aid student comprehension and give added flexibility to instructors as they construct their courses.

I have written the introductory material in an informal, engaging, and, I trust, clear manner. I hope to engage students in the thinking process by connecting the selections to questions and issues students have already begun to encounter. The selections themselves have been classroom-tested and represent different degrees of difficulty. Most will challenge beginning students to think in more depth and in a more precise way.

Acknowledgments

A book like this is written, edited, and revised by many people. Steve Wainwright, the philosophy editor at Wadsworth, made valuable suggestions. The staff at Wadsworth has been most accommodating and patient. Lee McCracken has provided valuable help and advice. Ruth Cottrell deserves special thanks for bringing clarity out of the messy prose academics sometimes write. Responsibility for whatever errors and infelicities remain rests on my doorstep.

Student response has been helpful. I have tried to keep students foremost in my mind as this fifth edition evolved. What will work in the classroom and what will stimulate students to engage philosophical issues is of fundamental importance. A special thanks goes to all those students who have shared their concerns, ideas, and suggestions.

The reviewers of my fifth edition were particularly helpful. I wish it were possible to follow all of their valuable suggestions. I would like to thank the following reviewers for their ideas and comments: Anne Benvenuti, Cerro Coso College; William Ferraiolo, San Joaquin Delta Community College; Elizabeth Hodge, Gavilan College; Robert Hood, Middle Tennessee State University; Joseph Prabhu, California State University, Los Angeles; M. Susan Rouse, Kennesaw State University; Steve Thomassin, Ventura College; and Lawrence Ulrich, University of Dayton.

A very special thanks goes to my wife Katy, whose ideas, insights, and loving support made this book possible. I also wish to thank all of you who used previous editions. Your responses have been gratifying and reinforce my hope that one day a multicultural approach to the study, teaching, and doing of philosophy will be commonplace. I would appreciate hearing your responses to this new edition—about how it works and how it can be improved.

Gary E. Kessler
California State University, Bakersfield
e-mail: gkessler@csub.edu

Introduction

Chapter 1

What Is Philosophy?

> . . . those who are eager to learn because they wonder at things are lovers of wisdom (*philosophoi*).
>
> ALEXANDER OF APHRODISIAS

1.1 A Definition of Philosophy

HAVE YOU EVER WONDERED about the purpose of life? Have you ever been curious about what you can reasonably believe? Have you ever marveled at the beauty of nature or been upset by suffering? Have you ever thought that life is unfair? Have you ever been puzzled about what you ought to do?

Perhaps you associate these kinds of questions with philosophy. If you do, why do you? What do you think is philosophical about these questions? When you hear the word *philosophy,* what do you think it means? Think about it awhile and write your answer.

The Greek philosopher Aristotle (384–322 BCE), who asserted that philosophy begins in wonder, was impressed by the ability of human beings to think. In fact, he defined humans as "rational animals." Aristotle maintained that philosophy arises from the human ability to reflect on experience, to wonder and be curious about what happens to us and to others.

Of course, wonder is not the sole cause of philosophizing. Sufficient leisure must be available to engage in reflection, and hence economic and cultural factors play an important role in promoting and influencing human curiosity. However, without the human capacity to wonder and be curious, it is doubtful that philosophical thinking would occur.

I hope this book will stimulate your natural ability to wonder, teach you something of the art of wondering, and help you learn how to live in wonder. Cultivating the art of wondering is important, Aristotle believed, because such an art leads us along the path toward wisdom.

The word *philosophy* comes from a combination of two Greek words—*philos,* meaning "loving" and *sophia,* meaning "wisdom." Etymologically, philosophy means the love of wisdom. To love something is to desire it. So, for many Greeks, the philosopher was the one who desired wisdom. The word *philos* also refers, for the Greeks, to the special kind of love found in close friendship. Hence the philosopher could also be characterized as the "friend of wisdom."

The historical origin of a word, however, often does not help us very much when we are searching for an adequate definition today. The meanings of words change. Also, meanings derived etymologically are sometimes unclear. If the philosopher is the lover or friend of wisdom, then what is wisdom? About that, philosophers—even Greek philosophers—disagree.

Philosophy in Western culture was born in the sixth century BCE among a group of thinkers called the Pre-Socratics. According to tradition, one of these thinkers, Pythagoras (about 570 BCE), coined the word *philosophy*. Along with other Pre-Socratics, he was intensely interested in nature, in knowing how the universe or cosmic order developed, and in figuring out what things were made of. These thinkers disagreed about the stuff out of which things are made (some said earth, some air, others fire, still others water or some combination of these elements), but many of them did think that wisdom consisted of knowledge about nature. To love wisdom, as far as they were concerned, was to search for knowledge about the universe.

A century later, another group of thinkers in Athens offered their services as teachers to those who could afford them. They claimed to teach virtue. The Greek word for virtue (*areté*) means "excellence or power." So to possess virtue is to possess power. Wisdom, they taught, is the possession of virtue. It is to have certain powers or abilities, especially in the social and political realm, to influence people and be successful. Since these teachers claimed to possess this wisdom, they came to be called "Sophists" or "The Wise Ones." For them, philosophy is not a search for knowledge about the universe, nor a *search* for wisdom. Rather, philosophy is the *possession* of wisdom and hence the possession of virtue or excellence, especially in the social and political dimensions of life.

Socrates (470–399 BCE) lived in Athens at the same time as the Sophists. He spent his days wandering around the marketplace, asking people questions about all kinds of things. He found himself perplexed by things other people claimed to know. For example, people claimed to know what knowledge, justice, virtue, and the right way to live are. The Sophists claimed to teach these things. However, under Socrates' relentless critical questioning, the definitions and grand theories that people held about these sorts of things collapsed.

The oracle at Delphi, a well-respected source of divine truth in the ancient world, said that Socrates was the wisest man in Athens. When word of this got to Socrates, he was greatly puzzled. How could he, who knew next to nothing and spent his days asking others, be the wisest? What about the Sophists, the teachers of wisdom? Were not they the wisest? Socrates did believe he knew what virtue is; it is knowledge. But what is knowledge? He had to confess he did not know, so how could he be wise? And yet, he reasoned, the oracle of Delphi could not be lying. It was, after all, the voice of the god Apollo. But the oracle was tricky. You had to figure out what it meant.

Finally, Socrates understood. Wisdom, the oracle was telling him, is knowing that he did not know! Wisdom is the awareness of our ignorance, an awareness of the limitations of knowledge. Let the Sophists claim to be wise; the best Socrates could do was to claim he was a lover of wisdom. He lived his life in the pursuit of wisdom as lovers live their lives in pursuit of the beloved. For him, philosophy was a critical examination of our pretensions to knowledge and the constant search for that final truth that always seems to be just beyond our grasp.

The Greeks were not the only ones to philosophize, for the pursuit of wisdom is common to all cultures. The Greeks were also not the only ones to disagree about the nature of wisdom. For example, in India some philosophers claimed that wisdom is coming to know one's true self as immortal. Yajnavalkya,* a wise man described in early Indian literature called the *Upanishads,* tells his wife Maitreyi that wealth will not gain one immortality; only the true self or *atman,* as he called it, is immortal. However, other Indian philosophers disagreed. Wisdom, they said, did not consist in the knowledge of a true immortal self or *atman.* Quite the opposite is the case. Genuine wisdom consists in knowing that there is no such thing as an eternal self or *atman.*

Clearly there are different understandings of what wisdom is and hence there are different understandings of what philosophy is about. No single definition can possibly capture all the nuances of the art of wondering in every place and time in which it appears. This does not mean, however, that we can define philosophy any way we wish, and it does not mean that some definitions are not better than others. Let me offer my definition, which, I think, states something important about philosophizing and helps us distinguish it from other types of thinking: **Philosophy** *is the rational attempt to formulate, understand, and answer fundamental questions.*

Many people think that philosophy is a body of doctrines and that philosophers are people who have answers to difficult questions about the meaning of life. My definition stresses that (1) philosophy is an activity rather than a body of set teachings and (2) philosophers are as concerned with formulating and understanding questions as they are with finding answers.

Formulating questions is very important. What we ask and how we ask it determine, in large part, where we look for answers and the kinds of answers we get. Progress in many fields consists, in part, of an ever-greater refinement of our questions and more precision and sophistication in our methods of interrogation. You will not get good answers if you do not ask the right questions.

For example, the title of this chapter is "What Is Philosophy?" and at the beginning of the chapter I asked you to think about the meaning of the word *philosophy* and to write your answer. Review your answer. Now think about the question, "What is it to philosophize?" If I had formulated the question about your understanding of philosophy as a question about what it is to philosophize and asked you to answer it, would your answer have been any different? If so, how would it have been different?

Understanding what we are after when we ask questions is as important as formulating questions. Words are often ambiguous and vague; we must be as clear as possible about what they mean. If I ask, "What is the meaning of life?" what do I mean? What am I looking for? Is this the best way to put it? What might count as a helpful answer? Where should I look for an answer? Am I asking about the purpose of life? Is life the sort of thing that has a purpose? Or am I interested in what makes life worthwhile? Is the purpose of life (if there is one) the same as what makes life valuable or worthwhile?

The purpose of formulating and understanding questions as precisely as we can is to find answers, but often our answers lead to further questions. Why assume some answer is final? Or why assume all questions we can ask have answers? Also, what counts as an answer? How do I know when I have a good one? Consider this conversation:

---

* For a pronunciation guide for Sanskrit, Chinese, and Arabic words see Appendix II. To facilitate reading, I have left out diacritical marks that indicate sounds in other languages that are not normally part of English.

Yolanda: What is the meaning of life?
José: What do you mean by that question?
Yolanda: I mean, what is the purpose of life?
José: Oh, that's easy, its purpose is survival and reproduction. That's what my biology textbook says.

Is José's answer a good one? Is it the sort of answer Yolanda is after? Can this question be answered with factual information, or is it about values? When Yolanda asks, "What is the meaning of life?" is she asking, "What makes life ultimately valuable?" And if she is asking that, then the answer José gives may well miss the mark (unless, of course, Yolanda thinks survival and reproduction are more valuable than anything else).

I said in my definition that philosophers are concerned with *fundamental* questions. The word *fundamental* means "basic" and has to do with what is primary. Fundamental questions are *radical* questions in the sense of pertaining to roots. They are the most basic questions we can ask. Therefore, they are often *abstract* questions that have to do with a wide area of human experience.

However, even though the sorts of questions that concern philosophers are abstract, they are about concepts we employ every day. We are constantly making judgments about good and bad, right and wrong, true and false, reality and fiction, beautiful and ugly, just and unjust. But what is good? By what norms can we distinguish right behavior from wrong? What is truth? How can I distinguish appearance from reality? Is beauty only in the eye of the beholder? What is justice, and is it ever possible to achieve it?

Some of the main branches of Western philosophy are distinguished by the kinds of fundamental questions they ask. Many philosophers have regarded "What is truly real?" as a fundamental question. Note the word *truly.* I did not ask, "What is real?" but "What is *truly* real?" In other words, I am assuming that not everything that appears to be real is real. Or, to put that another way, by asking, "What is truly real?" I am asking how we might distinguish appearance from reality. The branch of philosophy called **metaphysics** deals with this and related issues. One of its purposes, some philosophers have claimed, is to develop a theory of reality or a theory of what is genuinely real. It is also concerned with what might be the most fundamental question we can think of: "Why is there something rather than nothing?"

What is knowledge and what is truth? These seem to be good candidates for fundamental questions because the concepts of knowledge and truth are basic to so much of our thinking, including all that we call science. The branch of Western philosophy known as **epistemology** concerns itself with the issues of knowledge and truth. Epistemologists search for a theory of what knowledge is and how it might be distinguished from opinion. They look for a definition of truth and wonder how we might correctly distinguish truth from error.

Axiology, the third main branch of Western philosophy, has to do with the study of value and the distinction between value and fact. Traditionally, it is divided into two main subdivisions: aesthetics and ethics. **Aesthetics** deals with such questions as: Is beauty a matter of taste, or is it something objective? What standards should be used to judge artistic work? Can we define art? **Ethics** attempts to decide what values and principles we should use to judge human action as morally right or wrong. What is the greatest good? How should one live? Applied ethics applies these values and principles to such social concerns as human rights, racial justice, affirmative action, environmental ethics, and business ethics in order to determine what would be the morally right thing to do.

Fundamental questions are not only basic and abstract; they are also *universal* questions. They are the sorts of questions any thinking person might ask anywhere and at any time. They arise out of our capacity to wonder about ourselves and the world in which we live. They arise naturally, as it were, as we search for wisdom.

Although fundamental questions are universal, or nearly so, it should be noted that the way I have described the organization of the field of philosophy (metaphysics, epistemology, axiology) is decidedly Western. Different societies organize knowledge in different ways. Also, what may seem fundamental in one society may seem far less important in another. For example, some Buddhist philosophers have been suspicious of intellectual speculation about metaphysical matters, especially questions like "Does God exist?" This question, so important to many people, excites little interest among these Buddhist thinkers.

It should also be noted that each of the three main branches of Western philosophy deals with important distinctions that all of us learn to make based on the standards our society teaches us. Hence, metaphysics is concerned with the distinction between *appearance and reality,* epistemology with the distinction between *knowledge and opinion,* and axiology with the distinction between *fact and value.* One important question is whether we can discover criteria that are universal and not merely relative to our own particular time in history and our own particular cultural view for making these distinctions. Fundamental and abstract questions about reality, knowledge, and value—and the distinctions these questions imply—may be universal in the sense that most cultures have developed intellectual traditions concerned with these issues. However, the concrete way the questions are asked, understood, and answered varies a great deal from one tradition to another.

For example, Plato (428–348 BCE) made the distinction between knowledge and opinion, at least in part, by claiming that *opinion* has to do with beliefs about the world, which are based on our sensations, but *knowledge* has to do with the reality we discover through our reason. For him, logic and mathematics constituted examples of knowledge, but information about physical objects based on sensation did not. Under the influence of physical science, many people today would be inclined to say almost the opposite of what Plato said. For instance, many of my students have maintained that knowledge is what empirical science provides, and opinion is a product of abstract speculation like philosophy.

As twenty-first century students living in a highly technological and pluralistic society, we live in a very different world from the ancient Greeks or Indians. Yet we, like them, wonder about life and ask basic questions about what is real, what is true, what is good, and what is beautiful. This is not to say that there are not vast differences among philosophies. There are. You are about to experience something of this variety firsthand as you read different philosophers from different cultures and different eras.

In sum, I think philosophy is the activity of rationally attempting to formulate, understand, and answer fundamental questions. I have discussed most of the parts of that definition except the word *rational.* Why must it be a rational attempt? And what is it to be rational, anyway? If we cannot agree on what rationality is, how can we know what constitutes a rational attempt to formulate and answer basic questions?

1.2 What Is Rationality?

This fundamental question is one of the most hotly debated issues in philosophy to-day. I cannot hope to settle the puzzles about rationality here, but I can give you some idea about what the issues are, describe some of the different views, and offer a few thoughts of my own.

William James (1842–1910), an important American philosopher, said that "phi-losophy is the unusually stubborn attempt to think clearly." Now *thinking* is a word with a much broader meaning than the word *rational.* To be rational is to think, but all thinking is not necessarily rational thinking. James does add the qualification "clearly." That narrows the field somewhat. But what is clear thinking, and how do we know it when we see it?

Consider this passage from a Chinese philosopher named Zhuangzi (Chuang Tzu)* who lived about 350 BCE.

> Suppose you and I have had an argument. If you have beaten me instead of my beat-ing you, then are you necessarily right and am I necessarily wrong? If I have beaten you instead of your beating me, then am I necessarily right and are you necessarily wrong? Is one of us right and the other wrong? Are both of us right or are both of us wrong? If you and I don't know the answer, then other people are bound to be even more in the dark. Whom shall we get to decide what is right? Shall we get someone who agrees with me? But if he already agrees with me, how can he decide? Shall we get someone who disagrees with both of us? But if he already disagrees with both of us, how can he decide? Shall we get someone who agrees with both of us? But if he already agrees with both of us, how shall he decide? Obviously, then, neither you nor I nor anyone else can know the answer. Shall we wait for still another person?

Zhuangzi wonders how we might decide who is right and who is wrong. You and I are not in a good position to make such a decision, at least not an objective one, because the fact that we are arguing shows we disagree. To bring in a third party to settle the dispute does not seem to help much because he or she will either dis-agree with you or with me or with both of us, and what was a two-person argument will now become a three-person argument.

Zhuangzi is wondering how we might proceed to settle an argument. What procedures do we have that will eventuate in agreement? Should we appeal to au-thority? Perhaps some divine revelation? A long-standing tradition? Common sense? Force? Rationality? You might be tempted to say that we should settle it by applying rational standards. If we follow that course, then we can decide which argument is the most rational. Are there, however, objective and universal standards of rational-ity? Is rationality something entirely subjective or, at the very least, relative to par-ticular historical periods and cultural communities?

Fundamental disagreements about the nature of rationality are very difficult to settle because in initially proceeding to approach the topic we have already made assumptions about what is a rational way to proceed. *Rationality* has to do with the

---

*There are two methods in wide use today for romanticizing (translating into a Latin-based alphabetical system) Chinese words. One is called Wade-Giles and the other Pinyin. The first time a word or name is introduced, I have used the Pinyin spelling and provided the Wade-Giles spelling in parentheses. See the pronunciation guide for Chinese words in Appendix II. The quotation is from *Chuang Tzu: Basic Writings,* translated by Burton Watson (New York, NY: Columbia University Press, 1996, p. 43).

way we proceed to investigate matters, settle disputes, evaluate evidence, assess people's behaviors, practices, and beliefs. If we could get agreement about the standards of rationality, then the only thing left to argue about would be whether or not these standards were fairly and accurately applied. But how do we proceed if we cannot agree on the standards themselves?

Imagine Zhaungzi's imaginary arguers arguing about the nature of rationality. Not only would they and some third-party find an acceptable settlement of the dispute difficult to obtain, they would not even know how to go about reaching a settlement. What would count as a rational solution to their disagreement if the very nature of rationality is itself the subject of the disagreement? With Zhaungzi we might ask, with more than a mere hint of futility, "Shall we wait for still another person?"

To avoid the futility of endless disagreements, some philosophers maintain that there must be objective and universal standards of rationality. This position on the question of rationality is called **foundationalism**. Generally (there are many different varieties of foundationalism), foundationalists hold that we can decide what is rational by appealing to principles that are undeniable to any rational person. For example, if I maintain that my belief about extraterrestrials visiting Peru is rational, I, according to this view, should be able to present good reasons in support of my belief. The reasons I present will be good ones insofar as they ultimately rest on a set of ideas that are *self-evidently true* for any person who can properly understand them.

What are these foundational principles? Many philosophers have maintained that they are the basic laws of logic and the rules and procedures deducible from those laws. Aristotle, for example, claims that the **law of noncontradiction** (a statement cannot be both true and false) stands at the foundation of all rational reasoning. You cannot rationally assert p (where p stands for any statement) *and* not-p. If you claim p is true, you cannot also claim it is false and be rational. Furthermore, he argues, anyone who denies this law and who is prepared to defend that denial will be unable to advance her or his argument without relying on the very law supposedly rejected.

I must confess that people who argued that the law of noncontradiction is false, and thereby meant that all statements (including their own statement about the falsity of the law of noncontradiction) could be both true and false, I would think either perverse or irrational. You would probably agree with me. However, you might quickly point out that being logical and correctly applying the laws of logic are, at best, necessary conditions of rationality. These are not sufficient. We can imagine someone applying logical procedures and arriving at the most absurd conclusions. If I were clever enough, I could justify my belief in extraterrestrials visiting Peru without violating any logical laws, but is that enough for you to conclude that my belief is rational?

So it would seem we need some fundamental principles, besides the laws of logic, in order to know both the necessary and sufficient conditions of rationality.* And here is where the fight really breaks out among foundationalists. Some (usually called *rationalists*) claim that these foundational principles of rationality amount to "clear and distinct ideas" that are innate in the human mind or can be discovered by a careful and critical analysis of our beliefs. Others (usually called *empiricists*) argue that immediate sense impressions form the foundations of rational beliefs. You will

---

* Something can be sufficient without being necessary and vice versa. A rock hitting a window is sufficient to break it, but not necessary because a baseball might do as well. Milk is necessary to make yogurt, but not sufficient.

encounter something of this debate between rationalists and empiricists as you read this book, so I will not belabor the point here. I only wish you to understand that much philosophical energy has been expended in a search for the foundational principles of rational belief. If we can find such principles, then we will have agreed-upon procedures for sifting through the many different answers to metaphysical questions (What is real?), epistemological questions (What is knowledge?), and axiological questions (What is value?) and settling on those that prove the most rational.

I think you can see the attractiveness of the foundationalist position, especially if you have ever been in one of those arguments where someone keeps asking you, "How do you know that?" At first you are patient and display your reasons. But she or he persists. "How do you know those are good reasons?" You explain why. Again, "Well, how can you be so sure?" About now your blood pressure is rising because you are beginning to see an infinite, bottomless abyss opening up. This could go on forever! But have no fear. Foundationalism can ride to your rescue because foundationalism maintains that regress is not infinite, the pit is not bottomless, and there is a sure foundation of first principles that your questioner will recognize to be rational. There is a way, according to foundationalists, of settling Zhaungzi's imaginary dispute.

However, the foundation you reach on your descent may turn out to be a ledge that gives way under your weight. Why? Because all the philosophical energy that has been spent on the search for foundational principles has ended in disagreement. Thus, many philosophers have declared the modern search for fundamental rational principles bankrupt. Welcome to the postmodern age of *anti-foundationalism.*

Just as there are many varieties of foundationalism, there are also many varieties of anti-foundationalism. In order to remove the negative connotations of the "anti," let us call the critics of foundationalism **constructivists** because many of them maintain that rationality is a social construction.

Some constructivists point to the failure of agreement among foundationalists as proof that the search for objective, universal, self-evident, rational principles is fruitless. Others argue that the so-called self-evident, objective, universal, ahistorical, transcultural foundations of rationality have been shown again and again to be little more than the elevation of the prejudices of an elite class, or of males, or of white culture, or of Western civilization to the honorific title of "self-evident rational principles." What is alleged to be "rational" turns out, after careful critical analysis, to be what Anglo-American European white males value! Foundationalism, this line of criticism maintains, is merely a variety of ethnocentric imperialism disguised with the mask of rationality.

Many constructivists argue that we are all so embedded in our cultures, our traditions, our religions, and our historical situations that we can never find some neutral point, some god's-eye view from which to pass judgment. Not one of our limited viewpoints is privileged. We are hopelessly culture-bound. There is no culturally neutral "third party," as Zhaungzi pointed out so clearly centuries ago, who can settle once and for all our important disputes. There are, of course, cultural procedures for settling disputes. However, it is a grave mistake to elevate such procedures to self-evident, universal marks of rationality.

Still other critics of foundationalism point out that foundationalism is fatally flawed because it is itself based on a contradiction. Foundationalism claims that a rational belief is one supported by good reasons. This means that before I accept your beliefs as rational, I should expect you to be able to display, if questioned, good reasons for such beliefs. If, after you have given me your good reasons, I persist and ask for more, sooner or later I shall have to be content with a belief whose truth is, you claim, "self-evident." So it turns out that good reasons rest on principles that we are asked to accept as self-evidently true and in need of no further support. Such principles would be irrational given the criterion initially assumed to be the hallmark of a rational belief—that is, a belief supported by good reasons.

Displaying the evidence and exploring the subtleties and shifts of argument between foundationalists and constructivists would take us too far afield. However, I should mention one major issue that this debate has engendered because it is particularly relevant to what this book is about. That is the issue of cognitive and ethical relativism. The foundationalists charge the constructivists with both **cognitive relativism** (the denial of universal truths) and **ethical relativism** (the denial of universally valid moral principles). They claim that if one denies the existence of transcultural, universal, objective standards of rationality, then what one is maintaining amounts to the view that there is no such thing as rationality; all there are, are *rationalities*. Eventually, this will lead the constructivist to assert moral relativism as well. One will be led down a slippery slope resulting in the conclusion that any culture's values, any religious tradition, any morality, indeed any set of beliefs, is as good or as rational as anyone else's. However, such relativism is self-defeating. If your view is no better or worse than my view, then all views are of equal merit. Therefore, constructivists can have no justification to support their claim that foundationalism is wrong. Foundationalists' views of rationality as universal and ahistorical are no more rational nor any less rational than constructivists' views of rationalities as local and historical (see Table 1.1).

Table 1.1

FOUNDATIONALISM	CONSTRUCTIVISM
CLAIM	*CLAIM*
One rationality that is universal and objective.	Many rationalities that are local and based on intersubjective agreement.
ARGUMENT	*ARGUMENT*
Beliefs are rational if supported by good reasons.	Rationality is conditioned by history and culture.
If an infinite regress of reasons is to be avoided, there must be a foundation of self-evident beliefs.	Vast amounts of historical, cultural, anthropological, and linguistic evidence supports the above claim.
Such foundational beliefs are: the laws of logic or clear and distinct ideas or beliefs evident to the senses.	
CRITIQUE OF CONSTRUCTIVISM	*CRITIQUE OF FOUNDATIONALISM*
Constructivism amounts to a self-refuting relativism.	Foundationalism cannot agree on what counts as foundational beliefs hence they are not self-evident. Its definition of rational beliefs is contradictory, and its claims amount to ethnocentric imperialism.

This is a powerful response to the constructivist critique of foundationalism. Few of us would argue with others if we thought that all views of morality or all views of truth were of equal worth. Yet we do argue. Few of us would be willing to maintain that programs of "ethnic cleansing," which lamentably characterize so much of human political practice, are as rational or moral as programs that aim at getting human beings to live in peace with one another.

We seem to be caught on the horns of a dilemma. We do not wish to opt for either ethnocentric imperialism or a kind of relativism that advocates "anything goes." Is there any other choice? Is there a way out of this predicament? Much contemporary philosophy is presently concerned with finding a way out of this dilemma, a sort of middle ground that allows us to assert that some answers are better than others but stops short of imposing on others our own local views of what is rational and what is good.

One way to escape the horns of a dilemma is to make careful distinctions. There is a difference between ethnocentrism and ethnocentric *imperialism.* Perhaps it is impossible to totally escape an ethnocentric viewpoint, but we do not have to impose our views on others by presenting them as if they are the only true views.

Likewise some philosophers distinguish between different kinds of relativism. Not all relativism may be self-defeating, contrary to what some foundationalists believe. We must carefully distinguish between relativism in the *strong sense* (the claim there are no universally valid standards) and relativism In the *weak sense* (the claim that standards of rationality and morality are culturally diverse). It seems obvious that standards of rationality and morality are relative to historical and cultural conditions in the sense that they are related to such conditions (weak relativism). Standards of rationality do not float in some timeless, nonhuman space. However, to conclude from this that *all* standards of rationality are of equal value or are equally true (the sort of self-defeating relativism the foundationalists charge the constructivists with) requires a big leap. It does not follow from the fact that there exist different understandings of rationality and morality that all understandings are of equal value, any more than it follows from the fact that there are different understandings of science that all of them are equally good or useful.

However, you might argue that if there are no objective standards of rationality or, at the very least, if we must admit we do not know what they might be, then all we are left with are rationalities bound to historical conditions and local cultural communities, and we have no way of determining which are better. Perhaps you are right. However, I think that we do have some options. We can remain convinced that our community has the last word on the subject and all others are wrong. Or, as we encounter other communities and other cultures, we can listen to them (and they to us) and try to discover ways of settling our disputes *together.* We can expand our conversations, listen to other voices, and together with them ask, What is real? What is knowledge? What is good? As we listen, as we enter into a dialogue, yes, and even as we argue, our standards of rationality will grow and, although we may still disagree in the end, at least we can say we have understood.

Hans-Georg Gadamer, a contemporary German philosopher, argues that truth is an understanding that occurs when there is a "fusion of horizons." Authentic conversation or dialogue occurs when we can recognize our own understanding as a horizon resulting from the perspective or bias we have acquired and when we are willing to risk our horizon in order to allow the horizon of the "other" to appear.

This book is an attempt to expand the philosophical dialogue. A wide variety of sounds will be heard—African American, Latino, Native American, feminist, and even Anglo-American European white males—and hopefully these sounds will turn into meaningful voices of wisdom. We will not agree with all these voices, but we can learn from each, and we may discover wider areas of agreement than we thought possible.

My claim that agreement about what is rational can emerge out of dialogue and expanded cultural communication rests on the assumption that we can understand philosophical views held by people who live in times and places very different from our own and on the hope that learning about ourselves and others is a worthwhile enterprise. Some might argue that we can never understand what others who are very different from us are saying and that my hope is naive. I do not have the space to defend my assumption and my hope, but I do believe that good reasons can be given for them. In any case, we will never find out if we do not try.

Recall that I characterized philosophy as a rational activity of formulating, understanding, and answering fundamental questions. This activity, I wish to stress, relies heavily on the logical skills of analyzing, criticizing, and developing arguments. It is, however, more than this. If the goal of philosophy is to formulate, understand, and answer fundamental questions on both an intellectual and practical level, then we can determine how rational this activity is only by assessing how successfully this goal is achieved by all those who participate in this sort of activity. I do not believe we can rule out any of the profound thinking about fundamental problems that the many peoples of the world have to offer by imposing some predetermined model of rationality. Hence, the very process of assessment is something we must learn as we go.

The Jains of India have a teaching called *syad-vada,* which might be translated as the "perhaps method." This teaching holds that 353 different viewpoints can be held on any question; hence, dogmatic closed-mindedness is inappropriate. To any perspective or any issue, the thoughtful will reply, "Perhaps." This "method" is based on the assumption that no single philosophical view or system can say all there is to be said about reality. It does not mean we should remain silent, nor does it mean that everything that is said (however partial) is of equal worth.

There are times, I think, when we can be a bit more definite than "perhaps," but the flexibility and openness this method recommends is a virtue we all need to practice when we have no privileged viewpoint from which we might settle a matter once and for all. Not all answers are rational. Some are better than others. However, the range of rational responses may be far broader than we realize.

1.3 Why Study Multicultural Philosophy?

In 1987, Allan Bloom, a professor of philosophy at the University of Chicago, published what was to become a major best seller, *The Closing of the American Mind* (New York: Simon and Schuster). The book generated a firestorm of controversy because Bloom forcefully attacked the culture of relativism and its associated stance of openness to (in Bloom's interpretation) anything and everything. According to Bloom, the intellectual elite teaching at the universities of America inculcated this "anything goes" relativism in their students.

These intellectuals had abandoned teaching the great classics of Western civilization in favor of a bland, unthinking celebration of a multiculturalism that was undermining the very foundations of American democracy. They promoted the "openness of indifference" and thereby were actually closing American minds to the great and enduring truths of the Western philosophical tradition, particularly to the thinking of the Greeks. Bloom does not deny that there is value in studying non-Western ways of thought. However, he does doubt that such study will teach students the right kind of openness, which he characterizes as the desire to know "what is good for me" (41). As far as Bloom is concerned it is Plato, especially Plato's great work the *Republic,* that tells us what is good for us.

Presumably Allan Bloom would not like this book. He writes, appealing to Plato's allegory of the cave (see Chapter 8), that:

> A culture is a cave. He [Plato] did not suggest going around to other cultures as a solution to the limitations of the cave. Nature should be the standard by which we judge our own lives and the lives of peoples. That is why philosophy, not history or anthropology, is the most important human science (38).

Bloom believes that only those "Western nations" that are deeply influenced by Greek philosophy have been and can be self-critical. Philosopher Martha Nussbaum remarks that such a view shows "startling ignorance" of the philosophical self-criticism found in many parts of the world. She writes, "I have rarely seen such a cogent, though inadvertent, argument for making the study of non-Western civilization an important part of the university curriculum."*

Times have changed since 1987, and world events have made it abundantly clear that ignorance of the philosophical, political, moral, and religious ideas from around the globe is a luxury we cannot afford. We need all the wisdom and understanding we can find from wherever it may be found to determine what is good for *all* of us. Today the burden of proof is not on those who advocate studying philosophy in a multicultural context. Rather it is on those who advocate that we should concentrate exclusively on traditional Western philosophy when we introduce a new generation of students to the pleasures of the pursuit of wisdom.

Professor Joseph Prabhu, who teaches philosophy at California State University in Los Angeles, makes (in the following brief essay written especially for this volume) a case for openness and understanding through global dialogue. He points out that the events of September 11, 2001, make such a global dialogue all the more urgent.

Reading Questions

1. What is globalization?
2. According to Prabhu, what are the two different models to which the events of September 11 point?
3. How are openness, tolerance, and criticism related to a "deep understanding" of others?
4. Why cannot sincere dialogue take place in situations of injustice?
5. How do Prabhu's insights support the need to study philosophy in a multicultural context?

---

* "Undemocratic Vistas," *New York Review of Books* (November 5, 1987): 20–26 reprinted in *Essays on the Closing of the American Mind*. Robert Stone, ed. (Chicago: Chicago Review Press, 1989), 201–202.

The Clash or Dialogue of Civilizations?

JOSEPH PRABHU

TWO DISTINCTIVE PHENOMENA characterize the beginning of the twenty-first century—globalization and the associated challenge of multiculturalism. They are, of course, of older provenance, but they acquire special urgency in this new era. Globalization may be conceived as a set of processes that bring about a palpable sense of worldwide interconnectedness. The effects of distant events can be rapidly felt around the globe, and local developments often have global consequences.

Contemporary globalization is marked, however, by two seemingly contradictory tendencies: a centripetal movement toward greater economic and technological integration, of which the Internet is a prime example, and an opposite centrifugal movement toward ethnic nationalism and cultural particularisms, as evidenced by the breakup of the former Soviet Union and Yugoslavia.

In these circumstances the challenge of the different cultures of the world, which are now forced to interact, becomes pressing. In the summer of 1993, American political scientist Samuel Huntington published an article, which he subsequently expanded into a book, in which he argued that "culture and cultural identities are shaping the patterns of cohesion, disintegration and conflict in the post-Cold war world"[1] and that the most dangerous conflicts are those that occur across the fault lines running through the major civilizations. September 11, 2001, made Huntington into an instant prophet, because on the surface that event appears to mark a clash between militant Islam and the West. Even though Huntington and others presented that conflict as a primarily cultural and religious one, it is not

clear that it is not also a political and economic clash, as indicated, among other evidence, by the fact that the World Trade Center and the Pentagon were chosen as targets.

The events of September 11, I would argue, point in terms of interpretation and prescription toward two quite different models. One is that suggested by Huntington, which presents cultures as monolithic, homogeneous, and oppositional and sees politics in the dichotomous terms of "the West versus the rest" or of "us" versus "them." The other model—that of dialogue—is suggested by the German-Jewish philosopher, Martin Buber. It may appear as if the clash model looks superior in terms of descriptive accuracy. Whether that is true or not, in line with the well-known distinction between "is" and "ought," the prescription need not be full-scale military confrontation, as seems to be the preferred policy of the United States at present. As Gandhi reminded us, the ethic of "an eye for an eye" ends up making the whole world blind.

The twentieth century had more war casualties than all the other centuries combined. There *has* to be—and is—another way other than war to reconcile differences, and that way, I suggest, is dialogue within and across cultures. The German theologian, Hans Küng, put it succinctly in the form of a slogan: "There will be no peace between nations without peace between religions, and there will be no peace between religions without dialogue between religions," To Küng's formulation we could add the words "and cultures," given the close links that exist between religions and cultures.

The notion of dialogue betokens an attitude of openness and tolerance. It does not preclude criticism, but it requires that criticism be based on a deep understanding of the other, and acquiring such understanding is often a challenging task. Such dialogues are occurring willy-nilly

1. Samuel Huntington, *The Clash of Civilizations and the Remaking of World Order* (New York: Simon and Schuster, 1996), 20.

Used by permission of the author.

within the United States, given the pluralistic nature of the country. Whatever the differences of religion, culture, class, race, gender, or ethnicity, citizens are guaranteed rights. As the U.S. experience suggests, cultures are not monolithic and necessarily oppositional. Under the right circumstances, they can be heterogeneous and interactive and lead to the acceptance of differences. World peace requires the extension of such *intra*national dialogues to *inter*national dialogues. This extension can and should happen at two levels: at a manifest level of intercultural understanding and also at a latent level of institutions and practices. Unjust institutions vitiate the possibility of dialogue; it is difficult to have a dialogue with someone if he has his foot on your neck. Unfortunately, as the United Nations Human Development Reports (1990–present) have

clearly shown, the benefits of economic globalization in the last twelve years have been uneven, bringing great wealth and power to the rich countries of the world, while exacerbating the poverty and misery of already poor, and sometimes starving, populations. There can be no sincere efforts at dialogue and peace without also remedying some of these injustices.

When atom bombs were dropped over Hiroshima and Nagasaki in 1945, Einstein, who had participated in the efforts to build such bombs, remarked: "The splitting of the atom has changed everything, except our ways of thinking." After the bloody history of the twentieth century and the annihilating power of our present military arsenals, it is time for us to heed Einstein's warning and change our ways of thinking.

1.4 Does Philosophy Bake Bread?

"Why should I study philosophy?" That is a question I often hear my students ask. It may be a question you are asking. Today many people approach their education pragmatically. They ask, "How will learning this prepare me for a job?" The implication of such a question is that if it does not help me get a job, it is not worth studying. If philosophy bakes no bread, why study it?

In the first two sections you have read about how we might define philosophy and about some debates over the nature of rationality. What have you learned that is of any importance? When you are interviewed for that first job upon graduation, do you think the interviewer might ask, "All right then, who do you think is right, the foundationalists or the constructivists?"

"Well," you might say, "I certainly don't think that the value of a field of study is completely exhausted by whether or not it leads to gainful employment. However, isn't it the case that philosophy, unlike science, never really settles anything? Philosophers just spin their wheels in endless debate."

It is true that uncertainty haunts the philosopher's study. Indeed, it is uncertainty that keeps the philosophical fires burning. If science could answer all our questions, if putting bread on the table were all there is to a happy life, if religion could provide all the answers we need, then I fear the philosopher in us would soon cease to exist. However, the philosophic wonder of which Aristotle spoke keeps our minds stirring largely because there are so many things about life that are uncertain.

There is an important sense, I think, in which we cannot help but philosophize. Life's circumstances and experiences compel us to think about things beyond our daily bread. If this line of reasoning is right, if we cannot help but philosophize, then should we not learn to do it well? One way of learning how to do it is to listen carefully to others who have philosophized from many different times and places. We can learn by example even when we disagree with the views of those from whom we learn.

If helping you get a job or answering with certainty the "big questions" is not the most important reason to study philosophy, it does not follow that philosophical study is totally without commercial value. I encourage you to visit the Web site of the American Philosophical Association (http://www.apa.vdel.edu). There you will find all kinds of valuable information about philosophy and its study. Among other things you will find illustrations of both academic and nonacademic careers pursued by philosophy majors. These careers include educator, advertising executive, computer systems analyst, publisher, librarian, commodities broker, diplomat, attorney, TV producer, editor, minister, and so forth. The skills of critical thinking and clear expression that you can learn from the study of philosophy prove to be valuable in many different pursuits that *do* bake bread.

We continue with a Western example. Bertrand Russell (1872–1970) is the author of the following selection. He explicitly addressed the issue of the value of philosophy in a book called *The Problems of Philosophy* published in 1912. What he has to say may surprise you. Whatever you may think about his claims, it is clear that the questions about the usefulness of philosophy are neither new nor unimportant.

Russell has been one of the most influential philosophers in the English-speaking world. He helped to establish a type of philosophizing known as *analytic philosophy.* The analytic approach to philosophy is characterized by logical analysis, critique, and clarification of the language we use to express our ideas. Russell made significant contributions to the development of the philosophy of logic, mathematics, and science in the first two decades of the last century. He also became known for his unconventional views on ethical, social, and political issues. Although he came from a long line of privileged English aristocrats, he still lost his teaching appointment at Cambridge University in 1916 because of his opposition to Britain's entering World War I. Throughout his life he lent his considerable talent and brilliant pen to many an anti-war movement, including opposition to the Vietnam War.

As you read what Russell has to say, see if you can answer the following reading questions and identify the passages that support your answers. Discuss in class the questions you had difficulty answering and the ones that stimulated your own thinking about the value of philosophy.

Reading Questions

1. Where, according to Russell, is the value of philosophy to be found?
2. Why does Russell maintain that the "uncertainty of philosophy is more apparent than real"?
3. What does Russell mean when he asserts that the value of philosophy is to be sought in its "very uncertainty"?
4. According to Russell, what may be the chief value of philosophy?
5. What do you think Russell means when he characterizes "true philosophic contemplation" as finding satisfaction in the "enlargement of the not-Self"?
6. How does Russell sum up the value of philosophical study? Do you agree with Russell? Why or why not?

On the Value of Philosophy

BERTRAND RUSSELL

HAVING NOW COME TO THE END of our brief and very incomplete review of the problems of philosophy, it will be well to consider, in conclusion, what is the value of philosophy and why it ought to be studied. It is the more necessary to consider this question, in view of the fact that many men, under the influence of science or of practical affairs, are inclined to doubt whether philosophy is anything better than innocent but useless trifling, hair-splitting distinctions, and controversies on matters concerning which knowledge is impossible.

This view of philosophy appears to result, partly from a wrong conception of the ends of life, partly from a wrong conception of the kind of goods which philosophy strives to achieve. Physical science, through the medium of inventions, is useful to innumerable people who are wholly ignorant of it; thus the study of physical science is to be recommended, not only, or primarily, because of the effect on the student, but rather because of the effect on mankind in general. Thus utility does not belong to philosophy. If the study of philosophy has any value at all for others than students of philosophy, it must be only indirectly, through its effects upon the lives of those who study it. It is in these effects, therefore, if anywhere, that the value of philosophy must be primarily sought.

But further, if we are not to fail in our endeavour to determine the value of philosophy, we must first free our minds from the prejudices of what are wrongly called "practical" men. The "practical" man, as this word is often used, is one who recognizes only material needs, who realizes that men must have food for the body, but is oblivious of the necessity of providing food for the mind. If all men were well off, if poverty and disease had been reduced to their lowest possible point, there would still remain much to be done to produce a valuable society; and even in the existing world the goods of the mind are at least as important as the goods of the body. It is exclusively among the goods of the mind that the value of philosophy is to be found; and only those who are not indifferent to these goods can be persuaded that the study of philosophy is not a waste of time.

Philosophy, like all other studies, aims primarily at knowledge. The knowledge it aims at is the kind of knowledge which gives unity and system to the body of the sciences, and the kind which results from a critical examination of the grounds of our convictions, prejudices, and beliefs. But it cannot be maintained that philosophy has had any very great measure of success in its attempts to provide definite answers to its questions. If you ask a mathematician, a mineralogist, a historian, or any other man of learning, what definite body of truths has been ascertained by his science, his answer will last as long as you are willing to listen. But if you put the same question to a philosopher, he will, if he is candid, have to confess that his study has not achieved positive results such as have been achieved by other sciences. It is true that this is partly accounted for by the fact that, as soon as definite knowledge concerning any subject becomes possible, this subject ceases to be called philosophy, and becomes a separate science. The whole study of the heavens, which now belongs to astronomy, was once included in philosophy; Newton's great work was called "the mathematical principles of natural philosophy." Similarly, the study of the human mind, which was a part of philosophy, has now been separated from philosophy and has become the science of psychology. Thus, to a great extent, the uncertainty of philosophy is more apparent than real: those questions which are already capable of definite answers are placed

From Bertrand Russell, The Problems of Philosophy, *London: Oxford University Press, 1912, pp. 153–161.*

in the sciences, while those only to which, at present, no definite answer can be given, remain to form the residue which is called philosophy.

This is, however, only a part of the truth concerning the uncertainty of philosophy. There are many questions—and among them those that are of the profoundest interest to our spiritual life—which, so far as we can see, must remain insoluble to the human intellect unless its powers become of quite a different order from what they are now. Has the universe any unity of plan or purpose, or is it a fortuitous concourse of atoms? Is consciousness a permanent part of the universe, giving hope of indefinite growth in wisdom, or is it a transitory accident on a small planet on which life must ultimately become impossible? Are good and evil of importance to the universe or only to man? Such questions are asked by philosophy, and variously answered by various philosophers. But it would seem that, whether answers be otherwise discoverable or not, the answers suggested by philosophy are none of them demonstrably true. Yet, however slight may be the hope of discovering an answer, it is part of the business of philosophy to continue the consideration of such questions, to make us aware of their importance, to examine all the approaches to them, and to keep alive that speculative interest in the universe which is apt to be killed by confining ourselves to definitely ascertainable knowledge.

Many philosophers, it is true, have held that philosophy could establish the truth of certain answers to such fundamental questions. They have supposed that what is of most importance in religious beliefs could be proved by strict demonstration to be true. In order to judge of such attempts, it is necessary to take a survey of human knowledge, and to form an opinion as to its methods and its limitations. On such a subject it would be unwise to pronounce dogmatically; but if the investigations of our previous chapters have not led us astray, we shall be compelled to renounce the hope of finding philosophical proofs of religious beliefs. We cannot, therefore, include as part of the value of philosophy any definite set of answers to such questions. Hence, once more, the value of philosophy must not depend upon any supposed body of definitely ascertainable knowledge to be acquired by those who study it.

The value of philosophy is, in fact, to be sought largely in its very uncertainty. The man who has no tincture of philosophy goes through life imprisoned in the prejudices derived from common sense, from the habitual beliefs of his age or his nation, and from convictions which have grown up in his mind without the co-operation or consent of his deliberate reason. To such a man the world tends to become definite, finite, obvious; common objects rouse no questions, and unfamiliar possibilities are contemptuously rejected. As soon as we begin to philosophize, on the contrary, we find . . . that even the most everyday things lead to problems to which only very incomplete answers can be given. Philosophy, though unable to tell us with certainty what is the true answer to the doubts which it raises, is able to suggest many possibilities which enlarge our thoughts and free them from the tyranny of custom. Thus, while diminishing our feeling of certainty as to what things are, it greatly increases our knowledge as to what they may be; it removes the somewhat arrogant dogmatism of those who have never travelled into the region of liberating doubt, and it keeps alive our sense of wonder by showing familiar things in an unfamiliar aspect.

Apart from its utility in showing unsuspected possibilities, philosophy has a value—perhaps its chief value—through the greatness of the objects which it contemplates, and the freedom from narrow and personal aims resulting from this contemplation. The life of the instinctive man is shut up within the circle of his private interests: family and friends may be included, but the outer world is not regarded except as it may help or hinder what comes within the circle of instinctive wishes. In such a life there is something feverish and confined, in comparison with which the philosophic life is calm and free. The private world of instinctive interests is a small one, set in the midst of a great and powerful world which must, sooner or later, lay our private world in ruins. Unless we can so enlarge our interests as to include the whole outer world, we remain like a garrison in a beleaguered fortress, knowing that the enemy prevents escape and that ultimate surrender is inevitable. In such a life there is no peace, but a constant strife between the insistence of desire and the powerlessness of will. In one way or another, if our life is to be great and free, we must escape this prison and this strife.

One way of escape is by philosophic contemplation. Philosophic contemplation does not, in its widest survey, divide the universe into two hostile camps—friends and foes, helpful and hostile, good and bad—it views the whole impartially. Philosophic contemplation, when it is unalloyed, does not aim at proving that the rest of the universe is akin to man. All acquisition of knowledge is an enlargement of the Self, but this enlargement is best attained when it is not directly sought. It is obtained when the desire for knowledge is alone operative, by a study which does not wish in advance that its objects should have this or that character, but adapts the Self to the characters which it finds in its objects. This enlargement of Self is not obtained when, taking the Self as it is, we try to show that the world is so similar to this Self that knowledge of it is possible without any admission of what seems alien. The desire to prove this is a form of self-assertion and, like all self-assertion, it is an obstacle to the growth of Self which it desires, and of which the Self knows that it is capable. Self-assertion, in philosophic speculation as elsewhere, views the world as a means to its own ends; thus it makes the world of less account than Self, and the Self sets bounds to the greatness of its goods. In contemplation, on the contrary, we start from the not-Self, and through its greatness the boundaries of Self are enlarged; through the infinity of the universe the mind which contemplates it achieves some share in infinity.

For this reason greatness of soul is not fostered by those philosophies which assimilate the universe to Man. Knowledge is a form of union of Self and not-Self; like all union, it is impaired by dominion, and therefore by any attempt to force the universe into conformity with what we find in ourselves. There is a widespread philosophical tendency towards the view which tells us that Man is the measure of all things, that truth is man-made, that space and time and the world of universals are properties of the mind, and that,

if there be anything not created by the mind, it is unknowable and of no account for us. This view, if our previous discussions were correct, is untrue; but in addition to being untrue, it has the effect of robbing philosophic contemplation of all that gives it value, since it fetters contemplation to Self. What it calls knowledge is not a union with the not-Self, but a set of prejudices, habits, and desires, making an impenetrable veil between us and the world beyond. The man who finds pleasure in such a theory of knowledge is like the man who never leaves the domestic circle for fear his word might not be law.

The true philosophic contemplation, on the contrary, finds its satisfaction in every enlargement of the not-Self, in everything that magnifies the objects contemplated, and thereby the subject contemplating. Everything, in contemplation, that is personal or private, everything that depends upon habit, self-interest, or desire, distorts the object, and hence impairs the union which the intellect seeks. By thus making a barrier between subject and object, such personal and private things become a prison to the intellect. The free intellect will see as God might see, without a *here* and *now,* without hopes and fears, without the trammels of customary beliefs and traditional prejudices, calmly, dispassionately, in the sole and exclusive desire of knowledge—knowledge as impersonal, as purely contemplative, as it is possible for man to attain. Hence also the free intellect will value more the abstract and universal knowledge into which the accidents of private history do not enter, than the knowledge brought by the senses, and dependent, as such knowledge must be, upon an exclusive and personal point of view and a body whose sense-organs distort as much as they reveal.

The mind which has become accustomed to the freedom and impartiality of philosophic contemplation will preserve something of the same freedom and impartiality in the world of action and emotion. It will view its purposes and desires as parts of the whole, with the absence of insistence that results from seeing them as infinitesimal fragments in a world of which all the rest is unaffected by any one man's deeds. The impartiality which, in contemplation, is the unalloyed desire for truth, is the very same quality of mind which, in action, is justice, and in emotion is that universal love which can be given to all, and not only to those who are judged useful or admirable. Thus contemplation enlarges not only the objects of our thoughts, but also the objects of our actions and our affections: it makes us citizens of the universe, not only of one walled city at war with all the rest. In this citizenship of the universe consists man's true freedom, and his liberation from the thraldom of narrow hopes and fears.

Thus, to sum up our discussion of the value of philosophy: Philosophy is to be studied, not for the sake of any definite answers to its questions, since no definite answers can, as a rule, be known to be true, but rather for the sake of the questions themselves; because these questions enlarge our conception of what is possible, enrich our intellectual imagination and diminish the dogmatic assurance which closes the mind against speculation; but above all because, through the greatness of the universe which philosophy contemplates, the mind also is rendered great, and becomes capable of that union with the universe which constitutes its highest good.

1.5 Reading Philosophy

Reading philosophy is both exciting and rewarding. Philosophy provides intellectual stimulation: the pleasure of discovering new ideas, the fascination of following the thread of a provocative argument, the challenge of rethinking inherited beliefs. For these reasons, reading philosophy can be enjoyable, but often it is not easy. Sometimes when you read philosophy, you feel like Alice in wonderland, who remarked, "Somehow it fills my head with ideas—only I don't know exactly what they are."

Philosophical texts come in a wide variety of types, ranging from technical essays to dramatic dialogues. They come from different cultures and different historical periods, and they are written in different languages. It is not easy to adjust to this variety. It takes practice to appreciate and understand ancient Greek dialogues, Buddhist fables, seventeenth-century French essays, and Chinese poetry.

Many of us are accustomed to reading secondary sources that explain the ideas of others. Textbooks digest what others say, explain what isn't clear, underline the important points, present summaries, and define technical words. Because much of our education has been centered on reading textbooks, not everyone is accustomed to wrestling with primary sources—the original texts and words—even in translation. If you are not used to digesting material on your own, explaining it to yourself, learning how to do your own summaries, and looking up words and references you do not understand, then at first you will find it difficult to read primary sources. Like anything else that is new, it will take some practice and some help from your instructor.

Voices of Wisdom is a combination of secondary material (my introductions to each chapter and to each selection in the chapters) and primary material (selections from the writings of philosophers past and present). Reading the primary texts may, in some cases, prove a rather difficult task. You need to learn how to read analytically and critically.

The purpose of analytical reading is to find out what the text says and to understand it as best you can. To do so requires analysis on your part. To analyze something is to break it into parts or smaller units. Thus you need to distinguish main ideas from supporting ideas and to determine what the author is trying to accomplish.

Critical reading involves evaluation. Your evaluation may be positive, negative, or some mixture of the two. Criticism requires you to make the effort to think about the ideas, analogies, arguments, evidence, and metaphors presented in the text, as well as their implications and assumptions.

Here are some suggestions that will help you understand philosophical texts and develop critical analysis skills.

1. Read the material at least twice.
2. Read actively and with a purpose.
3. Read analytically and sympathetically.

Here are some analytical questions that you can ask and answer as you read.

- What is the thesis (the central idea or main point)?
- What are the major points made in developing and supporting the thesis?
- How are key terms defined?
- What are the basic assumptions made by the author?
- What are the important implications of the author's position?

4. Read critically.

Here are some critical questions that will help you evaluate the strengths and weaknesses of the selections.

- Is what is said clear? If not, how is it unclear?
- Are adequate definitions given for important concepts? Can you think of counterexamples?
- Are the arguments adequate to support the claims; for example, are the premises true? the assumptions dubious?
- Do the implications of the text lead to absurd or false consequences?
- Are important aspects of the issue overlooked?
- How well did the author accomplish her or his goal?

5. After you have finished, review what you have read.
6. It is a good idea to keep a "philosophical notebook" in which you record your notes on the readings.

Before each selection are reading questions that will help you to both analyze and criticize the readings. You can keep the answers to these questions in your philosophical notebook.

Visit the companion Web site for chapter specific quizzes, suggestions for further reading, video ideas, and other resources to assess and expand your understanding of the chapter material. Go to http://philosophy.wadsworth.com and select the companion Web site for *Voices of Wisdom*. You will also find more information on how to read philosophy.

 You can access many additional readings at the InfoTrac-College Edition Web site. To find the following suggested articles do a keyword search with the article title. Use the passcode that was packaged with your new book to enter the site at http://www.Infotrac-college.com/Wadsworth/. Here is a sampling.

Georges Faraklas, "Common and Proper: An Attempt to Answer the Question 'What is Philosophy?'" *Diogenes*, Winter 2000 v48 i192 p41(14), Article A81764880.

Robert C. Solomon, "'What Is Philosophy?': The Status of World Philosophy in the Profession." *Philosophy East and West,* January 2001 v51 i1 p100, Article A72272267.

James V. Schall, "Philosophy: Why What Is Useless Is the Best Thing About Us." *Vital Speeches,* August 1, 1999 v65 i20 p628(5), Article A55684009.

Miguel Morey and Diane H. Sharp. "The Man and the Child. (The Literature of Democratic Spain: 1975–1992)." *The Literary Review,* Spring 1993 v36 n3 p419(5), Article A13929657.

Margaret A. Miller, "Philosophy in the Public Interest: An Interview with Martha C. Nussbaum." *Change,* January-February 2002 v34 i1 p39(5). A81764486.

"Philosophy's Purpose." *The Wilson Quarterly Autumn* 2001 v25 i4 p123, A80089704.

Carine Defoort. "Is There Such a Thing as Chinese Philosophy? Arguments of an Implicit Debate." *Philosophy East and West,* July 2001 v51 i3 p393, A78545897.

Part 2

Ethics

Chapter 2

How Should One Live?

> The superior person is open-minded and not partisan.
>
> CONFUCIUS

2.1 Introduction

HAVE YOU EVER WONDERED about how one should live? Should we live compassionately, pursuing a wisdom that liberates us from suffering? Should we live a virtuous and sincere life of balance, harmony, and family loyalty? Perhaps we should live a life of critical reflection, searching for truth and following an argument wherever it may lead. Should we live in pursuit of happiness? What exactly is happiness? How can we attain it? Perhaps we must unselfishly do what duty demands in devotion to God. Few of us would deny that we should live a meaningful life. A life without meaning and purpose is not desirable. However, what is a meaningful life, and how can it be pursued in a world that constantly threatens boredom if not meaninglessness?

The question of how one should live is fundamental to human existence. It is a question that has concerned ancient and modern peoples, Eastern and Western cultures. What do you understand by the question? If you had to write an essay on the topic, how would you begin? "One should live the good life," you might say. That seems a sensible way to start. The next question is, of course, what is the good life? Notice that the term "the good life" is both **ambiguous** (it can mean many different things and often it is not clear precisely to what it refers) and **vague** because the line between a good life and a bad life is not always clear. Is the good life one that is personally satisfying or a life possessing moral merit? Can it be both? Should it be both?

Let us assume that the good life is both, namely a personally satisfying life and a life of moral worth. Proceeding on this assumption you can continue your essay by exploring what is most important to you. What sorts of things do you value the most? Health? Wealth? Pleasure? However, just because you desire certain things, does that mean you *ought* to desire them? Desiring something is one thing, but claiming you ought to desire it is something else. The search for what is personally satisfying sooner or later runs into the issue of moral merit, and, if we assume the good life should be both personally satisfying and morally worthwhile, we must now explore the question in more depth.

What does *ought* have to do with this question about conducting one's life? "How *should* one live?" is not the same question as "How *ought* one to live?" You might say "I should go to the store," but that does not mean that you "ought" to in the sense that you are morally obligated to do so. Even so your sense of what you are morally obligated to do often grows out of your sense of what you should do.

Who is the "one" whom this question addresses? It is an impersonal one. "How should *one* live?" is not the same question as "How should *I* live?" So does your answer hold good for you alone? What about others? Is there one way we all ought to live? Writing an essay about how you think you should live is one thing. Writing an essay about how you think everyone ought to live is another matter. For one thing, the latter essay is a lot more difficult to write.*

If you have ever wondered about how you or anyone else ought to live, you have been concerned with what philosophers call *ethics* or *moral philosophy*. Ethics comes from the Greek word *ethos*, which means "character." For the Greeks, ethics had to do with developing a virtuous character. They believed that if you develop such a character, you will not only know the right thing to do but also do it.

Today we use the word *ethics* in many different ways. Sometimes it refers to moral rules or a way of life based on a religiously inspired moral code. We speak of "Christian ethics" or "Buddhist ethics." However, sometimes it refers to the secular study of moral values and a search for the principles of right moral action. As a branch of philosophy, "ethics" is used in this latter sense to refer to reflection on or study of moral issues. It is concerned with such questions as: What is the morally right way to live? How can I know what is morally right? How can I decide morally difficult cases? What makes a society just?

We can answer moral questions in different ways. One way is **descriptive**. We might *describe* the kinds of values people have and the sorts of principles they use in making moral judgments. Another way is **normative**. Normative reflection has to do with trying to discover *norms* or principles by which we *ought* to live. Many philosophers maintain that ethics is primarily a normative study. It is not only a description of what people find morally good and morally bad; it also seeks to discover norms that ought to guide our actions.

Although we can distinguish the kinds of questions moral philosophers ask, the answers often blend into one another. An answer to the question about how one should live will sooner or later have to address such issues as how we can know what is right, whether justice is possible, whether God exists, whether there is life after death, and many more. The readings in this chapter directly address the question of how one should live, in a broad sense, but this same question is addressed, in one way or another, by many of the other readings in *Voices of Wisdom*.

One useful way to approach the brief sampling of answers (which follow) to the question about how one should live is to see if you can find, explicitly or implicitly, answers to a set of what, how, and why questions. *What* is the good life? That is, what, according to the philosophers sampled here, is the goal of human life? Is the good life understood to be one that is primarily personally fulfilling or one of moral value? Is it understood to be both? *How* is the good life attained? That is, what are

---

*See Chapter 1, "Socrates' Question," in *Ethics and the Limits of Philosophy* by Bernard Williams (Cambridge, MA: Harvard University Press, 1985) for a discussion of the various ways the question "How should one live?" can be understood and for Williams's recommendation that we *not* take it in the sense of a question about obligation. He argues that Western philosophy would do well to return to this question as the starting point of ethical reflection. Also see John Kekes, *The Morality of Pluralism* (Princeton, NJ: Princeton University Press, 1993) for an argument in support of moral pluralism (there are many good ways to live) and against moral monism (there is only one good way to live).

the means that the author recommends that would lead one (presumably) to the goal of living a good life. *Why* is the life as described a good one? That is, is the goal of human life the author envisions appropriate and right? Why is the means recommended appropriate? That is, what reasons (if any) does the author give for thinking that the means will in fact lead to the goal? The "why" question asks you to find out how the philosopher justifies his or her answer. At least two sorts of justification are called for: (1) a justification of the goal and (2) a justification of the means. You may wish to set up a grid like the one in Table 2.1 on which you can write brief answers to these questions based on your reading and then compare the answers that are given.

Table 2.1

	BUDDHA	CONFUCIUS	SOCRATES	ARISTOTLE	GITA	KOLAK & MARTIN
What						
How						
Why						

Analyzing the answers in this way not only allows you to discern differences and similarities among the answers but also provides an opportunity for you to evaluate the answers. Is the good life as described or presupposed truly good? Can you think of a better one? Are the justifications adequate? Why should we think that the way to live (the means) will result in a good life? Maybe there is something the authors have overlooked. What about luck? Maybe living a good life is not a matter of choice but dumb luck. Can we attain a good life if we live in a horrible society? Does social harmony or social disintegration have anything to do with it? What about illness or poverty? Are these significant factors?

As you read and think through these questions, your own understanding of the question and the issues should deepen, and your own answer should become clearer. What do you think the good life is, and how do you think it can be attained?

2.2 The Buddha and the Middle Way

The word *Buddha,* which means "the Enlightened One," is the title bestowed on Siddhartha Gautama, who was born into a royal family in Nepal around 563 BCE. He lived a life of luxury and pleasure in the palace. On a trip outside the palace, he became aware of the suffering (*dukkha*) of humans. He witnessed people experiencing disease, old age, and death. At the age of twenty-nine, he left his life of comfort and became an ascetic in search of the solution to the problem of suffering.

Siddhartha studied with the sages of his day and practiced extreme austerities. Ironically, he nearly starved himself to death in his search for the answer to suffering. However, he found no satisfactory answer, either from his teachers or from his extreme ascetic practices. Eventually, he went his own way. One evening, he seated himself under a tree (later called the Bo-tree, or Tree of Enlightenment) and resolved not to stir from meditation until he discovered how to overcome suffering. He attained enlightenment and henceforth was called the Buddha.

After his enlightenment, he taught the wisdom he had realized and the practice for attaining that wisdom because he wished to help others gain **nirvana**, the release from suffering. He was convinced, based on his experience, that human beings should live free from suffering and that such a life was possible. He taught for forty-five years and founded an order of monks. He died at the age of eighty, in **483** BCE, thirteen years before Socrates (see Section 2.4) was born. From his teachings, a religion called Buddhism has grown and spread throughout Asia and much of the rest of the world. It is divided into three main groups: Theravada (Way of the Elders), Mahayana (Greater Vehicle), and Vajrayana (Diamond Vehicle). His teachings also inspired philosophical reflection, and various philosophical schools have also developed. Here we are primarily interested in Buddha, the philosopher or lover of wisdom, rather than Buddha, the religious founder.

What follows is one selection from the "Long Discourses" (*Digha Nikaya*, Sutta 22:18–22), attributed to the Buddha himself, concerning the **Four Noble Truths**. These constitute the heart of his message and presumably express, in condensed form, what he learned under the Bo-tree. The second selection is a commentary, from a Theravadan viewpoint, on the Fourth Noble Truth (also called the **Middle Way** or the **Eightfold Path**) by a contemporary Sri Lankan Buddhist scholar, Dr. Walpola Rahula.

Reading Questions

As you read the first selection, see if you can answer these questions:

1. What is *suffering?*
2. What is the relationship between *craving* and *pleasure?*
3. Why does the Buddha teach that the cessation of suffering (Third Noble Truth) is the extinction of craving?
   As you read the commentary by Rahula, see if you can answer these questions:
4. Why is the Fourth Noble Truth called the Middle Path?
5. What is the relationship between compassion and wisdom?
6. What is the difference between *knowing accordingly* and *penetration?* Can you give an example of each from your own experience?
7. What is the good life, according to the Buddha, and how would he answer the question, "How should one live?" Do you agree? Why, or why not?

The Four Noble Truths

THE BUDDHA

17. "AGAIN, MONKS, a monk abides contemplating mind-objects as mind-objects in respect of the Four Noble Truths. How does he do so?

Here, a monk knows as it really is: 'This is suffering'; he knows as it really is: 'This is the origin of suffering'; he knows as it really is: 'This is

From Thus Have I Heard: The Long Discourses of the Buddha: Digha Nikaya, *translated by Maurice Walshe, 1987, pp. 344–349. Reprinted by permission of Wisdom Publications, Boston.*

the cessation of suffering'; he knows as it really is: 'This is the way of practice leading to the cessation of suffering.'

18. "And what, monks, is the Noble Truth of Suffering? Birth is suffering, aging is suffering, death is suffering, sorrow, lamentation, pain, sadness and distress are suffering. Being attached to the unloved is suffering, being separated from the loved is suffering, not getting what one wants is suffering. In short, the five aggregates of grasping are suffering. . . .

"And how, monks, in short, are the five aggregates of grasping suffering? They are as follows: the aggregate of grasping that is form, the aggregate of grasping that is feeling, the aggregate of grasping that is perception, the aggregate of grasping that is the mental formations, the aggregate of grasping that is consciousness. These are, in short, the five aggregates of grasping that are suffering.[1] And that, monks, is called the Noble Truth of Suffering.

19. "And what, monks, is the Noble Truth of the Origin of Suffering? It is that craving which gives rise to rebirth, bound up with pleasure and lust, finding fresh delight now here, now there: that is to say sensual craving, craving for existence, and craving for non-existence.

"And where does this craving arise and establish itself? Wherever in the world there is anything agreeable and pleasurable, there this craving arises and establishes itself.

"And what is there in the world that is agreeable and pleasurable? The eye in the world is agreeable and pleasurable, the ear . . . , the nose . . . , the tongue . . . , the body . . . , the mind in the world is agreeable and pleasurable, and there this craving arises and establishes itself. Sights, sounds, smells, tastes, tangibles, mind-objects in the world are agreeable and pleasurable, and there this craving arises and establishes itself.

"The craving for sights, sounds, smells, tastes, tangibles, mind-objects in the world is agreeable and pleasurable, and there this craving arises and establishes itself.[2]

"Thinking of sights, sounds, smells, tastes, tangibles, mind-objects in the world is agreeable and pleasurable, and there this craving arises and establishes itself.

"Pondering on sights, sounds, smells, tastes, tangibles and mind-objects in the world is agreeable and pleasurable, and there this craving arises and establishes itself. And that, monks, is called the Noble Truth of the Origin of Suffering.

20. "And what, monks, is the Noble Truth of the Cessation of Suffering? It is the complete fading-away and extinction of this craving, its forsaking and abandonment, liberation from it, detachment from it. And how does this craving come to be abandoned, how does its cessation come about? . . .

21. "And what, monks, is the Noble Truth of the Way of Practice Leading to the Cessation of Suffering? It is just this Noble Eightfold Path, namely:—Right View, Right Thought; Right Speech, Right Action, Right Livelihood; Right Effort, Right Mindfulness, Right Concentration.

"And what, monks, is Right View? It is, monks, the knowledge of suffering, the knowledge of the origin of suffering, the knowledge of the cessation of suffering, and the knowledge of the way of practice leading to the cessation of suffering. This is called Right View.

"And what, monks, is Right Thought? The thought of renunciation, the thought of non-ill-will, the thought of harmlessness. This, monks, is called Right Thought.

"And what, monks, is Right Speech? Refraining from lying, refraining from slander, refraining from harsh speech, refraining from frivolous speech. This is called Right Speech.

"And what, monks, is Right Action? Refraining from taking life, refraining from taking what is not given, refraining from sexual misconduct. This is called Right Action.

1. [The five aggregates constitute the components of the individual human being. *Form* refers to the physical, *feelings* to the sensations that arise from the operation of the senses, *perception* to the cognition or awareness of sensation, *mental formations* to the emotions and dispositions to act based on sensations, and *consciousness* to the product or result of the interaction of the other four aggregates.—Ed.]

2. [In the West, we classify five senses as sight, sound, smell, taste, and touch. Buddhism adds a sixth, the mind.—Ed.]

"And what, monks, is Right Livelihood? Here, monks, the Ariyan disciple, having given up wrong livelihood, keeps himself by right livelihood.

"And what, monks, is Right Effort? Here, monks, a monk rouses his will, makes an effort, stirs up energy, exerts his mind and strives to prevent the arising of unarisen evil unwholesome mental states. He rouses his will . . . and strives to overcome evil unwholesome mental states that have arisen. He rouses his will . . . and strives to produce unarisen wholesome mental states. He rouses his will, makes an effort, stirs up energy, exerts his mind and strives to maintain wholesome mental states that have arisen, not to let them fade away, to bring them to greater growth, to the full perfection of development. This is called Right Effort.

"And what, monks, is Right Mindfulness? Here, monks, a monk abides contemplating body as body, ardent, clearly aware and mindful, having put aside hankering and fretting for the world; he abides contemplating feelings as feelings . . . ; he abides contemplating mind as mind . . . ; he abides contemplating mind-objects as mind-objects, ardent, clearly aware and mindful, having put aside hankering and fretting for the world. This is called Right Mindfulness.

"And what, monks, is Right Concentration? Here, a monk, detached from sense-desires, detached from unwholesome mental states, enters and remains in the first jhāna,[3] which is with thinking and pondering, born of detachment, filled with delight and joy. And with the subsiding of thinking and pondering, by gaining inner tranquillity and oneness of mind, he enters and remains in the second jhāna, which is without thinking and pondering, born of concentration, filled with delight and joy. And with the fading away of delight, remaining imperturbable, mindful and clearly aware, he experiences in himself the joy of which the Noble Ones say: 'Happy is he who dwells with equanimity and mindfulness,' he enters the third jhāna. And, having given up pleasure and pain, and with the disappearance of former gladness and sadness, he enters and remains in the fourth jhāna, which is beyond pleasure and pain, and purified by equanimity and mindfulness. This is called Right Concentration. And that, monks, is called the way of practice leading to the cessation of suffering."

3. [*Jhāna* (or *dhyana*) refers to altered states of consciousness that occur in meditation.—Ed.]

The Fourth Noble Truth

WALPOLA RAHULA

THE FOURTH NOBLE TRUTH is that of the Way leading to the Cessation of *Dukkha* [suffering]. This is known as the "Middle Path," because it avoids two extremes: one extreme being the search for happiness through the pleasures of the senses, which is "low, common, unprofitable and the way of the ordinary people"; the other being the search for happiness through self-mortification in different forms of asceticism, which is "painful, unworthy and unprofitable." Having himself first tried these two extremes, and having found them to be useless, the Buddha discovered through personal experience the Middle Path "which gives vision and knowledge, which leads to Calm, Insight, Enlightenment, Nirvāna." This Middle Path is generally referred to as the Noble Eightfold Path, because it is composed of eight categories or divisions: namely,

1. Right Understanding,
2. Right Thought,
3. Right Speech,
4. Right Action,
5. Right Livelihood,
6. Right Effort,
7. Right Mindfulness,
8. Right Concentration.

Practically the whole teaching of the Buddha, to which he devoted himself during 45 years, deals in some way or other with this Path. He explained it in different ways and in different words to different people, according to the stage of their development and their capacity to understand and follow him. But the essence of those many thousand discourses scattered in the Buddhist Scriptures is found in the Noble Eightfold Path.

It should not be thought that the eight categories or divisions of the Path should be followed and practised one after the other in the numerical order as given in the usual list above. But they are to be developed more or less simultaneously, as far as possible according to the capacity of each individual. They are all linked together and each helps the cultivation of the others.

These eight factors aim at promoting and perfecting the three essentials of Buddhist training and discipline: namely: (*a*) Ethical Conduct, (*b*) Mental Discipline and (*c*) Wisdom. It will therefore be more helpful for a coherent and better understanding of the eight divisions of the Path, if we group them and explain them according to these three heads.

Ethical Conduct is built on the vast conception of universal love and compassion for all living beings, on which the Buddha's teaching is based. It is regrettable that many scholars forget this great ideal of the Buddha's teaching, and indulge in only dry philosophical and metaphysical divagations when they talk and write about Buddhism. The Buddha gave his teaching "for the good of the many, for the happiness of the many, out of compassion for the world."

According to Buddhism, for a man to be perfect there are two qualities that he should develop equally: compassion on one side, and wisdom on the other. Here compassion represents love, charity, kindness, tolerance and such noble qualities on the emotional side, or qualities of the heart, while wisdom would stand for the intellectual side or the qualities of the mind. If one develops only the emotional neglecting the intellectual, one may become a good-hearted fool; while to develop only the intellectual side neglecting the emotional may turn one into a hard-hearted intellect without feeling for others. Therefore, to be perfect one has to develop both equally. That is the aim of the Buddhist way of life: in it wisdom and compassion are inseparably linked together, as we shall see later.

Now, in Ethical Conduct, based on love and compassion, are included three factors of the Noble Eightfold Path: namely, Right Speech, Right Action and Right Livelihood. (Nos. 3, 4 and 5 in the list).

Right Speech means abstention (1) from telling lies, (2) from backbiting and slander and talk that may bring about hatred, enmity, disunity and disharmony among individuals or groups of people, (3) from harsh, rude, impolite, malicious and abusive language, and (4) from idle, useless and foolish babble and gossip. When one abstains from these forms of wrong and harmful speech one naturally has to speak the truth, has to use words that are friendly and benevolent, pleasant and gentle, meaningful and useful. One should not speak carelessly: speech should be at the right time and place. If one cannot say something useful, one should keep "noble silence."

Right Action aims at promoting moral, honourable and peaceful conduct. It admonishes us that we should abstain from destroying life, from stealing, from dishonest dealings, from illegitimate sexual intercourse, and that we should also help others to lead a peaceful and honourable life in the right way.

Right Livelihood means that one should abstain from making one's living through a profession that brings harm to others, such as trading in arms and lethal weapons, intoxicating drinks, poisons, killing animals, cheating, etc., and should live by a profession which is honourable, blameless and innocent of harm to others. One can clearly see here that Buddhism is strongly opposed to any kind of war, when it lays down that trade in arms and lethal weapons is an evil and unjust means of livelihood.

These three factors (Right Speech, Right Action and Right Livelihood) of the Eightfold Path constitute Ethical Conduct. It should be realized that the Buddhist ethical and moral conduct aims at promoting a happy and harmonious life both for the individual and for society. This moral conduct is considered as the indispensable foundation for all higher spiritual attainments. No spiritual development is possible without this moral basis.

Next comes Mental Discipline, in which are included three other factors of the Eightfold Path: namely, Right Effort, Right Mindfulness (or Attentiveness) and Right Concentration. (Nos. 6, 7 and 8 in the list).

Right Effort is the energetic will (1) to prevent evil and unwholesome states of mind from arising, and (2) to get rid of such evil and unwholesome states that have already arisen within a man, and also (3) to produce, to cause to arise, good and wholesome states of mind not yet arisen, and (4) to develop and bring to perfection the good and wholesome states of mind already present in a man.

Right Mindfulness (or Attentiveness) is to be diligently aware, mindful and attentive with regard to (1) the activities of the body, (2) sensations or feelings, (3) the activities of the mind and (4) ideas, thoughts, conceptions and things.

The practice of concentration on breathing is one of the well-known exercises, connected with the body, for mental development. There are several other ways of developing attentiveness in relation to the body—as modes of meditation.

With regard to sensations and feelings, one should be clearly aware of all forms of feelings and sensations, pleasant, unpleasant and neutral, of how they appear and disappear within oneself.

Concerning the activities of mind, one should be aware whether one's mind is lustful or not, given to hatred or not, deluded or not, distracted or concentrated, etc. In this way one should be aware of all movements of mind, how they arise and disappear.

As regards ideas, thoughts, conceptions and things, one should know their nature, how they appear and disappear, how they are developed, how they are suppressed, and destroyed, and so on. These four forms of mental culture or meditation are treated in detail in the *Setting-up of Mindfulness*.

The third and last factor of Mental Discipline is Right Concentration leading to the four stages of *Dhyāna,* generally called trance or *recueillement*. In the first stage of *Dhyāna,* passionate desires and certain unwholesome thoughts like sensuous lust, ill-will, languor, worry, restlessness, and sceptical doubt are discarded, and feelings of joy and happiness are maintained, along with certain mental activities. In the second stage, all intellectual activities are suppressed, tranquillity and "one-pointedness" of mind developed, and the feelings of joy and happiness are still retained. In the third stage, the feeling of joy, which is an active sensation, also disappears, while the disposition of happiness still remains in addition to mindful equanimity. In the fourth stage of *Dhyāna,* all sensations, even of happiness and unhappiness, of joy and sorrow, disappear, only pure equanimity and awareness remaining.

Thus the mind is trained and disciplined and developed through Right Effort, Right Mindfulness, and Right Concentration. The remaining two factors, namely Right Thought and Right Understanding, go to constitute Wisdom.

Right Thought denotes the thoughts of selfless renunciation or detachment, thoughts of love and thoughts of non-violence, which are extended to all beings. It is very interesting and important to note here that thoughts of selfless detachment, love and non-violence are grouped on the side of wisdom. This clearly shows that true wisdom is endowed with these noble qualities, and that all thoughts of selfish desire, ill-will, hatred and violence are the result of a lack of wisdom—in all spheres of life whether individual, social, or political.

Right Understanding is the understanding of things as they are, and it is the Four Noble Truths that explain things as they really are. Right Understanding, therefore, is ultimately reduced to the understanding of the Four Noble Truths.

This understanding is the highest wisdom which sees the Ultimate Reality. According to Buddhism there are two sorts of understanding: What we generally call understanding is knowledge, an accumulated memory, an intellectual grasping of a subject according to certain given data. This is called "knowing accordingly." It is not very deep. Real deep understanding is called "penetration," seeing a thing in its true nature, without name and label. This penetration is possible only when the mind is free from all impurities and is fully developed through meditation.

From this brief account of the Path, one may see that it is a way of life to be followed, practised and developed by each individual. It is self-discipline in body, word and mind, self-development and self-purification. It has nothing to do with belief, prayer, worship or ceremony. In that sense, it has nothing which may popularly be called "religious." It is a Path leading to the realization of Ultimate Reality, to complete freedom, happiness and peace through moral, spiritual and intellectual perfection.

In Buddhist countries there are simple and beautiful customs and ceremonies on religious occasions. They have little to do with the real Path. But they have their value in satisfying certain religious emotions and the needs of those who are less advanced, and helping them gradually along the Path.

With regard to the Four Noble Truths we have four functions to perform:

The First Noble Truth is *Dukkha,* the nature of life, its suffering, its sorrows and joys, its imperfection and unsatisfactoriness, its impermanence and insubstantiality. With regard to this, our function is to understand it as a fact, clearly and completely.

The Second Noble Truth is the Origin of *Dukkha,* which is desire, "thirst," accompanied by all other passions, defilements and impurities. A mere understanding of this fact is not sufficient. Here our function is to discard it, to eliminate, to destroy and eradicate it.

The Third Noble Truth is the Cessation of *Dukkha,* Nirvāna, the Absolute Truth, the Ultimate Reality. Here our function is to realize it.

The Fourth Noble Truth is the Path leading to the realization of Nirvāna. A mere knowledge of the Path, however complete, will not do. In this case, our function is to follow it and keep to it.

2.3 Confucius and the Life of Virtue

Twelve years after the Buddha was born in India, Confucius (551–479 BCE) was born in the state of Lu in China. ("Confucius" is the latinization of Kong Fuzi (K'ung Fu Tzu),* which means "Master Kong.") He lived at a time when Chinese society had disintegrated into social and political chaos. Because of these circumstances, he became interested in the question of how the well-being of society could best be achieved and how this was related to the good life.

Biographical information is uncertain, but tradition tells us that Confucius was from the nobility. When he was three years old, his father died. At age nineteen he married and sought a government career. However, he was to make his name as an educator, not as a politician. He provided what we today would call a "humanistic" education to commoners and nobles alike, and he taught what might be termed a "humanistic social philosophy"—"social" because of his concern for achieving a

---

*There are two widely used methods for romanticizing (translating into a Latin-based alphabetical system) Chinese words. One is called Wade-Giles and the other Pinyin. The first time a word or name is introduced, I have used the Pinyin spelling and provided the Wade-Giles spelling in parentheses. See the pronunciation guide for Chinese words in Appendix II.

good social order and "humanistic" because of his concern to cultivate humane qualities in the human spirit. His reputation in China became so immense that on the popular level he was deified, while among scholars he was venerated as a great sage.

Ren (*jen*) is one of the central ideas of his thought. It has been translated in a variety of ways: "goodness," "humanity," "benevolence," and "humanheartedness," to name only a few. The concept is so rich and used in such a variety of ways that no simple English translation captures its meaning. *Ren* is not something we are, but something we become by cultivating our aesthetic, moral, cognitive, and spiritual sensibilities. These qualities develop in social or community contexts involving ordered and ritualized relationships. *Ren* is closely related to the principle of reciprocity, which ought to govern relationships among humans. We should not, Confucius contended, do to others what we would not have them do to us. Long before Judaism and Christianity, Confucius had articulated a form of the "Golden Rule."

Li (pronounced "lee") is another central concept in Confucian philosophy. It can mean rules of proper behavior, ritual or rite, custom, etiquette, ceremony, worship, and propriety. Humans should behave appropriately. The models for appropriate behavior came, according to Confucius, from the traditional rites and customs handed down from the past Golden Age. He regarded himself as a traditionalist and spent much of his time teaching and interpreting the cultural classics (called the "Six Disciplines") from China's past. Tradition is important in his view because it provides an external check on what one may subjectively believe to be the right way to act and is a repository of the wisdom of the past with regard to proper conduct. However, tradition must be personally appropriated and made one's own. Otherwise rituals become dead ceremonies performed mechanically and without meaning.

One of the major traditional virtues in China associated with Confucianism is **xiao** (*hsiao*) (pronounced "shee-ow"). *Xiao* is often translated as filial piety and involves the practice of kindness, honor, respect, and loyalty among family members. Confucius believed that a strong family is the basis of a strong society. In fact, the family is the microcosmic version of society. Society ought to be one large family, and ultimately *xiao* should be extended to the whole human community. Family harmony contributes to a wider social harmony and a social harmony supports family harmony.

Yi (pronounced "yee") is often translated as "rightness" and sometimes as "morals" or "morality." Many interpreters of Confucius, including the author of our next selection, D. C. Lau, think *yi,* or morality, becomes the primary concern of Confucius as he searches for the best way to live. While there is no denying that Confucius was concerned with what we today would call moral issues, the concept of *yi* is broader than morality. *Yi* refers to what is appropriate or fitting to do in a given situation. Hence it has aesthetic, political, social, and religious implications as well as moral ones.

Although it is usual to interpret Confucius as primarily concerned with moral, social, and political values, the aesthetic dimension of his thought needs to be emphasized as well. Ethics has to do with moral value; aesthetics has to do with artistic value or beauty. The Confucian concern with balance, harmony, and appropriateness reflects aesthetic values. Indeed, the very division between moral and aesthetic value is something Confucius probably did not recognize. For him to call an action right was not merely to pass a moral judgment, but an aesthetic judgment as well. Moral order is aesthetic order. The good and the beautiful are one.

Education plays a key role in the process of becoming a virtuous person because knowledge of the past is a clue to proper action in the present. Since becoming a virtuous person or developing good character is a process, it is something we must *learn* how to do. Hence, proper instruction and good education are keys to self-cultivation.

Because of present-day concerns with individual self-realization associated with the human potential movement and because of the "cult of individual privacy and freedom" that has developed in U.S. society, it is tempting to read Confucius as if he were concerned exclusively with the self-improvement of the individual. However, the individual can never be abstracted from society. Ultimately, for Confucius, there could be no absolute separation between the public and private realms of life. If *ren* is the foundation of one's individual life, it is also the foundation of society. His vision of the ideal world is one in which the world is like a home shared by all. Trust among all prevails and "all people love and respect their parents and children . . . there is caring for the old . . . sharing replaces selfishness and materialistic greed . . . and the door to every home need never be locked and bolted by day or night" (*The Record of Rites*, Book IX).

I have chosen to use a secondary source to introduce Confucius because it is rather difficult for a modern reader who has little or no background in Confucian philosophy to understand primary sources. Our guide to Confucius is D. C. Lau, respected translator and interpreter of Confucian thought. The following comes from the introduction to his widely used translation of Confucius's *Analects*.

Reading Questions

(Note: I have used the Wade-Giles spelling of Chinese terms in my questions because Lau uses Wade-Giles.)

1. What, according to Lau, is the most fundamental message of Confucius?
2. What is the difference between the *chün tzu* and the *hsiao jen*?
3. Can anyone become a *chün tzu*?
4. What is *jen* and how is it related to *chung* and *shu*?
5. Why are the obligations we owe others proportionate to the closeness of our relationship to them?
6. If benevolence requires the overcoming of self-interest, then why should our obligations to others be proportionate to the benefits we receive from them?
7. What is the relationship between *jen* and *li*?

Confucius and Moral Character

D. C. LAU

BEFORE WE PROCEED to look at what Confucius has to say about moral character, it is convenient, first of all, to dispose of two concepts which were already current in Confucius'

From D. C. Lau, The Analects, *London: Penguin Books, 1979, pp. 11–22. Copyright © D. C. Lau, 1979. Reprinted by permission.*

time, viz., the Way (*tao*) and virtue (*te*). The importance Confucius attached to the Way can be seen from his remark, "He has not lived in vain who dies the day he is told about the Way" (IV.8). Used in this sense, the Way seems to cover the sum total of truths about the universe and man, and not only the individual but also the state is said either to possess or not to possess the Way. As it is something which can be transmitted from teacher to disciple, it must be something that can be put into words. There is another slightly different sense in which the term is used. The way is said also to be someone's way, for instance, "the ways of the Former Kings" (I.12), "the way of King Wen and King Wu" (XIX.22), or "the way of the Master" (IV.15). When thus specified, the way naturally can only be taken to mean the way followed by the person in question. As for the Way, rival schools would each claim to have discovered it even though what each school claimed to have discovered turned out to be very different. The Way, then, is a highly emotive term and comes very close to the term "Truth" as found in philosophical and religious writings in the West.

There seems to be little doubt that the word *te*, virtue, is cognate with the word *te*, to get. Virtue is an endowment men get from Heaven. The word was used in this sense when Confucius, facing a threat to his life, said, "Heaven is author of the virtue that is in me" (VII.23), but this usage is rare in the *Analects*. By the time of Confucius, the term must have already become a moral term. It is something one cultivates, and it enables one to govern a state well. One of the things that caused him concern was, according to Confucius, his failure to cultivate his virtue (VII.3). He also said that if one guided the common people by virtue they would not only reform themselves but have a sense of shame (II.3).

Both the Way and virtue were concepts current before Confucius' time and, by then, they must have already acquired a certain aura. They both, in some way, stem from Heaven. It is, perhaps, for this reason that though he said little of a concrete and specific nature about either of these concepts, Confucius, nevertheless, gave them high precedence in his scheme of things.

He said, "I set my heart on the Way, base myself on virtue, lean upon benevolence for support and take my recreation in the arts" (VII.6). Benevolence is something the achievement of which is totally dependent upon our own efforts, but virtue is partly a gift from Heaven.

Behind Confucius' pursuit of the ideal moral character lies the unspoken, and therefore, unquestioned, assumption that the only purpose a man can have and also the only worthwhile thing a man can do is to become as good a man as possible. This is something that has to be pursued for its own sake and with complete indifference to success or failure. Unlike religious teachers, Confucius could hold out no hope of rewards either in this world or in the next. As far as survival after death is concerned, Confucius' attitude can, at best, be described as agnostic. When Tzu-lu asked how gods and spirits of the dead should be served, the Master answered that as he was not able even to serve man how could he serve the spirits, and when Tzu-lu further asked about death, the Master answered that as he did not understand even life how could he understand death (XI.12). This shows, at least, a reluctance on the part of Confucius to commit himself on the subject of survival after death. While giving men no assurance of an after life, Confucius, nevertheless, made great moral demands upon them. He said of the Gentleman[1] of purpose and the benevolent man that "while it is inconceivable that they should seek to stay alive at the expense of benevolence, it may happen that they have to accept death in order to have benevolence accomplished" (XV.9). When such demands are made on men, little wonder that one of Confucius' disciples should have considered that a Gentleman's "burden is heavy and the road is long," for his burden was benevolence and the road came to an end only with death (VIII.7).

If a man cannot be assured of a reward after death, neither can he be guaranteed success in his moral endeavours in this life. The gatekeeper at

---

1. Throughout this book, "Gentleman" is used as an equivalent for *shih* while "gentleman" is mad for *chün tzu*. *Shih* was the lowest rank of officials while *chün tzu* denoted either a men of moral excellence or a man in authority. . . .

the Stone Gate asked Tzu-lu, "Is that the K'ung who keeps working towards a goal the realization of which he knows to be hopeless?" (XIV.38). On another occasion, after an encounter with a recluse, Tzu-lu was moved to remark, "The gentleman takes office in order to do his duty. As for putting the Way into practice, he knows all along that it is hopeless" (XVIII.7). Since in being moral one can neither be assured of a reward nor guaranteed success, morality must be pursued for its own sake. This is, perhaps, the most fundamental message in Confucius' teachings, a message that marked his teachings from other schools of thought in ancient China.

For Confucius there is not one single ideal character but quite a variety. The highest is the sage (*sheng jen*). This ideal is so high that it is hardly ever realized. Confucius claimed neither to be a sage himself nor even to have seen such a man. He said, "How dare I claim to be a sage or a benevolent man?" (VII.34) and, on another occasion, "I have no hopes of meeting a sage" (VII.26). The only time he indicated the kind of man that would deserve the epithet was when Tzu-kung asked him, "If there were a man who gave extensively to the common people and brought help to the multitude, what would you think of him? Could he be called benevolent?" Confucius' answer was, "It is no longer a matter of benevolence with such a man. If you must describe him, 'sage' is, perhaps, the right word" (VI.30).

Lower down the scale there are the good man (*shan jen*) and the complete man (*ch'eng jen*). Even the good man Confucius said he had not seen, but the term "good man" seems to apply essentially to men in charge of government, as he said, for instance, "How true is the saying that after a state has been ruled for a hundred years by good men it is possible to get the better of cruelty and to do away with killing" (XIII.11), and "After a good man has trained the common people for seven years, they should be ready to take up arms" (XIII.29). On the one occasion when he was asked about the way of the good man, Confucius' answer was somewhat obscure (XI.20). As for the complete man, he is described in terms applied not exclusively to him. He

"remembers what is right at the sight of profit," and "is ready to lay down his life in the face of danger" (XIV.12). Similar terms are used to describe the Gentleman (XIX.1).

There is no doubt, however, that the ideal moral character for Confucius is the *chün tzu* (gentleman), as he is discussed in more than eighty chapters in the *Analects*. *Chün tzu* and *hsiao jen* (small man) are correlative and contrasted terms. The former is used of men in authority while the latter of those who are ruled. In the *Analects*, however, *chün tzu* and *hsiao jen* are essentially moral terms. The *chün tzu* is the man with a cultivated moral character, while the *hsiao jen* is the opposite. It is worth adding that the two usages indicating the social and moral status are not exclusive, and, in individual cases, it is difficult to be sure whether, besides their moral connotations, these terms may not also carry their usual social connotations as well.

As the gentleman is the ideal moral character, it is not to be expected that a man can become a gentleman without a great deal of hard work or cultivation, as the Chinese called it. There is a considerable number of virtues a gentleman is supposed to have and the essence of these virtues is often summed up in a precept. In order to have a full understanding of the complete moral character of the gentleman, we have to take a detailed look at the various virtues he is supposed to possess.

Benevolence (*jen*) is the most important moral quality a man can possess. Although the use of this term was not an innovation on the part of Confucius, it is almost certain that the complexity of its content and the pre-eminence it attained amongst moral qualities were due to Confucius. That it is *the* moral quality a gentleman must possess is clear from the following saying.

> If the gentleman forsakes benevolence, in what way can he make a name for himself? The gentleman never deserts benevolence, not even for as long as it takes to eat a meal. If he hurries and stumbles, one may be sure that it is in benevolence that he does so. (IV.5)

In some contexts "the gentleman" and "the benevolent man" are almost interchangeable terms. For instance, it is said in one place that "a gentleman is free from worries and fears" (XII.4), while elsewhere it is the benevolent man who is said not to have worries (IX.29, XIV.28). As benevolence is so central a concept, we naturally expect Confucius to have a great deal to say about it. In this we are not disappointed. There are no less than six occasions on which Confucius answered direct questions about benevolence, and as Confucius had the habit of framing his answers with the specific needs of the inquirer in mind, these answers, taken together, give us a reasonably complete picture.

The essential point about benevolence is to be found in Confucius' answer to Chung-kung:

> Do not impose on others what you yourself do not desire. (XII.2)

These words were repeated on another occasion.

> Tzu-kung asked, "Is there a single word which can be a guide to conduct throughout one's life?" The Master said, "It is perhaps the word 'shu'. Do not impose on others what you yourself do not desire." (XV.24)

By taking the two sayings together we can see that *shu* forms part of benevolence and, as such, is of great significance in the teachings of Confucius. This is confirmed by a saying of Tseng Tzu's. To the Master's remark that there was a single thread binding his way together, Tseng Tzu added the explanation, "The way of the Master consists in *chung* and *shu*. That is all" (IV.15). There is another saying which is, in fact, also about *shu*. In answer to a question from Tzu-kung, Confucius said,

> A benevolent man helps others to take their stand in so far as he himself wishes to take his stand, and gets others there in so far as he himself wishes to get there. The ability to take as analogy what is near at hand can be called the method of benevolence. (VI.30)

From this we can see that *shu* is the method of discovering what other people wish or do not wish done to them. The method consists in taking oneself—"what is near at hand"—as an analogy[2] and asking oneself what one would like or dislike were one in the position of the person at the receiving end. *Shu*, however, cannot be the whole of benevolence as it is only its method. Having found out what the other person wants or does not want, whether we go on to do to him what we believe he wants and refrain from doing to him what we believe he does not want must depend on something other than *shu*. As the way of the Master consists of *chung* and *shu*, in *chung* we have the other component of benevolence. *Chung* is the doing of one's best and it is through *chung* that one puts into effect what one had found out by the method of *shu*. Tseng Tzu said on another occasion, "Every day I examine myself on three counts," and of these the first is "In what I have undertaken on another's behalf, have I failed to be *chung*?" (I.4). Again, when asked how a subject should serve his ruler, Confucius' answer was that he "should serve his ruler with *chung*" (III.19). Finally, it is also said that in dealing with others one should be *chung* (XIII.19). In all these cases there is no doubt at all that *chung* means "doing one's best."

Another answer Confucius gave to the question about benevolence was, "Love your fellow men" (XII.22). As he did not elaborate, his meaning is not very clear. But fortunately he used this phrase again on two other occasions. In I.5 he said, "In guiding a state of a thousand chariots . . . avoid excesses in expenditure and love your fellow men; employ the labour of the common people in the right seasons." Again, the Master, according to Tzu-yu, once said "that the gentleman instructed in the Way loves his fellow men and that the small man instructed in the Way is easy to command" (XVII.4). In the first case, the love for one's fellow men (*jen*) is contrasted with the employment of the common people (*min*) in the right seasons, while in the second the gentleman's loving his fellow men is contrasted with the small man's being easy to command. If we remember that the small man

---

2. There is a more explicit definition of *shu* in one of the philosophers of the Warring States period. The *Shih tzu* says, "By '*shu*' is meant using oneself as a measure." (*Ch'ün shu chih yao*, 36.19b).

was probably different from the common people, we cannot rule out the possibility that when Confucius defined benevolence in terms of loving one's fellow men he did not have the common people in mind as well. Even if this is the case, it is perhaps not as strange as it may seem at first sight, and in order to see it in perspective, we should first take a look at the basis of Confucius' system of morals.

Confucius had a profound admiration for the Duke of Chou who, as regent in the early part of the reign of his young nephew, King Ch'eng, was the architect of the Chou feudal system some five hundred years before Confucius' time. It is beyond the scope of this introduction to discuss in detail the influence of the Duke on Chinese society and the Chinese political system. It is sufficient simply to single out for mention his most important contribution, the clan inheritance system known as *tsung fa*. Under this system, succession passes to the eldest son by the principal wife. Younger sons or sons by concubines become founders of their own noble houses. Thus the feudal lord stands to the king in a double relationship. In terms of political relationship he is a vassal while in terms of blood ties he is the head of a cadet branch of the royal clan. Political allegiance has as its foundation family allegiance. This social system founded by the Duke of Chou proved its soundness by the durability of the Chou Dynasty.

Following the footsteps of the Duke of Chou, Confucius made the natural love and obligations obtaining between members of the family the basis of a general morality. The two most important relationships within the family are those between father and son and between elder and younger brother. The love one owes to one's parents is *hsiao* while the respect due one's elder brother is *t'i*. If a man is a good son and a good younger brother at home, he can be counted on to behave correctly in society. Tzu-yu said,

> It is rare for a man whose character is such that he is good as a son (*hsiao*) and obedient as a young man (*t'i*) to have the inclination to transgress against his superiors; it is unheard of for one who has no such inclination to be inclined to start a rebellion. (I.2)

He goes on to draw the logical conclusion that "being good as a son and obedient as a young man is, perhaps, the root of a man's character."

In later Confucianism an undue emphasis was put on being a good son, but we can see here that even in early Confucian teachings *hsiao* was one of the most basic virtues.

If being a good son makes a good subject, being a good father will also make a good ruler. Love for people outside one's family is looked upon as an extension of the love for members of one's own family. One consequence of this view is that the love, and so the obligation to love, decreases by degrees as it extends outwards. Geographically, one loves members of one's own family more than one's neighbours, one's neighbours more than one's fellow villagers, and so on. Socially, one loves members of one's own social class more than those of another class. Thus it would not be surprising if benevolence was confined to one's fellow men (*jen*), but what is much more important to remember is that this does not mean that one does not love the common people at all. One loves them, but to a lesser degree and, perhaps, in a different manner. In Confucius' terminology, one should be generous (*hui*) to the common people (V.16). This is in keeping with Confucius' general attitude towards obligations. Our obligation towards others should be in proportion to the benefit we have received from them. This seems to be the case even between parents and children. In commenting on Tsai Yü who wanted to cut short the three-year mourning period, Confucius said, "Was Yü not given three years' love by his parents?" (XVII.21). This may be taken to mean that the observance of the three-year mourning period is, in some sense, a repayment of the love received from one's parents in the first years of one's life. If this is so, it is not difficult to see why the obligations we owe to other people should also be in proportion to the closeness of our relationship to them. As to how a ruler should treat the common people, this is a topic to which we shall return.

Concerning the nature of benevolence, there is another answer given by Confucius which is of great importance because the question was put to him by his most talented disciple.

Yen Yüan asked about benevolence. The Master said, "To return to the observance of the rites through overcoming the self constitutes benevolence. If for a single day a man could return to the observance of the rites through overcoming himself, then the whole Empire would consider benevolence to be his. However, the practice of benevolence depends on oneself alone, and not on others." (XII.1)

There are two points in this definition of benevolence which deserve attention. First, benevolence consists in overcoming the self. Second, to be benevolent one has to return to the observance of the rites.

Take the first point first. It is a central tenet in the teachings of Confucius that being moral has nothing to do with self-interest. To be more precise, to say that two things have nothing to do with each other is to say that there is no relationship whatsoever between them, either positive or negative. If being moral has nothing to do with pursuing one's own interest, neither has it anything to do with deliberately going against it. Why, then, it may be asked, is it so important to emphasize this lack of relationship between the two? The answer is this. Of all the things that are likely to distort a man's moral judgement and deflect him from his moral purpose, self-interest is the strongest, the most persistent and the most insidious. Confucius was well aware of this. That is why he said, more than once, that at the sight of profit one should think of what is right (XIV.12, XVI.10 and XIX.1). In another context he warned men in their old age against acquisitiveness (XVI.7). He also asked, "Is it really possible to work side by side with a mean fellow in the service of a lord? Before he gets what he wants, he worries lest he should not get it. After he has got it, he worries lest he should lose it, and when that happens he will not stop at anything" (XVII.15). Confucius came to the conclusion that he would not remain in undeserved wealth or position in spite of their being desirable objects (IV.5).

The point about returning to the observance of the rites is equally important. The rites (*li*) were a body of rules governing action in every aspect of life and they were the repository of past insights into morality. It is, therefore, important that one should, unless there are strong reasons to the contrary, observe them. Though there is no guarantee that observance of the rites necessarily leads, in every case, to behaviour that is right, the chances are it will, in fact, do so. To this point we shall return. For the moment, it is enough to say that Confucius had great respect for the body of rules which went under the name of *li*. That is why when Yen Yüan pressed for more specific details, he was told not to look or listen, speak or move, unless it was in accordance with the rites (XII.1). This, in Confucius' view, was no easy task, so much so that "if for a single day a man could return to the observance of the rites through overcoming himself, then the whole Empire would consider benevolence to be his."

There are two occasions when answers are given which emphasize another aspect of benevolence. When Fan Ch'ih asked about benevolence, the Master said, "The benevolent man reaps the benefit only after overcoming difficulties" (VI.22). Similarly, when Ssu-ma Niu asked about benevolence, the Master said, "The mark of the benevolent man is that he is loath to speak," and then went on to explain, "When to act is difficult, is it any wonder that one is loath to speak?" (XII.3). That he considered benevolence difficult can be seen from his reluctance to grant that anyone was benevolent. He would not commit himself when asked whether Tzu-lu, Jan Ch'iu and Kung-hsi Ch'ih were benevolent (V.8). Nor would he grant that either Ling Yin Tzu-wen or Ch'en Wen Tzu was benevolent (V.19). He refused to claim benevolence for himself (VII.32). This is no more than one would expect from a man of modesty. However, he did say of Yen Yüan, "in his heart for three months at a time Hui does not lapse from benevolence," while "the others attain benevolence merely by fits and starts" (VI.7). This emphasis on the difficulty of practising benevolence is echoed, as we have seen, by Tseng Tzu who described benevolence as "a heavy burden" (VIII.7). But although Confucius emphasized the difficulty of practising benevolence, he also made it abundantly clear that whether we succeed or not depends solely on ourselves. As we have already seen, he said in answer to Yen Yüan's question that "the practice of benevolence depends on oneself alone, and not on others" (XII.1). He was quite clear that failure to practise benevolence was not due to lack of strength to carry it through. He said, "Is there a man who, for the space of a single day, is able to devote all his strength to benevolence? I have not come across such a man whose strength proves insufficient for the task" (IV.6). Thus when Jan Ch'iu excused himself by saying, "It is not that I am not pleased with your way, but rather that my strength gives out," Confucius' comment was, "A man whose strength gives out collapses along the course. In your case you set the limits before-

hand" (VI.12). Confucius stated his conviction unambiguously when he said, "Is benevolence really far away? No sooner do I desire it than it is here" (VII.30). On the lines of the *Odes*

> The flowers of the cherry tree,
> How they wave about!
> It's not that I do not think of you,
> But your home is so far away,

Confucius commented, "He did not really think of her. If he did, there is no such thing as being far away" (IX.31). He must have made this comment with its possible application to benevolence in mind. . . .

2.4 Socrates on Living the Examined Life

Socrates (470–399 BCE), born in Athens nine years after Confucius died, lived during the golden era of Greek culture in a city that had become the intellectual and cultural center of the Mediterranean world. Many consider him the father of Western philosophy.

We have inherited contradictory pictures of Socrates. Plato, his most famous student and author of the dialogues in which Socrates stars, portrays him as the ideal philosopher. Aristophanes, in his play *The Clouds,* pictures him as a buffoon. Unlike the Pre-Socratics, Socrates showed little interest in natural philosophy. Like the Sophists, he was intensely interested in ethical and political problems. To many, he appeared to be just another Sophist, teaching the youth virtue. Plato contrasts him with the Sophists, however, claiming that he took no fee for his instruction and that his instruction was not a matter of *telling* others the truth but, like the activity of a midwife, of helping others give birth to and critically examine their own ideas.

His method (the **Socratic method**) consisted of asking people questions about matters they presumably knew something about. Socrates would usually begin by asking for a definition of a concept like justice. Once a definition was offered, he analyzed its meaning and critically examined it. Some defect was found, and the definition was reformulated to avoid the defect. Then this new definition was critically examined until another defect appeared. The process went on as long as Socrates could keep the other parties talking.

As an example, let's consider the dialogue called *Euthyphro.* Socrates is at the courthouse in Athens because he has been charged with corrupting the youth and inventing new gods. The latter charge amounts to a charge of impiety, and so he is anxious to talk with Euthyphro, who has appeared at the courthouse on his way to prosecute his own father for the impious act of murder. He asks Euthyphro, who claims to be something of an expert in these matters, to define piety. Euthyphro responds by offering his own action of prosecuting his father for murder as an example of piety.

Socrates points out that this is an *example* of piety, but it is not the sort of definition he is seeking. He wants to know the *essential* characteristics of piety. So Euthyphro tries again and defines piety as whatever is pleasing to the gods. This definition is soon found wanting when Socrates points out that the gods are often pleased by different things. What pleases Zeus does not always please his wife, Hera. So Euthyphro amends his definition. Piety is what is pleasing to *all* the gods. Socrates responds to this reformulation by asking, "Do the gods love piety because it is pious, or is it pious because the gods love it?" What is at issue is whether piety has some intrinsic characteristic that accounts for the fact that the gods love it, or whether the essential trait that determines piety is simply the fact that the gods love it. Euthyphro replies that the gods love piety because it is pious. Then Socrates shows him that he has not yet offered a good definition of piety itself, but only stated an effect of piety—namely that, whatever it is essentially, piety has the effect of pleasing all the gods. So Euthyphro, getting rather upset, offers another definition. This one, too, proves inadequate, but Euthyphro manages to make an excuse and leave before Socrates can drag yet another definition from him and demolish it. The dialogue ends, as so many do, with the issue of what piety is still up in the air. However, progress has been made. We now know more about what piety is not, but no positive, agreed-on definition has been formulated.

This dialogue not only illustrates the Socratic method but also probes the interesting and complex problem of the foundation of ethics. If we substitute the word *good* for the word *piety* and the word *will* for the word *love,* then, following Socrates' lead, we can ask, "Does God will the good because it is good, or is something good because God wills it?" In other words, is moral goodness an independent value, or is it something that depends on something else (like the will or command of God)? Some Jewish, Christian, and Islamic theologians have argued in favor of the **divine command theory** of ethics. According to this theory, God's command or will makes something morally right. Such a theory implies that the Ten Commandments, for example, are good only because God decreed them. Hence murder is not morally wrong in itself, but only if God should happen to forbid it. However, this sort of theory appears to make morality a matter of divine whim. If God decides to command just the opposite of the Ten Commandments, then this new set of commandments would become morally right. Surely we want to say that there is something intrinsically wrong about certain actions like murder, no matter what God might happen to command.

Socrates got into trouble with the people of Athens and was brought to trial in 399 BCE. Three Athenians—Meletus, Anytus, and Lycon—brought charges. There were 501 citizens on the jury. *The Apology,* which you are about to read, is Plato's account of the trial and Socrates' defense. It provides a dramatic statement of why Socrates believed that the pursuit of truth by the critical methods of rational inquiry is the way one should live. However, we should be cautious about interpreting Socrates' views in a purely intellectual way. He was concerned with the pursuit of wisdom and truth through the critical use of reason; there can be no doubt about that. However, this way of living is not unrelated to moral concerns. As he said at one point, his teaching had always been "not to take thought of yourself or your properties, but to care about the improvement of your soul." This "improvement of soul" is not acquired by money but by the practice of virtue. Indeed, he claimed that "from virtue come money and every other good of man, public as well as private."

Reading Questions

1. What is the main point Socrates made by telling the story about the oracle of Delphi?
2. How did Socrates defend himself against the charge of corrupting the youth and the charge of atheism?
3. At one point Socrates compared himself to a gadfly (horsefly) and the Athenians to a thoroughbred horse. What is the point of this comparison?
4. Socrates asserted that the unexamined life is not worth living. Imagine living your life using the Socratic method to examine your own beliefs and actions as well as the beliefs and actions of others. Would this be a good way to live? Why, or why not?
5. What are some basic assumptions made by Socrates in his response to the verdict of death?
6. How do you think Socrates would answer the question, "How should one live?"

The Apology

PLATO

Socrates: How you have felt, O men of Athens, hearing the speeches of my accusers, I cannot tell. I know their persuasive words almost made me forget who I was, such was their effect. Yet they hardly spoke a word of truth. But many as their falsehoods were, there was one of them which quite amazed me—I mean when they told you to be on your guard and not let yourselves be deceived by the force of my eloquence. They ought to have been ashamed of saying this, because they were sure to be detected as soon as I opened my lips and displayed my deficiency. They certainly did appear to be most shameless in saying this, unless by the force of eloquence they mean the force of truth; for then I do indeed admit that I am eloquent. But in how different a way from theirs!

Well, as I was saying, they have hardly uttered a word, or not more than a word, of truth. You shall hear from me the whole truth: not, however, delivered in their manner, in an oration ornamented with words and phrases. No, indeed! I shall use the words and arguments which occur to me at the moment. I am certain this is right, and at my time of life I should not appear before you, O men of Athens, in the character of a juvenile orator—let no one expect this of me. And I must beg you to grant me one favor, which is this—if you hear me using the same words in my defense which I have been in the habit of using, and which most of you may have heard in the agora, and at the tables of the money-changers, or anywhere else, I ask you not to be surprised at this, and not to interrupt me. I am more than 70 years of age and this is the first time I have ever appeared in a court of law, and I am a stranger to the ways of this place. Therefore I would have you regard me as if I was really a stranger whom you would excuse if he spoke in his native tongue and after the fashion of his country. That, I think, is not an unfair request. Never mind the way I speak, which may or may not be good, but think only of the justice of my cause, and give heed to that. Let the judge decide justly and the speaker speak truly.

First, I have to reply to the older charges and to my first accusers, and then I will go on to the later ones. I have had many accusers who accused me in the past and their false charges have continued during many years. I am more afraid

The translation is based on Benjamin Jowett's nineteenth-century translation as updated and revised by Christopher Biffle, A Guided Tour of Five Works by Plato (Mountain View, CA: Mayfield, 1988), pp. 30–50. Reprinted by permission of Mayfield Publishing Company. Footnotes deleted.

of them than of Anytus and his associates, who are dangerous, too, in their own way. But far more dangerous are these, who began when you were children, and took possession of your minds with their falsehoods, telling of Socrates, a wise man, who speculated about the heavens above, and searched into the earth beneath, and made the worse argument defeat the better. These are the accusers whom I fear because they are the circulators of this rumor and their listeners are too likely to believe that speculators of this sort do not believe in the gods. My accusers are many and their charges against me are of ancient date. They made them in days when you were impressionable—in childhood, or perhaps in youth—and the charges went by unanswered for there was none to answer. Hardest of all, their names I do not know and cannot tell, unless in the chance case of a comic poet. But the main body of these slanderers who from envy and malice have convinced you—and there are some of them who are convinced themselves, and impart their convictions to others—all these, I say, are most difficult to deal with. I cannot have them up here and examine them. Therefore, I must simply fight with shadows in my own defense and examine when there is no one who answers. I will ask you then to assume with me that my opponents are of two kinds: one more recent, the other from the past. I will answer the latter first, for these accusations you heard long before the others, and much more often.

Well, then, I will make my defense, and I will try in the short time allowed to do away with this evil opinion of me which you have held for such a long time. I hope I may succeed, if this be well for you and me, and that my words may find favor with you. But I know to accomplish this is not easy—I see the nature of the task. Let the event be as the gods will; in obedience to the law I make my defense.

I will begin at the beginning and ask what the accusation is which has given rise to this slander of me and which has encouraged Meletus to proceed against me. What do the slanderers say? They shall be my prosecutors and I will sum up their words in an affidavit. "Socrates is an evildoer and a curious person, who searches into things under the earth and in the heavens. He makes the weaker argument defeat the stronger and he teaches these doctrines to others." That is the nature of the accusation, and that is what you have seen in the comedy of Aristophanes. He introduced a man whom he calls Socrates, going about and saying he can walk in the air, and talking a lot of nonsense concerning matters which I do not pretend to know anything about—however, I mean to say nothing disparaging of anyone who is a student of such knowledge. I should be very sorry if Meletus could add that to my charge. But the simple truth is, O Athenians, I have nothing to do with these studies. Very many of those here are witnesses to the truth of this and to them I appeal. Speak then, you who have heard me, and tell your neighbors whether any of you ever heard me hold forth in few words or in many upon matters of this sort. . . . You hear their answer. And from what they say you will be able to judge the truth of the rest.

There is the same foundation for the report I am a teacher, and take money; that is no more true than the other. Although, if a man is able to teach, I honor him for being paid. There is Gorgias of Leontium, Prodicus of Ceos, and Hippias of Elis, who go round the cities and are able to persuade young men to leave their own citizens, by whom they might be taught for nothing, and come to them, whom they not only pay but are thankful if they may be allowed to pay them.

There is actually a Parian philosopher residing in Athens who charges fees. I came to hear of him in this way: I met a man who spent a world of money on the sophists, Callias, the son of Hipponicus, and knowing he had sons, I asked him: "Callias," I said, "if your two sons were foals or calves, there would be no difficulty in finding someone to raise them. We would hire a trainer of horses, or a farmer probably, who would improve and perfect them in their own proper virtue and excellence. But, as they are human beings, whom are you thinking of placing over them? Is there anyone who understands human and political virtue? You must have thought about this because you have sons. Is there anyone?"

"There is," he said.

"Who is he?" said I. "And of what country? And what does he charge?"

"Evenus the Parian," he replied. "He is the man and his charge is five minae."

Happy is Evenus, I said to myself, if he really has this wisdom and teaches at such a modest charge. Had I the same, I would have been very proud and conceited; but the truth is I have no knowledge like this, O Athenians.

I am sure someone will ask the question, "Why is this, Socrates, and what is the origin of these accusations of you: for there must have been something strange which you have been doing? All this great fame and talk about you would never have come up if you had been like other men. Tell us then, why this is, as we should be sorry to judge you too quickly."

I regard this as a fair challenge, and I will try to explain to you the origin of this name of "wise," and of this evil fame. Please attend then and although some of you may think I am joking, I declare I will tell you the entire truth. Men of Athens, this reputation of mine has come from a certain kind of wisdom which I possess. If you ask me what kind of wisdom, I reply, such wisdom as is attainable by man, for to that extent I am inclined to believe I am wise. Whereas, the persons of whom I was speaking have a superhuman wisdom which I may fail to describe, because I do not have it. He who says I have, speaks false, and slanders me.

O men of Athens, I must beg you not to interrupt me, even if I seem to say something extravagant. For the word which I will speak is not mine. I will refer you to a wisdom which is worthy of credit, and will tell you about my wisdom—whether I have any, and of what sort—and that witness shall be the god of Delphi. You must have known Chaerephon. He was a friend of mine and also a friend of yours, for he shared in the exile of the people and returned with you. Well, Chaerephon, as you know, was very impetuous in all his doings, and he went to Delphi and boldly asked the oracle to tell him whether—as I said, I must beg you not to interrupt—he asked the oracle to tell him whether there was anyone wiser than I was. The Pythian prophetess

answered, there was no man wiser. Chaerephon is dead, himself, but his brother, who is in court, will confirm the truth of this story.

Why do I mention this? Because I am going to explain to you why I have such an evil name. When I heard the answer, I said to myself, "What can the god mean and what is the interpretation of this riddle? I know I have no wisdom, great or small. What can he mean when he says I am the wisest of men? And yet he is a god, and cannot lie; that would be against his nature." After long consideration, I at last thought of a method of answering the question.

I reflected if I could only find a man wiser than myself then I might go to the god with a refutation in my hand. I would say to him, "Here is a man who is wiser than I am, but you said I was the wisest." Accordingly I went to one who had the reputation of wisdom, and observed him—his name I need not mention; he was a politician whom I selected for examination. When I began to talk with him I could not help thinking he was not really wise, although he was thought wise by many, and wiser still by himself. I tried to explain to him that he thought himself wise, but was not really wise. The result was he hated me and his hatred was shared by several who were present who heard me. So I left him, saying to myself, as I went away: "Well, although I do not suppose either of us knows anything really beautiful and good, I am better off than he is—for he knows nothing and thinks that he knows. I neither know nor think that I know. In this latter, then, I seem to have an advantage over him." Then I went to another who had still higher philosophical pretensions and my conclusion was exactly the same. I made another enemy of him and of many others besides him.

After this I went to one man after another, being aware of the anger which I provoked and I lamented and feared this, but necessity was laid upon me. The word of the god, I thought, ought to be considered first. And I said to myself, "I must go to all who appear to know, and find out the meaning of the oracle." And I swear to you Athenians, by the dog, I swear!, the result of my mission was this: I found the men with the highest reputations were all nearly the most foolish and some inferior men were really wiser and better.

I will tell you the tale of my wanderings and of the Herculean labors, as I may call them, which I endured only to find at last the oracle was right. When I left the politicians, I went to the poets: tragic, dithyrambic, and all sorts. There, I said to myself, you will be detected. Now you will find out you are more ignorant than they are. Accordingly, I took them some of the most elaborate passages in their own writings, and asked what was the meaning of them—thinking the poets would teach me something. Will you believe me? I am almost ashamed to say this, but I must say there is hardly a person present who would not have talked better about their poetry than the poets did themselves. That quickly showed me poets do not write poetry by wisdom, but by a sort of inspiration. They are like soothsayers who also say many fine things, but do not understand the meaning of what they say. The poets appeared to me to be much the same and I further observed that upon the strength of their poetry they believed themselves to be the wisest of men in other things in which they were not wise. So I departed, conceiving myself to be superior to them for the same reason I was superior to the politicians.

At last I went to the artisans, because I was conscious I knew nothing at all and I was sure they knew many fine things. In this I was not mistaken, for they did know many things of which I was ignorant, and in this they certainly were wiser than I was. But I observed even the good artisans fell into the same error as the poets. Because they were good workmen, they thought they also knew all sorts of high matters and this defect in them overshadowed their wisdom. Therefore, I asked myself on behalf of the oracle whether I would like to be as I was, having neither their knowledge nor their ignorance, or like them in both. I answered myself and the oracle that I was better off as I was.

This investigation led to my having many enemies of the worst and most dangerous kind and has given rise also to many falsehoods. I am called wise because my listeners always imagine I possess the wisdom which I do not find in others.

The truth is, O men of Athens, the gods only are wise and in this oracle they mean to say wisdom of men is little or nothing. They are not speaking of Socrates, only using my name as an illustration, as if they said, "He, O men, is the wisest who, like Socrates, knows his wisdom is in truth worth nothing." And so I go my way, obedient to the gods, and seek wisdom of anyone, whether citizen or stranger, who appears to be wise. If he is not wise, then in support of the oracle I show him he is not wise. This occupation quite absorbs me, and I have no time to give either to any public matter of interest or to any concern of my own, but I am in utter poverty by reason of my devotion to the gods.

There is another thing. Young men of the richer classes, who have little to do, gather around me of their own accord. They like to hear the pretenders examined. They often imitate me and examine others themselves. There are plenty of persons, as they soon enough discover, who think they know something, but really know little or nothing. Then those who are examined by the young men instead of being angry with themselves are angry with me. "This confounded Socrates," they say, "this villainous misleader of youth!" Then if somebody asks them, "Why, what evil does he practice or teach?," they do not know and cannot tell. But so they may not appear ignorant, they repeat the readymade charges which are used against all philosophers about teaching things up in the clouds and under the earth, and having no gods, and making the worse argument defeat the stronger. They do not like to confess their pretense to knowledge has been detected, which it has. They are numerous, ambitious, energetic and are all in battle array and have persuasive tongues. They have filled your ears with their loud and determined slanders. This is the reason why my three accusers, Meletus and Anytus and Lycon, have set upon me. Meletus has a quarrel with me on behalf of the poets, Anytus, on behalf of the craftsmen, Lycon, on behalf of the orators. As I said at the beginning, I cannot expect to get rid of this mass of slander all in a moment.

This, O men of Athens, is the truth and the whole truth. I have concealed nothing. And yet,

I know this plainness of speech makes my accusers hate me and what is their hatred but a proof that I am speaking the truth? This is the reason for their slander of me, as you will find out either in this or in any future inquiry.

I have said enough in my defense against the first class of my accusers. I turn to the second class who are headed by Meletus, that good and patriotic man, as he calls himself. Now I will try to defend myself against them: These new accusers must also have their affidavit read. What do they say? Something of this sort: "Socrates is a doer of evil and corrupter of the youth, and he does not believe in the gods of the state. He has other new divinities of his own." That is their charge and now let us examine the particular counts. He says I am a doer of evil, who corrupts the youth but I say, O men of Athens, Meletus is a doer of evil and the evil is that he makes a joke of a serious matter. He is too ready to bring other men to trial from a pretended zeal and interest about matters in which he really never had the smallest interest. And the truth of this I will try to prove to you.

Come here, Meletus, and let me ask a question of you. You think a great deal about the improvement of youth?

Meletus: Yes I do.

Socrates: Tell the judges, then, who is their improver. You must know, as you have taken the pains to discover their corruptor and are accusing me before them. Speak then, and tell the judges who their improver is. Observe, Meletus, that you are silent and have nothing to say. But is this not rather disgraceful and a very great proof of what I was saying, that you have no interest in the matter? Speak up, friend, and tell us who their improver is.

Mel: The laws.

Soc: But that, my good sir, is not my meaning. I want to know who the person is, who, in the first place, knows the laws.

Mel: The jury, Socrates, who are present in court.

Soc: Do you mean to say, Meletus, they are able to instruct and improve youth?

Mel: Certainly they are.

Soc: All of them, or only some and not others?

Mel: All of them.

Soc: By the goddess Hera, that is good news! There are plenty of improvers, then. And what do you say of the audience—do they improve them?

Mel: Yes, they do.

Soc: And the senators?

Mel: Yes, the senators improve them.

Soc: But perhaps the members of the Assembly corrupt them? Or do they too improve them?

Mel: They improve them.

Soc: Then every Athenian improves and elevates them, all with the exception of myself. I alone am their corruptor? Is that what you say?

Mel: Most definitely.

Soc: I am very unfortunate if that is true. But suppose I ask you a question. Would you say that this also holds true in the case of horses? Does one man do them harm and everyone else good? Is not the exact opposite of this true? One man is able to do them good and not the many. The trainer of horses, that is to say, does them good, and others who deal with horses injure them? Is that not true, Meletus, of horses or any other animals? Yes, certainly. Whether you and Anytus say yes or no, that is no matter. Fortunate indeed would be the condition of youth if they had one corruptor only and all the rest of the world were their improvers. You, Meletus, have sufficiently shown you never had a thought about the young. Your carelessness is seen in your not caring about the matters spoken of in this very indictment.

And now, Meletus, I must ask you another question: Which is better, to live among bad citizens or among good ones? Answer, friend, I say, for that is a question which may be easily answered. Do not the good do their neighbors good and the bad do them evil?

Mel: Certainly.

Soc: And is there anyone who would rather be injured than benefited by those who associate with him? Answer, my good friend, the law requires you to answer—does anyone like to be injured?

Mel: Certainly not.

Soc: And when you accuse me of corrupting the youth, do you charge I corrupt them intentionally or unintentionally?

Mel: Intentionally, I say.

Soc: But you just admitted that the good do their neighbors good, and the evil do them evil. Now, is that a truth which your superior wisdom has recognized thus early in life, and am I, at my age, in such ignorance as not to know if a man with whom I associate is corrupted by me, I am very likely to be harmed by him? Yet you say I corrupt him, and intentionally too; of that you will never persuade me or any other human being. But either I do not corrupt them, or I corrupt them unintentionally, so that on either view of the case you lie. If my offense is unintentional, the law does not mention unintentional offenses. You ought to have taken me aside and warned me, because if I had been better advised, I should have stopped doing what I only did unintentionally—no doubt I should. Instead, you hated to talk with me or teach me and you indicted me in this court, which is a place not of instruction, but of punishment.

I have shown, Athenians, as I was saying, Meletus has no care at all, great or small, about the matter. But still I should like to know, Meletus, in what way do I corrupt the young. I suppose you mean, as I infer from your indictment, I teach them not to acknowledge the gods which the state acknowledges, but some other new divinities or spiritual agencies instead. These are the lessons which corrupt the youth, as you say.

Mel: Yes, I say that emphatically.

Soc: Then, by the gods, Meletus, of whom we are speaking, tell me and the court, in somewhat plainer terms, what you mean! I do not understand whether you charge I teach others to acknowledge some gods, and therefore do believe in gods, and am not an entire atheist— but only that they are not the same gods which the city recognizes, or, do you mean to say that I am atheist simply, and a teacher of atheism?

Mel: I mean the latter—that you are a complete atheist.

Soc: That is an extraordinary statement, Meletus. Why do you say that? Do you mean that I do not believe the sun or moon are gods, which is the common belief of all men?

Mel: I assure you, jurymen, he does not believe in them. He says the sun is stone and the moon, earth.

Soc: Friend Meletus, you think you are accusing Anaxagoras and you have a bad opinion of the jury, if you believe they do not know these doctrines are found in the books of Anaxagoras the Clazomenian. These are the doctrines which the youth are said to learn from Socrates, when these doctrines can be bought in the marketplace. The youth might cheaply purchase them and laugh at Socrates if he pretends to father such eccentricities. And so, Meletus, you really think that I do not believe in any god?

Mel: I swear by Zeus that you absolutely believe in none at all.

Soc: You are a liar, Meletus, not believed even by yourself. I cannot help thinking, O men of Athens, Meletus is reckless and impudent and has written this indictment in a spirit of wantonness and youthful bravado. He has made a riddle, thinking to fool me. He said to himself: "I shall see whether this wise Socrates will discover my ingenious contradiction, or whether I shall be able to deceive him and the rest of them." For he certainly does appear to me to contradict himself in the indictment as much as if he said that Socrates is guilty of not believing in the gods, and yet of believing in them—but this surely is a piece of nonsense.

I should like you, O men of Athens, to join me in examining what I conceive to be his inconsistency and you, Meletus, answer. And I must remind you not to interrupt me if I speak in my accustomed manner.

Did any man, Meletus, ever believe in the existence of human things, and not human beings? . . . I wish, men of Athens, that he would answer and not be always trying to create an interruption. Did ever any man believe in horsemanship and not in horses? Or in flute playing and not in flute players? No, my friend, I will answer for you and to the court, as you refuse to answer for yourself. There is no man who ever did. But now, please answer the next question. Can a man believe in spiritual and divine activities and not in divine beings?

Mel: He cannot.

Soc: I am glad I have extracted that answer, by the assistance of the court. Nevertheless you swear in the indictment that I teach and believe in divine activities (new or old, no matter for that). At any rate, I believe in divine activities, as you swear in the affidavit, but if I believe in divine activities, I must believe in divine beings. Is that not true? Yes, that is true, for I may assume that your silence gives assent to that. Now what are divine beings? Are they not either gods or the sons of gods? Is that true?

Mel: Yes, that is true.

Soc: But this is just the ingenious riddle of which I was speaking. The divine beings are gods and you say first that I don't believe in gods, and then again that I do believe in gods; that is, if I believe in divine beings. For if the divine beings are the illegitimate sons of gods, whether by the nymphs or by any other mothers, as is thought, that, as all men will agree, necessarily implies the existence of their parents. You might as well affirm the existence of mules, and deny the existence of horses and donkeys. Such nonsense, Meletus, could only have been intended by you as a test of me. You have put this into the indictment because you have no real charge against me. But no one who has a particle of understanding will ever be convinced by you that the same men can believe in divine and superhuman activities, and yet not believe that there are gods and demigods.

I have said enough in answer to the charge of Meletus. Any elaborate defense is unnecessary but, as I was saying before, I certainly have many enemies and this will be my destruction if I am destroyed; of that I am certain—not Meletus, nor Anytus, but the envy and slander of the world, which has been the death of many good men and will probably be the death of many more. I will not be the last of them.

Someone will say: Are you not ashamed, Socrates, of a way of life which is likely to bring you to an untimely end? To him I answer: There you are mistaken, a man who is good for anything should not calculate the chance of living or dying. He should only consider whether in doing anything he is doing right or wrong and acting the part of a good man or of a bad. Whereas,

according to your view, the heroes who fell at Troy were not good for much, and the son of Thetis above all, who altogether despised danger in comparison with disgrace. His goddess mother said to him, in his eagerness to slay Hector, that if he avenged his companion Patroclus, and slew Hector, he would die himself.

"Fate," as she said, "waits upon you next after Hector."

He, hearing this, utterly despised danger and death, and instead of fearing them, feared rather to live in dishonor and not to avenge his friend.

"Let me die next," he replied, "and be avenged of my enemy, rather than stay here by the beaked ships to be mocked and a burden on the earth."

Had Achilles any thought of death and danger? For wherever a man's place is, whether the place which he has chosen or that in which he has been placed by a commander, there he should remain in the hour of danger. He should not consider death or anything else but only disgrace. And this, O men of Athens, is a true saying.

My conduct would be strange, O men of Athens, if I, who was ordered by the generals you chose to command me at Potidaea, Amphipolis, and Delium, remained where they placed me, like any other man facing death, should know when, as I believe, God orders me to fulfil the philosopher's mission of searching into myself and other men, desert my post through fear of death, or any other fear. That would indeed be strange, and I might be justly arraigned in court for denying the existence of the gods, if I disobeyed the oracle because I was afraid of death. Then I should be supposing I was wise when I was not wise.

This fear of death is indeed the imitation of wisdom, and not real wisdom, being the appearance of knowing the unknown. No one knows whether death, which they in their fear believe to be the greatest evil, may not be the greatest good. Is there not here the pretense of knowledge, which is a disgraceful sort of ignorance? This is the point that, as I think, I am superior to men in general and in which I might believe myself wiser than other men. Whereas I know little of the other world, I do not suppose that I know. But I do know that injustice and disobedience to a better, whether god or man, is evil and dishonorable, and I will never fear or avoid a possible good rather than a certain evil. Therefore if you let me go now, reject the advice of Anytus, who said if I were not put to death I should not have been prosecuted, and that if I escape now, your sons will all be utterly ruined by listening to my words. If you say to me, Socrates, this time we will not listen to Anytus and will let you off, but upon one condition, you are not to inquire and speculate in this way any more and if you are caught doing this again you shall die. If this was the condition on which you let me go, I would reply: Men of Athens, I honor and love you but I shall obey the god rather than you. While I have life and strength I shall never cease from practicing and teaching philosophy, exhorting anyone whom I meet in my usual way and convincing him, saying: O my friend, why do you, who are a citizen of the great and wise city of Athens, care so much about laying up the greatest amount of money, honor and reputation, and so little about wisdom, truth and the greatest improvement of the soul, which you never regard or heed at all? Are you not ashamed of this? If the person with whom I am arguing says: Yes, but I do care; I do not depart or let him go at once. I question, examine and cross-examine him, and if I think he has no virtue, but only says he has, I reproach him with undervaluing the greater, and overvaluing the lesser. This I would say to everyone I meet, young and old, citizen and alien, but especially to the citizens, inasmuch as they are my brethren. This is the command of the god, as I would have you know and I believe that to this day no greater good has ever happened in the state than my service to the god.

I do nothing but go about persuading you all, old and young alike, not to take thought of yourself or your properties, but to care about the improvement of your soul. I tell you virtue is not acquired with money, but that from virtue come money and every other good of man, public as well as private. This is my teaching, and if this is the doctrine which corrupts the young, my influence is certainly ruinous. If anyone says this is not my teaching, he is speaking a lie. Therefore,

O men of Athens, I say to you, do as Anytus bids or not as Anytus bids, and either acquit me or not; but whatever you do, know that I shall never change my ways, not even if I have to die many times.

Men of Athens, do not interrupt, but hear me. There was an agreement between us that you should hear me out. I think what I am going to say will do you good: for I have something more to say, which you may be inclined to interrupt but I ask you not to do this.

I want you to know if you kill someone like me, you will injure yourselves more than you will injure me. Meletus and Anytus will not injure me. They cannot because it is not possible that a bad man should injure someone better than himself. I do not deny he may, perhaps, kill him, or drive him into exile, or deprive him of civil rights. He may imagine, and others may imagine, he is doing him a great injury but I do not agree with him. The evil of doing as Anytus is doing—of unjustly taking away another man's life is far greater.

Now, Athenians, I am not going to argue for my own sake, as you may think, but for yours, that you may not sin against the gods or lightly reject their favor by condemning me. If you kill me you will not easily find another like me, who, if I may use such a ludicrous figure of speech, am a sort of gadfly, given to the State by the gods. The State is like a great and noble steed who is slow in his motions owing to his very size and needs to be stirred into life. I am that gadfly which the gods have given the State and all day long and in all places am always fastening upon you, arousing, persuading, and reproaching you. As you will not easily find another like me, I would advise you to spare me. I believe you may feel irritated at being suddenly awakened when you are caught napping. You may think if you were to strike me dead, as Anytus advises, which you easily might, then you would sleep on for the remainder of your lives, unless the god in his care of you gives you another gadfly. That I am given to you by the god is proved by this: if I had been like other men, I should not have neglected my own concerns all these years, and been occupied with yours, coming to you individually like a father or elder brother, exhorting you to think about virtue. This, I say, would not be like human nature. If I had gained anything, or if my exhortations had been paid, there would be some sense in that; but now, as you see not even my accusers dare to say I have ever sought pay from anyone. They have no witnesses for that. I have a witness of the truth of what I say; my poverty is my witness.

Someone may wonder why I go about in private giving advice and busying myself with the concerns of others, but do not come forward in public and advise the state. I will tell you the reason for this. You have often heard me speak of an oracle or sign which comes to me and is the divinity which Meletus ridicules in the indictment. This sign I have had ever since I was a child. The sign is a voice which comes to me and always forbids me to do something which I am going to do, but never commands me to do anything. This is what stands in the way of my being a politician. And correctly I think. For I am certain, O men of Athens, if I had engaged in politics, I would have perished long ago, and done no good either to you or to myself. Do not be offended at my telling you the truth. The truth is no man who goes to war with you or any other multitude, honestly struggling against acts of unrighteousness in the state, will save his life. He who will really fight for the right, if he would live even for a little while, must have a private station and not a public one.

I can give you proofs of this, not words only, but deeds, which you value more than words. Let me tell you a part of my own life which will prove to you I would never have yielded to injustice from any fear of death, and that if I had not yielded I should have died at once. I will tell you a story—tasteless perhaps and commonplace, but nevertheless true. . . .

The only office of state which I ever held, O men of Athens, was when I served on the council. The clan Antiochis, which is my clan, had the presidency at the trial of the generals who had not taken up the bodies of the slain after the battle of Arginusae. You proposed to try them all together, which was illegal, as you all thought afterwards, but at the time I was the only one of the committee who was opposed to the illegality. I gave my vote against you. When the orators threatened to impeach and arrest me and have me taken away, and you called and shouted, I made up my mind I would run the risk, having law and justice with me, rather than take part in your injustice because I feared imprisonment and death. This happened in the days of the democracy. But when the oligarchy of the Thirty was in power, they brought me and four others into the rotunda, and told us to bring in Leon from Salamis because they wanted to execute him. This was an example of the sort of commands which they were always giving in order to implicate as many as possible in their crimes. Then I showed, not in word only but in deed, if I may be allowed to use such an expression, I cared not a straw for death, and my only fear was the fear of doing an unrighteous or unholy thing. The strong arm of that oppressive power did not frighten me into doing wrong. When we came out of the rotunda the other four went to Salamis and fetched Leon, but I went quietly home. For this I might have lost my life, had not the power of the Thirty shortly afterwards come to an end. And to this many will witness.

Now do you really imagine I could have survived all these years if I had led a public life, supposing that like a good man I always supported the right and made justice, as I should, the first thing? No indeed, men of Athens, neither I nor any other. I have been always the same in all my actions, public as well as private, and never have yielded to any base agreement with those who are slanderously termed my disciples, or to any other. The truth is I have no regular disciples but if anyone likes to come and hear me while I am pursuing my mission, whether he be young or old, he may freely come. Nor do I converse with those who pay only, and not with those who do not pay; but anyone, whether he be rich or poor, may question and answer me and listen to my words. If he turns out to be a bad man or a good one, I am not responsible, as I never taught him anything. If anyone says he has ever learned or heard anything from me in private which all the world has not heard, I would like you to know that he is lying.

I will be asked, why do people delight in continually conversing with you? I have told you already, Athenians, the whole truth about this. They like to hear the cross-examination of the pretenders to wisdom; there is amusement in this. This is a duty which the gods have imposed upon me, as I am assured by oracles, visions, and in every sort of way which the will of divine power was ever made plain to anyone. This is true, O Athenians or, if not true, would be soon refuted. If I am really corrupting the youth and have corrupted some of them already, those who have grown up and are aware I gave them bad advice in the days of their youth should come forward as accusers and take their revenge. If they do not like to come themselves, some of their relatives, fathers, brothers, or other kinsmen, should say what evil their families suffered at my hands. Now is their time. I see many of them in the court.

There is Crito, who is of the same age and of the same township as myself, and there is Critobulus, his son, whom I also see. There is Lysanias of Sphettus, who is the father of Aeschines—he is present; and also there is Antiphon of Cephisus, who is the father of Epigenes; and there are the brothers of several who have associated with me. There is Nicostratus, the son of Theosdotides, and the brother of Theodotus (not Theodotus himself—he is dead, and therefore, he will not seek to stop him). There is Paralus, the son of Demodocus, who had a brother Theages; and Adeimantus, the son of Ariston, whose brother Plato is present; and Aeantodorus, who is the brother of Apollodorus, whom I also see. I might mention a great many others, any of whom Meletus could have produced as witnesses in the course of his speech. Let him still produce them, if he has forgotten—I will make way for him. Let him speak, if he has any testimony of this sort which he can produce. Nay, Athenians, the very opposite is the truth. For all these are ready to witness on behalf of the corruptor, of the destroyer of their kindred, as Meletus and Anytus call me; not the corrupted youth only—there might have been a motive for that—but their uncorrupted elder relatives. Why should they, too, support me with their testimony? Why indeed, except for the reason of

truth and justice, and because they know I am speaking the truth and Meletus is lying.

Well, Athenians, this and similar to this is nearly all the defense I have to offer. Yet a word more. Perhaps there may be someone who is offended by me, when he calls to mind how he himself on a similar, or even a less serious occasion, had recourse to prayers and supplications with many tears, and how he produced his children in court, which was a moving spectacle, together with a group of his relations and friends. I, who am probably in danger of my life, will do none of these things. Perhaps this may come into his mind and he may be set against me, and vote in anger because he is displeased at this. Now if there is such a person among you I reply to him: My friend, I am a man, and like other men, a creature of flesh and blood and not of wood or stone, as Homer says. I have a family, yes, and sons, O Athenians, three in number, one of whom is growing up, and two others who are still young. Yet I will not bring any of them here in order to beg you for an acquittal. And why not? Not from any self-will or disregard of you. Whether I am, or am not, afraid of death is another question, of which I will not now speak. My reason is that I feel such conduct to be discreditable to myself, you and the whole state. One who has reached my years and who has a name for wisdom, whether deserved or not, should not lower himself. The world has decided that Socrates is in some way superior to other men. And if those among you who are said to be superior in wisdom, courage and any other virtue, lower themselves in this way, how shameful is their conduct!

I have seen men of reputation, when they have been condemned, behaving in the strangest manner. They seemed to believe they were going to suffer something dreadful if they died, and they could be immortal if you only allowed them to live. I think they were a dishonor to the state, and any stranger coming in would say the most eminent men of Athens, to whom the Athenians themselves give honor and command, are no better than women. I say these things ought not to be done by those of us who are of reputation; and if they are done, you ought not to permit them. You ought to show you are more inclined to condemn, not the man who is quiet, but the man who gets up a doleful scene and makes the city ridiculous.

Setting aside the question of dishonor, there seems to be something wrong in begging a judge and thus procuring an acquittal instead of informing and convincing him. For his duty is not to make a present of justice, but to give judgment. He has sworn he will judge according to the laws and not according to his own good pleasure. Neither he nor we should get into the habit of perjuring ourselves—there can be no piety in that. Do not require me to do what I consider dishonorable, impious and wrong, especially now, when I am being tried for impiety on the indictment of Meletus. For if, O men of Athens, by force of persuasion and entreaty, I could overpower your oaths, then I should be teaching you to believe there are no gods, and convict myself in my own defense of not believing in them. But that is not the case. I do believe there are gods and in a far higher sense than any of my accusers believe in them. To you and to the gods I commit my cause, to be determined by you as is best for you and me.

(The jury returns a guilty verdict and Meletus proposes death as a punishment.)

There are many reasons why I am not grieved, O men of Athens, at the vote of condemnation. I expected this and am only surprised the votes are so nearly equal. I thought the majority against me would have been far larger, but now, had thirty votes gone over to the other side, I would have been acquitted. And I may say I have escaped Meletus' charges. And I may say more; without the assistance of Anytus and Lycon, he would not have had a fifth part of the votes, as the law requires, in which case he would have incurred a fine of a thousand drachmae.

He proposes death as the penalty. What shall I propose on my part, O men of Athens? Clearly what is my due. What is that which I ought to pay or to receive? What shall be done to the man who has never been idle during his whole life, but has been careless of what the many care about—wealth, family interests, military offices and speaking in the Assembly, and courts, plots,

and parties. Believing I was really too honest a man to follow in this way and live, I did not go where I could do no good to you or to myself. I went where I could do the greatest good privately to every one of you. I sought to persuade every man among you that he must look to himself and seek virtue and wisdom before he looks to his private interests, and look to the welfare of the State before he looks to the wealth of the State. This should be the order which he observes in all his actions. What shall be done to someone like me? Doubtless some good thing, O men of Athens, if he has his reward and the good should be suitable to him. What would be a reward suitable to a poor man who is your benefactor, who desires to instruct you? There can be no more fitting reward than maintenance in the Prytaneum, O men of Athens, a reward which he deserves far more than the citizen who wins the prize at Olympia in the horse or chariot race, whether the chariots were drawn by two horses or many. For I am in need and he has enough. He only gives you the appearance of happiness and I give you the reality. Thus, if I am to estimate the penalty justly, I say maintenance in the Prytaneum is just.

Perhaps you think I am mocking you in saying this, as in what I said before about the tears and prayers. But that is not the case. I speak because I am convinced I never intentionally wronged anyone, although I cannot convince you of that—for we have had a short conversation only. If there were a law at Athens, such as there is in other cities, that a case involving the death penalty should not be decided in one day, then I believe I would have convinced you. Now the time is too short. I cannot quickly refute great slanders and, as I am convinced that I never wronged another, I will assuredly not wrong myself. I will not say of myself that I deserve any evil, nor propose any penalty. Why should I? Because I am afraid of the penalty of death which Meletus proposes? When I do not know whether death is a good or an evil, why should I propose a penalty which would certainly be an evil? Shall I say imprisonment? And why should I live in prison, and be the slave of the judges of the year—of the Eleven? Or shall the penalty be a fine, and imprisonment until the fine is paid? There is the same objection. I should have to stay in prison for I have no money and cannot pay. And if I say exile, and this may be the penalty which you will affix, I must indeed be blinded by love of life, if I do not realize that you, who are my own citizens, cannot endure my words and have found them so hateful you want to silence them, others are likely to endure me. No indeed, men of Athens, that is not very likely. And what a life should I lead, at my age, wandering from city to city, living in ever-changing exile and always being driven out! For I am quite sure that whatever place I go, the young men will come to me. If I drive them away, their elders will drive me out. And, if I let them come, their fathers and friends will drive me out for their sakes.

Someone will say: Yes, Socrates, but can you not hold your tongue, and then go into a foreign city, and no one will interfere with you? Now I have great difficulty in making you understand my answer to this. If I tell you this would be a disobedience to a divine command, and therefore I cannot hold my tongue, you will not believe I am serious. If I say again that greatest good is daily to converse about virtue, and all that concerning which you hear me examining myself and others, and that the life which is unexamined is not worth living—that you are still less likely to believe. And yet what I say is true, although it is hard for me to persuade you. Moreover, I am not accustomed to thinking I deserve any punishment. Had I money I might have proposed to give you what I had and would have been none the worse. But you see I have none and can only ask you to proportion the fine to my means. However, I think I could afford a mina, and therefore I propose that penalty. Plato, Crito, Critobulus, and Apollodorus, my friends here, bid me say 30 minae and they will pay the fine. Well, then, say 30 minae, let that be the penalty for that they will be ample security to you.

(The jury votes again to decide between Socrates' proposal of a fine and Meletus' proposal of the death penalty. The verdict is death.)

Not much time will be gained, O Athenians, in return for the evil name you will get from the enemies of the city, who will say you killed Socrates, a wise man. They will call me wise even though I am not wise when they want to reproach you. If you waited a little while, your desire would have been fulfilled in the course of nature. I am far advanced in years, as you may perceive, and not far from death. I am speaking now only to those of you who have condemned me to death. And I have another thing to say to them: You think I was convicted through deficiency of words—I mean, if I had thought fit to leave nothing undone, nothing unsaid, I might have gained an acquittal. Not so, the deficiency which led to my conviction was not of words—certainly not. I did not have the boldness or impudence or inclination to address you as you would have liked me to address you, weeping, wailing, and lamenting, and saying and doing many things which you have been accustomed to hear from others, and which, as I say, are unworthy of me. I believed I should not do anything common or cowardly in the hour of danger. I do not now repent the manner of my defense. I would rather die having spoken after my manner than speak in your manner and live. Neither in war nor yet at law ought any man to use every way of escaping death. Often in battle there is no doubt if a man will throw away his arms and fall on his knees before his pursuers, he may escape death. In other dangers there are other ways of escaping death, if a man is willing to say and do anything.

The difficulty, my friends, is not in avoiding death, but in avoiding evil; for evil runs faster than death. I am old and move slowly, and the slower runner has overtaken me, and my accusers are keen and quick, and the faster runner, who is evil, has overtaken them. And now I depart hence condemned by you to suffer the penalty of death, and they, too, go their ways condemned by the truth to suffer the penalty of wickedness. I must abide by my award—let them abide by theirs. I suppose these things may be regarded as fated—and I think things are as they should be.

And now, O men who have condemned me, I would prophesy to you. I am about to die and that is the hour in which men are gifted with prophetic power. I prophesy to you who are my murderers that, immediately after my death, punishment far heavier than you have inflicted on me will await you. You have killed me because you wanted to escape the accuser, and not to give an account of your lives. That will not be as you suppose. I say there will be more accusers of you than there are now, accusers I have restrained: and as they are younger they will be more severe with you and you will be more offended at them. For if you think that by killing men you can avoid the accuser censuring your lives, you are mistaken; that is not a way of escape which is either possible or honorable. The easiest, noblest way is not to be crushing others but to be improving yourselves. This is the prophecy which I utter before my departure to the members of the jury who have condemned me.

Friends, who have acquitted me, I would like also to talk with you about this thing which has happened, while the judges are busy, and before I go to the place where I must die. Stay awhile, for we may as well talk with one another while there is time. You are my friends and I would like to show you the meaning of this event which has happened to me. O my judges—for you I may truly call judges—I should like to tell you of a wonderful occurrence. Before this, the familiar oracle within me has constantly been in the habit of opposing me even about trifles, if I was going to make a slip or error about anything. Now, as you see there has come upon me that which may be thought, and is generally believed to be, the last and worst evil. But the oracle made no sign of opposition, either as I was leaving my house and going out in the morning, or when I was going up into this court, or while I was speaking at anything I was going to say. I have often been stopped in the middle of a speech, but now in nothing I either said or did has the oracle opposed me. Why is this? I will tell you. I regard this as a proof that what has happened to me is a good, and that those of us who think that death is an evil are in error. This is a great proof to me of what I am saying, for the customary sign would surely have opposed me had I been going to evil and not to good.

Let us reflect in another way, and we shall see there is great reason to hope that death is a good.

Either death is a state of nothingness and utter unconsciousness, or, as men say, there is a change and migration of the soul from this world to another. Now if you suppose there is no consciousness, but a sleep like the sleep of him who is undisturbed even by the sight of dreams, death will be an unspeakable gain. If a person were to select the night in which his sleep was undisturbed even by dreams and were to compare this with the other days and nights of his life, and then were to tell us how many days and nights he passed in the course of his life better and more pleasantly than this one, I think any man, even a great king, will not find many such days or nights, when compared with the others. Now if death is like this, I say to die is to gain, for eternity is then only a single night. But if death is the journey to another place, and there, as men say, all the dead are, what good, O my friends and judges, can be greater than this? If indeed when the traveler arrives in the other world, he is delivered from the false judges in this world, and finds the true judges who are said to give judgment there, Minos, Rhadamanthus, Aeacus, and Triptolemus, and other sons of the gods who were righteous in their own life, that journey will be worth making. What would a man give if he might converse with Orpheus and Masaeus and Hesiod and Homer? Nay, if this is true, let me die again and again. I, too, shall have a wonderful interest in a place where I can converse with Palamedes, and Ajax, the son of Telamon, and other heroes of old who have suffered death through an unjust judgment. I think there will be pleasure, in comparing my own sufferings with theirs. Above all, I shall be able to continue my search into true and false knowledge. As in this world, so also in that; I shall find out who is wise, and who pretends to be wise but is not. What would a man give, O judges, to be able to examine the leader of the great Trojan expedition; or Odysseus or Sisyphus, or numberless others, men and women too! What infinite delight would there be in conversing with them and asking them questions! For in that world they do not put a man to death for such investigations, certainly not. For besides being happier in that world than in this, they will be immortal, if what is said is true.

Wherefore, O judges, be of good cheer about death, and know this truth—no evil can happen to a good man, either in life or after death. He and his are not neglected by the gods nor has my own approaching end happened by mere chance. I see clearly that to die and be released was better for me and therefore the oracle gave no sign. Because of this also, I am not angry with my accusers or my condemners. They have done me no harm, although neither of them meant to do me any good; and for this I gently blame them.

Still I have a favor to ask of them. When my sons are grown up, I would ask you, O my friends, to punish them. I would have you trouble them, as I troubled you, if they seem to care about riches, or anything, more than virtue. Or, if they pretend to be something when they are really nothing, then chastise them, as I chastised you, for not caring about what they ought to care, and thinking they are something when they are really nothing. And if you do this, I and my sons will have received justice at your hands. The hour of departure has arrived, and we go on our different ways—I to die, and you to live. Which is better only the god knows.

2.5 Aristotle on Happiness and the Life of Moderation

Student of Plato

Aristotle (384–322 BCE) was a student of Plato and is recognized, along with Plato, as one of the greatest philosophic minds of the ancient Western world. He made significant contributions to all areas of philosophy, as well as to the natural sciences. He founded a school in Athens called the Lyceum. His students became known as the Peripatetics (which means "to walk around") because of his habit of strolling in the garden of the school while giving instruction.

Aristotle was from Macedonia and, while living there, tutored Alexander, the son of the king. Alexander the Great, as he was later called, established a vast empire. Legend has it that as he traveled toward India on his conquests, Alexander sent plant and animal specimens back to Aristotle. Alexander's death in 323 triggered anti-Macedonian sentiment in Athens. Realizing that his life might be in danger, Aristotle left in a hurry and, recalling what happened to Socrates, reputedly made the comment that he was leaving lest he provide an opportunity for the Athenians to "sin twice against philosophy."

Aristotle was a **teleologist**. He believed that all existing things have a purpose (in Greek the word for "end," "goal," or "purpose" is *telos*) and that their purpose constitutes their good. So, when seeking to answer the question "How should one live?" Aristotle naturally considered the issue of what is the good for humans. Notice he did not ask what is his good. He was not concerned with individual good but with the good for all humans. He called this good **eudaimonia**, which is here translated as "happiness." This translation is somewhat misleading because in English happiness refers to a feeling. For Aristotle happiness was more than a feeling; it was also a way of acting and living. Hence, some have translated it as human "flourishing." Since flourishing involves achieving excellence, any discussion of *eudaimonia* or human flourishing must pay attention to the notion of virtue.

The word *virtue* (*areté* in Greek) refers to an excellence. The excellence of a thing is the full development of the potentials of its essential nature. Because the human animal is essentially a "rational" animal according to Aristotle, the good for humans must involve the realization of their rational natures. For Aristotle, a life of moderation accords best with reason. He viewed moral virtue as a mean between extremes and vice as either a deficiency or an excess. For example, courage is the mean between rashness (the vice of excess in confidence) and cowardice (the vice of deficiency in confidence). However, Aristotle did recognize that some actions have no mean. For example, there is no mean for the act of murder. How do you murder someone with moderation?

The selection that follows is from the first two books of the *Nicomachean Ethics,* which consists of lectures on *ethos* (character, habit) supposedly edited by Aristotle's son, Nicomachus. In the first book, Aristotle presented an argument in support of his claim that happiness is the chief end of humans and searches for a precise definition. In the second, he examined the question of virtue and proposed a theory about the nature of moral virtue. He argued that living a morally virtuous life is essential to being happy. Unfortunately, there is not enough space to include the rest of what he had to say here, but the following summary will tell you where his discussion leads.

The third and fourth books continue the discussion of moral virtue and introduce the issue of whether humans are free to choose to live a virtuous life. Book 5 examines the virtue of justice. This is the highest social value because, Aristotle argued, the good life cannot be lived apart from a good society. In Book 6, Aristotle shifted his attention from moral virtue to intellectual virtue. Humans are concerned with both theoretical and practical wisdom. Practical wisdom is essential to happiness because in order to live our lives well we must exercise good judgment. Books 7–9 deal with issues of moral strength and weakness, pleasure, and friendship. Pleasure is not the highest good, he argued, but it is part of the highest good. We also need good friends to be happy. In the final chapter, Aristotle focused on theoretical wisdom and argued that the highest human happiness is the contemplation of truth. Hence, only theoretical wisdom can lead to "primary" happiness, while practical wisdom can lead to "secondary" happiness.

Reading Aristotle will test your reading skills. He is not easy to read, in part because you are reading the translation of lecture notes edited by someone else. However, he is also dealing with issues about how to live at a profound level, and one must get into his mind, so to speak, in order to follow his line of reasoning. The effort will, however, be repaid as you learn to think about the issue of how to conduct one's life at a deeper level.

Be sure to activate your "I-don't-understand" list and go over it with a classmate or in class for clarification.

Reading Questions

1. What, according to Aristotle, have others declared the good to be?
2. Why must the chief good be desired for its own sake?
3. Aristotle said that on a very abstract level, happiness can be considered as "living well and doing well." If so, the next question becomes "In what specifically does this consist?" Aristotle argued that whatever it is it must be something final, chosen for its own sake, self-sufficient, and an end of action. If this is so, why will not health or wealth or pleasure or honor (all of which are goods) count as the chief good or happiness?

4. How did Aristotle arrive at the conclusion that the human good (happiness) is an activity of soul in accordance with virtue? (*Hint:* His argument begins with the notion that human beings have a function.)

5. Given what Aristotle said in Book 1, Section 9, about how happiness is acquired, how do you think he would respond to the question "Can someone be happy even if he or she suffers bad luck?"

6. What are the two kinds of virtue, and do the moral virtues arise by nature (are we born with them?) or by learning and practice?

7. Why did Aristotle conclude that virtue must be a state of character?

8. State in your own words what Aristotle meant when he claims, "Virtue, then, is a state of character concerned with choice, lying in a mean, i.e., the mean relative to us, this being determined by a rational principle, and by that principle by which the man of practical wisdom would determine it."

9. What are the excesses, deficiencies, and the means with respect to (a) feelings of fear and confidence, (b) giving and taking of money, (c) honor and dishonor, and (d) anger?

10. In Book 2, Section 9, Aristotle gave some advice for those who wish to practice virtue (hit the mean). Summarize his advice.

11. What are the similarities and differences between how a Confucian (see Section 2.3) would answer the question "How should one live?" and how Aristotle would answer it?

Nicomachean Ethics

ARISTOTLE

Book I

1.

EVERY ART AND EVERY INQUIRY, and similarly every action and pursuit, is thought to aim at some good; and for this reason the good has rightly been declared to be that at which all things aim. But a certain difference is found among ends; some are activities, others are products apart from the activities that produce them. Where there are ends apart from the actions, it is the nature of the products to be better than the activities. Now, as there are many actions, arts, and sciences, their ends also are many; the end of the medical art is health, that of shipbuilding a vessel, that of strategy victory, that of economics wealth. But where such arts fall under a single capacity—as

bridlemaking and the other arts concerned with the equipment of horses fall under the art of riding, and this and every military action under strategy, in the same way other arts fall under yet others—in all of these the ends of the master arts are to be preferred to all the subordinate ends; for it is for the sake of the former that the latter are pursued. It makes no difference whether the activities themselves are the ends of the actions, or something else apart from the activities, as in the case of the sciences just mentioned.

2.

If, then, there is some end of the things we do, which we desire for its own sake (everything else being desired for the sake of this), and if we do

Reprinted from Nicomachean Ethics, *translated by W. D. Ross (1925) Oxford University Press. Footnotes deleted.*

not choose everything for the sake of something else (for at that rate the process would go on to infinity, so that our desire would be empty and vain), clearly this must be the good and the chief good. Will not the knowledge of it, then, have a great influence on life? Shall we not, like archers who have a mark to aim at, be more likely to hit upon what is right? If so, we must try, in outline at least to determine what it is, and of which of the sciences or capacities it is the object. . . .

4.

Let us resume our inquiry and state, in view of the fact that all knowledge and every pursuit aims at some good, . . . what is the highest of all goods achievable by action. Verbally there is very general agreement; for both the general run of men and people of superior refinement say that it is happiness, and identify living well and doing well with being happy; but with regard to what happiness is they differ, and the many do not give the same account as the wise. For the former think it is some plain and obvious thing, like pleasure, wealth, or honour; they differ, however, from one another—and often even the same man identifies it with different things, with health when he is ill, with wealth when he is poor; but, conscious of their ignorance, they admire those who proclaim some great ideal that is above their comprehension. Now some thought that apart from these many goods there is another which is self-subsistent and causes the goodness of all these as well. To examine all the opinions that have been held were perhaps somewhat fruitless; enough to examine those that are most prevalent or that seem to be arguable. . . .

5.

Let us, however, resume our discussion from the point at which we digressed. To judge from the lives that men lead, most men, and men of the most vulgar type, seem (not without some ground) to identify the good, or happiness, with pleasure; which is the reason why they love the life of enjoyment. For there are, we may say, three prominent types of life—that just mentioned, the political, and thirdly the contemplative life. Now the mass of mankind are evidently quite slavish in their tastes, preferring a life suitable to beasts, but they get some ground for their view from the fact that many of those in high places share the tastes of Sardanapallus. A consideration of the prominent types of life shows that people of superior refinement and of active disposition identify happiness with honour; for this is, roughly speaking, the end of the political life. But it seems too superficial to be what we are looking for, since it is thought to depend on those who bestow honour rather than on him who receives it, but the good we divine to be something proper to a man and not easily taken from him. Further, men seem to pursue honour in order that they may be assured of their goodness; at least it is by men of practical wisdom that they seek to be honoured, and among those who know them, and on the ground of their virtue; clearly, then, according to them, at any rate, virtue is better. And perhaps one might even suppose this to be, rather than honour, the end of the political life. But even this appears somewhat incomplete; for possession of virtue seems actually compatible with being asleep, or with life-long inactivity, and, further, with the greatest sufferings and misfortunes; but a man who was living so no one would call happy, unless he were maintaining a thesis at all costs. But enough of this; for the subject has been sufficiently treated even in the current discussions. Third comes the contemplative life, which we shall consider later. The life of money-making is one undertaken under compulsion, and wealth is evidently not the good we are seeking; for it is merely useful and for the sake of something else. And so one might rather take the aforenamed objects to be ends; for they are loved for themselves. But it is evident that not even these are ends; yet many arguments have been thrown away in support of them. Let us leave this subject, then. . . .

7.

Let us again return to the good we are seeking, and ask what it can be. It seems different in different actions and arts; it is different in medicine, in strategy, and in the other arts likewise. What then is the good of each? Surely that for whose sake everything else is done. In medicine this is health, in strategy victory, in architecture a house, in any other sphere something else, and in every action and pursuit the end; for it is for the sake of this that all men do whatever else they do. Therefore, if there is an end for all that we do, this will be the good achievable by action, and if there are more than one, these will be the goods achievable by action.

So the argument has by a different course reached the same point; but we must try to state this even more clearly. Since there are evidently more than one end, and we choose some of these (e.g., wealth, flutes, and in general instruments) for the sake of something else, clearly not all ends are final ends; but the chief good is evidently something final. Therefore, if there is only one final end, this will be what we are seeking, and if there are more than one, the most final of these will be what we are seeking. Now we call that which is in itself worthy of pursuit more final than that which is worthy of pursuit for the sake of something else, and that which is never desirable for the sake of something else more final than the things that are desirable both in themselves and for the sake of that other thing, and therefore we call final without qualification that which is always desirable in itself and never for the sake of something else.

Now such a thing happiness, above all else, is held to be; for this we choose always for itself and never for the sake of something else, but honour, pleasure, reason, and every virtue we choose indeed for themselves (for if nothing resulted from them we should still choose each of them), but we choose them also for the sake of happiness, judging that by means of them we shall be happy. Happiness, on the other hand, no one chooses for the sake of these, nor, in general, for anything other than itself.

From the point of view of self-sufficiency the same result seems to follow; for the final good is thought to be self-sufficient. Now by self-sufficient we do not mean that which is sufficient for a man by himself, for one who lives a solitary life, but also for parents, children, wife, and in general for his friends and fellow citizens, since man is born for citizenship. But some limit must be set to this; for if we extend our requirement to ancestors and descendants and friends' friends we are in for an infinite series. Let us examine this question, however, on another occasion; the self-sufficient we now define as that which when isolated makes life desirable and lacking in nothing; and such we think happiness to be; and further we think it most desirable of all things, without being counted as one good thing among others—if it were so counted it would clearly be made more desirable by the addition of even the least of goods; for that which is added becomes an excess of goods, and of goods the greater is always more desirable. Happiness, then, is something final and self-sufficient, and is the end of action.

Presumably, however, to say that happiness is the chief good seems a platitude, and a clearer account of what it is is still desired. This might perhaps be given, if we could first ascertain the function of man. For just as for a flute-player, a sculptor, or any artist, and, in general, for all things that have a function or activity, the good and the "well" is thought to reside in the function, so would it seem to be for man, if he has a function. Have the carpenter, then, and the tanner certain functions or activities, and has man none? Is he born without a function? Or as eye, hand, foot, and in general each of the parts evidently has a function, may one lay it down that man similarly has a function apart from all these? What then can this be? Life seems to be common even to plants, but we are seeking what is peculiar to man. Let us exclude, therefore, the life of nutrition and growth. Next there would be a life of perception, but it also seems to be common even to the horse, the ox, and every animal. There remains, then, an active life of the element that has a rational principle; of this, one part has such a principle in the sense of being obedient to one, the other in the sense of possessing one and exercising thought. And, as "life of the rational element" also has two meanings, we must state that life in the sense of activity is what we mean; for this seems to be the more proper sense of the term. Now if the function of man is an activity of soul which follows or implies a rational principle, and if we say "a so-and-so" and "a good so-and-so" have a function which is the same in kind, e.g., a lyre-player and a good lyre-player, and so without qualification in all cases, eminence in respect of goodness being added to the name of the function (for the function of a lyre-player is to play the lyre, and that of a good lyre-player is to do so well): if this is the case, [and we state the function of man to be a certain kind of life, and this to be an activity or actions of the soul implying a rational principle, and the function of a good man to be the good and noble performance of these, and if any action is well performed when it is performed in accordance with the appropriate excellence: if this is the case,] human good turns out to be activity of soul in accordance with virtue, and if there are more than one virtue, in accordance with the best and most complete.

But we must add "in a complete life." For one swallow does not make a summer, nor does one day; and so too one day, or a short time, does not make a man blessed and happy. . . .

[*Editor's Note:* In Section 8, here omitted, Aristotle compares his view of happiness as living well and doing well with what most people say. He finds that many who have expressed their views on this topic agree in general with his own views. He takes this as confirmation that he is on the right track. Many regard happiness as consisting of three kinds of goods: worldly goods, bodily goods, and goods of the soul. While Aristotle wishes to stress in his account that happiness resides primarily in goods of the soul (the virtues), he acknowledges that we are not likely to call someone happy if they lack entirely worldly goods (wealth, friends, political influence) and bodily goods (noble family, handsome appearance, long life, and children). But both worldly goods and bodily goods often depend on circumstances beyond one's control. Can one be happy, even if misfortune diminishes some worldly and bodily goods? Some would say that happiness depends on good fortune. Others that it is a matter of acquiring virtue or excellence.]

9.

For this reason also the question is asked, whether happiness is to be acquired by learning or by habituation or some other sort of training, or comes in virtue of some divine providence or again by chance. Now if there is any gift of the gods to men, it is reasonable that happiness should be god-given, and most surely god-given of all human things inasmuch as it is the best. But this question would perhaps be more appropriate to another inquiry; happiness seems, however, even if it is not god-sent but comes as a result of virtue and some process of learning or training, to be among the most god-like things; for that which is the prize and end of virtue seems to be the best thing in the world, and something god-like and blessed.

It will also on this view be very generally shared; for all who are not maimed as regards their potentiality for virtue may win it by a certain kind of study and care. But if it is better to be happy thus than by chance, it is reasonable that the facts should be so, since everything that depends on the action of nature is by nature as good as it can be, and similarly everything that depends on art or any rational cause, and especially if it depends on the best of all causes. To entrust to chance what is greatest and most noble would be a very defective arrangement.

The answer to the question we are asking is plain also from the definition of happiness; for it has been said to be a virtuous activity of soul, of a certain kind. Of the remaining goods, some must necessarily pre-exist as conditions of happiness, and others are naturally co-operative and useful as instruments. And this will be found to agree with what we said at the outset; for we stated the end of political science to be the best end, and political science spends most of its pains on making the citizens to be of a certain character, viz. good and capable of noble acts.

It is natural, then, that we call neither ox nor horse nor any other of the animals happy; for none of them is capable of sharing in such activity. For this reason also a boy is not happy; for he is not yet capable of such acts, owing to his age; and boys who are called happy are being congratulated by reason of the hopes we have for them. For there is required, as we said, not only complete virtue but also a complete life, since many changes occur in life, and all manner of chances, and the most prosperous may fall into great misfortunes in old age, as is told of Priam in the Trojan Cycle; and one who has experienced such chances and has ended wretchedly no one calls happy. . . .

13.

Since happiness is an activity of soul in accordance with perfect virtue, we must consider the nature of virtue; for perhaps we shall thus see better the nature of happiness. . . .

Book II

1.

Virtue, then, being of two kinds, intellectual and moral, intellectual virtue in the main owes both its birth and its growth to teaching (for which reason it requires experience and time), while moral virtue comes about as a result of habit, whence also its name *ethiké* is one that is formed by a slight variation from the word *ethos* (habit). From this it is also plain that none of the moral virtues arises in us by nature; for nothing that exists by nature can form a habit contrary to its nature. For instance the stone which by nature moves downwards cannot be habituated to move upwards, not even if one tries to train it by throwing it up ten thousand times; nor can fire be habituated to move downwards, nor can anything else that by nature behaves in one way be trained to behave in another. Neither by nature, then, nor contrary to nature do the virtues arise in us; rather we are adapted by nature to receive them, and are made perfect by habit.

Again, of all the things that come to us by nature we first acquire the potentiality and later exhibit the activity (this is plain in the case of the senses; for it was not by often seeing or often hearing that we got these senses, but on the contrary we had them before we used them, and did not come to have them by using them); but

the virtues we get by first exercising them, as also happens in the case of the arts as well. For the things we have to learn before we can do them, we learn by doing them, e.g., men become builders by building and lyre-players by playing the lyre; so too we become just by doing just acts, temperate by doing temperate acts, brave by doing brave acts.

This is confirmed by what happens in states; for legislators make the citizens good by forming habits in them, and this is the wish of every legislator, and those who do not effect it miss their mark, and it is in this that a good constitution differs from a bad one.

Again, it is from the same causes and by the same means that every virtue is both produced and destroyed, and similarly every art; for it is from playing the lyre that both good and bad lyre-players are produced. And the corresponding statement is true of builders and of all the rest; men will be good or bad builders as a result of building well or badly. For if this were not so, there would have been no need of a teacher, but all men would have been born good or bad at their craft. This, then, is the case with the virtues also; by doing the acts that we do in our transactions with other men we become just or unjust, and by doing the acts that we do in the presence of danger, and being habituated to feel fear or confidence, we become brave or cowardly. The same is true of appetites and feelings of anger; some men become temperate and good-tempered, others self-indulgent and irascible, by behaving in one way or the other in the appropriate circumstances. Thus, in one word, states of character arise out of like activities. This is why the activities we exhibit must be of a certain kind; it is because the states of character correspond to the differences between these. It makes no small difference, then, whether we form habits of one kind or of another from our very youth; it makes a very great difference, or rather *all* the difference. . . .

5.

Next we must consider what virtue is. Since things that are found in the soul are of three kinds—passions, faculties, states of character, virtue must be one of these. By passions I mean appetite, anger, fear, confidence, envy, joy, friendly feeling, hatred, longing, emulation, pity, and in general the feelings that are accompanied by pleasure or pain; by faculties the things in virtue of which we are said to be capable of feeling these, e.g., of becoming angry or being pained or feeling pity; by states of character the things in virtue of which we stand well or badly with reference to the passions, e.g., with reference to anger we stand badly if we feel it violently or too weakly, and well if we feel it moderately; and similarly with reference to the other passions.

Now neither the virtues nor the vices are *passions,* because we are not called good or bad on the ground of our passions, but are so called on the ground of our virtues and our vices, and because we are neither praised nor blamed for our passions (for the man who feels fear or anger is not praised, nor is the man who simply feels anger blamed, but the man who feels it in a certain way), but for our virtues and our vices we are praised or blamed.

Again, we feel anger and fear without choice, but the virtues are modes of choice or involve choice. Further, in respect of the passions we are said to be moved, but in respect of the virtues and the vices we are said not to be moved but to be disposed in a particular way.

For these reasons also they are not *faculties;* for we are neither called good nor bad, nor praised nor blamed, for the simple capacity of feeling the passions; again, we have the faculties by nature, but we are not made good or bad by nature; we have spoken of this before.

If, then, the virtues are neither passions nor faculties, all that remains is that they should be *states of character.*

Thus we have stated what virtue is in respect of its genus.

6.

We must, however, not only describe virtue as a state of character, but also say what sort of state it is. We may remark, then, that every virtue or excellence both brings into good condition the thing of which it is the excellence and makes the work of that thing be done well; e.g., the excellence of the eye makes both the eye and its work good; for it is by the excellence of the eye that we see well. Similarly the excellence of the horse makes a horse both good in itself and good at running and at carrying its rider and at awaiting the attack of the enemy. Therefore, if this is true in every case, the virtue of man also will be the state of character which makes a man good and which makes him do his own work well.

How this is to happen we have stated already, but it will be made plain also by the following consideration of the specific nature of virtue. In everything that is continuous and divisible it is possible to take more, less, or an equal amount, and that either in terms of the thing itself or relative to us; and the equal is an intermediate between excess and defect. By the intermediate in the object I mean that which is equidistant from each of the extremes, which is one and the same for all men; by the intermediate relative to us that which is neither too much nor too little—and this is not one, nor the same for all. For instance, if ten is many and two is few, six is the intermediate, taken in terms of the object; for it exceeds and is exceeded by an equal amount; this is intermediate according to arithmetical proportion. But the intermediate relative to us is not to be taken so; if ten pounds are too much for a particular person to eat and two too little, it does not follow that the trainer will order six pounds; for this also is perhaps too much for the person who is to take it, or too little—too little for Milo, too much for the beginner in athletic exercises. The same is true of running and wrestling. Thus a master of any art avoids excess and defect, but seeks the intermediate and chooses this—the intermediate not in the object but relative to us. If it is thus, then, that every art does its work well—by looking to the intermediate and judging its works by this standard (so that we often say of good works of art that it is not possible either to take away or to add anything, implying that excess and defect destroy the goodness of works of art, while the mean preserves it; and good artists, as we say, look to this in their work), and if, further, virtue is more exact and better than any art, as nature also is, then virtue must have the quality of aiming at the intermediate. I mean moral virtue; for it is this that is concerned with passions and actions, and in these there is excess, defect, and the intermediate. For instance, both fear and confidence and appetite and anger and pity and in general pleasure and pain may be felt both too much and too little, and in both cases not well; but to feel them at the right times, with reference to the right objects, towards the right people, with the right motive, and in the right way, is what is both intermediate and best, and this is characteristic of virtue. Similarly with regard to actions also there is excess, defect, and the intermediate. Now virtue is concerned with passions and actions, in which excess is a form of failure, and so is defect, while the intermediate is praised and is a form of success; and being praised and being successful are both characteristics of virtue. Therefore virtue is a kind of mean, since, as we have seen, it aims at what is intermediate.

Again, it is possible to fail in many ways (for evil belongs to the class of the unlimited, as the Pythagoreans conjectured, and good to that of the limited), while to succeed is possible only in one way (for which reason also one is easy and the other difficult—to miss the mark easy, to hit it difficult); for these reasons also, then, excess and defect are characteristic of vice, and the mean of virtue;

> For men are good in but one way, but bad in many.

Virtue, then, is a state of character concerned with choice, lying in a mean, i.e., the mean relative to us, this being determined by a rational principle, and by that principle by which the man of practical wisdom would determine it. Now it is a mean between two vices, that which depends on excess and that which depends on defect; and again it is a mean because the vices respectively fall short of or exceed what is right in both passions and actions, while virtue both finds and chooses that which is intermediate. Hence in respect of its substance and the definition which states its essence virtue is a mean, with regard to what is best and right an extreme.

But not every action nor every passion admits of a mean; for some have names that already imply badness, e.g., spite, shamelessness, envy, and in the case of actions adultery, theft, murder; for all of these and suchlike things imply by their names that they are themselves bad, and not the excesses or deficiencies of them. It is not possible, then, ever to be right with regard to them; one must always be wrong. Nor does goodness or badness with regard to such things depend on committing adultery with the right woman, at the right time, and in the right way, but simply to do any of them is to go wrong. It would be equally absurd, then, to expect that in unjust, cowardly, and voluptuous action there should be a mean, an excess, and a deficiency; for at that rate there would be a mean of excess and of deficiency, an excess of excess, and a deficiency of deficiency. But as there is no excess and deficiency of temperance and courage because what is intermediate is in a sense an extreme, so too of the actions we have mentioned there is no mean nor any excess and deficiency, but however they are done they are wrong; for in general there is neither a mean of excess and deficiency, nor excess and deficiency of a mean.

7.

We must, however, not only make this general statement, but also apply it to the individual facts. For among statements about conduct those which are general apply more widely, but those which are particular are more genuine, since conduct has to do with individual cases, and our statements must harmonize with the facts in these cases. We may take these cases from our table. With regard to feelings of fear and confidence courage is the mean; of the people who exceed, he who exceeds in fearlessness has no name (many of the states have no name), while the man who exceeds in confidence is rash, and he who exceeds in fear and falls short in confidence is a coward. With regard to pleasures and pains—not all of them, and not so much with regard to the pains—the mean is temperance, the excess self-indulgence. Persons deficient with regard to the pleasures are not often found; hence such persons also have received no name. But let us call them "insensible."

With regard to giving and taking of money, the mean is liberality, the excess and the defect prodigality and meanness. In these actions people exceed and fall short in contrary ways; the prodigal exceeds in spending and falls short in taking, while the mean man exceeds in taking and falls short in spending. (At present we are giving a mere outline or summary, and are satisfied with this; later these states will be more exactly determined.) With regard to money there are also other dispositions—a mean, magnificence (for the magnificent man differs from the liberal man; the former deals with large sums, the latter with small ones), and excess, tastelessness and vulgarity, and a deficiency, niggardliness; these differ from the states opposed to liberality, and the mode of their difference will be stated later.

With regard to honour and dishonour the mean is proper pride, the excess is known as a sort of "empty vanity," and the deficiency is undue humility; and as we said liberality was related to magnificence, differing from it by dealing with small sums, so there is a state similarly related to proper pride, being concerned with small honours while that is concerned with great. For it is possible to desire honour as one ought, and more than one ought, and less, and the man who exceeds in his desires is called ambitious, the man who falls short unambitious, while the intermediate person has no name. The dispositions also are nameless, except that that of the ambitious man is called ambition. Hence the people who are at the extremes lay claim to the middle place; and we ourselves sometimes call the intermediate person ambitious and sometimes unambitious, and sometimes praise the ambitious man and sometimes the unambitious. The reason of our doing this will be stated in what follows; but now let us speak of the remaining states according to the method which has been indicated.

With regard to anger also there is an excess, a deficiency, and a mean. Although they can scarcely be said to have names, yet since we call the intermediate person good-tempered let us call the mean good temper; of the persons at the extremes let the one who exceeds be called irascible, and his vice irascibility, and the man who falls short an inirascible sort of person, and the deficiency inirascibility. . . .

9.

That moral virtue is a mean, then, and in what sense it is so, and that it is a mean between two vices, the one involving excess, the other deficiency, and that it is such because its character is to aim at what is intermediate in passions and in actions, has been sufficiently stated. Hence also it is no easy task to be good. For in everything it is no easy task to find the middle, e.g., to find the middle of a circle is not for everyone but for him who knows; so, too, any one can get angry—that is easy—or give or spend money; but to do this to the right person, to the right extent, at the right time, with the right motive, and in the right way, *that* is not for everyone, nor is it easy; wherefore goodness is both rare and laudable and noble. Hence he who aims at the intermediate must first depart from what is the more contrary to it, as Calypso advises—

Hold the ship out beyond that surf and spray.

For of the extremes one is more erroneous, one less so; therefore, since to hit the mean is hard in the extreme, we must as a second best, as people say, take the least of the evils; and this will be done best in the way we describe.

But we must consider the things towards which we ourselves also are easily carried away; for some of us tend to one thing, some to another; and this will be recognizable from the pleasure and the pain we feel. We must drag ourselves away to the contrary extreme; for we shall get into the intermediate state by drawing well away from error, as people do in straightening sticks that are bent.

Now in everything the pleasant or pleasure is most to be guarded against; for we do not judge it impartially. We ought, then, to feel towards pleasure as the elders of the people felt towards Helen, and in all circumstances repeat their saying; for if we dismiss pleasure thus we are less likely to go astray. It is by doing this, then, (to sum the matter up) that we shall best be able to hit the mean.

But this is no doubt difficult, and especially in individual cases; for it is not easy to determine both how and with whom and on what provocation and how long one should be angry; for we too sometimes praise those who fall short and call them good-tempered, but sometimes we praise those who get angry and call them manly. The man, however, who deviates little from goodness is not blamed, whether he do so in the direction of the more or of the less, but only the man who deviates more widely; for *he* does not fail to be noticed. But up to what point and to what extent a man must deviate before he becomes blameworthy it is not easy to determine by reasoning, any more than anything else that is perceived by the senses; such things depend on particular facts, and the decision rests with perception. So much, then, is plain, that the intermediate state is in all things to be praised, but that we must incline sometimes towards the excess, sometimes towards the deficiency; for so shall we most easily hit the mean and what is right.

2.6 The Song of God

Have you ever faced a conflict of duties? For example, have you ever been torn between your duty to be loyal to a friend and your obligation to tell the truth? Have you ever confronted a situation in which, in order to do right, you had to do wrong? Have you ever been faced with options, neither of which were morally desirable? Have you ever felt sad because you live in a world where so often you must choose between doing the "lesser of two evils"?

In this same world, we are taught that we should strive for moral perfection. Reason demands that we should always do what is right and good, never what is wrong. Yes, we must face temptation and wrestle with evil, but in the end are we not expected to triumph over sin? Jesus reportedly said, "Be perfect, as your Father in heaven is perfect." But moral perfection, be it demanded by reason or by God, is impossible. Try as we might, we cannot make this a morally black-and-white world; too many choices are various shades of moral gray.

If you have ever faced moral conflicts or wondered how moral perfection is possible in a morally imperfect world, you ought to be able to identify with Arjuna, one of the main characters in the *Bhagavad-Gita* (*Song of God*). This Hindu poem forms part of India's greatest epic poem, *Mahabharata*. It was written sometime between the fourth and second centuries BCE. Much of the *Gita* is a conversation between Arjuna, who is a member of the warrior caste and a leader of the Pandava family, and Sri (Lord) Krishna, his cousin and the incarnation of the god Vishnu (Vishnu is the god responsible, according to traditional Hindu mythology, for sustaining the universe after it has been created by the god Brahman). This conversation is narrated by Sanjaya, a poet and charioteer. It takes place just before a horrendous battle, which is part of a civil war started by some of Arjuna's relatives. Krishna attempts to get Arjuna to do his duty, which, since he is a warrior and since he is on the side of right in this war, is to fight. However, Arjuna is reluctant because those whom he must fight and kill are his relatives and friends. We can formulate Arjuna's conflict as a dilemma:

1. Either Arjuna ought to fight or he ought not to fight.
2. If he fights, he will violate his duty to protect his relatives.

3. If he does not fight, he will violate his duty as a warrior and his obligation to fight in a just war.
4. Therefore, either he violates one set of duties or he violates another set of duties.

To appreciate the depth of this dilemma in the Indian context, we need some background information about Hinduism. The word for duty is **dharma**, which means, among other things, the order or law underlying the cosmos and embodied in social and ethical law codes. In this context, to violate one's duty is to violate *dharma* and thus to upset the natural, cosmic order. An immoral act has a negative impact on the whole universe. According to Hindu moral theory, there is a moral and natural law called the law of **karma**. Karma comes from the Sanskrit word *karman,* which means "action" or "the consequences of action." The law of *karma* states, "what you sow, so shall you reap." If you do good deeds, you will experience good things sometime in this or a future life; and if you act wrongly, you will suffer accordingly. The ultimate goal in life is to escape **samsara**, the cycle of rebirth, death, and suffering that characterizes human life. Our *karma* traps us in *samsara* because it determines our **reincarnation**, or rebirth into a new physical body. If the full consequences of our karma do not come in this life, we must live another life, and another, and another, and another, until there is no *karma* left and we get it right. In this context, the question of how one should live takes on added urgency because a wrong answer affects both the order of the universe and your future lives.

However, how can "getting it right" be possible? If, like Arjuna, we are faced with situations in which no matter what we do we will get bad *karma,* there seems no hope of breaking the cycle. Arjuna is doomed if he fights and doomed if he does not fight. We live in a morally imperfect world, and we can never hope to achieve moral perfection. However, even if we could, even if all our actions produced good *karma,* we would still be reborn. If we do evil, we are reborn to reap the bad consequences. If we do good, we are reborn to reap the good consequences.

We have now uncovered a more universal form of Arjuna's dilemma, what A. L. Herman calls the "dilemma of action." We can express it as follows:

1. Either you do good acts or you do bad acts.
2. If you do good acts, you are bound to be reborn to reap the good results.
3. If you do bad acts, you are bound to be reborn to reap the bad results.
4. Therefore, you reap good results or bad results, but, in either case, you are reborn.

We may not believe that transgressions of moral codes violate the natural order of things, and we may not believe in the law of *karma* or the idea of reincarnation. Nevertheless, each of us in his or her own way faces a form of Arjuna's dilemma—the conflict of duties, the necessity to do wrong in order to do right, the lack of moral perfection.

Is there a way out of these moral dilemmas? Krishna teaches that freedom from these dilemmas is found in the practice of disciplined action (*karmayoga*). All action is to be performed detached from the consequences of action. Or, to put it another way, act unselfishly. Do what is right because it is right, not because the consequences will bring benefit or harm. How can this be done? One can do this by first gaining knowledge (*jnanayoga*) of our true natures (an eternal, unchanging self) and by dedicating the fruits of our actions in devotion (*bhaktiyoga*) to God. These three yogas or disciplines (*karma, jnana,* and *bhakti*) are interconnected. To live the good life requires acting in an appropriate way (unselfishly), knowing who you really are (an eternal self), and being devoted to God.

The first book describes Arjuna's state of mind and the dilemma in which he finds himself. The second book states the assumptions on which Krishna's advice is based: (1) The self is eternal and survives bodily death, and (2) one must do one's moral duty. Although this selection ends with the second book, the rest of the *Gita* goes on to elaborate the themes found in the second book. The third and fourth books develop the relationship between sacrifice and action, and the fifth and sixth books examine the tension between a life of renunciation (withdrawal from action) and action. In the final six books, Krishna recapitulates his basic teaching and integrates it with the need for religious devotion. The climax comes with Krishna's awe-inspiring theophany (revelation of his divinity).

The *Gita* is the "Song of God." Hence it is meant to be sung aloud. Lacking the music, we can and should speak it aloud in order to appreciate its poetic qualities as well as its meaning. Read it aloud dramatically and its meaning will be clearer to you.

I have summarized Ramesh N. Patel's explanation of the philosophical implications of the *Gita*. Patel's ideas help us to understand the profound philosophy of the *Gita*. To find the summary, go to http://philosophy.wadsworth.com and select the companion Web site for *Voices of Wisdom*.

Reading Questions

1. Why does Arjuna declare, "We don't know which weight is worse to bear—our conquering them or their conquering us"?
2. What reasons does Krishna present to Arjuna in support of his advice to fight?
3. What is the method of "spiritual discipline" (*karmayoga*)?
4. What are the characteristics, according to Krishna, of a person "deep in contemplation whose insight and thought are sure"?
5. How would following Krishna's advice solve Arjuna's dilemma?
6. Do you think living the sort of life Krishna recommends (knowing the true nature of the self, doing one's moral duty, being unconcerned about the results of one's action, devotion to the divine) would be a good way to live? Why, or why not?

Bhagavad-Gita

I. The First Teaching: Arjuna's Dejection

Arjuna, his war flag a rampant monkey,
saw Dhritarashtra's sons assembled
as weapons were ready to clash,
and he lifted his bow.

He told his charioteer:
"Krishna,
halt my chariot
between the armies!

Far enough for me to see
these men who lust for war,

From The Bhagavad-Gita, *translated by Barbara Stoler Miller. Copyright © 1986 by Barbara Stoler Miller. Used by permission of Bantam Books, a division of Random House, Inc., pages 23–39.*

ready to fight with me
in the strain of battle.

I see men gathered here,
eager to fight,
bent on serving the folly
of Dhritarashtra's son."

When Arjuna had spoken,
Krishna halted
their splendid chariot
between the armies.

Facing Bhishma and Drona
and all the great kings,
he said, "Arjuna, see
the Kuru men assembled here!"

Arjuna saw them standing there:
fathers, grandfathers, teachers,
uncles, brothers, sons,
grandsons, and friends.

He surveyed his elders
and companions in both armies,
all his kinsmen
assembled together.

The greed that distorts their reason
blinds them to the sin they commit
in ruining the family, blinds them
to the crime of betraying friends.

How can we ignore the wisdom
of turning from this evil
when we see the sin
of family destruction, Krishna?

When the family is ruined,
the timeless laws of family duty
perish; and when duty is lost,
chaos overwhelms the family.

In overwhelming chaos, Krishna,
women of the family are corrupted;
and when women are corrupted,
disorder is born in society.

This discord drags the violators
and the family itself to hell;
for ancestors fall when rites
of offering rice and water lapse.

The sins of men who violate
the family create disorder in society
that undermines the constant laws
of caste and family duty.

Krishna, we have heard
that a place in hell
is reserved for men
who undermine family duties.

I lament the great sin
we commit when our greed
for kingship and pleasures
drives us to kill our kinsmen.

Dejected, filled with strange pity,
he said this:

"Krishna, I see my kinsmen
gathered here, wanting war.

My limbs sink,
my mouth is parched,
my body trembles,
the hair bristles on my flesh.

The magic bow slips
from my hand, my skin burns,
I cannot stand still,
my mind reels.

I see omens of chaos,
Krishna; I see no good
in killing my kinsmen
in battle.

Krishna, I seek no victory,
or kingship or pleasures.
What use to us are kingship,
delights, or life itself?

We sought kingship, delights,
and pleasures for the sake of those
assembled to abandon their lives
and fortunes in battle.

They are teachers, fathers, sons,
and grandfathers, uncles, grandsons,
fathers and brothers of wives,
and other men of our family.

I do not want to kill them
even if I am killed, Krishna;

not for kingship of all three worlds,
much less for the earth!

What joy is there for us, Krishna,
in killing Dhritarashtra's sons?
Evil will haunt us if we kill them,
though their bows are drawn to kill.

Honor forbids us to kill
our cousins, Dhritarashtra's sons;
how can we know happiness
if we kill our own kinsmen?

If Dhritarashtra's armed sons
kill me in battle when I am unarmed
and offer no resistance,
it will be my reward."

Saying this in the time of war,
Arjuna slumped into the chariot
and laid down his bow and arrows,
his mind tormented by grief.

The Second Teaching

PHILOSOPHY AND SPIRITUAL DISCIPLINE

Sanjaya

Arjuna sat dejected,
filled with pity,
his sad eyes blurred by tears.
Krishna gave him counsel.

Lord Krishna

Why this cowardice
in time of crisis, Arjuna?
The coward is ignoble, shameful,
foreign to the ways of heaven.

Don't yield to impotence!
It is unnatural in you!
Banish this petty weakness from your heart.
Rise to the fight, Arjuna!

Arjuna

Krishna, how can I fight
against Bhishma and Drona
with arrows
when they deserve my worship?

It is better in this world
to beg for scraps of food
than to eat meals
smeared with the blood
of elders I killed
at the height of their power
while their goals
were still desires.

We don't know which weight
is worse to bear—
our conquering them
or their conquering us.
We will not want to live
if we kill
the sons of Dhritarashtra
assembled before us.

The flaw of pity
blights my very being;
conflicting sacred duties
confound my reason.
I ask you to tell me
decisively—Which is better?
I am your pupil.
Teach me what I seek!

I see nothing
that could drive away
the grief
that withers my senses;
even if I won kingdoms
of unrivaled wealth
on earth
and sovereignty over gods.

Sanjaya

Arjuna told this
to Krishna—then saying,
"I shall not fight,"
he fell silent.

Mocking him gently,
Krishna gave this counsel
as Arjuna sat dejected,
between the two armies.

Lord Krishna

You grieve for those beyond grief;
and you speak words of insight;

but learned men do not grieve
for the dead or the living.

Never have I not existed,
nor you, nor these kings;
and never in the future
shall we cease to exist.

Just as the embodied self
enters childhood, youth, and old age,
so does it enter another body;
this does not confound a steadfast man.

Contacts with matter make us feel
heat and cold, pleasure and pain.
Arjuna, you must learn to endure
fleeting things—they come and go!

When these cannot torment a man,
when suffering and joy are equal
for him and he has courage,
he is fit for immortality.

Nothing of nonbeing comes to be,
nor does being cease to exist;
the boundary between these two
is seen by men who see reality.

Indestructible is the presence
that pervades all this;
no one can destroy
this unchanging reality.

Our bodies are known to end,
but the embodied self is enduring,
indestructible, and immeasurable;
therefore, Arjuna, fight the battle!

He who thinks this self a killer
and he who thinks it killed,
both fail to understand;
it does not kill, nor is it killed.

It is not born,
it does not die;
having been,
it will never not be;
unborn, enduring,
constant, and primordial,
it is not killed
when the body is killed.

Arjuna, when a man knows the self
to be indestructible, enduring, unborn,

unchanging, how does he kill
or cause anyone to kill?

As a man discards
worn-out clothes
to put on new
and different ones,
so the embodied self
discards
its worn-out bodies
to take on other new ones.

Weapons do not cut it,
fire does not burn it,
waters do not wet it,
wind does not wither it.

It cannot be cut or burned;
it cannot be wet or withered;
it is enduring, all-pervasive,
fixed, immovable, and timeless.

It is called unmanifest,
inconceivable, and immutable;
since you know that to be so,
you should not grieve!

If you think of its birth
and death as ever-recurring,
then too, Great Warrior,
you have no cause to grieve!

Death is certain for anyone born,
and birth is certain for the dead;
since the cycle is inevitable,
you have no cause to grieve!

Creatures are unmanifest in origin,
manifest in the midst of life,
and unmanifest again in the end.
Since this is so, why do you lament?

Rarely someone
sees it,
rarely another
speaks it,
rarely anyone
hears it—
even hearing it,
no one really knows it.

The self embodied in the body
of every being is indestructible;

you have no cause to grieve
for all these creatures, Arjuna!

Look to your own duty;
do not tremble before it;
nothing is better for a warrior
than a battle of sacred duty.

The doors of heaven open
for warriors who rejoice
to have a battle like this
thrust on them by chance.

If you fail to wage this war
of sacred duty,
you will abandon your own duty
and fame only to gain evil.

People will tell
of your undying shame,
and for a man of honor
shame is worse than death.

The great chariot warriors will think
you deserted in fear of battle;
you will be despised
by those who held you in esteem.

Your enemies will slander you,
scorning your skill
in so many unspeakable ways—
could any suffering be worse?

If you are killed, you win heaven;
if you triumph, you enjoy the earth;
therefore, Arjuna, stand up
and resolve to fight the battle!

Impartial to joy and suffering,
gain and loss, victory and defeat,
arm yourself for the battle,
lest you fall into evil.

Understanding is defined in terms
    of philosophy;
now hear it in spiritual discipline.
Armed with this understanding, Arjuna,
you will escape the bondage of action.

No effort in this world
is lost or wasted;
a fragment of sacred duty
saves you from great fear.

This understanding is unique
in its inner core of resolve;
diffuse and pointless are the ways
irresolute men understand.

Undiscerning men who delight
in the tenets of ritual lore
utter florid speech, proclaiming,
"There is nothing else!"

Driven by desire, they strive after heaven
and contrive to win powers and delights,
but their intricate ritual language
bears only the fruit of action in rebirth.

Obsessed with powers and delights,
their reason lost in words,
they do not find in contemplation
this understanding of inner resolve.

Arjuna, the realm of sacred lore
is nature—beyond its triad of qualities,
dualities, and mundane rewards,
be forever lucid, alive to your self.

For the discerning priest,
all of sacred lore
has no more value than a well
when water flows everywhere.

Be intent on action,
not on the fruits of action;
avoid attraction to the fruits
and attachment to inaction!

Perform actions, firm in discipline,
relinquishing attachment;
be impartial to failure and success—
this equanimity is called discipline.

Arjuna, action is far inferior
to the discipline of understanding;
so seek refuge in understanding—pitiful
are men drawn by fruits of action.

Disciplined by understanding,
one abandons both good and evil deeds;
so arm yourself for discipline—
discipline is skill in actions.

Wise men disciplined by understanding
relinquish the fruit born of action;

freed from these bonds of rebirth,
they reach a place beyond decay.

When your understanding passes beyond
the swamp of delusion,
you will be indifferent to all
that is heard in sacred lore.

When your understanding turns
from sacred lore to stand fixed,
immovable in contemplation,
then you will reach discipline.

Arjuna

Krishna, what defines a man
deep in contemplation whose insight
and thought are sure? How would he speak?
How would he sit? How would he move?

Lord Krishna

When he gives up desires in his mind,
is content with the self within himself,
then he is said to be a man
whose insight is sure, Arjuna.

When suffering does not disturb his mind,
when his craving for pleasures has vanished,
when attraction, fear, and anger are gone,
he is called a sage whose thought is sure.

When he shows no preference
in fortune or misfortune
and neither exults nor hates,
his insight is sure.

When, like a tortoise retracting
its limbs, he withdraws his senses
completely from sensuous objects,
his insight is sure.

Sensuous objects fade
when the embodied self abstains from food;
the taste lingers, but it too fades
in the vision of higher truth.

Even when a man of wisdom
tries to control them, Arjuna,
the bewildering senses
attack his mind with violence.

Controlling them all,
with discipline he should focus on me;

when his senses are under control,
his insight is sure.

Brooding about sensuous objects
makes attachment to them grow;
from attachment desire arises,
from desire anger is born.

From anger comes confusion;
from confusion memory lapses;
from broken memory understanding
    is lost;
from loss of understanding, he is ruined.

But a man of inner strength
whose senses experience objects
without attraction and hatred,
in self-control, finds serenity.

In serenity, all his sorrows
dissolve;
his reason becomes serene,
his understanding sure.

Without discipline,
he has no understanding or inner power;
without inner power, he has no peace;
and without peace where is joy?

If his mind submits to the play
of the senses,
they drive away insight,
as wind drives a ship on water.

So, Great Warrior, when withdrawal
of the senses
from sense objects is complete,
discernment is firm.

When it is night for all creatures,
a master of restraint is awake;
when they are awake, it is night
for the sage who sees reality.

As the mountainous depths
of the ocean
are unmoved when waters
rush into it,
so the man unmoved
when desires enter him
attains a peace that eludes
the man of many desires.

When he renounces all desires
and acts without craving,
possessiveness,
or individuality, he finds peace.

This is the place of the infinite spirit;
achieving it, one is freed from delusion;
abiding in it even at the time of death,
one finds the pure calm of infinity.

2.7 Does Life Have Meaning?

Most of you have probably seen a cartoon of someone climbing a mountain and reaching a bearded guru in order to ask, "What is the meaning of life?" The answer is usually unexpected and slightly humorous.

Imagine a variation. Imagine the seeker reaching the guru and asking, "Why must life have a meaning?" Perhaps the guru is suddenly dumbfounded in this new version so the seeker continues, "I mean, isn't it all right for life to be pointless?"

This second version may seem odd because we all assume that life must have a meaning and that it is important that it does. The second version does not make that assumption. Instead it wonders about why we think it necessary or important that life have a meaning.

Imagine a third version of the cartoon. The seeker reaches the guru and asks, "What does it mean to ask what is the meaning of life?" Perhaps this time the guru is not dumbfounded, but answers, "You have been studying too much philosophy." That may be true. You have already learned to question questions by asking how they might best be understood and formulated. So what are we to make of the question about the meaning of life? What does it mean?

If you think about it, it is a rather odd question. If what we do, think, and believe as we live our lives makes sense, why must life as a whole make sense? If there are good reasons for how I live my life in its details, why do I need a reason for my life taken as a whole? However, is the question even a question about *my* life? Is it not a question about every life? If we interpret the question this way, as a question about the whole of every human life (should we include animals and plants?), then the answer becomes both more difficult and more questionable. How could there be a good reason for every life that will ever be lived? Why should we think there is such a reason? Just because something supports my computer, why should I presume that there is something that supports everything in the universe?

I have assumed that the question about the meaning of life is a question about finding a good reason for living. Shift your focus a bit and think about what might be a "good reason" for living. Is there only one? Could there be many? How is the search for a good reason for living connected to the search for the good life? Does the answer to the question, "How should one live?" also provide an answer to the question, "What is the meaning of life?" If life has no meaning, no good reason, and no point, does it make any sense to worry about how we should conduct our lives?

Daniel Kolak, Director of the Cognitive Science Laboratory at William Paterson University, and Raymond Martin, professor of philosophy at the University of Maryland, explore questions about the meaning and purpose of human life in the following essay. They suggest that many of us often look in the wrong place for an answer.

Finding a satisfactory answer involves a reorientation in our thinking about how best to conduct our lives.

Reading Questions

1. What is the difference between the problem of the meaning of life and the problem of life?
2. What is the pattern of internal struggle?
3. What are two ways to stop internal struggle, and what are the advantages of accepting yourself just as you are?
4. Can you think of any counterexamples to the authors' claim that success depends upon pleasing others?
5. In what sense is our desire for independence the "glue of social cohesion"?
6. Give an example of connecting "directly to an activity."
7. What is the main point of this essay?
8. What are some of the assumptions made by the authors?
9. How well did the authors accomplish their goal?

Meaning

DANIEL KOLAK and RAYMOND MARTIN

WHAT IS IT ALL ABOUT? Why are we here? Is there some purpose, or meaning, to life?

At one time or another, everyone asks such questions. As children and as old people, especially, we wonder: Why? What does it all mean? Most of the rest of the time, we're so busy trying to be successful we don't worry about meaning. But even then, in the back of our minds, we may still wonder. And when we do, what is it we really want to know?

Suppose you're at a party. You love being with the people there; they love having you there. The music is terrific, the food and drinks are delicious, and everything is paid for. No one has to go anywhere, do anything, be any particular way. Everyone is having a wonderful time. Suddenly someone turns to you and asks, "Why are we here? What is the meaning of this party?" You'd probably consider the question irrelevant. Suppose,

on the other hand, the party is terrible. Then you might think the question has a point.

So also with the question "What is the meaning of life?" When life is wonderful, we don't ask what it means—we're too busy enjoying it. When life is a painful struggle, the question forces itself upon us not so much because we want to answer the question of the meaning of life but, rather, because we want to end our struggle. We don't then care about solving the problem of the *meaning* of life. We care about solving the problem of *life*.

Everyone wants to have a good time. And it seems everyone has a recipe. Yet nearly everyone is involved in a painful struggle. There must be something wrong with the recipes.

Nearly everyone *is* struggling, not only in the poorest parts of the world but everywhere. Poor people struggle just to survive, but even affluent people struggle. Everywhere, nearly everyone is

From Daniel Kolak and Raymond Martin, Wisdom Without Answers: A Guide to the Experience of Philosophy. *Belmont, CA: Wadsworth, 1989, pp. 80–90.*

always struggling. Why? What can we do about it? Isn't that what we usually want to know, when the question of the meaning of life bothers us?

Theoretical answers might be of theoretical interest. But even after all the philosophy books, novels, songs, poems, and movies, people are still struggling. Lots of answers have been given— some serious, some funny, some clever, some stupid—but they haven't ended the struggle. On the other hand, knowing *why* life is a struggle could change things a great deal. It might even lessen the struggle enough to enable us to live more meaningful lives.

Everyone knows it takes two to have a fight. You can't be involved in a struggle unless someone or something is resisting. The resistance might come from the outside or from the inside—either you are divided from someone else, or from your environment, or from yourself. Without division there can be no resistance. Without resistance there can be no struggle.

So the way to stop struggling is to end the fragmentation that leads to resistance. The problem is that we don't want to stop struggling at the cost of being dominated. If we drop all resistance, someone else is sure to dominate us. But even people who no one is trying to dominate, even those in control, are struggling. In some places in the world, and at some times, struggle comes from the outside. But at all places in the world, and at all times, struggle comes from the inside.

What is *your* internal struggle? You're reading this book. Chances are no one is trying to shoot you. Chances are, though, that you are bothered by some internal struggle. How can you live without internal struggle? When you're bothered by questions about the meaning of life, isn't that what you usually want to know?

External and internal struggle both can be stopped in the same way: Drop all resistance. The problem with this simple answer in the case of external struggle is that we're afraid of being dominated. But no such problem exists in the case of internal struggle. In fact, just the opposite is the case. The reason you're bothered by internal struggle in the first place is that you're trying to dominate yourself—one part of you is trying to dominate another part of you.

Consider the simplest possible example of internal struggle. Suppose you drink too much alcohol and it bothers you. Part of you wants to continue. Another part of you wants to quit. If *all* of you wants to continue drinking, there is no struggle, you just drink. If *all* of you wants to quit, there is no struggle, you just quit. The problem is how to decide which part of yourself should prevail—in this case, the drinker or the nondrinker—and then how to get the other part to stop resisting.

Almost all internal struggle follows the same pattern. There is what you *are* and there is what you think you *should* be. That is the essence of internal conflict. So, which part should prevail— the actual you, who exists right now, or the ideal you, who might exist sometime in the future?

You can end your internal struggle in two ways: by eventually becoming the ideal you, or by accepting yourself exactly as you are right now and dropping all notions of how you should be. The first way, you continue struggling with yourself in the hope your struggle will end some day. The second way, you stop struggling right away.

It is difficult to drop being the way you are. It is easier to drop all notions of how you should be. You might eventually be able to change the way you are, but "trying to change" is a sure formula for perpetuating the struggle.

So, in the simple case of the drinker versus the nondrinker, who wins? For the time being, the drinker wins. That doesn't necessarily mean that the drinker will *always* be a drinker. Maybe—but not necessarily. Accepting the fact of being a drinker, accepting it without condition that you might change, may, as we shall see, be an effective way to become a nondrinker. The evolution might not take place, but there is a *chance* it will. One thing is certain: If the evolution does take place, it will be effortless.

But what if the drinker is addicted? Won't surrendering all resistance mean oblivion and death? Perhaps. But continuing to struggle with addiction might also mean oblivion and death—after great effort and pain! If one must drink oneself to death, isn't it better to do it effortlessly, rather than with great struggle and pain?

We are all addicted to one thing or another. Accepting ourselves as we are without any condition that we change can give us insight into the causes of our addictions. For instance, one major reason people enjoy alcohol is that it makes them less inhibited. But why are they inhibited in the first place? Isn't that kind of inhibition just their own resistance against what they themselves really are? The alcohol takes away the inhibition and allows the inhibited part to come out. Often self-destructive behavior is the inhibited part of you, ordinarily repressed by the ideal you, finally exerting itself and saying, "If you don't let me out, I'll kill you!" So the drinker who allows self-acceptance might become less inhibited—even without alcohol—and, in turn, might be less prone to drug abuse.

But if we all cease struggling, won't we just lie around all day? What will move us to act? Perhaps nothing. We might lie around all day. But one thing that *could* move us to act is love of some activity. We don't need to be coerced into doing what we love to do.

So whatever your struggle, the way out of that struggle is to accept yourself as you are without any condition that you change. The alternative is to keep struggling. That's the alternative most of us take because, deep down, we believe that struggle is the price we must pay for success. Without struggle, we think, we could never go from being what we are now to being the successful person we would someday like to be. But there is something suspicious about this strategy: Nearly everyone is struggling, yet few are successful.

Ordinarily, when we call someone successful, we're talking about career. That is only one kind of success. You can also be successful as a person—for instance, by being happy and by contributing to the happiness of others. Professional and personal success don't necessarily go together. We all know people who are successful in their careers but failures as persons and people who have failed in their careers but are successful as persons. Struggling does not ensure either kind of success. Does anything?

There may be no single key to having a successful career. But there is a common element:

The farmer who becomes a successful farmer, the doctor who becomes a successful doctor, the playwright who becomes a successful playwright, and so on, all become successful, if they do, by pleasing others. To make money, for instance, you have to sell something or provide a service that someone else wants to buy. Somewhere down the line, all types of professional success require pleasing others.

What, then, of being successful as a person? Oddly enough, here too success requires pleasing others. Being happy at work, being a good friend, a good parent, a good lover, and so on, all ultimately involve pleasing others.

Few of us are hermits. Even pleasing ourselves involves pleasing others. We may like to think of ourselves as individualists. The truth is that being successful as a person—being happy and contributing to the happiness of others—almost always involves pleasing others. So a common element to both professional and personal success seems to be: pleasing others.

Instinctively we already know this. But we may not like to admit it. We tend to view ourselves through the lens of an idealized self-image, part of which is our belief that we are not dependent on the approval of others, that we are the masters of our own destinies. We don't like to think of ourselves as dependent, even for our happiness, upon other people's approval. We like to think that it doesn't matter what people think of us. The truth is it does matter.

We need the approval of others, but we don't want to need it. So we often pretend that we don't need it. We resist needing it. This creates a tension within us, an internal struggle between the part of us that wants approval and the part that wants independence from the need for approval.

There is an ironic twist to this tension within us. We think the way to independence is through success. But the way to success is almost always through the approval of others. The student, the architect, the actor, the grocer, the football player, are all dependent on the approval of bosses, clients, fans, and so on, to gain greater independence from their need for approval.

We're all in the same boat. For instance, the authors of this book think that if this book is a great success, they will become more independent and will be better able to go where they want, do what they want, write what they want, and so on, without having to worry about what others think. The authors want to free themselves from the need for approval. How are they going to do it? Like everyone else, they will gain their independence from the need for the approval of others by gaining the approval of others. How smart!

This truth about success cuts deeply into all of our lives. Consider, for example, the way power is distributed in a romantic relationship. The one who is more powerful is the one who is less dependent on the other. How do you get less dependent? Usually by having more choice as to who you are with. The better you are at pleasing others, all else being equal, the more choice you have as to who you are with. The more choice you have, the more independent you are. So even in romantic relationships the way to independence is through pleasing others. Ironically, the way to independence is through dependence.

Such are society's mechanisms for keeping all of us in line. Without our need to seek the approval of others, society would collapse. The very structure of society—no matter what the society's particular mores are—depends on social cohesion. One way society ensures this cohesion is by linking our need to be independent with our need for approval. Society breeds the desire for independence into us to ensure that, as individuals, we will be dependent on the approval of others, thereby ensuring social cohesion. We depend on approval because only through approval can we hope to achieve independence. Our desire for independence is part of the very glue of social cohesion.

It may seem, then, from what we've just said, that seeking approval is the key to success. If success is impossible without approval, then the way to success would seem to be to aim directly for it. That is what most of us do.

This strategy can't be completely wrong. After all, we've just seen that the approval of others is necessary for success. For instance, most students want to get good grades. That is their criterion of success. Students instinctively know that

the surest way to get good grades is to get approval from their teachers by agreeing with them. This strategy works—but only to a point. It often, but not always, ensures that the student gets good grades. But merely getting good grades is a mediocre level of success. As every good teacher knows, those students who reach a high level of success in school—academic excellence—develop the capacity for *independent* thought. Getting good grades, on the other hand, usually doesn't ensure that a student has developed this capacity.

Students who agree with their teachers tend to get good grades partly because imitating their teachers' views on the material they are studying is the first level of connecting to that material. The best students then go on to challenge the opinions of their teachers in creative ways. The best students, once they have achieved the initial connection between themselves and the subject matter through imitating the teacher, then go on to connect to the subject matter directly. This requires taking risks—in particular, risking the disapproval of their teachers. Ultimately, what must matter most to these students is not the connection between themselves and their teachers, but the connection between themselves and their subject matter.

Seeking approval is the first step to success. But it only goes so far. In the end, it is even limiting. If you want to reach the higher levels of success, you must win approval not by seeking it but rather by achieving some level of excellence through connecting directly to the activity you are involved in. The ironic twist is that such a level of excellence through direct connecting to an activity can never be attained so long as one is primarily concerned with seeking approval. One must drop the quest for approval in order to attain success in its fullest form.

In other words, people tend to think that success has something to do with pleasing others because that is itself an indirect way of connecting with an activity. But pleasing others is also a byproduct of connecting directly with an activity. In the end, what matters most is not approval but connecting directly with an activity, for that is the way to attain a high level of success. For instance, you might get a promotion by pleasing your boss, a job as an actor by pleasing a director, a lucrative business contract by pleasing a client, and so on. All these initial successes are like the student getting a good grade by pleasing the teacher. Whether or not you are successful in your new job once you have it, whether or not you are successful as an actor, grocer, teacher, or whatever, will ultimately depend on how you connect to whatever activity your job requires.

What does it mean to connect directly to an activity? First, consider professional success. The purpose of all professions is to make a product. For instance, doctors cultivate health, architects design buildings, playwrights write plays, and so on. Many people view their work-related activities merely as instruments for producing products. They don't value the process that leads to the product as an end in itself. The ones who do, however, are the ones who become most successful. The student who loves to study, the boxer who loves to box, the runner who loves to run, the farmer who loves to farm, all experience the same joy of activity. They love the *process,* not just the product, and so they succeed to a much greater degree.

Suppose you repair bicycles. Fixing bicycles is the process. A fixed bicycle is the product. You want to be a successful bicycle repairman. How? You can't be successful unless you please your clients. You must turn damaged or faulty bicycles into good ones, and you must do it efficiently and well. You can do this at a minimal level if you merely want to please your customers. You can do it much better if you love to repair bicycles.

But every activity, every process, it would seem, has its drudgery. In bicycle repair, you have to repack the ball bearings, grease the chains, adjust the cables. Ordinarily, such chores are drudgery because, as we do them, we focus on getting them done instead of on doing them. When we focus on getting them done we are not all there. Our hands are there and perhaps part of our minds are there, but another part of us constantly projects into the future. If we are completely there, focused on our activity, paying attention to everything we do, our activity, no matter what it is, will rarely be drudgery. Almost always, our desire to get it over with makes it drudgery.

Suppose, for instance, you are told to set up and then dismantle a toy city. It will take hours and hours of patient, detailed work to set up the city, only to destroy it in the end. How would you react? As you were doing it, you'd probably be thinking: What is the purpose of this? I want to finish, get some sleep before I have to go to work, and so on.

Yet when we were children, we played like that for hours on end. Did we worry then about the purpose of building toy cities, only to dismantle them as soon as we finished? What was the purpose of building them? Wasn't it simply the act of doing it? When we were children, we played games not to be done with them, but to do them. That's why we enjoyed them so much. Isn't that the very source of the magic of childhood?

Living is a series of activities that involves everything you do, including your job. Living is your activity. The product is *you.* Being connected to your life means, ultimately, being connected to all the activities of your life. These activities continually produce new versions of you. Being connected means valuing these activities not merely as a means to an end—as a means to producing a certain type of you—but rather as ends in themselves.

Consider, for example, the activity of keeping yourself physically fit. It can be done primarily as an end in itself. Or it can be done as a mere means to fitness. Ask yourself this: Who will be more physically fit after five years—the person who flogs himself into jogging every morning, or the person who so enjoys the physical act of running that she does it willingly every day?

If in all your activities the thing you focus on is the finished product—the read book, the fixed bicycle, the delivered mail, the ideal you—happiness will elude you. Happiness might surface after you have completed something, but then it is usually time to start something else. Then you rush through the next project, struggling with yourself because you don't really want to be doing it either. You just want to have done it, to be finished.

If you are connected to the process, the main reward isn't with the finishing. It's with the doing. The finishing may even have a sorrowful aspect to it because it will signify the end of a particular process. For the authors of this book, for instance, when the last word is written, when the final revision is sent off to the publisher, there will be joy. There will also be sorrow because a process they love will have ended. There might be other books, other processes. But *this* particular process will have ended forever.

So also with the process of being a person. When a life that has been good is nearing completion, there will be sorrow. There might also be the joy of completion. There might even be other lives. But *this* life, *this* particular process, will end forever.

The key to success in life, then, is connecting, not with a product, but with a process: ultimately, with the process of being ourselves. Where there is genuine connection to a process, there will be success.

Success, like a good party, has its own intrinsic value. It makes our lives rich and full of meaning. And where there is success, there will ultimately also be sorrow because it is the nature of all processes to change, and by changing they end.

Visit the companion Web site for chapter specific quizzes, suggestions for further reading, video ideas, and other resources to assess and expand your understanding of the chapter material. Go to http://philosophy.wadsworth.com and select the companion Web site for *Voices of Wisdom.*

 You can access many additional readings at the InfoTrac-College Edition Web site. To find the following suggested articles do a keyword search with the article title. Use the passcode that was packaged with your new book to enter the site at http://www.Infotrac-college.com/Wadsworth/. Here is a sampling.

Matthew Dillon, "Dialogues with Death: The Last Days of Socrates and the Buddha." *Philosophy East and West,* October 2000 v50 i4 p525. A68952124.

David Burton, "Knowledge and Liberation: Philosophical Ruminations on a Buddhist Conundrum." *Philosophy East and West,* July 2002 v52 i3 p326(20) A90753118.

A. T. Nuyen, "Confucianism and the Idea of Equality." *Asian Philosophy,* July 2001 v11 i2 p61(11) A80491461.

Sin Yee Chan, "Can Shu Be the One Word That Serves as the Guiding Principle of Caring Actions?" *Philosophy East and West,* October 2000 v50 i4 p507 A68952123.

Chandran Kukathas, "Passing the Unexamined Life." *Quadrant,* July 2001 p22 A76751444.

W. A. Borody, "The 'Trials' of Arjuna and Socrates: Physical Bodies, Violence and Sexuality." *Asian Philosophy,* November 1997 v7 n3 p221(13) A20412149.

Jiyuan Yu, "Virtue: Confucius and Aristotle." *Philosophy East and West,* April 1998 v48 n2 p323(25) A20653030.

Menaha Ganesathasan, "A Matter of Character: Vasistha and Aristotle on Moral Development." *Asian Philosophy,* July 2001 v11 i2 p103(21) A80491464.

Christine Swanton, "How Should One Live? Essays on the Virtues." *Mind,* July 1997 v106 n423 p596(3) A19635816.

Thaddeus Metz, "Recent Work on the Meaning of Life." *Ethics,* July 2002 v112 i4 p781(35) A90995763.

Chapter 3

How Can I Know What Is Right?

> **Ethics is limitations on freedom of action in the struggle for existence.**
> ALDO LEOPOLD

3.1 Introduction

HAVE YOU EVER WONDERED how you can know what is morally right? You have been told to do the right thing. But what is the *right* thing? Sometimes it is very hard to figure out. Sometimes our duties conflict. We know we should be loyal to our friends, but shouldn't we report them for cheating? Sometimes we must choose between alternatives, both of which seem wrong.

To know what is the right thing to do, we need to know what makes an action right. How can we know that? Do my motives make my actions right? If I intend to do my moral duty as best I understand it, isn't that enough? We call that acting out of a good will. However, maybe a good will is not enough. Maybe it is not my motives but the consequences of what I do that count. If my actions result in good things for most people, isn't that sufficient to justify my actions?

You might reply, "What about the act itself? It is surely either right or wrong in itself, no matter what my motives are or the consequences. Aren't some things just plain wrong? It is not right to steal even if my motives are good or the consequences will benefit some. Stealing is just plain wrong."

The philosopher wonders why it is "just plain wrong." What *makes* it wrong? How do I know that it is wrong?

We all know that people have different values and believe different things to be right. Are your moral beliefs any better than anyone else's? Some people are **ethical skeptics.** They doubt whether there is any such thing as moral truth. For them, there is no way we can know that stealing is wrong. It may be, but we cannot know that. To show that the ethical skeptic is mistaken, you would have to show how we can arrive at moral knowledge.

Some people are **ethical relativists.** They deny that there are any universally valid moral principles. Even stealing can be "right" if some culture recognizes it to be "right," even though others might think it "wrong." However, if we subscribe to ethical relativism, it appears that we must give up any basis for condemning someone like Hitler. Morally deplorable actions such as "ethnic cleansing" become "right" if some culture thinks them to be right. Surely there must be some moral absolutes.

While ethical skeptics doubt that we can know any moral absolutes, if there should happen to be any, and ethical relativists claim that there are, in fact, no such absolutes, **ethical absolutists** (also called universalists) claim there are. Moral values, they argue, are objective. They transcend time and place. What is right is right, regardless of what anyone may think. Stealing is wrong, even if it might be justified in some circumstances by some higher good and even if some culture might think it is "cool."

If you have wondered about these issues, you have been asking some important questions that have to do with the very foundations of morality. In this chapter, we explore some different answers to this question: How can we know what is right?

3.2 Kant and the Categorical Imperative

Immanuel Kant (1724–1804) was born, spent his entire life, and died in Königsberg, Prussia. He studied natural science, mathematics, history, and philosophy at the University of Königsberg. After graduation he worked for a while as a tutor to the children of Prussian aristocrats, eventually landing a job as *Privatdozent* at the university. This meant that he was licensed by the university to offer lectures, but the university did not pay him. Rather, he was paid by the students who attended his lectures. For more than a dozen years, Kant lectured on a wide variety of subjects for up to 21 hours a week in order to make enough money to live.

Kant's monetary fortunes improved when he was finally appointed professor of logic and metaphysics in 1770 and was paid a decent wage by the university. In 1781 one of his many books appeared, *The Critique of Pure Reason*, which was destined to revolutionize Western philosophy. It earned Kant the reputation of being one of the greatest philosophical minds of the modern period. In this book Kant was concerned with epistemological as well as metaphysical issues. Does the world conform to our ideas, or do our ideas conform to the world? Most people thought that true ideas are those that conform to the world. However, Kant argued just the opposite, namely, that the world conforms to our ideas.

We do not have time to go into Kant's complex proof nor the radical implications of this contention. I note it in passing to indicate that Kant made contributions to philosophy in other areas besides moral philosophy, even though we will be concerned here primarily with his ethical ideas. According to Kant, we cannot know what is the morally right thing to do unless we can know what *makes* an action morally right.

Before we can know what might make an action right, we have to do a little bit of thinking about the parts of an action. It is evident that actions have consequences. Thus we might wonder whether the consequences or the results of an action make it right. People who advocate the view that consequences determine the rightness of an action support what philosophers call **teleological ethical theories.**

There is more to action, however, than its consequences. There is also the motive for the action, and it is worth asking whether motives, not consequences, make an action morally right. We know that people can do something that has good results, but do it for the wrong reasons. I may refrain from cheating on a test because I am afraid I will get caught. Not cheating has good consequences because it makes the test fair for all. However, is it right to praise me for being morally good simply because I was afraid to cheat? Should I not do the right thing because it is the right thing? Moral theories that advocate doing what is good because it is good, regardless of the consequences, are called **deontological ethical theories** (from the Greek *deon,* meaning "duty," and *logos,* meaning "science" or "study of").

Kant wondered about the sorts of questions we have been discussing. His answers constitute a deontological theory. He argued that the only thing that is unconditionally good is a good will. What makes a good will good is not the consequences that result from its acts, nor the inclinations and desires that *in fact* influence it, but its freely willing to do what *duty* requires.

And what does duty require? It requires that we act in accord with the **categorical imperative,** which can be formulated, "Act only on that maxim through which you can at the same time will that it should become a universal law." For example, if you are wondering whether you should tell the truth, you should formulate a maxim, "Always tell the truth," and ask whether you can will that such a rule become a universal law—that is, a law everyone ought to obey. Note that this imperative, or command, is *categorical,* that is, unconditional. It is not a *hypothetical,* or conditional, command. Kant does *not* say, "Act only on that maxim *if.* . . ." Kant believed that this imperative is equivalent to a rule that requires us always to treat persons as ends in themselves rather than as means to some other end, such as the production of pleasure, happiness, or wealth.

An action is right, Kant argued, if it is done from a good will, and a will is good if it meets three conditions:

1. The maxim on which its action is based can be universalized.
2. It freely accepts (what Kant called *autonomy*) its duty.
3. It treats people as ends, not means.

Kant was looking for a rational foundation for morality. He opposed ethical relativism and disagreed with those who were skeptical of moral truth. Kant was an ethical absolutist. Moral truth is objective, he contended, and morality has a rational foundation revealing that some things are morally right no matter what anyone thinks or what any society claims.

The selection that follows is from *Groundwork of the Metaphysics of Morals,* which Kant published in 1785. He intended it to be a brief introduction to his theory, which he later elaborated in the *Critique of Practical Reason.* Even though this work is introductory, it is not easy to read. Take your time, think about what Kant is saying, and answer the following questions.

Reading Questions

1. What is good without qualification?
2. Do the consequences or results of a good will make it good?
3. According to Kant, a good will is manifested in acting for the sake of duty. He contends that "the worth of character begins to show" when a person "does good, not from inclination, but from duty." Why does Kant claim this? Do you agree? Why, or why not?
4. Where, according to Kant, does the moral value or worth of an action done from duty reside? In the results of the action? In the actual motive a person may in fact have (the *material principle*)? If not in these, where?
5. What do you think Kant meant when he said, "Duty is the necessity to act out of reverence for the law"?

6. What is the *categorical imperative?*

7. Kant claimed we can will to lie, but we cannot will a universal law of lying. Do you agree? Why, or why not?

8. Kant said that if you want to know whether an action is morally right, determine the maxim or subjective principle on which it is based and then ask, "Can I also will that my maxim should become a universal law?" If the answer is no, it is not the right thing to do. Apply Kant's advice to the following case: You are a bright individual who usually gets good grades. You want to go to law school, and you need good grades to get accepted at a good law school. You find yourself taking a philosophy test for which you are not well prepared, and you have an opportunity to cheat without being caught. By cheating, you will definitely improve your final grade for the course. Should you cheat? If you were a Kantian (a follower of Kant's theory), what would be your answer, and what would be your reasoning?

9. How did Kant answer the question "How can I know what is right?"

Groundwork of the Metaphysics of Morals

IMMANUEL KANT

The Good Will

IT IS IMPOSSIBLE to conceive anything at all in the world, or even out of it, which can be taken as good without qualification, except a *good will*. Intelligence, wit, judgment, and any other *talents* of the mind we may care to name, or courage, resolution, and constancy of purpose, as qualities of *temperament,* are without doubt good and desirable in many respects; but they can also be extremely bad and hurtful when the will is not good which has to make use of these gifts of nature, and which for this reason has the term "*character*" applied to its peculiar quality. It is exactly the same with *gifts of fortune.* Power, wealth, honour, even health and that complete well-being and contentment with one's state which goes by the name of "*happiness,*" produce boldness, and as a consequence often over-boldness as well, unless a good will is present by which their influence on the mind—and so, too, the whole principle of action—may be corrected and adjusted to universal ends; not to mention that a rational and impartial spectator can never feel approval in contemplating the uninterrupted prosperity of a being graced by no touch of a pure and good will, and that consequently a good will seems to constitute the indispensable condition of our very worthiness to be happy.

Some qualities are even helpful to this good will itself and can make its task very much easier. They have none the less no inner unconditioned worth, but rather presuppose a good will which sets a limit to the esteem in which they are rightly held and does not permit us to regard them as absolutely good. Moderation in affections and passions, self-control, and sober reflexion are not only good in many respects: they may even seem to constitute part of the *inner* worth of a person. Yet they are far from being properly described as good without qualification (however unconditionally they have been commended by the ancients). For without the principles of a good will they may become exceedingly bad; and the very coolness of a scoundrel makes him, not merely more dangerous, but also immediately more abominable in our eyes than we should have taken him to be without it.

From I. Kant, Groundwork of the Metaphysics of Morals, *translated by H. J. Paton (New York: Harper & Row, 1964), pp. 61–62; 64–71. Reprinted by permission of Unwin Hyman, Ltd. Translator's footnotes deleted.*

The Good Will and Its Results

A good will is not good because of what it effects or accomplishes—because of its fitness for attaining some proposed end: it is good through its willing alone—that is, good in itself. Considered in itself it is to be esteemed beyond comparison as far higher than anything it could ever bring about merely in order to favour some inclination or, if you like, the sum total of inclinations. Even if, by some special disfavour of destiny or by the niggardly endowment of step-motherly nature, this will is entirely lacking in power to carry out its intentions; if by its utmost effort it still accomplishes nothing, and only good will is left (not, admittedly, as a mere wish, but as the straining of every means so far as they are in our control); even then it would still shine like a jewel for its own sake as something which has its full value in itself. Its usefulness or fruitlessness can neither add to, nor subtract from, this value. Its usefulness would be merely, as it were, the setting which enables us to handle it better in our ordinary dealings or to attract the attention of those not yet sufficiently expert, but not to commend it to experts or to determine its value. . . .

The Good Will and Duty

We have now to elucidate the concept of a will estimable in itself and good apart from any further end. This concept, which is already present in a sound natural understanding and requires not so much to be taught as merely to be clarified, always holds the highest place in estimating the total worth of our actions and constitutes the condition of all the rest. We will therefore take up the concept of *duty,* which includes that of a good will, exposed, however, to certain subjective limitations and obstacles. These, so far from hiding a good will or disguising it, rather bring it out by contrast and make it shine forth more brightly.

The Motive of Duty

I will here pass over all actions already recognized as contrary to duty, however useful they may be with a view to this or that end; for about these the question does not even arise whether they could have been done *for the sake of duty* inasmuch as they are directly opposed to it. I will also set aside actions which in fact accord with duty, yet for which men have *no immediate inclination,* but perform them because impelled to do so by some other inclination. For there it is easy to decide whether the action which accords with duty has been done *from duty* or from some purpose of self-interest. This distinction is far more difficult to perceive when the action accords with duty and the subject has in addition an *immediate* inclination to the action. For example, it certainly accords with duty that a grocer should not overcharge his inexperienced customer; and where there is much competition a sensible shopkeeper refrains from so doing and keeps to a fixed and general price for everybody so that a child can buy from him just as well as anyone else. Thus people are served *honestly;* but this is not nearly enough to justify us in believing that the shopkeeper has acted in this way from duty or from principles of fair dealing; his interests required him to do so. We cannot assume him to have in addition an immediate inclination towards his customers, leading him, as it were out of love, to give no man preference over another in the matter of price. Thus the action was done neither from duty nor from immediate inclination, but solely from purposes of self-interest.

On the other hand, to preserve one's life is a duty, and besides this every one has also an immediate inclination to do so. But on account of this the often-anxious precautions taken by the greater part of mankind for this purpose have no inner worth, and the maxim of their action is without moral content. They do protect their lives *in conformity with duty,* but not *from the motive of duty.* When on the contrary, disappointments and hopeless misery have quite taken away the taste for life; when a wretched man, strong in soul and more angered at his fate than fainthearted or cast down, longs for death and still preserves his life without loving it—not from inclination or fear but from duty; then indeed his maxim has a moral content.

To help others where one can is a duty, and besides this there are many spirits of so sympathetic a temper that, without any further motive of vanity or self-interest, they find an inner pleasure in spreading happiness around them and can take delight in the contentment of others as their own work. Yet I maintain that in such a case an action of this kind, however right and however amiable it may be, has still no genuinely moral worth. It stands on the same footing as other inclinations—for example, the inclination for honour, which if fortunate enough to hit on something beneficial and right and consequently honorable, deserves praise and encouragement, but not esteem; for its maxim lacks moral content, namely, the performance of such actions, not from inclination, but *from duty*. Suppose then that the mind of this friend of man were overclouded by sorrows of his own which extinguished all sympathy with the fate of others, but that he still had power to help those in distress, though no longer stirred by the need of others because sufficiently occupied with his own; and suppose that, when no longer moved by any inclination, he tears himself out of this deadly insensibility and does the action without any inclination for the sake of duty alone; then for the first time his action has its genuine moral worth. Still further: if nature had implanted little sympathy in this or that man's heart; if (being in other respects an honest fellow) he were cold in temperament and indifferent to the sufferings of others—perhaps because, being endowed with the special gift of patience and robust endurance in his own sufferings, he assumed the like in others or even demanded it; if such a man (who would in truth not be the worst product of nature) were not exactly fashioned by her to be a philanthropist, would he not still find in himself a source from which he might draw a worth far higher than any that a good-natured temperament can have? Assuredly he would. It is precisely in this that the worth of character begins to show—a moral worth and beyond all comparison the highest—namely, that he does good, not from inclination, but from duty.

To assure one's own happiness is a duty (at least indirectly); for discontent with one's state, in a press of cares and amidst unsatisfied wants, might easily become a great *temptation to the transgression of duty*. But here also, apart from regard to duty, all men have already of themselves the strongest and deepest inclination towards happiness, because precisely in this idea of happiness all inclinations are combined into a sum total. The prescription for happiness is, however, often so constituted as greatly to interfere with some inclinations, and yet men cannot form under the name of "happiness" any determinate and assured conception of the satisfaction of all inclinations as a sum. Hence it is not to be wondered at that a single inclination which is determinate as to what it promises and as to the time of its satisfaction may outweigh a wavering idea; and that a man, for example, a sufferer from gout, may choose to enjoy what he fancies and put up with what he can—on the ground that on balance he has here at least not killed the enjoyment of the present moment because of some possibly groundless expectations of the good fortune supposed to attach to soundness of health. But in this case also, when the universal inclination towards happiness has failed to determine his will, when good health, at least for him, has not entered into his calculations as so necessary, what remains over, here as in other cases, is a law—the law of furthering his happiness, not from inclination, but from duty; and in this for the first time his conduct has a real moral worth.

It is doubtless in this sense that we should understand too the passages from Scripture in which we are commanded to love our neighbour and even our enemy. For love out of inclination cannot be commanded; but kindness done from duty—although no inclination impels us, and even although natural and unconquerable disinclination stands in our way—is *practical,* and not *pathological,* love, residing in the will and not in the propensions [propensity] of feeling, in principles of action and not of melting compassion; and it is this practical love alone which can be an object of command.

The Formal Principle of Duty

Our second proposition is this: An action done from duty has its moral worth, *not in the purpose* to be attained by it, but in the maxim in accordance with which it is decided upon; it depends therefore, not on the realization of the object of the action, but solely on the *principle of volition* in accordance with which, irrespective of all objects of the faculty of desire, the action has been performed. That the purposes we may have in our actions, and also their effects considered as ends and motives of the will, can give to actions no unconditioned and moral worth is clear from what has gone before. Where then can this worth be found if we are not to find it in the will's relation to the effect hoped for from the action? It can be found nowhere but *in the principle of the will,* irrespective of the ends which can be brought about by such an action; for between its *a priori* principle, which is formal, and its *a posteriori* motive, which is material, the will stands, so to speak, at a parting of the ways; and since it must be determined by some principle, it will have to be determined by the formal principle of volition when an action is done from duty, where, as we have seen, every material principle is taken away from it.

Reverence for the Law

Our third proposition, as an inference from the two preceding, I would express thus: *Duty is the necessity to act out of reverence for the law.* For an object as the effect of my proposed action I can have an *inclination,* but *never reverence,* precisely because it is merely the effect, and not the activity, of a will. Similarly for inclination as such, whether my own or that of another, I cannot have reverence: I can at most in the first case approve, and in the second case sometimes even love—that is, regard it as favourable to my own advantage. Only something which is conjoined with my will solely as a ground and never as an effect—something which does not serve my inclination, but outweighs it or at least leaves it entirely out of account in my choice—and therefore only bare law for its own sake, can be an object of reverence and therewith a command. Now an action done from duty has to set aside altogether the influence of inclination, and along with inclination every object of the will; so there is nothing left able to determine the will except

objectively the *law* and subjectively *pure reverence* for this practical law, and therefore the maxim[1] of obeying this law even to the detriment of all my inclinations.

Thus the moral worth of an action does not depend on the result expected from it, and so too does not depend on any principle of action that needs to borrow its motive from this expected result. For all these results (agreeable states and even the promotion of happiness in others) could have been brought about by other causes as well, and consequently their production did not require the will of a rational being, in which, however, the highest and unconditioned good can alone be found. Therefore nothing but the *idea of the law* in itself, *which admittedly is present only in a rational being*—so far as it, and not an expected result, is the ground determining the will—can constitute that pre-eminent good which we call moral, a good which is already present in the person acting on this idea and has not to be awaited merely from the result.[2]

1. A *maxim* is the subjective principle of a volition: an objective principle (that is, one which would also serve subjectively as a practical principle for all rational beings if reason had full control over the faculty of desire) is a practical *law*.
2. It might be urged against me that I have merely tried, under cover of the word "*reverence,*" to take refuge in an obscure feeling instead of giving a clearly articulated answer to the question by means of a concept of reason. Yet, although reverence is a feeling, it is not a feeling *received* through outside influence, but one *self-produced* by a rational concept, and therefore specifically distinct from feelings of the first kind, all of which can be reduced to inclination or fear. What I recognize immediately as law for me, I recognize with reverence, which means merely consciousness of the *subordination* of my will to a law without the mediation of external influences on my senses. Immediate determination of the will by the law and consciousness of this determination is called "*reverence,*" so that reverence is regarded as the *effect* of the law on the subject and not as the *cause* of the law. Reverence is properly awareness of a value which demolishes my self-love. Hence, there is something which is regarded neither as an object of inclination nor as an object of fear, though it has at the same time some analogy with both. The *object* of reverence is the *law* alone—that law which we impose *on ourselves* but yet as necessary in itself. Considered as a law, we are subject to it without any consultation of self-love; considered as self-imposed it is a consequence of our will. In the first respect it is analogous to fear, in the second to inclination. All reverence for a person is properly only reverence for the law (of honesty and so on) of which that person gives us an

The Categorical Imperative

But what kind of law can this be the thought of which, even without regard to the results expected from it, has to determine the will if this is to be called good absolutely and without qualification? Since I have robbed the will of every inducement that might arise for it as a consequence of obeying any particular law, nothing is left but the conformity of actions to universal law as such, and this alone must serve the will as its principle. That is to say, I ought never to act except in such a way *that I can also will that my maxim should become a universal law.* Here bare conformity to universal law as such (without having as its base any law prescribing particular actions) is what serves the will as its principle, and must so serve it if duty is not to be everywhere an empty delusion and a chimerical concept. The ordinary reason of mankind also agrees with this completely in its practical judgments and always has the aforesaid principle before its eyes.

Take this question, for example. May I not, when I am hard pressed, make a promise with the intention of not keeping it? Here I readily distinguish the two senses which the question can have—Is it prudent, or is it right, to make a false promise? The first no doubt can often be the case. I do indeed see that it is not enough for me to extricate myself from present embarrassment by this subterfuge: I have to consider whether from this lie there may not subsequently accrue to me much greater inconvenience than that from which I now escape, and also—since, with all my supposed *astuteness,* to foresee the consequences is not so easy that I can be sure there is no chance, once confidence in me is lost, of this proving far more disadvantageous than all the ills I now think to avoid—whether it may not be a *more prudent* action to proceed here on a general maxim and make it my habit not to give a promise except

with the intention of keeping it. Yet it becomes clear to me at once that such a maxim is always founded solely on fear of consequences. To tell the truth for the sake of duty is something entirely different from doing so out of concern for inconvenient results; for in the first case the concept of the action already contains in itself a law for me, while in the second case I have first of all to look around elsewhere in order to see what effects may be bound up with it for me. When I deviate from the principle of duty, this is quite certainly bad; but if I desert my prudential maxim, this can often be greatly to my advantage, though it is admittedly safer to stick to it. Suppose I seek, however, to learn in the quickest way and yet unerringly how to solve the problem "Does a lying promise accord with duty?" I have then to ask myself "Should I really be content that my maxim (the maxim of getting out of a difficulty by a false promise) should hold as a universal law (one valid both for myself and others)?" And could I really say to myself that everyone may make a false promise if he finds himself in a difficulty from which he can extricate himself in no other way? I then become aware at once that I can indeed will to lie, but I can by no means will a universal law of lying; for by such a law there could properly be no promises at all, since it would be futile to profess a will for future action to others who would not believe my profession or who, if they did so over-hastily, would pay me back in like coin; and consequently my maxim, as soon as it was made a universal law, would be bound to annul itself.

Thus I need no far-reaching ingenuity to find out what I have to do in order to possess a good will. Inexperienced in the course of world affairs and incapable of being prepared for all the chances that happen in it, I ask myself only "Can you also will that your maxim should become a universal law?" Where you cannot, it is to be rejected, and that not because of a prospective loss to you or even to others, but because it cannot fit as a principle into a possible enactment of universal law. For such an enactment reason compels my immediate reverence, into whose grounds (which the philosopher may investigate) I have as yet no *insight,* although I do at least understand

example. Because we regard the development of our talents as a duty, we see too in a man of talent a sort of *example of the law* (the law of becoming like him by practice), and this is what constitutes our reverence for him. All moral *interest,* so-called, consists solely in *reverence* for the law.

this much: reverence is the assessment of a worth which far outweighs all the worth of what is commended by inclination, and the necessity for me to act out of *pure* reverence for the practical law is what constitutes duty, to which every other motive must give way because it is the condition of a will good *in itself,* whose value is above all else.

3.3 Utilitarianism

Suppose you have to decide whether your loveable cat, who has been your companion for many years and is now very sick, should be "put to sleep," as we euphemistically say. How would you go about making the decision? Would you consider how much pain your cat (let's call her Jenny) is suffering? Would you consider Jenny's chances of recovery? Would and *should* you think about your own pain and loss if you put Jenny to sleep?

Now suppose that Jenny is your mother, not your cat. Suppose further that you lived in a state that allowed physician-assisted suicide. Suppose your mother is not able to tell a physician what she wants, and you must make a decision. How would you go about it? Would the same questions that occurred to you in the case of your cat also occur to you in this case? Would those questions be relevant? Should the decision-making process be essentially the same in both cases?

Now suppose that Jenny is the name you have selected for your newborn daughter who is so severely retarded and incapable of thought or action that she will be nothing but a burden to you and your family for as long as she may live. She will never know you, or have the capacity to love you. Suppose further that you live in a state that permits euthanasia. Should Jenny be "put to sleep"? How would you decide? Are the same sorts of considerations that you agonized about in the first two cases relevant to this case? Is there any way of thinking about these cases that might help us know what is right?

Jeremy Bentham (1748–1832), a British philosopher and social reformer, thought he could provide some help in deciding these difficult cases. He believed that a rational and scientific approach to social and moral issues is possible if we learn to apply what he called "the principle of utility."

Bentham's ethical theory is called **utilitarianism**. Classified as a teleological theory, it maintains that what makes an action right are its consequences. If the consequences are good, then the action is right. However, what are good consequences? Bentham answers that good consequences are those that result in the greatest amount of pleasure (happiness) for the "party whose interest is in question." The party may be the collection of individuals we call a community insofar as they share common interests or it may be a particular individual. Go to http://philosophy.wadsworth.com and select the companion Web site for *Voices of Wisdom* for a link to Bentham's writings.

John Stuart Mill (1806–1873), a follower of Bentham, interpreted Bentham's discussion of the interests of the community to mean that Bentham was talking about the greatest happiness for the greatest number of people who are affected by the action in question. Whether this is what Bentham meant is a matter of scholarly dispute. However, it is clear that Bentham's principle of utility is intended to guide legislative (and individual) decision making by focusing attention on the amount of pleasure that might result from a particular law or course of action.

Because Mill believed that the good is pleasure, his utilitarian theory is also a variety of **hedonism.** According to hedonistic theories, the highest good is pleasure. Morality is thus grounded in feelings that are natural to the human animal. We, like all animals, act in order to avoid pain and maximize pleasure.

The following selection is from Chapters 2 through 4 of Mill's work, *Utilitarianism*, which was published in 1861. In the first chapter (not included here), Mill made general remarks about ethics and attacked Kant's theory. Kant believed that it is illogical and hence irrational to will universal immoral laws. Thus, although we can will to lie, we cannot will that everyone ought to lie. Mill said that Kant never proved that the adoption of immoral laws by all rational beings is illogical in the sense that it somehow involves a contradiction. All he ever showed is that the consequences of adopting immoral laws as universal would be so undesirable that no one would choose to do so. That is, we do not advocate that everyone should lie because it is irrational to do so; rather, we do not advocate it because we do not wish to live in societies where no one can be trusted. Thus Kant, in spite of his rejection of teleological ethical theories, ended up having to appeal to consequences but refusing to acknowledge them, or so Mill contended.

Ethicists who follow a Kantian deontological theory (see the previous selection) usually criticize utilitarianism for its failure to provide an adequate theory of justice. Some argue, for example, that it would be possible to justify slavery on utilitarian grounds because that may give more pleasure to the community in general. In other words, Kantians argue that it would be possible to deny people their rights given the utilitarian viewpoint. An adequate theory of justice, they claim, can be based only on the recognition that people have rights simply because they are people. That is, rights are intrinsic, and Kant's categorical imperative acknowledges this. However, utilitarianism does not hold that people have rights just because they are people. People have rights only if granting them rights produces greater happiness to the community.

In his last chapter (not included here), Mill turned to the issue of justice, acknowledging that providing an adequate theory of justice is one of the hardest problems for utilitarianism. Nevertheless, he argued that the fair treatment of all people in society can be justified on utilitarian grounds because it is in the best interests of all to promote a feeling of security. Fair treatment, extended to all, promotes such a feeling.

But I am getting too far ahead. Before we can compare Kant's deontological theory with Mill's teleological theory, we need to learn more about Mill's theory. I think you will find Mill a lot easier to read than Kant, but answering the following questions will still prove helpful in understanding the main points of Mill's theory. The utilitarian viewpoint has sunk deeply into the value system of Western culture, so most of us will have a social framework that makes it easier to understand and accept this moral theory.

Reading Questions

1. What is the "greatest happiness principle" (also called the "principle of utility")?
2. What does Mill mean by happiness?
3. What is the theory of life on which the utilitarian theory is based?

4. How does Mill answer the objection that Epicureanism (a variety of hedonism) is a "doctrine only worthy of swine"? Do you think his answer is a good one? Why?

5. According to Mill, how can we determine whether one pleasure is more valuable than another?

6. Mill claims it is "better to be Socrates dissatisfied than a fool satisfied." Do you agree or not? Why?

7. How does Mill answer the question, "Why am I bound to promote the general happiness?"

8. Why, in your opinion, should people do what is morally right?

9. Summarize Mill's proof for the principle of utility. Some philosophers have argued that Mill's proof is faulty because it confuses the descriptive (what people *actually* desire) with the normative (what people *ought* to desire). Do you agree with this criticism or not? Why?

10. Refer back to the case of potential cheating I recounted in Question 8 in the section on Kant. If you were a utilitarian, how would you go about determining the right thing to do in this situation?

11. Some people object to utilitarianism on the grounds that it allows us to do things that are immoral. Can you think of an example of something that would be immoral that utilitarian theory would say is good?

12. How does Mill answer the question, "How can I know what is right?"

What Utilitarianism Is

JOHN STUART MILL

THE CREED WHICH ACCEPTS as the foundation of morals "utility" or the "greatest happiness principle" holds that actions are right in proportion as they tend to promote happiness; wrong as they tend to produce the reverse of happiness. By "happiness" is intended pleasure and the absence of pain; by "unhappiness," pain and the privation of pleasure. To give a clear view of the moral standard set up by the theory, much more requires to be said; in particular, what things it includes in the ideas of pain and pleasure, and to what extent this is left an open question. But these supplementary explanations do not affect the theory of life on which this theory of morality is grounded — namely, that pleasure and freedom from pain are the only things desirable as ends; and that all desirable things (which are as numerous in the utilitarian as in any other scheme) are desirable either for pleasure inherent in themselves or as means to the promotion of pleasure and the prevention of pain.

Now such a theory of life excites in many minds, and among them in some of the most estimable in feeling and purpose, inveterate dislike. To suppose that life has (as they express it) no higher end than pleasure — no better and nobler object of desire and pursuit — they designate as utterly mean and groveling, as a doctrine worthy only of swine, to whom the followers of Epicurus were, at a very early period, contemptuously likened; and modern holders of the doctrine are occasionally made the subject of equally polite comparisons by its German, French, and English assailants.

Excerpts from Chapters II, III, and IV of Utilitarianism *by J. S. Mill.* (*London:* Frasers Magazine, 1861).

When thus attacked, the Epicureans have always answered that it is not they, but their accusers, who represent human nature in a degrading light, since the accusation supposes human beings to be capable of no pleasures except those of which swine are capable. If this supposition were true, the charge could not be gainsaid, but would then be no longer an imputation; for if the sources of pleasure were precisely the same to human beings and to swine, the rule of life which is good enough for the one would be good enough for the other. The comparison of the Epicurean life to that of beasts is felt as degrading, precisely because a beast's pleasures do not satisfy a human being's conceptions of happiness. Human beings have faculties more elevated than the animal appetites and, when once made conscious of them, do not regard anything as happiness which does not include their gratification. I do not, indeed, consider the Epicureans to have been by any means faultless in drawing out their scheme of consequences from the utilitarian principle. To do this in any sufficient manner, many Stoic, as well as Christian elements require to be included. But there is no known Epicurean theory of life which does not assign to the pleasures of the intellect, of the feelings and imagination, and of the moral sentiments a much higher value as pleasures than to those of mere sensation. It must be admitted, however, that utilitarian writers in general have placed the superiority of mental over bodily pleasures chiefly in the greater permanency, safety, uncostliness, etc., of the former — that is, in their circumstantial advantages rather than in their intrinsic nature. And on all these points utilitarians have fully proved their case; but they might have taken the other and, as it may be called, higher ground with entire consistency. It is quite compatible with the principle of utility to recognize the fact that some kinds of pleasure are more desirable and more valuable than others. It would be absurd that, while in estimating all other things quality is considered as well as quantity, the estimation of pleasure should be supposed to depend on quantity alone.

If I am asked what I mean by difference of quality in pleasures, or what makes one pleasure more valuable than another, merely as a pleasure, except its being greater in amount, there is but one possible answer. Of two pleasures, if there be one to which all or almost all who have experience of both give a decided preference, irrespective of any feeling of moral obligation to prefer it, that is the more desirable pleasure. If one of the two is, by those who are competently acquainted with both, placed so far above the other that they prefer it, even though knowing it to be attended with a greater amount of discontent, and would not resign it for any quantity of the other pleasure which their nature is capable of, we are justified in ascribing to the preferred enjoyment a superiority in quality so far outweighing quantity as to render it, in comparison, of small account.

Now it is an unquestionable fact that those who are equally acquainted with and equally capable of appreciating and enjoying both do give a most marked preference to the manner of existence which employs their higher faculties. Few human creatures would consent to be changed into any of the lower animals for a promise of the fullest allowance of a beast's pleasures; no intelligent human being would consent to be a fool, no instructed person would be an ignoramus, no person of feeling and conscience would be selfish and base, even though they should be persuaded that the fool, the dunce, or the rascal is better satisfied with his lot than they are with theirs. They would not resign what they possess more than he for the most complete satisfaction of all the desires which they have in common with him. If they ever fancy they would, it is only in cases of unhappiness so extreme that to escape from it they would exchange their lot for almost any other, however undesirable in their own eyes. A being of higher faculties requires more to make him happy, is capable probably of more acute suffering, and certainly accessible to it at more points, than one of an inferior type; but in spite of these liabilities, he can never really wish to sink into what he feels to be a lower grade of existence. We may give what explanation we please of this unwillingness; we may attribute it to pride, a name which is given indiscriminately to some of the most and to some of the least estimable feelings of which mankind are capable; we may refer it to the love of liberty and personal independence, an appeal to which was with the Stoics one of the most effective means for the inculcation of it; to the love of power or to the love of excitement, both of which do really enter into and contribute to it; but its most appropriate appellation is a sense of dignity, which all human beings possess in one form or other, and in some, though by no means in exact, proportion to their higher faculties, and which is so essential a part of the happiness of those in whom it is strong that nothing which conflicts with it could be otherwise than momentarily an object of desire to them. Whoever supposes that this preference takes place at a sacrifice of happiness — that the superior being, in anything like equal circumstances, is not happier than the inferior — confounds the two very different ideas of happiness and content. It is indisputable that the being whose capacities of enjoyment are low has the greatest chance of having them fully satisfied; and a highly endowed being will always feel that any happiness which he can look for, as the world is constituted, is imperfect. But he can learn to bear its imperfections, if they are at all bearable; and they will not make him envy the being who is indeed unconscious of the imperfections, but only because he feels not at all the good which those imperfections qualify. It is better to be a human being dissatisfied than a pig satisfied; better to be Socrates dissatisfied than a fool satisfied. And if the fool or the pig are of a different opinion, it is because they only know their own side of the question. The other party to the comparison knows both sides.

It may be objected that many who are capable of the higher pleasures occasionally, under the influence of temptation, postpone them to the lower. But this is quite compatible with a full appreciation of the intrinsic superiority of the higher. Men often, from infirmity of character, make their election for the nearer good, though they know it to be the less valuable; and this no less when the choice is between two bodily pleasures than when it is between bodily and mental. They pursue sensual indulgences to the injury of health, though perfectly aware that health is the greater good. It may be further objected that many who begin with youthful enthusiasm for everything noble, as they advance in years, sink into indolence and selfishness. But I do not believe that those who undergo this very common change voluntarily choose the lower description of pleasures in preference to the higher. I believe that, before they devote themselves exclusively to the one, they have already become incapable of the other. Capacity for the nobler feelings is in most natures a very tender plant, easily killed, not only by hostile influences, but by mere want of sustenance; and in the majority of young persons it speedily dies away if the occupations to which their position in life has devoted them, and the society into which it has thrown them, are not favorable to keeping that higher capacity in exercise. Men lose their high aspirations as they lose their intellectual tastes, because they have not time or opportunity for indulging them; and they addict themselves to inferior pleasures, not because they deliberately prefer them, but because they are either the only ones to which they have access or the only ones which they are any longer capable of enjoying. It may be questioned whether anyone who has remained equally susceptible to both classes of pleasures ever knowingly and calmly preferred the lower, though many, in all ages, have broken down in an ineffectual attempt to combine both.

From this verdict of the only competent judges, I apprehend there can be no appeal. On a question which is the best worth having of two pleasures, or which of two modes of existence is the most grateful to the feelings, apart from its moral attributes and from its consequences, the judgment of those who are qualified by knowledge of both, or, if they differ, that of the majority among them, must be admitted as final. And there needs be the less hesitation to accept this judgment respecting the quality of pleasures, since there is no other tribunal to be referred to even on the question of quantity. What means are there of determining which is the acutest of two pains, or the intensest of two pleasurable sensations, except the general suffrage of those who are familiar with both? Neither pains nor pleasures are homogeneous, and pain is always heterogeneous with pleasure. What is there to decide whether a particular pleasure is worth purchasing at the cost of a particular pain, except the feelings and judgment of the experienced? When, therefore, those feelings and judgment declare the pleasures derived from the higher faculties to be preferable *in kind,* apart from the question of intensity, to those of which the animal nature, disjoined from the higher faculties, is susceptible, they are entitled on this subject to the same regard. . . .

Of the Ultimate Sanction of the Principle of Utility

The question is often asked, and properly so, in regard to any supposed moral standard —What is its sanction? what are the motives to obey? or, more specifically, what is the source of its obligation? whence does it derive its binding force? It is a necessary part of moral philosophy to provide the answer to this question, which, though frequently assuming the shape of an objection to the utilitarian morality, as if it had some special applicability to that above others, really arises in regard to all standards. It arises, in fact, whenever a person is called on to *adopt* a standard, or refer morality to any basis on which he has not been accustomed to rest it. For the customary morality, that which education and opinion have consecrated, is the only one which presents itself to the mind with the feeling of being *in itself* obligatory; and when a person is asked to believe that this morality *derives* its obligation from some general principle round which custom has not thrown the same halo, the assertion is to him a paradox; the supposed corollaries seem to have a more binding force than the original theorem; the superstructure seems to stand better without than with what is represented as its foundation. He says to himself, I feel that I am bound not to rob or murder, betray or deceive; but why am I bound to promote the general happiness? If my own happiness lies in something else, why may I not give that the preference? . . .

The ultimate sanction, therefore, of all morality (external motives apart) being a subjective feeling in our own minds, I see nothing embarrassing to those whose standard is utility in the question, What is the sanction of that particular standard? We may answer, the same as of all other moral standards — the conscientious feelings of mankind. Undoubtedly this sanction has no binding efficacy on those who do not possess the feelings it appeals to; but neither will these persons be more obedient to any other moral principle than to the utilitarian one. On them morality of any kind has no hold but through the external sanctions. Meanwhile the feelings exist, a fact in human nature, the reality of which, and the great power with which they are capable of acting on those in whom they have been duly cultivated, are proved by experience. No reason has ever been shown why they may not be cultivated to as great intensity in connection with the utilitarian as with any other rule of morals.

There is, I am aware, a disposition to believe that a person who sees in moral obligation a transcendental fact, an objective reality belonging to the province of "things in themselves," is likely to be more obedient to it than one who believes it to be entirely subjective, having its seat in human consciousness only. But whatever a person's opinion may be on this point of ontology, the force he is really urged by is his own subjective feeling, and is exactly measured by its strength. No one's belief that duty is an objective reality is stronger than the belief that God is so; yet the belief in God, apart from the expectation of actual reward and punishment, only operates on conduct through, and in proportion to, the subjective religious feeling. The sanction, so far as it is disinterested, is always in the mind itself; and the notion, therefore, of the transcendental moralists must be that this sanction will not exist *in* the mind unless it is believed to have its root out of the mind; and that if a person is able to say to himself, "That which is restraining me and which is called my conscience is only a feeling in my own mind," he may possibly draw the conclusion that when the feeling ceases the obligation ceases, and that if he find the feeling inconvenient, he may disregard it and endeavor to get rid of it. But is this danger confined to the utilitarian morality? Does the belief that moral obligation has its seat outside the mind make the feeling of it too strong to be got rid of? The fact is so far otherwise that all moralists admit and lament the ease with which, in the generality of minds, conscience can be silenced or stifled. The question, "Need I obey my conscience?" is quite as often put to themselves by persons who never heard of the principle of utility as by its adherents. Those whose conscientious feelings are so weak as to allow of their asking this question, if they answer it affirmatively, will not do so because they believe in the transcendental theory, but because of the external sanctions. . . .

It is not necessary, for the present purpose, to decide whether the feeling of duty is innate or implanted. Assuming it to be innate, it is an open question to what objects it naturally attaches itself; for the philosophic supporters of that theory are now agreed that the intuitive perception is of principles of morality and not of the details. If there be anything innate in the matter, I see no reason why the feeling which is innate should not be that of regard to the pleasures and pains of others. If there is any principle of morals which is intuitively obligatory, I should say it must be that. If so, the intuitive ethics would coincide with the utilitarian, and there would be no further quarrel between them. Even as it is, the intuitive moralists, though they believe that there are other intuitive moral obligations, do already believe this to be one; for they unanimously hold that a large *portion* of morality turns upon the consideration due to the interests of our fellow creatures. Therefore, if the belief in the transcendental origin of moral obligation gives any additional efficacy to the internal sanction, it appears to me that the utilitarian principle has already the benefit of it.

On the other hand, if, as is my own belief, the moral feelings are not innate but acquired, they are not for that reason the less natural. It is natural to man to speak, to reason, to build cities, to cultivate the ground, though these are acquired faculties. The moral feelings are not indeed a part of our nature in the sense of being in any perceptible degree present in all of us; but this, unhappily, is a fact admitted by those who believe the most strenuously in their transcendental origin. Like the other acquired capacities above referred to, the moral faculty, if not a part of our nature, is a natural outgrowth from it; capable,

like them, in a certain small degree, of springing up spontaneously; and susceptible of being brought by cultivation to a high degree of development. Unhappily it is also susceptible, by a sufficient use of the external sanctions and of the force of early impressions, of being cultivated in almost any direction, so that there is hardly anything so absurd or so mischievous that it may not, by means of these influences, be made to act on the human mind with all the authority of conscience. To doubt that the same potency might be given by the same means to the principle of utility, even if it had no foundation in human nature, would be flying in the face of all experience.

But moral associations which are wholly of artificial creation, when the intellectual culture goes on, yield by degrees to the dissolving force of analysis; and if the feeling of duty, when associated with utility, would appear equally arbitrary; if there were no leading department of our nature, no powerful class of sentiments, with which that association would harmonize, which would make us feel it congenial and incline us not only to foster it in others (for which we have abundant interested motives), but also to cherish it in ourselves — if there were not, in short, a natural basis of sentiment for utilitarian morality, it might well happen that this association also, even after it had been implanted by education, might be analyzed away.

But there *is* this basis of powerful natural sentiment; and this it is which, when once the general happiness is recognized as the ethical standard, will constitute the strength of the utilitarian morality. This firm foundation is that of the social feelings of mankind — the desire to be in unity with our fellow creatures, which is already a powerful principle in human nature, and happily one of those which tend to become stronger, even without express inculcation, from the influences of advancing civilization. The social state is at once so natural, so necessary, and so habitual to man, that, except in some unusual circumstances or by an effort of voluntary abstraction, he never conceives himself otherwise than as a member of a body; and this association is riveted more and more, as mankind are further removed from the state of savage independence.

Any condition, therefore, which is essential to a state of society becomes more and more an inseparable part of every person's conception of the state of things which he is born into, and which is the destiny of a human being. Now society between human beings, except in the relation of master and slave, is manifestly impossible on any other footing than that the interests of all are to be consulted. Society between equals can only exist on the understanding that the interests of all are to be regarded equally. And since in all states of civilization, every person, except an absolute monarch, has equals, everyone is obliged to live on these terms with somebody; and in every age some advance is made toward a state in which it will be impossible to live permanently on other terms with anybody. . . .

Of What Sort of Proof the Principle of Utility Is Susceptible

It has already been remarked that questions of ultimate ends do not admit of proof, in the ordinary acceptation of the term. To be incapable of proof by reasoning is common to all first principles, to the first premises of our knowledge, as well as to those of our conduct. But the former, being matters of fact, may be the subject of a direct appeal to the faculties which judge of fact — namely, our senses and our internal consciousness. Can an appeal be made to the same faculties on questions of practical ends? Or by what other faculty is cognizance taken of them?

Questions about ends are, in other words, questions about what things are desirable. The utilitarian doctrine is that happiness is desirable, and the only thing desirable, as an end; all other things being only desirable as means to that end. What ought to be required of this doctrine, what conditions is it requisite that the doctrine should fulfill — to make good its claim to be believed?

The only proof capable of being given that an object is visible is that people actually see it. The only proof that a sound is audible is that people hear it; and so of the other sources of our experience. In like manner, I apprehend, the sole evidence it is possible to produce that anything is desirable is that people do actually desire it. If the end which the utilitarian doctrine proposes to itself were not, in theory and in practice, acknowledged to be an end, nothing could ever convince any person that it was so. No reason can be given why the general happiness is desirable, except that each person, so far as he believes it to be attainable, desires his own happiness. This, however, being a fact, we have not only all the proof which the case admits of, but all which it is possible to require, that happiness is a good, that each person's happiness is a good to that person, and the general happiness, therefore, a good to the aggregate of all persons. Happiness has made out its title as *one* of the ends of conduct and, consequently, one of the criteria of morality.

But it has not, by this alone, proved itself to be the sole criterion. To do that, it would seem, by the same rule, necessary to show, not only that people desire happiness, but that they never desire anything else. Now it is palpable that they do desire things which, in common language, are decidedly distinguished from happiness. They desire, for example, virtue and the absence of vice no less really than pleasure and the absence of pain. The desire of virtue is not as universal, but it is as authentic a fact as the desire of happiness. And hence the opponents of the utilitarian standard deem that they have a right to infer that there are other ends of human action besides happiness, and that happiness is not the standard of approbation and disapprobation.

But does the utilitarian doctrine deny that people desire virtue, or maintain that virtue is not a thing to be desired? The very reverse. It maintains not only that virtue is to be desired, but that it is to be desired disinterestedly, for itself. Whatever may be the opinion of utilitarian moralists as to the original conditions by which virtue is made virtue, however they may believe (as they do) that actions and dispositions are only virtuous because they promote another end than virtue, yet this being granted, and it having been decided, from considerations of this description, what *is* virtuous, they not only place virtue at the very head of the things which are good as means to the ultimate end, but they also recognize as a psychological fact the possibility of its being, to the individual, a good in itself, without looking to any end beyond it; and hold that the mind is not in a right state, not in a state conformable to utility, not in the state most conducive to the general happiness, unless it does love virtue in this manner — as a thing desirable in itself, even although, in the individual instance, it should not produce those other desirable consequences which it tends to produce, and on account of which it is held to be virtue. This opinion is not, in the smallest degree, a departure from the happiness principle. The ingredients of happiness are very various, and each of them is desirable in itself, and not merely when considered as swelling an aggregate. The principle of utility does not mean that any given pleasure, as music, for instance, or any given exemption from pain, as for example health, is to be looked upon as means to a collective something termed happiness, and to be desired on that account. They are desired and desirable in and for themselves; besides being means, they are a part of the end. Virtue, according to the utilitarian doctrine, is not naturally and originally part of the end, but it is capable of becoming so; and in those who live it disinterestedly it has become so, and is desired and cherished, not as a means to happiness, but as a part of their happiness. . . .

It results from the preceding considerations that there is in reality nothing desired except happiness. Whatever is desired otherwise than as a means to some end beyond itself, and ultimately to happiness, is desired as itself a part of happiness, and is not desired for itself until it has become so. Those who desire virtue for its own sake desire it either because the consciousness of it is a pleasure, or because the consciousness of being without it is a pain, or for both reasons united; as in truth the pleasure and pain seldom exist separately, but almost always together — the same person feeling pleasure in the degree of

virtue attained, and pain in not having attained more. If one of these gave him no pleasure, and the other no pain, he would not love or desire virtue, or would desire it only for the other benefits which it might produce to himself or to persons whom he cared for.

We have now, then, an answer to the question, of what sort of proof the principle of utility is susceptible. If the opinion which I have now stated is psychologically true — if human nature is so constituted as to desire nothing which is not either a part of happiness or a means of happiness — we can have no other proof, and we require no other, that these are the only things desirable. If so, happiness is the sole end of human action, and the promotion of it the test by which to judge of all human conduct; from whence it necessarily follows that it must be the criterion of morality, since a part is included in the whole.

And now to decide whether this is really so, whether mankind does desire nothing for itself but that which is a pleasure to them, or of which the absence is a pain, we have evidently arrived at a question of fact and experience, dependent, like all similar questions, upon evidence. It can only be determined by practiced self-consciousness and self-observation, assisted by observation of others. I believe that these sources of evidence, impartially consulted, will declare that desiring a thing and finding it pleasant, aversion to it and thinking of it as painful, are phenomena entirely inseparable or, rather, two parts of the same phenomenon — in strictness of language, two different modes of naming the same psychological fact; that to think of an object as desirable (unless for the sake of its consequences) and to think of it as pleasant are one and the same thing; and that to desire anything except in proportion as the idea of it is pleasant is a physical and metaphysical impossibility. . . .

3.4 Revaluation of Values

Consideration of the question "How can I know what is right?" leads to thinking about other questions, such as what makes an action right. The "what" in both these questions initiates a search for a "something" that not only makes for moral rightness but also is something we can know. Pondering what this "something" might be sends our minds along a path searching for what some have called the foundations of morality. Where does morality come from? What supports it? Why, in our struggle for existence, should we limit our behavior in any way, or at least in any way that might be called moral? Why be moral?

Many people have found a close association between religion and morality. Not only are the moral values we hold historically derived from certain religions like Judaism, Christianity, Islam, Hinduism, Confucianism, and others, but many have held that there must be some sort of divine source or foundation for morality. So some might say that the shortest answer to the question "How can I know what is right?" is "What does God say?"

This line of thought reflects a divine command theory of ethics (see Section 2.4). What is good is what God commands. However, this short answer is problematic. Which "god" are we talking about? How do we know what are the divine commands? Wars have been fought with both sides claiming they were acting according to God's will. And, as Socrates pointed out, if God's command or will determines what is good, then nothing is good in itself, but only if God should happen to will it. If the meaning of the concept "moral goodness" is equivalent to the meaning "God commands," then we have no independent standards for judging whether what God commands is good. It is good by definition. So, for example, if I believe God has commanded me to allow my diabetic child to go without medical treatment, then that is a good thing to do—by definition.

Another problem arises if we ask, "How do we know the divine will won't change?" One day murder may be wrong (forbidden by God) and the next day right (commanded by God). One can always counter that God is unchanging. The divine mind will never change with respect to morality. Of course, saying this is one thing; proving it is quite another. Thus this divine foundation of morality is beginning to appear very unstable, and moral goodness is beginning to look like little more than obedience to a superior power.

Some might say that if there is no God, then anything is morally permissible. There is no reason at all to limit our freedom to do what we want. Both Kant and Mill (see the two previous sections) were concerned with the issue of the foundation of morality and wanted to make a rational case for morality. If we cannot rely entirely on a religious answer to our question, perhaps human reason itself, without relying on alleged revelations of God's will, can supply an answer.

What if human reason should fail? What if Kant's categorical imperative and Mill's principle of utility turn out to be inadequate answers? Where might we turn next? Perhaps there is <u>no answer</u> (a view some have <u>dubbed **ethical nihilism**</u>) or, if there is, <u>we cannot not know</u> it (ethical skepticism).

Friedrich <u>Nietzsche</u> (1844–1900), a German philosopher, thought both the religious answer and the reliance on human reason failed. If all religious and rational accounts of morality fail, what are we left with? Some have argued that Nietzsche gave a negative answer. <u>We are left with nothing (nihilism)</u>. Others have argued that Nietzsche tried to overcome ethical nihilism with a theory of his own. Exactly how to characterize this theory, however, is problematic. For some it amounts to a version of **ethical emotivism,** or the claim that moral judgments express the appraiser's attitudes of approval or disapproval. "A (where A is some action) is good" becomes, according to an emotivist theory, "I like A." It is a short step, some philosophers have argued, from this position to the view that people ought to do what is in their own self-interest (**ethical egoism**) since it is in our self-interest to do what we like. Ethical egoism is often contrasted with **altruism** (the view that people ought, at least sometimes, to do what is in the interest of others). Much of the morality we have inherited stresses an altruistic viewpoint and Kant, as we have seen, finds selfishness at the root of immorality.

In order to understand Nietzsche, we must make a distinction between morality and ethics. The word morality can be used in both a wide and a narrow sense. In its wider sense it refers to any code of conduct or system of values. In this sense it is equivalent to the term *ethics.* In its narrow sense morality refers to a specific code or value system. Thus we speak about "honor among thieves" as a moral code, albeit one beyond morality as we normally think of it. In other words, morality in the narrow sense is only one of the possibilities for an ethical life (morality in the wider sense).

Nietzsche's approach to morality is naturalistic in the sense that an explanation of its existence requires no reference to some world beyond nature, be that a supernatural world containing some god who gives commands to humans or a metaphysical world of elaborate rationalistic theories that explain good and evil. The practices and associated feelings that we call ethical are quite natural to the human species. How we interpret or understand those practices (morality in the narrow sense) changes with time. What has happened, according to Nietzsche, is that an ascetic ideal of self-denial has come to dominate morality as we think of it. This has come about because of what he calls a "slave revolt" led by priests that transformed a noble idea of virtue or excellence into our conventional or herd ideas of moral virtue. This ascetic ideal will no longer work as an adequate interpretation of human ethical practice. The religious and traditional moral establishment that has supported it is becoming (for a variety of very complex reasons) increasingly weak. Its capacity to convince us that it is the right interpretation of our ethical practices is waning. What is needed is a new interpretation, a new moral ideal, if you will, that takes us beyond the conventional moral understandings of good and evil.

Exactly what this new ideal would be, Nietzsche, I think, did not clearly see. It was something that was arriving, a future that he only had glimpses of prior to his death in 1900. What he did know was that it was not a divine command theory, or a categorical imperative, or a principle of utility, or a principle of asceticism. It was a principle of a new nobility, a new type of humanity, that we have yet to realize. This new moral ideal affirms not the pleasure principle of the utilitarians, or the English psychologists as Nietzsche calls them, but the "will to power" that affirms life, the whole of life with all its pleasures and all its pains.

The selection that follows incorporates material from two of Nietzsche's most influential books, *Beyond Good and Evil,* first published in 1886, and *On the Genealogy of Morality,* first published in 1887. According to Nietzsche, the *Genealogy* was a "clarification and supplement to my last book, *Beyond Good and Evil.*" In both books Nietzsche wanted to show how the values of a noble and ruling class were revaluated by the slave classes led by priests (Nietzsche singled out the role the Jews played early in this process, but his remarks should not be construed as anti-Semitic) and motivated by hatred directed at the ruling class. Once we realize that our own life-denying morality that counsels us to sacrifice our self for the sake of others is the product of a historical process of revaluation, the way will be opened for another revaluation and the creation of a life-affirming morality that counsels us to respect ourselves and all who affirm life.

Reading Questions

1. How did Nietzsche characterize the pre-moral, moral, and extra-moral periods of human history?
2. What is wrong, according to Nietzsche, with past philosophical attempts to find the rational ground of morality?
3. What do you think Nietzsche meant when he said, "moralities too are only *a sign-language of the emotions*"?
4. What is the difference between the "will to the denial of life" and the "will to power"?
5. What are some of the basic differences between *slave morality* and *master morality*?
6. What is noble?
7. What is the "English psychologists'" theory of the origin of the concept "good" and why is it wrong?
8. What, according to Nietzsche, is the real origin of the concepts good and bad?
9. Under what conditions does the opposition between unegoistic (altruistic) and egoistic (selfish) arise?
10. According to Nietzsche, what role does the priestly class play in the development of morality?
11. What role does *ressentiment* (grudge-bearing resentment) play in the creation of slave morality?
12. What do you think Nietzsche meant when he said that "bad" is of noble origin and "evil" is the "true *deed*" of a slave morality?
13. What do you think about some of the things Nietzsche said? Do you think he was right or wrong? Could the conventional morality we follow today have a history rooted in class conflict and resentment?

Beyond Good and Evil

FRIEDRICH NIETZSCHE

32.

THROUGHOUT THE LONGEST PART of human history—it is called prehistoric times—the value or non-value of an action was derived from its consequences: the action itself came as little into consideration as did its origin, but, in much the same way as today in China a distinction or disgrace reflects back from the child onto its parents, so it was the retroactive force of success or failure which led men to think well or ill of an action.

Let us call this period the *pre-moral* period of mankind: the imperative "know thyself" was then still unknown. Over the past ten thousand years, on the other hand, one has in a few large tracts of the earth come step by step to the point at which it is no longer the consequences but the origin of the action which determines its value: a great event, taken as a whole, a considerable refinement of vision and standard, the unconscious after-effect of the sovereignty of aristocratic

From Friedrich Nietzsche, Beyond Good and Evil: Prelude to a Philosophy of the Future, *translated by R. J. Hollingdale. London: Penguin Books, 1990. Copyright © R. J. Hollingdale, 1973, 1990.*

values and of belief in "origins," the sign of a period which may be called the *moral* in the narrower sense: the first attempt at self-knowledge has been made. Instead of the consequences, the origin: what an inversion of perspectives! And certainly one achieved only after protracted struggles and vacillations! To be sure, a fateful new superstition, a peculiar narrowness of interpretation therewith became dominant: men interpreted the origin of an action in the most definite sense as origin in an *intention;* men became *unanimous* in the belief that the value of an action resided in the value of the intention behind it. The intention as the whole origin and prehistory of an action: it is under the sway of this prejudice that one has morally praised, blamed, judged and philosophized on earth almost to the present day.—But ought we not today to have arrived at the necessity of once again determining upon an inversion and shift of values, thanks to another self-examination and deepening on the part of man—ought we not to stand on the threshold of a period which should be called, negatively at first, the *extra-moral:* today, when among us immoralists at least the suspicion has arisen that the decisive value of an action resides in precisely that which is *not intentional* in it, and that all that in it which is intentional, all of it that can be seen, known, "conscious," still belongs to its surface and skin—which, like every skin, betrays something but *conceals* still more? In brief, we believe that the intention is only a sign and symptom that needs interpreting, and a sign, moreover, that signifies too many things and which thus taken by itself signifies practically nothing—that morality in the sense in which it has been understood hitherto, that is to say the morality of intentions, has been a prejudice, a precipitancy, perhaps something provisional and precursory, perhaps something of the order of astronomy and alchemy, but in any event something that must be overcome. The overcoming of morality, in a certain sense even the self-overcoming of morality: let this be the name for that protracted secret labour which has been reserved for the subtlest, most honest and also most malicious consciences as living touchstones of the soul. . . .

Part Five: On the Natural History of Morals

186.

. . . Philosophers one and all have, with a strait-laced seriousness that provokes laughter, demanded something much higher, more pretentious, more solemn of themselves as soon as they have concerned themselves with morality as a science: they wanted to furnish the *rational ground* of morality—and every philosopher hitherto has believed he has furnished this rational ground; morality itself, however, was taken as "given." How far from their clumsy pride was that apparently insignificant task left in dust and mildew, the task of description, although the most delicate hands and senses could hardly be delicate enough for it! It was precisely because moral philosophers knew the facts of morality only somewhat vaguely in an arbitrary extract or as a chance abridgement, as morality of their environment, their class, their church, the spirit of their times, their climate and zone of the earth, for instance—it was precisely because they were ill informed and not even very inquisitive about other peoples, ages and former times, that they did not so much as catch sight of the real problems of morality—for these come into view only if we compare *many* moralities. Strange though it may sound, in all "science of morals" hitherto the problem of morality itself has been *lacking*: the suspicion was lacking that there was anything problematic here. What philosophers called "the rational ground of morality" and sought to furnish was, viewed in the proper light, only a scholarly form of *faith* in the prevailing morality, a new way of *expressing* it, and thus itself a fact within a certain morality, indeed even in the last resort a kind of denial that this morality *ought* to be conceived of as a problem—and in any event the opposite of a testing, analysis, doubting and vivisection of this faith. . . .

187.

Quite apart from the value of such assertions as "there exists in us a categorical imperative" one can still ask: what does such an assertion say of the man who asserts it? There are moralities which are intended to justify their authors before others; other moralities are intended to calm him and make him content with himself; with others he wants to crucify and humiliate himself; with others he wants to wreak vengeance, with others hide himself, with others transfigure himself and set himself on high; this morality serves to make its author forget, that to make him or something about him forgotten; many moralists would like to exercise power and their creative moods on mankind; others, Kant perhaps among them, give to understand with their morality: "what is worthy of respect in me is that I know how to obey—and things *ought* to be no different with you!"—in short, moralities too are only a *sign-language of the emotions*. . . .

259.

To refrain from mutual injury, mutual violence, mutual exploitation, to equate one's own will with that of another: this may in a certain rough sense become good manners between individuals if the conditions for it are present (namely if their strength and value standards are in fact similar and they both belong to *one* body). As soon as there is a desire to take this principle further, however, and if possible even as the *fundamental principle of society,* it at once reveals itself for what it is: as the will to the *denial* of life, as the principle of dissolution and decay. One has to think this matter thoroughly through to the bottom and resist all sentimental weakness: life itself is *essentially* appropriation, injury, overpowering of the strange and weaker, suppression, severity, imposition of one's own forms, incorporation and, at the least and mildest, exploitation—but why should one always have to employ precisely those words which have from of old been stamped with a slanderous intention? Even that body within which, as was previously assumed, individuals treat one another as equals—this happens in every healthy aristocracy—must, if it is a living and not a decaying body, itself do all that to other bodies which the individuals within it refrain from doing to one another: it will have to be the will to power incarnate, it will want to grow, expand, draw to itself, gain ascendancy—not out of any morality

or immorality, but because it *lives,* and because life *is* will to power. On no point, however, is the common European consciousness more reluctant to learn than it is here; everywhere one enthuses, even under scientific disguises, about coming states of society in which there will be "no more exploitation"—that sounds to my ears like promising a life in which there will be no organic functions. "Exploitation" does not pertain to a corrupt or imperfect or primitive society: it pertains to the *essence* of the living thing as a fundamental organic function, it is a consequence of the intrinsic will to power which is precisely the will of life.—Granted this is a novelty as a theory—as a reality it is the *primordial fact* of all history: let us be at least that honest with ourselves!—

260.

In a tour of the many finer and coarser moralities which have ruled or still rule on earth I found certain traits regularly recurring together and bound up with one another: until at length two basic types were revealed and a basic distinction emerged. There is *master morality* and *slave morality*—I add at once that in all higher and mixed cultures attempts at mediation between the two are apparent and more frequently confusion and mutual misunderstanding between them, indeed sometimes their harsh juxtaposition—even within the same man, within *one* soul. The moral value-distinctions have arisen either among a ruling order which was pleasurably conscious of its distinction from the ruled—or among the ruled, the slaves and dependants of every degree. In the former case, when it is the rulers who determine the concept "good," it is the exalted, proud states of soul which are considered distinguishing and determine the order of rank. The noble human being separates from himself those natures in which the opposite of such exalted proud states find expression: he despises them. It should be noted at once that in this first type of morality the antithesis "good" and "bad" means the same thing as "noble" and "despicable"—the antithesis "good" and "*evil*" originates elsewhere. The cowardly, the timid, the petty, and those who think only of narrow utility are despised; as are the mistrustful with their constricted glance, those who abase themselves, the dog-like type of man who lets himself be mistreated, the fawning flatterer, above all the liar—it is a fundamental belief of all aristocrats that the common people are liars. "We who are truthful"—thus did the nobility of ancient Greece designate themselves. It is immediately obvious that designations of moral value were everywhere first applied to *human beings,* and only later and derivatively to *actions:* which is why it is a grave error when moral historians start from such questions as "why has the compassionate action been praised?" The noble type of man feels *himself* to be the determiner of values, he does not need to be approved of, he judges "what harms me is harmful in itself," he knows himself to be that which in general first accords honour to things, he *creates values.* Everything he knows to be part of himself, he honours: such a morality is self-glorification. In the foreground stands the feeling of plenitude, of power which seeks to overflow, the happiness of high tension, the consciousness of a wealth which would like to give away and bestow—the noble human being too aids the unfortunate but not, or almost not, from pity, but more from an urge begotten by superfluity of power. The noble human being honours in himself the man of power, also the man who has power over himself, who understands how to speak and how to keep silent, who enjoys practising severity and harshness upon himself and feels reverence for all that is severe and harsh. "A hard heart has Wotan set in my breast," it says in an old Scandinavian saga: a just expression coming from the soul of a proud Viking. A man of this type is actually proud that he is *not* made for pity: which is why the hero of the saga adds as a warning: "he whose heart is not hard in youth will never have a hard heart." Brave and noble men who think that they are at the farthest remove from that morality which sees the mark of the moral precisely in pity or in acting for others or in *désintéressement;* belief in oneself, pride in oneself, a fundamental hostility and irony for "selflessness" belong just as definitely to noble morality as does a mild contempt for and caution against sympathy and the "warm heart."—It is

the powerful who *understand* how to honour, that is their art, their realm of invention. Deep reverence for age and the traditional—all law rests on this twofold reverence—belief in and prejudice in favour of ancestors and against descendants, is typical of the morality of the powerful; and when, conversely, men of "modern ideas" believe almost instinctively in "progress" and "the future" and show an increasing lack of respect for age, this reveals clearly enough the ignoble origin of these "ideas." A morality of the rulers is, however, most alien and painful to contemporary taste in the severity of its principle that one has duties only towards one's equals; that towards beings of a lower rank, towards everything alien, one may act as one wishes or "as the heart dictates" and in any case "beyond good and evil"—: it is here that pity and the like can have a place. The capacity for and the duty of protracted gratitude and protracted revenge—both only among one's equals—subtlety in requittal, a refined conception of friendship, a certain need to have enemies (as conduit systems, as it were, for the emotions of envy, quarrelsomeness, arrogance—fundamentally so as to be able to be a good *friend*): all these are typical marks of noble morality which, as previously indicated, is not the morality of "modern ideas" and is therefore hard to enter into today, also hard to unearth and uncover.—It is otherwise with the second type of morality, *slave morality.* Suppose the abused, oppressed, suffering, unfree, those uncertain of themselves and weary should moralize: what would their moral evaluations have in common? Probably a pessimistic mistrust of the entire situation of man will find expression, perhaps a condemnation of man together with his situation. The slave is suspicious of the virtues of the powerful: he is sceptical and mistrustful, *keenly* mistrustful, of everything "good" that is honoured among them—he would like to convince himself that happiness itself is not genuine among them. On the other hand, those qualities which serve to make easier the existence of the suffering will be brought into prominence and flooded with light: here it is that pity, the kind and helping hand, the warm heart, patience, industriousness, humility, friendliness come into honour—for here these are the most useful qualities and virtually the only means of enduring the burden of existence. Slave morality is essentially the morality of utility. Here is the source of the famous antithesis "good" and "*evil*"—power and danger were felt to exist in evil, a certain dreadfulness, subtlety and strength which could not admit of contempt. Thus, according to slave morality the "evil" inspire fear; according to master morality it is precisely the "good" who inspire fear and want to inspire it, while the "bad" man is judged contemptible. The antithesis reaches its height when, consistently with slave morality, a breath of disdain finally also comes to be attached to the "good" of this morality—it may be a slight and benevolent disdain—because within the slaves' way of thinking the good man has in any event to be a *harmless* man: he is good-natured, easy to deceive, perhaps a bit stupid, *un bonhomme.* Wherever slave morality comes to predominate, language exhibits a tendency to bring the words "good" and "stupid" closer to each other.—A final fundamental distinction: the longing for *freedom,* the instinct for the happiness and the refinements of the feeling of freedom, belong just as necessarily to slave morality and morals as the art of reverence and devotion and the enthusiasm for them are the regular symptom of an aristocratic mode of thinking and valuating.—This makes it clear without further ado why love *as passion*—it is our European speciality—absolutely must be of aristocratic origin: it was, as is well known, invented by the poet-knights of Provence, those splendid, inventive men of the "*gai saber*" to whom Europe owes so much and, indeed, almost itself.— . . .

287.

—What is noble? What does the word "noble" mean to us today? What, beneath this heavy, overcast sky of the beginning rule of the rabble which makes everything leaden and opaque, betrays and makes evident the noble human being?—It is not his actions which reveal him—actions are always ambiguous, always unfathomable—; neither is it his "works." One finds today among artists and scholars sufficient who reveal by their works that they are driven on by a profound desire for the noble: but precisely this need *for* the noble is fundamentally different from the needs of the noble soul itself, and in fact an eloquent and dangerous sign of its lack. It is not the works, it is the *faith* which is decisive here, which determines the order of rank here, to employ an old religious formula in a new and deeper sense: some fundamental certainty which a noble soul possesses in regard to itself, something which may not be sought or found and perhaps may not be lost either.—*The noble soul has reverence for itself.*— . . .

On the Genealogy of Morality

FRIEDRICH NIETZSCHE

First Treatise: "Good and Evil," "Good and Bad"

1.

—These English psychologists whom we also have to thank for the only attempts so far to produce a history of the genesis of morality—they themselves are no small riddle for us; I confess, in fact, that precisely as riddles in the flesh they have something substantial over their books—*they themselves are interesting!* These English psychologists—what do they actually want? One finds them, whether voluntarily or involuntarily, always at the same task, namely of pushing the *partie honteuse*[1] of our inner world into the foreground and of seeking that which is actually effective, leading, decisive for our development, precisely where the intellectual pride of man would least of all *wish* to find it (for example in the *vis inertiae*[2] of habit or in forgetfulness or in a blind and accidental interlacing and mechanism of ideas or in anything purely passive, automatic, reflexive, molecular, and fundamentally mindless)—what is it actually that always drives these psychologists in precisely *this* direction? Is it a secret, malicious, base instinct to belittle mankind, one that perhaps cannot be acknowledged even to itself? Or, say, a pessimistic suspicion, the mistrust of disappointed, gloomy idealists who have become poisonous and green? Or a little subterranean animosity and rancor against Christianity (and Plato) that has perhaps not yet made it past the threshold of consciousness? Or even a lascivious taste for the disconcerting, for the painful-paradoxical, for the questionable and nonsensical aspects of existence? Or finally—a little of everything, a little meanness, a little gloominess, a little anti-Christianity, a little tickle and need for pepper? . . . But I am told that they are simply old, cold, boring frogs who creep and hop around on human beings, into human beings, as if they were really in their element there, namely in a *swamp*. I resist this, still more, I don't believe it; and if one is permitted to wish where one cannot know, then I wish from my heart that the reverse may be the case with them—that these explorers and microscopists of the soul are basically brave, magnanimous, and proud animals who know how to keep a rein on their hearts as well as their pain and have trained themselves to sacrifice all desirability to truth, to *every* truth, even plain, harsh, ugly, unpleasant, unchristian, immoral truth . . . For there are such truths.—

1. *partie honteuse* shameful part (in the plural, this expression is the equivalent of the English "private parts").
2. *vis inertiae* force of inactivity. In Newtonian physics, this term denotes the resistance offered by matter to any force tending to alter its state of rest or motion.

2.

Hats off then to whatever good spirits may be at work in these historians of morality! Unfortunately, however, it is certain that they lack the *historical spirit* itself, that they have been left in the lurch precisely by all the good spirits of history! As is simply the age-old practice among philosophers, they all think *essentially* ahistorically; of this there is no doubt. The ineptitude of their moral genealogy is exposed right at the beginning, where it is a matter of determining the origins of the concept and judgment "good." "Originally"—so they decree—"unegoistic actions were praised and called good from the perspective of those to whom they were rendered, hence for whom they were *useful;* later one *forgot* this origin of the praise and, simply because unegoistic actions were *as a matter of habit* always praised as good, one also felt them to be good—as if they were something good in themselves." One sees immediately: this first derivation already contains all the characteristic traits of the idiosyncrasy of English psychologists—we have "usefulness," "forgetting," "habit," and in the end "error," all as basis for a valuation of which the higher human being has until now been proud as if it were some kind of distinctive prerogative of humankind. This pride *must* be humbled, this valuation devalued: has this been achieved? . . . Now in the first place it is obvious to me that the actual genesis of the concept "good" is sought and fixed in the wrong place by this theory: the judgment "good" does *not* stem from those to whom "goodness" is rendered! Rather it was "the good" themselves, that is the noble, powerful, higher-ranking, and high-minded who felt and ranked themselves and their doings as good, which is to say, as of the first rank, in contrast to everything base, low-minded, common, and vulgar. Out of this *pathos of distance* they first took for themselves the right to create values, to coin names for values: what did they care about usefulness! The viewpoint of utility is as foreign and inappropriate as possible, especially in relation to so hot an outpouring of highest rank-ordering, rank-distinguishing value judgments: for here feeling has arrived at an opposite of that low degree of warmth presupposed by every calculating prudence, every assessment of utility—and not just for once, for an hour of exception, but rather for the long run. As was stated, the pathos of nobility and distance, this lasting and dominant collective and basic feeling of a higher ruling nature in relation to a lower nature, to a "below"—*that* is the origin of the opposition "good" and "bad." (The right of lords to give names goes so far that we should allow ourselves to comprehend the origin of language itself as an expression of power on the part of those who rule: they say "this *is* such and such," they seal each thing and happening with a sound and thus, as it were, take possession of it.) It is because of this origin that from the outset the word "good" does *not* necessarily attach itself to "unegoistic" actions—as is the superstition of those genealogists of morality. On the contrary, only when aristocratic value judgments begin to *decline* does this entire opposition "egoistic" "unegoistic" impose itself more and more on the human conscience—to make use of my language, it is *the herd instinct* that finally finds a voice (also *words*) in this opposition. And even then it takes a long time until this instinct becomes dominant to such an extent that moral valuation in effect gets caught and stuck at that opposition (as is the case in present-day Europe: today the prejudice that takes "moral," "unegoistic," "*désintéressé*"[3] to be concepts of equal value already rules with the force of an "*idée fixe*"[4] and sickness in the head).

3.

In the second place, however: quite apart from the historical untenability of that hypothesis concerning the origins of the value judgment "good," it suffers from an inherent psychological absurdity. The usefulness of the unegoistic action is supposed to be the origin of its praise, and this origin is supposed to have been *forgotten:*—how is this forgetting even *possible?*

3. *désintéressé* disinterested, unselfish, selfless.
4. "*idée fixe*" obsession; literally: a fixed idea.

Did the usefulness of such actions cease at some point? The opposite is the case: this usefulness has been the everyday experience in all ages, something therefore that was continually underscored anew; accordingly, instead of disappearing from consciousness, instead of becoming forgettable, it could not help but impress itself upon consciousness with ever greater clarity. How much more reasonable is that opposing theory (it is not therefore truer—) advocated for example by Herbert Spencer—which ranks the concept "good" as essentially identical with the concept "useful," "purposive," so that in the judgments "good" and "bad" humanity has summed up and sanctioned its *unforgotten* and *unforgettable* experiences concerning what is useful-purposive, what is injurious-nonpurposive. Good, according to this theory, is whatever has proved itself as useful from time immemorial: it may thus claim validity as "valuable in the highest degree," as "valuable in itself." This path of explanation is also false, as noted above, but at least the explanation is in itself reasonable and psychologically tenable.

4.

—The pointer to the *right* path was given to me by the question: what do the terms coined for "good" in the various languages actually mean from an etymological viewpoint? Here I found that they all lead back to the *same conceptual transformation*—that everywhere the basic concept is "noble," "aristocratic" in the sense related to the estates, out of which "good" in the sense of "noble of soul," "high-natured of soul," "privileged of soul" necessarily develops: a development that always runs parallel to that other one which makes "common," "vulgar," "base" pass over finally into the concept "bad." The most eloquent example of the latter is the German word "*schlecht*" [bad] itself: which is identical with "*schlicht*" [plain, simple]—compare "*schlechtweg*," "*schlechterdings*" [simply or downright]—and originally designated the plain, the common man, as yet without a suspecting sideward glance, simply in opposition to the noble one. Around the time of the Thirty-Years'

War, in other words late enough, this sense shifts into the one now commonly used.—With respect to morality's genealogy this appears to me to be an *essential* insight; that it is only now being discovered is due to the inhibiting influence that democratic prejudice exercises in the modern world with regard to all questions of origins. And this influence extends all the way into that seemingly most objective realm of natural science and physiology, as I shall merely hint at here. But the nonsense that this prejudice—once unleashed to the point of hate—is able to inflict, especially on morality and history, is shown by Buckle's notorious case; the *plebeianism* of the modern spirit, which is of English descent, sprang forth there once again on its native ground, vehemently like a muddy volcano and with that oversalted, overloud, common eloquence with which until now all volcanoes have spoken.— . . .

7.

—One will already have guessed how easily the priestly manner of valuation can branch off from the knightly-aristocratic and then develop into its opposite; this process is especially given an impetus every time the priestly caste and the warrior caste confront each other jealously and are unable to agree on a price. The knightly-aristocratic value judgments have as their presupposition a powerful physicality, a blossoming, rich, even overflowing health, together with that which is required for its preservation: war, adventure, the hunt, dance, athletic contests, and in general everything which includes strong, free, cheerful-hearted activity. The priestly-noble manner of valuation—as we have seen—has other presuppositions: too bad for it when it comes to war! Priests are, as is well known, the *most evil enemies*—why is that? Because they are the most powerless. Out of their powerlessness their hate grows into something enormous and uncanny, into something most spiritual and most poisonous. The truly great haters in the history of the world have always been priests, also the most ingenious haters:—compared with the spirit of

priestly revenge all the rest of spirit taken together hardly merits consideration. Human history would be much too stupid an affair without the spirit that has entered into it through the powerless:—let us turn right to the greatest example. Of all that has been done on earth against "the noble," "the mighty," "the lords," "the power-holders," nothing is worthy of mention in comparison with that which the *Jews* have done against them: the Jews, that priestly people who in the end were only able to obtain satisfaction from their enemies and conquerors through a radical revaluation of their values, that is, through an act of *spiritual revenge*. This was the only way that suited a priestly people, the people of the most suppressed priestly desire for revenge. It was the Jews who in opposition to the aristocratic value equation (good = noble = powerful = beautiful = happy = beloved of God) dared its inversion, with fear-inspiring consistency, and held it fast with teeth of the most unfathomable hate (the hate of powerlessness), namely: "the miserable alone are the good; the poor, powerless, lowly alone are the good; the suffering, deprived, sick, ugly are also the only pious, the only blessed in God, for them alone is there blessedness,—whereas you, you noble and powerful ones, you are in all eternity the evil, the cruel, the lustful, the insatiable, the godless, you will eternally be the wretched, accursed, and damned!". . . We know *who* inherited this Jewish revaluation. . . . In connection with the enormous and immeasurably doom-laden initiative provided by the Jews with this most fundamental of all declarations of war, I call attention to the proposition which I arrived at on another occasion ("Beyond Good and Evil" section 195)—namely, that with the Jews *the slave revolt in morality* begins: that revolt which has a two-thousand-year history behind it and which has only moved out of our sight today because it—has been victorious. . . .

10.

The slave revolt in morality begins when *ressentiment* itself becomes creative and gives birth to values: the *ressentiment* of beings denied the true reaction, that of the deed, who recover their losses only through an imaginary revenge. Whereas all noble morality grows out of a triumphant yes-saying to oneself, from the outset slave morality says "no" to an "outside," to a "different," to a "not-self": and *this* "no" is its creative deed. This reversal of the value-establishing glance—this *necessary* direction toward the outside instead of back onto oneself—belongs to the very nature of *ressentiment:* in order to come into being, slave-morality always needs an opposite and external world; it needs, psychologically speaking, external stimuli in order to be able to act at all,—its action is, from the ground up, reaction. The reverse is the case with the noble manner of valuation: it acts and grows spontaneously, it seeks out its opposite only in order to say "yes" to itself still more gratefully and more jubilantly—its negative concept "low" "common" "bad" is only an after-birth, a pale contrast-image in relation to its positive basic concept, saturated through and through with life and passion: "we noble ones, we good ones, we beautiful ones, we happy ones!" When the noble manner of valuation lays a hand on reality and sins against it, this occurs relative to the sphere with which it is *not* sufficiently acquainted, indeed against a real knowledge of which it rigidly defends itself: in some cases it forms a wrong idea of the sphere it holds in contempt, that of the common man, of the lower people; on the other hand, consider that the affect of contempt, of looking down on, of the superior glance—assuming that it does *falsify* the image of the one held in contempt—will in any case fall far short of the falsification with which the suppressed hate, the revenge of the powerless, lays a hand on its opponent—in effigy, of course. Indeed there is too much carelessness in contempt, too much taking-lightly, too much looking-away and impatience mixed in, even too much of a feeling of cheer in oneself, for it to be capable of transforming its object into a real caricature. . . . For the *ressentiment* of the noble human being, when it appears in him, runs its course and exhausts itself in an immediate reaction, therefore it does not *poison*—on the

other hand it does not appear at all in countless cases where it is unavoidable in all the weak and powerless. To be unable for any length of time to take his enemies, his accidents, his *misdeeds* themselves seriously—that is the sign of strong, full natures in which there is an excess of formative, reconstructive, healing power that also makes one forget (a good example of this from the modern world is Mirabeau, who had no memory for insults and base deeds committed against him and who was only unable to forgive because he—forgot). Such a human is simply able to shake off with a single shrug a collection of worms that in others would dig itself in; here alone is also possible—assuming that it is at all possible on earth—the true "*love* of one's enemies." What great reverence for his enemies a noble human being has!—and such reverence is already a bridge to love. . . . After all, he demands his enemy for himself, as his distinction; he can stand no other enemy than one in whom there is nothing to hold in contempt and *a very great deal* to honor! On the other hand, imagine "the enemy" as the human being of *ressentiment* conceives of him—and precisely here is his deed, his creation: he has conceived of "the evil enemy," "*the evil one,*" and this indeed as the basic concept, starting from which he now also thinks up, as reaction and counterpart, a "good one"—himself! . . .

11.

Precisely the reverse, therefore, of the case of the noble one, who conceives the basic concept "good" in advance and spontaneously, starting from himself that is, and from there first creates for himself an idea of "bad"! This "bad" of noble origin and that "evil" out of the brewing cauldron of unsatiated hate—the first, an after-creation, something on the side, a complementary color; the second, in contrast, the original, the beginning, the true *deed* in the conception of a slave morality—how differently the two words "bad" and "evil" stand there, seemingly set in opposition to the same concept "good"! But it is *not* the same concept "good": on the contrary, just ask yourself *who* is actually "evil" in the sense of the morality of *ressentiment*. To answer in all strictness: *precisely* the "good one" of the other morality, precisely the noble, the powerful, the ruling one, only recolored, only reinterpreted, only reseen through the poisonous eye of *ressentiment*. There is one point we wish to deny least of all here: whoever encounters those "good ones" only as enemies encounters nothing but *evil enemies,* and the same humans who are kept so strictly within limits *inter pares,* by mores, worship, custom, gratitude, still more by mutual surveillance, by jealousy, and who on the other hand in their conduct towards each other prove themselves so inventive in consideration, self-control, tact, loyalty, pride, and friendship,—they are not much better than uncaged beasts of prey toward the outside world, where that which is foreign, the foreign world, begins. There they enjoy freedom from all social constraint; in the wilderness they recover the losses incurred through the tension that comes from a long enclosure and fencing-in within the peace of the community; they step *back* into the innocence of the beast-of-prey conscience, as jubilant monsters, who perhaps walk away from a hideous succession of murder, arson, rape, torture with such high spirits and equanimity that it seems as if they have only played a student prank, convinced that for years to come the poets will again have something to sing and to praise. . . .

3.5 Care versus Rights

In 1982, Carol Gilligan, a developmental psychologist, published a book entitled *In a Different Voice.* She pointed out that empirical research into moral reasoning and moral development used samples consisting of mostly male subjects. Thus, most of the major psychological theories of moral reasoning took male reasoning and male development as the norm.

Gilligan began to listen to women and discovered that their approach to moral issues was different from the male approach. The male perspective toward relationships tends to emphasize reciprocity. Equality, justice, rights, impartiality, objectivity, generalization, fair rules, and logical reasoning emerge as central concerns of males when dealing with moral dilemmas. For example, an 11-year-old boy, Jake, is given the Heinz dilemma. A man named Heinz considers whether to steal a drug that he cannot afford to buy because the drug is essential for saving the life of his wife. Jake is confident that Heinz should steal the drug because this is a clear-cut case of a conflict between the values of property and life. Logically, he argues, since life is irreplaceable, it must be given greater priority than property.

The female approach to moral problems, according to Gilligan, tends to be responsive. Care, love, trust, dealing with specific persons who have specific needs, compassion, mercy, forgiveness, the importance of not hurting anyone, and the authority of feeling in solving problems emerge as central concerns of females when dealing with moral issues. For example, Amy, also 11 years old, when given the Heinz dilemma, says she is not sure whether Heinz should steal the drug since that would harm the druggist. Also, Heinz might harm himself if he is caught and has to go to jail. That would also harm his wife who needs him to take care of her. Of course, she shouldn't be allowed to die either. Some other way needs to be found (borrow the money, work out installment payments), and she suggests they all get together, talk about the problem, and find a solution acceptable to all concerned.

Lawrence Kohlberg, who originally designed the study and developed the theory to which Gilligan is responding, construed the Heinz dilemma as a conflict between life and property and thus would regard Jake's response as indicative of a higher level of moral reasoning than Amy's. Gilligan remarks that one is not "higher" than the other—they are just different.

The major and most influential theories in moral philosophy have been developed by men. They reflect what Gilligan sees as the male concern with logical consistency, impartiality, rights, and obligations. Gilligan's work in descriptive psychology inspired the development of *feminist ethical theories* by philosophers. These feminist theories often begin with a critique of the sexism hidden in traditional moral theories and then go on to develop theories that take seriously caring and nurturing.

However, some feminist philosophers have been critical of this development for several reasons. First, an ethics of care may itself be sexist by elevating to philosophic status gender stereotypes of women as more self-sacrificing and more nurturing than men. This can work against women by reinforcing the idea that women are best suited to raising children and working in the "caring" professions, thereby restricting their opportunities. Second, an ethics of care cannot be divorced from an ethics of justice or rights without severe consequences. Justice demands that we treat people fairly, and this is an ethical notion that has played an important role in the women's movement for liberation. For example, the "Seneca Falls Declaration" that resulted from the 1848 conference convened by Elizabeth Cady Stanton and Lucretia Mott in Seneca Falls, New York, to consider the "rights of women" states that "these truths [are] self-evident: that all men and *women* are created equal. . . ." The implicit reference to the "Declaration of Independence" and the adding of the word *women* anchored the claim to equal rights in the values already widely accepted in the United States and thereby made it far more difficult for men to deny women fundamental rights (such as the right to vote). Whatever we may think about the ethical importance of caring for people, caring without justice leaves us with a very one-sided moral theory.

Joy Kroeger-Mappes, author of the next selection, teaches philosophy at Frostburg State University in Maryland. She is an assistant professor of philosophy and women's studies with a Ph.D. in philosophy from Georgetown University.

Reading Questions

1. What is the main point Kroeger-Mappes wishes to make?
2. Describe some of the main features of an "ethic of rights" (or justice) in contrast to the "ethics of care."
3. What two theses capture the meaning of the "one-system" conception?
4. What is "moral madness," and how does it reveal a "fatal flaw" in the system?
5. According to Kroeger-Mappes, what is needed and what is not needed?
6. Does anything the author says coincide with your experience?
   If so, what?

The Ethic of Care vis-à-vis the Ethic of Rights*

JOY KROEGER-MAPPES

I. Introduction

CAROL GILLIGAN HAS DELINEATED two ethics, the ethic of rights and the ethic of care. The implications of this work have reverberated throughout both academic and nonacademic circles. In this article I focus on the wider discussion and understanding of Gilligan's work and its implications rather than on the scholarship devoted specifically to Gilligan's writings. I argue that the two ethics are part of one system, the ethic of care functioning as a necessary base of the ethic of rights. I also argue that the system is seriously flawed in that it is biased in favor of men. Ethical theory thus functions, as it has in the past, to support the subordination of women. It may also and in similar ways support the subordination of one group by another in other dominant-subordinate relationships. Because women are held accountable to both ethics and because the two ethics frequently conflict, women recurrently find themselves in a moral double bind. This account of morality allows us to understand what many women describe as "moral madness" (Morgan 1987).

Why does Gilligan's work continue to receive attention when much of this attention has been quite negative? The reasons for the extensive debate are important in themselves. One reason given is that Gilligan's ethic of care has important implications for feminism, theory in the social sciences, and moral philosophy. It also generates discussion among both "specialists" interested in theory and "generalists" who can latch onto the concept of the ethic of care that by now is a "famous concept" (Davis, 1992, 222). Nevertheless, criticisms have come from all quarters and particularly from social scientists who have questioned Gilligan's methodology as well as the theoretical underpinnings of the ethic of care (Davis 1993; Kerber et al. 1986). In a recent article Kathy Davis attempts to explain why the debate about Gilligan's work arose in the first place and continues, despite the fact that much of the debate is repetitive. Davis describes Gilligan's work as a "successful" theory. Theories that are successful do not survive because they "provide an accurate reflection of reality"; rather they attract our interest because they deny our unexamined assumptions, appeal to our shared concerns, and provide a novel explanation (221).

Instead of providing a novel explanation of ethics, however, Gilligan has highlighted the ethic of rights and some of the difficulties with it, revealed a part of the ethic of care that had been present but largely invisible before, and suggested predictable ways of reforming this ethical system. In other words, Gilligan retells a particular official story (Upin 1992, 180–83), the story of ethical theory which is the ethic of rights, and modifies it slightly. As Davis says, Gilligan does deny some of our examined assumptions by asking how "girls" and "women" fit in and appeals to many of our shared concerns about our individual and collective well-being. What Gilligan does not do is significantly alter or transform the official story. Gilligan's discussion of the ethic of care can be seen as a female, that is, feminine, or a woman's ethic that is consistent with the subordination of women. Seen in this way, the modified official story is another false

* I wish to thank Tom Mappes, Elli Burkett, Shelley Drees, Jane Zembaty, Pat Altenbernd Johnson, Susan Allen, Philip Alien, Sara Chant, Pat Coward, and Mary Anne Lutz for comments and encouragement sustained through many drafts of this paper.

From Joy Kroeger-Mappes, "The Ethics of Care vis-à-vis the Ethics of Rights: A Problem for Contemporary Moral Theory." Hypatia, Vol. 9 (Summer, 1994), 108ff. Copyright © 1994 Indiana University Press. Reprinted by permission. Footnotes renumbered.

generalization. In the most recent version of the official story the ethic of rights was falsely generalized to apply to "women" as well as to "men." Gilligan, in slightly changing the official story, falsely generalizes about "women" in suggesting that there is a different voice, namely, a women's ethic. I address a variety of ways of thinking about the difficulties with regard to this generalization later in the article.[1]

In this article, I focus on the relation of the two ethics within moral philosophy and some of the real life implications of this relation. One assumption in modern moral philosophy (and in much common sense) in the late twentieth century has been that women are included in moral guidelines, categories, and contexts, so that moral admonitions or rules apply to women and men equally. Much of moral and political philosophy has consisted of worlds with no women in them and only some men, though some women received brief mention now and again. According to Marilyn Frye, "Most academic philosophical activity appears . . . to be almost untouched by feminism, either the political movement or the philosophy" (Frye 1992b, 130). Some philosophers claim that since women have been left out in the past, all that is needed now is to update the examples and to use more inclusive pronouns than, say, Kant used or would have been willing to use because of his bias. In words well known in the area of curriculum transformation, "just add women and stir." Many moral philosophers adhere to this view, though work in feminist ethics may have had some more significant effect. Work in feminist ethics raises questions that would alter moral theory considerably. Certainly, the comprehensiveness of past moral philosophy is in doubt; the view of moral life reflected in ethical theory must now be recognized as only a partial view. To use Marilyn Frye's imagery, ethical theorists dealt only with what was happening

among the players on stage and were led to conclude that the players alone accounted for bringing the play into existence and sustaining each performance (Frye 1983, 168–69). The ethic of care as we know it, however, has been functioning behind the scenes all along, or at least for a few centuries. In addition to briefly summarizing the two ethics as Gilligan presents them and in order to see how they form one system, it is necessary to show the difference between the ethic of rights, sometimes referred to as the justice approach, and rights theory as it is more narrowly understood in moral and political philosophy.

According to Gilligan, the logic of the ethic of rights posits individuals as opponents in contests of rights. In this logic, morality consists of a hierarchy of rights and rules used to resolve moral conflicts or problems by weighing claims and judging which is the heavier claim. Images of winning and losing are common. There is potential for violence resulting, in part, from seeing others as opponents and seeing oneself in contests to obtain, or win, one's rights and to maintain them. Individual rights are primary and universal. Actual moral dilemmas are conceived of as "math problems with humans," and the solution is rationally arrived at so that anyone following reason will arrive at more or less the same conclusion. Abstracting from the interpersonal situation and solving hypothetical dilemmas are means of arriving at objective criteria and objectively deciding who will win in the contest of rights. An underlying premise of the ethic of rights is that individuals are separate from one another. Relationships are viewed as derived from separation; connection with others is experienced as freely contracted. Involvement with others then qualifies identity.

The ethic of care, as Gilligan outlines it, understands responsibility within a context of relationship or connection. The image is that of a web which ultimately connects everyone. Responsibility is equated with the need to respond. Individuals need to respond when they recognize that others are counting on them and when they are in a position to help. The ideal of care is an activity of relationship, of seeing and

---

1. I believe that gender is an important analytical category and largely agree with Susan Bordo (1992, 197–205). However, I also agree with Maria Lugones and others that white, Anglo, European, middle class, heterosexual Christian women have perpetuated and created official stories that are destructive to many women.

responding to need. The moral imperative is to care, namely to discern and alleviate trouble in the world. Communication is the means of resolving conflict. Because the activity of care is seen as enhancing both others and self, and violence is viewed as destructive to all, conflict resolution is nonviolent. No single specific principle or set of principles, as moral principles are generally thought of, applies to situations or settles disputes. Rather a guiding principle relates responsibility to caring about others and yourself.

As contrasted to the ethic of care, the ethic of rights, when articulated philosophically, embodies an obligation theory. The ethic of rights, as Gilligan speaks of it and as discussed in much of the work by feminist philosophers in this area[2] is not synonymous with the narrower rights theory of social and political philosophy. Rather, the ethic of rights includes, but is not limited to, standard rights theory. It focuses on what moral theories, including political theory, since the seventeenth and eighteenth centuries have in common rather than on how they differ. Rights are symbols of attitudes built into modern moral theory which set out ways of determining what moral obligation individuals, supposedly whoever they might be, have toward one another. There are significant similarities among such modern moral theorists as Immanuel Kant, John Stuart Mill, John Rawls, and Robert Nozick. The differences among their theories and the distinctions among various mainstream deontologists and utilitarians and among various mainstream liberals and libertarians fill volumes and span centuries. In many contexts there is much to be gained by paying careful attention to these differences. It is also important, however, to view modern moral theories from the perspective of what they share. Paraphrasing Catharine MacKinnon, the history of ethical theory as it applies to men and women is fairly consistent. "Underneath all of these hills and valleys, these ebbs and flows, there is this bedrock, this tide that has not changed much, namely male supremacy and the subordination of women" (MacKinnon 1991, 6). Gilligan's general conception of the ethic of rights has provided an opening for understanding some of the impact of this ethic.

Are there two general ethics, one for women as compared to men, and, if so, how are they related to each other? Annette Baier, wary of generalizations, nevertheless thinks she hears a voice in the work of moral philosophers who are women that is different from the voice heard in men's "theory of obligation," a phrase she associates with Gilligan's ethic of rights. In Baier's view, the theory of obligation leaves out much that is important in morality. She believes that social contract theory in particular has misplaced the emphasis and has taken contractual obligations to be the model of moral obligations. As Baier points out, modern ethical theories seem to be "traffic rules for self-asserters" (Baier 1985, 62). She sees the concept of trust as a possible bridge between the ethic of care and obligation theory. . . .

In viewing the ethic of rights and the ethic of care as separate moral domains, which somehow only need to be linked, Baier makes an important mistake. To think that the two ethics are separate is in effect to take the roles and interaction of the two moral domains out of their context and to render the domains ahistorical. Baier herself clearly reveals the political nature of this interaction when she discusses the relative powerlessness of women. But this analysis is not sustained when she turns her attention to the relation of the ethic of care vis-à-vis the ethic of rights.

In asserting that the ethic of rights and the ethic of care are parts of one system, I certainly do not mean to deny the distinctiveness of the two ethics. To deny the distinctiveness of the ethic of care, in particular, would be tantamount to losing it once again. Caring and nurturance, for example, have been subsumed under the general heading of benevolence. As a result, their distinctiveness has been forgotten and ignored. To neglect the fact that many moral virtues still continue to bear the marks of their gender-related history is to run the risk of devaluation, distortion, or invisibility. Affirming the

2. For example, Margaret Urban Walker (1992) speaks of the theoretical model of ethics and earlier (1989) of the universalist/impersonalist tradition.

distinctiveness of the ethics, however, should not mislead us into thinking of them (as Baier does) as separate, as existing apart from one another. The two ethics are distinctive, but they jointly constitute part of one overall system. Not to see the two ethics as parts of one system is to miss the difference in relative power that was once so important in Baier's analysis. Unless the intimate connection of the two ethics operating within one system is acknowledged, the relative power-lessness of women who are assigned the ethic of care will continue to go unrecognized.

II. The One-System Conception

In this section I reveal the two ethics as elements of one system of morality by arguing for two theses that in large part express the meaning of the one-system conception. The first thesis, the supererogatory thesis, asserts that the activity of caring, which is perceived as supererogatory for most men, is perceived as obligatory for most women. The second thesis, the necessary-base thesis, holds that the ethic of care is a necessary base for the ethic of rights. The supererogatory thesis deals with our collective social perceptions and understandings, so empirical evidence will be recruited in its support. The necessary-base thesis is a philosophical thesis revealing at a theoretical level moral relationships within social reality. Since the truth of the necessary-base thesis follows in part from the truth of the supererogatory thesis and in part from other philosophical considerations, I begin with a consideration of the supererogatory thesis.

Can it really be that both the supererogatory and what is obligatory for men constitute what is obligatory for women? Consider the following. Women, whatever else they are to do, traditionally have been given the essential duties of the preservation and repair of human relations in general. Women's work, according to Adrienne Rich, has been the work of "world-protection, world-preservation, and world-repair," which includes "the invisible weaving of frayed and threadbare family life" (Rich 1977, 205). Women's distinctive labor consists largely of caring for others either inside the home or outside the home in

service jobs.[3] Women care for infants, children, the elderly, and the sick, handicapped, or help-less (Sommers et. al. 1987). Women, "by virtue of their position in the world vis-à-vis men, and by virtue of their special labor, have experienced a distinctive form of moral labor that (roughly) parallels the sexual division of labor" (Houston 1987, 258). Despite the fact that much of what women do is not considered work, as feminists have repeatedly pointed out, women have in fact been assigned a distinctive moral labor. It is understood by both men and women that women's responsibilities include the activity of caring. Women's distinctive moral labor is in essence obligatory for them and is at the same time supererogatory from the perspective of the ethic of rights. As the point is expressed in the supererogatory thesis, the activity of caring, which is perceived as supererogatory for most men, is perceived as obligatory for most women.

There is perhaps a shorter route by which the supererogatory thesis could be established. If it were simply acknowledged that men's obligations are commonly assessed solely in reference to the ethic of rights and women's obligations are commonly assessed in reference to the ethic of care — and the factual evidence surely supports this claim — we could directly derive the supererogatory thesis simply by reference to the content or meaning of the two ethics. Men are not obligated to care, because they are not bound by the ethic of care. Women, of course, are obligated to care because they are bound by the ethic of care, but caring is supererogatory in the sense that it is "above and beyond the call of duty" from the point of view of the ethic of rights.[4]

3. For example: "Women make up the majority of all categories of caregivers; they represent 77 percent of adult children who care for their parents. . . . And sons caring for aging parents get more help — both material and emotional — from their wives than daughters get from their husbands."

4. It should be noted that the concept of self is more relevant to a discussion of the supererogatory than is generally recognized in moral theory. The sense of self, as Gilligan was aware, is implicated in both the ethic of rights and the ethic of care. The notion of self in the ethic of rights and as viewed

According to the necessary-base thesis, the ethic of care is a necessary base for the ethic of rights. In other words, in order for any semblance of a decent society to be maintained in the face of one segment of society acting solely on the basis of the ethic of rights, another segment of society must act in accordance with the ethic of care. Though the ethic of rights gives the appearance of being a self-sustaining moral framework, in reality it is not.

Given the fundamental social reality expressed in the supererogatory thesis — the fact that the activity of caring is perceived by both women and men to be obligatory for women — it is implausible to think that the ethic of rights could be an adequate overall account of morality. Indeed, I want to argue, in conjunction with my effort to support the necessary-base thesis, that the ethic of rights, when taken alone as a moral guide for all human behavior, is inadequate in the extreme. The basic point of this argument is easily stated: solely following the ethic of rights would result in a place where none of us could thrive, endure, or perhaps even survive. For literally everyone to follow an ethic of rights would amount to the physical, psychological, and emotional neglect of

virtually everyone. In Naomi Scheman's words: "There is every reason to react with alarm to the prospect of a world filled with self-actualizing persons pulling their own strings, capable of guiltlessly saying "no" to anyone about anything, and freely choosing when to begin and end all their relationships. It is hard to see how, in such a world, children could be raised, the sick or disturbed could be cared for, or people could know each other through their lives and grow old together" (Scheman 1983, 240).

With individual autonomy at the center of the ethic of rights and the leading admonition "respect rights," the problem becomes who cares for those who are powerless, who are not recognized as being autonomous, or who are incapable of autonomy. Suppose that everyone, women as well as men, really did embrace the ethic of rights and acted solely in accordance with its dictates. Even if we believe that human existence could be sustained over the generations in such a circumstance, itself an arguable claim, we have to ask: Do we want to live in such a place? The answer, of course, is no. Human existence, were it to be cut asunder from the enormous amount of moral labor routinely performed by those who embrace the ethic of care, would be virtually unrecognizable to us. It would in any case be very different from the society pictured for us by the major moral theorists who focus on the one moral standard of an ethic of rights.[5] The ethic of rights, when it finds expression in moral theory, is typically presented as gender-neutral. In fact, what we encounter here is a male-centered morality, but it is a morality that is deceptively put forth as universal, thereby obstructing from view and thus failing to acknowledge (while at the same time in a crucial sense presuming) that women will perform the moral labor that is entailed by adherence to the ethic of care.

I will conclude my overall discussion of the necessary-base thesis with the following

---

generally in both philosophy and society is well defined and highly individuated. The notion of self in the ethic of care is linked to others in a web of interdependence. One's own well-being is closely connected to the well-being of others, a state of affairs which is not the case for a person with a highly individuated self. According to the ethic of rights then, since the welfare of only a few others affects you, paying heed to the welfare of most people necessitates only laying out clear obligations and rules to follow which will serve to protect the welfare of others. And going beyond what one is obligated to do to perform a supererogatory or "heroic" act would be rare. According to the ethic of care, on the other hand, since one's own well-being depends on the well-being of a significant number of others, obligations laying out what is necessary to assure the well-being of others is less important. Acting in the interest of others is also to act in the interest of oneself. The ethic of rights views actions in the interest of others as supererogatory, whereas the ethic of care does not. The notion of ego boundaries in psychology is helpful here as well. The well-defined ego boundaries more generally possessed by men lead them to view actions for others generally as altruistic whereas the "blurred" (again, by the male standard) ego boundaries of most women lead them to perform more actions that are considered altruistic from the perspective of the ethic of rights.

5. It might be objected that my argument in support of the necessary-base thesis is unsound because the ethic of rights can be articulated in such a way as to include a right of human beings "to be cared for." In discussing what I call the "assimilation" approach in the next section, I provide an answer to this objection.

considerations. In carrying out their responsibilities, women are expected to have the virtues of "gentleness, sensitivity, resilient cheerfulness, patience, and perhaps a sense of humility" (Exdell 1987, 183). The problem is that these very qualities or "virtues" are "also ideally suited for those who are obliged to serve and obey their superior" (Exdell 1987, 184). The ethic of care is the necessary base for the ethic of rights in the sense that if the ethic of rights is to continue intact, then womanly "virtues" and "women's morality" are required in those who serve others. Women's moral labor is essential to the operation of the system as a whole, and this fact is clearly reflected in the social reality (itself clearly articulated by the supererogatory thesis) that is understood to be morally obligatory for women.

An appropriate question to ask at this point is the one Claudia Card asks: In articulating the ethic of care is Gilligan picking up on something in women's voices genuinely analogous to what Nietzsche heard, or thought he heard, in Christianity — something he identified as a slave morality? (Card 1985, 11). Because the relationship of men and women has been elaborately disguised, it is surely not true that the subordinate role played by women in unquestioningly adhering to the ethic of care and taking on "womanly virtues" is in any sense the product of informed consent. By being humble and obedient helpmates and by protecting men through immunity from the independent, critical judgments of women, women make it possible for the system to remain intact. In espousing the ethic of care as it presently exists, women can be seen as contributing to our own oppression and powerlessness rather than contributing to our liberation or a transformation of the system.

III. A Fatal Flaw in the System

In the "one system" of morality that to a large extent exists as our present social reality, women are morally required to perform what is obligatory for everyone and in addition are morally required to perform actions that are supererogatory from the perspective of the ethic of rights. That women must bear an additional moral burden by being required to go "above and beyond the call of duty" reveals a major failing in the system. There is a fundamental unfairness in the way the system distributes the moral burden, requiring much more of women than of men. This is bad enough, but another aspect of the system is even more damaging to women: the system functions to generate in women a kind of "moral madness." The same behavior and qualities of women are recurrently viewed and judged as both morally praiseworthy and morally blameworthy: women recurrently find themselves in moral double binds.

The ethic of rights is not only the theory of ethics and obligations for men. It has been so widely universalized as to become the standard for human moral behavior. Women's ethic of care, then, is not only different from men's ethic but, perhaps more important, different from the standard. Indeed, the characteristics of the two ethics are so different — with women's ethical concerns centered on the concrete and men's on the abstract, for example — that women's ethical concerns might be seen as the opposite of the norm. When women's ethic of care is measured against the prevailing standard for ethical theories, it is by definition deficient. Women then are caught in an ethical catch-22: We can either be morally deficient as women when we adopt men's ethic of rights or morally deficient as human beings when we adopt women's ethic of care. Moreover, since women are in fact held accountable to both ethics, the standard of judgment can shift back and forth between the ethic of care and the ethic of rights at any moment. There is always a point of view from which women's behavior can be found wanting.

What is morally required for women? To begin with, whatever is required by the ethic of rights, namely, respecting and not interfering with the rights of others. In confronting ethical dilemmas within this framework, women are expected, as are men, to abstract from an interpersonal situation to decide who will win in the contest of rights. Connectedness is to be experienced as freely contracted. Moral behavior for women as well as for men then is seen as fulfilling obligations that correspond to rights. But as we have just seen, women are expected or required to do much more than simply fulfill these obligations. Merely staying out of the way of others and following rules and principles to minimize conflict, contact, and even connection are required of women at the very same time they are required to establish and maintain close connection with their children, members of families, neighborhood, and community.

Women, of course, typically receive praise for caring for others. Women receive praise especially for being mothers. This fact is perhaps not made explicit publicly except on Mother's Day, but it is a large part of our everyday lives. It is present in the media, in talk shows, commercials, drama, and sitcoms. Mothers too praise one another in nodding recognition of delightful surprises and the unanticipated antics of their children and by sharing concerns and problems. Praise also comes from grandparents, physicians, economists, politicians, and numerous other sources. To many people, a woman's choice not to be a mother is so blameworthy that it seems virtually incomprehensible, irrational;[6] to some, being told that a woman has chosen not to have a child is akin to being told that "health is bad, not good."[7] The connection between the concepts of "woman" and "mother" is so strong as to sometimes make any distinction difficult.

At the same time women receive praise for being mothers, the blame they receive is more than ample. "Mother-blaming" by psychiatrists and psychologists is well known (Caplan and Hall-McCorquodale 1985). A host of other experts such as physicians, teachers, and clergy can use accumulated data to support the blaming of mothers for any deficiencies in the health, education, and physical, psychological, and emotional development of their children. Direct and plentiful blame goes to mothers who are not married, are lesbian, and/or are poor. But more to my present point, a mother is commonly subjected to both praise and blame for the very same actions. This perhaps is not uncommon in moral dilemmas in general, but for women who are mothers, widely held views recurrently come into direct conflict. In mothering, because women are held to both the ethic of care and the ethic of rights, nearly every action is potentially a dilemma. For example, to care for a child (being responsive and giving attentive love) can be considered praiseworthy (a judgment derived from the ethic of care), while at the same time a mother can be criticized (a judgment derived from the ethic of rights) for not giving a child space or allowing the child to develop as an individual by making mistakes. The mother is blamed for smothering her child. Giving a child space of course in turn can be criticized as uncaring, inattentive, and nonresponsive. Women who work outside the home are subject to this blame as are "full-time" mothers — only the reasons vary. Mothers who are poor (particularly black mothers) are blamed for being on welfare and at the same time blamed for leaving their children for salaried work. Moreover, many psychiatrists and psychologists have fostered the view that difficulties (including psychopathology) experienced by children while young, and often as adults, are heavily influenced by the actions and behavior of the mother.[8] This belief contributes to a state of affairs in which mothers may come to feel that choosing how best to raise one's children is much like choosing a path across a mine field.

It is important to remember that moral judgments about nurturing vary depending on class, race, and ethnicity and that moral assessments are fluid and constantly changing. Nevertheless, whether in this century or this decade, mothers have been and still are put in the impossible moral position of simultaneously being judged morally right and morally wrong for the same behavior. To be "caring" can be, and often (or generally) is, seen as seriously damaging to one's child. On the other hand, "respecting and

---

6. See Lillian Rubin's thoughts about her daughter possibly deciding not to have children. . . .

7. Women who have children are generally unable to give reasons for having them. Women who choose not to have children are more able to give reasons for not having them (NBC Today Show, June 24, 1988).

8. I do not mean to imply that mothers are not blameworthy in many instances, but they are not as blameworthy as traditional psychoanalytic and psychological theories have claimed. The works of Alice Miller are directly relevant here, in particular *Banished Knowledge*.

fostering a child's autonomy" can be, and often is, seen as unresponsive and inattentive. Women who choose not to be mothers are also placed in the same impossible position. They can be seen as selfish, cold, uncaring (judgments arising out of the ethic of care) and at the same time as acting autonomously, thus valuing their freedom (judgments arising out of the ethic of rights). Divorced women with children are often placed in a double bind, and lesbian mothers who are divorced are often subjected to particularly severe and conflicting judgment. Women who give custody of their children to the fathers can be seen as blameworthy, as unresponsive, uncaring, and selfish with regard to their children (judgments arising out of the ethic of care). Women who retain custody of their children can be considered unresponsive, uncaring, and selfish with regard to the father of their children but also blameworthy for interfering with the rights of the father (a judgment arising out of the ethic of rights). Moral madness in women is the result of repeated no-win situations in which any given action is subject to judgment as both morally right and morally wrong.

The moral assessment of men's behavior seems different. For example, a middle class, heterosexual, European American father who gives his child space, say, to make mistakes, is not as likely as a mother to be considered uncaring, inattentive, and unresponsive. Also, men who choose not to be fathers or choose not to request custody of their children are not ordinarily considered blameworthy to the extent women in a parallel situation would be, and men do not typically experience themselves as recurrently caught in a moral double bind. However, fathers who are African American, Native American, Asian American, Hispanic, and/or poor[9] are often subject to criticism and also to moral double binds of a somewhat different sort.

In other spheres as well, gender often seems to mediate our moral assessments. In an administrative context, for example, certain behaviors are typically assessed in a praiseworthy

way when the moral agent is male and in a blameworthy way when the moral agent is female. The following still common assessments are by now familiar to many. "His style is praised for being aggressive and assertive; hers is denounced as pushy. He is praised for his attention to detail; she is reprimanded for her pickiness. He is seen as steadfast; she is seen as dogmatic and hard. He is valued for his firm judgments; she is deplored for her prejudices and biases. He is admired for his courageous frankness and straightforwardness; she is labeled mouthy and strident. He is seen as witty; she is . . . blamed for being sarcastic" (Cuplin 1984, 130). But again, because women are judged by both the ethic of care and the ethic of rights, the situation is more complex than simply assessing identical behavior of women and men differently. In the passage just quoted, for instance, women's behavior is being judged using the ethic of care as the standard. To be aggressive and frank is to be unresponsive or inattentive to others, hence blameworthy. On the other hand, if a woman administrator displays responsive and attentive behavior, she is likely to be found wanting (from the standpoint of the ethic of rights) on the grounds that she is overly involved and not sufficiently impartial. Empathic imagination can be "cited as a reason for eliminating women from positions that require sensitive moral reflection on the grounds that the alleged requisite of hyper-detachment cannot be achieved" (Morgan 1987, 215). Once again, as for women who are mothers, the fact that a woman's behavior is subject to judgment by the standards of the two different ethics produces the result that she is confronted with a moral catch-22.

The qualities women display can also be viewed as both vices and virtues. Stereotypical qualities of women such as altruism or having an open heart and a forgiving soul can be and are seen as servile and destructive of personal integrity. Nurturing, helping, and sustaining the growth of others has been cited as women's normal (even praiseworthy), but pathological, masochism (Morgan 1987, 215). Stereotypical qualities of men that women display, such as being aggressive, firm, straightforward, and frank, are generally blameworthy but on rare occasions,

---

9. I indicate possible ways of explaining this difference later in this article. . . .

in Margaret Thatcher or Indira Gandhi, for example, are praiseworthy. . . .

IV. What Is Needed and What Is Not

What direction should feminists take in an effort to address the problem of conflicting moral standards applied to women and to develop an adequate moral theory that addresses the bias and inadequacies of the current system of morality? The standard approaches, both the "assimilation" approach and the "valorization" approach, are inadequate, the former extremely so.

The basic strategy of the assimilation approach is to assimilate the ethic of care into the ethic of rights. It is taken for granted (wrongly) that the ethic of rights is itself unbiased in the sense of being gender neutral, and an effort is made to bring the categories of care and nurturance (so important in the ethic of care) into the ethic of rights, perhaps under the category of benevolence. The result is what might be called an unbiased, neutral, or objective ethic.

In support of the assimilation approach and its seemingly impartial conception of morality, it might be argued that the language of the ethic of care can in fact be translated into the "rights and obligations" language of the ethic of rights. For example, since obligations have correlating rights, it could be argued that parents have obligations to care for their children, and children have the correlating right to be cared for by their parents. But this account fails to capture the meaning and content of the ethic of care. To see care as an obligation or duty is a distortion of the maternal care many infants and children often receive. Some of Sara Ruddick's and Caroline Whitbeck's work is especially directed to this very point. It is true that many mothers and fathers do view their relationships with their children as simply a matter of fulfilling certain moral requirements. But it is precisely for this reason that we find these relationships lacking. They are deficient because there is little or no care, only a sense of duty.[10]

10. . . . According to recent discussions of child abuse, any "safety net" of even minimal duty or any sense of children's rights is also seriously lacking.

It might also be argued that contemporary moral philosophy assimilates the ethic of care into the ethic of rights, but this view cannot be sustained; it is challenged by the claim that people in prosperous countries have a moral obligation to provide famine relief for people in poor countries, that is, it might be said, to provide care. Starving people have a right to famine relief or to be cared for, and advantaged people have correlating obligations to give aid. Here, to care is viewed as meeting a need, in this case the need for food. In this spirit, a list of needs might be generated to which some people are said to have a right and which others have an obligation to meet. But again, this view does not capture the meaning and content of the ethic of care. It may be that meeting needs such as food, clothing, and shelter can be adequately addressed by reference to rights and obligations. But this is not true of all needs, and perhaps "needs" language here is itself inadequate.

For example, children have many needs. When virtually none of a child's needs have been met by her or his parents, the parents are morally blameworthy to be sure. But they are not primarily morally blameworthy because they have not met, what we might call in the language of the ethic of rights, their obligations to the child. They may well have given the child "the best of what money can buy," but there is no caring, no attachment. Being connected to a person, caring for someone, loving a child, cannot be imposed or placed on a person by an outside party in the way that obligations can. People can be made to meet their obligations by the law and by nonlegal sanctions. But people cannot be made to care, to love. To say that people have a right to another's caring is jarring and points to a gaping hole in the ethic of rights concerning the basic well-being of children and of those children as adults. There are, in fact, many people who deeply care about less fortunate others even though they are virtual strangers to them. But this care is not equivalent to a sense of obligation. Care isn't care unless it is freely chosen. Hence care cannot be part of any obligation theory.

The assimilation approach then is a dead end for feminist moral theory. Nothing really changes.

Women disappear; moral agents have pretty clearly identifiable masculine qualities; and the conflicting moral standards used to judge the behavior of women remain, albeit hidden. Women are left to deal with their moral madness in silence in part because the expression of anger is itself a taboo for women (Lerner 1977, 4–11). The system remains critically flawed, but it is possible to ignore the crisis because the problem is not experienced by those in positions of power, those relatively advantaged.[11]

Moral theories that bring in aspects of women's morality and/or womanly virtues and subsume them into a larger category or relabel them do not address the fatal flaw in the system. Such theories do not benefit women because they function to support the status quo and thus do not contribute to efforts to end the subordination and powerlessness of women.

In vivid contrast to the assimilation approach is the valorization approach. The basic strategy of this second approach, exemplified in some of the work of Gilligan, Whitbeck, Noddings, and Ruddick, is to develop and give support to the ethic of care. This ethic has been particularly important to many women moral theorists (and other women) because it serves to validate aspects of women's lives which otherwise are perceived to have no value. That validation or general support for women and what they do has been and is otherwise absent in society. So it is clear that the valorization approach offers an advance over the assimilation approach. In beginning the task of providing a clear and forceful articulation of the moral experience of women, the valorization approach provides the important service of pointing out what has long been hidden under the reign of modern moral theory. Yet there are nagging questions that remain. For example, Joan Ringelheim asks: "Is women's culture liberating? How can it be if it

was nourished in oppression? Can we ever forget the price we pay as oppressed women? Should we? If we glorify the feminine from a presumably feminist perspective, how do we avoid valorizing oppression in order to criticize and organize against it?" (Ringelheim 1985, 759).

Despite the fact that the valorization approach functions to validate women's moral experience, it is fundamentally unsatisfactory as a moral theory for feminists or anyone. Because this perspective is essentially ahistorical and fails to take account of women's social and political context, it unwittingly serves to maintain a status quo that the one-system view clearly reveals as incompatible with the best interests of women and, I think, men. According to Barbara Houston, it fails to give us a view of the enormous damage women suffer as a result of the particular position they hold. It does not encourage us to focus on the question of how we might alter women's condition; nor does it encourage us to ask whether the allegedly uniquely female moral virtues are a cause of women's subordination (Houston 1987; see also Young 1985).

The challenge for feminist ethics is both to take seriously women's moral experience and to arrive at a theory that will avoid the temptation to wind up endorsing the ongoing subordination of women. Or the challenge may be, as Marilyn Frye suggests, to help us learn how to do without ethics entirely (Frye 1990, 133). In any case, the valorization approach recommends to women that we embrace the ethic of care and proudly display it as a badge of honor. But for women to adopt it as it is would further our oppression rather than liberate us.

The valorization approach also fails to acknowledge the extent to which the ethic of care has been a coping strategy and identified as subordinate. In fact, to valorize the ethic of care is to repeat recent history. In the first women's movement women were assigned, and many women gladly assumed, the role of moral housekeepers. They along with many men viewed women's morality as superior. When men made a mess of things, women cleaned up. Many women, however, never gained (or sought) positions in politics, business, science, religion, or

---

11. This is a ubiquitous problem. To take only two of a great many examples, Martin Luther King Jr. and Gandhi used nonviolent demonstrations to make those relatively advantaged (white Americans and the British in India) aware that a problem existed. Nonviolent demonstrations are one way to make the problem felt among those who do not experience a problem because of their particular advantage.

academia to transform the society in order to prevent future messes. Identifying two ethics and labeling one masculine and one feminine is not new, nor is it helpful. There is no reason to believe that the feminine ethic would or should be adopted as the ethic for everyone. Although discerning the male bias in the dominant ethic and the resulting implications for women and men is important (Jaggar 1991, 90), we need to now move away from a system that has generated so much destruction.

V. Conclusion

How does what I have said here help us move away from this destructive ethical system?

I have argued that the ethic of care and the ethic of rights must be seen as parts of one system of morality, but what does this way of thinking explain? First, "the problem," namely, heavy and conflicting responsibility (the double bind), that emerges in the moral experience of many women now becomes comprehensible — itself a great relief for women.

More specifically, seeing the ethic of care and the ethic of rights as one system, with the former the necessary base of the latter, explains some of the social resistance on the part of both men and women to changes in women's lives and also explains some of the unexpected and often incomprehensible problems that arise when some women adopt the ethic of rights. While women have often maintained homes and have worked outside as well as inside the home, we have recently entered the public "working" world in increasingly larger numbers. In doing so, many women have asked that some of their traditional caring activities in all sorts of configurations that are families (e.g., caring for children, those who are sick, and the elderly) be assumed by others in addition to themselves. This change has provoked a cry from some for the return of the "traditional family," and the cry has come from men, as well as from women, who recognize or sense that something important is being lost.

The traditional family has been portrayed as "natural," and support for this view has been provided by biology, the social sciences, and religion. However, the real reason for stiff sanctions against women who seriously question their lot in word and deed is that, if women were to fail to perform their traditional functions, society would be radically changed and the dominant group as such would be in peril. Hence, the call for women (by both women and men) to fulfill their traditional role even while women are encouraged to enter and succeed in traditionally male fields.

Even more important, this way of thinking can begin to explain why serious social problems have been pushed aside. The existing theoretical framework, made up of the ethic of rights with the ethic of care as an often unrecognized presupposition, does not have resources adequate to address them. More important, it perpetuates, and in many cases generates, social problems. In addition to the social problems of battered women, rape, sexual harassment, pornography, and sexual abuse are ever present problems that make home, other workplaces, and the places in between inhospitable or unsafe environments for women. In biomedical ethics, for example, surrogate motherhood, reproductive technologies, abortion, and the nurse-physician relationship together with its impact on the quality of health care can be better understood if the relation of women's ethic of care to men's ethic of rights becomes an explicit part of the discussion.

Critiquing the present and the past alone will not help us move away from this destructive normative ethical system and on to increasingly less destructive ways of constituting our moral lives. Many women, and in particular lesbian, Jewish, African American, Native American, Hispanic American, Asian American, poor, rural, disabled women, and some men are currently saying things never said before. Their work helps us visualize new practices. Some of the most perplexing problems in female dominated salaried work such as nursing and teaching and in male dominated fields can be seen in new ways in order to develop new practices. I am putting this article forward with the hope that it in some small way contributes to that effort.

References

Abel, Emily. 1988. "Who really cares?" *The Women's Review of Books* 5(8): 12.

Auerbach, Judy, et al. 1985. "Commentary on Gilligan's In a different voice." *Feminist Studies* 11(1): 149–61.

Baier, Annette. 1985. "What do women want in a moral theory?" *Nous* 19 (March): 53–64.

———. 1986a. "Trust and anti-trust." *Ethics* 96(2): 231–60.

———. 1986b "Extending the limits of moral theory." *Journal of Philosophy* 83(10): 538–44.

———. 1987. "Hume, the women's moral theorist?" In *Women and moral theory,* ed. Eva Feder Kittay and Diane T. Meyers. Totowa, NJ: Rowman and Littlefield.

Beck, Evelyn Torton. 1988. "The politics of Jewish invisibility." *NWSA Journal* 1(1): 93–102.

Bernick, Susan E. 1992. "Philosophy and feminism: The case of Susan Bordo." *Hypatia* 7(3): 188–96.

———. 1990. "Caring and evil." *Hypatia* 5(1): 101–08.

———, ed. 1991. *Feminist ethics.* Lawrence: University Press of Kansas.

Collins, Patricia Hill. 1991. *Black feminist thought: Knowledge, consciousness, and the politics of empowerment.* New York: Routledge.

Davis, Kathy. 1992. "Toward a feminist rhetoric: The Gilligan debate revisited." *Women's Studies International Forum* 15(2): 219–31.

Di Stefano, Christine. 1983. "Masculinity as ideology in political theory." *Women's Studies International Forum* 6(6): 633–44.

Exdell, John. 1987. "Ethics, ideology, and feminine virtue." In *Science, morality, and feminist theory,* ed. Marsha Hanen and Kai Nielsen. Calgary, Alberta: University of Calgary Press.

Flanagan, Owen J. 1982. "Virtue, sex, and gender: Some philosophical reflections on the moral psychology debate." *Ethics* 92(3): 500–02.

Blum, Larry, Marcia Homiak, Judy Housman, and Naomi Scheman. 1973–74. "Altruism and women's oppression." *The Philosophical Forum* 5(1–2): 222–47.

Bordo, Susan. 1992. "Maleness" revisited. *Hypatia* 7(3): 197–207.

Broughton, John M. 1983. "Women's rationality and men's virtues." *Social Research* 50: 597–642.

Calhoun, Cheshire. 1988. "Justice, care, gender bias." *The Journal of Philosophy* 85(9): 451–63.

Caplan, Paula. 1984. "The myth of masochism." *American Psychologist* 39: 130–39.

Caplan, Paula, and Ivan Hall-McCorquodale. 1985. "Mother-blaming in major clinical journals." *American Journal of Orthopsychiatry* 55(3): 345–53.

Card, Claudia. 1985. "Virtues and moral luck." *Working Series* 1, no. 4, *Institute for Legal Studies,* University of Wisconsin, Madison, Law School.

———. 1988. "Women's voices and ethical ideals: Must we mean what we say?" *Ethics* 99(1): 125–35.

Flanagan, Owen J., and Kathryn Jackson. 1987. "Justice, care, and gender: The Kohlberg-Gilligan debate revisited." *Ethics* 97(3): 622–37.

Friedman, Marilyn. 1985. "Abraham, Socrates, and Heinz: Where are the women?" In *Moral dilemmas: Philosophical and psychological issues in the development of moral reasoning,* ed. Carol Harding. Chicago: Precedent Publishing.

———. 1987. "Beyond caring: The de-moralization of gender." In *Science, morality, and feminist theory,* ed. Marsha Hanen and Kai Nielsen. Calgary, Alberta: University of Calgary Press.

———. 1991a. "The social self and the partiality debates." In *Feminist ethics,* ed. Claudia Card. Lawrence: University Press of Kansas.

———. 1991b. "The practice of partiality." *Ethics* 101(4): 818–35.

Frye, Marilyn. 1983. *The politics of reality: Essays in feminist theory.* Trumansburg, NY: Crossing Press.

———. 1990. "A response to Lesbian ethics." *Hypatia* 5(3): 132–37.

———. 1992a. *Willful virgin: Essays in feminism.* Freedom, CA: Crossing Press.

———. 1992b. "The body philosophical." In *The knowledge explosion: Generations of feminist scholarship,* ed. Cheris Kramarae and Dale Spender. New York: Teachers College Press (Athene Series).

Gigueira-McDonough, Josefina, and Rosemarry Sarri. 1987. *The trapped woman: Catch-22 in deviance and control.* Newbury Park, CA: Sage Publications.

Gilligan, Carol. 1982. *In a different voice: Psychological theory and women's development.* Cambridge: Harvard University Press.

———. 1986. "Reply." *Signs* 11(2): 324–33.

———. 1987. "Moral orientation and moral development." In *Women and moral theory,* ed. Eva Feder Kittay and Diana T. Meyers. Totowa, NJ: Rowman and Littlefield.

Gilligan, Carol, and Grant Wiggins. 1986. *The origins of morality in early childhood relationships.* Unpublished manuscript.

Harding, Sandra. 1987. "The curious coincidence of feminine and African moralities: Challenges for feminist theory." In *Women and moral theory,* ed. Eva Feder Kittay and Diana T. Meyers. Totowa, NJ: Rowman and Littlefield.

Hardwig, John. 1984. "Should women think in terms of rights?" *Ethics* 94(3): 441–55.

Hoagland, Sara Lucia. 1990. "Some concerns about Nel Noddings' Caring." *Hypatia* 5(1): 109–13.

———. 1991. "Some thoughts about 'caring.'" In *Feminist ethics,* ed. Claudia Card. Lawrence: University Press of Kansas.

hooks, bell. 1981. *Ain't I a woman: Black women and feminism.* Boston: South End Press.

———. 1984. *Feminist theory: From margin to center.* Boston: South End Press.

———. 1989. *Talking back: Thinking feminist, thinking black.* Boston: South End Press.

Houston, Barbara. 1987. "Rescuing womanly virtues: Some dangers of moral reclamation." In *Science, morality, and feminist theory,* ed. Marsha Hanen and Kai Nielsen. Calgary, Alberta: University of Calgary Press.

———. 1988. "Gilligan and the politics of a distinctive women's morality." In *Feminist perspectives: Philosophical essays on methods and morals,* ed. Lorraine Code, Sheila Mullet, and Christine Overall. Toronto, Ontario: University of Toronto Press.

———. 1990. "Caring and exploitation." *Hypatia* 5(1): 115–19.

Jaggar, Alison. 1987. "Sex inequality and bias in sex differences research." In *Science, morality, and feminist theory,* ed. Marsha Hanen and Kai Nielsen. Calgary, Alberta: University of Calgary Press.

———. 1991. "Feminist ethics: Projects, problems, prospects." In *Feminist ethics,* ed. Claudia Card. Lawrence: University of Kansas Press.

Kerber, Linda K., Catherine C. Greens, Eleanore E. Maccoby, Zella Luria, Carol B. Stack, and Carol Gilligan. 1986. "On In a Different Voice: An interdisciplinary forum." *Signs* 11(2): 304–33.

Kohlberg, Lawrence. 1982. "A reply to Owen Flanagan and some comments on the Puka-Goodpaster exchange." *Ethics* 92(3): 513–28.

Larrabee, Mary Jeanne, ed. 1993. *An ethic of care: Feminist and interdisciplinary perspectives.* New York: Routledge.

Lugones, Maria. 1987. "Playfulness, 'world'-traveling, and loving perception." *Hypatia* 2(2): 3–19.

———. 1991. "On the logic of pluralist feminism." In *Feminist ethics,* ed. Claudia Card. Lawrence: University Press of Kansas.

Lugones, Maria, and Elizabeth V. Spelman. 1983. "Have we got a theory for you! Feminist theory, cultural imperialism, and the demand for the woman's view." *Hypatia* 1, published as *Women's Studies International Forum* 6(6): 573–81. Reprinted in *Hypatia reborn* (Indiana University Press), 1990.

Mackinnon, Catharine. 1991. "Does sexuality have a history?" *Michigan Quarterly Review* 30: 1–11.

Miller, Alice. 1983. *For your own good: Hidden cruelty in child-rearing and the roots of violence.* Translated by Hildegarde Hannum and Hunter Hannum. New York: Farrar, Straus, and Giroux.

———. 1990. *Banished knowledge: Facing childhood injuries.* New York: Doubleday.

Miller, Jean Baker. 1976. *Toward a new psychology of women.* Boston: Beacon Press.

Morgan, Kathryn Pauly. 1987. "Women and moral madness." In *Science, morality, and feminist theory,* ed. Marsha Hanen and Kai Nielsen. Calgary, Alberta: University of Calgary Press.

Noddings, Nel. 1984. *Caring: A feminine approach to ethics and moral education.* Berkeley: University of California Press.

O'Barr, Jean F., Deborah Pope, and Mary Wyer, eds. 1990. *Ties that bind: Essays on mothering and patriarchy.* Chicago: University of Chicago Press.

Rich, Adrienne. 1977. "The conditions for work: The common world of women." In *On lies, secrets, and silence.* New York: W. W. Norton.

Ringelheim, Joan. 1985. "Women and the holocaust: A reconsideration of research." *Signs* 10(4): 741–61.

Rubin, Lillian B. 1983. *Intimate strangers: Men and women together.* New York: Harper and Row.

Ruddick, Sara. 1984. "Maternal thinking." In *Mothering: Essays in feminist theory,* ed. Joyce Trebilcot. Totowa, NJ: Rowman and Allenheld.

———. 1989. *Maternal thinking.* Boston: Beacon Press.

Rumsey, Jean P. 1990. "Constructing maternal thinking." *Hypatia* 5(3): 125–31.

Ryan, William. 1971. *Blaming the victim.* New York: Random House.

Scheman, Naomi. 1983. "Individualism and the objects of psychology." In *Discovering reality: Feminist perspectives on epistemology, metaphysics, methodology, and philosophy of science,* ed. Sandra Harding and Merill B. Hintikka. Boston: D. Reidel.

Sichel, Betty, and Nancy Tuana, eds. 1991. "Feminism and morality." *APA Newsletter on Feminism and Philosophy* 90(2): 83–121.

Simons, Margaret A. 1984. "Motherhood, feminism, and identity." *Hypatia* 2, published as *Women's Studies International Forum* 7(5): 349–59. Reprinted in *Hypatia reborn* (Indiana University Press), 1990.

Singer, Linda. 1987. "Value, power, and gender: Do we need a different voice?" In *Power, gender, values,* ed. Judith Genova. Edmonton, Alberta: Academic Printing and Publishing.

Sommers, Tish, et al. 1987. *Women take care: The consequences of caregiving in today's society.* Gainesville, FL: Triad.

Spelman, Elizabeth. 1988. *Inessential woman: Problems of exclusion in feminist thought.* Boston: Beacon Press.

Trebilcot, Joyce, ed. 1984. *Mothering: Essays in feminist theory.* Totowa, NJ: Rowman and Allenheld.

Tronto, Joan C. 1987. "Beyond gender difference: Toward a theory of care." *Signs* 12(4): 644–63.

———. 1989. "Women and caring: What can feminists learn about morality from caring?" In *Gender/body/knowledge,* ed. Alison M. Jaggar and Susan R. Bordo. New Brunswick, NJ: Rutgers University Press.

Upin, Jane S. 1992. "Applying the concept of gender: Unsettled questions." *Hypatia* 7(3): 180–87.

Walker, Beverly M. 1981. "Psychology and feminism—If you can't beat them, join them." In *Men's studies modified,* ed. Dale Spender. New York: Pergamon Press.

Walker, Margaret Urban. 1989. "Moral understandings: Alternative 'epistemology' for a feminist ethics." *Hypatia* 4(2): 15–28.

———. 1992. "Feminism, ethics, and the question of theory." *Hypatia* 7(3): 23–38.

Whitbeck, Caroline. 1973–74. "Theories of sex differences." *The Philosophical Forum* 5(1–2): 54–80.

———. 1982. "Women and medicine: An introduction." *The Journal of Medicine and Philosophy* 7(2): 119–33.

———. 1983a. "A different reality: Feminist ontology." In

Beyond domination: New perspectives on women and philosophy, ed. Carol C. Gould. Totowa, NJ: Rowman and Allanheld.

———. 1983b. "The maternal instinct" (1972) and "Afterword" (1982). In *Mothering: Essays in feminist theory,* ed. Joyce Trebilcot. Totowa, NJ: Rowman and Allanheld.

———. 1983c. "The moral implications of regarding women as people: New perspectives on pregnancy and personhood." In *Abortion and the status of the fetus,* ed. William B. Bondeson et al. Boston: D. Reidel.

———. 1984. "Love, knowledge, and transformation." *Women's Studies International Forum* 7(5): 393–405.

Young, Iris Marion. 1985. "Humanism, gynocentrism, and feminist politics." *Women's Studies International Forum* 8(3): 173–83.

3.6 Moral Relativism

Does anything go? I mean, is any moral view with its associated actions acceptable? What about this: sacrificing humans by ripping their hearts out because some people believe that the Sun God requires it? What about this: killing Jews because some people believe Jews are somehow responsible for all the world's problems? What about this: beating and hanging Blacks because some believe Blacks are subhuman? What about this: sexually abusing boys and girls because some people sexually desire children and believe that having sex with them does no real harm?

Most of us (I would hope all of us) would condemn such actions and reject such beliefs as false. However, we often hear people say that we should not judge others or make them conform to our values. Many people support some version of moral relativism because they believe that the values of others are as valid as their own.

We must do some careful thinking when we wade into the waters of moral relativism. Precise distinctions are in order. It is true that moral values and codes differ with historical, cultural, and religious circumstances. Does it follow from this fact that it is wrong to render moral judgments about the rightness or wrongness of human action? (See the discussion of rationality in Chapter 1.) When conflicts in moral values and judgments arise, we rightly feel uncomfortable imposing our own values on others. However, we feel equally uncomfortable supporting an "anything goes" position. Are we forced to choose between a kind of moral relativism which holds that all human actions are of equal moral worth and a kind of moral universalism or absolutism which maintains that one and only one set of moral values is true?

David Wong (b. 1942), the author of the next selection and professor of philosophy at Duke University, seeks to find a way between the extremes of moral relativism (anything goes) and moral universalism (there is one and only one set of true moral values). His concern to find a middle way grows out of his personal experience as a Chinese American trying to reconcile the values of Confucianism with the values of contemporary American society.

Reading Questions

1. What are the differences among meta-ethical relativism, normative moral relativism, moral universalism, and moral absolutism?
2. Why, according to Wong, does the argument from diversity not support relativism "in any simple or direct way?"
3. What two universal human needs are served by morality?
4. Why are extreme forms of normative moral relativism indefensible?
5. Why does Wong think that a moderate rather than an extreme form of moral relativism is correct?
6. Has Wong persuaded you that he is right? Why, or why not?

Relativism

DAVID WONG

I. Introduction

MORAL RELATIVISM is a common response to the deepest conflicts we face in our ethical lives. Some of these conflicts are quite public and political, such as the apparently intractable disagreement in the United States over the moral and legal permissibility of abortion. Other conflicts inviting the relativistic response are of a less dramatic but more recurrent nature. This author's experience as a first-generation Chinese American exemplifies a kind of conflict that others have faced: that between inherited values and the values of the adopted country. As a child I had to grapple with the differences between what was expected of me as a good Chinese son and what was expected of my non-Chinese friends. Not only did they seem bound by duties that were much less rigorous in the matter of honouring parents and upholding the family name, but I was supposed to feel superior to them because of that. It added to my confusion that I sometimes felt envy at their freedom.

Moral relativism, as a common response to such conflicts, often takes the form of a denial that any single moral code has universal validity, and an assertion that moral truth and justifiability, if there are any such things, are in some way relative to factors that are culturally and historically contingent. This doctrine is *meta-ethical* relativism, because it is about the relativity of moral truth and justifiability. Another kind of moral relativism, also a common response to deep moral conflict, is a doctrine about how one ought to act toward those who accept values very different from one's own. This *normative* moral relativism holds that it is wrong to pass judgement on others who have substantially different values, or to try to make them conform to one's values, for the reason that their values are as valid as one's

own. Another common response to deep moral conflict, however, contradicts moral relativism in its two major forms. It is the universalist or absolutist position that both sides of a moral conflict cannot be equally right, that there can be only one truth about the matter at issue. This position is so common, in fact, that William James was led to call us "absolutists by instinct" (James, 1948). The term "universalism" will be used hereafter, because "absolutism" is used not only to refer to the denial of moral relativism, but also to the view that some moral rules or duties are absolutely without exception.

II. Meta-Ethical Relativism

The debate between moral relativism and universalism accounts for a significant proportion of philosophical reflection in ethics. In ancient Greece at least some of the "Sophists" defended a version of moral relativism, which Plato attempted to refute. Plato attributes to the first great Sophist, Protagoras, the argument that human custom determines what is fine and ugly, just and unjust. Whatever is communally judged to be the case, the argument goes, actually comes to be the case (*Theaetetus,* 172AB; it is unclear, however, whether the real Protagoras actually argued in this manner). Now the Greeks, through trade, travel, and war, were fully aware of wide variation in customs, and so the argument concludes with the relativity of morality. The question with this argument, however, is whether we can accept that custom determines in a strong sense what is fine and ugly, just and unjust. It may influence what people *think* is fine and just. But it is quite another thing for custom to determine what *is* fine and just. Customs sometimes change under the pressure of moral criticism,

David Wong, "Relativism," A Companion to Ethics, *edited by Peter Singer. Copyright © Basil Blackwell 1991,* Cambridge, MA: Basil Blackwell, Inc, pp. 442–450. Reprinted by permission.

and the argument seems to rely on a premise that contradicts this phenomenon.

Another kind of argument given for relativism is premised on the view that the customary ethical beliefs in any given society are functionally necessary for that society. Therefore, the argument concludes, the beliefs are true for that society, but not necessarily in another. The sixteenth-century essayist, Michel de Montaigne, sometimes makes this argument ("Of custom, and not easily changing an accepted law," in Montaigne, 1595), but it has had its greatest acceptance among anthropologists of the twentieth century who emphasize the importance of studying societies as organic wholes of which the parts are functionally interdependent. . . . The problem with the functional argument, however, is that moral beliefs are not justified merely on the grounds that they are necessary for a society's existence in anything like its present form. Even if a society's institutions and practices crucially depend on the acceptance of certain beliefs, the justifiability of those beliefs depends on the moral acceptability of the institutions and practices. To show that certain beliefs are necessary for maintaining a fascist society, for instance, is not to justify those beliefs.

Despite the weaknesses of these arguments for moral relativism, the doctrine has always had its adherents. Its continuing strength has always been rooted in the impressiveness of the variation in ethical belief to be found across human history and culture. In an ancient text (*Dissoi Logoi* or the *Contrasting Arguments;* Robinson, 1979) associated with the Sophists, it is pointed out that for the Lacedaemonians, it was fine for girls to exercise without tunics, and for children not to learn music and letters, while for the Ionians, these things were foul. Montaigne assembled a catalogue of exotic customs, such as male prostitution, cannibalism, women warriors, killing one's father at a certain age as an act of piety, and recites from the Greek historian Herodotus the experiment of Darius. Darius asked Greeks how much they would have to be paid before they would eat the bodies of their deceased fathers. They replied that no sum of money could get them to do such a thing. He then asked certain Indians who customarily ate the bodies of their deceased fathers what they would have to be paid to burn the bodies of their fathers. Amidst loud exclamations, they bade him not to speak of such a thing (Montaigne's "Of custom" (1595), and Herodotus, *Persian Wars,* Book III, 38).

But while many have been moved by such examples to adopt moral relativism, the argument from diversity does not support relativism in any simple or direct way. As the Socrates of Plato's dialogues observed, we have reason to listen only to the wise among us (*Crito,* 44CD). The simple fact of diversity in belief is no disproof of the possibility that there are some beliefs better to have than the others because they are truer or more justified than the rest. If half the world still believed that the sun, the moon, and the planets revolved around the earth, that would be no disproof of the possibility of a unique truth about the structure of the universe. Diversity in belief, after all, may result from varying degrees of wisdom. Or it may be that different people have their own limited perspectives of the truth, each perspective being distorted in its own way.

It is sometimes thought that the extent and depth of disagreement in ethics indicates that moral judgements are simply not judgements about facts, that they assert nothing true or false about the world but straightforwardly express our own subjective reactions to certain facts and happenings, whether these be collective or individual reactions (e.g. see C. L. Stevenson, *Ethics and Language* (1944). . . . A more complicated view is that moral judgements purport to report objective matters of fact, but that there are no such matters of fact (see J. L. Mackie, *Ethics: Inventing Right and Wrong,* 1977). The success of modern science in producing a remarkable degree of convergence of belief about the basic structure of the physical world probably reinforces these varieties of scepticism about the objectivity of moral judgements. It is hard to deny that there is a significant difference in the degree of convergence of belief in ethics and in science. Yet there are possible explanations for that difference that are compatible with claiming that moral judgements are ultimately about facts in the world. These explanations might stress, for instance, the special difficulties of acquiring knowledge of subjects that pertain to moral knowledge.

An understanding of human nature and human affairs is necessary for formulating an adequate moral code. The enormously difficult and complex task of reaching such an understanding could be a major reason for differences in moral belief. Furthermore, the subject matter of ethics is such that people have the most intense practical interest in what is established as truth about it, and surely this interest engenders the passions that becloud judgement (for a reply in this spirit see Nagel, 1986, pp. 185–88). Universalists could point out that many apparently exotic moral beliefs presuppose certain religious and metaphysical beliefs, and that these beliefs, rather than any difference in fundamental values, explain the apparent strangeness. Consider, for example, the way our view of Darius' Indians would change if we were to attribute to them the belief that eating the body of one's deceased father is a way of preserving his spiritual substance. Finally, some of the striking differences in moral belief across societies may not be rooted in differences in fundamental values but in the fact that these values may have to be implemented in different ways given the varying conditions that obtain across societies. If one society contains many more women than men (say, because men are killing each other off in warfare), it would not be surprising if polygamy were acceptable there, while in another society, where the proportion of women to men is equal, monogamy is required. The difference in accepted marriage practice may come down to that difference in the proportion of women to men, and not to any difference in basic moral ideals of marriage or of the proper relationships between women and men.

The mere existence of deep and wide disagreements in ethics, therefore, does not disprove the possibility that moral judgements can be objectively correct or incorrect judgements about certain facts. Moral relativists must chart some other more complicated path from the existence of diversity to the conclusion that there is no single true or most justified morality. I believe

(and have argued, in *Moral Relativity,* 1984) that the relativist argument is best conducted by pointing to particular kinds of differences in moral belief, and then by claiming that these particular differences are best explained under a theory that denies the existence of a single true morality. This would involve denying that the various ways that universalists have for explaining ethical disagreement are sufficient for explaining the particular differences in question. (For another strategy of argument that relies more on an analysis of the meaning of moral judgements, see Harman, 1975.)

One apparent and striking ethical difference that would be a good candidate for this sort of argument concerns the emphasis on individual rights that is embodied in the ethical culture of the modern West and that seems absent in traditional cultures found in Africa, China, Japan and India. The content of duties in such traditional cultures instead seems organized around the central value of a common good that consists in a certain sort of ideal community life, a network of relationships, partially defined by social roles, again, ideal, but imperfectly embodied in ongoing existing practice. The ideal for members is composed of various virtues that enable them, given their place in the network of relationships, to promote and sustain the common good.

Confucianism, for instance, makes the family and kinship groups the models for the common good, with larger social and political units taking on certain of their features, such as benevolent leaders who rule with the aim of cultivating virtue and harmony among their subjects. . . . Moralities centered on such values would seem to differ significantly from ones centred on individual rights to liberty and to other goods, if the basis for attributing such rights to persons does not seem to lie in their conduciveness to the common good of a shared life, but in a moral worth independently attributed to each individual. By contrast a theme frequently found in ethics of the common good is that individuals find their realization as human beings in promoting and sustaining the common good. Given this assumption of the fundamental harmony between the highest good of individuals and the common good, one might expect the constraints on freedom to have greater scope and to be more pervasive when compared to a tradition in which no such fundamental harmony between individual and common goods is assumed.

If the contrast between the two types of morality is real, it raises the question of whether one or the other type is truer or more justified than the other. The argument for a relativistic answer may start with the claim that each type focuses on a good that may reasonably occupy the centre of an ethical ideal for human life. On the one hand, there is the good of belonging to and contributing to a community; on the other, there is the good of respect for the individual apart from any potential contribution to community. It would be surprising, the argument goes, if there were just one justifiable way of setting a priority with respect to the two goods. It should not be surprising, after all, if the range of human goods is simply too rich and diverse to be reconciled in just a single moral ideal.

Such an argument could be supplemented by an explanation of why human beings have such a thing as a morality. Morality serves two universal human needs. It regulates conflicts of interest between people, and it regulates conflicts of interest within the individual born of different desires and drives that cannot all be satisfied at the same time. Ways of dealing with those two kinds of conflict develop in anything recognizable as human society. To the extent that these ways crystallize in the form of rules for conduct and ideals for persons, we have the core of a morality. Now in order to perform its practical functions adequately, it may be that a morality will have to possess certain general features. A relatively enduring and stable system for the resolution of conflict between people, for instance, will not permit the torture of persons at whim.

But given this picture of the origin and functions of morality, it would not be surprising if significantly different moralities were to perform the practical functions equally well, at least according to standards of performance that were common to these moralities. Moralities, on this picture, are social creations that evolve to meet certain needs. The needs place conditions on what could be an adequate morality, and if human nature has a definite structure, one would expect further constraining conditions on an adequate morality to derive from our nature. But the complexity of our nature makes it possible for us to prize a variety of goods and to order them in different ways, and this opens the way for a substantial relativism to be true.

The picture sketched above has the advantage of leaving it open as to how strong a version of relativism is true. That is, it holds that there is no single true morality, yet does not deny that some moralities might be false and inadequate for the functions they all must perform. Almost all polemics against moral relativism are directed at its most extreme versions: those holding that all moralities are equally true (or equally false, or equally lacking in cognitive content). Yet a substantial relativism need not be so radically egalitarian. Besides ruling out moralities that would aggravate interpersonal conflict, such as the one described above, relativists could also recognize that adequate moralities must promote the production of persons capable of considering the interests of others. Such persons would need to have received a certain kind of nurturing and care from others. An adequate morality, then, whatever else its content, would have to prescribe and promote the sorts of upbringing and continuing interpersonal relationships that produce such persons.

A moral relativism that would allow for this kind of constraint on what could be a true or most justified morality might not fit the stereotype of relativism, but would be a reasonable position to hold. One reason, in fact, that not much progress has been made in the debate between relativists and universalists is that each side has tended to define the opponent as holding the most extreme position possible. While this makes the debating easier, it does nothing to shed light on the vast middle ground where the truth indeed may lie. Many of the same conclusions could be drawn about the debate over normative moral relativism: much heat, and frequent identification of the opponent with the most extreme position possible.

III. *Normative Relativism*

The most extreme possible position for the normative relativist is that no-one should ever pass judgement on others with substantially different values, or try to make them conform to one's own values. Such a definition of normative relativism is usually given by its opponents, because it is an indefensible position. It requires self-condemnation by those who act according to it. If I pass judgement on those who pass judgement, I must condemn myself. I am trying to impose a value of tolerance on everyone, when not everyone has that value, but this is not what I am supposed to be doing under the most extreme version of normative relativism. Philosophers are usually content with such easy dismissals of the most extreme version of normative relativism, but there is reason to consider whether more moderate versions might be more tenable. The reason is that normative relativism is not just a philosophical doctrine but a stance adopted toward morally troubling situations.

Anthropologists are sometimes identified with this stance, and it is instructive to understand how this identification emerged from a historical and sociological context. The birth of cultural anthropology in the late nineteenth century was in part subsidized by colonizing governments needing to know more about the nature and status of "primitive" peoples. Influenced by Darwinian theory, early anthropological theory tended to arrange the peoples and social institutions of the world in an evolutionary series; from primordial man to the civilized human being of nineteenth-century Europe. Many anthropologists eventually reacted against the imperialism of their governments and to its rationalization supplied by their predecessors. More importantly, they came to see the peoples they studied as intelligent men and women whose lives had meaning and integrity. And this led to questioning the basis for implicit judgements of the inferiority of their ways of life, especially after the spectacle of the civilized nations in brutal struggle with one another in the First World War (see, for example, Ruth Benedict, *Patterns of Culture*, 1934, and more recently, Melville Herskovits, *Cultural Relativism: Perspectives in Cultural Pluralism*, 1972).

The normative relativism of some of the anthropologists of that period, then, was a response to real moral problems concerning the justifiability of colonization and more generally concerning intervention in another society so as to cause major changes in previously accepted values or in people's ability to act on those values. No simple version of normative relativism is the answer to these problems, as was illustrated by the fact that an ethic of non-judgemental tolerance would self-destruct when used to condemn the intolerant. The inadequacy of the simple versions also is illustrated by the swing in anthropology on the question of normative relativism after the Second World War. That war, many realized, was a battle against enormous evil. Such a realization brought vividly to the forefront the necessity of passing judgement at least sometimes and of acting on one's judgement. And accordingly there was a new trend within cultural anthropology toward finding a basis for making judgements that would depend on criteria to be applied to all moral codes.

A more reasonable version of normative relativism would have to permit us to pass judgement on others with substantially different values. Even if these different values are as justified as our own from some neutral perspective, we still are entitled to call bad or evil or monstrous what contradicts our most important values. What we are entitled to do in the light of such judgements, however, is another matter. Many of us who are likely to read this book would be reluctant to intervene in the affairs of others who have values substantially different from ours, when the reason for intervention is the enforcement of our own values, and when we think that we have no more of an objective case for our moral outlook than the others have for theirs. The source of this reluctance is a feature of our morality. A liberal, contractualist outlook is very much part of our ethical life in the postmodern West, whether we acknowledge it or not. . . . We want to act toward others in such a way that our actions could be seen as justified by them if they were fully reasonable and informed of all relevant facts. If we hold a meta-ethical moral relativism, however, then we must recognize that there will be occasions when some otherwise desirable course of action toward others with different values will violate this feature of our morality.

At that point, there is no general rule that will tell us what to do. It would seem to depend on what other values of ours are at stake. If a practice performed by others were to involve human sacrifice, for example, then the value of tolerance might indeed be outweighed, and we may decide to intervene to prevent it. The disagreement over the legal permissibility of abortion demonstrates how difficult the weighing can be, however. Consider the position of those who believe that abortion is morally wrong because it is the taking of life that has moral status. Within this group some seem undisturbed by the fact that there is deep disagreement over the moral status of the fetus. They wish to prohibit abortion. But others in this group, while holding that abortion is wrong, admit that reasonable persons could disagree with them and that human reason seems unable to resolve the question. For this reason they oppose legal prohibitions of abortion. The former believe that the latter do not take the value of human life seriously, while the latter believe that the former fail to recognize the depth and seriousness of the disagreement between reasonable persons. . . .

Each position has some force, and clearly normative relativism offers no simple solution to the dilemma. What the doctrine provides, however, is a set of reasons for tolerance and non-intervention that must be weighed against other reasons. The doctrine applies not only to proposed interventions by one society in another, but also, as in the case of abortion, to deep moral disagreements within pluralistic societies containing diverse moral traditions. If meta-ethical relativism is true, even if only with respect to a limited set of moral conflicts such as abortion, then our moral condition is immeasurably complicated. We must strive to find what will be for us the right or the best thing to do, and also deal with the feelings of unease caused by the recognition that there is no single right or best thing to do. This task, no matter how difficult, is not the end of moral reflection. It instead may be the beginning of a different sort of reflection that involves on the one hand an effort to reach an understanding with those who have substantially different values, and on the other the effort to stay true to one's own values. Some of those who believe that abortion is the taking of a life with moral status, for instance, have chosen to oppose it by placing their efforts into organizations that aim to lessen the perceived need for abortion, organizations that aid unwed mothers, for example.

One final issue regarding relativism needs addressing. Relativism has a bad name in some quarters because it is associated with a lack of moral conviction, with a tendency toward nihilism. Part of the reason for the bad name may be the identification of relativism with its most extreme forms. If these forms are true, then everything is permitted, on someone's morality. But another reason for the bad name is the assumption that one's moral confidence, one's commitment to act on one's values, is somehow dependent on maintaining the belief that one's morality is the only true or the most justified one. But surely some reflection will reveal that such a belief alone would not guarantee a commitment to act. The commitment to act involves a conception of what one's morality means to the self, whether it be the only true one or not. It involves making a connection between what one desires, what one aspires to, and the substantive content of one's moral values. It is being able to see morality as important to us in these ways that allows us to avoid nihilism. The belief that our morality is the only true or most justified one does not automatically create this kind of importance, nor is it a necessary condition for this kind of importance, because the values I may see as important and part of what makes life most meaningful to me may not have to be values that all reasonable persons would accept or recognize to be true.

Here, as in other matters concerning relativism, the emotion provoked by the mere name tends to muddle the issues and to polarize unnecessarily. When we get through defending and attacking what most people conceive as relativism or what they associate with it, then most of the real work remains to be done. What is left is a moral reality that is quite messy and immune to neat solutions. But why should we have expected anything else?

References

Benedict, R.: *Patterns of Culture* (New York: Penguin, 1934).

Harman, G.: "Moral relativism defended," *Philosophical Review* 84 (1975), 3–22.

Herodotus: *The Persian Wars,* trans. George Rawlinson (New York: Modern Library, 1942).

Herskovits, M.: *Cultural Relativism: Perspectives in Cultural Pluralism* (New York: Vintage, 1972).

James, W.: "The will to believe," *Essays in Pragmatism,* ed. Aubrey Castell (New York: Hafner, 1948).

Mackie, J.L.: *Ethics: Inventing Right and Wrong* (Harmondsworth: Penguin, 1977).

Montaigne, M. de: *Complete Essays* (1595); trans. Donald M. Frame (Stanford: Stanford University Press, 1973).

Nagel, T.: *The View from Nowhere* (New York: Oxford University Press, 1986).

Plato: *Crito* and *Theaetetus;* trans. E. Hamilton and H. Cairns, *Collected Dialogues of Plato* (Princeton: Princeton University Press, 1961).

Robinson, T. M., trans.: *Contrasting Arguments: An Edition of the Dissoi Logoi* (New York: Arno Press, 1979).

Stevenson, C. L.: *Ethics and Language* (New Haven: Yale University Press, 1944).

Wong, D. B.: *Moral Relativity* (Berkeley: University of California Press, 1984).

Visit the companion Web site for chapter specific quizzes, suggestions for further reading, video ideas, and other resources to assess and expand your understanding of the chapter material. Go to http://philosophy.wadsworth.com and select the companion Web site for *Voices of Wisdom.*

 You can access many additional readings at the Info Trac-College Edition Web site. To find the following suggested articles do a keyword search with the article title. Use the passcode that was packaged with your new book to enter the site at http://www.Infotrac-college.com/Wadsworth/. Here is a sampling.

J. David Velleman, "Love as a Moral Emotion." *Ethics,* January 1999 v109 i2 p338(1), A53985530.

Axel Honneth and John Farrell, "Recognition and Moral Obligation. (The Decent Society)." *Social Research,* Spring 1997 v64 n1 p16(20), A19382724.

Kok-Chor Tan, "Kantian Ethics and Global Justice." *Social Theory and Practice,* Spring 1997 v23 n1 p53(21), A19532591.

Elijah Millgram, "Mill's Proof of the Principle of Utility." *Ethics,* January 2000 v110 i2 p282, A60060293.

Brian Leiter, "Nietzsche and the Morality Critics." *Ethics,* January 1997 v107 n2 p250(36), A19206999.

Joan C. Tronto, "Care as a Basis for Radical Political Judgments." *Hypatia,* Spring 1995 v10 n2 p141(9), A17192674.

Alison M. Jaggar, "Globalizing Feminist Ethics. (Border Crossings: Multicultural and Postcolonial Feminist Challenges to Philosophy, Part 1)." *Hypatia,* Spring 1998 v13 n2 p7(25), A21107828.

Samantha Brennan, "Recent Work in Feminist Ethics." *Ethics,* July 1999 v109 i4 p858, A55266881.

Virginia Held, "The Meshing of Care and Justice." *Hypatia,* Spring 1995 v10 n2 p128(5), A17192670.

Alison Hornstein, "The Question That We Should Be Asking: Is Terrorism Wrong?" *Newsweek,* December 17, 2001 p14, A80784800.

Theodore Schick Jr., "Is Morality a Matter of Taste? Why Professional Ethicists Think That Morality Is Not Purely 'Subjective.'" *Inquiry,* Fall 1998 v18 n4 p32(3), A21231822.

Chapter 4

What Makes a Society Just?

> The problem of setting up a state can be solved even by a nation of devils.
>
> IMMANUEL KANT

4.1 Introduction

HAVE YOU EVER WONDERED, "What is justice?" Have you been curious about why we have governments? What is the best form of government? Who should rule? Where does the authority to rule come from? Have you ever thought, "Why should there be laws and why should we obey them? Are all people naturally wicked and do they need to be restrained from doing bad or forced to do good? Is it morally justifiable to break the law?" Have you noticed that we talk a lot about liberty, equality, and justice but have a hard time defining these concepts? Should liberty be sacrificed to promote equality? Or should liberty be protected at all costs, even if it means some people will not get an equal opportunity?

Have you wondered, "What should the government give the people—what they want or what is good for them? Who knows what is good for them? Should the state serve the interests of the individual, or should the interests of the individual be subordinate to the interests of the state?"

If you have thought about these sorts of questions, you have been concerned with the kinds of issues and problems that are normally studied by social and political philosophers. Political and social philosophy deal with issues of moral value at the level of the group. **Political philosophy** is primarily concerned with the justification of governmental authority to rule and with the nature of government or the state. **Social philosophy** is primarily concerned with who gets what and how.

Your pursuit of your own good occurs within a social context—that is, within a context in which others are also pursuing their own good. In such a social context, issues of fairness, social rights and responsibilities, the limits of political and economic power, and the welfare of your fellow human beings inevitably arise.

Like ethics, social-political philosophy is primarily *normative* rather than *descriptive.* For example, one goal of political philosophy is not just to describe the kinds of governments there are and how they function, but also to figure out which are the best forms of government and by what standards such a judgment can be made.

There are many issues and problems relating to social-political philosophy, and we can do no more than investigate a few of them in this chapter. However, two concepts are central to many of the debates in this field: authority and justice. A government is the exercise of power and coercive force by one person or group over the rest in a society. A fundamental political question has to do with what gives one group the authority to exercise such power. **Anarchism** is the position that governments are by nature immoral and should not be established. Those who argue in favor of anarchism maintain that each individual has the ultimate moral authority to live and act as he or she chooses. It is immoral for one group to rule another, and it is immoral of you, as an individual, to surrender your moral responsibility for the conduct of your own life to another. Of course, many people believe that anarchism would lead to social chaos, and so government of some kind seems necessary. But the question remains, by whose authority does one person or group rule another? And even if we grant that some kind of government is needed, the issues of what kind and the limits of its power must be answered.

Some people have argued that one of the purposes of government is to ensure justice. Philosophers often distinguish among **compensatory justice, retributive justice,** and **distributive justice.** Affirmative action programs, which may provide for preferential treatment, constitute examples of compensatory (also called "corrective") justice because they involve providing benefits to persons who have suffered undeserved hardships or who have been denied benefits they deserve. The imposition of legal penalties (e.g., putting someone in prison) is an example of retributive justice because it involves placing burdens on people who have enjoyed benefits they did not deserve or who are guilty of failing to fulfill their responsibilities. Distributive justice is the fair distribution of both burdens and benefits to persons in situations of conflict of interest and relative scarcity. For example, not everyone can get into medical school, so how can we decide who should be accepted in a manner fair to all?

These three notions—compensation, retribution, and fair distribution—indicate that the concepts of fairness and desert are central to the concept of justice. What about the notion of equality? Isn't treating everyone equally the same as treating them justly? **Egalitarians** argue that all persons, simply because they are persons, should share equally in the distribution of all benefits and burdens. Yet treating everyone equally may not always be the just thing to do. Paying Harry $50,000 and paying Chong the same, even though Harry has worked only 5 years for the company and has a poor performance record whereas Chong is a 15-year veteran with an excellent record, does not seem just. Harry and Chong are both persons, but in the case of salary should this be the primary consideration? However, allowing some people, because of good luck or birth, to become extremely wealthy and others, because of misfortune or birth, to become extremely poor does not seem fair either. Is there a fair way to distribute wealth?

4.2 God and Justice

Who ought to have the ultimate authority to rule? In other words, who is sovereign or has the right to exercise sovereignty? Should it be one person, several, or all people? If we need rulers, which type of rule is best? What criteria would help us decide the issue?

Plato, in the *Republic* (see Section 8.3), describes an ideal society in which only the lovers of wisdom (philosophers) rule. Justice is achieved, according to Plato, when each of the classes of his ideal republic do well what they are best suited to do. Justice shall reign when the rulers rule wisely, the guardians protect courageously, and the producers produce and consume goods moderately. Plato's vision of a just society has been widely influential. However, his pupil Aristotle modified his teacher's political ideas.

Aristotle divided governments into three types: rule of one, rule of some, and rule of all. He divided these types again into those that were good because they had the common good in view and those that were bad because they had only self-interest or special interests in mind.

TYPE	GOOD	BAD
One	Monarchy	Tyranny
Some	Aristocracy	Oligarchy
All	Polity	Democracy

It might surprise you to find **democracy** (rule by the people) listed as the bad form of the rule of all, but Aristotle believed that democracies did not promote the common good. Rather, they promote the special interests of those who are able to exercise the most influence. For Aristotle, the moral entitlement to rule derives from whether those in power have their own interest in view or the interests of all segments of society. In other words, good governments promote the common good, and they do this by making human flourishing possible.

Aristotle did not list **theocracy** (the theory that only God has the right to rule) among his governmental types, but this has been a widespread and long-lasting theory of sovereignty. The Hebrew Bible (called by Christians the Old Testament) endorses a theocratic state in which a king rules with God's proxy. The monarchs of the ancient world ruled as divine stand-ins, and the emperors of China had the mandate of heaven as their charter. During the Middle Ages, the divine right of kings was a widely held political theory, which said, in effect, that the moral entitlement to exercise the power to rule is a divine right, but this right can be granted by God to those of his (her?) choice. The great monarchies of Europe were founded on this principle, and their power maintained by the support of the Roman Catholic Church. Even today in the United States, one hears talk of the "restoration" of a theocratic state among fundamentalist Protestants, and the modern world is not without its theocracies.

The notion that God alone is sovereign is an idea that is found not only in ancient Judaism and Christianity but also in Islam. Muhammad (570–632) is considered by Muslims to be a prophet of **Allah** (God). A **Muslim** is one who submits to the will of Allah, and Islam is the name of a religious community that seeks to obey the commands of Allah. According to Islam, Allah revealed his will to the prophet Muhammad. Those revelations are recorded in the *Qur'an,* the holy book of Islam. Central to Islamic practice are the **five pillars of Islam:** witnessing that there is no God but Allah and that Muhammad is his Apostle; mandatory prayers, or *salat;* mandatory alms (*zakat*); fasting during the month of Ramadan; and *hajj,* or pilgrimage to Mecca.

Throughout Islamic history there has been and there continues to be considerable debate about the best type of government. The fundamental presupposition of this debate is that the right to rule belongs to God because only God is the perfectly just creator of all that exists. All parties agree on this theistic understanding of sovereignty. The disputes center on the political implications of divine sovereignty.

After the death of Muhammad, various schools of Islamic thought developed. Two of these schools—the **Sunni** and **Shi'i**—agreed that, since God does not rule human society directly, humans must devise governments that strive to realize as nearly as humans can the divine ideal of justice. According to the Sunni, a caliph (successor to the Prophet) should be selected or elected to provide political and military leadership. This caliphate would have, according to the Sunni, limited religious power although, ideally, the caliph himself would be a descendant from Muhammad's tribe if not from Muhammad himself. The Shi'i argued that leadership should be vested in an imam (leader) who is the direct descendant of the Prophet and his cousin and son-in-law Ali, who, according to the Shi'i, is the first true imam after the Prophet himself. The imam is a divinely inspired religious *and* political leader.

Islamic philosophers, while well aware of the debates within Islam over legitimate political succession, tended to take a different approach to the issue of what makes a society just. While acknowledging the sovereignty of Allah and the authority of revelation, philosophers such as Abu al-Walid Ibn Rushid (d. 595/1198), known in the West by his Latin name of Averroës, introduced ideas derived from both Aristotle and Plato into the debate. Criteria derived from reasonable reflection on the issues must also be considered. Proper genealogy is not enough. Just rulers are rational rulers, whatever may be their connection to the Prophet.

Majid Khadduri, author of the next selection, is professor emeritus of The School of Advanced International Studies of the Johns Hopkins University. After some general comments about the view of justice found in Islamic sources, he summarizes Ibn Rushid's views.

Reading Questions

1. What is the difference between positive justice and revelational justice?
2. What are the three sources of justice in Islamic tradition?
3. Why is it more accurate to call the Islamic state a divine nomocracy rather than a theocracy?
4. What is the literal meaning of *'adl*?
5. How does Ibn Rushd draw on the ideas of Plato and Aristotle?
6. According to Ibn Rushd, why should the ruler of a just state be a philosopher (lover of wisdom)?
7. What are unjust states like, and why does Ibn Rushd consider democracy one of them?

The Islamic Conception of Justice

MAJID KHADDURI

And fill up the measure when you measure, and with the just balance; that it better and fairer in the issue.

—Q. XVII, 37

And when you speak, be just, even if it should be to a kinsman.

—Q. VI, 153

JUSTICE IS ESSENTIALLY a relative concept. Whenever a man asserts that which he considers his just claim, were it to be valid, it must be relevant to an established public order under which a certain scale of justice is acknowledged. Scales of justice vary considerably from land to land, and each scale is defined and ultimately determined by society in accordance with the public order of that society. Yet no matter how scales differ one from another, they all seem to have certain elements in common and, broadly speaking, may be divided into two major categories.

One category is to be found in societies which assume that men are capable of determining their individual or collective interests and know that which they may need or to which they may aspire; they therefore can, individually or collectively, establish a public order under which a certain scale or scales of justice are likely to evolve by tacit agreement or by formal action. This kind of justice, a product of the interaction between expectations and existing conditions, may be called positive justice. It is admittedly imperfect and men always endeavor to refine and improve it by a continuing process of social change. The ideal or perfect justice is a mirage, and the real one develops by improvisation from generation to generation.

In a society which presupposes that man is essentially weak and therefore incapable of rising above personal failings, the idea that fallible human beings can determine what their collective interests are and lay down an impartial standard of justice is scarcely acceptable. In such a society a superhuman or divine authority is invoked to provide either the sources or the basic principles of the public order under which a certain standard of justice is established. Whether the superhuman authority is exercised by a gifted sage or an inspired prophet, the kind of justice that flows from such a source commands respect and can have a lasting impact on the administration of justice. Some of the ancient societies—the Hebrew, the Christian and the Islamic are but three examples—were committed to this viewpoint: God disclosed Himself through Revelations, communicated to men through prophets, in which His justice is embodied. The justice which flows from such a high divine source is considered applicable to all men and forms another category of justice. In contrast with positive justice, it may be called Divine or Revelational justice. It is the product of intuition, or divine inspiration, and is closely interwoven with religion and ethics. It coincides with Reason and may well fall in the category of natural justice. Aristotle used the term "natural justice" in the sense that it is the product not of social but of natural forces. Following Aristotle, scholars often equated Divine or God's justice with natural justice, but, unlike the natural-law scholars who were concerned with the relation of justice to society, Christian and Muslim scholars focused their primary concern on the concept of justice in relation to God's Will and related it to the destiny of man. Both held that Divine Justice is the ultimate objective of the Revelation, expressed in its early form in the sacred laws of Christianity and Islam. In the

From Majid Khadduri, The Islamic Conception of Justice. Baltimore, MD: The Johns Hopkins University Press, 1984, pp. 1–6, 8–11, 97–101. © 1984 by The Johns Hopkins University Press. Reprinted by permission. Notes deleted.

Summa Theologica, St. Thomas Aquinas termed the sacred law of Christianity the Eternal Law, and Muslim scholars called their Eternal Law simply the "pathway" (Sharī'a). The concept of justice embodied in the Religion and Law of Islam, not to speak of Christian justice, evoked an endless debate among scholars concerning both its scope and character and how its standard is to be realized on Earth.

The Sources of Justice

In Islam, Divine Justice is enshrined in the Revelation and Divine Wisdom which the Prophet Muhammad communicated to his people. The Revelation, transmitted in God's words, is to be found in the Qur'ān; and the Divine Wisdom, inspired to the Prophet, was uttered in the Prophet's own words and promulgated as the Sunna, which subsequently came to be known as the Hadīth, or the Prophet's Traditions. These two authoritative or "textual sources," the embodiment of God's Will and Justice, provided the raw material on the basis of which the scholars, through the use of a third "derivative source" of human reasoning called ijtihād, laid down the Law and the Creed. The fundamental principles of the Law and the Creed, and the creative works of succeeding generations, formed the foundation of the renowned Islamic public order. . . .

In Islamic theory, God is the Sovereign of the community of believers; He is its ultimate Ruler and Legislator. The Revelation and Divine Wisdom are the primary sources of the developing public order, presuming to meet the community's growing needs and expectations. The principles and maxims of justice derived from the Revelation and Divine Wisdom were considered infallible and inviolable, designed for all time and potentially capable of application to all men. In principle, the Law laid down by the Divine Legislator is an ideal and perfect system. But the public order, composed of the Law as well as state acts and the rulings (furū') and opinions of the scholars on all matters arrived at through human reasoning (ijtihād), are by necessity subject to adaptation and refinement to meet changing conditions and the growing needs of the community.

Since the Divine Legislator did not rule directly over the believers, the enthronement of a Ruler to represent God on Earth, to whom God's authority was delegated, had become necessary to put the Law into practice and to rule with Justice. A new form of government had thus been established based on Divine Law and Justice. This form of government, often called theocracy, is obviously not based on the principle that authority is exercised directly by God (whether as a Pharaoh or a Caesar) but by a representative who derives his authority not directly from God but from God's Law. It is therefore the Law, embodying the principles of Divine authority, which indeed rules and therefore the state becomes not, strictly speaking, a theocracy, but a form of nomocracy. The Islamic State, whose constitution and source of authority is a Divine Law, might be called a Divine nomocracy.

The textual sources, consisting of the Revelation and Divine Wisdom, are the Qur'ān and the Sunna. To these constitutional instruments, the proximate source of authority, all the political leaders and contending parties appealed to assert their conflicting claims to power. Likewise, on the strength of these sources, the scholars sought to legitimize one claim against another by diverse arguments—theological, legal, and others—on the grounds of justice. Although the scholars agreed on the Divine nature of justice, they disagreed on how it should be realized on Earth and formulated various doctrines of justice reflecting the conflicting interests, local traditions, and aspirations of rival leaders and groups in their struggle for power. Legitimacy and justice were often used interchangeably by political leaders, and the scholars, in an attempt to rationalize the legitimacy of rival groups, provided one scale of justice or another drawn from the emerging public order. . . .

At the outset the debate on justice began on the political level. In a community founded on religion, it was indeed in the nature of things that public concern should focus first on the question of legitimacy and the qualification of the Ruler whose primary task was to put God's Law and Justice into practice. Since the Prophet, the first Ruler, died without providing a rule for succession, the question of legitimacy became crucial. Should any pretender to the throne seize power without a valid claim, his act would naturally be considered a travesty to Divine Justice. The debate thus was bound to center on the procedural question of the choice of the person who would have a legitimate claim to succeed the Prophet in accordance with the standard of political justice embodied in the textual sources.

Once the debate on political justice started, it never really ended. Like Pandora's box, it became exceedingly difficult to bring political differences under control. It led to schism in the body politic and the rise of rival credal groups and sects, each seeking to rationalize its standard of political justice on one credal ground or another. From the political level the debate gradually shifted to other levels—theological, legal, and others—although ulterior political motivation continued to reassert itself in one form or another. As the Islamic public order advanced, the debate moved to higher levels of sophistication, and scholars in fields other than theology and law—philosophers and other men of learning—were very soon drawn into it. For no great thinker, whether in Islam or in any other community, could possibly remain indifferent to a debate on a subject as engaging and central as justice. But before we proceed further, perhaps a clarification of the literary meaning of justice and other related terms would be in order.

The Literary Meaning of Justice

The meaning of the common usage of words expressing the notions of justice or injustice is not only important in the abstract sense, but also illuminating for an understanding of the manifold aspects of justice; since the literal meaning of words is ultimately the outgrowth of their social or every-day meaning, the writers and thinkers are likely to be influenced by it in the articulation and rationalization of man's needs and expectations in the struggle to achieve justice and other human ideals. Classical Arabic is renowned for its richness in vocabulary and literary expressions. Indeed, it is no exaggeration to say that for every concept or action describing or identifying a particular human activity, perhaps a dozen words in the major lexicons are likely to be found, notwithstanding that each word is not necessarily a synonym, as it may often imply a slightly different shade of meaning from the other. For instance, for the name of God (although this is not a typical example), it may be interesting to note, there are ninety-nine words called the asmā' al-ḥusna (the beautiful names), each denoting or expressing the meaning of one of His manifold attributes.

For every aspect of justice there are several words and the most common in usage is the word "'adl." . . . The antonym of 'adl is not a modified spelling of the word 'adl denoting its negative meaning—as is the counter word "injustice" to "justice" in English—but an entirely different word called "jawr." . . .

Literally, the word 'adl is an abstract noun, derived from the verb 'adala, which means: First, to straighten or to sit straight, to amend or modify; second, to run away, depart or deflect from one (wrong) path to the other (right) one; third, to be equal or equivalent, to be equal or match, or to equalize; fourth, to balance or counterbalance, to weigh, or to be in a state of equilibrium. Finally, 'adl (or 'idl) may also mean example or alike (Q. V, 96), a literal expression which is indirectly related to justice. . . .

The literal meaning of 'adl in classical Arabic is thus a combination of moral and social values denoting fairness, balance, temperance and straightforwardness. Logically, Divine Justice would be a synthesis of all these values and virtues; indeed such a conceptual meaning is the theme of the debate among theologians, jurists and philosophers and will be the subject of our inquiry in the pages to follow.

The Notion of Justice in the Qur'ān and Traditions

The Prophet Muhammad, who seems to have been endowed with a deep sense of justice, found widespread inequity and oppression in the society in which he had grown up, and he sought to establish order and harmony within which a distinct standard of justice would be acknowledged.

As a Prophet, he naturally stressed religious values, but he was also a social reformer, and his decisions provided precedents on the strength of which the issues that were to arise in succeeding generations were resolved. The idea of justice was of particular interest to him, and he dealt with the problems of his day with uprightness, balance, and fairness. Nor was he indifferent to discrimination and inhuman acts, as exemplified in the legislation for the improvement of the status of women, emancipation of slaves (though slavery as a system was not abolished), and prohibition of infanticide and other unjust acts and practices. Moreover, he himself valued certain virtues honored by his followers and he incorporated them in his teachings. As he said in one of his often quoted utterances, his call was not to abolish but to "further the good morals" (li utammim makārim al-akhlāq) that had been in existence in society, and he felt compelled to confirm them.

In the tribal society of Arabia, where survival was perhaps the tribesman's primary concern, such virtues as honor, courage, and liberality were more highly prized than other virtues. These were epitomized in the word "muruwwa," consisting of everything that was taken to be praiseworthy and which may be called the Arab *summum bonum*. The muruwwa continued to be viewed so high in Arab eyes in subsequent centuries that al-Maqqarī (d. 770/1369) in his definition of justice, stated that no one could claim to be just were he to compromise the virtue of muruwwa. But in the exhibition of honor and courage the tribesmen were often brutal and oppressive, especially in the pursuit of *vendetta,* with the consequent subordination of the virtues of fairness and moderation to arbitrary rules of order. The poet 'Amr B. Kulthūm, composer of one of the well-known Seven Odes (al-Mu'allaqāt al-Sab'a) was not the only one who sang the praise of brutality and oppression attributed to his tribe. The absence of a coherent social order and political unity in the tribal society of Arabia necessarily subordinated the scale of justice to the requirements of survival, and consequently the appeal to justice took the negative form of retribution, such as retaliation and the payment of blood-money, rather than the positive forms of fairness, balance, and temperance.

The Prophet, while conceding the value of courage and other virtues, felt keenly the need to assert religious and moral values to temper cruelty and harshness. For this reason, the Qur'ān and Traditions often warned believers against bigotry and oppression, and admonished them that in the fulfillment of their religious obligations they must above all be just. In the Qur'ān there are over two hundred admonitions against injustice expressed in such words as zulm, ithm, dalāl, and others, and no less than almost a hundred expressions embodying the notion of justice, either directly in such words as 'adl, qist, mizān, and others . . . or in a variety of indirect expressions.

Second only to the existence of the One God, no other religious or moral principles are more emphasized in the Qur'ān and Traditions than the principles of uprightness, equity, and temperance, partly because of their intrinsic value but mainly because of the reaction against the pre-Islamic social order which paid little or no attention to justice. The most important Quranic references to justice are as follows:

> God commands justice and good-doing . . . and He forbids indecency, dishonor and insolence. (Q. XV, 92)
> God commands you to deliver trusts back to their owners, and when you judge among men, you should judge with justice. (Q. IV, 61)
> Of those We created are a people who guide by the truth, and by it act with justice. (Q. VIII, 180)

In the Traditions, the Prophet sought to explain the meaning of the abstract maxims of justice enunciated in the Qur'ān by specific examples, expressed in legal and ethical terms, to distinguish between just and unjust acts as well as to set underlying rules indicating what the scale of justice ought to be. Since the Prophet dealt essentially with practical questions, the theologians and other scholars found in the Traditions precedents on the strength of which they formulated their theories of justice. However, neither in the Qur'ān nor in the Traditions are there specific measures to indicate what are the constituent elements of justice or how justice can be realized on Earth. Thus the task of working out what the standard of justice ought to be fell upon the scholars who sought to draw its elements from the diverse authoritative sources and the rulings and acts embodied in the works of commentators.

The religious character of the public order, however, imposed by its very nature certain restraints, and the community of believers, distrustful of the capacity of fallible men to legislate for society, discouraged radical departure from the literal meaning of textual sources. Small wonder that many scholars, under popular pressures, were often forced to renounce doctrines seemingly inconsistent with the literal meaning of the authoritative sources, despite the growing needs of society for innovations. However, most scholars felt that they were duty-bound to accept the interpretation of the standard of justice laid down by their predecessors more strictly than by those who sought radical changes. . . .

Having established the harmony of Reason and Revelation, Ibn Rushd proceeded to discuss his ideas of justice making a distinction between the Divine and Human justice (Rational Justice). He made it clear that despite differences in sources (Greek and Islamic), the notion of justice embodied in both is ultimately the same. In setting forth his theory of human justice, Ibn Rushd has drawn on both Plato and Aristotle, making a distinction between the theoretical and practical forms of justice with an emphasis on the latter. Justice, like other virtues, does not exist in its perfect form in a vacuum, said Ibn Rushd; it attains its perfection only when men are citizens of the state. Just as virtues are faculties of the soul, he added, justice is the highest virtue of man as a citizen. But justice is not just one virtue; it is, as Plato said, the sum of all virtues. "It consists," he said, "in no more than every citizen following the activity for which he is best qualified by nature." He went on to explain that this is conceivable only when the state is functioning in accordance with the guidance provided by the speculative science (philosophy) and governed by its masters. These are the ruling classes of the state just as the intellect is the ruling part of the soul. So justice

means that each man (or class) does what he (or the class) has to do in proper measure and time.

Ibn Rushd distinguishes between virtues like wisdom and courage which are closely connected with one class only, and virtues like justice and temperance ('iffa) which are manifestly connected with all classes of the state. In agreement with Aristotle, he says that the virtue of temperance is connected with all, although Plato insists that temperance is a virtue confined to craftsmen. Justice is the virtue necessary for all.

In the realization of justice—indeed, in the realization of all virtues—Ibn Rushd said, in agreement with Aristotle, that three conditions are required. First, it is not only knowledge of the nature of virtues that is necessary; action is even more important. Second, the souls of the young must be inculcated with these virtues and cultivated to the point of perfection; if evil is ever in possession of some, it must be removed. Third, the qualities and virtues, whenever they are combined and render other virtues perfect, must be specified.

Ibn Rushd then turned to the question of how to inculcate and cultivate these virtues into the souls of the citizens. There are obviously two methods: First, by persuasion, either rhetorical and poetical for the multitude or the rational (speculative) for the elect; and second, by force. The first method is for the citizens who had already been accustomed to it from youth, and the other is for the adversaries and all those who are not sensitive to the appeals of virtue. The latter is evidently not for the citizens of the Virtuous State; it is for states whose public order is not based on virtues. In dealing with these states, whose rulers resort to force to correct their citizens, there is no other way than to resort to war. The Law, says Ibn Rushd, indicates how the two methods can be applied. If persuasion is not heeded, war becomes just (jihād) against rebels as well as unbelievers. Since preparation for war is impossible without the cultivation of the virtue of courage, the citizens should cultivate this virtue in preparedness for war when it becomes necessary. Just as wisdom is the virtue necessary for the realization of justice within the state, so courage is necessary for the realization of justice in the relationship between nations.

Ibn Rushd, in agreement with Plato, maintains that justice can be realized only in a state founded upon a set of virtues, namely, wisdom, courage, temperance, and justice. Whenever these virtues are fully cultivated, the state becomes an ideal state. A few words about each virtue may be called for.

Wisdom includes possession of theoretical and practical knowledge concerning governance and Law. Men who are endowed with this rare quality are very few; they may be found only among the philosophers and those who are capable of governing the State. The rulers of the Ideal State, said Ibn Rushd in agreement with Plato, "are necessarily the Philosophers."

Courage as a virtue is the quality of strength against such emotions as fear and desire, which can be attained by education, especially in music and gymnastics. This virtue is most needed by the guardians whose responsibility is to maintain order and protect the state from its enemies.

Temperance and justice are in a different category from wisdom and courage. Whereas the last two are ordinarily found among rulers and guardians, temperance and justice are virtues necessary for all men. Temperance may be defined as the middle or the mean in human behavior—in eating, drinking, sexual intercourse, and others—and the man who is temperate "is he who can, of his own accord, remain permanently in this middle position." He can control himself and restrain "the soul from pleasures and desire." "It is said," Ibn Rushd adds, "that the temperate man is the most courageous and master over himself." Just as the man who is by his intellect the master over the inferior, so is the temperate state more courageous than others and a master over itself. In order to attain such a quality, temperance should exist not only in one class but in all—the rulers and the ruled alike.

Finally, justice as a virtue is the quality of fairness and self-control. It is the quality by which the state can survive and claims to continue as long as the rulers and the multitude are in agreement "to keep that which the laws demand,"

namely, that "everyone . . . does that business for which he is fitted by nature, and does not long for what he does not possess." In other words, the ideal state is the Just State by reason of the quality of justness with which all its citizens are clothed, just as wrongdoings reduce other states to "states of injustice" or "erring states."

Justice is maintained in the state as long as each citizen pursues the virtue most fitting to his class. The Just State is characterized as wise, courageous, and temperate, provided that these virtues exist in the state in their true measure, so that the rational faculty (Reason) rules over the other faculties.

Justice, in order to endure, is dependent on the Ruler who presides over the destiny of the state. Such a Ruler must be a philosopher, because he is the only one who desires knowledge and investigates its nature (separated from matter) and is able to teach it. Knowledge may be taught to the few either by the rational or demonstrative argument; the multitude can be taught only by rhetorical and poetical methods. In order to succeed, the philosopher should master both the theoretical and the practical arts, just as the king, in order to perfect the art of governance, is in need of the qualities of wisdom and intellect. The lawgiver obviously needs the same qualities. Indeed, the qualities of the philosopher, the king, and the lawgiver are the same. The Imām, Ruler of the Islamic state, must possess all of these qualities.

Should the ruler be a prophet? Ibn Rushd's answer to this question in general is in the affirmative. Apart from being a prophet or a philosopher, however, the Ruler must be endowed with a set of natural qualifications such as disposition to theoretical knowledge, love for the truth, high-mindedness, courage, fluency in speech, good memory, control over desires that are not proper for rulers (like sensual desires and love for money), and—last but not least—justice. Since the existence of the prophet is a rarity, . . . Ibn Rushd stressed the personal qualities of the Ruler upon whom the survival of the state is dependent. Thus it would be tempting to conclude that were the state to be a just state it should be presided over by a Ruler possessing the theoretical and practical qualities without having first been ruled by a prophet. In such a state Rational Justice may be equated with the *jus naturale*.

The opposite of the Just State are the erring or wrongdoing states where injustice prevails. Like Plato, Ibn Rushd identifies four types of states apart from the Ideal State; in each a different scale of justice is maintained. The first is the state whose order is based on honor, which is called timocracy. In such a state, justice is subordinate to honor and to other qualities. As an end, honor may be combined with wealth and power and may tempt men to overpower each other and do evil and injustice. Men of honor are masters and their status corresponds generally to the degree of honor they attain. Rulers possess the ability to distribute honors in pursuit of the measures that preserve their control. This, says Ibn Rushd, is the kind of justice that exists in timocracy.

The second type, called plutocracy, is ruled by a few whose power rests on wealth. So wealth, not virtue, is the measure of the quality of men. The Ruler, the most powerful and perhaps the richest, combines with wealth an ability to govern successfully and consequently he is the master of the state, provided he allows his men to acquire wealth and let them enjoy it indefinitely. Wealth and power are the privilege of the few, but the majority, possessing no claim to privilege, are poor and oppressed.

The third type is the democratic state in which everybody is free from restraints and each is entitled to do whatever his heart desires. The aims and qualities of men vary—some love honor, others wealth, and still others tyranny. But there may be some who possess a few virtues and are moved by them. All arts and dispositions come into being, and it is possible that an "ideal state" as well as other types of states may emerge out of these varied dispositions. The man who is truly just is the one who has the power of leadership. The majority, at the mercy of whoever becomes the master, are plundered and oppressed by the more powerful, but these are often tempted to commit excesses "just as it happens in our own time and in our own state." When the conditions deteriorate and the rulers can no longer distribute wealth among supporters, they resort to imposing heavy taxes. Consequently the common run of men, encouraged by dissatisfied supporters, try to shake off the oppressors, but the masters seek control by force. The State, supported by a few (including religious leaders), becomes tyrannical. The end of such a state is reduced to nothing more than to serve the master and to fulfill his wishes. This state is obviously the opposite of the Just State. Only in the Just State can the citizen attain justice equal to his natural abilities. . . .

4.3 Capitalism and Exploitation

Should people be allowed to own property? That may be a startling question. We are so used to the notion of private property that it seems absurd to even ask such a question. Of course, we should be able to own property and, furthermore, do with it as we see fit. However, think a moment. Which society is better: One in which the wealthy are allowed to accumulate as much wealth as they can, or one in which the state regulates the distribution of wealth for the sake of the common good? Remember— we are *not* all born equal. Some of us are born into wealth and privilege. We can afford a good education, good medical care, excellent legal representation. Others of us are born into poverty. We cannot afford education, medical care, and legal counsel. Is that fair?

Adam Smith (1723–1790), in his influential book *The Wealth of Nations*, published in 1776, argued for an economic philosophy called **laissez-faire capitalism.**

He believed that, in the long run, a free competitive market would work for the common good. Smith thought that even though we are all selfish by nature, the laws that guided self-interested competitors would work like an "invisible hand" to the benefit of all.

Smith argued that the value of a commodity equals the amount of labor it commands (the labor theory of value). Those who acquire capital or "stock" can hire labor to produce a product. If a division of labor is efficiently established (in a famous example, Smith divided the process of making pins into eighteen different jobs, thereby increasing the number of pins per worker that could be produced), a *surplus* value over and above the expense of wages and materials will result. This profit is a repayment to the capitalists for their efforts and ingenuity.

Central to this theory is the concept of private property. John Locke (1632–1704), an English philosopher, articulated this concept long before Smith. He wrote in *Concerning Civil Government* that God gave "nature to humans to use for their benefit." The use of nature involves human labor. Once labor is mixed with the material God has given to humans, private property results. He wrote, "Whatsoever then, he [a human being] removes out of a state that nature hath provided and left it in, he hath mixed his labor with, and joined to it something that is his own, and thereby makes it his property." Since this property is private (owned by the individual), the individual should be free to use it as he or she sees fit. Thus, Locke argued for certain individual rights, among them the right to life, liberty, and the preservation of property. If those words sound at least partly familiar, it is because Thomas Jefferson (1743–1826) in the *Declaration of Independence* of the United States borrowed them from Locke but made one change, substituting the "pursuit of happiness" for "preservation of property."

The view that the freedom of the individual takes priority over the group is subject to some serious objections. For one thing, a community is more than an atomistic collection of individuals. It is an organic whole, and the good of each is not necessarily the good of all. In addition, the notion of "human rights" implies more than leaving people alone to compete with one another. Human rights include an equal opportunity to participate in and contribute to society. The right to work under safe conditions, to have access to education, to obtain adequate medical care, to enjoy a decent standard of living and a secure retirement—there is no provision for such rights in laissez-faire capitalism. And what about the intrinsic value of cooperation? Should not society promote cooperation? Laissez-faire capitalism promotes competition. Alienation, envy, corruption, greed—such can be the results when petty self-interest prevails.

Karl Marx (1818–1883) and Friedrich Engels (1820–1895) saw the results of Adam Smith's economic theory. They saw workers abused and degraded, children exploited, and society divided into two antagonistic classes: the proletariat (an urban population of wage-earning workers) and the bourgeoisie (the owners of production, along with bankers and financiers). All this was the result of the activity of capitalists whose primary interest was to maximize profits.

Marx and Engels argued that the division of labor results in meaningless repetitive jobs that alienate workers from the product of their labors. The workers, even though they have "mixed" their labor with natural materials, do not own the result. The capitalist owns the product and can dispose of it as she or he wishes. They also argued that wage labor is necessarily exploitation because workers give more than they receive. If this were not the case, it would be crazy for a capitalist to hire a worker because the value produced by an hour's labor would not be worth more than the money paid for that hour's worth of work (plus materials and overhead). The so-called "surplus value" from which the capitalist makes a profit is, in fact, created by paying workers less than full value for their efforts.

Marx and Engels advocated **socialism** in place of capitalism. All citizens should own the means of production, and there should be rational planning of economic investment and growth. Production should exist for the sake of human need, not private profit. There should be a just distribution of goods and services. At first, a strong governmental role is needed to create such a system. Eventually, however, as full equality and universal prosperity are achieved, the classes will disappear and a society of naturally cooperative individuals will emerge. The need for a state will simply wither away. When this happens, **communism,** in its ideal form, will be achieved.

There are some serious objections to this position. For one thing, socialism, at least in centrally planned, one-party **totalitarian** states, does not seem to work well. The collapse of the Soviet Union is a case in point. People do not work very hard when they lack economic incentives. Voluntary cooperation is one thing, but forced cooperation is entirely different. The notion that eventually a classless society will be in place and government will disappear seems to be wishful thinking. If anything, government may get stronger and more absolute. Abuse of power may increase as control increases. The state may become more totalitarian and, while the human rights to education, employment, medical care, and shelter are ensured, the human rights of free assembly, free speech, and freedom of religion are often denied.

Neither sacrificing the interests of the individual completely to the interests of the community nor sacrificing the interests of the community completely to the interests of the individual seems to be the best way to produce a just society. Perhaps this is why many economic systems have moved in a mixed direction—that is, creating a mixture of capitalism and socialism.

Both Marx and Engels believed that the revolution that could bring about economic justice needed to be led by the workers—those most exploited by capitalism. They wrote the *Manifesto of the Communist Party* in 1848, not only to explain their views and defend them, but also to call on the workers of the world to unite and throw off the chains of capitalistic exploitation. As you read parts of this manifesto, answer the questions and engage Marx and Engels in a critical dialogue about what makes a society just.

Reading Questions

1. Do you think that the description of bourgeois society as *essentially* exploitive is accurate? Why, or why not?
2. What is the *proletariat,* and how does it differ from the *bourgeoisie?*
3. What objections have been made to communism, and how do Marx and Engels answer those objections? Do you find their responses convincing? Why, or why not?
4. Do you think the measures Marx and Engels outline for wresting power from the bourgeoisie will eventually result in the end of class struggles and the arrival of a just society? Why, or why not?
5. How would Marx and Engels answer the question, "What makes a society just?"

Manifesto of the Communist Party

KARL MARX AND FRIEDRICH ENGELS

I. *Bourgeois and Proletarians*

THE HISTORY OF ALL HITHERTO EXISTING SOCIETY is the history of class struggles.

Freeman and slave, patrician and plebeian, lord and serf, guild master and journeyman, in a word, oppressor and oppressed, stood in constant opposition to one another, carried on an uninterrupted, now hidden, now open fight—a fight that each time ended either in a revolutionary reconstitution of society at large, or in the common ruin of the contending classes.

In the earlier epochs of history, we find almost everywhere a complicated arrangement of society into various orders, a manifold gradation of social rank. In ancient Rome, we have patricians, knights, plebeians, slaves; in the Middle Ages, feudal lords, vassals, guild masters, journeymen, apprentices, serfs; in almost all of these classes, again, subordinate gradations.

The modern bourgeois society that has sprouted from the ruins of feudal society has not done away with class antagonisms. It has but established new classes, new conditions of oppression, new forms of struggle in place of the old ones.

Our epoch, the epoch of the bourgeoisie, possesses, however, this distinctive feature: it has simplified the class antagonisms. Society as a whole is more and more splitting up into two great hostile camps, into two great classes directly facing each other: bourgeoisie and proletariat.

From the serfs of the Middle Ages sprang the chartered burghers of the earliest towns. From these burgesses the first elements of the bourgeoisie were developed.

The discovery of America, the rounding of the Cape, opened up fresh ground for the rising bourgeoisie. The East Indian and Chinese markets, the colonisation of America, trade with the colonies, the increase in the means of exchange and in commodities generally, gave to commerce, to navigation, to industry, an impulse never before known, and thereby, to the revolutionary element in the tottering feudal society, a rapid development.

The feudal system of industry, under which industrial production was monopolised by closed guilds, now no longer sufficed for the growing wants of the new markets. The manufacturing system took its place. The guild masters were pushed on one side by the manufacturing middle class; division of labour between the different corporate guilds vanished in the face of division of labour in each single workshop.

Meantime the markets kept ever growing, the demand ever rising. Even manufacture no longer sufficed. Thereupon, steam and machinery revolutionised industrial production. The place of manufacture was taken by the giant, modern industry; the place of the industrial middle class, by industrial millionaires, the leaders of whole industrial armies, the modern bourgeois.

Modern industry has established the world market, for which the discovery of America paved the way. This market has given an immense development to commerce, to navigation, to communication by land. This development has, in its turn, reacted on the extension of industry; and in proportion as industry, commerce, navigation, railways extended, in the same proportion the bourgeoisie developed, increased its capital, and pushed into the background every class handed down from the Middle Ages.

We see, therefore, how the modern bourgeoisie is itself the product of a long course of development, of a series of revolutions in the modes of production and of exchange. . . .

The bourgeoisie, historically, has played a most revolutionary part.

The bourgeoisie, wherever it has got the upper hand, has put an end to all feudal, patriarchal,

Selections from Manifesto of the Communist Party, *first published in English by Friedrich Engels in 1888.*

idyllic relations. It has pitilessly torn asunder the motley feudal ties that bound man to his "natural superiors," and has left remaining no other nexus between man and man than naked self-interest, than callous "cash payment." It has drowned the most heavenly ecstasies of religious fervour, of chivalrous enthusiasm, of philistine sentimentalism, in the icy water of egotistical calculation. It has resolved personal worth into exchange value, and in place of the numberless indefeasible chartered freedoms, has set up that single, unconscionable freedom—free trade. In one word, for exploitation veiled by religious and political illusions, it has substituted naked, shameless, direct, brutal exploitation.

The bourgeoisie has stripped of its halo every occupation hitherto honoured and looked up to with reverent awe. It has converted the physician, the lawyer, the priest, the poet, the man of science, into its paid wage-labourers.

The bourgeoisie has torn away from the family its sentimental veil, and has reduced the family relation to a mere money relation. . . .

The bourgeoisie cannot exist without constantly revolutionising the instruments of production, and thereby the relations of production, and with them the whole relations of society. Conservation of the old modes of production in unaltered form was, on the contrary, the first condition of existence for all earlier industrial classes. Constant revolutionising of production, uninterrupted disturbance of all social conditions, everlasting uncertainty and agitation, distinguish the bourgeois epoch from all earlier ones. All fixed, fast-frozen relations, with their train of ancient and venerable prejudices and opinions, are swept away; all new-formed ones become antiquated before they can ossify. All that is solid melts into air, all that is holy is profaned, and man is at last compelled to face with sober senses his real conditions of life and his relations with his kind.

The need of a constantly expanding market for its products chases the bourgeoisie over the whole surface of the globe. It must nestle everywhere, settle everywhere, establish connexions everywhere.

The bourgeoisie has through its exploitation of the world market given a cosmopolitan character to production and consumption in every country. To the great chagrin of reactionists, it has drawn from under the feet of industry the national ground on which it stood. All old-established national industries have been destroyed or are daily being destroyed. They are dislodged by new industries, whose introduction becomes a life and death question for all civilised nations, by industries that no longer work up indigenous raw material, but raw material drawn from the remotest zones; industries whose products are consumed not only at home, but in every quarter of the globe. In place of the old wants, satisfied by the productions of the country, we find new wants, requiring for their satisfaction the products of distant lands and climes. In place of the old local and national seclusion and self-sufficiency, we have intercourse in every direction, universal interdependence of nations. And as in material, so also in intellectual production. The intellectual creations of individual nations become common property. National onesidedness and narrow-mindedness become more and more impossible, and from the numerous national and local literatures there arises a world literature.

The bourgeoisie, by the rapid improvement of all instruments of production, by the immensely facilitated means of communication, draws all, even the most barbarian, nations into civilisation. The cheap prices of its commodities are the heavy artillery with which it batters down all Chinese walls, with which it forces the barbarians' intensely obstinate hatred of foreigners to capitulate. It compels all nations, on pain of extinction, to adopt the bourgeois mode of production; it compels them to introduce what it calls civilisation into their midst, that is, to become bourgeois themselves. In one word, it creates a world after its own image. . . .

Modern bourgeois society with its relations of production, of exchange, and of property, a society that has conjured up such gigantic means of production and of exchange, is like the sorcerer who is no longer able to control the powers of the nether world whom he has called up by his spells. For many a decade past, the history of industry and commerce is but the history of the revolt of modern productive forces against modern conditions of production, against the property relations that are the conditions for the existence of the bourgeoisie and of its rule. It is enough to mention the commercial crises that by their periodical return put on its trial, each time more threateningly, the existence of the entire bourgeois society. In these crises a great part not only of the existing products, but also of the previously created productive forces, are periodically destroyed. In these crises there breaks out an epidemic that, in all earlier epochs, would have seemed an absurdity—the epidemic of overproduction. Society suddenly finds itself put back into a state of momentary barbarism; it appears as if a famine, a universal war of devastation, had cut off the supply of every means of subsistence; industry and commerce seem to be destroyed. And why? Because there is too much civilisation, too much means of subsistence, too much industry, too much commerce. The productive forces at the disposal of society no longer tend to further the development of the conditions of bourgeois property; on the contrary, they have become too powerful for these conditions by which they are fettered, and so soon as they overcome these fetters, they bring disorder into the whole of bourgeois society, endanger the existence of bourgeois property. The conditions of bourgeois society are too narrow to comprise the wealth created by them. And how does the bourgeoisie get over these crises? On the one hand, by enforced destruction of a mass of productive forces; on the other, by the conquest of new markets and by the more thorough exploitation of the old ones. That is to say, by paving the way for more extensive and more destructive crises, and by diminishing the means whereby crises are prevented.

The weapons with which the bourgeoisie felled feudalism to the ground are now turned against the bourgeoisie itself.

But not only has the bourgeoisie forged the weapons that bring death to itself; it has also called into existence the men who are to wield those weapons—the modern working class, the proletarians.

In proportion as the bourgeoisie, that is, capital, is developed, in the same proportion is the proletariat, the modern working class, developed—a class of labourers who live only so long as they find work and who find work only so long as their labour increases capital. These labourers, who must sell themselves piecemeal, are a commodity like every other article of commerce, and are consequently exposed to all the vicissitudes of competition, to all the fluctuations of the market.

Owing to the extensive use of machinery and to division of labour, the work of the proletarians has lost all individual character and, consequently, all charm for the workman. He becomes an appendage of the machine, and it is only the most simple, most monotonous, and most easily acquired knack that is required of him. Hence, the cost of production of a workman is restricted, almost entirely, to the means of subsistence that he requires for his maintenance and for the propagation of his race. But the price of a commodity, and therefore also of labour, is equal to its cost of production. In proportion, therefore, as the repulsiveness of the work increases, the wage decreases. Nay more, in proportion as the use of machinery and division of labour increases, in the same proportion the burden of toil also increases, whether by prolongation of the working hours, by increase of the work exacted in a given time, or by increased speed of the machinery, etc. . . . .

But with the development of industry the proletariat not only increases in number; it becomes concentrated in greater masses, its strength grows, and it feels that strength more. The various interests and conditions of life within the ranks of the proletariat are more and more equalised, in proportion as machinery obliterates all distinctions of labour, and nearly everywhere reduces wages to the same low level. The growing competition among the bourgeois, and the resulting commercial crises, make the wages of the workers ever more fluctuating. The unceasing improvement of machinery, ever more rapidly developing, makes their livelihood more and more precarious; the collisions between individual workmen and individual bourgeois take more and more the character of collisions between two classes. Thereupon the workers begin to form combinations (Trades Unions) against the bourgeois; they club together in order to keep up the rate of wages; they found permanent associations in order to make provision beforehand for these occasional revolts. Here and there the contest breaks out into riots. . . .

In the conditions of the proletariat, those of old society at large are already virtually swamped. The proletarian is without property; his relation to his wife and children has no longer anything in common with the bourgeois family-relations; modern industrial labour, modern subjection to capital, the same in England as in France, in America as in Germany, has stripped him of every trace of national character. Law, morality, religion, are to him so many bourgeois prejudices, behind which lurk in ambush just as many bourgeois interests.

All the preceding classes that got the upper hand, sought to fortify their already acquired status by subjecting society at large to their conditions of appropriation. The proletarians cannot become masters of the productive forces of society, except by abolishing their own previous mode of appropriation, and thereby also every other previous mode of appropriation. They have nothing of their own to secure and to fortify; their mission is to destroy all previous securities for, and insurances of, individual property.

All previous historical movements were movements of minorities, or in the interests of minorities. The proletarian movement is the self-conscious, independent movement of the immense majority, in the interests of the immense majority. The proletariat, the lowest stratum of our present society, cannot stir, cannot raise itself up, without the whole superincumbent strata of official society being sprung into the air.

Though not in substance, yet in form, the struggle of the proletariat with the bourgeoisie is at first a national struggle. The proletariat of each country must, of course, first of all settle matters with its own bourgeoisie.

In depicting the most general phases of the development of the proletariat, we traced the more or less veiled civil war, raging within existing society, up to the point where that war breaks out into open revolution, and where the violent overthrow of the bourgeoisie lays the foundation for the sway of the proletariat. . . .

All property relations in the past have continually been subject to historical change consequent upon the change in historical conditions.

The French Revolution, for example, abolished feudal property in favour of bourgeois property.

The distinguishing feature of Communism is not the abolition of property generally, but the abolition of bourgeois property. But modern bourgeois private property is the final and most complete expression of the system of producing and appropriating products, that is based on class antagonisms, on the exploitation of the many by the few.

In this sense, the theory of the Communists may be summed up in the single sentence: Abolition of private property.

We Communists have been reproached with the desire of abolishing the right of personally acquiring property as the fruit of a man's own labour, which property is alleged to be the groundwork of all personal freedom, activity and independence.

Hard-won, self-acquired, self-earned property! Do you mean the property of the petty artisan and of the small peasant, a form of property that preceded the bourgeois form? There is no need to abolish that; the development of industry has to a great extent already destroyed it, and is still destroying it daily.

Or do you mean modern bourgeois private property?

But does wage-labour create any property for the labourer? Not a bit. It creates capital, *i.e.,* that kind of property which exploits wage-labour, and which cannot increase except upon condition of begetting a new supply of wage-labour for fresh exploitation. Property, in its present form, is based on the antagonism of capital and wage-labour. Let us examine both sides of this antagonism.

To be a capitalist, is to have not only a purely personal, but a social *status* in production. Capital is a collective product, and only by the united action of many members, nay, in the last resort, only by the united action of all members of society, can it be set in motion.

Capital is, therefore, not a personal, it is a social power.

When, therefore, capital is converted into common property, into the property of all members of society, personal property is not thereby transformed into social property. It is only the social character of the property that is changed. It loses its class-character.

Let us now take wage-labour.

The average price of wage-labour is the minimum wage, *i.e.,* that quantum of the means of subsistence, which is absolutely requisite to keep the labourer in bare existence as a labourer. What, therefore, the wage-labourer appropriates by means of his labour, merely suffices to prolong and reproduce a bare existence. We by no means intend to abolish this personal appropriation of the products of labour, an appropriation that is made for the maintenance and reproduction of human life, and that leaves no surplus wherewith to command the labour of others. All that we want to do away with, is the miserable character of this appropriation, under which the labourer lives merely to increase capital, and is allowed to live only in so far as the interest of the ruling class requires it.

In bourgeois society, living labour is but a means to increase accumulated labour. In Communist society, accumulated labour is but a means to widen, to enrich, to promote the existence of the labourer.

In bourgeois society, therefore, the past dominates the present; in Communist society, the present dominates the past. In bourgeois society capital is independent and has individuality, while the living person is dependent and has no individuality.

And the abolition of this state of things is called by the bourgeois, abolition of individuality and freedom! And rightly so. The abolition of bourgeois individuality, bourgeois independence, and bourgeois freedom is undoubtedly aimed at.

By freedom is meant, under the present bourgeois conditions of production, free trade, free selling and buying.

But if selling and buying disappears, free selling and buying disappears also. This talk about free selling and buying, and all the other "brave words" of our bourgeoisie about freedom in general, have a meaning, if any, only in contrast with restricted selling and buying, with the fettered traders of the Middle Ages, but have no meaning when opposed to the Communistic abolition of buying and selling, of the bourgeois conditions of production, and of the bourgeoisie itself.

You are horrified at our intending to do away with private property. But in your existing society, private property is already done away with for nine-tenths of the population; its existence for the few is solely due to its non-existence in the hands of those nine-tenths. You reproach us, therefore, with intending to do away with a form of property, the necessary condition for whose existence is the non-existence of any property for the immense majority of society.

In one word, you reproach us with intending to do away with your property. Precisely so; that is just what we intend.

From the moment when labour can no longer be converted into capital, money, or rent, into a social power capable of being monopolised, *i.e.,* from the moment when individual property can no longer be transformed into bourgeois property, into capital, from that moment, you say, individuality vanishes.

You must, therefore, confess that by "individual" you mean no other person than the bourgeois, than the middle-class owner of property. This person must, indeed, be swept out of the way, and made impossible.

Communism deprives no man of the power to appropriate the products of society; all that it does is to deprive him of the power to subjugate the labour of others by means of such appropriation.

It has been objected that upon the abolition of private property all work will cease, and universal laziness will overtake us.

According to this, bourgeois society ought long ago to have gone to the dogs through sheer idleness; for those of its members who work, acquire nothing, and those who acquire anything, do not work. The whole of this objection is but another expression of the tautology: that there can no longer be any wage-labour when there is no longer any capital.

All objections urged against the Communistic mode of producing and appropriating material products, have, in the same way, been urged against the Communistic modes of producing and appropriating intellectual products. Just as, to the bourgeois, the disappearance of class property is the disappearance of production itself, so the disappearance of class culture is to him identical with the disappearance of all culture.

That culture, the loss of which he laments, is, for the enormous majority, a mere training to act as a machine.

But don't wrangle with us so long as you apply, to our intended abolition of bourgeois property, the standard of your bourgeois notions of freedom, culture, law, &c. Your very ideas are but the outgrowth of the conditions of your bourgeois production and bourgeois property, just as your jurisprudence is but the will of your class made into a law for all, a will, whose essential character and direction are determined by the economical conditions of existence of your class.

The selfish misconception that induces you to transform into eternal laws of nature and of reason, the social forms springing from your present mode of production and form of property—historical relations that rise and disappear in the progress of production—this misconception you share with every ruling class that has preceded you. What you see clearly in the case of ancient property, what you admit in the case of feudal property, you are of course forbidden to admit in the case of your own bourgeois form of property.

Abolition of the family! Even the most radical flare up at this infamous proposal of the Communists.

On what foundation is the present family, the bourgeois family, based? On capital, on private gain. In its completely developed form this family exists only among the bourgeoisie. But this state of things finds its complement in the practical absence of the family among the proletarians, and in public prostitution.

The bourgeois family will vanish as a matter of course when its complement vanishes, and both will vanish with the vanishing of capital.

Do you charge us with wanting to stop the exploitation of children by their parents? To this crime we plead guilty.

But, you will say, we destroy the most hallowed of relations, when we replace home education by social.

And your education! Is not that also social, and determined by the social conditions under which you educate, by the intervention, direct or indirect, of society, by means of schools, etc.? The Communists have not invented the intervention of society in education; they do but seek to alter the character of that intervention, and to rescue education from the influence of the ruling class. The bourgeois clap-trap about the family and education, about the hallowed co-relation of parent and child, becomes all the more disgusting, the more, by the action of Modern Industry, all family ties among the proletarians are torn asunder, and their children transformed into simple articles of commerce and instruments of labour.

But you Communists would introduce community of women, screams the whole bourgeoisie in chorus.

The bourgeois sees in his wife a mere instrument of production. He hears that the instruments of production are to be exploited in common, and, naturally, can come to no other conclusion than that the lot of being common to all will likewise fall to the women.

He has not even a suspicion that the real point aimed at is to do away with the status of women as mere instruments of production.

For the rest, nothing is more ridiculous than the virtuous indignation of our bourgeois at the community of women, which, they pretend, is to be openly and officially established by the Communists. The Communists have no need to introduce community of women; it has existed almost from time immemorial.

Our bourgeois, not content with having the wives and daughters of their proletarians at their disposal, not to speak of common prostitutes, take the greatest pleasure in seducing each other's wives.

Bourgeois marriage is in reality a system of wives in common and thus, at the most, what the Communists might possibly be reproached with, is that they desire to introduce, in substitution for a hypocritically concealed, an openly legalised community of women. For the rest, it is self-evident that the abolition of the present system of production must bring with it the abolition of the community of women springing from that system, *i.e.*, of prostitution both public and private.

The Communists are further reproached with desiring to abolish countries and nationality.

The working men have no country. We cannot take from them what they have not got. Since the proletariat must first of all acquire political supremacy, must rise to be the leading class of the nation, must constitute itself *the* nation, it is, so far, itself national, though not in the bourgeois sense of the word.

National differences and antagonisms between peoples are daily more and more vanishing, owing to the development of the bourgeoisie, to freedom of commerce, to the world-market, to uniformity in the mode of production and in the conditions of life corresponding thereto.

The supremacy of the proletariat will cause them to vanish still faster. United action, of the leading civilised countries at least, is one of the first conditions for the emancipation of the proletariat.

In proportion as the exploitation of one individual by another is put an end to, the exploitation of one nation by another will also be put an end to. In proportion as the antagonism between classes within the nation vanishes, the hostility of one nation to another will come to an end.

The charges against Communism made from a religious, a philosophical, and, generally, from an ideological standpoint, are not deserving of serious examination.

Does it require deep intuition to comprehend that man's ideas, views and conceptions, in one word, man's consciousness, changes with every change in the conditions of his material existence, in his social relations and in his social life? What else does the history of ideas prove, than that intellectual production changes its character in proportion as material production is changed? The ruling ideas of each age have ever been the ideas of its ruling class.

When people speak of ideas that revolutionise society, they do but express the fact, that within the old society, the elements of a new one have been created, and that the dissolution of the old ideas keeps even pace with the dissolution of the old conditions of existence.

When the ancient world was in its last throes, the ancient religions were overcome by Christianity. When Christian ideas succumbed in the 18th century to rationalist ideas, feudal society fought its death battle with the then revolutionary bourgeoisie. The ideas of religious liberty and freedom of conscience merely gave expression to the sway of free competition within the domain of knowledge.

"Undoubtedly," it will be said, "religious, moral, philosophical and juridical ideas have been modified in the course of historical development. But religion, morality, philosophy, political science, and law, constantly survived this change."

"There are, besides, eternal truths, such as Freedom, Justice, etc., that are common to all states of society. But Communism abolishes eternal truths, it abolishes all religion, and all morality, instead of constituting them on a new basis; it therefore acts in contradiction to all past historical experience."

What does this accusation reduce itself to? The history of all past society has consisted in the development of class antagonisms, antagonisms that assumed different forms at different epochs.

But whatever form they may have taken, one fact is common to all past ages, *viz.*, the exploitation of one part of society by the other. No wonder, then, that the social consciousness of past ages, despite all the multiplicity and variety it displays, moves within certain common forms, or general ideas, which cannot completely vanish except with the total disappearance of class antagonisms.

The Communist revolution is the most radical rupture with traditional property relations; no wonder that its development involves the most radical rupture with traditional ideas.

But let us have done with the bourgeois objections to Communism.

We have seen above, that the first step in the revolution by the working class, is to raise the proletariat to the position of ruling class, to win the battle of democracy.

The proletariat will use its political supremacy to wrest, by degrees, all capital from the bourgeoisie, to centralise all instruments of production in the hands of the State, *i.e.*, of the proletariat organised as the ruling class; and to increase the total of productive forces as rapidly as possible.

Of course, in the beginning, this cannot be effected except by means of despotic inroads on the rights of property, and on the conditions of bourgeois production; by means of measures, therefore, which appear economically insufficient and untenable, but which, in the course of the movement, outstrip themselves, necessitate further inroads upon the old social order, and are unavoidable as a means of entirely revolutionising the mode of production.

These measures will of course be different in different countries.

Nevertheless in the most advanced countries, the following will be pretty generally applicable.

1. Abolition of property in land and application of all rents of land to public purposes.
2. A heavy progressive or graduated income tax.
3. Abolition of all right of inheritance.
4. Confiscation of the property of all emigrants and rebels.
5. Centralisation of credit in the hands of the State, by means of a national bank with State capital and an exclusive monopoly.
6. Centralisation of the means of communication and transport in the hands of the State.
7. Extension of factories and instruments of production owned by the State; the bringing into cultivation of wastelands, and the improvement of the soil generally in accordance with a common plan.
8. Equal liability of all to labour. Establishment of industrial armies, especially for agriculture.
9. Combination of agriculture with manufacturing industries; gradual abolition of the distinction between town and country, by a more equable distribution of the population over the country.
10. Free education for all children in public schools. Abolition of children's factory labour in its present form. Combination of education with industrial production etc., etc.

When, in the course of development, class distinctions have disappeared, and all production has been concentrated in the hands of a vast association of the whole nation, the public power will lose its political character. Political power, properly so called, is merely the organised power of one class for oppressing another. If the proletariat during its contest with the bourgeoisie is compelled, by the force of circumstances, to organise itself as a class, if, by means of a revolution, it makes itself the ruling class, and, as such, sweeps away by force the old conditions of production, then it will, along with these conditions, have swept away the conditions for the existence of class antagonisms and of classes generally, and will thereby have abolished its own supremacy as a class.

In place of the old bourgeois society, with its classes and class antagonisms, we shall have an association, in which the free development of each is the condition for the free development of all.

IV. Position of the Communists in Relation to the Various Existing Opposition Parties

. . . The Communists everywhere support every revolutionary movement against the existing social and political order of things.

In all these movements they bring to the front, as the leading question in each, the property question, no matter what its degree of development at the time.

Finally, they labour everywhere for the union and agreement of the democratic parties of all countries.

The Communists disdain to conceal their views and aims. They openly declare that their ends can be attained only by the forcible overthrow of all existing social conditions. Let the ruling classes tremble at a Communistic revolution. The proletarians have nothing to lose but their chains. They have a world to win.

WORKING MEN OF ALL COUNTRIES, UNITE!

4.4 The Original Position

What is the role of justice in a society? Is it very important or not so important? Is it more important than anything else? Should all the laws and all the major institutions of a society be changed or rejected if they are unjust?

You can imagine arguments on both sides of the issue. Someone might say that the promotion of law and order is of primary importance for any government. Justice must sometimes take a back seat to these more important goals. One could counter that law and order without justice is a sham. Peace and social stability at any price are just not worth it. There is no greater social good than justice.

If you read Kant, you might recognize a Kantian theme in the claim that justice is the highest social good. If you read Mill, you might recognize a utilitarian theme in the claim that justice must sometimes take a back seat to a greater good. So where do we go from here? How can we decide whether justice is the most important social good? Surely we must know what justice is before we can decide how important it is? What is justice?

Philosophers distinguish between the material principle of justice and the formal principle of justice. The **material principle of justice** is some particular trait that is used as a basis for distributing benefits and burdens. If someone claimed that race, ethnic background, sex, or sexual orientation is the basis on which he or she decided to deny (or give) someone a job, what would you say? Is this fair? If someone claimed that seniority, skill, or a record of good performance Is the basis on which she or he decided to deny (or give) someone a job, what would you say? Is this fair? The **formal principle of justice** requires that benefits and burdens be distributed fairly according to *relevant* differences and similarities. So if I decide to award an A to all my students who wear something red on the first Tuesday of each month, is that fair?

"But," you might properly retort, "that is not relevant."

Why isn't it?

"Because," you say, "it has nothing to do with how well they perform on the exams."

That is a reasonable response. However, why is performance on exams relevant? How do we decide what is relevant and fair?

Imagine that you are faced with the task of creating a new society. You are in the dark about your status in that new society. You do not know if you will be rich or poor. You do not know if you will be healthy or sick. You do not know your race or gender or sexual orientation or religion. Not knowing any of these things, what sort of society would you create? What sort of government would it have? How would its laws be enacted? What would its public policies be like?

The philosopher John Rawls thinks he knows what kind of society you would create in such a situation. You would create a just society. In 1971 Rawls, professor of philosophy at Harvard University, published a now famous and influential book called *A Theory of Justice.* Below you will read some selections from that book in which Rawls answers some of the questions we have been thinking about here.

Reading Questions

1. What is the role of justice?
2. What is the subject of justice?
3. What is the main idea of Rawls's theory of justice?
4. What role does the original position play in justifying different principles of justice?
5. What does Rawls mean by "reflective equilibrium"?
6. What two principles of justice would persons in the original position be likely to choose? How are these principles related?
7. What is the "veil of ignorance," and why is it important in developing a contractarian theory of justice?
8. Given what you have read, what do you think is wrong with Rawls's theory of justice? Why do you think it is wrong?
9. How would Rawls answer the question, "What makes a society just?"

A Theory of Justice

JOHN RAWLS

1. The Role of Justice

JUSTICE IS THE FIRST VIRTUE of social institutions, as truth is of systems of thought. A theory however elegant and economical must be rejected or revised if it is untrue; likewise laws and institutions no matter how efficient and well-arranged must be reformed or abolished if they are unjust. Each person possesses an inviolability founded on justice that even the welfare of society as a whole cannot override. For this reason justice denies that the loss of freedom for some is made right by a greater good shared by others. It does not allow that the sacrifices imposed on a few are outweighed by the larger sum of advantages enjoyed by many. Therefore in a just society the liberties of equal citizenship are taken as settled; the rights secured by justice are not subject to political bargaining or to the calculus of social interests. The only thing that permits us to acquiesce in an erroneous theory is the lack of a better one; analogously, an injustice is tolerable only when it is necessary to avoid an even greater injustice. Being first virtues of human activities, truth and justice are uncompromising.

These propositions seem to express our intuitive conviction of the primacy of justice. No doubt they are expressed too strongly. In any event I wish to inquire whether these contentions or others similar to them are sound, and if so how they can be accounted for. To this end, it is necessary to work out a theory of justice in the light of which these assertions can be interpreted and assessed. I shall begin by considering the role of the principles of justice. Let us assume, to fix ideas, that a society is a more or less self-sufficient association of persons who in their relations to one another recognize certain rules of conduct as binding and who for the most part act in accordance with them. Suppose further that these rules specify a system of cooperation designed to advance the good of those taking part in it. Then, although a society is a cooperative venture for mutual advantage, it is typically marked by a conflict as well as by an identity of interests. There is an identity of interests since social cooperation makes possible a better life for all than any would have if each were to live solely by his own efforts. There is a conflict of interests since persons are not indifferent as to how the greater benefits produced by their collaboration are distributed, for in order to pursue their ends they each prefer a larger to a lesser share. A set of principles is required for choosing among the various social arrangements which determine this division of advantages and for underwriting an agreement on the proper distributive shares. These principles are the principles of social justice: they provide a way of assigning rights and duties in the basic institutions of society and they define the appropriate distribution of the benefits and burdens of social cooperation.

Now let us say that a society is well-ordered when it is not only designed to advance the good of its members but when it is also effectively regulated by a public conception of justice. That is, it is a society in which (1) everyone accepts and knows that the others accept the same principles of justice, and (2) the basic social institutions generally satisfy and are generally known to satisfy these principles. In this case while men may put forth excessive demands on one another, they nevertheless acknowledge a common point of view from which their claims may be adjudicated. If men's inclination to self-interest makes their vigilance against one another necessary, their public sense of justice makes their secure association together possible. Among individuals with disparate aims and purposes a shared conception of justice establishes the bonds of civic friendship; the general desire for justice limits the pursuit of other ends. One may think of a public conception of justice as constituting the fundamental charter of a well-ordered human association. . . .

2. *The Subject of Justice*

Many different kinds of things are said to be just and unjust: not only laws, institutions, and social systems, but also particular actions of many kinds, including decisions, judgments, and imputations. We also call the attitudes and dispositions of persons, and persons themselves, just and unjust. Our topic, however, is that of social justice. For us the primary subject of justice is the basic structure of society, or more exactly, the way in which the major social institutions distribute fundamental rights and duties and determine the division of advantages from social cooperation. By major institutions I understand the political constitution and the principal economic and social arrangements. Thus the legal protection of freedom of thought and liberty of conscience, competitive markets, private property in the means of production, and the monogamous family are examples of major social institutions. Taken together as one scheme, the major institutions define men's rights and duties and influence their life-prospects, what they can expect to be and how well they can hope to do. The basic structure is the primary subject of justice because its effects are so profound and present from the start. The intuitive notion here is that this structure contains various social positions and that men born into different positions have different expectations of life determined, in part, by the political system as well as by economic and social circumstances. In this way the institutions of society favor certain starting places over others. These are especially deep inequalities. Not only are they pervasive, but they affect men's initial chances in life; yet they cannot possibly be justified by an appeal to the notions of merit or desert. It is these inequalities, presumably inevitable in the basic structure of any society, to which the principles of social justice must in the first instance apply. These principles, then, regulate the choice of a political constitution and the main elements of the economic and social system. The justice of a social scheme depends essentially on how fundamental rights and duties are assigned and on the economic opportunities and social conditions in the various sectors of society. . . .

3. The Main Idea of the Theory of Justice

My aim is to present a conception of justice which generalizes and carries to a higher level of abstraction the familiar theory of the social contract as found, say, in Locke, Rousseau, and Kant.[1] In order to do this we are not to think of the original contract as one to enter a particular society or to set up a particular form of government. Rather, the guiding idea is that the principles of justice for the basic structure of society are the object of the original agreement. They are the principles that free and rational persons concerned to further their own interests would accept in an initial position of equality as defining the fundamental terms of their association. These principles are to regulate all further agreements; they specify the kinds of social cooperation that can be entered into and the forms of government that can be established. This way of regarding the principles of justice I shall call justice as fairness.

Thus we are to imagine that those who engage in social cooperation choose together, in one joint act, the principles which are to assign basic rights and duties and to determine the division of social benefits. Men are to decide in advance how they are to regulate their claims against one another and what is to be the foundation charter of their society. Just as each person must decide by rational reflection what constitutes his good, that is, the system of ends which it is rational for him to pursue, so a group of persons must decide once and for all what is to count among them as just and unjust. The choice which rational men would make in this hypothetical situation of equal liberty, assuming for the present that this choice problem has a solution, determines the principles of justice.

In justice as fairness the original position of equality corresponds to the state of nature in the traditional theory of the social contract. This original position is not, of course, thought of as an actual historical state of affairs, much less as a primitive condition of culture. It is understood as a purely hypothetical situation characterized so as to lead to a certain conception of justice. Among the essential features of this situation is that no one knows his place in society, his class position or social status, nor does any one know his fortune in the distribution of natural assets and abilities, his intelligence, strength, and the like. I shall even assume that the parties do not know their conceptions of the good or their special psychological propensities. The principles of justice are chosen behind a veil of ignorance. This ensures that no one is advantaged or disadvantaged in the choice of principles by the outcome of natural chance or the contingency of social circumstances. Since all are similarly situated and no one is able to design principles to favor his particular condition, the principles of justice are the result of a fair agreement or bargain. For given the circumstances of the original position, the symmetry of everyone's relations to each other, this initial situation is fair between individuals as moral persons, that is, as rational beings with their own ends and capable, I shall assume, of a sense of justice. The original position is, one might say, the appropriate initial status quo, and thus the fundamental agreements reached in it are fair. This explains the

1. As the text suggests, I shall regard Locke's *Second Treatise of Government,* Rousseau's *The Social Contract,* and Kant's ethical works beginning with *The Foundations of the Metaphysics of Morals* as definitive of the contract tradition. For all of its greatness, Hobbes's *Leviathan* raises special problems. A general historical survey is provided by J. W. Gough, *The Social Contract,* 2nd ed. (Oxford, The Clarendon Press, 1957), and Otto Gierke, *Natural Law and the Theory of Society,* trans. with an introduction by Ernest Barker (Cambridge, The University Press, 1934). A presentation of the contract view as primarily an ethical theory is to be found in G. R. Grice, *The Grounds of Moral Judgment* (Cambridge, The University Press, 1967). . . .

propriety of the name "justice as fairness": it conveys the idea that the principles of justice are agreed to in an initial situation that is fair. The name does not mean that the concepts of justice and fairness are the same, any more than the phrase "poetry as metaphor" means that the concepts of poetry and metaphor are the same.

Justice as fairness begins, as I have said, with one of the most general of all choices which persons might make together, namely, with the choice of the first principles of a conception of justice which is to regulate all subsequent criticism and reform of institutions. Then, having chosen a conception of justice, we can suppose that they are to choose a constitution and a legislature to enact laws, and so on, all in accordance with the principles of justice initially agreed upon. Our social situation is just if it is such that by this sequence of hypothetical agreements we would have contracted into the general system of rules which defines it. Moreover, assuming that the original position does determine a set of principles (that is, that a particular conception of justice would be chosen), it will then be true that whenever social institutions satisfy these principles those engaged in them can say to one another that they are cooperating on terms to which they would agree if they were free and equal persons whose relations with respect to one another were fair. They could all view their arrangements as meeting the stipulations which they would acknowledge in an initial situation that embodies widely accepted and reasonable constraints on the choice of principles. The general recognition of this fact would provide the basis for a public acceptance of the corresponding principles of justice. No society can, of course, be a scheme of cooperation which men enter voluntarily in a literal sense; each person finds himself placed at birth in some particular position in some particular society, and the nature of this position materially affects his life prospects. Yet a society satisfying the principles of justice as fairness comes as close as a society can to being a voluntary scheme, for it meets the principles which free and equal persons would assent to under circumstances that are fair. In this sense its members are autonomous and the obligations they recognize self-imposed.

One feature of justice as fairness is to think of the parties in the initial situation as rational and mutually disinterested. This does not mean that the parties are egoists, that is, individuals with only certain kinds of interests, say in wealth, prestige, and domination. But they are conceived as not taking an interest in one another's interests. They are to presume that even their spiritual aims may be opposed, in the way that the aims of those of different religions may be opposed. Moreover, the concept of rationality must be interpreted as far as possible in the narrow sense, standard in economic theory, of taking the most effective means to given ends. I shall modify this concept to some extent, . . . but one must try to avoid introducing into it any controversial ethical elements. The initial situation must be characterized by stipulations that are widely accepted.

In working out the conception of justice as fairness one main task clearly is to determine which principles of justice would be chosen in the original position. To do this we must describe this situation in some detail and formulate with care the problem of choice which it presents. These matters I shall take up in the immediately succeeding chapters. It may be observed, however, that once the principles of justice are thought of as arising from an original agreement in a situation of equality, it is an open question whether the principle of utility would be acknowledged. Offhand it hardly seems likely that persons who view themselves as equals, entitled to press their claims upon one another, would agree to a principle which may require lesser life prospects for some simply for the sake of a greater sum of advantages enjoyed by others. Since each desires to protect his interests, his capacity to advance his conception of the good, no one has a reason to acquiesce in an enduring loss for himself in order to bring about a greater net balance of satisfaction. In the absence of strong and lasting benevolent impulses, a rational man would not accept a basic structure merely because it maximized the algebraic sum of advantages irrespective of its permanent effects on his own basic rights and interests. Thus it seems that the principle of utility is incompatible with the conception of social cooperation among equals for mutual advantage. It appears to be inconsistent with the idea of reciprocity implicit in the notion of a well-ordered society. Or, at any rate, so I shall argue.

I shall maintain instead that the persons in the initial situation would choose two rather different principles: the first requires equality in the assignment of basic rights and duties, while the second holds that social and economic inequalities, for example inequalities of wealth and authority, are just only if they result in compensating benefits for everyone, and in particular for the least advantaged members of society. These principles rule out justifying institutions on the grounds that the hardships of some are offset by a greater good in the aggregate. It may be expedient but it is not just that some should have less in order that others may prosper. But there is no injustice in the greater benefits earned by a few provided that the situation of persons not so fortunate is thereby improved. The intuitive idea is that since everyone's well-being depends upon a scheme of cooperation without which no one could have a satisfactory life, the division of advantages should be such as to draw forth the willing cooperation of everyone taking part in it, including those less well situated. Yet this can be expected only if reasonable terms are proposed. The two principles mentioned seem to be a fair agreement on the basis of which those better endowed, or more fortunate in their social position, neither of which we can be said to deserve, could expect the willing cooperation of others when some workable scheme is a necessary condition of the welfare of all. Once we decide to look for a conception of justice that nullifies the accidents of natural endowment and the contingencies of social circumstance as counters in quest for political and economic advantage, we are led to these principles. They express the result of leaving aside those aspects of the social world that seem arbitrary from a moral point of view. . . .

4. The Original Position and Justification

I have said that the original position is the appropriate initial status quo which insures that the fundamental agreements reached in it are fair. This fact yields the name "justice as fairness." It is clear, then, that I want to say that one conception of justice is more reasonable than another, or justifiable with respect to it, if rational persons in the initial situation would choose its principles over those of the other for the role of justice. Conceptions of justice are to be ranked by their acceptability to persons so circumstanced. Understood in this way the question of justification is settled by working out a problem of deliberation: we have to ascertain which principles it would be rational to adopt given the contractual situation. This connects the theory of justice with the theory of rational choice.

If this view of the problem of justification is to succeed, we must, of course, describe in some detail the nature of this choice problem. A problem of rational decision has a definite answer only if we know the beliefs and interests of the parties, their relations with respect to one another, the alternatives between which they are to choose, the procedure whereby they make up their minds, and so on. As the circumstances are presented in different ways, correspondingly different principles are accepted. The concept of the original position, as I shall refer to it, is that of the most philosophically favored interpretation of this initial choice situation for the purposes of a theory of justice.

But how are we to decide what is the most favored interpretation? I assume, for one thing, that there is a broad measure of agreement that principles of justice should be chosen under certain conditions. To justify a particular description of the initial situation one shows that it incorporates these commonly shared presumptions. One argues from widely accepted but weak premises to more specific conclusions. Each of the presumptions should by itself be natural and plausible; some of them may seem innocuous or even trivial. The aim of the contract approach is to establish that taken together they impose significant bounds on acceptable principles of justice. The ideal outcome would be that these conditions determine a unique set of principles; but I shall be satisfied if they suffice to rank the main traditional conceptions of social justice.

One should not be misled, then, by the somewhat unusual conditions which characterize the original position. The idea here is simply to make vivid to ourselves the restrictions that it seems reasonable to impose on arguments for principles of justice, and therefore on these principles themselves. Thus it seems reasonable and generally acceptable that no one should be advantaged or disadvantaged by natural fortune or social circumstances in the choice of principles. It also seems widely agreed that it should be impossible to tailor principles to the circumstances of one's own case. We should insure further that particular inclinations and aspirations, and persons' conceptions of their good do not affect the principles adopted. The aim is to rule out those principles that it would be rational to propose for acceptance, however little the chance of success, only if one knew certain things that are irrelevant from the standpoint of justice. For example, if a man knew that he was wealthy, he might find it rational to advance the principle that various taxes for welfare measures be counted unjust; if he knew that he was poor, he would most likely propose the contrary principle. To represent the desired restrictions one imagines a situation in which everyone is deprived of this sort of information. One excludes the knowledge of those contingencies which sets men at odds and allows them to be guided by their prejudices. In this manner the veil of ignorance is arrived at in a natural way. This concept should cause no difficulty if we keep in mind the constraints on arguments that it is meant to express. At any time we can enter the original position, so to speak, simply by following a certain procedure, namely, by arguing for principles of justice in accordance with these restrictions.

It seems reasonable to suppose that the parties in the original position are equal. That is, all have the same rights in the procedure for choosing principles; each can make proposals, submit reasons for their acceptance, and so on. Obviously the purpose of these conditions is to represent equality between human beings as moral persons, as creatures having a conception of their good and capable of a sense of justice. The basis of equality is taken to be similarity in these two respects. Systems of ends are not ranked in value; and each man is presumed to have the requisite ability to understand and to act upon whatever principles are adopted. Together with the veil of ignorance, these conditions define the principles of justice as those which rational persons concerned to advance their interests would consent to as equals when none are known to be advantaged or disadvantaged by social and natural contingencies.

There is, however, another side to justifying a particular description of the original position. This is to see if the principles which would be chosen match our considered convictions of justice or extend them in an acceptable way. We can note whether applying these principles would lead us to make the same judgments about the basic structure of society which we now make intuitively and in which we have the greatest confidence; or whether, in cases where our present judgments are in doubt and given with hesitation, these principles offer a resolution which we can affirm on reflection. There are questions which we feel sure must be answered in a certain way. For example, we are confident that religious intolerance and racial discrimination are unjust. We think that we have examined these things with care and have reached what we believe is an impartial judgment not likely to be distorted by an excessive attention to our own interests. These convictions are provisional fixed points which we presume any conception of justice must fit. But we have much less assurance as to what is the correct distribution of wealth and authority. Here we may be looking for a way to remove our doubts. We can check an interpretation of the initial situation, then, by the capacity of its principles to accommodate our firmest convictions and to provide guidance where guidance is needed.

In searching for the most favored description of this situation we work from both ends. We begin by describing it so that it represents generally shared and preferably weak conditions. We then see if these conditions are strong enough to yield a significant set of principles. If not, we look for further premises equally reasonable. But if so, and these principles match our considered convictions of justice, then so far well and good. But presumably there will be discrepancies. In this case we have a choice. We can either modify the account of the initial situation or we can revise our existing judgments, for even the judgments we take provisionally as fixed points are liable to revision. By going back and forth, sometimes altering the conditions of the contractual circumstances, at others withdrawing our judgments and conforming them to principle, I assume that eventually we shall find a description of the initial situation that both expresses reasonable conditions and yields principles which match our considered judgments duly pruned and adjusted. This state of affairs I refer to as reflective equilibrium. It is an equilibrium because at last our principles and judgments coincide; and it is reflective since we know to what principles our judgments conform and the premises of their derivation. At the moment everything is in order. But this equilibrium is not necessarily stable. It is liable to be upset by further examination of the conditions which should be imposed on the contractual situation and by particular cases which may lead us to revise our judgments. Yet for the time being we have done what we can to render coherent and to justify our convictions of social justice. We have reached a conception of the original position.

I shall not, of course, actually work through this process. Still, we may think of the interpretation of the original position that I shall present as the result of such a hypothetical course of reflection. It represents the attempt to accommodate within one scheme both reasonable philosophical conditions on principles as well as our considered judgments of justice. In arriving at the favored interpretation of the initial situation there is no point at which an appeal is made to self-evidence in the traditional sense either of general conceptions or particular convictions. I do not claim for the principles of justice proposed that they are necessary truths or derivable from such truths. A conception of justice cannot be deduced from self-evident premises or conditions on principles; instead, its justification is a matter of the mutual support of many considerations, of everything fitting together into one coherent view.

A final comment. We shall want to say that certain principles of justice are justified because they would be agreed to in an initial situation of equality. I have emphasized that this original position is purely hypothetical. It is natural to ask why, if this agreement is never actually entered into, we should take any interest in these principles, moral or otherwise. The answer is that the conditions embodied in the description of the original position are ones that we do in fact accept. Or if we do not, then perhaps we can be persuaded to do so by philosophical reflection. Each aspect of the contractual situation can be given supporting grounds. Thus what we shall do is to collect together into one conception a number of conditions on principles that we are ready upon due consideration to recognize as reasonable. These constraints express what we are prepared to regard as limits on fair terms of social cooperation. One way to look at the idea of the original position, therefore, is to see it as an expository device which sums up the meaning of these conditions and helps us to extract their consequences. On the other hand, this conception is also an intuitive notion that suggests its own elaboration, so that led on by it we are drawn to define more clearly the standpoint from which we can best interpret moral relationships. We need a conception that enables us to envision our objective from afar: the intuitive notion of the original position is to do this for us. . . .

11. *Two Principles of Justice*

I shall now state in a provisional form the two principles of justice that I believe would be chosen in the original position. . . .

The first statement of the two principles reads as follows.

First: each person is to have an equal right to the most extensive basic liberty compatible with a similar liberty for others.

Second: social and economic inequalities are to be arranged so that they are both (a) reasonably expected to be to everyone's advantage, and (b) attached to positions and offices open to all.

There are two ambiguous phrases in the second principle, namely "everyone's advantage" and "open to all." . . .

By way of general comment, these principles primarily apply, as I have said, to the basic structure of society. They are to govern the assignment of rights and duties and to regulate the distribution of social and economic advantages. As their formulation suggests, these principles presuppose that the social structure can be divided into two more or less distinct parts, the first principle applying to the one, the second to the other. They distinguish between those aspects of the social system that define and secure the equal liberties of citizenship and those that specify and establish social and economic inequalities. The basic liberties of citizens are, roughly speaking, political liberty (the right to vote and to be eligible for public office) together with freedom of speech and assembly; liberty of conscience and freedom of thought; freedom of the person along with the right to hold (personal) property; and freedom from arbitrary arrest and seizure as defined by the concept of the rule of law. These liberties are all required to be equal by the first principle, since citizens of a just society are to have the same basic rights.

The second principle applies, in the first approximation, to the distribution of income and wealth and to the design of organizations that make use of differences in authority and responsibility, or chains of command. While the distribution of wealth and income need not be equal, it must be to everyone's advantage, and at the same time, positions of authority and offices of command must be accessible to all. One applies the second principle by holding positions open, and then, subject to this constraint, arranges social and economic inequalities so that everyone benefits.

These principles are to be arranged in a serial order with the first principle prior to the second. This ordering means that a departure from the institutions of equal liberty required by the first principle cannot be justified by, or compensated for, by greater social and economic advantages. The distribution of wealth and income, and the hierarchies of authority, must be consistent with both the liberties of equal citizenship and equality of opportunity.

It is clear that these principles are rather specific in their content, and their acceptance rests on certain assumptions that I must eventually try to explain and justify. A theory of justice depends upon a theory of society in ways that will become evident as we proceed. For the present, it should be observed that the two principles (and this holds for all formulations) are a special case of a more general conception of justice that can be expressed as follows.

All social values—liberty and opportunity, income and wealth, and the bases of self-respect—are to be distributed equally unless an unequal distribution of any, or all, of these values is to everyone's advantage.

Injustice, then, is simply inequalities that are not to the benefit of all. Of course, this conception is extremely vague and requires interpretation.

As a first step, suppose that the basic structure of society distributes certain primary goods, that is, things that every rational man is presumed to want. These goods normally have a use whatever a person's rational plan of life. For simplicity, assume that the chief primary goods at the disposition of society are rights and liberties, powers and opportunities, income and wealth. . . . These are the social primary goods. Other primary goods such as health and vigor, intelligence and imagination, are natural goods; although their possession is influenced by the basic structure, they are not so directly under its control. Imagine, then, a hypothetical initial arrangement in which all the social primary goods are equally distributed: everyone has similar rights and duties, and income and wealth are evenly shared. This state of affairs provides a benchmark for judging improvements. If certain inequalities of wealth and organizational powers would make everyone better off than in this hypothetical starting situation, then they accord with the general conception.

Now it is possible, at least theoretically, that by giving up some of their fundamental liberties men are sufficiently compensated by the resulting social and economic gains. The general conception of justice imposes no restrictions on what sort of inequalities are permissible; it only requires that everyone's position be improved. We need not suppose anything so drastic as consenting to a condition of slavery. Imagine instead that men forego certain political rights when the economic returns are significant and their capacity to influence the course of policy by the exercise of these rights would be marginal in any case. It is this kind of exchange which the two principles as stated rule out; being arranged in serial order they do not permit exchanges between basic liberties and economic and social gains. The serial ordering of principles expresses an underlying preference among primary social goods. When this preference is rational so likewise is the choice of these principles in this order. . . .

24. The Veil of Ignorance

The idea of the original position is to set up a fair procedure so that any principles agreed to will be just. The aim is to use the notion of pure procedural justice as a basis of theory. Somehow we must nullify the effects of specific contingencies which put men at odds and tempt them to exploit social and natural circumstances to their own advantage. Now in order to do this I assume that the parties are situated behind a veil of ignorance. They do not know how the various alternatives will affect their own particular case and they are obliged to evaluate principles solely on the basis of general considerations.

It is assumed, then, that the parties do not know certain kinds of particular facts. First of all, no one knows his place in society, his class

position or social status; nor does he know his fortune in the distribution of natural assets and abilities, his intelligence and strength, and the like. Nor, again, does anyone know his conception of the good, the particulars of his rational plan of life, or even the special features of his psychology such as his aversion to risk or liability to optimism or pessimism. More than this, I assume that the parties do not know the particular circumstances of their own society. That is, they do not know its economic or political situation, or the level of civilization and culture it has been able to achieve. The persons in the original position have no information as to which generation they belong. These broader restrictions on knowledge are appropriate in part because questions of social justice arise between generations as well as within them, for example, the question of the appropriate rate of capital saving and of the conservation of natural resources and the environment of nature. There is also, theoretically anyway, the question of a reasonable genetic policy. In these cases too, in order to carry through the idea of the original position, the parties must not know the contingencies that set them in opposition. They must choose principles the consequences of which they are prepared to live with whatever generation they turn out to belong to.

As far as possible, then, the only particular facts which the parties know is that their society is subject to the circumstances of justice and whatever this implies. It is taken for granted, however, that they know the general facts about human society. They understand political affairs and the principles of economic theory; they know the basis of social organization and the laws of human psychology. Indeed, the parties are presumed to know whatever general facts affect the choice of the principles of justice. There are no limitations on general information, that is, on general laws and theories, since conceptions of justice must be adjusted to the characteristics of the systems of social cooperation which they are to regulate, and there is no reason to rule out these facts. It is, for example, a consideration against a conception of justice that, in view of the laws of moral psychology, men would not acquire a desire to act upon it even when the institutions of their society satisfied it. For in this case there would be difficulty in securing the stability of social cooperation. It is an important feature of a conception of justice that it should generate its own support. That is, its principles should be such that when they are embodied in the basic structure of society men tend to acquire the corresponding sense of justice. Given the principles of moral learning, men develop a desire to act in accordance with its principles. In this case a conception of justice is stable. This kind of general information is admissible in the original position.

The notion of the veil of ignorance raises several difficulties. Some may object that the exclusion of nearly all particular information makes it difficult to grasp what is meant by the original position. Thus it may be helpful to observe that one or more persons can at any time enter this position, or perhaps, better, simulate the deliberations of this hypothetical situation, simply by reasoning in accordance with the appropriate restrictions. In arguing for a conception of justice we must be sure that it is among the permitted alternatives and satisfies the stipulated formal constraints. No considerations can be advanced in its favor unless they would be rational ones for us to urge were we to lack the kind of knowledge that is excluded. The evaluation of principles must proceed in terms of the general consequences of their public recognition and universal application, it being assumed that they will be complied with by everyone. To say that a certain conception of justice would be chosen in the original position is equivalent to saying that rational deliberation satisfying certain conditions and restrictions would reach a certain conclusion. If necessary, the argument to this result could be set out more formally. I shall, however, speak throughout in terms of the notion of the original position. It is more economical and suggestive, and brings out certain essential features that otherwise one might easily overlook.

These remarks show that the original position is not to be thought of as a general assembly which includes at one moment everyone who will live at some time; or, much less, as an assembly of everyone who could live at some time. It is not a gathering of all actual or possible persons. To conceive of the original position in either of these ways is to stretch fantasy too far; the conception would cease to be a natural guide to intuition. In any case, it is important that the original position be interpreted so that one can at any time adopt its perspective. It must make no difference when one takes up this viewpoint, or who does so: the restrictions must be such that the same principles are always chosen. The veil of ignorance is a key condition in meeting this requirement. It insures not only that the information available is relevant, but that it is at all times the same.

It may be protested that the condition of the veil of ignorance is irrational. Surely, some may object, principles should be chosen in the light of all the knowledge available. There are various replies to this contention. Here I shall sketch those which emphasize the simplifications that need to be made if one is to have any theory at all. . . . To begin with, it is clear that since the differences among the parties are unknown to them, and everyone is equally rational and similarly situated, each is convinced by the same arguments. Therefore, we can view the choice in the original position from the standpoint of one person selected at random. If anyone after due reflection prefers a conception of justice to another, then they all do, and a unanimous agreement can be reached. We can, to make the circumstances more vivid, imagine that the parties are required to communicate with each other through a referee as intermediary, and that he is to announce which alternatives have been suggested and the reasons offered in their support. He forbids the attempt to form coalitions, and he informs the parties when they have come to an understanding. But such a referee is actually superfluous, assuming that the deliberations of the parties must be similar.

Thus there follows the very important consequence that the parties have no basis for bargaining in the usual sense. No one knows his situation in society nor his natural assets, and therefore no one is in a position to tailor principles to his advantage. We might imagine that one of the contractees threatens to hold out unless the others agree to principles favorable to him. But how does he know which principles are especially in his interests? The same holds for the formation of coalitions: if a group were to decide to band together to the disadvantage of the others, they would not know how to favor themselves in the choice of principles. Even if they could get everyone to agree to their proposal, they would have no assurance that it was to their advantage, since they cannot identify themselves either by name or description. The one case where this conclusion fails is that of saving. Since the persons in the original position know that they are contemporaries (taking the present time of entry interpretation), they can favor their generation by refusing to make any sacrifices at all for their successors; they simply acknowledge the principle that no one has a duty to save for posterity. Previous generations have saved or they have not; there is nothing the parties can now do to affect that. So in this instance the veil of ignorance fails to secure the desired result. Therefore I resolve the question of justice between generations in a different way by altering the motivation assumption. But with this adjustment no one is able to formulate principles especially designed to advance his own cause. Whatever his temporal position, each is forced to choose for everyone.

The restrictions on particular information in the original position are, then, of fundamental importance. Without them we would not be able to work out any definite theory of justice at all. We would have to be content with a vague formula stating that justice is what would be agreed to without being able to say much, if anything, about the substance of the agreement itself. The formal constraints of the concept of right, those applying to principles directly, are not sufficient for our purpose. The veil of ignorance makes possible a unanimous choice of a particular conception of justice. Without these limitations on knowledge the bargaining problem of the original position would be hopelessly complicated. Even if theoretically a solution were to exist, we would not, at present anyway, be able to determine it.

The notion of the veil of ignorance is implicit, I think, in Kant's ethics. . . . Nevertheless the problem of defining the knowledge of the parties and of characterizing the alternatives open to them has often been passed over, even by contract theories. Sometimes the situation definitive of moral deliberation is presented in such an indeterminate way that one cannot ascertain how it will turn out. Thus Perry's doctrine is essentially contractarian: he holds that social and personal integration must proceed by entirely different principles, the latter by rational prudence, the former by the concurrence of persons of good will. He would appear to reject utilitarianism on much the same grounds suggested earlier: namely, that it improperly extends the principle of choice for one person to choices facing society. The right course of action is characterized as that which best advances social aims as these would be formulated by reflective agreement given that the parties have full knowledge of the circumstances and are moved by a benevolent concern for one another's interests. No effort is made, however, to specify in any precise way the possible outcomes of this sort of agreement. Indeed, without a far more elaborate account, no conclusions can be drawn. I do not wish here to criticize others; rather, I want to explain the necessity for what may seem at times like so many irrelevant details.

Now the reasons for the veil of ignorance go beyond mere simplicity. We want to define the original position so that we get the desired solution. If a knowledge of particulars is allowed, then the outcome is biased by arbitrary contingencies. As already observed, to each according to his threat advantage is not a principle of justice. If the original position is to yield agreements that are just, the parties must be fairly situated and treated equally as moral persons. The arbitrariness of the world must be corrected for by adjusting the circumstances of the initial contractual situation. Moreover, if in choosing principles we required unanimity even when there is full information, only a few rather obvious cases could be decided. A conception of justice based on unanimity in these circumstances would indeed be weak and trivial. But once knowledge is excluded, the requirement of unanimity is not out of place and the fact that it can be satisfied is of great importance. It enables us to say of the preferred conception of justice that it represents a genuine reconciliation of interests.

A final comment. For the most part I shall suppose that the parties possess all general information. No general facts are closed to them. I do this mainly to avoid complications. Nevertheless a conception of justice is to be the public basis of the terms of social cooperation. Since common understanding necessitates certain bounds on the complexity of principles, there may likewise be limits on the use of theoretical knowledge in the original position. Now clearly it would be very difficult to classify and to grade for complexity the various sorts of general facts. I shall make no attempt to do this. We do however recognize an intricate theoretical construction when we meet one. Thus it seems reasonable to say that other things equal one conception of justice is to be preferred to another when it is founded upon markedly simpler general facts, and its choice does not depend upon elaborate calculations in the light of a vast array of theoretically defined possibilities. It is desirable that the grounds for a public conception of justice should be evident to everyone when circumstances permit. This consideration favors, I believe, the two principles of justice over the criterion of utility. . . .

4.5 Our Obligation to the State

In Chapter 2, we left Socrates condemned to death by the Athenian court. His execution was delayed because of a religious festival, and his friends made plans for his escape from prison. Crito went to Socrates in prison and tried to persuade him to escape. Socrates argued that the right thing for him to do was to obey the law. This argument was surprising because in the *Apology* he made it quite clear that his mission to search for the truth was of more value than conforming to the laws of Athens. Even if the Athenians should order him to stop his activities, he would continue because, as he so dramatically put it, "the unexamined life is not worth living."

So why did Socrates now argue that he should obey the laws of Athens and drink the hemlock? Should all laws be obeyed just because they are legally established? Where do governments get the authority to pass laws? Where do they get the authority to take a human life? If the laws are bad laws, isn't it right to break them? If someone is unjustly condemned, isn't it right to try to escape punishment? Or is it morally right to suffer the consequences of your actions, even if what you did was right?

At one point in his argument, Socrates made an allusion to an implied agreement that he had with the state. According to this agreement, the city-state of Athens had provided him and his family with certain benefits in return for his promise to keep the laws. By living in Athens, he had tacitly entered into a contract, and to break that contract now would be dishonest. Here we find the seeds for what has emerged as one of the dominant modern Western theories of political authority, the theory of the social contract (see Rawls's appeal to a contractarian position in the previous selection).

Social contract theory states that the authority of government derives from a voluntary agreement among all the people to form a political community and to obey the laws passed by a government they collectively select. Thomas Hobbes (1588–1679), in his book *Leviathan,* imagined a state of nature that was pre-social. This condition he characterized as a "war of all against all" in which people pursued their own self-interest and the only right was the right to self-preservation. The desire for self-preservation eventually made it clear that peace was a desirable goal and that the only way to secure this was to give the "sword of sovereignty" to someone who could guarantee order.

Jean-Jacques Rousseau (1712–1778), in his book *Social Contract,* rejected Hobbes's view that humans are by nature selfish and warlike. Human nature is basically good, he argued; evil arises with society. Civilization corrupts us. However, even though we are born free and good, we are bound together in a social contract and obliged to obey the decisions of the group to which our agreement has bound us. Individually, we have unique desires and interests that express our individual will. But as voting citizens of a community, we manifest the "general will" of the group, and it is this general will that forms the foundation of political authority.

Social contract theory makes clear how closely political theories are tied to theories of human nature. If we think humans are by nature evil, governments will be seen as necessary goods that restrain evil and prevent chaos. Governments provide law and order. The stronger the government, the better. If we think humans are by nature good, governments will be seen as necessary evils that hamper free and spontaneous expression. Governments restrict our freedom, and the less government, the better.

Notice how different social contract theory is from the theocratic and successionist theories of early Islam and the Platonically inspired philosophical theories of the philosopher king discussed in the first selection in this chapter. The right to rule derives not from God or wisdom, according to this view, but from an agreement of the people. If sovereignty derives from agreement of citizens, can not those citizens break such an agreement when they deem it necessary?

Reading Questions

1. What are Crito's main arguments in favor of Socrates' escape?
2. Socrates first responds by stating certain principles with which he gets Crito to agree. What are these principles?
3. Socrates imagines that the laws of Athens are speaking to him. In this speech, what are the most important points in support of not escaping?
4. Socrates asserts that "the really important thing is not to live, but to live well." Do you agree? Why, or why not?
5. Assume you are Crito. Offer Socrates your best argument for escaping that does not cause him to violate his principles.
6. Do you think the government is, as Socrates asserts, like your parents? Why?
7. Does living in a country amount to a tacit promise on your part to obey *all* its laws? Why, or why not?
8. What do you think Socrates should do and why?
9. Based on your reading of the *Crito,* how do you think Socrates would answer the question, "What makes a society just?"

Crito

PLATO

Socrates: Why have you come at this hour, Crito? It must be quite early?

Crito: Yes, it certainly is.

Soc: What time is it?

Cr: The dawn is breaking.

Soc: I am surprised the keeper of the prison let you in.

Cr: He knows me because I come often, Socrates, and he owes me a favor.

Soc: Did you just get here?

Cr: No, I came some time ago.

Soc: Why did you sit and say nothing instead of waking me at once?

Cr: Why, indeed, Socrates, I myself would rather not have all this sleeplessness and sorrow. I have been wondering at your peaceful slumber and that was the reason why I did not (wake) you. I wanted you to be out of pain. I always thought you fortunate in your calm temperament but I never saw anything like the easy, cheerful way you bear this calamity.

Soc: Crito, when a man reaches my age he should not fear approaching death.

Cr: Other men of your age in similar situations fear death.

Soc: That may be. But you have not told me why you come at this early hour.

Cr: I bring you a sad and painful message; not sad, as I believe, for you, but to all of us who are your friends and saddest of all to me.

Soc: Has the ship come from Delos, on the arrival of which I am to die?

Cr: No, the ship has not actually arrived, but it will probably be here today because people who came from Sunium tell me they left it there. Therefore tomorrow, Socrates, will be the last day of your life.

Soc: Very well, Crito. If it is the will of the gods, I am willing but I believe there will be a delay of a day.

Cr: Why do you say that?

Soc: I will tell you. I am to die on the day after the arrival of the ship?

Cr: Yes, that is what the authorities say.

Soc: I do not think the ship will be here until tomorrow. I had a dream last night, or rather only just now, when you fortunately allowed me to sleep.

Cr: What was your dream?

Soc: I saw the image of a wondrously beautiful woman, clothed in white robes, who called to me and said: "O Socrates, the third day hence to fertile Phthia shalt thou go."

Cr: What a strange dream, Socrates!

Soc: I think there can be no doubt about the meaning, Crito.

Cr: Perhaps the meaning is clear to you. But, oh my beloved Socrates, let me beg you once more to take my advice and escape! If you die I shall not only lose a friend who can never be replaced, but there is another evil: People who do not know you and me will believe I might have saved you if I had been willing to spend money, but I did not care to do so. Now, can there be a worse disgrace than this—that I should be thought to value money more than the life of a friend? The many will not be persuaded I wanted you to escape and you refused.

Soc: But why, my dear Crito, should we care about the opinion of the many? Good men, and they are the only persons worth considering, will think of these things as they happened.

Cr: But do you see, Socrates, the opinion of the many must be regarded, as is clear in your

The original translation is by Benjamin Jowett and has been revised and updated by Christopher Biffle, A Guided Tour of Five Works of Plato *(Mountain View, CA: Mayfield, 1988), pp. 57–67. Reprinted by permission of Mayfield Publishing Company.*

own case, because they can do the very greatest evil to anyone who has lost their good opinion.

Soc: I only wish, Crito, they could. Then they could also do the greatest good and that would be excellent. The truth is, they can do neither good nor evil. They cannot make a man wise or make him foolish and whatever they do is the result of chance.

Cr: Well, I will not argue about that. But please tell me, Socrates, if you are acting out of concern for me and your other friends. Are you afraid if you escape we may get into trouble with the informers for having stolen you away and lose either the whole or a great part of our property, or even a worse evil may happen to us? Now, if this is your fear, be at ease. In order to save you we should surely run this, or even a greater, risk. Be persuaded, then, and do as I say.

Soc: Yes, Crito, that is one fear which you mention, but by no means the only one.

Cr: Do not be afraid. There are persons who at no great cost are willing to save you and bring you out of prison. As for the informers, they are reasonable in their demands, a little money will satisfy them. My resources, which are ample, are at your service and if you are troubled about spending all mine, there are strangers who will give you theirs. One of them, Simmias the Theban, brought a sum of money for this very purpose. Cebes and many others are willing to spend their money, too. I say therefore, do not hesitate about making your escape and do not say, as you did in the court, you will have difficulty in knowing what to do with yourself if you escape. Men will love you in other places you may go and not only in Athens. There are friends of mine in Thessaly, if you wish to go to them, who will value and protect you and no Thessalian will give you any trouble. Nor can I think you are justified, Socrates, in betraying your own life when you might be saved. This is playing into the hands of your enemies and destroyers. Besides, I say you are betraying your children. You should bring them up and educate them; instead you go away and leave them, and they will have to grow up on their own. If they do not meet with the usual fate of orphans, there will be small thanks to you. No man should bring children

into the world who is unwilling to continue their nurture and education. You are choosing the easier part, as I think, not the better and manlier, which you should as one who professes virtue in all his actions. Indeed, I am ashamed not only of you, but of us, your friends, when I think this entire business of yours will be attributed to our lack of courage. The trial need never have started or might have been brought to another conclusion. The end of it all, which is the crowning absurdity, will seem to have been permitted by us, through cowardice and baseness, who might have saved you. You might have saved yourself, if we had been good for anything, for there was no difficulty in escaping, and we did not see how disgraceful, Socrates, and also miserable all this will be to us as well as to you. Make up your mind then. Or rather, have your mind already made up, for the time of deliberation is over. There is only one thing to be done, which must be done if at all this very night, and which any delay will render all but impossible. I plead with you therefore, Socrates, to be persuaded by me, and do as I say.

Soc: Dear Crito, your zeal is invaluable if right. If wrong, the greater the zeal, the greater the evil. Therefore we must consider whether these things should be done or not. I am, and always have been, someone who must be guided by reason, whatever the reason may be which, upon reflection, appears to me to be the best. Now that this misfortune has come upon me, I cannot put away my old beliefs. The principles I honored and revered I still honor and unless we can find other and better principles, I will not agree with you. I would not even if the power of the multitude could inflict many more imprisonments, confiscations and deaths, frightening us like children with foolish terrors.

What will be the best way of considering the question? Shall I return to your old argument about the opinions of men, some of which should be considered, and others, as we were saying, are not to be considered. Now were we right in maintaining this before I was condemned? And has the argument which was once good, now proved to be talk for the sake of talking—in fact an amusement only and altogether foolish?

That is what I want to consider with your help, Crito: whether, under my present circumstances, the argument appears to be in any way different or not and is to be followed by me or abandoned. That argument, I believe, is held by many who claim to be authorities, was to the effect, that the opinions of some men are to be considered and of other men not to be considered. Now you, Crito, are not going to die tomorrow—at least, there is no probability of this. You are therefore not likely to be deceived by the circumstances in which you are placed. Tell me, then, whether I am right in saying that some opinions are to be valued and other opinions are not to be valued. I ask you whether I was right in believing this?

Cr: Certainly.

Soc: The good opinions are to be believed and not the bad?

Cr: Yes.

Soc: And the opinions of the wise are good and the opinions of the foolish are evil?

Cr: Certainly.

Soc: And what was said about another matter? Is the gymnastics student supposed to attend to the praise and blame and opinion of every man, or of one man only—his physician or trainer, whoever that is?

Cr: Of one man only.

Soc: And he should fear the blame and welcome praise of that one only, and not of the many?

Cr: That is clear.

Soc: He should live and train, eat and drink in the way which seems good to his single teacher who has understanding, rather than according to the opinion of all other men put together?

Cr: True.

Soc: And if he disobeys and rejects the opinion and approval of the one, and accepts the opinion of the many who have no understanding, will he not suffer evil?

Cr: Certainly he will.

Soc: And how will the evil affect the disobedient student?

Cr: Clearly, it will affect his body; that is what is destroyed by the evil.

Soc: Very good. Is this not true, Crito, of other things which we need not separately consider? In the matter of the just and unjust, the fair and foul, the good and evil, which are the subjects of our present discussion, should we follow the opinion of the many and fear them, or the opinion of the one man who has understanding? Is he the one we ought to fear and honor more than all the rest of the world? If we leave him, we shall destroy and injure that principle in us which may be assumed to be improved by justice and deteriorated by injustice? Is there not such a principle?

Cr: Certainly there is, Socrates.

Soc: Take a similar case. If, acting under the advice of men who have no understanding, we ruined what is improved by health and destroyed by disease—when the body has been destroyed, I say, would life be worth having?

Cr: Yes.

Soc: Could we live having an evil and corrupted body?

Cr: Certainly not.

Soc: And will life be worth having, if the soul is crippled, which is improved by justice and harmed by injustice? Do we suppose the soul to be inferior to the body?

Cr: Certainly not.

Soc: More important, then?

Cr: Far more important.

Soc: Then, my friend, we must not consider what the many say of us, but what he, the one man who has understanding of the just and unjust will say, and what the truth will say. Therefore you begin in error when you suggest we should consider the opinion of the many about the just and unjust, the good and evil, the honorable and dishonorable, but what if someone says, "But the many can kill us."

Cr: Yes, Socrates, that will clearly be the answer.

Soc: Still I believe our old argument is unshaken. I would like to know whether I may say the same of another proposition—that not life, but a good life, is to be chiefly valued?

Cr: Yes, that is also true.

Soc: And a good life is equivalent to a just and honorable one—that is also true?

Cr: Yes, that is true.

Soc: From these beliefs I am ready to consider whether I should or should not try to escape without the consent of the Athenians. If I am clearly right in escaping, then I will make the attempt, but if not, I will remain here. The other considerations which you mention, of money and loss of reputation and the duty of educating children, are, I fear, only the beliefs of the many, who would be as ready to bring people to life, if they were able, as they are to put them to death. The only question remaining to be considered is whether we shall do right escaping or allowing others to aid our escape and paying them money and thanks or whether we shall not do right. If the latter, then death or any other calamity which may result from my remaining here must not be allowed to influence us.

Cr: I think you are right, Socrates. But, how shall we proceed?

Soc: Let us consider the matter together and either refute me if you can and I will be convinced; or else cease, my dear friend, from repeating to me that I ought to escape against the wishes of the Athenians. I am extremely eager to be persuaded by you, but not against my own better judgment. And now please consider my first position and do your best to answer me.

Cr: I will do my best.

Soc: Are we to say we are never intentionally to do wrong, or that in one way we should and in another way we should not do wrong? Or is doing wrong always evil and dishonorable, as I was just now saying? Are all our former admissions to be thrown away because of these last few days? Have we, at our age, been earnestly discoursing with one another all our life long only to discover we are no better than children? Or, are we convinced in spite of the opinion of the many and in spite of consequences of the truth of what we said, that injustice is always an evil and dishonor to him who acts unjustly? Shall we agree to that?

Cr: Yes.

Soc: Then we must do no wrong?

Cr: Certainly not.

Soc: Nor when injured should we injure in return, as the many imagine. We must injure no one at all?

Cr: Clearly not.

Soc: Again, Crito, can we do evil?

Cr: Surely not, Socrates.

Soc: And what of doing evil in return for evil, which is the morality of the many—is that just or not?

Cr: Not just.

Soc: For doing evil to another is the same as injuring him.

Cr: Very true.

Soc: Then we ought not to retaliate or render evil for evil to any one, whatever evil we may have suffered from him. But I would have you consider, Crito, whether you really mean what you are saying. For this opinion has never been held, and never will be held, by many people. Those who are agreed and those who are not agreed upon this point have no common ground, and can only despise one another when they see how widely they differ. Tell me, then, whether you agree with my first principle, that neither injury nor retaliation nor returning evil for evil is ever right. Shall that be the premise of our argument? Or do you disagree? For this has been and still is my opinion; but, if you are of another opinion, let me hear what you have to say. If, however, you remain of the same mind as formerly, I will go to the next step.

Cr: You may proceed, for I have not changed my mind.

Soc: The next step may be put in the form of a question: Ought a man to do what he admits to be right, or ought he to betray the right?

Cr: He ought to do what he thinks right.

Soc: But if this is true, what is the application? In leaving the prison against the will of the Athenians, do I wrong anyone? Or do I wrong those whom I ought least to wrong? Do I abandon the principles which were acknowledged by us to be just. What do you say?

Cr: I cannot tell, Socrates, because I do not know.

Soc: Then consider the matter in this way— imagine I am about to escape, and the Laws and the State come and interrogate me: "Tell us, Socrates," they say, "what are you doing? Are you going to overturn us—the Laws and the State, as far as you are able? Do you imagine that a State can continue and not be overthrown, in which the decisions of Law have no power, but are set aside and overthrown by individuals?"

What will be our answer, Crito, to these and similar words? Anyone, and especially a clever orator, will have a good deal to say about the evil of setting aside the Law which requires a sentence to be carried out. We might reply, "Yes, but the State has injured us and given an unjust sentence." Suppose I say that?

Cr: Very good, Socrates.

Soc: "And was that our agreement with you?" the Law would say, "Or were you to abide by the sentence of the State?" And if I was surprised at their saying this, the Law would probably add: "Answer, Socrates, instead of opening your eyes: you are in the habit of asking and answering questions. Tell us what complaint you have against us which justifies you in attempting to destroy us and the State? In the first place did we not bring you into existence? Your father married your mother by our aid and conceived you. Say whether you have any objection against those of us who regulate marriage?" None, I should reply. "Or against those of us who regulate the system of care and education of children in which you were trained? Were not the Laws, who have the charge of this, right in commanding your father to train you in the arts and exercise?" Yes, I should reply.

"Well then, since you were brought into the world, nurtured and educated by us, can you deny in the first place that you are our child and slave, as your fathers were before you? And if this is true you are not on equal terms with us. Nor can you think you have a right to do to us what we are doing to you. Would you have any right to strike or do any other evil to a father or to your master, if you had one, when you have been struck or received some other evil at his hands? And because we think it is right to destroy you, do you think that you have any right to destroy us in return, and your country so far as you are able? And will you, O expounder of virtue, say you are justified in this? Has a philosopher like you failed to discover your country is more to be valued and higher and holier by far than mother and father or any ancestor, and more regarded in the eyes of the gods and of men of understanding?

It should be soothed and gently and reverently entreated when angry, even more than a father, and if not persuaded, it should be obeyed. And when we are punished by the State, whether with imprisonment or whipping, the punishment is to be endured in silence. If the State leads us to wounds or death in battle, we follow as is right; no one can yield or leave his rank, but whether in battle or in a court of law, or in any other place, he must do what his city and his country order him. Or, he must change their view of what is just. If he may do no violence to his father or mother, much less may he do violence to his country." What answer shall we make to this, Crito? Do the Laws speak truly, or do they not?

Cr: I think that they do.

Soc: Then the Laws will say: "Consider, Socrates, if this is true, that in your present attempt you are going to do us wrong. For, after having brought you into the world, nurtured and educated you, and given you and every other citizen a share in every good we had to give, we further give the right to every Athenian, if he does not like us when he has come of age and has seen the ways of the city, he may go wherever else he pleases and take his goods with him. None of us Laws will forbid or interfere with him. Any of you who does not like us and the city, and who wants to go to a colony or to any other city, may go where he likes, and take his possessions with him. But he who has experience of the way we order justice and administer the State, and still remains, has entered into an implied contract to do as we command him. He who disobeys us is, as we maintain, triply wrong; first, because in disobeying us he is disobeying his parents; second, because we are the authors of his education; third, because he has made an agreement with us that he will duly obey our commands. He neither obeys them nor convinces us our commands are wrong. We do not rudely impose our commands but give each person the alternative of obeying or convincing us. That is what we offer and he does neither. These are the sort of accusations to which, as we were saying, Socrates, you will be exposed if you do as you were intending; you, above all other Athenians."

Suppose I ask, why is this? They will justly answer that I above all other men have acknowledged the agreement.

"There is clear proof," they will say, "Socrates, that we and the city were not displeasing to you. Of all Athenians you have been the most constant resident in the city, which, as you never leave, you appear to love. You never went out of the city either to see the games, except once when you went to the Isthmus, or to any other place unless you were on military service; nor did you travel as other men do. Nor had you any curiosity to know other States or their Laws: Your affections did not go beyond us and our State; we were your special favorites and you agreed in our government of you. This is the State in which you conceived your children, which is a proof of your satisfaction. Moreover, you might, if you wished, have fixed the penalty at banishment in the course of the trial—the State which refuses to let you go now would have let you go then. You pretended you preferred death to exile and that you were not grieved at death. And now you have forgotten these fine sentiments and pay no respect to us, the Laws, who you destroy. You are doing what only a miserable slave would do, running away and turning your back upon the agreements which you made as a citizen. First of all, answer this very question: Are we right in saying you agreed to be governed according to us in deed, and not in word only? Is that true or not?"

How shall we answer that, Crito? Must we not agree?

Cr: We must, Socrates.

Soc: Then will the Laws say: "You, Socrates, are breaking the agreements which you made with us at your leisure, not in any haste or under any compulsion or deception, but having had 70 years to think of them, during which time you were at liberty to leave the city, if we were not to your liking, or if our covenants appeared to you to be unfair. You might have gone either to Lacedaemon or Crete, which you often praise for their good government, or to some other Hellenic or foreign state. You, above all other Athenians, seemed to be so fond of the State and of us, her Laws, that you never left her. The lame, the blind, the maimed were not more stationary in the State than you were. Now you run away and forsake your agreements. Now, Socrates, if you will take our advice; do not make yourself ridiculous by escaping out of the city.

"Just consider, if you do evil in this way, what good will you do either yourself or your friends? That your friends will be driven into exile and lose their citizenship, or will lose their property, is reasonably certain. You yourself, if you fly to one of the neighboring cities, like Thebes or Megara, both of which are well-governed cities, will come to them as an enemy, Socrates. Their government will be against you and all patriotic citizens will cast suspicious eye upon you as a destroyer of the laws. You will confirm in the minds of the judges the justice of their own condemnation of you. For he who is a corruptor of the laws is more than likely to be corruptor of the young. Will you then flee from well-ordered cities and virtuous men? Is existence worth having on these terms? Or will you go to these cities without shame and talk to them, Socrates? And what will you say to them? Will you say what you say here about virtue, justice, institutions and laws being the best things among men? Would that be decent of you? Surely not.

"If you go away from well-governed states to Crito's friends in Thessaly, where there is a great disorder and immorality, they will be charmed to have the tale of your escape from prison, set off with ludicrous particulars of the manner in which you were wrapped in a goatskin or some other disguise and metamorphosed as the fashion of runaways is—that is very likely. But will there be no one to remind you in your old age you violated the most sacred laws from a miserable desire of a little more life. Perhaps not, if you keep them in a good temper. But if they are angry you will hear many degrading things; you will live, but how? As the flatterer of all men, and the servant of all men. And doing what? Eating and drinking in Thessaly, having gone abroad in order that you may get a dinner. Where will your fine sentiments about justice and virtue be then? Say that you wish to live for the sake of your children, that you may bring them up and educate them—will you take them into Thessaly and deprive them of Athenian citizenship? Is that the benefit which you would confer upon them? Or are you under the impression that they will be better cared for and educated here if you are still alive, although absent from them because your friends will take care of them? Do you think if you are an inhabitant of Thessaly they will take care of them, and if you are an inhabitant of the other world they will not take care of them? No, if they who call themselves friends are truly friends, they surely will.

"Listen, then, Socrates, to us who have brought you up. Think not of life and children first, and of justice afterwards, but of justice first, that you may be justified before the rulers of the other world. For neither will you nor your children be happier or holier in this life, or happier in another, if you do as Crito bids. Now you depart in innocence, a sufferer and not a doer of evil; a victim, not of the Laws, but of men. But if you escape, returning evil for evil and injury for injury, breaking the agreements which you have made with us, and wronging those whom you ought least to wrong, that is to say, yourself, your friends, your country, and us, we shall be angry with you while you live. Our brethren, the Laws in the other world, will receive you as an enemy because they will know you have done your best to destroy us. Listen, then, to us and not to Crito."

This is the voice which I seem to hear murmuring in my ears, like the sound of a divine flute in the ears of the mystic. That voice, I say, is humming in my ears and prevents me from hearing any other. I know anything more which you may say will be useless. Yet speak, if you have anything to say.

Cr: I have nothing to say, Socrates.

Soc: Then let me follow what seems to be the will of the gods.

4.6 Civil Disobedience

Are there times when disobeying the law is morally justified? What are the responsibilities of a citizen? The dialogue *Crito* raised these issues, but in one way or another we have been asking these questions whenever the issue of governmental authority has arisen. The issue of civil disobedience also raises fundamental questions about the rule of law. Why do we need laws?

A case against the rule of law might go something like this: Laws limit human freedom and hinder spontaneity; they are sometimes unfair and repressive; common sense, social custom, and religion already provide enough guidance; and morality can never be legislated.

Many of course believe that the rule of law is both good and necessary. Laws protect people, create social stability, and provide opportunities to develop rights that people might not otherwise enjoy. The rights to life, liberty, and the pursuit of happiness need to be protected and defined by laws. In pluralistic societies, we cannot depend on customs and traditions to unite people. Nor can we depend on the virtue and goodwill of our leaders.

Only the rule of law can prevent abuse of power, but how can we tell the difference between good laws and bad laws? Are there minimal conditions for good laws? We might argue that good laws guarantee access to the resources necessary to live, provide for enforcement of contracts, and give security from violence. Such laws should be fairly enforced, adjudicated in courts free from prejudice, provide for due process, and be free from vagueness and ambiguity. Should we also add that the right of civil disobedience be granted, or would such a right undermine entirely the rule of law?

Civil disobedience has played and continues to play a major role in effecting political and legal change. In the nineteenth century, Henry David Thoreau went to jail for refusing to pay taxes to a government that supported slavery. He argued that conscience constitutes a higher law than the law of any land. (Go to http://philosophy. wadsworth.com and select the companion Web site for *Voices of Wisdom* for a link to Thoreau's *On Civil Disobedience*.) We all have a moral duty to obey our consciences, but how many of us are willing to pay the legal penalty for disobeying the law?

Civil disobedience became a political strategy in many nations in the twentieth century. Gandhi used it to liberate India from British colonial rule. He carried a copy of Thoreau's *On Civil Disobedience* with him and used it as a blueprint for nonviolent resistance. Nelson Mandela used civil disobedience to change the apartheid system of South Africa. But when does civil disobedience become political revolution? When violence is used? Must one be willing to suffer the consequences of breaking the law in order to engage in a morally justifiable act of civil disobedience? Is *uncivil* disobedience morally justified? What makes disobedience civil rather than uncivil?

Martin Luther King, Jr. (1929–1968), a Baptist minister and winner of the Nobel Peace Prize, devoted his life to the struggle for racial justice in the United States. Like Thoreau and Gandhi, he argued for nonviolent methods. As a result, he found himself opposing those African Americans who did advocate the use of violence. He died from an assassin's bullet in Memphis, Tennessee.

A year before he won the Nobel Peace Prize and five years before his death, he served a sentence in the Birmingham, Alabama, jail for participating in a civil rights demonstration. Eight prominent Alabama clergy wrote an open letter critical of King's methods. In his famous "Letter from Birmingham Jail," King responded to their criticisms and, in the process, wrote a moving justification of civil disobedience.

In light of the first selection in this chapter on ideas of justice in Islam, it is interesting to note the role that a religious conception of justice plays in King's argument and the role religious institutions play in promoting or retarding racial justice in the United States. Some people often appeal to notions of a "higher law" that is explicitly linked to God when they engage in social criticism and reform.

Reading Questions

1. Do you agree with King's claim that "injustice anywhere is a threat to justice everywhere"? Why, or why not?
2. Do you think groups are more immoral than individuals? Why?
3. What are the differences, according to King, between unjust laws and just laws? Are all the differences compatible? For example, could not a law code passed and obeyed by the majority that respects the rights of the minority be unjust in the sense that it is not in harmony with God's law? Can you think of an example?
4. Under what conditions is it permissible, according to King, to break the law? Do you agree? Why?
5. According to King, what is the purpose of law and order? Do you agree?
6. According to King, what is the proper role of the Christian Church with respect to issues of social justice? Do you think he is right? Why, or why not?
7. Write a brief letter in response to King from the point of view of the clergy who originally criticized him.
8. How do you think King would answer the question, "What makes a society just?"

Letter from Birmingham Jail

MARTIN LUTHER KING, JR.

MY DEAR FELLOW CLERGYMEN,
While confined here in the Birmingham city jail, I came across your recent statement calling our present activities "unwise and untimely." Seldom, if ever, do I pause to answer criticism of my work and ideas. If I sought to answer all of the criticisms that cross my desk, my secretaries would be engaged in little else in the course of the day, and I would have no time for constructive work. But since I feel that you are men of genuine good will and your criticisms are sincerely set forth, I would like to answer your statement in what I hope will be patient and reasonable terms.

I think I should give the reason for my being in Birmingham, since you have been influenced by the argument of "outsiders coming in." I have the honor of serving as president of the Southern Christian Leadership Conference, an organization operating in every southern state, with headquarters in Atlanta, Georgia. We have some 85 affiliate organizations all across the South— one being the Alabama Christian Movement for Human Rights. Whenever necessary and possible we share staff, educational and financial resources with our affiliates. Several months ago our local affiliate here in Birmingham invited us to be on call to engage in a nonviolent direct-action program if such were deemed necessary. We readily consented and when the hour came we lived up to our promises. So I am here, along with several members of my staff, because we were invited here. I am here because I have basic organizational ties here.

Beyond this, I am in Birmingham because injustice is here. Just as the eighth century prophets left their little villages and carried their "thus saith the Lord" far beyond the boundaries of their hometowns; and just as the Apostle Paul left his little village of Tarsus and carried the gospel of Jesus Christ to practically every hamlet and city of the Graeco-Roman world, I too am compelled to carry the gospel of freedom beyond my particular hometown. Like Paul, I must constantly respond to the Macedonian call for aid.

Moreover, I am cognizant of the interrelatedness of all communities and states. I cannot sit idly by in Atlanta and not be concerned about what happens in Birmingham. Injustice anywhere is a threat to justice everywhere. We are caught in an inescapable network of mutuality, tied in a single garment of destiny. Whatever affects one directly affects all indirectly. Never again can we afford to live with the narrow, provincial "outside agitator" idea. Anyone who lives in the United States can never be considered an outsider anywhere in this country.

You deplore the demonstrations that are presently taking place in Birmingham. But I am sorry that your statement did not express a similar concern for the conditions that brought the demonstrations into being. I am sure that each of you would want to go beyond the superficial social analyst who looks merely at effects, and does not grapple with underlying causes. I would not hesitate to say that it is unfortunate that so-called demonstrations are taking place in Birmingham at this time, but I would say in more emphatic terms that it is even more unfortunate that the white power structure of this city left the Negro community with no other alternative.

In any nonviolent campaign there are four basic steps: (1) collection of the facts to determine whether injustices are alive, (2) negotiation,

(3) self-purification, and (4) direct action. We have gone through all of these steps in Birmingham. There can be no gainsaying of the fact that racial injustice engulfs this community.

Birmingham is probably the most thoroughly segregated city in the United States. Its ugly record of police brutality is known in every section of this country. Its unjust treatment of Negroes in the courts is a notorious reality. There have been more unsolved bombings of Negro homes and churches in Birmingham than any city in this nation. These are the hard, brutal and unbelievable facts. On the basis of these conditions Negro leaders sought to negotiate with the city fathers. But the political leaders consistently refused to engage in good faith negotiation.

Then came the opportunity last September to talk with some of the leaders of the economic community. In these negotiating sessions certain promises were made by the merchants—such as the promise to remove the humiliating racial signs from the stores. On the basis of these promises Rev. Shuttlesworth and the leaders of the Alabama Christian Movement for Human Rights agreed to call a moratorium on any type of demonstrations. As the weeks and months unfolded we realized that we were the victims of a broken promise. The signs remained. Like so many experiences of the past we were confronted with blasted hopes, and the dark shadow of a deep disappointment settled upon us. So we had no alternative except that of preparing for direct action, whereby we would present our very bodies as a means of laying our case before the conscience of the local and national community. We were not unmindful of the difficulties involved. So we decided to go through a process of self-purification. We started having workshops on nonviolence and repeatedly asked ourselves the questions, "Are you able to accept blows without retaliating?" "Are you able to endure the ordeals of jail?" We decided to set our direct-action program around the Easter season, realizing that with the exception of Christmas, this was the largest shopping period of the year. Knowing that a strong economic withdrawal program would be the by-product of direct action, we felt that this was the best time to bring pressure on the merchants for the needed changes. Then it occurred to us that the March election was ahead and so we speedily decided to postpone action until after election day. When we discovered that Mr. Connor was in the run-off, we decided again to postpone action so that the demonstrations could not be used to cloud the issues. At this time we agreed to begin our nonviolent witness the day after the run-off.

This reveals that we did not move irresponsibly into direct action. We, too, wanted to see Mr. Connor defeated; so we went through postponement after postponement to aid in this community need. After this we felt that direct action could be delayed no longer.

You may well ask, "Why direct action? Why sit-ins, marches, etc.? Isn't negotiation a better path?" You are exactly right in your call for negotiation. Indeed, this is the purpose of direct action. Nonviolent direct action seeks to create such a crisis and establish such creative tension that a community that has constantly refused to negotiate is forced to confront the issue. It seeks so to dramatize the issue that it can no longer be ignored. I just referred to the creation of tension as a part of the work of the nonviolent resister. This may sound rather shocking. But I must confess that I am not afraid of the word tension. I have earnestly worked and preached against violent tension, but there is a type of constructive nonviolent tension that is necessary for growth. Just as Socrates felt that it was necessary to create a tension in the mind so that individuals could rise from the bondage of myths and half-truths to the unfettered realm of creative analysis and objective appraisal, we must see the need of having nonviolent gadflies to create the kind of tension in society that will help men to rise from the dark depths of prejudice and racism to the majestic heights of understanding and brotherhood. So the purpose of the direct action is to create a situation so crisis-packed that it will inevitably open the door to negotiation. We, therefore, concur with you in your call for negotiation. Too long has our beloved Southland been bogged down in the tragic attempt to live in monologue rather than dialogue.

One of the basic points in your statement is that our acts are untimely. Some have asked, "Why didn't you give the new administration time to act?" The only answer that I can give to this inquiry is that the new administration must be prodded about as much as the outgoing one before it acts. We will be sadly mistaken if we feel that the election of Mr. Boutwell will bring the millennium to Birmingham. While Mr. Boutwell is much more articulate and gentle than Mr. Connor, they are both segregationists, dedicated to the task of maintaining the status quo. The hope I see in Mr. Boutwell is that he will be reasonable enough to see the futility of massive resistance to desegregation. But he will not see this without pressure from the devotees of civil rights. My friends, I must say to you that we have not made a single gain in civil rights without determined legal and nonviolent pressure. History is the long and tragic story of the fact that privileged groups seldom give up their privileges voluntarily. Individuals may see the moral light and voluntarily give up their unjust posture; but as Reinhold Niebuhr has reminded us, groups are more immoral than individuals.

We know through painful experience that freedom is never voluntarily given by the oppressor; it must be demanded by the oppressed. Frankly, I have never yet engaged in a direct action movement that was "well-timed," according to the timetable of those who have not suffered unduly from the disease of segregation. For years now I have heard the words "Wait!" It rings in the ear of every Negro with a piercing familiarity. This "Wait" has almost always meant "Never." It has been a tranquilizing thalidomide, relieving the emotional stress for a moment, only to give birth to an ill-formed infant of frustration. We must come to see with the distinguished jurist of yesterday that "justice too long delayed is justice denied." We have waited for more than 340 years for our constitutional and God-given rights. The nations of Asia and Africa are moving with jetlike speed toward the goal of political independence, and we still creep at horse and buggy pace toward the gaining of a cup of coffee at a lunch counter. I guess it is easy for those who have never felt the stinging darts of segregation to say, "Wait." But when you have seen vicious mobs lynch your mothers and fathers at will and drown your sisters and brothers at whim; when you have seen hate-filled policemen curse, kick, brutalize and even kill your black brothers and sisters with impunity; when you see the vast majority of your twenty million Negro brothers smothering in an airtight cage of poverty in the midst of an affluent society; when you suddenly find your tongue twisted and your speech stammering as you seek to explain to your six-year-old daughter why she can't go to the public amusement park that has just been advertised on television, and see tears welling up in her little eyes when she is told that Funtown is closed to colored children, and see the depressing clouds of inferiority begin to form in her little mental sky, and see her begin to distort her little personality by unconsciously developing a bitterness toward white people; when you have to concoct an answer for a five-year-old son asking in agonizing pathos: "Daddy, why do white people treat colored people so mean?"; when you take a cross-country drive and find it necessary to sleep night after night in the uncomfortable corners of your automobile because no motel will accept you; when you are humiliated day in and day out by nagging signs reading "white" and "colored"; when your first name becomes "nigger" and your middle name becomes "boy" (however old you are) and your last name becomes "John," and when your wife and mother are never given the respected title "Mrs."; when you are harried by day and haunted by night by the fact that you are a Negro, living constantly at tiptoe stance never quite knowing what to expect next, and plagued with inner fears and outer resentments; when you are forever fighting a degenerating sense of "nobodiness"; then you will understand why we find it difficult to wait. There comes a time when the cup of endurance runs over, and men are no longer willing to be plunged into an abyss of injustice where they experience the blackness of corroding despair. I hope, sirs, you can understand our legitimate and unavoidable impatience.

You express a great deal of anxiety over our willingness to break laws. This is certainly a legitimate concern. Since we so diligently urge people to obey the Supreme Court's decision of 1954 outlawing segregation in the public schools, it is rather strange and paradoxical to find us consciously breaking laws. One may well ask, "How can you advocate breaking some laws and obeying others?" The answer is found in the fact that there are two types of laws: there are *just* and there are *unjust* laws. I would agree with Saint Augustine that "An unjust law is no law at all."

Now what is the difference between the two? How does one determine when a law is just or unjust? A just law is a man-made code that squares with the moral law or the law of God. An unjust law is a code that is out of harmony with the moral law. To put it in the terms of Saint Thomas Aquinas, an unjust law is a human law that is not rooted in eternal and natural law. Any law that uplifts human personality is just. Any law that degrades human personality is unjust. All segregation statutes are unjust because segregation distorts the soul and damages the personality. It gives the segregator a false sense of superiority, and the segregated a false sense of inferiority. To use the words of Martin Buber, the great Jewish philosopher, segregation substitutes an "I–it" relationship for the "I–thou" relationship, and ends up relegating persons to the status of things. So segregation is not only politically, economically and sociologically unsound, but it is morally wrong and sinful. Paul Tillich has said that sin is separation. Isn't segregation an existential expression of man's tragic separation, an expression of his awful estrangement, his terrible sinfulness? So I can urge men to disobey segregation ordinances because they are morally wrong.

Let us turn to a more concrete example of just and unjust laws. An unjust law is a code that a majority inflicts on a minority that is not binding on itself. This is difference made legal. On the other hand a just law is a code that a majority compels a minority to follow that it is willing to follow itself. This is sameness made legal.

Let me give another explanation. An unjust law is a code inflicted upon a minority which that minority had no part in enacting or creating because they did not have the unhampered right to vote. Who can say that the legislature of Alabama which set up the segregation laws was democratically elected? Throughout the state of Alabama all types of conniving methods are used to prevent Negroes from becoming registered voters and there are some counties without a single Negro registered to vote despite the fact that the Negro constitutes a majority of the population. Can any law set up in such a state be considered democratically structured?

These are just a few examples of unjust and just laws. There are some instances when a law is just on its face and unjust in its application. For instance, I was arrested Friday on a charge of parading without a permit. Now there is nothing wrong with an ordinance which requires a permit for a parade, but when the ordinance is used to preserve segregation and to deny citizens the First Amendment privilege of peaceful assembly and peaceful protest, then it becomes unjust.

I hope you can see the distinction I am trying to point out. In no sense do I advocate evading or defying the law as the rabid segregationist would do. This would lead to anarchy. One who breaks an unjust law must do it *openly, lovingly* (not hatefully as the white mothers did in New Orleans when they were seen on television screaming, "nigger, nigger, nigger"), and with a willingness to accept the penalty. I submit that an individual who breaks a law that conscience tells him is unjust, and willingly accepts the penalty by staying in jail to arouse the conscience of the community over its injustice, is in reality expressing the very highest respect for law.

Of course, there is nothing new about this kind of civil disobedience. It was seen sublimely in the refusal of Shadrach, Meshach and Abednego to obey the laws of Nebuchadnezzar because a higher moral law was involved. It was practiced superbly by the early Christians who were willing to face hungry lions and the excruciating pain of chopping blocks, before submitting to certain unjust laws of the Roman Empire. To a degree academic freedom is a reality today because Socrates practiced civil disobedience.

We can never forget that everything Hitler did in Germany was "legal" and everything the Hungarian freedom fighters did in Hungary was "illegal." It was "illegal" to aid and comfort a Jew in Hitler's Germany. But I am sure that if I had lived in Germany during that time I would have aided and comforted my Jewish brothers even though it was illegal. If I lived in a Communist country today where certain principles dear to the Christian faith are suppressed, I believe I would openly advocate disobeying these antireligious laws. I must make two honest confessions to you, my Christian and Jewish brothers. First, I must confess that over the last few years I have been gravely disappointed with the white moderate. I have almost reached the regrettable conclusion that the Negro's great stumbling block in the stride toward freedom is not the White Citizen's Counciler or the Ku Klux Klanner, but the white moderate who is more devoted to "order" than to justice; who prefers a negative peace which is the absence of tension to a positive peace which is the presence of justice; who constantly says, "I agree with you in the goal you seek, but I can't agree with your methods of direct action"; who paternalistically feels that he can set the timetable for another man's freedom; who lives by the myth of time and who constantly advised the Negro to wait until a "more convenient season." Shallow understanding from people of good will is more frustrating than absolute misunderstanding from people of ill will. Lukewarm acceptance is much more bewildering than outright rejection.

I had hoped that the white moderate would understand that law and order exist for the purpose of establishing justice, and that when they fail to do this they become dangerously structured dams that block the flow of social progress. I had hoped that the white moderate would understand that the present tension of the South is merely a necessary phase of the transition from an obnoxious negative peace, where the Negro passively accepted his unjust plight, to a substance-filled positive peace, where all men will respect the dignity and worth of human personality. Actually, we who engage in nonviolent direct action are not the creators of tension. We merely bring to the surface the hidden tension that is already alive. We bring it out in the open where it can be seen and dealt with. Like a boil that can never be cured as long as it is covered up but must be opened with all its pus-flowing ugliness

to the natural medicines of air and light, injustice must likewise be exposed, with all of the tension its exposing creates, to the light of human conscience and the air of national opinion before it can be cured.

In your statement you asserted that our actions, even though peaceful, must be condemned because they precipitate violence. But can this assertion be logically made? Isn't this like condemning the robbed man because his possession of money precipitated the evil act of robbery? Isn't this like condemning Socrates because his unswerving commitment to truth and his philosophical delvings precipitated the misguided popular mind to make him drink the hemlock? Isn't this like condemning Jesus because His unique God-consciousness and never-ceasing devotion to His will precipitated the evil act of crucifixion? We must come to see, as federal courts have consistently affirmed, that it is immoral to urge an individual to withdraw his efforts to gain his basic constitutional rights because the quest precipitates violence. Society must protect the robbed and punish the robber.

I had also hoped that the white moderate would reject the myth of time. I received a letter this morning from a white brother in Texas which said: "All Christians know that the colored people will receive equal rights eventually, but it is possible that you are in too great of a religious hurry. It has taken Christianity almost two thousand years to accomplish what it has. The teachings of Christ take time to come to earth." All that is said here grows out of a tragic misconception of time. It is the strangely irrational notion that there is something in the very flow of time that will inevitably cure all ills. Actually time is neutral. It can be used either destructively or constructively. I am coming to feel that the people of ill will have used time much more effectively than the people of good will. We will have to repent in this generation not merely for the vitriolic words and actions of the bad people, but for the appalling silence of the good people. We must come to see that human progress never rolls in on wheels of inevitability. It comes through the tireless efforts and persistent work of men willing to be co-workers with God, and without this hard work time itself becomes an ally of the forces of social stagnation. We must use time creatively, and forever realize that the time is always ripe to do right. Now is the time to make real the promise of democracy, and transform our pending national elegy into a creative psalm of brotherhood. Now is the time to lift our national policy from the quicksand of racial injustice to the solid rock of human dignity.

You spoke of our activity in Birmingham as extreme. At first I was rather disappointed that fellow clergymen would see my nonviolent efforts as those of the extremist. I started thinking about the fact that I stand in the middle of two opposing forces in the Negro community. One is a force of complacency made up of Negroes who, as a result of long years of oppression, have been so completely drained of self-respect and a sense of "somebodiness" that they have adjusted to segregation, and, of a few Negroes in the middle class who, because of a degree of academic and economic security, and because at points they profit by segregation, have unconsciously become insensitive to the problems of the masses. The other force is one of bitterness and hatred, and comes perilously close to advocating violence. It is expressed in the various black nationalist groups that are springing up over the nation, the largest and best known being Elijah Muhammad's Muslim movement. This movement is nourished by the contemporary frustration over the continued existence of racial discrimination. It is made up of people who have lost faith in America, who have absolutely repudiated Christianity, and who have concluded that the white man is an incurable "devil." I have tried to stand between these two forces, saying that we need not follow the "do-nothingism" of the complacent or the hatred and despair of the black nationalist. There is the more excellent way of love and nonviolent protest. I'm grateful to God that, through the Negro church, the dimension of nonviolence entered our struggle. If this philosophy had not emerged, I am convinced that by now many streets of the South would be flowing with floods of blood. And I am further convinced that if our white brothers dismiss us as "rabble-rousers" and "outside agitators" those of us who are working through the channels of nonviolent direct action and refuse to support our non-violent efforts, millions of Negroes, out of frustration and despair, will seek solace and security in black nationalist ideologies, a development that will lead inevitably to a frightening racial nightmare.

Oppressed people cannot remain oppressed forever. The urge for freedom will eventually come. This is what happened to the American Negro. Something within has reminded him of his birthright of freedom; something without has reminded him that he can gain it. Consciously and unconsciously, he has been swept in by what the Germans call the *Zeitgeist,* and with his black brothers of Africa, and his brown and yellow brothers of Asia, South America and the Caribbean, he is moving with a sense of cosmic urgency toward the promised land of racial justice. Recognizing this vital urge that has engulfed the Negro community, one should readily understand public demonstrations. The Negro has many pent-up resentments and latent frustrations. He has to get them out. So let him march sometime; let him have his prayer pilgrimages to the city hall; understand why he must have sit-ins and freedom rides. If his repressed emotions do not come out in these nonviolent ways, they will come out in ominous expressions of violence. This is not a threat; it is a fact of history. So I have not said to my people "get rid of your discontent." But I have tried to say that this normal and healthy discontent can be channelized through the creative outlet of nonviolent direct action. Now this approach is being dismissed as extremist. I must admit that I was initially disappointed in being so categorized.

But as I continued to think about the matter, I gradually gained a bit of satisfaction from being considered an extremist. Was not Jesus an extremist in love—"Love your enemies, bless them that curse you, pray for them that despitefully use you." Was not Amos an extremist for justice—"Let justice roll down like waters and righteousness like a mighty stream." Was not Paul an extremist for the gospel of Jesus Christ—"I bear in my body the marks of the Lord Jesus." Was not Martin Luther an extremist—"Here I stand;

I can do none other so help me God." Was not John Bunyan an extremist—"I will stay in jail to the end of my days before I make a butchery of my conscience." Was not Abraham Lincoln an extremist—"This nation cannot survive half slave and half free." Was not Thomas Jefferson an extremist—"We hold these truths to be self-evident, that all men are created equal." So the question is not whether we will be extremist but what kind of extremist will we be. Will we be extremists for hate or will we be extremists for love? Will we be extremists for the preservation of injustice—or will we be extremists for the cause of justice? In that dramatic scene on Calvary's hill, three men were crucified. We must not forget that all three were crucified for the same crime—the crime of extremism. Two were extremists for immorality, and thusly fell below their environment. The other, Jesus Christ, was an extremist for love, truth and goodness, and thereby rose above his environment. So, after all, maybe the South, the nation and the world are in dire need of creative extremists.

I had hoped that the white moderate would see this. Maybe I was too optimistic. Maybe I expected too much. I guess I should have realized that few members of a race that has oppressed another race can understand or appreciate the deep groans and passionate yearnings of those that have been oppressed and still fewer have the vision to see that injustice must be rooted out by strong, persistent and determined action. I am thankful, however, that some of our white brothers have grasped the meaning of this social revolution and committed themselves to it. They are still all too small in quantity, but they are big in quality. Some like Ralph McGill, Lillian Smith, Harry Golden and James Dabbs have written about our struggle in eloquent, prophetic and understanding terms. Others have marched with us down nameless streets of the South. They have languished in filthy roach-infested jails, suffering the abuse and brutality of angry policemen who see them as "dirty nigger-lovers." They, unlike so many of their moderate brothers and sisters, have recognized the urgency of the moment and sensed the need for powerful "action" antidotes to combat the disease of segregation.

Let me rush on to mention my other disappointment. I have been so greatly disappointed with the white church and its leadership. Of course, there are some notable exceptions. I am not unmindful of the fact that each of you has taken some significant stands on this issue. I commend you, Rev. Stallings, for your Christian stance on this past Sunday, in welcoming Negroes to your worship service on a non-segregated basis. I commend the Catholic leaders of this state for integrating Springhill College several years ago.

But despite these notable exceptions I must honestly reiterate that I have been disappointed with the church. I do not say that as one of the negative critics who can always find something wrong with the church. I say it as a minister of the gospel, who loves the church; who was nurtured in its bosom; who has been sustained by its spiritual blessings and who will remain true to it as long as the cord of life shall lengthen.

I had the strange feeling when I was suddenly catapulted into the leadership of the bus protest in Montgomery several years ago that we would have the support of the white church. I felt that the white ministers, priests and rabbis of the South would be some of our strongest allies. Instead, some have been outright opponents, refusing to understand the freedom movement and misrepresenting its leaders; all too many others have been more cautious than courageous and have remained silent behind the anesthetizing security of the stained-glass windows.

In spite of my shattered dreams of the past, I came to Birmingham with the hope that the white religious leadership of this community would see the justice of our cause, and with deep moral concern, serve as the channel through which our just grievances would get to the power structure. I had hoped that each of you would understand. But again I have been disappointed. I have heard numerous religious leaders of the South call upon their worshippers to comply with a desegregation decision because it is the *law,* but I have longed to hear white ministers say, "Follow this decree because integration is morally *right* and the Negro is your brother." In the midst of blatant injustices inflicted upon the Negro,

I have watched white churches stand on the sideline and merely mouth pious irrelevancies and sanctimonious trivialities. In the midst of a mighty struggle to rid our nation of racial and economic injustice, I have heard so many ministers say, "Those are social issues with which the gospel has no real concern," and I have watched so many churches commit themselves to a completely otherworldly religion which made a strange distinction between body and soul, the sacred and the secular.

So here we are moving toward the exit of the twentieth century with a religious community largely adjusted to the status quo, standing as a taillight behind other community agencies rather than a headlight leading men to higher levels of justice.

I have traveled the length and breadth of Alabama, Mississippi and all the other southern states. On sweltering summer days and crisp autumn mornings I have looked at her beautiful churches with their lofty spires pointing heavenward. I have beheld the impressive outlay of her massive religious education buildings. Over and over again I have found myself asking: "What kind of people worship here? Who is their God? Where were their voices when the lips of Governor Barnett dripped with words of interposition and nullification? Where were they when Governor Wallace gave the clarion call for defiance and hatred? Where were their voices of support when tired, bruised and weary Negro men and women decided to rise from the dark dungeons of complacency to the bright hills of creative protest?"

Yes, these questions are still in my mind. In deep disappointment, I have wept over the laxity of the church. But be assured that my tears have been tears of love. There can be no deep disappointment where there is not deep love. Yes, I love the church; I love her sacred walls. How could I do otherwise? I am in the rather unique position of being the son, the grandson and the great-grandson of preachers. Yes, I see the church as the body of Christ. But, oh! How we have blemished and scarred that body through social neglect and fear of being nonconformists.

There was a time when the church was very powerful. It was during that period when the early Christians rejoiced when they were deemed worthy to suffer for what they believed. In those days the church was not merely a thermometer that recorded the ideas and principles of popular opinion; it was a thermostat that transformed the mores of society. Wherever the early Christians entered a town the power structure got disturbed and immediately sought to convict them for being "disturbers of the peace" and "outside agitators." But they went on with the conviction that they were "a colony of heaven," and had to obey God rather than man. They were small in number but big in commitment. They were too God-intoxicated to be "astronomically intimidated." They brought an end to such ancient evils as infanticide and gladiatorial contest.

Things are different now. The contemporary church is often a weak, ineffectual voice with an uncertain sound. It is so often the arch-supporter of the status quo. Far from being disturbed by the presence of the church, the power structure of the average community is consoled by the church's silent and often vocal sanction of things as they are.

But the judgment of God is upon the church as never before. If the church of today does not recapture the sacrificial spirit of the early church, it will lose its authentic ring, forfeit the loyalty of millions, and be dismissed as an irrelevant social club with no meaning for the twentieth century. I am meeting young people every day whose disappointment with the church has risen to outright disgust.

Maybe again, I have been too optimistic. Is organized religion too inextricably bound to the status quo to save our nation and the world? Maybe I must turn my faith to the inner spiritual church, the church within the church, as the true *ecclesia* and the hope of the world. But again I am thankful to God that some noble souls from the ranks of organized religion have broken loose from the paralyzing chains of conformity and joined us as active partners in the struggle for freedom. They have left their secure congregations and walked the streets of Albany, Georgia, with us. They have gone through the highways of the South on tortuous rides for freedom. Yes, they have gone to jail with us. Some have been kicked out of their churches, and lost support of their bishops and fellow ministers. But they have gone with the faith that right defeated is stronger than evil triumphant. These men have been the leaven in the lump of the race. Their witness has been the spiritual salt that has preserved the true meaning of the gospel in these troubled times. They have carved a tunnel of hope through the dark mountain of disappointment.

I hope the church as a whole will meet the challenge of this decisive hour. But even if the church does not come to the aid of justice, I have no despair about the future. I have no fear about the outcome of our struggle in Birmingham, even if our motives are presently misunderstood. We will reach the goal of freedom in Birmingham and all over the nation, because the goal of America is freedom. Abused and scorned though we may be, our destiny is tied up with the destiny of America. Before the Pilgrims landed at Plymouth, we were here. Before the pen of Jefferson etched across the pages of history the majestic words of the Declaration of Independence, we were here. For more than two centuries our foreparents labored in this country without wages; they made cotton king; and they built the homes of their masters in the midst of brutal injustice and shameful humiliation—and yet out of a bottomless vitality they continued to thrive and develop. If the inexpressible cruelties of slavery could not stop us, the opposition we now face will surely fail. We will win our freedom because the sacred heritage of our nation and the eternal will of God are embodied in our echoing demands.

I must close now. But before closing I am impelled to mention one other point in your statement that troubled me profoundly. You warmly commended the Birmingham police force for keeping "order" and "preventing violence." I don't believe you would have so warmly commended the police force if you had seen its angry violent dogs literally biting six unarmed, non-violent Negroes. I don't believe you would so quickly commend the policemen if you would observe their ugly and inhuman treatment of Negroes here in the city jail; if you would watch

them push and curse old Negro women and young Negro girls; if you would see them slap and kick old Negro men and young boys; if you will observe them, as they did on two occasions, refuse to give us food because we wanted to sing our grace together. I'm sorry that I can't join you in your praise for the police department.

It is true that they have been rather disciplined in their public handling of the demonstrators. In this sense they have been rather publicly "nonviolent." But for what purpose? To preserve the evil system of segregation. Over the last few years I have consistently preached that nonviolence demands that the means we use must be as pure as the ends we seek. So I have tried to make it clear that it is wrong to use immoral means to attain moral ends. But now I must affirm that it is just as wrong, or even more so, to use moral means to preserve immoral ends. Maybe Mr. Connor and his policemen have been rather publicly nonviolent, as Chief Pritchett was in Albany, Georgia, but they have used the moral means of nonviolence to maintain the immoral end of flagrant racial injustice. T. S. Eliot has said that there is no greater treason than to do the right deed for the wrong reason.

I wish you had commended the Negro sitinners and demonstrators of Birmingham for their sublime courage, their willingness to suffer and their amazing discipline in the midst of the most inhuman provocation. One day the South will recognize its real heroes. They will be the James Merediths, courageously and with a majestic sense of purpose facing jeering and hostile mobs and the agonizing loneliness that characterizes the life of the pioneer. They will be old, oppressed, battered Negro women, symbolized in a seventy-two-year-old woman of Montgomery, Alabama, who rose up with a sense of dignity and with her people decided not to ride the segregated buses, and responded to one who inquired about her tiredness with ungrammatical profundity: "My feet is tired, but my soul is rested." They will be the young high school and college students, young ministers of the gospel and a host of their elders courageously and nonviolently sitting-in at lunch counters and willingly going to jail for conscience's sake.

One day the South will know that when these disinherited children of God sat down at lunch counters they were in reality standing up for the best in the American dream and the most sacred values in our Judeo-Christian heritage, and thusly, carrying our whole nation back to those great wells of democracy which were dug deep by the Founding Fathers in the formulation of the Constitution and the Declaration of Independence.

Never before have I written a letter this long (or should I say a book?). I'm afraid that it is much too long to take your precious time. I can assure you that it would have been much shorter if I had been writing from a comfortable desk, but what else is there to do when you are alone for days in the dull monotony of a narrow jail cell other than write long letters, think strange thoughts, and pray long prayers?

If I have said anything in this letter that is an overstatement of the truth and is indicative of an unreasonable impatience, I beg you to forgive me. If I have said anything in this letter that is an understatement of the truth and is indicative of my having a patience that makes me patient with anything less than brotherhood, I beg God to forgive me.

I hope this letter finds you strong in the faith. I also hope that circumstances will soon make it possible for me to meet each of you, not as an integrationist or a civil rights leader, but as a fellow clergyman and a Christian brother. Let us all hope that the dark clouds of racial prejudice will soon pass away and the deep fog of misunderstanding will be lifted from our fear-drenched communities and in some not too distant tomorrow the radiant stars of love and brotherhood will shine over our great nation with all of their scintillating beauty.

Yours for the cause of Peace and Brotherhood,
Martin Luther King, Jr.

4.7 Sovereignty and Justice: An Indigenist's Viewpoint

Have you ever wondered why oppression exists? Have you wondered how oppression might be eliminated? Surely one of the features of societies that makes them unjust is the existence of oppression. Oppression can take many forms: economic, racial, sexual. The rich dominate the poor and get richer at their expense. In the United States and elsewhere, whites discriminate against blacks. Men limit the opportunities for women. Gays and lesbians are denied the rights and opportunities others enjoy. Native Americans have suffered near extinction and cultural destruction at the hands of the European invaders and their descendants. Mexican Americans have been brutally exploited as farm laborers, and prevented, until recently, from gaining any significant political power. Unfortunately, I could go on and on recounting example after example.

Oppressors need to justify their position, and so they convince themselves that those whom they oppress are inferior, immoral, heathen, lazy, stupid, dirty, or somehow deserving of their lot in life. In effect, they dehumanize the oppressed while keeping for themselves the image of full humanity. For example, during the westward expansion in the United States, it was often said that "The only good Indian is a dead Indian."

Oppressors also need to justify their positions by legal means. If what one does is immoral, that fact can be disguised by making it appear legal. Exactly how the U.S government has made it legal to take and occupy land once occupied by others is the subject of the next selection by Ward Churchill.

Ward Churchill (Creek/Cherokee Metis), one of the most influential voices of native resistance in North America, is a professor of Communications and Coordinator of American Indian Studies at the University of Colorado at Boulder. He is also co-director of the Colorado chapter of the American Indian Movement (AIM) that is active in seeking justice for the descendants of the first peoples to inhabit North America.

Before you read Churchill's argument, imagine that you are a judge and have been asked to rule in a case. The facts of the case appear simple enough. A group of people many years ago occupied land that was taken from them by force and fraud. This land has changed hands many times and today the descendants of those who took the land occupy it. Now the descendants of the original people are demanding that justice be done. Your task is to decide what constitutes justice in this case. What must be done now to make a society in which this happened a more just society?

Reading Questions

1. What is the "Discovery Doctrine"?
2. What is the "Norman Yoke," and how does it change the Discovery Doctrine?
3. What is the main point Churchill makes in the section on "Treaties as Tools of the State"?
4. Explain the logic supporting the "Marshall Doctrine."
5. What is the "Allotment Act," and what were its consequences?
6. According to Churchill, what was the purpose of the IRA?
7. What is the "Blue Water Thesis," and what role did it play in countering the claims of AIM?
8. What are some of Churchill's conclusions?
9. Assuming Churchill is right, how can justice be done with respect to indigenous peoples and to those who now occupy and control much of their former land and its wealth?

Perversions of Justice

WARD CHURCHILL

FROM THE OUTSET of the "Age of Discovery" precipitated by the Columbian voyages, the European powers, eager to obtain uncontested title to at least some portion of the lands their emissaries were encountering, quickly recognized the need to establish a formal code of juridical standards to legitimate what they acquired. This lent a patina of "civilized" legality to the actions of the European Crowns. More importantly, the system was envisioned to resolve disputes between the Crowns themselves, each vying with the others in a rapacious battle over the wealth accruing through ownership of given regions in the "New World."

In order for any such regulatory code to be considered effectively binding by all Old World

From Ward Churchill, Struggle for the Land. *Monroe, ME: Common Courage Press, 1993, pp. 34–49, 53– 54, 59–63. Copyright © 1993 Ward Churchill. Reprinted by permission. Footnotes omitted.*

parties, it was vital that it be sanctioned by the Church. A theme begun with a series of Papal Bulls begun by Pope Innocent IV during the late thirteenth century First Crusade was used to define the proper ("lawful") relationship between Christians and "Infidels" in worldly matters such as property rights. Beginning in the early sixteenth century, Spanish jurists in particular did much to develop this theory into what have come to be known as the "Doctrine of Discovery" and an attendant dogma, the "Rights of Conquest." Through the efforts of legal scholars such as Franciscus de Vitoria and Matías de Paz, Spanish articulations of Discovery Doctrine, endorsed by the Pope, rapidly evolved to hold the following as primary tenets of international law:

- Outright ownership of land accrued to the Crown represented by a given Christian (European) discoverer only when the land discovered proved to be uninhabited (territorium res nullius).
- Title to inhabited lands discovered by Crown representatives was recognized as belonging inherently to the indigenous people encountered, but rights to acquire land from, and to trade with the natives of the region accrued exclusively to the discovering Crown *vis-à-vis* other European powers. In exchange for this right, the discovering power committed itself to proselytizing the Christian gospel among the natives.
- Acquisition of land title from indigenous peoples could occur only by their consent—by an agreement usually involving purchase—rather than through force of arms, so long as the natives did not arbitrarily decline to trade with Crown representatives, refuse to admit missionaries among them, or inflict gratuitous violence upon citizens of the Crown.
- Absent these last three conditions, utilization of armed force to acquire aboriginally held territory was considered unjust and claims to land title accruing therefrom to be correspondingly invalid.
- Should one or more of the three conditions be present, then the Crown had a legal right to use whatever force was required to subdue native resistance and impound their property as compensation. Land title gained by prosecution of such "Just Wars" was considered valid.

Although this legal perspective was hotly debated at the time (it still is, in certain quarters), and saw considerable violation by European colonists, it was generally acknowledged as the standard against which international conduct would be weighed. By the early seventeenth century, the requirements of the Discovery Doctrine had led the European states, England in particular, to adopt a policy of entering into formal treaties with native nations. These full-fledged international instruments officially recognized the sovereignty of the indigenous parties to such agreements as equivalent to that of the respective Crowns. They became an expedient to obtaining legally valid land titles from American Indian peoples, first in what is now the state of Virginia, and then in areas further north. Treaties concerning trade, professions of peace and friendship, and to consummate military alliances were also quite common.

Undeniably, there is a certain overweening arrogance imbedded in the proposition that Europeans were somehow intrinsically imbued with an authority to unilaterally restrict the range of those to whom Native Americans might sell their property, assuming they wished to sell it at all. Nonetheless, the legal posture of early European colonialism in recognizing that indigenous peoples constituted bona fide nations holding essentially the same rights to land and sovereignty as any other, seems rather advanced and refined in retrospect. In these respects, the Doctrine of Discovery is widely viewed as one of the more important cornerstones of modern international law and diplomacy.

With its adoption of Protestantism, however, Britain had already begun to mark its independence from papal regulation by adding an element of its own, usually termed the "Norman Yoke," to the doctrine. Land rights were said to rest in large part upon the extent to which owners demonstrate a willingness and ability to "develop" their territories in accordance with a scriptural obligation to exercise "dominium" over nature. Thus, entitlement is restricted to the quantity of real estate which the individual or people can convert from "wilderness" to a "domesticated" state. This criterion bestowed on English settlers an inherent right to dispossess native people of all land other than that which the latter might be "reasonably expected" to put to such "proper" uses as cultivation. More importantly at this time, this doctrinal innovation automatically placed the British Crown on a legal footing from which it could contest the discovery rights of any European power not adhering to the requirement of "overcoming the wilderness."

This allowed England simultaneously to "abide by the law" and directly confront Catholic France for ascendancy in the Atlantic regions of North America. After a series of "French and Indian Wars" beginning in the late 1600s and lasting nearly a century, the British were victorious, but at a cost greater than the expected financial benefits to the Crown of launching its colonial venture in the first place. As one major consequence, King George II, in a move intended to preclude further warfare with indigenous nations, issued the Proclamation of 1763. This royal edict stipulated that all settlement or other forms of land acquisition by British subjects west of a line running along the Allegheny and Appalachian Mountains from Canada to the Spanish colony of Florida would be suspended indefinitely, and perhaps permanently. English expansion on the North American continent was thereby brought to an abrupt halt.

Treaties as Tools of the State

The new British proclamation conflicted sharply with the desires for personal gain growing among a voracious élite within the seaboard colonial population. Most of the colonies held some pretense of title to "western" lands, much of it conveyed by earlier Crown grant, and had planned to use it as a means of bolstering their respective economic positions. Similarly, members of the landed gentry such as George Washington, Thomas Jefferson, John Adams, James Madison and Anthony Wayne all possessed considerable speculative interests in land parcels on the far side of the 1763 demarcation line. The only way in which these could be converted into profit was for the parcels to be settled and developed. Vociferous contestation and frequent violation of the proclamation, eventually enforced by George III, became quite common. This dynamic became a powerful precipitating factor in the American Revolution, during which many rank-and-file rebels were convinced to fight against the Crown by promises of western land grants "for services rendered" in the event their revolt was successful.

But successful revolt does not necessarily bring legitimacy. The United States emerged from its decolonization struggle against Britain—perhaps the most grievous offense which could be perpetrated by any subject people under then prevailing law—as a pariah, an outlaw state that was shunned as an utterly illegitimate entity by most other countries. Desperate to establish itself as a legitimate nation, and lacking other viable alternatives with which to demonstrate its aptitude for complying with international legality, the new government was virtually compelled to observe the strictest of protocols in its dealings with Indians. Indeed, what the Continental Congress needed more than anything at the time was for indigenous nations, already recognized as respectable sovereignties via their treaties with the European states, to bestow a comparable recognition upon the fledgling U.S. by entering into treaties with *it*. The urgency of the matter was compounded by the fact that the Indians maintained military parity with, and in some cases superiority to, the U.S. Army all along the frontier.

As a result, both the Articles of Confederation and subsequent Constitution of the United States contained clauses explicitly and exclusively restricting relations with indigenous nations to the federal government, insofar as the former were recognized as enjoying the same politico-legal status as any other foreign power. The U.S. also officially renounced, in the 1789 Northwest Ordinance and elsewhere, any aggressive intent concerning indigenous nations, especially with regard to their respective landbases:

> The utmost good faith shall always be observed towards the Indians; their land and property shall never be taken from them without their consent; and in their property, rights, and liberty, they shall never be disturbed . . . but laws founded in justice and humanity shall from time to time be made, for wrongs done to them, and for peace and friendship with them.

This rhetorical stance, reflecting an impeccable observance of international legality, was also incorporated into agreements between the U.S. and European states during its formative years. For instance, in the 1803 "Louisiana" Purchase of much of North America west of the Mississippi from France, the federal government solemnly pledged itself to protect "the inhabitants of the ceded territory . . . in the free enjoyment of their liberty, property and the religion they profess." Other sections of the purchase agreement make it clear that federal authorities understood they were acquiring from the French, not the land itself, but France's monopolistic trade rights and prerogatives to buy any acreage within the area its indigenous owners wished to sell.

The same understanding certainly pertained to all unceded Indian Country claimed by Britain under Discovery Doctrine east of the Mississippi, once it was quit-claimed by George III in the Treaty of Paris concluding the Revolution. Even if English discovery rights somehow "passed" to the new republic by virtue of this royal action, an extremely dubious premise in itself, there still remained the matter of obtaining native consent to U.S. ownership of any area beyond the 1763 proclamation line. Hence, in addition to the legitimacy gained by signing treaties with the indigenous nations, and the military goals of some such instruments, the U.S. actively pursued treaties to procure indigenous agreement to land cessions. This comprised the main currency of American diplomacy throughout the immediate post-revolutionary period. Moreover, the need to secure valid land title from native people through treaties far outlasted the motivations of diplomatic and military necessity, these having been greatly diminished in importance after U.S. victories over Tecumseh's alliance in 1794 and 1811, Britain in the War of 1812, and the Red Stick Confederacy during 1813 and 1814. The treaties were and remain the basic real estate documents anchoring U.S. claims to land title—and thus to rights of occupancy—in North America.

But, while these treaties solved some issues such as legitimacy for the newly born state, they created new problems. In gaining diplomatic recognition and land cessions from indigenous nations through treaties, the U.S. was simultaneously admitting not only that Indians ultimately owned virtually all of the territory coveted by the U.S., but that they were also under no obligation to part with it. As William Wirt, an early attorney general, put it in 1821:

> [Legally speaking,] so long as a tribe exists and remains in possession of its lands, its title and possession are sovereign and exclusive. We treat with them as separate sovereignties, and while an Indian nation continues to exist within its acknowledged limits, we have no more right to enter upon their territory than we have to enter upon the territory of a foreign prince.

A few years later, Wirt amplified his point:

> The point, once conceded, that the Indians are independent to the purpose of treating, their independence is to that purpose as absolute as any other nation. Being competent to bind themselves by treaty, they are equally competent to bind the party that treats with them. Such party cannot take benefit of [a] treaty with the Indians, and then deny them the reciprocal benefits of the treaty on the grounds that they are not independent nations to all intents and purposes. . . . Nor can it be conceded that their independence as a nation is a limited independence. Like all other independent nations, they have the absolute power of war and peace. Like all other independent nations, their territories are inviolate by any other sovereignty. . . . They

are entirely self-governed, self-directed. They treat, or refuse to treat, at their pleasure; and there is no human power that can rightly control them in the exercise of their discretion in this respect.

For twenty years following the revolution (roughly 1790 to 1810), such acknowledgment of these genuine indigenous sovereign rights and status considerably retarded the acquisition of land grants by revolutionary soldiers, as well as consummation of the plans of the élite caste of prerevolutionary land speculators. Over the next two decades (1810 to 1830), the issue assumed an ever increasing policy importance: native sovereignty replaced Crown policy as the preeminent barrier to U.S. territorial consolidation east of the Mississippi. Worse, as Chief Justice John Marshall pointed out in 1822, any real adherence to the rule of law in regard to native rights might not only block U.S. expansion, but—since not all the territory therein had been secured through Crown treaties—cloud title to significant portions of the original thirteen states as well. Perhaps predictably, it was perceived in juridical circles that the only means of circumventing this dilemma was through construction of a legal theory—a subterfuge, as it were—by which the more inconvenient implications of international law might be voided even while the republic maintained an appearance of holding to its doctrinal requirements.

The Marshall Doctrine: "Legal" Justification of an Outlaw State

The task of forging the required "interpretation" of existing law fell to Chief Justice Marshall, widely considered one of the great legal minds of his time. Whatever his scholarly qualifications, the Chief Justice was hardly a disinterested party. His ideological advocacy of the rebel cause before and during the revolution was vociferous. More important, both he and his father were consequent recipients of 10,000 acre grants west of the Appalachians, in what is now the state of West Virginia. His first serious foray into land rights law thus centered in devising a conceptual basis to secure title for his own and similar grants.

In the 1810 *Fletcher v. Peck* case, he invoked the Norman Yoke tradition in a manner which far exceeded previous British applications, advancing the patently absurd contention that the areas involved were effectively "vacant" even though very much occupied—and in many instances stoutly defended—by indigenous inhabitants. On this basis, he declared individual Euroamerican deeds within recognized Indian territories might be considered valid whether or not native consent was obtained.

While *Peck* was obviously useful from the U.S. point of view, resolving a number of short-term difficulties in meeting obligations already incurred by the government with regard to individual citizens, it was a tactical opinion, falling far short of accommodating the country's overall territorial goals and objectives. In the 1823 *Johnson v. McIntosh* case, however, Marshall followed up with a more clearly strategic enunciation, reaching to the core issues. Here, he opined that, because Discovery Rights purportedly constricted native discretion in disposing of property, the sovereignty of discoverers was to that extent inherently superior to that of indigenous nations. From this point of departure, he then proceeded to invert all conventional understandings of the Discovery Doctrine, ultimately asserting that native people occupied land within discovered regions at the sufferance of their discoverers rather than the other way around. A preliminary rationalization was thus contrived by which to explain the fact that the U.S. had already begun depicting its borders as encompassing vast portions of unceded Indian Country.

Undoubtedly aware that neither *Peck* nor *McIntosh* was likely to withstand the gaze of even minimal international scrutiny, Marshall next moved to bolster the logic undergirding his position. In the two so-called "Cherokee Cases" of the early 1830s, he hammered out the thesis that native nations within North America were "nations like any other" in the sense that they possessed both territories they were capable of ceding, and recognizable governmental bodies empowered to cede these areas through treaties. However, he argued on the basis of the reasoning deployed in *McIntosh*, they were nations of a "peculiar type," both "domestic to" and "dependent upon" the United States, and therefore possessed of a degree of sovereignty intrinsically less than that enjoyed by the U.S. itself. Thus while native peoples are entitled to exercise some range of autonomy in managing their affairs within their own territories, both the limits of that autonomy and the extent of the territories involved can be "naturally" and unilaterally established by the federal government. At base, this is little more than a judicial description of the classic relationship between colonizer and colonized, put forth in such a way as to seem at first glance to be the exact opposite.

While it might be contended (and has been, routinely enough) that Marshall's framing of the circumstances pertaining to the Cherokee Nation, already completely surrounded by the territorality of the United States by 1830, bore some genuine relationship to then prevailing reality, he did not confine his observations to the situation of the Cherokees, or even to native nations east of the Mississippi. Rather, he purported to articulate the legal status of *all* indigenous nations, including those west of the Mississippi—the Lakota, Cheyenne, Arapaho, Comanche, Kiowa, Navajo and Chiricahua Apache, to name but a few—which had not yet encountered the U.S. in any appreciable way. Self-evidently, these nations could not have been described with the faintest accuracy as domestic to or dependent upon the United States. The clear intent belied by Marshall's formulation was that they be *made so* in the future. The doctrine completed with elaboration of the Cherokee Cases was thus the pivotal official attempt to rationalize and legitimate the future campaign of conquest and colonization which was absolutely contrary to the customary law of the period.

The doctrine was not complete without a final inversion of accepted international legal norms and definitions of "Just" and "Unjust" warfare. Within Marshall's convoluted and falsely premised reasoning, it became arguable that indigenous nations acted unlawfully whenever and wherever they attempted to physically prevent exercise of the U.S. "right" to expropriate their property. Resistance to invasion of indigenous homelands could then be construed as "aggression" against the United States. In this sense, the U.S. could declare itself to be waging a "Just"—and therefore lawful—War against native people on any occasion where force of arms was required to realize its territorial ambitions. *Ipso facto,* all efforts of native people to defend themselves against systematic dispossession and subordination could thereby be categorized as "unjust"—and thus unlawful—by the United States.

In sum, the Marshall Doctrine shredded significant elements of the existing Laws of Nations. Given the historical records of federal judicial officials such as Attorney General Wirt and Marshall himself, and the embodiment of such understandings in the Constitution and formative federal statutes, this breach was not unintentional or inadvertent. Instead, with calculated juridical cynicism, the Chief Justice deliberately confused and deformed accepted legal principles to "justify" his country's pursuit of a thoroughly illegitimate course of territorial acquisition. Insofar as federal courts and policymakers elected to adopt his doctrine as the predicate to all subsequent relations with American Indians, the posture of the United States as an outlaw state was rendered permanent.

From Treaty Violation to Extermination

The Cherokee Cases were followed by a half-century hiatus in important judicial determinations regarding American Indians. On the foundation provided by the Marshall Doctrine, the government felt confident in entering into the great bulk of the more than 370 treaties with indigenous nations by which it professed to have gained the consent of Indians in ceding huge portions of the native landbase. With its self-anointed position of superior sovereignty, it would be under "no legal obligation" to live up to its end of the various bargains struck. Well before the end of the nineteenth century, the United States stood in default on virtually every treaty agreement it had made with native people, and there is considerable evidence in many instances that this was intended from the outset.

Aside from the fraudulent nature of U.S. participation in the treaty process, there is an ample record that many of the instruments of cession were militarily coerced while the government implemented Marshall's version of Just Wars against Indians. As the U.S. Census Bureau put it in 1894:

> The Indian wars under the United States government have been about 40 in number [most of them occurring after 1835]. They have cost the lives of . . . about 30,000 Indians [at a minimum]. . . . The actual number of killed and wounded Indians must be very much greater than the number given, as they conceal, where possible, their actual loss in battle. . . . Fifty percent additional would be a safe number to add to the numbers given.

The same report noted that some number "very much more" than 8,500 Indians were known to have been killed by government-sanctioned private citizen action—dubbed "individual affairs"—during the course of U.S./Indian warfare. In fact, such citizen action was primarily responsible for reducing the native population of Texas from about 100,000 in 1828 to less than 10,000 in 1880. Similarly, in California, an aggregate indigenous population which still numbered approximately 300,000 had been reduced to fewer than 35,000 by 1860, mainly because of "the cruelties and wholesale massacres perpetrated by [American] miners and early settlers." Either of these illustrations offers a death toll several times the total number officially recognized as accruing through individual affairs in the 48 contiguous states.

Even while this slaughter was occurring, the government was conducting, by its own admission, a "policy of extermination" in its conduct of wars against those indigenous nations which proved "recalcitrant" in giving up their land and liberty. This manifested itself in a lengthy series of massacres of native people—men, women, children, and old people alike—at the hands of U.S. troops. Among the worst were those at Blue River (Nebraska, 1854), Bear River (Idaho, 1863), Sand Creek (Colorado, 1864), Washita River (Oklahoma, 1868), Sappa Creek (Kansas, 1875), Camp Robinson (Nebraska, 1878), and Wounded Knee (South Dakota, 1890). Somewhat different, but comparable, methods of destroying indigenous peoples included the forced march of the entire Cherokee Nation along the "Trail of Tears" to Oklahoma during the 1830s (55 percent did not survive), and the internment of the bulk of the Navajo Nation under abysmal conditions at the Bosque Redondo from 1864 to 1868 (35 to 50 percent died). Such atrocities were coupled with an equally systematic extermination of an entire animal species, the buffalo or North American Bison, as part of a military strategy to starve resistant Indians into submission by "destroying their commissary."

It is probable that more than a quarter-million Indians perished as a direct result of U.S. extermination campaigns. By the turn of the century, only 237,196 native people were recorded by census as still being alive with the United States, perhaps 2 percent of the total indigenous population of the U.S. portion of North America at the point of first contact with Europeans. Correlating rather precisely with this genocidal reduction in the number of native inhabitants was an erosion of Indian land holdings to approximately 2.5 percent of the "lower 48" states. Admiring its effectiveness, barely thirty years later, Adolf Hitler would explicitly anchor his concept of *lebensraumpolitik* ("politics of living space") directly upon U.S. practice against American Indians.

Justice as a "Pulverizing Engine"

Even as the census figures were being tallied, the United States had already moved beyond the "Manifest Destiny" embodied in the conquest phase of its continental expansion, and was emphasizing the development of colonial administration over residual indigenous land and lives through the Bureau of Indian Affairs (BIA), a subpart of the War Department which had been reassigned for this purpose to the Department of Interior.

This was begun as early as 1871, when Congress—having determined that the military capacity of indigenous nations had finally been sufficiently reduced by incessant wars of attrition—elected to consecrate Marshall's description of their "domestic" status by suspending further treaty-making with them. In 1885, the U.S. began for the first time to directly extend its internal jurisdiction over reserved Indian territories ("reservations") through passage of the Major Crimes Act. When this was immediately challenged as a violation of international standards, Supreme Court Justice Samuel F. Miller rendered an opinion which consolidated and extended Marshall's earlier assertion of federal plenary power over native nations, contending that the government held an "incontrovertible right" to exercise authority over Indians as it saw fit and "for their own good." Miller also concluded that Indians lacked legal recourse in matters of federal interest, their sovereignty being defined as whatever Congress did not remove through specific legislation. This decision opened the door to enactment of more than 5,000 statutes regulating affairs in Indian Country by the present day.

One of the first of these was the General Allotment Act of 1887, "which unilaterally negated Indian control over land tenure patterns within the reservations, forcibly replacing the traditional mode of collective use and occupancy with the Anglo-Saxon system of individual property ownership." The Act also imposed for the first time a formal eugenics code—dubbed "blood quantum"—by which American Indian identity would be federally defined on racial grounds rather than by native nations themselves on the basis of group membership/citizenship.

The Allotment Act stipulated that each officially recognized American Indian would receive an allotment of land according to the following formula: 160 acres for family heads, eighty acres for single persons over eighteen years of age and orphans under eighteen, and forty acres for non-orphan children under eighteen. "Mixed blood" Indians received title by fee simple patent; "full bloods" were issued "trust patents," meaning they had no control over their property for a period of 25 years. Once each person recognized by the government as belonging to a given

Indian nation had received his or her allotment, the "surplus" acreage was "opened" to non-Indian homesteading or conversion into the emerging system of national parks, forests, and grasslands. . . .

Given the contours of federal policy towards American Indians, how is it that the indigenous nations were not obliterated long ago? The answer is ironic. Unbeknownst to the policymakers who implemented allotment policy against Indians during the late nineteenth century, much of the ostensibly useless land to which native people were consigned turned out to be some of the most mineral rich on earth. It is presently estimated that as much as two-thirds of all known U.S. "domestic" uranium reserves lie beneath reservation lands, as well as perhaps a quarter of the readily accessible low sulphur coal and about a fifth of the oil and natural gas. In addition, the reservations are now known to hold substantial deposits of copper, zinc, iron, nickel, molybdenum, bauxite, zeolite and gold.

Such matters were becoming known by the early 1920s. Federal economic planners quickly discerned a distinct advantage in retaining these abundant resources within the framework of governmental trust control. In contrast to land held privately, this arrangement was an expedient to awarding extractive leases, mining licenses and the like to preferred corporate entities. Granting these rights might have proven impossible had the reservations been liquidated altogether. Hence, beginning in 1921, it was determined that selected indigenous nations should be maintained. Washington began to experiment with the creation of "tribal governments" intended to administer what was left of Indian Country on behalf of an emerging complex of interlocking federal/corporate interests. In 1934, this resulted in the passage of the Indian Reorganization Act (IRA), a bill which served to supplant virtually every remaining traditional indigenous government in the country, replacing them with federally designed "Tribal Councils" structured along the lines of corporate boards and empowered primarily to sign off on mineral leases and similar instruments.

The arrangement led to a recapitulation of the Marshall Doctrine's principle of indigenous "quasi-sovereignty" in slightly revised form: now, native nations were cast as being sovereign enough to legitimate Euroamerican mineral exploitation on their reservations, never sovereign enough to prevent it. Predictably, under such circumstances the BIA negotiated mining leases, duly endorsed by the puppet governments it had installed, "on behalf of" its "Indian wards" which have typically paid native people 15 percent or less of market royalty rates on minerals taken from their lands. The "super profits" thus generated for major corporations have had a significant positive effect on U.S. economic growth since 1950, a matter amplified by the BIA "neglecting" to include land restoration and other environmental cleanup clauses into contracts pertaining to reservation land. (Currently, Indians are construed as sovereign enough to waive environmental protection regulations but never sovereign enough to enforce them). One consequence of this trend is that, on reservations where uranium mining has occurred, Indian Country has become so contaminated by radioactive substances that the government has actively considered designating them as "National Sacrifice Areas" unfit for human habitation. Planning is also afoot to utilize several reservations as dump sites for high level nuclear wastes and toxic chemical substances which cannot be otherwise disposed of conveniently. . . .

A Legal Raft in Blue Water

During the 1970s, the American Indian Movement (AIM), an organization militantly devoted to the national liberation of Native North America, emerged in the United States. In part, the group attempted the physical decolonization of the Pine Ridge Reservation in South Dakota (home of the Oglala Lakota people), but was met with a counterinsurgency war waged by federal agencies such as the FBI and U.S. Marshals Service, and surrogates associated with the reservation's IRA Council. Although unsuccessful in achieving a resumption of indigenous self-determination at Pine Ridge, the tenacity of

AIM's struggle (and the ferocity of the government's repression of it) attracted considerable international attention. This led, in 1980, to the establishment of a United Nations Working Group on Indigenous Populations, under auspices of the U.N. Economic and Social Council (ECOSOC), an entity mandated to assess the situation of native peoples globally and produce a universal declaration of their rights as a binding element of international law.

Within this arena, the United States, joined by Canada, has consistently sought to defend its relations with indigenous nations by trotting out the Marshall Doctrine's rationalization that the U.S. has assumed a trust responsibility rather than outright colonial domination over Native North America. American Indian delegates have countered, correctly, that trust prerogatives, in order to be valid under international law, must be tied to some clearly articulated time interval after which the subordinate nations resume independent existence. This has been successfully contrasted to the federal (and Canadian) government's presumption that it enjoys a permanent trust authority over indigenous nations; assumption of *permanent* plenary authority over another nation's affairs and property is the essential definition of colonialism, it is argued, and is illegal under a number of international covenants.

The U.S. and Canada have responded with prevarication, contending that their relationship to Native North America cannot be one of colonialism insofar as United Nations Resolution 1541 (XV), the so-called "Blue Water Thesis," specifies that in order to be defined as a colony a nation must be separated from its colonizer by at least thirty miles of open ocean. The representatives of both countries have also done everything in their power to delay or prevent completion of the Universal Declaration of the Rights of Indigenous Peoples, arguing, among other things, that the term "peoples," when applied to native populations, should not carry the force of law implied by its use in such international legal instruments as the Universal Declaration of Human Rights (1948), Covenant on Civil and Political Rights (1978), and the International Convention on Elimination of All Forms of Racial

Discrimination (1978). The United States in particular has implied that it will not abide by any declaration of indigenous rights which runs counter to what it perceives as its own interests, a matter which would replicate its posture with regard to the authority of the International Court of Justice (the "World Court") and elements of international law such as the 1948 Convention on Prevention and Punishment of the Crime of Genocide.

Meanwhile, the U.S. has set out to "resolve things internally" through what may be intended as a capstone extrapolation of the Marshall Doctrine. This has assumed the shape of a drive to convince Indians to accept the premise that, rather than struggling to regain the self-determining rights to separate sovereign existence embodied in their national histories and treaty relationships, they should voluntarily merge themselves with the U.S. polity. In this scenario, the IRA administrative apparatus created during the 1930s would assume a position as a "third level of the federal government," finally making indigenous rights within the U.S. inseparable from those of the citizenry as a whole. This final assimilation of native people into the "American sociopolitical mainstream" would obviously void most (or perhaps all) potential utility for Indian rights which exist in or might emerge from international law over the next few years. The option is therefore being seriously pursued by a Senate Select Committee on Indian Affairs, chaired by Hawaii Senator Daniel Inouye (who has already done much to undermine the last vestiges of rights held by the native people of his own state).

The Marshall Doctrine on a Global Scale

During the fall of 1990, President George Bush stepped onto the world stage beating the drums for what he termed a "Just War" to roll back what he described as the "naked aggression" of Iraq's invasion and occupation of neighboring Kuwait. Claiming to articulate "universal principles of international relations and human decency," Bush stated that such aggression

"cannot stand," that "occupied territory must be liberated, legitimate governments must be reinstated, the benefits of their aggression must be denied to aggressive powers." Given the tone and tenor of this Bushian rhetoric—and the undeniable fact that Iraq had a far better claim to Kuwait (its nineteenth province, separated from the Iraqis by the British as an administrative measure following World War I), than the U.S. has to virtually any part of North America—one might logically expect the American president to call airstrikes in upon his own capitol as a means of forcing his government to withdraw from Indian Country. Since he did not, the nature of his "New World Order" is clear: it is based on the rule of force, not on the rule of law.

The United States does not now possess, nor has it ever had, a legitimate right to occupancy in at least half the territory it claims as its own on this continent. It began its existence as an outlaw state and, given the nature of its expansion to its present size, it has adamantly remained so through the present moment. In order to make things appear otherwise, its legal scholars and its legislators have persistently and often grotesquely manipulated and deformed accepted and sound legal principles, both internationally and domestically. They have done so in precisely the same fashion, and on the same basis, as the [N]azi leaders they stood at the forefront in condemning for Crimes Against Humanity at Nuremberg.

In no small part because of its past achievements in consolidating its position on other peoples' land in North America, the United States may well continue to succeed where the [N]azis failed. With the collapse of the Soviet Union, it has emerged as the ascendant military power on the planet during the late twentieth century. As the sheer margin of its victory over Iraq has revealed, it now possesses the capacity to extend essentially the same sort of relationships it has already imposed upon American Indians to the remainder of the world. And, given the experience it has acquired in Indian Affairs over the years, it is undoubtedly capable of garbing this process of planetary subordination in a legalistic attire symbolizing its deep-seated concern with international freedom and dignity, the sovereignty of other nations, and the human rights of all peoples. At a number of levels, the Marshall Doctrine reckons to become truly globalized in the years ahead.

This is likely to remain the case, unless and until significant numbers of people within and without the United States recognize the danger, and the philosophical system underpinning it, for what it is. More importantly, any genuine alternative to a consummation of the Bushian vision of world order is predicated upon these same people acting upon their insights, opposing the order implicit to the U.S. status quo both at home and abroad. Ultimately, the dynamic represented by the Marshall Doctrine must be reversed, and the structure it fostered dismantled, within the territorial corpus of the United States itself. In this, nothing can be more central than the restoration of indigenous land and indigenous national rights in the fullest sense of the term. The U.S.—at least as it has come to be known, and in the sense that it knows itself— must be driven from North America. In its stead resides the possibility, likely the only possibility, of a truly just and liberatory future for all humanity.

Visit the companion Web site for chapter specific quizzes, suggestions for further reading, video ideas, and other resources to assess and expand your understanding of the chapter material. Go to http://philosophy.wadsworth.com and select the companion Web site for *Voices of Wisdom.*

 You can access many additional readings at the Info Trac-College Edition Web site. To find the following suggested articles do a keyword search with the article title. Use the passcode that was packaged with your new book to enter the site at http://www.Infotrac-college.com/Wadsworth/. Here is a sampling.

Khaled Abou El Fadl, "Islamic Law and Ambivalent Scholarship." *Michigan Law Review,* May 2002 v100 i6 p1421(23), A92691866.

"What Islam Teaches about Ethics and Justice. (Interview)" *U.S. Catholic,* May 1996 v61 n5 p15(5), A18215033.

Hannah Arendt, "Karl Marx and the Tradition of Western Political Thought." *Social Research,* Summer 2002 v69 i2 p273(48), A90439534.

Roger Spalding, "The Communist Manifesto." *History Review,* September 2000 p8, A67407433.

Ellen Meiksins Wood, "Back to Marx." *Monthly Review,* June 1997 v49 n2 p1(9), A19979854.

Tamara M. Teale, "The Silko Road from Chiapas or Why Native Americans Cannot Be Marxists." *MELUS,* Winter 1998 v23 i4 p157, A55909807.

Peter Berkowitz, "John Rawls and the Liberal Faith." *The Wilson Quarterly,* Spring 2002 v26 i2 p60(10), A86056800.

Martha C. Nussbaum, "Conversing with the Tradition: John Rawls and the History of Ethics." *Ethics,* January 1999 v109 i2 p424(1), A53985533.

Barbara Allen, "Martin Luther King's Civil Disobedience and the American Covenant Tradition." *Publius,* Fall 2000 v30 i4 p71, A72986274.

Mark Tunick, "Hegel on Justified Disobedience." *Political Theory,* August 1998 v26 n4 p514(22), A20998440.

Rick Whaley, "The Centrality of Native Americans to Green Philosophy and Practice." *Synthesis/Regeneration,* Fall 2002 p32(2), A91469739.

Charlie Smoke, "Rumours of Borders: Refusing to Recognize the Existence of Imposed Boundaries Is an Important Part of Maintaining First Nations' Identity, but It Sure Shakes up the Colonial Government." *Briarpatch,* July–August 2002 v31 i6 p3(5), A89148730.

Brad Miller, "Bush's War on Sacred Lands." *Earth Island Journal,* Summer 2002 v17 i2 p22(1), A84867071.

Lucy Maddox, "Politics, Performance and Indian Identity." *American Studies International,* June 2002 v40 i2 p7(30), A90333509.

Chapter 5

Is Justice for All Possible?

> **Live compassionately.**
> THE BUDDHA

5.1 Introduction

WHEN I ASK STUDENTS to write a brief essay on whether they think a just society is possible, the responses I get are overwhelmingly negative. They do not think a just society is possible because, as one student put it, "Someone will always be unhappy with the way things are."

The United States, as well as other countries, faces a number of complex issues requiring some sort of legislation. Yet every time a law is passed or a judicial decision is made, someone is going to feel cheated. Even so, decisions must be made, and we can only hope that the decisions make good moral sense even if someone may be "unhappy."

The issue of human rights is a case in point. Do humans have certain rights just because they are human? Are such rights universal or local? Does some international agency have the right to enforce certain human rights in countries that do not recognize such rights? Should trade decisions be based on the "human rights record" of countries?

Racism and sexism have plagued many countries. Can they be eliminated? Is a society that tolerates racism and sexism a just society? Can there ever be justice for those who have been victims of racism and sexism? Are affirmative action programs justified? One often hears such programs justified on the grounds of compensatory justice. However, many argue that the correction of a past injustice leads to a present injustice.

Some hail the globalization of capitalism as the economic salvation of the world. Others take to the streets to protest violently what they see as yet another scheme on the part of the very rich to exploit the very poor. Policies of the International Monetary Fund (IMF) and the World Bank have reaped great benefits for rich countries like the United States and failed to improve in any significant way the economic status of the Third World. Twenty-three of the fifty countries with the lowest per annum incomes had lower average incomes in 1999 than they did in 1990, and twenty-seven had, on average, a positive growth rate of only 2.7 percent per annum (see Friedman, *New York Review of Books* XLIX, August 15, 2002, p. 48).

Terrorism, which has an ancient history, has recently emerged with a renewed fury in a frantic attempt to achieve justice by any means possible. If globalization is shrinking the world and spreading exploitation of the poor by the rich, terrorism is balkanizing the world, creating "us-versus-them" mentalities. Any serious consideration of the problems of achieving justice for all today must contend with both of these forces.

Environmental issues appear in the news almost daily. Many predict that in the twenty-first century a good portion of our time and resources will be spent cleaning up the mess left by the last century's insensitivity to the environment. As international businesses expand and globalization becomes more and more entrenched, the temptations to exploit humans, other-than-human animals, and our environment in the name of "progress" (read "profit") will multiply.

Social philosophy discusses these sorts of issues (and many more). Philosophers try to illuminate the issues, sort out the reasonable positions, and argue for policies that make moral sense. We will become a part of some of these discussions in this chapter, and, I trust, our thinking about them will deepen. We may, in some cases, still be uncertain about what is the best thing to do, and we still may realize that some people will be unhappy no matter what is done, but at least our vision of social justice in some areas may become clearer.

5.2 Universal Human Rights

If I asked you to come up with a list of universal human rights, could you? For example, does everyone have the right to life and liberty? Does everyone have the right to own property? Does everyone have the right to work?

Did you know that before the mid-twentieth century, there were very few restraints on what states could do to their citizens? The relationship between citizens and states was, for the most part, thought to be a domestic, internal affair. The genocide, ethnic cleansings, and other human atrocities that increased to an unprecedented degree in the last century eventually led to the adoption by the United Nations on December 10, 1948 of a Universal Declaration of Human Rights. Forty-eight nations ratified the Declaration and eight abstained (South Africa, Saudi Arabia, and six members of the Soviet bloc at that time).

Eleanor Roosevelt chaired the international commission that wrote the Declaration. She was deeply interested in social issues, particularly racial equality and women's rights. She represented the United States at the United Nations and worked tirelessly to get the Declaration drafted and passed.

Below you will find an edited version of the United Nations Declaration following a brief article by René Trujillo. Trujillo, a professor at San Jose State University, writes about the moral reflection that occurred as the Spanish conquered the indigenous peoples in the "New World." He points out that, contrary to what we might expect, issues of human rights and human dignity played an important role in the thinking of some Spanish philosophers of the day.

"Little good it did the native peoples," you might say. In the same vein, some have wondered whether the United Nations Declaration has done much good. Indeed it seems that a universal declaration of human rights will do little good because governments and greedy corporations ignore the human rights of others whenever it is to their advantage to do so. There is no doubt that some states have repeatedly violated many of the specific provisions of the Declaration. However, over the years many have come to see the Declaration as a useful gauge for progress on the issue of human rights. Virtually every national constitution incorporates some of its provisions, and human rights organizations refer to the Declaration as a standard of rights and freedoms.

For a perceptive discussion of the universal nature of human rights in light of the claim by some that Asian countries have their own view of human rights that appropriately reflects Asian values, go to http://philosophy.wadsworth.com and select the companion Web site for *Voices of Wisdom* for a link to Xiaorong Li's "Asian Values and the Universality of Human Rights."

Reading Questions

1. What do you think is left out of UN *Universal Declaration of Human Rights* that should be included, and what do you think is included that should be left out? Give reasons for your answer.
2. Do you see any links between these two selections? If so, what are they?

Human Rights in the "Age of Discovery"

RENÉ TRUJILLO

As we remember the "Age of Discovery" of the "New World," in terms of the brutality that attended it for the indigenous peoples of the Western Hemisphere, let us also remember what effect it had on conscientious European thinkers of the day. Let us learn not only from the mistakes of the conquest, but from the moral reflection that it occasioned.

In reply to the theology and philosophy of repression prevalent in his day, Francisco de Vitoria (1485–1546) proposed an alternative in his *Carta Constitucional de los Indios.* The major thesis of this work was expressed in three fundamental principles. First, the indigenous peoples had a fundamental right based on their humanity—that is, based on the fact that they were human beings—to be treated as free people. Second, they had a fundamental right to defend their own sovereignty. Third, and finally, they enjoyed the fundamental right of all peoples to

work toward and to make peace and international solidarity. It was in light of these three beliefs that Vitoria both determined and evaluated the rights and concomitant obligations of the Spanish Crown to be in and remain in the "new" world. Ultimately, considering the transgressions suffered by the indigenous peoples, he concluded that Spain owed restitution to the natives.

The dispute that ensued between Juan Gines de Sepulveda (1490–1573), the official defender of the monarch, and Vitoria was based on the concept of the just war. They were concerned with the justifications for the actions of the Spanish Crown against the integrity of the societies of indigenous peoples with whom the Spanish conquerors had contact. More broadly, these two men were concerned with the concept of "justice" in general as it pertained to human rights and obligations.

From Social Justice in a Diverse Society, *edited by Rita C. Manning and René Trujillo. Reprinted by permission of the McGraw-Hill Companies.*

The constitutional principles of Vitoria's alternative perspective can be understood on the basis of five points. In the first place, the Spaniards and indigenous peoples had to be understood as equal with regards to their humanity. This consideration spanned both actual and potential human characteristics. Second, any assertion of inhumanity in the indigenous peoples had to be understood as due to a lack of education and to their resultant barbaric customs. Some European thinkers of the day were enlightened enough to see that this same point might be leveled against the European communities within which they found themselves. Third, the indigenous peoples, in the same fashion as the Spanish, had property rights to their possessions and as such could not be dispossessed of them by virtue of any charge of lack of culture. This would follow for the same reasons as those which would serve to protect an uncultured individual in Spain. Fourth—and this might be very controversial today—the indigenous peoples might be entrusted to the tutelage of the Spaniards while still in an "underdeveloped state." This provision, of course, assumes that the aim of the tutelage would be the eventual autonomy of the indigenous peoples, and that the Spaniards had the requisite moral character and skill to undertake such a position. Finally, the consent of the indigenous peoples and their free choice were the ultimate grounds for any just Spanish intervention in the "new" world.

To better understand these assertions, and to see their relevance to us today, we must understand the motivation behind them. We might appropriately ask, What question do they answer? All demands placed on the indigenous peoples were justified in the minds of the Spanish based on their belief in the universal power of the Roman Catholic Church. Specifically, the appropriateness of their actions followed from the world authority of the pope, who, they thought, had sovereign power over all spiritual and temporal concerns. The papal "donation" of the Indies to the Catholic Kings (Fernando II el Catolico, king of Aragon and Castilla and Isabel I la Catolica, queen of Castilla) conferred the status of vassals (in a feudal sense) to the

indigenous peoples, and established sovereignty for Spain over the "new" world. This condition of servitude was understood in Spain as "natural" and as having ample historical precedent. The latter belief was certainly clearly true; however, the issue of servitude, natural or otherwise, was to create a significant theological and moral crisis.

Along with their papal authority to govern came the mandate to evangelize the indigenous peoples, that is, to seek their free conversion to Christendom. It was understood as the duty of the indigenous peoples to accept evangelization—but what would this imply about the nature and humanity of these peoples? The Spanish monarchy wished to justify its wars against the indigenous peoples by establishing papal authority, Spanish sovereignty, and the right to evangelize. It wanted to be able to establish the submission, occupation, and enslavement of these peoples as the natural and inevitable consequence of the just war waged against indigenous rebellion and resistance. Much of this policy, however, rested on the notion that these indigenous individuals had some *duty* to comply. The resistance to these ideas, as evidenced in Vitoria's position, was based on a reevaluation of the necessary preconditions for moral duty. What sort of being has moral duties?

The resounding answer was "human beings." But human beings have not only moral duties and responsibilities, they have moral rights. They have human rights. Can one be held responsible for one's moral duties in the face of the systematic infringement of one's moral rights? Can one be morally disenfranchised within the community of moral beings, and still be expected to comply with moral law? These were some of the questions that motivated the opposition to come out against the policies and actions of the crown.

Today it is true, as it was five hundred years ago, that duty and obligation imply rights and benefits if they are to be considered just. To have the duties of a human being, one must be able to enjoy the rights that attend the human condition. If there are any moral duties to be defined within such a state, there must also be a sense of moral rights. The conclusion I draw from these observations is that morality requires humanity, and humanity depends on the recognition and observance of dignity. In the case of human beings, dignity is achieved not only through our duties and obligations to others, but also through the obligations and duties of others to ourselves. Human duties to ourselves or others only make sense in a reflective equilibrium that defines the rights that follow from these duties.

In today's communities there is an overabundance of duties talk in the face of a paucity of rights talk. When we do speak of rights, it is overwhelmingly in terms of personal rights and not the rights of others. We may in word understand that these rights depend on each other, but our deeds rarely conform to this understanding. If we are to secure the rights of any individuals whatsoever, we must secure the rights of all. If we are to establish the duties of any one person, we must confirm the basis for such a duty as rooted in the enjoyment of some right or privilege. Otherwise, we commit ourselves to the irrational: we ask of all disenfranchised human beings that they act systematically and freely against their own interests and that they trust in the beneficence of those who force them into such a dilemma.

Until we recognize that humanity manifests itself variously, we are in no position to judge either ourselves or others. Race, gender, class, and sexual orientation have historically been used as the basis for different duties and rights. These duties and rights have always been determined by the politically strong and the duties exacted with vengeance from the politically subordinate. We see continued evidence of this trend today. Take the recent Colorado state initiative to repeal all antigay discrimination protection legislation (as currently on the books in Boulder, Denver, and Aspen). How can we ask individuals to fully participate in a community where they are not deemed worthy of their full human rights with all the protection society is willing to offer others? The answer is, we cannot. To support the quality of our lives, each and every one of us must be committed to the quality of all lives. Otherwise, we will suffer the consequences.

United Nations Universal Declaration of Human Rights

The General Assembly

PROCLAIMS

This universal declaration of human rights as a common standard of achievement for all peoples and all nations, to the end that every individual and every organ of society, keeping this Declaration constantly in mind, shall strive by teaching and education to promote respect for these rights and freedoms and by progressive measures, national and international, to secure their universal and effective recognition and observance, both among the peoples of Member States themselves and among the peoples of territories under their jurisdiction.

ARTICLE 1

All human beings are born free and equal in dignity and rights. They are endowed with reason and conscience and should act towards one another in a spirit of brotherhood.

ARTICLE 2

Everyone is entitled to all the rights and freedoms set forth in this Declaration, without distinction of any kind, such as race, colour, sex, language, religion, political or other opinion, national or social origin, property, birth or other status.

Furthermore, no distinction shall be made on the basis of the political, jurisdictional or international status of the country or territory to which a person belongs, whether it be independent, trust, non-self-governing or under any other limitation of sovereignty.

ARTICLE 3

Everyone has the right to life, liberty and security of person.

ARTICLE 4

No one shall be held in slavery or servitude; slavery and the slave trade shall be prohibited in all their forms.

ARTICLE 5

No one shall be subjected to torture or to cruel, inhuman or degrading treatment or punishment.

ARTICLE 6

Everyone has the right to recognition everywhere as a person before the law.

ARTICLE 7

All are equal before the law and are entitled without any discrimination to equal protection of the law. All are entitled to equal protection against any discrimination in violation of this Declaration and against any incitement to such discrimination.

ARTICLE 8

Everyone has the right to an effective remedy by the competent national tribunals for acts violating the fundamental rights granted him by the constitution or by law.

ARTICLE 9

No one shall be subjected to arbitrary arrest, detention or exile.

ARTICLE 10

Everyone is entitled in full equality to a fair and public hearing by an independent and impartial tribunal, in the determination of his rights and obligations and of any criminal charge against him.

ARTICLE 11

1. Everyone charged with a penal offence has the right to be presumed innocent until proved guilty according to law in a public trial at which he has had all the guarantees necessary for his defence.

2. No one shall be held guilty of any penal offence on account of any act or omission which did not constitute a penal offence, under national or international law, at the time when it was committed. Nor shall a heavier penalty be imposed than the one that was applicable at the time the penal offence was committed.

ARTICLE 12

No one shall be subjected to arbitrary interference with his privacy, family, home or correspondence, nor to attacks upon his honour and reputation. Everyone has the right to the protection of the law against such interference or attacks.

ARTICLE 13

1. Everyone has the right to freedom of movement and residence within the borders of each state.

2. Everyone has the right to leave any country, including his own, and to return to his country.

ARTICLE 14

1. Everyone has the right to seek and to enjoy in other countries asylum from persecution.

2. This right may not be invoked in the case of prosecutions genuinely arising from non-political crimes or from acts contrary to the purposes and principles of the United Nations.

ARTICLE 15

1. Everyone has the right to a nationality.

2. No one shall be arbitrarily deprived of his nationality nor denied the right to change his nationality.

ARTICLE 16

1. Men and women of full age, without any limitation due to race, nationality or religion, have the right to marry and to found a family. They are entitled to equal rights as to marriage, during marriage and at its dissolution.

2. Marriage shall be entered into only with the free and full consent of the intending spouses.

3. The family is the natural and fundamental group unit of society and is entitled to protection by society and the State.

ARTICLE 17

1. Everyone has the right to own property alone as well as in association with others.

2. No one shall be arbitrarily deprived of his property.

ARTICLE 18

Everyone has the right to freedom of thought, conscience and religion; this right includes freedom to change his religion or belief, and freedom, either alone or in community with others and in public or private, to manifest his religion or belief in teaching, practice, worship and observance.

ARTICLE 19

Everyone has the right to freedom of opinion and expression; this right includes freedom to hold opinions without interference and to seek, receive and impart information and ideas through any media and regardless of frontiers.

ARTICLE 20

1. Everyone has the right to freedom of peaceful assembly and association.

2. No one may be compelled to belong to an association.

ARTICLE 21

1. Everyone has the right to take part in the government of his country, directly or through freely chosen representatives.

2. Everyone has the right of equal access to public service in his country.

3. The will of the people shall be the basis of the authority of government; this will shall be expressed in periodic and genuine elections which shall be by universal and equal suffrage and shall be held by secret vote or by equivalent free voting procedures.

ARTICLE 22

Everyone, as a member of society, has the right to social security and is entitled to realization, through national effort and international cooperation and in accordance with the organization and resources of each State, of the economic, social and cultural rights indispensable for his dignity and the free development of his personality.

ARTICLE 23

1. Everyone has the right to work, to free choice of employment, to just and favourable conditions of work and to protection against unemployment.

2. Everyone, without any discrimination, has the right to equal pay for equal work.

3. Everyone who works has the right to just and favourable remuneration ensuring for himself and his family an existence worthy of human dignity, and supplemented, if necessary, by other means of social protection.

4. Everyone has the right to form and to join trade unions for the protection of his interests.

ARTICLE 24

Everyone has the right to rest and leisure, including reasonable limitation of working hours and periodic holidays with pay.

ARTICLE 25

Everyone has the right to a standard of living adequate for the health and well-being of himself and of his family, including food, clothing, housing and medical care and necessary social services, and the right to security in the event of unemployment, sickness, disability, widowhood, old age or other lack of livelihood in circumstances beyond his control.

1. Motherhood and childhood are entitled to special care and assistance. All children, whether born in or out of wedlock, shall enjoy the same social protection.

ARTICLE 26

1. Everyone has the right to education. Education shall be free, at least in the elementary and fundamental stages. Elementary education shall be compulsory. Technical and professional education shall be made generally available and higher education shall be equally accessible to all on the basis of merit.

2. Education shall be directed to the full development of the human personality and to the strengthening of respect for human rights and fundamental freedoms. It shall promote understanding, tolerance and friendship among all nations, racial or religious groups, and shall further the activities of the United Nations for the maintenance of peace.

3. Parents have a prior right to choose the kind of education that shall be given to their children.

ARTICLE 27

1. Everyone has the right freely to participate in the cultural life of the community, to enjoy the arts and to share in scientific advancement and its benefits.

2. Everyone has the right to the protection of the moral and material interests resulting from any scientific, literary or artistic production of which he is the author.

ARTICLE 28

Everyone is entitled to a social and international order in which the rights and freedoms set forth in this Declaration can be fully realized.

ARTICLE 29

1. Everyone has duties to the community in which alone the free and full development of his personality is possible.

2. In the exercise of his rights and freedoms, everyone shall be subject only to such limitations as are determined by law solely for the purpose of securing due recognition and respect for the rights and freedoms of others and of meeting the just requirements of morality, public order and the general welfare in a democratic society.

3. These rights and freedoms may in no case be exercised contrary to the purposes and principles of the United Nations.

ARTICLE 30

Nothing in this Declaration may be interpreted as implying for any State, group or person any right to engage in any activity or to perform any act aimed at the destruction of any of the rights and freedoms set forth herein.

5.3 Racism and Feminism

Suppose I ask you to list five types of the most common social injustices. I would wager that both racism and sexism are somewhere on that list. Both these social wrongs appear to be so widespread and difficult to eliminate because race and sex are such fundamental features of human existence. However, it clearly is not possible to achieve justice for all as long as racial prejudice and sexual discrimination exist.

It is important to distinguish individual racism and sexism from institutional forms. The first kind involves negative attitudes and beliefs about someone of another race or sex that often results in negative actions such as racial epithets and sexual harassment. The second kind, institutional racism and sexism, involves intitutions' traditional ways of doing things that mistreat people because of their race or sex. For example, for many years blacks and women were not allowed to serve on police forces or in the military in the United States and other countries. Women were not allowed to vote in the United States until 1920, and they are still not allowed to vote in Saudi Arabia. Institutional racism and sexism unfairly create disadvantages for some and advantages for others on irrelevant grounds and thus violate the formal principle of justice.

Combating both individual and institutional racism and sexism is the goal of various liberation movements. One thinks of the black power movement or the women's liberation movement of the 1960s and 1970s. Both were intended to empower the victims of racism and sexism. The ideas they spawned—racial equality and feminism—have continued to shape social policy in many countries to the present day.

It has proven very difficult to eliminate the injustices of racism and sexism. Just when we think progress is being made, new forms of both are discovered. In part this is due to our tendencies to see the world from an egocentric viewpoint. In part it is due to the power, prestige, and benefits that result from being in the advantaged group. In part, perhaps in large part, it is due to the elitism that infects all societies. Even efforts devoted to the liberation of one group can mask negative beliefs and attitudes toward other groups. Thus black men fighting for liberation have often excluded women from leadership positions, and white women fighting for sexual equality have discriminated against black women.

The author of our next selection is bell hooks, a professor of English at City College of New York. She was born Gloria Watkins but writes under the name of her great-grandmother in order to pay homage to the unheard voices of black women, past and present. She writes her name all in lowercase, thereby symbolizing her skepticism about the importance of fame even though her book, *Ain't I a Woman,* from which the following selection is taken, brought her fame as an author, activist, and important social critic.

Reading Questions

1. What is the main point hooks is making?
2. What did you learn from reading this selection that you did not know before?

Ain't I a Woman

BELL HOOKS

IN A RETROSPECTIVE EXAMINATION of the black female slave experience, sexism looms as large as racism as an oppressive force in the lives of black women. Institutionalized sexism—that is, patriarchy—formed the base of the American social structure along with racial imperialism. Sexism was an integral part of the social and political order white colonizers brought with them from their European homelands, and it was to have a grave impact on the fate of enslaved black women. In its earliest stages, the slave trade focused primarily on the importation of laborers; the emphasis at that time was on the black male. The black female slave was not as valued as the black male slave. On the average, it cost more money to buy a male slave than a female slave. The scarcity of workers coupled with the relatively few numbers of black women in American colonies caused some white male planters to encourage, persuade, and coerce immigrant white females to engage in sexual relationships with black male slaves as a means of producing new workers. In Maryland, in the year 1664, the first anti-amalgamation law was passed; it was aimed at curtailing sexual relationships between white women and enslaved black men. One part of the preamble of this document stated:

> That whatsoever freeborn woman shall intermarry with any slave, from and after the last day of the present assembly, shall serve the masters of such slaves during the life of her husband; and that all the issue of such free born women, so married shall be slaves as their fathers were.

The most celebrated case of this time was that of Irish Nell, an indentured servant sold by Lord Baltimore to a southern planter who encouraged her to marry a black man named Butler. Lord Baltimore, on hearing of the fate of Irish Nell, was so appalled that white women were either by choice or coercion co-habiting sexually with black male slaves that he had the law repealed. The new law stated that the offspring of relationships between white women and black men would be free. As efforts on the part of outraged white men to curtail inter-racial relationships between black men and white women succeeded, the black female slave acquired a new status. Planters recognized the economic gain they could amass by breeding black slave women. The virulent attacks on slave importation also led to more emphasis on slave breeding. Unlike the offspring of relationships between black men and white women, the offspring of any black slave woman regardless of the race of her mate would be legally slaves, and therefore the property of the owner to whom the female slave belonged. As the market value of the black female slave increased, larger numbers were stolen or purchased by white slave traders.

White male observers of African culture in the 18th and 19th centuries were astounded and impressed by the African male's subjugation of the African female. They were not accustomed to a patriarchal social order that demanded not only that women accept an inferior status, but that they participate actively in the community labor force. Amanda Berry Smith, a 19th century black missionary, visited African communities and reported on the condition of African women:

> The poor women of Africa, like those of India, have a hard time. As a rule, they have all the hard work to do. They have to cut and carry all the wood, carry all the water on their heads, and plant all the rice. The men and boys cut and burn the bush, with the help of the women; but

sowing the rice, and planting the cassava, the women have to do.

You will often see a great, big man walking ahead with nothing in his hand but a cutlass (as they always carry that or a spear), and a woman, his wife, coming on behind with a great big child on her back, and a load on her head.

No matter how tired she is, her lord would not think of bringing her a jar of water, to cook his supper with, or of beating the rice, no, she must do that.

The African woman schooled in the art of obedience to a higher authority by the tradition of her society was probably seen by the white male slaver as an ideal subject for slavery. As much of the work to be done in the American colonies was in the area of hoe-agriculture, it undoubtedly occurred to slavers that the African female, accustomed to performing arduous work in the fields while also performing a wide variety of tasks in the domestic household, would be very useful on the American plantation. While only a few African women were aboard the first ships bringing slaves to the new world, as the slave trade gathered momentum, females made up one-third of the human cargo aboard most ships. Because they could not effectively resist capture at the hands of thieves and kidnappers, African women became frequent targets for white male slavers. Slavers also used the capture of women important to the tribe, like the daughter of a king, as a means of luring African men into situations where they could be easily captured. Other African women were sold into slavery as punishment for breaking tribal laws. A woman found guilty of committing an act of adultery might be sold into bondage.

White male slavers did not regard the African female as a threat, so often aboard slave ships black women were stored without being shackled while black men were chained to one another. The slavers believed their own safety to be threatened by enslaved African men, but they had no such fear of the African female. The placing of African men in chains was to prevent possible uprisings. As white slavers feared resistance and retaliation at the hands of African men, they placed as much distance between themselves and black male slaves as was possible on board. It was only

in relationship to the black female slave that the white slaver could exercise freely absolute power, for he could brutalize and exploit her without fear of harmful retaliation. Black female slaves moving freely about the decks were a ready target for any white male who might choose to physically abuse and torment them. Initially every slave on board the ship was branded with a hot iron. A cat-o'-nine-tails was used by the slavers to lash those Africans that cried out in pain or resisted the torture. Women were lashed severely for crying. They were stripped of their clothing and beaten on all parts of their body. Ruth and Jacob Weldon, an African couple who experienced the horrors of the slave passage, saw "mothers with babes at their breasts basely branded and scarred, till it would seem as if the very heavens might smite the infernal tormentors with the doom they so richly merited." After the branding all slaves were stripped of any clothing. The nakedness of the African female served as a constant reminder of her sexual vulnerability. Rape was a common method of torture slavers used to subdue recalcitrant black women. The threat of rape or other physical brutalization inspired terror in the psyches of displaced African females. Robert Shufeldt, an observer of the slave trade, documented the prevalence of rape on slave ships. He asserts, "In those days many a negress was landed upon our shore already impregnated by someone of the demonic crew that brought her over."

Many African women were pregnant prior to their capture or purchase. They were forced to endure pregnancy without any care given to their diet, without any exercise, and without any assistance during the labor. In their own communities African women had been accustomed to much pampering and care during pregnancy, so the barbaric nature of childbearing on the slave ship was both physically harmful and psychologically demoralizing. Annals of history record that the American slave ship Pongas carried 250 women, many of them pregnant, who were squeezed into a compartment of 16 by 18 feet. The women who survived the initial stages of pregnancy gave birth aboard ship with their bodies exposed to either the scorching sun or the freezing cold. The numbers of black women who died during childbirth or the number of stillborn children will never be known. Black women with children on board the slave ships were ridiculed, mocked, and treated contemptuously by the slaver crew. Often the slavers brutalized children to watch the anguish of their mothers. In their personal account of life aboard a slave ship, the Weldons recounted an incident in which a child of nine months was flogged continuously for refusing to eat. When beating failed to force the child to eat, the captain ordered that the child be placed feet first into a pot of boiling water. After trying other torturous methods with no success, the captain dropped the child and caused its death. Not deriving enough satisfaction from this sadistic act, he then commanded the mother to throw the body of the child overboard. The mother refused but was beaten until she submitted. . . .

Chapter Three

THE IMPERIALISM OF PATRIARCHY

When the contemporary movement toward feminism began, there was little discussion of the impact of sexism on the social status of black women. The upper and middle class white women who were at the forefront of the movement made no effort to emphasize that patriarchal power, the power men use to dominate women, is not just the privilege of upper and middle class white men, but the privilege of all men in our society regardless of their class or race. White feminists so focused on the disparity between white male/white female economic status as an indication of the negative impact of sexism that they drew no attention to the fact that poor and lower-class men are as able to oppress and brutalize women as any other group of men in American society. The feminist tendency to make synonymous male possession of economic power with being an oppressor caused white men to be labeled "the" enemy. The labeling of the white male patriarch as "chauvinist pig" provided a convenient scapegoat for black male sexists. They could join with white and black women to protest against white male oppression and divert attention away from their sexism, their support

of patriarchy, and their sexist exploitation of women. Black leaders, male and female, have been unwilling to acknowledge black male sexist oppression of black women because they do not want to acknowledge that racism is not the only oppressive force in our lives. Nor do they wish to complicate efforts to resist racism by acknowledging that black men can be victimized by racism but at the same time act as sexist oppressors of black women. Consequently there is little acknowledgement of sexist oppression in black male/female relationships as a serious problem. Exaggerated emphasis on the impact of racism on black men has evoked an image of the black male as effete, emasculated, crippled. And so intensely does this image dominate American thinking that people are absolutely unwilling to admit that the damaging effects of racism on black men neither prevents them from being sexist oppressors nor excuses or justifies their sexist oppression of black women.

Black male sexism existed long before American slavery. The sexist politics of white-ruled and colonized America merely reinforced in the minds of enslaved black people existing beliefs that men were the superiors of women. In an earlier discussion of the slave sub-culture I noted that the patriarchal social structure gave the enslaved male higher status than the enslaved female. Historiographers have not been willing to acknowledge either the higher status of the enslaved male in the black sub-culture or the fact that sex-based differentiation of work roles as assigned by white masters reflected a bias towards the male (i.e., black women required to perform "male" tasks but black men not required to perform "female" tasks—women labor in fields but men do no childcare). In modern times, the emphasis on the sexist definition of the male role as that of protector and provider has caused scholars to argue that the most damaging impact of slavery on black people was that it did not allow black men to assume the traditional male role. But the inability of black men to assume the role of protector and provider did not change the reality that men in patriarchal society automatically have higher status than women—they are not obliged to earn that status. Consequently, the enslaved black male, though obviously deprived of the social status that would enable him to protect and provide for himself and others, had a higher status than the black female slave based solely on his being male. This higher status did not always lead to preferential treatment but it was overtly acknowledged by sex-role differentiation.

Sexist discrimination against all women in the labor force and in higher educational spheres throughout 19th century America meant that of those black people who aspired to leadership roles, either during slavery or at manumission, black men were the more likely candidates. As black men dominated leadership roles, they shaped the early black liberation movement so that it reflected a patriarchal bias. Courageous black women leaders like Sojourner Truth and Harriet Tubman did not represent the norm; they were exceptional individuals who dared to challenge the male vanguard to struggle for freedom. At public appearances, rallies, luncheons, and dinners black male leaders spoke in support of patriarchal rule. They did not talk directly about discriminating against women. Their sexism was shrouded in romantic visions of black men lifting black women to pedestals. Outspoken black nationalist leader Martin Delaney in his political treatise, *The Condition, Elevation, Emigration, and Destiny of the Colored People of the United States,* which was first published in 1852, advocated distinct sex role patterns for black women and men:

> Let our young men and women prepare themselves for usefulness and business; that the men may enter into merchandise, trading, and other things of importance; the young women may become teachers of various kinds, and otherwise fill places of usefulness. . . .

> Our females must be qualified, because they are to be the mothers of our children. As mothers are the first nurse and instructors of children; from them children consequently, get their first impression, which being always the most lasting, should be the more correct. Raise the mothers above the level of degradation, and the offspring is elevated with them. In a word, instead of our young men, transcribing in their blank books recipes for Cooking, we desire to see them making the transfer of Invoices and Merchandise.

Frederick Douglass saw the entire racial dilemma in America as a struggle between white men and black men. In 1865 he published an essay titled "What the Black Man Wants" which argued in favor of black men gaining the vote while women remained disenfranchised:

> Shall we at this moment justify the deprivation of the Negro of the right to vote, because some one else is deprived of that privilege? I hold that women, as well as men, have the right to vote, and my heart and my voice go with the movement to extend suffrage to women; but the question rests on another basis than that on which our rights rest. We may be asked, I say, why we want it. I will tell you why we want it. We want it because it is our right, first of all. No class of men can, without insulting their own nature, be content with any deprivation of their rights.

It is evident in this statement that to Douglass the "negro" was synonymous with the black male. And though he claims in his essay to support woman suffrage, he clearly believed it was more appropriate and fitting that men be given the right to vote. By emphasizing that the right to vote was more important to men than women, Douglass and other black male activists allied themselves with white male patriarchs on the basis of shared sexism. . . .

Chapter Four

RACISM AND FEMINISM: THE ISSUE OF ACCOUNTABILITY

American women of all races are socialized to think of racism solely in the context of race hatred. Specifically in the case of black and white people, the term racism is usually seen as synonymous with discrimination or prejudice against black people by white people. For most women, the first knowledge of racism as institutionalized oppression is engendered either by direct personal experience or through information gleaned from conversations, books, television, or movies.

Consequently, the American woman's understanding of racism as a political tool of colonialism and imperialism is severely limited. To experience the pain of race hatred or to witness that pain is not to understand its origin, evolution, or impact on world history. The inability of American women to understand racism in the context of American politics is not due to any inherent deficiency in woman's psyche. It merely reflects the extent of our victimization.

No history books used in public schools informed us about racial imperialism. Instead we were given romantic notions of the "new world," the "American dream," America as the great melting pot where all races come together as one. We were taught that Columbus *discovered* America; that "Indians" were scalphunters, killers of innocent women and children; that black people were enslaved because of the biblical curse of Ham, that God "himself" had decreed they would be hewers of wood, tillers of the field, and bringers of water. No one talked of Africa as the cradle of civilization, of the African and Asian people who came to America before Columbus. No one mentioned mass murders of Native Americans as genocide, or the rape of Native American and African women as terrorism. No one discussed slavery as a foundation for the growth of capitalism. No one described the forced breeding of white wives to increase the white population as sexist oppression.

I am a black woman. I attended all-black public schools. I grew up in the south where all around me was the fact of racial discrimination, hatred, and forced segregation. Yet my education as to the politics of race in American society was not that different from that of white female students I met in integrated high schools, in college, or in various women's groups. The majority of us understood racism as a social evil perpetuated by prejudiced white people that could be overcome through bonding between blacks and liberal whites, through militant protest, changing of laws or racial integration. Higher educational institutions did nothing to increase our limited understanding of racism as a political ideology. Instead professors systematically denied us truth, teaching us to accept racial polarity in the form of white supremacy and sexual polarity in the form of male dominance.

American women have been socialized, even brainwashed, to accept a version of American history that was created to uphold and maintain racial imperialism in the form of white supremacy and sexual imperialism in the form of patriarchy. One measure of the success of such indoctrination is that we perpetuate both consciously and unconsciously the very evils that oppress us. I am certain that the black female sixth grade teacher who taught us history, who taught us to identify with the American government, who loved those students who could best recite the pledge of allegiance to the American flag was not aware of the contradiction; that we should love this government that segregated us, that failed to send schools with all black students supplies that went to schools with only white pupils. Unknowingly she implanted in our psyches a seed of the racial imperialism that would keep us forever in bondage. For how does one overthrow, change, or even challenge a system that you have been taught to admire, to love, to believe in? Her innocence does not change the reality that she was teaching black children to embrace the very system that oppressed us, that she encouraged us to support it, to stand in awe of it, to die for it.

That American women, irrespective of their education, economic status, or racial identification, have undergone years of sexist and racist socialization that has taught us to blindly trust our knowledge of history and its effect on present reality, even though that knowledge has been formed and shaped by an oppressive system, is nowhere more evident than in the recent feminist movement. The group of college-educated white middle and upper class women who came together to organize a women's movement brought a new energy to the concept of women's rights in America. They were not merely advocating social equality with men. They demanded a transformation of society, a revolution, a change in the American social structure. Yet as they attempted to take feminism beyond the realm of radical rhetoric and into the realm of American life, they revealed that they had not changed, had not undone the sexist and racist brainwashing that had taught them to regard women unlike themselves as Others. Consequently, the Sisterhood they talked about has not become a reality, and the women's movement they envisioned would have a transformative effect on American culture has not emerged. Instead, the hierarchical pattern of race and sex relationships already established in American society merely took a different form under "feminism": the form of women being classed as an oppressed group under affirmative action programs further perpetuating the myth that the social status of all women in America is the same; the form of women's studies programs being established with all-white faculty teaching literature almost exclusively by white women about white women and frequently from racist perspectives; the form of white women writing books that purport to be about the experience of American women when in fact they concentrate solely on the experience of white women; and finally the form of endless argument and debate as to whether or not racism was a feminist issue.

If the white women who organized the contemporary movement toward feminism were at all remotely aware of racial politics in American history, they would have known that overcoming barriers that separate women from one another would entail confronting the reality of racism, and not just racism as a general evil in society but the race hatred they might harbor in their own psyches. Despite the predominance of patriarchal rule in American society, America was colonized on a racially imperialistic base and not on a sexually imperialistic base. No degree of patriarchal bonding between white male colonizers and Native American men overshadowed white racial imperialism. Racism took precedence over sexual alliances in both the white world's interaction with Native Americans and African Americans, just as racism overshadowed any bonding between black women and white women on the basis of sex. Tunisian writer Albert Memmi emphasizes in *The Colonizer and the Colonized* the impact of racism as a tool of imperialism:

> Racism appears . . . not as an incidental detail, but as a consubstantial part of colonialism. It is the highest expression of the colonial system

and one of the most significant features of the colonialist. Not only does it establish a fundamental discrimination between colonizer and colonized, a sine qua non of colonial life, but it also lays the foundation for the immutability of this life.

While those feminists who argue that sexual imperialism is more endemic to all societies than racial imperialism are probably correct, American society is one in which racial imperialism supersedes sexual imperialism.

In America, the social status of black and white women has never been the same. In 19th and early 20th century America, few if any similarities could be found between the life experiences of the two female groups. Although they were both subject to sexist victimization, as victims of racism black women were subjected to oppressions no white woman was forced to endure. In fact, white racial imperialism granted all white women, however victimized by sexist oppression they might be, the right to assume the role of oppressor in relationship to black women and black men. From the onset of the contemporary move toward feminist revolution, white female organizers attempted to minimize their position in the racial caste hierarchy of American society. In their efforts to disassociate themselves from white men (to deny connections based on shared racial caste), white women involved in the move toward feminism have charged that racism is endemic to white male patriarchy and have argued that they cannot be held responsible for racist oppression. Commenting on the issue of white female accountability in her essay "'Disloyal to Civilization': Feminism, Racism, and Gynephobia," radical feminist Adrienne Rich contends:

> If Black and White feminists are going to speak of female accountability, I believe the word racism must be seized, grasped in our bare hands, ripped out of the sterile or defensive consciousness in which it so often grows, and transplanted so that it can yield new insights for our lives and our movement. An analysis that places the guilt for active domination, physical and institutional violence, and the justifications embedded in myth and language, on white women not only compounds false consciousness; it

allows us all to deny or neglect the charged connection among black and white women from the historical conditions of slavery on, and it impedes any real discussion of women's instrumentality in a system which oppresses all women and in which hatred of women is also embedded in myth, folklore, and language.

No reader of Rich's essay could doubt that she is concerned that women who are committed to feminism work to overcome barriers that separate black and white women. However, she fails to understand that from a black female perspective, if white women are denying the existence of black women, writing "feminist" scholarship as if black women are not a part of the collective group American women, or discriminating against black women, then it matters less that North America was colonized by white patriarchal *men* who institutionalized a racially imperialistic social order than that white women who purport to be feminists support and actively perpetuate anti-black racism.

To black women the issue is not whether white women are more or less racist than white men, but that they are racist. If women committed to feminist revolution, be they black or white, are to achieve any understanding of the "charged connections" between white women and black women, we must first be willing to examine woman's relationship to society, to race, and to American culture as it is and not as we would ideally have it be. That means confronting the reality of white female racism. Sexist discrimination has prevented white women from assuming the dominant role in the perpetuation of white racial imperialism, but it has not prevented white women from absorbing, supporting, and advocating racist ideology or acting individually as racist oppressors in various spheres of American life. . . .

Chapter Five

BLACK WOMEN AND FEMINISM

More than a hundred years have passed since the day Sojourner Truth stood before an assembled body of white women and men at an anti-slavery rally in Indiana and bared her breasts to prove that she was indeed a woman. To Sojourner, who had traveled the long road from slavery to freedom, the baring of her breasts was a small matter. She faced her audience without fear, without shame, proud of having been born black and female. Yet the white man who yelled at Sojourner, "I don't believe you really are a woman," unwittingly voiced America's contempt and disrespect for black womanhood. In the eyes of the 19th century white public, the black female was a creature unworthy of the title woman; she was mere chattel, a thing, an animal. When Sojourner Truth stood before the second annual convention of the women's rights movement in Akron, Ohio, in 1852, white women who deemed it unfitting that a black woman should speak on a public platform in their presence screamed: "Don't let her speak! Don't let her speak! Don't let her speak!" Sojourner endured their protests and became one of the first feminists to call their attention to the lot of the black slave woman who, compelled by circumstance to labor alongside black men, was a living embodiment of the truth that women could be the work-equals of men.

It was no mere coincidence that Sojourner Truth was allowed on stage after a white male spoke against the idea of equal rights for women, basing his argument on the notion that woman was too weak to perform her share of manual labor—that she was innately the physical inferior to man. Sojourner quickly responded to his argument, telling her audience:

> . . . Well, children, whar dar is so much racket dar must be something out o' kilter. I tink dat 'twixt de niggers of de Souf and de women at de Norf all a talkin 'bout rights, de white men will be in a fix pretty soon. But what's all dis here talkin' 'bout? Dat man ober dar say dat women needs to be helped into carriages, and lifted ober ditches, and to have de best places . . . and ain't I a woman? Look at me! Look at my arm! . . . I have plowed, and planted, and gathered into barns, and no man could head me—and ain't I a woman? I could work as much as any man (when I could get it), and bear de lash as well—and ain't I a woman? I have borne five children and I seen 'em mos all sold off into slavery, and when I cried out with a mother's grief, none but Jesus hear—and ain't I a woman?

Unlike most white women's rights advocates, Sojourner Truth could refer to her own personal life experience as evidence of woman's ability to function as a parent; to be the work equal of man; to undergo persecution, physical abuse, rape, torture; and to not only survive but emerge triumphant.

Sojourner Truth was not the only black woman to advocate social equality for women. Her eagerness to speak publicly in favor of women's rights despite public disapproval and resistance paved the way for other politically-minded black women to express their views. Sexism and racism have so informed the perspective of American historiographers that they have tended to overlook and exclude the effort of black women in discussions of the American women's rights movement. White female scholars who support feminist ideology have also ignored the contribution of black women. In contemporary works, like *The Remembered Gate: Origins of American Feminism* by Barbara Berg; *Herstory* by June Sochen, *Hidden from History* by Sheila Rowbothan, *The Women's Movement* by Barbara Deckard, to name a few, the role black women played as advocates for women's rights in the 19th century is never mentioned. Eleanor Flexner's *Century of Struggle,* which was first published in 1959, remains one of the very few book-length historical works on the women's rights movement that documents the participation of black women.

Most women involved in the recent move toward a feminist revolution assume that white women have initiated all feminist resistance to male chauvinism in American society, and further assume that black women are not interested in women's liberation. While it is true that white women have led every movement toward feminist revolution in American society, their dominance is less a sign of black female disinterest in feminist struggle than an indication that the politics of colonization and racial imperialism have made it historically impossible for black women in the United States to lead a women's movement. . . .

Feminism is an ideology in the making. According to the Oxford English Dictionary the term "feminism" was first used in the latter part of the 19th century and it was defined as having the "qualities of females." The meaning of the term has been gradually transformed and the 20th century dictionary definition of feminism is a "theory of the political, economic, and social equality of the sexes." To many women this definition is inadequate. In the introduction to *The Remembered Gate: Origins of American Feminism* Barbara Berg defines feminism as a "broad movement embracing numerous phases of woman's emancipation." She further states:

> It is the freedom to decide her own destiny; freedom from sex-determined role; freedom from society's oppressive restrictions; freedom to express her thoughts fully and to convert them freely to actions. Feminism demands the acceptance of woman's right to individual conscience and judgment. It postulates that woman's essential worth stems from her common humanity and does not depend on the other relationships of her life.

Her expanded definition of feminism is useful but limited. Many women have found that neither the struggle for "social equality" nor the focus on an "ideology of woman as an autonomous being" are enough to rid society of sexism and male domination. To me feminism is not simply a struggle to end male chauvinism or a movement to ensure that women will have equal rights with men; it is a commitment to eradicating the ideology of domination that permeates Western culture on various levels—sex, race, and class, to name a few—and a commitment to reorganizing U.S. society so that the self-development of people can take precedence over imperialism, economic expansion, and material desires. Writers of a feminist pamphlet published anonymously in 1976 urged women to develop political consciousness:

> In all these struggles we must be assertive and challenging, combating the deep-seated tendency in Americans to be liberal, that is, to evade struggling over questions of principle for fear of creating tensions or becoming unpopular. Instead we must live by the fundamental dialectical principle: that progress comes only from struggling to resolve contradictions.

It is a contradiction that white females have structured a women's liberation movement that is racist and excludes many non-white women. However, the existence of that contradiction should not lead any woman to ignore feminist issues. Oftentimes I am asked by black women to explain why I would call myself a feminist and by using that term ally myself with a movement that is racist. I say, "The question we must ask again and again is how can racist women call themselves feminists." It is obvious that many women have appropriated feminism to serve their own ends, especially those white women who have been at the forefront of the movement; but rather than resigning myself to this appropriation I choose to re-appropriate the term "feminism," to focus on the fact that to be "feminist" in any authentic sense of the term is to want for all people, female and male, liberation from sexist role patterns, domination, and oppression.

Today masses of black women in the U.S. refuse to acknowledge that they have much to gain by feminist struggle. They fear feminism. They have stood in place so long that they are afraid to move. They fear change. They fear losing what little they have. They are afraid to openly confront white feminists with their racism or black males with their sexism, not to mention confronting white men with their racism and sexism. I have sat in many a kitchen and heard black women express a belief in feminism and eloquently critique the women's movement explaining their refusal to participate. I have witnessed their refusal to express these same views in a public setting. I know their fear exists because they have seen us trampled upon, raped, abused, slaughtered, ridiculed and mocked. Only a few black women have rekindled the spirit of feminist struggle that stirred the hearts and minds of our 19th century sisters. We, black women who advocate feminist ideology, are pioneers. We are clearing a path for ourselves and our sisters. We hope that as they see us reach our goal—no longer victimized, no longer unrecognized, no longer afraid—they will take courage and follow.

5.4 Globalization and Justice

Anyone who follows the news must be dismayed by the power of the two opposing forces now shaping global events. On the one hand, the world appears to be disintegrating into smaller and smaller units intent on pursuing their own agendas for self-determination. On the other hand, the forces of telecommunications and globalization render the world more interconnected and interdependent than it has ever been. Muslim women wear lipstick and nail polish under their black burkas while sipping Pepsi through straws in the openings of their veils.

How can both disintegration and integration be happening all at once? How can people around the world become both closer and further apart at the same time? What do these twin forces that Benjamin Barber, who is Whitman Professor of Political Science at Rutgers University, calls McWorld and Jihad, have to do with one another?

The selection that follows is the introduction to Barber's widely acclaimed book, *Jihad vs. McWorld.* Here Barber sounds the notes that he develops in more detail in later chapters. He is particularly concerned with the issue of the future of democracy. Can viable democracies that promote justice for all people be created and maintained as the world falls apart in violence and bloodshed, while simultaneously being brought together by an economic powerhouse of multinational capitalistic interests that put private drives to make a buck above concerns for public welfare? The final paragraph of the last chapter of *Jihad vs. McWorld* reads almost like a prayer:

> In a nation at war, Abraham Lincoln saw in democracy a last and best hope. On our paradoxical planet today, with nations falling apart and coming together at the same moment for some of the very same reasons, and with cowering national governments and toothless international law hardly able to bark, let alone bite, democracy may now have become our first and only hope (292).

What do you think? Is democracy our first and only hope as the world fragments into war, terrorism, hatred, and violence while greedy capitalists try to transform diverse peoples around the globe into a bland market of unreflective consumers?

Reading Questions

1. What does Barber mean by "Jihad *and* McWorld," and why do they need one another?
2. Why are both Jihad and McWorld bad for democracy?
3. How does Barber's use of the word *Jihad* differ from its theological meaning of "religious struggle on behalf of faith"?
4. What does the author mean when he characterizes Jihad as "multiculturalism turned cancerous," and what does this have to do with the quest for self-determination?
5. Why does Barber think, contrary to popular thinking, that capitalism does not necessarily promote democratic ideals?
6. Sum up in one sentence what you think is Barber's main point. Do you agree with him? Why, or why not?

Jihad vs. McWorld

BENJAMIN R. BARBER

HISTORY IS NOT OVER. Nor are we arrived in the wondrous land of techné promised by the futurologists. The collapse of state communism has not delivered people to a safe democratic haven, and the past, fratricide and civil discord perduring, still clouds the horizon just behind us. Those who look back see all of the horrors of the ancient slaughterbench reenacted in disintegral nations like Bosnia, Sri Lanka, Ossetia, and Rwanda and they declare that nothing has changed. Those who look forward prophesize commercial and technological interdependence — a virtual paradise made possible by spreading markets and global technology — and they proclaim that everything is or soon will be different. The rival observers seem to consult different almanacs drawn from the libraries of contrarian planets.

Yet anyone who reads the daily papers carefully, taking in the front page accounts of civil carnage as well as the business page stories on the mechanics of the information superhighway and the economics of communication mergers, anyone who turns deliberately to take in the whole 360-degree horizon, knows that our world and our lives are caught between what William Butler Yeats called the two eternities of race and soul: that of race reflecting the tribal past, that of soul anticipating the cosmopolitan future. Our secular eternities are corrupted, however, race reduced to an insignia of resentment, and soul sized down to fit the demanding body by which it now measures its needs. Neither race nor soul offers us a future that is other than bleak, neither promises a polity that is remotely democratic.

The first scenario rooted in race holds out the grim prospect of a retribalization of large swaths of humankind by war and bloodshed: a threatened balkanization of nation-states in which culture is pitted against culture, people against people, tribe against tribe, a Jihad in the name of a hundred narrowly conceived faiths against every kind of interdependence, every kind of artificial social cooperation and mutuality: against technology, against pop culture, and against integrated markets; against modernity itself as well as the future in which modernity issues. The second paints that future in shimmering pastels, a busy portrait of onrushing economic, technological, and ecological forces that demand integration and uniformity and that mesmerize peoples everywhere with fast music, fast computers, and fast food — MTV, Macintosh, and McDonald's — pressing nations into one homogenous global theme park, one McWorld tied together by communications, information, entertainment, and commerce. Caught between Babel and Disneyland, the planet is falling precipitously apart and coming reluctantly together at the very same moment.

Some stunned observers notice only Babel, complaining about the thousand newly sundered "peoples" who prefer to address their neighbors with sniper rifles and mortars; others — zealots in Disneyland — seize on futurological platitudes and the promise of virtuality, exclaiming "It's a small world after all!" Both are right, but how can that be?

We are compelled to choose between what passes as "the twilight of sovereignty" and an entropic end of all history; or a return to the past's most fractious and demoralizing discord; to "the menace of global anarchy," to Milton's capital of hell, Pandaemonium; to a world totally "out of control."

The apparent truth, which speaks to the paradox at the core of this book, is that the tendencies of both Jihad *and* McWorld are at work, both visible sometimes in the same country at the very same instant. Iranian zealots keep one ear tuned to the mullahs urging holy war and the other cocked to Rupert Murdoch's Star television beaming in *Dynasty, Donahue,* and *The Simpsons* from hovering satellites. Chinese entrepreneurs vie for the attention of party cadres in Beijing and simultaneously pursue KFC franchises in cities like Nanjing, Hangzhou, and Xian where twenty-eight outlets serve over 100,000 customers a day. The Russian Orthodox church, even as it struggles to renew the ancient faith, has entered a joint venture with California businessmen to bottle and sell natural waters under the rubric Saint Springs Water Company. Serbian assassins wear Adidas sneakers and listen to Madonna on Walkman headphones as they take aim through their gunscopes at scurrying Sarajevo civilians looking to fill family watercans. Orthodox Hasids and brooding neo-Nazis have both turned to rock music to get their traditional messages out to the new generation, while fundamentalists plot virtual conspiracies on the Internet.

Now neither Jihad nor McWorld is in itself novel. History ending in the triumph of science and reason or some monstrous perversion thereof (Mary Shelley's Doctor Frankenstein) has been the leitmotiv of every philosopher and poet who has regretted the Age of Reason since the Enlightenment. Yeats lamented "the center will not hold, mere anarchy is loosed upon the world," and observers of Jihad today have little but historical detail to add. The Christian parable of the Fall and of the possibilities of redemption that it makes possible captures the eighteenth-century ambivalence — and our own — about past and future. I want, however, to do more than dress up the central paradox of human history in modern clothes. It is not Jihad and McWorld but the relationship between them that most interests me. For, squeezed between their opposing forces, the world has been sent spinning out of control. Can it be that what Jihad and McWorld have in common is anarchy: the absence of common will and that conscious and collective human control under the guidance of law we call democracy?

Progress moves in steps that sometimes lurch backwards; in history's twisting maze, Jihad not only revolts against but abets McWorld, while McWorld not only imperils but re-creates and reinforces Jihad. They produce their contraries and need one another. My object here then is not simply to offer sequential portraits of McWorld and Jihad, but while examining McWorld, to keep Jihad in my field of vision, and while dissecting Jihad, never to forget the context of McWorld. Call it a dialectic of McWorld: a study in the cunning of reason that does honor to the radical differences that distinguish Jihad and McWorld yet that acknowledges their powerful and paradoxical interdependence.

There is a crucial difference, however, between my modest attempt at dialectic and that of the masters of the nineteenth century. Still seduced by the Enlightenment's faith in progress, both Hegel and Marx believed reason's cunning was on the side of progress. But it is harder to believe that the clash of Jihad and McWorld will issue in some overriding good. The outcome seems more likely to pervert than to nurture human liberty. The two may, in opposing each other, work to the same ends, work in apparent tension yet in covert harmony, but democracy is not their beneficiary. In East Berlin, tribal communism has yielded to capitalism. In Marx-Engelsplatz, the stolid, overbearing statues of Marx and Engels face east, as if seeking distant solace from Moscow: but now, circling them along the streets that surround the park that is their prison are chain eateries like T.G.I. Friday's, international hotels like the Radisson, and a circle of neon billboards mocking them with brand names like Panasonic, Coke, and Gold-Star. New gods, yes, but more liberty?

What then does it mean in concrete terms to view Jihad and McWorld dialectically when the tendencies of the two sets of forces initially appear so intractably antithetical? After all, Jihad and McWorld operate with equal strength in opposite directions, the one driven by parochial hatreds, the other by universalizing markets, the one re-creating ancient subnational and ethnic borders from within, the other making national borders porous from without. Yet Jihad and McWorld have this in common: they both make war on the sovereign nation-state and thus undermine the nation-state's democratic institutions. Each eschews civil society and belittles democratic citizenship, neither seeks alternative democratic institutions. Their common thread is indifference to civil liberty. Jihad forges communities of blood rooted in exclusion and hatred, communities that slight democracy in favor of tyrannical paternalism or consensual tribalism. McWorld forges global markets rooted in consumption and profit, leaving to an untrustworthy, if not altogether fictitious, invisible hand issues of public interest and common good that once might have been nurtured by democratic citizenries and their watchful governments. Such governments, intimidated by market ideology, are actually pulling back at the very moment they ought to be aggressively intervening. What was once understood as protecting the public interest is now excoriated as heavy-handed regulatory browbeating. Justice yields to markets, even though, as Felix Rohatyn has bluntly confessed, "there is a brutal Darwinian logic to these markets. They are nervous and greedy. They look for stability and transparency, but what they reward is not always our preferred form of democracy." If the traditional conservators of freedom were democratic constitutions and Bills of Rights, "the new temples to liberty," George Steiner suggests, "will be McDonald's and Kentucky Fried Chicken."

In being reduced to a choice between the market's universal church and a retribalizing politics of particularist identities, peoples around the globe are threatened with an atavistic return to medieval politics where local tribes and ambitious emperors together ruled the world entire, women and men united by the universal abstraction of Christianity even as they lived out isolated lives in warring fiefdoms defined by involuntary (ascriptive) forms of identity. This was a world in which princes and kings had little real power until they conceived the ideology of nationalism. Nationalism established government on a scale greater than the tribe yet less cosmopolitan than the universal church and in time gave birth to those intermediate, gradually more democratic institutions that would come to constitute the nation-state. Today, at the far end of this history, we seem intent on re-creating a world in which our only choices are the secular universalism of the cosmopolitan market and the everyday particularism of the fractious tribe.

In the tumult of the confrontation between global commerce and parochial ethnicity, the virtues of the democratic nation are lost and the instrumentalities by which it permitted peoples to transform themselves into nations and seize sovereign power in the name of liberty and the commonweal are put at risk. Neither Jihad nor McWorld aspires to resecure the civic virtues undermined by its denationalizing practices; neither global markets nor blood communities service public goods or pursue equality and justice. Impartial judiciaries and deliberative assemblies play no role in the roving killer bands that speak on behalf of newly liberated "peoples," and such democratic institutions have at best only marginal influence on the roving multinational corporations that speak on behalf of newly liberated markets. Jihad pursues a bloody politics of identity, McWorld a bloodless economics of profit. Belonging by default to McWorld, everyone is a consumer; seeking a repository for identity, everyone belongs to some tribe. But no one is a citizen. Without citizens, how can there be democracy?

From Self-Determination to Jihad

Not long ago, Daniel Patrick Moynihan predicted that the next half hundred states likely to come into existence over the next fifty years will all be defined by ethnic conflict: that is to say, by civil war. The Soviet Union and Yugoslavia have together already produced twenty or more new (old) "nations" or national fragments. In the most egregious cases, the United Nations sends peacekeeping forces, although its member nations are increasingly loath to put their soldiers at risk. Currently, it has stationed troops in eighteen countries — in nearly every case, arrayed against forces of domestic insurrection and civil discord. The Carter Center in Atlanta has a still more nuanced and thus expansive list that is more or less mirrored in the forty-eight trouble spots charted by *The New York Times* at the beginning of 1993. Amnesty International reports political prisoners and political executions in more than sixty countries.

In this tumultuous world, the real players are not nations at all but tribes, many of them at war with one another. Their aim is precisely to redraw boundaries in order to divide — say in Kurdish Iraq or Muslim Sudan or Serbian-populated sections of Croatia. Countries like Afghanistan, recently fighting a foreign invader in the name of its national independence, have been effectively dismembered: divided among Panthans, Hazaras, Uzbeks, and Tajiks. This is ethnic membership enhanced via national dismemberment — or by expulsion or expunction of unwanted contaminators, as has occurred in slaughter-happy Rwanda. Is this pandaemonium just an extension of benign efforts at multiculturalism? A natural consequence of a centuries-old impulse to self-determination? Or the appearance of a new disease that has corrupted integral nationalism and opened the way to ethnic and religious Jihad?

Jihad is, I recognize, a strong term. In its mildest form, it betokens religious struggle on behalf of faith, a kind of Islamic zeal. In its strongest political manifestation, it means bloody holy war on behalf of partisan identity that is metaphysically defined and fanatically defended. Thus, while for many Muslims it may signify only ardor in the name of a religion that can properly be regarded as universalizing (if not quite ecumenical), I borrow its meaning from those militants who make the slaughter of the "other" a higher duty. I use the term in its militant construction to suggest dogmatic and violent particularism of a kind known to Christians no less than Muslims, to Germans and Hindis as well as to Arabs. The phenomena to which I apply the phrase have innocent enough beginnings: identity politics and multicultural diversity can represent strategies of a free society trying to give expression to its diversity. What ends as Jihad may begin as a simple search for a local identity, some set of common personal attributes to hold out against the numbing and neutering uniformities of industrial modernization and the colonizing culture of McWorld.

America is often taken as the model for this kind of benign multiculturalism, although we too have our critics like Arthur Schlesinger, Jr., for whom multiculturalism is never benign and for whom it signals the inaugural logic of a long-term disintegration. Indeed, I will have occasion below to write about an "American Jihad" being waged by the radical Right. The startling fact is that less than 10 percent (about twenty) of the modern world's states are truly homogenous and thus, like Denmark or the Netherlands, can't get smaller unless they fracture into tribes or clans. In only half is there a single ethnic group that comprises even 75 percent of the population. As in the United States, multiculturalism is the rule, homogeneity the exception. Nations like Japan or Spain that appear to the outside world as integral turn out to be remarkably multicultural. And even if language alone, the nation's essential attribute, is made the condition for self-determination, a count of the number of languages spoken around the world suggests the community of nations could grow to over six thousand members.

The modern nation-state has actually acted as a cultural integrator and has adapted well to pluralist ideals: civic ideologies and constitutional faiths around which their many clans and tribes can rally. It has not been too difficult to contrive a civil religion for Americans or French or Swiss, since these "peoples" actually contain multitudes of subnational factions and ethnic tribes earnestly seeking common ground. But for Basques and Normans? What need have they for anything but blood and memory? And what of Alsatians, Bavarians, and East Prussians? Kurds, Ossetians, East Timorese, Quebecois, Abkhazians, Catalonians, Tamils, Inkatha Zulus, Kurile Islander Japanese — peoples without countries inhabiting nations they cannot call their own? Peoples trying to seal themselves off not just from others but from modernity? These are frightened tribes running not to but from civic faith in search of something more palpable and electrifying. How will peoples who define themselves by the slaughter of tribal neighbors be persuaded to subscribe to some flimsy artificial faith organized around abstract civic ideals or commercial markets? Can advertising divert warriors of blood from the genocide required by their ancient grievances?

Like McWorld, Jihad can of course be painted in bright as well as dark colors. Just as McWorld's sometimes rapacious markets have been advanced in the name of democratic free choice, so Jihad's combative interests can be touted in the name of self-determination. Indeed, the ideology of self-determination may be the source of more than a few of Jihad's pathologies. President Woodrow Wilson's own secretary of state, Robert L. Lansing, failed to share his chief's enthusiasm for the idea, asking would not self-determination "breed discontent, disorder and rebellion? The phrase is simply loaded with dynamite. It will raise hopes which can never be realized. It will, I fear, cost thousands of lives. What a calamity that the phrase was ever uttered! What misery it will cause!"

Lansing's anxieties seem well justified. In Wilson's own time, the politics of self-determination balkanized Europe, fanned nationalist wildfires, and created instabilities that contributed to the rise of fascism. Today there is no tribe, no faction or splinter group or neighborhood gang, that does not aspire to self-determination. "Don't dis me!" shouts the gangsta rapper, "I gotta get some respect." The futile Owen-Vance map for the partition of Bosnia, multiplying boundaries as it narrowed the compass of ethnic communities, finally seemed to give respectability to a gang logic, trying to write into law the absurdity of treating nearly each city block as a nation, almost every housing unit a potential sovereign. In other times, this bankrupt political arrangement, sanctioned for a considerable time by a desperate United Nations Security Council, would carry the name anarchy.

One cannot really blame the cartographers or peacemakers for Jihad's absurdity, however.

They do not rearrange the scene, they just take snapshots of it. Multiculturalism has in some places conjured anarchy. Self-determination has at times amounted to little more than other-extermination. Colonial masters did still worse in their time, drawing arbitrary lines across maps they could not read with consequences still being endured throughout the ex-colonial world, above all in Africa and the Middle East. Jihad is then a rabid response to colonialism and imperialism and their economic children, capitalism and modernity; it is diversity run amok, multiculturalism turned cancerous so that the cells keep dividing long after their division has ceased to serve the healthy corpus.

Even traditionally homogenous integral nations have reason to feel anxious about the prospect of Jihad. The rising economic and communications interdependence of the world means that such nations, however unified internally, must nonetheless operate in an increasingly multicultural global environment. Ironically, a world that is coming together pop culturally and commercially is a world whose discrete subnational ethnic and religious and racial parts are also far more in evidence, in no small part as a reaction to McWorld. Forced into incessant contact, post-modern nations cannot sequester their idiosyncracies. Post-Maastricht Europe, while it falls well short of earlier ambitions, has become integrated enough to force a continent-wide multicultural awareness whose consequences have by no means been happy, let alone unifying. The more "Europe" hoves into view, the more reluctant and self-aware its national constituents become. What Günter Grass said of Germany — "unified, the Germans were more disunited than ever" — applies in spades to Europe and the world beyond: integrated, it is more disintegral than ever.

Responding to McWorld, parochial forces defend and deny, reject and repel modernity wherever they find it. But they also absorb and assimilate, utilizing the native's strategy against every colonizer to have crossed a border since the Romans came to Gaul. When the Hilton came to the Hills of Buda, a local architect grafted the new structure onto a thirteenth-century monastery. When the French restored the Champs

Élysées to its former glory, they banished the arch from McDonald's. When American music invaded the Caribbean, Orlando Patterson reminds us, the Caribbean reacted with enormous music production of its own, of which reggae is only one well-known example. Yet to think that indigenization and globalization are entirely coequal forces that put Jihad and McWorld on an equal footing is to vastly underestimate the force of the new planetary markets. The Budapest Hilton's "monastery" houses a casino; Paris's McDonald's serves Big Macs and fries with or without the arch; reggae gets only a tiny percentage of MTV play time even in Latin markets. It's no contest.

A pattern of feudal relations does, however, persist. And so we are returned to the metaphor of feudalism, that puzzling world of fragments knit together by the abstraction of Christianity. Today's abstraction is the consumers' market, no less universal for all its insistent materialist secularism. Following McDonald's golden arch from country to country, the market traces a trajectory of dollars and bonds and ads and yen and stocks and currency transactions that reaches right around the globe. Grass's observation works the other way around as well: disunited, pulled apart by Jihad, the world is more united than ever. And more interdependent as well.

The Smalling World of McWorld

Even the most developed, supposedly self-sufficient nations can no longer pretend to genuine sovereignty. That is the meaning of *ecology*, a term that marks the final obsolescence of all man-made boundaries. When it comes to acid rain or oil spills or depleted fisheries or tainted groundwater or fluorocarbon propellants or radiation leaks or toxic wastes or sexually transmitted diseases, national frontiers are simply irrelevant. Toxins don't stop for customs inspections and microbes don't carry passports. North America became a water and air free-trade zone long before NAFTA loosened up the market in goods.

The environmental tocsin has been sounded, loudly and often, and there is little to add here to the prodigious literature warning of a biospherical Armageddon. We have learned well enough how easily the German forests can be devastated by Swiss and Italians driving gas-guzzling roadsters fueled by leaded gas (the Europeans are far behind the Americans in controlling lead). We know that the planet can be asphyxiated by greenhouse gases because Brazilian farmers want to be part of the twentieth century and are burning down their tropical rain forests to clear a little land to plow, and because many Indonesians make a living out of converting their lush jungles into toothpicks for fastidious Japanese diners, upsetting the delicate oxygen balance and puncturing our global lungs.

Ecological interdependence is, however, reactive: a consequence of natural forces we cannot predict or fully control. But McWorld's interdependence and the limits it places on sovereignty is more a matter of positive economic forces that have globalism as their conscious object. It is these economic and commercial forces — the latest round in capitalism's long-standing search for world markets and global consumers — that are the primary subject of this book.

Every demarcated national economy and every kind of public good is today vulnerable to the inroads of transnational commerce. Markets abhor frontiers as nature abhors a vacuum. Within their expansive and permeable domains, interests are private, trade is free, currencies are convertible, access to banking is open, contracts are enforceable (the state's sole legitimate economic function), and the laws of production and consumption are sovereign, trumping the laws of legislatures and courts. In Europe, Asia, and the Americas such markets have already eroded national sovereignty and given birth to a new class of institutions — international banks, trade associations, transnational lobbies like OPEC, world news services like CNN and the BBC, and multinational corporations — institutions that lack distinctive national identities and neither reflect nor respect nationhood as an organizing or a regulative principle. While mills and factories sit somewhere on sovereign territory under the eye and potential regulation of nation-states, currency markets and the Internet exist everywhere, but nowhere in particular. Without an address or

a national affiliation, they are altogether beyond the devices of sovereignty. Even products are becoming anonymous: whose national workforce do you fault on a defective integrated circuit labeled:

> Made in one or more of the following countries: Korea, Hong Kong, Malaysia, Singapore, Taiwan, Mauritius, Thailand, Indonesia, Mexico, Philippines. The exact country of origin is unknown.

How are the social and political demands of responsibility preserved under such remarkable circumstances?

The market imperative has in fact reinforced the quest for international peace and stability, requisites of an efficient international economy, without improving the chances for civic responsibility, accountability, or democracy, which may or may not benefit from commerce and free markets and which, although it depends on peace, is not synonymous with it. The claim that democracy and markets are twins has become a commonplace of statesmanship, especially in light of the demise of state socialism, which has left capitalism's zealots free to regard themselves not only as victors in the Cold War but as the true champions of a democracy that (they are certain) markets alone make possible. Thus have they managed to parlay the already controversial claim that markets are free into the even more controversial claim that market freedom entails and even defines democracy. President Clinton employed the phrase *democratic markets* as a mantra during his historic visit to Eastern Europe and Russia at the beginning of 1994. His foreign policy aides have consistently done the same.

This stealth rhetoric that assumes capitalist interests are not only compatible with but actively advance democratic ideals, translated into policy, is difficult to reconcile with the international realities of the last fifty years. Market economies have shown a remarkable adaptability and have flourished in many tyrannical states from Chile to South Korea, from Panama to Singapore. Indeed, the state with one of the world's least democratic governments — the People's Republic of

China—possesses one of the world's fastest-growing market economies. "Communist" Vietnam is not far behind, and was opened to American trade recently, presumably on the strength of the belief that markets ultimately defeat ideology. Capitalism requires consumers with access to markets and a stable political climate in order to succeed: such conditions may or may not be fostered by democracy, which can be disorderly and even anarchic, especially in its early stages, and which often pursues public goods costly to or at odds with private-market imperatives — environmentalism or full employment for example. On the level of the individual, capitalism seeks consumers susceptible to the shaping of their needs and the manipulation of their wants while democracy needs citizens autonomous in their thoughts and independent in their deliberative judgments. Aleksandr Solzhenitsyn wishes to "tame savage capitalism," but capitalism wishes to tame anarchic democracy and appears to have little problem tolerating tyranny as long as it secures stability.

Certainly the hurried pursuit of free markets regardless of social consequences has put democratic development in jeopardy in many nations recently liberated from communism. Social insecurity and rampant unemployment for peoples accustomed to the cradle-to-the-grave ministrations of paternalistic socialist bureacracies are unlikely to convert them to a system of democracy for which they have otherwise had no preparation. This is perhaps why majorities in all but a handful of ex-Soviet lands have been busy reelecting former Communist officials (usually wearing new party labels and carrying new ideological doctrines) to their new democratic legislatures. In economist Robert McIntyre's blunt words: "Communists and former Communists are winning because the Western economic advice has led to pointless, dysfunctional pain, while failing to set the foundations for politically and socially viable future growth." The right to choose between nine VCR models or a dozen automobile brands does not necessarily feel like freedom to workers whose monthly salaries can hardly keep up with the rising price of bread, let alone to women and men with no jobs at all.

Capitalists may be democrats but capitalism does not need or entail democracy. And capitalism certainly does not need the nation-state that has been democracy's most promising host.

This is not to criticize capitalism in and of itself: joint-stock, limited-liability corporations are quite properly interested primarily in profits and pursue civic liberty and social justice only where they do not interfere with the bottom line. Indeed, they have certain conspicuous virtues beyond their intrinsic economic utilities like efficiency, productivity, elasticity, profitability. They are enemies of parochialism, isolation, fractiousness, and war and are hostile to constraints on economic choice and social mobility, although this hardly makes them friends of justice. Market psychology also can attenuate the psychology of ideological and religious cleavages and nurture concord among producers and consumers, identities that ill-suit Jihad's narrowly conceived ethnic or religious cultures. But it also undermines the psychology of skeptical inquiry upon which autonomous judgment and resistance to manipulation are founded. In the world of McWorld, the alternative to dogmatic tradionalism may turn out to be materialist consumerism or relativistic secularism or merely a profitable corruption. Democracy's ties to McWorld are at best contingent. Shopping, it is true, has little tolerance for blue laws, whether dictated by pub-closing British paternalism, Sabbath-observing Jewish Orthodoxy, or no-Sunday-liquor-sales Massachusetts Puritanism; but intolerance for blue laws is hardly a condition for constitutional faith or a respect for due process. In the context of common markets, international law has largely ceased to be a vision of justice and has become a workaday framework for getting things done: enforcing contracts, certifying deals, regulating trade and currency relations, and supervising mergers or bankruptcies. Moralists used to complain that international law was impotent in curbing the injustices of nation-states, but it has shown even less capacity to rein in markets that, after all, do not even have an address to which subpoenas can be sent. As the product of a host of individual choices or singular corporate acts, markets offer no collective responsibility. Yet responsibility is the first obligation of both citizens and civic institutions.

While they produce neither common interests nor common law, common markets do demand, along with a common currency, a common language; moreover, they produce common behaviors of the kind bred by cosmopolitan city life everywhere. Commercial pilots, computer programmers, film directors, international bankers, media specialists, oil riggers, entertainment celebrities, ecology experts, movie producers, demographers, accountants, professors, lawyers, athletes — these compose a new breed of men and women for whom religion, culture, and ethnic nationality are marginal elements in a working identity. Although sociologists of everyday life will continue to distinguish a Japanese from an American mode, shopping has a common signature throughout the world. Cynics might even suggest that some of the recent revolutions in Eastern Europe had as their true goal not liberty and the right to vote but well-paying jobs and the right to shop. Shopping means consumption and consumption depends on the fabrication of needs as well as of goods in what I will call the infotainment telesector of the service economy.

McWorld is a product of popular culture driven by expansionist commerce. Its template is American, its form style. Its goods are as much images as matériel, an aesthetic as well as a product line. It is about culture as commodity, apparel as ideology. Its symbols are Harley-Davidson motorcycles and Cadillac motorcars hoisted from the roadways, where they once represented a mode of transportation, to the marquees of global market cafés like Harley-Davidson's and the Hard Rock where they become icons of lifestyle. You don't drive them, you feel their vibes and rock to the images they conjure up from old movies and new celebrities, whose personal appearances are the key to the wildly popular international café chain Planet Hollywood. Music, video, theater, books, and theme parks — the new churches of a commercial civilization in which malls are the public squares and suburbs the neighborless neighborhoods — are all constructed as image exports creating a common world taste around common logos, advertising slogans, stars, songs, brand names, jingles, and trademarks. Hard power yields to soft, while ideology is transmuted into a kind of videology that works through sound bites and film clips. Videology is fuzzier and less dogmatic than traditional political ideology: it may as a consequence be far more successful in instilling the novel values required for global markets to succeed.

McWorld's videology remains Jihad's most formidable rival, and in the long run it may attenuate the force of Jihad's recidivist tribalisms. Yet the information revolution's instrumentalities are also Jihad's favored weapons. Hutu or Bosnian Serb identity was less a matter of real historical memory than of media propaganda by a leadership set on liquidating rival clans. In both Rwanda and Bosnia, radio broadcasts whipped listeners into a killing frenzy. As *New York Times* rock critic Jon Pareles has noticed, "regionalism in pop music has become as trendy as microbrewery beer and narrowcasting cable channels, and for the same reasons." The global culture is what gives the local culture its medium, its audience, and its aspirations. Fascist pop and Hasid rock are not oxymorons; rather they manifest the dialectics of McWorld in particularly dramatic ways. Belgrade's radio includes stations that broadcast Western pop music as a rebuke to hardliner Milosevic's supernationalist government and stations that broadcast native folk tunes laced with antiforeign and anti-Semitic sentiments. Even the Internet has its neo-Nazi bulletin boards and Turk-trashing Armenian "flamers" (who assail every use of the word *turkey,* fair and fowl alike, so to speak), so that the abstractions of cyberspace too are infected with a peculiar and rabid cultural territoriality all their own.

The dynamics of the Jihad-McWorld linkage are deeply dialectical. Japan has, for example, become more culturally insistent on its own traditions in recent years even as its people seek an ever greater purchase on McWorld. In 1992, the number-one restaurant in Japan measured by volume of customers was McDonald's, followed in the number-two spot by the Colonel's Kentucky Fried Chicken. In France, where cultural purists complain bitterly of a looming Sixième République ("la République Américaine"), the government attacks "franglais" even as it funds EuroDisney park just outside of Paris. In the same spirit, the cinema industry makes war on American film imports while it bestows upon Sylvester Stallone one of France's highest honors, the Chevalier des arts et lettres. Ambivalence also stalks India. Just outside of Bombay, cheek by jowl with villages still immersed in poverty and notorious for the informal execution of unwanted female babies or, even, wives, can be found a new town known as SCEEPZ — the Santa Cruz Electronic Export Processing Zone — where Hindi-, Tamil-, and Mahratti-speaking computer programmers write software for Swissair, AT&T, and other labor-cost-conscious multinationals. India is thus at once a major exemplar of ancient ethnic and religious tensions and "an emerging power in the international software industry." To go to work at SCEEPZ, says an employee, is "like crossing an international border." Not into another country, but into the virtual nowhere-land of McWorld.

More dramatic even than in India, is the strange interplay of Jihad and McWorld in the remnants of Yugoslavia. In an affecting *New Republic* report, Slavenka Drakulic recently told the brief tragic love story of Admira and Bosko, two young star-crossed lovers from Sarajevo: "They were born in the late 1960's," she writes. "They watched Spielberg movies; they listened to Iggy Pop; they read John le Carré; they went to a disco every Saturday night and fantasized about traveling to Paris or London." Longing for safety, it seems they finally negotiated with all sides for safe passage, and readied their departure from Sarajevo. Before they could cross the magical border that separates their impoverished land from the seeming sanctuary of McWorld, Jihad caught up to them. Their bodies lay along the riverbank, riddled with bullets from anonymous snipers for whom safe passage signaled an invitation to target practice. The murdered young lovers, as befits émigrés to McWorld, were clothed in jeans and sneakers. So too, one imagines, were their murderers.

Further east, tourists seeking a piece of old Russia that does not take them too far from MTV can find traditional Matryoshka nesting dolls (that fit one inside the other) featuring the nontraditional visages of (from largest to smallest) Bruce Springsteen, Madonna, Boy George, Dave Stewart, and Annie Lennox.

In Russia, in India, in Bosnia, in Japan, and in France too, modern history then leans both ways: toward the meretricious inevitability of McWorld, but also into Jihad's stiff winds, heaving to and fro and giving heart both to the Panglossians and the Pandoras, sometimes for the very same reasons. The Panglossians bank on Euro-Disney and Microsoft, while the Pandoras await nihilism and a world in Pandaemonium. Yet McWorld and Jihad do not really force a choice between such polarized scenarios. Together, they are likely to produce some stifling amalgam of the two suspended in chaos. Antithetical in every detail, Jihad and McWorld nonetheless conspire to undermine our hard-won (if only half-won) civil liberties and the possibility of a global democratic future. In the short run the forces of Jihad, noisier and more obviously nihilistic than those of McWorld, are likely to dominate the near future, etching small stories of local tragedy and regional genocide on the face of our times and creating a climate of instability marked by multimicrowars inimical to global integration. But in the long run, the forces of McWorld are the forces underlying the slow certain thrust of Western civilization and as such may be unstoppable. Jihad's microwars will hold the headlines well into the next century, making predictions of the end of history look terminally dumb. But McWorld's homogenization is likely to establish a macropeace that favors the triumph of commerce and its markets and to give to those who control information, communication, and entertainment ultimate (if inadvertent) control over human destiny. Unless we can offer an alternative to the struggle between Jihad and McWorld, the epoch on whose threshold we stand — postcommunist, postindustrial, postnational, yet sectarian, fearful, and bigoted — is likely also to be terminally postdemocratic.

5.5 Terrorism and Morality

One day when we were having a lively discussion of terrorism in one of my classes, a student suddenly asked, "So what is really wrong with terrorism?" The room fell silent and after the initial shock wore off, someone said, "What a stupid question!"

Is it not the case that terrorism is self-evidently wrong? We don't have to figure out what is wrong about it; everyone knows it is morally reprehensible. If that is the case, then one wonders why so many people have been and are willing to engage in terrorist acts. The picture gets complicated when we realize that terrorists usually feel morally justified. They see themselves as doing the right thing, not the wrong thing. Of course we can always say that they are deluded, or insane, or gravely (no pun intended) misled. Somehow these responses seem inadequate when we confront the sincerity of terrorists' beliefs and the integrity, even to the point of suicide (or martyrdom depending on one's perspective), of their actions.

One reason terrorists, especially those who are politically or religiously motivated, feel morally justified in terrorizing others is because they approach terrorism from the "just war" tradition. According to that tradition, one of the conditions (among others) that justifies violence is that the use of force is in a "just cause." If the critics of terrorism also approach the issue of the morality of terrorism from the "just war" tradition, they share the same general moral framework as the terrorists. The major difference is that those who condemn terrorism do not see the cause of the terrorist as just, or at least just enough to warrant violence against innocent people.

Bat-Ami Bar On, a professor of philosophy at the State University of New York at Binghamton, argues in the next selection that philosophers and others who think about terrorism from the viewpoint of an ethic of justice or rights miss one of the most important features of terrorism, one that makes it immoral. If we morally assess terrorism from the ethic of care perspective, then it is cruelty, not unjust causes, that emerge as the central moral problem with terrorism. Bat-Ami Bar On wrote this essay before 9/11. However much the events of that dreaded day may have changed the world, her ideas about terrorism and violence are still relevant. Read it and see if you agree.

Reading Questions

1. How does the author define terrorism, and why does she reject any sharp conceptual difference between a terrorist and a freedom fighter?
2. What do terrorism, "seasoning," and torture have in common as a "formative process"?
3. Why is cruelty immoral?
4. What is the "just war" tradition, and why, according to Bat-Ami Bar On, is it inadequate for understanding what is morally problematic about terrorism?
5. Do you agree with the author that the essential fact about terrorism that makes it immoral is cruelty? Why, or why not?

Why Terrorism Is Morally Problematic *

BAT-AMI BAR ON

IN MY LIFE and in the lives of members of my family, terrorism has been a formative force. In this essay I will examine how terrorism forms the terrorized. I will argue that what is morally problematic about terrorism is that it produces people who are psychologically and morally diminished and it is, therefore, cruel. This brute fact is not addressed by the standard moral arguments offered by contemporary philosophers about terrorism. Those arguments appeal to the "just war" tradition and thus to abstract principles. Looking at the way in which terrorism forms the terrorized reveals that such appeals are insufficient to condemn and especially to condone terrorism.

That terrorism operates psychologically in certain ways became clearest for me just after the *intifada*[1] started. I was in Israel and talking with one of my cousins about the situation. I argued that the formation of an independent Palestinian state was the only realistic compromise solution to the Jewish-Israeli[2]–Palestinian conflict. I was told in response that the formation of an independent Palestinian state would endanger the state of Israel with a war. When I claimed that the *intifada* together with the militarily enforced

official Israeli repression constitute a war, I was told that at least this war is not happening within Israel's borders and thus does not endanger the majority of the Jewish-Israeli population.

I realized as the discussion developed that my cousin genuinely believed that for the Palestinians an independent state would be first and foremost a means to assert a destructive power against her and her family and against the Jewish-Israeli population. Motivating this belief was a deep-seated fear that also motivated a clinging to the Israeli military as the only shield against the expected destruction and a commitment to the deployment and use, including inhumane use, of the military against the Palestinians.

Since Jewish-Israeli life within the 1948 disengagement lines, which delineate what is popularly believed to form the pre-1967 Israeli borders, seemed undisturbed by the *intifada*, my cousin's fear can make sense only given the history of the Jewish-Israeli–Palestinian relationship. Looked at from the Jewish-Israeli perspective, this relationship has been colored by Palestinian terrorism ever since the beginning of Jewish settlement in the area at the end of the nineteenth century. My cousin's fear, a fear I recognize in myself, is a product of growing up under and living with the constant threat of terrorism. Although this threat was magnified by the Israeli government's official pronouncements and the official history of Israel,[3] it was nonetheless real.

---

* Versions of this chapter were read at the SUNY College at Oswego and at Le Moyne College. I would like to thank the Central New York Feminist Philosophers Study Group, Sandra Bartky, and Claudia Card for their insightful comments.

1. The *intifada* is the Palestinian uprising in the areas that were occupied by the state of Israel in the 1967 Six Days War. Following the Israeli War of Independence in 1948, these areas were held by Jordan (the West Bank, or Judaea and Samaria) and Egypt (the Gaza Strip), respectively. The *intifada* began in December 1988. Its declared end is the formation of an independent Palestinian state.

2. I am using the term "Jewish-Israeli" in order both to emphasize the multinational character of the Israeli population in which the Jews form the majority, and to locate the conflict more accurately.

3. Recent revisionist historical work is very suggestive. See, for example, Bernard Avishai, *The Tragedy of Zionism: Revolution and Democracy in the Land of Israel* (New York: Farrar, Straus, Giroux, 1985); Simha Flapan, *The Birth of Israel: Myths and Realities* (New York: Pantheon, 1987); Yosef Gorny, *The Arab Question and the Jewish Problem* (Tel-Aviv: Am Oved, 1985); and Michael Janson, *Dissonance in Zion* (London: Zed, 1987).

From Bat-Ami Bar On, "Why Terrorism Is Morally Problematic," Feminist Ethics, *edited by Claudia Card. Lawrence, KA: The University Press of Kansas, 1991, 107–125. ©1991 by the University Press of Kansas. Footnotes edited. Reprinted by permission.*

For the purpose of this essay the only salient fact about terrorism is that it is a practice of terrorization in which terror is a means to an end other than itself.[4] The means used to terrorize, the possible distinctions among the ends, and the practitioners of terrorism are all insignificant insofar as this essay is concerned. Knowing the means, ends, and practitioners may help one to list the different kinds of terrorism, to chart it historically and culturally, to understand the relation between it and technology, or to see its place in local or global social, political, or economic structures or power relations.[5] But knowledge of the means, ends, and practitioners of terrorism does not shed light on terrorism as a formative process.

Letting terrorism be understood as a practice of terrorization in which terror is a means to an end other than itself does not permit one to categorize as terroristic a random attack on a school by a psychotic person, no matter how violent and terrifying, since it is not a means to a further end. On the other hand, such a conception of terrorism does permit one to categorize as terroristic certain practices of nation-states — for example,

the repressive actions of the Argentinian junta during the "dirty war," the nuclear strategies of the United States and the USSR, the actions of criminal organizations such as the Colombian drug cartel, and the U.S. government's tactics of intimidation against organized crime — since they do have ends other than terrorization.

The inclusive conception of terrorism that I have adopted here would trouble anyone committed to a distinction between terrorism and freedom fighting, be the source of the commitment politically on the left or on the right — hence, a commitment to the work of groups such as the El Salvadoran Farabundo Marti National Liberation Front (FMLN), or the Afghan Mujahadin, respectively. Conor Cruise O'Brien, who believes that a distinction between freedom fighters and terrorists is viable, says:

> We reserve the use [of the words "terrorism" and "terrorist"] in practice for politically motivated violence *of which we disapprove*. The words imply a judgement about the political context in which those whom we decide to call terrorists operate, and above all about the nature of the regime under which and against which they operate. We imply that the regime itself is *legitimate*. If we call them "freedom fighters" we imply that the regime is illegitimate.

O'Brien's claims, which focus on what he calls "politically motivated violence," first suggest that in ordinary usage "terrorism" and "freedom fighting" are terms used not merely to describe but also to morally condemn and commend. His analysis then points out that the basis for the moral condemnation or commendation is the end of the "politically motivated violence" and that it is the ends with the moral meanings attached to them that are used to distinguish between terrorism and freedom fighting.

Although O'Brien's analysis of the ordinary usage of terrorism and freedom fighting is not wrong, the ordinary-language distinction between the two terms is not strong enough to be able to claim that the two are conceptually distinct. They are not. The ordinary-usage distinction between terrorism and freedom fighting presupposes that the ends of a practice are the necessary and sufficient criteria to distinguish

4. There are many discussions of the definition of terrorism and a consensus on the use of terrorization as a means to an end in terrorism. The following are a few examples of analyses of the concept of terrorism: Eugene Victor Walter, "Violence and the Process of Terror," *American Sociological Review* 29, no. 2 (April 1964): 248–257; Grant Wardlaw, "The Problem of Defining Terrorism," in Wardlaw, *Political Terrorism: Theory, Tactics, and Counter-Measures* (Cambridge: Cambridge University Press, 1982), 3–17; and Carl Wellman, "On Terrorism Itself," *Journal of Value Inquiry* 13 (1979): 250–258.

5. For attempts to list, chart, and understand the history, culture, and social, economic, and political place of terrorism, see H. Edward Price, Jr., "The Strategy and Tactics of Revolutionary Terrorism," *Comparative Studies in Society and History* 19 (1977): 52–66; Luigi Bonanate, "Some Unanticipated Consequences of Terrorism," *Journal of Peace Research* 16 (1979): 192–212; William Gutteridge (editor for the Institute for the Study of Conflict), *Contemporary Terrorism* (New York: Facts on File, 1986); Alberto Melucci, "New Movements, Terrorism, and the Political System: Reflections on the Italian Case," *Socialist Review* 11, no. 2 (March–April 1981): 97–136; Christopher Dobson and Ronald Payne, *The Terrorists: Their Weapons, Leaders, and Tactics* (New York: Facts on File, 1982); and Noel O'Sullivan, ed., *Terrorism, Ideology, and Revolution: The Origins of Modern Political Violence* (Brighton, England: Wheatsheaf Books, 1986).

among practices, and this is just not so. Furthermore, according to the ordinary usage, the terms "terrorism" and "freedom fighting" have certain normative connotations that are important for the distinction between them. Yet these connotations are simply the products of Western politics.

"Terrorism" as a negative term was coined in 1795 by the French Directory to refer specifically to the repressive measures practiced by Robespierre's government. It later was used to describe the activities of nineteenth-century clandestine oppositional groups in Russia. Not surprisingly, because these groups were considered revolutionary, "terrorism" retained its negative connotations in the dictionaries of the time even though these groups were different from the French revolutionaries, and their ends differed also. Furthermore, these groups did not necessarily consider themselves terroristic, and if they did, they viewed terrorism positively. As they saw it, they were freedom fighters.

I think this brief discussion shows that terrorism and freedom fighting are not conceptually distinct and thus that terrorists can be freedom fighters and freedom fighters can be terrorists. One could similarly show that other distinctions people attempt to make to save some action from being classified as terroristic will not work. If terrorism is a practice, then, as uncomfortable as it may be to think so, the Allies' strategic use of air raids against the German civilian population during the Second World War was as terroristic as the Germans' bombardment of London with V rockets. The Irish Republican Army relies on terrorism in its war of liberation, as did the Palestine Liberation Organization. And the South African and Salvadoran death squads, even if only covertly supported by their governments, are also terroristic.

Suppose, then, that terrorism is a practice of terrorization in which terror is a means to an end other than itself. What can be said about it as a process through which the terrorized are formed?

In *The Demon Lover: On the Sexuality of Terrorism,* Robin Morgan claims that terrorism democratizes violence and brings men to experience the world in relation to each other similarly, though not identically, to how women experience the world in relation to men. She begins with the description of the woman.

> Look closely at her. She crosses a city street, juggling her briefcase and her sack of groceries. Or she walks down the dirt road, balancing a basket on her head. Or she hurries toward her locked car, pulling a small child along with her. Or she trudges home from the fields, the baby strapped to her back. Suddenly there are footsteps behind her. Heavy, rapid. A man's footsteps. She knows this immediately, just as she knows that she must not look around. She quickens her pace in time to the quickening of her pulse. She is afraid. He could be a rapist. He could be a soldier, a harasser, a robber, a killer. He could be none of these. He could be a man in a hurry. He could be a man merely walking at his normal pace. But she fears him. She fears him because he is a man. She has reason to fear. She does not feel the same way — on a city street or dirt road, in parking lot or field — if she hears a woman's footsteps behind her.

Morgan later adds the comparable description of the man:

> Now look closely at him. He hurries through the airport to catch his plane. Or he pedals his bicycle, basket laden with books to the university. Or he mounts the steps to his embassy on official business. Or he snaps a fresh roll of film into his camera and starts out on an assignment. Suddenly, there are footsteps behind him. Heavy, rapid. A man's footsteps. In the split second before he turns around, he knows he's afraid. he tells himself he has no reason to fear. But he fears. *He does not feel the same way if he hears a woman's footsteps behind him.*

Morgan's descriptions make it vividly clear that as a formative process, terrorism produces people who are afraid. Terrorized people's fear is deep and easily triggered by the slightest indication of possible danger. Yet the fear is triggered by things and movements that are not extraordinary within an ordinary day-to-day context. And the day-to-day ordinariness of the terrorized circumstances does not dissipate the fear.

Morgan does not talk about the consequences of living a life in which fear is triggered so easily under what should be ordinary circumstances. Some of the consequences are described by Leo Lowenthal in his "Terror's Atomization of Man," an essay written in 1946 about fascist state terrorism. According to Lowenthal, terrorism interrupts the causal relation between what people do and what happens to them. As a result, the terrorized's sense of a continuous experience and memory weakens and even breaks down. This in turn leads to a shrinking or breakdown of personality.

How this happens can be clarified somewhat by a comparison of terrorism with seasoning, the process used by pimps to form prostitutes. Kathleen Barry discusses the process in *Female Sexual Slavery*, and Marilyn Frye elaborates on it in *The Politics of Reality*. Frye writes:

> While he holds her in captivity and isolation he brutalizes the victim in as many ways as there are to brutalize. . . . The abductor's brutality functions in several ways. By placing the victim in a life-threatening and absolutely aversive situation, he maximizes the urgency of the victim's taking action in her own behalf while making it utterly impossible for her to do so. This puts maximum force into the process of alienating her from herself through total helplessness. The result is radical loss of self-esteem, self-respect and any sense of capacity or agency. . . . After having been in a situation where her presence as agent has been reduced to nothing, she now has the opportunity to try to act in support of her physical survival. She can try to discover what pleases and what displeases the man, and try to please him and avoid displeasing him.

Like seasoning, terrorism places its victims in a life-threatening situation in which one feels both a need to do something to save oneself and a helplessness. The terrorized too will experience an alienation from self and a loss of the sense of oneself as an agent capable of acting on her or his own behalf and deserving of respect. The sense of alienation from self together with the lack of a sense of agency and dignity constitute a dissolution of the individual self. What is left is a will to survive, as evidenced in the case of the victim of

seasoning, who attempts to live through satisfying the pimp.

Another way to understand terrorism as a formative process is by comparing it with torture, which, like seasoning, is also a practice in which brutalization is used as a means to break a person down. In *The Body in Pain*, Elaine Scarry analyzes several aspects of torture. Like Morgan, Scarry begins with the transformation of the ordinary. Like Lowenthal, she emphasizes the consequences of torture, which also constitute the dissolution of the ordinary world. Scarry describes the transformation of a room:

> In torture the world is reduced to a single room or set of rooms. Called "guest rooms" in Greece and "safe houses" in the Philippines, the torture rooms are often given names that acknowledge and call attention to the generous, civilizing impulse normally present in the human shelter. They call attention to the impulse only as a prelude to announcing its annihilation. The torture room is not just the setting in which the torture occurs. . . . It is itself literally converted into another weapon, into an agent of pain. All aspects of the basic structure — walls, ceiling, window, doors — undergo this conversion.

Scarry proceeds from here to focus on the interrogation and its end — the confession — and calls attention to elements that Frye focuses on in her discussion of seasoning. Scarry writes: "Torture systematically prevents the prisoner from being the agent of anything and simultaneously pretends that he is the agent of some things. Despite the fact that in reality he has been deprived of all control over, and therefore all responsibility for, his world, his words, his body, he is to understand his confession as it will be understood by others, as an act of self-betrayal."

It is not only confession that will be experienced as self-betrayal. The torturer controls the tortured body and voice and can make the tortured act or stop acting, speak, sing, or scream or stop speaking, singing, or screaming. The torturer's control is a function of the ability to cause pain, and it is through the experience of pain that the tortured is formed into a self-betrayer because this experience dissolves the distinction between outside and inside the body, conflates the private and the public, destroys language, and obliterates the contents of consciousness.

Like the tortured, the terrorized may come to experience themselves as self-betrayers, and the possibility of self-betrayal is one of the things they fear most, because the terrorized, like the tortured, realize very quickly once their terrorization begins that what is at issue for their tormentors is the length of time it may take for them to break down and betray themselves by accepting the terrorists' demands. Indeed, from the point of view of the terrorist, as from the point of view of the torturer, terrorization consists of a series of tests of strength that are designed to reveal the weakness of their victims to the terrorist and to the victims.

When the victims feel tested, they know that what is being tested is the strength of their will. As they become aware of their weakness, they also become aware of the erosion of their will. This is accompanied by a diminishing sense of self, since under these conditions the self becomes the will. Everything else is stripped away. When the will erodes totally or when it feels as if it has been broken, nothing is left of the self.

One may want to claim that although a comparison of terrorism with seasoning or torture may provide some insight, terrorism actually differs significantly from both because it does not occur in circumstances that allow for the kind of intensity that takes place in seasoning or torture. After all, in the case of terrorism, the terrorized are not totally at the mercy of the terrorists. In fact, only some terrorized are not at the mercy of the terrorists, usually those living under the threat of some form of political terrorism, especially when it is an oppositional practice. When, for example, a state is in the business of terrorizing its citizenry and has in place the organizations necessary for carrying out the terrorizing — such as the Nicaraguan national guard during Somoza's rule — the people are very much at the mercy of their state. Under these conditions, people can usually find refuge from their government only by becoming exiles. Resistance is a viable alternative to exile only when the resistance movement has succeeded in occupying and maintaining a territory in which its members are relatively safe, as the Sandinistas did in Nicaragua.

Still, most torture happens within Goffmanian total institutions such as jails, prisons, concentration camps, and special torture camps. Seasoning has in common with torture the confinement and isolation of its victims. Being and feeling at the mercy of torturers and pimps is the function of the confinement and isolation. Terrorists, on the other hand, do not confine and isolate the terrorized.

Again, much too much is claimed about terrorism in general. But even in the case of those terrorized by oppositional political terrorism — the kind of terrorism that at the outset seems just not to take place in circumstances resembling the confinement and isolation of the tortured — the situation is much more complicated. This fact is testified to by the practices states institute to control terrorism (such as careful inspection of people and luggage in airports) and the general fear that terrorism endangers the liberal democratic state.

This general fear, noted by many contemporary experts on international oppositional political terrorism, causes liberal democratic states to risk violating civil liberties because of the practices they have to institute to prevent terrorism within their borders. To be effective they have to work like a screen that does not permit infiltration by terrorists into the state. They must also facilitate tracing an infiltration if and when it occurs.

Thus in Israel, for example, roads at certain intervals have checkpoints staffed by military personnel, who stop and inspect all cars. For buses, the armed soldiers get in and inspect the luggage racks, making sure that every item has an owner among the people on the bus. To maximize security on its campus, the University of Tel-Aviv is surrounded by a fence, and at the gates, security personnel check every bag that is brought in. Security personnel check every bag brought into every public building in Israel, including movie theaters. Helicopters patrol the seashores on the hour, and a civilian militia patrols them on foot. It also patrols the streets of every town twenty-four hours a day. Children at summer camps and at schools are always accompanied by armed guards on their field trips. Everyone in Israel is expected to carry officially issued identity papers and produce them upon the demand of the police, militia, or army. Everywhere in Israel there are posters that remind the public of terrorism and of the people's obligation to be alert and vigilant, to always survey their environment for suspicious items, movement, or individuals.

These various practices instituted by states to combat terrorism confine and isolate the citizenry and put it under constant surveillance. Surveillance makes one feel simultaneously safer and more vulnerable. One feels safer because one feels protected by it. But at the same time, one feels more exposed and not only to one's own government, especially if terrorists have been successful in their attempts, because this means that they are even better at surveillance than the government. The consequences of this state of affairs are best captured by Foucault's explanation of the workings of Bentham's panopticon in *Discipline and Punish*. According to him the panoptic mechanism arranges things so that it is possible to see everyone constantly and recognize everyone immediately, and anyone can use it at anytime. The effect is to induce in those who are observed a state of conscious and permanent visibility that assures the automatic functioning of power.

Thus even in the case of terrorists who do not confine and isolate their victims, circumstances are altered in response to their terrorism. The new situation has within it the elements needed to create for the terrorized an intense experience of feeling totally at the mercy of the terrorists. This suffices to start the process of the formation of the self as the self of a terrorized person, a fearful self that contracts and is organized more and more around its experience as a certain level of strength of will.

My description of terrorism can tempt one to argue that what is morally problematic with terrorism is that it is a coercive practice, a practice whose structure Marilyn Frye describes as follows: "The structure of coercion, then, is this: to coerce someone into doing something, one has to manipulate the situation so that the world as perceived by the victim presents the victim with

a range of options the least unattractive of which (or the most attractive of which) in the judgement of the victim is the act one wants the victim to do." But to argue this, though formally correct, requires the conceptual classification of terrorism with practices that do not involve the intentional erosion of selves and the intentional breaking of wills, such as a state's paternalistic imposition of seatbelts, helmets, or a 55-mile-per-hour speed limit. Conceiving terrorism as a practice of terrorization through which a self is intentionally eroded and a will is intentionally broken implies, I believe, that *what morally problematizes terrorism is that it is cruel.*

That cruelty is the crux of what is morally problematic with terrorism becomes clearer when one thinks about the things terrorists do when they terrorize: bombing a city, shooting indiscriminately in an airport, abducting and killing people. Such events provide the occasion for a variety of possible attitudes and moral dispositions toward those who suffer as a result of these terroristic acts. Some people are motivated to help the victims of terrorism. Others are motivated to increase their suffering. The latter disposition is cruelty. One expects people who intentionally induce and increase suffering either to take pleasure in other people's pain or to be indifferent to it. Tom Regan notes these two kinds of cruelty in "Cruelty, Kindness, and Unnecessary Suffering."

> The central case of cruelty appears to be the case where, in Locke's apt phase, one takes "a seeming kind of pleasure" in causing another to suffer. . . . Not all cruel people are cruel in this sense. Some cruel people do not take pleasure in making others suffer. Indeed, they seem not to feel anything. Their cruelty is manifested by a lack of what is judged as appropriate feeling . . . for the plight of the individual whose suffering they cause. . . . [T]hey are . . . insensitive to the suffering they inflict, unmoved by it, as if they were unaware of it or failed to appreciate it as suffering.

Terrorists intentionally intensify the suffering of people whom they intentionally victimize. And although they may not take pleasure in this, in some important sense they have to be indifferent to the pain they cause. Sergey Nechaev and Mikhail Bakunin express this clearly in their *Revolutionary Catechism,* written in 1869 for clandestine Russian oppositional groups. In this booklet, they say:

> 1. The revolutionary is a lost man; he has no interests of his own, no cause of his own, no feelings, no habits, no belongings, he does not even have a name. . . .
>
> 2. In the very depths of his being, not just in words but in deed, he has broken every tie with the civil order, with the educated world and all laws, conventions, and generally accepted conditions and with the ethics of this world. . . .
>
> . . .
>
> 6. Hard with himself, he must be hard toward others. All the tender feelings of family life, of friendship, love, gratitude, and even honour must be stifled in him by a single cold passion for the revolutionary cause. . . .
>
> . . .
>
> 13. . . . He is not a revolutionary if he feels pity for anything in this world. If he is able to, he must face the annihilation of a situation, of a relationship, or of any person who is part of this world — everything and everyone must be equally odious to him.

Terrorists are cruel, therefore, not only because they create and worsen in an obvious way the suffering that comes through the body but also because they create the anguish that the terrorized experience as they feel their selves erode and fear they will break.

So, if cruelty morally problematizes terrorism, what, then, is morally wrong with cruelty? It is not easy to capture what is morally wrong with cruelty. But cruelty horrifies, and Steven G. Smith suggests that the repugnance felt is a "protesting recoil from a violation" of normative, value-laden "shoulds" and "should nots." Given Smith's analysis, in the case of a terrorist's cruelty, the violated "should not" seems to be the Kantian categorical imperative prohibiting the use of people as means only. Yet there are also "shoulds" that seem to be violated by cruelty: the "shoulds" of compassion, kindness, and hospitality.

Lawrence Blum believes compassion is directed at "a person in a negative condition, suffering from harm, difficulty, or danger (past, present or future)." He points out that it characteristically involves "imaginative dwelling on the condition of another person, an active regard for his good, a view of him as a fellow human being, and emotional responses of a certain degree of intensity." Tom Regan contrasts cruelty with kindness: "A kind person is one who is inclined (disposed) to act with the intention of forwarding the interest of others, not for reasons of self-gain, but out of love, affection or compassion for the individuals whose interests are forwarded."

Philip Hallie contrasts cruelty with hospitality. In "From Cruelty to Goodness," he says that he learned that the two were opposites after reading about the Huguenot French village of Le Chambon de Ligon, which saved about six thousand people, many of them Jewish children, from the Nazis. The village, whose population was poor, had about thirty-five hundred people. Beginning in 1940, the villagers sheltered the refugees, taking many of them across the mountains to neutral Geneva. What was so special about the villagers of Le Chambon was that they sincerely welcomed the refugees, shared everything they had with them and were surprised when asked why they did it. According to them, even though this endangered them as individuals and as a community, this is what they should have done if they were to manifest their belief in a love for humanity.

Neither cruelty nor compassion, kindness nor hospitality, enters the standard moral discussions of terrorism with their limited focus on political and especially oppositional terrorism. These discussions are usually framed by the Western "just war" tradition. According to this tradition, one has to distinguish between the general question of whether some resort to force is morally justified and the particular question of whether this or that specific form of force is morally justified. The answers to these two questions, which are presumed to be independent of each other, can be found by following certain guidelines. These guidelines define the "just war" tradition.

To assess whether some resort to force is morally justified one needs to decide (1) whether there is a just cause for the use of force, that is, some wrong to be redressed through it; (2) whether there is a legitimate authority seeking to use it, popular support for it, and ways of controlling it; (3) whether force is being used as the last resort; and (4) whether the overall damage that will result from the use of force is at least balanced by the good that will be attained by it. On the other hand, to assess whether a specific form of the use of force is morally justified, one needs to decide (1) what is the balance of proximate good and bad that would result from using a specific form of force, and (2) whether this specific form of force discriminates between combatants and noncombatants.

Michael Walzer frames his discussion of political oppositional terrorism very strictly within the "just war" tradition. He argues that it is morally unjustifiable because it fails to discriminate between combatants and noncombatants. R. M. Hare argues that political oppositional terrorism, which he distinguishes from revolutionary violence, is morally unjustifiable because it leads to more destruction than good. Among the latest variations on both arguments is that of C. A. J. Coady. He argues that no form of political terrorism could be morally justified because it fails to discriminate between combatants and noncombatants and because it is ineffective

Those who morally object to terrorism are not the only ones who rely on the "just war" tradition. Robert Young appeals to this tradition by arguing that revolutionary terrorism is morally justifiable because of its just cause, because it is a tactic of last resort, and because it is more economical than a war, achieving the same results with less destruction. According to Young, even if revolutionary terrorism involves harming noncombatants, it is not ultimately morally unjustifiable. It just requires a more complex justification.

Though the "just war" tradition has provided a framework for the standard discussions of terrorism, most of the arguments either for or against terrorism do not use all of the criteria or guidelines for assessment that the tradition provides. In addition, they do not clearly distinguish between the assessment of use of force in general

and the assessment of a specific use of force. Thus, for example, both Hare and Young, while treating terrorism as a specific use of force, discuss it primarily in terms designed for assessing the use of force in general. And no one seems to bother to assess whether terrorism has a legitimate authority behind it.

For me, this problem of legitimate authority is not as important as the fact that from the beginning of its construction by Augustine, the "just war" tradition was designed to legitimate certain wars. A war's just cause was given priority to make this possible. Limitations on the legitimate use of force were put in place to mitigate its destructiveness. In using the "just war" framework to discuss terrorism, the issue becomes the possibility of its legitimation. Just cause is made the most important criterion of assessment. Destructiveness is a concern only in relation to the possible need to limit it.

I do not know why just cause was given priority over other criteria. I think that concern only about the physical destructiveness of certain forms of force — about the extent of injury, death, and rubble — is much too limited a moral worry, at least in the case of terrorism. The most important issue is not the balance between advantages gained and material destruction. The most important issue is the formation of persons through terrorization and the fact that terrorism requires terrorists to be cruel rather than compassionate, kind, and hospitable.

It could be said that my issue is addressed by concerns about destruction typical of the "just war" tradition because what I worry about is psychic injury, a worry that need not be restricted to the terrorized but can be extended to the terrorist. In the process of terrorization, terrorists also form themselves as psychically injured persons.

Further, if my concerns are seen as belonging to an "ethics of care," which gives precedence to empathy, their conflict with the standard moral discussions of terrorism, insofar as they are framed by the "just war" tradition, can be viewed as a conflict with justice. An "ethics of justice" gives precedence to abstract moral principles concerned with justice, and the "just war" tradition seems to be motivated by concerns situated within this kind of ethics.

However, my concern with how individuals are formed through terrorization, be it the terrorized or the terrorists, is not merely a concern with the physical damage inflicted, and I am not unconcerned with justice. Like others who have tried to argue that an ethics of care and an ethics of justice, though different, are not really in conflict, I am interested in challenging the prioritization of justice and not in its substitution by empathy. Both empathy and justice have to be accorded a serious place in moral thinking.

I am not certain how to accord both empathy and justice a serious place in moral thinking. Yet when I reflect on terrorism, I find that responses to the terrorism of organized crime or perhaps to covert right-wing state terrorism (for example, that practiced in Guatemala) are helpful in clarifying the relation between empathy and justice in the moral assessment of terrorism. As I see it, the difference between the responses to these two forms of terrorism is that though both horrify because both are cruel, the horror in the case of organized crime is not accompanied by surprise at or disillusionment with the cruelty of the criminals, whereas the horror in state terrorism is accompanied by surprise at and disillusionment with the cruelty of politicians. Unlike the terrorism of organized crime, the terrorism of a state against its citizens leaves the victims with a deep sense of betrayal.

I believe this difference in response can be accounted for by expectations from the relation between the ends and the means used to achieve them. The ends of organized crime — the accumulation of wealth and power — do not limit the means that can be used to obtain them. On the other hand, unless one is already disillusioned and corrupted by cynicism, one cannot view the means to the ends that politicians ought to have — the service and maintenance of communities for the good of their members — as independent of these ends. Organized crime can achieve its ends by all means necessary. Criminals need not be just or decent. However, politicians must be just and decent and so cannot use all means necessary to achieve their ends.

Moreover, there are means that would not fit organized crime's ends but would undermine them just as there are means that would not fit the ends that politicians ought to have but would undermine them. Terrorism is not a means that would undermine the ends of organized crime. Yet even if one could show, as the Guatemalan right-wing politicians try to, that terrorism may serve a greater communal good in the future (for example, increase the wealth available for distribution to all the members of the community, thereby making the community better and more just), it is very hard to see how this should count for more than what happens to the people who are terrorized and who terrorize. Terrorism produces fearful people with diminished selves organized around the experience of the fear of the loss of their strength of will. It also produces cruel people, people who feel no compassion or kindness and are inhospitable. Could such people enjoy the promised future goods?

If there is a promised future good whose value seems overwhelming, it is freedom from conditions in which people are formed as they are by terrorism. Contrary to Fanon and Sartre, I doubt very much that such a future can be brought about by terrorism. Fanon's patients are much more resilient than I think people really are, especially given the growing evidence on post-traumatic stress disorder. Post-traumatic stress shapes the lives not only of individuals whose experiences resulted in the stress but the young people who grow up with them as well. The children of Holocaust survivors have Holocaust nightmares.

So in the case of terrorism, it seems that one cannot fail to give precedence to empathy, to concern about what happens to people who are terrorized and to people who terrorize. Yet this concern has its foundation not merely in care for people as individuals and the possibility that they may be harmed but also in care for them as members of communities. As producers and distributors of wealth and power, communities can continue for a long time independently of the kind of people who populate them. But good communities — communities that are fairly just, that get along not only contractually but generously, that take each other concretely into consideration, and whose members are free of daily fears for their survival and physical well-being — these communities need people who care. Neither the terrorized nor the terrorists can care well enough — for themselves or for others.

5.6 *Justice and the Land*

Connect to www.earth.masa.gov. for a glimpse of our home from outer space. This planet earth that we call our home looks beautiful from afar, but looks can be deceiving because runaway pollution already threatens our lives and livelihoods. And what does the future hold? "Imagine a future of relentless storms and floods; islands and heavily inhabited coastal regions inundated by rising sea levels; fertile soils rendered barren by drought and the desert's advance; mass emigrations of environmental refugees; and armed conflicts over water and other precious natural resources."

The preceding quotation concerning a far from rosy future comes from page A18 of *Time*'s special report on the environment (August 26, 2002). The following facts also come from that special report, which was prepared in anticipation of the World Summit 2002 on Sustainable Development held in South Africa.

- By 2050 the earth's population will increase from its present 6.1 billion to 9.3 billion.
- The average temperature of the earth will climb eight degrees Fahrenheit by 2100.
- The United States produces more greenhouse gases per person than any other country.
- More than 15 percent of the Amazon rainforests have been destroyed in only 30 years.
- As much as 86 percent of Indonesia's coral reefs are severely damaged by pollution and overfishing.
- As many as half of all species presently alive could vanish in this century.
- In 25 years two-thirds of the human population may live in countries that are running dangerously short of fresh water.
- Presently one-third of the world goes hungry.
- Wild populations of orangutans have decreased by 50 percent since 1992.

I could go on, but more facts like these just add to the depression and helplessness most of us feel when we read about the environmental destruction of the only home we have. In spite of these less than happy facts, most of the contributors to *Time*'s special report, titled "How to Save the Earth," take a surprisingly optimistic viewpoint. The "future of relentless storms" quickly gives way to a future of "green technologies; livable cities; energy-efficient homes, transport, industry; and rising standards of living for all the world's people. . . ." (A18). The authors of this report devote large amounts of space to new technologies that will save us as well as positive ideas like "sustainable development." Little if any space is given to philosophic ideas that seriously and deeply revise our views concerning humans as part of an ecologically interdependent system that places special moral obligations on them (on us!) with respect to the land that sustains our lives and the lives of the other animals with which we share this beautiful planet. In other words, the notions associated with deep ecology (a term coined by the Norwegian philosopher Arne Naess) about the urgent need to shift from an anthropocentric to a biocentric perspective are overlooked when experts consider "pollution solutions."

Aldo Leopold (1887–1948), the author of the following selection, worked for many years for the U.S. Forestry Service and then taught at the University of Wisconsin, Madison. He is often called the father of wildlife conservation. His book, *A Sand County Almanac,* in which he developed his idea of a "land ethic," reminds us of other great literature on nature, such as the writings of Henry David Thoreau and John Muir.

Leopold's concern for the land extends to all the creatures, human and other-than-human, that the land sustains and nurtures. That concern has not only sparked a variety of movements like deep ecology but also reflections on the morality of humans' treatment of animals. The animal rights movement, for example, finds inspiration in Leopold's work, as well as in the work of the philosopher Peter Singer. For more on animal rights issues and the need to include other-than-human animals in our thinking about justice for *all,* go to http://philosophy.wadsworth.com and select the companion Web site for *Voices of Wisdom.*

Reading Questions

1. How does a land ethic change the role of humans?
2. How does Leopold's definition of conservation relate to his observations about "land as a community"?
3. What is one basic weakness of a conservation system based entirely on economic motives?
4. What is the land pyramid, and why is it important to realize its biotic character?
5. What "general deduction" does Leopold draw from his consideration of the land pyramid?
6. How does Leopold define right and wrong? If you accepted his definition, how might your change your present lifestyle?

The Land Ethic

ALDO LEOPOLD

WHEN GOD-LIKE ODYSSEUS returned from the wars in Troy, he hanged all on one rope a dozen slave-girls of his household whom he suspected of misbehavior during his absence.

This hanging involved no question of propriety. The girls were property. The disposal of property was then, as now, a matter of expediency, not of right and wrong.

Concepts of right and wrong were not lacking from Odysseus' Greece: witness the fidelity of his wife through the long years before at last his black-prowed galleys clove the wine-dark seas for

From Aldo Leopold, A Sand County Almanac. *New York: Oxford University Press, 1949, pp. 217–241. Copyright © 1949, 1977 by Oxford University Press, Inc. Reprinted by permission.*

home. The ethical structure of that day covered wives, but had not yet been extended to human chattels. During the three thousand years which have since elapsed, ethical criteria have been extended to many fields of conduct, with corresponding shrinkages in those judged by expediency only.

The Ethical Sequence

This extension of ethics, so far studied only by philosophers, is actually a process in ecological evolution. Its sequences may be described in ecological as well as in philosophical terms. An ethic, ecologically, is a limitation on freedom of action in the struggle for existence. An ethic, philosophically, is a differentiation of social from anti-social conduct. These are two definitions of one thing. The thing has its origin in the tendency of interdependent individuals or groups to evolve modes of co-operation. The ecologists calls these symbioses. Politics and economics are advanced symbioses in which the original free-for-all competition has been replaced, in part, by co-operative mechanisms with an ethical content.

The complexity of co-operative mechanisms has increased with population density, and with the efficiency of tools. It was simpler, for example, to define the anti-social uses of sticks and stones in the days of the mastodons than of bullets and billboards in the age of motors.

The first ethics dealt with the relation between individuals; the Mosaic Decalogue is an example. Later accretions dealt with the relation between the individual and society. The Golden Rule tries to integrate the individual to society; democracy to integrate social organization to the individual.

There is as yet no ethic dealing with man's relation to land and to the animals and plants which grow upon it. Land, like Odysseus' slave-girls, is still property. The land-relation is still strictly economic, entailing privileges but not obligations.

The extension of ethics to this third element in human environment is, if I read the evidence correctly, an evolutionary possibility and an ecological necessity. It is the third step in a sequence. The first two have already been taken. Individual thinkers since the days of Ezekiel and Isaiah have asserted that the despoliation of land is not only inexpedient but wrong. Society, however, has not yet affirmed their belief. I regard the present conservation movement as the embryo of such an affirmation.

An ethic may be regarded as a mode of guidance for meeting ecological situations so new or intricate, or involving such deferred reactions, that the path of social expediency is not discernible to the average individual. Animal instincts are modes of guidance for the individual in meeting such situations. Ethics are possibly a kind of community instinct in-the-making.

The Community Concept

All ethics so far evolved rest upon a single premise: that the individual is a member of a community of interdependent parts. His instincts prompt him to compete for his place in that community, but his ethics prompt him also to co-operate (perhaps in order that there may be a place to compete for).

The land ethic simply enlarges the boundaries of the community to include soils, waters, plants, and animals, or collectively, the land.

This sounds simple: do we not already sing our love for and obligation to the land of the free and the home of the brave? Yes, but just what and whom do we love? Certainly not the soil, which we are sending helter-skelter downriver. Certainly not the waters, which we assume have no function except to turn turbines, float barges, and carry off sewage. Certainly not the plants, of which we exterminate whole communities without batting an eye. Certainly not the animals, of which we have already extirpated many of the largest and most beautiful species. A land ethic of course cannot prevent the alteration, management, and use of these "resources," but it does affirm their right to continued existence, and, at least in spots, their continued existence in a natural state.

In short, a land ethic changes the role of *Homo sapiens* from conqueror of the land-community to plain member and citizen of it. It implies respect for his fellow-members, and also respect for the community as such.

In human history, we have learned (I hope) that the conqueror role is eventually self-defeating. Why? Because it is implicit in such a role that the conqueror knows, *ex cathedra,* just what makes the community clock tick, and just what and who is valuable, and what and who is worthless, in community life. It always turns out that he knows neither, and this is why his conquests eventually defeat themselves.

In the biotic community, a parallel situation exists. Abraham knew exactly what the land was for: it was to drip milk and honey into Abraham's mouth. At the present moment, the assurance with which we regard this assumption is inverse to the degree of our education.

The ordinary citizen today assumes that science knows what makes the community clock tick; the scientist is equally sure that he does not. He knows that the biotic mechanism is so complex that its workings may never be fully understood.

That man is, in fact, only a member of a biotic team is shown by an ecological interpretation of history. Many historical events, hitherto explained solely in terms of human enterprise, were actually biotic interactions between people and land. The characteristics of the land determined the facts quite as potently as the characteristics of the men who lived on it.

Consider, for example, the settlement of the Mississippi valley. In the years following the Revolution, three groups were contending for its control: the native Indian, the French and English traders, and the American settlers. Historians wonder what would have happened if the English at Detroit had thrown a little more weight into the Indian side of those tipsy scales which decided the outcome of the colonial migration into the cane-lands of Kentucky. It is time now to ponder the fact that the cane-lands, when subjected to the particular mixture of forces represented by the cow, plow, fire, and axe of the pioneer, became bluegrass. What if the plant succession inherent in this dark and bloody ground had, under the impact of these forces, given us some worthless sedge, shrub, or weed? Would Boone and Kenton have held out? Would there have been any overflow into Ohio, Indiana, Illinois, and Missouri? Any Louisiana Purchase? Any transcontinental union of new states? Any Civil War?

Kentucky was one sentence in the drama of history. We are commonly told what the human actors in this drama tried to do, but we are seldom told that their success, or the lack of it, hung in large degree on the reaction of particular soils to the impact of the particular forces exerted by their occupancy. In the case of Kentucky, we do not even know where the bluegrass came from — whether it is a native species, or a stowaway from Europe.

Contrast the cane-lands with what hindsight tells us about the Southwest, where the pioneers were equally brave, resourceful, and persevering. The impact of occupancy here brought no bluegrass, or other plant fitted to withstand the bumps and buffetings of hard use. This region, when grazed by livestock, reverted through a series of more and more worthless grasses, shrubs, and weeds to a condition of unstable equilibrium. Each recession of plant types bred erosion; each increment to erosion bred a further recession of plants. The result today is a progressive and mutual deterioration, not only of plants and soils, but of the animal community subsisting thereon. The early settlers did not expect this: on the ciénegas of New Mexico some even cut ditches to hasten it. So subtle has been its progress that few residents of the region are aware of it. It is quite invisible to the tourist who finds this wrecked landscape colorful and charming (as indeed it is, but it bears scant resemblance to what it was in 1848).

This same landscape was "developed" once before, but with quite different results. The Pueblo Indians settled the Southwest in pre-Columbian times, but they happened *not* to be equipped with range livestock. Their civilization expired, but not because their land expired.

In India, regions devoid of any sod-forming grass have been settled, apparently without wrecking the land, by the simple expedient of carrying the grass to the cow, rather than vice versa. (Was this the result of some deep wisdom, or was it just good luck? I do not know.)

In short, the plant succession steered the course of history; the pioneer simply demonstrated, for good or ill, what successions inhered in the land. Is history taught in this spirit? It will be, once the concept of land as a community really penetrates our intellectual life.

The Ecological Conscience

Conservation is a state of harmony between men and land. Despite nearly a century of propaganda, conservation still proceeds at a snail's pace; progress still consists largely of letterhead pieties and convention oratory. On the back forty we still slip two steps backward for each forward stride.

The usual answer to this dilemma is "more conservation education." No one will debate this, but is it certain that only the *volume* of education needs stepping up? Is something lacking in the *content* as well?

It is difficult to give a fair summary of its content in brief form, but, as I understand it, the content is substantially this: obey the law, vote right, join some organizations, and practice what conservation is profitable on your own land; the government will do the rest.

Is not this formula too easy to accomplish anything worthwhile? It defines no right or wrong, assigns no obligation, calls for no sacrifice, implies no change in the current philosophy of values. In respect to land-use, it urges only enlightened self-interest. Just how far will such education take us? An example will perhaps yield a partial answer.

By 1930 it had become clear to all except the ecologically blind that southwestern Wisconsin's topsoil was slipping seaward. In 1933 the farmers were told that if they would adopt certain remedial practices for five years, the public would donate CCC labor to install them, plus the necessary machinery and materials. The offer was widely accepted, but the practices were widely forgotten when the five-year contract period was up. The farmers continued only those practices that yielded an immediate and visible economic gain for themselves.

This led to the idea that maybe farmers would learn more quickly if they themselves wrote the rules. Accordingly the Wisconsin Legislature in 1937 passed the Soil Conservation District Law. This said to farmers, in effect: *We, the public, will furnish you free technical service and loan you specialized machinery, if you will write your own rules for land-use. Each county may write its own rules, and these will have the force of law.* Nearly all the counties promptly organized to accept the proffered help, but after a decade of operation, *no county has yet written a single rule.* There has been visible progress in such practices as strip-cropping, pasture renovation, and soil liming, but none in fencing woodlots against grazing, and none in excluding plow and cow from steep slopes. The farmers, in short, have selected those remedial practices which were profitable anyhow, and ignored those which were profitable to the community, but not clearly profitable to themselves.

When one asks why no rules have been written, one is told that the community is not yet ready to support them; education must precede rules. But the education actually in progress makes no mention of obligations to land over and above those dictated by self-interest. The net result is that we have more education but less soil, fewer healthy woods, and as many floods as in 1937.

The puzzling aspect of such situations is that the existence of obligations over and above self-interest is taken for granted in such rural community enterprises as the betterment of roads, schools, churches, and baseball teams. Their existence is not taken for granted, nor as yet seriously discussed, in bettering the behavior of the water that falls on the land, or in the preserving of the beauty or diversity of the farm landscape. Land-use ethics are still governed wholly by economic self-interest, just as social ethics were a century ago.

To sum up: we asked the farmer to do what he conveniently could to save his soil, and he has done just that, and only that. The farmer who clears the woods off a 75 per cent slope, turns his cows into the clearing, and dumps its rainfall, rocks, and soil into the community creek, is still (if otherwise decent) a respected member of society. If he puts lime on his fields and plants his crops on contour, he is still entitled to all the privileges and emoluments of his Soil Conservation District. The District is a beautiful piece of social machinery, but it is coughing along on two cylinders because we have been too timid, and too anxious for quick success, to tell the farmer the true magnitude of his obligations. Obligations have no meaning without conscience, and the problem we face is the extension of the social conscience from people to land.

No important change in ethics was ever accomplished without an internal change in our intellectual emphasis, loyalties, affections, and convictions. The proof that conservation has not yet touched these foundations of conduct lies in the fact that philosophy and religion have not yet heard of it. In our attempt to make conservation easy, we have made it trivial.

Substitutes for a Land Ethic

When the logic of history hungers for bread and we hand out a stone, we are at pains to explain how much the stone resembles bread. I now describe some of the stones which serve in lieu of a land ethic.

One basic weakness in a conservation system based wholly on economic motives is that most members of the land community have no economic value. Wildflowers and songbirds are examples. Of the 22,000 higher plants and animals native to Wisconsin, it is doubtful whether more than 5 per cent can be sold, fed, eaten, or otherwise put to economic use. Yet these creatures are members of the biotic community, and if (as I believe) its stability depends on its integrity, they are entitled to continuance.

When one of these non-economic categories is threatened, and if we happen to love it, we invent subterfuges to give it economic importance. At the beginning of the century songbirds were supposed to be disappearing. Ornithologists jumped to the rescue with some distinctly shaky evidence to the effect that insects would eat us up if birds failed to control them. The evidence had to be economic in order to be valid.

It is painful to read these circumlocutions today. We have no land ethic yet, but we have at least drawn nearer the point of admitting that birds should continue as a matter of biotic right, regardless of the presence or absence of economic advantage to us.

A parallel situation exists in respect of predatory mammals, raptorial birds, and fish-eating birds. Time was when biologists somewhat overworked the evidence that these creatures preserve the health of game by killing weaklings, or that they control rodents for the farmer, or that they prey only on "worthless" species. Here again, the evidence had to be economic in order to be valid. It is only in recent years that we hear the more honest argument that predators are members of the community, and that no special interest has the right to exterminate them for the sake of a benefit, real or fancied, to itself. Unfortunately this enlightened view is still in the talk stage. In the field the extermination of predators goes merrily on: witness the impending erasure of the timber wolf by fiat of Congress, the Conservation Bureaus, and many state legislatures.

Some species of trees have been "read out of the party" by economics-minded foresters because they grow too slowly, or have too low a sale value to pay as timber crops: white cedar, tamarack, cypress, beech, and hemlock are examples. In Europe, where forestry is ecologically more advanced, the non-commercial tree species are recognized as members of the native forest community, to be preserved as such, within reason. Moreover, some (like beech) have been found to have a valuable function in building up soil fertility. The interdependence of the forest and its constituent tree species, ground flora, and fauna is taken for granted.

Lack of economic value is sometimes a character not only of species or groups, but of entire biotic communities: marshes, bogs, dunes, and "deserts" are examples. Our formula in such cases is to relegate their conservation to government as refuges, monuments, or parks. The difficulty is that these communities are usually interspersed with more valuable private lands; the government cannot possibly own or control such scattered parcels. The net effect is that we have relegated some of them to ultimate extinction over large areas. If the private owner were ecologically minded, he would be proud to be the custodian of a reasonable proportion of such areas, which add diversity and beauty to his farm and to his community.

In some instances, the assumed lack of profit in these "waste" areas has proved to be wrong, but only after most of them had been done away with. The present scramble to reflood muskrat marshes is a case in point.

There is a clear tendency in American conservation to relegate to government all necessary jobs that private land-owners fail to perform. Government ownership, operation, subsidy, or regulation is now widely prevalent in forestry, range management, soil and watershed management, park and wilderness conservation, fisheries management, and migratory bird management, with more to come. Most of this growth in governmental conservation is proper and logical, some of it is inevitable. That I imply no disapproval of it is implicit in the fact that I have spent most of my life working for it. Nevertheless the question arises: What is the ultimate magnitude of the enterprise? Will the tax base carry its eventual ramifications? At what point will governmental conservation, like the mastodon, become handicapped by its own dimensions? The answer, if there is any, seems to be in a land ethic, or some other force which assigns more obligation to the private landowner.

Industrial landowners and users, especially lumbermen and stockmen, are inclined to wail long and loudly about the extension of government ownership and regulation to land, but (with notable exceptions) they show little disposition to develop the only visible alternative: the voluntary practice of conservation on their own lands.

When the private landowner is asked to perform some unprofitable act for the good of the community, he today assents only with outstretched palm. If the act costs him cash this is fair and proper, but when it costs only forethought, open-mindedness, or time, the issue is at least debatable. The overwhelming growth of land-use subsidies in recent years must be ascribed, in large part, to the government's own agencies for conservation education: the land bureaus, the agricultural colleges, and the extension services. As far as I can detect, no ethical obligation toward land is taught in these institutions.

To sum up: a system of conservation based solely on economic self-interest is hopelessly lopsided. It tends to ignore, and thus eventually to eliminate, many elements in the land community that lack commercial value, but that are (as far as we know) essential to its healthy functioning. It assumes, falsely, I think, that the economic parts of the biotic clock will function without the uneconomic parts. It tends to relegate to government many functions eventually too large, too complex, or too widely dispersed to be performed by government.

An ethical obligation on the part of the private owner is the only visible remedy for these situations.

The Land Pyramid

An ethic to supplement and guide the economic relation to land presupposes the existence of some mental image of land as a biotic mechanism. We can be ethical only in relation to something we can see, feel, understand, love, or otherwise have faith in.

The image commonly employed in conservation education is "the balance of nature." For reasons too lengthy to detail here, this figure of speech fails to describe accurately what little we know about the land mechanism. A much truer image is the one employed in ecology: the biotic pyramid. I shall first sketch the pyramid as a symbol of land, and later develop some of its implications in terms of land-use.

Plants absorb energy from the sun. This energy flows through a circuit called the biota, which may be represented by a pyramid consisting of layers. The bottom layer is the soil. A plant layer rests on the soil, an insect layer on the plants, a bird and rodent layer on the insects, and so on up through various animal groups to the apex layer, which consists of the larger carnivores.

The species of a layer are alike not in where they came from, or in what they look like, but rather in what they eat. Each successive layer depends on those below it for food and often for other services, and each in turn furnishes food and services to those above. Proceeding upward, each successive layer decreases in numerical abundance. Thus, for every carnivore there are hundreds of his prey, thousands of their prey, millions of insects, uncountable plants. The pyramidal form of the system reflects this numerical progression from apex to base. Man shares an intermediate layer with the bears, raccoons, and squirrels which eat both meat and vegetables.

The lines of dependency for food and other services are called food chains. Thus soil-oak-deer-Indian is a chain that has now been largely converted to soil-corn-cow-farmer. Each species, including ourselves, is a link in many chains. The deer eats a hundred plants other than oak, and the cow a hundred plants other than corn. Both, then, are links in a hundred chains. The pyramid is a tangle of chains so complex as to seem disorderly, yet the stability of the system proves it to be a highly organized structure. Its functioning depends on the co-operation and competition of its diverse parts.

In the beginning, the pyramid of life was low and squat, the food chains short and simple. Evolution has added layer after layer, link after link. Man is one of thousands of accretions to the height and complexity of the pyramid. Science has given us many doubts, but it has given us at least one certainty: the trend of evolution is to elaborate and diversify the biota.

Land, then, is not merely soil; it is a fountain of energy flowing through a circuit of soils, plants, and animals. Food chains are the living channels which conduct energy upward; death and decay return it to the soil. The circuit is not closed; some energy is dissipated in decay, some is added by absorption from the air, some is stored in soils, peats, and long-lived forests; but it is a sustained circuit, like a slowly augmented revolving fund of life. There is always a net loss by downhill wash, but this is normally small and offset by the decay of rocks. It is deposited in the ocean and, in the course of geological time, raised to form new lands and new pyramids.

The velocity and character of the upward flow of energy depend on the complex structure of the plant and animal community, much as the upward flow of sap in a tree depends on its complex cellular organization. Without this complexity, normal circulation would presumably not occur. Structure means the characteristic numbers, as well as the characteristic kinds and functions, of the component species. This interdependence between the complex structure of the land and its smooth functioning as an energy unit is one of its basic attributes.

When a change occurs in one part of the circuit, many other parts must adjust themselves to it. Change does not necessarily obstruct or divert the flow of energy; evolution is a long series of self-induced changes, the net result of which has been to elaborate the flow mechanism and to lengthen the circuit. Evolutionary changes, however, are usually slow and local. Man's invention of tools has enabled him to make changes of unprecedented violence, rapidity, and scope.

One change is in the composition of floras and faunas. The larger predators are lopped off the apex of the pyramid; food chains, for the first time in history, become shorter rather than longer. Domesticated species from other lands are substituted for wild ones, and wild ones are moved to new habitats. In this world-wide pooling of faunas and floras, some species get out of bounds as pests and diseases; others are extinguished. Such effects are seldom intended or foreseen; they represent unpredicted and often untraceable readjustments in the structure. Agricultural science is largely a race between the emergence of new pests and the emergence of new techniques for their control.

Another change touches the flow of energy through plants and animals and its return to the soil. Fertility is the ability of soil to receive, store, and release energy. Agriculture, by overdrafts on the soil, or by too radical a substitution of domestic for native species in the superstructure, may derange the channels of flow or deplete storage. Soils depleted of their storage, or of the organic matter which anchors it, wash away faster than they form. This is erosion.

Waters, like soil, are part of the energy circuit. Industry, by polluting waters or obstructing them with dams, may exclude the plants and animals necessary to keep energy in circulation.

Transportation brings about another basic change: the plants or animals grown in one region are now consumed and returned to the soil in another. Transportation taps the energy stored in rocks, and in the air, and uses it elsewhere; thus we fertilize the garden with nitrogen gleaned by the guano birds from the fishes of seas on the other side of the Equator. Thus the formerly localized and self-contained circuits are pooled on a world-wide scale.

The process of altering the pyramid for human occupation releases stored energy, and this often gives rise, during the pioneering period, to a deceptive exuberance of plant and animal life, both wild and tame. These releases of biotic capital tend to becloud or postpone the penalties of violence.

*   *   *

This thumbnail sketch of land as an energy circuit conveys three basic ideas:

1. That land is not merely soil.
2. That the native plants and animals kept the energy circuit open; others may or may not.
3. That man-made changes are of a different order than evolutionary changes, and have effects more comprehensive than is intended or foreseen.

These ideas, collectively, raise two basic issues: Can the land adjust itself to the new order? Can the desired alterations be accomplished with less violence?

Biotas seem to differ in their capacity to sustain violent conversion. Western Europe, for example, carries a far different pyramid than Caesar found there. Some large animals are lost; swampy forests have become meadows or plowland; many new plants and animals are introduced, some of which escape as pests; the remaining natives are greatly changed in distribution and abundance. Yet the soil is still there and, with the help of imported nutrients, still fertile; the waters flow normally; the new structure seems to

function and to persist. There is no visible stoppage or derangement of the circuit.

Western Europe, then, has a resistant biota. Its inner processes are tough, elastic, resistant to strain. No matter how violent the alterations, the pyramid, so far, has developed some new *modus vivendi* which preserves its habitability for man, and for most of the other natives.

Japan seems to present another instance of radical conversion without disorganization.

Most other civilized regions, and some as yet barely touched by civilization, display various stages of disorganization, varying from initial symptoms to advanced wastage. In Asia Minor and North Africa diagnosis is confused by climatic changes, which may have been either the cause or the effect of advanced wastage. In the United States the degree of disorganization varies locally; it is worst in the Southwest, the Ozarks, and parts of the South, and least in New England and the Northwest. Better land-uses may still arrest it in the less advanced regions. In parts of Mexico, South America, South Africa, and Australia a violent and accelerating wastage is in progress, but I cannot assess the prospects.

This almost world-wide display of disorganization in the land seems to be similar to disease in an animal, except that it never culminates in complete disorganization or death. The land recovers, but at some reduced level of complexity, and with a reduced carrying capacity for people, plants, and animals. Many biotas currently regarded as "lands of opportunity" are in fact already subsisting on exploitative agriculture, i.e. they have already exceeded their sustained carrying capacity. Most of South America is overpopulated in this sense.

In arid regions we attempt to offset the process of wastage by reclamation, but it is only too evident that the prospective longevity of reclamation projects is often short. In our own West, the best of them may not last a century.

The combined evidence of history and ecology seem to support one general deduction: the less violent the man-made changes; the greater the probability of successful readjustment in the pyramid. Violence, in turn, varies with human population density; a dense population requires a more violent conversion. In this respect, North America has a better chance for permanence than Europe, if she can contrive to limit her density.

This deduction runs counter to our current philosophy, which assumes that because a small increase in density enriched human life, an indefinite increase will enrich it indefinitely. Ecology knows of no density relationship that holds for indefinitely wide limits. All gains from density are subject to a law of diminishing returns.

Whatever may be the equation for men and land, it is improbable that we as yet know all its terms. Recent discoveries in mineral and vitamin nutrition reveal unsuspected dependencies in the up-circuit: incredibly minute quantities of certain substances determine the value of soils to plants, of plants to animals. What of the down-circuit? What of the vanishing species, the preservation of which we now regard as an esthetic luxury? They helped build the soil; in what unsuspected ways may they be essential to its maintenance? Professor Weaver proposes that we use prairie flowers to reflocculate the wasting soils of the dust bowl; who knows for what purpose cranes and condors, otters and grizzlies may some day be used?

Land Health and the A-B Cleavage

A land ethic, then, reflects the existence of an ecological conscience, and this in turn reflects a conviction of individual responsibility for the health of the land. Health is the capacity of the land for self-renewal. Conservation is our effort to understand and preserve this capacity.

Conservationists are notorious for their dissensions. Superficially these seem to add up to mere confusion, but a more careful scrutiny reveals a single plane of cleavage common to many specialized fields. In each field one group (A) regards the land as soil, and its function as commodity-production; another group (B) regards the land as a biota, and its function as something broader. How much broader is admittedly in a state of doubt and confusion.

In my own field, forestry, group A is quite content to grow trees like cabbages, with cellulose as the basic forest commodity. It feels no inhibition against violence; its ideology is agronomic. Group B, on the other hand, sees forestry as fundamentally different from agronomy because it employs natural species, and manages a natural environment rather than creating an artificial one. Group B prefers natural reproduction on principle. It worries on biotic as well as economic grounds about the loss of species like chestnut, and the threatened loss of the white pines. It worries about a whole series of secondary forest functions: wildlife, recreation, watersheds, wilderness areas. To my mind, Group B feels the stirrings of an ecological conscience.

In the wildlife field, a parallel cleavage exists. For Group A the basic commodities are sport and meat; the yardsticks of production are ciphers of take in pheasants and trout. Artificial propagation is acceptable as a permanent as well as a temporary recourse — if its unit costs permit. Group B, on the other hand, worries about a whole series of biotic side-issues. What is the cost in predators of producing a game crop? Should we have further recourse to exotics? How can management restore the shrinking species, like prairie grouse, already hopeless as shootable game? How can management restore the threatened rarities, like trumpeter swan and whooping crane? Can management principles be extended to wildflowers? Here again it is clear to me that we have the same A-B cleavage as in forestry.

In the larger field of agriculture I am less competent to speak, but there seem to be somewhat parallel cleavages. Scientific agriculture was actively developing before ecology was born; hence a slower penetration of ecological concepts might be expected. Moreover the farmer, by the very nature of his techniques, must modify the biota more radically than the forester or the wildlife manager. Nevertheless, there are many discontents in agriculture which seem to add up to a new vision of "biotic farming."

Perhaps the most important of these is the new evidence that poundage or tonnage is no measure of the food-value of farm crops; the products of fertile soil may be qualitatively as well as quantitatively superior. We can bolster poundage from depleted soils by pouring on imported fertility, but we are not necessarily bolstering food-value. The possible ultimate ramifications of this idea are so immense that I must leave their exposition to abler pens.

The discontent that labels itself "organic farming," while bearing some of the earmarks of a cult, is nevertheless biotic in its direction, particularly in its insistence on the importance of soil flora and fauna.

The ecological fundamentals of agriculture are just as poorly known to the public as in other fields of land-use. For example, few educated people realize that the marvelous advances in technique made during recent decades are improvements in the pump, rather than the well. Acre for acre, they have barely sufficed to offset the sinking level of fertility.

In all of these cleavages, we see repeated the same basic paradoxes: man the conqueror *versus* man the biotic citizen; science the sharpener of his sword *versus* science the searchlight on his universe; land the slave and servant *versus* land the collective organism. Robinson's injunction to Tristram may well be applied, at this juncture, to *Homo sapiens* as a species in geological time:

> Whether you will or not
> You are a King, Tristram, for you are one
> Of the time-tested few that leave the world,
> When they are gone, not the same place
>   it was.
> Mark what you leave.

The Outlook

It is inconceivable to me that an ethical relation to land can exist without love, respect, and admiration for land, and a high regard for its value. By value, I of course mean something far broader than mere economic value; I mean value in the philosophical sense.

Perhaps the most serious obstacle impeding the evolution of a land ethic is the fact that our educational and economic system is headed away from, rather than toward, an intense consciousness of land. Your true modern is separated from the land by many middlemen, and by innumerable physical gadgets. He has no vital relation to it; to him it is the space between cities on which crops grow. Turn him loose for a day on the land, and if the spot does not happen to be a golf links or a "scenic" area, he is bored stiff. If crops could be raised by hydroponics instead of farming, it would suit him very well. Synthetic substitutes for wood, leather, wool, and other natural land products suit him better than the originals. In short, land is something he has "outgrown."

Almost equally serious as an obstacle to a land ethic is the attitude of the farmer for whom the land is still an adversary, or a taskmaster that keeps him in slavery. Theoretically, the mechanization of farming ought to cut the farmer's chains, but whether it really does is debatable.

One of the requisites for an ecological comprehension of land is an understanding of ecology, and this is by no means co-extensive with "education"; in fact, much higher education seems deliberately to avoid ecological concepts. An understanding of ecology does not necessarily originate in courses bearing ecological labels; it is quite as likely to be labeled geography, botany, agronomy, history, or economics. This is as it should be, but whatever the label, ecological training is scarce.

The case for a land ethic would appear hopeless but for the minority which is in obvious revolt against these "modern" trends.

The "key-log" which must be moved to release the evolutionary process for an ethic is simply this: quit thinking about decent land-use as solely an economic problem. Examine each question in terms of what is ethically and esthetically right, as well as what is economically expedient. A thing is right when it tends to preserve the integrity, stability, and beauty of the biotic community. It is wrong when it tends otherwise.

It of course goes without saying that economic feasibility limits the tether of what can or cannot be done for land. It always has and it always will. The fallacy the economic determinists have tied around our collective neck, and which we now need to cast off, is the belief that economics determines *all* land-use. This is simply not true. An innumerable host of actions and attitudes, comprising perhaps the bulk of all land relations, is determined by the land-users' tastes and predilections, rather than by his purse. The bulk of all land relations hinges on investments of time, forethought, skill, and faith rather than on investments of cash. As a land-user thinketh, so is he.

I have purposely presented the land ethic as a product of social evolution because nothing so important as an ethic is ever "written." Only the most superficial student of history supposes that Moses "wrote" the Decalogue; it evolved in the minds of a thinking community, and Moses wrote a tentative summary of it for a "seminar." I say tentative because evolution never stops.

The evolution of a land ethic is an intellectual as well as emotional process. Conservation is paved with good intentions which prove to be futile, or even dangerous, because they are devoid of critical understanding either of the land, or of economic land-use. I think it is a truism that as the ethical frontier advances from the individual to the community, its intellectual content increases.

The mechanism of operation is the same for any ethic: social approbation for right actions; social disapproval for wrong actions.

By and large, our present problem is one of attitudes and implements. We are remodeling the Alhambra with a steam-shovel, and we are proud of our yardage. We shall hardly relinquish the shovel, which after all has many good points, but we are in need of gentler and more objective criteria for its successful use.

Visit the companion Web site for chapter specific quizzes, suggestions for further reading, video ideas, and other resources to assess and expand your understanding of the chapter material. Go to http://philosophy.wadsworth.com and select the companion Web site for *Voices of Wisdom.*

 You can access many additional readings at the InfoTrac-College Edition Web site. To find the following suggested articles do a keyword search with the article title. Use the passcode that was packaged with your new book to enter the site at http://www.Infotrac-college.com/Wadsworth/. Here is a sampling.

Joshua Muravchik, "The UN on the Loose" (United States chooses not to attend summit meeting of United Nations Commission on Human Rights, 2002). *Commentary* July–August 2002 v114 i1 p29(4), A89233651.

James H. Carr, "Discrimination in a Time of National Crisis: Lessons from September 11." *Vital Speeches,* July 1, 2002 v68 i18 p554(7), A89648437.

William Schulz, Robin Fox, and Francis Fukuyama, "The Ground and Nature of Human Rights: Another Round." *The National Interest,* Summer 2002 p113(11), A87720940.

bell hooks, "All Quiet on the Feminist Front." *Artforum International,* December 1996 v35 n4 p39(2), A19128242.

bell hooks, "Appearance Obsession: Is the Price Too High?" *Essence,* August 1995 v26 n4 p69(3) Mag. Coll.: 80H0718, A17320952.

Benjamin R. Barber, "Beyond Jihad vs. McWorld: On Terrorism and the New Democratic Realism." *The Nation,* January 21, 2002 v274 i2 p11, A81529481.

Adam L. Silverman, "Just War, Jihad, and Terrorism: A Comparison of Western and Islamic Norms for the Use of Political Violence." *Journal of Church and State,* Winter 2002 v44 i1 p73(20), A85033362.

Lewis H. Lapham, "American Jihad." *Harper's Magazine,* January 2002 v304 i1820 p7(3) Mag. Coll.: 109M0800, A81470325.

Lisa H. Newton, "Protection for the Biosphere: A Proposal for International Business Operations." *Global Virtue Ethics Review,* Oct 2000 v2 i4 p323, A76666512.

Dorothy Richardson, "Ethics and the Environment: Beyond Self-Interest." *Canadian Public Administration,* Spring 1991 v34 n1 p111(6), A10943666.

Michael E. Zimmerman, "Deep Ecology, Ecoactivism, and Human Evolution." *ReVision,* Spring 2002 v24 i4 p40(6), A89380355.

J. Baird Callicott, "Multicultural Environmental Ethics." *Daedalus,* Fall 2001 v130 i4 p77 Mag. Coll.: 110A3742, A79210526.

Epistemology

Chapter 6

Is Knowledge Possible?

6.1 Introduction

HAVE YOU EVER THOUGHT that people didn't really know what they were talking about? Have you ever wondered whether we can trust our intuition? Have you ever thought about the limits of human reason? Are there things that we cannot know? But how could we know that? Have you thought about how we can know what happened before we were born? Does everything we know come from experience? Have you been puzzled by the question, "What is truth?" Have you wondered whether we can be certain about any of our beliefs? Do we need evidence, and if so, what kind, to support our beliefs?

If you have wondered about these kinds of questions, you have been thinking about what philosophers call *epistemology* (the study of knowledge). The epistemologist wants to know how we can distinguish between opinion and knowledge.

We've all had the experience of listening to someone tell us something she thinks she knows. Perhaps we have dismissed what was said with the comment, "Oh, that's just *your* opinion." How do we know it is only her opinion? However we know it, the very fact that we call it opinion indicates that we assume that it is possible to distinguish between opinion and knowledge.

Let's start with a game. How do you know, if you know, the following?

You exist.	This book exists.
It will snow tomorrow.	All fat cats are fat.
It rained yesterday.	Two plus two equals four.
God exists.	Every event has a cause.

I imagine that you said you knew some of the things on this list because of sense experiences you've had. For example, you might have said that you know this book exists because you can see it and touch it. One important epistemological theory is called **empiricism.** According to this theory, we know things because we experience them with our senses. We see, touch, taste, smell, and hear things. That is how we gain knowledge about them. If someone tells me something is true, but what he says is based neither on experience nor verifiable by reference to experience, I would say, if I were an empiricist, "Oh, that's just a matter of opinion."

However, there are some things on the preceding list that you might say you knew because of reason. For example, you might have said that you know two plus two equals four because that's the way it works out when you add. Addition is a rational activity, one that requires you to reason, and you reason, in this case, by applying the rules of addition. If you apply the rules correctly, the answer has to be four.

If some of you identified reason as the source of knowledge, you would be reflecting the ideas of another important epistemological theory called **rationalism.** According to this theory, we know things by the use of reason. Reason tells us what is true. If someone says he knows there are some fat cats that are not fat because he has seen one, you might want to suggest that this is not merely a matter of opinion. Fat cats, by definition, are fat. Whatever he saw, he is mistaken.

Let us contrast these two basic theories of knowledge a bit more to be sure we grasp how they are different. Empiricism usually claims that the human mind, prior to sense experience, is like a blank slate (*tabula rasa*) or empty tablet. Sensations make impressions on this slate via our senses. It is from these impressions that we learn what is true and false and thereby, over the years, slowly build up a fund of knowledge. Hence, our knowledge is **a posteriori** (after experience). We cannot know anything until after we have had experiences, and if we wish to test or verify what we believe, we do so by checking it against further experiences. Knowledge, according to the empiricist, is also largely inductive because we induce some future events from past or present experiences. Of course our inductions may be wrong. The conclusions we draw are only probable, but probability is the best we can hope for if we want to know something about the world in which we live.

Rationalists reject the idea that the human mind is blank. We have, they usually claim, **innate ideas,** or ideas already built into our minds at birth, like the wiring built into a computer that allows it to compute. We use these innate ideas to make sense of our sensations. How do we know such innate ideas are true? By direct intellectual intuition (reason). Sensation does not tell us that every event has a cause since we cannot experience every event. Reason tells us that. We know it intuitively. Hence, knowledge is **a priori** (prior to or independent from experience). We do know things not learned from sensation, and we can prove things true without reference to sensation. Our proofs are deductive, and we can deduce that a fat cat is fat from the definition of "fat cat." It follows necessarily. It is certain.

Ponder the contrast between the following:

EMPIRICISM	RATIONALISM
tabula rasa	innate ideas
sensation	reason
a posteriori	a priori
inductive	deductive

"But wait," some of you might be saying, "what about those of us who are not sure that anything on that first list can be known at all? After all, you said, 'How do you know, *if you know?*' Well, I don't think some of these things can be known. For example, God. I think we just believe or we don't, but we can't know."

This response raises the issue of **skepticism.** The word *skepticism* comes from a Greek word that means "to reflect on," "consider," or "examine." We often associate the word with doubt or the suspension of judgment. The skeptic is a doubter.

There are various kinds of skepticism. One kind, what we might call **common-sense skepticism,** refers to the activity of doubting or suspending judgment about some things at one time or another. In this sense, we are all skeptics because we have all doubted. This sort of skepticism is healthy. It prevents an overly credulous attitude and is a good antidote to intellectual arrogance. If you are too gullible, you can be manipulated by others who claim to have knowledge when they do not.

Another kind of skepticism is **methodical skepticism.** This is the sort of skepticism that is used by some philosophers and scientists in their search for truth. If, for example, I want to be as certain as I can be that water freezes at 32 degrees Fahrenheit, I might doubt that hypothesis and conduct several experiments under differing circumstances to see if evidence supports it. Such doubt can be enormously constructive because it stimulates our intellectual curiosity and energizes our search for truth.

There is yet a third kind of skepticism, **absolute skepticism,** which, somewhat ironically, some philosophers have presented as a theory of knowledge. Unlike both rationalism and empiricism, this theory doubts the very possibility of knowledge. Pyrrho of Elis (about 300 BCE) founded a school of philosophers who advocated absolute skepticism. He claimed to be following Socrates and just asking questions. However, he also claimed that every argument cancels out its opposite. In other words, arguments on opposite sides of an issue balance out, thereby canceling any definitive conclusion. Try as we might, we cannot know what is true.

"Well," you might say, "that is ridiculous. If we cannot know what is true, then how can Pyrrho or any other skeptic know that we cannot know?" That is a good question. You are suggesting that absolute skepticism is self-refuting. If it is true that we cannot know anything, then how do we know that it is true that we cannot know anything? If absolute skepticism is true, then it must be false!

Pyrrho himself anticipated a similar criticism. He retorted that he was not certain that he was not certain of anything. Of course, one wonders whether he was not certain that he was not certain that. . . . This conversation could go on forever! Yet self-refuting propositions are puzzling and provocative things. Consider:

The sentence in this box is false.

Think about that. If "the sentence in the box is false" is false, then it must be true. And if it is true, it must be false. However, one claim central to two-valued logics is that sentences must be either true or false. They presumably cannot be both. Here we have, however, a sentence that seems to be both. What are we to make of this? Is the claim of the absolute skeptic another example of a proposition of this sort? Perhaps certainty is simply not possible for humans, and, if we mean by "knowledge" certainty (knowing without the possibility of doubt), then we may have to be more humble when we claim to know something.

6.2 Sufi Mysticism

Abu Hamid Muhammad al-Ghazali was born at Tus, Persia, in 450 AH (1058). He was appointed a professor of Islamic theology at the university in Baghdad at the early age of thirty-three. Four years later, he had an emotional and spiritual crisis and came to believe that his way of life was too worldly. He left his academic post and became an ascetic, studying both the teachings and the practices of Islamic mystics. He later returned to teaching; he died in 505 AH. *Deliverance from Error,* from which the following selection is taken, constitutes al-Ghazali's spiritual and intellectual autobiography.

Al-Ghazali was embarked on a quest for certainty. He studied theology but was disappointed with its intellectual achievements. His quest prompted him to study philosophy, but once again he was disappointed, especially with its unfounded metaphysical claims and with the fact that philosophers held beliefs contrary to Islamic revelation. He turned to the Batiniyah, who taught that truth is attained not by reason, but by accepting the pronouncements of the infallible imam (religious leader). At the time, this teaching had important political implications because it was the official ideology of the Fatimid caliphate with its center in Cairo. However, al-Ghazali found the teachings of the imams to be trivial. He characterized their knowledge as "feeble" and "emaciated." Finally he investigated **Sufism,** an Islamic mystical movement which taught that direct and immediate experience of Allah is possible. It was among the Sufis that his restless soul found peace.

Al-Ghazali was not satisfied with empiricism, rationalism, or skepticism. Hence, he sought to discover a source or means to knowledge that escapes the skeptic's doubts and provides a firmer foundation than either empiricism or rationalism. He believed he found such a source in mystical experience—that is, an experience of intimate union or contact with the Divine.

Of course, al-Ghazali's motivation was not entirely philosophical or scientific. He did not merely want to know about the world that sense experience could show him, nor about the abstract world of mathematics and metaphysics that reason could reveal. Nor was he content to be a doubter. His motivation was also spiritual; he wanted to know about the Divine. His quest may reveal to us something about the limited nature of epistemological theories. Each theory may be appropriate in a limited domain. If you want to know about the world, empiricism is attractive. If you want to know about mathematics or abstract realities, rationalism commends itself. However, what if you want to know about God? Is either empiricism or rationalism adequate?

Al-Ghazali's views are controversial because many would be skeptical about the claim that adequate knowledge can be grounded in some sort of mystical experience. How do we know that mystical experience is not an illusion, just like some sense experiences? Within Islamic philosophy, al-Ghazali was not without his critics. Another Islamic philosopher, Averrëos (Ibn Rushid, 1126–1198), wrote a book called *The Incoherence of the Incoherence,* referring to a book al-Ghazali wrote entitled *The Incoherence of the Philosophers.* Averroës attacked al-Ghazali's views, arguing that the philosophic reliance on reason and sense experience is an adequate method for knowing.

Reading Questions

1. How does al-Ghazali define *knowledge?*
2. What leads him to doubt beliefs based on sense perception and on intellect?
3. What is distinctive about mysticism?
4. What *credal principles* were firmly rooted in al-Ghazali after his study of theology and philosophy?

5. What is the *mystic way,* and what did al-Ghazali learn from following it?

6. How does the author distinguish among *knowledge, immediate experience,* and *faith?*

7. What does he mean by *prophetic revelation?* How is it related to other ways of obtaining knowledge? What is the proof of prophecy, and do you find the proof convincing? Why, or why not?

8. What method does he suggest we use to arrive at the knowledge that someone is a prophet? Why is this method better than relying on miracles as proof?

9. How does al-Ghazali answer the question, "Is knowledge possible?"

Deliverance from Error

AL-GHAZALI

To THIRST AFTER A comprehension of things as they really are was my habit and custom from a very early age. It was instinctive with me, a part of my God-given nature, a matter of temperament and not of my choice or contriving. Consequently as I drew near the age of adolescence the bonds of mere authority (*taqlid*) ceased to hold me and inherited beliefs lost their grip upon me, for I saw that Christian youths always grew up to be Christians, Jewish youths to be Jews and Muslim youths to be Muslims. I heard, too, the Tradition related of the Prophet of God according to which he said: "Everyone who is born is born with a sound nature; it is his parents who make him a Jew or a Christian or a Magian." My inmost being was moved to discover what this original nature really was and what the beliefs derived from the authority of parents and teachers really were. The attempt to distinguish between these authority-based opinions and their principles developed the mind, for in distinguishing the true in them from the false differences appeared.

I therefore said within myself: "To begin with, what I am looking for is knowledge of what things really are, so I must undoubtedly try to find what knowledge really is." It was plain to me that sure and certain knowledge is that knowledge in which the object is disclosed in such a fashion that no doubt remains along with it, that no possibility of error or illusion accompanies it, and that the mind cannot even entertain such a supposition. Certain knowledge must also be infallible; and this infallibility or security from error is such that no attempt to show the falsity of the knowledge can occasion doubt or denial, even though the attempt is made by someone who turns stones into gold or a rod into a serpent. Thus, I know that ten is more than three. Let us suppose that someone says to me: "No, three is more than ten, and in proof of that I shall change this rod into a serpent"; and let us suppose that he actually changes the rod into a serpent and that I witness him doing so. No doubts about what I know are raised in me because of this. The only result is that I wonder precisely how he is able to produce this change. Of doubt about my knowledge there is no trace.

After these reflections I knew that whatever I do not know in this fashion and with this mode

Extract taken from The Faith and Practice of Al-Ghazali, *trans. by W. Montgomery Watt. Copyright © 1953 by George Allen and Unwin, pp. 21–26, 54–57, 59, 60–68. Reproduced by kind permission of HarperCollins Publishers. Footnotes deleted.*

of certainty is not reliable and infallible knowledge; and knowledge that is not infallible is not certain knowledge.

Preliminaries: Scepticism and the Denial of All Knowledge

Thereupon I investigated the various kinds of knowledge I had, and found myself destitute of all knowledge with this characteristic of infallibility except in the case of sense-perception and necessary truths. So I said: "Now that despair has come over me, there is no point in studying any problems except on the basis of what is self-evident, namely, necessary truths and the affirmations of the senses. I must first bring these to be judged in order that I may be certain on this matter. Is my reliance on sense-perception and my trust in the soundness of necessary truths of the same kind as my previous trust in the beliefs I had merely taken over from others and as the trust most men have in the results of thinking? Or is it a justified trust that is in no danger of being betrayed or destroyed?"

I proceeded therefore with extreme earnestness to reflect on sense-perception and on necessary truths, to see whether I could make myself doubt them. The outcome of this protracted effort to induce doubt was that I could no longer trust sense-perception either. Doubt began to spread here and say: "From where does this reliance on sense-perception come? The most powerful sense is that of sight. Yet when it looks at the shadow (*sc.* of a stick or the gnomon of a sundial), it sees it standing still, and judges that there is no motion. Then by experiment and observation after an hour it knows that the shadow is moving and, moreover, that it is moving not by fits and starts but gradually and steadily by infinitely small distances in such a way that it is never in a state of rest. Again, it looks at the heavenly body (*sc.* the sun) and sees it small, the size of a shilling; yet geometrical computations show that it is greater than the earth in size."

In this and similar cases of sense-perception the sense as judge forms his judgements, but another judge, the intellect, shows him repeatedly to be wrong; and the charge of falsity cannot be rebutted.

To this I said: "My reliance on sense-perception also has been destroyed. Perhaps only those intellectual truths which are first principles (or derived from first principles) are to be relied upon, such as the assertion that ten are more than three, that the same thing cannot be both affirmed and denied at one time, that one thing is not both generated in time and eternal, nor both existent and non-existent, nor both necessary and impossible."

Sense-perception replied: "Do you not expect that your reliance on intellectual truths will fare like your reliance on sense-perception? You used to trust in me; then along came the intellect-judge and proved me wrong; if it were not for the intellect-judge you would have continued to regard me as true. Perhaps behind intellectual apprehension there is another judge who, if he manifests himself, will show the falsity of intellect in its judging, just as, when intellect manifested itself, it showed the falsity of sense in its judging. The fact that such a supra-intellectual apprehension has not manifested itself is no proof that it is impossible."

My ego hesitated a little about the reply to that, and sense-perception heightened the difficulty by referring to dreams. "Do you not see," it said, "how, when you are asleep, you believe things and imagine circumstances, holding them to be stable and enduring, and, so long as you are in that dream-condition, have no doubts about them? And is it not the case that when you awake you know that all you have imagined and believed is unfounded and ineffectual? Why then are you confident that all your waking beliefs, whether from sense or intellect, are genuine? They are true in respect of your present state; but it is possible that a state will come upon you whose relation to your waking consciousness is analogous to the relation of the latter to dreaming. In comparison with this state your waking consciousness would be like dreaming! When you have entered into this state, you will be certain that all the suppositions of your intellect are empty imaginings.

It may be that that state is what the Sufis claim as their special 'state' (*sc.* mystic union or ecstasy), for they consider that in their 'states' (or ecstasies), which occur when they have withdrawn into themselves and are absent from their senses, they witness states (or circumstances) which do not tally with these principles of the intellect. Perhaps that 'state' is death; for the Messenger of God (God bless and preserve him) says: 'The people are dreaming; when they die, they become awake.' So perhaps life in this world is a dream by comparison with the world to come; and when a man dies, things come to appear differently to him from what he now beholds, and at the same time the words are addressed to him: 'We have taken off thee thy covering, and thy sight today is sharp'" (Q. 50, 21).

When these thoughts had occurred to me and penetrated my being, I tried to find some way of treating my unhealthy condition; but it was not easy. Such ideas can only be repelled by demonstration; but a demonstration requires a knowledge of first principles; since this is not admitted, however, it is impossible to make the demonstration. The disease was baffling, and lasted almost two months, during which I was a sceptic in fact though not in theory nor in outward expression. At length God cured me of the malady; my being was restored to health and an even balance; the necessary truths of the intellect became once more accepted, as I regained confidence in their certain and trustworthy character.

This did not come about by systematic demonstration or marshalled argument, but by a light which God most high cast into my breast. That light is the key to the greater part of knowledge. Whoever thinks that the understanding of things Divine rests upon strict proofs has in his thought narrowed down the wideness of God's mercy. When the Messenger of God (peace be upon him) was asked about "enlarging" and its meaning in the verse, "Whenever God wills to guide a man, He enlarges his breast for *islām* (i.e. surrender to God)" (Q. 6, 125), he said, "It is a light which God most high casts into the heart." When asked, "What is the sign of it?," he said, "Withdrawal from the mansion of deception and return to the mansion of eternity." It was

about this light that Muhammad (peace be upon him) said, "God created the creatures in darkness, and then sprinkled upon them some of His light." From that light must be sought an intuitive understanding of things Divine. That light at certain times gushes from the spring of Divine generosity, and for it one must watch and wait—as Muhammad (peace be upon him) said: "In the days of your age your Lord has gusts of favour; then place yourselves in the way of them."

The point of these accounts is that the task is perfectly fulfilled when the quest is prosecuted up to the stage of seeking what is not sought (but stops short of that). For first principles are not sought, since they are present and to hand; and if what is present is sought for, it becomes hidden and lost. When, however, a man seeks what is sought (and that only), he is not accused of falling short in the seeking of what is sought. . . .

The Ways of Mysticism

I knew that the complete mystic "way" includes both intellectual belief and practical activity; the latter consists in getting rid of the obstacles in the self and in stripping off its base characteristics and vicious morals, so that the heart may attain to freedom from what is not God and to constant recollection of Him.

The intellectual belief was easier to me than the practical activity. I began to acquaint myself with their belief by reading their books. . . . I thus comprehended their fundamental teachings on the intellectual side, and progressed, as far as is possible by study and oral instruction, in the knowledge of mysticism. It became clear to me, however, that what is most distinctive of mysticism is something which cannot be apprehended by study, but only by immediate experience (*dhawq*—literally "tasting"), by ecstasy and by a moral change. What a difference there is between *knowing* the definition of health and satiety, together with their causes and presuppositions, and *being* healthy and satisfied! What a difference between being acquainted with the definition of drunkenness—namely, that it designates a state arising from the domination of the seat of the intellect by vapours arising from the stomach—and being drunk! Indeed, the drunken man while in that condition does not know the definition of drunkenness nor the scientific account of it; he has not the very least scientific knowledge of it. The sober man, on the other hand, knows the definition of drunkenness and its basis, yet he is not drunk in the very least. Again the doctor, when he is himself ill, knows the definition and causes of health and the remedies which restore it, and yet is lacking in health. Similarly there is a difference between knowing the true nature and causes and conditions of the ascetic life and actually leading such a life and forsaking the world.

I apprehended clearly that the mystics were men who had real experiences, not men of words, and that I had already progressed as far as was possible by way of intellectual apprehension. What remained for me was not to be attained by oral instruction and study but only by immediate experience and by walking in the mystic way.

Now from the sciences I had laboured at and the paths I had traversed in my investigation of the revelational and rational sciences (that is, presumably, theology and philosophy), there had come to me a sure faith in God most high, in prophethood (or revelation), and in the Last Day. These three credal principles were firmly rooted in my being, not through any carefully argued proofs, but by reason of various causes, coincidences and experiences which are not capable of being stated in detail.

It had already become clear to me that I had no hope of the bliss of the world to come save through a God-fearing life and the withdrawal of myself from vain desire. It was clear to me too that the key to all this was to sever the attachment of the heart to worldly things by leaving the mansion of deception and returning to that of eternity, and to advance towards God most high with all earnestness. It was also clear that this was only to be achieved by turning away from wealth and position and fleeing from all time-consuming entanglements.

Next I considered the circumstances of my life, and realized that I was caught in a veritable thicket of attachments. I also considered my activities, of which the best was my teaching and lecturing, and realized that in them I was dealing with sciences that were unimportant and contributed nothing to the attainment of eternal life.

After that I examined my motive in my work of teaching, and realized that it was not a pure desire for the things of God, but that the impulse moving me was the desire for an influential position and public recognition. I saw for certain that I was on the brink of a crumbling bank of sand and in imminent danger of hell-fire unless I set about to mend my ways.

I reflected on this continuously for a time, while the choice still remained open to me. One day I would form the resolution to quit Baghdad and get rid of these adverse circumstances; the next day I would abandon my resolution. I put one foot forward and drew the other back. If in the morning I had a genuine longing to seek eternal life, by the evening the attack of a whole host of desires had reduced it to impotence. Worldly desires were striving to keep me by their chains just where I was, while the voice of faith was calling, "To the road! to the road! What is left of life is but little and the journey before you is long. All that keeps you busy, both intellectually and practically, is but hypocrisy and delusion. If you do not prepare *now* for eternal life, when will you prepare? If you do not now sever these attachments, when will you sever them?" On hearing that, the impulse would be stirred and the resolution made to take to flight. . . .

I left Baghdad, then. I distributed what wealth I had, retaining only as much as would suffice myself and provide sustenance for my children. This I could easily manage, as the wealth of 'Iraq was available for good works, since it constitutes a trust fund for the benefit of the Muslims. Nowhere in the world have I seen better financial arrangements to assist a scholar to provide for his children. . . .

In general, then, how is a mystic "way" (*tariqah*) described? The purity which is the first condition of it (*sc.* as bodily purity is the prior condition of formal Worship for Muslims) is the purification of the heart completely from what is other than God most high; the key to it, which corresponds to the opening act of adoration in prayer, is the sinking of the heart completely in the recollection of God; and the end of it is complete absorption (*fanā'*) in God. At least this is its end relatively to those first steps which almost come within the sphere of choice and personal responsibility; but in reality in the actual mystic "way" it is the first step, what comes before it being, as it were, the ante-chamber for those who are journeying towards it.

With this first stage of the "way" there begin the revelations and visions. The mystics in their waking state now behold angels and the spirits of the prophets; they hear these speaking to them and are instructed by them. Later, a higher state is reached; instead of beholding forms and figures, they come to stages in the "way" which it is hard to describe in language; if a man attempts to express these, his words inevitably contain what is clearly erroneous.

In general what they manage to achieve is nearness to God; some, however, would conceive of this as "inherence," some as "union," and some as "connection." All that is erroneous. In my book, *The Noblest Aim,* I have explained the nature of the error here. Yet he who has attained the mystic "state" need do no more than say:

> Of the things I do not remember, what was, was;
> Think it good; do not ask an account of it.
> (Ibn al-Mu'tazz)

In general the man to whom He has granted no immediate experience at all, apprehends no more of what prophetic revelation really is than the name. The miraculous graces given to the saints are in truth the beginnings of the prophets; and that was the first "state" of the Messenger of God (peace be upon him) when he went out to Mount Hirā', and was given up entirely to his Lord, and worshipped, so that the bedouin said, "Muhammad loves his Lord passionately."

Now this is a mystical "state" which is realized in immediate experience by those who walk in the way leading to it. Those to whom it is not granted to have immediate experience can become assured of it by trial (*sc.* contact with mystics or observation of them) and by hearsay, if they have sufficiently numerous opportunities of associating with mystics to understand that (*sc.* ecstasy) with certainty by means of what accompanies the "states." Whoever sits in their company derives from them this faith; and none who sits in their company is pained.

Those to whom it is not even granted to have contacts with mystics may know with certainty the possibility of ecstasy by the evidence of demonstration, as I have remarked in the section entitled *The Wonders of the Heart* of my *Revival of the Religious Sciences.*

Certainty reached by demonstration is *knowledge* (*'ilm*); actual acquaintance with that "state" is *immediate experience* (*dhawq*); the acceptance of it as probable from hearsay and trial (or observation) is *faith* (*imān*). These are three degrees. "God will raise those of you who have faith and those who have been given knowledge in degrees (*sc.* of honour)" (Q. 58, 12).

Behind the mystics, however, there is a crowd of ignorant people. They deny this fundamentally, they are astonished at this line of thought, they listen and mock. "Amazing," they say. "What nonsense they talk!" About such people God most high has said: "Some of them listen to you, until, upon going out from you, they say to those to whom knowledge has been given, 'What did he say just now?' These are the people on whose hearts God sets a seal and they follow their passions" (Q. 47, 18). He makes them deaf, and blinds their sight.

Among the things that necessarily became clear to me from my practice of the mystic "way" was the true nature and special characteristics of prophetic revelation. The basis of that must undoubtedly be indicated in view of the urgent need for it.

The True Nature of Prophecy and the Compelling Need of All Creation for It

You must know that the substance of man in his original condition was created in bareness and simplicity without any information about the worlds of God most high. These worlds are many, not to be reckoned save by God most high Himself. As He said, "None knows the hosts of thy Lord save He" (Q. 74, 34). Man's information about the world is by means of perception; and every perception of perceptibles is created so that thereby man may have some acquaintance with a world (or sphere) from among existents. By "worlds (or spheres)" we simply mean "classes of existents."

The first thing created in man was the sense of *touch,* and by it he perceives certain classes of existents, such as heat and cold, moisture and dryness, smoothness and roughness. Touch is completely unable to apprehend colours and noises. These might be non-existent so far as concerns touch.

Next there is created in him the sense of *sight,* and by it he apprehends colours and shapes. This is the most extensive of the worlds of sensibles. Next *hearing* is implanted in him, so that he hears sounds of various kinds. After that *taste* is created in him; and so on until he has completed the world of sensibles.

Next, when he is about seven years old, there is created in him *discernment* (or the power of distinguishing). This is a fresh stage in his development. He now apprehends more than the world of sensibles; and none of these additional factors (*sc.* relations, etc.) exists in the world of sense.

From this he ascends to another stage, and *intellect* (or reason) is created in him. He apprehends things necessary, possible, impossible, things which do not occur in the previous stages.

Beyond intellect there is yet another stage. In this another eye is opened, by which he beholds the unseen, what is to be in the future, and other things which are beyond the ken of intellect in the same way as the objects of intellect are beyond the ken of the faculty of discernment and the objects of discernment are beyond the ken of sense. Moreover, just as the man at the stage of discernment would reject and disregard the objects of intellect were these to be presented to him, so some intellectuals reject and disregard the objects of prophetic revelation. That is sheer ignorance. They have no ground for their view except that this is a stage which they have not reached and which for them does not exist; yet they suppose that it is non-existent in itself. When a man blind from birth, who has not learnt about colours and shapes by listening to people's talk, is told about these things for the first time,

he does not understand them nor admit their existence.

God most high, however, has favoured His creatures by giving them something analogous to the special faculty of prophecy, namely dreams. In the dream-state a man apprehends what is to be in the future, which is something of the unseen; he does so either explicitly or else clothed in a symbolic form whose interpretation is disclosed.

Suppose a man has not experienced this himself, and suppose that he is told how some people fall into a dead faint, in which hearing, sight and the other senses no longer function, and in this condition perceive the unseen. He would deny that this is so and demonstrate its impossibility. "The sensible powers," he would say, "are the causes of perception (or apprehension); if a man does not perceive things (*sc.* the unseen) when these powers are actively present, much less will he do so when the senses are not functioning." This is a form of analogy which is shown to be false by what actually occurs and is observed. Just as intellect is one of the stages of human development in which there is an "eye" which sees the various types of intelligible objects, which are beyond the ken of the senses, so prophecy also is the description of a stage in which there is an eye endowed with light such that in that light the unseen and other supra-intellectual objects become visible.

Doubt about prophetic revelation is either (a) doubt of its possibility in general, or (b) doubt of its actual occurrence, or (c) doubt of the attainment of it by a specific individual.

The proof of the possibility of there being prophecy and the proof that there has been prophecy is that there is knowledge in the world the attainment of which by reason is inconceivable; for example, in medical science and astronomy. Whoever researches in such matters knows of necessity that this knowledge is attained only by Divine inspiration and by assistance from God most high. It cannot be reached by observation. For instance there are some astronomical laws based on phenomena which occur only once in a thousand years; how can these be arrived at by personal observation? It is the same with the properties of drugs.

This argument shows that it is possible for there to be a way of apprehending these matters which are not apprehended by the intellect. This is the meaning of prophetic revelation. That is not to say that prophecy is merely an expression for such knowledge. Rather, the apprehending of this class of extra-intellectual objects is *one* of the properties of prophecy; but it has many other properties as well. The said property is but a drop in the ocean of prophecy. It has been singled out for mention because you have something analogous to it in what you apprehend in dreaming, and because you have medical and astronomical knowledge belonging to the same class, namely, the miracles of the prophets, for the intellectuals cannot arrive at these at all by any intellectual efforts.

The other properties of prophetic revelation are apprehended only by immediate experience from the practice of the mystic way, but this property of prophecy you can understand by an analogy granted you, namely, the dream-state. If it were not for the latter you would not believe in that. If the prophet possessed a faculty to which you had nothing analogous and which you did not understand, how could you believe in it? Believing presupposes understanding. Now that analogous experience comes to a man in the early stages of the mystic way. Thereby he attains to a kind of immediate experience, extending as far as that to which he has attained, and by analogy to a kind of belief (or assent) in respect of that to which he has not attained. Thus this single property is a sufficient basis for one's faith in the principle of prophecy.

If you come to doubt whether a specific person is a prophet or not, certainty can only be reached by acquaintance with his conduct, either by personal observation, or by hearsay as a matter of common knowledge. For example, if you are familiar with medicine and law, you can recognise lawyers and doctors by observing what they are, or, where observation is impossible, by hearing what they have to say. Thus you are not unable to recognise that al-Shāfi'i (God have mercy upon him) is a lawyer and Galen a doctor; and your recognition is based on the facts and not on the judgment of someone else. Indeed, just because

you have some knowledge of law and medicine, and examine their books and writings, you arrive at a necessary knowledge of what these men are.

Similarly, if you understand what it is to be a prophet, and have devoted much time to the study of the Qur'an and the Traditions, you will arrive at a necessary knowledge of the fact that Muhammad (God bless and preserve him) is in the highest grades of the prophetic calling. Convince yourself of that by trying out what he said about the influence of devotional practices on the purification of the heart—how truly he asserted that "whoever lives out what he knows will receive from God what he does not know"; how truly he asserted that "if anyone aids an evil-doer, God will give that man power over him"; how truly he asserted that "if a man rises up in the morning with but a single care (*sc.* to please God), God most high will preserve him from all cares in this world and the next." When you have made trial of these in a thousand or several thousand instances, you will arrive at a necessary knowledge beyond all doubt.

By this method, then, seek certainty about the prophetic office, and not from the transformation of a rod into a serpent or the cleaving of the moon. For if you consider such an event by itself, without taking account of the numerous circumstances accompanying it—circumstances readily eluding the grasp of the intellect—then you might perhaps suppose that it was magic and deception and that it came from God to lead men astray; for "He leads astray whom He will, and guides whom He will." Thus the topic of miracles will be thrown back upon you; for if your faith is based on a reasoned argument involving the probative force of the miracle, then your faith is destroyed by an ordered argument showing the difficulty and ambiguity of the miracle.

Admit, then, that wonders of this sort are one of the proofs and accompanying circumstances out of the totality of your thought on the matter; and that you attain necessary knowledge and yet are unable to say specifically on what it is based. The case is similar to that of a man who receives from a multitude of people a piece of information which is a matter of common belief. . . . He is unable to say that the certainty is derived from the remark of a single specific person; rather, its source is unknown to him; it is neither from outside the whole, nor is it from specific individuals. This is strong, intellectual faith. Immediate experience, on the other hand, is like actually witnessing a thing and taking it in one's hand. It is only found in the way of mysticism.

This is a sufficient discussion of the nature of prophetic revelation for my present purpose.

6.3 Is Certainty Possible?

Have you ever been plagued by doubt? Would you like to be certain about something? Have you ever longed for an absolute truth that would never let you down? Have you ever gotten tired of questions, questions, questions?

You might be inclined to answer, "Yes, especially when studying philosophy." Uncertainty is not a pleasant state for anyone, even philosophers. It leaves us up in the air, juggling things that might fall and break at any moment. Uncertainty is unsettling. However, if we really want to know what is true, if we really want absolutely certain knowledge, must we not question and doubt until we find it?

René Descartes (sounds like "day kart") was born in France in 1596 and died in Sweden in 1650. He was a brilliant philosopher and mathematician who has been called "the father" of modern philosophy. Like many of you, and like al-Ghazali (see the previous selection), he sought something about which he could be absolutely certain. He was willing to undergo the turmoil of doubt to find it because he believed that we should accept as true only that which is supported by sound arguments.

Descartes was a methodical skeptic because he employed the method of doubt in his quest for certainty. This method deals with *logical possibility*. He was not concerned with beliefs that people actually doubt or with beliefs that are in fact false. Rather, he was concerned with those beliefs that are logically possible to doubt. If it is possible for a belief to be false, then it is capable of being doubted, whether or not, as a matter of fact, anyone has ever doubted it and whether or not, as a matter of fact, it is false.

However, Descartes could not be content with skepticism. Ultimately he sought knowledge firmly grounded in reason. Like Plato he was a rationalist, holding that beliefs based on sensations are little more than opinions, but beliefs based on reason constitute genuine knowledge. He refined Plato's distinction between opinion and knowledge. By *certainty* he meant that about which logical doubt is impossible. A belief is certain (or "clear and distinct" as Descartes liked to put it) if it is *not* logically possible to doubt its truth. Only such beliefs constitute knowledge. Because it is logically possible to doubt the truth of beliefs based on sensations, such beliefs must constitute opinion, not knowledge.

To grasp Descartes's philosophical project, we must take a brief look at the historical context. Descartes lived at the time when modern science was replacing medieval science, which had been based on the philosophies of Aristotle and Plato. Medieval science assumed as true a theory (ultimately derived from Aristotle) called **direct realism.** According to this theory, there is a reality that exists apart from human sensations, and our senses put us *directly* in touch with this reality.

This theory of direct realism had proved increasingly problematic because it seemed to lead to all sorts of contradictions. I see a house as small from a distance and as large when close up. Is the house both small and large? "Hardly," you say. If, however, our senses put us *directly* in touch with the *real* house, then what else can we conclude?

Galileo Galilei (1564–1642), who had reintroduced the atomistic theory of matter into physical science, also rejected direct realism because it was rather obvious that we do not directly sense atoms. If what is really out there are atoms and if we don't sense them, then we cannot be directly in touch with physical reality via our senses.

So what role do our senses play? Galileo proposed a theory called **indirect** or **representational realism.** According to this theory, our sensations represent physical reality. We are not directly in touch with physical reality; we are only directly in touch with our sensations *of* physical reality.

How did Galileo know that? How did he know, or how does anyone know, that our sensations represent an external reality? We cannot get outside of sensations to see. We cannot compare our image of a fat cat with the real fat cat as we can compare a picture of a fat cat with our sensations of a fat cat. Here we have a problem that seems to undermine the epistemic certainty the new science promises.

Descartes believed that science ought to provide us with certainty. Its great promise was to give us knowledge. Knowledge is certainty as far as Descartes was concerned, but how can science provide us with knowledge if the theory on which it is built, the theory of indirect or representational realism, cannot be proved true? Without a proof of representational realism, science is without a firm foundation, or so Descartes thought.

Descartes wrote his famous *Meditations on First Philosophy* in order to arrive at certainty and to prove representational realism correct. Here you will read only the first two *Meditations* because they deal directly with his epistemological theory.

In the first *Meditation,* Descartes employed the method of doubt to show that all our beliefs based on sensations can be doubted and that we cannot even be sure we have not made a mistake in calculation when we do mathematics. In the second *Meditation,* he showed that one thing cannot be doubted: "I exist as a thinking thing when I think." This is the famous *"cogito, ergo sum"* ("I think, therefore I am") argument (although Descartes did not use that exact language here), and Descartes maintained this is an absolutely certain truth that cannot be doubted. In later *Meditations,* Descartes attempted to rationally deduce the existence of God from his own existence as a thinking thing and to show that God is perfectly good and hence no deceiver.

"So what?" you say. Well, if we can be certain that we exist and if we can be certain that God exists and if we can be certain that God is no deceiver, we can also be certain that our sensations must truly represent an external reality. If they did not, we would live in constant error and ignorance, like Plato's prisoners in the cave, and this, surely, a good and gracious God would not allow.

Reading Questions

1. What was Descartes's goal, and what method did he employ to get there?
2. Many of our beliefs are based on sensation. Descartes offered two arguments, the arguments from deception and dreaming, to show that beliefs based on sensations are not trustworthy. State these arguments in your own words.
3. List some examples of occasions when you have been deceived by your senses.
4. Have you ever had a dream that you were totally convinced was true? How do you know you are not now dreaming?

5. Some of our beliefs—for example, that two plus three equals five—are based on reasoning, not sensation. Descartes argued that even arithmetic calculations can be doubted. What is his argument?

6. Descartes ended the first *Meditation* with the famous evil demon argument. What is the point of this argument?

7. Play Descartes's game for a moment and imagine there is an all-powerful force that has nothing better to do than to deceive you. Give this force a name and imagine it, like some mad puppeteer pulling the strings behind the scenes, constantly arranging things so that your beliefs are false. Now ask yourself, "Is there anything about which this wicked force could not deceive me?" If there is anything you can think of, what is it?

8. Descartes concluded that the statement "I am, I exist" must be true whenever he thought it. Why? What reasons support this conclusion?

9. The next step in Descartes's argument is to reach the conclusion that he is a thinking thing. How did he reach that conclusion? Why did he not conclude instead that he was a physical thing?

10. In the final paragraph of *Meditation II*, Descartes listed several things he had learned from his consideration of a piece of wax. What are they, and how did he arrive at these conclusions?

11. If you studied the previous selection, what similarities and differences do you notice between al-Ghazali's quest for knowledge and Descartes's quest?

12. How did Descartes answer the question, "Is knowledge possible?"

Meditations I and II

RENÉ DESCARTES

Meditation I

ON WHAT CAN BE
CALLED INTO DOUBT

FOR SEVERAL YEARS NOW, I've been aware that I accepted many falsehoods as true in my youth, that what I built on the foundations of those falsehoods was dubious, and accordingly that once in my life I would need to tear down everything and begin anew from the foundations if I wanted to establish any stable and lasting knowledge. But the task seemed enormous, and I waited until I was so old that no better time for undertaking it would be likely to follow. I have thus delayed so long that it would be wrong for

me to waste in indecision the time left for action. Today, then, having rid myself of worries and having arranged for some peace and quiet, I withdraw alone, free at last earnestly and wholeheartedly to overthrow all my beliefs.

To do this, I don't need to show each of them to be false: I may never be able to do that. But, since reason now convinces me that I ought to withhold my assent just as carefully from what isn't obviously certain and indubitable as from what's obviously false, I can justify the rejection of all my beliefs if in each I can find some ground for doubt. And, to do this, I need not run through my beliefs one by one, which would be an endless task. Since a building collapses

From René Descartes' Meditations on First Philosophy, *translated by Ronald Rubin (Claremont, CA: Areté Press, 1986), pp. 1–13. Reprinted by permission of Areté Press.*

when its foundation is cut out from under it, I will go straight to the principles on which all my former beliefs rested.

Of course, whatever I have so far accepted as supremely true I have learned either from the senses or through the senses. But I have occasionally caught the senses deceiving me, and it's prudent never completely to trust those who have cheated us even once.

But, while my senses may deceive me about what is small or far away, there may still be other things which I take in by the senses but which I cannot possibly doubt—like that I am here, sitting before the fire, wearing a dressing gown, touching this paper. And on what grounds might I deny that my hands and the other parts of my body exist?—unless perhaps I liken myself to madmen whose brains are so rattled by the persistent vapors of melancholy that they are sure that they're kings when in fact they are paupers, or that they wear purple robes when in fact they're naked, or that their heads are clay, or that they are gourds, or made of glass. But these people are insane, and I would seem just as crazy if I were to apply what I say about them to myself.

This would be perfectly obvious—if I weren't a man accustomed to sleeping at night whose experiences while asleep are at least as far-fetched as those that madmen have while awake. How often, at night, I've been convinced that I was here, sitting before the fire, wearing my dressing gown, when in fact I was undressed and between the covers of my bed! But now I am looking at this piece of paper with my eyes wide open; the head that I am shaking has not been lulled to sleep; I put my hand out consciously and deliberately and feel. None of this would be as distinct if I were asleep. As if I can't remember having been tricked by similar thoughts while asleep! When I think very carefully about this, I see so plainly that there are no reliable signs by which I can distinguish sleeping from waking that I am stupefied—and my stupor itself suggests that I am asleep!

Suppose, then, that I am dreaming. Suppose, in particular, that my eyes are not open, that my head is not moving, and that I have not put out my hand. Suppose that I do not have hands, or

even a body. I must still admit that the things I see in sleep are like painted images which must have been patterned after real things and, hence, that things like eyes, heads, hands, and bodies are real rather than imaginary. For, even when painters try to give bizarre shapes to sirens and satyrs, they are unable to give them completely new natures; they only jumble together the parts of various animals. And, even if they were to come up with something so novel that no one had ever seen anything like it before, something entirely fictitious and unreal, at least there must be real colors from which they composed it. Similarly, while things like eyes, heads, and hands may be imaginary, it must be granted that some simpler and more universal things are real—the "real colors" from which the true and false images in our thoughts are formed.

Things of this sort seem to include general bodily nature and its extension, the shape of extended things, their quantity (that is, their size and number), the place in which they exist, the time through which they endure, and so on.

Perhaps we can correctly infer that, while physics, astronomy, medicine, and other disciplines that require the study of composites are dubious, disciplines like arithmetic and geometry, which deal only with completely simple and universal things without regard to whether they exist in the world, are somehow certain and indubitable. For, whether we are awake or asleep, two plus three is always five, and the square never has more than four sides. It seems impossible even to suspect such obvious truths of falsity.

Nevertheless, the traditional view is fixed in my mind that there is a God who can do anything and by whom I have been made to be as I am. How do I know that He hasn't brought it about that, while there is in fact no earth, no sky, no extended thing, no shape, no magnitude, and no place, all of these things seem to me to exist, just as they do now? I think that other people sometimes err in what they believe themselves to know perfectly well. Mightn't I be deceived when I add two and three, or count the sides of a square, or do even simpler things, if we can even suppose that there is anything simpler? Maybe it will be denied that God deceives me, since He is said to be supremely good. But, if God's being good is incompatible with His having created me so that I am deceived always, it seems just as out of line with His being good that He permits me to be deceived sometimes—as he undeniably does.

Maybe some would rather deny that there is an omnipotent God than believe that everything else is uncertain. Rather than arguing with them, I will grant everything I have said about God to be fiction. But, however these people think I came to be as I now am—whether they say it is by fate, or by accident, or by a continuous series of events, or in some other way—it seems that he who errs and is deceived is somehow imperfect. Hence, the less power that is attributed to my original creator, the more likely it is that I am always deceived. To these arguments, I have no reply. I'm forced to admit that nothing that I used to believe is beyond legitimate doubt—not because I have been careless or playful, but because I have valid and well-considered grounds for doubt. Hence, I must withhold my assent from my former beliefs as carefully as from obvious falsehoods if I want to arrive at something certain.

But it's not enough to have noticed this: I must also take care to bear it in mind. For my habitual views constantly return to my mind and take control of what I believe as if our longstanding, intimate relationship has given them the right to do so, even against my will. I'll never break the habit of trusting and giving in to these views while I see them for what they are—things somewhat dubious (as I have just shown) but nonetheless probable, things that I have much more reason to believe than to deny. That's why I think it will be good deliberately to turn my will around, to allow myself to be deceived, and to suppose that all my previous beliefs are false and illusory. Eventually, when I have counterbalanced the weight of my prejudices, my bad habits will no longer distort my grasp of things. I know that there is no danger of error here and that I won't overindulge in skepticism, since I'm now concerned, not with action, but only with gaining knowledge.

I will suppose, then, not that there is a supremely good God who is the source of all truth, but that there is an evil demon, supremely powerful and cunning, who works as hard as he can to deceive me. I will say that sky, air, earth, color, shape, sound, and other external things are just dreamed illusions which the demon uses to ensnare my judgment. I will regard myself as not having hands, eyes, flesh, blood, and senses—but as having the false belief that I have all these things. I will obstinately concentrate on this meditation and will thus ensure by mental resolution that, if I do not really have the ability to know the truth, I will at least withhold assent from what is false and from what a deceiver may try to put over on me, however powerful and cunning he may be. But this plan requires effort, and laziness brings me back to my ordinary life. I am like a prisoner who happens to enjoy the illusion of freedom in his dreams, begins to suspect that he is asleep, fears being awakened, and deliberately lets the enticing illusions slip by unchallenged. Thus, I slide back into my old views, afraid to awaken and to find that after my peaceful rest I must toil, not in the light, but in the confusing darkness of the problems just raised.

Meditation II

ON THE NATURE OF THE HUMAN MIND, WHICH IS BETTER KNOWN THAN THE BODY

Yesterday's meditation has hurled me into doubts so great that I can neither ignore them nor think my way out of them. I am in turmoil, as if I have accidentally fallen into a whirlpool and can neither touch bottom nor swim to the safety of the surface. I will struggle, however, and try to follow the path that I started on yesterday. I will reject whatever is open to the slightest doubt just as though I have found it to be entirely false, and I will continue until I find something certain—or at least until I know for certain that nothing is certain. Archimedes required only one fixed and immovable point to move the whole earth from its place, and I too can hope for great things if I can find even one small thing that is certain and unshakable.

I will suppose, then, that everything I see is unreal. I will believe that my memory is unreliable and that none of what it presents to me ever happened. I have no senses. Body, shape, extension, motion, and place are fantasies. What then is true? Perhaps just that nothing is certain.

But how do I know that there isn't something different from the things just listed which I do not have the slightest reason to doubt? Isn't there a God, or something like one, who puts my thoughts into me? But why should I say so when I may be the author of those thoughts? Well, isn't it at least the case that I am something? But I now am denying that I have senses and a body. But I stop here. For what follows from these denials? Am I so bound to my body and to my senses that I cannot exist without them? I have convinced myself that there is nothing in the world—no sky, no earth, no minds, no bodies. Doesn't it follow that I don't exist? No, surely I must exist if it's me who is convinced of something. But there is a deceiver, supremely powerful and cunning, whose aim is to see that I am always deceived. But surely I exist, if I am deceived. Let him deceive me all he can, he will never make it the case that I am nothing while I think that I am something. Thus having fully weighed every consideration, I must finally conclude that the statement "I am, I exist" must be true whenever I state it or mentally consider it.

But I do not yet fully understand what this "I" is that must exist. I must guard against inadvertently taking myself to be something other than I am, thereby going wrong even in the knowledge that I put forward as supremely certain and evident. Hence, I will think once again about what I believed myself to be before beginning these meditations. From this conception, I will subtract everything challenged by the reasons for doubt which I produced earlier, until nothing remains except what is certain and indubitable.

What, then, did I formerly take myself to be? A man, of course. But what is a man? Should I say a rational animal? No, because then I would need to ask what an animal is and what it is to be rational. Thus, starting from a single question, I would sink into many which are more difficult, and I do not have the time to waste on such subtleties. Instead, I will look here at the thought which occurred to me spontaneously and naturally when I reflected on what I was. The first thought to occur to me was that I have a face, hands, arms, and all the other equipment (also found in corpses) which I call a body. The next thought to occur to me was that I take nourishment, move myself around, sense, and think—that I do things which I trace back to my soul. Either I didn't stop to think about what this soul was, or I imagined it to be a rarified air, or fire, or ether permeating the denser parts of my body. But, about physical objects, I didn't have any doubts whatever: I thought that I distinctly knew their nature. If I had tried to describe my conception of this nature, I might have said this: "When I call something a physical object, I mean that it is capable of being bounded by a shape and limited to a place; that it can fill a space so as to exclude other objects from it; that it can be perceived by touch, sight, hearing, taste, and smell; that it can be moved in various ways, not by itself, but by something else in contact with it." I judged that the powers of self-movement, of sensing, and of thinking did not belong to the nature of physical objects, and, in fact, I marveled that there were some physical objects in which these powers could be found.

But what should I think now, while supposing that a supremely powerful and "evil" deceiver completely devotes himself to deceiving me? Can I say that I have any of the things that I have attributed to the nature of physical objects? I concentrate, think, reconsider—but nothing comes to me; I grow tired of the pointless repetition. But what about the things that I have assigned to soul? Nutrition and self-movement? Since I have no body, these are merely illusions. Sensing? But I cannot sense without a body, and in sleep I've seemed to sense many things that I later realized I had not really sensed. Thinking? It comes down to this: Thought and thought alone cannot be taken away from me. I am, I exist. That much is certain. But for how long? As long as I think—for it may be that, if I completely stopped thinking, I would completely cease to exist. I am not now admitting anything unless it must be true, and I am therefore not admitting that I am anything at all other than a thinking thing—that is, a mind, soul, understanding, or reason (terms whose meaning I did not previously know). I know that I am a real, existing thing, but what kind of thing? As I have said, a thing that thinks.

What else? I will draw up mental images. I'm not the collection of organs called a human body. Nor am I some rarified gas permeating these organs, or air, or fire, or vapor, or breath—for I have supposed that none of these things exist. Still, I am something. But couldn't it be that these things, which I do not yet know about and which I am therefore supposing to be nonexistent, really aren't distinct from the "I" that I know to exist? I don't know, and I'm not going to argue about it now. I can only form judgments on what I do know. I know that I exist, and I ask what the "I" is that I know to exist. It's obvious that this conception of myself doesn't depend on anything that I do not yet know to exist and, therefore, that it does not depend on anything of which I can draw up a mental image. And the words "draw up" point to my mistake. I would truly be creative if I were to have a mental image of what I am, since to have a mental image is just to contemplate the shape or image of a physical object. I now know with certainty that I exist and at the same time that all images—and, more generally, all things associated with the nature of physical objects—may just be dreams. When I keep this in mind, it seems just as absurd to say "I use mental images to help me understand what I am" as it would to say "Now, while awake, I see something true—but, since I don't yet see it clearly enough, I'll go to sleep and let my dreams present it to me more clearly and truly." Thus I know that none of the things that I can comprehend with the aid of mental images bear on my knowledge of myself. And I must carefully draw my mind away from such things if it is to see its own nature distinctly.

But what then am I? A thinking thing. And what is that? Something that doubts, understands, affirms, denies, wills, refuses, and also senses and has mental images.

That's quite a lot, if I really do all of these things. But don't I? Isn't it me who now doubts nearly everything, understands one thing, affirms this thing, refuses to affirm other things, wants to know much more, refuses to be deceived, has mental images (sometimes involuntarily), and is aware of many things "through his senses?" Even if I am always dreaming, and even if my creator does what he can to deceive me, isn't it just as true that I do all these things as that I exist? Are any of these things distinct from my thought? Can any be said to be separate from me? That it's me who doubts, understands, and wills is so obvious that I don't see how it could be more evident. And it's also me who has mental images. While it may be, as I am supposing, that absolutely nothing of which I have a mental image really exists, the ability to have mental images really does exist and is a part of my thought. Finally, it's me who senses—or who seems to gain awareness of physical objects through the senses. For example, I am now seeing light, hearing a noise, and feeling heat. These things are unreal, since I am dreaming. But it is still certain that I seem to see, to hear, and to feel. This seeming cannot be unreal, and it is what is properly called sensing. Strictly speaking, sensing is just thinking.

From this, I begin to learn a little about what I am. But I still can't stop thinking that I apprehend physical objects, which I picture in mental images and examine with my senses, much more distinctly than I know this unfamiliar "I," of which I cannot form a mental image. I think this, even though it would be astounding if I comprehended things which I've found to be doubtful, unknown, and alien to me more distinctly than the one which I know to be real: my self. But I see what's happening. My mind enjoys wandering, and it won't confine itself to the truth. I will therefore loosen the reins on my mind for now so that later, when the time is right, I will be able to control it more easily.

Let's consider the things commonly taken to be the most distinctly comprehended: physical objects that we see and touch. Let's not consider physical objects in general, since general conceptions are very often confused. Rather, let's consider one, particular object. Take, for example, this piece of wax. It has just been taken from the honeycomb; it hasn't yet completely lost the taste of honey; it still smells of the flowers from which it was gathered; its color, shape, and size are obvious; it is hard, cold, and easy to touch; it makes a sound when rapped. In short, everything seems to be present in the wax that is required for me to know it as distinctly as possible. But, as I speak, I move the wax towards the fire; it loses what was left of its taste; it gives up its smell; it changes color; it loses its shape; it gets bigger; it melts; it heats up; it becomes difficult to touch; it no longer makes a sound when struck. Is it still the same piece of wax? We must say that it is: no one denies it or thinks otherwise. Then what was there in the wax that I comprehended so distinctly? Certainly nothing that I reached with my senses—for, while everything having to do with taste, smell, sight, touch, and hearing has changed, the same piece of wax remains.

Perhaps what I distinctly knew was neither the sweetness of honey, not the fragrance of flowers, nor a sound, but a physical object which once appeared to me one way and now appears differently. But what exactly is it of which I now have a mental image? Let's pay careful attention, remove everything that doesn't belong to the wax, and see what's left. Nothing is left except an extended, flexible, and changeable thing. But what is it for this thing to be flexible and changeable? Is it just that the wax can go from round to square and then to triangular, as I have mentally pictured? Of course not. Since I understand that the wax's shape can change in innumerable ways, and since I can't run through all the changes in my imagination, my comprehension of the wax's flexibility and changeability cannot have been produced by my ability to have mental images. And what about the thing that is extended? Are we also ignorant of its extension? Since the extension of the wax increases when the wax melts, increases again when the wax boils, and increases still more when the wax gets hotter, I will be mistaken about what the wax is unless I believe that it can undergo more changes in extension than I can ever encompass with mental images. I must therefore admit that I do not have an image of what the wax is—that I grasp what it is with only my mind. (While I am saying this about a particular piece of wax, it is even more clearly true about wax in general.) What then is this piece of

wax that I grasp only with my mind? It is something that I see, feel, and mentally picture—exactly what I believed it to be at the outset. But it must be noted that, despite the appearances, my grasp of the wax is not visual, tactile, or pictorial. Rather, my grasp of the wax is the result of a purely mental inspection, which can be imperfect and confused, as it was once, or clear and distinct, as it is now, depending on how much attention I pay to the things of which the wax consists.

I'm surprised by how prone my mind is to error. Even when I think to myself non-verbally, language stands in my way, and common usage comes close to deceiving me. For, when the wax is present, we say that we see the wax itself, not that we infer its presence from its color and shape. I'm inclined to leap from this fact about language to the conclusion that I learn about the wax by eyesight rather than by purely mental inspection. But, if I happen to look out my window and see men walking in the street, I naturally say that I see the men just as I say that I see the wax. What do I really see, however, but hats and coats that could be covering robots? I *judge* that there are men. Thus I comprehend with my judgment, which is in my mind, objects that I once believed myself to see with my eyes.

One who aspires to wisdom above that of the common man disgraces himself by deriving doubt from common ways of speaking. Let's go on, then, to ask when I most clearly and perfectly grasped what the wax is. Was it when I first looked at the wax and believed my knowledge of it to come from the external senses—or at any rate from the so-called "common sense," the power of having mental images? Or is it now, after I have carefully studied what the wax is and how I come to know it? Doubt would be silly here. For what was distinct in my original conception of the wax? How did that conception differ from that had by animals? When I distinguish the wax from its external forms—when I "undress" it and view it "naked"—there may still be errors in my judgments about it, but I couldn't possibly grasp the wax in this way without a human mind.

What should I say about this mind—or, in other words, about myself? (I am not now admitting that there is anything to me but a mind.) What is this "I" that seems to grasp the wax so distinctly? Don't I know myself much more truly and certainly, and also much more distinctly and plainly, than I know the wax? For, if I base my judgment that the wax exists on the fact that I see it, my seeing it much more obviously implies that I exist. It's possible that what I see is not really wax, and it's even possible that I don't have eyes with which to see—but it clearly is not possible that, when I see (or, what now amounts to the same thing, when I think I see), the "I" which thinks is not a real thing. Similarly, if I base my judgment that the wax exists on the fact that I feel it, the same fact makes it obvious that I exist. If I base my judgment that the wax exists on the fact that I have a mental image of it or on some other fact of this sort, the same thing can obviously be said. And what I've said about the wax applies to everything else that is outside me. Moreover, if I seem to grasp the wax more distinctly when I detect it with several senses than when I detect it with just sight or touch, I must know myself even more distinctly—for every consideration that contributes to my grasp of the piece of wax or to my grasp of any other physical object serves better to reveal the nature of my mind. Besides, the mind has so much in it by which it can make its conception of itself distinct that what comes to it from physical objects hardly seems to matter.

And now I have brought myself back to where I wanted to be. I now know that physical objects are grasped, not by the senses or the power of having mental images, but by understanding alone. And, since I grasp physical objects in virtue of their being understandable rather than in virtue of their being tangible or visible, I know that I can't grasp anything more easily or plainly than my mind. But, since it takes time to break old habits of thought, I should pause here to allow the length of my contemplation to impress the new thoughts more deeply into my memory.

6.4 Empiricism and Limited Skepticism

David Hume (1711–1776) was a Scottish philosopher regarded by some as the greatest philosopher to write in the English language. There is little doubt about his brilliance. He graduated from the University of Edinburgh at the ripe old age of fifteen and headed for law school. Deciding he did not like law, he began writing a philosophical work called *A Treatise on Human Nature* (1739–1740), which he hoped would bring him fame and fortune. It did not. Very few people understood what he was talking about. Disappointed, he wrote a more popular version called *An Enquiry Concerning Human Understanding* (1748) from which the following selection is taken. You can judge for yourself how popular this version might have been.

Hume presented an empiricist theory of knowledge: Everything we can know about the world is ultimately derived from our senses. He developed empiricism into a critical tool for checking ideas. If you want to know what an idea or concept means, said Hume, trace it back to the impressions from which it came. For example, in a famous section (VII, not included here) Hume sought to find out what the concept of cause means. This is a basic idea because so much of science and, for that matter, common sense presupposes the law of cause and effect.

Usually people mean three things by *cause*—namely, that event *A* is the cause of event *B* if *A* occurs *before B, A* is *contiguous* to *B* in some way, and *A* is *necessarily connected* with *B*. It is this last idea that puzzled Hume. What is a necessary connection? From what impression does it arise? The only impression Hume could find was the impression of *constant conjunction*. We say *A* is the cause of *B* because in our experience *A* and *B* are constantly conjoined. Yet the concept of a necessary connection goes far beyond constant conjunction. If *A* and *B* are necessarily connected, then whenever *A* occurs, *B* will necessarily occur. However, from the fact that *A* and *B* have been constantly conjoined in the past, can we conclude that they will be so connected in the future? It is likely that they will be connected, even highly probable, but high probability is not the same as necessity.

This conclusion shocked the intellectual community of Hume's day because, if Hume was right, a fundamental law of thought and of science was without foundation in experience. This issue of the foundation of knowledge was of central importance to Hume. The rationalists claimed there was a foundation found in reason; the empiricists claimed there was a foundation found in experience. Hume, while sympathetic to empiricism, questioned whether there are in fact any firm foundations on which knowledge rests other than customary and habitual associations of ideas.

Hume brought the assumption that knowledge had a foundation into question by discovering the problem of induction. Although Hume did not call it by this name, the **problem of induction,** simply stated, is the problem of discovering rational foundations for all the conclusions we draw based on experience.

Later philosophers, inspired by Hume, drew a distinction between **analytic statements** such as "All bachelors are unmarried men" and **synthetic statements** such as "My cat is fat." Hume used the terms *relations of ideas* and *matters of fact* for these two kinds of statements because analytic statements are about how ideas are related and synthetic statements are about facts. You can test to see if any given statement is analytic by applying this rule: "If it is not logically possible for the negation of the statement to be true, the statement is analytic." For example, the claim that "some bachelors are married" cannot be true because the word *bachelor* means "unmarried man." You can test to see if a statement is synthetic by applying this rule: "If it is logically possible for the negation of the statement to be true, the statement is synthetic." For example, it is quite possible that, in fact, my cat is not fat.

See if you understand these rules by determining which of these statements are analytic and which synthetic.

1. The sun is round.
2. The lights are on.
3. $2 + 2 = 4$
4. Philosophy is fun.
5. Blind bats cannot see.

Note that statements about the relation of ideas (analytic) are *necessarily true.* That is, they are true by virtue of the meaning of the terms. Statements about matters of fact (synthetic) are *contingently true* because their truth depends on a certain state of affairs actually obtaining. Philosophers have also maintained that the truth of analytic statements is justified a priori by deductive reasoning, whereas the truth of synthetic statements is justified a posteriori by inductive reasoning.

Let us return to the problem of induction. Conclusions based on experience presuppose, according to Hume, that the future will resemble the past. Now how is this presupposition justified?

There are two types of proof: deductive and inductive. We cannot justify the statement "The future will resemble the past" deductively because it is not an analytic statement, but a synthetic statement. It is logically possible that the future will not resemble the past. So what about induction? Well, according to Hume, we cannot justify it inductively because that would be to beg the question (argue in a circle). It amounts to circular reasoning because the inductive method itself *presupposes* this rule (that the future will resemble the past) to be true.

The question of whether there is a foundation of knowledge remains a major philosophical problem. In fact, philosophy today is deeply embroiled in this issue. For Hume, it was important because the then-new physical sciences claimed to provide knowledge of the world based on conclusions drawn from experience. Can such scientific knowledge be philosophically justified?

In the last section (XII, "On the Academical or Skeptical Philosophy") of the *Enquiry* (not included here), Hume admitted it is our natural instinct to believe that our senses provide us with information about an external world. This, however, is a philosophically naive attitude because serious objections can be raised that would lead us to doubt whether we do have access to an external world through our senses. Our senses do not put us directly in touch with external objects. We never see a chair per se, only visual images that we infer to be *of* a chair.

There are two ways to overcome such objections. One way is to argue that assertions about matters of fact (synthetic statements) are justified a posteriori by reference to sense experience or impressions. However, all such proofs are bound to fail because all they can ever prove is that we have sensations. The other way is to try to prove deductively the existence of an external world (remember Descartes?). However, this line of argument is also bound to fail because the most it can prove is that certain relations among ideas (analytic statements) are true a priori. Such arguments tell us what words mean but do not tell us what the world is like.

If critical objections to the naive attitude cannot be overcome by either inductive or deductive reasoning, then skepticism about all claims to knowledge of the external world seems the only logical conclusion to draw. Absolute skepticism, however, can be shown to lead to absurdities. If we really were totally skeptical about all our beliefs based on sensation, then we would never move because there is no proof that we can, nor would we ever eat because there is no proof that food exists or is good for us. Besides, absolute skepticism appears to be self-refuting. So if inductive and deductive arguments fail and if absolute skepticism leads to absurdities, what are we to do?

Hume ends up advocating a limited or *mitigated* skepticism, much like the commonsense skepticism I mentioned in the introduction. We should take claims to knowledge with a grain of salt. We should accept what seems reasonable and useful but keep an open mind. We should avoid dogmatism and beware of a naive credulity. And we should limit our inquiries to subjects that are useful. These include mathematics, which provides us with useful analytic statements justified a priori, and the physical and social sciences, which provide us with synthetic statements justified a posteriori. All other subjects such as metaphysical speculations and theology are best left alone.

Reading Questions

1. Into what two categories can the "perceptions of the mind" be divided, and how are they distinguished from one another? Give an example of each.
2. Hume presented two arguments to prove "all our ideas . . . are copies of our impressions." State these arguments in your own words. What do you think of them? Are they convincing? Why, or why not?

3. What is the difference between *matters of fact* and *relations of ideas?* Provide your own example of each.

4. According to Hume, all reasoning concerning matters of fact is founded on the relation of cause and effect. This relation, Hume argued, is not discoverable by reason, only by experience. Summarize the argument Hume used to support this claim.

5. In answer to the question "What is the foundation of all conclusions from experience?" Hume challenged the reader to supply the foundation for the inference from the fact that I have found objects (like bread) to produce certain effects (like nourishment) in the past to the conclusion that the same will occur in the future. Can you supply the basis for the connection or inference between these two statements? If so, what is it?

6. Why can we not prove the principle "the future will resemble the past" deductively (Hume's term was "by demonstrative reasoning")?

7. Why can we not prove this principle inductively ("by moral reasoning")?

8. How do you think Hume would have answered the question, "Is knowledge possible?" How would his answer differ from the answers given by al-Ghazali and Descartes?

An Enquiry Concerning Human Understanding

DAVID HUME

Section II

OF THE ORIGIN OF IDEAS

EVERY ONE WILL READILY allow, that there is a considerable difference between the perceptions of the mind, when a man feels the pain of excessive heat, or the pleasure of moderate warmth, and when he afterwards recalls to his memory this sensation, or anticipates it by his imagination. These faculties may mimic or copy the perceptions of the senses; but they never can entirely reach the force and vivacity of the original sentiment. The utmost we say of them, even when they operate with greatest vigour, is, that they represent their object in so lively a manner, that we could *almost* say we feel or see it: But, except the mind be disordered by disease or madness, they never can arrive at such a pitch of vivacity, as to render these perceptions altogether indistinguishable. All the colours of poetry, however splendid, can never paint natural objects in such a manner as to make the description be taken for a real landscape. The most lively thought is still inferior to the dullest sensation.

We may observe a like distinction to run through all the other perceptions of the mind. A man in a fit of anger, is actuated in a very different manner from one who only thinks of that emotion. If you tell me, that any person is in love, I easily understand your meaning, and form a just conception of his situation; but never can mistake that conception for the real disorders and agitations of the passion. When we reflect on our past sentiments and affections, our thought is a faithful mirror, and copies its objects truly; but the colours which it employs are faint and dull, in comparison of those in which our original perceptions were clothed. It requires no nice discernment or metaphysical head to mark the distinction between them.

Excerpts from Sections II and IV of David Hume's An Enquiry Concerning Human Understanding *(Oxford: Clarendon Press, 1748).*

Here therefore we may divide all the perceptions of the mind into two classes or species, which are distinguished by their different degrees of force and vivacity. The less forcible and lively are commonly denominated *Thoughts* or *Ideas.* The other species want a name in our language, and in most others; I suppose, because it was not requisite for any, but philosophical purposes, to rank them under a general term or appellation. Let us, therefore, use a little freedom, and call them *Impressions;* employing that word in a sense somewhat different from the usual. By the term *impression,* then, I mean all our more lively perceptions, when we hear, or see, or feel, or love, or hate, or desire, or will. And impressions are distinguished from ideas, which are the less lively perceptions, of which we are conscious, when we reflect on any of those sensations or movements above mentioned.

Nothing, at first view, may seem more unbounded than the thought of man, which not only escapes all human power and authority, but is not even restrained within the limits of nature and reality. To form monsters, and join incongruous shapes and appearances, costs the imagination no more trouble than to conceive the most natural and familiar objects. And while the body is confined to one planet, along which it creeps with pain and difficulty; the thought can in an instant transport us into the most distant regions of the universe; or even beyond the universe, into the unbounded chaos, where nature is supposed to lie in total confusion. What never was seen, or heard of, may yet be conceived; nor is any thing beyond the power of thought, except what implies an absolute contradiction.

But though our thought seems to possess this unbounded liberty, we shall find, upon a nearer examination, that it is really confined within very narrow limits, and that all this creative power of the mind amounts to no more than the faculty of compounding, transposing, augmenting, or diminishing the materials afforded us by the senses and experience. When we think of a golden mountain, we only join two consistent ideas, *gold,* and *mountain,* with which we were formerly acquainted. A virtuous horse we can conceive; because, from our own feeling, we can conceive virtue; and this we may unite to the figure and shape of a horse, which is an animal familiar to us. In short, all the materials of thinking are derived either from our outward or inward sentiment: the mixture and composition of these belongs alone to the mind and will. Or, to express myself in philosophical language, all our ideas or more feeble perceptions are copies of our impressions or more lively ones.

To prove this, the two following arguments will, I hope, be sufficient. First, when we analyze our thoughts or ideas, however compounded or sublime, we always find that they resolve themselves into such simple ideas as were copied from a precedent feeling or sentiment. Even those ideas, which, at first view, seem the most wide of this origin, are found, upon a nearer scrutiny, to be derived from it. The idea of God, as meaning an infinitely intelligent, wise, and good Being, arises from reflecting on the operations of our own mind, and augmenting, without limit, those qualities of goodness and wisdom. We may prosecute this enquiry to what length we please; where we shall always find, that every idea which we examine is copied from a similar impression. Those who would assert that this position is not universally true nor without exception, have only one, and that an easy method of refuting it; by producing that idea, which, in their opinion, is not derived from this source. It will then be incumbent on us, if we would maintain our doctrine, to produce the impression, or lively perception, which corresponds to it.

Secondly. If it happen, from a defect of the organ, that a man is not susceptible of any species of sensation, we always find that he is as little susceptible of the correspondent ideas. A blind man can form no notion of colours; a deaf man of sounds. Restore either of them that sense in which he is deficient; by opening this new inlet for his sensations, you also open an inlet for the ideas; and he finds no difficulty in conceiving these objects. The case is the same, if the object, proper for exciting any sensation, has never been applied to the organ. A Laplander or Negro has no notion of the relish of wine. And though there are few or no instances of a like deficiency in the mind, where a person has never felt or is wholly incapable of a sentiment or passion that belongs to his species; yet we find the same observation to take place in a less degree. A man of mild manners can form no idea of inveterate revenge or cruelty; nor can a selfish heart easily conceive the heights of friendship and generosity. It is readily allowed, that other beings may possess many senses of which we can have no conception; because the ideas of them have never been introduced to us in the only manner by which an idea can have access to the mind, to wit, by the actual feeling and sensation. . . .

Section IV

SCEPTICAL DOUBTS CONCERNING THE OPERATIONS OF THE UNDERSTANDING

PART 1. All the objects of human reason or enquiry may naturally be divided into two kinds, to wit, *Relations of Ideas,* and *Matters of Fact.* Of the first kind are the sciences of Geometry, Algebra, and Arithmetic; and in short, every affirmation which is either intuitively or demonstratively certain. *That the square of the hypothenuse is equal to the square of the two sides,* is a proposition which expresses a relation between these figures. *That three times five is equal to the half of thirty,* expresses a relation between these numbers. Propositions of this kind are discoverable by the mere operation of thought, without dependence on what is anywhere existent in the universe. Though there never were a circle or triangle in nature, the truths demonstrated by Euclid would for ever retain their certainty and evidence.

Matters of fact, which are the second objects of human reason, are not ascertained in the same manner; nor is our evidence of their truth, however great, of a like nature with the foregoing. The contrary of every matter of fact is still possible; because it can never imply a contradiction, and is conceived by the mind with the same facility and distinctness, as if ever so conformable to reality. *That the sun will not rise to-morrow* is no less intelligible a proposition, and implies no more contradiction than the affirmation, *that it will rise.* We should in vain, therefore, attempt to demonstrate its falsehood. Were it demonstratively false, it would imply a contradiction, and could never be distinctly conceived by the mind.

It may, therefore, be a subject worthy of curiosity, to enquire what is the nature of that evidence which assures us of any real existence and matter of fact, beyond the present testimony of our senses, or the records of our memory. This part of philosophy, it is observable, has been little cultivated, either by the ancients or moderns; and therefore our doubts and errors, in the prosecution of so important an enquiry, may be the more excusable; while we march through such difficult paths without any guide or direction. They may even prove useful, by exciting curiosity, and destroying that implicit faith and security, which is the bane of all reasoning and free enquiry. The discovery of defects in the common philosophy, if any such there be, will not, I presume, be a discouragement, but rather an incitement, as is usual, to attempt something more full and satisfactory than has yet been proposed to the public.

All reasonings concerning matter of fact seem to be founded on the relation of *Cause and Effect.* By means of that relation alone we can go beyond the evidence of our memory and senses. If you were to ask a man, why he believes any matter of fact, which is absent; for instance, that his friend is in the country, or in France; he would give you a reason; and this reason would be some other fact; as a letter received from him, or the knowledge of his former resolutions and promises. A man finding a watch or any other machine in a desert island, would conclude that there had once been men in that island. All our reasonings concerning fact are of the same nature. And here it is constantly supposed that there is a connexion between the present fact and that which is inferred from it. Were there nothing to bind them together, the inference would be entirely precarious. The hearing of an articulate voice and rational discourse in the dark assures us of the presence of some person: Why? because these are the effects of the human make and fabric, and closely connected with it. If we anatomize all the other reasonings of this nature, we shall find that they are founded on the relation of cause and effect, and that this relation is either near or remote, direct or collateral. Heat and light are collateral effects of fire, and the one effect may justly be inferred from the other.

If we would satisfy ourselves, therefore, concerning the nature of that evidence, which assures us of matters of fact, we must enquire how we arrive at the knowledge of cause and effect.

I shall venture to affirm, as a general proposition, which admits of no exception, that the knowledge of this relation is not, in any instance, attained by reasonings *a priori;* but arises entirely from experience, when we find that any particular objects are constantly conjoined with each other. Let an object be presented to a man of ever so strong natural reason and abilities; if that object be entirely new to him, he will not be able, by the most accurate examination of its sensible qualities, to discover any of its causes or effects. Adam, though his rational faculties be supposed, at the very first, entirely perfect, could not have inferred from the fluidity and transparency of water that it would suffocate him, or from the light and warmth of fire that it would consume him. No object ever discovers, by the qualities which appear to the senses, either the causes which produced it, or the effects which will arise from it; nor can our reason, unassisted by experience, ever draw any inference concerning real existence and matter of fact. . . .

We fancy, that were we brought on a sudden into this world, we could at first have inferred that one Billiard-ball would communicate motion to another upon impulse; and that we needed not to have waited for the event, in order to pronounce with certainty concerning it. Such is the influence of custom, that, where it is strongest, it not only covers our natural ignorance, but even conceals itself, and seems not to take place, merely because it is found in the highest degree.

But to convince us that all the laws of nature, and all the operations of bodies without exception, are known only by experience, the following reflections may, perhaps, suffice. Were any object presented to us, and were we required to pronounce concerning the effect, which will result from it, without consulting past observation; after what manner, I beseech you, must the mind proceed in this operation? It must invent or imagine some event, which it ascribes to the object as its effect; and it is plain that this invention must be entirely arbitrary. The mind can never possibly find the effect in the supposed cause, by the most accurate scrutiny and examination. For the effect is totally different from the cause, and consequently can never be discovered in it. Motion in the second Billiard-ball is a quite distinct event from motion in the first; nor is there anything in the one to suggest the smallest hint of the other. A stone or piece of metal raised into the air, and left without any support, immediately falls: but to consider the matter *a priori,* is there anything we discover in this situation which can beget the idea of a downward, rather than an upward, or any other motion, in the stone or metal?

And as the first imagination or invention of a particular effect, in all natural operations, is arbitrary, where we consult not experience; so must we also esteem the supposed tie or connexion between the cause and effect, which binds them together, and renders it impossible that any other effect could result from the operation of that cause. When I see, for instance, a Billiard-ball moving in a straight line towards another; even suppose motion in the second ball should by accident be suggested to me, as the result of their contact or impulse; may I not conceive, that a hundred different events might as well follow from that cause? May not both these balls remain at absolute rest? May not the first ball return in a straight line, or leap off from the second in any line or direction? All these suppositions are consistent and conceivable. Why then should we give the preference to one, which is no more consistent or conceivable than the rest? All our reasonings *a priori* will never be able to show us any foundation for this preference. . . .

PART II. But we have not yet attained any tolerable satisfaction with regard to the question first proposed. Each solution still gives rise to a new question as difficult as the foregoing, and leads us on to farther enquiries. When it is asked, *What is the nature of all our reasonings concerning matter of fact?* the proper answer seems to be, that they are founded on the relation of cause and effect. When again it is asked, *What is the foundation of all our reasonings and conclusions concerning that relation?* it may be replied in one word, Experience. But if we still carry on our sifting humour, and ask, *What is the foundation of all conclusions from experience?* this implies a new question, which may be of more difficult solution and explication. Philosophers, that give themselves airs of superior wisdom and sufficiency, have a hard task when they encounter persons of inquisitive dispositions, who push them from every corner to which they retreat, and who are sure at last to bring them to some dangerous dilemma. The best expedient to prevent this confusion, is to be modest in our pretensions; and even to discover the difficulty ourselves before it is objected to us. By this means, we may make a kind of merit of our very ignorance.

I shall content myself, in this section, with an easy task, and shall pretend only to give a negative answer to the question here proposed. I say then, that, even after we have experience of the operations of cause and effect, our conclusions from that experience are *not* founded on reasoning, or any process of the understanding. This answer we must endeavour both to explain and to defend.

It must certainly be allowed, that nature has kept us at a great distance from all her secrets, and has afforded us only the knowledge of a few superficial qualities of objects; while she conceals from us those powers and principles on which the influence of those objects entirely depends. Our senses inform us of the colour, weight, and consistence of bread; but neither sense nor reason can ever inform us of those qualities which fit it for the nourishment and support of a human body. Sight or feeling conveys an idea of the actual motion of bodies; but as to that wonderful force or power, which would carry on a moving body for ever in a continued change of place, and which bodies never lose but by communicating it to others; of this we cannot form the most distant conception. But notwithstanding this

ignorance of natural powers and principles, we always presume, when we see like sensible qualities, that they have like secret powers, and expect that effects, similar to those which we have experienced, will follow from them. If a body of like colour and consistence with that bread, which we have formerly [eaten], be presented to us, we make no scruple of repeating the experiment, and foresee, with certainty, like nourishment and support. Now this is a process of the mind or thought, of which I would willingly know the foundation. It is allowed on all hands that there is no known connexion between the sensible qualities and the secret powers; and consequently, that the mind is not led to form such a conclusion concerning their constant and regular conjunction, by anything which it knows of their nature. As to past *Experience,* it can be allowed to give *direct* and *certain* information of those precise objects only, and that precise period of time, which fell under its cognizance: but why this experience should be extended to future times, and to other objects, which for aught we know, may be only in appearance similar; this is the main question on which I would insist. The bread, which I formerly [ate], nourished me; that is, a body of such sensible qualities was, at that time, endued with such secret powers: but does it follow, that other bread must also nourish me at another time, and that like sensible qualities must always be attended with like secret powers? The consequence seems nowise necessary. At least, it must be acknowledged that there is here a consequence drawn by the mind; that there is a certain step taken; a process of thought, and an inference, which wants to be explained. These two propositions are far from being the same, *I have found that such an object has always been attended with such an effect,* and *I foresee, that other objects, which are, in appearance, similar, will be attended with similar effects.* I shall allow, if you please, that the one proposition may justly be inferred from the other: I know, in fact, that it always is inferred. But if you insist that the inference is made by a chain of reasoning, I desire you to produce that reasoning. The connexion between these propositions is not intuitive. There is required a medium, which may enable the mind to draw such an inference, if indeed it be drawn by reasoning and argument. What that medium is, I must confess, passes my comprehension; and it is incumbent on those to produce it, who assert that it really exists; and is the origin of all our conclusions concerning matter of fact.

This negative argument must certainly, in process of time, become altogether convincing, if many penetrating and able philosophers shall turn their enquiries this way and no one be ever able to discover any connecting proposition or intermediate step, which supports the understanding in this conclusion. But as the question is yet new, every reader may not trust so far to his own penetration, as to conclude, because an argument escapes his enquiry, that therefore it does not really exist. For this reason it may be requisite to venture upon a more difficult task; and enumerating all the branches of human knowledge, endeavour to show that none of them can afford such an argument.

All reasonings may be divided into two kinds, namely, demonstrative reasoning, or that concerning relations of ideas, and moral reasoning, or that concerning matter of fact and existence. That there are no demonstrative arguments in the case seems evident; since it implies no contradiction that the course of nature may change, and that an object, seemingly like those which we have experienced, may be attended with different or contrary effects. May I not clearly and distinctly conceive that a body, falling from the clouds, and which, in all other respects, resembles snow, has yet the taste of salt or feeling of fire? Is there any more intelligible proposition than to affirm, that all the trees will flourish in December and January, and decay in May and June? Now whatever is intelligible, and can be distinctly conceived, implies no contradiction, and can never be proved false by any demonstrative argument or abstract reasoning *a priori*.

If we be, therefore, engaged by arguments to put trust in past experience, and make it the standard of our future judgment, these arguments must be probable only, or such as regard matter of fact and real existence, according to the division above mentioned. But that there is no argument of this kind, must appear, if our explication of that species of reasoning be admitted as solid and satisfactory. We have said that all arguments concerning existence are founded on the relation of cause and effect; that our knowledge of that relation is derived entirely from experience; and that all our experimental conclusions proceed upon the supposition that the future will be conformable to the past. To endeavour, therefore, the proof of this last supposition by probable arguments, or arguments regarding existence, must be evidently going in a circle, and taking that for granted, which is the very point in question.

In reality, all arguments from experience are founded on the similarity which we discover among natural objects, and by which we are induced to expect effects similar to those which we have found to follow from such objects. And though none but a fool or madman will ever pretend to dispute the authority of experience, or to reject that great guide of human life, it may surely be allowed a philosopher to have so much curiosity at least as to examine the principle of human nature, which gives this mighty authority to experience, and makes us draw advantage from that similarity which nature has placed among different objects. From causes which appear *similar* we expect similar effects. This is the sum of all our experimental conclusions. Now it seems evident that, if this conclusion were formed by reason, it would be as perfect at first, and upon one instance, as after ever so long a course of experience. But the case is far otherwise. Nothing so like as eggs; yet no one, on account of this appearing similarity, expects the same taste and relish in all of them. It is only after a long course of uniform experiments in any kind, that we attain a firm reliance and security with regard to a particular event. Now where is that process of reasoning which, from one instance, draws a conclusion, so different from that which it infers from a hundred instances that are nowise different from that single one? This question I propose as much for the sake of information, as with an intention of raising difficulties. I cannot find, I cannot imagine any such reasoning. But I keep my mind still open to instruction, if any one will vouchsafe to bestow it on me.

6.5 Should We Believe Beyond the Evidence?

Should you believe something to be true even though you have insufficient evidence that it is true? Do you have a moral obligation to refrain from believing something true or false if the available evidence is not sufficient? Suppose you loan your old car to a friend. You have not checked the brakes in some time, but you dismiss all doubts about the brakes from your mind, confident that they will work because they have in the past. Suppose your friend crashes and dies due to faulty brakes. Are you to blame? Suppose your friend does not crash and die. Are you to blame for putting her life in danger? According to William K. Clifford (1845–1879), if you do not have sufficient evidence that the brakes are in working order, then you are to blame no matter what happens.

Clifford, a British mathematician interested in philosophical and religious topics, wrote an essay entitled "The Ethics of Belief." Clifford's argument reflects an epistemological position called evidentialism. **Evidentialism** holds that we should not accept any statement as true unless we have good evidence to support its truth. Our beliefs about the truth of things—be they moral, religious, or scientific beliefs—must meet appropriate *epistemic* standards. *Practical* standards, such as aiding me in accomplishing certain goals or possibly resulting in my eternal happiness, will not do. William James (1842–1910), an American philosopher, wrote a famous essay in reply to Clifford, called "The Will To Believe." James advocated a philosophy called **pragmatism.**

James characterized pragmatism (from the Greek word *pragma*, meaning "action") as a method for settling philosophical disputes. This method was based on a distinctive theory of truth, called the **pragmatic theory of truth.** According to this theory, some proposition *p* is true if and only if the belief that "*p* is true" works.

"And what does *works* mean"? you ask. James used words like "useful," "adaptive," "serviceable," "satisfying," "verifiable," and "agreeing with reality" to try to explain what it means. He also asserted that for any proposition to "work" and hence to be taken as true, it must be consistent with what we already take to be true, and it must be in agreement with our sense experience. Thus, my belief that "my fat, blind cat is on the rug by the fire" works as long as it is consistent with my other beliefs (he is not outside, he is not in the kitchen eating my dinner, he is not in the pool practicing his backstroke, etc.), and when I look at the rug I get "fat-blind-cat" type sensations.

We can grasp James's theory better by contrasting it with two other theories of truth, both of which derive from Plato. They have been the two dominant theories of truth in Western thought. The first is called the **correspondence theory of truth.** According to this theory, *p* is true if and only if *p* corresponds to the facts. My believing *p* to be true or false has nothing to do with the matter of its truth, or so this theory would maintain. "My cat is on the rug" is true if, indeed, that is where the cat is and is false if the cat is not there. Even if I don't look and no matter how I feel or what I believe, it is true or false independent of my actions or beliefs.

The second theory of truth is called the **coherence theory of truth.** According to this view, *p* is true if and only if *p* is logically implied by *q*, where *q* is a true statement, and *q* in turn is logically implied by *r*, and so on. Truth, on this account, is the coherence of a whole system of statements in which each statement is entailed by all the others. We have only fragments of this whole, but when and if we ever discover the entire system, we will have arrived at absolute truth. Thus, "My fat, blind cat is on the rug" is true if a whole host of other propositions are true such as "My cat is blind," "The rug exists," "Cats exist," and so on.

James ascribed both the correspondence and coherence theories to philosophers he called "intellectualists and rationalists." He objected to these theories on the grounds that they present truth as a static property existing prior to and independent of human experience and investigation. James saw truth as something dynamic, something that happens to ideas when they lead humans into ever more satisfactory experiences. The rationalists accused James, in turn, of denying objectivity, reducing truth to a matter of what we want to believe, and making it relative to the context in which we verify propositions.

From James's point of view, Clifford's argument rests in part on a reliance on a static theory of truth, which too narrowly confines our thinking. His insistence on purely epistemic standards, and his refusal to admit practical standards, not only denies the facts involved in how humans come to hold many of their beliefs, but also restricts us to a very narrow range of beliefs and forbids us to have beliefs about some of the most important matters that make human life worth living.

James's argument against evidentialism is often misunderstood because readers ignore the conditions James placed on believing beyond the evidence. In at least three situations, James contended, belief beyond the evidence is justified. First, when you are confronted with what he called a "genuine option" that *cannot be decided on evidential grounds,* you have a right to decide the issue according to your "passional nature." Second, when faced with a situation when belief in a fact is necessary for the existence of that fact, you have the right to believe beyond the evidence. And finally, in a situation when belief in a true proposition is necessary for getting at the evidence in support of its truth, you are entitled to believe.

What follows are brief selections from both Clifford's essay and James's. Read their arguments and decide for yourself whether we have a right to believe beyond the evidence.

Reading Questions

1. What do the examples of the shipowner and the commission show?
2. Do you agree with Clifford's contention that all of us have a duty to question our beliefs? Why, or why not?
3. Do you agree with Clifford's claim that it is "wrong always, everywhere, and for anyone, to believe anything upon insufficient evidence"? Why, or why not?
4. What do you think Clifford means by "sufficient evidence"? How much evidence is sufficient?
5. What, according to James, is a *genuine option?* Give an example.
6. What is James's thesis?
7. How, according to James, does Clifford's attitude differ from James's with respect to "our first and great commandments as would-be knowers"?
8. How did James support his own attitude? What examples did he use? Do his examples support his thesis? Why, or why not?
9. Who do you think is right, Clifford or James? Why?

The Ethics of Belief

WILLIAM K. CLIFFORD

A SHIPOWNER WAS ABOUT to send to sea an emigrant-ship. He knew that she was old, and not over-well built at the first; that she had seen many seas and climes, and often had needed repairs. Doubts had been suggested to him that possibly she was not seaworthy. These doubts preyed upon his mind, and made him unhappy; he thought that perhaps he ought to have her thoroughly overhauled and refitted, even though this should put him to great expense. Before the ship sailed, however, he succeeded in overcoming these melancholy reflections. He said to himself that she had gone safely through so many voyages and weathered so many storms that it was idle to suppose she would not come safely home from this trip also. He would put his trust in providence, which could hardly fail to protect all these unhappy families that were leaving their fatherland to seek for better times elsewhere. He would dismiss from his mind all ungenerous suspicions about the honesty of builders and contractors. In such ways he acquired a sincere and comfortable conviction that his vessel was thoroughly safe and seaworthy; he watched her departure with a light heart, and benevolent wishes for the success of the exiles in their strange new home that was to be; and he got his insurance-money when she went down in mid-ocean and told no tales.

What shall we say of him? Surely this, that he was verily guilty of the death of those men. It is admitted that he did sincerely believe in the soundness of his ship; but the sincerity of his conviction can in no wise help him, because *he had no right to believe on such evidence as was before him.* He had acquired his belief not by honestly earning it in patient investigation, but by stifling his doubts. And although in the end he may have felt so sure about it that he could not think otherwise, yet inasmuch as he had knowingly and willingly worked himself into that frame of mind, he must be held responsible for it.

Let us alter the case a little, and suppose that the ship was not unsound after all; that she made her voyage safely, and many others after it. Will that diminish the guilt of her owner? Not one jot. When an action is once done, it is right or wrong for ever; no accidental failure of its good or evil fruits can possibly alter that. The man would not have been innocent, he would only have been not found out. The question of right or wrong has to do with the origin of his belief, not the matter of it; not what it was, but how he got it; not whether it turned out to be true or false, but whether he had a right to believe on such evidence as was before him.

There was once an island in which some of the inhabitants professed a religion teaching neither the doctrine of original sin nor that of eternal punishment. A suspicion got abroad that the professors of this religion had made use of unfair means to get their doctrines taught to children. They were accused of wresting the laws of their country in such a way as to remove children from the care of their natural and legal guardians; and even of stealing them away and keeping them concealed from their friends and relations. A certain number of men formed themselves into a society for the purpose of agitating the public about this matter. They published grave accusations against individual citizens of the highest position and character, and did all in their power to injure these citizens in the exercise of their professions. So great was the noise they made, that a Commission was appointed to investigate the facts; but after the Commission had carefully inquired into all the evidence that could be got, it appeared that the accused were innocent. Not only had they been accused on insufficient evidence, but the evidence of their innocence was such as the agitators might easily have obtained, if they had attempted a fair inquiry. After these disclosures the inhabitants of that country looked upon the

From Lectures and Essays, *Vol. 2 (London: Macmillan, 1897), pp. 177–188. Footnotes deleted.*

members of the agitating society, not only as persons whose judgment was to be distrusted, but also as no longer to be counted honourable men. For although they had sincerely and conscientiously believed in the charges they had made, yet *they had no right to believe on such evidence as was before them.* Their sincere convictions, instead of being honestly earned by patient inquiring, were stolen by listening to the voice of prejudice and passion.

Let us vary this case also, and suppose, other things remaining as before, that a still more accurate investigation proved the accused to have been really guilty. Would this make any difference in the guilt of the accusers? Clearly not; the question is not whether their belief was true or false, but whether they entertained it on wrong grounds. . . .

In the two supposed cases which have been considered, it has been judged wrong to believe on insufficient evidence, or to nourish belief by suppressing doubts and avoiding investigation. The reason of this judgment is not far to seek: it is that in both these cases the belief held by one man was of great importance to other men. But forasmuch as no belief held by one man, however seemingly trivial the belief, and however obscure the believer, is ever actually insignificant or without its effect on the fate of mankind, we have no choice but to extend our judgment to all cases of belief whatever. . . .

It is not only the leader of men, statesman, philosopher, or poet, that owes this bounden duty to mankind. Every rustic who delivers in the village alehouse his slow, infrequent sentences, may help to kill or keep alive the fatal superstitions which clog his race. Every hard-worked wife of an artisan may transmit to her children beliefs which shall knit society together, or rend it in pieces. No simplicity of mind, no obscurity of station, can escape the universal duty of questioning all that we believe. . . .

The harm which is done by credulity in a man is not confined to the fostering of a credulous character in others, and consequent support of false beliefs. Habitual want of care about what I believe leads to habitual want of care in others about the truth of what is told to me. Men speak the truth to one another when each reveres the truth in his own mind and in the other's mind; but how shall my friend revere the truth in my mind when I myself am careless about it, when I believe things because I want to believe them, and because they are comforting and pleasant? Will he not learn to cry, "Peace," to me, when there is no peace? By such a course I shall surround myself with a thick atmosphere of falsehood and fraud, and in that I must live. It may matter little to me, in my cloud-castle of sweet illusions and darling lies; but it matters much to Man that I have made my neighbours ready to deceive. The credulous man is father to the liar and the cheat; he lives in the bosom of this his family, and it is no marvel if he should become even as they are. So closely are our duties knit together, that whoso shall keep the whole law, and yet offend in one point, he is guilty of all.

To sum up: it is wrong always, everywhere, and for anyone, to believe anything upon insufficient evidence. . . .

The Will to Believe

WILLIAM JAMES

LET US GIVE the name of *hypothesis* to anything that may be proposed to our belief; and just as the electricians speak of live and dead wires, let us speak of any hypothesis as either *live* or *dead*.

From William James, The Will to Believe and Other Essays in Popular Philosophy *(New York: Henry Holt, 1912), pp. 1–31.*

A live hypothesis is one which appeals as a real possibility to him to whom it is proposed. If I ask you to believe in the Mahdi, the notion makes no electric connection with your nature—it refuses to scintillate with any credibility at all. As an hypothesis it is completely dead. To an Arab, however (even if he be not one of the Mahdi's followers), the hypothesis is among the mind's possibilities: it is alive. This shows that deadness and liveness in an hypothesis are not intrinsic properties, but relations to the individual thinker. They are measured by his willingness to act. The maximum of liveness in an hypothesis means willingness to act irrevocably. Practically, that means belief; but there is some believing tendency wherever there is willingness to act at all.

Next, let us call the decision between two hypotheses an *option*. Options may be of several kinds. They may be—1, *living* or *dead;* 2, *forced* or *avoidable;* 3, *momentous* or *trivial;* and for our purposes we may call an option a *genuine* option when it is of the forced, living and momentous kind.

1. A living option is one in which both hypotheses are live ones. If I say to you: "Be a theosophist or be a mahomedan," it is probably a dead option, because for you neither hypothesis is likely to be alive. But if I say "Be an agnostic or be a Christian," it is otherwise: trained as you are, each hypothesis makes some appeal, however small, to your belief.

2. Next, if I say to you: "Choose between going out with your umbrella or without it," I do not offer you a genuine option, for it is not forced. You can easily avoid it by not going out at all. Similarly, if I say "Either love me or hate me," "Either call my theory true or call it false," your option is avoidable. You may remain indifferent to me, neither loving nor hating, and you may decline to offer any judgment as to my theory. But if I say "Either accept this truth or go without it," I put on you a forced option, for there is no standing place outside of the alternative. Every dilemma based on a complete logical disjunction, with no possibility of not choosing, is an option of this forced kind.

3. Finally, if I were Dr. Nansen and proposed to you to join my North Pole expedition, your option would be momentous; for this would probably be your only similar opportunity, and your choice now would either exclude you from the North Pole sort of immortality altogether or put at least the chance of it into your hands. He who refuses to embrace a unique opportunity loses the prize as surely as if he tried and failed. *Per contra,* the option is trivial when the opportunity is not unique, when the stake is insignificant, or when the decision is reversible if it later prove unwise. Such trivial options abound in the scientific life. A chemist finds an hypothesis live enough to spend a year in its verification: he believes in it to that extent. But if his experiments prove inconclusive either way, he is quit for his loss of time, no vital harm being done. . . .

The thesis I defend is, briefly stated, this: *Our passional nature not only lawfully may, but must, decide an option between propositions, whenever it is a genuine option that cannot by its nature be decided on intellectual grounds; for to say, under such circumstances, "Do not decide, but leave the question open," is itself a passional decision—just like deciding yes or no—and is attended with the same risk of losing the truth. . . .*

There are two ways of looking at our duty in the matter of opinion—ways entirely different, and yet ways about whose difference the theory of knowledge seems hitherto to have shown very little concern. *We must know the truth;* and *we must avoid error*—these are our first and great commandments as would-be knowers; but they are not two ways of stating an identical commandment, they are two separable laws. Although it may indeed happen that when we believe the truth *A,* we escape as an incidental consequence from believing the falsehood *B,* it hardly ever happens that by merely disbelieving *B* we necessarily believe *A.* We may in escaping *B* fall into believing other falsehoods, *C* or *D,* just as bad as *B;* or we may escape *B* by not believing anything at all, not even *A.*

Believe truth! Shun error!—these, we see, are two materially different laws; and by choosing between them we may end by colouring differently our whole intellectual life. We may regard the chase for truth as paramount, and the avoidance of error as secondary; or we may, on the other hand, treat the avoidance of error as more imperative, and let truth take its chance. Clifford . . . exhorts us to the latter course. Believe nothing, he tells us, keep your mind in suspense forever, rather than by closing it on insufficient evidence incur the awful risk of believing lies. You, on the other hand, may think that the risk of being in error is a very small matter when compared with the blessings of real knowledge, and be ready to be duped many times in your investigation rather than postpone indefinitely the chance of guessing true. I myself find it impossible to go with Clifford. We must remember that these feelings of our duty about either truth or error are in any case only expressions of our passional life. Biologically considered, our minds are as ready to grind out falsehood as veracity, and he who says "Better go without belief forever than believe a lie!" merely shows his own preponderant private horror of becoming a dupe. He may be critical of many of his desires and fears, but this fear he slavishly obeys. He cannot imagine anyone questioning its binding force. For my own part, I have also a horror of being duped; but I can believe that worse things than being duped may happen to a man in this world: so Clifford's exhortation has to my ears a thoroughly fantastic sound. It is like a general informing his soldiers that it is better to keep out of battle forever than to risk a single wound. Not so are victories either over enemies or over nature gained. Our errors are surely not such awfully solemn things. In a world where we are so certain to incur them in spite of all our caution, a certain lightness of heart seems healthier than this excessive nervousness on their behalf. . . .

Wherever the option between losing truth and gaining it is not momentous, we can throw the chance of *gaining truth* away, and at any rate save ourselves from any chance of *believing falsehood,* by not making up our minds at all till objective evidence has come. In scientific questions, this is almost always the case; and even in human affairs in general, the need of acting is seldom so urgent that a false belief to act on is better than no belief at all. Law courts, indeed, have to decide on the best evidence attainable for the moment, because a judge's duty is to make law as well as to

ascertain it, and (as a learned judge once said to me) few cases are worth spending much time over: the great thing is to have them decided on *any* acceptable principle, and got out of the way. But in our dealings with objective nature we obviously are recorders, not makers, of the truth; and decisions for the mere sake of deciding promptly and getting on to the next business would be wholly out of place. Throughout the breadth of physical nature facts are what they are quite independently of us, and seldom is there any such hurry about them that the risks of being duped by believing a premature theory need be faced. The questions here are always trivial options, the hypotheses are hardly living (at any rate not living for us spectators), the choice between believing truth or falsehood is seldom forced. The attitude of sceptical balance is therefore the absolutely wise one if we would escape mistakes. . .

[But] are there not somewhere forced options in our speculative questions, and can we (as men who may be interested at least as much in positively gaining truth as in merely escaping dupery) always wait with impunity till the coercive evidence shall have arrived? . . .

Moral questions immediately present themselves as questions whose solution cannot wait for sensible proof. A moral question is a question not of what sensibly exists, but of what is good, or would be good if it did exist. Science can tell us what exists; but to compare the *worths,* both of what exists and of what does not exist, we must consult not science, but what Pascal calls our heart. Science herself consults her heart when she lays it down that the infinite ascertainment of fact and correction of false belief are the supreme goods for man. Challenge the statement and science can only repeat it oracularly, or else prove it by showing that such ascertainment and correction bring man all sorts of other goods which man's heart in turn declares. The question of having moral beliefs at all or not having them is decided by our will. Are our moral preferences true or false, or are they only odd biological phenomena, making things good or bad for *us,* but in themselves indifferent? How can your pure intellect decide? If your heart does not *want* a world of moral reality, your head will assuredly never make you believe in one. . . .

Turn now from these wide questions of good to a certain class of questions of fact, questions concerning personal relations, states of mind between one man and another. *Do you like me or not?*—for example. Whether you do or not depends, in countless instances, on whether I meet you half-way, am willing to assume that you must like me, and show you trust and expectation. The previous faith on my part in your liking's existence is in such cases what makes your liking come. But if I stand aloof, and refuse to budge an inch until I have objective evidence, . . . ten to one your liking never comes. How many women's hearts are vanquished by the mere sanguine insistence of some man that they *must* love him! he will not consent to the hypothesis that they cannot. The desire for a certain kind of truth here brings about that special truth's existence; and so it is in innumerable cases of other sorts. Who gains promotions, boons, appointments, but the man in whose life they are seen to play the part of live hypotheses, who discounts them, sacrifices other things for their sake before they have come, and takes risks for them in advance? His faith acts on the powers above him as a claim, and creates its own verification.

A social organism of any sort whatever, large or small, is what it is because each member proceeds to his own duty with a trust that the other members will simultaneously do theirs. Wherever a desired result is achieved by the co-operation of many independent persons, its existence as a fact is a pure consequence of the precursive faith in one another of those immediately concerned. A government, an army, a commercial system, a ship, a college, an athletic team, all exist on this condition, without which not only is nothing achieved, but nothing is even attempted. A whole train of passengers (individually brave enough) will be looted by a few highwaymen, simply because the latter can count on one another, while each passenger fears that if he makes a movement of resistance, he will be shot before anyone else backs him up. If we believed that the whole car-full would rise at once with us, we should each severally rise, and train-robbing

would never even be attempted. There are, then, cases where a fact cannot come at all unless a preliminary faith exists in its coming. *And where faith in a fact can help create the fact,* that would be an insane logic which should say that faith running ahead of scientific evidence is the "lowest kind of immorality" into which a thinking being can fall. Yet such is the logic by which our scientific absolutists pretend to regulate our lives!

In truths dependent on our personal action, then, faith based on desire is certainly a lawful and possibly an indispensable thing.

But now, it will be said, these are all childish human cases, and have nothing to do with great cosmical matters, like the question of religious faith. Let us then pass on to that. Religions differ so much in their accidents that in discussing the religious question we must make it very generic and broad. What then do we now mean by the religious hypothesis? Science says things are; morality says some things are better than other things; and religion says essentially two things.

First, she says that the best things are the most eternal things, the overlapping things, the things in the universe that throw the last stone, so to speak, and say the final word. "Perfection is eternal"—this phrase of Charles Secrétan seems a good way of putting this first affirmation of religion, an affirmation which obviously cannot yet be verified scientifically at all.

The second affirmation of religion is that we are better off even now if we believe her first affirmation to be true.

Now let us consider what the logical elements of this situation are *in case the religious hypothesis in both its branches be really true.* (Of course, we must admit that possibility at the outset. If we are to discuss the question at all, it must involve a living option. If for any of you religion be a hypothesis that cannot, by any living possibility be true, then you need go no farther. I speak to the "saving remnant" alone.) So proceeding, we see, first, that religion offers itself as a *momentous* option. We are supposed to gain, even now, by our belief, and to lose by our non-belief, a certain vital good. Secondly, religion is a *forced* option, so far as that good goes. We cannot escape the issue by remaining sceptical and waiting for more light, because, although we do avoid error in that way *if religion be untrue,* we lose the good, *if it be true,* just as certainly as if we positively chose to disbelieve. It is as if a man should hesitate indefinitely to ask a certain woman to marry him because he was not perfectly sure that she would prove an angel after he brought her home. Would he not cut himself off from that particular angel-possibility as decisively as if he went and married someone else? Scepticism, then, is not avoidance of option; it is option of a certain particular kind of risk. *Better risk loss of truth than chance of error*—that is your faith-vetoer's exact position. He is actively playing his stake as much as the believer is; he is backing the field against the religious hypothesis, just as the believer is backing the religious hypothesis against the field. To preach scepticism to us as a duty until "sufficient evidence" for religion be found, is tantamount therefore to telling us, when in presence of the religious hypothesis, that to yield to our fear of its being error is wiser and better than to yield to our hope that it may be true. It is not intellect against all passions, then; it is only intellect with one passion laying down its law. And by what, forsooth, is the supreme wisdom of this passion warranted? Dupery for dupery, what proof is there that dupery through hope is so much worse than dupery through fear? I, for one, can see no proof; and I simply refuse obedience to the scientist's command to imitate his kind of option, in a case where my own stake is important enough to give me the right to choose my own form of risk. If religion be true and the evidence for it be still insufficient, I do not wish, by putting your extinguisher upon my nature (which feels to me as if it had after all some business in this matter), to forfeit my sole chance in life of getting upon the winning side—that chance depending, of course, on my willingness to run the risk of acting as if my passional need of taking the world religiously might be prophetic and right.

All this is on the supposition that it really may be prophetic and right, and that, even to us who are discussing the matter, religion is a live hypothesis which may be true. Now to most of us religion comes in a still farther way that makes a veto on our active faith even more illogical. The more perfect and more eternal aspect of the universe is represented in our religions as having personal form. The universe is no longer a mere *It* to us, but a *Thou,* if we are religious; and any relation that may be possible from person to person might be possible here. For instance, although in one sense we are passive portions of the universe, in another we show a curious autonomy, as if we were small active centres on our own account. We feel, too, as if the appeal of religion to us were made to our own active goodwill, as if evidence might be forever withheld from us unless we met the hypothesis half-way. To take a trivial illustration: just as a man who in a company of gentlemen made no advances, asked a warrant for every concession, and believed no one's word without proof, would cut himself off by such churlishness from all the social rewards that a more trusting spirit would earn—so here, one who should shut himself up in snarling logicality and try to make the gods extort his recognition willy-nilly, or not get it at all, might cut himself off forever from his only opportunity of making the gods' acquaintance. This feeling, forced on us we know not whence, that by obstinately believing that there are gods (although not to do so would be so easy both for our logic and our life) we are doing the universe the deepest service we can, seems part of the living essence of the religious hypothesis. If the hypothesis *were* true in all its parts, including this one, then pure intellectualism, with its veto on our making willing advances, would be an absurdity; and some participation of our sympathetic nature would be logically required. I, therefore, for one, cannot see my way to accepting the agnostic rules for truth-seeking, or wilfully agree to keep my willing nature out of the game. I cannot do so for this plain reason, that *a rule of thinking which would absolutely prevent me from acknowledging certain kinds of truth if those kinds of truth were really there, would be an irrational rule.* That for me is the long and short of the formal logic of the situation, no matter what the kinds of truth might materially be.

I confess I do not see how this logic can be escaped. But sad experience makes me fear that some of you may still shrink from radically saying with me, *in abstracto,* that we have the right to believe at our own risk any hypothesis that is live enough to tempt our will. I suspect, however, that if this is so, it is because you have got away from the abstract logical point of view altogether, and are thinking (perhaps without realizing it) of some particular religious hypothesis which for you is dead. The freedom to "believe what we will" you apply to the case of some patent superstition; and the faith you think of is the faith defined by the schoolboy when he said, "Faith is when you believe something that you know ain't true." I can only repeat that this is misapprehension. *In concreto,* the freedom to believe can only cover living options which the intellect of the individual cannot by itself resolve; and living options never seem absurdities to him who has them to consider. When I look at the religious question as it really puts itself to concrete men, and when I think of all the possibilities which both practically and theoretically it involves, then this command that we shall put a stopper on our heart, instincts and courage, and *wait*—acting of course meanwhile more or less as if religion were *not* true—till doomsday, or till such time as our intellect and senses working together may have

raked in evidence enough—this command, I say, seems to me the queerest idol ever manufactured in the philosophic cave. Were we scholastic absolutists, there might be more excuse. If we had an infallible intellect with its objective certitudes, we might feel ourselves disloyal to such a perfect organ of knowledge in not trusting to it exclusively, in not waiting for its releasing word. But if we are empiricists, if we believe that no bell in us tolls to let us know for certain when truth is in our grasp, then it seems a piece of idle fantasticality to preach so solemnly our duty of waiting for the bell. Indeed we *may* wait if we will—I hope you do not think that I am denying that— but if we do so, we do so at our peril as much as if we believed. In either case we *act,* taking our life in our hands. No one of us ought to issue vetoes to the other, nor should we bandy words of abuse. We ought, on the contrary, delicately and profoundly to respect one another's mental freedom—then only shall we bring about the intellectual republic; then only shall we have that spirit of inner tolerance without which all our outer tolerance is soulless, and which is empiricism's glory; then only shall we live and let live, in speculative as well as in practical things. . . .

6.6 *Classical Indian Epistemology*

Some people think of Indian philosophy as "spiritual" and unconcerned with technical issues relating to truth and knowledge. Popular culture associates India with mysticism, meditation, and religion. Students often study about India in religious studies courses but seldom in philosophy classes.

This picture of Indian thought as spiritual is misleading. Among the various schools of Indian philosophy, careful attention is given to logical and epistemological issues. For example, Udayana, an Indian philosopher who lived about 1000, combined two previous schools of philosophy, the Vaisesika and the **Nyaya** ("nyah-yah") schools, into what is usually called **Naiyayika.** This philosophic school advanced an epistemological theory (first developed in Nyaya philosophy) that influenced much of Indian philosophy. According to this theory, the correct causes of knowledge (called **pramā nas**) can be analyzed into four kinds: perception, inference, comparison (analogy), and reliable testimony.

Perceptual knowledge arises from the contact of the senses (eye, ear, nose, etc.) with an object external to the senses, and such contact correctly represents the way the object is. *Inferential knowledge* arises from the inference from a bit of perceptual knowledge (I see smoke) to a correct conclusion concerning what is not immediately seen (there is a fire). *Analogical knowledge* derives from drawing a correct conclusion about an unknown object from the similarities between it and a known object. *Testimonial knowledge* occurs when the person telling you something is honest and reliable, knows what she or he is talking about, and you understand correctly what is said.

Naiyayika philosophers were very much concerned with epistemological issues. They viewed knowledge as a relation between self (subject) and nonself (object). Knowledge, they claimed, is like the light of a lamp that reveals objects. The light is not the object nor the subject, but it makes it possible for an object to be seen by a subject.

Other schools of Indian philosophy also developed epistemological theories. For example, Advaita Vedanta argued that we do perceive the absence of things. If the Naiyayika theory is correct that perception is dependent upon the contact of the sense organs with an object, then when an object is absent, we can never correctly know this. However, we do perceive, and correctly perceive, things as absent. Hence the Advaitins added nonperception or the perception of the absence of something to the list of *pranamas.*

There were debates, however, not just about the causes of knowledge, but about the nature of knowledge itself. What are the marks of knowledge? If you had to state the characteristics that differentiate knowledge from opinion, what might you say? One thing you might say is that any cognition (thought or perception) that is going to count as knowledge must be true. In other words, truth is an essential feature of knowledge. Of course this leads to the question "What is truth?" and, as we saw in the last section, there are different theories of truth. However, is truth the only essential feature of knowledge? Some Indian philosophers have maintained that it is not. Not only must a cognition be true in order to count as knowledge, it must also be novel or new. If novelty were accepted as an essential mark of knowledge, what sort of conceptual difficulties might it cause when we consider cases of memory or cases of persistent true perceptions of the same object over a period of time?

In the next selection, D. M Datta (1916–   ), former professor of philosophy at Patna University, discusses some of the controversies in classical Indian philosophy surrounding the question of the marks of knowledge. He compares some of this debate to Western theories of truth (see the previous section) and shows you how complicated these debates can become as one question leads to an answer that in turn produces another question.

Reading Questions

1. What is *pramā?*
2. What are the four different views of truth?
3. What are the problems and their solutions associated with the claim that novelty is an essential mark of knowledge?
4. What do you think are the essential marks of knowledge, and why do you think so?

Knowledge and the Methods of Knowledge

D. M. DATTA

THE SANSKRIT WORD JÑĀNA stands for all kinds of cognition irrespective of the question of truth and falsehood. But the word pramā is used to designate only a true cognition . . . as distinct from a false one. . . . In English the word knowledge implies a cognition attended with belief. If, therefore, a cognition turns out to be false, belief in it is immediately withdrawn and as such it should cease to be called knowledge. Consequently knowledge, strictly speaking, should always stand only for a cognition that is true, uncontradicted or unfalsified. The ordinary division of knowledge into true knowledge and false knowledge should, therefore, be considered as an instance of loose thinking; the word true as applied to knowledge would then be a tautology, and the word false positively contradictory—false knowledge being only a name for falsified knowledge, which is another name for no knowledge.

If this logical meaning of the word knowledge be consistently and rigidly adhered to, knowledge will exactly correspond to the word pramā. Pramā is generally defined as a cognition having the twofold characteristics of truth and novelty. . . .

As regards the first characteristic, truth, all schools of Indian philosophy are unanimous. Every philosopher holds that truth should be the differentia of knowledge or pramā. But views as regards the meaning of truth vary, and consequently the mark of a pramā is variously expressed. Broadly speaking there are at least four different views about truth.

According to one view the truth of knowledge consists in its practical value. A true cognition is, therefore, variously defined as that which reveals an object that serves some purpose . . . or leads to the achievement of some end, or which favours a successful volition. . . . This view will at once be seen to resemble the modern pragmatic theory of the West. It is mostly held by the Buddhists, but other writers also occasionally support it.

Another view, that we find chiefly in the Nyāya works, regards truth as the faithfulness with which knowledge reveals its object. True knowledge is, therefore, defined as that which informs us of the existence of something in a place where it really exists, or which predicates of something a character really possessed by it. This view resembles the correspondence theory of Western realists.

A third view, which is incidentally referred to by many writers, regards truth as a harmony of experience. . . . A true knowledge, according to this view, would be one which is in harmony with other experiences. This view again resembles the Western theory of coherence.

The Advaita school of Vedānta, however, favours a fourth view according to which the truth of knowledge consists in its noncontradictedness. . . . The correspondence view of truth cannot directly prove itself. The only way to prove correspondence is to fall back on the foreign method of consilience or coherence . . . —that is to infer the existence of a real correspondence between knowledge and reality from the facts of the harmony of experience. But all that we can legitimately infer from the harmony of knowledge with the rest of our experience up to that time, is not that the knowledge is absolutely free from error, but that it is not yet contradicted. For we do not know that we shall not have in future any experience that can falsify our present knowledge. As regards the pragmatic test of causal efficiency . . . the Advaitins argue that even a false cognition may, and sometimes does, lead to the fulfilment of a purpose. One of the examples they cite to support their view is the case of a distant bright jewel which emits lustre. We mistake the lustre for the jewel and, desiring to get the mistaken object of our

From D. M. Datta, The Six Ways of Knowing: A Critical Study of the Vedanta Theory of Knowledge, *revised edition, Calcutta: University of Calcutta, 1960, pp. 19–28. Footnotes omitted.*

knowledge, approach it and actually get the jewel. In this case, therefore, the knowledge of lustre as the jewel—which is clearly a false cognition—leads to the attainment of the jewel and thereby satisfies our purpose, though eventually we come also to know that the initial cognition which caused our action was itself false. We can multiply instances of this kind. The hypothesis that the earth is stationary and the sun is moving has been working quite satisfactorily for ages; on the basis of this cognition many of our actions are performed and purposes attained. It is only its conflict with astronomical phenomena that enables us to detect its falsity.

It is found, therefore, that the pragmatic view of truth is not tenable. The correspondence view has ultimately to fall back on the consilience or coherence theory which, when subjected to strict scrutiny, has to yield the result that truth, as ascertained by it, consists only in its noncontradictedness.

According to the Advaitins, therefore, pramā or knowledge must have as one of its characteristics truth; and the truth of pramā consists in its content being uncontradicted. . . .

The second characteristic of pramā or knowledge is, as we have already said, novelty. It is not sufficient that knowledge should be true, it is also necessary that the content of knowledge should be new or previously unacquired—anadhigata. On this point, however, not all authorities are unanimous; while some . . . consider it to be an essential part of the differentia of knowledge, others think it unnecessary as unduly narrowing the scope of knowledge. The Vedāntists seem to be rather indifferent to this controversy and unwilling to take sides. The material part of the controversy turns upon the question whether memory should be admitted to have the status of knowledge. If truth be the sole characteristic of knowledge, memory, in so far as it is uncontradicted or undoubted, has to be called knowledge. But there is a peculiarity about memory that deserves special consideration. The only claim of memory to belief lies in its explicit reference to a past experience which it professes to reproduce faithfully. A remembered fact is believed to be true just because it is regarded as identical with the content of a past experience which it claims to represent. This confessed and explicit falling back on the past experience means its self-abdication in favour of its archetype. Thus the question of treating memory as a distinct type of knowledge does not at all arise, being barred *ex hypothesi*. The only kind of knowledge is then the knowledge of the already unacquired. But though memory is not a distinct source of knowledge, it is still a distinct experience that has to be distinguished from knowledge and given a separate name. The experience which reveals the new (i.e. knowledge proper) is called anubhūti, whereas reproduced knowledge is called smṛti. Thus novelty comes to be considered an essential quality of knowledge.

If this be the conception of knowledge (pramā), the question then arises whether in the case of a persistent knowledge of the same object, our experience at every moment during that time can be regarded as knowledge. When I keep looking at a table for some moments continuously, my experience of the first moment, as an acquisition of the "new," is of course to be called knowledge. But what about the experiences of the subsequent moments? Can they also be rightly called knowledge, seeing that they only reveal to me what has been already acquired at the first moment and lack thereby the quality of novelty?

This question is answered in the affirmative by all schools of thinkers. But different reasons are assigned in justification of this answer.

Some say that in a persistent knowledge . . . say of a table, the object is not the same at different moments, as it is ordinarily supposed to be. For even if we grant that the same table persists without any spatial change for a certain period, yet the inevitable temporal change has to be taken into consideration. In other words the table, the object of our knowledge, is determined both spatially and temporally to our consciousness. By perceiving its spatial properties we judge it to be big or small, high or low. Similarly by perceiving its temporal property we judge it to be "present." Without perceiving this time-quality it would be difficult for us to distinguish present knowledge of a table, or its perception, from the past knowledge of a table or its memory. So the table as determined by the first moment of the persistent knowledge is not the same as that determined by the second moment. Every moment we have the knowledge of an object that is different from the object of the previous moment and is, therefore, as good as a new object. The definition of knowledge (pramā), therefore, applies to the case of a persistent cognition as well, the quality of novelty being present also in that case.

This reply is regarded by others as unsatisfactory. These thinkers, while admitting that the time-quality of a percept is also directly perceived, hold that in a persistent perception the different moments, which are infinitely small, are never perceived as such. What we perceive as "present" is not an atomic point of time but a finite span of time. So it is difficult to say that in a persistent perception the time-quality of the object is perceived as new at every moment. The atomic moments are obtained not perceptually, but logically, i.e. by a continuous conceptual analysis of the perceived span. Knowledge remains, therefore, the same during the moments composing this finite span of time, and consequently at each one of these moments, except the first, there is only a repetition of the old knowledge obtained at the first moment.

The disqualification that is pressed against memory is, therefore, equally present in the case of a persistent cognition, and the difficulty in including the latter in the definition of knowledge (pramā), while excluding the former, remains as great as before.

The solution of the difficulty, however, lies in understanding the exact sense of "novelty" . . . as present in the case of knowledge and absent in the case of memory. In memory novelty is said to be absent, in the sense that memory is wholly a reproduction of a past knowledge; it is solely caused by the impression of a past experience. . . . In a persistent knowledge the knowledge of the second moment is not a reproduction of the knowledge of the previous moment; it is caused not by the impression of the previous experience, but by the very objective conditions which cause the first knowledge. So while memory by its very nature falls back on a past experience, and entirely

rests thereon for its validity, the knowledge at subsequent moments of a persistent cognition stands by its own right and makes a demand for its independent validity. It is in this important respect that memory has to be distinguished from a persistent cognition, and it is in virtue of this very important distinction that the one has to be excluded from the definition of knowledge and the other has to be included therein. This is the Nyāya solution of the problem.

The Advaitins however hold that in their theory of knowledge, such a problem or difficulty does not at all arise; no defence or explanation, therefore, is necessary. According to them, knowledge persists so long as fresh knowledge does not come to replace it. Whether knowledge changes or remains the same can only be ascertained by determining whether the logical activity of the self, i.e. the judgment affirming the knowledge ("The pot is" or "The pot is perceived"), changes or remains the same.

This problem assumes that in persistent cognition there is separate knowledge at every moment (during the time of persistence), while the content or object of these distinct elements of knowledge is the same, and therefore at every subsequent moment there is only a repetition or reproduction of the knowledge of the first moment. But this assumption is wrong. For if the object of the so-called different elements of knowledge be judged to be identical, they are themselves indistinguishable from each other, i.e. they are but one identical process of knowledge. Thus the question of repetition or reproduction does not arise at all.

This question and the Vedāntin's answer require the consideration of the fundamental problem how one perception is to be distinguished from another. One way of distinguishing one perception from another is, of course, the ascertaining of a distinction between their respective objects. This would mean that the characteristic that distinguishes one perception from another must remain in the object of that knowledge, i.e. the distinguishing characteristic must itself become the object of that very perception. But is this the sole way of distinguishing one perception from another? The Vedāntins say "yes." But those who raise the original question seem to think that there may be some other way of making a distinction; as, for example, by the distinction of their times of happening. In such a case the time characteristic may not have been originally known as an element qualifying the object of the knowledge. At a subsequent time we may infer that as the knowledge persisted for a length of time which was composed of so many different moments, the knowledge of the first moment must differ from the knowledge of the second moment, since the two pieces of knowledge possess two distinct qualifications (viz. "of the first moment" and "of the second moment"). This would be distinguishing knowledge by an external adjective, while the former case consisted in distinguishing knowledge by an essential or internal quality. But it should be noted that a mere distinction based on an external mark does not argue separateness in existence. Edward VII as the King of England can be, for certain purposes, distinguished from Edward VII as the Emperor of India, or the father of George V; but this does not mean that the three as distinguishable must also be separate. Similarly the knowledge of the first moment, though in language or thought distinguishable from the knowledge of the second moment, is not necessarily separate from the second. In order that time-quality may serve as the basis of an inference as to the separateness of one knowledge from another, that quality must enter the knowledge itself as characterising its object. The perception of the table "now" is known to be different or separate from the perception of the table I had an hour ago, from the fact that the "presence" and "pastness" characterize respectively the object of the present perception and that of the past perception. In such a case the second perception contains a novelty (in virtue of its time-quality, viz. "presence") and is, therefore, a full-fledged knowledge.

To return to the original discussion, then, we find that even if "novelty" be regarded as an essential characteristic of knowledge, any real case of knowledge, such as persistent perception, or repeated perception, is not excluded from the definition of knowledge. A pramā or knowledge, therefore, can be accurately regarded as a cognition the object of which is neither contradicted nor already known as an object. . . .

The special source of a particular pramā or knowledge is called pramāna. Pramāna is defined as the karana of a pramā. A karana is conceived as the *unique* or special cause through the *action* of which a particular effect is produced. In the case of perceptual knowledge or pratyaksa pramā, for example, a sense-organ (in the case of an external perception) or the mind (in the case of an internal perception) is said to be the karana or instrumental cause. There are many causes, e.g. the mind, the sense-organ, etc., the existence of which is necessary for the production of perceptual knowledge of an external object. But of these, the mind is a cause the existence of which is common to all sorts of knowledge, perceptual and inferential; so it cannot be regarded as a special cause. The special cause here is the particular sense-organ involved in that perception, because it is not common to other kinds of knowledge; it is peculiar to external perception alone.

A cause, to be called a karana, must not be merely unique . . . it must also possess some active function. . . . The contact of the sense-organ with its object is undeniably a cause (kārana) of perception. It is also unique; the instrumentality of sense-contact is present in perception alone. But still it is not called the karana of perception, because it is itself a function or action of the sense-organ and as such does not possess a further function. . . .

A pramāna is, then, such an active and unique cause (kārana) of a pramā or knowledge.

6.7 Afrocentric Feminist Epistemology

Is knowledge universal? If we know what it means to know something in one culture, do we know what it means in all cultures? Who is the subject of knowledge? Who is the knower? Is knowing the knower at all relevant to knowing what knowledge is or whether it is possible? How does the social position of the knower make an impact on the production and transmission of knowledge? Is all knowledge expressible in the form of propositions? Is knowledge the result of the exercise of social power?

These questions are not easy to answer, and even to raise them is somewhat unsettling because they introduce political and social questions into philosophic reflection on the nature and possibility of knowledge. Feminist epistemology, however, has not shied away from asking such questions or from interjecting moral and political considerations into the epistemological project.

Feminist epistemology began as a critique of existing theories of knowledge. This critique revealed and continues to reveal how large a role gender has played in supposedly universal and objective theories of knowledge. Genevieve Lloyd (1984) documents how rationality has been associated with males and with masculine qualities in the development of Western philosophy. Men, supposedly, are rational whereas women are emotional. Thus, not only are women excluded from the sacred halls of knowers, but also an unwarranted division is created between knowledge and emotion.

Janice Moulton (1983) argues that philosophy has relied heavily on the *adversary paradigm.* This model pictures rational activity aimed at producing knowledge as one of an opponent defending a belief against an attacker. According to this model, the best way to arrive at the truth is to subject our beliefs to the strongest possible objections.

Undoubtedly, there are advantages to this method, especially in courts of law, but it has severe limitations if it is transposed into a universal model of knowledge-production. Not only is it tainted with sexism insofar as it assumes that aggressive (male-type) thinking is the best thinking, but also the adversary paradigm leads to bad reasoning. By restricting reasoning to an adversarial situation, we ignore the sorts of reasoning that might be appropriate in different situations, such as figuring something out for oneself, exploring a topic among like-minded people, or trying to show how two apparently opposed positions might be in harmony.

It is not enough, however, to unmask the ways traditional theories of knowledge have been tainted by male bias. We must go on, feminist philosophers maintain, to find new frameworks for thinking about problems relating to knowledge. So some feminists argue that a "standpoint" epistemology that frankly acknowledges that all knowing substantially involves the social and historical context of the knowers is a better place to begin our philosophical reflection on the possibility of knowledge. Others point out how the community—as the place where knowledge is generated, stored, and communicated—has been neglected in favor of the traditional views that the "isolated individual" is the epistemic agent. Still others call for a recognition of the significant role that emotions play in the production of knowledge. One thing that all the diverse feminist views on knowledge have in common is the conviction that philosophical reflection on the nature and possibility of knowledge must begin with and remain rooted in the experience of women.

However, in the search for a new starting point, one which recognizes the importance of the experience of women for doing epistemology, many women have come to see that they cannot presume to speak for all women. If concrete human experiences of coming to know must be the starting point, if feminist theories are to be constructed from the bottom up rather than from the top down, then the experiences of white, middle-class, educated, elite women can no more be used to create a "universal" theory of knowledge than the experiences of white, middle-class, educated, elite males can be.

Patricia Hill Collins, author of our next selection and a professor of Afro-American studies at the University of Cincinnati, is a sociologist. Hence, she approaches the question of knowledge from a perspective often referred to as the "sociology of knowledge." Whereas many philosophers have ignored the social conditions of knowledge-production and validation, sociologists of knowledge argue that these social conditions are essential. Philosophers have sought some sort of "pure" theory—some universal and objective picture of the knowing process untainted by the everyday and peculiar experiences of socially and historically situated people. Sociologists want to know the role that class, race, and gender play in the process of coming to know.

Dr. Collins is a sociologist, but she is also an *African-American woman* doing sociology. Hence, she cannot ignore her own experiences, both as a woman and as a Black. The result is a fascinating and provocative inquiry into the dimensions of an Afrocentric feminist epistemology.

Reading Questions

1. What is one key epistemological concern facing Black female intellectuals?
2. What is wrong with the "Eurocentric, masculinist knowledge validation process" according to Collins?
3. What are, according to Collins, the dimensions of an Afrocentric feminist epistemology?
4. Are the arguments Collins presents adequate to support her claims? Why, or why not?
5. How do you think Collins would answer the question, "Is knowledge possible?"

Toward an Afrocentric Feminist Epistemology

PATRICIA HILL COLLINS

EPISTEMOLOGY IS THE STUDY of the philosophical problems in concepts of knowledge and truth. The techniques I use in this volume to rearticulate a Black women's standpoint and to further Black feminist thought may appear to violate some of the basic epistemological assumptions of my training as a social scientist. In choosing the core themes in Black feminist thought that merited investigation, I consulted established bodies of academic research. But I also searched my own experiences and those of African-American women I know for themes we thought were important. My use of language signals a different relationship to my material than that which currently prevails in social science literature. For example, I often use the pronoun "our" instead

Reprinted from Black Feminist Thought: Knowledge, Consciousness, and the Politics of Empowerment, *by Patricia Hill Collins (1990). Reproduced by permission of Routledge, Inc., part of the Taylor & Francis Group. Footnotes and references deleted.*

of "their" when referring to African-American women, a choice that embeds me in the group I am studying instead of distancing me from it. In addition, I occasionally place my own concrete experiences in the text. To support my analysis, I cite few statistics and instead rely on the voices of Black women from all walks of life. These conscious epistemological choices signal my attempts not only to explore the thematic content of Black feminist thought but to do so in a way that does not violate its basic epistemological framework.

One key epistemological concern facing Black women intellectuals is the question of what constitutes adequate justifications that a given knowledge claim, such as a fact or theory, is true. In producing the specialized knowledge of Black feminist thought, Black women intellectuals often encounter two distinct epistemologies: one representing elite white male interests and the other expressing Afrocentric feminist concerns. Epistemological choices about who to trust, what to believe, and why something is true are not benign academic issues. Instead, these concerns tap the fundamental question of which versions of truth will prevail and shape thought and action.

The Eurocentric, Masculinist Knowledge Validation Process

Institutions, paradigms, and other elements of the knowledge validation procedure controlled by elite white men constitute the Eurocentric masculinist knowledge validation process. The purpose of this process is to represent a white male standpoint. Although it reflects powerful white males' interest, various dimensions of the process are not necessarily managed by white men themselves. Scholars, publishers, and other experts represent specific interests and credentialing processes, and their knowledge claims must satisfy the political and epistemological criteria of the contexts in which they reside.

Two political criteria influence the knowledge validation process. First, knowledge claims are evaluated by a community of experts whose members represent the standpoints of the groups from which they originate. Within the Eurocentric

masculinist process this means that a scholar making a knowledge claim must convince a scholarly community controlled by white men that a given claim is justified. Second, each community of experts must maintain its credibility as defined by the larger group in which it is situated and from which it draws its basic, taken-for-granted knowledge. This means that scholarly communities that challenge basic beliefs held in the culture at large will be deemed less credible than those which support popular perspectives.

When white men control the knowledge validation process, both political criteria can work to suppress Black feminist thought. Given that the general culture shaping the taken-for-granted knowledge of the community of experts is permeated by widespread notions of Black and female inferiority, new knowledge claims that seem to violate these fundamental assumptions are likely to be viewed as anomalies. Moreover, specialized thought challenging notions of Black and female inferiority is unlikely to be generated from within a white-male-controlled academic community because both the kinds of questions that could be asked and the explanations that would be found satisfying would necessarily reflect a basic lack of familiarity with Black women's reality.

The experiences of African-American women scholars illustrate how individuals who wish to rearticulate a Black women's standpoint through Black feminist thought can be suppressed by a white-male-controlled knowledge validation process. Exclusion from basic literacy, quality educational experiences, and faculty and administrative positions has limited Black women's access to influential academic positions. While Black women can produce knowledge claims that contest those advanced by the white male community, this community does not grant that Black women scholars have competing knowledge claims based in another knowledge validation process. As a consequence, any credentials controlled by white male academicians can be denied to Black women producing Black feminist thought on the grounds that it is not credible research. . . .

African-American women academicians who persist in trying to rearticulate a Black women's standpoint also face potential rejection of our knowledge claims on epistemological grounds. Just as the material realities of the powerful and the dominated produce separate standpoints, each group may also have distinctive epistemologies or theories of knowledge. Black women scholars may know that something is true but be unwilling or unable to legitimate our claims using Eurocentric, masculinist criteria for consistency with substantial knowledge and criteria for methodological adequacy. For any body of knowledge, new knowledge claims must be consistent with an existing body of knowledge that the group controlling the interpretive context accepts as true. The methods used to validate knowledge claims must also be acceptable to the group controlling the knowledge validation process.

The criteria for the methodological adequacy of positivism illustrate the epistemological standards that Black women scholars would have to satisfy in legitimating Black feminist thought using a Eurocentric masculinist epistemology. While I describe Eurocentric masculinist approaches as a single process, many schools of thought or paradigms are subsumed under this one process. Moreover, my focus on positivism should be interpreted neither to mean that all dimensions of positivism are inherently problematic for Black women nor that nonpositivist frameworks are better. For example, most traditional frameworks that women of color internationally regard as oppressive to women are not positivist, and Eurocentric feminist critiques of positivism may have less political importance for women of color, especially those in traditional societies than they have for white feminists.

Positivist approaches aim to create scientific descriptions of reality by producing objective generalizations. Because researchers have widely differing values, experiences, and emotions, genuine science is thought to be unattainable unless all human characteristics except rationality are eliminated from the research process. By following strict methodological rules, scientists aim to distance themselves from the values, vested interests, and emotions generated by their class, race, sex, or unique situation. By decontextualizing

themselves, they allegedly become detached observers and manipulators of nature. Moreover, this researcher decontextualization is paralleled by comparable efforts to remove the objects of study from their contexts. The result of this entire process is often the separation of information from meaning.

Several requirements typify positivist methodological approaches. First, research methods generally require a distancing of the researcher from her or his "object" of study by defining the researcher as a "subject" with full human subjectivity and by objectifying the "object" of study. A second requirement is the absence of emotions from the research process. Third, ethics and values are deemed inappropriate in the research process, either as the reason for scientific inquiry or as part of the research process itself. Finally, adversarial debates, whether written or oral, become the preferred method of ascertaining truth: the arguments that can withstand the greatest assault and survive intact become the strongest truths.

Such criteria ask African-American women to objectify ourselves, devalue our emotional life, displace our motivations for furthering knowledge about Black women, and confront in an adversarial relationship those with more social, economic and professional power. It therefore seems unlikely that Black women would use a positivist epistemological stance in rearticulating a Black women's standpoint. Black women are more likely to choose an alternative epistemology for assessing knowledge claims, one using different standards that are consistent with Black women's criteria for substantiated knowledge and with our criteria for methodological adequacy. If such an epistemology exists, what are its contours? Moreover, what is its role in the production of Black feminist thought?

The Contours of an Afrocentric Feminist Epistemology

Africanist analyses of the Black experience generally agree on the fundamental elements of an Afrocentric standpoint. Despite varying histories, Black societies reflect elements of a core African value system that existed prior to and independently of racial oppression. Moreover, as a result of colonialism, imperialism, slavery, apartheid, and other systems of racial domination, Black people share a common experience of oppression. These two factors foster shared Afrocentric values that permeate the family structure, religious institutions, culture, and community life of Blacks in varying parts of Africa, the Caribbean, South America, and North America. This Afrocentric consciousness permeates the shared history of people of African descent through the framework of a distinctive Afrocentric epistemology.

Feminist scholars advance a similar argument by asserting that women share a history of gender oppression, primarily through sex/gender hierarchies. These experiences transcend divisions among women created by race, social class, religion, sexual orientation, and ethnicity and form the basis of a women's standpoint with a corresponding feminist consciousness and epistemology.

Because Black women have access to both the Afrocentric and the feminist standpoints, an alternative epistemology used to rearticulate a Black women's standpoint should reflect elements of both traditions. The search for the distinguishing features of an alternative epistemology used by African-American women reveals that values and ideas Africanist scholars identify as characteristically "Black" often bear remarkable resemblance to similar ideas claimed by feminist scholars as characteristically "female." This similarity suggests that the material conditions of race, class, and gender oppression can vary dramatically and yet generate some uniformity in the epistemologies of subordinate groups. Thus the significance of an Afrocentric feminist epistemology may lie in how such an epistemology enriches our understanding of how subordinate groups create knowledge that fosters resistance. . . .

Like a Black women's standpoint, an Afrocentric feminist epistemology is rooted in the everyday experiences of African-American women. In spite of diversity that exists among women, what are the dimensions of an Afrocentric feminist epistemology?

Concrete Experience as a Criterion of Meaning

"My aunt used to say, 'A heap see, but a few know,'" remembers Carolyn Chase, a 31-year-old inner-city Black woman. This saying depicts two types of knowing—knowledge and wisdom—and taps the first dimension of an Afrocentric feminist epistemology. Living life as Black women requires wisdom because knowledge about the dynamics of race, gender, and class oppression has been essential to Black women's survival. African-American women give such wisdom high credence in assessing knowledge.

Allusions to these two types of knowing pervade the words of a range of African-American women. Zilpha Elaw, a preacher of the mid-1800s, explains the tenacity of racism: "The pride of a white skin is a bauble of great value with many in some parts of the United States, who readily sacrifice their intelligence to their prejudices, and possess more knowledge than wisdom." In describing differences separating African-American and white women, Nancy White invokes a similar rule: "When you come right down to it, white women just *think* they are free. Black women *know* they ain't free." Geneva Smitherman, a college professor specializing in African-American linguistics, suggests that "from a black perspective, written documents are limited in what they can teach about life and survival in the world. Blacks are quick to ridicule 'educated fools,' . . . they have 'book learning' but no 'mother wit,' knowledge, but not wisdom." Mabel Lincoln eloquently summarizes the distinction between knowledge and wisdom: "To black people like me, a fool is funny—you know, people who love to break bad, people you can't tell anything to, folks that would take a shotgun to a roach."

African-American women need wisdom to know how to deal with the "educated fools" who would "take a shotgun to a roach." As members of a subordinate group, Black women cannot afford to be fools of any type, for our objectification as the Other denies us the protections that white skin, maleness, and wealth confer. This distinction between knowledge and wisdom, and the use of experience as the cutting edge dividing them, has been key to Black women's survival. In the context of race, gender, and class oppression, the distinction is essential. Knowledge without wisdom is adequate for the powerful, but wisdom is essential to the survival of the subordinate. . . .

Experience as a criterion of meaning with practical images as its symbolic vehicles is a fundamental epistemological tenet in African-American thought systems. "Look at my arm!" Sojourner Truth proclaimed: "I have ploughed, and planted, and gathered into barns, and no man could head me! And ain't I a woman?" By invoking concrete practical images from her own life to symbolize new meanings, Truth deconstructed the prevailing notions of woman. Stories, narratives, and Bible principles are selected for their applicability to the lived experiences of African-Americans and become symbolic representations of a whole wealth of experience. Bible tales are often told for the wisdom they express about everyday life, so their interpretation involves no need for scientific historical verification. The narrative method requires that the story be told, not torn apart in analysis, and trusted as core belief, not "admired as science." . . .

Some feminist scholars offer a similar claim that women as a group are more likely than men to use concrete knowledge in assessing knowledge claims. For example, a substantial number of the 135 women in a study of women's cognitive development were "connected knowers" and were drawn to the sort of knowledge that emerges from first-hand observation. Such women felt that because knowledge comes from experience, the best way of understanding another person's ideas was to develop empathy and share the experiences that led the person to form those ideas.

In valuing the concrete, African-American women invoke not only an Afrocentric tradition but a women's tradition as well. Some feminist theorists suggest that women are socialized in complex relational nexuses where contextual rules versus abstract principles govern behavior. This socialization process is thought to stimulate characteristic ways of knowing. These theorists suggest that women are more likely to experience two modes of knowing: one located in the body and the space it occupies and the other passing beyond it. Through their child-rearing and nurturing activities, women mediate these two modes and use the concrete experiences of their daily lives to assess more abstract knowledge claims.

Although valuing the concrete may be more representative of women than men, social class differences among women may generate differential expression of this women's value. One study of working-class women's ways of knowing found that both white and African-American women rely on common sense and intuition. These forms of knowledge allow for subjectivity between the knower and the known, rest in the women themselves (not in higher authorities), and are experienced directly in the world (not through abstractions). . . .

In traditional African-American communities Black women find considerable institutional support for valuing concrete experience. Black women's centrality in families, churches, and other community organizations allows us to share our concrete knowledge of what it takes to be self-defined Black women with younger, less experienced sisters. "Sisterhood is not new to Black women," asserts Bonnie Thornton Dill, but "while Black women have fostered and encouraged sisterhood, we have not used it as the anvil to forge our political identities." Though not expressed in explicitly political terms, this relationship of sisterhood among Black women can be seen as a model for a whole series of relationships African-American women have with one another.

Given that Black churches and families are both woman-centered, Afrocentric institutions, African-American women traditionally have found considerable institutional support for this dimension of an Afrocentric feminist epistemology. While white women may value the concrete, it is questionable whether white families— particularly middle-class nuclear ones—and white community institutions provide comparable types of support. Similarly, while Black men are supported by Afrocentric institutions, they cannot participate in Black women's sisterhood. In terms of Black women's relationships with one another, African-American women may find it easier than others to recognize connectedness as a primary way of knowing, simply because we are encouraged to do so by a Black women's tradition of sisterhood.

The Use of Dialogue in Assessing Knowledge Claims

"Dialogue implies talk between two subjects, not the speech of subject and object. It is a humanizing speech, one that challenges and resists domination," asserts bell hooks. For Black women new knowledge claims are rarely worked out in isolation from other individuals and are usually developed through dialogues with other members of a community. A primary epistemological assumption underlying the use of dialogue in assessing knowledge claims is that connectedness rather than separation is an essential component of the knowledge validation process.

This belief in connectedness and the use of dialogue as one of its criteria for methodological adequacy has Afrocentric roots. In contrast to Western, either/or dichotomous thought, the traditional African worldview is holistic and seeks harmony. "One must understand that to become human, to realize the promise of becoming human, is the only important task of the person," posits Molefi Asante. People become more human and empowered only in the context of a community, and only when they "become seekers of the type of connections, interactions, and meetings that lead to harmony." The power of the word generally, and dialogues specifically, allows this to happen.

Not to be confused with adversarial debate, the use of dialogue has deep roots in an African-based oral tradition and in African-American culture. Ruth Shays describes the importance of dialogue in the knowledge validation process of enslaved African-Americans:

They would find a lie if it took them a year. . . . The foreparents found the truth because they listened and they made people tell their part many times. Most often you can hear a lie. . . .

Those old people was everywhere and knew the truth of many disputes. They believed that a liar should suffer the pain of his lies, and they had all kinds of ways of bringing liars to judgement.

The widespread use of the call-and-response discourse mode among African-Americans illustrates the importance placed on dialogue. Composed of spontaneous verbal and nonverbal interaction between speaker and listener in which all of the speaker's statements, or "calls," are punctuated by expressions, or "responses," from the listener, this Black discourse mode pervades African-American culture. The fundamental requirement of this interactive network is active participation of all individuals. For ideas to be tested and validated, everyone in the group must participate. To refuse to join in, especially if one really disagrees with what has been said, is seen as "cheating." . . .

Black women's centrality in families and community organizations provides African-American women with a high degree of support for invoking dialogue as a dimension of an Afrocentric feminist epistemology. However, when African-American women use dialogues in assessing knowledge claims, we might be invoking a particularly female way of knowing as well. Feminist scholars contend that men and women are socialized to seek different types of autonomy—the former based on separation, the latter seeking connectedness—and that this variation in types of autonomy parallels the characteristic differences between male and female ways of knowing. For instance, in contrast to the visual metaphors (such as equating knowledge with illumination, knowing with seeing, and truth with light) that scientists and philosophers typically use, women tend to ground their epistemological premises in metaphors suggesting finding a voice, speaking, and listening. The words of the Black woman who struggled for her education at Medgar Evers College resonate with the importance placed on voice: "I was basically a shy and reserved person prior to the struggle at Medgar, but I found my voice—and I used it! Now, I will never lose my voice again!"

While significant differences exist between Black women's family experiences and those of middle-class white women, African-American women clearly are affected by general cultural norms prescribing certain familial roles for women. Thus in terms of the role of dialogue in an Afrocentric feminist epistemology, Black women may again experience a convergence of the values of the African-American community and women's experiences.

The Ethic of Caring

"Ole white preachers used to talk wid dey tongues widdout sayin' nothin', but Jesus told us slaves to talk wid our hearts." These words of an ex-slave suggest that ideas cannot be divorced from the individuals who create and share them. This theme of talking with the heart taps the ethic of caring, another dimension of an alternative epistemology used by African-American women. Just as the ex-slave used the wisdom in his heart to reject the ideas of the preachers who talked "wid dey tongues widdout sayin' nothin'," the ethic of caring suggests that personal expressiveness, emotions, and empathy are central to the knowledge validation process.

One of three interrelated components comprising the ethic of caring is the emphasis placed on individual uniqueness. Rooted in a tradition of African humanism, each individual is thought to be a unique expression of a common spirit, power, or energy inherent in all life. When Alice Walker "never doubted her powers of judgment because her mother assumed they were sound," she invokes the sense of individual uniqueness taught to her by her mother. The polyrhythms in African-American music, in which no one main beat subordinates the others, is paralleled by the theme of individual expression in Black women's quilting. Black women quilters place strong color and patterns next to one another and see the individual differences not as detracting from each piece but as enriching the whole quilt. This belief in individual uniqueness is illustrated by the value placed on personal expressiveness in African-American communities. Johnetta Ray, an inner-city resident, describes this Afrocentric emphasis on individual uniqueness: "No matter how hard we try, I don't think black people will ever develop much of a herd instinct. We are profound individualists with a passion for self-expression."

A second component of the ethic of caring concerns the appropriateness of emotions in dialogues. Emotion indicates that a speaker believes in the validity of an argument. Consider Ntozake Shange's description of one of the goals of her work: "Our [Western] society allows people to be absolutely neurotic and totally out of touch with their feelings and everyone else's feelings, and yet be very respectable. This, to me, is a travesty. . . . I'm trying to change the idea of seeing emotions and intellect as distinct faculties." The Black women's blues tradition's history of personal expressiveness heals this either/or dichotomous rift separating emotion and intellect. For example, in her rendition of "Strange Fruit," Billie Holiday's lyrics blend seamlessly with the emotion of her delivery to render a trenchant social commentary on southern lynching. Without emotion, Aretha Franklin's cry for "respect" would be virtually meaningless.

A third component of the ethic of caring involves developing the capacity for empathy. Harriet Jones, a 16-year-old Black woman, explains to her interviewer why she chose to open up to him: "Some things in my life are so hard for me to bear, and it makes me feel better to know that you feel sorry about those things and would change them if you could." Without her belief in his empathy, she found it difficult to talk. Black women writers often explore the growth of empathy as part of an ethic of caring. For example, the growing respect that the Black slave woman Dessa and the white woman Rufel gain for one another in Sherley Anne William's *Dessa Rose* stems from their increased understanding of each other's positions. After watching Rufel fight off the advances of a white man, Dessa lay awake thinking: "The white woman was subject to the same ravishment as me; this the thought that kept me awake. I hadn't knowed white mens could use a white woman like that, just take her by force same as they could with us." As a result of her new-found empathy, Dessa observed, "it was like we had a secret between us."

These components of the ethic of caring—the value placed on individual expressiveness, the appropriateness of emotions, and the capacity for empathy—pervade African-American culture. One of the best examples of the interactive nature of the importance of dialogue and the ethic of caring in assessing knowledge claims occurs in the use of the call-and-response discourse mode in traditional Black church services. In such services both the minister and the congregation routinely use voice rhythm and vocal inflection to convey meaning. The sound of what is being said is just as important as the words themselves in what is, in a sense, a dialogue of reason and emotion. As a result it is nearly impossible to filter out the strictly linguistic-cognitive abstract meaning from the sociocultural psychoemotive meaning. While the ideas presented by a speaker must have validity (i.e., agree with the general body of knowledge shared by the Black congregation), the group also appraises the way knowledge claims are presented.

There is growing evidence that the ethic of caring may be part of women's experience as well. Certain dimensions of women's ways of knowing bear striking resemblance to Afrocentric expressions of the ethic of caring. Belenky et al. point out that two contrasting epistemological orientations characterize knowing: one an epistemology of separation based on impersonal procedures for establishing truth and the other, an epistemology of connection in which truth emerges through care. While these ways of knowing are not gender specific, disproportionate numbers of women rely on connected knowing.

The emphasis placed on expressiveness and emotion in African-American communities bears marked resemblance to feminist perspectives on the importance of personality in connected knowing. Separate knowers try to subtract the personality of an individual from his or her ideas because they see personality as biasing those ideas. In contrast, connected knowers see personality as adding to an individual's ideas and feel that the personality of each group member enriches a group's understanding. The significance of individual uniqueness, personal expressiveness, and empathy in African-American communities thus resembles the importance that some feminist analyses place on women's "inner voice."

The convergence of Afrocentric and feminist values in the ethic of caring seems particularly acute. White women may have access to a women's tradition valuing emotion and expressiveness, but few Eurocentric institutions except the family validate this way of knowing. In contrast, Black women have long had the support of the Black church, an institution with deep roots in the African past and a philosophy that accepts and encourages expressiveness and an ethic of caring. Black men share in this Afrocentric tradition. But they must resolve the contradictions that confront them in searching for Afrocentric models of masculinity in the face of abstract, unemotional notions of masculinity imposed on them. The differences among race/gender groups thus hinge on differences in their access to institutional supports valuing one type of knowing over another. Although Black women may be denigrated within white-male-controlled academic institutions, other institutions, such as Black families and churches, which encourage the expression of Black female power seem to do so, in part, by way of their support for an Afrocentric feminist epistemology.

The Ethic of Personal Accountability

An ethic of personal accountability is the final dimension of an alternative epistemology. Not only must individuals develop their knowledge claims through dialogue and present them in a style proving their concern for their ideas, but people are expected to be accountable for their knowledge claims. Zilpha Elaw's description of slavery reflects this notion that every idea has an owner and that the owner's identity matters: "Oh, the abominations of slavery! . . . Every case of slavery, however lenient its inflictions and mitigated its atrocities, indicates an oppressor, the oppressed, and oppression." For Elaw abstract definitions of slavery mesh with the concrete identities of its perpetrators and its victims. African-Americans consider it essential for individuals to have personal positions on issues and assume full responsibility for arguing their validity.

Assessments of an individual's knowledge claims simultaneously evaluate an individual's character, values, and ethics. African-Americans reject the Eurocentric, masculinist belief that probing into an individual's personal viewpoint is outside the boundaries of discussion. Rather, all views expressed and actions taken are thought to derive from a central set of core beliefs that cannot be other than personal. "Does Aretha really *believe* that Black women should get 'respect,' or is she just mouthing the words?" is a valid question in an Afrocentric feminist epistemology. Knowledge claims made by individuals respected for their moral and ethical connections to their ideas will carry more weight than those offered by less respected figures.

An example drawn from an undergraduate course composed entirely of Black women which I taught might help to clarify the uniqueness of this portion of the knowledge validation process. During one class discussion I asked the students to evaluate a prominent Black male scholar's analysis of Black feminism. Instead of severing the scholar from his context in order to dissect the rationality of his thesis, my students demanded facts about the author's personal biography. They were especially interested in concrete details of his life, such as his relationships with Black women, his marital status, and his social class background. By requesting data on dimensions of his personal life routinely excluded in positivist approaches to knowledge validation, they invoked concrete experience as a criterion of meaning. They used this information to assess whether he really cared about his topic and drew on this ethic of caring in advancing their knowledge claims about his work. Furthermore, they refused to evaluate the rationality of his written ideas without some indication of his personal credibility as an ethical human being. The entire exchange could only have occurred as a dialogue among members of a class that had established a solid enough community to employ an alternative epistemology in assessing knowledge claims.

The ethic of personal accountability is clearly an Afrocentric value, but is it feminist as well?

While limited by its attention to middle-class, white women, Carol Gilligan's work suggests that there is a female model for moral development whereby women are more inclined to link morality to responsibility, relationships, and the ability to maintain social ties. If this is the case, then African-American women again experience a convergence of values from Afrocentric and female institutions.

The use of an Afrocentric feminist epistemology in traditional Black church services illustrates the interactive nature of all four dimensions and also serves as a metaphor for the distinguishing features of an Afrocentric feminist way of knowing. The services represent more than dialogues between the rationality used in examining biblical texts and stories and the emotion inherent in the use of reason for this purpose. The rationale for such dialogues involves the task of examining concrete experiences for the presence of an ethic of caring. Neither emotion nor ethics is subordinated to reason. Instead, emotion, ethics, and reason are used as interconnected, essential components in assessing knowledge claims. In an Afrocentric feminist epistemology, values lie at the heart of the knowledge validation process such that inquiry always has an ethical aim.

Alternative knowledge claims in and of themselves are rarely threatening to conventional knowledge. Such claims are routinely ignored, discredited, or simply absorbed and marginalized in existing paradigms. Much more threatening is the challenge that alternative epistemologies offer to the basic process used by the powerful to legitimate their knowledge claims. If the epistemology used to validate knowledge comes into question, then all prior knowledge claims validated under the dominant model become suspect. An alternative epistemology challenges all certified knowledge and opens up the question of whether what has been taken to be true can stand the test of alternative ways of validating truth. The existence of a self-defined Black women's standpoint using an Afrocentric feminist epistemology calls into question the content of what currently passes as truth and simultaneously challenges the process of arriving at the truth.

Visit the companion Web site for chapter specific quizzes, suggestions for further reading, video ideas, and other resources to assess and expand your understanding of the chapter material. Go to http://philosophy.wadsworth.com and select the companion Web site for *Voices of Wisdom.*

 You can access many additional readings at the Info Trac-College Edition Web site. To find the following suggested articles do a keyword search with the article title. Use the passcode that was packaged with your new book to enter the site at http://www.Infotrac-college.com/Wadsworth/. Here is a sampling.

Gail Fine, "Descartes and Ancient Skepticism: Reheated Cabbage?" *The Philosophical Review,* April 2000 v109 i2 p195, A67710131.

Michael Rowan, "Stove on the Rationality of Induction and the Uniformity Thesis." *The British Journal for the Philosophy of Science,* September 1993 v44 n3 p561(6), A14940355.

Timothy J. Madian, "The Virtues of 'The Ethics of Belief': W. K. Clifford's Continuing Relevance." *Free Inquiry,* Spring 1997 v17 n2 p29(5), A19417762.

Jeff Jordan, "Pragmatic Arguments and Belief." *American Philosophical Quarterly,* October 1996 v33 n4 p409(12) A19098070.

Douglas McDermid, "Pragmatism and Truth: The Comparison Objection to Correspondence." *The Review of Metaphysics,* June 1998 v51 n4 p775(37), A21257643.

Jayandra Soni, "Basic Jaina Epistemology." *Philosophy East and West,* July 2000 v50 i3 p367, A65863563.

Janice D. Hamlet, "Assessing Womanist Thought: The Rhetoric of Susan L. Taylor." *Communication Quarterly,* Fall 2000 v48 i4 p420(17), A92805646.

Ward E. Jones, "Why Do We Value Knowledge?" *American Philosophical Quarterly,* October 1997 v34 n4 p423(17), A20150878.

Susan Hekman, "Truth and Method: Feminist Standpoint Theory Revisited." *Signs,* Winter 1997 v22 n2 p341(25) A19149616.

Chapter 7

Does Science Tell Us the Whole Truth and Nothing but the Truth?

> "[F]alsehood is as likely to follow truth as the reverse."
>
> JORGE J. E. GRACIA

7.1 Introduction

AS IS OUR PHILOSOPHICAL CUSTOM, a custom I trust you have all become accustomed to, let us begin by asking some questions about science. What makes a theory scientific? What is the difference between superstition and science? Does science progress at a steady pace, carefully building on previous discoveries? Is science objective? Is it value-free? What is the place of science in human life? Should it be subordinated to ethical and religious concerns? What is the relationship between scientific thinking and traditional modes of problem solving? Are scientific explanations and religious explanations logically similar?

These questions raise some of the issues we will explore in this chapter and some of the issues associated with an area of philosophical research known as the **philosophy of science**. This branch of philosophy centers on a critical analysis of the various sciences, such as the physical, life, and behavioral sciences. To the extent that all of these sciences (physics, biology, psychology, and so on) share certain assumptions about the production of knowledge, the philosophy of science often focuses on methodological issues generally associated with all the sciences. Philosophers of science concern themselves with such topics as theory formation, the nature of hypotheses, the role of observation and experiment in the processes of verification and falsification, and the nature of explanation.

Clearly the philosophy of science is closely related to epistemology because of its concern with the role science plays in generating true statements that constitute knowledge about ourselves and the world in which we live. Questions about the nature of truth and the nature of knowledge inevitably arise as philosophical reflection on science proceeds. One cannot long ponder what is meant by such talk as "verifying a hypothesis" without wondering about truth and its possibility.

We live in a time and a place that puts a great deal of trust in science to tell us the truth and nothing but the truth. Many of our decisions, both public and private, are based on scientific information. We are wowed and amazed at the technological spin-offs scientific research engenders. Today we can do what only yesterday seemed like magic. We can travel in outer space and communicate within seconds with people on the other side of the earth.

Many people also mistrust science. They are uncertain about how reliable scientific theory is, what the limits of science are, and whether the technological marvels are ultimately conducive to living a better life. Some scholars warn of **scientism**, a kind of blind faith in the power of science to determine all truth. Still others worry about the religious and moral implications of the trust many have in science.

I do not know how much interest you have in science or in the philosophy of science. It is, I think, very interesting from a theoretical point of view. Questions about the nature of scientific truth (if there is any) and questions about the differences between superstition and science can be fascinating in their own right. But the pursuit of answers to such questions may seem remote from the business of everyday life.

Studying the philosophy of science may seem irrelevant to our daily concerns, but it is not. We face a host of public policy debates, from global warming to genetic engineering, in which scientific evidence often plays a crucial role. The more we understand about the nature of scientific theories and the procedures of science, the better informed we will be when we make the difficult judgments we must make as we create public policy that will have a significant impact on our own future, as well as on the future of our children.

Is it a mark of scientific objectivity to present, as the media supposedly does, "all sides of the issue"? Or is it more objective to follow scientific consensus even when some scientists disagree with that consensus? How important is scientific consensus when it comes to matters of truth? Would good science counsel us to adopt a precautionary principle when it comes to new technologies? We require drug companies to prove scientifically that a new drug is safe before it is introduced to the public. However, we do not apply the same principle to environmental concerns. We allow the release of all kinds of chemicals into the atmosphere without any requirements that such actions be proved scientifically safe ahead of time. Why? Why do we trust science sometimes and reject it at other times? Why do we treat the controversies between creationists and evolutionists differently from conflicting claims between the Flat Earth Society and contemporary astronomers?

7.2 The Growth of Scientific Knowledge

What exactly is science? What do we mean when we call an idea or a theory scientific? How does a scientific idea differ from the ideas of common sense? Certainly one can make a case that science is nothing but just plain, good common sense. Do not both science and common sense share the same goals?

In thinking about these questions I am sure the concept of explanation came to your mind. Science explains things. It answers the "why" and the "how" questions about natural events. It explains what causes what. In good philosophical fashion, however, we must press further and ask what an explanation is.

Many (but not all) philosophers of science subscribe to the **deductive-nomological model** (also called the **covering law model**) of explanation. According to this model, an explanation of an event consists in "covering" or "subsuming" the event under some law. In other words, explaining something requires that a description of it is deducible from the relevant laws of nature. One might explain, for example, the expansion of some metal by appealing to some law such as "metal expands when heated." (Note: this is a highly simplified and nontechnical version of the physical laws involved. One can still ask why heat causes expansion.)

So science is concerned with laws, the laws of nature as some would say. Here science seems to go beyond common sense. Scientists discover and formulate natural laws, and science allows us to accomplish much more than common sense allows. The concept of law is important in science because it makes predictions possible, and predictions make control possible. If I can predict exactly how much a metal will expand when heated to such and such a degree, I have much greater control over the behavior of, let us say, a combustion engine, than I would otherwise. So philosophers of science need to ponder the nature of natural laws and how they are discovered. They must explore how scientists construct scientific concepts.

In addition to problems about the nature of explanation and the construction of scientific concepts like natural law, the philosopher of science must give some account of how scientific conclusions are validated. How do we know when we have arrived at a scientific truth? Is it significantly different from how we know when we have arrived at a commonsense truth?

Karl Popper (1902–1994) was an Austrian-born British philosopher who took issue with the notion that scientific progress consists in extending the laws of nature to explain more and more hitherto unexplained events. Although Popper did not totally reject the deductive-nomological model, he did try to refocus the attention of philosophers of science on issues surrounding the testability of what he liked to call *conjectures.* Science grows not so much by deducing hypotheses from some known laws as it does by making interesting guesses and then subjecting those guesses to rigorous criticism. It is more fruitful, Popper maintained, to try to disprove or falsify a conjecture than to verify or confirm it. We can verify that crows are black by observing many crows, but that does not mean that the next crow we see will be black. It not only saves us time but also gets us closer to the truth if we construct clever experiments designed to refute conjectures about the color of crows. Attempts to falsify theories make a greater contribution to the growth of science than attempts to verify them.

Reading Questions

1. What is Popper's first thesis, and what does it imply?
2. What is the difference between the verificationists and the falsificationists?
3. According Popper, what makes scientific theorizing rational?
4. What did Popper mean when he asserted "*truth is not the only aim of science*"?
5. What are the three requirements of a good scientific theory?
6. How does the third requirement differ from the first two?
7. Why did Popper think that "every refutation should be regarded as a great success"?
8. If we adopt Popper's view of science, how can we distinguish science from superstition?

Conjectures and Refutations

KARL POPPER

I

MY AIM IN THIS LECTURE is to stress the significance of one particular aspect of science — its need to grow, or, if you like, its need to progress. I do not have in mind here the practical or social significance of this need. What I wish to discuss is rather its intellectual significance. I assert that continued growth is essential to the rational and empirical character of scientific knowledge; that if science ceases to grow it must lose that character. It is the way of its growth which makes science rational and empirical; the way, that is, in which scientists discriminate between available theories and choose the better one or (in the absence of a satisfactory theory) the way they give reasons for rejecting all the available theories, thereby suggesting some of the conditions with which a satisfactory theory should comply.

You will have noticed from this formulation that it is not the accumulation of observations which I have in mind when I speak of the growth of scientific knowledge, but the repeated overthrow of scientific theories and their replacement by better or more satisfactory ones. This, incidentally, is a procedure which might be found worthy of attention even by those who see the most important aspect of the growth of scientific knowledge in new experiments and in new observations. For our critical examination of our theories leads us to attempts to test and to overthrow them; and these lead us further to experiments and observations of a kind which nobody would ever have dreamt of without the stimulus and guidance both of our theories and of our criticism of them. For indeed, the most interesting experiments and observations were carefully designed by us in order to *test* our theories, especially our new theories.

In this paper, then, I wish to stress the significance of this aspect of science and to solve some of the problems, old as well as new, which are connected with the notions of scientific progress and of discrimination among competing theories. The new problems I wish to discuss are mainly those connected with the notions of objective truth, and of getting nearer to the truth — notions which seem to me of great help in analysing the growth of knowledge.

Although I shall confine my discussion to the growth of knowledge in science, my remarks are applicable without much change, I believe, to the growth of pre-scientific knowledge also — that is to say, to the general way in which men, and even animals, acquire new factual knowledge about the world. The method of learning by trial and error — of learning from our mistakes — seems to be fundamentally the same whether it is practised by lower or by higher animals, by chimpanzees or by men of science. My interest is not merely in the theory of scientific knowledge, but rather in the theory of knowledge in general. Yet the study of the growth of scientific knowledge is, I believe, the most fruitful way of studying the growth of knowledge in general. For the growth of scientific knowledge may be said to be the growth of ordinary human knowledge *writ large* (as I have pointed out in the 1958 Preface to my *Logic of Scientific Discovery*).

But is there any danger that our need to progress will go unsatisfied, and that the growth of scientific knowledge will come to an end? In particular, is there any danger that the advance of science will come to an end because science has completed its task? I hardly think so, thanks to the infinity of our ignorance. Among the real dangers to the progress of science is not the likelihood of its being completed, but such things as lack of imagination (sometimes a consequence of lack of real interest); or a misplaced faith in formalization and precision . . . ; or authoritarianism in one or another of its many forms.

Since I have used the word "progress" several times, I had better make quite sure, at this point, that I am not mistaken for a believer in a historical law of progress. Indeed I have before now struck various blows against the belief in a law of progress, and I hold that even science is not subject to the operation of anything resembling such a law. The history of science, like the history of all human ideas, is a history of irresponsible dreams, of obstinacy, and of error. But science is one of the very few human activities—perhaps the only one — in which errors are systematically criticized and fairly often, in time, corrected. This is why we can say that, in science, we often learn from our mistakes, and why we can speak clearly and sensibly about making progress there. In most other fields of human endeavour there is change, but rarely progress (unless we adopt a very narrow view of our possible aims in life); for almost every gain is balanced, or more than balanced, by some loss. And in most fields we do not even know how to evaluate change.

Within the field of science we have, however, a *criterion of progress:* even before a theory has ever undergone an empirical test we may be able to say whether, provided it passes certain specified tests, it would be an improvement on other theories with which we are acquainted. This is my first thesis.

To put it a little differently, I assert that we *know* what a good scientific theory should be like, and—even before it has been tested—what kind of theory would be better still, provided it passes certain crucial tests. And it is this (meta-scientific) knowledge which makes it possible to speak of progress in science, and of a rational choice between theories.

II

Thus it is my first thesis that we can know of a theory, even before it has been tested, that *if* it passes certain tests it will be better than some other theory.

My first thesis implies that we have a criterion of relative *potential* satisfactoriness, or of *potential* progressiveness, which can be applied to a theory even before we know whether or not it will turn out, by the passing of some crucial tests, to be satisfactory *in fact*.

This criterion of relative potential satisfactoriness (which I formulated some time ago, and which, incidentally, allows us to grade theories according to their degree of relative potential satisfactoriness) is extremely simple and intuitive. It characterizes as preferable the theory which tells us more; that is to say, the theory which contains the greater amount of empirical information or *content;* which is logically stronger; which has the greater explanatory and predictive power; and which can therefore be *more severely tested* by comparing predicted facts with observations. In short, we prefer an interesting, daring, and highly informative theory to a trivial one.

All these properties which, it thus appears, we desire in a theory can be shown to amount to one and the same thing: to a higher degree of empirical *content* or of testability. . . .

IX

Like many other philosophers I am at times inclined to classify philosophers as belonging to two main groups—those with whom I disagree, and those who agree with me. I also call them the verificationists or the justificationist philosophers of knowledge (or of belief), and the falsificationists or fallibilists or critical philosophers of knowledge (or of conjectures). I may mention in passing a third group with whom I also disagree. They may be called the disappointed justificationists — the irrationalists and sceptics.

The members of the first group — the verificationists or justificationists — hold, roughly speaking, that whatever cannot be supported by positive reasons is unworthy of being believed, or even of being taken into serious consideration.

On the other hand, the members of the second group—the falsificationists or fallibilists—say, roughly speaking, that what cannot (at present) in principle be overthrown by criticism is (at present) unworthy of being seriously considered; while what can in principle be so overthrown and yet resists all our critical efforts to do so may quite possibly be false, but is at any rate not unworthy of being seriously considered and perhaps even of being believed—though only tentatively.

Verificationists, I admit, are eager to uphold that most important tradition of rationalism—the fight of reason against superstition and arbitrary authority. For they demand that we should accept a belief *only if it can be justified by positive evidence;* that is to say, *shown* to be true, or, at least, to be highly probable. In other words, they demand that we should accept a belief only if it can be *verified,* or probabilistically *confirmed.*

Falsificationists (the group of fallibilists to which I belong) believe—as most irrationalists also believe—that they have discovered logical arguments which show that the programme of the first group cannot be carried out: that we can never give positive reasons which justify the belief that a theory is true. But, unlike irrationalists, we falsificationists believe that we have also discovered a way to realize the old ideal of distinguishing rational science from various forms of superstition, in spite of the breakdown of the original inductivist or justificationist programme. We hold that this ideal can be realized, very simply, by recognizing that the rationality of science lies not in its habit of appealing to empirical evidence in support of its dogmas—astrologers do so too—but solely in the *critical approach*—in an attitude which, of course, involves the critical use, among other arguments, of empirical evidence (especially in refutations). For us, therefore, science has nothing to do with the quest for certainty or probability or reliability. We are not interested in establishing scientific theories as secure, or certain, or probable. Conscious of our fallibility we are only interested in

criticizing them and testing them, in the hope of finding out where we are mistaken; of learning from our mistakes; and, if we are lucky, of proceeding to better theories.

Considering their views about the positive or negative function of argument in science, the first group—the justificationists—may be also nicknamed the "positivists" and the second—the group to which I belong—the critics or the "negativists." These are, of course, mere nicknames. Yet they may perhaps suggest some of the reasons why some people believe that only the positivists or verificationists are seriously interested in truth and in the search for truth, while we, the critics or negativists, are flippant about the search for truth, and addicted to barren and destructive criticism and to the propounding of views which are clearly paradoxical.

This mistaken picture of our views seems to result largely from the adoption of a justificationist programme, and of the mistaken subjectivist approach to truth which I have described.

For the fact is that we too see science as the search for truth, and that, at least since Tarski, we are no longer afraid to say so. Indeed, it is only with respect to this aim, the discovery of truth, that we can say that though we are fallible, we hope to learn from our mistakes. It is only the idea of truth which allows us to speak sensibly of mistakes and of rational criticism, and which makes rational discussion possible—that is to say, critical discussion in search of mistakes with the serious purpose of eliminating as many of these mistakes as we can, in order to get nearer to the truth. Thus the very idea of error—and of fallibility—involves the idea of an objective truth as the standard of which we may fall short. (It is in this sense that the idea of truth is a *regulative* idea.)

Thus we accept the idea that the task of science is the search for truth, that is, for true theories (even though as Xenophanes pointed out we may never get them, or know them *as true* if we get them). Yet we also stress that *truth is not the only aim of science.* We want more than mere truth: what we look for is *interesting truth*—truth which is hard to come by. And in the natural sciences (as distinct from mathematics) what we look for is truth which has a high degree of explanatory power, which implies that it is logically improbable.

For it is clear, first of all, that we do not merely want truth — we want more truth, and new truth. We are not content with "twice two equals four," even though it is true: we do not resort to reciting the multiplication table if we are faced with a difficult problem in topology or in physics. Mere truth is not enough; what we look for are *answers to our problems.* The point has been well put by the German humorist and poet Busch, of Max-and-Moritz fame, in a little nursery rhyme — I mean a rhyme for the episte-mological nursery:

Twice two equals four: 'tis true,
But too empty, and too trite.
What I look for is a clue
To some matters not so light.

Only if it is an answer to a problem — a difficult, a fertile problem, a problem of some depth — does a truth, or a conjecture about the truth, become relevant to science. This is so in pure mathematics, and it is so in the natural sciences. And in the latter, we have something like a logical measure of the depth or significance of the problem in the increase of logical improba-bility or explanatory power of the proposed new answer, as compared with the best theory or con-jecture previously proposed in the field. This logical measure is essentially the same thing which I have described above as the logical crite-rion of potential satisfactoriness and of progress.

My description of this situation might tempt some people to say that truth does not, after all, play a very big role with us negativists even as a regulative principle. There can be no doubt, they will say, that negativists (like myself) much pre-fer an attempt to solve an interesting problem by a bold conjecture, *even if it soon turns out to be false,* to any recital of a sequence of true but un-interesting assertions. Thus it does not seem, af-ter all, as if we negativists had much use for the idea of truth. Our ideas of scientific progress and of attempted problem-solving do not seem very closely related to it.

This, I believe, would give quite a mistaken impression of the attitude of our group. Call us negativists, or what you like: but you should re-alize that we are as much interested in truth as anybody — for example, as the members of a court of justice. When the judge tells a witness that he should speak "The truth, the *whole truth,* and nothing but the truth," then what he looks for is as much of the *relevant truth* as the witness may be able to offer. A witness who likes to wan-der off into irrelevancies is unsatisfactory as a wit-ness, even though these irrelevancies may be tru-isms, and thus part of "the whole truth." It is quite obvious that what the judge — or anybody else — wants when he asks for "the whole truth" is as much *interesting and relevant* true informa-tion as can be got; and many perfectly candid witnesses have failed to disclose some important information simply because they were unaware of its relevance to the case.

Thus when we stress, with Busch, that we are not interested in mere truth but in interesting and relevant truth, then, I contend, we only em-phasize a point which everybody accepts. And if we are interested in bold conjectures, even if these should soon turn out to be false, then this interest is due to our methodological conviction that only with the help of such bold conjectures can we hope to discover interesting and relevant truth.

There is a point here which, I suggest, it is the particular task of the logician to analyse. "Inter-ests," or "relevance," in the sense here intended, can be *objectively* analysed; it is relative to our problems; and it depends on the explanatory power, and thus on the content or improbability, of the information. The measures alluded to ear-lier . . . are precisely such measures as take ac-count of some *relative content* of the informa-tion — its content relative to a hypothesis or to a problem.

I can therefore gladly admit that falsification-ists like myself much prefer an attempt to solve an interesting problem by a bold conjecture, *even (and especially) if it soon turns out to be false,* to any recital of a sequence of irrelevant truisms. We prefer this because we believe that this is the way in which we can learn from our mistakes;

and that in finding that our conjecture was false, we shall have learnt much about the truth, and shall have got nearer to the truth.

I therefore hold that both ideas — the idea of truth, in the sense of correspondence with the facts and the idea of content (which may be measured by the same measure as testability) — play about equally important roles in our considerations, and that both can shed much light on the idea of progress in science. . . .

XVIII

. . . What is the general problem situation in which the scientist finds himself? He has before him a scientific problem: he wants to find a new theory capable of explaining certain experimental facts; facts which the earlier theories successfully explained; others which they could not explain; and some by which they were actually falsified. The new theory should also resolve, if possible, some theoretical difficulties (such as how to dispense with certain *ad hoc* hypotheses, or how to unify two theories). Now if he manages to produce a theory which is a solution to all these problems, his achievement will be very great.

Yet it is not enough. I have been asked, "What more do you want?" My answer is that there are many more things which I want; or rather, which I think are required by the logic of the general problem situation in which the scientist finds himself; by the task of getting nearer to the truth. I shall confine myself here to the discussion of three such requirements.

The first requirement is this. The new theory should proceed from some *simple, new, and powerful, unifying idea* about some connection or relation (such as gravitational attraction) between hitherto unconnected things (such as planets and apples) or facts (such as inertial and gravitational mass) or new "theoretical entities" (such as field and particles). This *requirement of simplicity* is a bit vague, and it seems difficult to formulate it very clearly. It seems to be intimately connected with the idea that our theories should describe the structural properties of the world — an idea which it is hard to think out fully without getting involved in an infinite regress. (This is so because any idea of a particular structure of the world — unless, indeed, we think of a purely *mathematical* structure — already presupposes a universal theory; for example, explaining the laws of chemistry by interpreting molecules as structures of atoms, or of subatomic particles, presupposes the idea of universal laws that regulate the properties and the behaviour of the atoms, or of the particles.) Yet one important ingredient in the idea of simplicity can be logically analysed. It is the idea of testability. This leads us immediately to our second requirement.

For, secondly, we require that the new theory should be *independently testable*. That is to say, apart from explaining all the *explicanda* which the new theory was designed to explain, it must have new and testable consequences (preferably consequences of a *new kind*); it must lead to the prediction of phenomena which have not so far been observed.

This requirement seems to me indispensable since without it our new theory might be *ad hoc;* for it is always possible to produce a theory to fit any given set of explicanda. Thus our two first requirements are needed in order to restrict the range of our choice among the possible solutions (many of them uninteresting) of the problem in hand.

If our second requirement is satisfied then our new theory will represent a potential step forward, whatever the outcome of the new tests may be. For it will be better testable than the previous theory: the fact that it explains all the explicanda of the previous theory, and that, in addition, it gives rise to new tests, suffices to ensure this.

Moreover, the second requirement also ensures that our new theory will, to some extent, be fruitful as an instrument of exploration. That is to say, it will suggest to us new experiments, and even if these should at once lead to the refutation of the theory, our factual knowledge will have grown through the unexpected results of the new experiments. Moreover, they will confront us with new problems to be solved by new explanatory theories.

Yet I believe that there must be a third requirement for a good theory. It is this. We require that the theory should pass some new, and severe, tests.

XIX

Clearly, this requirement is totally different in character from the previous two. These could be seen to be fulfilled, or not fulfilled, largely by analysing the old and the new theories logically. (They are "formal requirements." The third requirement, on the other hand, can be found to be fulfilled, or not fulfilled, only by testing the new theory empirically. (It is a "material requirement," a requirement of *empirical success.*)

Moreover, the third requirement clearly cannot be indispensable in the same sense as are the two previous ones. For these two are indispensable for deciding whether the theory in question should be at all accepted as a serious candidate for examination by empirical tests; or in other words, whether it is an interesting and promising theory. Yet on the other hand, some of the most interesting and most admirable theories ever conceived were refuted at the very first test. And why not? The most promising theory may fail if it makes predictions of a new kind. . . .

Refutations have often been regarded as establishing the failure of a scientist, or at least of his theory. It should be stressed that this is an inductivist error. Every refutation should be regarded as a great success; not merely a success of the scientist who refuted the theory, but also of the scientist who created the refuted theory and who thus in the first instance suggested, if only indirectly, the refuting experiment.

Even if a new theory (such as the theory of Bohr, Kramers, and Slater) should meet an early death, it should not be forgotten; rather its beauty should be remembered, and history should record our gratitude to it — for bequeathing to us new and perhaps still unexplained experimental facts and, with them, new problems; and for the services it has thus rendered to the progress of science during its successful but short life.

All this indicates clearly that our third requirement is not indispensable: even a theory which fails to meet it can make an important contribution to science. Yet in a different sense, I hold, it is indispensable none the less. (Bohr, Kramers and Slater rightly aimed at more than making an important contribution to science.)

In the first place, I contend that further progress in science would become impossible if we did not reasonably often manage to meet the third requirement; thus if the progress of science is to continue, and its rationality not to decline, we need not only successful refutations, but also positive successes. We must, that is, manage reasonably often to produce theories that entail new predictions, especially predictions of new effects, new testable consequences, suggested by the new theory and never thought of before. Such a new prediction was that planets would under certain circumstances deviate from Kepler's laws; or that light, in spite of its zero mass, would prove to be subject to gravitational attraction (that is, Einstein's eclipse-effect). Another example is Dirac's prediction that there will be an anti-particle for every elementary particle. New predictions of these kinds must not only be produced, but they must also be reasonably often corroborated by experimental evidence, I contend, if scientific progress is to continue. . . .

7.3 Scientific Revolutions

If I asked you to tell me something about scientific procedure, you might start talking about the scientific method of observation, which leads to theories from which predictive hypotheses are deduced and then tested by making further observations. This is called the **hypothetico-deductive method** because it involves deducing consequences (predictions) that should hold if the hypothesis is correct and then designing experiments to see if they do indeed hold true.

Your version of the scientific method might also include a belief that science is incremental in the sense that truth slowly accumulates over time. Scientists build on past discoveries and theories. Many people working very carefully, but slowly and surely, add to an ever growing understanding of the way the world operates. Present theories absorb past theories, and each generation makes progress toward the ideal of understanding everything scientifically.

This picture of science is what philosophers often call **normal science** or standard science. It can be contrasted with a picture of science that might be new to you, a picture called **revolutionary science**. According to this picture, scientists sometimes reject traditional, time-honored, and well-established theories of how the world runs in favor of new and incompatible theories. Old problems and puzzles that people worked on so carefully now seem irrelevant, and a host of new problems emerges, clamoring for attention. **Anomalies** or new events that do not fit with prevailing beliefs generate new and deep questions about accepted scientific views. Theories once thought true now appear inadequate, and new theories must be invented.

According to Thomas Kuhn (1922–1996), one of the most influential and controversial philosophers of science in the last century, one of the main differences between normal science and revolutionary science has to do with what he calls paradigms. A **paradigm** is a scientific achievement so deep and impressive that it defines the daily practice for a particular community of scientists. It settles fundamental issues, provides a general set of assumptions, and offers a kind of basic model, thereby generating research puzzles with definite solutions. Normal science works within a paradigm, solving slowly but surely the puzzles and problems the paradigm generates. Within the boundaries of the paradigm, we may speak of scientific progress. Then anomalies occur. Unexpected experimental results that are incompatible with prevailing theory generate a crisis that leads to a paradigm shift. This shift in paradigms is the work of revolutionary science, which tears down established frameworks and creates something new. Once revolutionary science has done its work, a new paradigm reigns and a new round of normal science begins, now operating within the bounds of the new paradigm.

I think you can see that if Kuhn is right, science does not always make gradual and smooth progress. Crises generated by anomalies create shifts in vision. What people see and how they see it changes very much like gestalt shifts in vision that occur when one suddenly sees a figure that first appeared to be a rabbit, now appears to be a duck (or vice versa). These shifts are not built on the old paradigm. In fact the old and new paradigms are **incommensurable**, not only in the sense of being incompatible, but also in the sense that given any two paradigms, we would not be able to say which one is better or more accurate because we lack paradigm-transcending criteria for making such extra-paradigmatic judgments. From the point of view of revolutionary science, science does not progress in a traditional sense: It changes direction.

The following selection comes from Kuhn's most influential book, *The Structure of Scientific Revolutions*. To present the key ideas, I have edited many of the examples that Kuhn uses to support his views (examples that give a thickness to his ideas) so the resulting version may seem overly thin, abstract, and unconnected to familiar scientific theories. Even so, what Kuhn has to say will get you to think about science and its ability to generate knowledge in a way you have not thought about it before.

Reading Questions

1. How does Kuhn describe normal science?
2. What, according to Kuhn, are two essential characteristics of a paradigm?
3. How does the emergence of a new paradigm in a particular field of science affect the structure of the group that practices that field?
4. What is the nature of normal science in relationship to a paradigm?
5. Why are anomalies important in science?
6. What influences the decision to reject a paradigm?
7. What are scientific revolutions, and what is their function in scientific development?
8. What sorts of parallels are there between scientific and political revolutions?
9. In Section X, do you think Kuhn is claiming that both the way the scientist sees the world and the world itself change when a paradigm shift occurs? Why, or why not?
10. How does Kuhn explain scientific progress? Do you think his answer is better than the traditional picture of science as progressing by drawing closer to the truth about the way things are? Why, or why not?
11. Do you think Kuhn's ideas about science imply that knowledge is relative? Why, or why not?

The Structure of Scientific Revolutions

THOMAS S. KUHN

II. *The Route to Normal Science*

IN THIS ESSAY, "normal science" means research firmly based upon one or more past scientific achievements, achievements that some particular scientific community acknowledges for a time as supplying the foundation for its further practice. Today such achievements are recounted, though seldom in their original form, by science textbooks, elementary and advanced. These textbooks expound the body of accepted theory, illustrate many or all of its successful applications, and compare these applications with exemplary observations and experiments. Before such books became popular early in the nineteenth century (and until even more recently in the newly matured sciences), many of the famous classics of science fulfilled a similar function. Aristotle's *Physica*, Ptolemy's *Almagest*, Newton's *Principia* and *Opticks*, Franklin's *Electricity*, Lavoisier's *Chemistry*, and Lyell's *Geology*—these and many other works served for a time implicitly to define the legitimate problems and methods of a research field for succeeding generations of practitioners. They were able to do so because they shared two essential characteristics. Their achievement was sufficiently unprecedented to attract an enduring group of adherents away from competing modes of scientific activity. Simultaneously, it was sufficiently open-ended to leave all sorts of problems for the redefined group of practitioners to resolve.

Achievements that share these two characteristics I shall henceforth refer to as "paradigms,"

From *Thomas S. Kuhn,* The Structure of Scientific Revolutions, *2nd Edition, enlarged. Chicago, IL: The University of Chicago Press, 1970, pp. 10–11, 18–19, 23–24, 52–53, 64–65, 77–78, 92–96, 109–112, 160–173. Footnotes omitted.* © *1962, 1970 by the University of Chicago Press. Reprinted by permission.*

a term that relates closely to "normal science." By choosing it, I mean to suggest that some accepted examples of actual scientific practice—examples which include law, theory, application, and instrumentation together—provide models from which spring particular coherent traditions of scientific research. These are the traditions which the historian describes under such rubrics as "Ptolemaic astronomy" (or "Copernican"), "Aristotelian dynamics" (or "Newtonian"), "corpuscular optics" (or "wave optics"), and so on. The study of paradigms, including many that are far more specialized than those named illustratively above, is what mainly prepares the student for membership in the particular scientific community with which he will later practice. Because he there joins men who learned the bases of their field from the same concrete models, his subsequent practice will seldom evoke overt disagreement over fundamentals. Men whose research is based on shared paradigms are committed to the same rules and standards for scientific practice. That commitment and the apparent consensus it produces are prerequisites for normal science, i.e., for the genesis and continuation of a particular research tradition. . . .

We shall be examining the nature of this highly directed or paradigm-based research in the next section, but must first note briefly how the emergence of a paradigm affects the structure of the group that practices the field. When, in the development of a natural science, an individual or group first produces a synthesis able to attract most of the next generation's practitioners, the older schools gradually disappear. In part their disappearance is caused by their members' conversion to the new paradigm. But there are always some men who cling to one or another of the older views, and they are simply read out of the profession, which thereafter ignores their work. The new paradigm implies a new and more rigid definition of the field. Those unwilling or unable to accommodate their work to it must proceed in isolation or attach themselves to some other group. Historically, they have often simply stayed in the departments of philosophy from which so many of the special sciences have been spawned. As these indications hint, it is sometimes just its reception of a paradigm that transforms a group previously interested merely in the study of nature into a profession or, at least, a discipline. In the sciences (though not in fields like medicine, technology, and law, of which the principal *raison d'être* is an external social need), the formation of specialized journals, the foundation of specialists' societies, and the claim for a special place in the curriculum have usually been associated with a group's first reception of a single paradigm. At least this was the case between the time, a century and a half ago, when the institutional pattern of scientific specialization first developed and the very recent time when the paraphernalia of specialization acquired a prestige of their own.

III. *The Nature of Normal Science*

What then is the nature of the more professional and esoteric research that a group's reception of a single paradigm permits? If the paradigm represents work that has been done once and for all, what further problems does it leave the united group to resolve? Those questions will seem even more urgent if we now note one respect in which the terms used so far may be misleading. In its established usage, a paradigm is an accepted model or pattern, and that aspect of its meaning has enabled me, lacking a better word, to appropriate "paradigm" here. But it will shortly be clear that the sense of "model" and "pattern" that permits the appropriation is not quite the one usual in defining "paradigm." In grammar, for example, *"amo, amas, amat"* is a paradigm because it displays the pattern to be used in conjugating a large number of other Latin verbs, e.g., in producing *"audo, laudas, laudat."* In this standard application, the paradigm functions by permitting the replication of examples any one of which could in principle serve to replace it. In a science, on the other hand, a paradigm is rarely an object for replication. Instead, like an accepted judicial decision in the common law, it is an object for further articulation and specification under new or more stringent conditions.

To see how this can be so, we must recognize how very limited in both scope and precision a paradigm can be at the time of its first appearance. Paradigms gain their status because they are more successful than their competitors in solving a few problems that the group of practitioners has come to recognize as acute. To be more successful is not, however, to be either completely successful with a single problem or notably successful with any large number. The success of a paradigm—whether Aristotle's analysis of motion, Ptolemy's computations of planetary position, Lavoisier's application of the balance, or Maxwell's mathematization of the electromagnetic field—is at the start largely a promise of success discoverable in selected and still incomplete examples. Normal science consists in the actualization of that promise, an actualization achieved by extending the knowledge of those facts that the paradigm displays as particularly revealing, by increasing the extent of the match between those facts and the paradigm's predictions, and by further articulation of the paradigm itself.

Few people who are not actually practitioners of a mature science realize how much mop-up work of this sort a paradigm leaves to be done or quite how fascinating such work can prove in the execution. And these points need to be understood. Mopping-up operations are what engage most scientists throughout their careers. They constitute what I am here calling normal science. Closely examined, whether historically or in the contemporary laboratory, that enterprise seems an attempt to force nature into the preformed and relatively inflexible box that the paradigm supplies. No part of the aim of normal science is to call forth new sorts of phenomena; indeed those that will not fit the box are often not seen at all. Nor do scientists normally aim to invent new theories, and they are often intolerant of those invented by others. Instead, normal-scientific research is directed to the articulation of those phenomena and theories that the paradigm already supplies. . . .

VI. Anomaly and the Emergence of Scientific Discoveries

Normal science, the puzzle-solving activity we have just examined, is a highly cumulative enterprise, eminently successful in its aim, the steady extension of the scope and precision of scientific knowledge. In all these respects it fits with great precision the most usual image of scientific work. Yet one standard product of the scientific enterprise is missing. Normal science does not aim at novelties of fact or theory and, when successful, finds none. New and unsuspected phenomena are, however, repeatedly uncovered by scientific research, and radical new theories have again and again been invented by scientists. History even suggests that the scientific enterprise has developed a uniquely powerful technique for producing surprises of this sort. If this characteristic of science is to be reconciled with what has already been said, then research under a paradigm must be a particularly effective way of inducing paradigm change. That is what fundamental novelties of fact and theory do. Produced inadvertently by a game played under one set of rules, their assimilation requires the elaboration of another set. After they have become parts of science, the enterprise, at least of those specialists in whose particular field the novelties lie, is never quite the same again.

We must now ask how changes of this sort can come about, considering first discoveries, or novelties of fact, and then inventions, or novelties of theory. That distinction between discovery and invention or between fact and theory will, however, immediately prove to be exceedingly artificial. Its artificiality is an important clue to several of this essay's main theses. Examining selected discoveries in the rest of this section, we shall quickly find that they are not isolated events but extended episodes with a regularly recurrent structure. Discovery commences with the awareness of anomaly, i.e., with the recognition that nature has somehow violated the paradigm-induced expectations that govern normal science. It then continues with a more or less extended exploration of the area of anomaly. And it closes only when the paradigm theory has been adjusted so that the anomalous has become the expected. Assimilating a new sort of fact demands a more than additive adjustment of theory, and until that adjustment is completed—until the scientist has learned to see nature in a different way—the new fact is not quite a scientific fact at all. . . .

In the development of any science, the first received paradigm is usually felt to account quite successfully for most of the observations and experiments easily accessible to that science's practitioners. Further development, therefore, ordinarily calls for the construction of elaborate equipment, the development of an esoteric vocabulary and skills, and a refinement of concepts that increasingly lessens their resemblance to their usual common-sense prototypes. That professionalization leads, on the one hand, to an immense restriction of the scientist's vision and to a considerable resistance to paradigm change. The science has become increasingly rigid. On the other hand, within those areas to which the paradigm directs the attention of the group, normal science leads to a detail of information and to a precision of the observation-theory match that could be achieved in no other way. Furthermore, that detail and precision of match have a value that transcends their not always very high intrinsic interest. Without the special apparatus that is constructed mainly for anticipated functions, the results that lead ultimately to novelty could not occur. And even when the apparatus exists, novelty ordinarily emerges only for the man who, knowing *with precision* what he should expect, is able to recognize that something has gone wrong. Anomaly appears only against the background provided by the paradigm. The more precise and far-reaching that paradigm is, the more sensitive an indicator it provides of anomaly and hence of an occasion for paradigm change. In the normal mode of discovery, even resistance to change has a use that will be explored more fully in the next section. By ensuring that the paradigm will not be too easily surrendered, resistance guarantees that scientists will not be lightly distracted and that the anomalies that lead to paradigm change will penetrate existing knowledge to the core. The very fact that a significant scientific novelty so often emerges simultaneously from several laboratories is an index both to the strongly traditional nature of normal science and to the completeness with which that traditional pursuit prepares the way for its own change. . . .

VIII. *The Response to Crisis*

Let us then assume that crises are a necessary precondition for the emergence of novel theories and ask next how scientists respond to their existence. Part of the answer, as obvious as it is important, can be discovered by noting first what scientists never do when confronted by even severe and prolonged anomalies. Though they may begin to lose faith and then to consider alternatives, they do not renounce the paradigm that has led them into crisis. They do not, that is, treat anomalies as counterinstances, though in the vocabulary of philosophy of science that is what they are. In part this generalization is simply a statement from historic fact, based upon examples like those given above and, more extensively, below. These hint what our later examination of paradigm rejection will disclose more fully: once it has achieved the status of paradigm, a scientific theory is declared invalid only if an alternate candidate is available to take its place. No process yet disclosed by the historical study of scientific development at all resembles the methodological stereotype of falsification by direct comparison with nature. That remark does not mean that scientists do not reject scientific theories, or that experience and experiment are not essential to the process in which they do so. But it does mean— what will ultimately be a central point—that the act of judgment that leads scientists to reject a previously accepted theory is always based upon more than a comparison of that theory with the world. The decision to reject one paradigm is always simultaneously the decision to accept another, and the judgment leading to that decision involves the comparison of both paradigms with nature *and* with each other.

There is, in addition, a second reason for doubting that scientists reject paradigms because confronted with anomalies or counterinstances. In developing it my argument will itself foreshadow another of this essay's main theses. The reasons for doubt sketched above were purely factual; they were, that is, themselves counterinstances to a prevalent epistemological theory. As such, if my present point is correct, they can at best help to create a crisis or, more accurately, to reinforce one that is already very much in existence. By themselves they cannot and will not falsify that philosophical theory, for its defenders will do what we have already seen scientists doing when confronted by anomaly. They will devise numerous articulations and *ad hoc* modifications of their theory in order to eliminate any apparent conflict. Many of the relevant modifications and qualifications are, in fact, already in the literature. If, therefore, these epistemological counterinstances are to constitute more than a minor irritant, that will be because they help to permit the emergence of a new and different analysis of science within which they are no longer a source of trouble. Furthermore, if a typical pattern, which we shall later observe in scientific revolutions, is applicable here, these anomalies will then no longer seem to be simply facts. From within a new theory of scientific knowledge, they may instead seem very much like tautologies, statements of situations that could not conceivably have been otherwise. . . .

IX. *The Nature and Necessity of Scientific Revolutions*

These remarks permit us at last to consider the problems that provide this essay with its title. What are scientific revolutions, and what is their function in scientific development? Much of the answer to these questions has been anticipated in earlier sections. In particular, the preceding discussion has indicated that scientific revolutions are here taken to be those non-cumulative developmental episodes in which an older paradigm is replaced in whole or in part by an incompatible new one. There is more to be said, however, and an essential part of it can be introduced by asking one further question. Why should a change of paradigm be called a revolution? In the face of the vast and essential differences between political and scientific development, what parallelism can justify the metaphor that finds revolutions in both?

One aspect of the parallelism must already be apparent. Political revolutions are inaugurated by a growing sense, often restricted to a segment of the political community, that existing institutions have ceased adequately to meet the problems posed by an environment that they have in part created. In much the same way, scientific revolutions are inaugurated by a growing sense, again often restricted to a narrow subdivision of the scientific community, that an existing paradigm has ceased to function adequately in the exploration of an aspect of nature to which that paradigm itself had previously led the way. In both political and scientific development the sense of malfunction that can lead to crisis is prerequisite to revolution. Furthermore, though it admittedly strains the metaphor, that parallelism holds not only for the major paradigm changes, like those attributable to Copernicus and Lavoisier, but also for the far smaller ones associated with the assimilation of a new sort of phenomenon, like oxygen or X-rays. Scientific revolutions . . . seem revolutionary only to those whose paradigms are affected by them. To outsiders they may, like the Balkan revolutions of the early twentieth century, seem normal parts of the developmental process. Astronomers, for example, could accept X-rays as a mere addition to knowledge, for their paradigms were unaffected by the existence of the new radiation. But for men like Kelvin, Crookes, and Roentgen, whose research dealt with radiation theory or with cathode ray tubes, the emergence of X-rays necessarily violated one paradigm as it created another. That is why these rays could be discovered only through something's first going wrong with normal research.

This genetic aspect of the parallel between political and scientific development should no longer be open to doubt. The parallel has, however, a second and more profound aspect upon which the significance of the first depends. Political revolutions aim to change political institutions in ways that those institutions themselves prohibit. Their success therefore necessitates the partial relinquishment of one set of institutions in favor of another, and in the interim, society is not fully governed by institutions at all. Initially it is crisis alone that attenuates the role of political institutions as we have already seen it attenuate the role of paradigms. In increasing numbers individuals become increasingly estranged from political life and behave more and more eccentrically within it. Then, as the crisis deepens, many of these individuals commit themselves to some concrete proposal for the reconstruction of society in a new institutional framework. At that point the society is divided into competing camps or parties, one seeking to defend the old institutional constellation, the others seeking to institute some new one. And, once that polarization has occurred, *political recourse fails.* Because they differ about the institutional matrix within which political change is to be achieved and evaluated, because they acknowledge no supra-institutional framework for the adjudication of revolutionary difference, the parties to a revolutionary conflict must finally resort to the techniques of mass persuasion, often including force. Though revolutions have had a vital role in the evolution of political institutions, that role depends upon their being partially extrapolitical or extrainstitutional events.

The remainder of this essay aims to demonstrate that the historical study of paradigm change reveals very similar characteristics in the evolution of the sciences. Like the choice between competing political institutions, that between competing paradigms proves to be a choice between incompatible modes of community life. Because it has that character, the choice is not and cannot be determined merely by the evaluative procedures characteristic of normal science, for these depend in part upon a particular paradigm, and that paradigm is at issue. When paradigms enter, as they must, into a debate about paradigm choice, their role is necessarily circular. Each group uses its own paradigm to argue in that paradigm's defense.

The resulting circularity does not, of course, make the arguments wrong or even ineffectual. The man who premises a paradigm when arguing in its defense can nonetheless provide a clear exhibit of what scientific practice will be like for those who adopt the new view of nature. That exhibit can be immensely persuasive, often compellingly so. Yet, whatever its force, the status of the circular argument is only that of persuasion. It cannot be made logically or even probabilistically compelling for those who refuse to step into

the circle. The premises and values shared by the two parties to a debate over paradigms are not sufficiently extensive for that. As in political revolutions, so in paradigm choice—there is no standard higher than the assent of the relevant community. To discover how scientific revolutions are effected, we shall therefore have to examine not only the impact of nature and of logic, but also the techniques of persuasive argumentation effective within the quite special groups that constitute the community of scientists.

To discover why this issue of paradigm choice can never be unequivocally settled by logic and experiment alone, we must shortly examine the nature of the differences that separate the proponents of a traditional paradigm from their revolutionary successors. That examination is the principal object of this section and the next. We have, however, already noted numerous examples of such differences, and no one will doubt that history can supply many others. What is more likely to be doubted than their existence—and what must therefore be considered first—is that such examples provide essential information about the nature of science. Granting that paradigm rejection has been a historic fact, does it illuminate more than human credulity and confusion? Are there intrinsic reasons why the assimilation of either a new sort of phenomenon or a new scientific theory must demand the rejection of an older paradigm?

First notice that if there are such reasons, they do not derive from the logical structure of scientific knowledge. In principle, a new phenomenon might emerge without reflecting destructively upon any part of past scientific practice. Though discovering life on the moon would today be destructive of existing paradigms (these tell us things about the moon that seem incompatible with life's existence there), discovering life in some less well-known part of the galaxy would not. By the same token, a new theory does not have to conflict with any of its predecessors. It might deal exclusively with phenomena not previously known, as the quantum theory deals (but, significantly, not exclusively) with subatomic phenomena unknown before the twentieth century. Or again, the new theory might be simply a higher level theory than those known before, one that linked together a whole group of lower level theories without substantially changing any. Today, the theory of energy conservation provides just such links between dynamics, chemistry, electricity, optics, thermal theory, and so on. Still other compatible relationships between old and new theories can be conceived. Any and all of them might be exemplified by the historical process through which science has developed. If they were, scientific development would be genuinely cumulative. New sorts of phenomena would simply disclose order in an aspect of nature where none had been seen before. In the evolution of science new knowledge would replace ignorance rather than replace knowledge of another and incompatible sort.

Of course, science (or some other enterprise, perhaps less effective) might have developed in that fully cumulative manner. Many people have believed that it did so, and most still seem to suppose that cumulation is at least the ideal that historical development would display if only it had not so often been distorted by human idiosyncrasy. There are important reasons for that belief. In Section X we shall discover how closely the view of science-as-cumulation is entangled with a dominant epistemology that takes knowledge to be a construction placed directly upon raw sense data by the mind. . . . Nevertheless, despite the immense plausibility of that ideal image, there is increasing reason to wonder whether it can possibly be an image of *science*. After the preparadigm period the assimilation of all new theories and of almost all new sorts of phenomena has in fact demanded the destruction of a prior paradigm and a consequent conflict between competing schools of scientific thought. Cumulative acquisition of unanticipated novelties proves to be an almost non-existent exception to the rule of scientific development. The man who takes historic fact seriously must suspect that science does not tend toward the ideal that our image of its cumulativeness has suggested. Perhaps it is another sort of enterprise. . . .

By shifting emphasis from the cognitive to the normative functions of paradigms, the preceding examples enlarge our understanding of the ways in which paradigms give form to the scientific life. Previously, we had principally examined the paradigm's role as a vehicle for scientific theory. In that role it functions by telling the scientist about the entities that nature does and does not contain and about the ways in which those entities behave. That information provides a map whose details are elucidated by mature scientific research. And since nature is too complex and varied to be explored at random, that map is as essential as observation and experiment to science's continuing development. Through the theories they embody, paradigms prove to be constitutive of the research activity. They are also, however, constitutive of science in other respects, and that is now the point. In particular, our most recent examples show that paradigms provide scientists not only with a map but also with some of the directions essential for map-making. In learning a paradigm the scientist acquires theory, methods, and standards together, usually in an inextricable mixture. Therefore, when paradigms change, there are usually significant shifts in the criteria determining the legitimacy both of problems and of proposed solutions.

That observation returns us to the point from which this section began, for it provides our first explicit indication of why the choice between competing paradigms regularly raises questions that cannot be resolved by the criteria of normal science. To the extent, as significant as it is incomplete, that two scientific schools disagree about what is a problem and what a solution, they will inevitably talk through each other when debating the relative merits of their respective paradigms. In the partially circular arguments that regularly result, each paradigm will be shown to satisfy more or less the criteria that it dictates for itself and to fall short of a few of those dictated by its opponent. There are other reasons, too, for the incompleteness of logical contact that consistently characterizes paradigm debates. For example, since no paradigm ever solves all the problems it defines and since no two paradigms leave all the same problems unsolved, paradigm debates always involve the question: Which problems is it more significant to have solved? Like the issue of competing standards, that question of values can be answered only in terms of criteria that lie outside of normal science altogether, and it is that recourse to external criteria that most obviously makes paradigm debates revolutionary. Something even more fundamental than standards and values is, however, also at stake. I have so far argued only that paradigms are constitutive of science. Now I wish to display a sense in which they arc constitutive of nature as well.

X. Revolutions as Changes of World View

Examining the record of past research from the vantage of contemporary historiography, the historian of science may be tempted to exclaim that when paradigms change, the world itself changes with them. Led by a new paradigm, scientists adopt new instruments and look in new places. Even more important, during revolutions scientists see new and different things when looking with familiar instruments in places they have looked before. It is rather as if the professional community had been suddenly transported to another planet where familiar objects are seen in a different light and are joined by unfamiliar ones as well. Of course, nothing of quite that sort does occur: there is no geographical transplantation; outside the laboratory everyday affairs usually continue as before. Nevertheless, paradigm changes do cause scientists to see the world of their research-engagement differently. In so far as their only recourse to that world is through what they see and do, we may want to say that after a revolution scientists are responding to a different world.

It is as elementary prototypes for these transformations of the scientist's world that the familiar demonstrations of a switch in visual gestalt prove so suggestive. What were ducks in the scientist's world before the revolution are rabbits afterwards. The man who first saw the exterior of the box from above later sees its interior from below. Transformations like these, though usually more gradual and almost always irreversible, are common concomitants of scientific training. Looking at a contour map, the student sees lines on paper, the cartographer a picture of a terrain.

Looking at a bubble-chamber photograph, the student sees confused and broken lines, the physicist a record of familiar subnuclear events. Only after a number of such transformations of vision does the student become an inhabitant of the scientist's world, seeing what the scientist sees and responding as the scientist does. The world that the student then enters is not, however, fixed once and for all by the nature of the environment, on the one hand, and of science, on the other. Rather, it is determined jointly by the environment and the particular normal-scientific tradition that the student has been trained to pursue. Therefore, at times of revolution, when the normal-scientific tradition changes, the scientist's perception of his environment must be re-educated—in some familiar situations he must learn to see a new gestalt. After he has done so the world of his research will seem, here and there, incommensurable with the one he had inhabited before. That is another reason why schools guided by different paradigms are always slightly at cross-purposes.

In their most usual form, of course, gestalt experiments illustrate only the nature of perceptual transformations. They tell us nothing about the role of paradigms or of previously assimilated experience in the process of perception. But on that point there is a rich body of psychological literature, much of it stemming from the pioneering work of the Hanover Institute. An experimental subject who puts on goggles fitted with inverting lenses initially sees the entire world upside down. At the start his perceptual apparatus functions as it had been trained to function in the absence of the goggles, and the result is extreme disorientation, an acute personal crisis. But after the subject has begun to learn to deal with his new world, his entire visual field flips over, usually after an intervening period in which vision is simply confused. Thereafter, objects are again seen as they had been before the goggles were put on. The assimilation of a previously anomalous visual field has reacted upon and changed the field itself. Literally as well as metaphorically, the man accustomed to inverting lenses has undergone a revolutionary transformation of vision. . . .

XIII. *Progress through Revolutions*

The preceding pages have carried my schematic description of scientific development as far as it can go in this essay. Nevertheless, they cannot quite provide a conclusion. If this description has at all caught the essential structure of a science's continuing evolution, it will simultaneously have posed a special problem: Why should the enterprise sketched above move steadily ahead in ways that, say, art, political theory, or philosophy does not? Why is progress a perquisite reserved almost exclusively for the activities we call science? The most usual answers to that question have been denied in the body of this essay. We must conclude it by asking whether substitutes can be found.

Notice immediately that part of the question is entirely semantic. To a very great extent the term "science" is reserved for fields that do progress in obvious ways. Nowhere does this show more clearly than in the recurrent debates about whether one or another of the contemporary social sciences is really a science. These debates have parallels in the pre-paradigm periods of fields that are today unhesitatingly labeled science. Their ostensible issue throughout is a definition of that vexing term. Men argue that psychology, for example, is a science because it possesses such and such characteristics. Others counter that those characteristics are either unnecessary or not sufficient to make a field a science. Often great energy is invested, great passion aroused, and the outsider is at a loss to know why. Can very much depend upon a *definition* of "science"? Can a definition tell a man whether he is a scientist or not? If so, why do not natural scientists or artists worry about the definition of the term? Inevitably one suspects that the issue is more fundamental. Probably questions like the following are really being asked: Why does my field fail to move ahead in the way that, say, physics does? What changes in technique or method or ideology would enable it to do so? These are not, however, questions that could respond to an agreement on definition. Furthermore, if precedent from the natural sciences serves, they will cease to be a source of concern not when a definition is found, but when the groups that now doubt their own status achieve consensus about their past and present accomplishments. It may, for example, be significant that economists argue less about whether their field is a science than do practitioners of some other fields of social science. Is that because economists know what science is? Or is it rather economics about which they agree?

That point has a converse that, though no longer simply semantic, may help to display the inextricable connections between our notions of science and of progress. For many centuries, both in antiquity and again in early modern Europe, painting was regarded as *the* cumulative discipline. During those years the artist's goal was assumed to be representation. Critics and historians, like Pliny and Vasari, then recorded with veneration the series of inventions from foreshortening through chiaroscuro that had made possible successively more perfect representations of nature. But those are also the years, particularly during the Renaissance, when little cleavage was felt between the sciences and the arts. Leonardo was only one of many men who passed freely back and forth between fields that only later became categorically distinct. Furthermore, even after that steady exchange had ceased, the term "art" continued to apply as much to technology and the crafts, which were also seen as progressive, as to painting and sculpture. Only when the latter unequivocally renounced representation as their goal and began to learn again from primitive models did the cleavage we now take for granted assume anything like its present depth. And even today, to switch fields once more, part of our difficulty in seeing the profound differences between science and technology must relate to the fact that progress is an obvious attribute of both fields.

It can, however, only clarify, not solve, our present difficulty to recognize that we tend to see as science any field in which progress is marked. There remains the problem of understanding why progress should be so noteworthy a characteristic of an enterprise conducted with the techniques and goals this essay has described. That question proves to be several in one, and we shall have to consider each of them separately. In all cases but the last, however, their resolution will depend in part upon an inversion of our normal view of the relation between scientific activity and the community that practices it. We must learn to recognize as causes what have ordinarily been taken to be effects. If we can do that, the phrases "scientific progress" and even "scientific objectivity" may come to seem in part redundant. In fact, one aspect of the redundancy has just been illustrated. Does a field make progress because it is a science, or is it a science because it makes progress?

Ask now why an enterprise like normal science should progress, and begin by recalling a few of its most salient characteristics. Normally, the members of a mature scientific community work from a single paradigm or from a closely related set. Very rarely do different scientific communities investigate the same problems. In those exceptional cases the groups hold several major paradigms in common. Viewed from within any single community, however, whether of scientists or of non-scientists, the result of successful creative work *is* progress. How could it possibly be anything else? We have, for example, just noted that while artists aimed at representation as their goal, both critics and historians chronicled the progress of the apparently united group. Other creative fields display progress of the same sort. The theologian who articulates dogma or the philosopher who refines the Kantian imperatives contributes to progress, if only to that of the group that shares his premises. No creative school recognizes a category of work that is, on the one hand, a creative success, but is not, on the other, an addition to the collective achievement of the group. If we doubt, as many do, that non-scientific fields make progress, that cannot be because individual schools make none. Rather, it must be because there are always competing schools, each of which constantly questions the very foundations of the others. The man who argues that philosophy, for example, has made no progress emphasizes that there are still Aristotelians, not that Aristotelianism has failed to progress.

These doubts about progress arise, however, in the sciences too. Throughout the pre-paradigm period when there is a multiplicity of competing schools, evidence of progress, except within schools, is very hard to find. This is the period described in Section II as one during which individuals practice science, but in which the results of their enterprise do not add up to science as we know it. And again, during periods of revolution when the fundamental tenets of a field are once more at issue, doubts are repeatedly expressed about the very possibility of continued progress if one or another of the opposed paradigms is adopted. Those who rejected Newtonianism proclaimed that its reliance upon innate forces would return science to the Dark Ages. Those who opposed Lavoisier's chemistry held that the rejection of chemical "principles" in favor of laboratory elements was the rejection of achieved chemical explanation by those who would take refuge in a mere name. A similar, though more moderately expressed, feeling seems to underlie the opposition of Einstein, Bohm, and others, to the dominant probabilistic interpretation of quantum mechanics. In short, it is only during periods of normal science that progress seems both obvious and assured. During those periods, however, the scientific community could view the fruits of its work in no other way.

With respect to normal science, then, part of the answer to the problem of progress lies simply in the eye of the beholder. Scientific progress is not different in kind from progress in other fields, but the absence at most times of competing schools that question each other's aims and standards makes the progress of a normal-scientific community far easier to see. That, however, is only part of the answer and by no means the most important part. We have, for example, already noted that once the reception of a common paradigm has freed the scientific community from the need constantly to re-examine its first principles, the members of that community can concentrate exclusively upon with precision and detail. In the process the community will sustain losses. Often some old problems must be banished. Frequently, in addition, revolution narrows the scope of the community's professional concerns, increases the extent of its specialization, and attenuates its communication with other groups, both scientific and lay. Though science surely grows in depth, it may not grow in breadth as well. If it does so, that breadth is manifest mainly in the proliferation of scientific specialties, not in the scope of any single specialty alone. Yet despite these and other losses to the individual communities, the nature of such communities provides a virtual guarantee that both the list of problems solved by science and the precision of individual problem-solutions will grow and grow. At least, the nature of the community provides such a guarantee if there is any way at all in which it can be provided. What better criterion than the decision of the scientific group could there be?

These last paragraphs point the directions in which I believe a more refined solution of the problem of progress in the sciences must be sought. Perhaps they indicate that scientific progress is not quite what we had taken it to be. But they simultaneously show that a sort of progress will inevitably characterize the scientific enterprise so long as such an enterprise survives. In the sciences there need not be progress of another sort. We may, to be more precise, have to relinquish the notion, explicit or implicit, that changes of paradigm carry scientists and those who learn from them closer and closer to the truth.

It is now time to notice that until the last very few pages the term "truth" had entered this essay only in a quotation from Francis Bacon. And even in those pages it entered only as a source for the scientist's conviction that incompatible rules for doing science cannot coexist except during revolutions when the profession's main task is to eliminate all sets but one. The developmental process described in this essay has been a process of evolution *from* primitive beginnings—a process whose successive stages are characterized by an increasingly detailed and refined understanding of nature. But nothing that has been or will be said makes it a process of evolution *toward* anything. Inevitably that lacuna will have

disturbed many readers. We are all deeply accustomed to seeing science as the one enterprise that draws constantly nearer to some goal set by nature in advance.

But need there be any such goal? Can we not account for both science's existence and its success in terms of evolution from the community's state of knowledge at any given time? Does it really help to imagine that there is some one full, objective, true account of nature and that the proper measure of scientific achievement is the extent to which it brings us closer to that ultimate goal? If we can learn to substitute evolution-from-what-we-do-know for evolution-toward-what-we-wish-to-know, a number of vexing problems may vanish in the process. Somewhere in this maze, for example, must lie the problem of induction.

I cannot yet specify in any detail the consequences of this alternate view of scientific advance. But it helps to recognize that the conceptual transposition here recommended is very close to one that the West undertook just a century ago. It is particularly helpful because in both cases the main obstacle to transposition is the same. When Darwin first published his theory of evolution by natural selection in 1859, what most bothered many professionals was neither the notion of species change nor the possible descent of man from apes. The evidence pointing to evolution, including the evolution of man, had been accumulating for decades, and the idea of evolution had been suggested and widely disseminated before. Though evolution, as such, did encounter resistance, particularly from some religious groups, it was by no means the greatest of the difficulties the Darwinians faced. That difficulty stemmed from an idea that was more nearly Darwin's own. All the well-known pre-Darwinian evolutionary theories—those of Lamarck, Chambers, Spencer, and the German *Naturphilosophen*—had taken evolution to be a goal-directed process. The "idea" of man and of the contemporary flora and fauna was thought to have been present from the first creation of life, perhaps in the mind of God. That idea or plan had provided the direction and the guiding force to the entire evolutionary process. Each new stage of evolutionary development was a more perfect realization of a plan that had been present from the start.

For many men the abolition of that teleological kind of evolution was the most significant and least palatable of Darwin's suggestions. The *Origin of Species* recognized no goal set either by God or nature. Instead, natural selection, operating in the given environment and with the actual organisms presently at hand, was responsible for the gradual but steady emergence of more elaborate, further articulated, and vastly more specialized organisms. Even such marvelously adapted organs as the eye and hand of man—organs whose design had previously provided powerful arguments for the existence of a supreme artificer and an advance plan—were products of a process that moved steadily *from* primitive beginnings but *toward* no goal. The belief that natural selection, resulting from mere competition between organisms for survival, could have produced man together with the higher animals and plants was the most difficult and disturbing aspect of Darwin's theory. What could "evolution," "development," and "progress" mean in the absence of a specified goal? To many people, such terms suddenly seemed self-contradictory.

The analogy that relates the evolution of organisms to the evolution of scientific ideas can easily be pushed too far. But with respect to the issues of this closing section it is very nearly perfect. The process described in Section XII as the resolution of revolutions is the selection by conflict within the scientific community of the fittest way to practice future science. The net result of a sequence of such revolutionary selections, separated by periods of normal research, is the wonderfully adapted set of instruments we call modern scientific knowledge. Successive stages in that developmental process are marked by an increase in articulation and specialization. And the entire process may have occurred, as we now suppose biological evolution did, without benefit of a set goal, a permanent fixed scientific truth, of which each stage in the development of scientific knowledge is a better exemplar.

Anyone who has followed the argument this far will nevertheless feel the need to ask why the evolutionary process should work. What must nature, including man, be like in order that science be possible at all? Why should scientific communities be able to reach a firm consensus unattainable in other fields? Why should consensus endure across one paradigm change after another? And why should paradigm change invariably produce an instrument more perfect in any sense than those known before? From one point of view those questions, excepting the first, have already been answered. But from another they are as open as they were when this essay began. It is not only the scientific community that must be special. The world of which that community is a part must also possess quite special characteristics, and we are no closer than we were at the start to knowing what these must be. That problem— What must the world be like in order that man may know it?—was not, however, created by this essay. On the contrary, it is as old as science itself, and it remains unanswered. But it need not be answered in this place. Any conception of nature compatible with the growth of science by proof is compatible with the evolutionary view of science developed here. Since this view is also compatible with close observation of scientific life, there are strong arguments for employing it in attempts to solve the host of problems that still remain.

7.4 Feminism and Science

Reading this title may make you wonder what feminism has to do with science. You may think that feminism is a political movement designed to improve the status of women and that science has nothing to do with politics. Good science is value-free and objective. Bad science is value-laden and subjective. Surely, you may think, to import political concerns about the status of women into the actual doing of science would be to introduce biases that would taint the results.

We need to pause a moment and think about what it means to "import" value judgments into the "actual doing of science." On one level, it is clear that the context in which science is done is often male oriented (androcentric) in contrast to female oriented (gynocentric). Feminist scholars have shown that a good deal of biological, medical, and social research has taken place in an androcentric context that has tainted the results (see Anne Fausto-Sterling's *Myths of Gender: Biological Theories about Women and Men,* 1985). It has been shown that more money is routinely spent on the medical problems men face rather than on the medical problems women face.

You may say that this is not really science, but rather the politics of science. We do not really need to rethink the nature of science, but rather its social context. Thus better control of funding and research may solve the problem. Or you may say that insofar as androcentric value-judgments have tainted scientific results, it is just bad science. Good science is free from all political and moral values, be they androcentric or gynocentric.

Imagine a situation in which all possible observational evidence is compatible with mutually incompatible theories. This situation is frequent enough in science to warrant a name. It is called **underdetermination of theory**. Theories are underdetermined precisely to the extent that available evidence cannot support a choice between them. This constitutes an epistemological impasse. If evidence does not and cannot guide our choice of theories, what can? Some scientists have suggested criteria like accuracy, fruitfulness, breadth, simplicity, and scope. In other words, you pick the one that works best given a whole variety of considerations. Should moral and political interests be part of those considerations? Is, for example, seeking justice a proper goal of science?

You may argue that value-laden inquiry is just plain dishonest. Being true is the best mark, indeed the only trustworthy mark, of a good theory. Science has one and only one goal—the truth. If other sorts of considerations—considerations like justice—are introduced in situations of underdetermination, then theory choice becomes hopelessly subjective, and science will cease its focus on the single goal of truth. It will become oriented toward multiple goals, thereby degenerating into camps of conflicting ideologies. But will it?

Elizabeth Anderson, professor of philosophy at the University of Michigan, gives what may be a surprising answer to that question. In the following selection she makes a case for value-laden scientific inquiry that supports women's concerns. Such inquiry, she maintains, can be both good science and sensitive to issues of justice if it is done properly.

Reading Projects

1. List two background assumptions and two implications of Anderson's ideas.
2. Summarize Anderson's main argument and critique it.

Knowledge, Human Interests, and Objectivity in Feminist Epistemology

ELIZABETH ANDERSON

> Apparatchik (impatiently): How much is 2 + 2?
> Mathematician (cautiously): How much do you want it to be?
>
> —*Soviet joke*

1. Making Room for Values in Feminist Epistemology

THIS JOKE from the former Soviet Union aptly captures the dominant view about what happens when social, political, and moral interests shape inquiry: the result is totalitarian thought control, in which those in power force beliefs to conform to their demands and wishes rather than to the facts. No wonder, then, that attempts by feminist epistemologists to legitimate important roles for social and moral values in academic inquiry have been greeted with such alarm in the recent wars over "political correctness." This paper aims to defuse the hysteria over value-laden inquiry by showing how it is based on a misapprehension of the arguments of the most careful advocates of such inquiry, an impoverished understanding of the goals of science, a mistaken model of the interaction of normative and evidential considerations in science, and a singular inattention to the empirical facts about how responsible inquirers go about their business.

Yet, the task of defending value-laden inquiry is a formidable one. For its most careful recent advocates in feminist epistemology have advanced an ambitious agenda. Feminists have long argued that scientific practice[1] should promote women's interests by removing discriminatory barriers that prevent women from participating in research, by developing technologies that empower women (such as safe, inexpensive birth control), and by paying due regard to women's actual achievements in science and other endeavors. Many who attack the idea of value-laden inquiry are willing to accept such political influences on the conduct of inquiry, because such influences are not thought to touch what they see as the core of scientific integrity: the methods and standards of justification for theoretical claims. These influences affect the context of discovery (where the choice of subjects of investigation and of colleagues is open to influence by the interests of the inquirer or of those who fund the research) or the context of practical application (which, involving action, is always subject to moral scrutiny), not the context of justification. But feminist epistemologists argue that feminist values may properly influence scientific method and theory choice. This ambition challenges the core commitments of many scientists and defenders of the ideal of value-neutral science.

Helen Longino has developed the most careful and closely reasoned recent arguments in favor of using "contextual values"—political, moral, and other values taken from the social context in which science is practiced—to guide scientific method and theory choice.[2] Longino observes that hypotheses are logically underde-

---

1. I use "science" in the inclusive sense of the German "Wissenschaft," which comprehends not just "science" in the English sense of the natural and social sciences, but all disciplined inquiry found in the academy, including the humanities, mathematics, law, public health, and engineering. I often use "science" rather than the generic "inquiry" to signify that my primary interest is in disciplined, systematic inquiry subject to institutionalized means of quality control (e.g., peer review). 2. Helen Longino, *Science as Social Knowledge* (Princeton, N.J.: Princeton University Press, 1980). See also Lynn Hankinson Nelson, *Who Knows: From Quine to a Feminist Empiricism* (Philadelphia: Temple University Press, 1990).

From Elizabeth Anderson, "Knowledge, Human Interests, and Objectivity in Feminist Epistemology," Philosophical Topics, *Volume 23 (Fall 1995): 27–42, 52–58. Footnotes edited. Copyright © 1995 by Elizabeth Anderson. Reprinted by permission of the author.*

termined by the data cited in their support. A particular fact provides evidential support for a given hypothesis only in conjunction with other background assumptions. Thus, two inquirers who accept different background assumptions may take the same fact as evidence for conflicting hypotheses. The failure to observe stellar parallax in the seventeenth century was taken as evidence that the earth did not move around the sun by those who assumed that the stars were not far away. But this same fact was taken as evidence that the stars were very far away by those who believed that the earth did move around the sun. In some cases empirical support, independent of the hypothesis being investigated, can be offered for the background assumptions—although only in conjunction with yet further background assumptions. But in many other cases independent evidence for the background assumptions is not available. Furthermore, as we trace back the sources of support for the interlocking background assumptions of a theory, we find that they do not rest on factual claims alone.

This fact is most dramatically revealed in cases where the available data in conjunction with the shared background assumptions of rival researchers are insufficient to justify the choice of one theory or research program over another. In these cases, dissenting scientists often criticize the background assumptions of their rivals and support their own contested background assumptions by appealing to conceptual, epistemological, methodological, or metaphysical considerations that often rest upon contextually specific norms of inquiry.[3] Thus, Einstein initially appealed to thought experiments grounded in empiricist epistemological norms to argue for the superiority of the theory of relativity over classical Newtonian mechanics. Watson appealed to the methodological norm that we ought to count as evidence only interpersonally accessible observations to argue for the superiority of behaviorism over introspectionist psychology. Functionalist explanation in sociology was discredited

partly because it was incompatible with the non-teleological metaphysical framework of modern science: for those who accept this framework, merely pointing out that a social phenomenon promotes social stability does not provide a satisfactory explanation for why it exists. Marginal utility theory in economics triumphed over classical economic theory partly because its hypotheses could be modeled using calculus, which made many economic problems mathematically tractable for the first time. In these cases, normative considerations about the conduct of inquiry, normative constraints on the form of acceptable data and of satisfactory explanations, and normative desiderata of calculative ease proved to be powerful arguments for theory choice. Where the data run out, values legitimately step in to take up the "slack" between observation and theory.[4]

These arguments show that values embedded in background assumptions help determine what counts as evidence and an explanation, how the evidence should be represented, and what direction the evidence points to. So values play a legitimate role in guiding science that is not reducible to the prescription to simply follow where the facts lead. But this is not enough to show that any sort of value may permissibly guide science. A prominent branch of mainstream philosophy of science accepts the argument that underdetermination leaves room for values to play a legitimate role in theory choice, but it insists that the admissible values must be epistemic or cognitive, rather than, say, moral, political, or economic. Acceptable values are "internal" to science; unacceptable ones are "contextual," or borrowed from the social context in which science is practiced. Thus, Kuhn argues that the values that properly guide theory choice are accuracy, consistency, fruitfulness, breadth of scope, and simplicity.[5] These cognitive values don't have any obvious moral or political content.

A crucial question for feminist epistemologists, then, is whether the sharp division between

3. Thomas Kuhn, *The Structure of Scientific Revolutions,* 2d ed. (Chicago: University of Chicago Press, 1970).

4. Nelson, op. cit., 173–174, 248.

5. Thomas Kuhn, "Objectivity, Value Judgment, and Theory Choice," in his *The Essential Tension* (Chicago: University of Chicago Press, 1977), 320–339.

epistemic and moral or political values is tenable. Longino argues that this division breaks down once we look beyond the content of the standards for theory choice and focus attention on the grounds for supporting them.[6] Here we see that epistemic, metaphysical, and practical interests may all help support a given standard of theory choice. Empirical adequacy is important not just on epistemic grounds but because an empirically inadequate theory cannot satisfy our practical interests in predicting and controlling phenomena.[7] What's more, the content of our practical interests helps determine what dimensions of empirical adequacy are demanded of science. This is not surprising if we keep in mind that theories do more than represent facts—they organize them for our use. The interest in control puts a premium on theories that accurately track in quantitative terms the behavior of objects in experimental and technological contexts, where background "interfering" conditions are tightly constrained and objects are manipulated by one or very few factors under the control of the knower. The Aristotelian interest in leading a life devoted to contemplating the natures of things (rather than asserting mastery over them) put a premium on accurately accounting for the qualitative characters of objects in unmanipulated contexts, where things can display their "true natures."[8] The interest in self-understanding and successful communication puts a premium on theories that accurately account for subjects' behavior in terms that the subjects themselves can recognize, affirm, and act on.[9]

Consider, in this light, two of the theoretical virtues that Longino identifies as among those that may properly guide theory choice for feminists.[10] One is "ontological heterogeneity." This is a preference for "splitting" over "lumping"—for emphasizing the qualitative diversity and individuality of subjects of study and the distinctions among properties commonly classified together. One purely cognitive motivation for this is to seek fine-grained descriptive accuracy. Barbara McClintock's revolutionary discovery of genetic transposition, which was based on close observation of the cytological differences among individual seeds on corn cobs, demonstrates that such a focus can yield huge theoretical advances.[11] But there are political reasons for emphasizing heterogeneity as well. Ideologies that purport to scientifically demonstrate the inevitability of male dominance often appeal to theories that assimilate disparate phenomena under vague, global classifications. Feminist primatologist Linda Fedigan showed that the common idea that male primates "dominate" females is ill-conceived, by pointing out that the numerous distinct measures of individual dominance (social rank, aggressiveness, winning conflicts, strength, initiating group movement, directing group movement, suppressing conflicts among others, mobilizing cooperation) do not correlate, shift over time and context, and in some cases apply only to within-sex rather than between-sex interactions. There is no global, unitary sense of "dominance" in which the generalization "male primates dominate females" is true.[12] Another political reason for emphasizing heterogeneity is to reinforce the self-critical practices of feminism itself. Feminist theories that focus on generalizations about "women" all too often have ignored important differences among women. In the U.S. context, this has meant that characteristics common among white, middle-class, heterosexual women have been represented as the norm for women generally, such that other women either are invisible or appear deviant within the theory.[13] What are we to make of the idea that there is something about "women's" cognitive styles that attracts them more to the life sciences then to the physical sciences or mathematics, once we

6. Helen Longino, "In Search of Feminist Epistemology," *Monist* 77 (1994): 472–485.

7. Ibid., 481.

8. Mary Tiles, "A Science of Mars or of Venus?" *Philosophy* 62 (1987): 293—306.

9. Jürgen Habermas, *Knowledge and Human Interests*, tr. Jeremy Shapiro (Boston: Beacon Press, 1971).

10. Longino, "In Search," 477—478.

11. See Evelyn Fox Keller, *A Feeling for the Organism* (New York: Freeman, 1983).

12. Linda Fedigan, *Primate Paradigms* (Chicago: University of Chicago Press, 1992), ch. 7.

13. bell hooks, *Feminist Theory from Margin to Center* (Boston: South End Press, 1983).

consider that black women scientists are twice as likely as white women scientists to choose a mathematical specialty and only half as likely to choose the life sciences?[14] Emphasizing heterogeneity enables feminist theorists to represent diversity among women and humans generally as a potential resource rather than as deviance.

Both cognitive and political reasons can also be offered in support of a second feminist theoretical virtue: "complexity of relationship." This value supports a preference for dynamic, interactive causal models that emphasize multiple causes of phenomena over single-factor linear or reductionist models. For some theorists, this preference is motivated by a metaphysical conviction that the world is complex, multifaceted, and messy. A cognitive interest in capturing the real causal structure of the world would then concur with this preference. But feminist political interests lend other support to the value of complexity. The preference for complexity encourages historians and social theorists to represent an individual's social power as a feature of context or role supported by others rather than as an individual trait. This representation enables the recognition and appreciation of women's activities, by making visible the role of private, domestic work in maintaining the activity and institutions of the "public" sphere.[15] It also opens up opportunities for activists to imagine strategies of resistance to oppression that involve changing the social structure rather than attacking individuals.

Feminists are not the only ones to justify methodological and theoretical standards by appeal to moral or political considerations. Functional explanation in sociology was discredited not just because it didn't offer a satisfactory scheme of explanation but because, by representing phenomena as functional for the social order, it underplayed the significance of social conflict and discouraged criticism of the status quo. A humanist interest in acknowledging and promoting the dignity and freedom of persons has influenced many social scientists. An emerging methodological norm among interpretive anthropologists is to show one's research to the subjects of study and respond to their criticisms. This norm serves the moral interest of respecting the dignity of those one studies. Chomsky argued for the superiority of cognitive psychology over behaviorism on the ground that the behaviorist explanatory framework left no room for representing human creativity in language use, a core ground of our own self-understandings as dignified free agents.[16] Others have launched a similar critique of behaviorist *methods,* arguing that behaviorism's experimental framework is coercive and demeaning, depriving people of opportunities to express their potentialities for taking initiatives and forging creative solutions to problems.[17]

With all of these moral and political interests shaping methodology and standards of theory choice in so many fields and schools of thought, is there any way to salvage some conception of objectivity in science? Longino argues that there is. In the first place, empirical adequacy is not an optional standard for any research program. Although, as we have seen, moral and political interests may help delineate the domains of evidence which a theory must account for or at least be consistent with, every empirical theory is accountable to some body of evidence.[18] In the second place, all scientists are accountable to other scientists. The evidence to which they appeal must be interpersonally accessible. The methodological standards and criteria of theory choice to which they appeal must be justified to and accepted by others. The entire research community must be open to criticism by others, provide opportunities for such criticism, and respond to it by appropriately modifying its methods, claims, and background assumptions when they fall short of commonly recognized

14. Donna Haraway, *Primate Visions* (New York: Routledge, 1989), 296.
15. Longino, "In Search," 478.

16. Noam Chomsky, "Review of B. F. Skinner's *Verbal Behavior,*" *Language* 35 (1959): 26–58.
17. Barry Schwartz and Hugh Lacey, *Behaviorism, Science, and Human Nature* (New York: W. W. Norton, 1982).
18. Helen Longino, "Essential Tensions—Phase Two: Feminist, Philosophical, and Social Studies of Science," in Louise M. Antony and Charlotte Witt, eds., *A Mind of One's Own* (Boulder, Colo.: Westview Press, 1993), 261–263.

standards. Furthermore, the research community must recognize the equality of inquirers, which is to say that it may not censor or disregard what others say simply on account of their social identity or relative lack of social power.[19] These social aspects of scientific practice—the ways in which it makes each inquirer accountable to others' observations and criticism—are what secure the objectivity of science. They are what prevent inquiry from degenerating into a free play of idiosyncratic preference and subjective bias.[20]

2. *The Critique of Politically Value-Laden Science*

Longino's defense of morally and politically value-laden inquiry strikes at the core self-understandings of many practicing scientists and at the core legitimation stories told about modern science to insulate it from political criticism. Thus it is no surprise that scientists and traditional epistemologists have subjected her work to pointed attacks. Susan Haack's critiques of Longino articulate better than any other the core assumptions behind the ideal of value-neutral inquiry and provide the sharpest response yet to Longino's proposals.[21]

Haack, like other defenders of value-neutral inquiry, sees many great dangers in permitting moral and political values to shape the criteria of theory choice in inquiry. Such a move would allow inquiry to be infected by wishful thinking: people would feel entitled to infer from the fact

that they wanted something to be true that it was actually true.[22] It would invite dogmatism: people would feel entitled to attack as pernicious any reasoning or evidence that did not reach a foregone conclusion supported by their political preferences.[23] It would provide a license for dishonest or less than candid research: researchers would be allowed to focus only on evidence that supports "politically correct" conclusions. The result would be the politicization of research along the lines of Nazi science, Lysenkoism, or *1984*, in which disinterested, honest researchers would be hounded out of the academy, which would henceforth be staffed by political propagandists.[24]

Why does Haack think these are the implications of introducing moral and political values into the context of justification? Behind her alarm lies a particular model of the interaction of evidential and political considerations in shaping inquiry. The model supposes that these considerations necessarily *compete* for control of inquiry. Either theory choice is guided by the facts, by observation and evidence, *or* it is guided by moral values and social influences, construed as wishes, desires, or social-political demands. To the extent that moral values and social influences shape theory choice, they *displace* attention to evidence and valid reasoning and hence *interfere* with the discovery of truth. This model depends upon a particular conception of the goals of theoretical inquiry and the nature of the considerations that can justify theory choice. The basic idea is to limit the goals of theory to the articulation of truths, and then to argue that value judgments have no evidential bearing on whether any claim is true. Therefore, value judgments cannot figure in the justification of theoretical claims or in the criteria for theory choice. It is natural to conclude that to the extent that value judgments influence theory choice, they must be diverting attention from the actual evidential support of theories. A simple logical argument supports this model:

1. Significant truth is the sole aim of theoretical inquiry.

---

19. Critics of the equality requirement assume that it tells us to disregard individual differences in expertise and cognitive ability. But the requirement only tells us not to rank the worth of inquirers' contributions on the basis of their social status. For further defense of the equality requirement and its relation to claims of expertise, see Elizabeth Anderson "The Democratic University: The Role of Justice in the Production of Knowledge," *Social Philosophy and Policy* 12 (1995): 186–219.
20. Longino, *Science as Social Knowledge*, ch. 4.
21. Susan Haack, "Epistemological Reflections of an Old Feminist," *Reason Papers* 18 (1993): 31–43 (reprinted, without footnotes, as "Knowledge and Propaganda: Reflections of an Old Feminist," *Partisan Review* 60 [1993]: 556–564); "Science as Social?—Yes and No," in Jack Nelson and Lynn Nelson, eds., *Dialogue on Feminism, Science, and Philosophy of Science* (Netherlands: Kluwer).

22. Haack, "Epistemological Reflections," 35.
23. Haack, "Science as Social?" 9.
24. Haack, "Epistemological Reflections," 38.

2. Whether a theory is justified depends only on features indicative of its truth, not its significance.

3. One shows that a theory is (most probably) true by showing that it is (best) supported by the evidence.

4. A theoretical proposition is supported by the evidence only if there is some valid inference from the evidence (in conjunction with background information) to it.

5. Value judgments take the form "*P* ought to be the case."

6. There is no valid inference from "*P* ought to be the case" to "*P* is the case" (or any other factual truths).

7. There is no valid inference from value judgments to factual truths (5, 6).

8. Value judgments can provide no evidential support for theories (4, 7).

9. Value judgments can play no role in indicating the truth of theories (3, 8).

10. Value judgments can play no role in justifying theories (1, 2, 9).

I believe this argument captures the core assumptions supporting the ideal of value-neutral science.[25] The debate over the value-neutrality of science has traditionally taken (6) as the crux of the argument. But the argument is not valid as it stands. In fact, it is remarkably hard to find a valid argument against using value judgments to justify theories that hangs on (6). Particular claims are evidence for theories only in conjunction with other background assumptions [premise (4)]. Premise (6), at most, supports the conclusion that value judgments all by themselves cannot provide evidence for theories. In conjunction with background teleological laws of the form "If *P* ought to be the case, then *P* is the case," it would be easy to license an inference from value judgments to factual claims. So the argument covertly relies on a background metaphysical assumption that the universe is not governed by teleological laws. Furthermore, despite Haack's insistence that no one has ever produced a counterexample to (6), many theorists hold that "ought" implies "can"—that is, that one may validly infer from "*M* ought to do *x*" that "*M* can do *x*," which is a factual claim about *M*'s capabilities.

These flaws in the argument are not worth pursuing, however. For few contemporary defenders of value-laden inquiry stake their case on the existence of teleological laws or on the inference from "ought" to "can."[26] And no defender

---

25. I am less confident that it accurately represents Haack's views. See Susan Haack, *Evidence and Inquiry* (Oxford: Basil Blackwell, 1993). Haack explicitly endorses premises (1), (2), (3), (5), and (6) [premises (1) and (2): *Evidence and Inquiry,* 199, 203–5; premise (3): ibid., 74, 203–5; premises (5) and (6) "Epistemological Reflections," 35, 42 n. 19]. She seems to think, along with most other defenders of value-neutrality, that (6) is crucial to her case. Premise (6) can play a role in the argument only if something like (4) is accepted. For unless the evidentiary relation can be explicated in logical oaths, the lack of any valid logical inference from "ought" to "is" would be irrelevant to the question of whether "ought" claims can provide evidential support for factual claims. But Haack appears to reject the view that logical inference is the basis of evidential relations. She speaks rather of "fitness" between evidence, background information, and conclusions (See "Science as Social?" 4; *Evidence and Inquiry,* 81–84). Haack might reach (8), not via (4)–(7), but through the assumption that value judgments express something like wishes or desires. Then all she needs for (8) is the claim that the wish or desire that *P* provides no evidential support for *P* or for any other proposition. I render the argument using (4)–(7)

because this captures the concerns of those who take (6) to be crucial and because Longino also accepts (4). The argument diverges from Haack's views in a second way. Haack speaks in the idiom of epistemology, Longino in the idiom of philosophy of science. To bring their views into contact, I have cast Haack's premises in terms of "theory," where Haack herself talks of "inquiry" in general. The argument works only if theories are construed in the logical empiricist sense, as sets of propositions which have truth-values. Many theorists, including Longino, construe theories as nonlinguistic models that can't have truth-values. See Longino, "The Fate of Knowledge in Social Theories of Science," in Frederick Schmitt, ed., *Socializing Epistemology* (Lanham, Md.: Rowman and Littlefeld, 1994), 146–8. This raises the larger issue, beyond the scope of my paper, of whether truth is an aim of theory-building at all. I set aside this issue and focus on whether truth is the only target of theoretical justification, assuming the logical empiricist picture of theories for the sake of argument.

26. See, however, Peter Railton, "Moral Realism," *Philosophical Review* 95 (1986): 163–207. No one argues any more that teleological laws govern the natural world. But some,

of value-laden inquiry has ever suggested that values figure in inquiry by licensing any direct inference from "*P* ought to be the case" to "*P*."[27] To focus the debates over values in science on premise (6) is therefore to follow a gigantic red herring. The real contests are over premises (1) and (2): the goals of theory and the relation of justification (criteria of theory choice) to those goals. I shall argue that contextual values properly enter into criteria for theory choice because the constitutive goals of scientific theory-building extend beyond the simple accumulation of bare truths and are themselves properly subject to moral and political evaluation.

But I get ahead of myself. Before we scrutinize Haack's key premises, let us consider whether the alarming conclusions she draws about the implications of contextually value-laden inquiry would follow even if her argument were sound. Haack claims that to allow contextual values to shape theory choice would be to invite wishful thinking, dogmatism, dishonesty, and totalitarianism into science. But the most her argument can so far show is that morally value-laden inquiry will not reliably track the truth. What it *will* track depends on one's further understandings of what value judgments are. Here Haack expresses a remarkable, unexamined cynicism about the nature of value judgments. Her claim that value-laden inquiry leads to wishful thinking makes sense only if value judgments express nothing more than idle wishes or desires: propositions one would like to be true, quite independently of whether they or any other propositions are likely or possible. No serious contemporary theorist accepts such a crude account of value judgments. Even

those who believe that value judgments express something more like emotional states than beliefs argue that emotional states can be warranted or not, depending on the facts.[28] So warranted value judgments, too, must be attentive to the facts. Haack's assumption that value-laden inquiry leads to dogmatism makes sense only if value judgments are essentially matters of blind, overbearing assertion, not subject to critical scrutiny or revision in light of arguments and evidence. Again, no serious moral theorist accepts this primitive emotivist view any more. Haack's assumption that value-laden inquiry will be dishonest comes from the thought that morally value-laden inquiry can only be inquiry designed to reach a foregone conclusion, hence inquiry that will neglect, cover up, or misrepresent evidence tending to show that the conclusion is false. Yet, this supposes that honesty is not itself an important moral value that should guide inquiry. Finally, Haack's charge that politically value-laden inquiry will invite totalitarianism supposes that political values are essentially totalitarian. But feminist empiricists, including Longino, are virtually all democrats and aim to extend principles of democracy to scientific practice, notably in insisting on tolerance of diverse value-laden research programs and on the equality of inquirers. Haack's alarm seems based on the nihilistic view that there is no such thing as moral inquiry at all, only arbitrary moral commitment. . . .

None of the alarmist implications Haack wishes to draw from Longino's advocacy of value-laden inquiry follow from her arguments. Longino's own normative constraints on research communities guard against them. Nevertheless, Haack's central argument does express a fundamental challenge to Longino's views. Even if Longino's recommendations don't lead to a totalitarian abyss, they may lead to false belief, and that is bad enough. Longino rests her case for value-laden inquiry on a logical analysis of the evidential relation between data and theory. If, as Haack suggests, this evidential relation is something like the relation "supporting the

---

like Railton, defend the thought that teleological laws might account for human actions—that is, that sometimes the reason why people do things is just because they are right or good or ought to be done.

27. Why do the critics of value-laden inquiry focus so narrowly on the imagined inference from "*P* ought to be the case" to "*P*"? I think the critics obsess over this single possibility because they imagine only one route by which value judgments could ever influence theory acceptance—via the mechanism of wishful thinking. They therefore overlook the possibility that there could be other routes by which value judgments can influence theory choice.

28. See, for example, Allan Gibbard, *Wise Choices, Apt Feelings* (Cambridge, Mass.: Harvard University Press, 1990).

claim to truth," then it is hard to see how value judgments can figure in this relation unless one accepts some kind of inference from "ought" to "is." Thus, Haack reads Longino as arguing that when the choice between rival theories is underdetermined by the available evidence in conjunction with shared background assumptions, then "we should decide which disjunct to accept by asking which would be politically preferable."[29] But surely Haack is right to insist that the fact that the world would be a better place if a theory were true, or the fact that one would like one theory to be true, offers no evidence for the conclusion that it really is true. Haack argues that in such cases of underdetermination one should suspend judgment rather than plump for one side for bad reasons. Even if practical considerations demand that we act on some theory, this does not justify belief in it, merely acceptance of it as if it were true.[30] Longino claims that underdetermination leaves open the permanent possibility that unarticulated moral judgments may be covertly influencing scientists' assessments of the evidence. But Haack argues that even if this is true, it argues for rigorously exposing and expunging these judgments from inquiry, not for allowing them in explicitly.[31]

Longino's arguments thus stand in need of clarification and further defense. We need an account of how value judgments can properly figure in theory choice which does not just come down to choosing a theory because it is politically preferable. Longino argues that criteria of theory choice can be simultaneously supported by epistemic and political considerations. But if epistemic considerations already support the choice of criteria, then aren't the political considerations superfluous?

I shall argue that the key dispute between Haack and Longino concerns the aims of theoretical inquiry. If these aims are broader than the bare accumulation of truths, and the justification of theories is relative to all these aims, then there is an opening for moral, social, and political

values to enter into theory choice. In fact, Haack already admits that theoretical inquiry aims for more than a bare accumulation of truths. Idle inquiry has no need for theory to accumulate trivial truths. Theoretical inquiry aims at some *organized* body of truths that can lay claim to *significance* [premise (1)]. Thus, it is possible for contextual values to figure in determining what counts as significant, even if they don't figure in determining what is true. Haack forestalls this move by claiming that justification is addressed only to the question of truth, not significance [premise (2)]. Against this view, I shall argue in the following section that theoretical justification cannot avoid questions of significance. For not every set of true statements *about* a given phenomenon constitutes an acceptable theory *of* that phenomenon. Some sets offer a distorted, biased representation of the whole. This can make them unworthy representations of a phenomenon even if they contain no falsehoods. But what constitutes an adequate, unbiased representation of the whole is relative to our values, interests, and aims, some of which have moral and political import. Thus, even the project of defining the boundaries of significant phenomena may involve contextual value judgments.

3. *Why Being True May Be No Defense of a Theory*

If epistemologists took murder mysteries and courtroom dramas as seriously as they take their image of science, they would learn a thing or two about the limitations of truth as a defense of an account of events. Mysteries tease theoretical reason by revealing the facts about crucial events in a sequence designed to turn readers' minds first in one direction, then in another, then in another. Although many characters in mysteries lie, the most interesting characters deceive by telling the truth—but only part of it. It is no accident that in the ritual formula of the courtroom oath one swears not only to tell the truth and nothing but the truth, but the "whole" truth. The significance of most truths can be adequately grasped only in the context of the whole truth. Consider, in this light, the controversy over the role of Jews

29. Haack, "Science as Social?" 12.
30. Ibid., 12–13; Haack, "Epistemological Reflections," 35.
31. Haack, "Epistemological Reflections," 36.

in the Atlantic slave system, sparked by the Nation of Islam's notorious book *The Secret Relationship between Blacks and Jews*.[32] The book stresses such claims as these: that Jews had considerable investments in the Dutch West India Company, which played a significant role in the seventeenth-century Atlantic slave trade; that Marranos (people forced by the Portuguese to convert from Judaism to Christianity) were among the major slaveowning sugar planters in Northeast Brazil; that Jews were prominent among the white colonists of Dutch Brazil and bought a large share of the slaves traded by the Dutch from the 1630s to the 1650s; and that a larger percentage of Jews living [in] the U.S. South owned slaves than did Southern whites as a whole.[33] These claims are all true. Yet, put together, these and the many other true claims in *The Secret Relationship* do not add up to an acceptable account of the role of Jews in the Atlantic slave system. As the historian David Brion Davis argues, even if every purported fact in the book were true, it would still offer a biased and distorted picture of the role of Jews in Atlantic slavery.[34]

The problem is not so much falsehood (although this is also present in *The Secret Relationship*) as the failure to put the facts into the larger context that would be required to assess their significance. The share of Jewish investment in the Dutch West India Company was small, and the Dutch played a significant role in the Atlantic slave trade only in the seventeenth century, when the trade was small. Slaveowning Marranos were not in Northeast Brazil by choice: Portugal had forced them to colonize the area and take up sugar production. Nor is there any reason to call them Jews, as their forced conversion had long since eliminated whatever connections they once had to Jewish culture and religion. Jews owned

slaves in Dutch Brazil for only a few decades and were expelled by the Portuguese in the 1650s.[35] A greater proportion of U.S. Southern Jews owned slaves than other Southern whites only because they were concentrated in urban areas, where rates of slave ownership were higher. Moreover, Jewish slaveowners owned fewer slaves per household than the average slaveowner, because urban slaveowners owned fewer slaves than their rural counterparts. And the vast majority of U.S. Jews lived in the nonslaveholding North. Finally, the absolute numbers of Jews involved in U.S. slavery were vanishingly small: the 1830 census records only 120 Jews among the 45,000 individuals owning 20 or more slaves, and it records only 20 Jews among the 12,000 owning 50 or more slaves.[36] How are we to assess the significance of the facts cited in *The Secret Relationship*? Taken in isolation, they suggest that Jews played a special or disproportionate role in the Atlantic slave system or that their participation was more intense than that of other ethnic and religious groups. But in the context of additional facts, such as those just cited, they show that Jewish participation in the slave system was minor in absolute terms and was no different in intensity from similarly situated ethnic and religious groups. The larger context exposes a serious bias or distortion in the way *The Secret Relationship* characterizes the significance of Jewish participation in the Atlantic slave system. The characterization is "partial" in the literal sense that it tells only part of the truth needed to assess the significance of the matters at hand. What matters for assessing significance, then, is not just that an account be true but that it in some sense represent the whole truth, that it be unbiased. Furthermore, the fact that an account is biased or distorted is a good reason to reject it, even if it contains only true statements. Haack's premise (2) is therefore false: to justify acceptance of a theory one must defend its significance, not just its truth.

32. Historical Research Department, Nation of Islam, *The Secret Relationship between Blacks and Jews* (Chicago: Nation of Islam Press, 1991).

33. Ibid., 23, 20, 28–30, 180.

34. David Brion Davis, "The Slave Trade and the Jews," *The New York Review of Books*, 22 December 1994, 14–16.

35. Ibid.

36. Winthrop Jordon. "Slavery and the Jews," *Atlantic Monthly*, September 1995, 109–112, 114.

I have argued that significance, bias, and partiality are features of theories, relevant to their justification, that need to be judged in relation to the "whole" truth and that cannot be judged simply by testing the truth-value of each claim a given theory upholds. For in offering T as an adequate theory or an account of a phenomenon, one purports something more than that the constitutive sentences of T are true. Theories don't just state facts; they organize them into patterns that purport to be representative of the phenomenon being theorized, patterns that are adequate to answer some question or satisfy some explanatory demand.[37] But what would be the "whole" historical truth about the Atlantic slave system and about the roles of different ethnic groups in it? What would be an "unbiased" representation of this phenomenon?

One might try to offer a value-neutral account of significance and bias, arguing that an unbiased theory—one that does justice to the whole truth—is one that disregards all contextual values in deciding which facts to represent or how to represent them. But what would such an account look like? The whole truth can't be an account that literally represents every fact about the phenomenon being studied. No theory offers anything close to that. Nor should any theory try. Such a representation would end up burying the significant truths in a mass of irrelevant and trivial detail (e.g., how many waves did each slave ship surmount? how many times did each slave blink?). The whole truth can't be one that rules out in advance all facts that bear on the moral assessment of slavery or of those involved in it, or that describes the phenomenon in terms that evade moral judgment. Such a representation would plainly omit most of the features of slavery that arouse our interest in studying it or else would misrepresent these features by Orwellian euphemism (e.g., by describing whipping as a "labor mobilization technique"). Such a representation would constitute collusion with those who wish to evade moral judgment themselves.

I see no contextually value-neutral way to characterize the whole truth, or the significant truths, about slavery.

To get a grip on the notions of significance and wholeness, we need a fuller understanding of the goals and context of theoretical inquiry. Theoretical inquiry does not just seek any random truth. It seeks answers to questions. What counts as a significant truth is any truth that bears on the answer to the question being posed. The whole truth consists of all the truths that bear on the answer, or, more feasibly, it consists of a representative enough sample of such truths that the addition of the rest would not make the answer turn out differently. Many of the questions we ask science to answer are motivated by contextual values and interests—that is, moral, political, cultural, economic, and other concerns drawn from the social context in which science is practiced. When these are the interests that motivate the questions we ask, then what counts as a significant truth, and the whole truth, can only be judged in relation to these interests. Thus, when the question driving inquiry is motivated by concerns with moral content, what counts as a significant truth will be whatever is *morally* relevant to addressing those concerns.

Before we can judge whether a theory is biased, then, we need to specify the question it purports to answer in such a form that we can tell whether the answer satisfactorily addresses the motivations for asking the question in the first place. The question that *The Secret Relationship* purports to answer is thus not adequately specified by such seemingly value-neutral questions as "What was the role of the Jews in the Atlantic slave system?" or even "How did Jewish roles in the slave system compare with the roles of other ethnic groups?" For these do not specify which roles and which comparisons are of interest. The question that *The Secret Relationship* implicitly purports to answer is rather "Do Jews deserve special moral opprobrium or blame for their roles in the Atlantic slave system or bear special moral responsibility for that system's operations?" The whole truth about the role of Jews in the Atlantic slave system, relative to this question, therefore consists of all the facts morally relevant

---

37. It follows that one could be justified in believing every sentence of T but not justified in accepting T as an adequate theory of the phenomenon it purports to be about.

to answering this question about blame and responsibility, or enough of them that adding the rest would not change the answer. *The Secret Relationship* offers a biased account with respect to this question, because it ignores facts morally relevant to answering it—for instance, facts that show that the Jews behaved no differently, from a moral point of view, than anyone else who had the opportunity to profit from the slave system.

When the questions driving inquiry are motivated by contextual values, judgments of significance and bias can only be made in relation to these values. Since significance and lack of bias are legitimate criteria of theory choice, it follows that contextual values play a legitimate role in justifying theories. It follows, also, that theories of phenomena can be criticized on the ground that the background value judgments that organize the theory's conception of significant facts are themselves unjustified. Thus, if it is a moral mistake to pass judgments of collective guilt or merit on whole ethnic groups, then there is no justification even to make "Jewish" a significant classification in historical studies of the slave trade that are aimed at addressing questions of responsibility. What justification could there be for singling out Jews as a comparison class in such studies, rather than, say, the class of people who have drooping eyelids? . . .

Historians sometimes contrast biased inquiry with inquiry that does justice to the events bring narrated and to the people involved in them. That the virtue of doing justice corrects bias expresses a superior understanding of the demands of inquiry than the ideal of value-neutrality. To adopt a stance of value-neutrality is to disregard contextual values in assessing the merits of theories. We have seen that insofar as science is driven by contextually value-laden questions, the ideal of value-neutrality leaves one incapable of coherently directed inquiry at all, because it leaves one incapable of distinguishing a significant from an insignificant fact, a biased account from one that does justice to the phenomena. One does justice not by adopting a stance of value-neutrality but by being impartial. Impartiality is not a commitment to disregard all evaluative standards but is a commitment to pass judgment in relation to a set of evaluative standards that transcends the competing interests of those who advocate rival answers to a question: These standards include honesty and fairness in judgment. To the extent that significance is judged in relation to highly contested political and moral questions, fairness demands attention to all the facts and arguments that support or undermine each side's value judgments, not a pose of value-neutrality. . . .

6. A Cooperative Model of the Interaction of Normative and Evidential Considerations in Theory Choice

The critique of contextually value-laden science depends on the assumption that truth is the only goal of science—or at least the only goal relevant to justifying theories. On this assumption, it is practically inevitable that any influence on theory choice other than evidence (considerations that support the claim to truth) must be viewed as *competing* with the evidence for our beliefs. Value judgments, social interests, wishes, and political demands in themselves have no evidentiary status. They do not support claims to truth. Therefore, to the extent that they influence theory choice, they must be seen as displacing attention to the evidence and diverting the search for truth.

I have defended an alternative conception of science, which holds that there are many goals of scientific inquiry. Multiple goals support multiple grounds for criticizing, justifying, and choosing theories besides truth.[38] Because modern science exists in large part to serve human interests, some of these goals and grounds are based on contextual values. I have identified three ways in which contextual values may shape legitimate grounds for theory choice.

38. As Longino also stresses, in her own dual-track model of justification. See her "Subjects, Power, and Knowledge," in Linda Alcoff and Elizabeth Potter, eds., *Feminist Epistemologies* (New York: Routledge, 1993), 101–120, 116.

First, all inquiry begins with a question. Questions direct inquiry by defining what is to count as a significant fact and what is a complete or adequate account of a phenomenon. A significant fact is one that bears on the answer to the question; an adequate account (one that represents the whole truth) is one that captures enough of the phenomenon that the addition of further detail will not change the answer. Many of the questions we ask science to answer come from the social context of science, not from its internal puzzle-generating activities. The constitutive goals of many sciences, such as engineering, medicine, and economics, are so contextually value-laden that it hardly makes sense to suppose that they have an "internal" source of questions independent from the social context in which they operate. When a theory or account of some phenomenon is taken to address some contextually value-laden question, it is therefore subject to criticism on at least three contextually value-laden grounds. The theory, although it asserts nothing but truths, may be trivial, insignificant, or beside the point: it doesn't address the contextual interests motivating the question. Or, although it asserts nothing but truths, it may be biased: it offers an incomplete account, one that pays disproportionate attention to those pieces of significant evidence that incline toward one answer, ignoring significant facts that support rival answers. When the question which the theory seeks to answer has moral or political import, the charge of bias can only be made relative to an assessment of the moral and political relevance of the evidence the theory cites. Such assessments of course depend upon moral and political value judgments. Finally, the theory may be objectionable for trying to answer a question that has illegitimate normative presuppositions.

Second, questions based on contextual interests require answers expressed in terms that track those interests. Contextual values come to directly inform the content of theories not simply by delineating the body of significant truths but by shaping how we ought to describe them. Purely epistemic criteria of significance are not sufficient to define our theoretical classifications.

The world is complex and messy enough that it is all too easy to come up with taxonomies that meet basic standards of epistemic significance. So which classifications should we pick? The interests behind the questions' driving inquiry tell us which classifications to use: ones that group phenomena that bear a common relation to these interests. It follows that theories embodying such classifications can be criticized on at least two normative grounds. They may misconceive the relevant, legitimate interests, and thereby classify together phenomena that should be separated or exclude phenomena that should be included in a class. Or a theoretical classification may be based on illegitimate contextual values and for that reason should be rejected altogether.

Third, questions based on contextual interests can only be answered by methods adequate to reveal the phenomena those interests classify as significant. A theory can therefore be criticized for relying on methods that foreclose the possibility of discovering that we have certain valuable potentialities or that certain important differences or similarities exist among the subjects being studied.

The introduction of multiple goals of inquiry allows us to model the interaction of normative and evidential considerations as cooperative rather than competitive. Contextual values aid empirical inquiry by identifying relevant facts and sources of evidence, shaping conceptual schemes for describing observations, and inspiring methodological innovations that open new avenues for empirical discovery adequate for answering contextually value-laden questions. This cooperative model of inquiry supports a dual-track model of theoretical justification. On this view, theory choice is properly based on both normative and evidential considerations. Contextual values set the standards of significance and completeness (impartiality, lack of bias) for a theory, and evidence determines whether the theory meets the standards. Contextual values help define what counts as a meaningful classification and the empirical criteria for identifying things falling under it, and evidence determines what, if anything meets these criteria. Contextual values help determine what methods are needed to answer a question, and evidence gathered in accordance with those methods helps answer it. In each case, evidential and normative considerations cooperate; neither usurps the role of the other.

The need for dual justification prevents wishful thinking and dogmatic insistence from counting as evidence for belief. Contextual value judgments do not play the same role that evidence does in supporting truth claims. But they do play a role in determining what the evidence means: what it points to, how it should be described. No advocate of value-laden inquiry argues that when the evidence is insufficient to justify belief in one of two rival theories, one may take the desirability of one conclusion as evidence for its truth. But contextual values do provide grounds for preferring theories that leave open the possibility of representing certain claims as true and for methods that leave open the possibility of discovering that we have certain valuable capacities.

My defense of value-laden inquiry suggests that good science is morally value-laden in a more global sense as well: it embodies the virtue of justice. Not value-neutrality, but justice, offers the proper model of objectivity in science. Justice includes the demand to do justice to the subjects of study as well as the demand to do justice to other inquirers: to respect them as equals, to respond to their arguments, evidence, and criticisms, to tolerate the diversity of views needed to secure the objectivity of science as a social practice. The lesson of this defense of value-laden science is not totalitarian, but pluralistic and tolerant.

7.5 Japanese Views of Western Science

Is science the foundation of all genuine knowledge? Would the alleged knowledge produced by science be less trustworthy if science were subordinated to moral and spiritual values?

These two questions return us to themes on which we have already touched. I mentioned scientism in my introduction to this chapter. Scientism holds that science is indeed the foundation of all genuine knowledge. Science is primary and privileged when it comes to knowing things, or so scientism maintains. In the last section we explored some issues related to science and knowing from a feminist viewpoint. This led to an investigation of the relationship between science and value. In the following selection we return to these themes, but in a different context. The context is cultural, and the questions under investigation by Thomas P. Kasulis, professor of philosophy at the Ohio State University in Columbus, have to do with how differing cultural values influence our understanding of science.

Before we look at what Kasulis says, we need to spend a little time thinking about fact and value. David Hume drew a distinction between fact and value when he argued that one cannot derive an "ought" from an "is." From the fact that *x does y,* we cannot infer that *x ought* to do *y* because the first judgment is descriptive whereas the second judgment is evaluative. To describe something is to state how it is (or is not) with respect to some context. To evaluate something is to find it valuable (or not) with respect to some context. Facts involve how things actually are. Values have to do with the worth of things. If Hume is right, facts and values are irreducibly distinct. Facts are objective. Values are subjective. Facts reflect the way the world is. Values reflect human interest and desire. Values cannot be inferred from facts, and facts cannot be inferred from values.

This distinction between fact and value is reflected in empiricist or (as they are sometimes called) positivist views of the nature of science. According to positivism, science has to do with facts, not values. Indeed, any knowledge claiming the exalted title *scientific* must be value-free. If it is not, then subjective human interests and desires have distorted our thinking about the way things really are. In short, science deals in facts, not values. Religion and morality deal with values, not facts. Hence science is objective, whereas religion and morality are subjective. Science is neutral with respect to human interests. Morality and religion are determined by human interests.

This sort of contrast may seem familiar to you and, perhaps, quite right. The fact that it may seem right indicates the extent to which the positivist or empiricist view of science has permeated our culture. However, since the work of Thomas Kuhn and the feminist analysis of people like Elizabeth Anderson, the maxim that scientific knowledge is value-laden, not value-free, has come to be accepted among many philosophers of science in Western cultures. The is/ought gap that Hume so skillfully opened up now seems like a myth or strange dream. Facts and values are not nearly as distinct as they once seemed.

This more recent viewpoint among philosophers of science in the West finds advocates among Eastern philosophers as well. In fact, two of the most influential Japanese philosophers of the last century provide valuable insights into how facts and values are interrelated. These insights are not just theory (as some say); they have important implications, not only for the way we live but also for alternative medical technologies.

Reading Questions

1. What conditions had to be met for Japan to assimilate Western ideas and science?
2. Why did the first phase of Westernization in the sixteenth century fail?
3. What has been an issue of major importance in modern Japanese philosophy, arising out of the modern phase of Westernization?
4. What is scientism, and how did the Japanese attitude toward science differ from scientism?
5. In his early philosophy, how does Nishida "solve" the separation of fact and value characteristic of Western science?
6. What are the three *basho,* how do they relate to one another, and how does Nishida's analysis of their logic lead to revealing the unity of science and value?
7. According to Yuasa, what two major assumptions in the Western view of the body need to be rethought?
8. What is the difference between a relativistic and a pluralistic understanding of truth?
9. In your view, would the subordination of science to moral and religious concerns lead to good science or bad science? Why, or why not?

Sushi, Science, and Spirituality*

THOMAS P. KASULIS

JAPAN SEEMS TO PRESENT two profiles to the West. One is that of a Westernized nation that is a major economic power in the world. Seeing the skyscrapers of Tokyo's downtown districts, hearing Western rock or classical music even in village coffee shops, or tasting the French cuisine of its fine restaurants, it is easy for one to think of Japan as part of the Western-based family of cultures. This face of Japan seems to confirm the interpretation of Habermas and others that European rationality is dominating the world. We might be led to expect that with the passage of time, Japan will become, if anything, even more like the West.

Yet, there is also the other, non-Western, profile as well. It appears to the consternation of foreign business people trying to establish Western-like contractual relations with Japanese corporations. It appears to the frustration of social scientists in their attempts to apply to the Japanese context Western models of social, political, or economic analysis. It appears even to philosophers who have tried to study Japanese thought. Charles Moore, the founder of the East-West Philosophers' Conferences half a century ago, felt able to write authoritatively about the "Chinese mind" and the "Indian mind." When he tried to write about the "Japanese mind,"

however, he could do no better than call it "enigmatic."[1] These reactions raise serious questions about how really "Western" Japanese rationality has become.

In short, Japan is a striking example of an Asian nation that has been successful at Western-style industrialization, technological development, and capitalistic expansion. Still, it has somehow also kept much of its own values and modes of behavior. How can this Western thinking and Japanese thinking exist in the same culture? Part of the answer is undoubtedly social or historical and best left to the analyses of specialists in those fields. Part of it is also philosophical, however. Since the major influx of Western ideas and technology into Japan in the latter half of the nineteenth century, Japanese philosophers have often addressed these very issues. In particular, they have asked (1) what the Western form of scientific and technological thinking is and (2) how it might function in Japan without eroding spiritual and moral values traditional to East Asia.

In this essay we will briefly examine two philosophical strategies representative of trends in modern Japanese philosophy. First, we will examine the early twentieth-century thought of Nishida Kitarō and his attempt to put Western

---

*Japanese personal names that appear in both the text and the notes may be in either traditional Japanese order (family name first) or in Western order (family name last). Also, conventional usage sometimes requires that historical personages be referred to by their *given* rather than their family names. Here are the names as they appear with *given* name for each in italics: *Masao* Abe, *Setsuko* Aihara, Inoue *Enryō*, Inoue *Tetsujirō*, Kuki *Shūzō*, Nagatomo *Shigenori*, Nakayama *Shigeru*, Nishida *Kitarō*, Nishitani *Keiji*, Oda *Nobunaga*, Sakuma *Shōzan*, *Masayoshi* Sugimoto, Takeuchi *Yoshinori*, Tanabe *Hajime*, *Kazuaki* Tanahashi, Tanizaki *Jun'ichirō*, Tokugawa *Ieyasu*, Toyotomi *Hideyoshi*, Yamamoto *Seisaku*, Yuasa *Yasuo*.

1. See Charles A. Moore, ed., *The Indian Mind: Essentials of Indian Philosophy and Culture, The Chinese Mind: Essentials of Chinese Philosophy and Culture,* and *The Japanese Mind: Essentials of Japanese Philosophy* (all Honolulu: East-West Center Press, University of Hawaii Press, 1967). Moore's "Introductions" to each volume are titled, respectively: "The Comprehensive Indian Mind," "The Humanistic Chinese Mind," and simply "Introduction." The first sentence of the Japanese volume starts: "The Japanese thought-and-culture is probably the most enigmatic and paradoxical of all major traditions. . ." (p. 1). The length of the introductions are perhaps also revealing. The Indian volume is sixteen pages of text, the Chinese ten, and the Japanese three.

From Thomas P. Kasulis, "Sushi, Science, and Spirituality: Modern Japanese Philosophy and its Views of Western Science, Philosophy East and West, *Volume 45 (April 1995): 227–248. Reprinted by permission from University of Hawaii Press.*

science into its place, a logical realm subordinate to that of ethics, spirituality, and aesthetics. Second, we will explore how a contemporary Japanese philosopher, Yuasa Yasuo, has seen a possible complementarity between modern Western science, especially medicine, and traditional Asian thought about the mind-body complex. Before discussing either philosophical approach, however, we need a sketch of the historical and cultural context of the Japanese encounter with Western thought. Only against that background can we clearly frame the problematics of modern Japanese philosophy.

To frame the specifics of the historical circumstances under which Western thought entered modern Japan, it is first useful to consider generally how ideas move from one culture to the next. Often, of course, they are imposed on a culture by a foreign military occupation. Until 1945, Japan was not in such a situation, however, and by then its internal processes of modernization (or Westernization) were already well under way. For that reason, there has been no prominent modern Japanese philosophy of "decolonization" as there has been in twentieth-century Indian, African, Islamic, and (to a lesser extent) Chinese thought. Even among Japanese critics of Westernization, the rhetoric has usually not been what "they" (Westerners) have done to "us" (Japanese), but what "we" have done to "ourselves."[2]

In short, Westernization was somewhat like an import item for Japan in the free marketplace of ideas. The issue may have been conditioned by external circumstances (most notably, the expansion of Western imperialist powers into Asia and the Pacific), but to some extent, at least, the Japanese welcomed the imported product. The question is: under what circumstances does a culture freely accept foreign ideas? This is too complex an issue to address fully here. It is easy to let such a question drift off into abstract dialectics concerning the logic of intercultural (mis-)understanding, however. So, for our background purposes, let us simply pursue for a bit the marketplace analogy. How does a product penetrate a foreign market? First, there must be a system of distribution: the product must be made available to the foreign market. Second, the product must develop an attractive image in the new culture. Third, the product must meet some need, or generate some need, in the perception of the potential consumers. Last, the product must suit the tastes of its new cultural home.[3]

To explain these basic categories further, let us consider an extended analogy: the rapidly growing number of sushi restaurants in U.S. urban areas. How can we understand this phenomenon in terms of the marketplace principles just outlined?

It is not simply the inherent taste of sushi that has given it its market niche in the American restaurant industry. Since the 1950s it has been common knowledge in the United States that the Japanese eat raw fish, yet few Americans wanted to try it. The issue, therefore, is what motivated Americans to want to try it. What changed between the 1950s and the 1980s such that a broadening spiral of supply and demand could develop?

The most obvious difference, of course, was the emergence of Japan as a powerful economic presence in the world generally and in the U.S. specifically. This economic change caused more Japanese business executives to reside temporarily in the United States, thereby establishing the demographic base in large cities for economically supporting a small number of local sushi restaurants. At the same time, more Americans visited Japan for business reasons, often sampling the local fare as part of the hospitality extended by Japanese business associates. Hence, availability increased. Furthermore, as Japan became one of

---

2. A good example of this ambivalence among Japanese intellectuals about the process of modernization is Tanizaki Jun'ichirō's essay, *"In'ei raisan,"* written in 1933. A fine translation is the short book by Tanizaki, *In Praise of Shadows*, trans. Thomas J. Harper and Edward G. Seidensticker (New Haven, Connecticut: Leete's Island Books, 1977).

3. As Tanizaki's *In Praise of Shadows* suggests, there is an aesthetic dimension to the acceptance of foreign ways. Similarly, in his *Iki no kōzō* (The structure of *iki*) (Tokyo: Iwanami Shoten, 1930), Kuki Shūzō typically characterized cultural influences in terms of "hue" and "tint." These examples suggest that Japanese thinkers often thought of the impact of culture in terms of aesthetic rather than logical categories.

the richest countries in the world, Americans came to admire its power. Americans began to think it worthwhile to emulate the Japanese, not merely observe them from afar as a land of exotica. Hence, we find the principles of availability/distribution and positive image.

One Japanese quality Americans admired was their health. The average Japanese male's life expectancy was almost a decade longer than the average American's. One factor in maintaining that health might be the Japanese low-fat, low-cholesterol diet. As the young American professionals of the baby boom years approached middle age and began to worry about heart disease, the "power lunch" of raw beef and egg so fashionable on Wall Street in the early 1980s was increasingly replaced by foods like sushi. This data shows that sushi was perceived as fitting a societal need to shift dietary habits. The third criterion of the marketplace was met.

The first three factors combined to create a context in which a significant number of Americans would try eating sushi. Then, the fourth condition could be met. If the Americans would acquire a taste for the new food—if they found sushi to be a desirable dietary option—it would become possible for sushi bars to establish a market niche in the American restaurant business. That is what seems to have happened.

Similar conditions had to be met for Japan to assimilate Western ideas, science, and technology. There were two major periods of influx from the West: the sixteenth century and the modern period starting in the mid- to late nineteenth century. In the first case, Westernization was eventually rejected, whereas in the modern period, it has been accepted. Let us briefly examine each case in terms of the four conditions just outlined.

The first factor is availability. In the sixteenth century, Westernization was offered to Japan primarily via Spanish and Portuguese Jesuits and Franciscans. Following the arrival of the missionaries, there was a moderate amount of trade between those European countries (including the Dutch shortly later) and Japan.

The second factor is the positive image of the host culture. The power trappings of Europeanization and Christianity were dual. First, they

brought knowledge of the outside world. Maps helped explain the geopolitical constitution of the lands beyond Asia. These were relevant to assessing the opportunities and dangers of future contact with Europe. The Japanese also found the foreigners fascinating: the aristocrats and samurai experimented with things European, including Portuguese dress. The Japanese admired the European worldliness, including the news, ideas, and goods they brought from afar. It might be noted, however, that the Japanese did find the Europeans rather crude culturally. There was some interest in Western foods (sukiyaki, for example, apparently developed as an attempt to make a Portuguese stew with native ingredients) and some exposure to Western art, but in general the Japanese felt more consternation than admiration for the unbathed, bearded barbarians. Most importantly, however, the Europeans brought new technology: some medical and scientific knowledge, but also the military technology of rifles and cannon. This brings us to the third condition—internal need.

For centuries preceding the arrival of the Westerners, Japan had been in a state of civil war, in which various barons were jockeying for territory and political power. There was the need for unification under a new military-political order. The strife ended with the rise to power of three successive military dictators: Oda Nobunaga (1534–1582), Toyotomi Hideyoshi (1536–1598), and Tokugawa Ieyasu (1542–1616). His mastery of Western firearms helped Nobunaga dominate the country militarily, for example. The new leaders initially respected and encouraged Christianity as an aid to unification. They feared the political and military power of the Buddhist sects, many of them having their own militia of armed monks, often numbering in the thousands. Therefore, conversion of the populace to Christianity was not only tolerated, but to some extent encouraged. In short, the introduction of both Western weaponry and Western religious ideas together served the need of unifying the country under the hegemony of the respective military dictators.

The support for these Western influences soon eroded, however. Ironically, this happened because Christianity and weapons technology no longer served the purposes of protecting the sovereignty of the military elite. Hideyoshi learned that the history of the world outside Japan showed that where European missionaries went, European navies and armies soon followed. That hundreds of thousands of Japanese might have a spiritual bond with priests connected to the imperialist courts of Europe was not an idea that Hideyoshi and Ieyasu relished. Christianity was, therefore, first persecuted and then proscribed.

The Tokugawa shōguns also realized that guns did not serve the purpose of a unified state under an iron-fisted rule. A peasant can be taught to fire a rifle in a few hours and kill a samurai swordsman who has spent decades perfecting his skill. Furthermore, ten men with rifles and cannon could kill a hundred archers and swordsmen. Hence, by the 1630s guns were, in effect, banned.[4] If the Tokugawas could ensure that only the samurai had power and that this power was strictly controlled by regulating the numbers and locations of the samurai, they could effectively rule the country through a central bureaucracy. They did so for over 250 years. During most of that time, with the exception of a few Dutch traders who visited an outlying island under scrupulous supervision, Japan closed itself off from European contact. Hence, the Europeanization process lasted for less than a century, and its effects were intentionally restricted severely.[5]

The influx of Western scientific ideas nurtured a burgeoning Japanese interest in studying the material world. It might be thought that Japanese intellectuals would be hesitant to relinquish that interest. It is significant, however, that Neo-Confucianism, especially that of Zhu Xi, also entered Japan in the fifteenth and sixteenth centuries, primarily via Zen Buddhist monks who brought back to Japan texts acquired during their pilgrimages to China. In that Neo-Confucian tradition there was also the notion of investigating natural things to understand their laws or principles. So, although there was not the mathematical dimension emergent in the contemporary Western science, Neo-Confucianism did offer an empirical interest in the ways of nature.[6] The Tokugawa shōguns opted to support that East Asian empiricism over its Western counterpart. Why? Partly because Neo-Confucianism framed its naturalism within a social ethic, a dimension of its system that the shōgunate could use as part of its state ideology. In short, although Western science and technology were available in the sixteenth century and although they often had the right image, their practical need was limited and temporary. They also lacked the ethical orientation to fit the image of the state that the Tokugawa shōguns had wanted to foster. So, it was marginalized.

The second Europeanizing phase in Japan is more pertinent to our philosophical purposes. When Commodore Perry forced Japan to open its ports to trade with the West in 1853, Japan once again encountered Westernization in a dynamic and disturbing way. Accessibility to the West had suddenly become a given. The West was at Japan's doorstep, and unlike the early seventeenth century, Japan was no longer in a position to tell it to go away. Japan felt squeezed and threatened. The United States had expanded across North America and into the Pacific; Britain and France were sweeping across the Asian and African continents; and Japan's nearest mainland neighbors, China and Russia, were countries of continental dimension.

---

4. For a general account of the initial acceptance and later prohibition of firearms in Japan, see Noel Perrin, *Giving Up the Gun: Japan's Reversion to the Sword, 1543–1879* (Boulder, Colorado: Shambala Publications, Inc., 1979).

5. The shōguns did allow and even endorsed a very limited influx of Western scientific works, so-called *rangaku* or "Dutch Learning." These were primarily limited to anatomy, medicine, astronomy (for calendar-making), and gunnery.

6. It is noteworthy that the first translated work of Dutch Learning related to mathematics did not appear until 1857, after the period of seclusion was over. See the table in Masayoshi Sugimoto and David L. Swain, *Science and Culture in Traditional Japan* (Cambridge: MIT Press, 1978; Rutland, Vermont: Charles E. Tuttle Company, 1989), p. 331. The book discusses the influx of Chinese science to Japan in two "waves:" 600–894 and 1401–1639. The two premodern Western "waves" were 1543–1639 and 1720–1854. This detailed study adds important nuance to many of the necessarily generalized historical statements in this essay.

The second condition for developing a taste for the foreign was also clearly present—a respect for the foreign culture. Western technology, including the technology of warfare, had developed enormously since Japan's last direct contact. The Tokugawa shōguns had kept Japan in a basically feudal mode for about 250 years. Japan envisioned two possible destinies: either be a pawn in the imperialist power plays of European and North American expansion or be an imperialist power in its own right through extensive economic, political, social, and technological reconstruction. It chose the latter course. It undertook an extensive program to modernize all sectors of the society: the government, education, industry, and the economy. Much of this movement was obviously a response to the outside threat of imperialist encroachment. At the same time, however, it was a response to an internally generated need—our third condition for accepting the foreign.

The Western intrusion came toward the end of a process of national change. The power of the shōguns had waned over the decades, and thoughts of revolutionary change had been brewing for some time. Through information leaking into the country via the heavily restricted trade with the Dutch, intellectuals were at least peripherally aware of the scientific, medical, and technological revolution occurring in the West. Hence, the internal desire for political and social reform dovetailed with the fear of foreign encroachment. Together, they supported the modernization movement.

By the early twentieth century, Japan had achieved a marked success. It had defeated both China and Russia in wars and had signed a major pact with Great Britain that treated the two countries more as equals. The development of science and technology had become a high priority in education, politics, and the economy.[7] There could be no turning back. The new Japanese industrial society had an enormous appetite for natural resources not available within its own archipelago. Modeling itself on its Western imperialist mentors, Japan looked to secure its supply of resources overseas on the Asian mainland and throughout the Pacific Basin. Japan had become an imperialist power and had set into motion a sequence of events that would result in the Pacific theater of World War II.

It is clear, therefore, that the first three conditions—accessibility, respect for the foreign culture, and internal need—were met. Japan had had a profound taste of Westernization. The issue was now whether that taste was palatable and desirable. In the early part of the Meiji period (1868–1912), intellectuals had expressed the hope that Japan could modernize without changing its underlying cultural value system. This ideal had been expressed in the slogan "Eastern morality and Western techniques" (*tōyōdōtoku to seiyōgeijutsu*) popularized by Sakuma Shōzan (1811–1864), for example. The more the Japanese intellectuals studied Western culture, however, the more skeptical they grew about the possibility of changing their country's social, economic, and political system without also changing its religious and moral values. Toward the end of the nineteenth century, for example, there was even an idea that science and Christianity had developed together so intimately in the West that it might be advisable for the Japanese emperor to convert to Christianity. The pro-Christian contingent did not win out in the end, and the emperor remained the chief priest of Shintō. Still, many prominent families in the modernization movement did convert. Even today, although Japan is only one percent Christian, Christianity's influence among higher social and economic classes is inordinately strong.

The examples of Sakuma's slogan and the plan to baptize the emperor are revealing. Obviously, even early on, the Japanese were acutely aware of two philosophically significant points. First, Western science and technology seemed to be packaged with a value system, one that at least appeared inimical to traditional Japanese values. Second, many intellectuals sensed that the historical development of the Western economy and the technological world it governed were

---

7. For an excellent institutional history of the development of modern Western science in Japan, see James R. Bartholomew, *The Formation of Science in Japan* (New Haven, Connecticut: Yale University Press, 1989).

somehow related to Christianity. Yet, they also sensed, much to their credit, that the connection between Western science and Western values and the connection between Western economics or politics and Western religion were contingent historical facts, not logical necessities. That is, they did not make the common mistake of assuming that what had happened had to have happened. They would, almost from the start, hope that they could have Western economic and technological development without adopting Western values in religion, ethics, and aesthetics. Was this hope justified? This has been a major issue in modern Japanese philosophy.

In exploring this issue, we must be wary of Western cultural assumptions about science. In the West, one often thinks of scientific thinking as acultural, a universal form of theory and practice transcending national boundaries. Unlike art, religion, society, and even morals, we do not tend to speak of, say, French physics as opposed to Indian physics, or German biology as opposed to Chinese biology. Certainly, there may have been indigenous Asian ideas about physical things or life, but they were not "scientific" in the modern Western sense of a science involving empirical observation, controlled experiment, and mathematical modeling.[8]

Certainly, there is much truth in that view of science. (Only in the past couple of decades has the West undertaken a postmodern critique of science, increasingly treating it as a social and cultural construction.) Yet, it is also true that the view of modern technology in Japan is quite different from the one dominant in the West. We must remember that it is the West that invented the modern scientific method of discovery and the technological principles for applying what was learned. Japan, as it has with so many other things that have become important to itself, imported the very idea of modern Western science. For the West, scientific thinking was a natural culmination of a sequence of ideas and trends in its history. It developed science originally as a way of discovering the laws, at first assumed to be the divine laws, of the universe. Assuming God gave humans the rationality to find the divine pattern, early modern Western scientists reasoned that it was their destiny to use that knowledge to complete the act of creation, to modify the world, to make it a better place.

For the Japanese, however, the modern scientific and technological mode of thinking came from outside only about 150 years ago. With their traditional Buddhist and *yin-yang* notions that the world is always in a process of change, technological alteration was accepted as part of the natural order. Nature is changing, so we must adapt to it. Indeed, we are part of the natural change itself. From the traditional Japanese perspective, human technology is as natural as, say, the technology of a beaver. It is not part of a divine plan.[9]

---

8. Of course, cultural historians of science have generally pointed out the qualifications that must be made about this view of science as Western. In the case of Chinese science, for example, there has been extensive research by such scholars as Joseph Needham and Nathan Sivin. See, for example, Needham's multivolume *Science and Civilisation in China* (Cambridge: Cambridge University Press, 1954–) and Sivin's *Chinese Alchemy: Preliminary Studies* (Cambridge: Harvard University Press, 1968). Also, see Nakayama Shigeru and Nathan Sivin, eds., *Chinese Science: Explorations of an Ancient Tradition* (Cambridge: The M.I.T. Press, 1973).

9. A contemporary example illustrates this poignantly. At some major intersections in many large Japanese cities, there are electronic billboards giving readings of the time of day, the temperature, and the levels of noise and carbon monoxide. As the traffic light changes and the vehicles move, one can see the noise and carbon monoxide numbers zoom upward. If such a sign were to appear on most American or European street corners, it would be a political statement about the danger of pollution. In Japan, however, it seems to be taken often as simply an indicator of what is the case. There is the temperature and there is the carbon monoxide level—two givens. This, I think, is one reason the Japanese, despite their love of nature, were slow to address environmental pollution. Technology was seen as natural, not the human intervention into the natural. Of course, Japan did eventually respond to the environmental crisis and has made tremendous strides, in some cases outstripping the West. But even the cleanup campaign was never posed in the humanity-nature dichotomy. It was simply humans taking part in the natural process of purification. Humanity acted out of the need for self-preservation and health, not out of any sense of moral responsibility to the environment.

This raises doubts about the common Western presupposition that science and technology must destroy traditional, nonmodern, non-Western forms of human rationality, values, and spirituality. We often forget what modern science's own ideology is supposed to maintain: science is essentially value-free. The problem is that the Western tradition has intimately connected science with scientism, that is, with the belief that the scientific way of knowing is somehow primary, foundational, or privileged. We should also note that in our scientism, we tend to collapse science into the realm of physics, that is, the discipline which gives a mathematical model for the forces of the universe. The Galileos, Keplers, and Newtons were interested in finding the key to explaining the universe. Mathematics became that key. To go from the idea that mathematics is the key for all scientific knowledge to the idea that scientific knowledge is the key for all knowledge in general was obviously a great leap, but one that enthusiasm could span. Westerners were seeking a replacement for the medieval science of theology; they wanted a single, holistic theory that would yield the one great, uppercase Truth.[10]

The Japanese, on the other hand, were not traditionally looking for that. They were often interested in having a set of lowercase truths, each getting the job done for the task at hand. For them, truths were not monolithic but plural, not holistic but partial. The truth varies with the context. Without context, there is no truth.[11] As Zen Master Dōgen (1200–1253) argued in the "Genjōkōan" chapter of his *Shōbōgenzō,* the fish is correct to see the ocean as a translucent emerald palace. The human being far out at sea is correct to see the ocean as a great circle. The celestial deities are correct to see the ocean as shining like a string of jewels in the sunlight. They are incorrect only if they claim that their

10. That the enterprise of technological development can differ in Japan from the West is illustrated by the following anecdote, related to me by a research and development officer of a major U.S. electronics company. Japanese corporations hold all the major patents on the technology for the home videocassette recorder. How did this technological advantage occur? In the 1970s the major American electronics companies held a joint meeting concerning the future of home video equipment. At that time, two possible formats had been developed. First, there was the videotape format: it had the advantage of being able to record as well as to play back prerecorded materials. The second was the videodisk format, which was somewhat better in reproductive quality but lacked the capacity to record. Obviously, the videotape system would be more marketable. The problem, however, was the complexity of the videotape mechanism. In a video recorder, unlike an audio recorder, both the tape heads and the tape surface must be in constant movement. Hence, the mechanism was very fragile and the tape tended to get wound around the tape heads causing a breakdown. Although rugged machines had been developed for professional use, the engineers were skeptical about the prospect of an affordable machine that would stand up to the rough use found in the typical American home. They exchanged data about the physics of the mechanical problem and decided that there could be no practical solution.

Meanwhile, the Sony Corporation engineers were tackling the same problem. Instead of swapping formulas, however, they assigned a team of engineers to study the situation. Their approach was to examine the prototype machine for hours, days, and weeks on end, watching how the tape continually got entangled. Then one of the engineers bent a little piece of wire into an odd shape and inserted it into a crucial point in the tape path. The problem was resolved. The production cost of the piece of wire that made the VCR possible, I was told, is about nineteen cents. The interesting part of the story for our purposes is how the Japanese engineer explained to my informant how they came to their sophisticated, technical solution of the problem. He said that they just watched the tape get entangled over and over again until they saw the way to "help the tape go where it wanted to go." The home VCR was the offspring of a marriage between technology and animism.

Another way of posing this is that the Japanese engineers took the attitude of invention rather than pure science. They "tinkered" with the physical object instead of first placing it under the universal categories of mathematical physics. Ironically, this used to be called "Yankee ingenuity."

11. There were exceptions to this general tendency to seek contextual truths over a single, comprehensive, systematic Truth. In the early Heian period, for example, Kūkai's esoteric Buddhism tried to develop a comprehensive philosophical system including metaphysics, epistemology, a theory of language, and aesthetics. It did not develop much after him as a continuing tradition, however. In the Tokugawa period, Zhu Xi's Neo-Confucian philosophy also had some tendencies toward developing a single, comprehensive system of truth. It was undermined almost immediately, though, by the more antirationalistic, indigenous development of *kogaku* and *kokugaku.*

view is the only correct view.[12] Therefore, the Japanese had the tendency to accept science without its being a scientism. Science is true within its own context; traditional Japanese values in religion, ethics, and aesthetics are also true within their own contexts. This interpretation of science as no more than one example of multiple, equally valid contextual systems was sometimes found in turn-of-the-century Japanese philosophy.[13]

As students of Western philosophy, however, Japanese thinkers began to see difficulties in a theory of contextual truth that did not articulate any hierarchy or criterion of appropriateness for the different contexts. In such a philosophy, there could be no overall consistency, nor any dialectic progress toward an ever more inclusive system. Surely, it was thought, some forms of rationality necessarily evolve out of others; some forms of thinking are simply of a higher order than others. Once a culture develops science, it does not go back to animism. At least such was the argument of Western thinkers like Comte and Hegel, and the early twentieth-century Japanese philosophers were acutely aware of their theories. Is scientific knowledge somehow higher than, say, religious ways of explaining and assimilating reality? Is scientism—a possible byproduct of Westernization—philosophically justified? If so, Western technique could not logically exist alongside Asian morality.

These concerns were anticipated by Japanese philosophers early in this century. Nishida Kitarō (1870–1945), the founder of the Kyōto School, ruminated about this problem throughout his career. We will consider two major phases of his thought. The first phase was developed mainly in his first book, *An Inquiry into the Good* (*Zen no kenkyū*), written in 1911.[14] *Inquiry into the Good* was written at the very end of the Meiji period, a time when Japanese national confidence was on the upswing and the country had the opportunity to reflect seriously on the full implication of Westernization. In that pioneering work, indeed in all his works to follow, Nishida struggled with the great philosophical issue of his time—the juxtaposition of Western science and technology with traditional Japanese values. If Japanese values were to coexist alongside Western empiricism, there would have to be a common philosophical structure embracing and grounding the two. Otherwise, Japan would, intellectually, at least, suffer a cultural schizophrenia.

As a philosopher, Nishida was able to take the issue out of its culture-bound form (such as the question of whether the emperor should become Christian in order to help modernization) and universalize it into the classic Western problem of the relation between fact (*is*) and value (*ought*). In this way, Nishida saw himself addressing a fundamental philosophical question, not just a cultural problem. One option open to Nishida was to follow the route of Hume and Kant, bifurcating fact and value into two separate domains and (for Kant) two different kinds of reasoning. This approach would, of course, affirm the possibility of separating Western science from Japanese values. But at what cost? Nishida knew that such a separation of *is* and *ought* was itself a divergence from the Eastern tradition. It was, in the final analysis, a Western approach to the problem, and it would

---

12. This work has appeared in various translations. See, for example, Kazuaki Tanahashi, ed., *Moon in a Dewdrop: Writings of Zen Master Dōgen* (San Francisco: North Point Press, 1985). The fascicle "*Genjōkōan*" is translated as "Actualizing the Fundamental Point," and the passage cited is found on page 71.

We may also note in passing that Dōgen's position on this point is akin to the pragmatism of Hilary Putnam's "internal realism," for example. For Putnam, truth or meaning is relative to the concepts in which it is framed. As the conceptual systems change, different propositions or theories will be true, even propositions that, if they had shared the same conceptual system, would be incompatible. Putnam develops this view in, for example, his book *The Many Faces of Realism: The Paul Carus Lectures* (LaSalle, Illinois: Open Court Publishing, 1987). This parallel exemplifies the extent to which Dōgen's type of philosophical stance cannot be discounted as merely "premodern" in the Western sense.

13. On trying to set the contextual domains for realism vs. idealism or science vs. spirituality, see the discussion of Inoue Enryō and Inoue Tetsujirō, in chapter 1 of the dissertation by Robert J. J. Wargo, "The Logic of Basho and the Concept of Nothingness in the Philosophy of Nishida Kitarō" (Ann Arbor: University of Michigan, 1972).

14. Nishida Kitarō, *An Inquiry into the Good,* trans. Masao Abe and Christopher Ives (New Haven, Connecticut: Yale University Press, 1990).

indeed seem strange that only a foreign way of thinking could justify preserving Japanese values.

So Nishida tried to bring fact and value, empiricism and morality (or religion or art), back together in a way consonant with the Asian tradition. At the same time, he thought his theory should be Western enough in form to serve the needs of an increasingly Westernized society. Here Nishida, like his childhood and lifelong friend D. T. Suzuki, found the writing of William James particularly provocative.[15] Rather than analyze science and value as two unrelated systems of reason, Nishida used James' notion of "pure experience" to articulate the common experiential flow toward unity underlying both the scientific and valuational enterprises. The surface differences notwithstanding, on a deeper level, science, morality, art, and religion share a single preconceptual drive (or "will") to unity. On the intellectual level, Nishida called this process "the intellectual intuition." Such was the basic thrust of his maiden philosophical work.

This solution to the fact/value, or is/ought, dilemma also satisfied Nishida as a practicing Zen Buddhist. Zen's ideal is the achievement of a preconceptual state of experiential purity ("no-mind") that becomes enacted pragmatically in various concrete ways, including thought.[16] For both James and Zen, thought is the temporary response to a break in the original unity of experience, a response which is itself intended to bring back the original unity of the experience. As Nishida put it, "pure experience is the alpha and omega of thought."

Inquiry into the Good became immediately popular among Japanese intellectuals and is probably today still the best-known work in modern philosophy among the Japanese. It is questionable how many of those intellectuals actually fathomed the nuances of Nishida's theory, but the major point for them was that Nishida had made Western-style philosophizing into something Japanese. His writing style had a Western ring to it, yet its fundamental insights were consistent with Japanese tradition. With *Inquiry into the Good,* modern Japanese philosophy—the so-called Kyōto or Nishida School—was born.

As Nishida's philosophical thinking further matured, however, he grew dissatisfied with *Inquiry into the Good*—not with its purpose, but with its philosophical form, its structural presuppositions. In particular, he criticized its psychologism (or "mysticism," as he sometimes called it). At the heart of his uneasiness was that *Inquiry into the Good* had attempted to solve the problem of the science/value split by appealing to a kind of experience, asserting it to be the ground of both the *is* and the *ought*. Nishida's readings in the Neo-Kantians during the period shortly after the publication of *Inquiry into the Good* made him sensitive to the problem of how forms of judgment, rather than strata of experience, interrelate.[17] That is, his concerns shifted from philosophical psychology to epistemology.

Throughout his life, Nishida constructed and subsequently razed his own attempts at systematic philosophy. He was an adamant critic of his own work and never seemed satisfied with the mode of explanations he had developed thus far. So the second phase of his thought rejected the idea that *Inquiry into the Good* had explained anything at all; it had simply described the drive of consciousness toward unification. One problem was that the psychologistic standpoint could only trace the evolution of thought in the individual's experiential process. It could, for example, describe how the desire for unity would lead to the emergence of scientific, moral, and religious thinking. But what about the fields of science, morality, and religion themselves? How can we analyze the interrelation of their claims without

15. Suzuki tended to focus on James' *Varieties of Religious Experience,* whereas Nishida was more interested in the *Psychology* and *Essays on Radical Empiricism.* This suggests the fundamental difference in their orientations: Suzuki was more religious and mystical, Nishida more psychological and epistemological.

16. For an account of Zen Buddhism that emphasizes this aspect, see my *Zen Action/Zen Person* (Honolulu: University of Hawaii Press, 1981).

17. For a highly edited translation of Nishida's journals on his reading of the Neo-Kantians, see his *Intuition and Reflection in Self-consciousness,* trans. Valdo H. Viglielmo with Takeuchi Yoshinori and Joseph S. O'Leary (Albany, New York: State University of New York Press, 1987).

limiting them to modes in the biography of a particular person's own experience? It is, after all, one matter to say that my empirical, moral, aesthetic, and religious experiences relate to each other, and quite another matter to say that science, morality, art, and religion are related. The first is to connect experiences within myself, the latter to connect kinds of judgments about what is right. Nishida was impressed with the Neo-Kantian attempts to articulate and explain the rationale of judgments and came to believe his earlier, Jamesian view to be overly subjectivistic.

This new interest led Nishida to examine more closely the structure of judgmental form, what he called its "logic" (*ronri*). The fundamental insight he explored was that any judgment necessarily arises out of a particular contextual field, place, or *topos*. The Japanese word for this contextual field is *basho*. There may be a plurality of truths and contexts, but how do those contexts interrelate? In effect, Nishida wanted to argue for the priority of the religious over both the idealist and empiricist, over both the psychologistic and the scientific. Although his argument was complex and refined or revised over many years, we can briefly summarize his point here in order at least to suggest how his line of thought developed.

Nishida analyzed closely the logical structure of judgmental form. Because he believed that any judgment necessarily arises out of a particular contextual field or place, his task in his later years was to explain the logic of those fields (*basho no ronri*). One way this system came to be formulated was in terms of the three *basho* of being, relative nothingness, and absolute nothingness. Roughly speaking, these corresponded to the judgmental fields of empiricism, idealism, and what he called the field of the "acting intuition" (*kōiteki chokkan*).[18]

Nishida's "logic of *basho*" is a complex system always in flux and under revision. Still, it represents Nishida's most integrated and systematic

attempt to deal with the issues of fact and value. To see the overall structure of Nishida's logic of *basho*, we can consider a simple empirical judgment—for example, "this table is brown." Scientific statements are generally of this form. They seem to express pure objectivity; the observer is so neutralized that he or she does not even enter into the judgment per se. They are statements about what is, statements about being (hence, the nomenclature "*basho* of being").

Yet, Nishida asked in what contextual field (*basho*) is such an objective judgment made? Where does one stand in making such a judgment about being? Nishida argued that such a judgment actually also makes judgments about our own consciousness. To neutralize the role of the observer as ordinary empirical judgments do is to say something about the observer—its role can be neutralized and ignored. This is an odd thing to say, however, since the larger contextual field of the judgment "the table is brown" is something more like "I see a brown table, and because what I see is real and external to my self, I can delete any reference to the self." So, Nishida maintains, the field or place of empirical judgments is really within the encompassing field of judgments about self-consciousness. Empiricism is actually dependent on, stands within, a field of judgments about self and its relation to the objects of experience. Since empirical judgments, as empirical judgments, ignore the being of the self, treating it as a nothing, this encompassing field can be called the "*basho* of relative nothingness." The self is, relative to empirical judgments, treated as a nothing. Of course, from the standpoint of the *basho* of relative nothingness, the self is very much a something, the very thing empiricism assumes, yet ignores. This insight, when taken literally, becomes the basis for idealism, theories that maintain that all knowledge is based in the mind.

Yet, Nishida was no idealist either. He criticized idealists (including Kant, Hegel, and Husserl) for not recognizing the true character of the *basho* within which their theories were formulated. The mistake of the idealists, according to Nishida, is that they think of the self as a thing, either a substance or a transcendental ego.

---

18. The best treatment of this aspect of Nishida's thought is the dissertation by Robert J. J. Wargo, cited in note 13 above. The dissertation's Appendix includes a translation of Nishida's "General Summary" in his *The System of Self Consciousness of the Universal*, a crucial formulation of Nishida's position at this stage of his thought.

Nishida claimed that the "I" in the previously stated judgment "I see a brown table and . . ." is not an agent, but an action, what he called the "acting intuition." So the *basho* of idealism that sees the self as both subject and object is itself encompassed by a third *basho,* the contextual field of "absolute nothingness." The acting intuition is both an active involvement in the world and an intuitive reception of information about that world. It is a process, not a thing, so it can never be either the subject or the object of itself. It can never be the gist of judgment—it is absolutely a nothing when it comes to any judgment. Hence, it is called "absolute nothingness."

The acting-intuiting process (the absolute nothingness) is, therefore, the true basis of judgments about both fact and value. On the surface level, fact is, as it were, the intuiting side, whereas value is the acting side. Yet, one never exists without the other. The two are moments or profiles of a single process. The facts we discover are influenced by what we value, and what we value is influenced by what we discover. Thus, as Yuasa Yasuo has explained in his analysis of Nishida,[19] the intuition is also active (informed by value) and the acting is also passive (as response to data received). The two poles of the process are totally inseparable.

For Nishida, therefore, science cannot replace spirituality, nor can it be separated from questions of value. Within its own terms, in its own *basho,* science can advocate an impersonal, value-free objectivity. But what makes science possible is the scientist—a person with interests, values, and creativity. It is human intention that cordons off a place within which science can function.

Furthermore, human intentionality can he explained within its own mentalistic or idealistic terms, as we do in phenomenology, psychoanalysis, and some forms of psychology. In taking the self as their starting point, these disciplines have a clearly demarcated field within which to function. Yet, Nishida asks, what makes that field

possible? Even "self" is a construction. It is not a given, but a product. As the idealists recognize, the self creates values that direct human activities like science. Nishida noted, however, that focusing an analysis on the self, indeed the very idea that there is a self, is itself a value. Nishida maintains that there is something more basic than self that constitutes the self—a responsive and creative process. That there is something more basic than self is a fundamental insight related to religious, ethical, and (sometimes) aesthetic values. It is this ineffable ground that is the basis for both self and the empirical world as known through science. At least such was Nishida's argument.

To sum up, in Japan, science did not have to break free of religious roots. It did not have to establish its hegemony. Rather, science and technology were foreign imports used to meet a set of practical needs related to political, military, and economic necessity. The traditional Japanese understanding of religion in terms of responsiveness and creativity was not displaced or successfully challenged by a new way of knowing. It did not have to be. The spiritual could continue to be a cornerstone of Japanese values, and, as Nishida tried to show, science could be seen as a special contextual extension of it, rather than a challenger to it.

Of course, not every Japanese philosopher agreed with Nishida. Yet, his impact has continued to be significant in Japan. In preparation for the college entrance examinations, only one book of Japanese philosophy is required reading: Nishida's *Inquiry into the Good*. Nishida's philosophical system is significant as an early, prewar philosophical struggle to articulate how it was possible to maintain "Asian values" and still develop "Western technique." His theory, in effect, justified what was already the social practice of giving science its "place" alongside the "places" of traditional religious and moral values. His philosophical theory showed, if nothing else, a distinctively Japanese way of accepting science without paying homage to the totem of scientism.

Has this tradition continued into more recent Japanese philosophy? The Kyōto School of philosophy founded by Nishida remains one of

19. Yuasa Yasuo, *The Body: Toward an Eastern Mind-Body Theory,* ed. T. P. Kasulis, trans. Nagatomo Shigenori and T. P. Kasulis (Albany, New York: State University of New York Press, 1987), chap. 2.

the most vigorous traditions in Japanese thought today.[20] Even philosophers who are not directly connected with the school still appreciate Nishida's pioneering work. We may wonder, therefore, whether there can be some fruitful interaction between Japanese and Western thought in the future. Yuasa Yasuo (1925–) is a Japanese philosopher who has been giving this issue some extensive thought over the past two decades, especially in terms of philosophical and medical views of the body. Since his works are beginning to be available in English translation,[21] let us briefly discuss his theory and its implications for our present theme.

Yuasa notes that, like science in general, Western and Asian medical traditions arose out of a radically different set of assumptions. He especially focuses on contrasting models of the body. With the birth of modern science in the West, the metaphor of the body as mechanism has become highly influential. Against this background, the West has tended to understand the living body's relation to the dead body as analogous to a machine that is either operative or turned off. Hence, modern Western medicine derives to a great extent from the anatomical information learned through the dissection of corpses or vivisection of animals, neither of which allows access to the functions of the conscious human body. More

recently, the model was enhanced by the study of physiology in terms of organs and their biochemical functions. For Yuasa, what is significant is that most of this information was amassed under the assumption that the body can be understood independently of the mind, the physical mechanism independently of consciousness.

Asian forms of medicine such as Chinese acupuncture, on the other hand, developed out of the study of living, conscious human beings. The operative assumption is that the mind-body forms a single energy system responsive to the field in which it functions. To a traditional Asian medical theorist, it would be counterintuitive to study a dead or unconscious human body. It would be like trying to study electromagnetism with the electric current turned off.

Because of this difference in philosophical assumptions, Asian and Western medical traditions developed expertise in radically different aspects of human health and disease. Acupuncture developed highly sophisticated procedures for controlling pain, for example. (It is hard to study pain by dissecting a corpse.) On the other hand, Western medicine became expert at the physical manipulation of the body through surgery, for instance. (Surgery would not develop very far in a culture where patients were conscious and unanesthetized.)

In recent decades, Western medicine has developed increasingly sophisticated instruments for studying the living, conscious human being. There has been, therefore, a concurrent interest in psychosomatic and holistic approaches to medicine. Conversely, Asians have been learning Western medical techniques and have shown an interest in Western surgical, pharmaceutical, and diagnostic approaches. So, we are finding a situation in which two different conceptual schemes—and their correspondingly different claims about the body—are being brought into conjunction. Can the two systems influence and enrich each other? Yuasa claims they can, but only if each side is willing to call into question some of its most treasured assumptions. Since the Western tradition is more familiar to most of us, let us list just two major assumptions that Yuasa believes must be rethought in the Western view of the body.

20. Two other prominent members of the Kyōto School interested in the place of science were Tanabe Hajime (1885–1962) and Nishitani Keiji (1900–1990). Some of their works have become available in English: Tanabe Hajime, *Philosophy as Metanoetics,* trans. Takeuchi Yoshinori (Berkeley: University of California Press, 1986); Nishitani Keiji, *Religion and Nothingness,* trans. Jan Van Bragt (Berkeley: University of California Press, 1982); Nishitani Keiji, *The Self-Overcoming of Nihilism,* trans. Graham Parkes and Setsuko Aihara (Albany, New York: State University of New York Press, 1990); and Nishitani Keiji, *Nishida Kitarō,* trans. Yamamoto Seisaku and James W. Heisig (Berkeley: University of California Press, 1991).

21. So far, three book-length works have appeared: Yuasa Yasuo, *The Body* (see note 19 above); David Edward Shaner, Shigenori Nagatomo, and Yuasa Yasuo, *Science and Comparative Philosophy: Introducing Yuasa Yasuo* (Leiden: E. J. Brill, 1989); and Yuasa Yasuo, *The Body, Self-cultivation, and Ki-energy,* trans. Shigenori Nagatomo and Monte S. Hull (Albany, New York: State University of New York Press, 1993).

According to Yuasa, the modern West has generally tended to assume that the relationship between the mind and the body is fixed and universal. That is, Western theorists tend to ask, "What is *the* relationship between the mind and the body?" Yuasa points out that, in contrast, most Asian traditions assume there is a range of interaction and integration between mind and body. For example, as I learned to type or play the piano, the relationship between my mind and my fingers changed. Originally, my mind had to "tell" my fingers what to do in a separate, self-conscious act. The fingers responded slowly, awkwardly, and imprecisely. Now my fingers are more the extension of my mind when I type or play the piano. This suggests modification in the mind-body system.

Yuasa also points out that traditional Asian medicine retained its intimate relation with Asian spiritual disciplines. The Indian yogin is a good example of how the integration of mind and body is considered to be both a spiritually and medically healthy goal. As we noted already, modern Western science had to separate itself from religion in order to develop. Fasting, contemplation, prayer, chanting, and repetitive ritual exercises can all shed light on aspects of our bodies as well as our souls, but these activities have fallen outside the concerns of the Western scientific study of the body. Modern Western medicine has only recently begun to explore the therapeutic benefits of biofeedback, relaxation exercises, visualization techniques, and so forth. In effect, these originally spiritual exercises are beginning to find their way back into our Western understanding of the body.

The second assumption that Yuasa believes Western mind-body theories should reexamine concerns what he sometimes calls the "third entity" that is neither mental nor somatic, but the basis of both. Taking physics for its paradigm, modern Western science has drawn too strong a bifurcation between matter and energy. If we were to take biology, not physics, to be the ground of science (as Asian cultures did, in many respects), then we would see the need for this third term. In fact, we would be asking not about matter and energy's applicability to biology, but rather about this third term's relation to non-human phenomena. Yuasa believes that in East Asia, the Chinese concept of *qi* (*ki* in Japanese) is just such a third term. It is interesting that it is foundational to East Asian theories of acupuncture, artistry, electricity, and cosmology alike. What Yuasa calls for is a more Western physical study of this phenomenon that is not even as yet recognized as a category in the West. Such research is, in fact, under way in both China and Japan.

From the examples of Nishida and Yuasa, what summary statements can we make about the modern Japanese philosophical views of science and technology?

1. A non-European culture can accept Western science and technology without necessarily destroying the roots of its traditional value systems. The opposition of science and spirituality, the bifurcation of *is* and *ought,* is a consequence of historical developments in the West and need not apply to other cultural traditions with different histories. For these oppositions not to occur, however, science must not degenerate into a scientism, the belief that only the scientific form of knowledge is valid or that scientific knowledge is the ground of all legitimate forms of knowing. The evidence suggests that the Japanese have been able to accept science without falling prey to scientism. Nishida's and Yuasa's philosophies give two prominent rationales for keeping science distinct from the assumptions of scientism.

2. The Japanese philosophical tradition for centuries has resisted the idea of developing a single monolithic ontology implying the existence of a single, all-embracing Truth. Rather, the Japanese have traditionally emphasized a world of multiple truths, each dependent on its context. This is not, it should be noted, a relativism, but a pluralism. Relativism would maintain that there is no standpoint by which to judge truth. Pluralism maintains that truth can only be judged from one standpoint at a time, and the standpoints themselves can be judged as appropriate to the questions asked. Within a given context, things are absolutely true or false, not just relatively so.

The Japanese view lends itself to seeing Western logic and scientific thinking as a pragmatic tool for addressing certain problems, rather than as an attempt to explain all things within one supersystem. The god of Western logic and empiricism can only be a henotheistic god, not the monotheistic god that scientism tries to make of it.

3. Following on the previous point, we can wonder about the relation between pluralism and philosophy or religion. Today there seems a need to express our philosophical and religious commitments within a pluralistically open context. Does the Japanese view of truth better lend itself to that enterprise than do the more monolithic, system-building approaches inherited from our Christian and modern Western philosophical traditions? Is part of the success of the Japanese economy related to the culture's capacity to recognize the dependence of truth on context and to move freely and flexibly among different contexts and seemingly different truths? As the world becomes economically, politically, and even philosophically and scientifically more interdependent, the alternatives seem to be either the enforcement of a hegemonic uniformity or the development of the capacity to live within an increasingly pluralistic context. If the latter alternative is preferred—and I would argue it is—might the West learn something from the Japanese experience and the philosophies developing out of it?

7.6 Science and Traditional Thought

Do you believe in spirits? Do you think that if you got ill, you could go to a shrine, have a priest sacrifice a chicken, and get well? If you think this would work, why? If you do not think going to spirit-shrines and sacrificing chickens would cure illness, why not?

Do you think false beliefs can survive for long periods of time? If you think there are no spirits who cure people in response to sacrificed chickens, why do you think some people believe there are? Let us suppose that the people who believe there are indeed such spirits have held this view for centuries, and that in fact there are no such spirits. What sustains false beliefs in healing spirits over centuries? Why do they persist if they are false?

I am going to call something a traditional religious belief if it is based on positing spirit-agents as causes of events. You go to the priest, she sacrifices a chicken, and you get well. The priest, who holds traditional religious beliefs, would say that the spirit of the shrine healed you. Is this traditional religious belief scientific? Why, or why not?

Suppose you go to a medical doctor and, instead of the doctor sacrificing a chicken, she gives you a shot and you get well. The medical doctor, who holds scientific beliefs, tells you that you have a bacterial infection and that the antibiotic she has just given you will destroy the bacteria. How is this scientific belief different from a traditional religious belief? Is there a significant difference between the two explanations of why you got well?

Some African people build granaries on poles to store their harvests above the ground so mice will not get into the grain. When it is hot, people sometimes sit under these granaries to get shade and sometimes, because termites weaken the supports, these granaries fall and kill or injure some of the people. If you ask why the granaries fell and people were injured, you would be told it was because of witchcraft. Witches did it! Everyone knows about the termites, and they know what termites have done to the supports, yet they still explain this unfortunate event by appealing to witchcraft. Witchcraft is their **theodicy** or answer to the problem of evil. It explains why bad things happen. Is it a scientific explanation? Why, or why not?

Suppose a friend, a religious and good person, is suddenly killed in an auto accident caused by a drunk driver. At the funeral the minister asks why bad things happen to good people and answers, "I believe this tragic event is part of God's plan." Everyone knows the accident was caused by a drunk driver, yet the minister says it is part of God's plan. Is this a scientific explanation of the tragic accident? Is it an explanation at all? If it is, what kind of explanation is it?

Kwame Anthony Appiah, professor of philosophy at Harvard University and author of the following selection, is a person of "two worlds." Before earning his Ph.D. from Cambridge University, he was trained in Africa to be a leader of the Asante. His farther, a British barrister, was from the royal house of the Asante, the most powerful kinship group in Ghana, and his mother, a published author, a member of the British establishment. One of his worlds is the world of traditional African belief and thought. The other world is the world of modern European scientific belief and thought. Here he offers some intriguing philosophical reflections on the relationship between these worlds.

Reading Questions

1. What is Durkheim's argument for treating religion as symbolic?
2. Why, according to Appiah, is Durkheim wrong?
3. Why are the concepts of "underdetermination" and "theory-laden" important in this context?
4. What is the analogy between traditional religion and natural science?
5. How, according to Horton, do traditional religious beliefs differ from natural science, and why?
6. Which sort of explanation is missing in Horton's account, and why?
7. Explain what Appiah means when he says that the "differences between traditional religious theory and the theories of the sciences reside in the social organization of inquiry." Do you think he is right about this? Why, or why not?
8. What is the difference between an "adversarial style" and an "accommodative style," and why is this difference important?
9. According to Appiah, what accounts for modern scientific cultures being adversarial and traditional religious cultures being accommodative?

Old Gods, New Worlds

KWAME ANTHONY APPIAH

IN COMING TO TERMS with what it means to be modern, Western and African intellectuals have interests they should share. . . . [A]s I shall suggest, neither of us will understand what modernity is until we understand each other. . . .

From Kwame Anthony Appiah, In My Father's House: Africa in the Philosophy of Culture. Oxford: Oxford University Press, © 1992 by Anthony Appiah, pp. 107–136. Reprinted by permission of the author and Oxford University Press, Inc. Notes edited.

[O]ne of the marks of traditional life is the extent to which beliefs, activities, habits of mind, and behavior in general are shot through with what Europeans and Americans would call "religion." . . . Most intellectuals outside . . . [traditional societies] think they know, after all, that there are no such spirits [as can be summoned by sacrificing, for example, gold or sheep and chickens at a shrine]. That, for all the requests in the priest's prayer, no unseen agent will come to inhabit the shrine; no one will answer the questions "What made this person ill?" or "Would we win if we went to war?" or "How should we cure the king's elder?" Yet here is a culture [Asante] where, for at least several hundred years, people have been setting up just such shrines and asking them just such questions and asking the spirits they believe are in them to perform just such tasks. Surely by now they should know, if they are rational, that it won't work? . . . And if we press the question how these beliefs can be sustained in the face of a falsity that is obvious, at least to us, we shall return, in the end, to the question whether we have really understood what is going on. . . .

[W]e need, I think, to bear in mind at least these three separate types of understanding: first, understanding the ritual and the beliefs that underlie it; second, understanding the historical sources of both ritual and belief; and, third, understanding what sustains them.

[T]o understand these ritual acts what is necessary is what is necessary in the understanding of any acts: namely to understand what beliefs and intentions underlie them, so that we know what the actors think they are doing, what they are trying to do. Indeed if we cannot do this we cannot even say what the ritual is. To say that what is going on here is that these people are inviting a spirit to take up its place in a shrine is already to say something about their beliefs and their intentions. It is to say, for example, that they believe that there is a spirit, Ta Kwesi, and believe too that asking the spirit to do something is a way of getting that spirit to do it; it is to say that they want the spirit to inhabit the shrine. . . .

But if we are to face the question of the rationality of traditional belief we must turn, finally, to my third set of questions: those about what keeps these beliefs, which outsiders judge so obviously false, alive.

It is in asking these questions that some have been led by another route to treating religion symbolically. The British anthropologist John Beattie, for example, has developed a "symbolist" view of Africa's traditional religions, whose "central tenet," as Robin Horton (a philosopher-anthropologist, who is a British subject and a longtime Nigerian resident) puts it, "is that traditional religious thought is basically different from and incommensurable with Western scientific thought"; so that the symbolists avoid "comparisons with science and turn instead to comparisons with symbolism and art. . . .[1] Simply put, the symbolists are able to treat traditional believers as reassuringly rational only because they deny that traditional people mean what they say. Now Robin Horton has objected—correctly—that . . . [i]t is peculiarly unsatisfactory to treat a system of propositions as symbolic when those whose propositions they are appear to treat them literally and display, in other contexts, a clear grasp of the notion of symbolic representation.

I have mentioned Durkheim . . . and it is in his work that we can find the clearest statement of the connection between the urge to treat religion as symbolic and the question why such patently false beliefs survive. For Durkheim cannot allow that religious beliefs are false, because he thinks that false beliefs could not survive. Since if they are false they would not have survived, it follows that they must be true: and since they are not literally true, they must be symbolically true.[2] This argument is based on a misunderstanding of the relationship between the rationality of beliefs, their utility and their truth; it is important to say why.

1. Robin Horton, "Spiritual Beings and Elementary Particles—A Reply to Mr. Pratt," *Second Order* 1, No. 1 (1972), p. 30.
2. John Skorupski has persuaded me that Durkheim does indeed offer this apparently crude argument; see Skorupski's *Symbol and Theory* (Cambridge: Cambridge University Press, 1976), chap. 2, for an excellent discussion.

Rationality is best conceived of as an ideal, both in the sense that it is something worth aiming for and in the sense that it is something we are incapable of realizing. It is an ideal that bears an important internal relation to that other great cognitive ideal, Truth. And, I suggest, we might say that rationality in belief consists in being disposed so to react to evidence and reflection that you change your beliefs in ways that make it more likely that they are true. . . .[3]

With such an account of reasonableness, we can see why the apparently obvious falsehood of the beliefs of the Asante priest might be regarded as evidence of his unreasonableness. For how could he have acquired and maintained such beliefs if he was following the prescription always to try to change his beliefs in ways that made it more likely that they were true? The answer is simple. The priest acquired his beliefs in the way we all acquire the bulk of our beliefs: by being told things as he grew up. As Evans-Pritchard says of the Zande people, they are "born into a culture with ready-made patterns of belief which have the weight of tradition behind them."[4] And of course, so are we. On the whole, little has happened in his life to suggest they are not true. So too, in our lives.

Now it may seem strange to suggest that accepting beliefs from one's culture and holding onto them in the absence of countervailing evidence can be reasonable, if it can lead to having

beliefs that are, from the point of view of Western intellectuals, so wildly false. And this is especially so if you view reasonableness as a matter of trying to develop habits of belief acquisition that make it likely that you will react to evidence and reflection in ways that have a tendency to produce truth. . . .

We may also fail to see how reasonable the priest's views should seem, because, in assessing the religious beliefs of other cultures, we start, as is natural enough, from our own. But it is precisely the absence of this, our alien, alternative point of view in traditional culture, that makes it reasonable to adopt the "traditional" worldview. The evidence that spirits exist is obvious: priests go into trance, people get better after the application of spiritual remedies, people die regularly from the action of inimical spirits. The reinterpretation of this evidence, in terms of medical-scientific theories or of psychology, requires that there be such alternative theories and that people have some reason to believe in them; but again and again, and especially in the area of mental and social life, the traditional view is likely to be confirmed. We have theories explaining some of this, the theory of suggestion and suggestibility, for example, and if we were to persuade traditional thinkers of these theories, they might become skeptical of the theories held in their own culture. But we cannot begin by asking them to assume their beliefs are false, for they can always make numerous moves in reasonable defense of their beliefs. [Blaming some extant auxiliary hypothesis or adding some excusing auxiliary, for example.] It is this fact that entitles us to oppose the thesis that traditional beliefs are simply unreasonable. . . .

Philosophers of science have names for this: they say that theory is "underdetermined" by observation, and that observation is "theory-laden." And they mean by underdetermination the fact that French philosopher-physicist Pierre Duhem noticed in the early part of this century: that the application of theory to particular cases relies on a whole host of other beliefs, not all of which can be checked at once. By the theory-ladenness of observation, relatedly, they mean that our theories both contribute to forming our experience

---

3. . . . This conception of rationality belongs to a family of recent proposals that treat a concept as being defined by the *de re* relations of agents to the world. . . . As Gettler [1963] showed, a belief can be justified and true, but not a piece of knowledge, because the justification fails to be appropriately related *de re* to the facts. . . . Similarly, I want to say a belief can be reasonable (subjectively), but irrational (objectively). Since questions of rationality, therefore, raise questions about how other people stand in relation to reality; and since these questions cannot be answered while leaving open, as I wish to do, questions about who is right, I shall talk from now on about reasonableness rather than rationality. Someone is reasonable, on my view, if they are trying to be rational: if they are trying to act só as to maximize the chance of their beliefs being true.

4. Evans-Pritchard, *Witchcraft, Oracles and Magic among the Azande* (Oxford: Oxford University Press, 1976), p. 202.

and give meaning to the language we use for reporting it. Sir Karl Popper's claim that science should proceed by attempts at falsification, as we all know after reading Thomas Kuhn, is incorrect. If we gave up every time an experiment failed, scientific theory would get nowhere. The underdetermination of our theories by our experience means that we are left even by the most unsuccessful experiment with room for maneuver. The trick is not to give up too soon or go on too long. In science, as everywhere else, there are babies and there is bathwater. . . .

[T]raditional religious theory is in certain respects more like modern natural science . . . which we may summarize in the slogan "explanation, prediction, and control." It is his systematic development of the analogy between natural science and traditional religion that has made the work of Robin Horton so important in the philosophy of African traditional religions, and it will be useful to begin with him.[5]

Horton's basic point is just the one I made earlier: the fundamental character of these religious systems is that the practices arise from the belief, literal and not symbolic, in the powers of invisible agents. Horton argues persuasively, and I believe correctly, that spirits and such function in explanation, prediction, and control much as do other theoretical entities: they differ from those of natural science in being persons and not material forces and powers, but the logic of their function in explanation and prediction is the same.

Horton's view, then, is that religious beliefs of traditional peoples constitute explanatory theories and that traditional religious actions are reasonable attempts to pursue goals in the light of these beliefs—attempts, in other words, at prediction and control of the world. In these respects, Horton argues, traditional religious belief and action are like theory in the natural sciences and the actions based on it. . . . Horton's thesis

is not that traditional religion is a kind of science but that theories in the two domains are similar in these crucial respects. The major difference in the contents of the theories, he argues, is that traditional religious theory is couched in terms of personal forces, while natural scientific theory is couched in terms of impersonal forces. The basic claim strikes me as immensely plausible. . . .

Horton himself is, of course, aware that traditional religious beliefs are certainly unlike those of natural science in at least two important respects. First of all, as I have already insisted, he points out that the theoretical entities invoked are agents and not material forces. . . . And he offers us an account of why this might be. He suggests that this difference arises out of the fundamental nature of explanation as the reduction of the unfamiliar to the familiar. In traditional cultures nature, the wild, is untamed, alien, and a source of puzzlement and fear. Social relations and persons are, on the contrary, familiar and well understood. Explaining the behavior of nature in terms of agency is thus reducing the unfamiliar forces of the wild to the familiar explanatory categories of personal relations.

In the industrial world, on the other hand, industrialization and urbanization have made social relations puzzling and problematic. We move between social environments—the rural and the urban, the workplace and the home—in which different conventions operate; in the new, urban, factory, market environment we deal with people whom we know only through our common productive projects. As a result the social is relatively unfamiliar. On the other hand, our relations with objects in the city are relations that remain relatively stable across all these differing social relations. Indeed, if factory workers move between factories, the skills they take with them are precisely those that depend on a familiarity not with other people but with the workings of material things. It is no longer natural to try to understand nature through social relations; rather, we understand it through machines, through matter whose workings we find comfortably familiar. It is well known that the understanding of gases in the nineteenth-century was modeled

5. Horton's most famous paper is his "African Traditional Religion and Western Science." . . . All my thought on these questions has been stimulated and enlivened by reading and talking with him, and so many of the ideas I shall be offering are his that I make now a general acknowledgement.

on the behavior of miniature billiard balls—for nineteenth-century scientists in Europe know the billiard table better than they knew, for example, their servants. Alienation is widely held to be the characteristic state of modern man: the point can be overstated, but it cannot be denied. . . . [Horton's] story works so well that is it hard not to feel that there is something right about it; it would indeed explain the preference for agency over matter, the first of the major differences Horton acknowledges between traditional religion and science.

And yet this *cannot* be quite right. All cultures—in modest mood, I might say, all the cultures I have knowledge of—have the conceptual resources for at least two fundamental sorts of explanation. On the one hand, all have some sort of notion of what Aristotle called "efficient" causation: the causality of push and pull through which we understand the everyday interactions of material objects and forces. On the other, each has a notion of explanation that applies paradigmatically to human action, the notion that the American philosopher Daniel Dennett has characterized as involving the "intentional stance."[6] This sort of explanation relates actions to beliefs, desires, intentions, fears, and so on—the so-called propositional attitudes—and is fundamental . . . to folk psychology. We might say, analogously, that efficient causality is central to what cognitive psychologists now call "naive" or "folk physics."

These kinds of explanations are, of course, interconnected: when I explain the death of the elephant by talking of your need for food, your hunt, your firing the gun, there are elements of folk physics and of folk psychology involved in each stage on this narrative. To say that mechanical explanation is unfamiliar to preindustrial peoples is, of course, to say something true. Mechanical explanation is explanation in terms of machines, which are, of course, exactly what preindustrial cultures do not have. But mechanical explanation is by no means the only kind of nonintentional explanation: there is more to folk physics than a view of machines. And the fact is that the stability of the causal relations of objects in the preindustrial world is surely quite substantial: not only do people make tools and utensils, using the concepts of efficient causation, but their regular physical interactions with the world—in digging, hunting, walking, dancing—are as stable and as well understood as their familial relations. More than this, preindustrial Homo is already Homo Faber, and the making of pots and of jewelry, for example, involves intimate knowledge of physical things and an expectation of regularity in their behavior. . . .

What we need to bring back into view here is a kind of explanation that is missing from Horton's story: namely, functional explanation, which we find centrally (but by no means uniquely) in what we might call "folk biology." Functional explanation is the sort of explanation that we give when we say that the flower is there to attract the bee that pollinates it; that the liver is there to purify the blood; that the rain falls to water the crops.

This sort of explanation is missing from Horton's story for a very good reason—namely, that the positivist philosophy of science on which Horton relies sought either to eradicate functional explanation or to reduce it to other sorts of explanation, in large part because it reeked of teleology—of the sort of Aristotelian "final" causation that positivism took to have been shown to be hopeless by the failure of vitalism in nineteenth-century biology. And, surely, what is most striking about the "unscientific" explanations that most precolonial African cultures offer is not just that they appeal to agency but that they are addressed to the question "Why?" understood as asking what the event in question was for. Evans-Pritchard in his account of Zande belief insists that the Azande do not think that "unfortunate events" ever happen by chance:[7] their

---

6. See Daniel Dennett's *The Intentional Stance* (Cambridge, Mass.: Bradford Books, 1987).

7. See Evans-Pritchard, *Witchcraft, Oracles and Magic among the Azande,* chap. 2.

frequent appeal to witchcraft—in the absence of other acceptable explanations of misfortunate—demonstrates their unwillingness to accept the existence of contingency. But to reject the possibility of the contingent is exactly to insist that everything that happens serves some purpose: a view familiar in Christian tradition in such formulas as "And we know that all things work together for good to them that love God" (Rom. 8:28), or in the deep need people feel—in Europe and America as in Africa—for answers to the question "Why do bad things happen to good people?" Zande witchcraft beliefs depend on an assumption that the universe is in a certain sort of evaluative balance; in short, on the sort of assumption that leads monotheistic theologians to develop theodicies.

What Zande people will not accept, as Evans-Pritchard's account makes clear, is not that "unfortunate events" have no explanation—the granary falls because the termites have eaten through the stilts that support it—but that they are meaningless; that there is no deeper reason why the person sitting in the shade of the granary was injured. And in that sense they share an attitude that we find in Christian theodicy from Irenaeus to Augustine to Karl Barth: that the cosmos works to a plan. Precolonial African cultures, pre- and nonscientific thinkers everywhere, are inclined to suppose that events in the world have meaning; they worry not about the possibility of the unexplained (what has no efficient cause nor agent explanation) but of the meaningless (what has no function, no point). And this marks those who accept the scientific worldview—a minority, of course, even in the industrialized world—from almost all other humans throughout history. For it is a distinctive feature of that scientific worldview that it accepts that not everything that happens has a human meaning. To explain this difference between scientific and nonscientific visions we need, I think, to begin with the fact that the world, as the sciences conceive of it, extends so hugely far beyond the human horizon, in time as in space. As Alexandre Korye indicated in the title of his well-known study of the birth of modern celestial

physics, the Newtonian revolution took the intellectual path *From the Closed World to the Infinite Universe,* and the Victorian dispute between science and religion had at its center a debate about the age of the earth, with geology insisting that the biblical time scale of thousands of years since the creation radically underestimated the age of our planet. Copernicus turned European scientists away from a geocentric to a heliocentric view of the universe and began a process, which Darwin continued, that inevitably displaced humankind from the center of the natural sciences. A recognition that the universe does not seem to have been made simply for us is the basis of the radically nonanthropocentric character of scientific theories of the world. This nonanthropocentrism is part of the change in view that develops with the growth of capitalism, of science, and of the modern state. The change to which, for example, Weber's account of modernization was addressed, and it contributes profoundly to the sense of the universe as disenchanted that Weberians have taken to be so central a feature of modernity (a claim that makes more sense as a claim about the life of professional intellectuals than as one about the culture as a whole). . . .

But Horton in his original work made, as I said, a second important claim for difference: he summarized it by calling the cognitive world of traditional cultures "closed" and that of modern cultures "open." "What I take to be the key difference is a very simple one," he writes. "It is that in traditional cultures there is no developed awareness of alternatives to the established body of theoretical tenets; whereas in scientifically oriented cultures, such an awareness is highly developed." . . . And it is here, when we turn from questions about the content and logic of traditional and scientific explanation to the social contexts in which those theories are constructed and mobilized, that Horton's account begins to seem less adequate. . . .

Remember the answer the priest gave to the question about the gold dust . . . "We do it because the ancestors did it." In the open society this will no longer do as a reason. The early modern natural scientists, the natural philosophers of the Renaissance, stressed often the unreasonableness of appeals to authority. And if modern scholarship suggests that they overstressed the extent to which their predecessors were bound by a hidebound traditionalism, it is still true that there is a difference—if only in degree—in the extent to which modernity celebrates distance from our predecessors, while the traditional world celebrates cognitive continuity.

Now Horton's account of the sense in which the traditional worldview is closed has—rightly—been challenged. The complexities of war and trade, dominance and clientage, migration and diplomacy, in much of precolonial Africa are simply not consistent with the image of peoples unaware that there is a world elsewhere. . . .

It is also possible to find first-rate speculative thinkers in traditional societies whose individual openness is not to be denied. I think here of Ogotemmêli, whose cosmology Griaule has captured . . . and Barry Hallen has provided evidence from Nigerian sources of the existence, within African traditional modes of thought, of styles of reasoning that are open neither to Wiredu's stern strictures nor to Horton's milder ones. . . .[8] Horton's original stress on the "closed" nature of traditional modes of thought does look less adequate in the face of Africa's complex history of cultural exchanges and of Hallen's babalawo, or in the presence of the extraordinary metaphysical synthesis of the Dogon elder, Ogotemmêli. . . . In a recent book—written with the Nigerian philosopher J. O. Sodipo—Hallen insists on the presence among Yoruba doctors of theories of witchcraft rather different from those of their fellow countrymen.[9] Here, then, among doctors, speculation inconsistent with ordinary folk belief occurs. . . .

Horton has recently come—in response, in part, to Hallen's critique—to speak not of the closedness of traditional belief systems but, borrowing a term from Wole Soyinka, of their being "accommodative." He discusses work by students of Evans-Pritchard that not only addresses the kind of static body of belief that is captured in Evans-Pritchard's picture of the Azande thought world but also stresses the dynamic and—as Horton admits—"open" way in which they "devise explanations for novel elements in . . . experience," and "their capacity to borrow, re-work and integrate alien ideas in the course of elaborating such explanations." "Indeed" he continues, "it is this 'open-ness' that has given the traditional cosmologies such tremendous durability in the face of immense changes that the 20th century has brought to the African scene." Horton then contrasts this accommodative style with the "adversary" style of scientific theory, which is characterized by the way in which the main stimulus to change of belief is not "novel experience but rival theory."[10]

And it seems to me that this change from the Popperian terminology of "open" and "closed" allows Horton to capture something important about the difference between traditional religion and science; something to do not with individual cognitive strategies but with social ones. If we want to understand the significance of social organization in differentiating traditional religion and natural science, we can do no better than to begin with those of Evans-Pritchard's answers to the question why the Azande do not see the falsity of their magic beliefs that mention social facts about the organization of those beliefs.

Evans-Pritchard wrote:

> Scepticism, far from being smothered, is recognized, even inculcated. But it is only about certain medicines and certain magicians. By contrast it tends to support other, medicines and other magicians. . . . Each man and each

8. Barry Hallen, "Robin Horton on Critical Philosophy and Traditional Thought." . . . Wiredu, of course, does not deny the existence of skeptics in traditional cultures. See pp. 20–21, 37, 143 of *Philosophy and an African Culture* (London: Cambridge University Press, 1980).

9. Barry Hallen and J. Sodipo, *Knowledge, Belief and Witchcraft: Analytic Experiments in African Philosophy* (London: Ethnographica, 1986)—summarized here in Chapter 9.

10. This work is in the paper, "Traditional Thought and the Emerging African Philosophy Department: A Reply to Dr. Hallen," unpublished manuscript.

kinship group acts without cognizance of the actions of others. People do not pool their ritual experiences. . . . They are not experimentally inclined. . . . Not being experimentally inclined, they do not test the efficacy of their medicines.[11]

And, he added, "Zande beliefs are generally vaguely formulated. A belief, to be easily contradicted by experience . . . must be clearly shared and intellectually developed."[12]

Whatever the practices of imperfect scientists are actually like, none of these things is supposed to be true of natural science. In our official picture of the sciences, skepticism is encouraged even about foundational questions—indeed, that is where the best students are supposed to be directed. . . . The scientific community is experimentally inclined, and, of course, scientific theory is formulated as precisely as possible in order that those experiments can be carried out in a controlled fashion. . . . [S]cience *is*, crucially, adversarial, and the norms of publication and reproducibility of results, even though only imperfectly adhered to, are explicitly intended to lay theories and experimental claims open to attack by one's peers, and thus make competition from the adventurous "young Turk" possible.

More important than the hugely oversimplified contrast between an experimental,

skeptical, science and an unexperimental, "dogmatic" traditional mode of thought is the difference in images of knowledge that are represented in the differences in the social organization of inquiry in modern as opposed to "traditional" societies. Scientists, like the rest of us, hold onto theories longer than they may be entitled to; suppress, unconsciously or half consciously, evidence they do not know how to handle; lie a little. In precolonial societies there were, we can be sure, individual doubters who kept their own counsel, resisters against the local dogma. But what is interesting about modern modes of theorizing is that they are organized around an image of constant change: we expect new theories, we reward and encourage the search for them, we believe that today's best theories will be revised beyond recognition if the enterprise of science survives. My ancestors in Asante never organized a specialized activity that was based around this thought. They knew that some people know more than others, and that there are things to be found out. But they do not seem to have thought it necessary to invest social effort in working out new theories of how the world works, not for some practical end (this they did constantly) but, as we say, for its own sake.

The differences between traditional religious theory and the theories of the sciences reside in the social organization of inquiry, as a systematic business, and it is differences in social organization that account, I think, both for the difference we feel in the character of natural scientific and traditional religious theory—they are products of different kinds of social process—and for the spectacular expansion of the domain of successful prediction and control, an expansion that characterizes natural science but is notably absent in traditional society. Experimentation, the publication and reproduction of results, the systematic development of alternative theories in precise terms, all these ideals, however imperfectly they are realized in scientific practice, are intelligible only in an organized social enterprise of knowledge.

But what can have prompted this radically different approach to knowledge? Why have the practitioners of traditional religion, even the

---

11. This is not to say that they do not have the concepts necessary to understand the idea of an experiment, merely to say that they are not interested in disinterested experimentation simply to find out how things work. For the Azande are very aware, for example, that an oracle needs to be run carefully if it is to be reliable. They therefore test its reliability on every occasion of its use. There are usually two tests: *bambata sima* and *gingo;* the first and second tests. Generally, in the first test, the question is asked so the death of a chicken means yes and in the second so that death means no; but it may be the other way round. Inconsistent results invalidate the procedure. The Azande also have a way of confirming that an oracle is not working; namely to ask it a question to which they already know the answer. Such failures can be explained by one of the many obstacles to an oracle's functioning properly: breach of taboo; witchcraft; the fact that the benge poison used in the oracle has been "spoiled" (as the Azande believe) because it has been near a menstruating woman.

12. Evans-Pritchard, *Witchcraft, Oracles and Magic and Magic among the Azande,* 202–4.

priests, who are the professionals, never developed the organized "adversarial" methods of the sciences? There are, no doubt, many historical sources. A few, familiar suggestions strike one immediately.

Social mobility leads to political individualism, of a kind that is rare in the traditional polity; political individualism allows cognitive authority to shift, also, from priest to king to commoner; and social mobility is a feature of industrial societies.

Or, in traditional societies, accommodating conflicting theoretical views is part of the general process of accommodation necessary for those who are bound to each other as neighbors for life. . . . In Ghana, but not in America, it is impolite to disagree, to argue, to confute. And this accommodating approach to conversation is part of the same range of attitudes that leads to theoretical accommodations. . . .

[I]t seems to me that there is one other fundamental difference between traditional West African culture and the culture of the industrial world, and that it plays a fundamental role in explaining why the adversarial style never established itself in West Africa. And it is that these cultures were largely nonliterate.

Now literacy has, as Jack Goody has pointed out in his influential book *The Domestication of the Savage Mind,* important consequences; among them is the fact that it permits a kind of consistency that oral culture cannot and does not demand. Write down a sentence and it is there,

in principle, forever; that means that if you write down another sentence inconsistent with it, you can be caught out. It is this fact that is at the root of the possibility of the adversarial style. How often have we seen Perry Mason—on television in Ghana or the United States or England (for television, at least, there is only one world)—ask the stenographer to read back from the record? In the traditional culture the answer can only be: "What record?" In the absence of written records, it is not possible to compare the ancestors' theories in their actual words with ours; nor, given the limitations of quantity imposed by oral transmission, do we have a detailed knowledge of what those theories were. We know more about the thought of Isaac Newton on one or two subjects than we know about the entire population of his Asante contemporaries.

The accommodative style is possible because orality makes it hard to discover discrepancies. And so it is possible to have an image of knowledge as unchanging lore, handed down from the ancestors. It is no wonder, with this image of knowledge, that there is no systematic research: nobody need ever notice that the way that traditional theory is used requires inconsistent interpretations. It is literacy that makes possible the precise formulation of questions that we have just noticed as one of the characteristics of scientific theory, and it is precise formulation that points up inconsistency. This explanation, which we owe to Horton, is surely very plausible. . . .

Visit the companion Web site for chapter specific quizzes, suggestions for further reading, video ideas, and other resources to assess and expand your understanding of the chapter material. Go to http://philosophy.wadsworth.com and select the companion Web site for *Voices of Wisdom.*

 You can access many additional readings at the Info Trac-College Edition Web site. To find the following suggested articles do a keyword search with the article title. Use the passcode that was packaged with your new book to enter the site at http://www.Infotrac-college.com/Wadsworth/. Here is a sampling.

G. G. Pinter and Vera Pinter, "From Epistemology to Rational Science Policy: Popper versus Kuhn." *Perspectives in Biology and Medicine.* Winter 1998 v41 n2 p291(8), A20585607.

Fritz Rohrlich, "Cognitive Scientific Realism." *Philosophy of Science,* June 2001 v68 i2 p185, A76134414.

William F. Brewer and Bruce L. Lambert, "The Theory-Ladenness of Observation and the Theory-Ladenness of the Rest of the Scientific Process." *Philosophy of Science,* September 2001 v68 i3 pS176, A79515269.

Kristen Intemann, "Science and Values: Are Value Judgments Always Irrelevant to the Justification of Scientific Claims?" *Philosophy of Science* September 2001 v68 i3 pS506, A79515294.

Barbara Friedberg, "Francis Bacon and the True Ends of Skepticism." *Skeptical Inquirer,* November 2000 v24 i6 p32, A66496164.

Tad Clements, "Are Science and Religion Compatible?" *Free Inquiry,* Summer 2000 v20 i3 p58, A64263122.

Kristin S. Shrader-Frechette, "Science, Environmental Risk Assessment, and the Frame Problem." *BioScience,* September 1994 v44 n8 p548(4), A16075441.

Harold I. Brown, "A Theory-Laden Observation Can Test the Theory." *The British Journal for the Philosophy of Science,* September 1993 v44 n3 p555(5), A8525417.

Part 4

Metaphysics

Chapter 8

What Is Really Real?

> If the doors of perception were cleansed everything would appear to man as it is, infinite.
>
> WILLIAM BLAKE

8.1 Introduction

HAVE YOU EVER WONDERED if what you *think* is real is *actually* real? Someone has undoubtedly asked you, with a smile, "If a tree falls in a forest and no one is there, does it make a sound?" What do you think? Have you ever thought about the question, "Why is there something rather than nothing?" Have you ever thought, "Is the world we experience real or an illusion?" Have you ever been puzzled by the question, "What are time and space?" Do you think something can come from nothing? What are ideas made of? Is nature all there is, or is there some sort of supernatural reality?

If you have wondered about these sorts of questions, you have been concerned with what philosophers call *metaphysics.* Metaphysics has to do with the construction and criticism of theories about what is truly real. Metaphysics deals with abstract issues, but its concerns arise out of everyday experiences. For example, you may have been traveling down a road and seen, ahead on the highway, what looked like an animal; but when you got closer, you discovered that it was really a bush. It appeared to be one thing and turned out to be another. The question about what is *genuinely or really* real presupposes a distinction between appearance and reality. Metaphysics generalizes that distinction and asks, "If some things in the world appear to be real but turn out not to be, what about the world itself? Is the universe appearance or reality?"

Some philosophers maintain that the chief part of metaphysics is what they call **ontology** (literally, "the study of being"). One ontological concern has to do with the *kinds* of things that exist. For example, try to categorize the items in the following list into two general groups, material and immaterial:

chairs	trees	cats	ideas
seeing	anger	stones	atoms
God	space	time	you

Did you have a hard time sorting these? One problem is that some things seem to be a mixture of the material and the immaterial. For example, you have a body, which is material, but you also have a mind, which some would claim to be immaterial. Another problem has to do with definitions. What do we mean by *material* and *immaterial?* How can we classify things until we know how to distinguish between them?

This last question leads us directly into a second concern of ontology, namely the *definition* of different kinds of being. For example, some philosophers have argued that material beings can be distinguished from immaterial beings according to the following characteristics:

MATERIAL	IMMATERIAL
spatial	nonspatial
public	private
mechanical	teleological

According to this list, material things like chairs take up space (hence are spatial), but immaterial things like ideas do not take up space (hence are nonspatial). It makes good sense to ask how wide a chair is, but does it make any sense to ask how wide my *idea* of a chair is? Material things are also public in the sense that they can be viewed by different people. I can see a chair or a tree, and so can you. However, I can not see your *idea* of a chair or a tree. Your idea is private; it is not open to public inspection. Finally, material objects are causally determined in a purely **mechanistic** way. They are nonintentional—that is, they behave not according to purposes but according to the laws of physics. That chair is in the corner of the room not because it *wants* to be there, but because it was *placed* there by external forces. But what about you? Is your behavior purely mechanistic (machinelike)? Or is your behavior teleological, that is, governed by goals and purposes? Are you in the corner of the room because of external forces, or are you there because you want to leave and the door is located there?

A third concern of ontology has to do with what is *ultimately* real. Once we have discovered all the kinds of beings that seem to exist and have adequately defined each of the kinds, which if any of these kinds are really real? Is matter the really real? If you answer yes, you would be an advocate of materialism. **Materialism** is the metaphysical theory that matter is truly real and immaterial things are not. Note that we should not confuse materialism with physical science. Physical science is clearly concerned with matter and the study of physical things. The claim, however, that *only* physical things are real is not a scientific claim, it is a metaphysical claim. It is a claim about the *whole* of reality.

Some of you might be inclined to argue that being, or reality, is fundamentally immaterial. One widespread philosophical version of this theory is called idealism. The metaphysical theory of **idealism** asserts that ideas (in the broad sense of thoughts, concepts, minds) are ultimately real. Do not confuse idealism as a metaphysical doctrine with idealism as a moral theory about ideals. Idealism, as I am using that term here, has to do with ideas, not ideals.

One major problem with idealism, as you might expect, is to explain our experience of things that seem both material and real. The chair I am sitting on seems physical, solid, and real to me, and I certainly hope it is. Could it be that this chair is nothing more than a bundle of sensations or ideas? If materialism needs to explain the mental in terms of the physical, idealism must explain the physical in terms of the mental.

Maybe you want to suggest that both these sorts of things (the material and the immaterial) are genuinely real. This dualistic approach seems reasonable. It certainly escapes the problems of explaining away chairs, bodies, minds, and ideas. **Dualism** is the theory that reality is both material and immaterial. My body is real, and the material chair it is sitting on is real (what a relief), but my mind and its ideas are also real (that's good to know, too). However, if reality is both material and immaterial, how are the two related? How, for example, are our minds related to our brains? The major problem of dualism is to relate the material and the immaterial.

Those who argue that being, or reality, is fundamentally of one nature avoid this problem. They are called monists, and their theory (in contrast to dualism) is called monism. **Monism** holds that there is a single reality. Notice that a monist can be either a materialist or an idealist. The contrast here is between monism and dualism, not between materialism and idealism.

Discussions of dualism versus monism soon lead to the **problem of the one and the many.** Is there one reality, or are there many different real things that cannot be reduced to a single thing? **Pluralism** is the position that there are many different real things. This question of one or many, along with the question about what is really real, constitute two fundamental metaphysical problems.

Metaphysics may seem abstract and totally unrelated to real world problems. What difference does it make whether reality is one undivided whole or is made up of many parts? Although it may not seem like it, metaphysical assumptions (largely unexamined and often unconscious) influence our lives on a daily basis. They also play a vital role in moral debates. For example, arguments about stem cell research and abortion depend on a variety of metaphysical ideas about the existence or nonexistence of souls and the nature of human beings. Debates about environmental policies rely on metaphysical assumptions about individuals, communities, ecosystems, and so forth. How we treat others with whom we share this planet depends, in part, on metaphysical assumptions about how all things are related (or not related). Although some philosophers have argued that metaphysical speculation is a meaningless activity because we cannot discover any solid, verifiable answers to metaphysical questions about the nature of reality, most philosophers realize that we cannot escape thinking about what is really real.

8.2 The Dao

The name "Daoism" (Wade-Giles spelling is Taoism) was first coined by Han scholars to refer to the philosophy developed by Laozi. As the name implies, central to this philosophical view is the notion of **Dao,** often translated as the "way of nature." Laozi is the alleged author of a book popularly known as the *Dao De Jing* (Wade-Giles *Tao Te Ching*).

We have legends about Laozi and when he lived, but we have very little firm historical information. According to tradition he was a contemporary of Confucius

(551–479 BCE), but most scholars have placed his book later, during the Warring States Period (403–221 BCE).

The *Dao De Jing* is a classic of world literature. Each time you come back to it, you will find something new and profound. However, the first time you read it you are likely to find it obscure. This is why I have included the translator's comments along with the translation.

You may find it obscure for a variety of reasons. First, it is written in a poetic and cryptic style. Poetry employs symbols and metaphors, uses paradoxes and unexpected contrasts in order to stimulate thought. It thrives on ambiguity. Second, this is a translation from ancient Chinese, and our English words often do not convey the richness of the Chinese concepts. Third, although 80 percent of the book deals with ethics (how one should live) and politics (what is the best way to govern), the rest deals with difficult metaphysical issues about the basic principles of reality, and it is these metaphysical portions of the text that are included here.

According to Aristotelian logic, a good definition should be positive and not negative. You should state what something is, not what it is not. Telling you that a pencil is "not a cat" does not help much if you do not know what a pencil is. However, what if there are realities that transcend the definitional abilities of human language? In such cases (and the *Dao* is such a case), the best we might hope for are negative indications, analogies, metaphors, and symbols.

Daoism has been characterized as a process ontology in contrast to a substance ontology. **Process ontologies** emphasize change and becoming as fundamentally real. In addition, they often emphasize the interrelatedness of an everflowing reality in which nothing is totally independent. **Substance ontologies** emphasize permanence and unchanging being as fundamentally real. Reality, a substantialist asserts, is made up of one or more substances that can exist independently.

Before you plunge into this bewildering, fascinating, and thought-provoking book about the *Dao*, it may be helpful to say something about some of the key concepts of Daoism. Let us begin with the word *Dao* itself.

The word *Dao* means "road" or "way" in Chinese. Before Laozi, the word had been used by the Confucians to refer to the way of humans, that is, the proper way that human beings ought to live. Laozi extends the term and gives it a cosmic and metaphysical meaning (at least according to some interpreters). It now becomes the way of the universe and the source of all reality. Reality consists of all the sorts of things we think exist (which we can classify as being) as well as what we take to be nonexistent (which we can classify as nonbeing). Already we encounter something odd from a traditional Western perspective. How can the nonexistent be real? Where we tend to identify the real with what exists (being) and the unreal with what does not (nonbeing), the Daoist distinguishes between reality and existence so that both the existent and nonexistent can be classified as real.

The *Dao*, because it is the source of all reality, is not *a* thing (a being or a substance). It is beyond distinctions and hence beyond the definitional powers of language. To define is to distinguish. However, how do you define that which is the source of all distinctions? So the *Dao* is called "the nameless," that is, the indefinable.

This negative designation suggests that the *Dao* is closer to nonbeing than to being, and indeed, Daoists say that the *Dao* is nonbeing. It is, however, not nonbeing in the Western sense of total nothingness. It is nonbeing in the sense of "no-thingness."

It is real, but not *a* thing. Laozi compares it to a *positive emptiness,* that is, an emptiness (like the hollow of a bowl) that makes being (the usefulness of the bowl) possible. This notion of nonbeing as positive and creative is a unique insight of the *Dao De Jing.* For the Greeks, and much of the Western tradition since the Greeks, something cannot come from nothing. Nothing is absolute nothingness. It is a totally negative void. Laozi sees things differently. Something *can* come from nothing; indeed, this whole marvelous universe did come from the *no-thing* that is the way of *all things.*

De can be translated as "virtue," "power," or "excellence," so the title of Laozi's mind-expanding poem has been translated as "The Book of the Way and Its Power." It is a book (*jing*) about the excellence or power of the *Dao. De* is sometimes thought of as the *Dao* itself viewed from the perspective of individual things. The excellence (perfection, power) of each thing is called its *de,* and this is the *Dao* manifesting itself on the individual level. To actualize the potential of one's nature in an excellent way is to exhibit *de.* For humans (as for all natural things), this actualization occurs by living in accord with the *Dao.*

Wuwei literally means "no action" and refers to the manner in which the *Dao* acts. The way that is no-thing acts by not acting. Now there is a bit of philosophy on which to chew! Let me repeat it. The way that is no-thing acts by not acting. This rather mysterious claim can be elucidated somewhat by looking at the various levels of meaning of *wuwei.* Laozi provides advice to rulers in his book. He tells them to govern according to *wuwei.* In this political context, *wuwei* means that rulers should not interfere unnecessarily in the lives of the people. In other words, the less government, the better. On a moral level, *wuwei* means acting unselfishly and spontaneously, free of all selfish attachment to the consequences of our actions. And on the cosmic level, *wuwei* refers to the way nature acts—spontaneously, freely, and naturally. There is nothing artificial in natural events. Nature does not calculate how to act, it just acts.

Finally, we need to speak of the Daoist use of the **yin/yang** concept. The Daoists adopted this concept to characterize the universe that stems from the *Dao. Yin* and *yang* stand for complementary opposites: *yin* for all things that manifest a passive or receptive force; *yang* for all things that manifest an active or aggressive force. The passive and the active are complementary opposites; you cannot have one without the other.

There is a little bit of *yang* in *yin* and a little bit of *yin* in *yang.* In time, opposites will change into each other. Hence, the universe is essentially a vast, harmonious process. This can be illustrated by the seasonal cycle. Winter is the most *yin* season because it is cold and dark, and life processes are slow. However, winter contains an element of *yang,* which expands over time until we reach spring with its warmth, light, and flourishing life. *Yang* continues to expand and reaches its zenith in summer. Yet summer contains an element of *yin,* which expands into fall and eventually winter again. Such is the operation of *Dao* by means of *yin* and *yang.*

So the *Dao,* which is not a thing, acts naturally, freely, spontaneously, unselfishly, without force, thereby producing and sustaining a universe of harmonious processes in such a way that it is possible for each individual thing to manifest its own excellence. This is the way of nature, the way of genuine reality. I hope this profound vision of reality whets your appetite for more. Read on, and as you do, see if you can answer the following questions.

Reading Questions

1. What does it mean to say that the *Dao* (*Tao*) is nameless, and why do you think it is "named" that?
2. What is the main idea that Chapter 2 in the *Dao* conveys about the nature of opposites?
3. How is it possible for the sage (wise person) to act without acting and teach without speaking?
4. What do you think the comparison between the *Dao* and a bowl implies about the relationship between the substance of a thing and its function?
5. Analogies are drawn between the *Dao* and a valley, a female, water, the hub of a wheel, a utensil, and a room. What do these analogies tell us about the *Dao*?
6. If the *Dao* is invisible, inaudible, and formless, how can it be known?
7. How does the *Dao* "run" the universe?
8. What does it mean to say that "reversion is the action of *Dao*"?
9. Is Daoist metaphysics a materialism, idealism, dualism, monism, or something that these categories fail to express adequately? Provide evidence to support your answer.

Dao De Jing

LAOZI

1

The Tao that can be told of is not the eternal Tao;
The name that can be named is not the eternal
*   name.*
The Nameless is the origin of Heaven and Earth;
The Named is the mother of all things.

Therefore let there always be non-being, so we may
*   see their subtlety,*
And let there always be being, so we may see their
*   outcome.*
The two are the same,
But after they are produced, they have different
*   names.*
They both may be called deep and profound.
Deeper and more profound,
The door of all subtleties!

COMMENT

This is the most important of all chapters, for in one stroke the basic characteristics of Tao as the eternal, the nameless, the source, and the substance of all things are explicitly or implicitly affirmed. It is no wonder the opening sentences are among the most often quoted or even chanted sayings in Chinese.

The key Taoist concepts of the named and the nameless are also introduced here. The concept of name is common to all ancient Chinese philosophical schools, but Taoism is unique in this respect. Most schools insist on the correspondence of names and actualities and accept names as necessary and good; Taoism, on the contrary, rejects names in favor of the nameless. This, among other things, shows its radical and unique character. To Lao Tzu, Tao is nameless and is the simplicity without names; when names arise, that is, when the simple oneness of Tao is split up into individual things with names, it is time to stop.

The cardinal ideas of being and non-being are also important here, for in Taoism the nameless (*wu-ming*) is equivalent to non-being and the named (*yu-ming*) is equivalent to being. For this reason, when he comments on the saying about the named and the nameless, Wang Pi says, "All being originated in non-being." As students of Chinese thought well know, the ideas of being and non-being have been dominant throughout the history of Chinese philosophy. They are central concepts in Neo-Taoism, Chinese Buddhism, and also Neo-Confucianism. It was the importance of these concepts, no doubt, that led the Neo-Confucianist Wang An-shih to deviate from tradition and punctuate the phrases "always be no desires" and "always be desires" to read "Let there always be non-being, so we may . . . ," and "Let there always be being, so we may. . . ."

Wang's punctuation not only underlines the importance of these ideas; it also shows the new metaphysical interest in Neo-Confucianism. Confucianism had been fundamentally ethical in tradition, but under the impact of Buddhist and Taoist metaphysics, the Neo-Confucianists developed Confucianism along metaphysical lines. In this case, in substituting the ideas of being and non-being for the ideas of having desires and having no desires, Wang shows a greater recognition of the philosophical content of the *Lao Tzu,* as it deserves.

2

> When the people of the world all know beauty as
>   beauty,
> There arises the recognition of ugliness.
> When they all know the good as good,
> There arises the recognition of evil.
> Therefore:
>   Being and non-being produce each other;
>   Difficult and easy complete each other;
>   Long and short contrast each other;
>   High and low distinguish each other;
>   Sound and voice harmonize each other;
>   Front and behind accompany each other.
>
>   Therefore the sage manages affairs without
>   action
>   And spreads doctrines without words.
>   All things arise, and he does not turn away
>   from them.

> He produces them but does not take possession
>   of them.
> He acts but does not rely on his own ability.
> He accomplishes his task but does not claim credit
>   for it.
> It is precisely because he does not claim credit
>   that his
> accomplishment remains with him.

COMMENT

That everything has its opposite, and that these opposites are the mutual causations of each other, form a basic part of Chuang Tzu's philosophy and later Chinese philosophy. It is important to note that opposites are here presented not as irreconcilable conflicts but as complements. The traditional Chinese ideal that opposites are to be synthesized and harmonized can be said to have originated with Lao Tzu.

The idea of teaching without words anticipated the Buddhist tradition of silent transmission of the mystic doctrine, especially in the Zen (Ch'an) school. This is diametrically opposed to the Confucian ideal, according to which a superior man acts and thus "becomes the model of the world," and speaks and thus "becomes the pattern for the world." It is true that Confucianists say that a superior man "is truthful without any words," but they would never regard silence itself as a virtue. . . .

4

> Tao is empty (like a bowl).
>   It may be used but its capacity is never exhausted.
> It is bottomless, perhaps the ancestor of all things.
> It blunts its sharpness,
> It unties its tangles.
> It softens its light.
> It becomes one with the dusty world.
> Deep and still, it appears to exist forever.
> I do not know whose son it is.
> It seems to have existed before the Lord.

COMMENT

This chapter, on the substance and function of Tao, shows clearly that in Taoism function is no less important than substance. Substance is further described in chapters 14 and 21, but here, as in chapters 11 and 45, function (*yung*, also meaning "use") is regarded with equal respect. There is no deprecation of phenomena, as is the case with certain Buddhist schools. To describe the world as dusty may suggest a lack of enthusiasm for it; indeed both Buddhism and later Taoism employ the word "dust" to symbolize the dirty world from which we should escape. It is significant to note, however, that Taoism in its true sense calls for identification with, not escape from, such a world. . . .

6

The spirit of the valley never dies.
   It is called the subtle and profound female.
The gate of the subtle and profound female
   Is the root of Heaven and Earth.
It is continuous, and seems to be always existing.
Use it and you will never wear it out.

COMMENT

The valley and the female, like the infant and water, are Lao Tzu's favorite symbols for Tao. The symbol of the valley is employed again and again. There is nothing mysterious about it or its spirit; it simply stands for vacuity, vastness, openness, all-inclusiveness, and lowliness or humility, all of which are outstanding characteristics of Tao. This is the interpretation of Wang Pi, and commentators, with only a few exceptions, have followed him. To understand the "continuous" operation as breathing, or the valley as the belly or the Void, and then to interpret the whole passage as one on the yoga technique of breathing, or to single out the characteristic of stillness of the valley and then to present it as an evidence of Taoist quietism, is to fail to interpret the passages in the context of the whole. These interpretations are not supported by the symbolic meaning of the valley elsewhere in the book.

The spirit of the chapter is far from quietism. Instead, it involves the idea of natural transformation and continuous creation. As Chu Hsi has said, "The valley is vacuous. As sound reaches it,

it echoes. This is the spontaneity of spiritual transformation. To be subtle and profound means to be wonderful. The female is one who receives something and produces things. This is a most wonderful principle and it has the meaning of production and reproduction." . . .

8

The best (man)[1] *is like water.*
   Water is good; it benefits all things and does not
      compete with them.
It dwells in (lowly) places that all disdain.
This is why it is so near to Tao.
(The best man) in his dwelling loves the earth.
In his heart, he loves what is profound.
In his associations, he loves humanity.
In his words, he loves faithfulness.
In government, he loves order.
In handling affairs, he loves competence.
In his activities, he loves timeliness.
It is because he does not compete that he is without
   reproach.

COMMENT

Water is perhaps the most outstanding among Lao Tzu's symbols for Tao. The emphasis of the symbolism is ethical rather than metaphysical or religious. It is interesting to note that, while early Indian philosophers associated water with creation and the Greek philosophers looked upon it as a natural phenomenon, ancient Chinese philosophers, whether Lao Tzu or Confucius, preferred to learn moral lessons from it. Broadly speaking, Western thought, derived chiefly from

---

1. Most commentators and translators have understood the Chinese phrase literally as the highest good, but some commentators and translators, including Lin Yutang, Cheng Lin, and Bynner, have followed Wang Pi and taken the phrase to mean the best man. Both interpretations are possible. The former interpretation has a parallel in chapter 38, which talks about the highest virtue, while the latter has a parallel in chapter 17, where both Wang Pi and Ho-shang Kung interpret "the best" to mean the best ruler. I have followed Wang Pi, not only because his commentary on the text is the oldest and most reliable, but also because the *Lao Tzu* deals with man's way of life more than abstract ideas.

the Greeks, has been largely interested in meta-physical and scientific problems, Indian thought largely interested in religious problems, and Chinese thought largely interested in moral problems. It is not too much to say that these different approaches to water characterize the Western, the Indian, and the Chinese systems of thought. . . .

11

> *Thirty spokes are united around the hub to make a*
> *   wheel,*
> *   But it is on its non-being that the utility of the*
> *   carriage depends.*
> *Clay is molded to form a utensil,*
> *   But it is on its non-being that the utility of the*
> *   utensil depends.*
> *Doors and windows are cut out to make a room,*
> *   But it is on its non-being that the utility of the*
> *   room depends.*
> *Therefore turn being into advantage, and turn*
> *   non-being into utility.*

COMMENT

Nowhere else in Chinese philosophy is the concept of non-being more strongly emphasized. This chapter alone should dispel any idea that Taoism is negativistic, for non-being—the hole in the hub, the hollowness of a utensil, the empty space in the room—is here conceived not as nothingness but as something useful and advantageous.

The Taoist interest in non-being has counteracted the positivistic tendency in certain Chinese philosophical schools, especially the Legalist and Confucian, which often overlook what seems to be nonexistent. It has prepared the Chinese mind for the acceptance of the Buddhist doctrine of Emptiness, although neither the Taoist concept of non-being nor that of vacuity is identical with that of the Buddhist Void. In addition, it was because of the Taoist insistence on the positive value of non-being that empty space has been utilized as a constructive factor in Chinese landscape painting. In this greatest art of China, space is used to combine the various elements into an organic whole and to provide a setting in which the onlooker's imagination may work. By the same

token, much is left unsaid in Chinese poetry, for the reader must play a creative role to bring the poetic idea into full realization. The Zen Buddhists have developed to the fullest the themes that real existence is found in the nonexistent and that true words are spoken in silence, but the origin of these themes must be traced to early Taoism. . . .

14

> *We look at it and do not see it;*
> *   Its name is The Invisible.*
> *We listen to it and do not hear it;*
> *   Its name is The Inaudible.*
> *We touch it and do not find it;*
> *   Its name is The Subtle (formless).*
>
> *These three cannot be further inquired into,*
> *And hence merge into one.*
> *Going up high, it is not bright, and coming down*
> *   low, it is not dark.*
> *Infinite and boundless, it cannot be given any name;*
> *It reverts to nothingness.*
> *This is called shape without shape,*
> *Form without objects.*
> *It is The Vague and Elusive.*
> *Meet it and you will not see its head.*
> *Follow it and you will not see its back.*
> *Hold on to the Tao of old in order to master the*
> *   things of the present.*
> *From this one may know the primeval beginning (of*
> *   the universe).*
> *This is called the bond[2] of Tao.*

COMMENT

Subtlety is an important characteristic of Tao and is more important than its manifestations. The Confucianists, on the other hand, emphasize manifestation. There is nothing more manifest than the hidden (subtle), they say, and "a man who knows that the subtle will be manifested can enter into virtue." The Buddhists and Neo-Confucianists eventually achieved a synthesis, saying that "there is no distinction between the manifest and the hidden."

2. *Chi,* literally, "a thread," denotes tradition, discipline, principle, order, essence, etc. Generally it means the system, principle, or continuity that binds things together.

To describe reality in terms of the invisible, the inaudible, and the subtle is an attempt to describe it in terms of non-being. Because the three Chinese words are pronounced *i, hsi,* and *wei,* respectively, they have been likened to *Jod, Heh, Vav,* indicating the name Jehovah, and to the Hindu god Ishvara, but any similarity is purely accidental. The threefold description does not suggest any idea of trinity either. Basically, Taoist philosophy is naturalistic, if not atheistic, and any idea of a god is alien to it. . . .

16

Attain complete vacuity.
Maintain steadfast quietude.

All things come into being,
And I see thereby their return.
All things flourish,
But each one returns to its root.
This return to its root means tranquillity.
It is called returning to its destiny.
To return to destiny is called the eternal (Tao).
To know the eternal is called enlightenment.
Not to know the eternal is to act blindly to result in
  disaster.
He who knows the eternal is all-embracing.
Being all-embracing, he is impartial.
Being impartial, he is kingly (universal).
Being kingly, he is one with Nature.
Being one with Nature, he is in accord with Tao.
Being in accord with Tao, he is everlasting
And is free from danger throughout his lifetime.

COMMENT

The central idea here is returning to the root, which is to be achieved through tranquillity. Generally speaking, in Taoist philosophy Tao is revealed most fully through tranquillity rather than activity. Under its influence, Wang Pi has commented on the hexagram *fu* (to return) in the *Book of Changes* in the same light. He says, "Although Heaven and Earth are vast, possessing the myriad things in abundance, where thunder moves and winds circulate, and while there is an infinite variety of changes and transformations, yet its original [substance] is absolutely quiet and perfect non-being. Therefore only with the cessation of activities within Earth can the mind of Heaven and Earth be revealed."

This Taoistic position is directly opposed by the Neo-Confucianists, who insist that the mind of Heaven and Earth is to be seen in a state of activity. As Ch'eng I says, "Former scholars all said that only in a state of tranquillity can the mind of Heaven and Earth be seen. They did not realize that the mind of Heaven and Earth is found in the beginning of activity." . . .

22

To yield is to be preserved whole.
To be bent is to become straight.
To be empty is to be full.
To be worn out is to be renewed.
To have little is to possess.
To have plenty is to be perplexed.
Therefore the sage embraces the One
And becomes the model of the world.
He does not show himself; therefore he is luminous.
He does not justify himself; therefore he becomes
  prominent.
He does not boast of himself; therefore he is given
  credit.
He does not brag; therefore he can endure for long.

It is precisely because he does not compete that the
  world cannot compete with him.
Is the ancient saying, "To yield is to be preserved
  whole," empty words?
Truly he will be preserved and (prominence and
  credit) will come to him.

COMMENT

Taoism seems to be advocating a negative morality. In this respect, it is not much different from the Christian doctrine taught in the Sermon on the Mount, which extols meekness, poverty, and so forth. Whatever negativism there may seem to be, it pertains to method only; the objective is entirely positive. . . .

25

There was something undifferentiated and yet
  complete,
Which existed before heaven and earth.

Soundless and formless, it depends on nothing and
does not change.
It operates everywhere and is free from danger.
It may be considered the mother of the universe.
I do not know its name; I call it Tao.
If forced to give it a name, I shall call it Great.
Now being great means functioning everywhere.
Functioning everywhere means far-reaching.
Being far-reaching means returning to the original
point.

Therefore Tao is great.
Heaven is great.
Earth is great.
And the king³ is also great.
There are four great things in the universe, and the
king is one of them.
Man models himself after Earth.
Earth models itself after Heaven.
Heaven models itself after Tao.
And Tao models itself after Nature.

COMMENT

Taoist cosmology is outlined here simply but clearly. In the beginning there is something undifferentiated, which is forever operating; it produces heaven and earth and then all things. In essence this cosmology is strikingly similar to that of the *Book of Changes*. In the system of Change, the Great Ultimate produces the Two Modes (yin and yang), which in turn produce all things. We don't know to what extent Taoist thought has influenced the *Book of Changes,* which the Confucians have attributed to their ancient sages, chiefly Confucius. At any rate, this naturalistic philosophy has always been prominent in Chinese thought, and later contributed substantially to the naturalistic pattern of Neo-Confucian cosmology, especially through Chou Tun-i. As will be noted, he has added the concept of the Non-ultimate to the philosophy of the *Book of Changes* in order better to explain the originally

3. The Fu I and Fan Ying-yüan texts have "man" in place of "king." This substitution has been accepted by Hsi T'ung, Ma Hsü-lun, Ch'en Chu, Jen Chi-yü, and Ch'u Ta-kao. They have been influenced, undoubtedly, by the concept of the trinity of Heaven, Earth, and man, without realizing that the king is considered here as representative of men. Moreover, in chapters 16 and 39, Heaven, Earth, and the king are spoken of together.

undifferentiated. It is to be noted that the term "Non-ultimate" comes from the *Lao Tzu.* . . .

34

The Great Tao flows everywhere.
It may go left or right.
All things depend on it for life, and it does not turn
away from them.
It accomplishes its task, but does not claim credit
for it.
It clothes and feeds all things but does not claim to
be master over them.
Always without desires, it may be called The Small.
All things come to it and it does not master them; it
may be called The Great.
Therefore (the sage) never strives himself for the
great, and thereby the great is achieved.

COMMENT

In commenting on this chapter, Yen Fu says that the left and the right, the small and the great, are relative terms, and that Tao in its original substance transcends all these relative qualities. Of greater significance, however, is the paradoxical character of Tao. This character is affirmed more than once in the *Lao Tzu.* In Neo-Confucianism, principle is both immanent and transcendent, as is the Christian God. Ultimate being or reality is by nature paradoxical. . . .

37

Tao invariably takes no action, and yet there is
nothing left undone.
If kings and barons can keep it, all things will
transform spontaneously.
If, after transformation, they should desire to be
active,
I would restrain them with simplicity, which has
no name.
Simplicity, which has no name, is free of desires.
Being free of desires, it is tranquil.
And the world will be at peace of its own accord.

COMMENT

"Transform spontaneously" seems to be a passing remark here, but the idea became a key concept in the *Chuang Tzu* and later formed a key tenet in the Neo-Taoism of Kuo Hsiang. In the *Lao Tzu,* things transform themselves because Tao takes no action or leaves things alone. Chuang Tzu goes a step further, saying that everything is in incessant change and that is self-transformation. In his commentary on the *Chuang Tzu,* Kuo Hsiang goes even further, stressing that things transform themselves spontaneously because they are self-sufficient, and there is no Nature behind or outside of them. Nature, he says, is but a general name for things. . . .

40

Reversion is the action of Tao.
Weakness is the function of Tao.
All things in the world come from being.
And being comes from non-being.[4]

COMMENT

The doctrine of returning to the original is a prominent one in the *Lao Tzu.*[5] It has contributed in no small degree to the common Chinese cyclical concept, according to which the Chinese believe that both history and reality operate in cycles. . . .

4. Cf. chapter 1. This seems to contradict the saying, "Being and non-being produce each other," in chaper 2, But to produce means not to originate but to bring about.
5. The doctrine is also encountered in one sense or another in chapters 14, 16, 25, 28, 30, and 52. To D. C. Lau, returning to the root is not a cyclical process. According to him, the main doctrine of the *Lao Tzu* is the preservation of life, which is to be achieved through "abiding by softness." Softness is real strength, because when strength is allowed to reach its limit, it falls, whereas softness preserves itself. Thus opposites are neither relative nor paradoxical, and their process is not circular but a gradual development to the limit and then an inevitable and sudden decline. This idea may be implied in the *Lao Tzu* but there is no explicit passage to support Lau's theory. See his "The Treatment of Opposites in Lao Tzu," *Bulletin of the School of Oriental and African Studies,* XXI (1958), 349–50, 352–7.

42

Tao produced the One.
The One produced the two.
The two produced the three.
And the three produced the ten thousand things.
The ten thousand things carry the yin and embrace the yang, and through the blending of the material force they achieve harmony.

People hate to be children without parents, lonely people without spouses, or men without food to eat,
And yet kings and lords call themselves by these names.
Therefore it is often the case that things gain by losing and lose by gaining.

What others have taught, I teach also:
"Violent and fierce people do not die a natural death."
I shall make this the father of my teaching.

COMMENT

It is often understood that the One is the original material force of the Great Ultimate, the two are yin and yang, the three arc their blending with the original material force, and the ten thousand things are things carrying yin and embracing yang. The similarity of this process to that of the *Book of Changes,* in which the Great Ultimate produces the Two Forces (yin and yang) and then the myriad things, is amazing. The important point, however, is not the specific similarities, but the evolution from the simple to the complex. This theory is common to nearly all Chinese philosophical schools.

It should be noted that the evolution here, as in the *Book of Changes,* is natural. Production (*sheng*) is not personal creation or purposeful origination, but natural causation.

8.3 Platonic Dualism

We have encountered Plato and Socrates before (see Chapter 2). Plato (428–347 BCE) was Socrates' star pupil and one of the most creative and influential minds in the whole history of Western philosophy. He lived in Athens, founded the first "university" (called the Academy) in the West, and wrote a number of dialogues in which Socrates frequently appeared.

Alfred North Whitehead, a twentieth-century British-American philosopher, remarked that "all Western philosophy is but a footnote to Plato." This might be overstating the case for Plato's importance, but there can be little doubt that his ideas have influenced and still influence the thoughts and values of people who do not even know his name.

Do you believe in the immortality of the soul? Do you think that there is a material reality and an immaterial or spiritual reality and that the latter is more important than the former? Do you think logical and mathematical methods of reasoning are ideal models for arriving at truth? Do you believe that things have an essential nature? Do you believe you ought to control your passions by the use of reason? Do you think politicians ought to have the good of the people in mind? Do you think virtue is its own reward? If you answered some of these questions in the affirmative, you are reflecting ideas that Plato articulated almost twenty-four centuries ago.

Plato wrote on almost every aspect of philosophy. Here we are concerned primarily with his metaphysical ideas. Plato's metaphysics has been classified as dualistic because he argued that reality could be divided into two radically different sorts of things. There is the reality of matter characterized by change (becoming) and the reality of what he called the **Forms,** or Ideas characterized by permanence (being). Being is immaterial and of greater value than the material.

Along with this general ontological dualism between being and becoming, Plato taught a soul–body dualism. Human beings are composed of bodies and souls. One power that our souls have is the power of thought (the mind), and this is by far our most valuable thing. Our minds and souls are immaterial in contrast to our material bodies.

Plato's metaphysics is also classified as an idealism because it centers on the **theory of Forms** (Ideas) and because, although the reality of matter is not denied, matter is regarded as less real than the immaterial Forms. What is the theory of Forms? The English word *form* is often used to translate the Greek word for idea or concept. So, in the first instance, a form is the mental concept or idea we have of something. For example, how do you recognize a table as a table when you see one? After all, each table is different. How are you able to classify a whole group of different-looking objects into the class "table"? Well, you can do this, we might say, because you have the concept or idea of a table. If someone asked you what a table is, you could give a definition. This definition would constitute the expression of your concept.

Your definition (if it were the "correct" definition in Socrates' sense) would also express the essential nature of table. That is, it would not tell us what this or that *particular* table is, but it would tell us what *all* tables are insofar as they are tables. So, in the second place, a form is an essence.

Now most of us think that the concepts of things exist only in human minds and the essences of things (if there are such) either exist in our minds or somehow exist in the things themselves. If we might use the word *tableness* to designate the Form of tables, then most of us would be inclined to say that if there were no tables, there would be no tableness. Not so Plato. Or at least, not so Plato as interpreted by his star pupil, Aristotle. For Plato, according to Aristotle, essences (Forms) exist objectively apart from the minds that think them and the objects that instantiate them. They constitute ideals, perfect models if you will, that are even more real than the material things that reflect them.

Think of a square. Any particular material square you can draw will be imperfect. Its angles and lines will not be exact. But the square as such (squareness or the pure abstract geometric shape that we can define with mathematical precision) is another matter. It is perfect, and its definition will never change. Is not that which is perfect and permanent more real than that which is imperfect and ever-changing? Plato answers yes.

The selection that follows is from Plato's most famous dialogue, *The Republic*. This is one of the masterpieces of Western literature, and someday you should read all of it. It is filled with stories, myths, striking analogies, and political ideas that are still debated. For now, we will have to be content with just a little bit. However, to appreciate this little bit, some idea of what the whole is about will help.

Socrates, along with others, has been invited to the home of Cephalus. The question "What is justice?" arises and after examining and finding fault with several definitions, Thrasymachus (pronounced Thra-*sim*-a-kus) argued that justice is whatever is in the interest of the stronger party. Socrates disagreed and argued that power and knowledge must be combined because the art of government, like other arts, requires skill and knowledge. In particular, it requires knowledge of what is good for people because government ought to serve the needs of those who are governed, not merely the interests of the strongest.

In Book 2, Glaucon and Adeimantus pressed Socrates to prove that the just life is worth living. Socrates argued that virtue is its own reward and began an analysis of political justice. The ideal state needs philosopher-kings (wisdom-loving rulers), guardians (soldiers and police), and producers (artisans, tradesmen, farmers). When each class does its proper business without interfering with the others, political justice is achieved. By analogy with the state, Socrates argued that the just person is one in whom the three basic elements of human nature—the rational, the spirited, and the appetitive—are properly ordered. Proper order consists of the rule of rationality or reason over the spirited and appetitive parts of the soul.

Books 3–5 describe in some detail Socrates' vision of the ideal state. In the ideal republic, the classes are carefully controlled by breeding, education, and selection. Just as reason should rule in the individual if personal justice is to be realized, so the "lovers of wisdom" (philosophers) should rule the state. This means that the rulers (philosopher-kings) need to know what is good and so must be properly educated. These ideas lead to a discussion of what the good is and what the proper education of the guardians should be. This discussion takes place in Books 6 and 7, from which the following selection comes.

Socrates admitted that the good itself is the proper object of the philosopher's quest, but he could not say directly what the good is. He offered three analogies. The first compares the good to the Sun. The second, called the simile of the divided line, compares *opinion* (which derives from sensations of material objects) with *knowledge* (which derives from knowing the Forms via reason and understanding). The third, called the allegory of the cave, compares the philosopher to a prisoner who has escaped from a cave and seen the light of the real world.

The last three books of *The Republic* deal with political change, the decline of the state, and various forms of government. *The Republic* closes with an argument for the immortality of the soul. By loving justice (i.e., by harmonizing reason, spirit, and appetite under the rule of rationality), we can keep our souls healthy and thereby prosper forever.

You should read what follows slowly and carefully, pausing to think about what Socrates is saying. Socrates is the main speaker. In this translation, the words of the speaker who responds to Socrates are sometimes indicated only by a dash (—). The following questions should help you catch the main ideas.

Reading Questions

1. What is the difference between the *many things* and the *Forms?*
2. In what ways are the Sun and the Good alike?
3. Give examples of what Socrates means by *images* and by *objects of sense.*
4. What is the difference between *reasoning* and *understanding?*
5. What do you think the allegory of the cave means?
6. What is the relationship between the image of the divided line and the story about the cave?
7. What conclusion about education does Socrates draw from the allegory of the cave?
8. Are you inclined to agree with Plato about the existence of some higher, immaterial, intelligible reality beyond this material world? Why, or why not?
9. How would Plato answer the question, "What is really real?"

The Republic

PLATO

. . . But you also, Socrates, must tell us whether you consider the good to be knowledge, or pleasure, or something else.

What a man! I said. It has been clear for some time that the opinion of others on this subject would not satisfy you.

Well, Socrates, he said, it does not seem right to me to be able to tell the opinions of others and not one's own, especially for a man who has spent so much time as you have occupying himself with this subject.

Why? said I. Do you think it right to talk about things one does not know as if one knew them? Not as if one knew them, he said, but for a man who has an opinion to say what that opinion is.

And have you not noticed that opinions not based on knowledge are ugly things? The best of them are blind; or do you think that those who express a true opinion without knowledge are any different from blind people who yet follow the right road?—They are no different.

Do you want to contemplate ugly, blind, and crooked things when you can hear bright and beautiful things from others?

By Zeus, Socrates, said Glaucon, do not stand off as if you had come to the end. We shall be satisfied if you discuss the Good in the same fashion as you did justice, moderation, and the other things.

That, my friend, I said, would also quite satisfy me, but I fear I shall not be able to do so, and that in my eagerness I shall disgrace myself and make myself ridiculous. But, my excellent friends, let us for the moment abandon the

From Plato's Republic, *translated by G. M. A. Grube, Hackett Publishing Co., Inc. Copyright © 1974, pp. 161–172. Reprinted with permission of Hackett Publishing Company, Inc. All rights reserved. Translator's footnotes have been retained but renumbered.*

quest for the nature of the Good itself, for that I think is a larger question than what we started on, which was to ascertain my present opinion about it. I am willing to tell you what appears to be the offspring of the Good and most like it, if that is agreeable to you. If not, we must let the question drop.

Well, he said, tell us. The story of the parent remains a debt which you will pay us some other time.

I wish, I said, that I could pay it in full now, and you could exact it in full and not, as now, only receive the interest.[1] However, accept then this offspring and child of the Good. Only be careful that I do not somehow deceive you unwillingly by giving a counterfeit account of this offspring.—We shall be as careful as we can. Only tell us.

I will, I said, after coming to an agreement with you and reminding you of the things we said before, and also many times elsewhere.—What are these things?

We speak of many beautiful things and many good things, and we say that they are so and so define them in speech.—We do.

And Beauty itself and Goodness itself, and so with all the things which we then classed as many; we now class them again according to one Form of each, which is one and which we in each case call that which is.—That is so.

And we say that the many things are the objects of sight but not of thought, while the Forms are the objects of thought but not of sight.—Altogether true.

With what part of ourselves do we see the objects that are seen?—With our sight.

And so things heard are heard by our hearing, and all that is perceived is perceived by our other senses?—Quite so.

Have you considered how very lavishly the maker of our senses made the faculty of seeing and being seen?—I cannot say I have.

Look at it this way: do hearing and sound need another kind of thing for the former to hear and the latter to be heard, and in the absence of this

third element the one will not hear and the other not be heard.—No, they need nothing else.

Neither do many other senses, if indeed any, need any such other thing, or can you mention one?—Not I.

But do you not realize that the sense of sight and that which is seen do have such a need?—How so?

Sight may be in the eyes, and the man who has it may try to use it, and colours may be present in the objects, but unless a third kind of thing is present, which is by nature designed for this very purpose, you know that sight will see nothing and the colours remain unseen.—What is this third kind of thing?

What you call light, I said.—Right.

So to no small extent the sense of sight and the power of being seen are yoked together by a more honourable yoke than other things which are yoked together, unless light is held in no honour.—That is far from being the case.

Which of the gods in the heavens can you hold responsible for this, whose light causes our sight to see as beautifully as possible, and the objects of sight to be seen?—The same as you would, he said, and as others would; obviously the answer to your question is the sun.

And is not sight naturally related to the sun in this way?—Which way?

Sight is not the sun, neither itself nor that in which it occurs which we call the eye.—No indeed.

But I think it is the most sunlike of the organs of sense.—Very much so.

And it receives from the sun the capacity to see as a kind of outflow.— Quite so.

The sun is not sight, but is it not the cause of it, and is also seen by it?—Yes.

Say then, I said, that it is the sun which I called the offspring of the Good, which the Good begot as analogous to itself. What the Good itself is in the world of thought in relation to the intelligence and things known, the sun is in the visible world, in relation to sight and things seen.—How? Explain further.

You know, I said, that when one turns one's eyes to those objects of which the colours are no longer in the light of day but in the dimness of

---

1. Plato is punning on the Greek word *tokos* which means a child, and in the plural was used also of the interest on capital, a pleasant and common metaphor.

the night, the eyes are dimmed and seem nearly blind, as if clear vision was no longer in them.—Quite so.

Yet whenever one's eyes are turned upon objects brightened by sunshine, they see clearly, and clear vision appears in those very same eyes?—Yes indeed.

So too understand the eye of the soul: whenever it is fixed upon that upon which truth and reality shine, it understands and knows and seems to have intelligence, but whenever it is fixed upon what is mixed with darkness—that which is subject to birth and destruction—it opines and is dimmed, changes its opinions this way and that, and seems to have no intelligence.—That is so.

Say that what gives truth to the objects of knowledge, and to the knowing mind the power to know, is the Form of Good. As it is the cause of knowledge and truth, think of it also as being the object of knowledge. Both knowledge and truth are beautiful, but you will be right to think of the Good as other and more beautiful than they. As in the visible world light and sight are rightly considered sun-like, but it is wrong to think of them as the sun, so here it is right to think of knowledge and truth as Good-like, but wrong to think of either as the Good, for the Good must be honoured even more than they.

This is an extraordinary beauty you mention, he said, if it provides knowledge and truth and is itself superior to them in beauty. You surely do not mean this to be pleasure!

Hush! said I, rather examine the image of it in this way.—How?

You will say, I think, that the sun not only gives to the objects of sight the capacity to be seen, but also that it provides for their generation, increase, and nurture, though it is not itself the process of generation.—How could it be?

And say that as for the objects of knowledge, not only is their being known due to the Good, but also their reality being, though the Good is not being but superior to and beyond being in dignity and power.

Glaucon was quite amused and said: By Apollo, a miraculous superiority!

It is your own fault, I said, you forced me to say what I thought about it.

Don't you stop, he said, except for a moment, but continue to explain the similarity to the sun in case you are leaving something out.

I am certainly leaving out a good deal, I said.—Don't omit the smallest point.

Much is omitted, I said. However, as far as the explanation can go at present, I will not omit anything.—Don't you!

Understand then, I said, that, as we say, there are those two, one reigning over the intelligible kind and realm, the other over the visible (not to say heaven, that I may not appear to play the sophist about the name [2]). So you have two kinds, the visible and the intelligible.—Right.

It is like a line divided [3] into two unequal parts, and then divide each section in the same ratio, that is, the section of the visible and that of the intelligible. You will then have sections related to each other in proportion to their clarity and obscurity. The first section of the visible consists of images—and by images I mean shadows in the first instance, then the reflections in water and all those on close-packed, smooth, and bright

2. He means play on the similarity of sound between *ouranos*, the sky, and *horaton*, visible.

3. It is clear that Plato visualizes a vertical line . . . with *B* as the highest point in the scale of reality and *A* as the lowest form of existence. The main division is at *C*. *AC* is the visible, *CB* being the intelligible world, *AD* is the world of images (and perhaps, though Plato does not say so, works of art), mathematical realities are contained in *CE*, the Platonic Forms in *EB*, with the Good presumably at *B*.

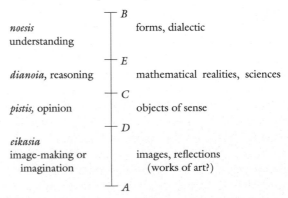

The names of the four mental processes—*noesis, dianoia, pistis,* and *eikasia*—are more or less arbitrary, and Plato does not use them regularly in these precise senses in the rest of the *Republic*.

materials, and all that sort of thing, if you understand me.—I understand.

In the other section of the visible, place the models of the images, the living creatures around us, all plants, and the whole class of manufactured things.—I so place them.

Would you be willing to say that, as regards truth and untruth, the division is made in this proportion: as the opinable is to the knowable so the image is to the model it is made like?—Certainly.

Consider now how the section of the intelligible is to be divided.—How?

In such a way that in one section the soul, using as images what before were models, is compelled to investigate from hypotheses, proceeding from these not to a first principle but to a conclusion. In the second section which leads to a first principle that is not hypothetical, the soul proceeds from a hypothesis without using the images of the first section, by means of the Forms themselves and proceeding through these.—I do not, he said, quite understand what you mean.

Let us try again, I said, for you will understand more easily because of what has been said. I think you know that students of geometry, calculation, and the like assume the existence of the odd and the even, of figures, of three kinds of angles, and of kindred things in each of their studies, as if they were known to them. These they make their hypotheses and do not deem it necessary to give any account of them either to themselves or to others as if they were clear to all; these are their starting points, and going through the remaining steps they reach an agreed conclusion on what they started out to investigate.— Quite so, I understand that.

You know also that they use visible figures and talk about them, but they are not thinking about them but about the models of which these are likenesses; they are making their points about the square itself, the diameter itself, not about the diameter which they draw, and similarly with the others. These figures which they fashion and draw, of which shadows and reflections in the water are images, they now in turn use as images, in seeking to understand those others in

themselves, which one cannot see except in thought.—That is true.

This is what I called the intelligible class, and said that the soul is forced to use hypotheses in its search for it, not travelling up to a first principle, since it cannot reach beyond its hypotheses, but it uses as images those very things which at a lower level were models and which, in comparison with their images, were thought to be clear and honoured as such.—I understand, he said, that you mean what happens in geometry and kindred sciences.

Understand also that by the other section of the intelligible I mean that which reason itself grasps by the power of dialectic. It does not consider its hypotheses as first principles, but as hypotheses in the true sense of stepping stones and starting points, in order to reach that which is beyond hypothesis, the first principle of all that exists. Having reached this and keeping hold of what follows from it, it does come down to a conclusion without making use of anything visible at all, but proceeding by means of Forms and through Forms to its conclusions which are Forms.

I understand, he said, but not completely, for you seem to be speaking of a mighty task—that you wish to distinguish the intelligible reality contemplated by the science of dialectic as clearer than that viewed by the so-called sciences, for which their hypotheses are first principles. The students of these so-called sciences are, it is true, compelled to study them by thought and not by sense perception, yet because they do not go back to a first principle but proceed from hypotheses, you do not think that they have any clear understanding of their subjects, although these can be so understood if approached from a first principle. You seem to me to call the attitude of mind of geometers and such reasoning but not understanding, reasoning being midway between opinion and understanding.

You have grasped this very satisfactorily, I said. There are four such processes in the soul, corresponding to the four sections of our line: understanding for the highest, reasoning for the second; give the name of opinion to the third, and imagination to the last. Place these in the due terms of a proportion and consider that each has as much clarity as the content of its particular section shares in truth.—I understand, and I agree and arrange them as you say.

Book VII

Next, I said, compare the effect of education and the lack of it upon our human nature to a situation like this: imagine men to be living in an underground cave-like dwelling place, which has a way up to the light along its whole width, but the entrance is a long way up. The men have been there from childhood, with their neck and legs in fetters, so that they remain in the same place and can only see ahead of them, as their bonds prevent them turning their heads. Light is provided by a fire burning some way behind and above them. Between the fire and the prisoners, some way behind them and on a higher ground, there is a path across the cave and along this a low wall has been built, like the screen at a puppet show in front of the performers who show their puppets above it.—I see it.

See then also men carrying along that wall, so that they overtop it, all kinds of artifacts, statues of men, reproductions of other animals in stone or wood fashioned in all sorts of ways, and, as is likely, some of the carriers are talking while others are silent.—This is a strange picture, and strange prisoners.

They are like us, I said. Do you think, in the first place, that such men could see anything of themselves and each other[4] except the shadows which the fire casts upon the wall of the cave in front of them?—How could they, if they have to keep their heads still throughout life?

And is not the same true of the objects carried along the wall?—Quite.

---

4. These shadows of themselves and each other are never mentioned again. A Platonic myth or parable, like a Homeric simile, is often elaborated in considerable detail. These contribute to the vividness of the picture but often have no other function, and it is a mistake to look for any symbolic meaning in them. It is the general picture that matters.

If they could converse with one another, do you not think that they would consider these shadows to be the real things?—Necessarily.

What if their prison had an echo which reached them from in front of them? Whenever one of the carriers passing behind the wall spoke, would they not think that it was the shadow passing in front of them which was talking? Do you agree?—By Zeus I do.

Altogether then, I said, such men would believe the truth to be nothing else than the shadows of the artifacts?—They must believe that.

Consider then what deliverance from their bonds and the curing of their ignorance would be if something like this naturally happened to them. Whenever one of them was freed, had to stand up suddenly, turn his head, walk, and look up toward the light, doing all that would give him pain, the flash of the fire would make it impossible for him to see the objects of which he had earlier seen the shadows. What do you think he would say if he was told that what he saw then was foolishness, that he was now somewhat closer to reality and turned to things that existed more fully, that he saw more correctly? If one then pointed to each of the objects passing by, asked him what each was, and forced him to answer, do you not think he would be at a loss and believe that the things which he saw earlier were truer than the things now pointed out to him?—Much truer.

If one then compelled him to look at the fire itself, his eyes would hurt, he would turn round and flee toward those things which he could see, and think that they were in fact clearer than those now shown to him.— Quite so.

And if one were to drag him thence by force up the rough and steep path, and did not let him go before he was dragged into the sunlight, would he not be in physical pain and angry as he was dragged along? When he came into the light, with the sunlight filling his eyes, he would not be able to see a single one of the things which are now said to be true.—Not at once, certainly.

I think he would need time to get adjusted before he could see things in the world above; at first he would see shadows most easily, then reflections of men and other things in water, then the things themselves. After this he would see objects in the sky and the sky itself more easily at night, the light of the stars and the moon more easily than the sun and the light of the sun during the day.—Of course.

Then, at last, he would be able to see the sun, not images of it in water or in some alien place, but the sun itself in its own place, and be able to contemplate it.—That must be so.

After this he would reflect that it is the sun which provides the seasons and the years, which governs everything in the visible world, and is also in some way the cause of those other things which he used to see.—Clearly that would be the next stage.

What then? As he reminds himself of his first dwelling place, of the wisdom there and of his fellow prisoners, would he not reckon himself happy for the change, and pity them?—Surely.

And if the men below had praise and honours from each other, and prizes for the man who saw most clearly the shadows that passed before them, and who could best remember which usually came earlier and which later, and which came together and thus could most ably prophesy the future, do you think our man would desire those rewards and envy those who were honoured and held power among the prisoners, or would he feel, as Homer put it, that he certainly wished to be "serf to another man without possessions upon the earth"[5] and go through any suffering, rather than share their opinions and live as they do?—Quite so, he said, I think he would rather suffer anything.

Reflect on this too, I said. If this man went down into the cave again and sat down in the same seat, would his eyes not be filled with darkness, coming suddenly out of the sunlight?— They certainly would.

And if he had to contend again with those who had remained prisoners in recognizing

those shadows while his sight was affected and his eyes had not settled down—and the time for this adjustment would not be short—would he not be ridiculed? Would it not be said that he had returned from his upward journey with his eyesight spoiled, and that it was not worthwhile even to attempt to travel upward? As for the man who tried to free them and lead them upward, if they could somehow lay their hands on him and kill him, they would do so.—They certainly would.

This whole image, my dear Glaucon, I said, must be related to what we said before. The realm of the visible should be compared to the prison dwelling, and the fire inside it to the power of the sun. If you interpret the upward journey and the contemplation of things above as the upward journey of the soul to the intelligible realm, you will grasp what I surmise since you were keen to hear it. Whether it is true or not only the god knows, but this is how I see it, namely that in the intelligible world the Form of the Good is the last to be seen, and with difficulty; when seen it must be reckoned to be for all the cause of all that is right and beautiful, to have produced in the visible world both light and the fount of light, while in the intelligible world it is itself that which produces and controls truth and intelligence, and he who is to act intelligently in public or in private must see it.—I share your thought as far as I am able.

Come then, share with me this thought also: do not be surprised that those who have reached this point are unwilling to occupy themselves with human affairs, and that their souls are always pressing upward to spend their time there, for this is natural if things are as our parable indicates.— That is very likely.

Further, I said, do you think it at all surprising that anyone coming to the evils of human life from the contemplation of the divine behaves awkwardly and appears very ridiculous while his eyes are still dazzled and before he is sufficiently adjusted to the darkness around him, if he is compelled to contend in court or some other place about the shadows of justice or the objects of which they are shadows, and to carry

5. *Odyssey* 11, 489–90, where Achilles says to Odysseus, on the latter's visit to the underworld, that he would rather be a servant to a poor man on earth than king among the dead.

through the contest about these in the way these things are understood by those who have never seen Justice itself?—That is not surprising at all.

Anyone with intelligence, I said, would remember that the eyes may be confused in two ways and from two causes, coming from light into darkness as well as from darkness into light. Realizing that the same applies to the soul, whenever he sees a soul disturbed and unable to see something, he will not laugh mindlessly but will consider whether it has come from a brighter life and is dimmed because unadjusted, or has come from greater ignorance into greater light and is filled with a brighter dazzlement. The former he would declare happy in its life and experience, the latter he would pity, and if he should wish to laugh at it, his laughter would be less ridiculous than if he laughed at a soul that has come from the light above.—What you say is very reasonable.

We must then, I said, if these things are true, think something like this about them, namely that education is not what some declare it to be; they say that knowledge is not present in the soul and that they put it in, like putting sight into blind eyes.—They surely say that.

Our present argument shows, I said, that the capacity to learn and the organ with which to do so are present in every person's soul. It is as if it were not possible to turn the eye from darkness to light without turning the whole body; so one must turn one's whole soul from the world of becoming until it can endure to contemplate reality, and the brightest of realities, which we say is the Good.—Yes.

Education then is the art of doing this very thing, this turning around, the knowledge of how the soul can most easily and most effectively be turned around; it is not the art of putting the capacity of sight into the soul; the soul possesses that already but it is not turned the right way or looking where it should. This is what education has to deal with.—That seems likely.

Now the other so-called virtues of the soul seem to be very close to those of the body—they really do not exist before and are added later by habit and practice—but the virtue of intelligence belongs above all to something more divine, it seems, which never loses its capacity but, according to which way it is turned, becomes useful and beneficial or useless and harmful. Have you never noticed in men who are said to be wicked but clever, how sharply their little soul looks into things to which it turns its attention? Its capacity for sight is not inferior, but it is compelled to serve evil ends, so that the more sharply it looks the more evils it works.—Quite so.

Yet if a soul of this kind had been hammered at from childhood and those excrescences had been knocked off it which belong to the world of becoming and have been fastened upon it by feasting, gluttony, and similar pleasures, and which like leaden weights draw the soul to look downward—if, being rid of these, it turned to look at things that are true, then the same soul of the same man would see these just as sharply as it now sees the things towards which it is directed.—That seems likely.

Further, is it not likely, I said, indeed it follows inevitably from what was said before, that the uneducated who have no experience of truth would never govern a city satisfactorily, nor would those who are allowed to spend their whole life in the process of educating themselves; the former would fail because they do not have a single goal at which all their actions, public and private, must aim; the latter because they would refuse to act, thinking that they have settled, while still alive, in the faraway islands of the blessed.—True.

It is then our task as founders, I said, to compel the best natures to reach the study which we have previously said to be the most important, to see the Good and to follow that upward journey. When they have accomplished their journey and seen it sufficiently, we must not allow them to do what they are allowed to do today.—What is that?

To stay there, I said, and to refuse to go down again to the prisoners in the cave, there to share both their labours and their honours, whether these be of little or of greater worth.

8.4 Nondualism

Shankara (ca. 788–820) is one of the most important figures in Indian philosophy. In his short life, he traveled extensively, founded four monasteries, and made major contributions to the development of philosophical and religious ideas. He wrote extensive commentaries interpreting important Hindu scriptures and became the leading advocate for a school of philosophy known as **Advaita** (nondual) **Vedanta** (end of the *Vedas*). Shankara preferred to be thought of as a *nondualist* rather than a monist because he taught that ultimate reality is an undifferentiated unity beyond all positive predication. Hence, it can be defined only by saying what it is not.

Brahman was the word used by Shankara for ultimate reality. The word **Atman** had been used for the true Self (the real identity behind our individual egos). Shankara thought of the Atman as pure consciousness (consciousness per se) and identified it with the Brahman. Hence, Atman is the word used for the Brahman "within," and Brahman is the word used for the Atman "without." But, of course, since they are identical and since there is no other absolute reality, ultimately there is no division between within and without. Philosophically, Shankara struggled to articulate more precisely what these ideas mean and to understand how they are related. Religiously, he sought to discover the way to experience the identity of Atman and Brahman.

Like Plato, Shankara believed that the more permanent something is, the more real it is. That which is absolutely permanent is absolutely real. Everything else is but an appearance of this eternal reality. The supposed "reality" of the impermanent is nothing but an illusion. We must learn how to discriminate between the permanent and the impermanent if we want to know what is really real.

To distinguish things, we need a principle of discrimination, which we can term *sublation.* **Sublation** is the act of correcting a previous judgment in light of a subsequent one. For example, when I think the shiny surface up ahead on the road is water but decide, as I get closer, that it is only the sun reflecting off the asphalt, I am engaging in an act of sublation and thereby discriminating appearance from reality. Sublatability is the quality a thing has that allows us to correct our judgment about it. If something is sublatable, it must be impermanent. If the "water" I saw up ahead were permanent, when I got closer I would still see water. It would not be a temporary mirage.

Shankara defines *reality* as that which cannot be sublated, *appearance* as that which can be sublated, and *unreality* as neither sublatable nor unsublatable because it does not exist. Armed with these distinctions and the principle of sublation, our task is to examine all the sorts of things we think are real to see if they really are real or just the appearance of what is real.

In the selection from *The Crest-Jewel of Discrimination* that follows, Shankara, speaking as the master, leads a disciple through an examination of various "coverings" in search of the true Self (Atman). The master then claims that the Atman, which is unsublatable, is the same as the Brahman, the really real.

Some scholars do not believe Shankara is the author of this text. Nevertheless, tradition has attributed it to him, and it undoubtedly expresses ideas associated with his philosophy, even if he did not write it.

Read the text slowly and carefully, keeping in mind that to qualify as really real, something must be permanent and unsublatable. I have added footnotes at key points to explain technical terms. Be sure to read them; they will help.

Reading Questions

1. What does *discrimination* mean?
2. Why do you think renunciation, tranquillity, self-control, faith, self-surrender, the longing for liberation, and devotion are necessary to gain knowledge of the Atman?
3. Shankara says all kinds of things about the Atman and yet claims that it cannot be defined. Is this a contradiction? Why?
4. What is *ignorance,* and how is it overcome?
5. Why is your body (physical covering) not your true Self?
6. What are the differences among the fool, the intelligent person, and the wise person?
7. Why are the vital covering, the mental covering, and the covering of the intellect not the Atman?
8. Do you agree that the "mind of the experiencer creates all the objects which he experiences" while in the waking *and* the dreaming state? Why?
9. How does the master answer the disciple's question, "How, then, can there be an existence which the wise man may realize as one with his Atman?" Do you find the answer convincing? Why?
10. How is the universe related to Brahman?
11. If you were in a debate with Shankara, what would be the major objection you would make to his ideas? How do you think he would defend himself?

The Crest-Jewel of Discrimination

SHANKARA

A MAN SHOULD BE intelligent and learned, with great powers of comprehension, and able to overcome doubts by the exercise of his reason. One who has these qualifications is fitted for knowledge of the Atman.

He alone may be considered qualified to seek Brahman who has discrimination, whose mind is turned away from all enjoyments, who possesses tranquillity and the kindred virtues, and who feels a longing for liberation.

In this connection, the sages have spoken of four qualifications for attainment. When these are present, devotion to the Reality will become complete. When they are absent, it will fail.

First is mentioned discrimination between the eternal and the non-eternal. Next comes renunciation of the enjoyment of the fruits of action,

here and hereafter. Then come the six treasures of virtue, beginning with tranquillity. And last, certainly, is the longing for liberation.

Brahman is real; the universe is unreal. A firm conviction that this is so is called *discrimination* between the eternal and the non-eternal.

Renunciation is the giving-up of all the pleasures of the eyes, the ears, and the other senses, the giving-up of the desire for a physical body as well as for the highest kind of spirit-body of a god.

To detach the mind from all objective things by continually seeing their imperfection, and to direct it steadfastly toward Brahman, its goal—this is called *tranquillity*.

To detach both kinds of sense-organs—those of perception and those of action—from objective things, and to withdraw them to rest in their

From Shankara's Crest-Jewel of Discrimination with a Garland of Questions and Answers, *translated by Swami Prabhavananda and Christopher Isherwood (New York: New American Library, 1970), pp. 37–39; 52–61; 65–69. Reprinted by permission of Vedanta Press, 1946 Vedanta Pl., Hollywood, CA 90068.*

respective centers—this is called *self-control*. True *mental poise* consists in not letting the mind react to external stimuli.

To endure all kinds of afflictions without rebellion, complaint or lament—this is called *forbearance*.

A firm conviction, based upon intellectual understanding that the teachings of the scriptures and of one's master are true—this is called by the sages the *faith* which leads to realization of the Reality.

To concentrate the intellect repeatedly upon the pure Brahman and to keep it fixed there always—this is called *self-surrender*. This does not mean soothing the mind, like a baby, with idle thoughts.

Longing for liberation is the will to be free from the fetters forged by ignorance—beginning with the ego-sense and so on, down to the physical body itself—through the realization of one's true nature.

Even though this longing for liberation may be present in a slight or moderate degree, it will grow intense through the grace of the teacher, and through the practice of renunciation and of virtues such as tranquillity, etc.: And it will bear fruit.

When renunciation and the longing for liberation are present to an intense degree within a man, then the practice of tranquillity and the other virtues will bear fruit and lead to the goal.

Where renunciation and longing for liberation are weak, tranquillity and the other virtues are a mere appearance, like the mirage in the desert.

Among all means of liberation, devotion is supreme. To seek earnestly to know one's real nature—this is said to be devotion.

In other words, devotion can be defined as the search for the reality of one's own Atman. The seeker after the reality of the Atman, who possesses the above-mentioned qualifications, should approach an illumined teacher from whom he can learn the way to liberation from all bondage. . . .

Now I shall tell you the nature of the Atman. If you realize it, you will be freed from the bonds of ignorance, and attain liberation.

There is a self-existent Reality, which is the basis of our consciousness of ego. That Reality is the witness of the three states of our consciousness, and is distinct from the five bodily coverings.[1]

That Reality is the knower in all states of consciousness—waking, dreaming and dreamless sleep. It is aware of the presence or absence of the mind and its functions. It is the Atman.

That Reality sees everything by its own light. No one sees it. It gives intelligence to the mind and the intellect, but no one gives it light.

That Reality pervades the universe, but no one penetrates it. It alone shines. The universe shines with its reflected light.

Because of its presence, the body, senses, mind and intellect apply themselves to their respective functions, as though obeying its command.

Its nature is eternal consciousness. It knows all things, from the sense of ego to the body itself. It is the knower of pleasure and pain and of the sense-objects. It knows everything objectively—just as a man knows the objective existence of a jar.

This is the Atman, the Supreme being, the ancient. It never ceases to experience infinite joy. It is always the same. It is consciousness itself. The organs and vital energies function under its command.

Here, within this body, in the pure mind, in the secret chamber of intelligence, in the infinite universe within the heart, the Atman shines in its captivating splendour, like a noonday sun. By its light, the universe is revealed.

It is the knower of the activities of the mind and of the individual man. It is the witness of all the actions of the body, the sense-organs and the vital energy. It seems to be identified with all these, just as fire appears identified with an

---

1. [The five bodily coverings will be discussed later. They are the physical, the vital, the mental, the intellectual, and the covering of bliss. These are called "coverings" because Shankara pictures them as progressively thinner bodies or sheaves (like those dolls within dolls) that cover the Atman. This is based on the idea that matter extends from a gross level (the physical body as we think of it) to subtler or finer levels. Notice that things like mind and intellect, which in the West have usually been thought of as immaterial, are here thought of as material (but matter of a finer sort).—Ed.]

iron ball. But it neither acts nor is subject to the slightest change.

The Atman is birthless and deathless. It neither grows nor decays. It is unchangeable, eternal. It does not dissolve when the body dissolves. Does the ether cease to exist when the jar that enclosed it is broken?

The Atman is distinct from Maya,[2] the primal cause, and from her effect, the universe. The nature of the Atman is pure consciousness. The Atman reveals this entire universe of mind and matter. It cannot be defined. In and through the various states of consciousness—the waking, the dreaming and the sleeping—it maintains our unbroken awareness of identity. It manifests itself as the witness of the intelligence.

The Mind

With a controlled mind and an intellect which is made pure and tranquil, you must realize the Atman directly, within yourself. Know the Atman as the real I. Thus you cross the shoreless ocean of worldliness, whose waves are birth and death. Live always in the knowledge of identity with Brahman, and be blessed.

Man is in bondage because he mistakes what is non-Atman for his real Self. This is caused by ignorance. Hence follows the misery of birth and death. Through ignorance, man identifies the Atman with the body, taking the perishable for the real. Therefore he nourishes this body, and anoints it, and guards it carefully. He becomes enmeshed in the things of the senses like a caterpillar in the threads of its cocoon.

Deluded by his ignorance, a man mistakes one thing for another. Lack of discernment will cause a man to think that a snake is a piece of rope. When he grasps it in this belief he runs a great risk. The acceptance of the unreal as real constitutes the state of bondage. Pay heed to this, my friend.

The Atman is indivisible, eternal, one without a second. It is eternally made manifest by the power of its own knowledge. Its glories are infinite. The veil of tamas[3] hides the true nature of the Atman, just as an eclipse hides the rays of the sun.

When the pure rays of the Atman are thus concealed, the deluded man identifies himself with his body, which is non-Atman. Then rajas, which has the power of projecting illusory forms, afflicts him sorely. It binds him with chains of lust, anger and the other passions.

His mind becomes perverted. His consciousness of the Atman is swallowed up by the shark of total ignorance. Yielding to the power of rajas, he identifies himself with the many motions and changes of the mind. Therefore he is swept hither and thither, now rising, now sinking, in the boundless ocean of birth and death, whose waters are full of the poison of sense-objects. This is indeed a miserable fate.

The sun's rays bring forth layers of cloud. By them, the sun is concealed; and so it appears that the clouds alone exist. In the same way, the ego, which is brought forth by the Atman, hides the true nature of the Atman; and so it appears that the ego alone exists.

On a stormy day the sun is swallowed up by thick clouds; and these clouds are attacked by sharp, chill blasts of wind. So, when the Atman is enveloped in the thick darkness of tamas, the terrible power of rajas attacks the deluded man with all kinds of sorrows.

Man's bondage is caused by the power of these two—tamas and rajas. Deluded by these, he mistakes the body for the Atman and strays on to the path that leads to death and rebirth.

Man's life in this relative world may be compared to a tree. Tamas is the seed. Identification of the Atman with the body is its sprouting forth.

---

2. [*Maya* is sometimes translated as "illusion" and sometimes as "appearance." It refers to the illusions done by magicians, and Shankara uses this analogy to indicate the nature of the pluralistic universe we usually experience. In general, *Maya* is the impermanent that appears to be real but is not. It stands in contrast to the permanence of Atman-Brahman, which is what is truly real.—Ed.]

3. [*Tamas* are one of the three *gunas* that make up all material things. *Gunas* are qualities. In ancient Hindu cosmology, it was thought that everything material is made up of some combination or mixture of the *gunas*. *Tamas* is the quality of stupor, laziness, stupidity, heaviness, and inaction in general. *Rajas*, another *guna*, is the active principle and hence the opposite of *tamas*. *Sattva*, the third *guna*, is associated with the pure, the fine, and the calm.—Ed.]

The cravings are its leaves. Work is its sap. The body is its trunk. The vital forces are its branches. The sense-organs are its twigs. The sense-objects are its flowers. Its fruits are the sufferings caused by various actions. The individual man is the bird who eats the fruit of the tree of life.

The Atman's bondage to the non-Atman springs from ignorance. It has no external cause. It is said to be beginningless. It will continue indefinitely until a man becomes enlightened. As long as a man remains in this bondage it subjects him to a long train of miseries—birth, death, sickness, decrepitude, and so forth.

This bondage cannot be broken by weapons, or by wind, or by fire, or by millions of acts. Nothing but the sharp sword of knowledge can cut through this bondage. It is forged by discrimination and made keen by purity of heart, through divine grace.

A man must faithfully and devotedly fulfill the duties of life as the scriptures prescribe. This purifies his heart. A man whose heart is pure realizes the supreme Atman. Thereby he destroys his bondage to the world, root and all.

Wrapped in its five coverings, beginning with the physical, which are the products of its own Maya, the Atman remains hidden, as the water of a pond is hidden by a veil of scum.

When the scum is removed, the pure water is clearly seen. It takes away a man's thirst, cools him immediately and makes him happy.

When all the five coverings are removed, the pure Atman is revealed. It is revealed as God dwelling within; as unending, unalloyed bliss; as the supreme and self-luminous Being.

The wise man who seeks liberation from bondage must discriminate between Atman and non-Atman. In this way, he can realize the Atman, which is Infinite Being, Infinite Wisdom and Infinite Love. Thus he finds happiness.

The Atman dwells within, free from attachment and beyond all action. A man must separate this Atman from every object of experience, as a stalk of grass is separated from its enveloping sheath. Then he must dissolve into the Atman all those appearances which make up the world of name and form. He is indeed a free soul who can remain thus absorbed in the Atman alone.

The Body

This body is the "physical covering." Food made its birth possible; on food it lives; without food it must die. It consists of cuticle, skin, flesh, blood, bone and water. It cannot be the Atman, the ever-pure, the self-existent.

It did not exist before birth, it will not exist after death. It exists for a short while only, in the interim between them. Its very nature is transient, and subject to change. It is a compound, not an element. Its vitality is only a reflection. It is a sense-object, which can be perceived, like a jar. How can it be the Atman—the experiencer of all experiences?

The body consists of arms, legs and other limbs. It is not the Atman—for when some of these limbs have been cut off, a man may continue to live and function through his remaining organs. The body is controlled by another. It cannot be the Atman, the controller.

The Atman watches the body, with its various characteristics, actions and states of growth. That this Atman, which is the abiding reality, is of another nature than the body, must be self-evident.

The body is a bundle of bones held together by flesh. It is very dirty and full of filth. The body can never be the same as the self-existent Atman, the knower. The nature of the Atman is quite different from that of the body.

It is the ignorant man who identifies himself with the body, which is compounded of skin, flesh, fat, bone and filth. The man of spiritual discrimination knows the Atman, his true being, the one supreme reality, as distinct from the body.

The fool thinks, "I am the body." The intelligent man thinks, "I am an individual soul united with the body." But the wise man, in the greatness of his knowledge and spiritual discrimination, sees the Atman as reality and thinks, "I am Brahman."

O fool, stop identifying yourself with this lump of skin, flesh, fat, bones and filth. Identify yourself with Brahman, the Absolute, the Atman in all beings. That is how you can attain the supreme peace.

The intelligent man may be learned in Vedanta and the moral laws. But there is not the least hope of his liberation until he stops mistakenly identifying himself with the body and the sense-organs. This identification is caused by delusion.

You never identify yourself with the shadow cast by your body, or with its reflection, or with the body you see in a dream or in your imagination. Therefore you should not identify yourself with this living body, either.

Those who live in ignorance identify the body with the Atman. This ignorance is the root-cause of birth, death and rebirth. Therefore you must strive earnestly to destroy it. When your heart is free from this ignorance, there will no longer be any possibility of your rebirth. You will reach immortality.

That covering of the Atman which is called "the vital covering" is made up of the vital force and the five organs of action. The body is called "the physical covering." It comes to life when it is enveloped by the vital covering. It is thus that the body engages in action.

This vital covering is not the Atman—for it is merely composed of the vital airs. Air-like, it enters and leaves the body. It does not know what is good or bad for itself, or for others. It is always dependent upon the Atman.

Purification

The mind, together with the organs of perception, forms the "mental covering." It causes the sense of "I" and "mine." It also causes us to discern objects. It is endowed with the power and faculty of differentiating objects by giving them various names. It is manifest, enveloping the "vital covering."

The mental covering may be compared to the sacrificial fire. It is fed by the fuel of many desires. The five organs of perception serve as priests. Objects of desire are poured upon it like a continuous stream of oblations. Thus it is that this phenomenal universe is brought forth.

Ignorance is nowhere, except in the mind. The mind is filled with ignorance, and this causes the bondage of birth and death. When, in the enlightenment of the Atman, a man transcends the mind, the phenomenal universe disappears from him. When a man lives in the domain of mental ignorance, the phenomenal universe exists for him.

In dream, the mind is emptied of the objective universe, but it creates by its own power a complete universe of subject and object. The waking state is only a prolonged dream. The phenomenal universe exists in the mind.

In dreamless sleep, when the mind does not function, nothing exists. This is our universal experience. Man seems to be in bondage to birth and death. This is a fictitious creation of the mind, not a reality.

The wind collects the clouds, and the wind drives them away again. Mind creates bondage, and mind also removes bondage.

The mind creates attachment to the body and the things of this world. Thus it binds a man, as a beast is tied by a rope. But it is also the mind which creates in a man an utter distaste for sense-objects, as if for poison. Thus it frees him from his bondage.

The mind, therefore, is the cause of man's bondage and also of his liberation. It causes bondage when it is darkened by rajas. It causes liberation when it is freed from rajas and tamas, and made pure.

If discrimination and dispassion are practiced, to the exclusion of everything else, the mind will become pure and move toward liberation. Therefore the wise man who seeks liberation must develop both these qualities within himself.

That terrible tiger called an impure mind prowls in the forest of the sense-objects. The wise man who seeks liberation must not go there.

The mind of the experiencer creates all the objects which he experiences, while in the waking or the dreaming state. Ceaselessly, it creates the differences in men's bodies, color, social condition and race. It creates the variations of the gunas. It creates desires, actions and the fruits of actions.

Man is pure spirit, free from attachment. The mind deludes him. It binds him with the bonds of the body, the sense-organs and the life-breath. It creates in him the sense of "I" and "mine." It makes him wander endlessly among the fruits of the actions it has caused.

The error of identifying Atman with non-Atman is the cause of man's birth, death and rebirth. This false identification is created by the mind. Therefore, it is the mind that causes the misery of birth, death and rebirth for the man who has no discrimination and is tainted by rajas and tamas.

Therefore the wise, who know Reality, have declared that the mind is full of ignorance. Because of this ignorance, all the creatures of the universe are swept helplessly hither and thither, like masses of cloud before the wind.

Therefore, the seeker after liberation must work carefully to purify the mind. When the mind has been made pure, liberation is as easy to grasp as the fruit which lies in the palm of your hand.

Seek earnestly for liberation, and your lust for sense-objects will be rooted out. Practice detachment toward all actions. Have faith in the Reality. Devote yourself to the practice of spiritual disciplines, such as hearing the word of Brahman, reasoning and meditating upon it. Thus the mind will be freed from the evil of rajas.

The "mental covering," therefore, cannot be the Atman. It has a beginning and an end, and is subject to change. It is the abode of pain. It is an object of experience. The seer cannot be the thing which is seen.

The Covering of Intellect

The discriminating faculty with its powers of intelligence, together with the organs of perception, is known as the "covering of intellect." To be the doer is its distinguishing characteristic. It is the cause of man's birth, death and rebirth.

The power of intelligence that is in the "covering of intellect" is a reflection of the Atman, the pure consciousness. The "covering of intellect" is an effect of Maya. It possesses the faculty of knowing and acting. It always identifies itself entirely with the body, sense-organs, etc.

It has no beginning. It is characterized by its sense of ego. It constitutes the individual man. It is the initiator of all actions and undertakings. Impelled by the tendencies and impressions formed in previous births, it performs virtuous or sinful actions and experiences their results.

It gathers experiences by wandering through many wombs of higher or lower degree. The states of waking and dreaming belong to this "covering of intellect." It experiences joy and sorrow.

Because of its sense of "I" and "mine," it constantly identifies itself with the body, and the physical states, and with the duties pertaining to the different stages and orders of life. This "covering of intellect" shines with a bright light because of its proximity to the shining Atman. It is a garment of the Atman, but man identifies himself with it and wanders around the circle of birth, death and rebirth because of his delusion.

The Atman, which is pure consciousness, is the light that shines in the shrine of the heart, the center of all vital force. It is immutable, but it becomes the "doer" and "experiencer" when it is mistakenly identified with the "covering of intellect."

The Atman assumes the limitations of the "covering of intellect" because it is mistakenly identified with that covering, which is totally different from itself. This man, who is the Atman, regards himself as being separate from it, and from Brahman, who is the one Atman in all creatures. An ignorant man, likewise, may regard a jar as being different from the clay of which it was made.

By its nature, the Atman is forever unchanging and perfect. But it assumes the character and nature of its coverings because it is mistakenly identified with them. Although fire is formless, it will assume the form of red-hot iron. . . .

Atman Is Brahman

The Disciple: Master, if we reject these five coverings as unreal, it seems to me that nothing remains but the void. How, then, can there be an existence which the wise man may realize as one with his Atman?

The Master: That is a good question, O prudent one. Your argument is clever. Nevertheless, there must be an existence, a reality, which perceives the ego-sense and the coverings and is also aware of the void which is their absence. This reality by itself remains unperceived. Sharpen your discrimination that you may know this Atman, which is the knower.

He who experiences is conscious of himself. Without an experiencer, there can be no self-consciousness.

The Atman is its own witness, since it is conscious of itself. The Atman is no other than Brahman.

The Atman is pure consciousness, clearly manifest as underlying the states of waking, dreaming and dreamless sleep. It is inwardly experienced as unbroken consciousness, the consciousness that I am I. It is the unchanging witness that experiences the ego, the intellect and the rest, with their various forms and changes. It is realized within one's own heart as existence, knowledge and bliss absolute. Realize this Atman within the shrine of your own heart.

The fool sees the reflection of the sun in the water of a jar, and thinks it is the sun. Man in the ignorance of his delusion sees the reflection of Pure Consciousness upon the coverings, and mistakes it for the real I.

In order to look at the sun, you must turn away from the jar, the water, and the sun's reflection in the water. The wise know that these three are only revealed by the reflection of the self-luminous sun. They are not the sun itself.

The body, the covering of intellect, the reflection of consciousness upon it—none of these is the Atman. The Atman is the witness, infinite consciousness, revealer of all things but distinct from all, no matter whether they be gross or subtle. It is the eternal reality, omnipresent, all-pervading, the subtlest of all subtleties. It has neither inside nor outside. It is the real I, hidden in the shrine of the heart. Realize fully the truth of the Atman. Be free from evil and impurity, and you shall pass beyond death.

Know the Atman, transcend all sorrows, and reach the fountain of joy. Be illumined by this knowledge, and you have nothing to fear. If you wish to find liberation, there is no other way of breaking the bonds of rebirth.

What can break the bondage and misery of this world? The knowledge that the Atman is Brahman. Then it is that you realize Him who is one without a second, and who is the absolute bliss.

Realize Brahman, and there will be no more returning to this world—the home of all sorrows. You must realize absolutely that the Atman is Brahman.

Then you will win Brahman for ever. He is the truth. He is existence and knowledge. He is absolute. He is pure and self-existent. He is eternal, unending joy. He is none other than the Atman.

The Atman is one with Brahman: this is the highest truth. Brahman alone is real. There is none but He. When He is known as the supreme reality there is no other existence but Brahman.

The Universe

Brahman is the reality—the one existence, absolutely independent of human thought or idea. Because of the ignorance of our human minds, the universe seems to be composed of diverse forms. It is Brahman alone.

A jar made of clay is not other than clay. It is clay essentially. The form of the jar has no independent existence. What, then, is the jar? Merely an invented name!

The form of the jar can never be perceived apart from the clay. What, then, is the jar? An appearance! The reality is the clay itself.

This universe is an effect of Brahman. It can never be anything else but Brahman. Apart from Brahman, it does not exist. There is nothing beside Him. He who says that this universe has an independent existence is still suffering from delusion. He is like a man talking in his sleep.

"The universe is Brahman"—so says the great seer of the Atharva Veda. The universe, therefore, is nothing but Brahman. It is superimposed upon Him. It has no separate existence, apart from its ground.

If the universe, as we perceive it, were real, knowledge of the Atman would not put an end to our delusion. The scriptures would be untrue. The revelations of the Divine Incarnations would make no sense. These alternatives cannot be considered either desirable or beneficial by any thinking person.

Sri Krishna, the Incarnate Lord, who knows the secret of all truths, says in the Gita: "Although I am not within any creature, all creatures exist within me. I do not mean that they exist within me physically. That is my divine mystery. My Being sustains all creatures and brings them to birth, but has no physical contact with them."

If this universe were real, we should continue to perceive it in deep sleep. But we perceive nothing then. Therefore it is unreal, like our dreams.

The universe does not exist apart from the Atman. Our perception of it as having an independent existence is false, like our perception of blueness in the sky. How can a superimposed attribute have any existence, apart from its substratum? It is only our delusion which causes this misconception of the underlying reality.

No matter what a deluded man may think he is perceiving, he is really seeing Brahman and nothing else but Brahman. He sees mother-of-pearl and imagines that it is silver. He sees Brahman and imagines that it is the universe. But this universe, which is superimposed upon Brahman, is nothing but a name.

I Am Brahman

Brahman is supreme. He is the reality—the one without a second. He is pure consciousness, free from any taint. He is tranquillity itself. He has neither beginning nor end. He does not change. He is joy for ever.

He transcends the appearance of the manifold, created by Maya. He is eternal, for ever beyond reach of pain, not to be divided, not to be measured, without form, without name, undifferentiated, immutable. He shines with His own light. He is everything that can be experienced in this universe.

The illumined seers know Him as the uttermost reality, infinite, absolute, without parts—the pure consciousness. In Him they find that knower, knowledge and known have become one.

They know Him as the reality which can neither be cast aside (since He is ever-present within the human soul) nor grasped (since He is beyond the power of mind and speech). They know Him immeasurable, beginningless, endless, supreme in glory. They realize the truth: "I am Brahman."

8.5 Subjective Idealism

George Berkeley was born in 1685 in Kilkenny, Ireland. At age fifteen he went to Trinity College, Dublin, where he studied classics, mathematics, and the then-new and controversial physics of Newton. In 1704, after graduation, he became a Fellow of his college and was ordained to the ministry. By the age of twenty-five, he had worked out the basic ideas of his philosophy in reaction to the philosophy of John Locke (1632–1704). He saw himself as a defender of common sense in a skeptical age and a defender of religion against a science that pictured the universe as a vast machine operating according to blind natural laws. Berkeley lived in the American colonies for a while, married in 1728, and was appointed Bishop of Cloyne in south Ireland in 1734 after his attempt to found a college in Bermuda to educate colonists, Native Americans, and Africans failed due to lack of funding. He died at Oxford in 1753.

Berkeley's metaphysics is called **subjective idealism.** His views constitute a variety of idealism because he argued that reality consists of finite or created minds, an infinite mind (God), and the ideas (thoughts, feelings, and sensations) these minds have. All of these things are immaterial. This idealism is termed *subjective* because physical objects do not exist apart from some subject (mind) who perceives them. This kind of idealism stands in contrast to **objective idealism,** which holds that although reality is mental, it does exist independently of the human knower because it is a manifestation of an absolute mind. Objective idealism is usually monistic (or at least nondualistic), maintaining that there is one absolute mind and the universe is a manifestation of it. Berkeley's subjective idealism, though nondualistic in the sense of asserting that all reality is mental or immaterial, is pluralistic in the sense that there are many finite minds independent of God's mind.

The denial of the objective or independent existence of physical objects seems so utterly fantastic that one wonders how Berkeley could view himself as a champion of common sense. Indeed, when he published his views in 1710, many thought him insane. However, Berkeley's rejection of matter seems more plausible if we understand the historical circumstances that led him to that conclusion.

We must return, for a moment, to Plato. Plato was a dualist, arguing that reality is twofold: material and immaterial. This dualism was revived and given a modern formulation by the French philosopher René Descartes in the early seventeenth century. Descartes argued for a position known as indirect or representational realism. His position is called **realism** because he believed objects can exist apart from any knower or mind. It is called *indirect* or *representational* because he also argued that sensations indirectly represent objects that exist outside the mind. This sort of realism stands in contrast to direct or naive realism, which holds that we are directly in touch with real objects via our senses.

John Locke, an English philosopher, combined Descartes's realism with empiricism. Empiricism is the view that knowledge derives from sense experience and that knowledge claims are tested by reference to sense experience. If empiricism is true, then all we can know *directly* or immediately are the ideas or sensations that occur in our minds. Although these ideas are themselves mental, they resemble and are caused by nonmental or physical objects existing outside the mind, or so the indirect realist claims. Hence, according to Locke, there are two substances: *immaterial substances* or minds, that have ideas *caused* by *material substances*.

This distinction between ideas and the physical objects they represent was accompanied by a distinction between primary and secondary qualities. **Primary qualities** are characteristics that constitute the properties of physical objects. Locke believed them to be extension, figure, motion, rest, solidity, and number. **Secondary qualities** are characteristics of our *sensation* of physical objects: color, flavor, odor, texture, sound, hot, cold, and the like. The theory of indirect realism combined with the distinction between secondary and primary qualities allowed Locke to explain, for example, how it is that an object looks a different color in different light or feels cold to one person but hot to another. Direct realism was unable to explain such common experiences, because if we are *directly* in touch with real physical objects via our senses, an object would have to be both blue and green or hot and cold if it were so experienced. However, if we are *indirectly* in touch with objects, and if color and heat are secondary qualities, then we can say that the object *appears* both blue and green or feels both hot and cold, but *in fact* it is simply in a certain state of motion.

Berkeley pondered Locke's ideas as an undergraduate and found them nonsensical. He felt that since all we can really know are immaterial ideas, there is no way of knowing that they represent anything at all outside the mind. To know that this picture is a likeness of my friend, I can look at my friend and compare that image to the picture image. However, I cannot do that with sensations because I can never get outside of sensations to compare them with the physical objects that supposedly caused them.

Locke, Berkeley thought, had created a duplex world. We have a world of physical objects duplicated by a world of mental images. It also turns out that there are problems involved in trying to explain how physical objects can cause nonphysical sensations. Why not just simplify things by getting rid of physical objects? Isn't it true that we only know for sure that ideas or sensations exist, but we have no way of knowing for sure that physical objects do? What we *do* know is that what we call a physical object is for us a bundle of sensations (colors, odors, flavors, etc.). Because sensations cannot exist without being sensed, why not say the obvious, that nothing can exist without being experienced. Hence, Berkeley concluded that *"esse* is *percipi"*—that is, *to be is to be perceived.* We don't really need the materialistic hypothesis—or so Berkeley argued.

Notice how Berkeley's argument is heavily dependent on an empirical epistemological theory. This may surprise you, because many people associate empiricism with materialism. Berkeley argued that this association is wrong. If empiricism is right in claiming that the only thing we can know are things that appear to our minds such as sensations, feelings, and ideas, then why assume we can know matter or some physical reality apart from what appears to our minds. Notice further how epistemological arguments and metaphysical assertions come together. The philosophical concern with knowledge will, sooner or later, lead us into metaphysical territory and theories of reality.

Reading Questions

1. Give an example of each of the three kinds of ideas that constitute, according to Berkeley, the objects of human knowledge.
2. What is the difference between *ideas* and the *mind*?
3. Why did Berkeley assert that the existence (*esse*) of the objects of knowledge consists in their being perceived (*percipi*)?
4. How would Berkeley answer that old question, "If a tree fell in the forest and no one was there to hear it, would it make a sound?"
5. How did Berkeley respond to the claim that things exist apart from minds (unthinking or material substances), which our ideas copy or resemble? Do you find his response convincing? Why, or why not?
6. Why did Berkeley reject the distinction between primary and secondary qualities, and why did he claim that the very notion of matter is contradictory?
7. In Sections 16–20, Berkeley advanced a series of arguments against the idea that material objects exist outside our minds. Briefly summarize the main ideas of these arguments.
8. Do you find any of these arguments convincing? If so, which ones, and why? If you find them all unconvincing, why?
9. If you got into a debate with Berkeley, what sort of objections would you raise against his claim that matter does not exist? How do you think he would respond to your objections?
10. Formulate and answer a question comparing Berkeley's views with any of the other metaphysical views you have studied in this chapter. How are they the same, and how are they different?

The Principles of Human Knowledge

GEORGE BERKELEY

Part I

1. IT IS EVIDENT to anyone who takes a survey of the objects of human knowledge, that they are either *ideas* actually imprinted on the senses; or else such as are perceived by attending to the passions and operations of the mind; or lastly, *ideas* formed by help of memory and imagination— either compounding, dividing, or barely representing those originally perceived in the aforesaid ways.—By sight I have the ideas of light and colours, with their several degrees and variations. By touch I perceive hard and soft, heat and cold, motion and resistance, and of all these more and less either as to quantity or degree. Smelling furnishes me with odours; the palate with tastes; and hearing conveys sounds to the mind in all their variety of tone and composition.—And as several of these are observed to accompany each other, they come to be marked by one name, and so to be reputed as one thing. Thus, for example, a certain colour, taste, smell, figure and consistence having been observed to go together, are accounted one distinct thing, signified by the name *apple;* other collections of ideas constitute a stone, a tree, a book, and the like sensible things—which as they are pleasing or disagreeable excite the passions of love, hatred, joy, grief, and so forth.

2. But, besides all that endless variety of ideas or objects of knowledge, there is likewise something which knows or perceives them; and exercises divers operations, as willing, imagining, remembering, about them. This perceiving, active being is what I call mind, spirit, soul, or myself. By which words I do not denote any one of my ideas, but a thing entirely distinct from them, wherein they exist, or, which is the same thing, whereby they are perceived—for the existence of an idea consists in being perceived.

3. That neither our thoughts, nor passions, nor ideas formed by the imagination, exist without the mind, is what everybody will allow.—And to me it is no less evident that the various sensations, or *ideas imprinted on the sense,* however blended or combined together (that is, whatever *objects* they compose), cannot exist otherwise than in a mind perceiving them—I think an intuitive knowledge may be obtained of this by anyone that shall attend to *what is meant by the term exist when applied to sensible things*. The table I write on I say exists, that is, I see and feel it; and if I were out of my study I should say it existed— meaning thereby that if I was in my study I might perceive it, or that some other spirit actually does perceive it. There was an odour, that is, it was smelt; there was a sound, that is, it was heard; a colour or figure, and it was perceived by sight or touch. This is all that I can understand by these and the like expressions.—For as to what is said of the absolute existence of unthinking things without any relation to their being perceived, that is to me perfectly unintelligible. Their *esse* is *percipi*, nor is it possible they should have any existence out of the minds or thinking things which perceive them.

4. It is indeed an opinion strangely prevailing amongst men, that houses, mountains, rivers, and in a word all sensible objects, have an existence, natural or real, distinct from their being perceived by the understanding. But, with how great an assurance and acquiescence soever this principle may be entertained in the world, yet whoever shall find in his heart to call it in question may, if I mistake not, perceive it to involve a manifest contradiction. For, what are the forementioned objects but the things we perceive by sense? and what do we perceive besides our own ideas or sensations? and is it not plainly repugnant

From *George Berkeley,* A Treatise Concerning the Principles of Human Knowledge *(1710), Sections 1–10; 14–20.*

that any one of *these,* or any combination of them, should exist unperceived?

5. If we thoroughly examine this tenet it will, perhaps, be found at bottom to depend on the doctrine of *abstract ideas.* For can there be a nicer strain of abstraction than to distinguish the *existence* of sensible objects from their *being perceived,* so as to conceive them existing unperceived? Light and colours, heat and cold, extension and figures—in a word the things we see and feel—what are they but so many sensations, notions, ideas, or impressions on the sense? and is it possible to separate, even in thought, any of these from perception? For my part, I might as easily divide a thing from itself. I may, indeed, divide in my thoughts, or conceive apart from each other, those things which, perhaps, I never perceived by sense so divided. Thus, I imagine the trunk of a human body without the limbs, or conceive the smell of a rose without thinking on the rose itself. So far, I will not deny, I can abstract—if that may properly be called *abstraction* which extends only to the conceiving separately such objects as it is possible may really exist or be actually perceived asunder. But my conceiving or imagining power does not extend beyond the possibility of real existence or perception. Hence, as it is impossible for me to see or feel anything without an actual sensation of that thing, so is it impossible for me to conceive in my thoughts any sensible thing or object distinct from the sensation or perception of it.

6. Some truths there are so near and obvious to the mind that a man need only open his eyes to see them. Such I take this important one to be, viz. that all the choir of heaven and furniture of the earth, in a word all those bodies which compose the mighty frame of the world, have not any subsistence without a mind—that their *being* is *to be perceived or known;* that consequently so long as they are not actually perceived by me, or do not exist in my mind or that of any other created spirit, they must either have no existence at all, or else subsist in the mind of some Eternal Spirit—it being perfectly unintelligible, and involving all the absurdity of abstraction, to attribute to any single part of them an existence independent of a spirit. To be convinced of which, the reader need only reflect, and try to separate in his own thoughts the *being* of a sensible thing from its *being perceived.*

7. From what has been said it is evident there is not any other Substance than SPIRIT, or *that which perceives.* But, for the fuller demonstration of this point, let it be considered the sensible qualities are colour, figure, motion, smell, taste, &c., *i.e.* the ideas perceived by sense. Now, for an idea to exist in an unperceiving thing is a manifest contradiction; for to have an idea is all one as to perceive; that therefore wherein colour, figure, &c. exist must perceive them; hence it is clear there can be no unthinking substance or *substratum* of those ideas.

8. But, say you, though the ideas themselves do not exist without the mind, yet there may be things like them, whereof they are copies or resemblances, which things exist without the mind in an unthinking substance. I answer, an idea can be like nothing but an idea; a colour or figure can be like nothing but another colour or figure. If we look but never so little into our own thoughts, we shall find it impossible for us to conceive a likeness except only between our ideas. Again, I ask whether those supposed originals or external things, of which our ideas are the pictures or representations, be themselves perceivable or no? If they are, then they are ideas and we have gained our point; but if you say they are not, I appeal to anyone whether it be sense to assert a colour is like something which is invisible; hard or soft, like something which is intangible; and so of the rest.

9. Some there are who make a distinction betwixt *primary* and *secondary* qualities. By the former they mean extension, figure, motion, rest, solidity or impenetrability, and number; by the latter they denote all other sensible qualities, as colours, sounds, tastes, and so forth. The ideas we have of these they acknowledge not to be the resemblances of anything existing without the mind, or unperceived, but they will have our ideas of the primary qualities to be patterns or images of things which exist without the mind, in an unthinking substance which they call *matter.* By *matter,* therefore, we are to understand an inert, senseless substance, in which extension, figure, and motion do actually subsist. But it is

evident, from what we have already shewn, that extension, figure, and motion are only ideas existing in the mind, and that an idea can be like nothing but another idea, and that consequently neither they nor their archetypes can exist in an unperceiving substance. Hence, it is plain that the very notion of what is called *matter* or *corporeal substance,* involves a contradiction in it.

10. They who assert that figure, motion, and the rest of the primary or original qualities do exist without the mind in unthinking substances, do at the same time acknowledge that colours, sounds, heat, cold, and such like secondary qualities, do not—which they tell us are sensations existing in the mind alone, that depend on and are occasioned by the different size, texture, and motion of the minute particles of matter. This they take for an undoubted truth, which they can demonstrate beyond all exception. Now, if it be certain that those original qualities are inseparably united with the other sensible qualities, and not, even in thought, capable of being abstracted from them, it plainly follows that they exist only in the mind. But I desire any one to reflect and try whether he can, by any abstraction of thought, conceive the extension and motion of a body without all other sensible qualities. For my own part, I see evidently that it is not in my power to frame an idea of a body extended and moving, but I must withal give it some colour or other sensible quality which is acknowledged to exist only in the mind. In short, extension, figure, and motion, abstracted from all other qualities, are inconceivable. Where therefore the other sensible qualities are, there must these be also, to wit, in the mind and nowhere else. . . .

14. I shall farther add, that, after the same manner as modern philosophers prove certain sensible qualities to have no existence in matter, or without the mind, the same thing may be likewise proved of all other sensible qualities whatsoever. Thus, for instance, it is said that heat and cold are affections only of the mind, and not at all patterns of real beings, existing in the corporeal substances which excite them, for [the reason] that the same body which appears cold to one hand seems warm to another. Now, why may we

not as well argue that figure and extension are not patterns or resemblances of qualities existing in matter, because to the same eye at different stations, or eyes of a different texture at the same station, they appear various, and cannot therefore be the images of anything settled and determinate without the mind? Again, it is proved that sweetness is not really in the sapid [tasty] thing, because the thing remaining unaltered the sweetness is changed into bitter, as in case of a fever or otherwise vitiated palate. Is it not as reasonable to say that motion is not without the mind, since if the succession of ideas in the mind become swifter, the motion, it is acknowledged, shall appear slower without any alteration in any external object?

15. In short, let any one consider those arguments which are thought manifestly to prove that colours and tastes exist only in the mind, and he shall find they may with equal force be brought to prove the same thing of extension, figure, and motion. Though it must be confessed this method of arguing does not so much prove that there is no extension or colour in an outward object, as that we do not know by sense which is the true extension or colour of the object. But the arguments foregoing plainly shew it to be impossible that any colour or extension at all, or other sensible quality whatsoever, should exist in an unthinking subject without the mind, or in truth, that there should be any such thing as an outward object.

16. But let us examine a little the received opinion.—It is said extension is a mode or accident of Matter, and that Matter is the *substratum* that supports it. Now I desire that you would explain to me what is meant by Matter's *supporting* extension. Say you, I have no idea of Matter and therefore cannot explain it. I answer, though you have no positive, yet, if you have any meaning at all, you must at least have a relative idea of Matter; though you know not what it is, yet you must be supposed to know what relation it bears to accidents, and what is meant by its supporting them. It is evident "support" cannot here be taken in its usual or literal sense—as when we say that pillars support a building; in what sense therefore must it be taken?

17. If we inquire into what the most accurate philosophers declare themselves to mean by *material substance,* we shall find them acknowledge they have no other meaning annexed to those sounds but the idea of *being in general,* together with the relative notion of its *supporting accidents.* The general idea of Being appeareth to me the most abstract and incomprehensible of all other; and as for its supporting accidents, this, as we have just now observed, cannot be understood in the common sense of those words; it must therefore be taken in some other sense, but what that is they do not explain. So that when I consider the two parts or branches which make the signification of the words *material substance,* I am convinced there is no distinct meaning annexed to them. But why should we trouble ourselves any farther, in discussing this material *substratum* or "support" of figure, and motion, and other sensible qualities? Does it not suppose *they* have an existence without the mind? And is not this a direct repugnancy, and altogether inconceivable?

18. But, though it were possible that solid, figured, moveable *substances* may exist without the mind, corresponding to the ideas we have of bodies, yet how is it possible for us to know this? Either we must know it by Sense or by Reason.— As for our senses, by them we have the knowledge only of our sensations, ideas, or those things that are immediately perceived by sense, call them what you will: but they do not inform us that things exist without the mind, or unperceived, like to those which are perceived. This the Materialists themselves acknowledge.—It remains therefore that if we have any knowledge at all of external things, it must be by Reason inferring their existence from what is immediately perceived by sense. But what reason can induce us to believe the existence of bodies without the mind, from what we perceive, since the very patrons of Matter themselves do not pretend there is any *necessary* connexion betwixt them and our ideas? I say it is granted on all hands—and what happens in dreams, frenzies, and the like, puts it beyond dispute—that it is possible we might be affected with all the ideas we have now, though there were no bodies existing without resembling them. Hence, it is evident the supposition of external bodies is not necessary for producing our ideas; since it is granted they are produced sometimes, and might possibly be produced always in the same order we see them in at present, without their concurrence.

19. But, though we might possibly have all our sensations without them, yet perhaps it may be thought easier to conceive and explain the manner of their production, by supposing external bodies in their likeness rather than otherwise; and so it might be at least probable there are such things as bodies that excite their ideas in our minds. But neither can this be said; for, though we give the materialists their external bodies, they by their own confession are never the nearer knowing *how* our ideas are produced; since they own themselves unable to comprehend in what manner body can act upon spirit, or how it is possible it should imprint any idea in the mind. Hence it is evident the production of ideas or sensations in our minds can be no reason why we should suppose Matter or corporeal substances, since *that* is acknowledged to remain equally inexplicable with or without this supposition. If therefore it were possible for bodies to exist without the mind, yet to hold they do so must needs be a very precarious opinion; since it is to suppose, without any reason at all, that God has created innumerable beings that are entirely useless, and serve to no manner of purpose.

20. In short, if there were external bodies, it is impossible we should ever come to know it; and if there were not, we might have the very same reasons to think there were that we have now. Suppose—what no one can deny possible—an intelligence *without the help of external bodies,* to be affected with the same train of sensations or ideas that you are, imprinted in the same order and with like vividness in his mind. I ask whether that intelligence hath not all the reason to believe the existence of corporeal substances, represented by his ideas, and exciting them in his mind, that you can possibly have for believing the same thing? Of this there can be no question—which one consideration were enough to make any reasonable person suspect the strength of whatever arguments he may think himself to have, for the existence of bodies without the mind.

8.6 Pre-Columbian Cosmologies

Cultural critiques have often lamented the fragmentation of modern life. Many think this fragmentation stems from modern scientific developments that have slowly chipped away at a more integrated view of the cosmos. Others lay the blame at the doorstep of modern metaphysical views, which deny the interconnectedness of fact and values, mind and matter, faith and science.

Comparisons can be illuminating. In fact, comparing one thing to another is one of the primary ways we add depth to our understanding. However helpful comparisons can be, they can also be misleading. Sometimes we view the "other" in the comparison as inferior to ourselves or to some viewpoint we prefer. Sometimes we view the "other" as superior, romanticizing a past no longer existent, but one for which we long. Comparisons are particularly difficult when comparing the views of a culture that has conquered another culture or when comparing existing cultural viewpoints with those that no longer exist. In such situations we must imagine the "other," and imagination—as we all know—can be both helpful and misleading.

Jorge Valadez, author of the next selection, teaches philosophy at Marquette University. His research focuses on ontology, social and political philosophy, and pre-Columbian philosophy. The selection that follows is part of a larger essay that includes a discussion of the Maya, Aztec, and Inca worldviews along with the changes that took place in the colonial and post-colonial period in Latin America.

Valadez is convinced that the metaphysical views of ancient Mesoamerican cultures have not been fully appreciated because of the Eurocentrism brought by the conquering Spanish. When we think of these cultures we think of wild-eyed priests in feathered headdresses brutally sacrificing humans to their sun god. However dreadful the practice of human sacrifice may be, it was embedded in a metaphysical view that we need to understand. We must not lose sight of the more positive elements that may be found in this ancient metaphysic, especially when compared with modern views.

Reading Questions

1. How did the metaphysical views of the Spanish influence their treatment of the Aztecs?
2. What four different kinds of integration characterized Mesoamerican metaphysics?
3. How do the Mesoamerican views of space and time, the divine, and death differ from your own?
4. Why, according to Valadez, did the conflict between science and religion that characterizes modern Western thought not occur among the Mesoamericans?
5. How is the Legend of the Four Suns related to human sacrifice and the need for a warrior class?
6. Can you think of a modern practice as morally objectionable as human sacrifice? If you can, how is it linked to our metaphysical views?

Pre-Columbian Philosophical Perspectives

JORGE VALADEZ

NOTHING IN THE EXPERIENCE of the much-traveled soldiers of Hernán Cortés's invading army could have prepared them for what they saw when they marched into Tenochtitlán, the ancient site of present-day Mexico City, in 1519. They encountered great buildings and ceremonial centers, vast and beautiful floating gardens, splendid murals, impressive sculptures and other works of art, and large and well-organized markets. The Spaniards were witnessing the splendors of one of the greatest civilizations in history. Their amazement was magnified by the fact that this civilization was so utterly foreign and unexpected. The Spaniards were denizens of the Old World, where diverse cultures had interacted and influenced one another for thousands of years. But here was a civilization that had evolved in isolation from the rest of the world and yet was highly advanced in astronomy and agriculture, had created architectural wonders, practiced sophisticated types of surgery, and developed complex and unique systems of religious belief and social organization.

This unprecedented and extraordinary encounter of two diverse cultures was destined to have catastrophic consequences for the people of the Americas. In less than two centuries diseases like smallpox and diphtheria, which the inhabitants of the New World had no defenses against because of their genetic isolation, decimated approximately two-thirds of the population of the Americas. In Mesoamerica (a region covering the southern two-thirds of Mexico and Guatemala, El Salvador, Belize, and certain areas of Nicaragua, Honduras, and Costa Rica), tens of millions of native people died either in battles with the technologically superior invading army

or, more commonly, as the result of infection with these new diseases. The Spaniards eventually conquered the Aztec capital, Tenochtitlán, plundered it for its gold and silver (melting many pieces of jewelry and religious figurines into gold bullion), and enslaved many of its inhabitants.

But there was another kind of destruction that the Spaniards were to wreak on the Aztecs and other people of Mesoamerica—the almost wholesale destruction of their culture. The social, religious, and political organization of early Mesoamerican society—including the structure of its large urban centers, forms of religious ritual, cultural customs, artistic styles, philosophy of education, and architectural forms—were all based on a religious and cosmological perspective that was completely foreign and incomprehensible to the Europeans.

The worldview of the Spaniards was determined by their Christian beliefs, and hence they were at once amazed and repulsed by what they saw: human sacrifices, rituals involving bloodletting, adoration of pagan gods, cannibalism, sculptures of what they considered monstrous creatures, and so on. According to their Christian metaphysical perspective there was a clear and straightforward way to categorize these practices; they were to be considered evil and the work of the Devil. One of the most famous chroniclers of the native culture, the Spanish Franciscan priest Bernardino de Sahagun, firmly believed that the existence of Aztec religious beliefs and customs was an ingenious and elaborate manifestation of the power of Satan's influence. Thus, the religious practices of the Aztecs not only had no claim to cultural legitimacy, they had to be stopped at whatever cost. Bolstered by such

From Jorge Valadez, "Pre-Columbian and Modern Philosophical Perspectives in Latin America," in From Africa to Zen: An Invitation to World Philosophy, edited by Robert C. Solomon and Kathleen M Higgins, Lanham, MD: Rowman and Littlefield, 1993, pp.81-89. Copyright © 1993 by Rowman and Littlefield Publishers, Inc. Reprinted by permission.

ethical and cultural chauvinism, the Spaniards undertook what is perhaps the most extensive and systematic (and certainly the most large-scale) destruction of a civilization in the world's history. In that the civilizations of Mesoamerica were essentially grounded in a radically different religious and cosmological vision, this conquest was nothing less than an attempt at metaphysical annihilation, that is, an attempt to destroy the worldviews of the native people. Nevertheless, despite the efforts of the Spaniards to eradicate the cosmological roots of these cultures, we shall see that some important features of the ancient worldviews can still be found in some contemporary Mesoamerican cultures.

Given their imperialistic orientations and the closed nature of their religious perspective, it was perhaps inevitable that the Spaniards would fail so completely to understand the Aztec culture and the other cultures of ancient Mesoamerica. In fact, it is only in the latter half of the twentieth century that it has been possible, through a variety of archaeological sources and different kinds of interpretive techniques, to understand the religious and metaphysical worldview of early Mesoamerican cultures.

This essay will present a systematic exposition of some of the central concepts and principles of the early Mesoamerican cosmological perspectives, . . . I will draw contrasts and comparisons between the Mesoamerican metaphysical perspectives and some perspectives that have been of predominant importance in the Western philosophical tradition. These comparisons will help us to appreciate more fully the uniqueness and depth of the ancient Mesoamerican worldviews and will further our understanding of some of the Western European philosophical perspectives by placing them within a wider global cultural context.

Precolonial Latin American Cosmologies

Cultures throughout history have developed a variety of answers to certain fundamental and perennial questions: What place do human beings have in the universe? What is the structure of the cosmos? How can we explain or account for the origin of the world? The cultures of Mesoamerica developed complex and fascinating answers to such questions. In order to provide a general understanding of how they approached these questions, we will look first at some central metaphysical principles common to the Mayan and Aztec cosmologies, and then examine the structure of each of these worldviews in more detail.

One of the most striking features of the Meso-american metaphysical perspective was the remarkable degree to which it interconnected or integrated different aspects or components of reality. Four different kinds of integration characterized its cosmology: (1) the internal structural interconnection of the different components of the universe, (2) the integration of fundamental dualities that were perceived as complementary instead of oppositional, (3) the holistic integration of astronomical science and religious beliefs, and, most important, (4) the integration of everyday life with the cycles and rhythms of the cosmos through the practice of rituals that were perceived as necessary for sustaining the very existence of the universe. To arrive at a unified view of the Mesoamerican metaphysical perspective, we must understand each of these four aspects of Mesoamerican cosmology. . . .

THE INTERACTIVE UNIVERSE

The people of Mesoamerica believed that the universe consisted of three different planes or levels: a celestial plane, a terrestrial plane, and an underworld plane. There were further divisions within the celestial and underworld levels. (The Aztecs, for example, believed that there were thirteen celestial levels and nine underworld levels.) There was also a constant interaction of supernatural forces or powers among these levels, which was made possible by the existence of spiral-shaped channels called *mallinalis*. These supernatural forces were thought to enter the terrestrial level through caves, sunlight, fire, and animals. Some of the rituals of the Mesoamerican cultures were designed to tap and redirect or harness these supernatural cosmic forces. Thus their universe was not a static universe, but rather an interactive one, with three dynamic levels of reality.

Time itself also existed at different planes or levels: human or terrestrial time; the time of myth; and the transcendent time in which the gods dwelled. Terrestrial time originated in the interaction of cosmic forces from the celestial and underworld levels converging at the terrestrial level. In other words, human time originated in the interaction of forces from two distinct spatial planes.

Myth time existed prior to terrestrial time, and in it the actions of the gods, as they were depicted in their myths, took place. For example, in one of the Mayan myths about death, two heroic twin brothers descend to the underworld to challenge the Lords of Death. After a long series of trials and ordeals, the brothers defeat the Lords of the Underworld and emerge victorious. This myth is an expression of the Mayan belief that death represents a challenge which, through courage and fortitude, can be overcome. It was also during this myth time, which still progresses and has not ceased to be, that many supernatural beings who exert cyclical influences on humans at the terrestrial level were born or created.

In transcendent time lived the most powerful gods at the apex of the divine hierarchy who created and grounded the universe. (Apparently these powerful creator gods existed in two temporal dimensions, namely, mythic and transcendent time.) The gods and supernatural beings that inhabited transcendent time, like those that lived in mythic time, had periodic or cyclical influences on the events and beings that existed in terrestrial time. The early Mesoamerican calendars marked the occasions during the year when these periodic influences occurred.

Thus, in the Mesoamerican worldview, space and time were not understood as existing independently of one another; instead, they formed a complex, unified whole. . . . For the ancient Mesoamericans, the world was replete with cosmic forces resulting from the intersection of the various spatial and temporal levels that comprised the universe.

In addition, their universe did not consist of isolated, discrete entities; rather, it consisted of entities, events, and forces that were in constant interaction with one another and that existed in different spaciotemporal planes. Absolute space, conceived as an empty vacuum in which entities exist and events take place, and absolute time, understood as an infinite linear progression of moments, had no reality in the Mesoamerican cosmological perspective. For the people of early Mesoamerica, space and time constituted the very fabric of existence; that is, they affected, shaped, and determined everything that exists. This is why Mesoamerican cultures were so preoccupied with developing accurate calendars and astronomical techniques for measuring time, determining the spatial location of celestial bodies, and anticipating the occurrence of astronomical events. The capacity to measure and predict the solar, lunar, planetary, and astral cycles enabled them to understand the various complex cosmic forces that they believed affected human events at the terrestrial level. By knowing the particular times at which certain cosmic forces affected events at the human level, they tried to mediate and channel these forces through rituals. From such observations we can appreciate the great extent to which the different components of the Mesoamerican universe were interrelated and interconnected with one another.

COMPLEMENTARY DUALITIES

The second kind of integration in Mesoamerican cosmology concerns the complementary nature of fundamental dualities. Dualities such as life/death, celestial world/underworld, male/female, night/day, and so forth were of central importance in the Mesoamerican worldview. These dualities were not conceived as being oppositional in nature; instead, they were understood as being different and necessary aspects of reality. One of the clearest examples of this type of nonoppositional duality was the supreme dual god of the Aztecs, Ometeotl. This supreme deity, who was the ultimate originator of all that exists, had a dual male and female nature. Ometeotl was sometimes called Tonacatecuhtli-Tonacacihuatl, which means "lord and lady of our maintenance," and often he/she was referred to as "our mother, our father." The dual nature of Ometeotl enabled him/her to beget other beings and the universe from his/her own essence. It is clear that the Aztecs wanted to incorporate both the male and the female principle within a single supreme entity and that they saw no contradiction in a deity who was simultaneously male and female.

It is interesting and instructive to compare the conception of a male/female dual god with the monotheistic God of the Judeo-Christian tradition. Traditionally, the Christian god has been characterized primarily as having male qualities and has been referred to in explicitly male terms. For example, the first two substantive terms in the expression "the father, the son, and the holy ghost" refer to God in terms that are unequivocally male, while the third substantive term, "the holy ghost," has traditionally never been spoken of in female terms. And historically, rarely if ever have we heard the Christian God referred to by the female pronoun "she" or by the phrase "holy mother." He is usually characterized by predominantly male qualities that emphasized his power and authority instead of, say, his nurturance and unconditional acceptance. Some contemporary theologians have argued that these gender-specific characterizations of the Christian God deny women full spiritual participation in the Christian religious tradition. In any case, we can see that the Aztec conceptualization of the supreme deity Ometeotl incorporates the two aspects of the male/female duality into a single divine entity.

We find another case of the Mesoamerican tendency to think in terms of nonoppositional dualities in the Mayan understanding of the life/death duality. From the Mayan perspective, death, whether of humans or of plants, was an integral part of a never-ending life cycle of birth, death, and regeneration. Death was not seen as the discontinuity of life, but rather as a necessary phase in the regeneration of life. Upon death, humans went to the underworld of Xibalba, where they experienced various ordeals and struggles with the supernatural entities of the underworld.

Then they would be reborn and ascend to the celestial or terrestrial level, where they might become a part of a heavenly body, an ancestral spiritual entity, or a maize plant. Through this transformation and process of rebirth, individuals would be integrated into one of the eternal life cycles of the universe. In similar fashion, the death of plant life in the seasonal and agricultural cycles was merely one phase in the recurring pattern of sowing, sprouting, dying, and regenerating. One of the central ideas in the Mayan cosmology was that the earth was a living entity that was continually in the process of regeneration, and that the death of plant life was an integral part of this process.

In short, death was not seen as the negation, or as the polar opposite, of life. Rather, death was a process that either (1) made possible the continuation of the life process or (2) allowed for the integration of the life of the individual into the eternal cosmic cycles. In the plant world, the death of plants enabled new vegetation to sprout and develop; that is, death was an integral part of the process of regeneration. In the human realm, death was, as we have seen, a process in which the individual would eventually become a part of the astral or earthly cycles of the universe. In contrast to some Western views on death, in which the soul of the individual continues to exist in an otherworldly spiritual realm, in the early Mesoamerican cosmology the spirits of the dead return to become a part of the world we can see, touch, and feel. That is, they became part of the world of everyday experience.

A SCIENTIFIC-RELIGIOUS WORLDVIEW

The third kind of structural integration that characterizes the Mesoamerican cosmology concerns the intimate linkage between Mesoamerican scientific and religious perspectives. Astronomy was by far the most fully developed science of the cultures of Mesoamerica. The accuracy of their calendars equaled or surpassed those of other cultures in the world at that time, and their astronomical observations were as extensive and accurate as those of any other civilization. Insofar as they possessed a scientific, empirically validated form of knowledge, it was their astronomy. This was the knowledge that allowed them to correctly predict celestial events, carry out extensive and accurate calendrical computations (some of which involved dates many millions of years into the future), and measure agricultural cycles. But their astronomical science was also closely interconnected with their religious ideas and beliefs, especially the fundamentally important concept of the renewal or regeneration of agricultural and human life cycles. They believed that the influences of the supernatural forces and beings that permeated the earth and supported these life cycles could be tracked and predicted by their calendars. In addition, they maintained that through religious rituals they could harness and successfully mediate these cosmic forces.

Thus, the intense interest of the people of ancient Mesoamerica in astronomical observation and the measurement of time was not motivated merely by the desire to acquire knowledge for its own sake; the continuation of the life cycles of the universe depended on the performance of the appropriate religious rituals at specific points in time. Their scientifically validated observations were united with their fundamental religious ideas and with the rituals they believed were crucial for the continued existence of the cosmos. This unification of their two most basic kinds of knowledge gave rise to a holistic conceptual unity in their thinking that is difficult for us to understand and appreciate. The reason this conceptual integration is so foreign to us is that there is a fundamental fragmentation in modern thought between scientific knowledge and religious belief.

Science tells us that reality consists of physical entities and forces that exist independently of human consciousness and that are utterly indifferent to the human search for meaning and cosmic significance. According to the contemporary scientific worldview, everything that occurs in the universe is explainable in terms of universal physical laws, not in terms of the acts of a divine will. Because according to this worldview it is physics, and not the will of God, that explains why events

occur, modern scientific knowledge conflicts with the age-old reliance on a supernatural, spiritual being to explain what happens in the universe. And if, as the modern scientific perspective tells us, reality consists exclusively of impersonal physical forces and entities governed by universal laws, where in such a universe can we find a basis for human spiritual meaning and significance? This scientific perspective has also deeply influenced nonreligious, philosophical attempts to find a basis for the meaning of human existence. For the past several centuries (a period coinciding with the emergence of modern science and the decline of the religious worldview), Western philosophers have wrestled with questions concerning the meaning of life. Here again the problem has been to find a basis for grounding existential significance and human values in an indifferent, impersonal universe consisting solely of objective physical forces and entities. In short, a basic dilemma has arisen in modern Western thought as a result of the scientific view of the universe as an objectively existing physical realm in which there is no room for the principles of human subjective experience as expressed in religious and philosophic thought. By contrast, in the Mesoamerican cosmological view there was no conflict between science and religion; on the contrary, Mesoamerican scientific and religious worldviews complemented and reinforced one another.

COSMIC RESPONSIBILITY

We have already alluded to the fourth kind of integration characteristic of the Mesoamerican metaphysical perspective. It concerns the belief that religious rituals were of central importance for maintaining the existence of the cosmos. Perhaps the clearest expression of this belief can be found in the Aztec Legend of the Four Suns. According to this legend, there have been four ages that have been dominated by four different suns. Each of these ages—which correspond to each of the four directions, east, south, west, and north—had ended in a catastrophic manner with the destruction of the human race and the world. The Aztecs believed that they lived in the age of the Fifth Sun, which was created at Tenochtitlán, the ancient site of Mexico City, as the result of the self-sacrifice of the gods Nanahuatzin and Tecuciztecatl. After the destruction of the Fourth Sun, all was darkness except for the divine hearth (the *teotexcalli*), where the gods gathered to create the new sun that would usher in the new age. The gods ordered Tecuciztecatl to leap into the great fire, but he was unable to do so out of fear. After Tecuciztecatl attempted and failed four times to leap into the fire, the gods ordered Nanahuatzin to sacrifice himself in the giant blaze. Nanahuatzin braced himself, closed his eyes, and threw himself in. Upon seeing this, Tecuciztecatl finally gained enough courage to jump into the fire. As the result of his courage and sacrifice, Nanahuatzin reemerges from the east as the new, blazing red sun.

The Legend of the Suns expresses some central ideas of the Aztec cosmology. One of these is the centrality of cataclysmic change in the evolution of the universe. Each of the previous four ages had been destroyed by sudden, catastrophic disasters and the present age was also susceptible to an abrupt, massive destruction. The Aztec universe was thus highly unstable and vulnerable to extinction. Another prominent theme in this myth is that of sacrifice. The Aztecs believed that the present age began with a sacrifice by the gods, and that in order to prevent this age from ending they had continually to provide the sun with life-sustaining blood and with the energy concentrated in certain parts of the body of sacrificial victims. This is the primary explanation for the religious rituals involving human sacrifice.

The need for sacrificial victims demanded the continued capture of enemy warriors and the creation of a warrior class to satisfy this need. This sense of cosmic responsibility reinforced certain authoritarian orientations in Aztec culture. Theirs was a society that did not tolerate a great deal of individual freedom or challenges to the established social order.

Human actions had great significance in the cosmology of the Aztecs, because the very existence of the universe depended on the proper performance of religious rituals, including human sacrifice. Without a doubt, most of us would find the practice of human sacrifice, and the extent to which it was practiced by the Aztecs, to be morally objectionable and repugnant in the extreme. Nevertheless, this practice was based on a religious doctrine that was of central importance in the Aztec cosmological perspective. Within their worldview, human sacrifice was not only justified, it was absolutely essential. Indeed, the profound sense of cosmic responsibility that was so central to the Aztec worldview was a double-edged sword. It provided them with an unquestioned faith in their relevance and importance as a people, but it also burdened them with the heavy obligation of maintaining the existence of the cosmos. It can truly be said that the Aztecs elaborated a highly imaginative, though severe, answer to the question concerning the role and relevance of human existence in the universe. . . .

8.7 So What Is Real?

Philosophers from around the world have wondered about whether there is some Archimedian point, some firm and solid foundation, some privileged perspective from which we can distinguish with confidence dreaming from waking, good from bad, reality from appearance. Some have claimed to have found such a foundation; others have claimed it does not exist. Is there some sort of "God's-eye view" that humans can adopt that will allow them to see things as they really are? What do you think?

"Not that question again," I hear some of you say. Wondering can be frustrating business, and being constantly challenged to think for ourselves can be intimidating.

Yet thinking is what philosophy is about. Of course, from time to time we all wonder what we have accomplished by all this thought. Sometimes it seems we just go in circles, but the circles get bigger and after a while begin to form a spiral. New ideas arise. Fresh distinctions emerge. Questions are refined and plateaus of clarity reached. You may not be in a position to say with absolute certainty exactly what is really real, but think about all you have learned in thinking about metaphysical issues in conversation with others from around the world.

I do hope that this experience encourages you to continue to wonder because wondering has given birth to some of the greatest of human accomplishments. I also hope that you have come to value the ideas and insights from different countries and cultural groups. It is good to learn what the world looks like from a different perspective. Different viewpoints enrich our own and open up new paths for further exploration. As we move deeper into the twenty-first century, it will become ever more necessary to understand the perspectives and values of others. Philosophy needs to become a global conversation that is stimulating, productive, and edifying. Each of you has something of value to contribute to this emerging global conversation, and I hope what you have learned has helped you begin to find your voice in these matters.

I close this chapter with a tale of dreaming by Jorge Luis Borges (1899–1986), Argentina's greatest writer and a man with an active, ever-probing mind and imagination who lived in constant wonder. He uses fiction to raise philosophical issues worth pondering. Can we ever be certain that our perspective is the right one? Can we ever be confident that our way of distinguishing appearance from reality is the one correct way? And if we cannot, then what?

Reading Questions

1. Write a one-page interpretative essay on what you think the tale of "The Circular Ruins" means. What is Borges' point?
2. Compare your interpretative essay with one written by a classmate and discuss the differences in your interpretations.

The Circular Ruins

JORGE LUIS BORGES

And if he left off dreaming about you . . .
  —*Through the Looking Glass,* VI

NO ONE SAW HIM DISEMBARK in the unanimous night. No one saw the bamboo canoe running aground on the sacred mud. But within a few days no one was unaware that the taciturn man had come from the South and that his home had been one of the infinity of hamlets which lie upstream, on the violent flank of the mountain, where the Zend language is uncontaminated by Greek, and where leprosy is infrequent. The certain fact is that the anonymous gray man kissed

From A Personal Anthology *by Jorge Luis Borges, translated by Anthony Kerrigan, pp. 68–74. Copyright ©
1967 by Grove Press, Inc. Used by permission of Grove/Atlantic, Inc.*

the mud, scaled the bank without pushing aside (probably without even feeling) the sharp-edged sedges lacerating his flesh, and dragged himself, bloody and sickened, up to the circular enclosure whose crown is a stone colt or tiger, formerly the color of fire and now the color of ash. This circular clearing is a temple, devoured by ancient conflagration, profaned by the malarial jungle, its god unhonored now of men. The stranger lay beneath a pedestal. He was awakened, much later, by the sun at its height. He was not astonished to find that his wounds had healed. He closed his pale eyes and slept, no longer from weakness of the flesh but from a determination of the will. He knew that this temple was the place required by his inflexible purpose; he knew that the incessant trees had not been able to choke the ruins of another such propitious temple down river, a temple whose gods also were burned and dead; he knew that his immediate obligation was to dream. The disconsolate shriek of a bird awoke him about midnight. The prints of bare feet, some figs, and a jug told him that the people of the region had reverently spied out his dreaming and solicited his protection or feared his magic. He felt the cold chill of fear, and sought in the dilapidated wall for a sepulchral niche where he concealed himself under some unfamiliar leaves.

The purpose which impelled him was not impossible though it was supernatural. He willed to dream a man. He wanted to dream him in minute totality and then impose him upon reality. He had spent the full resources of his soul on this magical project. If anyone had asked him his own name or about any feature of his former life, he would have been unable to answer. The shattered and deserted temple suited his ends, for it was a minimum part of the visible world, and the nearness of the peasants was also convenient, for they took it upon themselves to supply his frugal needs. The rice and fruits of the tribute were nourishment enough for his body, given over to the sole task of sleeping and dreaming.

At first his dreams were chaotic. A little later they were dialectical. The stranger dreamt he stood in the middle of a circular amphitheater which was in some measure the fired temple; clouds of taciturn students wearied the tiers; the

faces of the last rows looked down from a distance of several centuries and from a stellar height, but their every feature was precise. The dreamer himself was delivering lectures on anatomy, cosmography, magic: the faces listened anxiously and strove to answer with understanding, as if they guessed the importance of that examination, which would redeem one of them from his insubstantial state and interpolate him into the real world. In dreams or in waking the man continually considered the replies of his phantoms; he did not let himself be deceived by the impostors; in certain paradoxes he sensed an expanding intelligence. He was seeking a soul worthy of participating in the universe.

At the end of nine or ten nights he realized, with a certain bitterness, that he could expect nothing from those students who accepted his teaching passively, but that he could of those who sometimes risked a reasonable contradiction. The former, though deserving of love and affection, could never rise to being individuals; the latter already existed to a somewhat greater degree. One afternoon (now even the afternoons were tributaries of the dream; now he stayed awake for only a couple of hours at daybreak) he dismissed the entire vast illusory student body for good and retained only one pupil. This pupil was a silent, sallow, sometimes obstinate boy, whose sharp features repeated those of his dreamer. The sudden elimination of his fellow students did not disconcert him for very long; his progress, at the end of a few private lessons, made his master marvel. And nevertheless, catastrophe came. One day the man emerged from sleep as from a viscous desert, stared about at the vain light of evening, which at first he took to be dawn, and realized he had not dreamt. All that night and all the next day the intolerable lucidity of insomnia broke over him in waves. He was impelled to explore the jungle, to wear himself out; he barely managed some quick snatches of feeble sleep amid the hemlock, shot through with fugitive visions of a rudimentary type: altogether unserviceable. He strove to assemble the student body, but he had scarcely uttered a few words of exhortation before the college blurred, was erased. Tears of wrath scalded his old eyes in his almost perpetual vigil.

He realized that the effort to model the inchoate and vertiginous stuff of which dreams are made is the most arduous task a man can undertake, though he get to the bottom of all the enigmas of a superior or inferior order: much more arduous than to weave a rope of sand or mint coins of the faceless wind. He realized that an initial failure was inevitable. He vowed to forget the enormous hallucination by which he had been led astray at first, and he sought out another approach. Before essaying it, he dedicated a month to replenishing the forces he had squandered in delirium. He abandoned all premeditation concerned with dreaming, and almost at once managed to sleep through a goodly part of the day. The few times he did dream during this period he took no notice of the dreams. He waited until the disk of the moon should be perfect before taking up his task again. Then, on the eve, he purified himself in the waters of the river, worshiped the planetary gods, pronounced the lawful syllables of a powerful name and went to sleep. Almost at once he dreamt of a beating heart.

He dreamt it active, warm, secret, the size of a closed fist, garnet-colored in the half-light of a human body that boasted as yet no sex or face. He dreamt this heart with meticulous love, for fourteen lucid nights. Each night he saw it more clearly. He never touched it, but limited himself to witnessing it, to observing it or perhaps rectifying it with a glance. He watched it, lived it, from far and from near and from many angles. On the fourteenth night he ran his index finger lightly along the pulmonary artery, and then over the entire heart, inside and out. The examination satisfied him. The next night, he deliberately did not dream. He then took up the heart again, invoked the name of a planet, and set about to envision another one of the principal organs. Before the year was up he had reached the skeleton, the eyelids. The most difficult task, perhaps, proved to be the numberless hairs. He dreamt a whole man, a fine lad, but one who could not stand nor talk nor open his eyes. Night after night he dreamt him asleep.

In the Gnostic cosmogonies, demiurges fashion a red Adam who never manages to get to his feet: as clumsy and equally as crude and elemental as this dust Adam was the dream Adam forged by the nights of the wizard. One afternoon, the man almost destroyed all his work, but then changed his mind. (It would have been better for him had he destroyed it.) Having expended all the votive offerings to the numina of the earth and the river, he threw himself at the feet of the effigy, which was perhaps a tiger or perhaps a colt, and implored its unknown help. That evening, at twilight, he dreamt of the statue. He dreamt it alive, tremulous: it was no atrocious bastard of a tiger and a colt, but both these vehement creatures at once and also a bull, a rose, a tempest. This multiple god revealed to him that its terrestrial name was Fire, that in this same circular temple (and in others like it) it once had been offered sacrifices and been the object of a cult, and that now it would magically animate the phantom dreamt by the wizard in such wise that all creatures—except Fire itself and the dreamer—would believe the phantom to be a man of flesh and blood. It directed that once the phantom was instructed in the rites, he be sent to the other broken temple, whose pyramids persisted down river, so that some voice might be raised in glorification in that deserted edifice. In the dream of the man who was dreaming, the dreamt man awoke.

The wizard carried out the directives given him. He dedicated a period of time (which amounted, in the end, to two years) to revealing the mysteries of the universe and the cult of Fire to his dream creature. In his intimate being, he suffered when he was apart from his creation. And so every day, under the pretext of pedagogical necessity, he protracted the hours devoted to dreaming. He also reworked the right shoulder, which was perhaps defective. At times, he had the uneasy impression that all this had happened before. . . . In general, though, his days were happy ones: as he closed his eyes he would think: *Now I shall be with my son.* Or, more infrequently: *The son I have engendered is waiting for me and will not exist if I do not go to him.*

Little by little he got his creature accustomed to reality. Once, he ordered him to plant a flag on a distant mountain top. The next day the flag was fluttering on the peak. He tried other analogous experiments, each one more audacious than the last. He came to realize, with a certain bitterness, that his son was ready—and perhaps impatient—to be born. That night he kissed his child for the first time, and sent him to the other temple, whose remains were whitening down river, many leagues across impassable jungle and swamp. But first, so that his son should never know he was a phantom and should think himself a man like other men, he imbued him with total forgetfulness of his apprentice years.

His triumph and his respite were sapped by tedium. In the twilight hours of dusk or dawn he would prostrate himself before the stone figure, imagining his unreal child practicing identical rites in other circular ruins downstream. At night he did not dream, or dreamt as other men do. The sounds and forms of the universe reached him wanly, pallidly: his absent son was being sustained on the diminution of the wizard's soul. His life's purpose had been achieved; the man lived on in a kind of ecstasy. After a time—which some narrators of his story prefer to compute in years and others in lustra—he was awakened one midnight by two boatmen: he could not see their faces, but they told him of a magical man at a temple in the North, who walked on fire and was not burned. The wizard suddenly recalled the words of the god. He remembered that of all the creatures composing the world, only Fire knew his son was a phantom. This recollection, comforting at first, ended by tormenting him. He feared lest his son meditate on his abnormal privilege and somehow discover his condition of mere simulacrum. Not to be a man, to be the projection of another man's dream—what incomparable humiliation, what vertigo! Every father is concerned with the children he has procreated (which he has permitted) in mere confusion or felicity: it was only natural that the wizard should fear for the future of his son, thought out entrail by entrail and feature by feature on a thousand and one secret nights.

The end of his caviling was abrupt, but not without forewarnings. First (after a long drought) a remote cloud, light as a bird, appeared over a hill. Then, toward the South, the sky turned the rosy color of a leopard's gums. Smoke began to rust the metallic nights. And then came the panic flight of the animals. And the events of several centuries before were repeated. The ruins of the fire god's sanctuary were destroyed by fire. One birdless dawn the wizard watched the concentric conflagration close around the walls: for one instant he thought of taking refuge in the river, but then he understood that death was coming to crown his old age and to absolve him of further work. He walked against the florid banners of the fire. And the fire did not bite his flesh but caressed and engulfed him without heat or combustion. With relief, with humiliation, with terror, he understood that he, too, was all appearance, that someone else was dreaming him.

Visit the companion Web sites for chapter specific quizzes, suggestions for further reading, video ideas, and other resources to assess and expand your understanding of the chapter material. Go to http://philosophy.wadsworth.com and select the companion Web site for *Voices of Wisdom.*

 You can access many additional readings at the Info Trac-College Edition Web Site. To find the following suggested articles do a keyword search with the article title. Use the passcode that was packaged with your new book to enter the site at http://www.Infotrac-college.com/Wadsworth/. Here is a sampling.

Stuart Rosenbaum, "Abortion, the Constitution, and Metaphysics." *Journal of Church and State,* Autumn 2001 v43 i4 p707(17), A82094387.

Francis J. Beckwith, "Law, Religion, and the Metaphysics of Abortion: A Reply to Simmons." *Journal of Church and State,* Winter 2001 v43 i1 p19, A73064914.

Joseph Grange, "Dao, Technology, and American Naturalism." *Philosophy East and West,* July 2001 v51 i3 p363, A7854895.

Hector Sabelli, "The Union of Opposites: From Taoism to Process Theory." *Systems Research and Behavioral Science,* September 1998 p429(1), A53383915.

Paul St. John Mackintosh, "Lao Tzu and Modern Western Philosophy." *Contemporary Review,* June 1992 v260 n1517 p305(7), A13553524.

Eric D. Perl, "The Presence of the Paradigm: Immanence and Transcendence in Plato's Theory of Forms." *The Review of Metaphysics,* December 1999 v53 i2 p339, A64426385.

Stephen H. Phillips," Could There Be Mystical Evidence for a Nondual Brahman?" *Philosophy East and West,* October 2001 v51 i4 p492(15), A80309984.

Frederic F. Fost, "Playful Illusion: The Making of Worlds in Advaita Vedanta." *Philosophy East and West,* July 1998 v48 n3 p387(19), A21035582.

Dale Jacquette, "Reconciling Berkeley's Microscopes in God's Infinite Mind." *Religious Studies,* Dec 1993 v29 n4 p453(11), A14683360.

Michel Graulich, "Aztec Human Sacrifice as Expiation." *History of Religions,* May 2000 v39 i4 p352, A63186406.

Edward Hirsch, "Jorge Luis Borges." *The Wilson Quarterly,* Autumn 1998 v22 n4 p109(2), A21240885.

Chapter 9

Are We Free or Determined?

> "Freedom is a state of mind"
>
> ANONYMOUS

9.1 Introduction

DETERMINISM (SOMETIMES CALLED SIMPLE DETERMINISM in order to distinguish it from other types) refers to the idea that all events are caused. For every event there is a set of conditions such that if the conditions were repeated, the event would recur. Simple determinism implies that the universe and what happens in it is lawful, that is, that the law of causality (or law of cause and effect) governs events. Hence, we can assume that any given event is determined (caused) by some set of antecedent events even if we are not fully aware of what those antecedent events are.

Simple determinism should not be confused with fatalism nor with predestination. **Fatalism** is the belief that events are predetermined by some impersonal cosmic force or power; **predestination** is the belief that events are predetermined by some personal power. Although fatalism and predestination differ about what predetermines events, they share the idea that if an event or action is fated or predestined, it will happen *no matter what.*

Simple determinism does not claim that events or actions are predetermined by personal or impersonal cosmic powers, nor does it claim that events will happen no matter what. Rather, it holds that events happen *only if* particular causes of those events occur. If the causes of a possible event do not occur, that event will not occur.

Although there are important differences among simple determinism, fatalism, and predestination, all three positions clearly raise questions about human freedom. If all events are caused (whether their cause be fate, a god, or some set of antecedent events), how can any human actions (assuming human actions are events), like your act of reading these words, be free? This is one way of formulating what philosophers call the **problem of freedom and determinism** (sometimes called the *problem of free will*).

This problem is important for a number of reasons. One of the most important has to do with moral responsibility. If the choices we make and the actions we perform are not free, it seems to make no sense to praise or blame people for what they do. Indeed, why bother to search for how one should live, or how to make correct moral choices, or how to create a just society if, in fact, all our choices are determined by antecedent factors over which we have no control?

The issue of moral responsibility allows us to probe more deeply the problem of freedom and determinism by formulating that problem as a dilemma.

1. Human choice is either free, or it is not free.
2. If it is free, then the law of causality is false.
3. If it is not free, then people are not responsible for their actions.
4. Therefore, either the law of causality is false, or people are not responsible for their actions.

Neither of the choices given in conclusion (4) is very attractive. On the one hand, we want to believe in the law of causality. All of science and technology depend on it. Surely, if there are uncaused events, then there are events that can never be explained, or predicted. So why search for a cure for cancer, or why try to eliminate crime, or why try to invent a pollution-free form of rapid transportation? There may be no causes for these things and hence no means of prediction or control. If the law of causality is false, the universe appears chaotic, disordered, unreliable, and events seem unexplainable.

On the other hand, we want to hold people morally responsible for what they do. What sense would praise or blame make if we aren't responsible? If you are not free and hence not responsible for what you do, then what sense does it make to say you *earned* a good grade in philosophy, or you *merited* a promotion, or you *ought* to be punished for behaving badly? Indeed, what sense would morality make if people cannot freely choose what they do?

In this chapter, we explore some of the solutions people have proposed to the problem of freedom and determinism. As we explore these solutions, our understanding of the problem will grow, and alternatives that may not have occurred to us will present themselves.

9.2 We Are Determined

One proposed solution to the problem of freedom and determinism is called **hard determinism.** Hard determinism holds that every event has a cause and that this fact is *incompatible* with free will. Nothing happens for which there is no sufficient reason; hence, free will is an illusion. People should not be held morally responsible for their actions since a given act is unavoidable if the appropriate antecedent conditions obtain. If we want to change people's behavior, we need to develop a science of behavior that will show us how to manipulate the causes of human behavior.

Notice that hard determinism is a form of simple determinism insofar as it holds that every event has a cause. However, *unlike* simple determinism, hard determinism claims, in addition, that determinism and free will are *incompatible,* that free will is an illusion, and that humans are *not* in fact responsible for what they do in the sense that they could have made choices other than they did.

Supporters of this position usually appeal to the physical sciences and concepts like "natural law" to back up their views. Science seeks to give a description of objective facts. It also seeks to discover uniformity in nature. That is, it seeks to explain facts by discovering the networks of cause and effect according to which events are ordered.

The debate about free will is not merely academic. It hovers in the background and sometimes comes to the foreground when arguments about the role heredity and environment play in causing human behavior to erupt violently. It also comes to the fore when horrific and perplexing crimes get national attention. Susan Smith locked her two little boys in a car, rolled it into a lake, and drowned them. At her trial in 1995 the prosecution portrayed her as a scheming monster, deserving of nothing less than the death penalty. The defense argued that she was a victim of destructive relationships, including sexual abuse by her stepfather. She suffered from depression and mental instability but was not, at the time she drowned her children, legally insane because she did know right from wrong. More recently the case of Andrea Yates made headlines when she drowned her five children in the bathtub. Once again the prosecution sought the death penalty, pointing to the deliberate manner in which she committed the murders. We wonder, when we hear about such cases, what made these people do such terrible things? Were they totally in control of their actions?

Two opposing tendencies drive our thoughts. On the one hand, we want to believe that some inner agent called the "I" controls what we do no matter what our genetic inheritance or life experiences. On the other hand, we want to know what makes us and others tick. We want science to tell us what accounts for addiction, intelligence, sexual preference, crime, and a host of other behaviors. Can we have it both ways? Can we believe both that some free agent called the self is responsible for people's actions *and* that there are factors beyond people's control that cause them to do what they do?

The hard determinist says we cannot have it both ways. Free will and determinism are incompatible. The idea of a free agent who is in control of what we do so that we could have done otherwise at many choice points in our lives is an illusion. It is a convenient fiction we maintain out of our desire to punish and blame others for wrong doing and to congratulate ourselves for doing the right thing.

In the following selection, Laura Waddell Ekstrom, who teaches philosophy at the College of William and Mary, describes what she calls "simple arguments" for the incompatibility of free will and determinism. This brief selection is one small part of a larger argument that explores the complexity of the philosophical debate about solutions to the problem of freedom and determinism.

Reading Questions

1. What, according to Ekstrom, is "*the minimal supposition of human free will*"? Why does it imply that what you or I do is not all that we can do?
2. What, according to the author, is causal determinism?
3. What is the first simple argument for incompatibilism? In your view, what is the key premise in the argument?
4. Explain the "consequence argument." What is the inference rule on which it depends?
5. Do you think these two arguments for incompatibilism are strong arguments or weak arguments? Why, or why not?

Arguments for Incompatibilism

LAURA WADDELL EKSTROM

ALTHOUGH WIDESPREAD PHILOSOPHICAL agreement on any topic is rare, there is broad-based support among philosophers for the claim that a person's having free will requires that he at least sometimes have the ability to act otherwise than he does. To appreciate the point of the condition, consider the many acts and series of acts you carry out each day, from tying your shoes to phoning your friend to deciding whether to purchase the white shirt or the black one to composing a philosophical argument. Suppose that not only these actions but *all* of the actions you ever performed in your lifetime were such that they were, at the time you did them, *the only acts you could have done.* A natural reaction is: Then I do not have any free will. For if what I do is always the only thing I can possibly do, how could I have any free rein in conducting my life?

Alternative Possibilities

Many philosophers from diverse periods make explicit note of this "alternative possibilities" condition of free will. Aristotle apparently requires the condition when, in his discussion of the voluntary in *Nicomachean Ethics,* he observes that "where it is in our power to act it is also in our power not to act" (1113b6). David Hume defines liberty as "a power of acting or not acting according to the determinations of the will; that is, if we choose to remain at rest, we may; if we choose to move, we also may." Thomas Reid proposes that the "power to produce any effect implies the power not to produce it" (1983: 523). Kant likewise maintains that for an act to be truly free, "the act as well as its opposite must be within the power of the subject at the moment of its taking place" (1960: 45).

The thought echoes among contemporary thinkers. According to A. J. Ayer, "When I am said to have done something of my own free will it is implied that I could have acted otherwise." Bernard Williams describes the claim that free will exists as consisting in "something to the effect that agents sometimes act voluntarily, and that when they do so they have a real choice between more than one course of action; or more than one course is open to them; or it is up to them which of several actions they perform." Similarly, Peter van Inwagen writes: "When I say of a man that he 'has free will' I mean that very often, if not always, when he has to choose between two or more mutually incompatible courses of action—that is, courses of action that it is impossible for him to carry out more than one of—each of these courses of action is such that he can, or is able to, or has it within his power to carry it out."

Hence it has become a philosophical commonplace that the possession of free will requires sometimes being able to do otherwise. Of course, how exactly to *interpret* the requisite ability is not uncontroversial, and in particular whether causal determinism precludes or does not preclude a person's ever having the ability rightly understood is a matter vigorously contested. We need not require that every free act is one for which the agent has at the precise time of acting multiple available options for acting in order to generate the question at the center of the controversy. For if it is true, as is plausible and prevalently supposed, that a person has no free will (or no power ever to act freely) if she cannot *ever* in her lifetime act otherwise than she does, then the question arises as to whether the alternative possibilities required for the possession of free will are or are not compatible with the truth of causal determinism.

Let us say that an agent has free will only if some of the actions she performs during her lifetime are such that she can do (or could have done) otherwise with respect to them. I will call *the minimal supposition of human free will* the thesis that, for some human person, this necessary condition—the ability at some time to act otherwise—is met. Thus if no human person can ever do otherwise than act precisely as he or she does act, then the minimal supposition of human free will is false. The minimal supposition requires that at least on occasion what some human person *can* do is not exhausted by what she *does* do.

The Compatibility Question

Does the truth of determinism imply the falsity of the minimal supposition of human free will? Causal determinism is the doctrine that there is at every instant exactly one physically possible future. Put differently, the doctrine maintains that, for every instant, a proposition expressing all of the facts about the universe at that time, together with a proposition expressing all of the actual laws of nature, entails every truth as to what happens after that time. According to the determinist, the laws of nature are wholly deterministic, and every event is covered by or falls under a law. Thus, according to determinism, the prevailing laws of nature are such that there do not exist any two "possible worlds" that are exactly alike up to some time, that differ thereafter, and in which those laws are never violated. If the minimal supposition of human free will and the thesis of determinism are compatible, then there is no logical contradiction in supposing them both to be true at once. If they are incompatible, then at most one of the claims can be true.

The compatibility question has been the centerpiece of free will debates for the past twenty-five years. Lining up on the side of incompatibilism are van Inwagen (1975, 1983), Ginet (1966, 1990), Wiggins (1973), Lamb (1977), Kane (1985, 1996a, 1996b), and Fischer (1983, 1994), with kindred-minded philosophical ancestors in (arguably) Aristotle, Aquinas, Leibniz, Kant, John Bramhall, Thomas Reid, and C. A. Campbell. On the other side, compatibilism—the position that if determinism is true, it does not rule out persons' having free will—has been recently defended by Lehrer (1966), Davidson (1973), Lewis (1981), Dennett (1984), and Wolf (1990), with historical support from such figures as Hobbes, Spinoza, Hume, Mill, Jonathan Edwards, and Moritz Schlick. This chapter examines arguments for incompatibilism: Why would a person think that *either* the thesis of determinism is true *or* persons have free will, but not both?

Simple Arguments for Incompatibilism

I will begin with a simple version of an argument for the incompatibilist position and proceed to arguments for the view that are more complex. I will then examine the major lines of response to incompatibilist arguments and assess what one should conclude after considering the metaphysical issues pertinent to free will.

CLASHING IMAGES OF PERSONAL LIFE

Consider first a straightforward line of reasoning in favor of incompatibilism. Here is the argument: A deep-rooted and pervasive understanding of ourselves as agents with free will assumes two things. First, it assumes that we are disengaged from the past in a way that makes us not "pushed" into doing precisely what we do by previous events or states of affairs. The thought that all of my behavior is the causally necessary outcome of my genetic blueprint, environment, and social conditioning—in short, the thought that I am pushed into doing what I do by what has come before me—undermines the idea that some of the acts I perform are genuinely "up to me," determined by a self with some causal autonomy from the past. Second, the understanding assumes a forking-paths model of the future (representing a natural interpretation of "the ability to do otherwise") that may be represented as [in figure 2.1].

On this model of the "path of life" of a free agent, as one lives through time facing various choices about what to do, one has open to oneself at a number of points in time multiple possible futures, multiple options for what to decide. As depicted in Figure 2.1, if one is a free agent, then as time proceeds from left to right and as one lives one's life traversing a path from left to right, there are at various junctures "forks in the road"—a number of alternative ways one might choose that, once chosen, alter the course of one's life from that point on. We might think, for instance, of your choice of spouse. The assumption that you have free will regarding whom to marry incorporates a forking-paths model of the future according to which there are a number of possible ways your life might unfold, depending upon exactly which among the several persons under consideration you actually choose. Which person you choose alters your life path significantly, and at the juncture of choice it was in your power to make actual any one of several possible futures.

But both of these aspects of the common understanding of ourselves as free agents are rather straightforwardly at odds with the thesis of scientific determinism as defined above. The doctrine of determinism maintains that every event occurs as the necessary unfolding of events of the past. But if so, then nothing we think or prefer or do (each instance of these being an event) is sufficiently "disengaged" from the past. Again, determinism claims that there is at every instant exactly one physically possible future. Yet the picture inherent in the practical deliberative point of view under the assumption of free agency is of a future involving multiple accessible branching paths. The following diagram makes the point clear. If determinism is true, then the course of events composing the history of the world and its future can be represented as shown in Figure 2.2.

As Figure 2.2 illustrates, there may be *apparent* "forks in the road" from the perspective of a person living in a deterministic universe, but exactly one of the "alternatives" is one that an agent can actually take, since there is only *one* way, given the past and the natural laws, that the course of events can proceed. From the point of view of the agent, there may at times appear to be available options for acting at the next moment. Yet if the thesis of causal determinism is true, then the agent cannot *get to* any of the alternative paths from the path he is on. But this model of the path of one's life through time is incongruous with the model incorporated into the assumption of agential free will. Hence, it cannot be true both that we have free will and that the doctrine of determinism is correct. One or the other of the suppositions is false.

The above is one way of putting the intuitive case in favor of the position of incompatibilism. It represents a very natural way of thinking about the matter of free will and determinism. In fact, by far the most common reaction among those

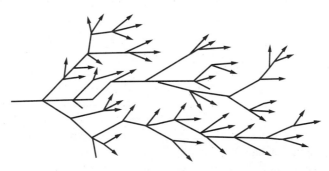

FIGURE 2.1
Forking-Paths Model of the Future

FIGURE 2.2
Deterministic Model of the Future

first hearing of the compatibility problem is an incompatibilist reaction. A large number of compatibilist philosophers, however, have alleged that lines of reasoning leading to incompatibilism are flawed, a charge I will examine further on in this chapter.

THE CONSEQUENCE ARGUMENT

Consider a different and more succinct way of expressing a simple argument for incompatibilism. In the most sustained recent defense of the incompatibilist thesis, *An Essay on Free Will* (1983), Peter van Inwagen presents three arguments for incompatibilism, each a proposed refinement of a certain basic line of reasoning. The basic line of reasoning, which van Inwagen calls "the Consequence Argument," is as follows:

> If determinism is true, then our acts are the consequences of the laws of nature and events in the remote past. But it is not up to us what went on before we were born, and neither is it up to us what the laws of nature are. Therefore, the consequences of these things (including our present acts) are not up to us.

Since only acts that are "up to us" are free, the argument shows that, if determinism is true, then we can never act freely. A natural initial reaction to this informal argument is the following: There must be something wrong with the argument because obviously our present acts *are* (contrary to the conclusion of the argument) "up to us." A present action seems the epitome of something that is "up to oneself," as opposed to, say, what the weather is today, to which parents you or I were born, what someone unknown and unrelated to me in another country decides to do today (for instance, whether a Pakistani political leader acts to escalate a nuclear arms race with India). These latter events and states of affairs are not at all up to me; they are beyond my sphere of influence, out of my control. But what I do today—how I think, how I react emotionally, what I plan to accomplish, what overt actions I commit—unless I unwittingly am manipulated from the outside or I let someone else control me, is up to me and not up to anybody else, or so it is natural to believe.

But, of course, this reaction does not necessarily impugn the consequence argument itself. Instead, it simply underscores the intuitive implausibility of an alleged result of supposing determinism to be true. The consequence argument is meant obviously to focus our attention on the *implications* of the doctrine of determinism. That doctrine maintains that every event is the causally necessary outcome of previous events, so that a chain of deterministically linked events stretches backward into history. We can envision the matter this way: Suppose that determinism is true. Then pick any past event in roughly your space-time region. From that past event, given determinism, one can trace a line forward in time through necessarily linked events up to each present event, including the events of your own acts. But then the consequence argument just states what seems intuitively compelling: Since past events are now out of your control and the laws of nature are out of your control, what happens now as the necessary outcome of those events and laws is also out of your control, if determinism is indeed true.

One can discern even before this argument is made more precise that the reasoning involved in it employs some sort of inference rule concerning what is under our control (what is "up to us," what we have the *power* to do, what we are *able* to do). Namely, if something is the necessary result of factors that are not under our control (not "up to us," not *within our power*, or factors such that we are not now able to affect them), then that result itself is likewise not under our control (not "up to us," not within our power, or something that we are not now able to affect). And it is at the point of the argument's reliance on this sort of inference rule that many compatibilists focus their attack on arguments for incompatibilism. Incompatibilists, for their part, defend the "transference of power" inference rules as impeccable and thus take the consequence argument, or at least one of the several alternate ways of setting out the line of reasoning that the consequence argument roughly embodies, as demonstrating the inconsistency of supposing both that persons have free will and that scientific determinism is true. . . .

9.3 We Are Free

Some of you may find hard determinism unconvincing. Some of you might still be wondering whether we are free in the sense that our choices are *not* always caused or determined by heredity or environment.

Libertarianism is the position that some human choices, in particular moral choices for which we are responsible, are not determined by antecedent events. (Note: This kind of libertarianism should *not* be confused with the political movement and theory of the same name.) One version of this theory holds that the self (sometimes called "soul") is an agent with a power to choose that transcends heredity and environment in the sense that the self can choose contrary to these factors. Another version holds that humans are radically free in the sense that they are free to create their own selves. The self is not a fixed essence determined by heredity, environment, or any other factor except our capacity for choice. We create who we are (our selves) by the choices we make. It follows that humans, when freely deciding to act in a particular way, not only can be but also ought to be held responsible for what they do.

Jean-Paul Sartre (1905–1980) was a French novelist, playwright, and philosopher. In 1939 he was called up by the French army to fight the German invasion. He was captured by the Germans in 1940 but returned to France after the armistice and became active in the resistance movement. After the war, he emerged as a leading French intellectual, a major figure in the philosophical movement called **existentialism,** and he became involved in a number of radical causes. His major philosophical work is *Being and Nothingness* (1943).

In 1945 Sartre gave a lecture that was published the following year as *L'Existentialisme est un Humanisme.* The selection that follows is from that lecture. Sartre was not only concerned with defining existentialism and defending it against its critics, but he was also concerned with free choice. Sartre realized that, if human nature is not something determined beforehand but is something we create as we make the decisions that come to constitute our lives, we are radically free. This is central to the existentialist view of human beings and, as Sartre also clearly realized, has important implications for ethics. If you are free to do whatever you wish, if for you everything is permissible, then what will you do?

Reading Questions

1. What does *existence precedes essence* mean?
2. What is the first principle of existentialism?
3. Why did Sartre claim that "In choosing myself, I choose man"?
4. What is meant by *anguish?*
5. What does *forlornness* mean?
6. Do you agree with the contention that "everything is permissible if God does not exist"? Why, or why not?
7. Why did Sartre say we are *condemned* to be free?
8. What is meant by *despair?*
9. If we create moral value and there is no guarantee that our values are correct or will produce good results, why bother to become socially and politically involved at all? How did Sartre answer this question? Do you agree with his answer? Why, or why not?

Existentialism

JEAN-PAUL SARTRE

WHAT IS MEANT BY THE TERM EXISTEN-TIALISM? Most people who use the word would be rather embarrassed if they had to explain it, since, now that the word is all the rage, even the work of a musician or painter is being called existentialist. A gossip columnist in *Clartés* signs himself *The Existentialist,* so that by this time the word has been so stretched and has taken on so broad a meaning that it no longer means anything at all. It seems that for want of an advance-guard doctrine analogous to surrealism, the kind of people who are eager for scandal and flurry turn to this philosophy which in other respects does not at all serve their purposes in this sphere.

Actually, it is the least scandalous, the most austere of doctrines. It is intended strictly for specialists and philosophers. Yet it can be defined easily. What complicates matters is that there are two kinds of existentialist; first, those who are Christian, among whom I would include Jaspers and Gabriel Marcel, both Catholic; and on the other hand the atheistic existentialists, among whom I class Heidegger, and then the French existentialists and myself. What they have in common is that they think that existence precedes essence, or, if you prefer, that subjectivity must be the starting point.

Just what does that mean? Let us consider some object that is manufactured, for example, a book or a paper-cutter: here is an object which has been made by an artisan whose inspiration came from a concept. He referred to the concept of what a paper-cutter is and likewise to a known method of production, which is part of the concept, something which is, by and large, a routine. Thus, the paper-cutter is at once an object produced in a certain way and, on the other hand, one having a specific use; and one can not postulate a man who produces a paper-cutter but does not know what it is used for. Therefore, let us say that, for the paper-cutter, essence—that is, the ensemble of both the production routines and the properties which enable it to be both produced and defined—precedes existence. Thus, the presence of the paper-cutter or book in front of me is determined. Therefore, we have here a technical view of the world whereby it can be said that production precedes existence.

When we conceive God as the Creator, He is generally thought of as a superior sort of artisan. Whatever doctrine we may be considering, whether one like that of Descartes or that of Leibniz, we always grant that will more or less follows understanding or, at the very least, accompanies it, and that when God creates He knows exactly what He is creating. Thus, the concept of man in the mind of God is comparable to the concept of paper-cutter in the mind of the manufacturer, and, following certain techniques and a conception, God produces man, just as the artisan, following a definition and a technique, makes a paper-cutter. Thus, the individual man is the realization of a certain concept in the divine intelligence.

In the eighteenth century, the atheism of the *philosophes* discarded the idea of God, but not so much for the notion that essence precedes existence. To a certain extent, this idea is found everywhere; we find it in Diderot, in Voltaire, and even in Kant. Man has a human nature; this human nature, which is the concept of the human, is found in all men, which means that each man is a particular example of a universal concept, man. In Kant, the result of this universality is that the wild-man, the natural man, as well as the bourgeois, are circumscribed by the same definition and have the same basic qualities. Thus, here too the essence of man precedes the historical existence that we find in nature.

Jean-Paul Sartre, Existentialism, *translated by Bernard Frechtman (New York: The Philosophical Library, 1947), pp. 14–42. Reprinted by permission of The Philosophical Library, Inc.*

Atheistic existentialism, which I represent, is more coherent. It states that if God does not exist, there is at least one being in whom existence precedes essence, a being who exists before he can be defined by any concept, and that this being is man, or, as Heidegger says, human reality. What is meant here by saying that existence precedes essence? It means that, first of all, man exists, turns up, appears on the scene, and, only afterwards, defines himself. If man, as the existentialist conceives him, is indefinable, it is because at first he is nothing. Only afterward will he be something, and he himself will have made what he will be. Thus, there is no human nature, since there is no God to conceive it. Not only is man what he conceives himself to be, but he is also only what he wills himself to be after this thrust toward existence.

Man is nothing else but what he makes of himself. Such is the first principle of existentialism. It is also what is called subjectivity, the name we are labeled with when charges are brought against us. But what do we mean by this, if not that man has a greater dignity than a stone or table? For we mean that man first exists, that is, that man first of all is the being who hurls himself toward a future and who is conscious of imagining himself as being in the future. Man is at the start a plan which is aware of itself, rather than a patch of moss, a piece of garbage, or a cauliflower; nothing exists prior to this plan; there is nothing in heaven; man will be what he will have planned to be. Not what he will want to be. Because by the word "will" we generally mean a conscious decision, which is subsequent to what we have already made of ourselves. I may want to belong to a political party, write a book, get married; but all that is only a manifestation of an earlier, more spontaneous choice that is called "will." But if existence really does precede essence, man is responsible for what he is. Thus, existentialism's first move is to make every man aware of what he is and to make the full responsibility of his existence rest on him. And when we say that a man is responsible for himself, we do not only mean that he is responsible for his own individuality, but that he is responsible for all men.

The word subjectivism has two meanings, and our opponents play on the two. Subjectivism means, on the one hand, that an individual chooses and makes himself; and, on the other, that it is impossible for man to transcend human subjectivity. The second of these is the essential meaning of existentialism. When we say that man chooses his own self, we mean that every one of us does likewise; but we also mean by that that in making this choice he also chooses all men. In fact, in creating the man that we want to be, there is not a single one of our acts which does not at the same time create an image of man as we think he ought to be. To choose to be this or that is to affirm at the same time the value of what we choose, because we can never choose evil. We always choose the good, and nothing can be good for us without being good for all. If, on the other hand, existence precedes essence, and if we grant that we exist and fashion our image at one and the same time, the image is valid for everybody and for our whole age. Thus, our responsibility is much greater than we might have supposed, because it involves all mankind. If I am a working man and choose to join a Christian trade-union rather than be a communist, and if by being a member I want to show that the best thing for man is resignation, that the kingdom of man is not of this world, I am not only involving my own case—I want to be resigned for everyone. As a result, my action has involved all humanity. To take a more individual matter, if I want to marry, to have children; even if this marriage depends solely on my own circumstances or passion or wish, I am involving all humanity in monogamy and not merely myself. Therefore, I am responsible for myself and for everyone else. I am creating a certain image of man of my own choosing. In choosing myself, I choose man.

This helps us understand what the actual content is of such rather grandiloquent words as anguish, forlornness, despair. As you will see, it's all quite simple.

First, what is meant by anguish? The existentialists say at once that man is anguish. What that means is this: the man who involves himself and who realizes that he is not only the person he chooses to be, but also a law-maker who is, at the same time, choosing all mankind as well as himself, can not help escape the feeling of his total and deep responsibility. Of course, there are many people who are not anxious; but we claim that they are hiding their anxiety, that they are fleeing from it. Certainly, many people believe that when they do something, they themselves are the only ones involved, and when someone says to them, "What if everyone acted that way?" they shrug their shoulders and answer, "Everyone doesn't act that way." But really, one should always ask himself, "What would happen if everybody looked at things that way?" There is no escaping this disturbing thought except by a kind of double-dealing. A man who lies and makes excuses for himself by saying "not everybody does that," is someone with an uneasy conscience, because the act of lying implies that a universal value is conferred upon the lie.

Anguish is evident even when it conceals itself. This is the anguish that Kierkegaard called the anguish of Abraham. You know the story: an angel has ordered Abraham to sacrifice his son; if it really were an angel who has come and said, "You are Abraham, you shall sacrifice your son," everything would be all right. But everyone might first wonder, "Is it really an angel, and am I really Abraham? What proof do I have?"

There was a madwoman who had hallucinations; someone used to speak to her on the telephone and give her orders. Her doctor asked her, "Who is it who talks to you?" She answered, "He says it's God." What proof did she really have that it was God? If an angel comes to me, what proof is there that it's an angel? And if I hear voices, what proof is there that they come from heaven and not from hell, or from the subconscious, or a pathological condition? What proves that they are addressed to me? What proof is there that I have been appointed to impose my choice and my conception of man on humanity? I'll never find any proof or sign to convince me of that. If a voice addresses me, it is always for me to decide that this is the angel's voice; if I consider that such an act is a good one, it is I who will choose to say that it is good rather than bad. Now, I'm not being singled out as an Abraham, and yet at every moment I'm obliged to perform exemplary acts. For every man, everything happens as if all mankind had its eyes fixed on him and were guiding itself by what he does. And every man ought to say to himself, "Am I really the kind of man who has the right to act in such a way that humanity might guide itself by my actions?" And if he does not say that to himself, he is masking his anguish.

There is no question here of the kind of anguish which would lead to quietism, to inaction. It is a matter of a simple sort of anguish that anybody who has had responsibilities is familiar with. For example, when a military officer takes the responsibility for an attack and sends a certain number of men to death, he chooses to do so, and in the main he alone makes the choice. Doubtless, orders come from above, but they are too broad; he interprets them, and on this interpretation depend the lives of ten or fourteen or twenty men. In making a decision he can not help having a certain anguish. All leaders know this anguish. That doesn't keep them from acting; on the contrary, it is the very condition of their action. For it implies that they envisage a number of possibilities, and when they choose one, they realize that it has value only because it is chosen. We shall see that this kind of anguish, which is the kind that existentialism describes, is explained, in addition, by a direct responsibility to the other men whom it involves. It is not a curtain separating us from action, but is part of action itself.

When we speak of forlornness, a term Heidegger was fond of, we mean only that God does not exist and that we have to face all the consequences of this. The existentialist is strongly opposed to a certain kind of secular ethics which would like to abolish God with the least possible expense. About 1880, some French teachers tried to set up a secular ethics which went something like this: God is a useless and costly hypothesis; we are discarding it; but, meanwhile, in order for there to be an ethics, a society, a civilization, it is essential that certain values be taken seriously and that they be considered as having an *a priori* existence. It must be obligatory, *a priori,* to be honest, not to lie, not to beat your wife, to have children, etc. So we're going to try a little device which will make it possible to show that values exist all the same, inscribed in a heaven of ideas, though otherwise God does not exist. In other words—and this, I believe, is the tendency of everything called reformism in France—nothing will be changed if God does not exist. We shall find ourselves with the same norms of honesty, progress, and humanism, and we shall have made of God an outdated hypothesis which will peacefully die off by itself.

The existentialist, on the contrary, thinks it very distressing that God does not exist, because all possibility of finding values in a heaven of ideas disappears along with Him; there can no longer be an *a priori* Good, since there is no infinite and perfect consciousness to think it. Nowhere is it written that the Good exists, that we must be honest, that we must not lie; because the fact is we are on a plane where there are only men. Dostoievsky said, "If God didn't exist, everything would be possible." That is the very starting point of existentialism. Indeed, everything is permissible if God does not exist, and as a result man is forlorn, because neither within him or without does he find anything to cling to. He can't start making excuses for himself.

If existence really does precede essence, there is no explaining things away by reference to a fixed and given human nature. In other words, there is no determinism, man is free, man is freedom. On the other hand, if God does not exist, we find no values or commands to turn to which legitimize our conduct. So, in the bright realm of values, we have no excuse behind us, nor justification before us. We are alone, with no excuses.

That is the idea I shall try to convey when I say that man is condemned to be free. Condemned, because he did not create himself, yet, in other respects is free; because, once thrown into the world, he is responsible for everything he does. The existentialist does not believe in the power of passion. He will never agree that a sweeping passion is a ravaging torrent which fatally leads a man to certain acts and is therefore an excuse. He thinks that man is responsible for his passion.

The existentialist does not think that man is going to help himself by finding in the world some omen by which to orient himself. Because he thinks that man will interpret the omen to suit himself. Therefore, he thinks that man, with no support and no aid, is condemned every moment to invent man. Ponge, in a very fine article, has said, "Man is the future of man." That's exactly it. But if it is taken to mean that this future is recorded in heaven, that God sees it, then it is false, because it would really no longer be a future. If it is taken to mean that, whatever a man may be, there is a future to be forged, a virgin future before him, then this remark is sound. But then we are forlorn.

To give you an example which will enable you to understand forlornness better, I shall cite the case of one of my students who came to see me under the following circumstances: His father was on bad terms with his mother, and, moreover, was inclined to be a collaborationist; his older brother had been killed in the German offensive of 1940, and the young man, with somewhat immature but generous feelings, wanted to avenge him. His mother lived alone with him, very much upset by the half-treason of her husband and the death of her older son; the boy was her only consolation.

The boy was faced with the choice of leaving for England and joining the Free French Forces—that is, leaving his mother behind—or remaining with his mother and helping her to carry on. He was fully aware that the woman lived only for him and that his going-off—and perhaps his death—would plunge her into despair. He was also aware that every act that he did for his mother's sake was a sure thing, in the sense that it was helping her to carry on, whereas every effort he made toward going off and fighting was an uncertain move which might run aground and prove completely useless; for example, on his way to England he might, while passing through Spain, be detained indefinitely in a Spanish camp; he might reach England or Algiers and be stuck in an office at a desk job. As a result, he was faced with two very different kinds of action: one, concrete, immediate, but concerning only one individual; the other concerned an incomparably vaster group, a national collectivity, but for that very reason was dubious, and might be interrupted en route. And, at the same time, he was wavering between two kinds of ethics. On the one hand, an ethics of sympathy, of personal devotion; on the other, a broader ethics, but one whose efficacy was more dubious. He had to choose between the two.

Who could help him choose? Christian doctrine? No. Christian doctrine says, "Be charitable, love your neighbor, take the more rugged path, etc." But which is the more rugged path? Whom should he love as a brother? The fighting man or his mother? Which does the greater good, the vague act of fighting in a group, or the concrete one of helping a particular human being to go on living? Who can decide *a priori*? Nobody. No book of ethics can tell him. The Kantian ethics says, "Never treat any person as a means, but as an end." Very well, if I stay with my mother, I'll treat her as an end and not as a means; but by virtue of this very fact, I'm running the risk of treating the people around me who are fighting, as means; and, conversely, if I go to join those who are fighting, I'll be treating them as an end, and, by doing that, I run the risk of treating my mother as a means.

If values are vague, and if they are always too broad for the concrete and specific case that we are considering, the only thing left for us is to trust our instincts. That's what this young man tried to do; and when I saw him, he said, "In the end, feeling is what counts. I ought to choose whichever pushes me in one direction. If I feel that I love my mother enough to sacrifice everything else for her—my desire for vengeance, for action, for adventure—then I'll stay with her. If, on the contrary, I feel that my love for my mother isn't enough, I'll leave."

But how is the value of a feeling determined? What gives his feeling for his mother value? Precisely the fact that he remained with her. I may say that I like so-and-so well enough to sacrifice a certain amount of money for him, but I may say so only if I've done it. I may say "I love my mother well enough to remain with her" if I have remained with her. The only way to determine the value of this affection is, precisely, to perform an act which confirms and defines it. But, since I require this affection to justify my act, I find myself caught in a vicious circle.

On the other hand, Gide has well said that a mock feeling and a true feeling are almost indistinguishable; to decide that I love my mother and will remain with her, or to remain with her by putting on an act, amount somewhat to the same thing. In other words, the feeling is formed by the acts one performs; so, I can not refer to it in order to act upon it. Which means that I can neither seek within myself the true condition which will impel me to act, nor apply to a system of ethics for concepts which will permit me to act. You will say, "At least, he did go to a teacher for advice." But if you seek advice from a priest, for example, you have chosen this priest; you already knew, more or less, just about what advice he was going to give you. In other words, choosing your adviser is involving yourself. The proof of this is that if you are a Christian, you will say, "Consult a priest." But some priests are collaborating, some are just marking time, some are resisting. Which to choose? If the young man chooses a priest who is resisting or collaborating, he has already decided on the kind of advice he's going to get. Therefore, in coming to see me he knew the answer I was going to give him, and I had only one answer to give: "You're free; choose, that is, invent." No general ethics can show you what is to be done; there are no omens in the world. The Catholics will reply, "But there are." Granted—but, in any case, I myself choose the meaning they have.

When I was a prisoner, I knew a rather remarkable young man who was a Jesuit. He had entered the Jesuit order in the following way: he had had a number of very bad breaks; in childhood, his father died, leaving him in poverty, and he was a scholarship student at a religious institution where he was constantly made to feel that he was being kept out of charity; then, he failed to get any of the honors and distinctions that children like; later on, at about eighteen, he bungled a love affair; finally, at twenty-two, he failed in military training, a childish enough matter, but it was the last straw.

This young fellow might well have felt that he had botched everything. It was a sign of something, but of what? He might have taken refuge in bitterness or despair. But he very wisely looked upon all this as a sign that he was not made for secular triumphs, and that only the triumphs of religion, holiness, and faith were open to him. He saw the hand of God in all this, and so he entered the order. Who can help seeing that he alone decided what the sign meant?

Some other interpretation might have been drawn from this series of setbacks; for example, that he might have done better to turn carpenter or revolutionist. Therefore, he is fully responsible for the interpretation. Forlornness implies that we ourselves choose our being. Forlornness and anguish go together.

As for despair, the term has a very simple meaning. It means that we shall confine ourselves to reckoning only with what depends upon our will, or on the ensemble of probabilities which make our action possible. When we want something, we always have to reckon with probabilities. I may be counting on the arrival of a friend. The friend is coming by rail or street-car; this supposes that the train will arrive on schedule, or that the street-car will not jump the track. I am left in the realm of possibility; but possibilities are to be reckoned with only to the point where my action comports with the ensemble of these possibilities, and no further. The moment the possibilities I am considering are not rigorously involved by my action, I ought to disengage myself from them, because no God, no scheme, can adapt the world and its possibilities to my will. When Descartes said, "Conquer yourself rather than the world," he meant essentially the same thing.

The Marxists to whom I have spoken reply, "You can rely on the support of others in your action, which obviously has certain limits because you're not going to live forever. That means: rely on both what others are doing elsewhere to help you, in China, in Russia, and what they will do later on, after your death, to carry on the action and lead it to its fulfillment, which will be the revolution. You even *have* to rely upon that, otherwise you're immoral." I reply at once that I will always rely on fellow-fighters insofar as these comrades are involved with me in a common struggle, in the unity of a party or a group in which I can more or less make my weight felt; that is, one whose ranks I am in as a fighter and whose movements I am aware of at every moment. In such a situation, relying on the unity and will of the party is exactly like counting on the fact that the train will arrive on time or that the car won't jump the track. But, given that man is free and that there is no human nature for me to depend on, I can not count on men whom I do not know by relying on human goodness or man's concern for the good of society. I don't know what will become of the Russian revolution; I may make an example of it to the extent that at the present time it is apparent that the proletariat plays a part in Russia that it plays in no other nation. But I can't swear that this will inevitably lead to a triumph of the proletariat. I've got to limit myself to what I see.

Given that men are free and that tomorrow they will freely decide what man will be, I can not be sure that, after my death, fellow-fighters will carry on my work to bring it to its maximum perfection. Tomorrow, after my death, some men may decide to set up Fascism, and the others may be cowardly and muddled enough to let them do it. Fascism will then be the human reality, so much the worse for us.

Actually, things will be as man will have decided they are to be. Does that mean that I should abandon myself to quietism? No. First, I should involve myself; then, act on the old saw, "Nothing ventured, nothing gained." Nor does it mean that I shouldn't belong to a party, but rather that I shall have no illusions and shall do what I can. For example, suppose I ask myself, "Will socialization, as such, ever come about?" I know nothing about it. All I know is that I'm going to do everything in my power to bring it about. Beyond that, I can't count on anything. Quietism is the attitude of people who say, "Let others do what I can't do." The doctrine I am presenting is the very opposite of quietism, since it declares, "There is no reality except in action." Moreover, it goes further, since it adds, "Man is nothing else than his plan; he exists only to the extent that he fulfills himself; he is therefore nothing else than the ensemble of his acts, nothing else than his life."

According to this, we can understand why our doctrine horrifies certain people. Because often the only way they can bear their wretchedness is to think, "Circumstances have been against me. What I've been and done doesn't show my true worth. To be sure, I've had no great love, no great friendship, but that's because I haven't met a man or woman who was worthy. The books I've written haven't been very good because I haven't had the proper leisure. I haven't had children to devote myself to because I didn't find a man with whom I could have spent my life. So there remains within me, unused and quite viable, a host of propensities, inclinations, possibilities, that one wouldn't guess from, the mere series of things I've done."

Now, for the existentialist there is really no love other than one which manifests itself in a person's being in love. There is no genius other than one which is expressed in works of art; the genius of Proust is the sum of Proust's works; the genius of Racine is his series of tragedies. Outside of that, there is nothing. Why say that Racine could have written another tragedy, when he didn't write it? A man is involved in life, leaves his impress on it, and outside of that there is nothing. To be sure, this may seem a harsh thought to someone whose life hasn't been a success. But, on the other hand, it prompts people to understand that reality alone is what counts, that dreams, expectations, and hopes warrant no more than to define a man as a disappointed dream, as miscarried hopes, as vain expectations. In other words, to define him negatively and not positively. However, when we say, "You are nothing else than your life," that does not imply that the artist will be judged solely on the basis of his works of art; a thousand other things will contribute toward summing him up. What we mean is that a man is nothing else than a series of undertakings, that he is the sum, the organization, the ensemble of the relationships which make up these undertakings.

When all is said and done, what we are accused of, at bottom, is not our pessimism, but an optimistic toughness. If people throw up to us our works of fiction in which we write about people who are soft, weak, cowardly, and sometimes even downright bad, it's not because these people

are soft, weak, cowardly, or bad; because if we were to say, as Zola did, that they are that way because of heredity, the workings of environment, society, because of biological or psychological determinism, people would be reassured. They would say, "Well, that's what we're like, no one can do anything about it." But when the existentialist writes about a coward, he says that this coward is responsible for his cowardice. He's not like that because he has a cowardly heart or lung or brain; he's not like that on account of his physiological makeup; but he's like that because he has made himself a coward by his acts. There's no such thing as a cowardly constitution; there are nervous constitutions; there is poor blood, as the common people say, or strong constitutions. But the man whose blood is poor is not a coward on that account, for what makes cowardice is the act of renouncing or yielding. A constitution is not an act; the coward is defined on the basis of the acts he performs. People feel, in a vague sort of way, that this coward we're talking about is guilty of being a coward, and the thought frightens them. What people would like is that a coward or a hero be born that way.

One of the complaints most frequently made about *The Ways of Freedom*[1] can be summed up as follows: "After all, these people are so spineless, how are you going to make heroes out of them?" This objection almost makes me laugh, for it assumes that people are born heroes. That's what people really want to think. If you're born cowardly, you may set your mind perfectly at rest; there's nothing you can do about it; you'll be cowardly all your life, whatever you may do. If you're born a hero, you may set your mind just as much at rest; you'll be a hero all your life; you'll drink like a hero and eat like a hero. What the existentialist says is that the coward makes himself cowardly, that the hero makes himself heroic. There's always a possibility for the coward not to be cowardly any more and for the hero to stop

---

[1] *Les Chemins de la Liberté*. M. Sartre's projected trilogy of novels, two of which, *L'Age de Raison* (*The Age of Reason*) and *Le Sursis* (*The Reprieve*) have already appeared.—Translator's note.

being heroic. What counts is total involvement; some one particular action or set of circumstances is not total involvement.

Thus, I think we have answered a number of the charges concerning existentialism. You see that it can not be taken for a philosophy of quietism, since it defines man in terms of action; nor for a pessimistic description of man—there is no doctrine more optimistic, since man's destiny is within himself; nor for an attempt to discourage man from acting, since it tells him that the only hope is in his acting and that action is the only thing that enables a man to live. Consequently, we are dealing here with an ethics of action and involvement. . . .

9.4 Karma and Freedom

The contemporary Western discussion of the problem of freedom and determinism usually takes place in the context of the natural and social sciences. Many philosophers believe that some type of determinism is one of the basic assumptions of science. If it is, then the scene is set for a conflict between a scientific view and the moral or religious view of human freedom and responsibility. The law of causality, as understood by science, is an amoral law. That is, it operates regardless of moral considerations. The social or behavioral sciences (psychology, sociology, anthropology, economics, and history) have extended this view to human behavior. They assume that human action, like physical action, is understandable only when the causal factors determining such action are described and explained by reference to some kind of "natural" law.

In the Asian (primarily Indian) context, the discussion of the problem of freedom and determinism often takes place in a moral and religious context. The law of causality that concerns much Indian and Buddhist philosophy is moral, not amoral. Very early in Indian philosophy (500 BCE?), the idea of the *law of karma* developed. This law states that as each of us sows, so shall we reap. If this law is valid, then your past and present actions determine your future spiritual, moral, and physical conditions. If there is a life beyond this one, then your actions also determine it.

The teaching of karma posits the existence of a perfect law of moral justice that operates automatically within the universe. Habitual liars in this life, for example, will pay for lying in the future. Perhaps they will be falsely accused at some future date or, when reborn, will have relatives who lie, cheat, and deceive them. In contrast, an honest person will be treated honestly by others.

The law of karma provides a good deal of comfort. It assures us that the universe is a just place. It tells us that evil people and good people will eventually get their just deserts. However, the notion of karma also raises questions about human freedom. If what is happening to me now is the effect of my own actions in the past, how can I be free? Are not my life and the circumstances of my life determined? It seems to be the case, according to the law of karma, that, for example, if you are poor, this condition is due to what you did in the past, and hence, it would seem, you are no more in control of your poverty than you are in control of the orbit of Earth.

Some Indian philosophers have drawn fatalistic conclusions from the doctrine of karma and have denied human freedom. The majority of Indian philosophers, however, have affirmed human freedom and argued that freedom and karma are compatible ideas. One such philosopher was Sarvepalli Radhakrishnan (1888–1975), a scholar and statesman who held chairs of philosophy at several Indian universities and was president of India from 1962 until 1967. He was a leading exponent of neo-Hinduism, maintaining that all religions are but different expressions of one truth and that spiritual reality is more fundamental than material reality. The following selection comes from his book *An Idealist View of Life,* which contains his Hibbert lectures given in 1929 and 1930.

Radhakrishnan supports a type of libertarianism. Though he believes that human action is determined to a large extent (and hence would not subscribe to Sartre's radical libertarianism), he also believes in self-determination. If a choice is caused by the whole self, rather than part of the self (such as character or environment), such choice is free. In other words, he subscribes to what is often called *agent causation.* When your self (not a part of your self but your whole self) is the agent that causes you to choose and act, then you are free. A crucial question now becomes, what is the self?

Reading Questions

1. According to Radhakrishnan, what is the law of karma?
2. What are the two aspects of karma?
3. How did Radhakrishnan define *freedom of the will?*
4. What did he mean by *self-determination?*
5. How did he respond to the argument that self-determination is not really freedom?
6. How did he define *choice?*
7. Does the author's assertion that even though "the self is not free from the bonds of determination, it can subjugate the past to a certain extent and turn it into a new course" make sense?
8. Do you think Radhakrishnan's analogy with a game of bridge is a good one? Why, or why not?
9. Name one thing you learned from reading this selection that you did not know before.

Karma and Freedom

SARVEPALLI RADHAKRISHNAN

THE TWO PERVASIVE features of all nature, connection with the past and creation of the future, are present in the human level. The connection with the past at the human stage is denoted by the word "Karma" in the Hindu systems. The human individual is a self-conscious, efficient portion of universal nature with his own uniqueness. His history stretching back to an indefinite period of time binds him with the physical and vital conditions of the world. Human life is an organic whole where each successive phase grows out of what has gone before. We are what we are on account of our affinity with the past. Human growth is an ordered one and its orderedness is indicated by saying that it is governed by the law of Karma.

From S. Radhakrishnan's An Idealist View of Life *(London: George Allen & Unwin, 1932), pp. 218–223. Reproduced by kind permission of HarperCollins Publishers Limited. Copyright S. Radhakrishnan 1932. Footnotes deleted.*

Karma literally means action, deed. All acts produce their effects which are recorded both in the organism and the environment. Their physical effects may be short-lived but their moral effects (samsskāra) are worked into the character of the self. Every single thought, word and deed enters into the living chain of causes which makes us what we are. Our life is not at the mercy of blind chance or capricious fate. The conception is not peculiar to the Oriental creeds. The Christian Scriptures refer to it. "Be not deceived; God is not mocked: for whatsoever a man soweth, that shall he also reap." Jesus is reported to have said on the Mount, "Judge not that ye be not judged, for with what judgment ye judge, ye shall be judged, and with what measure ye mete, it shall be measured to you again."

Karma is not so much a principle of retribution as one of continuity. Good produces good, evil, evil. Love increases our power of love, hatred our power of hatred. It emphasizes the great importance of right action. Man is continuously shaping his own self. The law of Karma is not to be confused with either a hedonistic or a juridical theory of rewards and punishments. The reward for virtue is not a life of pleasure nor is the punishment for sin pain. Pleasure and pain may govern the animal nature of man but not his human. Love which is a joy in itself suffers; hatred too often means a perverse kind of satisfaction. Good and evil are not to be confused with material well-being and physical suffering.

All things in the world are at once causes and effects. They embody the energy of the past and exert energy on the future. Karma or connection with the past is not inconsistent with creative freedom. On the other hand it is implied by it. The law that links us with the past also asserts that it can be subjugated by our free action. Though the past may present obstacles, they must all yield to the creative power in man in proportion to its sincerity and insistence. The law of Karma says that each individual will get the return according to the energy he puts forth. The universe will respond to and implement the demands of the self. Nature will reply to the insistent call of spirit. "As is his desire, such is his purpose; as is his purpose, such is the action he performs; what action he

performs, that he procures for himself." "Verily I say unto you that whoever shall say to this mountain, 'Be lifted up and cast into the sea,' and shall not doubt in his heart but believe fully that what he says shall be, it shall be done for him." When Jesus said, "Destroy this temple and I will raise it again in three days" he is asserting the truth that the spirit within us is mightier than the world of things. There is nothing we cannot achieve if we want it enough. Subjection to spirit is the law of universal nature. The principle of Karma has thus two aspects, a retrospective and a prospective, continuity with the past and creative freedom of the self.

The urge in nature which seeks not only to maintain itself at a particular level but advance to a higher becomes conscious in man who deliberately seeks after rules of life and principles of progress. "My father worketh hitherto, and I work." Human beings are the first among nature's children who can say "I" and consciously collaborate with the "father," the power that controls and directs nature, in the fashioning of the world. They can substitute rational direction for the slow, dark, blundering growth of the subhuman world. We cannot deny the free action of human beings however much their origin may be veiled in darkness. The self has conative tendencies, impulses to change by its efforts the given conditions, inner and outer, and shape them to its own purpose.

The problem of human freedom is confused somewhat by the distinction between the self and the will. The will is only the self in its active side and freedom of the will really means the freedom of the self. It is determination by the self.

It is argued that self-determination is not really freedom. It makes little difference whether the self is moved from without or from within. A spinning top moved from within by a spring is as mechanical as one whipped into motion from without. The self may well be an animated automaton. A drunkard who takes to his glass habitually does so in obedience to an element in his nature. The habit has become a part of his self. If we analyze the contents of the self, many of them are traceable to the influence of the environment and the inheritance from the past.

If the individual's view and character are the product of a long evolution, his actions which are the outcome of these cannot be free. The feeling of freedom may be an illusion of the self which lives in each moment of the present, ignoring the determining past. In answer to these difficulties, it may be said that the self represents a form of relatedness or organization, closer and more intimate than that which is found in animal, plant or atom. Self-determination means not determination by any fragment of the self's nature but by the whole of it. Unless the individual employs his whole nature, searches the different possibilities and selects one which commends itself to his whole self, the act is not really free.

Sheer necessity is not to be found in any aspect of nature; complete freedom is divine and possible only when the self becomes co-extensive with the whole. Human freedom is a matter of degree. We are most free when our whole self is active and not merely a fragment of it. We generally act according to our conventional or habitual self and sometimes we sink to the level of our subnormal self.

Freedom is not caprice, nor is Karma necessity. Human choice is not unmotivated or uncaused. If our acts were irrelevant to our past, then there would be no moral responsibility or scope for improvement. Undetermined beginnings, upstart events are impossible either in the physical or the human world. Free acts cannot negate continuity. They arise within the order of nature. Freedom is not caprice since we carry our past with us. The character, at any given point, is the condensation of our previous history. What we have been enters into the "me" which is now active and choosing. The range of one's natural freedom of action is limited. No man has the universal field of possibilities for himself. The varied possibilities of our nature do not all get a chance and the cosmic has its influence in permitting the development of certain possibilities and closing down others. Again, freedom is dogged by automatism. When we make up our mind to do a thing, our mind is different from what it was before. When a possibility becomes an actuality, it assumes the character of necessity. The past can never be cancelled, though it may be utilized. Mere defiance of the

given may mean disaster, though we can make a new life spring up from the past. Only the possible is the sphere of freedom. We have a good deal of present constraint and previous necessity in human life. But necessity is not to be mistaken for destiny which we can neither defy nor delude. Though the self is not free from the bonds of determination, it can subjugate the past to a certain extent and turn it into a new course. Choice is the assertion of freedom over necessity by which it converts necessity to its own use and thus frees itself from it. "The human agent is free." He is not the plaything of fate or driftwood on the tide of uncontrolled events. He can actively mould the future instead of passively suffering the past. The past may become either an opportunity or an obstacle. Everything depends on what we make of it and not what it makes of us. Life is not bound to move in a specific direction. Life is a growth and a growth is undetermined in a measure. Though the future is the sequel of the past, we cannot say what it will be. If there is no indetermination, then human consciousness is an unnecessary luxury.

Our demand for freedom must reckon with a universe that is marked by order and regularity. Life is like a game of bridge. The cards in the game are given to us. We do not select them. They are traced to past Karma but we are free to make any call as we think fit and lead any suit. Only we are limited by the rules of the game. We are more free when we start the game than later on when the game has developed and our choices become restricted. But till the very end there is always a choice. A good player will see possibilities which a bad one does not. The more skilled a player the more alternatives does he perceive. A good hand may be cut to pieces by unskillful play and the bad play need not be attributed to the frowns of fortune. Even though we may not like the way in which the cards are shuffled, we like the game and we want to play. Sometimes wind and tide may prove too strong for us and even the most noble may come down. The great souls find profound peace in the consciousness that the stately order of the world, now lovely and luminous, now dark and terrible, in which man finds his duty and destiny, cannot be subdued to known aims. It seems to have a purpose of its own of which we are ignorant. Misfortune is not fate but providence.

The law of Karma does not support the doctrine of predestination. There are some who believe that only the predestination of certain souls to destruction is consistent with divine sovereignty. God has a perfect right to deal with his creatures even as a potter does with his clay. St. Paul speaks of "vessels of wrath fitted to destruction." Life eternal is a gracious gift of God. Such a view of divine sovereignty is unethical. God's love is manifested in and through law.

In our relations with human failures, belief in Karma inclines us to take a sympathetic attitude and develop reverence before the mystery of misfortune. The more understanding we are, the less do we pride ourselves on our superiority. Faith in Karma induces in us the mood of true justice or charity which is the essence of spirituality. We realize how infinitely helpless and frail human beings are. When we look at the warped lives of the poor, we see how much the law of Karma is true. If they are lazy and criminal, let us ask what chance they had of choosing to be different. They are more unfortunate than wicked. Again, failures are due not so much to "sin" as to errors which lead us to our doom. In Greek tragedy man is held individually less responsible and circumstances or the decisions of Moira [Fate] more so. The tale of Oedipus Rex tells us how he could not avoid his fate to kill his father and marry his mother, in spite of his best efforts. The parting of Hector and Andromache in Homer is another illustration. In Shakespeare again, we see the artist leading on his characters to their destined ends by what seems a very natural development

of their foibles, criminal folly in Lear or personal ambition in Macbeth. The artist shows us these souls in pain. Hamlet's reason is puzzled, his will confounded. He looks at life and at death and wonders which is worse. Goaded by personal ambition, Macbeth makes a mess of it all. Othello kills his wife and kills himself because a jealous villain shows him a handkerchief. When these noble souls crash battling with adverse forces we feel with them and for them; for it might happen to any of us. We are not free from the weaknesses that broke them, whatever we call them, stupidity, disorder, vacillation or, if you please, insane ambition and self-seeking. Today the evil stars of the Greek tragedians are replaced by the almighty laws of economics. Thousands of young men the world over are breaking their heads in vain against the iron walls of society like trapped birds in cages. We see in them the essence of all tragedy, something noble breaking down, something sublime falling with a crash. We can only bow our heads in the presence of those broken beneath the burden of their destiny. The capacity of the human soul for suffering and isolation is immense. Take the poor creatures whom the world passes by as the lowly and the lost. If only we had known what they passed through, we would have been glad of their company. It is utterly wrong to think that misfortune comes only to those who deserve it. The world is a whole and we are members one of another, and we must suffer one for another. In Christianity, it needed a divine soul to reveal how much grace there is in suffering. To bear pain, to endure suffering, is the quality of the strong in spirit. It adds to the spiritual resources of humanity.

9.5 We Are Both Free and Determined

You might be thinking, "Hard determinism seems awfully hard. Human beings are not just pawns in the hands of heredity and environment. We are free. I am free. Indeed, right now, I can continue reading this book or I can stop, whichever is my pleasure. Yet Sartre's views seem unrealistic. I am not totally free. Heredity and environment clearly play some role. However, Radhakrishnan's ideas, though less radical than Sartre's with respect to the scope of human freedom, require me to believe in some kind of metaphysical notions about the self and reincarnation. I don't find that attractive. I don't, however, want to deny the law of causality. There must be some way to reconcile freedom and determinism."

If these are your thoughts, then you may like another answer that has been proposed to the problem of freedom and determinism, an answer called **soft determinism.** This position holds that every event has a cause, and this fact is *compatible* with human freedom. Hence, another name for soft determinism is **compatibilism.** According to the compatibilist, even if determinism is true, people ought to be held morally responsible for those actions they do voluntarily. Indeed, many compatibilists argue that moral responsibility makes no sense unless determinism is true because it makes no sense to hold anyone responsible for uncaused (undetermined) actions.

Notice that soft determinism is, like hard determinism, a kind of determinism. Both the soft and hard determinists agree that every event has a cause. However, they disagree about whether this is compatible with human freedom and about the implications for moral responsibility.

As you might imagine, the harmony between freedom and determinism that the compatibilist wishes to defend is based on a particular understanding of human freedom. Compatibilists do *not* define a free event as an uncaused event. The issue, according to many compatibilists, is not a question of events being caused or uncaused, rather it is a question of what kind of cause we are talking about. If my behavior is coerced or forced by circumstances over which I have no control, then I am not free and my behavior is involuntary. But if my behavior is caused by circumstances over which I do have control, it is free or voluntary.

Raymond M. Smullyan, author of the next selection, gives a slightly different twist to the compatibilist argument. In an imaginative dialogue between a "mortal" and "God" (here used to symbolize *Dao*), Smullyan applies his understanding of Daoism to the issue of free will and determinism. Daoism maintains that the Dao is the way of nature that harmonizes all opposites. If we follow this idea to its logical conclusion, then, Smullyan thinks, it makes sense to say that free choice is just built into the causal order of the universe. The so-called laws of nature do not literally "determine" anything in the sense of forcing events. They simply describe the regularities we can observe in nature. Hence, there can be no conflict between our wills and the way of nature because one of the ways nature operates is via the human will. In the final analysis, there is no problem of free will at all!

Is this a reasonable solution? Does it really answer the question, "Could we have done other that we did, all other conditions remaining the same?" Some philosophers argue that this is really the crucial question in the debate and that compatibilistic answers do not adequately address it. Read this fun dialogue and freely (?) decide for yourself.

Reading Questions

1. The dialogue opens with the mortal requesting that God take away its free will. But very soon the mortal is refusing to let God take its free will away. What happened to cause such a reversal?
2. What is the "double bind" the mortal finds himself in?
3. What is the "double bind" God finds herself in?
4. What argument does the mortal present supporting the conclusion that God should not have given free will to humans in the first place?

5. Why does the mortal finally wish that a replica of himself be created with free will?
6. What is wrong with the word *determined* as used in the controversy over free will?
7. How does God show determinism and free will compatible? What do you think of the argument? Is it convincing? Why, or why not?

Is God a Taoist?

RAYMOND M. SMULLYAN

Mortal: AND THEREFORE, O God, I pray thee, if thou hast one ounce of mercy for this thy suffering creature, absolve me of *having* to have free will!

God: You reject the greatest gift I have given thee?

Mortal: How can you call that which was forced on me a gift? I have free will, but not of my own choice. I have never freely chosen to have free will. I have to have free will, whether I like it or not!

God: Why would you wish not to have free will?

Mortal: Because free will means moral responsibility, and moral responsibility is more than I can bear!

God: Why do you find moral responsibility so unbearable?

Mortal: Why? I honestly can't analyze why; all I know is that I do.

God: All right, in that case suppose I absolve you from all moral responsibility but leave you still with free will. Will this be satisfactory?

Mortal (after a pause): No, I am afraid not.

God: Ah, just as I thought! So moral responsibility is not the only aspect of free will to which you object. What else about free will is bothering you?

Mortal: With free will I am capable of sinning, and I don't want to sin!

God: If you don't want to sin, then why do you?

Mortal: Good God! I don't know why I sin, I just do! Evil temptations come along, and try as I can, I cannot resist them.

God: If it is really true that you cannot resist them, then you are not sinning of your own free will and hence (at least according to me) not sinning at all.

Mortal: No, no! I keep feeling that if only I tried harder I could avoid sinning. I understand that the will is infinite. If one wholeheartedly wills not to sin, then one won't.

God: Well now, you should know. Do you try as hard as you can to avoid sinning or don't you?

Mortal: I honestly don't know! At the time, I feel I am trying as hard as I can, but in retrospect, I am worried that maybe I didn't!

God: So in other words, you don't really know whether or not you have been sinning. So the possibility is open that you haven't been sinning at all!

Mortal: Of course this possibility is open, but maybe I have been sinning, and this thought is what so frightens me!

God: Why does the thought of your sinning frighten you?

Mortal: I don't know why! For one thing, you do have a reputation for meting out rather gruesome punishments in the afterlife!

God: Oh, that's what's bothering you! Why didn't you say so in the first place instead of all this peripheral talk about free will and responsibility? Why didn't you simply request me not to punish you for any of your sins?

Mortal: I think I am realistic enough to know that you would hardly grant such a request!

God: You don't say! *You* have a realistic knowledge of what requests I will grant, eh? Well, I'll tell you what I'm going to do! I will grant you a very, very special dispensation to sin as much as you like, and I give you my divine word of honor that I will never punish you for it in the least. Agreed?

Mortal (in great terror): No, no, don't do that!

God: Why not? Don't you trust my divine word?

Mortal: Of course I do! But don't you see, I don't want to sin! I have an utter abhorrence of sinning, quite apart from any punishments it may entail.

God: In that case, I'll go you one better. I'll remove your abhorrence of sinning. Here is a magic pill! Just swallow it, and you will lose all *abhorrence* of sinning. You will joyfully and merrily sin away, you will have no regrets, no abhorrence and I still promise you will never be punished by me, or yourself, or by any source whatever. You will be blissful for all eternity. So here is the pill!

Mortal: No, no!

God: Are you not being irrational? I am even removing your abhorrence of sin, which is your last obstacle.

Mortal: I still won't take it!

God: Why not?

Mortal: I believe that the pill will indeed remove my future abhorrence for sin, but my present abhorrence is enough to prevent me from being willing to take it.

God: I command you to take it!

Mortal: I refuse!

God: What, you refuse of your own free will?

Mortal: Yes!

God: So it seems that your free will comes in pretty handy, doesn't it?

Mortal: I don't understand!

God: Are you not glad now that you have the free will to refuse such a ghastly offer? How would you like it if I forced you to take this pill, whether you wanted it or not?

Mortal: No, no! Please don't!

God: Of course I won't; I'm just trying to illustrate a point. All right, let me put it this way. Instead of forcing you to take the pill, suppose I grant your original prayer of removing your free will—but with the understanding that the moment you are no longer free, then you *will* take the pill.

Mortal: Once my will is gone, how could I possibly choose to take the pill?

God: I did not say you would choose it; I merely said you would take it. You would act, let us say, according to purely deterministic laws which are such that you would as a matter of fact take it.

Mortal: I still refuse.

God: So you refuse my offer to remove your free will. This is rather different from your original prayer, isn't it?

Mortal: Now I see what you are up to. Your argument is ingenious, but I'm not sure it is really correct. There are some points we will have to go over again.

God: Certainly.

Mortal: There are two things you said which seem contradictory to me. First you said that one cannot sin unless one does so of one's own free will. But then you said you would give me a pill which would deprive me of my own free will, and then I could sin as much as I liked. But if I no longer had free will, then, according to your first statement, how could I be capable of sinning?

God: You are confusing two separate parts of our conversation. I never said the pill would deprive you of your free will, but only that it would remove your abhorrence of sinning.

Mortal: I'm afraid I'm a bit confused.

God: All right, then let us make a fresh start. Suppose I agree to remove your free will, but with the understanding that you will then commit an enormous number of acts which you now regard as sinful. Technically speaking, you will not then be sinning since you will not be doing these acts of your own free will. And these acts will carry no moral responsibility, nor moral culpability, nor any punishment whatsoever. Nevertheless, these acts will all be of the type which you presently regard as sinful; they will all have this quality which you presently feel as abhorrent, but your abhorrence will disappear; so you will not *then* feel abhorrence toward the acts.

Mortal: No, but I have present abhorrence toward the acts, and this present abhorrence is sufficient to prevent me from accepting your proposal.

God: Hm! So let me get this absolutely straight. I take it you no longer wish me to remove your free will.

Mortal (reluctantly): No, I guess not.

God: All right, I agree not to. But I am still not exactly clear as to why you now no longer wish to be rid of your free will. Please tell me again.

Mortal: Because, as you have told me, without free will I would sin even more than I do now.

God: But I have already told you that without free will you cannot sin.

Mortal: But if I choose now to be rid of free will, then all my subsequent evil actions will be sins, not of the future, but of the present moment in which I choose not to have free will.

God: Sounds like you are pretty badly trapped, doesn't it?

Mortal: Of course I am trapped! You have placed me in a hideous double bind! Now whatever I do is wrong. If I retain free will, I will continue to sin, and if I abandon free will (with your help, of course), I will now be sinning in so doing.

God: But by the same token, you place me in a double bind. I am willing to leave you free will or remove it as you choose, but neither alternative satisfies you. I wish to help you, but it seems I cannot.

Mortal: True!

God: But since it is not my fault, why are you still angry with me?

Mortal: For having placed me in such a horrible predicament in the first place!

God: But, according to you, there is nothing satisfactory I could have done.

Mortal: You mean there is nothing satisfactory you can now do, but that does not mean that there is nothing you could have done.

God: Why? What could I have done?

Mortal: Obviously you should never have given me free will in the first place. Now that you have given it to me, it is too late—anything I do will be bad. But you should never have given it to me in the first place.

God: Oh, that's it! Why would it have been better had I never given it to you?

Mortal: Because then I never would have been capable of sinning at all.

God: Well, I'm always glad to learn from my mistakes.

Mortal: What!

God: I know, that sounds sort of self-blasphemous, doesn't it? It almost involves a logical paradox! On the one hand, as you have been taught, it is morally wrong for any sentient being to claim that I am capable of making mistakes. On the other hand, I have the right to do anything. But I am also a sentient being. So the question is, Do I or do I not have the right to claim that I am capable of making mistakes?

Mortal: That is a bad joke! One of your premises is simply false. I have not been taught that it is wrong for any sentient being to doubt your omniscience, but only for a mortal to doubt it. But since you are not mortal, then you are obviously free from this injunction.

God: Good, so you realize this on a rational level. Nevertheless, you did appear shocked when I said, "I am always glad to learn from my mistakes."

Mortal: Of course I was shocked. I was shocked not by your self-blasphemy (as you jokingly called it), not by the fact that you had no right to say it, but just by the fact that you did say it, since I have been taught that as a matter of fact you don't make mistakes. So I was amazed that you claimed that it is possible for you to make mistakes.

God: I have not claimed that it is possible. All I am saying is that *if* I make mistakes, I will be happy to learn from them. But this says nothing about whether the *if* has or ever can be realized.

Mortal: Let's please stop quibbling about this point. Do you or do you not admit it was a mistake to have given me free will?

God: Well now, this is precisely what I propose we should investigate. Let me review your present predicament. You don't want to have free will because with free will you can sin, and you don't want to sin. (Though I still find this puzzling; in a way you must want to sin, or else you wouldn't. But let this pass for now.) On the other hand, if you agreed to give up free will, then you would now be responsible for the acts of the future. Ergo, I should never have given you free will in the first place.

Mortal: Exactly!

God: I understand exactly how you feel. Many mortals—even some theologians—have complained that I have been unfair in that it was I, not they, who decided that they should have free will, and then I hold *them* responsible for their actions. In other words, they feel that they are expected to live up to a contract with me which they never agreed to in the first place.

Mortal: Exactly!

God: As I said, I understand the feeling perfectly. And I can appreciate the justice of the complaint. But the complaint arises only from an unrealistic understanding of the true issues involved. I am about to enlighten you as to what these are, and I think the results will surprise you! But instead of telling you outright, I shall continue to use the Socratic method.

To repeat, you regret that I ever gave you free will. I claim that when you see the true ramifications you will no longer have this regret. To prove my point, I'll tell you what I'm going to do. I am about to create a new universe—a new space-time continuum. In this new universe will be born a mortal just like you—for all practical purposes, we might say that you will be reborn. Now, I can give this new mortal—this new you—free will or not. What would you like me to do?

Mortal (in great relief): Oh, please! Spare him from having to have free will!

God: All right, I'll do as you say. But you do realize that this new *you* without free will, will commit all sorts of horrible acts.

Mortal: But they will not be sins since he will have no free will.

God: Whether you call them sins or not, the fact remains that they will be horrible acts in the sense that they will cause great pain to many sentient beings.

Mortal (after a pause): Good God, you have trapped me again! Always the same game! If I now give you the go-ahead to create this new creature with no free will who will nevertheless commit atrocious acts, then true enough he will not be sinning, but I again will be the sinner to sanction this.

God: In that case, I'll go you one better! Here, I have already decided whether to create this new *you* with free will or not. Now, I am writing my decision on this piece of paper and I won't show it to you until later. But my decision is now made and is absolutely irrevocable. There is nothing you can possibly do to alter it; you have no responsibility in the matter. Now, what I wish to know is this: Which way do you hope I have decided? Remember now, the responsibility for the decision falls entirely on my shoulders, not yours. So you can tell me perfectly honestly and without any fear, which way do you hope I have decided?

Mortal (after a very long pause): I hope you have decided to give him free will.

God: Most interesting! I have removed your last obstacle! If I do not give him free will, then no sin is to be imputed to anybody. So why do you hope I will give him free will?

Mortal: Because sin or no sin, the important point is that if you do not give him free will, then (at least according to what you have said) he will go around hurting people, and I don't want to see people hurt.

God (with an infinite sigh of relief): At last! At last you see the real point!

Mortal: What point is that?

God: That sinning is not the real issue! The important thing is that people as well as other sentient beings don't get hurt!

Mortal: You sound like a utilitarian!

God: I am a utilitarian!

Mortal: What!

God: Whats or no whats, I am a utilitarian. Not a unitarian, mind you, but a utilitarian.

Mortal: I just can't believe it!

God: Yes, I know, your religious training has taught you otherwise. You have probably thought of me more like a Kantian than a utilitarian, but your training was simply wrong.

Mortal: You leave me speechless!

God: I leave you speechless, do I! Well, that is perhaps not too bad a thing—you have a tendency to speak too much as it is. Seriously, though, why do you think I ever did give you free will in the first place?

Mortal: Why did you? I never have thought much about why you did; all I have been arguing for is that you shouldn't have! But why did you? I guess all I can think of is the standard religious explanation: Without free will, one is not capable of meriting either salvation or damnation. So without free will, we could not earn the right to eternal life.

God: Most interesting! *I* have eternal life; do you think I have ever done anything to merit it?

Mortal: Of course not! With you it is different. You are already so good and perfect (at least allegedly) that it is not necessary for you to merit eternal life.

God: Really now? That puts me in a rather enviable position, doesn't it?

Mortal: I don't think I understand you.

God: Here I am eternally blissful without ever having to suffer or make sacrifices or struggle against evil temptations or anything like that. Without any of that type of "merit," I enjoy blissful eternal existence. By contrast, you poor mortals have to sweat and suffer and have all sorts of horrible conflicts about morality, and all for what? You don't even know whether I really exist or not, or if there really is any afterlife, or if there is, where you come into the picture. No matter how much you try to placate me by being "good," you never have any real assurance that your "best" is good enough for me, and hence you have no real security in obtaining salvation. Just think of it! I already *have* the equivalent of "salvation"—and

have never had to go through this infinitely lugubrious process of earning it. Don't you ever envy me for this?

Mortal: But it is blasphemous to envy you!

God: Oh come off it! You're not now talking to your Sunday school teacher, you are talking to *me*. Blasphemous or not, the important question is not whether you have the right to be envious of me but whether you are. Are you?

Mortal: Of course I am!

God: Good! Under your present world view, you sure should be most envious of me. But I think with a more realistic world view, you no longer will be. So you really have swallowed the idea which has been taught you that your life on earth is like an examination period and that the purpose of providing you with free will is to test you, to see if you merit blissful eternal life. But what puzzles me is this: If you really believe I am as good and benevolent as I am cracked up to be, why should I require people to merit things like happiness and eternal life? Why should I not grant such things to everyone regardless of whether or not he deserves them? . . .

God: [But] [w]e have gotten sidetracked as it is, and I would like to return to the question of what you believed my purpose to be in giving you free will. Your first idea of my giving you free will in order to test whether you merit salvation or not may appeal to many moralists, but the idea is quite hideous to me. You cannot think of any nicer reason—any more humane reason—why I gave you free will?

Mortal: Well now, I once asked this question to an Orthodox rabbi. He told me that the way we are constituted, it is simply not possible for us to enjoy salvation unless we feel we have earned it. And to earn it, we of course need free will.

God: That explanation is indeed much nicer than your former but still is far from correct. According to Orthodox Judaism, I created angels, and they have no free will. They are in actual sight of me and are so completely attracted by goodness that they never have even the slightest temptation towards evil. They really have no choice in the matter. Yet they are eternally happy even though they have never earned it. So if your rabbi's explanation were correct, why wouldn't I have simply created only angels rather than mortals?

Mortal: Beats me! Why didn't you?

God: Because the explanation is simply not correct. In the first place, I have never created any ready made angels. All sentient beings ultimately approach the state which might be called "angelhood." But just as the race of human beings is in a certain stage of biologic evolution, so angels are simply the end result of a process of Cosmic Evolution. The only difference between the so-called *saint* and the so-called *sinner* is that the former is vastly older than the latter. Unfortunately it takes countless life cycles to learn what is perhaps the most important fact of the universe—evil is simply painful. All the arguments of the moralists—all the alleged reasons why people *shouldn't* commit evil acts—simply pale into insignificance in light of the one basic truth that *evil is suffering*. No, my dear friend, I am not a moralist. I am wholly a utilitarian. That I should have been conceived in the role of a moralist is one of the great tragedies of the human race. My role in the scheme of things (if one can use this misleading expression) is neither to punish nor reward, but to aid the process by which all sentient beings achieve ultimate perfection. . . .

Mortal: Anyway, putting all these pieces together, it occurs to me that the only reason you gave free will is because of your belief that with free will, people will tend to hurt each other—and themselves—less than without free will.

God: Bravo! That is by far the best reason you have yet given! I can assure you that had I *chosen* to give free will that would have been my very reason for so choosing.

Mortal: What! You mean to say you did not choose to give us free will?

God: My dear fellow, I could no more choose to give you free will than I could choose to make an equilateral triangle equiangular. I could choose to make or not to make an equilateral triangle in the first place, but having chosen to make one, I would then have no choice but to make it equiangular.

Mortal: I thought you could do anything!

God: Only things which are logically possible. As St. Thomas said, "It is a sin to regard the fact that God cannot do the impossible, as a limitation on His powers." I agree, except that in place of his using the word *sin* I would use the term *error*.

Mortal: Anyhow, I am still puzzled by your implication that you did not choose to give me free will.

God: Well, it is high time I inform you that the entire discussion—from the very beginning—has been based on one monstrous fallacy! We have been talking purely on a moral level—you originally complained that I gave you free will, and raised the whole question as to whether I should have. It never once occurred to you that I had absolutely no choice in the matter.

Mortal: I am still in the dark!

God: Absolutely! Because you are only able to look at it through the eyes of a moralist. The more fundamental *metaphysical* aspects of the question you never even considered.

Mortal: I still do not see what you are driving at.

God: Before you requested me to remove your free will, shouldn't your first question have been whether as a matter of fact you *do* have free will?

Mortal: That I simply took for granted.

God: But why should you?

Mortal: I don't know. Do I have free will?

God: Yes.

Mortal: Then why did you say I shouldn't have taken it for granted?

God: Because you shouldn't. Just because something happens to be true, it does not follow that it should be taken for granted.

Mortal: Anyway, it is reassuring to know that my natural intuition about having free will is correct. Sometimes I have been worried that determinists are correct.

God: They are correct.

Mortal: Wait a minute now, do I have free will or don't I?

God: I already told you you do. But that does not mean that determinism is incorrect.

Mortal: Well, are my acts determined by the laws of nature or aren't they?

God: The word *determined* here is subtly but powerfully misleading and has contributed so much to the confusions of the free will versus determinism controversies. Your acts are certainly in accordance with the laws of nature, but to say they are *determined* by the laws of nature creates a totally misleading psychological image which is that your will could somehow be in conflict with the laws of nature and that the latter is somehow more powerful than you, and could "determine" your acts whether you liked it or not. But it is simply impossible for your will to ever conflict with natural law. You and natural law are really one and the same.

Mortal: What do you mean that I cannot conflict with nature? Suppose I were to become very stubborn, and I *determined* not to obey the laws of nature. What could stop me? If I became sufficiently stubborn, even you could not stop me!

God: You are absolutely right! *I* certainly could not stop you. Nothing could stop you. But there is no need to stop you, because you could not even start! As Goethe very beautifully expressed it, "In trying to oppose Nature, we are in the very process of doing so, acting according to the laws of nature!" Don't you see, that the so-called "laws of nature" are nothing more than a description of how in fact you and other beings *do* act. They are merely a description of how you act, not a prescription of how you should act, nor a power or force which compels or determines your acts. To be valid a law of nature must take into account how in fact you do act, or, if you like, how you choose to act.

Mortal: So you really claim that I am incapable of determining to act against natural law?

God: It is interesting that you have twice now used the phrase "determined to act" instead of "chosen to act." This identification is quite common. Often one uses the statement "I am determined to do this" synonymously with "I have chosen to do this." This very psychological identification should reveal that determinism and choice are much closer than they might appear. Of course, you might well say that the doctrine of free will says that it is *you* who are doing

the determining, whereas the doctrine of determinism appears to say that your acts are determined by something apparently outside you. But the confusion is largely caused by your bifurcation of reality into the "you" and the "not you." Really now, just where do you leave off and the rest of the universe begin? Or where does the rest of the universe leave off and you begin? Once you can see the so-called "you" and the so-called "nature" as a continuous whole, then you can never again be bothered by such questions as whether it is you who are controlling nature or nature who is controlling you. Thus the muddle of free will versus determinism will vanish. If I may use a crude analogy, imagine two bodies moving toward each other by virtue of gravitational attraction. Each body, if sentient, might wonder whether it is he or the other fellow who is exerting the "force." In a way it is both, in a way it is neither. It is best to say that it is the configuration of the two which is crucial.

Mortal: You said a short while ago that our whole discussion was based on a monstrous fallacy. You still have not told me what this fallacy is.

God: Why, the idea that I could possibly have created you without free will! You acted as if this were a genuine possibility, and wondered why I did not choose it! It never occurred to you that a sentient being without free will is no more conceivable than a physical object which exerts no gravitational attraction. (There is, incidentally, more analogy than you realize between a physical object exerting gravitational attraction and a sentient being exerting free will!) Can you honestly even imagine a conscious being without free will? What on earth could it be like? I think that one thing in your life that has so misled you is your having been told that I gave man the *gift* of free will. As if I first created man, and then as an afterthought endowed him with the extra property of free will. Maybe you think I have some sort of "paint brush" with which I daub some creatures with free will, and not others. No, free will is not an "extra"; it is part and parcel of the very essence of consciousness. A conscious being without free will is simply a metaphysical absurdity. . . .

Visit the companion Web site for chapter specific quizzes, suggestions for further reading, video ideas, and other resources to assess and expand your understanding of the chapter material. Go to http://philosophy.wadsworth.com and select the companion Web site for *Voices of Wisdom.*

 You can access many additional readings at the Info Trac-College Edition Web site. To find the following suggested articles do a keyword search with the article title. Use the passcode that was packaged with your new book to enter the site at http://www.Infotrac-college.com/Wadsworth/. Here is a sampling.

Rachel J. Littman, "Adequate Provocation, Individual Responsibility, and the Deconstruction of Free Will." *Albany Law Review,* Summer 1997 v60 n4 p1127–1170, A19509306.

Thomas W. Clark, "The Freedom of Susan Smith." *The Humanist,* March–April 1996 v56 n2 p8(5), A18047673.

John Martin Fischer, "Recent Work on Moral Responsibility." *Ethics,* October 1999 v110 i1 p93, A57829382.

Lewis Vaughn and Theodore Schick Jr., "Do We Have Free Will?" *Free Inquiry,* Spring 1998 v18 n2 p43(5), A20633114.

Steven Goetz, "The Choice-Intention Principle." *American Philosophical Quarterly,* April 1995 v32 n2 p177(9), A17156498.

Bruce Glymour, "Selection, Indeterminism, and Evolutionary Theory." *Philosophy of Science,* December 2001 v68 i4 p518(18), A80748171.

Mary Paquette, "This Is Insane!" *Perspectives in Psychiatric Care,* July–September 2002 v38 i3 p77(2), A93204528.

Kenton Machina, "Challenges for Compatibilitism." *American Philosophical Quarterly,* July 1994 v31 n3 p213(10), A15723026.

Tom Settle, "How Determinism Refutes Compatibilism." *Religious Studies,* September 1993 v29 n3 p353(10), A13274659.

Chapter 10

What Am I?

> *I think, therefore I am* **is the statement of an intellectual who underrates toothaches.** *I feel, therefore I am* **is a truth much more universally valid, and it applies to everything that's alive.**
>
> MILAN KUNDERA

10.1 Introduction

TO WHAT DOES THE WORD I REFER? You might want to say that the word *I* refers to your body. This would mean that you are your body, and I am my body. That seems simple enough. Notice, however, the words *your* body or *my* body. Why do we say *my* body as if the body were something the *I* possessed? This way of talking seems to imply that we make a distinction between ourselves and our bodies. And, of course, we can lose parts of our bodies or even have parts of them replaced without losing or replacing ourselves.

Maybe "I" doesn't refer to the body but to something that goes on inside the body, like thoughts or sensations. So you are what you think, perceive, and feel. However, we run into the same problem, don't we? We speak of *my* thoughts, *my* perceptions, and *my* feelings. Also, these things are constantly changing, but is the "I" constantly changing? Are you a different person every time you have a different thought, feeling, or sensation?

If "I" does not refer to my body or my thoughts, perceptions, and feelings, maybe it refers to my mind. My mind is what *has* thoughts, perceptions, and feelings, so you might say it possesses them. And since my mind tells my body what to do, you might even say that my body is possessed by my mind. Or, at least, my mind inhabits my body.

As the above bit of thinking about the question "What am I?" indicates, the discussion sooner or later leads one to talk about the mind and the body. This seems natural enough since we normally think of ourselves as human beings, and we commonly think of humans as having minds and bodies. However, what precisely are the mind and the body, and how are they related to each other? These questions constitute what philosophers call the **mind–body problem.**

Generally speaking, the proposed solutions to the mind–body problem fall into two groups: dualistic and monistic. Dualistic theories hold that the mind and the body are two different substances. The mind is conscious, nonspatial, and private (only you have direct access to your own mind). The body is unconscious, spatial, and public (it can be viewed by others). How do these two substances, so defined, relate?

One theory, usually associated with René Descartes, is called **interactionism.** According to this theory, mind and body causally interact in the sense that mental events (e.g., thoughts) can cause physical events (e.g., walking) and physical events (e.g., taking a sleeping pill) can cause mental events (e.g., feeling sleepy). This seems plausible enough at first, but the problem of how two substances so radically different can causally affect each other has led to considerable controversy as well as to the development of other theories.

Some dualists who reject the idea of causal interactionism subscribe to **parallelism.** The German philosopher Gottfried Leibniz (1646–1716), for example, argued that a preestablished harmony exists between mental and physical events so that they run in parallel, like two clocks set to tick together. Mind and body appear to interact, but in fact they do not. A physical event occurs (e.g., a blow to the arm), and parallel to that event, but uncaused by it, a mental event (e.g., pain) occurs.

This seems somewhat fantastic, so other dualists have been led to yet a third theory called **epiphenomenalism.** According to this theory, mental events are by-products of physical events, as smoke is a by-product of fire. This means that physical events cause mental events, but mental events cannot cause physical events. Mental events are just things that happen when certain brain activities take place. The brain activity is what is primary; the mental activity is secondary.

Monistic solutions to the mind–body problem deny that the mind and the body are two different substances. For example, *materialism,* or *physicalism* as it is sometimes called, holds that so-called mental events are not different from physical events. There is no such thing as a mental substance above and beyond the physical. There are several varieties of materialism, but a popular version, called the **identity theory**, proposes that mental events are identical with brain processes in much the same way as lightning flashes are identical with electrical discharges.

Whereas some versions of materialism attempt to reduce mind to matter, *idealism* attempts to reduce matter to mind. If you read Berkeley, you may recall how such an argument progresses. Berkeley argued that because all we ever experience are sensations and because sensations are mental, matter is an unwarranted and unneeded inference. Only minds and mental events exist.

A third kind of monism is called the **double-aspect theory.** This view, maintained by the Dutch philosopher Baruch Spinoza (1632–1677), proposes that we rethink what we mean by mind and body (matter). Instead of thinking of these as things or *substances,* we should think of them as qualities, characteristics, or aspects. There is one substance, Spinoza argued, that in itself is neither mental nor physical but has at least two different aspects or qualities called mind and body. A modern version of this theory was suggested by the famous British philosopher Bertrand Russell (see Section 1.4). Russell called his theory **neutral monism** and characterized it as the view that what exists is neither mental nor physical but neutral with respect to these distinctions.

Perhaps the mind–body problem arises only because we begin with faulty assumptions. If we focus on our normal experiences we notice that we experience ourselves as embodied. Our bodies are not irrelevant to what we think and feel. We raise our arms without thinking about how to do it, and when someone kicks us we yell. Our bodies seem to be more than mere shells or irrelevant dwelling places where our true selves just happen to be, sort of by accident.

Our brains are part of our bodies. They are an important part. I might accidentally cut off my finger, and although that unfortunate event would change me, it would not change me nearly as much as accidentally losing my brain. The relationship between brains and conscious minds is particularly close, and it is important to know how the brain works.

After the advent of the computer age it did not take long for people to start suggesting that brains work like computers. Computers compute all sorts of information very rapidly. Perhaps the brain does the same thing. Maybe our minds are simply products of a very complex computing system we happen to call the brain. Then again, maybe not. Read further and see.

10.2 You Are Your Mind

We return once again to Descartes, in particular to the last chapter of his *Meditations.* Let me remind you of his argument so far. Descartes was concerned with proving representational realism true. That is, he wanted to show for certain that physical objects really do exist outside our minds. He began by using his method of doubt to show that all our beliefs about an external world based on our sensations can be doubted. Hence, the most direct way to know the external world—namely, by sensation—is blocked by doubt. He then discovered that he could not doubt that he existed as a thinking thing as long as he was thinking because every time he doubted (thought) that he existed he proved that he existed (thought). So he found a certain foundation from which to begin, but he was trapped in his own mind.

Our selection in Section 6.3 ended with the second meditation and with Descartes knowing for certain that he existed as a thinking thing, but knowing nothing else. In the subsequent meditations, he sought a way out of his own mind by showing that God exists. If he could prove that God exists, he could be certain that at least one thing outside his own mind exists. He attempted this proof in *Meditation V* with his famous argument from perfection. Descartes argued that by God we mean a perfect being. A perfect being has all perfections. Existing is a perfection and, because a perfect being has all perfections, God must exist. Furthermore, God cannot be a deceiver because a perfect being must also have the perfection of goodness and a perfectly good being would not deceive.

Along the way Descartes also tried to establish a rule for distinguishing true ideas from false. Ideas that are clear and distinct are true. He also thought he discovered the cause of error. We can use our will to choose to believe things that our understanding does not completely grasp. Hence, we can be confident that God is good and not the source of error. He also tried to show that material things are essentially different from mental things. Matter is extended in space and mind is not. So Descartes believed he had established with absolute certainty the existence of his own mind as a mental substance and the existence of a perfectly good God. How did he get from there to a world made up of physical objects external to our minds? In the *Meditation* that follows, Descartes made that move.

He argued that physical objects outside his mind exist because there are only three possible causes of his perception of such objects:

1. His mind caused the perceptions.
2. God caused them.
3. Physical objects caused them.

We have, Descartes argued, a strong inclination to believe that (3) is true. If it were not true, then God who is perfectly good and who has given us this strong inclination, would be a deceiver because it is neither evident nor certain that our mind causes our perceptions of physical objects or that God does. Because he proved (at least to his satisfaction) that God is perfectly good, then it follows that God is not a deceiver, and hence (3) is true.

Central to Descartes's view is a sharp distinction between the mind, which is a nonphysical substance (not extended in space and private), and objects outside the mind, which are physical substances (extended in space and public). One of these outside objects is our own body. However, unlike rocks (so far as we know), persons are a unique combination of the nonphysical (the mind) and the physical (the body). In addition, it appears that human minds can cause their bodies to act in certain ways and that bodies can cause certain mental events.

The standard interpretation of Descartes is that he not only establishes a mind–body dualism but also supports a theory of interactionism. According to this theory, the mind and body can causally interact even though one is a mental substance and the other is a physical substance. Recently, some philosophers have questioned whether Descartes did in fact support interactionism. Descartes corresponded about this very issue with Princess Elisabeth of Bohemia in May and June of 1643. Elisabeth was puzzled about how interactive causation might happen because causation is a mechanical process requiring contact between bodies extended in space. But the mind is not extended in space and hence can have no contact with a physical body. So *how* do you raise your arm if your mind can have no contact with the muscles in your arm?

Reading Questions

1. What is the difference between having a *mental image* and having a *pure understanding*? Give an example of each.
2. According to Descartes, how does the mind or soul (what he here calls "a thinking thing") differ from the body?
3. What did Descartes mean when he said that he could "conceive of my whole self" as something that lacks the power or ability to have mental images and to sense?
4. Restate in your own words the argument Descartes provided that led him to the conclusion that physical objects exist.
5. What did Descartes mean when he said that his mind was indivisible but his body was divisible?
6. In the first *Meditation*, Descartes was skeptical about how confident we can be in distinguishing dreaming from waking. Then he became more confident about making the distinction. According to Descartes, how can dreaming be distinguished from waking? Do you agree? Why, or why not?

7. Has Descartes convinced you that you are made of two substances, a mental substance or mind—which is unextended in space, indivisible, and capable of pure understanding—and a body—which is extended in space, divisible, and is capable of sensation? Why, or why not?

Meditation VI

RENÉ DESCARTES

On the Existence of Material Objects and the Real Distinction of Mind from Body

IT REMAINS FOR ME to examine whether material objects exist. Insofar as they are the subject of pure mathematics, I now know at least that they can exist, because I grasp them clearly and distinctly. For God can undoubtedly make whatever I can grasp in this way, and I never judge that something is impossible for Him to make unless there would be a contradiction in my grasping the thing distinctly. Also, the fact that I find myself having mental images when I turn my attention to physical objects seems to imply that these objects really do exist. For, when I pay careful attention to what it is to have a mental image, it seems to me that it's just the application of my power of thought to a certain body which is immediately present to it and which must therefore exist.

To clarify this, I'll examine the difference between having a mental image and having a pure understanding. When I have a mental image of a triangle, for example, I don't just understand that it is a figure bounded by three lines; I also "look at" the lines as though they were present to my mind's eye. And this is what I call having a mental image. When I want to think of a chiliagon, I understand that it is a figure with a thousand sides as well as I understand that a triangle is a figure with three, but I can't imagine its sides or "look" at them as though they were present.

Being accustomed to using images when I think about physical objects, I may confusedly picture some figure to myself, but this figure obviously is not a chiliagon—for it in no way differs from what I present to myself when thinking about a myriagon or any other many sided figure, and it doesn't help me to discern the properties that distinguish chiliagons from other polygons. If it's a pentagon that is in question, I can understand its shape, as I can that of the chiliagon, without the aid of mental images. But I can also get a mental image of the pentagon by directing my mind's eye to its five lines and to the area that they bound. And it's obvious to me that getting this mental image requires a special mental effort different from that needed for understanding—a special effort which clearly reveals the difference between having a mental image and having a pure understanding.

It also seems to me that my power of having mental images, being distinct from my power of understanding, is not essential to my self or, in other words, to my mind—for, if I were to lose this ability, I would surely remain the same thing that I now am. And it seems to follow that this ability depends on something distinct from me. If we suppose that there is a body so associated with my mind that the mind can "look into" it at will, it's easy to understand how my mind might get mental images of physical objects by means of my body. If there were such a body, the mode of thinking that we call imagination would only differ from pure understanding in one way: when

From René Descartes's Meditations on First Philosophy, *translated by Ronald Rubin (Claremont, CA: Areté Press, 1986), pp. 40–53. Reprinted by permission of Areté Press.*

the mind understood something, it would turn "inward" and view an idea that it found in itself, but, when it had mental images, it would turn to the body and look at something there which resembled an idea that it had understood by itself or had grasped by sense. As I've said, then, it's easy to see how I get mental images, if we suppose that my body exists. And, since I don't have in mind any other equally plausible explanation of my ability to have mental images, I conjecture that physical objects probably do exist. But this conjecture is only probable. Despite my careful and thorough investigation, the distinct idea of bodily nature that I get from mental images does not seem to have anything in it from which the conclusion that physical objects exist validly follows. . . .

Now that I've begun to know myself and my creator better, I still believe that I oughtn't blindly to accept everything that I seem to get from the senses. Yet I no longer believe that I ought to call it all into doubt. . . .

Accordingly, from the fact that I have gained knowledge of my existence without noticing anything about my nature or essence except that I am a thinking thing, [mind or soul] I can rightly conclude that my essence consists solely in the fact that I am a thinking thing. It's possible (or, as I will say later, it's certain) that I have a body which is very tightly bound to me. But, on the one hand, I have a clear and distinct idea of myself insofar as I am just a thinking and unextended thing, and, on the other hand, I have a distinct idea of my body insofar as it is just an extended and unthinking thing. It's certain, then, that I am really distinct from my body and can exist without it. In addition, I find in myself abilities for special modes of awareness, like the abilities to have mental images and to sense. I can clearly and distinctly conceive of my whole self as something that lacks these abilities, but I can't conceive of the abilities' existing without me, or without an understanding substance in which to reside. Since the conception of these abilities includes the conception of something that understands, I see that these abilities are distinct from me in the way that a thing's properties are distinct from the thing itself.

I recognize other abilities in me, like the ability to move around and to assume various postures. These abilities can't be understood to exist apart from a substance in which they reside any more than the abilities to imagine and sense, and they therefore cannot exist without such a substance. But it's obvious that, if these abilities do exist, the substance in which they reside must be a body or extended substance rather than an understanding one—for the clear and distinct conceptions of these abilities contain extension but not understanding.

There is also in me, however, a passive ability to sense—to receive and recognize ideas of sensible things. But, I wouldn't be able to put this ability to use if there weren't, either in me or in something else, an active power to produce or make sensory ideas. Since this active power doesn't presuppose understanding, and since it often produces ideas in me without my cooperation and even against my will, it cannot exist in me. Therefore, this power must exist in a substance distinct from me. And, for reasons that I've noted, this substance must contain, either formally or eminently, all the reality that is contained subjectively in the ideas that the power produces. Either this substance is a physical object (a thing of bodily nature which contains formally the reality that the idea contains subjectively), or it is God or one of His creations which is higher than a physical object (something which contains this reality eminently). But, since God isn't a deceiver, it's completely obvious that He doesn't send these ideas to me directly or by means of a creation which contains their reality eminently rather than formally. For, since He has not given me any ability to recognize that these ideas are sent by Him or by creations other than physical objects, and since He has given me a strong inclination to believe that the ideas come from physical objects, I see no way to avoid the conclusion that He deceives me if the ideas are sent to me by anything other than physical objects. It follows that physical objects exist. These objects may not exist exactly as I comprehend them by sense; in many ways, sensory comprehension is obscure and confused. But these objects must at least have in them everything that I clearly and distinctly understand them to have—every general property within the scope of pure mathematics. . . .

I'll note that mind differs importantly from body in that body is by its nature divisible while mind is indivisible. When I think about my mind—or, in other words, about myself insofar as I am just a thinking thing—I can't distinguish any parts in me; I understand myself to be a single, unified thing. Although my whole mind seems united to my whole body, I know that cutting off a foot, arm, or other limb would not take anything away from my mind. The abilities to will, sense, understand, and so on can't be called parts, since it's one and the same mind that wills, senses, and understands. On the other hand, whenever I think of a physical or extended thing, I can mentally divide it, and I therefore understand that the object is divisible. This single fact would be enough to teach me that my mind and my body are distinct, if I hadn't already learned that in another way.

Next, I notice that the mind isn't directly affected by all parts of the body, but only by the brain—or maybe just by the small part of the brain containing the so-called "common sense." Whenever this part of the brain is in a given state, it presents the same thing to the mind, regardless of what is happening in the rest of the body (as is shown by innumerable experiments that I need not review here). . . .

I know that sensory indications of what is good for my body are more often true than false; I can almost always examine a given thing with several senses; and I can also use my memory (which connects the present to the past) and my understanding (which has now examined all the causes of error). Hence, I need no longer fear that what the senses daily show me is unreal. I should reject the exaggerated doubts of the past few days as ridiculous. This is especially true of the chief ground for these doubts—namely, my inability to distinguish dreaming from being awake. For I now notice that dreaming and being awake are importantly different: the events in dreams are not linked by memory to the rest of my life like those that happen while I am awake. If, while I'm awake, someone were suddenly to appear and then immediately to disappear without my seeing where he came from or went to (as happens in dreams), I would justifiably judge that he was not a real man but a ghost—or, better, an apparition created in my brain. But, if I distinctly observe something's source, its place, and the time at which I learn about it, and if I grasp an unbroken connection between it and the rest of my life, I'm quite sure that it is something in my waking life rather than in a dream. And I ought not to have the slightest doubt about the reality of such things if I have examined them with all my senses, my memory, and my understanding without finding any conflicting evidence. For, from the fact that God is not a deceiver, it follows that I am not deceived in any case of this sort. Since the need to act does not always allow time for such a careful examination, however, we must admit the likelihood of men's erring about particular things and acknowledge the weakness of our nature.

10.3 You Are an Embodied Self

Descartes's notion that the mind causally interacts with the body has been criticized for a variety of reasons. One has to do with the mysterious nature of the supposed causality. How can an immaterial substance that is nonspatial cause a material substance (the spatial body) to do anything? Causality requires some sort of contact. But how can this contact take place?

Another problem has to do with a physical law called the *conservation of energy*. According to this well-established law in current physical theory, the amount of energy in the universe is constant. However, if minds can act on physical bodies, new energy is created every time the mind causes the body to act. So interactionism appears to stand in direct contradiction to known physical laws.

A more recent line of criticism derives from mounting evidence about the brain and how it operates. Many scientists and philosophers now believe that it is only a matter of time until we can explain human behavior in physical terms. The more we learn about the brain and how it works, the more it seems evident that so-called mental states totally depend on the way the brain functions. If we had never seen a computer and suddenly discovered one, we might suppose that it was operated by some little person inside. However, as we learn more about the computer and how it works, we realize that there is no little person, or self, inside. The computations it performs are due to a complex mechanical arrangement and a program that provides instructions. So too, the argument goes, is the human brain.

Another recent criticism of Descartes's notion of the self as mind does not focus on the issue of interactionism but attacks the very idea of the self that underlies the theory of interaction. Cartesian dualism is a refined and sophisticated version of Plato's soul–body dualism (see Section 8.3). Both types of dualism have been immensely influential in Western culture. In fact, most of us were raised to believe in some kind of dualism. The very way we talk about ourselves reflects a dualistic viewpoint. We talk and think about our bodies as if they were shells or containers we just happen to inhabit. In other words, being in a body is not a necessary or essential characteristic of who we are.

However, imagine a world in which we had no eyes or ears, no sense of touch or smell or taste. What would such a world be like? "We would be very isolated," you might plausibly respond. Quite so. And isn't Descartes's mind quite isolated as well?

In the next selection, Eve Browning Cole, professor of philosophy at the University of Minnesota, Duluth, summarizes a critique of Descartes that stems from feminist philosophy. She argues that Descartes's procedure and his notion of the self pays insufficient attention to the fact that the self is embodied and exists in a network of relations with others. This fault has led to sexism insofar as it has reinforced a masculine notion of the self as autonomous, detached, and dominant over matter.

Reading Questions

1. What are some of the motivations, according to Cole, behind the philosophical discomfort with the physical body?
2. In what sense, according to Cole, is Descartes setting himself an artificial task?
3. Cole claims that if Descartes were working in collaboration with others, he could not easily entertain such radical doubts. Why?
4. What is the main point of the section entitled "The Uncertain Body"?
5. What is meant by "the relational self," and what difference would it have made if Descartes had begun his thought there?
6. In what sense is the concept of a radically isolated subject incoherent?
7. What does it mean to say that "the Cartesian ego is quintessentially *masculine*" and to say that "the relational self . . . is more aligned with feminine identity development"? What do you think about these two claims?
8. According to Cole, how is the "appearance obsession" related to Descartes's views about the relationship between mind and body?
9. What does Cole mean by the "embodied self"?

Body, Mind, and Gender

EVE BROWNING COLE

WE HAVE ALREADY had occasion to observe that much of Western philosophy has displayed a definite discomfort with the fact that human minds come in human *bodies,* that consciousness and the thought processes it underlies are embodied in more or less gross matter. It is not very difficult to understand some of the motivations behind this discomfort. For thoughts do not seem to be subject to the same limitations as ordinary physical objects; in imagination, I can accomplish things which seem to transcend the limits of space and time. Vivid memories defy the irrecoverability of the past, seeming to bring to life dead friends, bringing into the present past scenes, meals, and dreams. Dreams themselves are a powerful impetus toward regarding the mind as something more than or different from the physical "container" which it "inhabits" (though we shall soon see reasons to question these terms). And personal identity, the "I" who is the location of my consciousness, stretches back in time to embrace the child I was, the adolescent I became, and the woman I am now, even though in the physical sense I can only claim to be exactly what I now am (the past being no longer present).

Thus there are certain *prima facie* reasons for at least questioning how consciousness, thought, dreams, and identity relate to the physical world. But we will see that quite often philosophers have gone much further than questioning the relationship, to the extent of privileging the mental over the physical, derogating the physical and the human body along with it to a secondary ontological status, counseling efforts to transcend the body in order to apprehend truth, and even regarding the fact that mental events can cause physical events as a miracle performed by God on a daily basis! While this last, far from being a majority view, seems to have been instead a desperate expedient recommended only by one philosopher (Malebranche), it is symptomatic of something having gone badly wrong at the philosophical starting point.

Let us look more closely at the way in which the relation between body and mind, and the status of the body in the grand scheme of things, become problematic for philosophy. As our companion in this inquiry we will choose René Descartes—whose philosophical outlook, especially as represented in the designedly popular work *Meditations on First Philosophy* (published in 1641), proved enormously influential and remains a standard component of introductory studies of Western philosophy today.

Solitary Meditations, Radical Doubts

Descartes's work came at an extremely crucial juncture for Western philosophy. He entered a philosophical milieu still largely dominated by the medieval scholastic tradition, itself based heavily on a theologized and incomplete digestion of the legacy of the ancient Greeks. Studying with the Jesuits at the college of La Flèche, he received a "classical" and rather intellectually conservative education. Descartes made a radical break with this tradition, however, and set institutional philosophy off in a wholly new direction. Seeking to provide a philosophical method which would be accessible to all who possess common sense, providing a set of "rules for the direction of the mind" which would be so simple that "even women" would be able to follow them, his contributions to philosophy were revolutionary and of inestimable worth and influence. His contribution to the topic of this chapter, however, is highly problematic; and the difficulties he bequeathed to subsequent modern Western thought are enormous.

The full title of Descartes's *Meditations* is *Meditations on First Philosophy: In Which the Existence of God and the Distinction Between Mind and Body Are Demonstrated.* This full title is instructive as to how Descartes himself viewed his purpose in the work, which is often read in modern terms as a refutation of skepticism or an essay in foundationalism. By his own description, it is a work of *metaphysics.*

Descartes begins by confessing that he has long been aware that false beliefs have formed a part of his world view, and that a general and total mental "housecleaning" would need to be undertaken, in order to discover which of his views should be retained and which discarded. The procedure for this belief-testing, which he now proposes to undertake (since he is at present free "from every care" and "happily agitated by no passions") is that of *doubting.* He will attempt to cast doubt on each of his present beliefs; only those that survive the doubt ordeal will be retained. Rather than holding up individual beliefs for scrutiny, however, he proposes to address their general bases:

> . . . [I]t will not be requisite that I should examine each [belief] in particular, which would be an endless undertaking; for owing to the fact that the destruction of the foundations of necessity brings with it the downfall of the rest of the edifice, I shall only in the first place attack those principles upon which all my former opinions rested.

This project raises several interesting issues. First, Descartes is firmly committed to a *hierarchical* view of the structure of his belief system. The metaphor of the edifice of opinion, an ordered structure in which there is a top-down organization of architectural form, is an epistemological image to which we return . . . when we discuss images of belief systems, and the power of the metaphors we choose to represent cognition.

But note also the extreme *solitude* of Descartes's project here. He is proposing to take apart and rebuild his entire belief structure in isolation from the rest of the world, and particularly from other human beings. The idea that an epistemological value test could reliably be applied in complete isolation from other knowers, that one's own relations of knowing the world could be tested through demolition and then rebuilt to stringent specifications entirely of one's own devising, is extraordinary. When we consider the contexts in which knowing takes place, in which knowledge is sought and constructed, few of these appear to be ones in which isolation is afforded or even desirable (we might think of archeological digs, science labs, classrooms, reading groups, research institutes, fact-finding missions to other countries, courtrooms, and other typical situations in which knowledge is found and formed in human minds; none is an individual-based project).

Thus Descartes is setting himself an *artificial* kind of task, in the dual sense that his knowledge-seeking environment is atypical and that the envisioned "new and improved" cognitive structure or edifice of opinion will be his *own* individual artifact.

But the solitariness of Descartes's project has also another implication/motivation. Only in radical isolation from the rest of the human social world can Descartes *fully* explore the reliability of his entire belief system. For if he were exploring in collaboration with others, if the meditations he undertakes were the work of a Cartesian task force, he would have to make concessions to the reliability of certain beliefs before the task force could begin its work. He would have to trust that the others were thinkers, perhaps even thinkers on a par with himself; that they were working with him rather than against him, that they could have and work toward a common goal, that their words could be understood, trusted, believed, taken more or less at face value. In other words, the Cartesian project could not motivate total doubt if it were not so solitary. The powerful skeptical doubts which Descartes is about to summon into existence will answer only to the call of an isolated individual human mental voice. They are creatures of solitude. Descartes's individualistic starting point has lasting and dramatic effects on his total project and its overall outcomes.

The Uncertain Body

As the doubt program progresses, Descartes discards his trust in his senses as a source of reliable belief. Since (he reasons) the senses have deceived him in the past, it is advisable to suspend belief in sensory information for the duration of his meditations until he can uncover some justification for their occasional reliable operations. But the senses have been the source of his belief that he is an embodied creature, that he exists in or as a physical organism, in addition to being an originator of thoughts. Thus he must suspend his belief in the existence of the embodied Descartes and conceive of himself only as a locus of thoughts and other mental events, possibly not embodied at all, possibly embodied very differently from the way he has always pictured and experienced himself:

> I shall . . . suppose, not that God who is supremely good and the fountain of truth, but some evil genius not less powerful than deceitful, has employed his whole energies in deceiving me; I shall consider that the heavens, the earth, colors, figures, sound, and all the other external things are nought but the illusions and dreams of which this genius has availed himself in order to lay traps for my credulity; I shall consider myself as having no hands, no eyes, no flesh, no blood, nor any senses, yet falsely believing myself to possess all these things; I shall remain obstinately attached to this idea. . . .

Descartes will conceive of "himself" as something independent of his body, and will discover in this incorporeal consciousness the one indubitable truth which will function for him as an Archimedean immovable point, from which his belief structure can be rebuilt. This point is the certain truth of his own existence.

Descartes has effectively divided himself, and his belief structure, into two components: the certain mind, the component in which he will repose confidence at least as to its existence, and the uncertain body, about whose reality he will remain in a state of doubt until complex argumentation proves a limited trustworthiness, a constricted and carefully policed reliability.

Armed with the certainty of his own existence (as an insular node of consciousness which may or may not be embodied), Descartes goes on to demonstrate the existence of God, the fact that God is neither a grand deceiver nor the kind of being who would tolerate such massive deception of his creatures, and finally infers that the senses' urgings toward belief are not in themselves so awfully unreliable after all.

But the body, on Descartes's showing, remains forever only a probability, never a certainty. Since certainty is the Cartesian Holy Grail, this means that the body is irredeemably a second-class citizen in the metaphysical scheme of things. First rank in Descartes's universe is held by "thinking things," nodes of consciousness that can through purely rational processes follow deductive argumentation to absolutely certain conclusions. The body cannot participate in this process with its own humble abilities, here conceived as sensation and perception; it either impedes the rational process or, tamed and disciplined, stands dumbly by and lets knowledge happen. Highest epistemological honors go to the elements of deductive reasoning processes: mathematical laws, logical principles, indubitable truths. These construct the knowable core of the world, and to them in human experience is superadded a "flesh" of more dubious nature: bodies, colors, touches, smells, and the entire organic contents of the universe.

This theme, the privileging of the mental over the physical, does not originate with Descartes by any means. It is familiar to readers of Plato, who describes the relationship of soul to body in vivid terms:

> . . . [W]hen the soul uses the instrumentality of the body for any inquiry, whether through sight or hearing or any other sense—because using the body implies using the senses—it is drawn away by the body into the realm of the variable, and loses its way and becomes confused and dizzy, as though it were fuddled, through contact with things of a similar nature. . . . But when it investigates by itself, it passes into the realm of the pure and everlasting and immortal and changeless. . . . [*Phaedo* 79c–d]

Here the body is cast in the role of a bad companion, bad company for the soul to keep, company that drags it down to its own level and impedes its effective functioning. A nonphysical form of knowing, in which the soul or mind operates "by itself," is much to be preferred.

Two features of this way of discussing the relation of mind to body, common to Plato and Descartes, should be noted. First, it is striking how easily both drop into the mode of thought in which a human being becomes not one but two, and two *different,* kinds of entity. There quickly emerges a kind of logical and metaphysical distance between mind and body, an alienation that provokes disagreement about what to believe, what to seek, how to behave. But secondly, this is not a disagreement among equals. The mind or soul is in Descartes's view the locus of certainty and value, in Plato's view the part of the human composite akin to the "pure" and "divine." Its relationship to the body is to be one of dominance; the body is to be subordinated and ruled.

An individual human being contains within the self, therefore, a fundamental power dialectic in which mind must triumph over body and must trumpet its victory in flourishes of "pure" rationality by means of which its soundness is demonstrated and ratified. Far from being an isolated peculiarity of a small handful of philosophers, moreover, this general dialectic is seen being set up and played out in many theaters of Western culture, from religion to popular morality, from Neoplatonism to existentialism. . . .

Feminist Critiques

We have already noted the extraordinary isolation of Descartes's metaphysical musings; he cuts off not only the instructions of his perceptive faculties, but also the entirety of his human social surroundings, to seek a certainty accessible only to the lone and insular conscious node "I." A feminist critique of Cartesian method might well begin with just this feature of his project.

The Cartesian ego, rather than being the ground for certainty and the Archimedean point which some philosophers have taken it to be,

may in fact be the result of a mistaken abstraction. Feminist philosophers such as Caroline Whitbeck and Lorraine Code have convincingly argued that a preferable starting point for understanding the contents of human consciousness is *the relational self,* the self presented as involved in and importantly constituted by its connectedness to others. Each of us at this moment is connected as it were by invisible threads to an indefinite number of specific other human beings. In some cases, these connections are relatively remote; for example, we are all members of the same species and have biological similarities. Similarity is a relationship; therefore we are all related. Western culture has not tended to place much weight on this species relationship, however, and in some notorious institutions such as chattel slavery the reality of the relationship has been implicitly or explicitly denied. In other cases, the relationships in which we now stand are of deep significance in defining who we are, how we think, and how we act.

Starting with the concept of the relational self would greatly have changed the course of Descartes's meditations. If other persons are not just colorful wallpaper the design of which I contemplate from inside a mental fishbowl but actually part of who I am, then distancing myself from them in thought and supposing that I am the only consciousness in the universe becomes, if not impossible, extremely illogical. What would I hope to accomplish? If on the other hand I begin by granting them mentality and humanity, I will proceed by considering the specific ways in which their contributions to my mental life are made.

Paula Gunn Allen writes that, in Native American cultures, the question "Who is your mother?" is another and more profound way of asking who one is. In asking, one is inquiring about one of the most significant parts of a person's identity, for the influence of the mother and the mother's contribution to the child's self is considerable. In much the same way, we might begin a metaphysics of the self by asking "To whom am I related? In what ways? What contributions to my consciousness are presently being made, and by whom?" Such a beginning acknowledges the fundamental importance of sociality in human existence.

Here it might be objected that Descartes's . . . methodological skepticism about the existence and reality of other minds remains a possible position even for a relational self. Haven't we merely sidestepped the skeptical possibility by granting the mentality and humanity of the others? Doesn't it really still seem possible that they are all phantasms, or robots, or results of direct C-fiber stimulation by a mad scientist on a distant planet?

Yes, skeptical possibilities remain and cannot be ruled out. But taking the standpoint of the relational self allows us to affirm that such possibilities *do not matter.* What matters is that relationships are granted metaphysical priority over isolated individuals, so that the embeddedness of the self in a social world becomes its primary reality. The exact nature of the individuals involved becomes a matter of secondary importance. I grant at the outset that others make constitutive contributions to my experience, and I to theirs. This mutual interrelation becomes the ground for any further inquiry rather than functioning as a more or less uncertain inductive conclusion. Thus, to return to the problem of other minds, we can see that the philosopher's uncertainty about the mentality of the "foreign body" at the bus stop is a symptom of a flawed starting point rather than a genuine puzzle attending our reflective lives. The philosopher's mistake is to begin from isolation and attempt to reason himself back into society; we in fact begin in society and this is not an accidental but a deep truth about us.

We might go even further and argue that the concept of a radically isolated subject as the seat of consciousness is simply incoherent. We do not begin to think and speak in solitude, but in concert with our culture and with the specific representatives of the culture in whose care we find ourselves. We form ourselves in a collective process that is ongoing; our thoughts are never entirely our own, intersubjectivity is basic, while individual subjectivity is secondary and an abstraction.

Some feminist philosophers have analyzed the isolation of the ego and the "fishbowl" syndrome of some philosophy of mind in terms of differences between masculine and feminine gender

socialization. Developmental psychologists have suggested that the structure and dynamics of relationships with other human beings differ profoundly for traditionally socialized men and women. Due largely to the fact that, in most cultures and historical epochs, women function as the primary caregiver for children of both sexes while men enter into the life of the family in a more intermittent way, it is to be expected that male children will form their earliest sense of themselves by *distinguishing* themselves from their female caregiver, realizing that they are members of the group from which the (distant, absent, or intermittently present) male family members derive. Female children will form their sense of themselves by *identifying* with the female caregiver, realizing that they share with her membership in the group of female family members. This early direction of the sense of self, either to distinguish oneself and differ from, or to identify oneself and resemble, leaves a lasting legacy in the child's heart and mind. The adult character which emerges from the socialization process is marked by the tendency toward either clear and stark ego boundaries (if male) or flexible and mobile ego boundaries (if female). A whole constellation of dispositions and traits goes alongside this basic distinction. The masculine ego, formed at a distance from its primary role exemplar, displays a lifelong tendency toward independence, distancing from others, and endless acts of "proving" the masculinity which it modeled, with some uncertainty, on the distant fellow *man*. The feminine ego, formed in close proximity to its primary role exemplar, has lifelong tendencies toward identifying with others, reciprocating feelings, being dependent on others and relating to them easily even confusing its own needs with those of others—since it early on perceived that part of being a woman was to place others first, as a primary caregiver must frequently do.

This developmental thesis about gender identity, though impossible to demonstrate empirically and almost certainty *not* cross-culturally or cross-racially, offers a tempting explanation for the philosophical model of the isolated self we have traced in Descartes and seen lurking behind the problem of other minds. The Cartesian ego is quintessentially *masculine* in its solitary doubting program, in its self-confidence about its quest, in its ambition ("proving" itself all on its own resources), and in its uneasiness. . . .

By contrast, the relational self which some feminist philosophers have proposed as an alternative starting point for philosophy of mind, and for grounding our understanding of human experience generally, is more aligned with feminine identity development.

In addition to proposing that philosophers start from a conception of the human self as relational, as situated within a web of cultural and personal relationships which not only shape but do much to constitute its being and its thought, feminist philosophers have also criticized the Cartesian legacy for the relation between mind and body which it conveys.

We saw above that Descartes (and others) operate from a position that separates mind, self, consciousness, ego from the physical body these are said to "inhabit" or . . . "animate." In Descartes, the distinction is so drastic that mind and body are said to share no attributes whatsoever; they are oppositionally defined and thus, metaphysically speaking, mutually exclusive. Consciousness is nonphysical, nonextended, and inhabits an order of being completely distinct from that in which the body lives. The body is a machine, operated by the mind in the case of the human being, mindless and purely mechanical in the case of other animals.

This drastic dualism is vulnerable to criticism from many different directions; feminist critics begin with the observation that in Western culture and throughout its history, we can observe a tendency to identify women with the natural, the physical, the bodily. Nature is personified as a female, a "mother"; women are portrayed as more closely linked to nature, less completely integrated into civilization and the cultural order, than men. Men are rational agents, makers of order and measure, controllers of history; women are emotional vessels, subjects of orders and measures, passive observers of history. No one describes this more clearly or more influentially for modern psychology than Sigmund Freud, who writes:

> The fact that women must be regarded as having little sense of justice is no doubt related to the predominance of envy in their mental life; for the demand for justice is a modification of envy and lays down the condition subject to which we can lay envy aside. We also regard women as weaker in their social interests and as having less capacity for sublimating their instincts than men.

Freud subsumes women into the domain of the natural, where instinct rules and justice is foreign.

Now, if man is to mind as woman is to body, as appears from much of the literature and iconography of Western culture throughout historical time, and if we adhere to a generally Cartesian view of the self as a purely mental entity, then the self of the woman becomes deeply problematic. Can women have Cartesian egos? Genuine selves? It would appear to be impossible if woman's essence is located in the domain of the bodily. Clearly some other and less dichotomously dualistic conception of the self must be sought. The associations between woman and body in Western culture have had a decidedly negative aspect, which feminist critics have stressed. The reduction of a woman's value to the culturally inscribed value of a certain feminine appearance and protest against that reduction have been strong themes of feminist criticism for several decades. Nevertheless, the appearance obsession which women are encouraged to develop in our culture, according to which a more-or-less single standard of feminine beauty applies to all women, no matter their age, race, build, or lifestyle, is as strong as ever and, some argue, gaining strength. In addition now to being slim, youthful, cosmetically adorned to the correct degree, fashionably dressed, and as light-skinned as possible (with of course a healthy tan to indicate white-skinned class-privilege), women must ideally have "hard bodies" with muscle-definition acquired by hours of grueling workouts and aerobic routines. That this formula cannot be met by the poor, those who don't have the time to devote to the pursuit of beauty, or those whose bodies resist the mold for whatever reason, does not mean that the standard does not hold its pristine severity over all women's heads equally. (Sadly, the appearance obsession does seem to be extending to men as well, but still seems to pertain to them in lesser degree.)

In a recent classroom discussion of trends in advertising, one young female student spoke out with sincere enthusiasm: "I can't wait till I get older! I'm going to eat whatever I want, wear whatever I want, and just not care!" An older female student turned to her and said, "Why wait? It isn't any easier to look different at age fifty than at age twenty." This exchange was instructive in many ways. There was anger in the second woman's voice; she heard herself as older being dismissed somehow from the class of viable potential beauties. There was a strange assumption behind the first woman's statements, to the effect that until some unspecified age, women are under an obligation to eat and to dress in ways other than those they would choose if not constrained. And there was in the second speaker's choice of the word *different* to describe an undisciplined woman the implicit admission that the *norm,* what it means to be *non*different, is precisely the cultural ideal of the dieting and carefully dressed youthful appearance. But this is clearly false, as a simple glance at the immense variety of actual women's bodies in any real-life situation will immediately confirm. The so-called *norm* is in fact extremely rare. Yet an enormous amount of women's energy is devoted to its pursuit. Constant dieting, eating disorders such as anorexia and bulimia, compulsive exercising, and (not least of all) enormous cash investments in beauty and fashion, are all symptomatic of the power of the cultural ideal.

To connect with our previous discussion of the gendered distinction between mind and body, men generally do not in our culture tend to identify themselves and their worth as persons with the details of their physical bodies' appearances. While in recent years the standards of male attractiveness have undoubtedly become more exacting, men clearly feel more relaxed about not meeting these standards.

Let us summarize the contribution which the dualistic Platonic–Cartesian model of the self has made to our cultural conceptions of body and mind: (1) The body's relationship to the mind, in any given human being, is one of unruly bondage or servitude; mind properly dominates its body and directs its actions, while body properly obeys. (2) Mind's behavior and dispositions are, however, described in terms more appropriate to masculine gender identity (activity, ruling or hegemony, capacity for abstraction and objectivity, distanced contemplation, dispassionate analysis), while body's configurations tend toward feminine (passivity, subordination, unconscious physicality, sensuous and emotional implication, confusion). (3) Thus, while rationality becomes defined as a mostly masculine project, an adorned and disciplined physicality becomes the feminist project—leading to the contemporary obsession of middle-class women with weight and appearance generally. Women are given the cultural prescription to be docile bodies, adorned and available for participation in the rational schemes of the male dominated social order. Thus the fact that in some basic respects the Cartesian ego is a masculine ego can be seen to have enormous reverberations throughout modern life. It is of no small significance to recognize that a certain outlook in the philosophy of mind provides a perfect recipe for male dominance and women's subordination.

Several important qualifications need to be made here, however. First, the neat gender dichotomy we have drawn in the ratio of proportion:

Male : Mind :: Female : Body

does not appear to hold cross-racially. That is, nonwhite males in a white-dominated culture will be treated in much the same way as bodies are treated by minds in the Cartesian framework: They will be dominated, ruled, directed, used. Furthermore, white females will participate in this domination and rule, functioning as "minds" in a bureaucratic manner; and white women will benefit from skin privilege at the expense of the dominated nonwhite men and women. The nonwhite populations will be accorded *mental* attributes that correspond to the physical attributes of the body in the Cartesian scheme; they will be considered less than fully rational, emotional, "natural" or savage, sensuous, weak-willed, and so forth. So the factor of race does much to complicate a mind–body value map which takes *only* gender into account. This has led some feminist philosophers to hypothesize that *both* sexism and racism are more about power than they are about either sex or race.

A second qualification concerns the relationship between what, for want of a clearer word, we could call ideology and social reality. The rational man and the physical woman, intellectual masculinity and corporeal femininity, are creatures of ideology. This means that they are intensely value-laden concepts structuring culture and its expectations, rather than empirical generalizations drawn from observation of real women and real men. But ideology and reality touch one another at multiple points and reciprocally influence each other at these points of contact. It may be a strange-sounding philosophical thesis that rationality has been interpreted in terms defined as masculine, but it takes on a gruesomely real shape when a Berkeley philosophy professor announces to his classes that women can't do logic, or when another philosophy professor writes to the secretary of the American Philosophical Association that white women and black people of both sexes display analytical capabilities inferior to those of white men. This is ideology shaping social reality with a vengeance.

Believing that the drastic dualism of the traditional picture of body's relation to mind, along with the inbuilt evaluatively hierarchical model of dominance and subordination which gives the model its working directives, are both deeply flawed, feminist philosophers look for alternatives.

A beginning point is to conceive of the human self as intrinsically embodied: An *embodied self* can displace the only questionably embodied Cartesian ego, the uncomfortably body-trapped Platonic soul, as a foundation for further inquiry into the nature of human experience. To conceive of the self as essentially or intrinsically embodied means to acknowledge the centrality of the physical in human psychology and cognition, for one thing. It means opening the door to the possibility of a bodily wisdom, to revaluing the physical human being, in ways that promise both better metaphysical schemes and more ethical models for human interaction. Breaking down the valuational hierarchy between mind and body, attempting to think of them as woven and melded together into what constitutes who we are and who we ought to be, eliminates the perhaps primary internal oppression model of mind over body. As a culture, however, we have learned to think of the body, and of those primarily identified with it, in terms of scorn (even when those latter people are ourselves). We have learned to privilege the "rational" over the emotional (conceived as proceeding from physical sources), the basely corporeal, the manual and tactile; to weigh technorationality over the mute testimony of nature and our own bodies. Those of us who are women have at times been encouraged to view our bodies with contempt when we perceive them as falling short of the beauty ideal or when we are addressed rudely in sexual terms by strangers. How can we begin to approach the relation of mind and body not as a *problem* but as a source of liberatory insight and joy?

French feminist philosophers, building on their national intellectual tradition, which placed the phenomenology of *lived experience* at center stage, have made exciting progress in constructing the basis for a liberatory philosophy of the body. They have argued that the dominant tradition in Western philosophy has made women's bodies problematic in two contradictory ways: In one way, woman and body are equated as essentially physical, and women's entire personalities become sexualized (think of the late Victorian habit of referring to women as a group with the phrase "the sex," as if men were "the non-sex"). In another direction, however, the sexualized woman is either ignored in philosophy, so complete is her subsumption under the rubric *Nature,* or she is philosophized about in male terms, and her (now highlighted in neon) sexuality is described in terms appropriate only to a certain specific cultural construction of *male* sexuality. She is thus obscured as a subject, discussed as an object.

This means that, for a genuinely liberatory philosophy of the body to be developed, women must reclaim in theory and in practice their own physicality, their own sexuality. . . .

10.4 You Are a Computing Machine

You probably don't like to think of yourself as a machine. After all, a machine is a thing, a mere "it," whereas you are a human being with a mind. I know I don't normally think of myself as a machine, and, like you, I think of myself as something more than an impersonal thing. But what if we are "virtual" machines? That is, what if our conscious life is the result of a particular pattern of rules (software) being imposed on fixed structures (hardware)?

Alan Turing, a brilliant mathematician and computer scientist, proposed an operational test for deciding whether a computer can think. Turing argued that we can conclude that a computer can think if it can regularly beat a human opponent in the "imitation game." Two "contestants," according to this "game" show, are hidden from a human judge. One is a human and the other is a computer. They can communicate with the judge by typing messages on computer terminals. Both the human and the computer try to convince the judge, by their responses to questions posed by the judge, that they are human, conscious thinkers. If the judge cannot regularly spot the difference (pick out the computer responses from the human responses), the computer "wins" (is judged to have a mind!). If it quacks like a duck, it is a duck even if it doesn't look like one or walk like one or is made of the same stuff.

Turing's test reflects a view called **behaviorism,** which is a materialistic theory of the mind. According to this theory, so-called mental events are the same thing as behaviors or dispositions to behave. Thus, if I have a pain in my leg, I am disposed (have a tendency) to say, "ouch" and rub the spot where it hurts. My behavior or my disposition to behave in such a fashion is the same as "experiencing pain in my leg." If a computer behaves like a conscious mind in the Turing test, why not say it is conscious?

And why not work it the other way around? If a computing machine can behave in the same way a mind does, then perhaps a mind is a computing machine, or at least the brain that produces a mind is a computing machine. Perhaps it is just lingering prejudices about souls, or a kind of egocentric arrogance, that prevents us from recognizing that the brain is a very complex organic computing machine and our conscious life is a product of this complex computing system.

Bruce Hinrichs, author of the next article, is a professor of psychology and humanities at Century College in Minnesota. He not only argues that the brain, which creates the mind, is a computing machine but also argues that this idea should not be as nearly upsetting to people as it often is.

Reading Questions

1. What are two reasons why some people resist the brain-computer analogy, and how does Hinrichs counter those objections?
2. What are some important differences between a brain and a computer? In your opinion, what is the most important difference? Why do you think so?

3. How does Hinrichs deal with the issue of how a brain creates a mind, and why does he think some people find his answer unsatisfactory?

4. Do you agree with Hinrichs that there is no good reason for people to feel "threatened or dehumanized" by scientific studies concerning how the brain produces a mind or consciousness? Explain your answer and support it with reasons.

Computing the Mind

BRUCE H. HINRICHS

FOR CENTURIES, PHILOSOPHERS have puzzled over the mind–body problem—the captivating enigma that asks how subjective mental states are connected to our objective physical biology. In this century, neuroscientists have made spectacular achievements in describing the cellular and molecular actions of the nervous system, while cognitive psychologists have indirectly observed and measured mental and psychological functions, sometimes with ingenious experimental methodology and often borrowing brain-imaging techniques from neuroscience.

The most recent contributors to the mind–body topic are computer network experts who study how individual elements interact in a systematic way, producing computational processes which give rise to information processing and artificial intelligence. Pioneers such as Alan Turing, John von Neumann, Warren McCulloch and Walter Pitts, and, more recently, Patricia Churchland and Terrence Sejnowski have provided an analysis of systems at a higher level than the typical biomedical approaches of neuroscience and at a lower level than the macro states and behaviors favored by psychologists. By examining neural networks, these researchers hope to uncover just how individual cells combine to create emergent phenomena which are more than the sum of their parts.

Of course, in each cast the attention is on the human brain as the locus of mental and psychological functions. Computer guru Marvin Minsky has called the brain a "meat machine" and a machine that "clanks softly." Viewing the brain as a soft computational machine allows an interesting commentary on the recent chess match lost by Garry Kasparov to the IBM computer sometimes called Deeper Blue (because it is an improved version of Deep Blue beaten by Kasparov the previous year). In this view, it was not man against machine as much as it was one type of machine—or process, if you prefer—against another. As was shown, one process happened to be better at chess than the other.

Critics complain that a digital computer lacks awareness or understanding, that it is just making unconscious computations. But a brain is a type of computer and it has awareness and understanding. A brain also just makes subconscious computations—by neurons creating electrical current and squirting transmitter chemicals. This, of course, is the essential mystery: how can these singularly objective cellular brain events transform into psychological states, moods, and behaviors? The consciousness we experience is apparently achieved via the interaction of billions of unconscious computational events, which in themselves have no awareness or understanding.

Certainly Deeper Blue was made and programmed by humans, but so was Kasparov! If we're giving credit to Deeper Blue's programmers, then let's give credit to the programmers

Bruce H. Hinrichs, "Computing the Mind: A Scientific Approach to the Philosophy of Mind and Brain," The Humanist, *March–April (1998), Volume 58, 26–31.* Copyright © 1998 American Humanist Association. *Reprinted by permission of the author.*

of Kasparov: his parents, teachers, previous opponents, authors of books he read, and so forth. Also, some machines today are made by other machines, and someday computers will likely be made and programmed by other computers. So what? None of these truths diminishes human integrity, dignity, worth, goals, values, or self-actualization. There is no threat. Brains are better at some things, while silicon digital computers excel at others.

Analogies

Years ago we were told that a human brain functions like a telephone switchboard. I still remember the scratchy 16mm movie that illustrated brain activity as a sequence of switchboard plugs being methodically pulled from and inserted into an impressive array of holes. This analogy was readily embraced throughout society, in and out of schools, and it even sprouted in pedestrian places such as the silly 1972 Woody Allen movie *Everything You Always Wanted to Know About Sex But Were Afraid to Ask.* Allen depicts the brain as a command center for body actions (sex, in this case), which are initiated and regulated via telephone communication.

The days when a brain was likened to a telephone switchboard are thankfully long gone. In the modern zeitgeist, the idea seems humorously antiquated, belonging more properly to an era of bobby-soxers, air raid drills, and bomb shelters. But contemporary society need not go metaphorless because—as is usually the case—when one analogy grows passe, another elbows its way into our collective hearts. The au courant brain metaphor, which is both ubiquitous and appropriate for the "information age," is that a brain is like a computer.

Our popular culture absorbs and reflects this analogy regularly—through such television characters as Commander Data of *Star Trek: The Next Generation,* who achieves consciousness with a "positronic" electronic matrix brain; through popular fiction like *The Terminal Man,* which features a man with epilepsy who has electrodes inserted into his brain; through newscasts which regularly report findings that certain traits are "hardwired" into the brain; and through movies such as *Brainstorm* (1983), *Total Recall* (1990), and *Until the End of the World* (1991), which envision machines that are able to interface with a living human brain and thereby access various mental functions, such as memories and dreams. Apparently, the brain–computer analogy is widespread and implicitly accepted throughout our culture. The brain has gone cyber.

Is a Brain Like a Computer?

When first proposed in the 1960s, the brain–computer analogy was widely criticized, quite unfairly, on the basis that brains do very different tasks from computers. For example, it was noted that a brain is exquisitely excellent at visually recognizing a face or an object, while a computer is clunky and exceedingly slow at pattern recognition. On the other hand, a computer can do complex mathematical calculations at extremely high speed, while a brain is stumped by such tasks. While these indeed were and still are accurate observations, what makes this criticism a red herring is that it isn't the particular content of a computation that determines if something is like a computer; rather, it is the process used. In other words, it isn't what is done but how it's done that matters.

A more valid complaint of the brain–computer analogy is regarding the word *like.* The brain is not like a computer; it is a computer. Certainly a brain does not compute the same information that a PC does, but in the method—the manner in which it processes information—the brain is computing. For better or worse, your brain is a computer. Greetings, Data.

Not surprisingly, the idea that a brain is a computer receives a good deal of resistance and scoffing. One reason for this is that the term *computer* is often wrongly interpreted to exclusively denote serial digital computers. But the PC, like the slide rule, is just one example of a device that makes computations. A brain also is a computational device.

A second reason for resistance is that most nonexperts and even a few experts believe that a brain is more than a mere computer; that brain functioning in some way—perhaps at a subatomic or metaphysical level—results in the creation of emergent mental and emotional properties that would not be possible simply through computational processes. When this idea is presented with a rationale, it commonly is accompanied by quasiscientific jargon. References to chaos theory and particle physics are currently in vogue, as if brains were the only substances on Earth that involve principles of quantum physics.

Arcane and illogical philosophical arguments are also often given. These imply that brains are somehow different than other matter in the universe and only brains can experience metaphysical transformations. Although these contentions certainly stimulate entertaining discussions, they are grossly speculative, controversial—even volatile when linked with religious beliefs—and extremely unlikely to be resolved in the near future. So far, a materialist view is completely complementary to today's wide-ranging multidisciplinary empirical data.

What seems clear is that, whatever other qualities it may possess, a brain appears to be a kind of computer, a nature-made computer. Through a series of complex interactions, a brain takes incoming sensory signals, processes that information, and achieves a computational product, an output. Think of your senses as the keyboard or modem and your conscious mind as the monitor. The output of the brain includes regulation of body systems, emotions, behaviors, and thoughts, both conscious and unconscious. A brain does compute. Of course, exactly what it computes varies significantly from a PC or Macintosh.

This idea is typically a frightening one to people, although not to a majority of brain researchers and artificial intelligence experts who have calmly accepted it, at least at some fundamental level, despite disagreements over nuances. For our part, although we may have some trepidation, if we are willing to take an open-minded view, then it seems reasonable, even fun, to agree with the experts that a brain is a natural computer, the world's first computer, the best and brightest computer. There should be

nothing threatening nor dehumanizing about this view. In fact, adopting this insight may help us to better understand and accept emotional, behavioral, and cognitive differences between people and the mental problems that beset us. However, even if we accept this framework, there are significant clarifications necessary, lest unwarranted conclusions be drawn.

What Kind of Computer Do You Have?

A brain may be a computer, but it is a distinctly different sort of computer than the silicon chip models on our desks. The complex networking that is characteristic of both a PC and a brain is achieved in each case through the use of entirely different substances and different systems of organization. The cells (neurons) which permit communication within a brain are alive; a brain is a living computer. Brain cells require oxygen and involve complex biological processes driven by genetic codes. They are subject to malformations, irregularities, and damage via biological mechanisms (consider, for example, Alzheimer's disease). This simple realization leads us to the most enlightening fact that, since brain cells are alive and therefore are malleable and dynamic, it becomes difficult, perhaps impossible, to distinguish between hardware and software within the brain.

In contrast, a semiconductor computer uses cells that are essentially static, unchanged by the signals they carry; in a PC or Mac, the hardware is not significantly altered by the software program it runs. When the software is removed, the hardware is unchanged, back to normal, ready for more software. Brains don't work like that. A brain's hardware is pivotally changed by its software—a process that is at the heart of how a brain stores information (that is, remembers) and maintains continuity. As a brain takes in information through the senses, the cells which comprise the hardware are physically changed by the process.

Take language, for example. One brain may run an "English" program while another runs a "French" one. Each brain has been programmed through experience, and the software programs are now integral parts of the hardware of the brain. The hardware of each brain is importantly different from the other at the cellular level. They are different in a physical/chemical way that would be extremely difficult, if not impossible, to undo without doing damage to their structures; in a brain, the software is intricately intertwined with the hardware. The program (in this example, language) cannot be removed without altering the hardware. Even while asleep (and not dreaming), when one's conscious mind is "turned off," the nature of the software program is retained within the hardware so that, when one awakens, the same old memories, thoughts, and feelings are booted up and running.

Make Up Your Mind!

This insight may lead us to wonder what exactly it is about brains that allows them to create thoughts, memories, awareness, emotions—that is, a mind. Where in the brain's biological processes are the key elements that give us consciousness? Are mental and emotional experiences a product of the brain's cellular interactions and therefore might be reproducible using inorganic networks that replicate brain networks? Or are conscious experiences dependent upon the biological characteristics of brain cells themselves? Does a mental experience—such as seeing, hearing, or feeling—depend on some particular quality of the individual cells of the brain, or is the computational interaction between the cells sufficient to produce awareness?

If it is the brain cells that are crucial for creating consciousness, then we may wonder which specific properties or characteristics of the cells are the necessary ones. Do other cells that have those properties then also have a mental life? Could mental experiences be replicated in a laboratory by reproducing those special cellular characteristics?

On the other hand, if mental experiences are produced not by particular aspects of the cells but instead by their interacting networks doing some sort of computing, then it should be possible to build a machine that could generate mental phenomena. If a silicon chip computer were built to exactly simulate brain connections, would it not feel? If not, why? What would be missing?

Of course, it is entirely possible—in fact, it is likely—that the creation of mental and emotional experiences depends on a unique combination of cellular characteristics and their interactions—that both biological cellular mechanisms and neural networks are necessary. In that event, it would take information about both neural nets and cell biology to understand and to artificially create a conscious mind.

When a brain creates a mind—when thoughts and emotions are formed by brain properties, states, conditions, and actions—then precisely what are the particular, distinctive elements involved? Are thinking, feeling, dreaming, and consciousness unique to humans or are these subjective experiences shared on some continuum with animals, insects, amoebae, perhaps even inorganic materials? In other words, are mental phenomena reproducible? Could a non-living machine, if properly constructed, conceive a thought, feel, think, dream?

A Scientific Answer

When we ask how it is that a brain creates a mind, it is somewhat similar to asking how any observed quality is created by its physical constituents. For example, how is it that rocks are hard, iron is magnetic, ice is cold, or, for illustrative purposes, water creates wetness? Just as wetness is a property or quality of water, the mind is a property or quality of the brain. Wetness is a state or condition that is created by the physical nature of water, and similarly we can conceptualize mental experiences as states or conditions created by the physical nature of the brain. Although this is not a perfect comparison—in fact, there are no perfect comparisons since a mind is the only thing we know to have subjectivity or awareness—still, we can use this comparison to help us achieve a better conceptual paradigm of the mind–brain connection.

When we attempt to explain a certain phenomenon, a scientific answer is one that describes the physical/chemical properties and interactions underlying the quality to be explained. For example, wetness is a quality that is scientifically explained by reference to certain properties and interactions of hydrogen and oxygen atoms. Following this paradigm, mental experiences can similarly be scientifically explained by detailing the specific brain substances and activities which generate them. Since the mind is one of the things a brain does, a scientific explanation of the mind would thus consist of a detailed description of the physical/chemical brain states and networks associated with each mental experience.

Though most people find this form of answer acceptable for explaining other things, it is typically found unsatisfactory for the question of how a brain creates a mind, since people want an answer of a different sort: one invoking the metaphysical or supernatural. Although the scientific approach may seem inadequate, it is how we explain other phenomena, and in those cases it is accepted. We don't ask how it is that water creates wetness; the how doesn't make sense, other than explaining wetness with reference to its underlying physical features. Perhaps this is the best approach to understanding the mind: to reduce mental experiences to their underlying physical features and not ask how it is that these features produce the mind.

It is disconcerting to hear critics reject a scientific approach to the mind because it doesn't include nonscientific ideas, such as the metaphysical, paranormal, or spiritual. But in any way that the mind can be examined empirically, a scientific approach is appropriate. This does not dehumanize us or diminish the value of the arts, emotions, self-discovery, and so on. Other valid approaches to understanding human experiences are, of course, welcomed. But science can provide one powerful piece of the puzzle.

It is likewise disconcerting to hear quasi-scientific explanations of the mind, which often are seductive enough to gain the favor of listeners. For example, Deepak Chopra often says that "a thought is a quantum event." Because of his use of scientific terminology, the hypothesis seems plausible. However, this is a confused idea. A thought is a personal, subjective experience produced by the brain, while quantum events are activities occurring at a subatomic level (for example, the interaction between an electron and a photon) which occur regularly in all physical matter in the universe, in and outside of our bodies. A thought is no more or less a quantum event than is wetness. The subjective experience of thinking is produced by actions of brain cells, which naturally include quantum events as do all physical acts.

We need to get over the idea that humans—and, in particular, the human mind—are somehow mysteriously or miraculously outside of nature. How a brain creates a mind is no more or less a mystery or a miracle than how rocks are hard, how magnets create fields, how electrons produce current, how light is both particle and wave, or how water is wet. Those who study the mind scientifically are interested in this area because it is one way of examining the human equation. It is a very practical approach that offers hope for people who have mental problems, such as Alzheimer's, Parkinson's, depression, or schizophrenia.

Basics of Brain and Mind

The brain is a physical thing within the natural world, not a supernatural or metaphysical entity. Minds are not supernatural entities but personal experiences produced when brains are in a state of awareness of their own functioning, most probably a state created through the complex intercommunication between and among brain subcomputers for vision, hearing, language, attention, and other cognitive and perceptual functions. Minds are not substances; they are subjective experiences which the brain creates as a window into certain aspects of its own functioning. A brain, or a particular subdivision of the brain, is able to create an awareness of certain of its own states or functions—a kind of self-monitoring.

This concept of the mind may help us in speculating about why the mind exists. Why didn't a brain evolve without consciousness? What was the evolutionary impetus for the development of awareness? Viewing mental experiences as self-monitoring events helps us initiate some hypotheses about why consciousness would have evolutionary survival advantages over a nonconscious brain.

Although some experts have proposed that minds and brains are the same thing (in fact, some writers have recently begun to use the term brain–mind), minds, of course, are not brains any more than wetness is water. Minds are a quality or product of certain brain activity—one of the many things that a brain does, along with control of muscles, organs, and body housekeeping functions. While asleep, for example, a brain can be performing many functions, although consciousness (the mind) is temporarily turned off.

A brain has many tasks. One of the most interesting is the creation of thoughts, feelings, dreams, choices, personal identity, and awareness of the environment and the self—in other words, a conscious mind. The specific details of how the mind is created by the brain are yet to be unraveled and are likely to be complex and difficult to uncover and elucidate. Still, there is no reason to believe that these details are conceptually any more inaccessible to scientific investigation and scrutiny than any other complex phenomena. Nor is there any reason to feel threatened or dehumanized by such studies. In fact, people who scientifically study the mind are demonstrating a central focus of humanism: a high regard for understanding human nature and experience without supernatural biases. One thing on which it is easy to agree is that how the brain creates the mind is one of the most fascinating and exhilarating of all questions.

As you read these final words, consider for a moment the idea that an abundance of intricate electrical and chemical signals surging through your brain at this very moment is responsible right now for your awareness and attention; your seeing and understanding; your memories and emotions; your questions, concerns, and doubts; your creative impulses, curiosity, and emerging ideas; and any excitement you may now feel as the computer in your head invites you to explore its cyberspace. Happy computing!

10.5 You Are Not a Machine

Have you ever wondered whether computers can think? Of course, they can think in the sense that they can process information. But I mean *really* think—that is, can they be conscious? If they can, perhaps our brains are like complex computers, vastly intricate machines that can process information in such a way that consciousness is the result.

As I pointed out in the introduction to this chapter, one set of answers to the mind–body problem is called *monism* because it denies that humans are made up of two radically different things, minds and bodies. One version of monism, usually called *materialism* or *physicalism,* claims that only bodies (matter) exist. The problem this answer must explain is why we have a conscious mental life (thoughts, feelings, sensations) that appears to be nonphysical in nature. Various kinds of physicalistic theories have been proposed in an attempt to solve this problem. I briefly mentioned the identity theory in the introduction. According to this theory, mental states are identical with brain states. When we think certain kinds of thoughts or dream certain sorts of dreams, certain sorts of physical events are happening in various parts of our brains, which can be observed and studied by science. One problem with this theory is that mental states seem to have characteristics different from those of physical states. For one thing, they are private whereas physical states are publically observable. For another, it appears unlikely that the same kind of brain state accompanies the same kind of thought or sensation. For example, I feel pain, you feel pain, and the other day Peanut, my fat blind cat, also felt pain when I accidentally stepped on his tail. Now my brain and your brain may be sufficiently alike so that our brain states may also be sufficiently alike. But the brain of my cat, and indeed the brains of many other animals, is quite different, and it seems unlikely that—even though we might have similar mental states (e.g., feeling pain)—we would have identical brain states. Also, for two things to be identical, they must have identical properties. A brain state, being physical, is located in space. But where in space is my feeling of being sorry that I stepped on my cat's tail? Is it 3 inches to the right of my left ear? Is it possible for a brain scientist to observe some kind of electrical event in my brain (a brain state) and read my thoughts? When I see Arthur the dog chasing Peanut the cat, can some scientist looking at my brain activity see the same thing? Hardly!

Materialists have their answers to these sorts of questions, but these kinds of problems with the identity theory have led some materialists to develop a different sort of theory, a theory called **functionalism.** There are different varieties of functionalism, but in general this theory holds that mental states are defined completely by their functions or causal relations. A mind is what a brain creates. Theoretically, something other than a brain could function as a mind—for example, a computer.

The slogan of functionalism is *not* the cry of the identity theorist that "the mind is nothing but the brain." Rather, drawing an analogy with computers, the slogan is "the mind is to the brain as a computer's software is to its hardware." The behavior of a computer is not explained, or at least not explained completely, by its physics and chemistry (hardware). It is explained by its program or "software" that manages the tasks the computer performs. The software of a computer is not identical with its hardware, and hence our minds are not identical with our brains. Nevertheless, the brain is a kind of computing machine, and the mind is the brain's program.

John Searle is professor of philosophy at the University of California, Berkeley. In the following selection, taken from the 1984 Reith Lectures, Searle argues that machines cannot think (be conscious) and thus, by implication, that functionalistic theories of the mind fail. He offers what has become a classic example of a thought experiment in the field, the Chinese room argument, in order to show that no matter how complex and sophisticated digital computers may become, they will never be able to produce consciousness and hence the human brain must be significantly unlike a computer because the brain can cause consciousness.

Central to Searle's argument is a distinction between *syntax* (the grammatical rules that govern the arrangement of words in a sentence) and *semantics* (the meaning of a word or a sentence). Computers manipulate symbols according to syntax (a set of rules for their arrangement), but it does not follow that computers are aware of the meaning (semantics) of those symbols. If I knew only the syntax of Chinese, but not the semantics, could I be said to know Chinese?

Reading Questions

1. According to Searle, what causes mental processes?
2. According to Searle, what is the "strong artificial intelligence (AI)" view?
3. What is one consequence of the strong AI view?
4. Why is Searle's refutation of the strong AI view independent of developments in computer technology?

5. What does Searle mean when he says, "the mind has more than a syntax, it has a semantics"?
6. What is the point of Searle's example of the Chinese room?
7. Describe the two types of responses that Searl's argument received and his counterresponse.
8. What four conclusions does Searle draw, and what are the premises on which they are based?
9. Has Searle made his case to your satisfaction—that is, has he proved to you that a digital computer, in principle, cannot think or have a mind like a human mind? Why, or why not?

Can Computers Think?

JOHN SEARLE

. . . THOUGH WE DO NOT KNOW in detail how the brain functions, we do know enough to have an idea of the general relationships, between brain processes and mental processes. Mental processes are caused by the behavior of elements of the brain. At the same time, they are realized in the structure that is made up of those elements. I think this answer is consistent with the standard biological approaches to biological phenomena. Indeed, it is a kind of commonsense answer to the question, given what we know about how the world works. However, it is very much a minority point of view. The prevailing view in philosophy, psychology, and artificial intelligence is one which emphasizes the analogies between the functioning of the human brain and the functioning of digital computers. According to the most extreme version of this view, the brain is just a digital computer and the mind is just a computer program. One could summarize this view—I call it "strong artificial intelligence," or "strong AI"—by saying that the mind is to the brain, as the program is to the computer hardware.

This view has the consequence that there is nothing essentially biological about the human mind. The brain just happens to be one of an indefinitely large number of different kinds of hardware computers that could sustain the programs which make up human intelligence. On this view, any physical system whatever that had the right program with the right inputs and outputs would have a mind in exactly the same sense that you and I have minds. So, for example, if you made a computer out of old beer cans powered by windmills; if it had the right program, it would have to have a mind. And the point is not that for all we know it might have thoughts and feelings, but rather that it must have thoughts and feelings, because that is all there is to having thoughts and feelings: implementing the right program.

Most people who hold this view think we have not yet designed programs which are minds. But there is pretty much general agreement among them that it's only a matter of time until computer scientists and workers in artificial intelligence design the appropriate hardware and programs which will be the equivalent of human brains and minds. These will be artificial brains and minds which are in every way the equivalent of human brains and minds.

Many people outside of the field of artificial intelligence are quite amazed to discover that anybody could believe such a view as this. So, before criticizing it, let me give you a few examples of the things that people in this field have actually said. Herbert Simon of Carnegie-Mellon University says that we already have machines that can literally think. There is no question of waiting for some future machine, because existing digital computers already have thoughts in exactly the same sense that you and I do. Well, fancy that! Philosophers have been worried for centuries about whether or not a machine could think, and now we discover that they already have such machines at Carnegie-Mellon. Simon's colleague Alan Newell claims that we have now discovered (and notice that Newell says "discovered" and not "hypothesized" or "considered the possibility," but we have *discovered*) that intelligence is just a matter of physical symbol manipulation; it has no essential connection with any specific kind of biological or physical wetware or hardware. Rather, any system whatever that is capable of manipulating physical symbols in the right way is capable of intelligence in the same literal sense as human intelligence of human beings. Both Simon and Newell, to their credit, emphasize that there is nothing metaphorical about these claims; they mean them quite literally. Freeman Dyson is quoted as having said that computers have an advantage over the rest of us when it comes to evolution. Since consciousness is just a matter of formal processes, in computers these formal processes can go on in substances that are much better able to survive in a universe that is cooling off than beings like ourselves made of our wet and messy materials. Marvin Minsky of MIT says that the next generation of computers will be so intelligent that we will "be lucky if they are willing to keep us around the house as household pets." My all-time favorite in the literature of exaggerated claims on behalf of the digital computer is from John McCarthy, the inventor of the term "artificial intelligence." McCarthy says even "machines as simple as thermostats can be said to have beliefs." And indeed, according to him, almost any machine capable of problem-solving can be said to have beliefs. I admire McCarthy's courage. I once asked him: "What beliefs does your thermostat have?" And he said: "My thermostat has three beliefs—it's too hot in here, it's too cold in here, and it's just right in here." As a philosopher, I like all these claims for a simple reason. Unlike most philosophical theses, they are reasonably clear, and they admit of a simple and decisive refutation. It is this refutation that I am going to undertake in this chapter.

The nature of the refutation has nothing whatever to do with any particular stage of computer technology. It is important to emphasize this point because the temptation is always to think that the solution to our problems must wait on some as yet uncreated technological wonder. But in fact, the nature of the refutation is completely independent of any state of technology. It has to do with the very definition of a digital computer, with what a digital computer is.

It is essential to our conception of a digital computer that its operations can be specified purely formally; that is, we specify the steps in the operation of the computer in terms of abstract symbols—sequences of zeros and ones printed on a tape, for example. A typical computer "rule" will determine that when a machine is in a certain state and it has a certain symbol on its tape, then it will perform a certain operation such as erasing the symbol or printing another symbol and then enter another state such as moving the tape one square to the left. But the symbols have no meaning; they have no semantic content; they are not about anything. They have to be specified purely in terms of their formal or syntactical structure. The zeros and ones, for example, are just numerals; they don't even stand for numbers. Indeed, it is this feature of digital computers that makes them so powerful. One and the same type of hardware, if it is appropriately designed, can be used to run an indefinite range of different programs. And one and the same program can be run on an indefinite range of different types of hardwares.

But this feature of programs, that they are defined purely formally or syntactically, is fatal to the view that mental processes and program processes are identical. And the reason can be stated quite simply. There is more to having a mind than having formal or syntactical processes. Our internal mental states, by definition, have certain sorts of contents. If I am thinking about Kansas City or wishing that I had a cold beer to drink or wondering if there will be a fall in interest rates, in each case my mental state has a certain mental content in addition to whatever formal features it might have. That is, even if my thoughts occur to me in strings of symbols, there must be more to the thought than the abstract strings, because strings by themselves can't have any meaning. If my thoughts are to be *about* anything, then the strings must have a *meaning* which makes the thoughts about those things. In a word, the mind has more than a syntax, it has a semantics. The reason that no computer program can ever be a mind is simply that a computer program is only syntactical, and minds are more than syntactical. Minds are semantical, in the sense that they have more than a formal structure, they have a content.

To illustrate this point I have designed a certain thought-experiment. Imagine that a bunch of computer programmers have written a program that will enable a computer to simulate the understanding of Chinese. So, for example, if the computer is given a question in Chinese, it will match the question against its memory, or data base, and produce appropriate answers to the questions in Chinese. Suppose for the sake of argument that the computer's answers are as good as those of a native Chinese speaker. Now then, does the computer, on the basis of this, understand Chinese, does it literally understand Chinese, in the way that Chinese speakers understand Chinese? Well, imagine that you are locked in a room, and in this room are several baskets full of Chinese symbols. Imagine that you (like me) do not understand a word of Chinese, but that you are given a rule book in English for manipulating these Chinese symbols. The rules specify the manipulations of the symbols purely formally, in terms of their syntax, not their semantics. So the rule might say: "Take a squiggle-squiggle sign out of basket number one and put it next to a squoggle-squoggle sign from basket number two." Now suppose that some other Chinese symbols are passed into the room, and that you are given further rules for passing back Chinese symbols out of the room. Suppose that unknown to you the symbols passed into the room are called "questions" by the people outside the room, and the symbols you pass back out of the room are called "answers to the questions." Suppose, furthermore, that the programmers are so good at designing the programs and that you are so good at manipulating the symbols, that very soon your answers are indistinguishable from those of a native Chinese speaker. There you are locked in your room shuffling your Chinese symbols and passing out Chinese symbols in response to incoming Chinese symbols. On the basis of the situation as I have described it, there is no way you could learn any Chinese simply by manipulating these formal symbols.

Now the point of the story is simply this: by virtue of implementing a formal computer program from the point of view of an outside observer, you behave exactly as if you understood Chinese, but all the same you don't understand a word of Chinese. But if going through the appropriate computer program for understanding Chinese is not enough to give *you* an understanding of Chinese, then it is not enough to give *any other digital computer* an understanding of Chinese. And again, the reason for this can be stated quite simply. If you don't understand Chinese, then no other computer could understand Chinese because no digital computer, just by virtue of running a program, has anything that you don't have. All that the computer has, as you have, is a formal program for manipulating uninterpreted Chinese symbols. To repeat, a computer has a syntax, but no semantics. The whole point of the parable of the Chinese room is to remind us of a fact that we knew all along. Understanding a language, or indeed, having mental states at all, involves more than just having a bunch of formal symbols. It involves having an interpretation, or a meaning attached to those symbols. And a digital computer, as defined, cannot have more than just formal symbols because the operation of the computer, as I said earlier, is defined in terms of its ability to implement programs. And these programs are purely formally specifiable—that is, they have no semantic content.

We can see the force of this argument if we contrast what it is like to be asked and to answer questions in English, and to be asked and to answer questions in some language where we have no knowledge of any of the meanings of the words. Imagine that in the Chinese room you are also given questions in English about such things as your age or your life history, and that you answer these questions. What is the difference between the Chinese case and the English case? Well again, if like me you understand no Chinese and you do understand English, then the difference is obvious. You understand the questions in English because they are expressed in symbols whose meanings are known to you. Similarly, when you give the answers in English you are producing symbols which are meaningful to you. But in the case of the Chinese, you have none of that. In the case of the Chinese, you simply manipulate formal symbols according to a computer program, and you attach no meaning to any of the elements.

Various replies have been suggested to this argument by workers in artificial intelligence and in psychology, as well as philosophy. They all have something in common; they are all inadequate. And there is an obvious reason why they have to be inadequate, since the argument rests on a very simple logical truth, namely, syntax alone is not sufficient for semantics, and digital computers insofar as they are computers have, by definition, a syntax alone.

I want to make this clear by considering a couple of the arguments that are often presented against me.

Some people attempt to answer the Chinese room example by saying that the whole system understands Chinese. The idea here is that though I, the person in the room manipulating the symbols, do not understand Chinese, I am just the central processing unit of the computer system. They argue that it is the whole system, including the room, the baskets full of symbols and the ledgers containing the programs and perhaps other items as well, taken as a totality, that understands Chinese. But this is subject to exactly the same objection I made before. There is no way that the system can get from the syntax to the semantics. I, as the central processing unit, have no way of figuring out what any of these symbols means; but then neither does the whole system. Another common response is to imagine that we put the Chinese understanding program inside a robot. If the robot moved around and interacted causally with the world, wouldn't that be enough to guarantee that it understood Chinese? Once again the inexorability of the semantics–syntax distinction overcomes this maneuver. As long as we suppose that the robot has only a computer for a brain then, even though it might behave exactly as if it understood Chinese, it would still have no way of getting from the syntax to the semantics of Chinese. You can see this if you imagine that I am the computer. Inside a room in the robot's skull I shuffle symbols without knowing that some of them come in to me from television cameras attached to the robot's head and others go out to move the robot's arms and legs. As long as all I have is a formal computer program, I have no way of attaching any meaning to any of the symbols. And the fact that the robot is engaged in causal interactions with the outside world won't help me to attach any meaning to the symbols unless I have some way of finding out about that fact. Suppose the robot picks up a hamburger and this triggers the symbol for hamburger to come into the room. As long as all I have is the symbol with no knowledge of its causes or how it got there, I have no way of knowing what it means. The causal interactions between the robot and the rest of the world are irrelevant unless those causal interactions are represented in some mind or other. But there is no way they can be if all that the so-called mind consists of is a set of purely formal, syntactical operations.

It is important to see exactly what is claimed and what is not claimed by my argument. Suppose we ask the question that I mentioned at the beginning: "Could a machine think?" Well, in one sense, of course, we are all machines. We can construe the stuff inside our heads as a meat machine. And of course, we can all think. So, in one sense of "machine," namely that sense in which a machine is just a physical system which is capable of performing certain kinds of operations, in that sense, we are all machines, and we can think. So, trivially, there are machines that can think. But that wasn't the question that bothered us. So let's try a different formulation of it. Could an artifact think? Could a man-made machine think? Well, once again, it depends on the kind of artifact. Suppose we designed a machine that was molecule-for-molecule indistinguishable from a human being. Well then, if you can duplicate the causes, you can presumably duplicate the effects. So once again, the answer to that question is, in principle at least, trivially yes. If you could build a machine that had the same structure as a human being, then presumably that machine would be able to think. Indeed, it would be a surrogate human being. Well, let's try again.

The question isn't: "Can a machine think?" or: "Can an artifact think?" The question is: "Can a digital computer think?" But once again we have to be very careful in how we interpret the question. From a mathematical point of view, anything whatever can be described *as if* it were a digital computer. And that's because it can be described as instantiating or implementing a computer program. In an utterly trivial sense, the pen that is on the desk in front of me can be described as a digital computer. It just happens to have a very boring computer program. The program says: "Stay there." Now since in this sense, anything whatever is a digital computer, because anything whatever can be described as implementing a computer program, then once again, our question gets a trivial answer. Of course our brains are digital computers, since they implement any number of computer programs. And of course our brains can think. So once again, there is a trivial answer to the question. But that wasn't really the question we were trying to ask. The question we wanted to ask is this: "Can a digital computer, as defined, think?" That is to say: "Is instantiating or implementing the right computer program with the right inputs and outputs, sufficient for, or constitutive of, thinking?" And to this question, unlike its predecessors, the answer is clearly "no." And it is "no" for the reason that we have spelled out, namely, the computer program is defined purely syntactically. But

thinking is more than just a matter of manipulating meaningless symbols, it involves meaningful semantic contents. These semantic contents are what we mean by "meaning."

It is important to emphasize again that we are not talking about a particular stage of computer technology. The argument has nothing to do with the forthcoming, amazing advances in computer science. It has nothing to do with the distinction between serial and parallel processes, or with the size of programs, or the speed of computer operations, or with computers that can interact causally with their environment, or even with the invention of robots. Technological progress is always grossly exaggerated, but even subtracting the exaggeration, the development of computers has been quite remarkable, and we can reasonably expect that even more remarkable progress will be made in the future. No doubt we will be much better able to simulate human behavior on computers than we can at present, and certainly much better than we have been able to in the past. The point I am making is that if we are talking about having mental states, having a mind, all of these simulations are simply irrelevant. It doesn't matter how good the technology is, or how rapid the calculations made by the computer are. If it really is a computer, its operations have to be defined syntactically, whereas consciousness, thoughts, feelings, emotions, and all the rest of it involve more than a syntax. Those features, by definition, the computer is unable to *duplicate* however powerful may be its ability to *simulate*. The key distinction here is between duplication and simulation. And no simulation by itself ever constitutes duplication.

What I have done so far is give a basis to the sense that those citations I began this talk with are really as preposterous as they seem. There is a puzzling question in this discussion though, and that is: "Why would anybody ever have thought that computers could think or have feelings and emotions and all the rest of it?" After all, we can do computer simulations of any process whatever that can be given a formal description. So, we can do a computer simulation of the flow of money in the British economy, or the pattern of power distribution in the Labour party. We can do computer simulation of rain storms in the home counties, or warehouse fires in East London. Now, in each of these cases, nobody supposes that the computer simulation is actually the real thing; no one supposes that a computer simulation of a storm will leave us all wet, or a computer simulation of a fire is likely to burn the house down. Why on earth would anyone in his right mind suppose a computer simulation of mental processes actually had mental processes? I don't really know the answer to that, since the idea seems to me, to put it frankly, quite crazy from the start. But I can make a couple of speculations.

First of all, where the mind is concerned, a lot of people are still tempted to some sort of behaviorism. They think if a system behaves as if it understood Chinese, then it really must understand Chinese. But we have already refuted this form of behaviorism with the Chinese room argument. Another assumption made by many people is that the mind is not a part of the biological world, it is not a part of the world of nature. The strong artificial intelligence view relies on that in its conception that the mind is purely formal; that somehow or other, it cannot be treated as a concrete product of biological processes like any other biological product. There is in these discussions, in short, a kind of residual dualism. AI partisans believe that the mind is more than a part of the natural biological world; they believe that the mind is purely formally specifiable. The paradox of this is that the AI literature is filled with fulminations against some view called "dualism," but in fact, the whole thesis of strong AI rests on a kind of dualism. It rests on a rejection of the idea that the mind is just a natural biological phenomenon in the world like any other.

I want to conclude this chapter by putting together the thesis of the last chapter and the thesis of this one. Both of these theses can be stated very simply. And indeed, I am going to state them with perhaps excessive crudeness. But if we put them together I think we get a quite powerful conception of the relations of minds, brains and computers. And the argument has a very simple logical structure, so you can see whether it is valid or invalid. The first premise is:

1. *Brains cause minds.*

Now, of course, that is really too crude. What we mean by that is that mental processes that we consider to constitute a mind are caused, entirely caused, by processes going on inside the brain. But let's be crude, let's just abbreviate that as three words—brains cause minds. And that is just a fact about how the world works. Now let's write proposition number two:

2. *Syntax is not sufficient for semantics.*

That proposition is a conceptual truth. It just articulates our distinction between the notion of what is purely formal and what has content. Now, to these two propositions—that brains cause minds and that syntax is not sufficient for semantics—let's add a third and a fourth:

3. *Computer programs are entirely defined by their formal, or syntactical, structure.*

That proposition, I take it, is true by definition; it is part of what we mean by the notion of a computer program.

4. *Minds have mental contents; specifically, they have semantic contents.*

And that, I take it, is just an obvious fact about how our minds work. My thoughts, and beliefs, and desires are about something, or they refer to something, or they concern states of affairs in the world; and they do that because their content directs them at these states of affairs in the world. Now, from these four premises, we can draw our first conclusion; and it follows obviously from premises 2, 3 and 4:

CONCLUSION I

No computer program by itself is sufficient to give a system a mind. Programs, in short, are not minds, and they are not by themselves sufficient for having minds.

Now, that is a very powerful conclusion, because it means that the project of trying to create minds solely by designing programs is doomed from the start. And it is important to re-emphasize that this has nothing to do with any particular state of technology or any particular state of the complexity of the program. This is a purely formal, or logical, result from a set of axioms which are agreed to by all (or nearly all) of the disputants concerned. That is, even most of the hardcore enthusiasts for artificial intelligence agree that in fact, as a matter of biology, brain processes cause mental states, and they agree that programs are defined purely formally. But if you put these conclusions together with certain other things that we know, then it follows immediately that the project of strong AI is incapable of fulfillment.

However, once we have got these axioms, let's see what else we can derive. Here is a second conclusion:

CONCLUSION 2

The way that brain functions cause minds cannot be solely in virtue of running a computer program.

And this second conclusion follows from conjoining the first premise together with our first conclusion. That is, from the fact that brains cause minds and that programs are not enough to do the job, it follows that the way that brains cause minds can't be solely by running a computer program. Now that also I think is an important result, because it has the consequence that the brain is not, or at least is not just, a digital computer. We saw earlier that anything can trivially be described as if it were a digital computer, and brains are no exception. But the importance of this conclusion is that the computational properties of the brain are simply not enough to explain its functioning to produce mental states. And indeed, that ought to seem a commonsense scientific conclusion to us anyway because all it does is remind us of the fact that brains are biological engines; their biology matters. It is not, as several people in artificial intelligence have claimed, just an irrelevant fact about the mind that it happens to be realized in human brains.

Now, from our first premise, we can also derive a third conclusion:

CONCLUSION 3

Anything else that caused minds would have to have causal powers at least equivalent to those of the brain.

And this third conclusion is a trivial consequence of our first premise. It is a bit like saying that if my petrol engine drives my car at seventy-five miles an hour, then any diesel engine that was capable of doing that would have to have a power output at least equivalent to that of my petrol engine. Of course, some other system might cause mental processes using entirely different chemical or biochemical features from those the brain in fact uses. It might turn out that there are beings on other planets, or in other solar systems, that have mental states and use an entirely different biochemistry from ours. Suppose that Martians arrived on earth and we concluded that they had mental states. But suppose that when their heads were opened up, it was discovered that all they had inside was green slime. Well still, the green slime, if it functioned to produce consciousness and all the rest of their mental life, would have to have causal powers equal to those of the human brain. But now, from our first conclusion, that programs are not enough, and our third conclusion, that any other system would have to have causal powers equal to the brain, conclusion four follows immediately:

CONCLUSION 4

For any artifact that we might build which had mental states equivalent to human mental states, the implementation of a computer program would not by itself be sufficient. Rather the artifact would have to have powers equivalent to the powers of the human brain.

The upshot of this discussion I believe is to remind us of something that we have known all along: namely, mental states are biological phenomena. Consciousness, intentionality, subjectivity, and mental causation are all a part of our biological life history, along with growth, reproduction, the secretion of bile, and digestion.

Visit the companion Web site for chapter specific quizzes, suggestions for further reading, video ideas, and other resources to assess and expand your understanding of the chapter material. Go to http://philosophy.wadsworth.com and select the companion Web site for *Voices of Wisdom.*

 You can access many additional readings at the Info Trac-College Edition Web site. To find the following suggested articles do a keyword search with the article title. Use the passcode that was packaged with your new book to enter the site at http://www.Infotrac-college.com/Wadsworth/. Here is a sampling.

E. D. Watt, "Souls, Bodies and Embryos: What Has Athens to Do with Jerusalem?" *Quadrant,* September 2002 v46 i9 p21(3), A92134158.

Jon Mills, "Five Dangers of Materialism." *Genetic, Social, and General Psychology Monographs,* February 2002 v128 il p5(23), A86470414.

Yair Neuman, "On Turing's Carnal Error: Some Guidelines for a Contextual Inquiry into the Embodied Mind." *Systems Research and Behavioral Science,* November–December 2001 v18 i6 p557(8), A80678912.

Steve Bunk, "Mind–Body Research Matures." *The Scientist,* June 11, 2001 v15 i12 p8, A76284621.

Roy W. Perrett, "Computationality, Mind and Value: The Case of Samkhya-Yoga." *Asian Philosophy,* March 2001 v11 i1 p5, A75121693.

Brook Ziporyn, "Setup, Punch Line, and the Mind–Body Problem: A Neo-Tiantai Approach." *Philosophy East and West,* October 2000 v50 i4 p584, A68952126.

William A. Dembski, "Are We Spiritual Machines?" *First Things: A Monthly Journal of Religion and Public Life,* October 1999 p25, A55981197.

Deborah Tollefsen, "Princess Elisabeth and the Problem of Mind–Body Interaction." *Hypatia,* Summer 1999 v14 i3 p59, A55842946.

Chapter 11

Who Am I?

11.1 Introduction

THE QUESTION ABOUT WHAT I AM leads to questions about the nature of human beings, about what they are made of or what constitutes their being. It also leads to other questions, in particular questions about what a person is. It is here that the question of what begins to shade off into the question of who? Who are we? We are persons. Simple enough, right?

We must be careful to distinguish the concept of "person" from the concept "human being." Human being refers to a biological species, one to which we happen to belong. Person, on the other hand, is not a biological concept. We can bring out the distinction by pointing to the example of the space alien E.T. It would appear that E.T. is a person, but certainly not a human being in the biological sense. This distinction is central to much of the debate about abortion because many claim that whereas a fetus belongs to the biological species human being, it is not a person, but only potentially a person.

To say that something is potentially a person indicates that personhood is something that may not always be present. Of course we all know that persons can and do change. The fact that being a person is dynamic (a changing and developing process) leads to the issue of the identity of persons through time. Consider this puzzle: Are you the same person today as you were when you were five years old? If we mean by "same" a kind of strict identity such that if *A* is identical with *B,* then *A* and *B* have the same characteristics, the answer is obviously no. You have a different set of qualities today (such as size and age) than you did when you were five years old. If we mean by "same" similar, but not absolutely identical characteristics, then the answer is yes.

But is similarity good enough? If I am only similar to my former self, then I have changed. And if I have changed, how much have I changed? For example, does it make sense to hold the person I am today responsible for the act of stealing cookies at age five? If my mother suddenly discovered that I, not my sister, stole the cookies and I lied about it, should she call me up and scold me many years later?

If we accept Descartes's views (see Chapter 10), then we might say that my identity consists in my soul substance, and because my soul has remained the same even though my body has changed, my mother should indeed scold me now no matter how different I am from what I (my soul) was at five.

Many people believe in the soul. It is very popular. It not only takes care of the problem of identity through time but also gives the assurance of life beyond the death of the body. This belief does all that and makes us feel very special, important, and different from all those other living things with which we happen to share the planet. My identity is a soul. My person is a spiritual being. I am special.

But what if there were no souls? What if human identities (persons, if you will) were not everlasting special and unique souls but bundles of sensations, thoughts, memories, and experiences? What if the word "I" was merely a convenient way of talking about that bundle?

Puzzles about personal identity are closely related to other concerns about identity, such as how our sense of who we are is constructed in a social setting. Whether we are souls or not, we are social animals. We are born, we live, and we die in a social/cultural setting that is vitally important to who we are. If you were born in another country to a different family, you would be a very different person than you are now. Your religion might be different, along with many of your beliefs and values. Talk to people from other countries or other ethnic groups and see what I mean.

Social identity is closely tied to gender identity because how society treats us depends, in part, on our gender. Suppose you were born a different sex. Can you imagine yourself, if you are female, as a male? How might you be different? Can those of you who are male imagine yourselves as female? Would you like to be female? Would a sex-change operation make any real difference to who you are? Could you be a female in a male body? Could you be a male in a female body? Who are you? Think about it.

11.2 There Is No Self

Buddhism developed in India around 500 BCE and quickly came into conflict with some of the basic ideas of Hindu philosophy. Among the areas of conflict was the issue of the existence of the self. Hinduism and Buddhism gave very different answers to the question "Who am I?" Some Hindu philosophers answered, "You are the Atman" (for a discussion of the Atman, see Section 8.4), and Buddhism responded with the assertion "There is no Atman." This is called **anatta** (also *Anatman*), or the no-self doctrine.

To understand this teaching, we must back up a moment to another Buddhist teaching called **anicca,** or impermanence. The doctrine of impermanence is a logical implication of the doctrine of dependent origination. If everything that exists is dependent on something else for its existence (as the thesis of dependent origination holds), there can be no independently existing things. This amounts to a denial of the existence of substances because substances are usually thought of as independently existing things. It also amounts to a denial of eternally permanent essences. And it is quite clear that some Indian philosophers regarded the Atman as an independently existing thing that is eternal and permanent.

If there are no substances and if everything is impermanent, it follows that what exists is in constant process. In contrast to Plato's essentialist metaphysics (see Section 8.3), Buddhism teaches a process view of reality. There are no Forms or essences, only ever-changing processes. Hence, according to Buddhist thought, we are wrong if we think of the *jiva* (individual soul or ego) as a permanent substance the way Plato did, or if we think of the Atman (universal Self) as a permanent substance the way some Hindu thinkers did. There is no soul, no ego, no Self, if we mean by any of those terms some independently existing substance or essence.

Note that Buddhists are not denying that you or I exist. They are only denying a particular philosophical view about our natures, the view that the word *I* refers to some unchanging substance called the self or soul. According to Buddhist philosophy, humans are made up of what they call the **five aggregates.** These consist of physical form, sensation, conceptualization, dispositions to act [Karmic constituents], and consciousness. There is no substance over and above these aggregates.

"What," I hear you say, "I am nothing but a collection of elements! How disappointing." It seems so to those of us raised with the idea that what is most important about us is our souls. If we have no souls, then we have no value, or so our culture has taught us. However, our cultural conditioning in this regard may blind us to the value of the Buddhist concept of *anatta.*

The no-self teaching had particular moral and religious value for Buddhism because once we are clear about the fact that there is no substantial self, we can be released from suffering and motivated to act with compassion. Suffering and selfishness arise from desiring things and clinging to them. However, if there is no self, then selfish desiring and clinging amount to one vast illusion, a dream from which those who know the truth about the self can awake. What appears at first glance to be a negative doctrine becomes positive once its moral and religious implications are understood.

The first selection in this section comes from the *Digha Nikaya* and is attributed to the Buddha himself. It deals with teachings about the permanence and existence of the soul found in Hindu philosophy. Buddhist monks found themselves in debate with Hindus on these issues, and this selection instructs them on how they can argue with their opponents and thereby show their opponents' views about the soul to be false. It is the classic expression of the sorts of arguments refined and elaborated in latter Buddhism.

Note that this selection ends with a statement about the afterlife. Clearly one advantage of the doctrine that there is a soul is that one can explain life after death and reincarnation in terms of this soul persisting after the death of the body. However, if there is no soul, what, if anything, persists? Interestingly, the Buddhists affirmed a doctrine of continuity from one life to the next but denied there is a soul that is reborn or reincarnated. Rather what connects this life to the past or to the future is *karma.* You are the result of what you have done.

The second selection is the famous simile of the chariot found in the *Milindapanha.* It would seem that if there is no soul, then all kinds of absurd things follow. King Menander, a Greek who ruled northwestern India in the second century BCE, was quick to point out these absurdities when the Buddhist monk Nagasena denied that his personal name referred to a permanent individual substance. Nagasena counterargued, using the king's own logic and the example of a chariot, to show that the king himself believed there is no chariot above and beyond its parts, yet he saw no problem in using the term *chariot* as a practical designation. So too with the word *I*. It is just a convenient way of talking, a mere sound, without any reference to something substantial.

As an interesting multicultural footnote on this ancient debate, I should call your attention to the fact that here Greek culture (represented by King Menander) encountered Indian Buddhist culture (represented by Nagasena) in public debate (there was an audience of Greeks and Indian monks who witnessed the exchange). Greek philosophers were fond of an argument called "turning the tables." One turns the table on one's debate opponents by using their own assumptions and arguments against them. So Socrates turned the table on a famous sophist named Protagoras by showing that his relativistic principle that stated "Man is the measure of all things" led to the conclusion that Protagoras's philosophical principle was false because Socrates (a man) thought (measures) it false. Supposedly the Greeks invented the technique of "turning the tables," but in this passage a Buddhist monk successfully used it on a Greek, much to the pleasure of the other monks and the grudging admiration of the assembled Greeks.

Reading Questions

1. What is wrong with maintaining that the soul is sensation?
2. What is wrong with maintaining that the soul is not sensation?
3. What is wrong with maintaining that sensation is a faculty of the soul?
4. Because the notions of the soul and of surviving death are closely related, what must a Buddhist monk who rejects these theories of the soul believe about a perfected being who has died?
5. How did King Menander argue against Nagasena's assertion that the name Nagasena is only a practical designation and does not refer to any permanent individual?
6. How did Nagasena counter the King's argument?
7. Who do you think wins this debate, Nagasena or King Menander? Why?
8. What unanswered questions do these readings leave you with? Can you figure out how to answer them?

False Doctrines about the Soul

IN REGARD TO THE SOUL, what are the views held concerning it?

It seems that either one holds the view that sensation is the soul or one holds the view that sensation is not the soul. One might also hold the view that the soul, while not identical to sensation, possesses the faculty or ability of sensation.

Where it is said, "Sensation is my soul," you should reply, "Brother, there are three sensations: the pleasant sensation, the unpleasant sensation, and the indifferent sensation. Which of these three sensations do you hold to be the soul? Whenever a person experiences a pleasant sensation, he does not at the same time experience an unpleasant sensation, nor does he experience an indifferent sensation; only the pleasant sensation does he then feel. This is also true of the others, for when one feels one

I have revised the translation of the Digha-Nikaya *256:21 by Henry Clarke Warren as found in* Buddhism in Translation *(Harvard University Press, 1896).*

sensation whether it be pleasant, unpleasant, or indifferent one does not feel the others."

Now all these sensations—pleasant, unpleasant, indifferent—are transitory, are due to causes, originate by dependence, and are subject to decay, disappearance, and cessation. While someone is experiencing a pleasant sensation, he thinks, "This is my soul." And after the cessation of this same pleasant sensation, he thinks, "My soul has passed away." The same is true of unpleasant and indifferent sensations. They are all subject to rise and disappearance. Accordingly, it is not possible to hold the view that sensation is my soul and that the soul is eternal.

If someone argues that sensation is not my soul, one should reply, "But, brother, where there is no sensation, is there any existence?" The answer is obviously no. Accordingly, it is not possible to hold the view that the soul has no sensation.

So, if sensation is the soul, then the soul is impermanent and not eternal and if sensation is not the soul, then the soul does not exist.

Suppose someone says that the soul has or possesses sensation as an ability but is not identical to it. In this case, a reply should be made as follows: "Suppose, brother, that utterly and completely, and without remainder, all sensation were to cease—if there were nowhere any sensation, pray, would there be anything, after the end of sensation, of which it could be said, "This am I?"

Accordingly, it is not possible to hold the views that the soul is sensation, the soul is not sensation, and that the soul possesses the faculty of sensation and still maintain that the soul is eternal.

From the time a monk no longer holds the view that sensation is the soul, no longer holds the view that the soul has no sensation, and no longer holds the view that the soul possesses the faculty of sensation, he ceases to attach himself to anything in the world, and being free from attachment, he is never agitated, and being never agitated, he attains to Nirvana [release from suffering]. He knows that rebirth is exhausted, that he has lived the holy life, that he has done what is required, and that he is no more for this world or any other. Now it is impossible that a monk whose mind is so freed should think that a perfect being exists after death, or does not exist after death, or both exists and does not exist after death, or neither exists nor does not exist after death.

And why do I say so?

I say so because a perfected being is released and in a state that goes beyond all expression, all communication, and all knowledge.

The Simile of the Chariot

THEN KING MILINDA DECLARED: "Listen to me, you five hundred . . . lords and you eighty thousand monks! This Nāgasena says, 'There is no Person to be found here!' Is it possible to agree to that?"

And addressing the Venerable Nāgasena, he said: "If, Venerable Nāgasena, no Person [soul] is to be found, who then is it who gives you robes, food, lodgings, medicine—all the requisites for a mendicant? Who is it who enjoys the use of these things? Who keeps the precepts? Who practices meditation? Who experiences the path, the fruits, nirvāṇa? Who kills living beings? Who takes what is not given? Who engages in sinful pleasures? Who tells lies? Who drinks intoxicants? Who commits the five evil deeds that have karmic effects in this lifetime?

"From what you say it follows that there is no such thing as merit or demerit; there is neither doer nor causer of meritorious or demeritorious

The translation of the "Simile of the Chariot" (from The Milindapanho*) is by John S. Strong,* The Experience of Buddhism: Sources and Interpretations, *Belmont, CA: Wadsworth Publishing Company, 1995, pp. 92–94. Copyright © 1995 by Wadsworth, Inc.*

actions; there is no reward or punishment for good or evil deeds. If, Nāgasena, a man were to kill you, there would be no murder in that! Moreover, Nāgasena, you monks would have neither teacher nor preceptor: you are not even ordained! You say, 'Your majesty, my co-practitioners call me Nāgasena'; well, what is this 'Nāgasena'? Tell me, is the hair of the head 'Nāgasena'?"

"No, it is not, your majesty."

"Is the hair of the body 'Nāgasena'?"

"No, your majesty."

"What about nails, teeth, skin, flesh, sinews, bones, marrow, kidneys, heart, liver, pleura, spleen, lungs, colon, intestines, stomach, feces, bile, phlegm, pus, blood, sweat, fat, tears, lymph, saliva, snot, synovia, urine, brain—are any of these 'Nāgasena'?"

"No, your majesty."

"Well, then, sir, is your physical form (rūpa) 'Nāgasena'?"

"No, your majesty."

"Are feelings (vedanā) 'Nāgasena'?"

"No, your majesty."

"Are perceptions (saññā) 'Nāgasena'?"

"No, your majesty."

"Are karmic constituents (sankhārā) 'Nāgasena'?"

"No, your majesty."

"Is consciousness (viññāṇa) 'Nāgasena'?"

"No, your majesty."

"Perhaps the five skandhas all together—form, feelings, perceptions, karmic constituents and consciousness—are they 'Nāgasena'?"

"No, your majesty."

"Then is it something other than physical form, feelings, perceptions, karmic constituents, and consciousness that is 'Nāgasena'?"

"No, your majesty."

"Well, my friend, though I question you repeatedly, I do not find any 'Nāgasena.' 'Nāgasena' is but a sound! Who is this 'Nāgasena'? You are lying, my friend, you are telling falsehoods. There is no Nāgasena!"

Then the Venerable Nāgasena said to King Milinda: "Your majesty, you are a delicate, refined nobleman. If, in the middle of the day, you were to walk on the hot, burning, sandy ground and tread on rough, gritty, pebbly sand, your feet would hurt, your body would get tired, your mind would be distressed, and there would arise in you a consciousness of bodily suffering. Tell me, did you come on foot, or did you ride?"

"I did not come on foot, sir, I rode in a chariot."

"If that is the case, your majesty, tell me what is the chariot. Is the pole the chariot?"

"No, it is not, sir."

"Is the axle the chariot?"

"No, sir."

"Are the wheels the chariot?"

"No, sir."

"Is the frame the chariot?"

"No, sir."

"Is the banner staff the chariot?"

"No, sir."

"Is the yoke the chariot?"

"No, sir."

"Are the reins the chariot?"

"No, sir."

"Is the goad the chariot?"

"No, sir."

"Perhaps, your majesty, the pole, the axle, the wheels, the frame, the banner staff, the yoke, the reins, and the goad all together—are they the chariot?"

"No, sir, they are not."

"Then, your majesty, is it something other than the pole, the axle, the wheels, the frame, the banner staff, the yoke, the reins, and the goad that is the chariot?"

"No, sir, it is not."

"Well, your majesty, though I question you repeatedly, I do not find any chariot. 'Chariot' is but a sound! What is this chariot? You are lying, your majesty, you are telling falsehoods. There is no chariot! Your majesty, you are the supreme ruler over the whole of India, who are you afraid of that you should tell a lie? Listen to me, you five hundred . . . lords and you eighty thousand monks! This King Milinda says, 'I came in a chariot!' But when I ask him to tell me what the chariot is, he cannot produce a chariot. Is it possible to agree to such a thing?"

When he had thus spoken, the five hundred . . . lords applauded the Venerable Nāgasena, and said to King Milinda: "Now, your majesty, answer that if you can!"

And King Milinda said to the Venerable Nāgasena: "Good Nāgasena, I did not lie. The word *chariot* comes into existence, dependent on the pole, dependent on the axle, the wheels, the frame, the banner staff, the yoke, the reins, the goad; it is a designation, a description, an appellation, a name."

"Well said, your majesty! You truly understand the chariot! In the same way, your majesty, in my case, the word *Nāgasena* comes into existence, dependent on the hair of the head, dependent on the hair of the body, . . . dependent on the brain, dependent on physical form, on feelings, on perceptions, on karmic constituents, on consciousness. It is a designation, a description, an appellation, nothing but a name. But in the final analysis, the ultimate sense, there is no Person [soul] to be found herein. . . ."

11.3 Down with the Ego

Suppose you found yourself in the following situation. You have agreed to participate in a psychological experiment. You are blindfolded and an object is placed in your left hand. When asked what the object is, you are unable to identify it. Your left hand is now placed in a box with a number of objects in it. You are still blindfolded so you cannot see them. You are asked to pick out the object that had been placed in your left hand, and you have no difficulty doing it. Now your right hand is put in the box, and you are asked to retrieve the object. You cannot. Now the blindfold is removed so that you can see which objects the right hand is picking up. Much to your astonishment, your left hand slaps your right hand whenever it picks up the wrong object. What would you make of this situation? What is going on here?

Those were the questions Roger Sperry and his colleagues asked in the 1960s when they began to get results like the ones above while they were conducting experiments with split-brain patients at the California Institute of Technology. Human brains are divided into two hemispheres. Each hemisphere controls and receives information from opposite sides of the body. The right hemisphere governs and gets information from the left side of the body, and the left hemisphere governs and gets information from the right side of the body. A large bundle of millions of nerves known as the *corpus callosum* connects these hemispheres and permits communication between the two sides of the brain. Neurosurgeons discovered that they could prevent seizures from moving from one hemisphere to another by cutting the *corpus callosum* without causing any obvious disruption in the cognitive life of the patients. However, controlled experiments like the one described above revealed differences between split-brain people and people whose *corpus callosum* was intact.

Researchers discovered that the information given to one hemisphere was unavailable to the other hemisphere in split-brain cases. In most people the left hemisphere controls speech, and people could not name an object placed in the left hand and communicated to the right hemisphere alone. The left hand could, however, select the object from among other objects because the right hemisphere remembered how it felt. The left hemisphere had no idea what the object was and so the right hand could not select the correct object. Once the blindfold was removed, the left hand (right hemisphere) could communicate to the right hand (left hemisphere) only by slapping it because the *corpus callosum* had been severed.

These experiments appear to indicate that there are two different streams of consciousness operating in a single brain. Are there two persons as well? Odd as it may sound, some people have argued that there are. Do we have two different minds associated with the two different hemispheres, but communicating with each other so quickly that we don't notice? If we have two different minds, are we two different persons? If so, who is the real me?

In the next selection Derek Parfit (b. 1942), a British philospher who has taught at Oxford and in the United States, reflects on the implications of split-brain research for notions of what a person is. He argues that the split-brain experiments are inconsistent with an "ego theory" of self but are consistent with a "bundle theory." He discovers a remarkable similarity between his ideas of personal identity and ancient Buddhist notions of the "No-Self" (see Section 11.2).

Reading Questions

1. According to Parfit, why do the split-brain cases support the view that there are two streams of consciousness?
2. What is the difference between the ego theory and the bundle theory of personal identity?
3. What point does Parfit make in his imaginary cases of teletransportation?
4. Explain what Parfit means when he says, "*Ordinary survival is about as bad a being destroyed and having a Replica.*"
5. Why does Parfit believe that the split-brain cases support the bundle theory?

Divided Minds and the Nature of Persons

DEREK PARFIT

IT WAS THE SPLIT-BRAIN CASES which drew me into philosophy. Our knowledge of these cases depends on the results of various psychological tests, as described by Donald MacKay. These tests made use of two facts. We control each of our arms, and see what is in each half of our visual fields, with only one of our hemispheres. When someone's hemispheres have been disconnected, psychologists can thus present this person two different written questions in the two halves of his visual field, and can receive two different answers written by this person's two hands.

Here is a simplified imaginary version of the kind of evidence that such tests provide. One of

these people looks fixedly at the centre of a wide screen, whose left half is red and right half is blue. On each half in a darker shade are the words, 'How many colours can you see?' With both hands the person writes, "Only one." The words are now changed to read, "Which is the only colour that you can see?" With one of his hands the person writes "Red," with the other he writes "Blue."

If this is how such a person responds, I would conclude that he is having two visual sensations—that he does, as he claims, see both red and blue. But in seeing each colour he is not aware of seeing the other. He has two streams of

From Derek Parfit, "Divided Minds and the Nature of Persons," Mindwaves: Thoughts on Intelligence, Identity and Consciousness, *edited by Colin Blakemore and Susan Greenfield. Oxford: Basil Blackwell, 1987, 19–25. Footnotes deleted.*

consciousness, in each of which he can see only one colour. In one stream he sees red, and at the same time, in his other stream, he sees blue. More generally, he could be having at the same time two series of thoughts and sensations, in having each of which he is unaware of having the other.

This conclusion has been questioned. It has been claimed by some that there are not *two* streams of consciousness, on the ground that the subdominant hemisphere is a part of the brain whose functioning involves no consciousness. If this were true, these cases would lose most of their interest. I believe that it is not true, chiefly because, if a person's dominant hemisphere is destroyed, this person is able to react in the way in which, in the split-brain cases, the sub-dominant hemisphere reacts, and we do not believe that such a person is just an automaton, without consciousness. The sub-dominant hemisphere is, of course, much less developed in certain ways, typically having the linguistic abilities of a three-year-old. But three-year-olds are conscious. This supports the view that, in split-brain cases, there *are* two streams of consciousness.

Another view is that, in these cases, there are two persons involved, sharing the same body. Like Professor MacKay, I believe that we should reject this view. My reason for believing this is, however, different. Professor MacKay denies that there are two persons involved because he believes that there is only one person involved. I believe that, in a sense, the number of persons involved is none.

The Ego Theory and the Bundle Theory

To explain this sense I must, for a while, turn away from the split-brain cases. There are two theories about what persons are, and what is involved in a person's continued existence over time. On the *Ego Theory,* a person's continued existence cannot be explained except as the continued existence of a particular *Ego,* or *subject of experiences.* An Ego Theorist claims that, if we ask what unifies someone's consciousness at any

time—what makes it true, for example, that I can now both see what I am typing and hear the wind outside my window—the answer is that these are both experiences which are being had by me, this person, at this time. Similarly, what explains the unity of a person's whole life is the fact that all of the experiences in this life are had by the same person, or subject of experiences. In its best-known form, the *Cartesian view,* each person is a persisting purely mental thing—a soul, or spiritual substance.

The rival view is the *Bundle Theory.* Like most styles in art—Gothic, baroque, rococo, etc.—this theory owes its name to its critics. But the name is good enough. According to the Bundle Theory, we can't explain either the unity of consciousness at any time, or the unity of a whole life, by referring to a person. Instead we must claim that there are long series of different mental states and events—thoughts, sensations, and the like—each series being what we call one life. Each series is unified by various kinds of causal relation, such as the relations that hold between experiences and later memories of them. Each series is thus like a bundle tied up with string.

In a sense, a Bundle Theorist denies the existence of persons. An outright denial is of course absurd. As Reid protested in the eighteenth century, "I am not thought, I am not action, I am not feeling; I am something which thinks and acts and feels." I am not a series of events, but a person. A Bundle Theorist admits this fact, but claims it to be only a fact about our grammar, or our language. There are persons or subjects in this language-dependent way. If, however, persons are believed to be more than this—to be separately existing things, distinct from our brains and bodies, and the various kinds of mental states and events—the Bundle Theorist denies that there are such things.

The first Bundle Theorist was Buddha, who taught "anatta," or the *No Self view.* Buddhists concede that selves or persons have "nominal existence," by which they mean that persons are merely combinations of other elements. Only what exists by itself, as a separate element, has instead what Buddhists call "actual existence." Here are some quotations from Buddhist texts:

> At the beginning of their conversation the king politely asks the monk his name, and receives the following reply: "Sir, I am known as 'Nagasena'; my fellows in the religious life address me as 'Nagasena.' Although my parents gave me the name . . . it is just an appellation, a form of speech, a description, a conventional usage. 'Nagasena' is only a name, for no person is found here."

> A sentient being does exist, you think, O Mara? You are misled by a false conception. This bundle of elements is void of Self, In it there is no sentient being. Just as a set of wooden parts Receives the name of carriage, So do we give to elements The name of fancied being.

> Buddha has spoken thus: "O Brethren, actions do exist, and also their consequences, but the person that acts does not. There is no one to cast away this set of elements, and no one to assume a new set of them. There exists no Individual, it is only a conventional name given to a set of elements."

Buddha's claims are strikingly similar to the claims advanced by several Western writers. Since these writers knew nothing of Buddha, the similarity of these claims suggests that they are not merely part of one cultural tradition, in one period. They may be, as I believe they are, true.

What We Believe Ourselves to Be

Given the advances in psychology and neurophysiology, the Bundle Theory may now seem to be obviously true. It may seem uninteresting to deny that there are separately existing Egos, which are distinct from brains and bodies and the various kinds of mental states and events. But this is not the only issue. We may be convinced that the Ego Theory is false, or even senseless. Most of us, however, even if we are not aware of this, also have certain beliefs about what is involved in our continued existence over time. And these beliefs would only be justified if something like the Ego Theory was true. Most of us therefore have false beliefs about what persons are, and about ourselves.

These beliefs are best revealed when we consider certain imaginary cases, often drawn from science fiction. One such case is *teletransportation*. Suppose that you enter a cubicle in which, when you press a button, a scanner records the states of all of the cells in your brain and body, destroying both while doing so. This information is then transmitted at the speed of light to some other planet, where a replicator produces a perfect organic copy of you. Since the brain of your Replica is exactly like yours, it will seem to remember living your life up to the moment when you pressed the button, its character will be just like yours, and it will be in every other way psychologically continuous with you. This psychological continuity will not have its normal cause, the continued existence of your brain, since the causal chain will run through the transmission by radio of your "blueprint."

Several writers claim that, if you chose to be teletransported, believing this to be the fastest way of travelling, you would be making a terrible mistake. This would not be a way of travelling, but a way of dying. It may not, they concede, be quite as bad as ordinary death. It might be some consolation to you that, after your death, you will have this Replica, which can finish the book that you are writing, act as parent to your children, and so on. But, they insist, this Replica won't be you. It will merely be someone else, who is exactly like you. This is why this prospect is nearly as bad as ordinary death.

Imagine next a whole range of cases, in each of which, in a single operation, a different proportion of the cells in your brain and body would be replaced with exact duplicates. At the near end of this range, only 1 or 2 per cent would be replaced; in the middle, 40 or 60 per cent; near the far end, 98 or 99 per cent. At the far end of this range is pure teletransportation, the case in which all of your cells would be "replaced."

When you imagine that some proportion of your cells will be replaced with exact duplicates, it is natural to have the following beliefs. First, if you ask, "Will I survive? Will the resulting person be me?," there must be an answer to this question. Either you will survive, or you are about to die. Second, the answer to this question must be either a simple "Yes" or a simple "No." The person who wakes up either will or will not be you. There cannot be a third answer, such as that the person waking up will be half you. You can imagine yourself later being half-conscious. But if the resulting person will be fully conscious, he cannot be half you. To state these beliefs together: to the question, "Will the resulting person be me?," there must always *be* an answer, which must be all-or-nothing.

There seem good grounds for believing that, in the case of teletransportation, your Replica would not be you. In a slight variant of this case, your Replica might be created while you were still alive, so that you could talk to one another. This seems to show that, if 100 per cent of your cells were replaced, the result would merely be a Replica of you. At the other end of my range of cases, where only 1 per cent would be replaced, the resulting person clearly *would* be you. It therefore seems that, in the cases in between, the resulting person must be either you, or merely a Replica. It seems that one of these must be true, and that it makes a great difference which is true.

How We Are Not What We Believe

If these beliefs were correct, there must be some critical percentage, somewhere in this range of cases, up to which the resulting person would be you, and beyond which he would merely be your Replica. Perhaps, for example, it would be you who would wake up if the proportion of cells replaced were 49 per cent, but if just a few more cells were also replaced, this would make all the difference, causing it to be someone else who would wake up.

That there must be some such critical percentage follows from our natural beliefs. But this conclusion is most implausible. How could a few cells make such a difference? Moreover, if there is such a critical percentage, no one could ever discover where it came. Since in all these cases the resulting person would believe that he was you, there could never be any evidence about where, in this range of cases, he would suddenly cease to be you.

On the Bundle Theory, we should reject these natural beliefs. Since you, the person, are not a separately existing entity, we can know exactly what would happen without answering the question of what will happen to you. Moreover, in the cases in the middle of my range, it is an empty question whether the resulting person would be you, or would merely be someone else who is exactly like you. These are not here two different possibilities, one of which must be true. These are merely two different descriptions of the very same course of events. If 50 per cent of your cells were replaced with exact duplicates, we could call the resulting person you, or we could call him merely your Replica. But since these are not here different possibilities, this is a mere choice of words.

As Buddha claimed, the Bundle Theory is hard to believe. It is hard to accept that it could be an empty question whether one is about to die, or will instead live for many years.

What we are being asked to accept may be made clearer with this analogy. Suppose that a certain club exists for some time, holding regular meetings. The meetings then cease. Some years later, several people form a club with the same name, and the same rules. We can ask, "Did these people revive the very same club? Or did they merely start up another club which is exactly similar?" Given certain further details, this would be another empty question. We could know just what happened without answering this question. Suppose that someone said: "But there must be an answer. The club meeting later must either be, or not be, the very same club." This would show that this person didn't understand the nature of clubs.

In the same way, if we have any worries about my imagined cases, we don't understand the nature of persons. In each of my cases, you would know that the resulting person would be both psychologically and physically exactly like you, and that he would have some particular proportion of the cells in your brain and body—90 per cent, or 10 per cent, or, in the case of teletransportation, 0 per cent. Knowing this, you know everything. How could it be a real question what would happen to you, unless you are a separately existing Ego, distinct from a brain and body, and the various kinds of mental state and event? If there are no such Egos, there is nothing else to ask a real question about.

Accepting the Bundle Theory is not only hard; it may also affect our emotions. As Buddha claimed, it may undermine our concern about our own futures. This effect can be suggested by redescribing this change of view. Suppose that you are about to be destroyed, but will later have a Replica on Mars. You would naturally believe that this prospect is about as bad as ordinary death, since your Replica won't be you. On the Bundle Theory, the fact that your Replica won't be you just consists in the fact that, though it will be fully psychologically continuous with you, this continuity won't have its normal cause. But when you object to teletransportation you are not objecting merely to the abnormality of this cause. You are objecting that this cause won't get *you* to Mars. You fear that the abnormal cause will fail to produce a further and all-important fact, which is different from the fact that your Replica will be psychologically continuous with you. You do not merely want there to be psychological continuity between you and some future person. You want to *be* this future person. On the Bundle Theory, there is no such special further fact. What you fear will not happen, in this imagined case, *never* happens. You want the person on Mars to be you in a specially intimate way in which no future person will ever be you. This means that, judged from the standpoint of your natural beliefs, even ordinary survival is about as bad as teletransportation. *Ordinary survival is about as bad as being destroyed and having a Replica.*

How the Split-Brain Cases Support the Bundle Theory

The truth of the Bundle Theory seems to me, in the widest sense, as much a scientific as a philosophical conclusion. I can imagine kinds of evidence which would have justified believing in the existence of separately existing Egos, and believing that the continued existence of these Egos is what explains the continuity of each mental life. But there is in fact very little evidence in favour of this Ego Theory, and much for the alternative Bundle Theory.

Some of this evidence is provided by the split-brain cases. On the Ego Theory, to explain what unifies our experiences at any one time, we should simply claim that these are all experiences which are being had by the same person. Bundle Theorists reject this explanation. This disagreement is hard to resolve in ordinary cases. But consider the simplified split-brain case that I described. We show to my imagined patient a placard whose left half is blue and right half is red. In one of this person's two streams of consciousness, he is aware of seeing only blue, while at the same time, in his other stream, he is aware of seeing only red. Each of these two visual experiences is combined with other experiences, like that of being aware of moving one of his hands. What unifies the experiences, at any time, in each of this person's two streams of consciousness? What unifies his awareness of seeing only red with his awareness of moving one hand? The answer cannot be that these experiences are being had by the same person. This answer cannot explain the unity of each of this person's two streams of consciousness, since it ignores the disunity between these streams. This person is now having all of the experiences in both of his two streams. If this fact was what unified these experiences, this would make the two streams one.

These cases do not, I have claimed, involve two people sharing a single body. Since there is only one person involved, who has two streams of consciousness, the Ego Theorist's explanation would have to take the following form. He would have to distinguish between persons and subjects of experiences, and claim that, in split-brain cases, there are *two* of the latter. What unifies the experiences in one of the person's two streams would have to be the fact that these experiences are all being had by the same subject of experiences. What unifies the experiences in this person's other stream would have to be the fact that they are being had by another subject of experiences. When this explanation takes this form, it becomes much less plausible. While we could assume that "subject of experiences," or "Ego," simply meant "person," it was easy to believe that there are subjects of experiences. But if there can be subjects of experiences that are not persons, and if in the life of a split-brain patient there are at any time two different subjects of experiences—two different Egos—why should we believe that there really are such things? This does not amount to a refutation. But it seems to me a strong argument against the Ego Theory.

As a Bundle Theorist, I believe that these two Egos are idle cogs. There is another explanation of the unity of consciousness, both in ordinary cases and in split-brain cases. It is simply a fact that ordinary people are, at any time, aware of having several different experiences. This awareness of several different experiences can be helpfully compared with one's awareness, in short-term memory, of several different experiences. Just as there can be a single memory of just having had several experiences, such as hearing a bell strike three times, there can be a single state of awareness both of hearing the fourth striking of this bell, and of seeing, at the same time, ravens flying past the bell-tower.

Unlike the Ego Theorist's explanation, this explanation can easily be extended to cover split-brain cases. In such cases there is, at any time, not one state of awareness of several different experiences, but two such states. In the case I described, there is one state of awareness of both seeing only red and of moving one hand, and there is another state of awareness of both seeing only blue and moving the other hand. In claiming that there are two such states of awareness, we are not postulating the existence of unfamiliar entities, two separately existing Egos which are not the same as the single person whom the case involves. This explanation appeals to a pair of mental states which would have to be described anyway in a full description of this case.

I have suggested how the split-brain cases provide one argument for one view about the nature of persons. I should mention another such argument, provided by an imagined extension of these cases, first discussed at length by David Wiggins.

In this imagined case a person's brain is divided, and the two halves are transplanted into a pair of different bodies. The two resulting people live quite separate lives. This imagined case shows that personal identity is not what matters. If I was about to divide, I should conclude that neither of the resulting people will be me. I will have ceased to exist. But this way of ceasing to exist is about as good—or as bad—as ordinary survival.

Some of the features of Wiggins's imagined case are likely to remain technically impossible. But the case cannot be dismissed, since its most striking feature, the division of one stream of consciousness into separate streams, has already happened. This is a second way in which the actual split-brain cases have great theoretical importance. They challenge some of our deepest assumptions about ourselves.

11.4 Where Am I?

Location, location, location. This real estate slogan might well be the slogan of philosophers searching for the necessary and sufficient conditions that allow us to say that a person existing at one time (the five-year-old) is the same person existing at another time (the sixty-two-year-old).

It is natural to locate personal identity in the body. I am the same person just insofar as I am in the same body. This "body identity theory" works perfectly well most of the time. If we see someone who looks like our friend Sonia, we assume that she is Sonia. But things can go wrong. Sonia may have an identical twin or a remarkable look-a-like. There are at least three serious problems with the body identity theory. First, looks can be deceiving, as we just noted. Second, bodies change with time, so that the body of the sixty-two-year-old is very different from the body of the five-year-old. Third, our psychological life is left out of the picture. We are more than bodies. We are psychologies. So if someone looks like Sonia but has none of Sonia's memories or personality characteristics, we may doubt that she is Sonia.

We may be able to overcome these problems in a variety of ways. One way is to deny that incidents of deception amount to serious objections to the theory. The fact that I can be deceived does not invalidate my theory unless, of course, my theory claims that deception is not possible. Another way is to build into the "body identity theory" the notion of continuity. If my sixty-two-year-old body is physically continuous in important ways with my five-year-old body, then we can say I am the same person. Although I am not the same in any numerical sense, I am the same in the sense that I am the closest continuer of that other body. But what do we do about my psychological life? Is that located in my body in such a way that where my body is, there my psychological life is?

At this point we may wish to modify my body identity theory by including the brain. Because the brain appears to be the home of my conscious life, along with my memories and personality traits, we might say that it would be better to call the body identity theory a brain identity theory. Where my brain is, there is my home. There, in the brain, is where my psychological life takes place. Of course the physiology of the brain changes as much as the physiology of the body as we age, and surely we can just as easily (and probably more accurately) speak of different psychological lives associated with the same person. I have different bodies over time, but I also have different psychologies over time. Once again, now that we have a "body-brain-psychology" theory of identity, we have to build in some idea of continuity and thereby give up the idea of strict numerical identity. It seems that we should speak instead of similarities connected by continuous physical and psychological streams.

Just when we think we are out of the woods, science fiction steps in to complicate matters. Let's suppose that in the future, brain transplantations become as routine as heart transplantations are today. My body is dying from cancer. If a suitable recipient is found, my brain can be transplanted into that body. Assuming that my psychology will go with my brain, which is now located in a new body, where am I? "You are where your brain is," you might reply. Quite so. Now let's assume that bodies are in short supply, so my brain has to be kept alive in a vat, apart from any body, and constantly bathed with life-supporting fluids. So I am in the vat. Now suppose that our technology is such that we can keep organic brains alive that way for only so long. When time is running out, scientists decide to create a computer replica of my brain. They duplicate my psychology "line for line" as it were. Now where am I?

Don't panic. We are on a roll here. Suppose that now the computer replica brain and my biological brain both exist. Then, just as time is running out, a suitable recipient is found and my biological brain is transplanted into a new body. But there is still this computer replica brain out there in Sci-Fi-Land, bearing the exact same psychology as the newly transplanted biological brain. Where am I?

Daniel C. Dennett (b. 1942) is currently the director of the Center for Cognitive Studies at Tufts University. In addition to being a philosopher, he is a sculptor, farmer, wine maker, and designer of museum computer exhibits. In the following selection, Dennett uses science fiction to explore conundrums about personal identity.

Reading Questions

1. Would you, like Dennett, initially conclude that you are where your body is and not where your brain is? Why?

2. How does the idea of a "*point of view*" support the notion that Dennett is "*wherever he thinks he is*"?

3. What philosophical "revelation" occurs to Dennett when the radio links between his brain and body are broken?

4. Would you, like Dennett, be upset about the possibility of one of your brains becoming connected to another body?

5. Where is your "self" located? Is it in your body or outside of your body? Is it in your brain and not in your body? Is it in your brain-body or some other place? Does it even make sense to ask where your "self" is located? Support whatever answers you give with reasons.

6. Does the popular idea that our self is our soul solve any of Dennett's problems about where he is located? If so, how does it? If not, why not?

Brainstorms

DANIEL DENNETT

NOW THAT I'VE WON MY SUIT under the Freedom of Information Act, I am at liberty to reveal for the first time a curious episode in my life that may be of interest not only to those engaged in research in the philosophy of mind, artificial intelligence and neuroscience but also to the general public.

Several years ago I was approached by Pentagon officials who asked me to volunteer for a highly dangerous and secret mission. In collaboration with NASA and Howard Hughes, the Department of Defense was spending billions to develop a Supersonic Tunneling Underground Device, or STUD. It was supposed to tunnel through the earth's core at great speed and deliver a specially designed atomic warhead "right up the Red's missile silos," as one of the Pentagon brass put it.

The problem was that in an early test they had succeeded in lodging a warhead about a mile deep under Tulsa, Oklahoma, and they wanted me to retrieve it for them. "Why me?" I asked. Well, the mission involved some pioneering applications of current brain research, and they had heard of my interest in brains and of course

my Faustian curiosity and great courage and so forth. . . . Well, how could I refuse? The difficulty that brought the Pentagon to my door was that the device I'd been asked to recover was fiercely radioactive, in a new way. According to monitoring instruments, something about the nature of the device and its complex interactions with pockets of material deep in the earth had produced radiation that could cause severe abnormalities in certain tissues of the brain. No way had been found to shield the brain from these deadly rays, which were apparently harmless to other tissues and organs of the body. So it had been decided that the person sent to recover the device should *leave his brain behind*. It would be kept in a safe place where it could execute its normal control functions by elaborate radio links. Would I submit to a surgical procedure that would completely remove my brain, which would then be placed in a life-support system at the Manned Spacecraft Center in Houston? Each input and output pathway, as it was severed, would be restored by a pair of microminiaturized radio transceivers, one attached precisely to the brain, the other to the nerve stumps in the

Daniel C. Dennett, Brainstorms: Philosophical Essays on Mind and Psychology, *310–323. Reprinted by permission of MIT Press. Footnotes deleted.*

empty cranium. No information would be lost, all the connectivity would be preserved. At first I was a bit reluctant. Would it really work? The Houston brain surgeons encouraged me. "Think of it," they said, "as a mere *stretching* of the nerves. If your brain were just moved over an *inch* in your skull, that would not alter or impair your mind. We're simply going to make the nerves indefinitely elastic by splicing radio links into them."

I was shown around the life-support lab in Houston and saw the sparkling new vat in which my brain would be placed, were I to agree. I met the large and brilliant support team of neurologists, hematologists, biophysicists, and electrical engineers, and after several days of discussions and demonstrations, I agreed to give it a try. I was subjected to an enormous array of blood tests, brain scans, experiments, interviews, and the like. They took down my autobiography at great length, recorded tedious lists of my beliefs, hopes, fears, and tastes. They even listed my favorite stereo recordings and gave me a crash session of psychoanalysis.

The day for surgery arrived at last and of course I was anesthetized and remember nothing of the operation itself. When I came out of anesthesia, I opened my eyes, looked around, and asked the inevitable, the traditional, the lamentably hackneyed post-operative question: "Where am I?" The nurse smiled down at me. "You're in Houston," she said, and I reflected that this still had a good chance of being the truth one way or another. She handed me a mirror. Sure enough, there were the tiny antennae poling up through their titanium ports cemented into my skull.

"I gather the operation was a success," I said, "I want to go see my brain." They led me (I was a bit dizzy and unsteady) down a long corridor and into the life-support lab. A cheer went up from the assembled support team, and I responded with what I hoped was a jaunty salute. Still feeling lightheaded, I was helped over to the life-support vat. I peered through the glass. There, floating in what looked like ginger-ale, was undeniably a human brain, though it was almost covered with printed circuit chips, plastic tubules, electrodes, and other paraphernalia. "Is that mine?" I asked. "Hit the output transmitter switch there on the side of the vat and see for yourself," the project director replied. I moved the switch to OFF, and immediately slumped, groggy and nauseated, into the arms of the technicians, one of whom kindly restored the switch to its ON position. While I recovered my equilibrium and composure, I thought to myself: "Well, here I am, sitting on a folding chair, staring through a piece of plate glass at my own brian. . . . But wait," I said to myself, "shouldn't I have thought, 'Here I am, suspended in a bubbling fluid, being stared at by my own eyes'?" I tried to think this latter thought. I tried to project it into the tank, offering it hopefully to my brain, but I failed to carry off the exercise with any conviction. I tried again. "Here am *I*, Daniel Dennett, suspended in a bubbling fluid, being stared at by my own eyes." No, it just didn't work. Most puzzling and confusing. Being a philosopher of firm physicalist conviction, I believed unswervingly that the tokening of my thoughts was occurring somewhere in my brain: yet, when I thought "Here I am," where the thought occurred to me was *here*, outside the vat, where I, Dennett, was standing staring at my brain.

I tried and tried to think myself into the vat, but to no avail. I tried to build up to the task by doing mental exercises. I thought to myself, "The sun is shining *over there*," five times in rapid succession, each time mentally ostending a different place: in order, the sun-lit corner of the lab, the visible front lawn of the hospital, Houston, Mars, and Jupiter. I found I had little difficulty in getting my "there's" to hop all over the celestial map with their proper references. I could loft a "there" in an instant through the farthest reaches of space, and then aim the next "there" with pinpoint accuracy at the upper left quadrant of a freckle on my arm. Why was I having such trouble with "here"? "Here in Houston" worked well enough, and so did "here in the lab," and even "here in this part of the lab," but "here in the vat" always seemed merely an unmeant mental mouthing. I tried closing my eyes while thinking it. This seemed to help, but still I couldn't manage to pull it off, except perhaps for a fleeting instant. I couldn't be sure. The discovery that I couldn't be sure was also unsettling. How did I know *where* I meant by "here" when I thought "here"? Could I *think* I meant one place when in fact I meant another? I didn't see how that could be admitted without untying the few bonds of intimacy between a person and his own mental life that had survived the onslaught of the brain scientists and philosophers, the physicalists and behaviorists. Perhaps I was incorrigible about where I *meant* when I said "here." But in my present circumstances it seemed that either I was doomed by sheer force of mental habit to thinking systematically false indexical thoughts, or where a person is (and hence where his thoughts are tokened for purposes of semantic analysis) is not necessarily where his brain, the physical seat of his soul, resides. Nagged by confusion, I attempted to orient myself by falling back on a favorite philosopher's ploy. I began naming things.

"Yorick," I said aloud to my brain, "you are my brain. The rest of my body, seated in this chair, I dub 'Hamlet.'" So here we all are: Yorick's my brain, Hamlet's my body, and I am Dennett. *Now,* where am I? And when I think "where am I?" where's that thought tokened? Is it tokened in my brain, lounging about in the vat, or right here between my ears where it *seems* to be tokened? Or nowhere? Its *temporal* coordinates give me no trouble; must it not have spatial coordinates as well? I began making a list of the alternatives.

(1) *Where Hamlet goes, there goes Dennett.* This principle was easily refuted by appeal to the familiar brain transplant thought-experiments so enjoyed by philosophers. If Tom and Dick switch brains, Tom is the fellow with Dick's former body—just ask him; he'll claim to be Tom, and tell you the most intimate details of Tom's autobiography. It was clear enough, then, that my current body and I could part company, but not likely that I could be separated from my brain. The rule of thumb that emerged so plainly from the thought experiments was that in a braintransplant operation, one wanted to be the *donor,* not the recipient. Better to call such an operation a *body*-transplant, in fact. So perhaps the truth was,

(2) *Where Yorick goes, there goes Dennett.* This was not at all appealing, however. How could I be in the vat and not about to go anywhere, when I was so obviously outside the vat looking in and beginning to make guilty plans to return to my room for a substantial lunch? This begged the question I realized, but it still seemed to be getting at something important. Casting about for some support for my intuition, I hit upon a legalistic sort of argument that might have appealed to Locke.

Suppose, I argued to myself, I were now to fly to California, rob a bank, and be apprehended. In which state would I be tried: In California, where the robbery took place, or in Texas, where the brains of the outfit were located? Would I be a California felon with an out-of-state brain, or a Texas felon remotely controlling an accomplice of sorts in California? It seemed possible that I might beat such a rap just on the undecidability of that jurisdictional question, though perhaps it would be deemed an inter-state, and hence Federal, offense. In any event, suppose I were convicted. Was it likely that California would be satisfied to throw Hamlet into the brig, knowing that Yorick was living the good life and luxuriously taking the waters in Texas? Would Texas incarcerate Yorick, leaving Hamlet free to take the next boat to Rio? This alternative appealed to me. Barring capital punishment or other cruel and unusual punishment, the state would be obliged to maintain the life-support system for Yorick though they might move him from Houston to Leavenworth, and aside from the unpleasantness of the opprobrium, I, for one, would not mind at all and would consider myself a free man under those circumstances. If the state has an interest in forcibly relocating persons in institutions, it would fail to relocate me in any institution by locating Yorick there. If this were true, it suggested a third alternative.

(3) *Dennett is wherever he thinks he is.* Generalized, the claim was as follows: At any given time a person has a *point of view,* and the location of the point of view (which is determined

internally by the content of the point of view) is also the location of the person.

Such a proposition is not without its perplexities, but to me it seemed a step in the right direction. The only trouble was that it seemed to place one in a heads-I-win/tails-you-lose situation of unlikely infallibility as regards location. Hadn't I myself often been wrong about where I was, and at least as often uncertain? Couldn't one get lost? Of course, but getting lost *geographically* is not the only way one might get lost. If one were lost in the woods one could attempt to reassure oneself with the consolation that at least one knew where one was: one was right *here* in the familiar surroundings of one's own body. Perhaps in this case one would not have drawn one's attention to much to be thankful for. Still, there were worse plights imaginable, and I wasn't sure I wasn't in such a plight right now.

Point of view clearly had something to do with personal location, but it was itself an unclear notion. It was obvious that the content of one's point of view was not the same as or determined by the content of one's beliefs or thoughts. For example, what should we say about the point of view of the Cinerama viewer who shrieks and twists in his seat as the roller-coaster footage overcomes his psychic distancing? Has he forgotten that he is safely seated in the theater? Here I was inclined to say that the person is experiencing an illusory shift in point of view. In other cases, my inclination to call such shifts illusory was less strong. The workers in laboratories and plants who handle dangerous materials by operating feedback-controlled mechanical arms and hands undergo a shift in point of view that is crisper and more pronounced than anything Cinerama can provoke. They can feel the heft and slipperiness of the containers they manipulate with their metal fingers. They know perfectly well where they are and are not fooled into false beliefs by the experience, yet it is as if they were inside the isolation chamber they are peering into. With mental effort, they can manage to shift their point of view back and forth, rather like making a transparent Neckar cube or an Escher drawing change orientation

before one's eyes. It does seem extravagant to suppose that in performing this bit of mental gymnastics, they are transporting *themselves* back and forth.

Still their example gave me hope. If I was in fact in the vat in spite of my intuitions, I might be able to train myself to adopt that point of view even as a matter of habit. I should dwell on images of myself comfortably floating in my vat, beaming volitions to that familiar body *out there*. I reflected that the ease or difficulty of this task was presumably independent of the truth about the location of one's brain. Had I been practicing before the operation, I might now be finding it second nature. You might now yourself try such a *tromp d'oeil*. Imagine you have written an inflammatory letter which has been published in the *Times,* the result of which is that the Government has chosen to impound your brain for a probationary period of three years in its Dangerous Brain Clinic in Bethesda, Maryland. Your body of course is allowed freedom to earn a salary and thus to continue its function of laying up income to be taxed. At this moment, however, your body is seated in an auditorium listening to a peculiar account by Daniel Dennett of his own similar experience. Try it. Think yourself to Bethesda, and then hark back longingly to your body, far away, and yet *seeming* so near. It is only with long-distance restraint (yours? the Government's?) that you can control your impulse to get those hands clapping in polite applause before navigating the old body to the rest room and a well-deserved glass of evening sherry in the lounge. The task of imagination is certainly difficult, but if you achieve your goal the results might be consoling.

Anyway, there I was in Houston, lost in thought as one might say, but not for long. My speculations were soon interrupted by the Houston doctors, who wished to test out my new prosthetic nervous system before sending me off on my hazardous mission. As I mentioned before, I was a bit dizzy at first, and not surprisingly, although I soon habituated myself to my new circumstances (which were, after all, well nigh indistinguishable from my old circumstances). My accommodation was not perfect, however, and to this day I continue to be plagued by minor coordination difficulties. The speed of light is fast, but finite, and as my brain and body move farther and farther apart, the delicate interaction of my feedback systems is thrown into disarray by the time lags. Just as one is rendered close to speechless by a delayed or echoic hearing of one's speaking voice so, for instance, I am virtually unable to track a moving object with my eyes whenever my brain and my body are more than a few miles apart. In most matters my impairment is scarcely detectable, though I can no longer hit a slow curve ball with the authority of yore. There are some compensations of course. Though liquor tastes as good as ever, and warms my gullet while corroding my liver, I can drink it in any quantity I please, without becoming the slightest bit inebriated, a curiosity some of my close friends may have noticed (though I occasionally have *feigned* inebriation, so as not to draw attention to my unusual circumstances). For similar reasons, I take aspirin orally for a sprained wrist, but if the pain persists I ask Houston to administer codeine to me *in vitro*. In times of illness the phone bill can be staggering.

But to return to my adventure. At length, both the doctors and I were satisfied that I was ready to undertake my subterranean mission. And so I left my brain in Houston and headed by helicopter for Tulsa. Well, in any case, that's the way it seemed to me. That's how I would put it, just off the top of my head as it were. On the trip I reflected further about my earlier anxieties and decided that my first post-operative speculations had been tinged with panic. The matter was not nearly as strange or metaphysical as I had been supposing. Where was I? In two places, clearly: both inside the vat and outside it. Just as one can stand with one foot in Connecticut and the other in Rhode Island, I was in two places at once. I had become one of those scattered individuals we used to hear so much about. The more I considered this answer, the more obviously true it appeared. But, strange to say, the more true it appeared, the less important the question to which it could be the true answer seemed. A sad, but not unprecedented, fate for a

philosophical question to suffer. This answer did not completely satisfy me, of course. There lingered some question to which I should have liked an answer, which was neither "Where are all my various and sundry parts?" nor "What is my current point of view?" Or at least there seemed to be such a question. For it did seem undeniable that in some sense *I* and not merely *most of me* was descending into the earth under Tulsa in search of an atomic warhead.

When I found the warhead, I was certainly glad I had left my brain behind, for the pointer on the specially built Geiger counter I had brought with me was off the dial. I called Houston on my ordinary radio and told the operation control center of my position and my progress. In return, they gave me instructions for dismantling the vehicle, based upon my on-site observations. I had set to work with my cutting torch when all of a sudden a terrible thing happened. I went stone deaf. At first I thought it was only my radio earphones that had broken, but when I tapped on my helmet, I heard nothing. Apparently the auditory transceivers had gone on the fritz. I could no longer hear Houston or my own voice, but I could speak, so I started telling them what had happened. In mid-sentence, I knew something else had gone wrong. My vocal apparatus had become paralyzed. Then my right hand went limp—another transceiver had gone. I was truly in deep trouble. But worse was to follow. After a few more minutes, I went blind. I cursed my luck, and then I cursed the scientists who had led me into this grave peril. There I was, deaf, dumb, and blind, in a radioactive hole more than a mile under Tulsa. Then the last of my cerebral radio links broke, and suddenly I was faced with a new and even more shocking problem: whereas an instant before I had been buried alive in Oklahoma, now I was disembodied in Houston. My recognition of my new status was not immediate. It took me several very anxious minutes before it dawned on me that my poor body lay several hundred miles away, with heart pulsing and lungs respiring, but otherwise as dead as the body of any heart transplant donor, its skull packed with useless, broken electronic gear. The shift in perspective

I had earlier found well nigh impossible now seemed quite natural. Though I could think myself back into my body in the tunnel under Tulsa, it took some effort to sustain the illusion. For surely it was an illusion to suppose I was still in Oklahoma: I had lost all contact with that body.

It occurred to me then, with one of those rushes of revelation of which we should be suspicious, that I had stumbled upon an impressive demonstration of the immateriality of the soul based upon physicalist principles and premises. For as the last radio signal between Tulsa and Houston died away, had I not changed location from Tulsa to Houston at the speed of light? And had I not accomplished this without any increase in mass? What moved from A to B at such speed was surely myself, or at any rate my soul or mind—the massless center of my being and home of my consciousness. My *point of view* had lagged somewhat behind, but I had already noted the indirect bearing of point of view on personal location. I could not see how a physicalist philosopher could quarrel with this except by taking the dire and counter-intuitive route of banishing all talk of persons. Yet the notion of personhood was so well entrenched in everyone's world view, or so it seemed to me, that any denial would be as curiously unconvincing, as systematically disingenuous, as the Cartesian negation, "non sum."

The joy of philosophic discovery thus tided me over some very bad minutes or perhaps hours as the helplessness and hopelessness of my situation became more apparent to me. Waves of panic and even nausea swept over me, made all the more horrible by the absence of their normal body-dependent phenomenology. No adrenalin rush of tingles in the arms, no pounding heart, no premonitory salivation. I did feel a dread sinking feeling in my bowels at one point, and this tricked me momentarily into the false hope that I was undergoing a reversal of the process that landed me in this fix—a gradual undisembodiment. But the isolation and uniqueness of that twinge soon convinced me that it was simply the first of a plague of phantom body hallucinations that I, like any other amputee, would be all too likely to suffer.

My mood then was chaotic. On the one hand, I was fired up with elation of my philosophic discovery and was wracking my brain (one of the few familiar things I could still do), trying to figure out how to communicate my discovery to the journals; while on the other, I was bitter, lonely, and filled with dread and uncertainty. Fortunately, this did not last long, for my technical support team sedated me into a dreamless sleep from which I awoke, hearing with magnificent fidelity the familiar opening strains of my favorite Brahms piano trio. So that was why they had wanted a list of my favorite recordings! It did not take me long to realize that I was hearing the music without ears. The output from the stereo stylus was being fed through some fancy rectification circuitry directly into my auditory nerve. I was mainlining Brahms, an unforgettable experience for any stereo buff. At the end of the record it did not surprise me to hear the reassuring voice of the project director speaking into a microphone that was now my prosthetic ear. He confirmed my analysis of what had gone wrong and assured me that steps were being taken to re-embody me. He did not elaborate, and after a few more recordings, I found myself drifting off to sleep. My sleep lasted, I later learned, for the better part of a year, and when I awoke, it was to find myself fully restored to my senses. When I looked into the mirror, though, I was a bit startled to see an unfamiliar face. Bearded and a bit heavier, bearing no doubt a family resemblance to my former face, and with the same look of spritely intelligence and resolute character, but definitely a new face. Further self-explorations of an intimate nature left me no doubt that this was a new body and the project director confirmed my conclusions. He did not volunteer any information on the past history of my new body and I decided (wisely, I think in retrospect) not to pry. As many philosophers unfamiliar with my ordeal have more recently speculated, the acquisition of a new body leaves one's *person* intact. And after a period of adjustment to a new voice, new muscular strengths and weaknesses, and so forth, one's *personality* is by and large also preserved. More dramatic changes in personality have been routinely observed in people who have under-gone extensive plastic surgery, to say nothing of sex change operations, and I think no one con-tests the survival of the person in such cases. In any event I soon accommodated to my new body, to the point of being unable to recover any of its novelties to my consciousness or even memory. The view in the mirror soon became utterly familiar. That view, by the way, still re-vealed antennae, and so I was not surprised to learn that my brain had not been moved from its haven in the life-support lab.

I decided that good old Yorick deserved a visit. I and my new body, whom we might as well call Fortinbras, strode into the familiar lab to another round of applause from the techni-cians, who were of course congratulating them-selves, not me. Once more I stood before the vat and contemplated poor Yorick, and on a whim I once again cavalierly flicked off the out-put transmitter switch. Imagine my surprise when nothing unusual happened. No fainting spell, no nausea, no noticeable change. A techni-cian hurried to restore the switch to ON, but still I felt nothing. I demanded an explanation, which the project director hastened to provide. It seems that before they had even operated on the first occasion, they had constructed a com-puter duplicate of my brain, reproducing both the complete information processing structure and the computational speed of my brain in a giant computer program. After the operation, but before they had dared to send me off on my mission to Oklahoma, they had run this computer system and Yorick side by side. The in-coming signals from Hamlet were sent simulta-neously to Yorick's transceivers and to the com-puter's array of inputs. And the outputs from Yorick were not only beamed back to Hamlet, my body; they were recorded and checked against the simultaneous output of the computer program, which was called "Hubert" for reasons obscure to me. Over days and even weeks, the outputs were identical and synchronous, which of course did not *prove* that they had suc-ceeded in copying the brain's functional struc-ture, but the empirical support was greatly encouraging.

Hubert's input, and hence activity, had been kept parallel with Yorick's during my disembod-ied days. And now, to demonstrate this, they had actually thrown the master switch that put Hubert for the first time in on-line control of my body—not Hamlet, of course, but Fortinbras. (Hamlet, I learned, had never been recovered from its underground tomb and could be as-sumed by this time to have largely returned to the dust. At the head of my grave still lay the magnificent bulk of the abandoned device, with the word STUD emblazoned on its side in large letters—a circumstance which may provide archeologists of the next century with a curious insight into the burial rites of their ancestors.)

The laboratory technicians now showed me the master switch, which had two positions, la-beled *B,* for Brain (they didn't know my brain's name was Yorick) and *H,* for Hubert. The switch did indeed point to *H,* and they explained to me that if I wished, I could switch it back to *B.* With my heart in my mouth (and my brain in its vat), I did this. Nothing happened. A click, that was all. To test their claim, and with the master switch now set at *B,* I hit Yorick's output trans-mitter switch on the vat and sure enough, I be-gan to faint. Once the output switch was turned back on and I had recovered my wits, so to speak, I continued to play with the master switch, flipping it back and forth. I found that with the exception of the transitional click, I could detect no trace of a difference. I could switch in mid-utterance, and the sentence I had begun speaking under the control of Yorick was finished without a pause or hitch of any kind un-der the control of Hubert. I had a spare brain, a prosthetic device which might some day stand me in very good stead, were some mishap to be-fall Yorick. Or alternatively, I could keep Yorick as a spare and use Hubert. It didn't seem to make any difference which I chose, for the wear and tear and fatigue on my body did not have any debilitating effect on either brain, whether or not it was actually causing the motions of my body, or merely spilling its output into thin air.

The one truly unsettling aspect of this new development was the prospect, which was not long in dawning on me, of someone detaching the spare—Hubert or Yorick, as the case might be—from Fortinbras and hitching it to yet another body—some Johnny-come-lately Rosencrantz or Guildenstern. Then (if not before) there would be *two* people, that much was clear. One would be me, and the other would be a sort of super-twin brother. If there were two bodies, one under the control of Hubert and the other being controlled by Yorick, then which would the world recognize as the true Dennett? And whatever the rest of the world decided, which one would be *me*? Would I be the Yorick-brained one, in virtue of Yorick's causal priority and former intimate relationship with the original Dennett body, Hamlet? That seemed a bit legalistic, a bit too redolent of the arbitrariness of consanguinity and legal possession, to be convincing at the metaphysical level. For, suppose that before the arrival of the second body on the scene, I had been keeping Yorick as the spare for years, and letting Hubert's output drive my body—that is, Fortinbras—all that time. The Hubert–Fortinbras couple would seem then by squatter's rights (to combat one legal intuition with another) to be the true Dennett and the lawful inheritor of everything that was Dennett's. This was an interesting question, certainly, but not nearly so pressing as another question that bothered me. My strongest intuition was that in such an eventuality *I* would survive so long as *either* brain–body couple remained intact, but I had mixed emotions about whether I should want both to survive.

I discussed my worries with the technicians and the project director. The prospect of two Dennetts was abhorrent to me, I explained, largely for social reasons. I didn't want to be my own rival for the affections of my wife, nor did I like the prospect of the two Dennetts sharing my modest professor's salary. Still more vertiginous and distasteful, though, was the idea of knowing *that much* about another person, while he had the very same goods on me. How could we ever face each other? My colleagues in the lab argued that I was ignoring the bright side of the matter. Weren't there many things I wanted to do but, being only one person, had been unable to do? Now one Dennett could stay at home and be the

professor and family man, while the other could strike out on a life of travel and adventure—missing the family of course, but happy in the knowledge that the other Dennett was keeping the home fires burning. I could be faithful and adulterous at the same time. I could even cuckold myself—to say nothing of other more lurid possibilities my colleagues were all too ready to force upon my overtaxed imagination. But my ordeal in Oklahoma (or was it Houston?) had made me less adventurous, and I shrank from this opportunity that was being offered (though of course I was never quite sure it was being offered to *me* in the first place).

There was another prospect even more disagreeable—that the spare, Hubert or Yorick as the case might be, would be detached from any input from Fortinbras and just left detached. Then, as in the other case, there would be two Dennetts, or at least two claimants to my name and possessions, one embodied in Fortinbras, and the other sadly, miserably disembodied. Both selfishness and altruism bade me take steps to prevent this from happening. So I asked that measures be taken to ensure that no one could ever tamper with the transceiver connections or the master switch without my (our? no, *my*) knowledge and consent. Since I had no desire to spend my life guarding the equipment in Houston, it was mutually decided that all the electronic connections in the lab would be carefully locked: both those that controlled the life-support system for Yorick and those that controlled the power supply for Hubert would be guarded with fail-safe devices, and I would take the only master switch, outfitted for radio remote control, with me wherever I went. I carry it strapped around my waist and—wait a moment—*here it is*. Every few months I reconnoiter the situation by switching channels. I do this only in the presence of friends of course, for if the other channel were, heaven forbid, either dead or otherwise occupied, there would have to be somebody who had my interests at heart to switch it back, to bring me back from the void. For while I could feel, see, hear and otherwise sense whatever befell my body, subsequent to such a switch, I'd be unable to control it. By the way, the two positions on the switch are intentionally unmarked, so I never have the faintest idea whether I am switching from Hubert to Yorick or *vice versa*. (Some of you may think that in this case I really don't know *who* I am, let alone where I am. But such reflections no longer make much of a dent on my essential Dennettness, on my own sense of who I am. If it is true that in one sense I don't know who I am then that's another one of your philosophical truths of underwhelming significance.)

In any case, every time I've flipped the switch so far, nothing has happened. *So let's give it a try. . . .*

"THANK GOD! I THOUGHT YOU'D NEVER FLIP THAT SWITCH! You can't imagine how horrible it's been these last two weeks—but now you know, it's your turn in purgatory. How I've longed for this moment! You see, about two weeks ago—excuse me, ladies and gentlemen, but I've got to explain this to my . . . um, brother, I guess you could say, but he's just told you the facts, so you'll understand—about two weeks ago our two brains drifted just a bit out of synch. I don't know whether *my* brain is now Hubert or Yorick, any more than you do, but in any case, the two brains drifted apart, and of course once the process started, it snowballed, for I was in a slightly different receptive state for the input we both received, a difference that was soon magnified. In no time at all the illusion that I was in control of my body—our body—was completely dissipated. There was nothing I could do—no way

to call you. YOU DIDN'T EVEN KNOW I EXISTED! It's been like being carried around in a cage, or better, like being possessed—hearing my own voice say things I didn't mean to say, watching in frustration as my own hands performed deeds I hadn't intended. You'd scratch our itches, but not the way I would have, and you kept me awake, with your tossing and turning. I've been totally exhausted, on the verge of a nervous breakdown, carried around helplessly by your frantic round of activities, sustained only by the knowledge that some day you'd throw the switch.

"Now it's your turn, but at least you'll have the comfort of knowing *I* know you're in there. Like an expectant mother, I'm eating—or at any rate tasting, smelling, seeing—for *two* now, and I'll try to make it easy for you. Don't worry. Just as soon as this colloquium is over, you and I will fly to Houston, and we'll see what can be done to get one of us another body. You can have a female body—your body could be any color you like. But let's think it over. I tell you what—to be fair, if we both want this body, I promise I'll let the project director flip a coin to settle which of us gets to keep it and which then gets to choose a new body. That should guarantee justice, shouldn't it? In any case, I'll take care of you, I promise. These people are my witnesses.

"Ladies and gentlemen, this talk we have just heard is not exactly the talk *I* would have given, but I assure you that everything he said was perfectly true. And now if you'll excuse me, I think I'd—we'd—better sit down."

11.5 Social Identity

How many languages do you speak? One? Two? Three or more? You probably speak more than you think.

"So why do you ask?" you may be thinking. I ask because when we focus on the question, "Who am I?" the issues relating to personal identity arise. This means that issues of ethnic and linguistic identity must soon be explored because our personal identities are shaped in a cultural and linguistic environment.

Recall that Eve Cole (see Section 10.3) takes Descartes to task for not only ignoring the embodied nature of the self but also for ignoring the relational self. She suggests that we might even begin a "metaphysics of the self" by asking, "To whom am I related?" Communication of some kind is essential to establishing relationships, and, for most of us, that means language is the vehicle by which we relate. You have all heard the slogan, "You are what you eat." Is it going to far to say, "You are your language?"

If you have grown up monolinguistic and securely centered within clear cultural borders, the slogan about you being your language may seem strange. However, if you have grown up in a borderland, between cultures, and multilinguistic, the slogan may not seem so strange. If we add to that experiences that have made you feel ashamed of your native tongue, then you can see more clearly how identity and language can be so closely related.

In the selection that follows, Gloria Anzaldúa explores issues of identity and language based on her own personal experience as a Chicana. In the preface to the book from which this selection is taken, the author writes, "I am a border woman. I grew up between two cultures, the Mexican (with a heavy Indian influence) and the Anglo (as a member of a colonized people in our own territory). I have been straddling that *tejas*-Mexican border, and others, all my life."

As a poet and writer of fiction who has taught at various universities, Anzaldúa brings a particular insightful passion to her explorations of identity in a borderland. As you can imagine, borderlands are not always comfortable places. The discomfort and contradictions that often characterize life on the border not only shape one's identity, they make one more aware of the subtle ways our personal self is a social self.

Reading Questions

1. How, according to Anzaldúa, did Chicano Spanish arise?
2. What is linguistic terrorism, and what makes it so bad?
3. What did you learn about identity from reading this selection that you had not thought about before?

How to Tame a Wild Tongue

GLORIA ANZALDÚA

"WE'RE GOING TO HAVE TO CONTROL your tongue," the dentist says, pulling out all the metal from my mouth. Silver bits plop and tinkle into the basin. My mouth is a motherlode.

The dentist is cleaning out my roots. I get a whiff of the stench when I gasp. "I can't cap that tooth yet, you're still draining," he says.

"We're going to have to do something about your tongue," I hear the anger rising in his voice. My tongue keeps pushing out the wads of cotton, pushing back the drills, the long thin needles. "I've never seen anything as strong or as stubborn," he says. And I think, how do you tame a wild tongue, train it to be quiet, how do you bridle and saddle it? How do you make it lie down?

> "Who is to say that robbing a people of
> its language is less violent than war?"
> —Ray Gwyn Smith[1]

I remember being caught speaking Spanish at recess—that was good for three licks on the knuckles with a sharp ruler. I remember being sent to the corner of the classroom for "talking back" to the Anglo teacher when all I was trying to do was tell her how to pronounce my name. "If you want to be American, speak 'American.' If you don't like it, go back to Mexico where you belong."

"I want you to speak English. *Pa' hallar buen trabajo tienes que saber hablar el inglés bien. Qué vale toda tu educación si todavía hablas inglés con un* 'accent,'" my mother would say, mortified that I spoke English like a Mexican. At Pan American University, I, and all Chicano students were required to take two speech classes. Their purpose: to get rid of our accents.

Attacks on one's form of expression with the intent to censor are a violation of the First Amendment. *El Anglo con cara de inocente nos arrancó la lengua.* Wild tongues can't be tamed, they can only be cut out.

Overcoming the Tradition of Silence

Ahogadas, escupimos el oscuro.
Peleando con nuestra propia sombra
el silencio nos sepulta.

En boca cerrada no entran moscas. "Flies don't enter a closed mouth" is a saying I kept hearing when I was a child. *Ser habladora* was to be a gossip and a liar, to talk too much. *Muchachitas bien criadas,* well-bred girls don't answer back. *Es una falta de respeto* to talk back to one's mother or father. I remember one of the sins I'd recite to the priest in the confession box the few times I went to confession: talking back to my mother, *hablar pa' 'tras, repelar. Hocicona, repelona, chismosa,* having a big mouth, questioning, carrying tales are all signs of being *mal criada.* In my culture they are all words that are derogatory if applied to women—I've never heard them applied to men.

The first time I heard two women, a Puerto Rican and a Cuban, say the word *"nosotras,"* I was shocked. I had not known the word existed. Chicanas use *nosotros* whether we're male or female. We are robbed of our female being by the masculine plural. Language is a male discourse.

> And our tongues have become
> dry   the wilderness has
> dried out our tongues   and
> we have forgotten speech.
> —Irena Klepfisz[2]

Even our own people, other Spanish speakers *nos quieren poner candados en la boca.* They would hold us back with their bag of *reglas de academia.*

> *Oyé como ladra: el lenguaje de la frontera*
> *Quien tiene boca se equivoca.*
> —Mexican saying

"*Pocho,* cultural traitor, you're speaking the oppressor's language by speaking English, you're ruining the Spanish language," I have been accused by various Latinos and Latinas. Chicano Spanish is considered by the purist and by most Latinos deficient, a mutilation of Spanish.

But Chicano Spanish is a border tongue which developed naturally. Change, *evolución, enriquecimiento de palabras nuevas por invención o adopción* have created variants of Chicano Spanish, *un nuevo lenguaje. Un lenguaje que corresponde a un modo de vivir.* Chicano Spanish is not incorrect, it is a living language.

For a people who are neither Spanish nor live in a country in which Spanish is the first language; for a people who live in a country in which English is the reigning tongue but who are not Anglo; for a people who cannot entirely identify with either standard (formal, Castillian) Spanish nor standard English, what recourse is left to them but to create their own language? A language which they can connect their identity to, one

---

1. Ray Gwyn Smith, *Moorland Is Cold Country,* unpublished book.

2. Irena Klepfisz, "*Di rayze aheym/* The Journey Home," in *The Tribe of Dina; A Jewish Women's Anthology,* Melanie Kaye/Kantrowitz and Irena Klepfisz, eds. (Montpelier, VT: Sinister Wisdom Books, 1986), 49.

capable of communicating the realities and values true to themselves—a language with terms that are neither *español ni inglés,* but both. We speak a patois, a forked tongue, a variation of two languages.

Chicano Spanish sprang out of the Chicanos' need to identify ourselves as a distinct people. We needed a language with which we could communicate with ourselves, a secret language. For some of us, language is a homeland closer than the Southwest—for many Chicanos today live in the Midwest and the East. And because we are a complex, heterogeneous people, we speak many languages. Some of the languages we speak are:

1. Standard English
2. Working class and slang English
3. Standard Spanish
4. Standard Mexican Spanish
5. North Mexican Spanish dialect
6. Chicano Spanish (Texas, New Mexico, Arizona and California have regional variations)
7. Tex-Mex
8. *Pachuco* (called *caló*)

My "home" tongues are the languages I speak with my sister and brothers, with my friends. They are the last five listed, with 6 and 7 being closest to my heart. From school, the media and job situations, I've picked up standard and working class English. From Mamagrande Locha and from reading Spanish and Mexican literature, I've picked up Standard Spanish and Standard Mexican Spanish. From *los recién llegados,* Mexican immigrants, and *braceros,* I learned the North Mexican dialect. With Mexicans I'll try to speak either Standard Mexican Spanish or the North Mexican dialect. From my parents and Chicanos living in the Valley, I picked up Chicano Texas Spanish, and I speak it with my mom, younger brother (who married a Mexican and who rarely mixes Spanish with English), aunts and older relatives.

With Chicanas from *Nuevo México* or *Arizona* I will speak Chicano Spanish a little, but often they don't understand what I'm saying. With most California Chicanas I speak entirely in English (unless I forget). When I first moved to San Francisco, I'd rattle off something in Spanish, unintentionally embarrassing them. Often it is only with another Chicana *tejana* that I can talk freely.

Words distorted by English are known as anglicisms or *pochismos.* The *pocho* is an anglicized Mexican or American of Mexican origin who speaks Spanish with an accent characteristic of North Americans and who distorts and reconstructs the language according to the influence of English.[3] Tex-Mex, or Spanglish, comes most naturally to me. I may switch back and forth from English to Spanish in the same sentence or in the same word. With my sister and my brother Nune and with Chicano *tejano* contemporaries I speak in Tex-Mex.

From kids and people my own age I picked up *Pachuco. Pachuco* (the language of the zoot suiters) is a language of rebellion, both against Standard Spanish and Standard English. It is a secret language. Adults of the culture and outsiders cannot understand it. It is made up of slang words from both English and Spanish. *Ruca* means girl or woman, *vato* means guy or dude, *chale* means no, *simón* means yes, *churro* is sure, talk is *periquiar, pigionear* means petting, *que gacho* means how nerdy, *ponte águila* means watch out, death is called *la pelona.* Through lack of practice and not having others who can speak it, I've lost most of the *Pachuco* tongue.

Chicano Spanish

Chicanos, after 250 years of Spanish/Anglo colonization have developed significant differences in the Spanish we speak. We collapse two adjacent vowels into a single syllable and sometimes shift the stress in certain words such as *maíz/maiz, cohete/cuete.* We leave out certain consonants when they appear between vowels: *lado/lao, mojado/mojao.* Chicanos from South Texas pronounce *f* as *j* as in *jue (fue).* Chicanos use "archaisms," words that are no longer in the Spanish language, words that have been evolved out. We say *semos, truje, haiga, ansina,* and *naiden.* We retain the "archaic" *j,* as in *jalar,* that derives

3. R. C. Ortega, *Dialectología Del Barrio,* trans. Hortencia S. Alwan (Los Angeles, CA: R. C. Ortega Publisher & Bookseller, 1977), 132.

from an earlier *h* (the French *halar* or the Germanic *halon* which was lost to standard Spanish in the 16th century), but which is still found in several regional dialects such as the one spoken in South Texas. (Due to geography, Chicanos from the Valley of South Texas were cut off linguistically from other Spanish speakers. We tend to use words that the Spaniards brought over from Medieval Spain. The majority of the Spanish colonizers in Mexico and the Southwest came from Extremadura—Hernán Cortés was one of them—and Andalucía. Andalucians pronounce *ll* like a *y*, and their *d*'s tend to be absorbed by adjacent vowels: *tirado* becomes *tirao*. They brought *el lenguaje popular, dialectos y regionalismos*.[4])

Chicanos and other Spanish speakers also shift *ll* to *y* and *z* to *s*.[5] We leave out initial syllables, saying *tar* for *estar, toy* for *estoy, hora* for *ahora* (*cubanos* and *puertorriqueños* also leave out initial letters of some words). We also leave out the final syllable such as *pa* for *para*. The intervocalic *y*, the *ll* as in *tortilla, ella, botella*, gets replaced by *tortia* or *tortiya, ea, botea*. We add an additional syllable at the beginning of certain words: *atocar* for *tocar, agastar* for *gastar*. Sometimes we'll say *lavaste las vacijas*, other times *lavates* (substituting the *ates* verb endings for the *aste*).

We use anglicisms, words borrowed from English: *bola* from ball, *carpeta* from carpet, *máchina de lavar* (instead of *lavadora*) from washing machine. Tex-Mex argot, created by adding a Spanish sound at the beginning or end of an English word such as *cookiar* for cook, *watchar* for watch, *parkiar* for park, and *rapiar* for rape, is the result of the pressures on Spanish speakers to adapt to English.

We don't use the word *vosotros/as* or its accompanying verb form. We don't say *claro* (to mean yes), *imagínate*, or *me emociona*, unless we picked up Spanish from Latinas, out of a book,

or in a classroom. Other Spanish-speaking groups are going through the same, or similar, development in their Spanish.

Linguistic Terrorism

Deslenguadas. Somos los del español deficiente. We are your linguistic nightmare, your linguistic aberration, your linguistic *mestisaje*, the subject of your *burla*. Because we speak with tongues of fire we are culturally crucified. Racially, culturally and linguistically *somos huérfanos—we speak an orphan tongue.*

Chicanas who grew up speaking Chicano Spanish have internalized the belief that we speak poor Spanish. It is illegitimate, a bastard language. And because we internalize how our language has been used against us by the dominant culture, we use our language differences against each other.

Chicana feminists often skirt around each other with suspicion and hesitation. For the longest time I couldn't figure it out. Then it dawned on me. To be close to another Chicana is like looking into the mirror. We are afraid of what we'll see there. *Pena.* Shame. Low estimation of self. In childhood we are told that our language is wrong. Repeated attacks on our native tongue diminish our sense of self. The attacks continue throughout our lives.

Chicanas feel uncomfortable talking in Spanish to Latinas, afraid of their censure. Their language was not outlawed in their countries. They had a whole lifetime of being immersed in their native tongue; generations, centuries in which Spanish was a first language, taught in school, heard on radio and TV, and read in the newspaper.

If a person, Chicana or Latina, has a low estimation of my native tongue, she also has a low estimation of me. Often with *mexicanas y latinas* we'll speak English as a neutral language. Even among Chicanas we tend to speak English at parties or conferences. Yet, at the same time, we're afraid the other will think we're *agringadas* because we don't speak Chicano Spanish. We oppress each other trying to out-Chicano each other, vying to be the "real" Chicanas, to speak like

4. Eduardo Hernandéz-Chávez, Andrew D. Cohen, and Anthony F. Beltramo, *El Lenguaje de los Chicanos: Regional and Social Characteristics of Language Used by Mexican Americans* (Arlington, VA: Center for Applied Linguistics, 1975), 39.

5. Hernández-Chávez, xvii.

Chicanos. There is no one Chicano language just as there is no one Chicano experience. A monolingual Chicana whose first language is English or Spanish is just as much a Chicana as one who speaks several variants of Spanish. A Chicana from Michigan or Chicago or Detroit is just as much a Chicana as one from the Southwest. Chicano Spanish is as diverse linguistically as it is regionally.

By the end of this century, Spanish speakers will comprise the biggest minority group in the U.S., a country where students in high schools and colleges are encouraged to take French classes because French is considered more "cultured." But for a language to remain alive it must be used.[6] By the end of this century English, and not Spanish, will be the mother tongue of most Chicanos and Latinos.

So, if you want to really hurt me, talk badly about my language. Ethnic identity is twin skin to linguistic identity—I am my language. Until I can take pride in my language, I cannot take pride in myself. Until I can accept as legitimate Chicano Texas Spanish, Tex-Mex and all the other languages I speak, I cannot accept the legitimacy of myself. Until I am free to write bilingually and to switch codes without having always to translate, while I still have to speak English or Spanish when I would rather speak Spanglish, and as long as I have to accommodate the English speakers rather than having them accommodate me, my tongue will be illegitimate.

I will no longer be made to feel ashamed of existing. I will have my voice: Indian, Spanish, white. I will have my serpent's tongue—my woman's voice, my sexual voice, my poet's voice. I will overcome the tradition of silence.

> My fingers
> move sly against your palm
> Like women everywhere, we speak in
>   code. . . .
>   —Melanie Kaye/Kantrowitz[7]

6. Irena Klepfisz, "Secular Jewish Identity: Yidishkayt in America," in *The Tribe of Dina*, Kaye/Kantrowitz and Klepfisz, eds., 43.

7. Melanie Kaye/Kantrowitz, "Sign," in *We Speak in Code: Poems and Other Writings* (Pittsburgh, PA: Motheroot Publications, Inc., 1980), 85.

"Vistas," corridos, y comida: *My Native Tongue*

In the 1960s, I read my first Chicano novel. It was *City of Night* by John Rechy, a gay Texan, son of a Scottish father and a Mexican mother. For days I walked around in stunned amazement that a Chicano could write and could get published. When I read *I Am Joaquín*[8] I was surprised to see a bilingual book by a Chicano in print. When I saw poetry written in Tex-Mex for the first time, a feeling of pure joy flashed through me. I felt like we really existed as a people. In 1971, when I started teaching High School English to Chicano students, I tried to supplement the required texts with works by Chicanos, only to be reprimanded and forbidden to do so by the principal. He claimed that I was supposed to teach "American" and English literature. At the risk of being fired, I swore my students to secrecy and slipped in Chicano short stories, poems, a play. In graduate school, while working toward a Ph.D., I had to "argue" with one advisor after the other, semester after semester, before I was allowed to make Chicano literature an area of focus.

Even before I read books by Chicanos or Mexicans, it was the Mexican movies I saw at the drive-in—the Thursday night special of $1.00 a carload—that gave me a sense of belonging. "*Vámonos a las vistas*," my mother would call out and we'd all—grandmother, brothers, sister and cousins—squeeze into the car. We'd wolf down cheese and bologna white bread sandwiches while watching Pedro Infante in melodramatic tearjerkers like *Nosotros los pobres,* the first "real" Mexican movie (that was not an imitation of European movies). I remember seeing *Cuando los hijos se van* and surmising that all Mexican movies played up the love a mother has for her children and what ungrateful sons and daughters suffer when they are not devoted to their mothers. I remember the singing-type "westerns" of Jorge Negrete and Miquel Aceves Mejía. When watching Mexican movies, I felt a

8. Rodolfo Gonzales, *I Am Joaquín/Yo Soy Joaquín* (New York, NY: Bantam Books, 1972). It was first published in 1967.

sense of homecoming as well as alienation. People who were to amount to something didn't go to Mexican movies, or *bailes* or tune their radios to *bolero, rancherita,* and *corrido* music.

The whole time I was growing up, there was *norteño* music sometimes called North Mexican border music, or Tex-Mex music, or Chicano music, or *cantina* (bar) music. I grew up listening to *conjuntos,* three- or four-piece bands made up of folk musicians playing guitar, *bajo sexto,* drums and button accordion, which Chicanos had borrowed from the German immigrants who had come to Central Texas and Mexico to farm and build breweries. In the Rio Grande Valley, Steve Jordan and Little Joe Hernández were popular, and Flaco Jiménez was the accordian king. The rhythms of Tex-Mex music are those of the polka, also adapted from the Germans, who in turn had borrowed the polka from the Czechs and Bohemians.

I remember the hot, sultry evenings when *corridos*—songs of love and death on the Texas-Mexican borderlands—reverberated out of cheap amplifiers from the local *cantinas* and wafted in through my bedroom window.

Corridos first became widely used along the South Texas/Mexican border during the early conflict between Chicanos and Anglos. The *corridos* are usually about Mexican heroes who do valiant deeds against the Anglo oppressors. Pancho Villa's song, "*La cucaracha,*" is the most famous one. *Corridos* of John F. Kennedy and his death are still very popular in the Valley. Older Chicanos remember Lydia Mendoza, one of the great border *corrido* singers who was called *la Gloria de Tejas.* Her "*El tango negro,*" sung during the Great Depression, made her a singer of the people. The everpresent *corridos* narrated one hundred years of border history, bringing news of events as well as entertaining. These folk musicians and folk songs are our chief cultural mythmakers, and they made our hard lives seem bearable.

I grew up feeling ambivalent about our music. Country-western and rock-and-roll had more status. In the 50s and 60s, for the slightly educated and *agringado* Chicanos, there existed a sense of shame at being caught listening to our music. Yet I couldn't stop my feet from thumping to the music, could not stop humming the words, nor hide from myself the exhilaration I felt when I heard it.

There are more subtle ways that we internalize identification, especially in the forms of images and emotions. For me food and certain smells are tied to my identity, to my homeland. Woodsmoke curling up to an immense blue sky; woodsmoke perfuming my grandmother's clothes, her skin. The stench of cow manure and the yellow patches on the ground; the crack of a .22 rifle and the reek of cordite. Homemade white cheese sizzling in a pan, melting inside a folded *tortilla.* My sister Hilda's hot, spicy *menudo, chile colorado* making it deep red, pieces of *panza* and hominy floating on top. My brother Carito barbequing *fajitas* in the backyard. Even now and 3,000 miles away, I can see my mother spicing the ground beef, pork and venison with *chile.* My mouth salivates at the thought of the hot steaming *tamales* I would be eating if I were home.

Si le preguntas a mi mamá, "¿Qué eres?"

> "Identity is the essential core of who we are as individuals, the conscious experience of the self inside."
>
> —Kaufman[9]

Nosotros los Chicanos straddle the borderlands. On one side of us, we are constantly exposed to the Spanish of the Mexicans, on the other side we hear the Anglos' incessant clamoring so that we forget our language. Among ourselves we don't say *nosotros los americanos, o nosotros los españoles, o nosotros los hispanos.* We say *nosotros los mexicanos* (by *mexicanos* we do not mean citizens of Mexico; we do not mean a national identity, but a racial one). We distinguish between *mexicanos del otro lado* and *mexicanos de este lado.* Deep in our hearts we believe that being Mexican has nothing to do with which country one lives in. Being Mexican is a state of soul—not one of mind, not one of citizenship. Neither eagle nor

9. Kaufman, 68.

serpent, but both. And like the ocean, neither animal respects borders.

> *Dime con quien andas y te diré quien eres.*
> (Tell me who your friends are and I'll tell you who you are.)
>
> —Mexican saying

Si le preguntas a mi mamá, "¿Qué eres?" te dirá, "Soy mexicana." My brothers and sister say the same. I sometimes will answer *"soy mexicana"* and at others will say *"soy Chicana" o "soy tejana."* But I identified as *"Raza"* before I ever identified as *"mexicana"* or "Chicana."

As a culture, we call ourselves Spanish when referring to ourselves as a linguistic group and when copping out. It is then that we forget our predominant Indian genes. We are 70–80% Indian.[10] We call ourselves Hispanic[11] or Spanish-American or Latin American or Latin when linking ourselves to other Spanish-speaking peoples of the Western hemisphere and when copping out. We call ourselves Mexican-American[12] to signify we are neither Mexican nor American, but more the noun "American" than the adjective "Mexican" (and when copping out).

Chicanos and other people of color suffer economically for not acculturating. This voluntary (yet forced) alienation makes for psychological conflict, a kind of dual identity—we don't identify with the Anglo-American cultural values and we don't totally identify with the Mexican cultural values. We are a synergy of two cultures with various degrees of Mexicanness or Angloness. I have so internalized the borderland conflict that sometimes I feel like one cancels out the other and we are zero, nothing, no one. *A veces no soy nada ni nadie. Pero hasta cuando no lo soy, lo soy.*

When not copping out, when we know we are more than nothing, we call ourselves Mexican, referring to race and ancestry; *mestizo* when affirming both our Indian and Spanish (but we hardly ever own our Black ancestry); Chicano when referring to a politically aware people born and/or raised in the U.S.; *Raza* when referring to Chicanos; *tejanos* when we are Chicanos from Texas.

Chicanos did not know we were a people until 1965 when Caesar Chavez and the farmworkers united and *I Am Joaquín* was published and *la Raza Unida* party was formed in Texas. With that recognition, we became a distinct people. Something momentous happened to the Chicano soul—we became aware of our reality and acquired a name and a language (Chicano Spanish) that reflected that reality. Now that we had a name, some of the fragmented pieces began to fall together—who we were, what we were, how we had evolved. We began to get glimpses of what we might eventually become.

Yet the struggle of identities continues, the struggle of borders is our reality still. One day the inner struggle will cease and a true integration take place. In the meantime, *tenémos que hacer la lucha. ¿Quién está protegiendo los ranchos de mi gente? ¿Quién está tratando de cerrar la fisura entre la india y el blanco en nuestra sangre? El Chicano, si, el Chicano que anda como un ladrón en su propia casa.*

Los Chicanos, how patient we seem, how very patient. There is the quiet of the Indian about us.[13] We know how to survive. When other races have given up their tongue, we've kept ours. We know what it is to live under the hammer blow of the dominant *norteamericano* culture. But more than we count the blows, we count the days the weeks the years the centuries the eons until the white laws and commerce and customs will rot in the deserts they've created, lie bleached. *Humildes* yet proud, *quietos* yet wild, *nosotros los mexicanos-Chicanos* will walk by the crumbling ashes as we go about our business. Stubborn, persevering, impenetrable as stone, yet possessing a malleability that renders us unbreakable, we, the *mestizas* and *mestizos,* will remain.

---

10. Chávez, 88–90.

11. "Hispanic" is derived from *Hispanis* (*España,* a name given to the Iberian Peninsula in ancient times when it was a part of the Roman Empire) and is a term designated by the U.S. government to make it easier to handle us on paper.

12. The Treaty of Guadalupe Hidalgo created the Mexican-American in 1848.

13. Anglos, in order to alleviate their guilt for dispossessing the Chicano, stressed the Spanish part of us and perpetrated the myth of the Spanish Southwest. We have accepted the fiction that we are Hispanic, that is Spanish, in order to accommodate ourselves to the dominant culture and its abhorrence of Indians. Chávez, 88–91.

11.6 Gender Identity

Gloria Anzaldúa (see previous section) grew up on a border. Deirdre (Donald) N. Mc-Closkey crossed a border. The border was gender. Donald McCloskey became Deirdre McCloskey at the age of fifty-two. Donald had achieved fame as a professor of history and economics at the University of Iowa where Deirdre now teaches. In a book titled *Crossing: A Memoir,* Deirdre McCloskey tells her story, a story that raises basic questions about gender and identity.

Theories of gender and identity fall into two camps. Essentialist theories maintain that gender is determined by nature. According to this view, gender is fixed and stable. It is something given, if not by evolutionary development then by God. Nonessentialist theories maintain that gender is a social construction. It is fluid and unstable. It is not something given, but something constructed. One of the major breakthroughs of feminist theory was to separate the social from the biological in such a way that what was formerly thought to be relatively unchangeable was recognized as changeable. Then liberation became possible.

While it is fairly common today to see gender (femininity and masculinity) as social constructions and not biological (female and male) determinates, it is less common to see sexuality in the same way. We speak of sexual preference, as if our sexual orientation is a matter of choice. We also speak about innate physiological factors that supposedly determine whether someone is homosexual or heterosexual. Is sexuality as well as gender a social construction?

Gay/lesbian theory, building on the insights of feminist theory, focused not only on the way sexuality is socially constructed but also on the way categories such as normal and deviant are used in a normative way to assert and maintain social control. To label something deviant, be it sexual or not, is to attach a negative value. Normal is good; deviant is bad. Once behaviors are labeled bad, then the many practices of social control, from denying legal rights to encouraging violence toward those labeled deviant, appear justified. People often link the normal and the deviant labels to essentialist theories. Thus certain sorts of sexuality become "natural" and other kinds become "unnatural."

Queer theory, an area of academic study, emerged in the early 1990s. The word *queer,* as used in Queer Theory, does not refer to homosexuality per se. The primary meaning of queer is "peculiar," or "odd." Queer theory extends the concerns of feminist theory and gay/lesbian theory to all sorts of sexual activities and identities (homosexual, bisexual, heterosexual, transsexual, and so forth) in order to explore the ways in which such identities are constructed and valorized by societies and ideologies. Sexuality can now be seen, thanks to the contributions of queer theory, as an elaborate system of signs and codes that define what is "normal" and what is "deviant" for a given society at a particular moment of history. In addition, this system of signs establishes identities. People come to think of themselves at a deep level in terms of both gender and sexuality.

Is Deirdre the same person as Donald? Donald was male, married, a father who existed in a complex web of social and professional relationships that reinforced his gender and sexual identity. Donald had certain gestures, interests, ways of sitting and walking, tastes, and more that Deirdre does not. Yet Deirdre liberated Donald. She allowed Donald to be what he always wanted to be: a woman.

The following selection, from the Preface to *Crossing,* provides an occasion for us to think not only about issues of gender and sexuality but also about issues of identity, nature, and the ways society constructs such categories as normal and deviant.

Reading Questions

1. What do you think McCloskey means when she says, "My gender crossing was motivated by identity, not to be a balance sheet of utility?"
2. What does McCloskey mean when she writes, "Gender is not in every way natural"? Do you think this statement contradicts the claim that her gender crossing was motivated by identity?
3. Why was McCloskey attracted to Christianity?
4. In your view, is gender identity natural or is it socially constructed? Why, or why not?

Crossing

DEIRDRE (DONALD) N. MCCLOSKEY

I WANT TO TELL YOU the story of a crossing from fifty-two-year-old man to fifty-five-year-old woman, Donald to Deirdre.

"A strange story," you say.

Yes, it's strange, statistically. All the instruments agree that what's usually called "transsexuality," permanently crossing the gender boundary, is rare. (The Latin in "transsexuality" makes it sound sexual, which is mistaken; or medical, which is misleading; or scientific, which is silly. I'll use plain English "crossing.") Only three in ten thousand want to cross the boundary of gender, a few of them in your own city neighborhood or small town. Gender crossing is no threat to male/female sex ratios or the role of women or the stability of the dollar. Most people are content with their birth gender.

But people do after all cross various boundaries. I've been a foreigner a little, in England and Holland and on shorter visits elsewhere. If you've been a foreigner you can understand somewhat, because gender crossing is a good deal like foreign travel. Most people would like to go to Venice on vacation. Most people, if they could magically do it, would like to try out the other gender for a day or a week or a month. The Venice visitors as a group can be thought of as all the "crossgendered," from stone butch dykes to postoperative male-to-female gender crossers, all the traversers, permanent or temporary, somber or ironic. A few people go to Venice regularly, and you can think of them as the crossdressers among these, wearing the clothing of the opposite gender once in a while. But only a tiny fraction of the crossgendered are permanent gender crossers, wanting to *become* Venetians. Most people are content to stay mainly at home. A tiny minority are not. They want to cross and stay.

On a trip to New York to see a friend after my own crossing I stood in the hall of photographs at Ellis Island and wept at the courage. Crossing cultures from male to female is big; it highlights some of the differences between men and women, and some of the similarities too. That's

From Deirdre N. McCloskey, Crossing: A Memoir, *Chicago, IL: The University of Chicago Press, 1999, xi–xvi.*
©*1999 by The University of Chicago. Reprinted by permission.*

interesting. My crossing was costly and opposed, which is too bad. But my crossing has been dull, easy, comfortable compared with Suyuan's or Giuseppi's outer migrations.

Or compared with some people's inner migrations. Some people cross this or that inner boundary so radically that it would look bizarre, a slippage in the normal order of the universe, Stephen King material, if it were not so common. The most radical one is the crossing from child to adult, a crossing similar to mine that we all experience. I once saw a spoof scientific paper titled "Short Stature Syndrome: A Nationwide Problem." The strange little people, whose thoughts and actions were so different from normal, requiring the compulsory intervention of psychiatrists, and lots more money for the National Institute of Mental Health, were . . . children.

The word "education" means just "leading out." People are always leading themselves out of one life and into another, such as out of childhood and into each new version of adulthood. Not everyone likes to keep doing it, but the women I most admire have. My mother educated herself to earning her income and writing poetry after my father died. My roomer for a year in Iowa educated herself as a hospital chaplain after a third of a century teaching elementary school. My sister got a second degree in psychology, my former wife made herself into a distinguished professor. May Sarton, so glad to become by forced crossing an American rather than a Belgian woman, an English rather than a French poet and novelist and memoirist, kept crossing, crossing and looked forward at age seventy to "what is ahead—to clear my desk, sow the annuals, plant perennials, get back to the novel . . . like a game of solitaire that is coming out."

It's strange to have been a man and now to be a woman. But it's no stranger perhaps than having once been a West African and now being an American, or once a priest and now a businessman. Free people keep deciding to make strange crossings, from storekeeper to monk or from civilian to soldier or from man to woman.

Crossing boundaries is a minority interest, but human.

My crossing—change, migration, growing up, self-discovery—took place from 1994 to 1997, beginning in my home in Iowa, then a year in Holland, then back in Iowa, with travels in between. As Donald and then as Deirdre I was and am a professor of economics and of history at the University of Iowa. From age eleven I had been a secret crossdresser, a few times a week. Otherwise I was normal, just a guy. My wife had known about the crossdressing since the first year of our marriage, when we were twenty-two. No big deal, we decided. Lots of men have this or that sexual peculiarity. Relax, we said. By 1994, age fifty-two, I had been married those three decades, had two grown children, and thought I might crossdress a little more. Visit Venice more too.

I visited womanhood and stayed. It was not for the pleasures, though I discovered many I had not imagined, and many pains too. But calculating pleasures and pains was not the point. The point was who I am. Here the analogy with migration breaks down. One moves permanently from Sicily to New York because one imagines the streets of New York are paved with gold, or at least better paved than the streets at home, not mainly because back in Catania since age eleven one had dreamed of being an American. Migration can be modeled as a matter of cost and benefit, and it has been by economic historians. But I did not change gender because I liked colorful clothing (Donald did not) or womanly grace (Donald viewed it as sentimentality). The "decision" was not utilitarian. In our culture the rhetoric of the very word "decision" suggests cost and benefit. My gender crossing was motivated by identity, not by a balance sheet of utility.

Of course you can ask what psychological reasons explain my desire to cross and reply with, say, a version of Freud. Some researchers think there is a biological explanation for gender crossing, because parts of the brains of formerly male gender crossers in postmortems are notably female. But a demand for an answer to why carries with it in our medicalized culture an agenda of treatment. If a gender crosser is "just" a guy who gets pleasure from it, that's one thing (laugh at him, jail him, murder him). If it's brain chemistry, that's another (commit him to a madhouse and try to "cure" him).

I say in response to your question Why? "Can't I just be?" You, dear reader, are. No one gets indignant if you have no answer to why you are an optimist or why you like peach ice cream. These days most people will grant you an exemption from the why question if you are gay: in 1960 they would not and were therefore eager to do things to you, many of them nasty. I want courtesy and the safety of a why-less treatment extended to gender crossers. I want the medical models of gender crossing (and of twenty other things) to fall. That's the politics. I am ashamed that from the 1960s and 1990s, in the political movements for black civil rights, women's liberation, gay rights, and opposition to the war in Vietnam, I had sound opinions but never really took a chance on them. Telling you my story is my last chance to be counted.

And incidentally, Why *do* you think you are the gender you were officially assigned to at birth? Prove it. How odd.

Ah. I think you need some treatment.

After a year of hesitation, and two years from well beginning, I found to my delight that I had crossed. Look by look, smile by smile, I was accepted. That doesn't make me a 100 percent, essential woman—I'll never have XX chromosomes, never have had the life of a girl and woman up to age fifty-two. But the world does not demand 100 percents and essences, thank God. An agnostic since adolescence, in my second year of crossing I came tentatively to religion and then could thank God in person, who made me inside in my comfort a woman.

I get weepy sometimes as I walk to the office, pick up my dry cleaning, shop at Prairie Lights bookstore, so pleased to Be. It's like someone who thought herself more French than American and one day was able to be French; or someone who always hoped to be a professional athlete and finally became one; or someone who felt herself a businesswoman and at last was seen as one. My game of solitaire came out.

I apologize for romanticizing sometimes the goodness of women and criticizing sometimes the badness of men. It's how I felt at the time. Forgive me, new to this place and starry-eyed. Perhaps my stories of Donald and then Dee and then Deirdre show enough bad women and good men to offset my romantic theories. In contrasting how men and women "are" I do not mean to recruit stereotypes or essentialisms that have been used to the disadvantage of other women. Women are not always more loving, or less interested in career. And certainly they are what in detail they "are" not on account of some eternal Platonic ideal or the imperatives of genetics. I am reporting how the difference in social practice seemed to me, admitting always that the difference might be, as the professors say, "socially constructed." Gender is not in every way "natural." "Feminine" gestures, for example, are not God's own creation. This of course I know. The social construction of gender is, after all, something a gender crosser comes to know with unusual vividness. She does it for a living.

I apologize, too, for any inaccuracies that remain despite my earnest attempts to get them out. I have tried to tell a true story. Yet none of the conversations and descriptions in the book are court transcripts. Each is something I believe I remember, ordered in the sequence I believe I remember, and intended to show how I heard and saw and thought at the time—my recollections, my ardent opinions, how I felt as I remember how I felt. I have been as careful as I can and have offered to show the manuscript to the main parties, some of whom could help.

The world does not tell stories. Men and women do, and I am merely a woman telling. It would be impossible to recount every single thing about your hour just passed, tiny things that illustrate character or position, much less to tell every single thing about three crowded years, or one side of a tangled life. Whether the result is God's own truth I don't know. Telling any story, from physics to fiction, is like placing stepping-stones through a garden, choosing what spots to miss in showing the path.

After the crossing I was eating lunch in Iowa City with a woman friend, another academic, and we spoke about how talk normalizes. She said, "This is the age of the candid memoir." So it seems. It's a good thing, we agreed, because talking to each other about who we are can make us mutually all human. Demonizing Others is the first stop on the railway to the gas chambers. Nowadays there are many books about the cross-gendered. Movies and television have stopped portraying them as dangerous lunatics in the mold of Anthony Perkins in *Psycho*. Since the 1960s, detested by those who value order above freedom, many kinds of people have spoken up: the raped women who kept their secrets, the unmarried mothers who kept theirs. In the 1950s a lot of people were keeping secrets, personal and state: the obedient wives, the hidden handicapped, the closeted homosexuals, the silenced socialists, the blacks under Jim Crow. After the liberation and the talk that followed they are no longer disgraceful Others or pathetic victims, or merely invisibles—"We don't have any homosexuals in Oklahoma"—but people whose stories are heard and talked about and might even be imagined as one's own. It's the difference between shame and life.

For this age of openness I praise the Lord, blessed be her holy name. I began to see that Christianity resembles the secular stoicism circa the 1930s in which I was raised, A. E. Housman to Hemingway, in that it promises no bed of roses. The world is mysterious from a human point of view, as both the stoic Housman and the Christian Gerard Manley Hopkins would say, and it contains bad news as well as good. I found Christianity in this way grown up, admitting sin. That *is* God's own truth.

And slowly as the story ended I began to hear the good news of forgiveness, the duty to offer it and the grace to receive.

Visit the companion Web site for chapter specific quizzes, suggestions for further reading, video ideas, and other resources to assess and expand your understanding of the chapter material. Go to http://philosophy.wadsworth.com and select the companion Web site for *Voices of Wisdom*.

 You can access many additional readings at the Info Trac-College Edition Web site. To find the following suggested articles do a keyword search with the article title. Use the passcode that was packaged with your new book to enter the site at http://www.Infotraccollege.com/Wadsworth/. Here is a sampling.

Roy W. Perrett, "Personal Identity, Minimalism, and Madhyamaka." *Philosophy East and West,* July 2002 v52 i3 p373(13), A90753120.

Gereon Kopf, "Temporality and Personal Identity in the Thought of Nishida Kitaro." *Philosophy East and West,* April 2002 v52 i2 p224(22), A86048935.

Maria Szadziuk, "Culture as Transition: Becoming a Woman in Bi-ethnic Space." *Mosaic* (Winnipeg), September 1999 v32 i3 p110, A56750206.

Andrew M. Gordus, "Silence and Celebration: Queer Markings in the Poetry of Abigail Bohorquez." *Mexican Studies–Estudios Mexicanos,* Winter 1999 v15 i1 p131(2), A54710004.

Teresa Kay Williams and Michael C. Thornton, "Social Construction of Ethnicity Versus Personal Experience: The Case of Afro-Amerasians." *Journal of Comparative Family Studies,* Summer 1998 v29 i2 p255, A57590476.

Walter Glannon, "Moral Responsibility and Personal Identity." *American Philosophical Quarterly,* July 1998 v35 n3 p231(19), A21130608.

Michael B. Burke, "Persons and Bodies: How to Avoid the New Dualism." *American Philosophical Quarterly,* October 1997 v34 n4 p457(11), A20150880.

Marya Schechtman, "The Same and the Same: Two Views of Psychological Continuity." *American Philosophical Quarterly,* July 1994 v31 n3 p199(14), A15723024.

Eugene Mills, "Dividing Without Reducing: Bodily Fission and Personal Identity." *Mind,* January 1993 v102 n405 p37(15), A13634949.

Chapter 12

Is There a God?

12.1 Introduction

HAVE YOU EVER WONDERED whether God exists? Of course. Most people have. But have you wondered whether God's existence can be proved? Are there arguments that would convince any reasonable person? Is there evidence, I mean real hard-core scientific evidence, that God exists? When I ask my students how many of them believe God exists, almost all of them raise their hands. But when I ask them how many think God's existence can be *proved,* most are skeptical. "It is," they say, "a matter of faith."

The existence of God is a metaphysical question central to a branch of philosophy called the **philosophy of religion.** As the name implies, this area of philosophy applies philosophical methods to the study of a wide variety of religious issues, including the existence of God. Philosophy of religion should be clearly distinguished from a type of theology called revealed theology. **Theology** literally means the "study of God." **Revealed theology** is a type of theology that claims human knowledge of God comes through special revelations such as the Bible or the Qur'an. St. Thomas Aquinas (see Section 12.2) said that revealed theology provides "saving knowledge"—that is, knowledge that will result in our salvation.

Another kind of theology, called **natural theology,** has to do with the knowledge of God that is possible based on the use of "natural" reason—that is, reason unaided by special revelations. St. Thomas says that this sort of theology can provide us with some knowledge of God's nature and can demonstrate that God exists, but it cannot provide saving knowledge because, after all, even devils know that God exists.

Natural theology is sometimes called *rational theology* or *philosophical theology.* As this last name indicates, this kind of theology is more closely related to the philosophy of religion than is revealed theology. Both natural theology and the philosophy of religion rely solely on the use of human reason in their attempts to discover something about the divine. They do not assume the truth of some special revelation; they allow only what reason can prove.

Although both philosophy of religion and natural theology rely on reason rather than on revelation, they differ in the range of topics considered. Philosophy of religion studies a wide range of religious issues and different notions of what constitutes ultimate reality. Theism is just one sort of religious notion of ultimate reality. The *Tao* or Brahman-Atman, for example (see Chapter 8), both present conceptions of ultimate reality that appear quite different from theistic ideas. Needless to say, *nontheistic* philosophies have not been overly concerned with the issue of God's existence even though they have been concerned with the nature and existence of some kind of ultimate reality. However, *theistic* philosophies and the cultures—both Eastern and Western—influenced by theistic religions have regarded the topic of God's existence as an issue of immense significance.

Although the questions "What is God like?" and "Does God exist?" are different, nevertheless they are closely related. The answer to the first question tells us something about God's nature; for example, that God or the Divine, if there is such a being, is the creator of the universe, is all-powerful and all-knowing, is perfectly good and loving, and so on. The answer to the second question tells us whether a being of this sort exists. But these answers blend into each other because every argument for God's existence or nonexistence is an argument for the existence or nonexistence of a God *of a certain sort.* So, for example, those who argue that the existence of complex order and beauty in the universe is evidence that God created it and hence exists imply that God's nature is that of an intelligent being capable of producing beauty and complex order.

The philosophy of religion is concerned with a wide range of questions. It is concerned with issues about how religion and science are related. Do both provide genuine knowledge about what is real? It is also concerned with how evil and suffering can be explained. One of the strongest arguments for the nonexistence of God is the apparent incompatibility between the existence of evil and the existence of an all-powerful and infinitely good God. Can such a God not prevent evil? Would he not want to?

Why he? Why use the masculine pronoun when referring to God? Is our concept of God hopelessly patriarchal? Is it a hangover from a past when men dominated societies and cultures, playing the role—often quite literally—of the divine? There are many different conceptions of God, including ideas about Goddesses. There are many different religions. Can they all be true? Are they all different but equally valid paths to salvation?

12.2 Arguments for God's Existence

How many of you have thought "there must be a God because the universe just couldn't happen by itself? Something must have caused it. Things don't just pop into existence out of nothing." If you have had thoughts like this, you have been thinking along the lines of a cosmological argument. **Cosmological arguments** (there are several varieties) argue from the existence of the universe (world or cosmos) to the existence of God as its cause, its creator, or its explanation.

Cosmological arguments are very old, being found among ancient Greek and Indian philosophers. The Greek versions were most influential on Western thought. Since the Greeks believed the universe was eternal (that is, it had no beginning and has no end), they did not believe that God created it out of nothing. However, they did believe that there had to be an explanation for the universe. After all, why should there be something, even if that something is not created and has been around forever? They especially thought that motion, a basic characteristic of the universe, needed an explanation.

Aristotle (see Section 2.5) argued from the existence of motion to the existence of an Unmoved Mover as the explanation of motion. This Unmoved Mover he called "*ho theos*" (the god), in part because it was unmoved (that is, nothing caused it to move) but was responsible for the motion of other things. It is, if you will, a *prime* mover. Aristotle's argument was based on three principles that operate as assumptions in practically all cosmological arguments: (1) Something cannot be the cause of itself, (2) something cannot come from nothing, and (3) there cannot be an infinite series of causes and effects.

Christian and Islamic theologians inherited the Greek thinking on these matters, but most could not accept the notion that the universe was uncreated and hence eternal. God, they believed, must be absolute, and the existence of the world must be completely dependent on him. God alone is uncreated. Therefore, they interpreted the story of creation found in Genesis (the first book of the Bible) in a manner compatible with the doctrine of *creatio ex nihilo*, creation out of nothing. God, they argued, created the universe out of nothing, and hence the universe is not eternal but began to exist at some point.

Kalam, which means "speech" in Arabic, came to denote the statement of points in theological doctrine. Eventually, it was used as a name for a movement in Islamic thought, which, among other things, was much concerned with the problems involved in demonstrating God's existence. Islamic theologians rejected the Greek idea that the world is uncreated and so formulated the cosmological argument to explicitly recognize a created universe.

It is natural for theistic religions that assert the existence of a creator God to be interested in arguments for such a God's existence. But not all religions are theistic. Early Buddhists, for example, were skeptical about the existence of a creator God. The world, or cosmos, for these early Buddhists needed no cause outside of itself to explain its existence.

Three different selections follow. The first comes from the *Summa Theologica* by Thomas Aquinas (ca. 1225–1274). Aquinas was one of the most influential thinkers of the Christian tradition, and in the first part of his massive summation of theology he presents not one but five arguments for the existence of God. The first three are versions of the cosmological argument and the fifth one is a version of what has come to be known as the teleological argument (see Section 12.4).

The second selection provides a modern version of the *kalam* argument by William Lane Craig who teaches at the Talbot School of Theology. The argument, as presented here, is incomplete. It ends with the conclusion that the existence of the universe has a cause. Assuming that this can be established, the question still remains whether that cause is the personal God of theism. Craig thinks it is, but he is well aware that establishing that God is the first cause of the universe requires further argument.

The third selection comes from the pen of Gunapala Dharmasiri, a professor of philosophy at the University of Sri Lanka. According to Dharmasiri, the Buddha did not think that one needed the idea of a creator God to explain the existence of the world. The causes of what exists can be found within the world itself.

One important philosophical issue that is raised by these arguments centers on the principle of sufficient reason. According to this principle, there must be a sufficient explanation for everything. Assuming that an explanation amounts to stating the cause of something and assuming that the universe is the kind of something that needs an explanation, what explains it sufficiently? Is that explanation found within the universe itself or outside of it?

Reading Questions

1. Summarize each of Aquinas's five ways as concisely as you can in premise and conclusion form.
2. Which of the five ways do you find the most plausible, and which do you find the least plausible? Why?
3. In the second way, Aquinas claims that it is not possible for efficient causes (by which he means the agent or agency that brings about an effect) to "go on to infinity." Why is that not possible?
4. Which of the premises of the *kalam* argument as presented by Craig do you find the strongest, and which do you find the weakest? Why?
5. If I asked you to complete the *kalam* argument as Craig presents it and to demonstrate that the cause of the universe is God, how would you go about doing it?
6. Why, according to Dharmasiri, do Buddhists think that "once the empirical facts have been explained causally it would be positively wrong to ask the cause of the whole of it"?

The Five Ways

ST. THOMAS AQUINAS

Third Article.
Whether God Exists?

We proceed thus to the Third Article:—

Objection 1. IT SEEMS THAT GOD does not exist; because if one of two contraries be infinite, the other would be altogether destroyed. But the word "God" means that He is infinite goodness. If, therefore, God existed, there would be no evil discoverable; but there is evil in the world. Therefore God does not exist.

Obj. 2. Further, it is superfluous to suppose that, what can be accounted for by a few principles has been produced by many. But it seems that everything that appears in the world can be accounted for by other principles, supposing God did not exist. For all natural things can be reduced to one principle, which is nature; and all things that happen intentionally can be reduced to one principle, which is human reason, or will. Therefore there is no need to suppose God's existence.

On the contrary, It is said in the person of God: *I am Who am* (Exod. iii. 14).

I answer that, The existence of God can be proved in five ways.

The first and more manifest way is the argument from motion. It is certain and evident to our senses that some things are in motion. Whatever is in motion is moved by another, for nothing

From The Summa Theologica of St. Thomas Aquinas *Part 1. Translated by the Fathers of the English Dominican Province. Copyright © 1911. New York: Genziger Brothers.*

can be in motion except it have a potentiality for that towards which it is being moved; whereas a thing moves inasmuch as it is in act. By "motion" we mean nothing else than the reduction of something from a state of potentiality into a state of actuality. Nothing, however, can be reduced from a state of potentiality into a state of actuality, unless by something already in a state of actuality. Thus that which is actually hot as fire, makes wood, which is potentially hot to be actually hot, and thereby moves and changes it. It is not possible that the same thing should be at once in a state of actuality and potentiality from the same point of view, but only from different points of view. What is actually hot cannot simultaneously be only potentially hot; still, it is simultaneously potentially cold. It is therefore impossible that from the same point of view and in the same way anything should be both moved and mover, or that it should move itself. Therefore whatever is in motion must be put in motion by another. If that by which it is put in motion be itself put in motion, then this also must needs be put in motion by another, and that by another again. This cannot go on to infinity, because then there would be no first mover, and, consequently, no other mover—seeing that subsequent movers only move inasmuch as they are put in motion by the first mover; as the staff only moves because it is put in motion by the hand. Therefore it is necessary to arrive at a First Mover, put in motion by no other; and this everyone understands to be God.

The second way is from the formality of efficient causation. In the world of sense we find there is an order of efficient causation. There is no case known (neither is it, indeed, possible) in which a thing is found to be the efficient cause of itself; for so it would be prior to itself, which is impossible. In efficient causes it is not possible to go on to infinity, because in all efficient causes following in order, the first is the cause of the intermediate cause, and the intermediate is the cause of the ultimate cause, whether the intermediate cause be several, or one only. To take away the cause is to take away the effect. Therefore, if there be no first cause among efficient causes, there will be no ultimate cause, nor any

intermediate. If in efficient causes it is possible to go on to infinity, there will be no first efficient cause, neither will there be an ultimate effect, nor any intermediate efficient causes; all of which is plainly false. Therefore it is necessary to put forward a First Efficient Cause, to which everyone gives the name of God.

The third way is taken from possibility and necessity, and runs thus. We find in nature things that could either exist or not exist, since they are found to be generated, and then to corrupt; and, consequently, they can exist, and then not exist. It is impossible for these always to exist, for that which can one day cease to exist must at some time have not existed. Therefore, if everything could cease to exist, then at one time there could have been nothing in existence. If this were true, even now there would be nothing in existence, because that which does not exist only begins to exist by something already existing. Therefore, if at one time nothing was in existence, it would have been impossible for anything to have begun to exist; and thus even now nothing would be in existence —which is absurd. Therefore, not all beings are merely possible, but there must exist something the existence of which is necessary. Every necessary thing either has its necessity caused by another, or not. It is impossible to go on to infinity in necessary things which have their necessity caused by another, as has been already proved in regard to efficient causes. Therefore we cannot but postulate the existence of some being having of itself its own necessity, and not receiving it from another, but rather causing in others their necessity. This all men speak of as God.

The fourth way is taken from the gradation to be found in things. Among beings there are some more and some less good, true, noble, and the like. But "more" and "less" are predicated of different things, according as they resemble in their different ways something which is in the degree of "most," as a thing is said to be hotter according as it more nearly resembles that which is hottest; so that there is something which is truest, something best, something noblest, and, consequently, something which is uttermost being; for the truer things are, the more truly they exist. What is most complete in any genus is the cause of all in that genus; as fire, which is the most complete form of heat, is the cause whereby all things are made hot. Therefore there must also be something which is to all beings the cause of their being, goodness, and every other perfection; and this we call God.

The fifth way is taken from the governance of the world; for we see that things which lack intelligence, such as natural bodies, act for some purpose, which fact is evident from their acting always, or nearly always, in the same way, so as to obtain the best result. Hence it is plain that not fortuitously, but designedly, do they achieve their purpose. Whatever lacks intelligence cannot fulfil some purpose, unless it be directed by some being endowed with intelligence and knowledge; as the arrow is shot to its mark by the archer. Therefore some intelligent being exists by whom all natural things are ordained towards a definite purpose; and this being we call God.

Reply Obj. 1. As Augustine says: *Since God is wholly good, He would not allow any evil to exist in His works, unless His omnipotence and goodness were such as to bring good even out of evil.* This is part of the infinite goodness of God, that He should allow evil to exist, and out of it produce good.

Reply Obj. 2. Since nature works out its determinate end under the direction of a higher agent, whatever is done by nature must needs be traced back to God, as to its first cause. So also whatever is done designedly must also be traced back to some higher cause other than human reason or will, for these can suffer change and are defective; whereas things capable of motion and of defect must be traced back to an immovable and self-necessary first principle.

The Kalam Argument from Islam

WILLIAM CRAIG

IN MY OPINION the cosmological argument which is most likely to be a sound and persuasive proof for the existence of God is the *kalām* cosmological argument based on the impossibility of an infinite temporal regress of events. We have seen that the argument rests essentially on two contentions: (1) some form of the principle of efficient causality and (2) the impossibility of an infinite regress of events. In this chapter I shall attempt to formulate and defend such a cosmological argument, taking into account the modern developments in both philosophy and science that have a bearing on the proof's cogency.

We may present the basic argument in a variety of ways. Syllogistically, it can be displayed in this manner:

1. Everything that begins to exist has a cause of its existence.

2. The universe began to exist.
3. Therefore the universe has a cause of its existence.

Or, alternatively, we may present the argument as a series of disjunctions about the universe, the existence of which is taken as given:

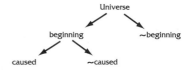

The point of the argument is to demonstrate the existence of a first cause which transcends and creates the entire realm of finite reality. Having reached that conclusion, one may then inquire into the nature of this first cause and assess its significance for theism.

From William Lane Craig, The Kalam Cosmological Argument. *London: The Macmillan Press, 1979, 63–64. Reprinted by Permission of Palgrave Macmillan.*

Problems with the Cosmological Argument

GUNAPALA DHARMASIRI

2.4   THE STARTING POINT of the argument for a creator is the idea of contingency, or "existence" as another for contingency. The assumption behind the argument is that existence cannot be explained by itself. Smart clarifies, ". . . in attempting to argue ourselves beyond the cosmos we seem to be going beyond the observable, and outside space and time. This provides us with another lesson—namely that any attempted explanation of the cosmos is nonscientific." This permits one to speak of God as the Cosmos-Explaining-Being: "We can argue that somehow 'beyond' or 'behind' the cosmos there exists a Being which explains the existence of the cosmos."

2.5   It is here that the Buddha would strongly disagree with the theist. He was conversant with the view of creation and said that some "believed as their traditional doctrine that the beginning of things was the work of God or Brahma." But he did not think that such a view could explain anything about the world. Buddhism does not call the world contingent but only impermanent. Its central thesis emphasizes that everything is subject to an unceasing flow of change (*vipariṇā-madhamma*). One of his disciples once questioned the Buddha: "'The world! The world!' is the saying, lord. How far, lord, does this saying go? It crumbles away, brethren. Therefore it is called 'the world.' What crumbles away? The eye . . . objects . . . eye-consciousness . . . tongue . . . body . . . mind etc. It crumbles away, brethren. Therefore it is called 'the world.'" What distinguishes the Buddha from the theist is that the former strongly believed the world to be explainable in its own terms. To him the world was not a 'thing' but only a vast series of evanescent changes. The law of causation (*idappaccayatā*) as affecting the physical and mental realms was

regarded to be fully sufficient to explain this cosmic series of changes. But the question as to what is the cause of this causal series still remains. Buddhaghosa thinks that when the idea of a creator God is rejected this question remains yet to be answered. But he maintains that empirical causation and causal regularities, in turn, can explain the causal series. "To begin with, he considers thus: 'Firstly this mentality-materiality is not causeless, because if that were so, it would follow that (having no causes to differentiate it), it would be identical everywhere always and for all. It has no Overlord [God] etc., because of the non-existence of any Overlord, etc., over and above mentality-materiality. And because, if people then argue that mentality-materiality itself is its Overlord etc., then it follows that their mentality-materiality, which they call the Overlord, etc., would itself be causeless. Consequently there must be a cause and a condition for it. What are they?

"Having thus directed his attention to mentality-materiality's cause and condition, he first discerns the cause and condition for the material body in this way . . . When it is born thus, its causes (root-causes) are the four things namely, ignorance, craving, clinging, and Kamma: since it is they that bring about its birth; and nutriment is its condition, since it is that that consolidates it. So five things constitute its cause and condition." In the same way, as we shall see later, Buddhism maintains that one can give a self-sufficient casual account in empirical terms of the physical and mental aspects of the world. . . .

2.21   The Buddha emphasized that one has to stop at the fundamental laws of nature and regularities of causation. To go beyond that would be

From Gunapala Dharmasiri, A Buddhist Critique of the Christian Concept of God. *Antioch, CA: Golden Leaves, 1988, pp. 25–26, 36–37. Copyright © 1988 by Gunapala Dharmasiri. Footnotes deleted.*

both unnecessary and wrong. Buddhaghosa states, "... knowledge of (causal) origin forestalls wrong theories of cause that occur as finding a reason where there is none, such as 'The world occurs owing to an Overlord . . .' etc." Here we can ask three questions: (i) Is it necessary to go beyond this point of explanation? (ii) Is it meaningful to go beyond this point? (iii) Is it correct to go beyond this point? Flew thinks that it is not necessary to go beyond this point of explanation because it is not a deficiency to stop at some fundamentals when one is giving an explanation. "In each and every case we must necessarily find at the end of every explanatory road some ultimates which have simply to be accepted as the fundamental truths about the way things are. And this itself is a contention, not about the lamentable contingent facts of the human condition, but about what follows necessarily from the nature of explanation." Is it meaningful to go beyond this point? If the theist goes beyond this point he will have to stop at some other ultimate which seems arbitrary, enigmatic and abrupt. For example, to stop at a necessary God is an arbitrary conclusion. Even before proceeding to that point he has to accept or stop at more enigmatic and uneasy ultimates. C.B. Martin points out one such ultimate: "This is one law of nature or one way of the world that would be beyond the power of God, namely, that the world should in fact go according to the will of God. God cannot ordain or will that his ordinations and will are effective. That, God's will is effective is just a fact (though a basic one) about how things happen. To ask why God's will is effective is to invite the answer 'That is just the way things are'." The theist's ultimates become more and more meaningless as he proceeds further. Hence, to proceed beyond the empirical ultimates is progressively meaningless. Then we come to the third question. Is it correct to go beyond the ultimates of empirical explanation?

Hume explains: "In such a chain too, or succession of objects, each part is caused by that which preceded it, and causes that which succeds it. Where then is the difficulty? But the *whole,* you say, wants a cause . . . Did I show you the particular causes of each individual in a collection of twenty particles of matter, I should think it very unreasonable, should you afterwards ask me, what was the cause of the whole twenty." Similarly, the Buddhist would say that once the empirical facts have been explained causally it would be positively wrong to ask the cause of the whole of it. That was why Buddhaghosa, as we saw above, maintained that the knowledge of the causal origin of things forestalls the theories of a creator God.

2.22   Now, coming to the second question of the theist, he can still ask "Why does anything exist at all?" The Buddhist can give four answers to this question. One is that, as he accepts the possibility of an everlasting cosmos, this question does not, in an important sense, arise to him. Here it should be emphatically stated that we should not drag in the idea of logical contingency into this context because it does not have any meaning as applied to empirical and factual contexts. Of existential propositions one can speak only of an empirical necessity. So, if the world is everlasting the fact that anything exists at all is an empirical necessity. One can *logically* think the world away, but it is not important at all because we are not talking about the realm of logic. The important thing is that one cannot *practically* think the world away because it exists as an empirical necessity. Therefore, to the Buddhist "why does anything exist at all?" does not pose any problem. One might still insist on a logical kind of explanation in terms of the idea of necessity, but such an explanation would not mean anything and therefore would fail to be an explanation at all. . . .

12.3 Hinduism and Science

There is much to be said in favor of a sharp distinction between religion and science. They are very different. And yet, throughout history, especially modern history, they have repeatedly come into conflict. For example, Galileo (1564–1642) was prosecuted for heresy by the Roman Catholic Church for teaching heliocentrism (the view that the Sun, not Earth, is the center of our solar system). And most of you are probably aware of the present-day conflict between fundamentalist Christians and biologists over evolution and creationism.

Modern science is strongly influenced by **naturalism,** the theory that the universe is a self-existing, self-regulating, and homogeneous system (its parts differ in degree but not in kind). Pierre Laplace (1749–1827), the famous and influential French mathematician and astronomer, when asked why God played no role in scientific theories about the origin of the universe, remarked, "We have no need of that hypothesis." He believed that science can explain the universe quite well without recourse to anything outside the universe. This is a good example of a naturalistic attitude.

Of course, there have been attempts to develop ideas of God that are compatible with scientific theories. Many scientists have been attracted, for example, to a deistic theory of God. **Deism** is the view that God started the universe and established natural laws (the laws of physics) according to which it operates. It now runs on its own without God's interference or help. Such a view of God implies that there are no miracles, if what you mean by a miracle is God intervening in world affairs in violation of natural laws. Still others have been attracted to **pantheism,** the theory that nature is God. According to pantheism, God does not transcend the universe; God is the universe. Both deistic and pantheistic views of God appear to conflict with theism. **Theism** is the view that God is an infinite, self-existent, all-powerful, all-knowing, perfectly good, and personal being who created the universe out of nothing and controls it.

Many of you may have heard of the Big Bang. This is the notion that the universe began as a huge explosion. The Big Bang has been treated as a physical singularity, that is, as an occurrence whose physics is not understood. A physical singularity marks the limits of the conceptual resources of a theory. Singularities must be thought of as a kind of arbitrary initial condition or as a phenomenon awaiting explanation.

Could that explanation be found in religious ideas about a creator God? According to P. Venugopala Rao, a physicist conducting research at Emory University and author of the next selection, the modern scientific view of the universe is not incompatible with the religious ideas associated with Hinduism. According to Rao, Hinduism considers nature to be an expression of a divine order. If it is, then modern science and at least one kind of religious vision are not necessarily opposed. Yet how can we know that the universe rests on some sort of divine foundation? Could this idea ever be a conclusion reached by scientific investigations of the origin and development of the universe?

Reading Questions

1. According to Rao, what is Hinduism?
2. Why can the creation hymn (*Nasdiya Sukta*) be seen as both a weakness and a strength of the Hindu faith?
3. What is a *darsana*?
4. What are the central concepts (*mahavakyas*) of the Upanishads?
5. What does Rao mean by "downward" versus "upward" causation, and how does this difference reveal a difference between Darwinian evolution and the Hindu concept of evolution?
6. Has Rao persuaded you of the compatibility of Hinduism and science? Why, or why not?

Science and Dharma

P. VENUGOPALA RAO

FROM A HINDU PHYSICIST'S PERSPECTIVE, scientific methods and discoveries can find a comfortable place within Hinduism's diverse, evolving metaphysics, but profound differences remain to be reconciled.

I consider myself a religious person whose spiritual bearings are firmly embedded in a tradition that dates back thousands of years. In common terminology, I am a Hindu and my religion is Hinduism. But among non-Hindus, the meaning of Hinduism is often misunderstood. It is not a single religious tradition, nor is it a religion revealed through one founding prophet. What, then, is Hinduism?

Historically, the Hindus of India have subscribed to various schools of thought, which have relied on intuition. While many Hindus did (and still do) share certain beliefs and sacred texts, there has been no single authoritative text for all Hindus. It is only in recent times, under pressure from modernizing influences from around the world, that the word *Hinduism* has been applied as a blanket term to those differing religious traditions of ancient India.

A person is a Hindu by virtue of being born into a Hindu family. Rarely does one receive a formal education in the faith. It is through a process of osmosis, from cultural and social interactions, that a Hindu evolves into a spiritually sensitive being.

During my childhood, the rituals, ceremonies, and customs practiced by my parents and grandparents provided me with a set of beliefs and principles of faith. I naturally used this frame of reference when looking at the world and my relationship to it. My faith consisted of devotion to a personal God (conceptualized in different forms) with unlimited qualities, immeasurable powers, incalculable patience, and

unquestionable commitment to the welfare of His (or Her) devotees.

During my education, I was led from a position of faith to that of inquiring into the reasons underlying that faith. And experience joined hands with education to induce doubt and uncertainty. Even during my early life, the faith I held dearly did not always remain firm and unshaken. There were deaths and serious illnesses in the family, and certain events were inexplicable by normal, commonsense reasoning. These and other occurrences raised questions with no ready answers in any of the sacred texts of Hinduism.

Having noted the diversity of thinking among Hindus, I should point out that most religious Hindus—whatever their economic, social, or educational level—would hold to at least some of the following beliefs:

- There exists a personal deity who is immanent as well as transcendent.
- We are but tiny specks in one of an infinite number of worlds that populate the universe.
- Our world is inhabited by many beings, human and nonhuman, sentient and insentient, corporeal and perhaps incorporeal.
- All our actions (karma) become part of our identity. They are registered in a cosmic account book and determine the eternal cycle of lives that we may have.
- We can, if we wish, modify our own destiny through a determined course of action.
- Action is the basic mode of existence of all beings, and we humans are expected to work according to our duty (dharma).

On Becoming a Scientist

In the course of becoming a physicist, I learned that science is a special way of discovering

From P. Venugopala Rao, "Science and Dharma," World and I, April 2001, vol. 16, 150ff. Copyright © 2001 News World Communications, Inc. Reprinted by permission.

structures and properties of the physical and biological worlds. The discoveries are often codified into lawlike propositions, and these in turn can be used predictively. But these laws are not permanent rules etched on sacred stones; they are extrapolations. To quote Richard Feynman, "Every scientific law, every scientific principle, every statement of the results of an observation is some kind of summary which leaves out details, because nothing can be stated precisely."

Nonetheless, aided by our intelligence and imagination, we continue to formulate laws that are valid over larger and larger domains of natural occurrences. We hold onto these laws with respectful faith until we encounter an observation that forces a modification. As an experimental physicist, I learned that an essential part of being a scientist is the habit of testing and correcting a concept by observing its consequences in experience. Moreover, the practice of experimentation and observation inculcates a range of values: independence, originality, dissent, tolerance, and respect, leading to a sense of human dignity.

The most exciting part of participating in this scientific activity is coming face to face with the grand and mysterious vision of our universe. Certainly, the science of cosmology—with its deep insights into the structure of the universe and its imaginative scenarios of the working of its parts—reigns supreme. Even as I write these words, theoretical physicists and cosmologists are hard at work to interpret our accumulating scientific knowledge about the universe, constructing models that were inconceivable just a few decades ago. According to the currently accepted model, the universe began with a sudden "big bang," followed by a continuing state of expansion. But we must keep our options open to observations that could force us to alter our views.

Recent speculations that attempt to explain the origin of the universe draw on the principles of quantum mechanics—a branch of science that was developed to explain the microcosm (the subatomic world). It has been proposed that our universe may have come into existence from a "quantum fluctuation"—a cosmic application of Heisenberg's uncertainty principle. If so, our universe might be just one among an infinite number of worlds, all born at different times and with different physical constants governing their development.

The possibility of multiple universes leads to the grand concept of a "multiverse." I am inevitably reminded of the opening words of a Sanskrit verse that a devout Hindu is expected to recite at the beginning of any puja (devotional ceremony): "In our universe, which is one among the billions of other universes floating in the great expanse of cosmic water, . . .".

What role does the personal God of Hindu religion have in this great architecture of the cosmos? To satisfy the curiosity of a seeker, many creation stories have been told and retold in various Hindu mythologies. But they leave us with a sense of uncertainty and a feeling that no one knows for sure how it all began. The Vedas—the ultimate scriptural source of profound thoughts for a Hindu—have posed only questions. The most inquiring philosophical hymn, the creation hymn (*Nasdiya Sukta*) in the Rig Veda, concludes with the following query:

> The flow of creation, from where it did arise?
> Whether it was ordered or not,
> He, the observer, in the highest heaven
> He alone knows, unless—he knows not.

These expressions of inability to comprehend the origin of the universe may be taken as a weakness in the Hindu faith. But they also imply that a Hindu may keep an open mind to entertain new creation stories, including those that cosmologists speculate upon. This attitude can be counted as a strength of the faith.

Hindu Metaphysics

Yet, questions about origins and creation were not what aroused the intense curiosity of the wise men and women of ancient India. Their questions were directed more toward understanding the meaning of life and the nature of reality. The answers and speculations resulting from such discussions constitute the primary narrative, while myths about creation and chronologies of cosmic and terrestrial events constitute a secondary narrative.

We are concerned here with the primary narratives, which are articulated in the vast literature of the *darsanas*—the philosophical traditions of India. A *darsana* is a theory of reality and is meant to provide an understanding of what one is, what one ought to become, what one can become, and what the nature of the world is. It is also a narrative that defines the ideal way of life for a Hindu.

Early religion in India, as evident from the Vedas, was a religion of action, taking the form of performing sacrifices and serving the family and community. The *darsana* that supplied the metaphysics and philosophy of action is known as Mimamsa. This school of thought, based on earlier parts of the Vedas, viewed the world as being real but did not accept the existence of God. It gave primacy to karma and dharma.

A separate group of people, belonging to the Charvaka school of thought, denied the authority of the Vedas and adopted a materialistic way of thinking. They doubted the value of sacrifice, the existence of God and the soul.

In addition, there were other independent thinkers who founded the Nyaya, Vaiseshika, Samkhya, and Yoga *darsanas*. They did not deny the authority and sacredness of the Vedas, but each group had its own system of thought.

In the Samkhya system, the world is to be understood from the standpoint of a person's inner being, which is identified as Atman (or *purusha*). Atmans are believed to be infinite in number and their nature is existence and consciousness. The manifested world is thought to be derived from a single entity called Prakriti. Independent of any Atman but not mere matter, it is the origin of both mental and physical aspects of our being. But the Samkhya system has no place for God.

Yoga *darsana* adopted the metaphysics of Samkhya but added the concept of a Supreme Purusha, a Special Atman, or God (Isvara), who supervises the process of Prakriti. Yoga teaches how the processes of Prakriti can be controlled. The Nyaya and Vaiseshika systems believe in God and objective reality—that is, the existence of objects independent of (and in addition to) the mind and the Atman.

In the later parts of the Vedas, known as the Upanishads, we find thoughtful reflections on inner spiritual experiences. It is said that one's internal spiritual reality can be realized through prayer and meditation. The *darsana* that is devoted to this philosophical quest is known as Vedanta. To understand the central concept of the Upanishads, a frame of reference is given in four important statements (*mahavakyas*):

1. I am the Brahman.
2. The Atman is the Brahman.
3. Thou art That. (You are the Brahman.)
4. Brahman is Consciousness.

Brahman is the Supreme Spirit, the ground of all beings. If one recognizes that a human being can exist in various states—waking, dreaming, and deep sleep—that differ in degree of ignorance and bondage, then by extension one may derive a fourth state, Atman. (The highest level of ignorance and bondage is thought to occur in the waking state, when the Atman identifies itself with the physical being.) With a leap of imagination and extrapolation, this fourth state is thought to have the same essence as Brahman and is the self (*jiva*) in the individual being. The relationship between Atman and Brahman has been defined in various ways, giving rise to different subdivisions of the Vedanta school.

Brahman is said to be indescribable. Through a process we cannot comprehend, Brahman becomes Prakriti—the support and origin of the entire manifested world. In that creative role, Brahman is known as Isvara.

As a religious philosophy, the Vedanta system of thought got the upper hand and absorbed the essentials from almost every other school. Contemporary Indian thinkers generally belong to the Vedanta tradition. They are also influenced by the religious thought of Christianity, the rational philosophies, and the sciences.

No account of the Hindu tradition can omit reference to the well-known sacred text, the Bhagavad Gita. This text presents a dialogue between God (in the form of Krishna) and man (in the form of Arjuna), putting forth a great synthesis of ideas established in the *darsanas*.

In the Gita, Krishna emphasizes the importance of karma when he tells Arjuna, "No one exists for even an instant without performing action: however unwilling, every being is forced to act by the qualities of Nature. . . . Seeing the way to preserve the world, you should act" (Gita III.5,20). But Krishna also sounds a warning: "Be intent on action, not on fruits (results) of action; avoid attraction to the results and attachment to inaction" (Gita II.47).

The teachings of the Gita incorporate a dual purpose. They emphasize that the processes of the human world must be maintained through action without regard for its result, and they teach the pathway toward salvation.

In today's world, a typical Hindu thinker who subscribes to the Vedanta tradition may express his metaphysical outlook as follows:

1. There exists Brahman, the ground of all beings, with both immanent and transcendent aspects. Unmanifested Brahman cannot be described in any way, except to say that Brahman is "being," "consciousness," and "bliss" (*sat-chit-ananda*).

2. Out of Brahman emerges Prakriti (unmanifested nature), which, through an unknown process, produces the entire world. In terms of this creative power, Brahman is referred to as Isvara. Isvara is also known as Brahma (in the role of creator), Vishnu (in the role of preserver), and Siva (in the role of destroyer). The processes of creation, preservation, and dissolution continue eternally, probably in cyclical fashion.

3. Living and nonliving beings evolve through the manifestation of Prakriti, which has three basic attributes (*gunas*), known as Sattva, Rajas, and Tamas. These attributes are in a state of equilibrium in the unmanifested stage of Prakriti. But when they are disturbed by Atman (Brahman), manifestation and evolution begin, and the biological and physical worlds become distinguished. Isvara may control this process—or he may just be a witness to the transformation.

4. In the biological world, the sentient individual—also known as *jiva*—has the same essence as Brahman. The physical body of the *jiva* has evolved from a number of categories or elements present in the manifested Prakriti. The human mind is one of these categories.

5. The *jiva* is ignorant of his (or her) own nature and seeks to understand the nature of reality, while performing karma to keep the world going according to God's desire. Karma is an essential quality of existence. The seeker who experiences his own true nature attains salvation.

These are the articles of faith that a learned and searching Hindu is expected to hold. Faith, however, is never meant to be blind; it is meant to be guided by truths that are revealed through the lives of honest beings.

Hinduism and Science

Let us now examine whether the findings of science are compatible with the metaphysics outlined above. As already noted, the cosmologist's vision of multiple universes readily meets the expectations of a Hindu. But the most intriguing questions raised in today's scientific community are about the conscious mind: How does the sense of self emerge? What is the relationship between mind and body, or mind and brain?

In attempting to find answers, neuroscientists and their colleagues have been working at an ever-accelerating pace. Consequently, we probably learned more about the brain in the 1990s than in all of history before then. Researchers anticipate that in another four or five decades, the dualistic separation of mind and brain will be wiped out. In the case of Hindu philosophies, both theistic and atheistic (other than materialistic ones), it is generally assumed that the mind belongs to a primary category, while the brain or body is secondary.

Darwin's theory of evolution, which has shaken some other faiths, is compatible with Hindu thinking in the sense that both see this complex world as having developed from an original unity, call it by whatever name. In Hindu thought, humanity is treated as part of manifested Prakriti (nature), and the sentient being (*jiva*) is the result of a process of evolution. But the physical world is said to have evolved out of mindlike substance rather than the other way around. Thus, Hindu metaphysics postulates downward causation, whereas modern science tries to provide explanations that call for upward causation. In this sense, the Hindu concept of evolution differs from the Darwinian one.

Scientific theories that range from quantum physics to cosmology have convinced us that our entire universe is interconnected. This total connectedness of nature cannot be articulated completely in any formal language, but this concept is included in Hindu teachings. Nonetheless, how do we comprehend our own finiteness in this larger picture? Perhaps we need to ask, "Is there a Brahman of physics?"

The scientific enterprise is continually seeking a unified description of the world, based on investigations of "objective" reality. But scientists also acknowledge that we have no means to observe and describe 90 percent (or more) of the contents of our universe. And, as quantum physics informs us, there are limitations to a view of reality that is beyond the ken of an observer. As a result, scientific investigation leads us to an incomplete understanding of reality.

In the Hindu metaphysics outlined above, there is the notion of an indescribable, immanent, and transcendent Brahman, who is the support and substratum of all that exists. This concept implies a realization of our smallness in the total scheme of things and the limited scope of the knowledge we gather. It is not surprising, therefore, that conflicts between scientific and religious ideas arise when science claims more than its share in the body of knowledge or when religion overrides the discoveries of science.

Hinduism considers that nature is an expression of a cosmic, divine order. The Vedas speak of this order as *Rta*. On the other hand, as science has successfully fueled the growth of technology in service of humanity, it has transformed this view of nature and emboldened many to become atheistic. As a result, our relationship with the divine, as nurtured by the spiritual teachings of various religions, has also been adversely affected.

A historical survey would show that Hindu philosophical views are continually revised, assimilating various types of new knowledge. And it may not be an overstatement to say that to be a good Hindu, it is part of one's dharma to participate in scientific activity—that is, the search for the true nature of our world. From an overall perspective, then, Hinduism's evolving metaphysics can comfortably accommodate scientific methods and discoveries, but there are major hurdles that need to be crossed.

12.4 Creationism vs. Evolution

In addition to the cosmological argument (see above) another type of argument for God's existence is the **teleological argument,** or the argument from design. This kind of argument begins with the premise that the universe exhibits order and draws the conclusion that a supreme, divine intelligence is responsible for the order of the universe.

Versions of the teleological argument are very old, but William Paley (1743–1805), a defender of the Christian evangelical cause in England, popularized it in his 1802 publication *Natural Theology.* Paley was under the influence of Newtonian physics, which pictured the universe as a vast machine operating in accord with well-known laws. In addition, he was much taken by the naturalist's descriptions of the complex order of various plant and animal life. It seemed to Paley that the universe was one vast, harmonious, interconnected order designed for a purpose. It seemed to him much like a watch, an intricately designed machine with all its parts working in harmony for a common goal.

Although David Hume (see Section 6.4) lived before Paley and published posthumously in 1779 his *Dialogues Concerning Natural Religion,* in which he severely criticized the teleological argument, Paley seems to be unaware of his work. Among Hume's several objections to the argument, three stand out. First Hume argues, through a fictional character named Philo, a skeptic, that the universe is not sufficiently like the productions of human design to support the argument. The things between which the analogy is drawn (the world and designed objects) are the same in some respects and different in others. Although the universe may share some things in common with houses, ships, watches, and the like, it is also vastly different. For one thing it is bigger than anything any human has ever made. Second, Philo points out that we have no other universes with which to compare this one, and we would need to make comparisons in order to decide if it were the kind of thing that was designed or simply grew on its own. Would you know, if you had never seen a cut diamond and found one by accident on a beach, that this stone was designed (cut according to a pattern) and the other stones were not? Third, Philo argues that an effect must be proportionate to its cause. Because the universe is imperfect (evil and suffering occur), its cause must be imperfect. But no theologian wishes to admit that God is anything less than perfect.

Although many philosophers thought Hume's objections to the teleological argument fatal, the argument, in one form or another, continued to be popular. Perhaps its continued popularity was due to the fact that Hume could provide no convincing alternative explanations for the observed order because there was no body of scientific evidence or theory to which Hume could point. At least there was no evidence or theory until the nineteenth century.

In 1859, some 58 years after Paley's *Natural Theology* was published, Charles Darwin published *On the Origin of the Species.* This book revolutionized the biological sciences by showing how the order nature exhibits is the result of evolutionary processes. According to Aristotle, species are fixed. This idea supported the sort of creationism Paley promoted: that God is the original creator and designer of species, which then proliferate by reproductive means. However, by Darwin's time, the fossil record and mounting biological evidence no longer supported the fixed-species idea. Species change, develop, and evolve, Darwin claimed, and they do so by a mechanism he called *natural selection.*

The theory of evolution has undergone considerable refinement since Darwin first formulated it. In one form or another, it has emerged as the dominant theory of modern biology. Since Paley had argued that only a divine intelligence was a sufficient explanation for the order found in nature, evolutionary theory appears to offer a direct challenge to his views. It provides not only an alternative explanation, but also one far more sufficient from a scientific viewpoint.

The reaction to the theory of evolution on the part of those who believe in a divine creative intelligence has been both varied and intense. A theory of *instantaneous creation* has been advanced by those who reject the theory of evolution. According to this view, God is responsible for the immediate and direct creation of all distinct forms of life. Supporters of this outlook have been very persistent in attempting to get the public schools to teach what they call "creation science" in addition to evolution. *Guided evolution* is a theory advanced by those who wish to combine evolution and belief in a creator God. In this view, God creates and designs the order in the world, but the means God uses is natural selection.

Evolutionary theory has had an impact on the way modern versions of the teleological argument are formulated. Recent versions of the argument tend to emphasize the idea of probability. In effect, they claim that evolutionary explanations ultimately boil down to notions of chance. The next move is to point out the tremendous odds against the complexity of life evolving by chance. Someone has suggested, for example, that the odds against life evolving on this planet in its present form by chance alone are about as great as the chances of a tornado assembling the parts of a Boeing 747 scattered over a field into a functioning airplane. If your choice is between chance and intelligent design and if the odds are against chance and in favor of design, which constitutes the most plausible explanation?

How much does chance have to do with the order we find? The next selection is by Richard Dawkins, a zoologist who has taught at Berkeley and Oxford. He was born in Nairobi, Kenya, in 1941 and moved to England in 1949. He is best known for his book *The Selfish Gene* (1976). Dawkins argues against Paley and in support of neo-Darwinian views of evolution. He maintains that the critics of evolution have misunderstood the mechanism by which life evolves. It does not evolve by chance (or at least the more complex forms do not), but by a nonrandom process he calls *cumulative selection* in contrast to *single-step selection.* Single-step selection sorts or filters all items once and for all. It is like filtering sand through a sieve once and looking at the formation that results. Cumulative selection filters repeatedly, thus passing on some of the first results of the filtering to the next process of selection. In other words, the first pile of sand resulting from the first filtering is filtered again, with a finer sieve. Hence, the result will be different from the first result (smaller bits of sand will result). If this process is repeated over and over again, the result will be that the finest bits of sand survive each filtering, and the larger pieces do not. If natural selection operated as single-step selection, then the odds *against* getting a heap of the finest sand the first time around would be very high. It would largely be a matter of chance. But if natural selection operates as a cumulative selection (and it does according to evolutionary theory), the odds of eventually getting a heap of the finest sand would greatly increase.

As the genetic traits of one generation are filtered by natural selection and passed on to the next, and again filtered and passed on to the next, and so on for many many generations, the chances of ending up with a complex, adaptive order increase greatly. Dawkins also argues that the major alternatives to neo-Darwinism are fatally flawed. Evolution remains the only viable scientific hypothesis for explaining the natural order.

You may have noted how discussions of both the cosmological and teleological arguments seem to return again and again to the issue of what constitutes a sufficient explanation. All parties agree that the existence of the universe and the order of life on Earth require an explanation, but they disagree about what constitutes a sufficient one. Perhaps there can be no agreement on this matter, because what counts as sufficient depends on the conceptual scheme (see Kuhn's idea of a paradigm in Section 7.3) from which you approach the issue. Or does it?

Reading Project and Questions

1. Write a brief summary of Dawkins's argument.
2. What do you find most puzzling about what Dawkins says?
3. What do you find most plausible about what Dawkins says?

The Blind Watchmaker

RICHARD DAWKINS

THIS BOOK IS WRITTEN in the conviction that our own existence once presented the greatest of all mysteries, but that it is a mystery no longer because it is solved. Darwin and Wallace solved it, though we shall continue to add footnotes to their solution for a while yet. I wrote the book because I was surprised that so many people seemed not only unaware of the elegant and beautiful solution to this deepest of problems but, incredibly, in many cases actually unaware that there was a problem in the first place!

The problem is that of complex design. The computer on which I am writing these words has an information storage capacity of about 64 kilobytes (one byte is used to hold each character of text). The computer was consciously designed and deliberately manufactured. The brain with which you are understanding my words is an array of some ten million kiloneurones. Many of these billions of nerve cells have each more than a thousand "electric wires" connecting them to other neurones. Moreover, at the molecular genetic level, every single one of more than a trillion cells in the body contains about a thousand times as much precisely-coded digital information as my entire computer. The complexity of living organisms is matched by the elegant efficiency of their apparent design. If anyone doesn't agree that this amount of complex design cries out for an explanation, I give up. No, on second thought I don't give up, because one of my aims in the book is to convey something of the sheer wonder of biological complexity to those whose eyes have not been opened to it. But having built up the mystery, my other main aim is to remove it again by explaining the solution.

Explaining is a difficult art. You can explain something so that your reader understands the words, and you can explain something so that the reader feels it in the marrow of his bones. To do the latter, it sometimes isn't enough to lay the evidence before the reader in a dispassionate way. You have to become an advocate and use the tricks of the advocate's trade. This book is not a dispassionate scientific treatise. Other books on Darwinism are, and many of them are excellent and informative and should be read in conjunction with this one. Far from being dispassionate, it has to be confessed that in parts this book is written with a passion which, in a professional scientific journal, might excite comment. Certainly it seeks to inform, but it also seeks to persuade and even—one can specify *aims* without presumption—to inspire. I want to inspire the reader with a vision of our own existence as, on the face of it, a spine-chilling mystery; and simultaneously to convey the full excitement of the fact that it is a mystery with an elegant solution which is within our grasp. More, I want to persuade the reader, not just that the Darwinian world-view *happens* to be true, but that it is the only known theory that *could*, in principle, solve the mystery of our existence. This makes it a doubly satisfying theory. A good case can be made that Darwinism is true, not just on this planet but all over the universe wherever life may be found.

In one respect I plead to distance myself from professional advocates. A lawyer or a politician is paid to exercise his passion and his persuasion on behalf of a client or a cause in which he may not privately believe. I have never done this and I never shall. I may not always be right, but I care passionately about what is true and I never say anything that I do not believe to be right. I remember being shocked when visiting a university debating society to debate with creationists. At dinner after the debate, I was placed next to a young woman who had made a relatively powerful speech in favour of creationism. She clearly couldn't *be* a creationist, so I asked her to tell me honestly why she had done it. She freely admitted that she was simply practising her debating skills, and found it more challenging to advocate a position in which she did not believe. Apparently it is common practice in university debating societies for speakers simply to be *told* on which side they are to speak. Their own beliefs don't come into it. I had come a long way to perform the disagreeable task of public speaking, because I believed in the truth of the motion that I had been asked to propose. When I discovered that members of the society were using the motion as a vehicle for playing arguing games, I resolved to decline future invitations from debating societies that encourage insincere advocacy on issues where scientific truth is at stake.

For reasons that are not entirely clear to me, Darwinism seems more in need of advocacy than similarly established truths in other branches of science. Many of us have no grasp of quantum theory, or Einstein's theories of special and general relativity, but this does not in itself lead us to *oppose* these theories! Darwinism, unlike "Einsteinism," seems to be regarded as fair game for critics with any degree of ignorance. I suppose one trouble with Darwinism is that, as Jacques Monod perceptively remarked, everybody *thinks* he understands it. It is, indeed, a remarkably simple theory; childishly so, one would have thought, in comparison with almost all of physics and mathematics. In essence, it amounts simply to the idea that nonrandom reproduction, where there is hereditary variation, has consequences that are far-reaching if there is time for them to be cumulative. But we have good grounds for believing that this simplicity is deceptive. Never forget that, simple as the theory may seem, nobody thought of it until Darwin and Wallace in the mid-nineteenth century, nearly 200 years after Newton's *Principia,* and more than 2,000 years after Eratosthenes measured the Earth. How could such a simple idea go so long undiscovered by thinkers of the calibre of Newton, Galileo, Descartes, Leibniz, Hume and Aristotle? Why did it have to wait for two Victorian naturalists? What was *wrong* with philosophers and mathematicians that they overlooked it? And

how can such a powerful idea go still largely unabsorbed into popular consciousness?

It is almost as if the human brain were specifically designed to misunderstand Darwinism, and to find it hard to believe. Take, for instance, the issue of "chance," often dramatized as *blind* chance. The great majority of people that attack Darwinism leap with almost unseemly eagerness to the mistaken idea that there is nothing other than random chance in it. Since living complexity embodies the very antithesis of chance, if you think that Darwinism is tantamount to chance you'll obviously find it easy to refute Darwinism! One of my tasks will be to destroy this eagerly believed myth that Darwinism is a theory of "chance." Another way in which we seem predisposed to disbelieve Darwinism is that our brains are built to deal with events on radically different *timescales* from those that characterize evolutionary change. We are equipped to appreciate processes that take seconds, minutes, years or, at most, decades to complete. Darwinism is a theory of cumulative processes so slow that they take between thousands and millions of decades to complete. All our intuitive judgments of what is probable turn out to be wrong by many orders of magnitude. Our well-tuned apparatus of scepticism and subjective probability-theory misfires by huge margins, because it is tuned—ironically, by evolution itself—to work within a lifetime of a few decades. It requires effort of the imagination to escape from the prison of familiar timescale, an effort that I shall try to assist.

A third respect in which our brains seem predisposed to resist Darwinism stems from our great success as creative designers. Our world is dominated by feats of engineering and works of art. We are entirely accustomed to the idea that complex elegance is an indicator of premeditated, crafted design. This is probably the most powerful reason for the belief, held by the vast majority of people that have ever lived, in some kind of supernatural deity. It took a very large leap of the imagination for Darwin and Wallace to see that, contrary to all intuition, there is another way and, once you have understood it, a far more plausible way, for complex "design" to arise out of primeval simplicity. A leap of the imagination so large that, to this day, many people seem still unwilling to make it. It is the main purpose of this book to help the reader to make this leap. . . .

The watchmaker of my title is borrowed from a famous treatise by the eighteenth-century theologian William Paley. His *Natural Theology—or Evidences of the Existence and Attributes of the Deity Collected from the Appearances of Nature,* published in 1802, is the best-known exposition of the "Argument from Design," always the most influential of the arguments for the existence of a God. It is a book that I greatly admire, for in his own time its author succeeded in doing what I am struggling to do now. He had a point to make, he passionately believed in it, and he spared no effort to ram it home clearly. He had a proper reverence for the complexity of the living world, and he saw that it demands a very special kind of explanation. The only thing he got wrong—admittedly quite a big thing!—was the explanation itself. He gave the traditional religious answer to the riddle, but he articulated it more clearly and convincingly than anybody had before. The true explanation is utterly different, and it had to wait for one of the most revolutionary thinkers of all time, Charles Darwin.

Paley begins *Natural Theology* with a famous passage:

> In crossing a heath, suppose I pitched my foot against a *stone,* and were asked how the stone came to be there; I might possibly answer, that, for anything I knew to the contrary, it had lain there for ever: nor would it perhaps be very easy to show the absurdity of this answer. But suppose I had found a *watch* upon the ground, and it should be inquired how the watch happened to be in that place; I should hardly think of the answer which I had before given, that for anything I knew, the watch might have always been there.

Paley here appreciates the differences between natural physical objects like stones, and designed and manufactured objects like watches. He goes on to expound the precision with which the cogs and springs of a watch are fashioned, and the intricacy with which they are put together. If we

found an object such as a watch upon a heath, even if we didn't know how it had come into existence, its own precision and intricacy of design would force us to conclude

> that the watch must have had a maker: that there must have existed, at some time, and at some place or other, an artificer or artificers, who formed it for the purpose which we find it actually to answer; who comprehended its construction, and designed its use.

Nobody could reasonably dissent from this conclusion, Paley insists, yet that is just what the atheist, in effect, does when he contemplates the works of nature, for:

> every indication of contrivance, every manifestation of design, which existed in the watch, exists in the works of nature; with the difference, on the side of nature, of being greater or more, and that in a degree which exceeds all computation.

Paley drives his point home with beautiful and reverent descriptions of the dissected machinery of life, beginning with the human eye, a favourite example which Darwin was later to use and which will reappear throughout this book. Paley compares the eye with a designed instrument such as a telescope, and concludes that "there is precisely the same proof that the eye was made for vision, as there is that the telescope was made for assisting it." The eye must have had a designer, just as the telescope had.

Paley's argument is made with passionate sincerity and is informed by the best biological scholarship of his day, but it is wrong, gloriously and utterly wrong. The analogy between telescope and eye, between watch and living organism, is false. All appearances to the contrary, the only watchmaker in nature is the blind forces of physics, albeit deployed in a very special way. A true watchmaker has foresight: he designs his cogs and springs, and plans their interconnections, with a future purpose in his mind's eye. Natural selection, the blind, unconscious, automatic process which Darwin discovered, and which we now know is the explanation for the existence and apparently purposeful form of all life, has no purpose in mind. It has no mind and no mind's eye. It does not plan for the future. It has no vision, no foresight, no sight at all. If it can be said to play the role of watchmaker in nature, it is the *blind* watchmaker.

I shall explain all this, and much else besides. But one thing I shall not do is belittle the wonder of the living "watches" that so inspired Paley. On the contrary, I shall try to illustrate my feeling that here Paley could have gone even further. When it comes to feeling awe over living "watches" I yield to nobody. I feel more in common with the Reverend William Paley than I do with the distinguished modern philosopher, a well-known atheist, with whom I once discussed the matter at dinner. I said that I could not imagine being an atheist at any time before 1859, when Darwin's *Origin of Species* was published. "What about Hume?" replied the philosopher. "How did Hume explain the organized complexity of the living world?" I asked. "He didn't," said the philosopher. "Why does it need any special explanation?"

Paley knew that it needed a special explanation; Darwin knew it, and I suspect that in his heart of hearts my philosopher companion knew it too. In any case it will be my business to show it here. As for David Hume himself, it is sometimes said that that great Scottish philosopher disposed of the Argument from Design a century before Darwin. But what Hume did was criticize the logic of using apparent design in nature as *positive* evidence for the existence of a God. He did not offer any *alternative* explanation for apparent design, but left the question open. An atheist before Darwin could have said, following Hume: "I have no explanation for complex biological design. All I know is that God isn't a good explanation, so we must wait and hope that somebody comes up with a better one." I can't help feeling that such a position, though logically sound, would have left one feeling pretty unsatisfied, and that although atheism might have been *logically* tenable before Darwin, Darwin made it possible to be an intellectually fulfilled atheist. I like to think that Hume would agree, but some of his writings suggest that he underestimated the complexity and beauty of biological design. The boy

naturalist Charles Darwin could have shown him a thing or two about that, but Hume had been dead 40 years when Darwin enrolled in Hume's university of Edinburgh. . . .

We have seen that living things are too improbable and too beautifully "designed" to have come into existence by chance. How, then, did they come into existence? The answer, Darwin's answer, is by gradual, step-by-step transformations from simple beginnings, from primordial entities sufficiently simple to have come into existence by chance. Each successive change in the gradual evolutionary process was simple enough, *relative to its predecessor,* to have arisen by chance. But the whole sequence of cumulative steps constitutes anything but a chance process, when you consider the complexity of the final end-product relative to the original starting point. The cumulative process is directed by nonrandom survival. The purpose of this chapter is to demonstrate the power of this *cumulative selection* as a fundamentally nonrandom process.

If you walk up and down a pebbly beach, you will notice that the pebbles are not arranged at random. The smaller pebbles typically tend to be found in segregated zones running along the length of the beach, the larger ones in different zones or stripes. The pebbles have been sorted, arranged, selected. A tribe living near the shore might wonder at this evidence of sorting or arrangement in the world, and might develop a myth to account for it, perhaps attributing it to a Great Spirit in the sky with a tidy mind and a sense of order. We might give a superior smile at such a superstitious notion, and explain that the arranging was really done by the blind forces of physics, in this case the action of waves. The waves have no purposes and no intentions, no tidy mind, no mind at all. They just energetically throw the pebbles around, and big pebbles and small pebbles respond differently to this treatment so they end up at different levels of the beach. A small amount of order has come out of disorder, and no mind planned it.

The waves and the pebbles together constitute a simple example of a system that automatically generates nonrandomness. The world is full of such systems. The simplest example I can think of is a hole. Only objects smaller than the hole can pass through it. This means that if you start with a random collection of objects above the hole, and some force shakes and jostles them about at random, after a while the objects above and below the hole will come to be nonrandomly sorted. The space below the hole will tend to contain objects smaller than the hole, and the space above will tend to contain objects larger than the hole. Mankind has, of course, long exploited this simple principle for generating nonrandomness, in the useful device known as the sieve.

The solar system is a stable arrangement of planets, comets and debris orbiting the Sun, and it is presumably one of many such orbiting systems in the universe. The nearer a satellite is to its sun, the faster it has to travel if it is to counter the sun's gravity and remain in stable orbit. For any given orbit, there is only one speed at which a satellite can travel and remain in that orbit. If it were travelling at any other velocity, it would either move out into deep space, or crash into the Sun, or move into another orbit. And if we look at the planets of our solar system, lo and behold, every single one of them is travelling at exactly the right velocity to keep it in its stable orbit around the Sun. A blessed miracle of provident design? No, just another natural "sieve." Obviously all the planets that we see orbiting the Sun must be travelling at exactly the right speed to keep them in their orbits, or we wouldn't see them there because they wouldn't be there! But equally obviously this is not evidence for conscious design. It is just another kind of sieve.

Sieving of this order of simplicity is not, on its own, enough to account for the massive amounts of nonrandom order that we see in living things. Nowhere near enough. Remember the analogy of the combination lock. The kind of nonrandomness that can be generated by simple sieving is roughly equivalent to opening a combination lock with one dial: it is easy to open it by sheer luck. The kind of nonrandomness that we see in living systems, on the other hand, is equivalent to a gigantic combination lock with an almost uncountable number of dials. To generate a biological molecule like haemoglobin, the red pigment in blood, by simple sieving would be equivalent to taking all the amino-acid building blocks of haemoglobin, jumbling them up at random, and hoping that the haemoglobin molecule would reconstitute itself by sheer luck. The amount of luck that would be required for this feat is unthinkable, and has been used as a telling mind-boggler by Isaac Asimov and others.

A haemoglobin molecule consists of four chains of amino acids twisted together. Let us think about just one of these four chains. It consists of 146 amino acids. There are 20 different kinds of amino acids commonly found in living things. The number of possible ways of arranging 20 kinds of thing in chains 146 links long is an inconceivably large number, which Asimov calls the "haemoglobin number." It is easy to calculate, but impossible to visualize the answer. The first link in the 146-long chain could be any one of the 20 possible amino acids. The second link could also be any one of the 20, so the number of possible 2-link chains is 20×20, or 400. The number of possible 3-link chains is $20 \times 20 \times 20$, or 8,000. The number of possible 146-link chains is 20 times itself 146 times. This is a staggeringly large number. A million is a 1 with 6 noughts after it. A billion (1,000 million) is a 1 with 9 noughts after it. The number we seek, the "haemoglobin number," is (near enough) a 1 with 190 noughts after it! This is the chance against happening to hit upon haemoglobin by luck. And a haemoglobin molecule has only a minute fraction of the complexity of a living body. Simple sieving, on its own, is obviously nowhere near capable of generating the amount of order in a living thing. Sieving is an essential ingredient in the generation of living order, but it is very far from being the whole story. Something else is needed. To explain the point, I shall need to make a distinction between "single-step" selection and "cumulative" selection. The simple sieves we have been considering so far in this chapter are all examples of single-step selection. Living organization is the product of cumulative selection.

The essential difference between single-step selection and cumulative selection is this. In single-step selection the entities selected or sorted, pebbles or whatever they are, are sorted once and for all. In cumulative selection, on the other hand, they "reproduce"; or in some other way the results of one sieving process are fed into a subsequent sieving, which is fed into . . . , and so on. The entities are subjected to selection or sorting over many "generations" in succession. The end-product of one generation of selection is the starting point for the next generation of selection, and so on for many generations. It is natural to borrow such words as "reproduce" and "generation," which have associations with living things, because living things are the main examples we know of things that participate in cumulative selection. They may in practice be the only things that do. But for the moment I don't want to beg that question by saying so outright.

Sometimes clouds, through the random kneading and carving of the winds, come to look like familiar objects. There is a much published photograph, taken by the pilot of a small aeroplane, of what looks a bit like the face of Jesus, staring out of the sky. We have all seen clouds that reminded us of something—a sea horse, say, or a smiling face. These resemblances come about by single-step selection, that is to say by a single coincidence. They are, consequently, not very impressive. The resemblance of the signs of the zodiac to the animals after which they are named, Scorpio, Leo, and so on, is as unimpressive as the predictions of astrologers. We don't feel overwhelmed by the resemblance, as we are by biological adaptations—the products of cumulative selection. We describe as weird, uncanny or spectacular, the resemblance of, say, a leaf insect to a leaf or a praying mantis to a cluster of pink flowers. The resemblance of a cloud to a weasel is only mildly diverting, barely worth calling to the attention of our companion. Moreover, we are quite likely to change our mind about exactly what the cloud most resembles.

Hamlet: Do you see yonder cloud that's almost in shape of a camel?
Polonius: By the mass, and 'tis like a camel, indeed.
Hamlet: Methinks it is like a weasel.
Polonius: It is backed like a weasel.
Hamlet: Or like a whale?
Polonius: Very like a whale.

I don't know who it was first pointed out that, given enough time, a monkey bashing away at random on a typewriter could produce all the works of Shakespeare. The operative phrase is, of course, given enough time. Let us limit the task facing our monkey somewhat. Suppose that he has to produce, not the complete works of Shakespeare but just the short sentence "Methinks it is like a weasel," and we shall make it relatively easy by giving him a typewriter with a restricted keyboard, one with just the 26 (capital) letters, and a space bar. How long will he take to write this one little sentence?

The sentence has 28 characters in it, so let us assume that the monkey has a series of discrete "tries," each consisting of 28 bashes at the keyboard. If he types the phrase correctly, that is the end of the experiment. If not, we allow him another "try" of 28 characters. I don't know any monkeys, but fortunately my 11-month-old daughter is an experienced randomizing device, and she proved only too eager to step into the role of monkey typist. Here is what she typed on the computer.

UMMK JK CDZZ F ZD DSDSKSM
S SS FMCV PU I DDRGLKDXRRDO
RDTE QDWFDVIOY UDSKZWDCCVYT
H CHVY NMGNBAYTDFCCVD D
RCDFYYYRM N DFSKD LD K WDWK
JJKAUIZMZI UXDKIDISFUMDKUDXI

She has other important calls on her time, so I was obliged to program the computer to simulate a randomly typing baby or monkey:

WDLDMNLT DTJBKWIRZREZLMQCO P
Y YVMQKZPGJXWVHGLAWFVCHQYOPY
MWR SWTNUXMLCDLEUBXTQHNZVJQF
FU OVAODVYKDGXDEKYVMOGGS VT
HZQZDSFZIHIVPHZPETPWVOVPMZGF
GEWRGZRPBCTPGQMCKHFDBGW ZCCF

And so on and on. It isn't difficult to calculate how long we should reasonably expect to wait for the random computer (or baby or monkey) to type METHINKS IT IS LIKE A WEASEL. Think about the total number of *possible* phrases of the right length that the monkey or baby or random computer *could* type. It is the same kind of calculation as we did for haemoglobin, and it produces a similarly large result. There are 27 possible letters (counting "space" as one letter) in the first position. The chance of the monkey happening to get the first letter—M—right is therefore 1 in 27. The chance of it getting the first two letters—ME—right is the chance of it getting the second letter—E—right (1 in 27) *given that* it has also got the first letter—M—right, therefore $1/27 \times 1/27$, which equals $1/729$. The chance of it getting the first word—METHINKS—right is $1/27$ for each of the 8 letters, therefore $(1/27) \times (1/27) \times (1/27) \times (1/27) \ldots$, etc. 8 times, or $(1/27)$ to the power 8. The chance of it getting the entire phrase of 28 characters right is $(1/27)$ to the power 28, i.e. $(1/27)$ multiplied by itself 28 times. These are very small odds, about 1 in 10,000 million million million million million million. To put it mildly, the phrase we seek would be a long time coming, to say nothing of the complete works of Shakespeare.

So much for single-step selection of random variation. What about cumulative selection; how much more effective should this be? Very very much more effective, perhaps more so than we at first realize, although it is almost obvious when we reflect further. We again use our computer monkey, but with a crucial difference in its program. It again begins by choosing a random sequence of 28 letters, just as before:

WDLMNLT DTJBKWIRZREZLMQCO P

It now "breeds from" this random phrase. It duplicates it repeatedly, but with a certain chance of random error—"mutation"—in the copying. The computer examines the mutant nonsense phrases, the "progeny" of the original phrase, and chooses the one which, *however slightly*, most resembles the target phrase, METHINKS IT IS LIKE A WEASEL. In this instance the winning phrase of the next "generation" happened to be:

WDLTMNLT DTJBSWIRZREZLMQCO P

Not an obvious improvement! But the procedure is repeated, again mutant "progeny" are

"bred from" the phrase, and a new "winner" is chosen. This goes on, generation after generation. After 10 generations, the phrase chosen for "breeding" was:

MDLDMNLS ITJISWHRZREZ MECS P

After 20 generations it was:

MELDINLS IT ISWPRKE Z WECSEL

By now, the eye of faith fancies that it can see a resemblance to the target phrase. By 30 generations there can be no doubt:

METHINGS IT ISWLIKE B WECSEL

Generation 40 takes us to within one letter of the target:

METHINKS IT IS LIKE I WEASEL

And the target was finally reached in generation 43. A second run of the computer began with the phrase:

Y   YVMQKZPFJXWVHGLAWFVCHQXYOPY,

passed through (again reporting only every tenth generation):

Y YVMQKSPFTXWSHLIKEFV HQYSPY
YETHINKSPITXISHLIKEFA WQYSEY
METHINKS IT ISSLIKE A WEFSEY
METHINKS IT ISBLIKE A WEASES
METHINKS IT ISJLIKE A WEASEO
METHINKS IT IS LIKE A WEASEP

and reached the target phrase in generation 64. In a third run the computer started with:

GEWRGZRPBCTPGQMCKHFDBGW ZCCF

and reached METHINKS IT IS LIKE A WEASEL in 41 generations of selective "breeding."

The exact time taken by the computer to reach the target doesn't matter. If you want to know, it completed the whole exercise for me, the first time, while I was out to lunch. It took about half an hour. (Computer enthusiasts may think this unduly slow. The reason is that the program was written in BASIC, a sort of computer baby-talk. When I rewrote it in Pascal, it took 11 seconds.) Computers are a bit faster at this kind of thing than monkeys, but the difference really isn't significant. What matters is the difference between the time taken by *cumulative* selection, and the time which the same computer, working flat out at the same rate, would take to reach the target phrase if it were forced to use the other procedure of *single-step selection:* about a million million million million million years. This is more than a million million million times as long as the universe has so far existed. Actually it would be fairer just to say that, in comparison with the time it would take either a monkey or a randomly programmed computer to type our target phrase, the total age of the universe so far is a negligibly small quantity, so small as to be well within the margin of error for this sort of back-of-an-envelope calculation. Whereas the time taken for a computer working randomly but with the constraint of *cumulative selection* to perform the same task is of the same order as humans ordinarily can understand, between 11 seconds and the time it takes to have lunch.

There is a big difference, then, between cumulative selection (in which each improvement, however slight, is used as a basis for future building), and single-step selection (in which each new "try" is a fresh one). If evolutionary progress had had to rely on single-step selection, it would never have got anywhere. If, however, there was any way in which the necessary conditions for *cumulative* selection could have been set up by the blind forces of nature, strange and wonderful might have been the consequences. As a matter of fact that is exactly what happened on this planet, and we ourselves are among the most recent, if not the strangest and most wonderful, of those consequences.

It is amazing that you can still read calculations like my haemoglobin calculation, used as though they constituted arguments *against* Darwin's theory. The people who do this, often expert in their own field, astronomy or whatever it may be, seem sincerely to believe that Darwinism explains living organization in terms of chance—"single-step selection"—alone. This belief, that Darwinian evolution is "random," is not merely false. It is

the exact opposite of the truth. Chance is a minor ingredient in the Darwinian recipe, but the most important ingredient is cumulative selection which is quintessentially *non*random. . . .

We have dealt with all the alleged alternatives to the theory of natural selection except the oldest one. This is the theory that life was created, or its evolution master-minded, by a conscious designer. It would obviously be unfairly easy to demolish some particular version of this theory such as the one (or it may be two) spelled out in Genesis. Nearly all peoples have developed their own creation myth, and the Genesis story is just the one that happened to have been adopted by one particular tribe of Middle Eastern herders. It has no more special status than the belief of a particular West African tribe that the world was created from the excrement of ants. All these myths have in common that they depend upon the deliberate intentions of some kind of supernatural being.

At first sight there is an important distinction to be made between what might be called "instantaneous creation" and "guided evolution." Modern theologians of any sophistication have given up believing in instantaneous creation. The evidence for some sort of evolution has become too overwhelming. But many theologians who call themselves evolutionists, for instance the Bishop of Birmingham quoted in Chapter 2, smuggle God in by the back door: they allow him some sort of supervisory role over the course that evolution has taken, either influencing key moments in evolutionary history (especially, of course, *human* evolutionary history), or even meddling more comprehensively in the day-to-day events that add up to evolutionary change.

We cannot disprove beliefs like these, especially if it is assumed that God took care that his interventions always closely mimicked what would be expected from evolution by natural selection. All that we can say about such beliefs is, firstly, that they are superfluous and, secondly, that they *assume* the existence of the main thing we want to *explain,* namely organized complexity. The one thing that makes evolution such a neat theory is that it explains how organized complexity can arise out of primeval simplicity.

If we want to postulate a deity capable of engineering all the organized complexity in the world, either instantaneously or by guiding evolution, that deity must already have been vastly complex in the first place. The creationist, whether a naive Bible-thumper or an educated bishop, simply *postulates* an already existing being of prodigious intelligence and complexity. If we are going to allow ourselves the luxury of postulating organized complexity without offering an explanation, we might as well make a job of it and simply postulate the existence of life as we know it! In short, divine creation, whether instantaneous or in the form of guided evolution, joins the list of other theories we have considered in this chapter. All give some superficial appearance of being alternatives to Darwinism, whose merits might be tested by an appeal to evidence. All turn out, on closer inspection, not to be rivals of Darwinism at all. The theory of evolution by cumulative natural selection is the only theory we know of that is in principle *capable* of explaining the existence of organized complexity. Even if the evidence did not favour it, it would *still* be the best theory available! In fact the evidence does favour it. But that is another story.

Let us hear the conclusion of the whole matter. The essence of life is statistical improbability on a colossal scale. Whatever is the explanation for life, therefore, it cannot be chance. The true explanation for the existence of life must embody the very antithesis of chance. The antithesis of chance is nonrandom survival, properly understood. Nonrandom survival, improperly understood, is not the antithesis of chance, it is chance itself. There is a continuum connecting these two extremes, and it is the continuum from single-step selection to cumulative selection. Single-step selection is just another way of saying pure chance. This is what I mean by nonrandom survival improperly understood. *Cumulative selection,* by slow and gradual degrees, is the explanation, the only workable explanation that has ever been proposed, for the existence of life's complex design.

The whole book has been dominated by the idea of chance, by the astronomically long odds against the spontaneous arising of order, complexity and apparent design. We have sought a way of taming chance, of drawing its fangs. "Untamed chance," pure, naked chance, means ordered design springing into existence from nothing, in a single leap. It would be untamed chance if once there was no eye, and then, suddenly, in the twinkling of a generation, an eye appeared, fully fashioned, perfect and whole. This is possible, but the odds against it will keep us busy writing noughts till the end of time. The same applies to the odds against the spontaneous existence of any fully fashioned, perfect and whole beings, including—I see no way of avoiding the conclusion—deities.

To "tame" chance means to break down the very improbable into less improbable small components arranged in series. No matter how improbable it is that an X could have arisen from a Y in a single step, it is always possible to conceive of a series of infinitesimally graded intermediates between them. However improbable a large-scale change may be, smaller changes are less improbable. And provided we postulate a sufficiently large series of sufficiently finely graded intermediates, we shall be able to derive anything from anything else, without invoking astronomical improbabilities. We are allowed to do this only if there has been sufficient time to fit all the intermediates in. And also only if there is a mechanism for guiding each step in some particular direction, otherwise the sequence of steps will career off in an endless random walk.

It is the contention of the Darwinian worldview that both these provisos are met, and that slow, gradual, cumulative natural selection is the ultimate explanation for our existence. If there are versions of the evolution theory that deny slow gradualism, and deny the central role of natural selection, they may be true in particular cases. But they cannot be the whole truth, for they deny the very heart of the evolution theory, which gives it the power to dissolve astronomical improbabilities and explain prodigies of apparent miracle.

12.5 The Mystery of Evil

Can you imagine the terror and physical suffering of the people killed or maimed in the attacks of 9/11? Can you imagine the continuing sorrow and suffering of those who lost loved ones in that tragedy? This example is but one of the many evils that plague human existence. Famine, disease, poverty, injustices of all sorts, torture, the Holocaust, slavery, rape, murder, earthquakes, floods — the list seems almost endless.

The **problem of evil** has many facets. In the *broad sense,* we are concerned with the problem of why evil exists. In the theological sense, the problem of evil involves the difficulties of harmonizing the existence of evil with the existence of a perfectly good, all-powerful, and all-knowing God who created the universe and governs it. If God is perfectly good, then God must not want evil things to happen to good people, and if God is all-powerful, God must be able to do something about evil. If God is the all-knowing creator and ruler of the world, then God must know about evil. So why do we experience evil? What good reason could God have for permitting the *kind* and *amount* of evil that exists in divinely created order?

When we consider suffering that appears to serve no good purpose, we can understand why Aquinas (see Section 12.2) began his presentation of the five arguments for God's existence by stating the argument from evil for the nonexistence of God. We can also understand why he closed that section of the *Summa Theologica* by asserting that because God is infinitely good and all-powerful, he can bring good "even out of evil." Ironically, the same divine qualities (perfect goodness and power) that contribute to the theological problem of evil in the first place also, at least for Aquinas, lead to a solution.

However, are there any really good solutions to the problem of evil? Can we find a plausible account that banishes the mystery of why evil exists and explains why God would permit evil to occur? Both the kind of evil in the world (intense seemingly pointless suffering) and the amount of evil raise severe problems for those who affirm that a perfectly good and powerful God governs the affairs of the universe.

Louis Pojman, professor of philosophy at the United States Military Academy, explains the problem of evil and critically examines some proposed solutions in the following reading. Pojman wants to get you to think about the problem and enter into the discussion of how, if at all, it might be solved.

Reading Questions

1. What paradox gives rise to the problem of evil?
2. What do process philosophers hold with respect to the claim that God is omnipotent and all-knowing? Why does Pojman reject their position?
3. What is the difference between moral and natural evil?
4. Why does Pojman reject the argument that "evil is the necessary counterpart to goodness"?
5. What is the free-will defense, and what is wrong with it?
6. What is the theodicy defense, and what are some problems with it?
7. How does evolution explain evil? In your view, is this a more reasonable explanation than theistic attempts to explain evil? Why, or why not?

The Problem of Evil

LOUIS P. POJMAN

Is he willing to prevent evil, but not able? Then he is impotent.

 Is he able, but not willing? Then he is malevolent.

 Is he both able and willing? Whence then is evil?

     —EPICURUS'S PARADOX

The Mystery of Evil

WHY IS THERE EVIL in the world? Why do bad things happen to good people? "The whole earth is cursed and polluted," says Philo in David Hume's (1711–1776) famous dialogue on natural religion. He continues:

> A perpetual war is kindled among all living creatures. Necessity, hunger, want, stimulate the strong and courageous; fear, anxiety, terror agitate the weak and infirm. The first entrance into life gives anguish to the new-born infant and to its wretched parent; weakness, impotence, distress attend each stage of that life, and it is, at last, finished in agony and horror. Man is the greatest enemy of man. Oppression, injustice, contempt, contumely, violence, sedition, war, calumny, treachery, fraud — by these they mutually torment each other, and they would soon dissolve that society which they had formed were it not for the dread of still greater ills which must attend their separation.

In Fyodor Dostoevsky's (1821–1881) *The Brothers Karamazov,* Ivan relates the following story to his religious brother Alyosha. There was an aristocratic Russian general who had two thousand serfs and hundreds of hunting dogs. One day an eight-year-old serf boy threw a stone in play and hurt the paw of the general's favorite hound. "Why is my favorite lame?" the general inquires. He is told that the boy threw a stone that hurt the dog's paw. "So you did it!" the general exclaimed and ordered the boy taken away from his mother and kept shut up all night.

Early the next morning, the general came out on horseback with his hounds, servants, and huntsmen all mounted, ready for a hunt. The eight-year-old boy is summoned from his cell, undressed. He shivers in the cold, numb with terror. "Make him run," commands the general. The boy runs. "At him!" yells the general, and he sets the pack of one hundred hounds loose. The hounds catch him and tear the boy to pieces before his mother's eyes.

Ivan cannot accept a world where such incidents occur. No amount of utility can justify the torture of a child. He cannot accept God's entrance ticket:

> And so I hasten to give back my entrance ticket, and if I am an honest man I am bound to give it back as soon as possible. . . . Tell me yourself, I challenge you. Imagine that you are creating a fabric of human destiny with the object of making men happy in the end, giving them peace and rest at last, but that it was essential and inevitable to torture to death only one tiny creature — that baby beating its breast with its fist, for instance — and to found that edifice on its unavenged tears, would you consent to be the architect on those conditions? Tell me, and tell me the truth.

. . . The agnostic and atheist usually base their case on the alleged unsoundness of the arguments for God's existence. But they have one arrow in their own quiver, an argument for disbelief. It is the problem of evil. From it the "atheologian" (one who argues against the existence of God) hopes either to neutralize any positive evidence for God's existence based on whatever in the traditional arguments survives their criticism or to demonstrate that it is unreasonable to believe in God. We will examine ways in which moral and natural evil are thought to provide evidence against the existence of a wholly

From Louis P. Pojman, Philosophy of Religion. *Mountain View, CA: Mayfield Publishing Company, 2001, pp. 67–79. Footnotes deleted.*

good, omnipotent God, including the argument from evolution, which provides an alternative explanatory account of evil. We shall also consider the two main defenses against the argument from evil: the free-will defense and the theodicy defense. But first let us examine the core argument from evil against the existence of God.

The Argument from Evil

The problem of evil arises because of the paradox, cited at the beginning of this chapter, presented by an omnibenevolent, omnipotent deity allowing the existence of evil. The Judeo-Christian tradition has affirmed these three propositions:

1. God is all-powerful (including omniscient).
2. God is perfectly good.
3. Evil exists.

But if God is perfectly good, why does he allow evil to exist? Why didn't he create a better world, if not with no evil, then at least with substantially less evil than in this world? Many have contended that this paradox, first schematized by Epicurus (341–270 B.C.), is worse than a paradox. It is an implicit contradiction, for it contains premises that are inconsistent with one another. They argue something like the following:

4. If God (an all-powerful, omniscient, omnibenevolent being) exists, there would be no (or no unnecessary) evil in the world.
5. There is evil (or unnecessary evil) in the world.
6. Therefore ∴ God does not exist. To see whether they are right, let us review each of the basic propositions that generate the paradox.

PROPOSITION I
God is all-powerful.

"God is all-powerful" has been a cornerstone of Christian theology since the early centuries of the Church. Although it is debatable whether one can show that the biblical writers had such a strong concept (or whether the exact formulation is derived from a Platonic and Aristotelian metaphysics), most Judeo-Christian theologians have seen it as entailed by any adequate view of deity. Some philosophers and theologians, such as John Stuart Mill, William James, Alfred North Whitehead, Charles Hartshorne, and John Cobb, have relinquished this attribute of omnipotence to get God "off the hook" with regard to evil. They accept a *limited* God. God is perfectly good and the greatest possible being, but not omnipotent or omniscient. He cannot do many things, nor does he know the future. They argue that if God knew the future, we would not be free to act, for his knowledge would determine the future. I think this is fallacious, for the epistemic domain does not affect ontological ones. My knowing that you will decide not to cheat on a test when you get a chance does not determine your decision not to cheat. Similarly, God could simply know how we will use our free will. Because he exists in eternity beyond time, it seems reasonable to suppose that he knows what we regard as the future without causing it. But these philosophers, called *process philosophers,* suppose that God's knowledge is somehow determining, so that it is reasonable to relinquish the claim of omniscience. God, like other finite beings, is still learning. But because he is neither all-powerful or all-knowing, he cannot eliminate all evil from the world. God simply does the best he can. Does this argument work? Many think that this is too desperate a move. Other critics point out that, even if God is not all-powerful, he certainly must be exceedingly powerful (and knowledgeable), and, if so, he should have been able to prevent evil (or most of the evil) in the world. On the other hand, if he is not so powerful, why do we call him "God" rather than "demiurge" and worship, instead, the *ideal* of moral goodness? This is not to say that such process theologians and philosophers do not have a case but that their case may not be any better than some of the alternative solutions. Many will find it too radical altogether.

Finally, when theists speak of God being omnipotent, they usually mean that God can do anything that is logically possible. God cannot make a stone heavier than he can lift, will that he never existed, or make $2 + 2 = 5$. This will be important with regard to the defense of theism from the charge of the atheologian.

PROPOSITION 2

God is perfectly good.

The Judeo-Christian, Muslim, and Hindu traditions all subscribe to the doctrine of complete divine benevolence. Take the property of benevolence from God, and what is the difference between God and a supreme devil? If mere power constitutes God's essence, why should we love and worship him? We might fear him, but he would hardly deserve our adoration or love. No, it is not mere power or knowledge but his complete goodness, his omnibenevolence, that makes God worthy of our worship. God cannot do evil and still remain God. All the major religions — Hinduism, Islam, Judaism, and Christianity — agree on this point. As the Psalmist exclaims, "Oh that men would praise the Lord for his goodness, and for his wonderful works to the children of men" (Psalms 107).

PROPOSITION 3

There is evil.

"There is evil" may be denied by some Eastern religions, which view it as an illusion, but the Judeo-Christian tradition has always taken it as a fundamental datum to be overcome, if not explained. Suffering and pain, disease and death, cruelty and violence, rape and murder, poverty and natural havoc have all been viewed as the enemy of the good. The millions of humans who have starved to death or died victims of torture, bloody battle, and brutal wars, the myriads who have been abandoned, abused, and aborted all testify to the tragedy of the human condition: Evil exists in abundance.

Generally, Western thought has distinguished between two types of evil: moral and natural. *Moral evil* covers all those bad things for which humans are morally responsible. *Natural evil,* or *surd (irrational) evil,* stands for all those terrible events that nature does of her own accord — for example, hurricanes, tornadoes, earthquakes, volcanic eruptions, and natural diseases, which bring suffering to humans and animals. However, some defenses of theism affirm that all evil is essentially moral evil. Here the devil is brought in as the cause of natural evil.

Sometimes students argue that evil is logically necessary for the good, so God could not remove all evil without removing all good. Evil is the necessary counterpart to goodness, as the tail of a coin is the necessary complement of the head of a coin. Without evil, there could not be good. This seems fallacious reasoning. A property need not have an actual opposite in order to exist, though we might not be able to appreciate the good without some contrasting experiences. First of all, Christian and Muslim doctrine has always taught that no evil exists in heaven, which is the paradigm of perfect goodness, so goodness apparently can exist without evil in these traditions. But even if we waive this point and concede the contrast to the counterpart theorist, this doesn't get him very far. For God could equip us with enormous imaginative powers, so that we can imagine great evil without really experiencing it. So although some people may not be able to appreciate the good without some evil, evil is not necessary to the good.

Let us turn to the two main defenses against the argument from evil. The first is the free-will defense.

The Free-Will Defense

The main defense of theism in the light of evil is the free-will defense, going back as far as St. Augustine (354–430) and receiving modern treatment in the works of John Hick, Alvin Plantinga, and Richard Swinburne. The free-will defense adds an additional premise (3A) to Epicurus's paradox in order to show that propositions 1 through 3 are consistent and not contradictory:

PROPOSITION 3A

It is logically impossible for God to create free creatures and guarantee that they will never do evil.

Because it is a good thing to create free creatures who are morally responsible agents, there is no assurance that they will not also do evil. Free agency is so important that it is worth the price of the evil it may cause or permit. As Plantinga puts it:

> God has actualized a possible world A containing significantly free creatures (angels, human beings, other kinds, what have you) with respect to whose actions there is a balance of good over evil (so that A on balance is a very good world); some of these creatures are responsible for moral and natural evil; and it was not within God's power to create significantly free creatures with respect to whose actions there would be a better balance of good over evil than that displayed in A.

Imagine that God viewed an infinite set of possible worlds. In some of them, he saw humans as not sinning but also not free. In some he saw humans as free and doing less evil than in this world, but he chose to create this world with its enormous amount of good and evil. Perhaps he could have created other worlds with more good or less evil, but he could not create a world with a lesser proportion of good over evil than this one has, and no world he could have created could have a better proportion of good over evil. This world, though not perfect, is the best an omnipotent, omnibenevolent God could do.

This defense assumes a libertarian view of freedom of the will. That is, humans are free to choose between good and evil acts. They are not caused (though they may be influenced) to do one deed rather than the other, but rather they are causally underdetermined. Given two identically similar situations with identical causal antecedents, an agent could do act A at one time and act B at the other. This view is opposed to determinism, as well as compatibilism (a view that tries to reconcile freedom of action with determinism). If you are committed to compatibilism or determinism, the free-will defense will not be effective against the argument from evil. The theologian Marilyn McCord Adams thinks that the free-will defense overestimates the level of free agency in humans. She holds that humans have diminished agency before God, analogous to a small child's ability to act freely against an adult, so that humans cannot be held responsible for the amount and quality of evil.

Many philosophers go even further than Adams and argue that metaphysical libertarianism is unsupported by any sound arguments. Every event in the world, including every action, is either the product of cause or chance. If the event is the result of mere chance, it is not a deliberative act for which we can be held accountable. On the other hand, if it is the effect of prior causes, we are not fully or strongly responsible for it — though we could be said to be responsible in a weak sense (we did the deed voluntarily).

If this is sound, then the problem with the free-will defense discussion is that the same arguments against libertarian freedom can be used to undermine or diminish divine agency. The crucial argument against libertarian free will and responsibility consists in a dilemma:

1. To be really free and responsible for our actions, we must be the cause of what we are (our states of mind).
2. No one is the cause of one's self. Not even God is *causa sui*.
3. So no one is really free and responsible.

As far as I can see, no one has explained what free will is (how it functions), let alone how it is possible. Roderick Chisholm calls it a mysterious *miracle*. Compatibilism, a form of *soft determinism*, toward which Adams seems to lean, may well be successful in reconciling determinism and responsibility, but this is not the robust kind of freedom needed for the free-will defense. The fact that I voluntarily do X makes me only the *proximate*, but not the *ultimate*, cause of X. Even my attitude of voluntariness is determined. But if God does not create himself, he is not free to do otherwise than he does. His actions are as causally determined as ours. Either he acts out of his basic character for determining reasons or he acts in an arbitrary manner. Either way, he is not omnipotent in the robust way the orthodox tradition supposes. Is there a way between the horns of this dilemma?

To return to the main issue, the proponent of the free-will defense claims that all moral evil derives from creature freedom of the will. But what about natural evil? How does the theist account for it? There are two different ways. The first one, favored by Plantinga and Stephen Davis, is to attribute natural evil to the work of the devil and his angels. Disease and tornadoes are caused by the devil and his minions. The second way, favored by Swinburne and Hick, argues that natural evil is part and parcel of the nature of things: a result of the combination of deterministic physical laws that are necessary for consistent action and the responsibility given to humans to exercise their freedom.

The Theodicy Defense

Whereas the free-will defense is concerned to show that Epicurus's original argument from evil is not decisive and that the problem of evil does not prove that God does not exist, the theodicy defense, first set forth by the German idealist Gottfried Wilhelm Leibniz (1646–1716), goes even further and argues that all evil will contribute to the greater good, so that this world, despite appearances, is the *best of all possible worlds*. The most prominent proponent of the theodicy defense is the British theologian John Hick.

Hick's thesis is particularly interesting because he endeavors to put forth a full-scale justification for God's permitting the evil in the world. Why does God allow natural evil and not normally intervene in either natural or moral evil? Hick answers: in order that human beings, as free responsible agents, may use this world as a place of "soul making," which involves the spiritual perfection of our character and persons. The skeptic errs in complaining about the recalcitrant structure of the world because he or she makes the assumption that God created humanity as a completed creation. The skeptic mistakenly thinks:

> that God's purpose in making the world was to provide a suitable dwelling-place for this fully-formed creature. Since God is good and loving, the environment which he has created for human life to inhabit is naturally as pleasant and comfortable as possible. The problem is essentially similar to that of a man who builds a cage for some pet animal. Since our world, in fact, contains sources of hardship, inconvenience,

and danger of innumerable kinds, the conclusion follows that this world cannot have been created by a perfectly benevolent and all-powerful deity.

Hick, drawing on the work of the second-century theologian Irenaeus, argues that humanity was made in the *image,* but not the *likeness,* of God. Incomplete beings, we must aim at full and perfect likeness. Our world, with all its rough edges and obstacles, "is the sphere in which this second and harder stage of the creative process is taking place."

Suppose that the world were a paradise, without the possibility of suffering, pain, and death. In that case, we would not be seriously accountable for our deeds:

> No one could ever injure anyone else; the murderer's knife would turn to paper or his bullets to thin air; the bank safe, robbed of a million dollars, would miraculously become filled with another million dollars; fraud, deceit, conspiracy, and treason would somehow always leave the fabric of society undamaged. . . . The reckless driver would never meet with disaster. There would be no need to work, since no harm could result from avoiding work; there would be no call to be concerned for others in time of need or danger, for in such a world there could be no real needs or dangers.

Our present ethical concepts would not apply in such a safe "playpen paradise"; concepts like courage, honesty, love, benevolence, and kindness would make no sense because no one could do any harm, nor would there be need for heroism or saintliness. Such a world would certainly promote pleasure, but it would be wholly inadequate for character development. But our world is not such a hedonistic romper room. It is a place where we must take full responsibility for our actions, for they have serious consequences. It is a place where we can and should develop our characters into the full likeness of God.

Problems with the Theodicy Defense

I will leave it to you to analyze Hick's challenging argument fully, but a few questions are in order. First, if this world with "the heartache, and the thousand natural shocks that flesh is heir to" is useful for suffering, couldn't a world with less suffering and evil than this one be adequate for the task? Were Auschwitz, My Lai, and Buchenwald and the torture chamber really necessary for soul building? While in training, astronauts are allowed to make mistakes, but built-in feedback mechanisms correct their mistakes before disaster sets in, while allowing the trainees to learn from their mistakes. Couldn't God have given us free will, allowed us to learn from our mistakes, and still constructed a world in which feedback mechanisms prevented the kind of monstrous disasters that occur around the world every day? Hick's theodicy may overestimate human capacity to use evil for good. It also seems inefficient. Why could God not aid us in our soul building without resorting to horrendous evils, perhaps in the way that astronauts are trained? A good teacher can educate and help build character without resorting to torture and brutality.

With or without the free-will defense, many philosophers maintain that the problem of evil still persists. Some, like J. L. Mackie and William Rowe, contend that the burden of proof is on the theist to explain why God does not intervene in the suffering of the world. If, by the mere pressing of a button, I could have caused Hitler to have had a heart attack before starting World War II, I would have been obliged to do so. Why did God not intervene in 1939 and prevent the evil of World War II, including the Holocaust? Why didn't he intervene in the event, described by Dostoevsky, in which the mad general set his hounds on the eight-year-old boy? Why does he not intervene in the sufferings of millions all over the world? Perhaps some evil is impossible to prevent, but why is there so much of it? Couldn't an all-knowing God have foreseen the evil in this world and created one in which people do not commit the amount of evil that occurs in our world? Couldn't he have seen another possible world in which humans are free but do much better than we do? Couldn't he have created a world with less natural evil, with less gratuitous pain in humans and animals? Couldn't an all-powerful, all-knowing deity do

better than this? We could formulate the argument this way:

1. A morally good being will eliminate evil as much as possible unless he has good reason to allow it.
2. If there is evil in the world, God must have a good reason to allow it.
3. There is evil in the world.
4. Therefore ∴ God must have a good reason for allowing evil.

But the atheologian points out that even if God has such a reason, unless he communicates it to us, we are not in the epistemic position to appreciate that reason, and hence in no position to believe that he has a sufficient reason to allow seemingly gratuitous evil. If God does not intervene in human and animal suffering, don't we have grounds to suspect that he doesn't exist, doesn't care, or is severely limited? Or perhaps God is not omnibenevolent, but only partly good and partly bad? If this is sound, the problem of evil seems to be a strong argument against belief in the God of classical theism.

Of course, theists counter each of these objections. Some, we have noted, maintain that God is not all-powerful but limited in what he can do. Others argue that it is simply a mystery why God, although all-powerful, doesn't intervene to prevent more evil than he does. How do we know that he hasn't prevented much more evil than there is? Or perhaps in heaven there will be due recompense for the suffering here on Earth. Perhaps the lesson of evil is to show us just how serious our moral responsibilities are. Why blame God for evil, when it is we humans who are producing it?

With regard to natural evil (e.g., genetic deformities, diseases, earthquakes, and volcanic eruptions that kill innocent people), the theist argues that this is simply part of an orderly process of nature. The laws of nature are necessarily such that the good is interconnected with the bad. The same rain that causes one farmer's field to germinate floods and ruins another farmer's field. Although there are, no doubt, limits to the amount of evil God will allow, he cannot constantly intervene without eroding human responsibility or the laws of nature. Where those limits of evil are, not one of us can know. And yet we wonder. Couldn't an all-powerful God have created a better world than this, a world with a significantly greater proportion of good over evil?

Finally, theists argue that in heaven God will thank us for enduring the evil we have suffered and compensate us for it. The lame will walk with special ability and the blind see with acuity. This thesis rests on the coherence and plausibility of the notion of survival in an afterlife. . . . I must leave you to deliberate on how the debate should continue, but there is one more argument from evil that we should consider before leaving the topic — that is the argument from evolution.

Evolution and Evil

. . . [W]hen discussing the argument from design, theists may have good reason to fear evolutionary theory and support creationist accounts of the origin of life and human beings, for evolution proposes a radical alternative paradigm to a theistic, purposive creation. This point can now be employed to undermine theism with regard to evil. Evolution holds that evil is not the result of Satan's sin or Adam's fall or human misuse of free will but rather the consequence of the species developing adaptive strategies that tend to be accompanied by pain, suffering, unhappiness, and conflicts of interest, the major categories of evil. It is our evolution first from nonsentient to sentient beings that enables us to experience pain. Pain serves as a warning mechanism, but extreme contingencies can utilize the capacity for no protective reason. The sensation of pain may cause us to withdraw our hand from a fire, but being immolated in a burning building or funeral pyre serves no warning purpose at all and seems entirely gratuitous. Much of our physical suffering is simply the failure of evolution's adaptive strategies. For example, bipedalism, the ability to walk upright on two limbs, enables "higher" primates, including humans, to free up their forelimbs for other purposes, like grasping and thrusting, but it incurs several liabilities — including the loss of speed of its quadrupedal ancestors, an imbalanced vertebral column, which increases the likelihood of lower back pain, troublesome birth pangs, and even stomach problems and herniation, as the center of balance shifts and more pressure is placed on the abdominal region. On a more local scale, sickle-shaped red blood cells are adaptive in areas in which malaria is rampant, but where it is not, they are lethal: Children born with sickle-cell anemia have only one-fifth the chance of other children of surviving to maturity. Similarly, human aggression may be adaptive in hunting and defending oneself against predators, but in social groups, in the face of conflicts of interest, it tends to be maladaptive, causing suffering, injury, and death. Use of reason is necessary for social cooperation and coexistence, but the instincts of our ancestor species are more reliable and efficient. Reason leads to institutions such as morality and law, which are necessary for civilization but create their own liabilities in terms of guilt, shame, litigation, and frustration. No lion deliberates as to whether he should kill an antelope or copulate with an available lioness, nor are his forays followed by guilt or remorse. He enjoys his conquests without worrying about whether he has violated antelope rights. He simply follows his instincts and usually gets away with it.

The point is not that we should go back to the state of the "noble savage." We couldn't, even if we tried. The point I'm trying to make is that each evolutionary adaptive strategy tends to incur a loss of some other virtue or capability, and this is what accounts for evil. What we call evil is simply part of the natural evolutionary process, which, as Tennyson pointed out, "is red in tooth and claw." Much, if not most, of moral or manmade evil is the "unintended" result of nature's making us creatures with insatiable wants but limited resources and sympathies.

This evolutionary account of the origins of evil fits within the broader framework of human biology and animal ethology. To that extent it is confirmable by scientific research, whereas the religious accounts of the origin of evil have less impressive credentials. How do we recreate or confirm the record of the fall of Adam and Eve? The naturalistic account holds that we don't need myths or dogmas about the fall or original sin. Simply investigating evolutionary processes of adaptation is sufficient as an explanation for our greatest problems. Evil has a biological basis, being simply the inextricable concomitant of characteristics that served an adaptive function.

The theist has responses to this account of evil. She may either reject evolution in favor of a creationist account or absorb the evolutionary account within a theistic framework. The first strategy seems a lost cause, because evolution is supported by all we know about animal biology and genetics. The second strategy is more promising, but it is haunted by problems of explaining why God wasn't more efficient and benevolent in developing the species. Couldn't he have avoided the waste (sacrificing the millions of less fit individuals and species) and done things more benevolently — for example, made carnivorous animals herbivores and so avoided the predator–prey cycle of death and destruction?

So the problem of evil persists in haunting theism, and theists continue to devise strategies to ward off the attacks. On which side do the best reasons lie?

Summary

The problem of evil has to do with three propositions that, at first glance, seem incompatible: God's benevolence, God's omnipotence, and evil in the world. Why did an all-powerful and omnibenevolent God permit evil in the first place, and, once established, why did he not eliminate it? The theist generally replies that it is better that God creates free beings who sin but who can be redeemed than for God to create a paradise in which only automatons mechanically do good. John Hick provides a second argument in terms of evil being necessary for soul building, so that humans may perfect themselves by developing into full spiritual beings, into the likeness of God. The skeptic objects to both of these proposals, arguing that it is implausible to suppose that an all-powerful, omnibenevolent God couldn't do better than make a world with this much evil in it.

Finally, we noted how an evolutionary explanation of the origins of evil competes with a theological account. Not Adam's fall but the evolution of the species is the best explanation of evil in the world.

12.6 The Gender of God

There is an old story about the reporter who was granted an interview with God. When the reporter returned, people eagerly asked, "Well, tell us. What is God like?"

"You will have to wait until I write my article," the reporter replied, "but I can tell you this much, she is black."

The punch line makes us smile because it is unexpected. But why is it unexpected? Why shouldn't God be female and black?

We have all been raised with certain images of God and the dominant one in Western culture has been the image of a white male (usually old and bearded!). Although the arguments for God's existence make no mention of God's sex, many who read the arguments undoubtedly imagine a male deity as the reference of these arguments. How many of you, as you read the arguments and read the word *God* thought of a male deity? If you did, you can understand how these arguments reinforce, perhaps unconsciously and unintentionally, the idea that masculinity is creative, powerful, perfect, and intelligent.

Mary Daly, professor of theology at Boston College until her forced retirement because of a controversy about allowing males to take some of her classes, understands the goal of Christianity as the liberation of all humans. She thinks that traditional Christian images of God as Father do not promote the liberation of females. Therefore, she argues, we must get beyond the notion of God as Father. In the introduction to the book from which this selection is taken (a book that has become a classic statement in the field), she sets forth her presuppositions as follows:

1. Women exist in a sexual "caste" system subordinate to and dominated by men.
2. Sex-role socialization perpetuates this system by convincing women to accept their "inferior" status and men to accept their "superior" status.
3. Women's lower status is disguised by sex-role segregation ("women are 'equal' but different") and by providing them derivative status as a consequence of their relationships with men (Mr. and *Mrs. John* Gibbons).
4. Judaism, Christianity, and Islam (to mention only three of the major world religions) have helped maintain women's subordination to men by their teachings about marriage, reproduction, and the roles women can assume in their respective religious organizations.
5. People try to avoid acknowledging the issue of sexual caste by trivializing it ("After all there are more important issues, like war or racism"), by particularizing it ("It's a problem for Muslims or Hindus or Jews, but not for Christians"), or by universalizing it ("The real problem is *human* liberation, so let's concentrate on that").

Daly's purpose is to show that the women's movement is a "spiritual revolution" that points us beyond the idolatries of a sexist society and religion. Her method, she writes, derives from the Biblical insight that "to exist humanly is to name the self, the world, and God. The method of evolving spiritual consciousness of women is nothing less than this beginning to speak humanly—reclaiming of the right to name. The liberation of language is rooted in the liberation of ourselves." For Daly, feminism is the attempt to gain equal opportunity and status for women. She does *not* believe God causes sexism, but she does believe human symbols and concepts of God have reinforced sexism.

Daly is not concerned with arguments for God's existence. Rather she is concerned with what humans think about the nature of God and how they conceptualize God. We express our concepts in language, so God-talk becomes a natural focus for those who would argue, as Daly does, that our ordinary concepts of God are sexist.

Reading Questions

1. How has the symbol of God as Father rendered service to male-dominated (patriarchal) societies?
2. How does Daly respond to the criticism that the liberation of women will not basically change the structures, ideologies, and values of society?
3. What are the differences between the masculine and the feminine stereotypes?
4. What do you think Daly means by "androgynous human persons"?
5. What is inadequate about popular preaching about God?
6. Why won't calling God "she" and stressing God's maternal qualities help the situation?
7. Why does the women's revolution even need to speak about God at all?
8. How does Daly interpret the "image of God"?
9. Who are the false deities (idols), and why are they false? Do you agree with Daly that there are false images of God? Why, or why not?
10. What are some of the important implications of Daly's argument?

Beyond God the Father

MARY DALY

> The first step in the elevation of women under all systems of religion is to convince them that the great Spirit of the Universe is in no way responsible for any of these absurdities.
>
> —Elizabeth Cady Stanton

THE BIBLICAL AND POPULAR image of God as a great patriarch in heaven, rewarding and punishing according to his mysterious and seemingly arbitrary will, has dominated the imagination of millions over thousands of years. The symbol of the Father God, spawned in the human imagination and sustained as plausible by patriarchy, has in turn rendered service to this type of society by making its mechanisms for the oppression of women appear right and fitting. If God in "his" heaven is a father ruling "his" people, then it is in the "nature" of things and according to divine plan and the order of the universe that society be male-dominated.

Within this context a mystification of roles takes place: the husband dominating his wife represents God "himself." The images and values of a given society have been projected into the realm of dogmas and "Articles of Faith," and these in turn justify the social structures which have given rise to them and which sustain their plausibility. The belief system becomes hardened and objectified, seeming to have an unchangeable independent existence and validity of its own. It resists social change that would rob it of its plausibility. Despite the vicious circle, however, change can occur in society, and ideologies can die, though they die hard.

As the women's movement begins to have its effect upon the fabric of society, transforming it from patriarchy into something that never existed before—into a diarchal situation that is radically new—it can become the greatest single challenge to the major religions of the world, Western and Eastern. Beliefs and values that have held sway for thousands of years will be questioned as never before. This revolution may well be also the greatest single hope for survival of spiritual consciousness on this planet.

The Challenge: Emergence of Whole Human Beings

There are some who persist in claiming that the liberation of women will only mean that new characters will assume the same old roles, and that nothing will change essentially in structures, ideologies, and values. This supposition is often based on the observation that the very few women in "masculine" occupations often behave much as men do. This kind of reasoning is not at all to the point, for it fails to take into account the fact that tokenism does not change stereotypes or social systems but works to preserve them, since it dulls the revolutionary impulse. The minute proportion of women in the United States who occupy such roles (such as senators, judges, business executives, doctors, etc.) have been trained by men in institutions defined and designed by men, and they have been pressured subtly to operate according to male rules. There are no alternate models. As sociologist Alice Rossi has suggested, this is not what the women's movement in its most revolutionary potential is all about.

What *is* to the point is an emergence of woman-consciousness such as has never before taken place. It is unimaginative and out of touch with what is happening in the women's movement to assume that the becoming of women will simply mean uncritical acceptance of structures, beliefs, symbols, norms, and patterns of behavior that have been given priority by society under male domination. Rather, this becoming will act as catalyst for radical change in our culture. It has been argued cogently by Piaget that structure is maintained by an interplay of transformation laws that never yield results beyond the system and never tend to employ elements external to the system. This is indicative of what *can* effect basic alteration in the system, that is, a potent influence *from without*. Women who reject patriarchy have this power and indeed *are* this power of transformation that is ultimately threatening to things as they are.

The roles and structures of patriarchy have been developed and sustained in accordance with an artificial polarization of human qualities into the traditional sexual stereotypes. The image of the person in authority and the accepted understanding of "his" role has corresponded to the eternal masculine stereotype, which implies hyperrationality (in reality, frequently reducible to pseudo-rationality), "objectivity," aggressivity, the possession of dominating and manipulative attitudes toward persons and the environment, and the tendency to construct boundaries between the self (and those identified with the self) and "the Other." The caricature of human being which is represented by this stereotype depends for its existence upon the opposite caricature—the eternal feminine. This implies hyperemotionalism, passivity, self-abnegation, etc. By becoming whole persons women can generate a counterforce to the stereotype of the leader, challenging the artificial polarization of human characteristics into sex-role identification. There is no reason to assume that women who have the support of each other to criticize not only the feminine stereotype but the masculine stereotype as well will simply adopt the latter as a model for ourselves. On the contrary, what is happening is that women are developing a wider range of qualities and skills. This is beginning to encourage and in fact demand a comparably liberating process in men—a phenomenon which has begun in men's liberation groups and which is taking place every day within the context of personal relationships. The becoming of androgynous human persons implies a radical change in the fabric of human consciousness and in styles of human behavior.

This change is already threatening the credibility of the religious symbols of our culture. Since many of these have been used to justify oppression, such a challenge should be seen as redemptive. Religious symbols fade and die when the cultural situation that gave rise to them and supported them ceases to give them plausibility. Such an event generates anxiety, but it is part of the risk involved in a faith which accepts the relativity of all symbols and recognizes that clinging to these as fixed and ultimate is self-destructive and idolatrous.

The becoming of new symbols is not a matter that can be decided arbitrarily around a conference table. Rather, symbols grow out of a changing communal situation and experience. This does not mean that we are confined to the role of passive spectators. The experience of the becoming of women cannot be understood merely conceptually and abstractly but through active participation in the overcoming of servitude. Both activism and creative thought flow from and feed into the evolving woman-consciousness. The cumulative effect is a surge of awareness beyond the symbols and doctrines of patriarchal religion.

The Inadequate God of Popular Preaching

The image of the divine Father in heaven has not always been conducive to humane behavior, as any perceptive reader of history knows. The often cruel behavior of Christians toward unbelievers and toward dissenters among themselves suggests a great deal not only about the values of the society dominated by that image, but also about how that image itself functions in relation to behavior. There has been a basic ambivalence in the image of the heavenly patriarch—a split between the God of love and the jealous God who represents the collective power of "his" chosen people. As historian Arnold Toynbee has indicated, this has reflected and perpetuated a double standard of behavior. Without debating the details of his historical analysis, the insight is available on an experiential level. The character of Vito Corleone in *The Godfather* is a vivid illustration of the marriage of tenderness and violence so intricately blended in the patriarchal ideal. The worshippers of the loving Father may in a sense love their neighbors, but in fact the term applies only to those within a restricted and unstable circumference, and these worshippers can "justifiably" be intolerant and fanatic persecutors of those outside the sacred circle.

How this God operates is illustrated in contemporary American civil religion. In one of the White House sermons given during the first term of Richard Nixon, Rabbi Louis Finkelstein expressed the hope that a future historian may say "that in the period of great trials and great tribulations, the finger of God pointed to Richard Milhous Nixon, giving the vision and the wisdom to save the world and civilization; and also to open the way for our country to realize the good that the twentieth century offers mankind." Within this context, as Charles Henderson has shown, God is an American and Nixon is "his" anointed one. The preachers carefully selected for the White House sermons stress that this nation is "under God." The logical conclusion is that its politics are right. Under God, the President becomes a Christ figure. In 1969, the day the astronauts would set foot on the moon, and when the President was preparing to cross the Pacific "in search of peace," one of these preachers proclaimed:

> And my hope for mankind is strengthened in the knowledge that our intrepid President himself will soon go into orbit, reaching boldly for the moon of peace. God grant that he, too, may return in glory and that countless millions of prayers that follow him shall not have been in vain.

A fundamental dynamic of this "theology" was suggested by one of Nixon's speech writers, Ray Price, who wrote:

> Selection of a President has to be an act of faith. . . . This faith isn't achieved by reason: it's achieved by charisma, by a feeling of trust. . . .

Price also argued that the campaign would be effective only "if we can get people to make the *emotional* leap, or what theologians call 'leap of faith.'" This is, of course, precisely the inauthentic leap that Camus labeled as philosophical suicide. It is the suicide demanded by a civil religion in which "God," the Savior-President, and "our nation" more or less merge. When the "leap" is made, it is possible simply not to see what the great God-Father and his anointed one are actually doing. Among the chosen ones are scientists and professors who design perverse methods of torture and death such as flechette pellets that shred the internal organs of "the enemy" and other comparable inhumane "antipersonnel" weapons. Also among the elect are politicians and priests who justify and bestow their blessing upon the system that perpetrates such atrocities. "Under God" are included the powerful industrialists who are making the planet uninhabitable.

Sophisticated thinkers, of course, have never intellectually identified God with a Superfather in heaven. Nevertheless it is important to recognize that even when very abstract conceptualizations of God are formulated in the mind, images survive in the imagination in such a way that a person can function on two different and even apparently contradictory levels at the same time. Thus one can speak of God as spirit and at the same time imagine "him" as belonging to the male sex. Such primitive images can profoundly affect conceptualizations which appear to be very refined and abstract. So too the Yahweh of the future, so cherished by the theology of hope, comes through on an imaginative level as exclusively a He-God, and it is consistent with this that theologians of hope have attempted to develop a political theology which takes no explicit cognizance of the devastation wrought by sexual politics.

The widespread conception of the "Supreme Being" as an entity distinct from this world but controlling it according to plan and keeping human beings in a state of infantile subjection has been a not too subtle mask of the divine patriarch. The Supreme Being's plausibility and that of the static worldview which accompanies this projection has of course declined, at least among the more sophisticated, as Nietzsche prophesied. This was a projection grounded in specifically patriarchal societal structures and sustained as subjectively real by the usual processes of producing plausibility such as preaching, religious indoctrination, and cult. The sustaining power of the social structure has been eroded by a number of developments in recent history, including the general trend toward democratization of society and the emergence of technology. However, it is the women's movement which appears destined to play the key role in the overthrow of such oppressive elements in traditional theism, precisely because it strikes at the source of the societal dualism that is reflected in traditional beliefs. It presents a growing threat to the plausibility of the inadequate popular "God" not so much by attacking "him" as by leaving "him" behind. Few major feminists display great interest in institutional religion. Yet this disinterest can hardly be equated with lack of spiritual consciousness. Rather, in our present experience the woman-consciousness is being wrenched free to find its own religious expression.

It can legitimately be pointed out that the Judeo-Christian tradition is not entirely bereft of elements that can foster intimations of transcendence. Yet the liberating potential of these elements is choked off in the surrounding atmosphere of the images, ideas, values, and structures of patriarchy. The social change coming from radical feminism has the potential to bring about a more acute and widespread perception of qualitative differences between the conceptualizations of "God" and of the human relationship to God which have been oppressive in their connotations, and the kind of language that is spoken from and to the rising woman-consciousness.

Castrating "God"

I have already suggested that if God is male, then the male is God. The divine patriarch castrates women as long as he is allowed to live on in the human imagination. The process of cutting away the Supreme Phallus can hardly be a merely "rational" affair. The problem is one of transforming the collective imagination so that this distortion of the human aspiration to transcendence loses its credibility.

Some religious leaders, notably Mary Baker Eddy and Ann Lee, showed insight into the problem to some extent and tried to stress the "maternal" aspect of what they called "God." A number of feminists have referred to "God" as "she." While all of this has a point, the analysis has to reach a deeper level. The most basic change has to take place in women—in our being and self-image. Otherwise there is danger of settling for mere reform, reflected in the phenomenon of "crossing," that is, of attempting to use the oppressor's weapons against him. Black theology's image of the Black God illustrates this. It can legitimately be argued that a transsexual operation upon "God," changing "him" to "her," would be a far more profound alteration than a mere pigmentation change. However, to stop at this level of discourse would be a trivialization of the deep problem of human becoming in women. . . .

Why Speak About "God"?

It might seem that the women's revolution should just go about its business of generating a new consciousness, without worrying about God. I suggest that the fallacy involved in this would be an overlooking of a basic question that is implied in human existence and that the pitfall in such an oversight is cutting off the radical potential of the movement itself.

It is reasonable to take the position that sustained effort toward self-transcendence requires keeping alive in one's consciousness the question of ultimate transcendence, that is, of God. It implies recognition of the fact that we have no power *over* the ultimately real, and that whatever authentic power we have is derived from *participation in* ultimate reality. This awareness, always hard to sustain, makes it possible to be free of idolatry even in regard to one's own cause, since it tells us that all presently envisaged goals, life-styles, symbols, and societal structures may be transitory. This is the meaning that the question of God should have for liberation, sustaining a concern that is really open to the future, in other words, that is really ultimate. Such a concern will not become fixated upon limited objectives. Feminists in the past have in a way been idolatrous about such objectives as the right to vote. Indeed, this right is due to women in justice and it is entirely understandable that feminists' energies were drained by the efforts needed to achieve even such a modicum of justice. But from the experience of such struggles we are in a position now to distrust token victories within a societal and structural framework that renders them almost meaningless. The new wave of feminism desperately needs to be not only many faceted but cosmic and ultimately religious in its vision. This means reaching outward and inward toward the God beyond and beneath the gods who have stolen our identity.

The idea that human beings are "to the image of God" is an intuition whose implications could hardly be worked through under patriarchal conditions. If it is true that human beings have projected "God" in their own image, it is also true that we can evolve beyond the projections of earlier stages of consciousness. It is the creative potential itself in human beings that is the image of God. As the essential victims of the archaic God-projections, women can bring this process of creativity into a new phase. This involves iconoclasm—the breaking of idols. Even—and perhaps especially—through the activity of its most militantly atheistic and areligious members, the movement is smashing images that obstruct the becoming of the image of God. The basic idol-breaking will be done on the level of internalized images of male superiority, on the plane of exorcising them from consciousness and from the cultural institutions that breed them.

One aspect of this expurgation is dethronement of false Gods—ideas and symbols of God that religion has foisted upon the human spirit (granted that the human spirit has created the religions that do this). I have already discussed this to some extent, but it might be well to focus specifically upon three false deities who still haunt the prayers, hymns, sermons, and religious education of Christianity. The three usurpers I have in mind have already been detected and made the targets of attack by liberal male theologians, but the point in mentioning them here is to indicate the specific relevance of feminism to their demise.

One of the false deities to be dethroned is the God of explanation, or "God as a stop-gap for the incompleteness of our knowledge," as Bonhoeffer called him. This serves sometimes as the legitimation of anomic occurrences such as the suffering of a child, a legitimation process which Peter Berger lucidly analyzes in discussing the problem of theodicy. Such phenomena are "explained" as being God's will. So also are socially prevailing inequalities of power and privilege, by a justifying process which easily encourages masochistic attitudes. Clearly, this deity does not encourage commitment to the task of analyzing and eradicating the social, economic, and psychological roots of suffering. As marginal beings who are coming into awareness, women are in a situation to see that "God's plan" is often a front for men's plans and a cover for inadequacy, ignorance, and evil. Our vantage point offers opportunities for dislodging this deity from its revered position on the scale of human delusions.

Another idol is the God of otherworldliness. The most obvious face of this deity in the past has been that of the Judge whose chief activity consists in rewarding and punishing after death. As de Beauvoir indicated, women have been the major consumers of this religious product. Since there has been so little self-realization possible by the female sex "in this life," it was natural to focus attention on the next. As mass consumers of this image, women have the power to remove it from the market, mainly by living full lives here and now. I do not mean to advocate a mere re-utterance of the "secularization" theology that was so popular in the sixties. This obvious shape of the God of otherworldliness has after all been the target of male theologians for some time, and the result has often been a kind of translation of religion into humanism to such an extent that there is a kind of "self-liquidation of theology." What I see beginning to happen with women coming into their own goes beyond this secularization. The rejection of the simplistic God of otherworldliness does not mean necessarily reduction to banal secularism. If women can sustain the courage essential to liberation this can give rise to a deeper "otherworldliness"—an awareness that the process of creating a counter-world to the counterfeit "this world" presented to consciousness by the societal structures that oppress us is participation in eternal life.

It should be noted that the God lurking behind some forms of Protestant piety has functioned similarly to the otherworldly God of popular Roman Catholic piety. In his analysis of the effects of Luther's doctrine of salvation by faith alone, Max Weber uncovers serious problems of ethical motivation, involving a complicated series of phenomena: "Every rational and planned procedure for achieving salvation, every reliance on good works, and above all every effort to surpass normal ethical behavior by ascetic achievement is regarded by religion based on faith as a wicked preoccupation with purely human powers." Transworldly asceticism and monasticism tend to be rejected when salvation by faith is stressed, and as a result there may be an increased emphasis upon vocational activity within the world. However, as Weber explains, emphasis upon personal religious relationship to God tends to be accompanied by an attitude of individualism in pursuit of such worldly vocational activity. One consequence is an attitude of patient resignation

regarding institutional structures, both worldly and churchly. It is precisely this schizophrenic attitude that combines personal vocational ambition within the prevailing set of social arrangements and passive acceptance of the system that radical feminism recognizes as destructive.

A third idol, intimately related to those described above, is the God who is the Judge of "sin," who confirms the rightness of the rules and roles of the reigning system, maintaining false consciences and self-destructive guilt feelings. Women have suffered both mentally and physically from this deity, in whose name they have been informed that birth control and abortion are unequivocally wrong, that they should be subordinate to their husbands, that they must be present at rituals and services in which men have all the leadership roles and in which they are degraded not only by enforced passivity but also verbally and symbolically. Although this is most blatant in the arch-conservative religions, the God who imposes false guilt is hardly absent from liberal Protestantism and Judaism, where his presence is more subtle. Women's growth in self-respect will deal the death blow to this as well as to the other demons dressed as Gods.

12.7 Are All Religions True?

Suppose there were only one religion in the world. Let's call it the religion of Bliss. Suppose further that most people were Blissians. They participated in its rituals and conducted their lives, for the most part, according to its teachings. There were some dissenters, some anti-Blissians, but very few.

One consequence of this imaginary situation would probably be that the teachings of Bliss would seem true. There would be no real alternatives, no other religions teaching different doctrines or disputing the truth of Bliss. No one would have to worry about what attitude to take toward rival religions. It would not be necessary. Blissians would have a monopoly on religious truth.

We do not live in such a world. Instead we live in a world with diverse religious traditions that have been and are in conflict. We cannot avoid contact with people of other faiths and the very existence of such religious pluralism calls into question the truth of each. In the diverse religious world in which we live, we must develop some view about how our religion, if we profess one, relates to the others.

One possibility is to claim that only members of our religion will be saved because only our religion teaches the true path to salvation. Truth belongs to us exclusively. Another possibility is to claim that, although other religions teach some truth and although others can be saved, *our* religion teaches the *full* truth. It is the fulfillment of what the others have only dimly glimpsed. This sort of *inclusivism* seems more charitable than the *exclusive* attitude, but it is not as charitable as a third possibility, which is often called *pluralism*. According to pluralism, all religions are valid paths to salvation.

If we adopt a pluralistic attitude, we need some sort of explanation of why the teachings of all these valid religions appear so different and often seem to conflict. One possibility is to argue that the differences are real but relate to trivial matters. On important issues there is basic agreement. Another possibility is to argue that the differences are not real but apparent. On the surface the different religions seem to contradict each other, but when properly understood, they do not. Or one might admit that these are real differences, even on important matters, but claim that these differences do not affect the salvific value of each of the great traditions.

In addition to the attitudes of exclusivism, inclusivism, and pluralism, one might argue that today religions interpenetrate one another. Religions no longer exist isolated from one another, but in mutual relationship. What others believe and do helps us to better understand our own religions.

We live, as it were, in a religious supermarket with competing brand names and products. Suppose we are shopping. How do we decide what to buy? Do we judge all the other religions by the standards of our own religion? Do we judge the other religions by their own standards? Do we develop some neutral set of rational criteria that allow us to judge impartially and fairly the truth claims of each?

Perhaps this whole business of judging the truth of other religions is misguided. Perhaps it simply cannot be done or, even if it could, it misses the point. Perhaps we should concentrate on cooperation among the various religions on important moral and social issues, like helping the poor and stopping violence and war.

Maybe the question, "Are all religions true?" is misleading. It is certainly ambiguous. Does it mean that the teachings of the various religions are true? Does it mean that the rituals and rites practiced by the various religions are effective? Does it mean that the social organizations of the various religions are conducive to building community? If we restrict its meaning only to the teachings, does the question mean that before a religion is true all (every single one) of its teachings (however trivial) must be true? Further, the question seems to presuppose that there is some sort of religious truth that humans are capable of discovering. Perhaps there is no such thing as objective, absolute truth. What we call "truth" is nothing more than human constructions and conventions that reflect cultural values and biases. Perhaps truth is localized and relative to particular historical periods. After all, many different religions and societies have managed to flourish and survive on this planet while responding to the problems of human existence in very different ways. Perhaps what works for each is the only truth there is.*

John B. Cobb, Jr., the author of the next selection, is Ingraham Professor at the Claremont School of Theology and Avery Professor of Religion at the Claremont Graduate School. Along with Masao Abe, he organized the Buddhist-Christian Theological Encounter and has written extensively on issues relating to religious

* This introductory material comes from Gary E. Kessler, *Philosophy of Religion: Toward a Global Perspective.* Belmont, CA: Wadsworth Publishing Company, 1999, pp. 529–530. Copyright © 1999 by Wadsworth Publishing Company. Reprinted by permission.

dialogue. In Chapter 1 we spoke about the importance of philosophical dialogue among different traditions for enlarging our vision of what might be true and for overcoming the dilemma posed by the impasse between foundationalism and constructivism. Professor Cobb touches on some of these themes in the context of religious dialogue. We can learn from others, but only if we respect the differences between ourselves and others who think differently.

Reading Questions

1. Why does Cobb reject the idea that there is an essence to religion, and how does that rejection relate to the value and validity of different religious traditions?
2. What are the two modes of evaluation of religious traditions?
3. How can the alternatives of essentialism and conceptual relativism be overcome?
4. What "relatively objective" norm can be used to evaluate religious traditions from an external point of view?
5. In what ways have the Chinese, Hindu, and Buddhist traditions opened themselves to other religions, and how, according to Cobb, might the Christian tradition open itself to other religious traditions?
6. Why does Cobb think that trying to sort out conflicting religious claims to truth by determining which are true and which are false is not "the most productive approach"?
7. Briefly summarize Cobb's argument in your own words and evaluate it. Is it a good argument? Why, or why not?

Beyond Pluralism

JOHN B. COBB, JR.

I DECLINED TO WRITE A PAPER for the conference that led to the publication of the book, *The Myth of Christian Uniqueness,* because I did not share in the consensus that conference was supposed to express and promote. In the minds of the organizers, that consensus was to be around the view that the several major religions are, for practical purposes, equally valid ways of embodying what religion is all about. The uniqueness that is rejected is any claim that Christianity achieves something fundamentally different from other religions. From my point of view, the assumptions underlying these formulations are mistaken and have misled those who have accepted them.

Probably the most basic assumption is that there is an essence of religion. This essence is thought to be both a common characteristic of all "religions" and their central or normative feature. Hence, once it is decided that Buddhism, Confucianism, or Christianity is a religion, one knows what it is all about and how it is to be evaluated. The next step is then the one about which the consensus was to be formed. Given the common essence, let us agree to acknowledge that it is realized and expressed more or less equally

From Christian Uniqueness Reconsidered: The Myth of a Pluralistic Theology of Religions, *edited by Gavin D'Costa. Maryknoll, NY: Orbis Books, 1990, pp. 81–94. Copyright © 1990 by Orbis Books. Reprinted by permission. Footnotes deleted.*

well in all the great religions. It is hoped in this way to lay to rest once and for all Christian arrogance and offensive efforts to proselytize. Christians could then contribute to that peace among religions that is an indispensable part of the peace the world so badly needs.

If, as in my case, one rejects this whole view of religion, then it is very difficult to take part in the discussion as thus posed. I do believe there is a family of traits or characteristics that guides the use of the term *religion* for most people. But the term is used even when only some, not all, the traits are present. For example, most people in the sphere of dominance of the Abrahamic faiths think of worship of a Supreme Being or deity as a religious trait. Yet when they find this absent in most Buddhist traditions, they do not automatically deny that Buddhism is a religion. They notice that it is permeated by a spirit of deep reverence or piety, that it aims to transform the quality and character of experience in a direction that appears saintly, that it manifests itself in such institutions as temples and monasteries in which there are ritual observances, and so forth. The overlap of characteristics suffices for most people, so that Buddhism is almost always included among the world's religions.

If one turns to Confucianism one finds a different set of overlaps with Abrahamic assumptions about religion and a different set of discrepancies. By a certain stretch of terms one can find in it a worship of a Supreme Being, but the function this plays is far less central than in Judaism, Christianity, and Islam. There is great concern for the right ordering of human behavior, but much less interest in transforming the quality and character of experience. So is Confucianism a religion? This question divided Jesuits and their opponents in the seventeenth century, and the vacillation by Rome prevented what might otherwise have been the conversion of the Chinese court to Catholicism. . . .

It would be possible to draw up a long list of characteristics that one person or another associates with the word *religion*. A list drawn up by a Buddhist would be likely to overlap with, but differ from, a list drawn up by a Muslim. Does that mean that one list would be more accurate than the other? That would imply that there is some objective reality with which the lists more or less correspond. But there is no Platonic idea "Religion" to which the use of the term *ought* to conform. The term means what it has come to mean through use in varied contexts. Each user should be at some pains to clarify his or her meaning. But arguments as to what religion truly is are pointless. There is no such thing as religion. There are only traditions, movements, communities, people, beliefs, and practices that have features that are associated by many people with what they mean by religion.

One meaning of religion derived from its Latin root deserves special attention here. *Religion* can mean "a binding together"; it can be thought of as a way of ordering the whole of life. All the great traditions *are*, or can be, religions in this sense. So is communism. All are, or can be, ways of being in the world. In most instances they designate themselves, or are readily designated, as Ways. If this were all that were meant by calling them religions, I would have no objection to designating them as such. But we would need to recognize that this use does not capture all the meanings of religion that are important to people. In fact, we do not cease thinking of these traditions as religious when they fail to function as the overarching ways of life for people who identify themselves with them. In the case of Buddhism in China, most people who identified themselves as Buddhists also identified themselves as Confucianists. Neither constituted an inclusive way of being in the world. For many people, being Chinese provided the comprehensive unity of meaning, the basic way of being, in the context of which they could adopt Buddhism for certain purposes and Confucianism for others. When religion is taken to mean the most foundational way of being in the world, then being Chinese is the religion of most of the Chinese people. This meaning of religion needs to be kept in mind along with others, but in most discourse it functions more as one of the characteristics that may or may or may not be present than as the decisive basis of use of the term.

If one views the situation in this way, as I do, the question, so important to the editors of

The Myth of Christian Uniqueness, can still arise as to whether all the great traditions are of roughly equal value and validity. But the requisite approach to an answer to this question is then much more complex than it is for those who assume that all these traditions have a common essence or purpose just because they are religions. The issue, in my view, is not whether they all accomplish the same goal equally well—however the goal may be defined. It is first of all whether their diverse goals are equally well-realized.

Consider the case of Buddhism and Confucianism in China. What of their relative value and validity? They coexisted there through many centuries, not primarily as alternate routes to the same goal, but as complementary. In crude oversimplification, Confucianism took care of public affairs, while Buddhism dealt with the inner life. Perhaps one might go on to say that they were about equally successful in fulfilling their respective roles, but that statement would be hard to support and does not seem especially important.

Questions about the relative value of the great religious traditions can all be asked, and asked with less confusion, if the category "religion" is dropped. Both Buddhism and Confucianism are traditions that are correctly characterized in a variety of ways. By most, but not all, definitions of "religious," both can be characterized as religious. But to move from the fact that they are, among other things, "religious," to calling them religions is misleading and has in fact misdirected most of the discussion. . . .

I oppose the "pluralism" of the editors of (and some of the contributors to) *The Myth of Christian Uniqueness,* not for the sake of claiming that only in Christianity is the end of all religion realized, but for the sake of affirming a much more fundamental pluralism. Confucianism, Buddhism, Hinduism, Islam, Judaism, and Christianity, among others, are religious traditions, but they are also many other things. Further, of the family of characteristics suggested by "religious," they do not all embody the same ones. . . .

I see no a priori reason to assume that religion has an essence or that the great religious traditions are well understood as religions, that is, as traditions for which being religious is the central

goal. I certainly see no empirical evidence in favor of this view. I see only scholarly habit and the power of language to mislead. I call for a pluralism that allows each religious tradition to define its own nature and purposes and the role of religious elements within it.

II

If we give up the notion of an essence of religion, there remain two modes of evaluation of individual religious traditions: internal and external. I will consider these in that order.

If a religious tradition claims to provide a way of life that leads to a just, peaceable, and stable social order, then we can ask whether, when its precepts have been most faithfully followed, the result has been a just, peaceable, and stable social order. If a religious tradition claims to provide a way to attain personal serenity and compassion toward all, then we can ask whether, when its precepts are most fully followed, the result has been personal serenity and compassion toward all.

These evaluations are not easy, but they can be made with some reasonable justification. On the other hand, when goals are stated in less factual ways, the evaluation becomes more difficult or even impossible. For example, if it is claimed that dramatic historical changes would occur if for one day all members of a community perfectly observed all the precepts, and if such perfect observance has never occurred and is highly unlikely ever to occur, evaluation cannot be empirical. Even more clearly, when the results of following the precepts are located in another world and another life, no evaluation is possible. Nevertheless, most religious traditions make *some* claims that are realistically examinable.

My own judgment is that no religious tradition would long survive if it failed to accomplish in the course of history and personal lives some measure of its goal. Hence, on the whole, religious traditions fare relatively well based on the norms to which they themselves are committed. Generally, by its own norms, each succeeds better than do any of the others. No doubt some do better than others even measured by their own norms, and within all of them there are massive failures as well as successes. Whether rough equality is a useful generalization is hard to say, but as people from different traditions meet, it is a good assumption with which to begin.

The second form of evaluation is external. These external judgments can be based on the norms of other religious traditions or secular communities. Here, of course, chaos ensues. Each does well by some norms and badly by others. The more important question is whether any of these norms have validity outside the communities that are committed to them. Is there any way in which one or another norm can claim validity of a universal sort?

This is where the essentialist view is so handy, and it may be one reason why it is clung to with such persistence. If religion has an essence, and if embodying that essence well is the primary goal of every religious tradition, then it becomes objectively meaningful to evaluate all religions by this normative essence. Since I have rejected that, I have no ready access to any universal norm. It seems that pluralists of my stripe are condemned to a pluralism of norms such that each tradition is best by its own norm and there is no normative critique of norms. This is the doctrine of conceptual relativism. It seems to do justice to each tradition, but in fact it vitiates the claims of all, since all claim at least some elements of universality.

Are we forced to choose between an essentialist view of religion, on the one hand, and conceptual relativism, on the other? I think not. The actual course of dialogue does not support either theory. One enters dialogue both as a believer convinced of the claims of one religious tradition and as a human being open to the possibility that one has something to learn from representatives of another religious tradition. Furthermore, this duality of attitudes is often united. In many instances, precisely *as* a believer one is open to learn from others, believing that the fullness of wisdom goes beyond what any tradition already possesses.

The belief that there is more to truth and wisdom than one's own tradition has thus far attained is the basis for overcoming the alternatives of essentialism and conceptual relativism. It entails belief that while one's own tradition has grasped important aspects of reality, reality in its entirety is always more. This means also that the ultimately true norm for life, and therefore also for religious traditions, lies beyond any extant formulation. As dialogue proceeds, glimpses of aspects of reality heretofore unnoticed are vouchsafed the participants. This is not felt as a threat to the religious traditions from which the participants come but as an opportunity for enrichment and even positive transformation.

The problem with conceptual relativism is not that it sees a circularity between beliefs and the norms by which they are judged. This is the human condition. The weakness is that it pictures this as a static, self-enclosed system, whereas the great religious traditions can be open and dynamic. This does not justify someone claiming to stand outside all the relative positions and to be able to establish a neutral, objective norm over all. But it does mean that normative thinking within each tradition can be expanded and extended through openness to the normative thinking of others. For example, in dialogue with Buddhists, Christians can come to appreciate the normative value of the realization of Emptiness, and can expand the way they have thought of the purpose and meaning of life. The norm by which they then judge both Christianity and Buddhism is thereby expanded. Similarly, in dialogue with Christians, Buddhists may come to appreciate the normative value of certain forms of historical consciousness, and the resultant norm by which they judge both Buddhism and Christianity is changed.

Of course, the enlarged norms of the Christians and the Buddhists that result from this dialogue are not universal and objective. When a Buddhist who has gained from dialogue with Christians enters dialogue with Hindus, quite different issues arise. If the dialogue is successful, there will be further expansions in the apprehensions of norms. But again, such expansion, however far it goes, does not detach itself from its historical conditions. It becomes more inclusive and more appropriate to use over a broader range. It does not become ultimate and absolute.

There is one relatively objective norm that can be abstracted from this process. It is relatively objective in that it follows from features that characterize all the traditions to the extent that they acknowledge the pluralistic situation in which all are plunged today. I will summarize these.

First, all the great religious traditions make some claim to the universal value of their particular insights and affirmations. This makes unacceptable a sheer conceptual relativism.

Second, most of the great religious traditions teach a certain humility with regard to human understanding of reality in its depth and fullness. Hence, they discourage the tendency, present in all, to identify ideas that are now possessed and controlled with final expression of all important truth.

Third, as the great religious traditions become more aware of one another, there is a tendency for some mutual appreciation to develop among them. They acknowledge that they learn something from mutual contact. They may claim that what they learn is to value neglected aspects of their own traditions, for in this way they can maintain the tendency to claim the perfection of their own sacred sources. But in fact the understanding that emerges is not the one that obtains when only their own tradition is studied. Some adherents are willing to acknowledge this.

Fourth, as they are in fact transformed by interaction, the norms by which they judge both themselves and others are enlarged. The universal relevance of their own insights is vindicated as other traditions acknowledge their value. The comprehensiveness and human adequacy of their traditions is enlarged as they assimilate the insights of others.

It is important to reemphasize that the points above are drawn from the actual experience of dialogue. They do not characterize those sections of each of the traditions that are unwilling to engage in dialogue at all. The pluralistic situation can lead to fundamentalist self-isolation in all the traditions. What I am seeking in this paper is a way of thinking about the situation appropriate for those who are committed to dialogue. Fortunately, there are many of these in all the traditions, and it is among them that new ways of understanding the relations among the traditions can arise. It is to this understanding that the editors of *The Myth of Christian Uniqueness* want to contribute. My intention is to offer a different proposal.

The implication of this summary of what happens in dialogue, then, is that one norm that can be applied with relative objectivity to the great religious traditions has to do with their ability, in faithfulness to their heritage, to expand their understanding of reality and its normative implications. A tradition that cannot do this is torn between several unsatisfactory options in this pluralistic world. One option is to claim that despite all appearances, it already possesses the fullness of truth so that all who disagree or make different points are to that extent simply wrong. A second option is to accept its own relativization after the fashion of conceptual relativism, asserting that its message is truth for its believers but irrelevant to others. A third option is to detach itself from its own heritage in part, acknowledging that this heritage absolutizes itself in a way that is not acceptable in a pluralistic world, and then to operate at two levels — one, of acceptance of the heritage, the other, of relativizing it. The distaste most persons who engage in dialogue feel for all three of these options is the basis for claiming relative objectivity for the proposed norm.

It may be that judged by this norm, all the great religious traditions are roughly equal. On the other hand, it may be that some are more favorably situated than others to benefit from the radically pluralistic situation in which we are now immersed. Certainly the readiness for dialogue and learning depends in all of the great religious traditions on the subtraditions in which people stand. All traditions have fundamentalist subtraditions that reject all new learning, insisting on the total adequacy and accuracy of what has been received from the past. Even participants in those other subtraditions that are most ready and eager to take advantage of the new pluralistic situation are not equally open to everything. The traditional understanding they bring to bear has a great effect on what they can receive through interaction. There are profound differences in the way the several traditions prepare their participants to hear what others are really saying. Whether they do this equally well is a question to be discussed and examined rather than set aside out of false courtesy.

III

In the first section I expounded my view that there is a radical pluralism of religious traditions. In the second section I argued that this view need not lead to relativism, because most traditions are open to being influenced by the truth and wisdom contained in others. In this third section I will consider first some ways in which Chinese and Indian religious traditions open themselves to others. I will then describe the way in which Abrahamic traditions approach this matter and argue for the peculiar capacity of Christianity to become increasingly inclusive in its understanding.

In the previous sections I noted how in China different religious traditions could function in a complementary fashion, in a context that was determined by a more inclusive horizon, that of being Chinese. This is one strategy for dealing with religious pluralism. Being Chinese opens one to learning whatever can be incorporated into that culture and way of being in the world. Confucianism springs out of that culture, and the fit is excellent. Buddhism was imported and adjusted itself so that it too could play a large role, but one subordinate to the Chinese ethos. Of course, its presence also changed that ethos. The Abrahamic faiths have been much more difficult to assimilate into a fundamentally Chinese ethos.

The method of the Indian religious traditions is somewhat different. Hinduism means little more than the traditional religions of the Indian people, but it does suggest a way of allowing this multiplicity of faiths and attitudes to co-exist. They are all viewed as ways in which people respond to the ultimate reality or Brahman. Hindus in general celebrate the diversity of approaches to Brahman, with some subtraditions worshipping various deities taken to be manifestations of Brahman and others seeking to realize oneness with Brahman through strenuous spiritual disciplines. The image of many paths up the same mountain expresses the way in which Hindus of many subtraditions have been able to accept and affirm one another with a remarkable degree of tolerance. As Hindus have met other religious traditions, they have typically been prepared to extend this same accepting attitude toward them. They are willing to listen and learn about other paths up the mountain.

Hindus such as Radhakrishnan, who have given thought to the world religions, are convinced that Hinduism already has the embracing vision that is needed for all the religions to live with one another and to learn from one another. Unfortunately, this approach has not worked well in relation to the Abrahamic faiths. Hindus are prepared to accept these if they will understand themselves as paths up the mountain already well-known to Hindus. But on the whole, representatives of the Abrahamic faiths cannot understand themselves in this way. They often express their refusal in exclusivistic terms, arguing that they alone have the way of salvation, so that Hinduism is a false guide. But even those representatives of Islam and Christianity who are not so arrogantly exclusivist resist being viewed as offering only another way to the goal already fully realized by the profoundest Hindu saints and mystics. This seems to entail viewing the God of Abraham, Isaac, and Jacob as only one among many manifestations of that one absolute reality known so much more fully and adequately by Hindus.

Buddhists can also think of many paths up the same mountain, but another image may be more illuminating for them. Buddhism has only one commitment, namely, to enlightenment. Enlightenment may occur in various traditions in various ways. One need not be a Buddhist in order to be enlightened. Indeed, enlightenment liberates one from all identification with historical or cultural movements. These are all superficial. Masao Abe characterizes the enlightened perspective as the "positionless position." From this perspective one can be open to whatever truth and wisdom is discoverable in any tradition. Thus there is complete openness to learning through dialogue with others. At every level except the ultimate level there is willingness to change or be transformed through the dialogue. But all of this must be for the sake of an enlightenment that relativizes everything else.

It is because it relativizes Buddhism itself that the Buddhist can be so free. The question is whether others can accept that relativization of their insights and wisdom. In the case of the Abrahamic faiths, this does not seem to be possible. They can accept relativization of every specific formulation. But their faith in God cannot be subordinated to something else without abandoning the heritage.

My point in the above is simply to note a limitation in the forms of openness that characterize the Indian religious traditions. They can be open to a great deal, but it does not seem they can be open to the ultimate claims of the Abrahamic traditions about faith in God. The question is now whether the openness that is possible from the side of the Abrahamic faiths can deal any better with the wisdom of India.

If we quickly scan the history of these faiths, the answer seems to be that their record is much worse than that of the Indian traditions. Belief in one God and in that God's unique revelation has led these traditions to exclusivism and intolerance. Of the three, Judaism has been most willing to live and let live, but its core teaching is not inherently so tolerant. The tolerance comes from its preoccupation with the people Israel, such that the destiny of others is of less concern. When, as in both Christianity and Islam, the core teaching about a God who is revealed in specific historical ways and calls for obedience to that revelation is separated from the ethnocentric features of Judaism, the zeal to bring the message to all has led both to heroic self-sacrifice and to brutal intolerance.

Yet there are features of this belief in God that have also led to openness to learning from others. It is generally believed that the God who is revealed in quite specific ways has also been present and active in the world always and everywhere. The believer can expect to see some signs of that activity throughout creation and especially among human beings. When members of the Abrahamic faiths have encountered what seemed good and true in other traditions, they have typically held that this, too, was the work of God. For example, all three traditions borrowed extensively from Greek philosophy. Especially in the case of Christianity and Islam, this borrowing involved, for good and ill, a profound transformation. In the case of Christianity it can be argued that its ultimate victory over Neo-Platonism for the commitment of the intelligentsia of the late Roman Empire was due to its ability to assimilate the wisdom of Neo-Platonism, while the Neo-Platonic philosophers were not equally able to assimilate the wisdom of the Hebrew and Christian scriptures.

One way of viewing the Christian advantage in this case is that Christians believed in a God who acted in history. For this reason they could believe that new developments expressed God's intention and purpose. It is more difficult to give religious meaning to current events when the ultimate is conceived as related in one and the same unchanging way with all events in the world. Then the truth is static and the way of coming to that truth is not through the changing course of events but through pure thought or religious experience.

The openness to being led into new truth in the course of events is accentuated in the Abrahamic traditions, and especially in Christianity, by the focus on the future. Christians know that they now see dimly, that the fullness of light is yet to come. The truth is what will be known, not what is already grasped. Of course, even in Christianity this future-orientation is always in tension with affirmations about the fullness of the revelation that is already given in Jesus Christ. Centering on Jesus or on Christ often functions as a form of closure, as an insistence that nothing more needs to be learned. Christians at times have wanted to purify the church from everything that was assimilated from the Greeks and Romans so as to be more purely biblical. The deeper question is whether centering ourselves on Jesus or on Christ truly has this effect of closure or whether this is itself a misunderstanding of the meaning of Christocentrism.

It is my conviction that Christocentrism provides the deepest and fullest reason for openness to others. I have argued that thesis at some length elsewhere, and it would not be appropriate to repeat the arguments here. I will only make a few simple points. It is hard to see how one can be truly centered on the historical Jesus if one does not share his hope for the coming realm of God. To claim to be Jesus-centered without sharing his future-orientation is, at least, paradoxical. This does not mean that we ignore everything about Jesus except for his future orientation. In his own ministry the coming realm is already manifest. Hence we know something of the character of the future for which we hope, and we order our lives now to realize that character as best we can. That character is above all love, not only of those like ourselves, but of those we are prone to count as opponents as well. Surely that includes love of adherents of other religious traditions, and surely also that love expresses itself both in sharing the Good News with which we are entrusted and in sensitive listening to what they have to say.

If we shift our focus to Christ, understood as the divine reality as incarnate, foremost in Jesus, but also in some measure in the church and the world, then the focus on the actual course of historical events and the presence of Christ in those events seems necessary. The question is then what Christ is doing in the world today. It is not hard to think of that work as reminding us of our finitude and breaking our tendency to think that our own opinions are final and adequate. It is easy to think of that work as calling us to listen to the truth and wisdom of others. Many Christians certainly feel more faithful when they listen in love and respect to what others have to say than when they insist only on restating the ideas that they bring from the past. To learn from others whatever truth they have to offer and to integrate that with the insights and wisdom we have learned from our Christian heritage appears to be faithful to Christ.

The test is whether in fact one *can* integrate the wisdom of alien traditions into one's Christian vision. This is not easy and there is no simple recipe. St. Augustine's Neo-Platonic Christianity was a major intellectual achievement that required personal genius and disciplined work. To do equally well today in relationship to Hindu and Buddhist wisdom will take equal daring and sustained effort. My point is not that it is easy. It is only that it is faithful to Christ and precedented

in our history. I have attempted myself to make some contributions to describing what a Christianity deeply informed by Buddhism may be like. A number of others are working on this project. I am convinced that it is a task whose time has come and that Christian faith offers us unique motivation and unique resources for the task.

IV

So am I affirming Christian uniqueness? Certainly and emphatically so! But I am affirming the uniqueness also of Confucianism, Buddhism, Hinduism, Islam, and Judaism. With the assumption of radical pluralism, nothing else is possible. Further, the uniqueness of each includes a unique superiority, namely, the ability to achieve what by its own historic norms is most important.

The question is whether there are any norms that transcend this diversity, norms that are appropriately applied to all. I have argued that the contemporary situation of pluralism does generate one such norm for those who are committed to dialogue—one that in this situation has relative objectivity. This is the ability of a tradition in faithfulness to its past to be enriched and transformed in its interaction with the other traditions.

I have qualified my claim about this norm by saying that it is relevant only to those who are committed to dialogue. But I have implied that interest in dialogue is characteristic of important segments of all the great religious traditions today. Indeed, it is my view that the dynamic subtraditions in the religious world today are finding it increasingly difficult to maintain a stance of indifference toward the presence of other religious traditions or even one of mere opposition. Hence I find it easy to move from a norm relevant to those involved in dialogue to one with broad implications for the religious world today.

I may be claiming too much. Some traditions may understand their primary task to be maintaining the separateness of their people from others or keeping their inherited wisdom intact and unaffected. For them the ability to be enriched and transformed is not a norm at all. It is only insofar as a tradition claims universal relevance that its exclusion of the insights of others is problematic in terms of its own norms. Of course, the claim for universal validity can continue to be made while ignoring the similar claims of others. But in this form it remains a mere claim. To demonstrate the validity of the claim requires that the claims of others also be understood and the relation among them explained. The ability, in faithfulness to one's heritage, to display the universal relevance of the wisdom of all traditions in a coherent way has a certain relative advantage once the aim at universal relevance is thought through in a pluralistic context.

The argument of the previous section is that Christianity is well-equipped to move forward to the fuller universality I believe to be desirable. I have not said enough to establish that no other tradition is equally well-equipped for this task. Negative argumentation of this sort is an ungracious work. I hope that other traditions will compete vigorously with Christianity. Whereas much past competition among the traditions has been mutually destructive, competition in learning from one another and being transformed by what is learned will prove constructive. I hope that the Christian advantage in this competition is less than I have supposed.

I am making a claim to Christian superiority. It is not a claim that Christians are better people than others, or that Christian history has made a more positive contribution to the planet than have other traditions, or that Christian institutions are superior. The claim is only that a tradition in which Jesus Christ is the center has in principle no need for exclusive boundaries, that it can be open to transformation by what it learns from others, that it can move forward to become a community of faith that is informed by the whole of human history, that its theology can become truly global.

I have avoided in the foregoing the issue of conflicting truth claims. This is because I do not find this the most productive approach. Of course, there are such conflicts. There are conflicting views of the natural world, of human nature, and of God. It is not possible that everything that has been said on these topics can correspond with reality, and for this reason many thinkers regard the sorting out of these

claims and adjudication among them as crucial for religious thought.

My view is that none of the central claims made by any of the traditions are likely to be literally and exactly correct. Indeed, in many traditions there is an internal emphasis on the difficulty, if not the impossibility, of grasping the truth and expressing its language. Laying out the conflicting doctrines and developing arguments for and against each is a questionable preoccupation. Instead, it is best to listen to the deep, even ultimate, concerns that are being expressed in these diverse statements. Here I am at one with those in opposition to whom this paper is written. They, too, seek to go beyond what is said to something deeper. We differ only in that what they find is something common to all the traditions, whereas I believe that what we find is diverse. My goal is to transform contradictory statements into different but not contradictory ones. My assumption is that what is positively intended by those who have lived, thought, and felt deeply is likely to be true, whereas their formulations are likely to exclude other truths that should not be excluded.

I will illustrate what I mean by the clearly contradictory statements: "God exists." and "No God exists." If we approach these statements with the assumption that the words *God* and *exists* have clear and exact meanings that are identical in the two statements, we have no choice but to say that at least one of them is wrong. But surely we are past this point in our reflections about religious discourse. We have to ask who is speaking and what concerns are being expressed. When a Buddhist says that no God exists, the main point is that there is nothing in reality to which one should be attached. When a Christian says that God exists, the meaning may be that there is that in reality that is worthy of trust and worship. *If* those translations are correct, at least in a particular instance, then it is not impossible that both be correct. Of course, the Buddhist is likely to believe that the Christian is wrong, and the Christian is likely to see no problem with attachment to God. There are then real disagreements between them. But the Buddhist could in principle acknowledge the reality of something worthy of trust and worship without abandoning the central insight that attachment blocks the way to enlightenment. And the Christian could come to see that real trust is not attachment in the Buddhist sense. Both would thereby have learned what is most important to the other without abandoning their central concerns.

Of course, there are many grossly erroneous statements that have been affirmed with great seriousness by adherents of the great religious traditions. It is not true that the world is flat. There is no point in seeking some deeper meaning behind such statements, since we know how they arose from a literalistic reading of certain passages of scripture. There are similar ideas in all the traditions. There are also far more damaging ideas, such as misogynist ones, in most of the religious traditions. These, too, should be condemned as false. But my assumption is that alongside all the errors and distortions that can be found in all our traditions there are insights arising from profound thought and experience that are diverse modes of apprehending diverse aspects of the totality of reality. They are true, and their truth can become more apparent and better formulated as they are positively related to one another.

Visit the companion Web site for chapter specific quizzes, suggestions for further reading, video ideas, and other resources to assess and expand your understanding of the chapter material. Go to http://philosophy.wadsworth.com and select the companion Web site for *Voices of Wisdom.*

 You can access many additional readings at the Info Trac-College Edition Web site. To find the following suggested articles do a keyword search with the article title. Use the passcode that was packaged with your new book to enter the site at http://www.Infotrac-college/com/Wadsworth/. Here is a sampling.

Tony Rothman, "A 'What You See Is What You Beget' Theory." *Discover,* May 1987 v8 p90(9), A4790864.

Mark T. Nelson, "Bertrand Russell's Defence of the Cosmological Argument." *American Philosophical Quarterly,* January 1998 v35 n1 p87(14) A20355295.

Quentin Smith, "Big Bang Cosmology and Atheism: Why the Big Band Is No Help to Theists." *Free Inquiry,* Spring 1998 v18 n2 p35(2), A2063311.

Victor J. Stenger, "Has Science Found God?" *Free Inquiry,* Winter 1998 v19 i1 p56(3), A53520115.

Frederick Turner, "The Phony War Between Science and Religion over Evolution." *The American Enterprise,* September–October 1998 v9 n5 p30(3), A21154903.

Antony Flew, "Revisiting Arguments to Design." *Free Inquiry,* Summer 1999 v19 i3 p52(2), A55503291.

Mark Bernstein, "Explaining Evil." *Religious Studies,* May 1998 v34 n2 p151(13), A209919740.

David Silver, "Religious Experience and the Evidential Argument from Evil." *Religious Studies,* September 2002 v38 i3 p339(15), A92042307.

Karen Armstrong, "Divinity and Gender: A God for Both Sexes." *The Economist,* December 21, 1996 v341 n7997 p65(5), A18975941.

Grace M. Jantzen, "What's the Difference? Knowledge and Gender in (Post) Modern Philosophy of Religion." *Religious Studies,* December 1996 v32 n4 p431(18), A19178933.

Owen C. Thomas, "Religious Plurality and Contemporary Philosophy: A Critical Survey." *Harvard Theological Review,* April 1994 v87 n2 p197(17), A15977796.

Judson B. Trapnell, "Indian Sources on the Possibility of a Pluralist View of Religions." *Journal of Ecumenical Studies,* Spring 1998 v35 i2 p210(2), A53590332.

Glossary

absolute skepticism. *See* skepticism.

Advaita Vedanta. A school of Hindu philosophy that teaches that reality is nondual (*advaita*).

aesthetics. A subdivision of the field of axiology (value theory) that has to do with philosophical reflection on a range of concepts relevant to art, such as beauty, harmony, structure, plot, texture, narrative, fiction, composition, and so on.

Allah. The Muslim name for God. Allah is viewed as a unitary sovereign, creator God of infinite mercy and goodness whose will is absolute.

altruism. The view holding that one ought to do what is in the best interest of others.

ambiguity. The word *ambiguity* refers to instances when linguistic meaning is unclear. For example, the word "bank" is ambiguous because without specified context it is unclear whether it refers to a place to keep money, the side of a river, or a type of shot in pool.

analytic statement. A statement that is necessarily true by virtue of the meaning of the words. According to Hume, such statements are about the relations of ideas, and it is not logically possible for their negation to be true. They are the opposite of synthetic statements.

anarchism. The political theory that governments, by their very nature, are immoral and should not be formed. It is based on the idea that only the individual has ultimate moral authority.

anatta (Anatman). A Buddhist term meaning "no-self," refers to the Buddhist doctrine that there is no Atman. It is the denial of the notion that a substance exists that constitutes the human self or soul.

anicca. A Buddhist term meaning "impermanence." According to this teaching, there are no eternal substances, essences, or ideal Forms (as in Plato's theory of Forms).

anomalies. New events that are inconsistent with prevailing laws and theories.

a posteriori. Latin meaning "following from" or "after," characterizes reasoning based on sense experience and identifies human experience as the place from which ideas come. Knowledge that comes from experience is called a posteriori.

a priori. Latin meaning "prior to" or "before," refers to reasoning based on reason (in contrast to sense experience) and identifies ideas as innate (acquired *prior* to sense experience) or as valid independent of experience. Mathematical knowledge is frequently characterized as a priori because its truth does not depend on sense experience.

Atman. Usually translated "Self." According to some schools of Hindu philosophy, it is pure consciousness or consciousness itself and constitutes the essence of all reality. It is to be distinguished from the ego, or individual self.

axiology. A branch of philosophy concerned with developing a theory of value. Ethics (moral value) and aesthetics (artistic value) are two main subdivisions.

behaviorism. The view that mental states are either equivalent to the behaviors of an organism or the dispositions to behave.

Brahman. A Sanskrit term that can refer to the creator God or, as in Shankara, to the source and essence of all reality. Sometimes translated as "Godhead," indicating the essence of the divine.

categorical imperative. A command or law that is unconditional. Such a law instructs us to do something regardless of the consequences. According to Kant, this is the principle of all morality. Kant characterized it as the highest moral law and formulated it in several ways, one of which states that humans should be treated as ends, not means.

cognitive relativism. The view that truth and standards of knowledge are relative rather than absolute. (*See* relativism.)

coherence theory of truth. *See* truth.

commonsense skepticism. *See* skepticism.

communism. A political and economic theory that rejects private ownership and maintains that the ideal society is classless.

compatibilism. *See* soft determinism.

compensatory justice. The sort of justice that demands the correct distribution of benefits to those who have suffered unfair hardship. Affirmative action programs are often justified on these grounds.

constructivists. Critics of foundationalism (see below) who maintain that rationality is a social construction.

correspondence theory of truth. *See* truth.

cosmological argument. An a posteriori argument from the existence of the universe (cosmos) to God as the cause, creator, or explanation of the universe's existence.

covering law model. A concept of explanation in the philosophy of science which holds that science explains events by reference to some natural law that includes (covers) the events.

Dao (Tao). A concept central to Chinese philosophy, usually translated as "The Way." It has a variety of meanings but often refers to the way of nature or the way reality functions.

de (te). A Chinese word meaning "excellence" or "power," often translated as "virtue."

deductive-nomological model. Another name for the covering law model (see above).

deism. A view of God that emphasizes God's remoteness from the creation. God is a first cause who starts the universe running according to natural laws and does not interfere in its operation.

democracy. The political theory stating that the people are sovereign and have the right to rule.

deontological ethical theory. A theory (such as Kant's) that stresses the importance of the motive of doing one's duty as a determining factor in assessing the moral value of actions. It is the motive for, not the consequences of, actions that morally count.

descriptive. A concept that is usually contrasted with normative (what ought to be) and is used to refer to a type of reflection that seeks to describe the way things are in *fact*.

determinism. Also called simple determinism, the belief that every event has a cause—that is, for every event, there is a set of conditions such that, if the conditions are repeated, the event is repeated.

dharma. A Sanskrit term meaning "duty," "teachings," or "doctrines." In Hindu philosophy, it often refers to the moral law and order believed to be inherent in nature.

direct realism. *See* realism.

distributive justice. The fair distribution of benefits such as wealth, privileges, rights, and honors among the members of a society.

divine command theory. A position holding that what makes an action morally right is the fact that God commands or wills it.

double-aspect theory. The view that the mind and body are two different aspects of one substance, which is itself neither mental nor physical. *See* neutral monism.

dualism. A metaphysical theory that two fundamentally different things, usually characterized as mind and matter (body), are real.

egalitarianism. The view that all persons, just because they are persons, should share equally in all benefits and burdens.

Eightfold Path. The way of attaining enlightenment as taught by Buddhism; this path consists of right views, right thought, right speech, right action, right livelihood, right effort, right mindfulness, and right concentration.

empiricism. An epistemological theory holding that (1) knowledge derives from sense experience and (2) knowledge claims are verified by reference to sense experience.

epiphenomenalism. Refers to a theory that mental events are by-products of physical events.

epistemology. A branch of philosophy concerned with developing a theory of knowledge and truth.

ethical absolutism. *See* objectivism.

ethical egoism. The belief that what is good for oneself is of primary moral value and ought to be chosen over what is primarily good for others (ethical altruism).

ethical emotivism. The view that moral value derives from how people feel.

ethical nihilism. The view that moral value has no basis.

ethical relativism. *See* relativism.

ethical skepticism. The position that the existence of moral truth and the possibility of ethical knowledge is doubtful.

ethics. A subdivision of axiology concerned with the study of moral value.

eudaimonia. Usually translated as "happiness" or "living well" and can be thought of as self-realization. Aristotle uses the concept to refer to the final good or purpose of human action, namely, to realize or actualize essential human nature.

evidentialism. The view that we should have good evidence in support of a position before we accept it as true.

existentialism. A philosophical movement that takes as its starting point reflection on the concrete existence of humans and what it means to be a human being living in the sort of world in which we actually live.

fatalism. The view that some or all events are predetermined by an impersonal force or power.

five aggregates. These are physical form, sensation, conceptualization, dispositions to act, and consciousness. According to Buddhism, they constitute the processes that make up the individual.

five pillars of Islam. These are the five central practices of Islam: (1) witnessing that there is no God but Allah and that Muhammad is his Apostle; (2) *salat,* or mandatory prayers; (3) *zakat,* or mandatory alms; (4) fasting during the holy month of Ramadan; and (5) *hajj,* or pilgrimage to Mecca.

formal principle of justice. People ought to be treated fairly with respect to relevantly similar (or relevantly different) traits.

Forms. *See* theory of Forms.

foundationalism. The claim that rationality and knowledge rest on a firm foundation of self-evident truths.

Four Noble Truths. The name for the heart of the Buddha's teaching: (1) life is suffering; (2) the cause of suffering is craving; (3) suffering can be overcome; and (4) the Eightfold Path, or the Middle Way, of right understanding, thought, speech, action, livelihood, effort, mindfulness, and concentration is the way to attain release from suffering.

functionalism. A theory about the mind, holding that mental states are completely defined as functions of physical processes.

hard determinism. The theory that every event has a cause and that this fact is incompatible with the existence of free will. Hence, human beings should not be held morally responsible for their actions because it is impossible for them to do other than what they do.

hedonism. A moral theory holding that the highest or greatest good is pleasure.

hypothetico-deductive method. Sometimes called the "scientific method" because it involves deducing predictions that can be experimentally tested in order to check some hypothesis.

incommensurable. A term that means not only incompatibility but also a degree of difference so fundamental that no value judgments are possible about incompatible views because they are based on a completely different set of assumptions.

idealism. A metaphysical theory that only ideas (minds and mental events) are real or that they are more real, valuable, and enduring than material things. In an ethical context, *idealistic* is sometimes used to refer to a person who lives by ideals or to a view based on principle.

identity theory. The view that mental events are identical with brain events.

indirect realism. *See* realism.

innate ideas. Refers to ideas we are born with, a concept used by rationalists to characterize the state of the human mind prior to sense experience.

interactionism. The theory that the mind and body, though they are two distinct and different substances, nevertheless can causally affect one another.

kalam. An Arabic word used to refer to theology in general and, in particular, that part of theology concerned with cosmological arguments for God's existence.

karma. From a Sanskrit word meaning "action"; it often refers to the consequences of actions and the natural moral law that governs actions called the law of karma ("You reap what you sow").

laissez-faire capitalism. An economic theory based on the idea of a totally free market.

law of noncontradiction. A cannot be A *and* not-A in the same respect and at the same time.

li. A Confucian concept meaning order, ceremony, custom, and propriety.

libertarianism. The theory that human choice is not caused (determined) by antecedent events. Human beings are free agents with the power to decide contrary to the influence of character and inclination. Hence, when deciding freely, humans can and should be held morally responsible. This term is also used in a political context to name a movement that supports the idea that the role of government ought to be severely restricted and individual freedom ought to be maximized.

materialism. Also called physicalism, the metaphysical view holding that matter alone is real. Negatively, it is the denial of the existence of immaterial, mental, and spiritual reality. In an ethical context, also refers to a value system that prizes material goods and possessions above other things.

material principle of justice. Refers to some specific trait on which decisions of distribution, retribution, and compensation are made—for example, all those who work 2 years get a 10 percent bonus.

mechanism. The view that the universe operates like a machine according to the law of cause and effect. It is the opposite of a teleological view.

metaphysics. A major branch of philosophy concerned with developing a theory of what is genuinely real.

methodical skepticism. *See* skepticism.

Middle Way. This term is used in general to characterize Buddhist teaching and practice as a middle way between extremes. It also has a variety of specialized meanings, such as specific reference to the Fourth Noble Truth or the Eightfold Path.

mind–body problem. The problem of defining what mind and body are and stating clearly how they are related.

monism. A metaphysical theory holding that reality is one.

Muslim. Literally it means "one who submits to Allah's will" and refers to the members of the Islamic religion.

Naiyayika. An Indian school of philosophy concerned with a whole range of philosophical issues, but most often associated with advancing a theory of knowledge called *pramana* (*see pramana*).

naturalism. The view that the universe is a self-existing, self-regulating, homogeneous system.

natural theology. *See* theology.

neutral monism. The view that what exists is neither mental nor physical, but neutral with respect to these properties. (*See* double-aspect theory.)

nirvana. A Buddhist term meaning "release from suffering." Attaining nirvana is the goal of life for a Buddhist.

normal science. A term referring to the practice of accumulating knowledge by careful applications of scientific methods working within a given model or paradigm.

normative. This concept, often contrasted with descriptive, refers to a type of reflection that seeks to discover the way things *ought* to be. It has to do with norms (rules for correct behavior).

Nyaya. A school of Hindu philosophy that emphasizes logic and holds that there are four sources of knowledge: correct perception, correct inference, correct comparison, and correct testimony.

objective idealism. The view that reality is a manifestation of an absolute mind.

ontology. A major subdivision of metaphysics, the study of being as such.

pantheism. The view that God is the infinite, unitary, and self-existing cause of all existence and is the same as nature.

paradigm. A scientific achievement so deep and impressive that it defines the daily practice for a particular community of scientists.

parallelism. The theory that mental and physical events parallel one another in a coordinated manner but do not causally interact.

philosophy. From the Greek word for "love of wisdom," it has been defined in a variety of ways, one of which is the notion that philosophy is the rational attempt to formulate, understand, and answer fundamental questions.

philosophy of religion. The use of philosophical methods to study a variety of religious issues such as the relation of faith to reason, God's existence, life after death, and the nature of religious experience.

philosophy of science. The use of philosophical methods to critically analyze the assumptions and key concepts of science.

pluralism. The metaphysical theory holding that there are many different realities and that they are not reducible to a single reality or to only two basic realities. Also used in a different context to refer to a society characterized by a variety of different cultural groups.

political philosophy. Philosophical reflection on the nature and justification of government.

positivism. A view holding that modern science and its methods are the sole trustworthy guide to the truth.

pragmatic theory of truth. *See* truth.

pragmatism. A philosophical movement, which developed in the United States, stressing that, in determining both the meaning and truth of our beliefs, we must pay attention to their implications for our behavior.

pramāna. The means of knowledge developed in Indian philosophy: correct perception, correct inference, correct comparison (analogy), and reliable testimony.

predestination. The belief that some or all events (including the salvation of some people) are predetermined by a personal divine power.

primary qualities. *See* secondary qualities.

problem of evil. In the broad sense, the problem of explaining and making sense of evil. In the theological sense, the difficulty of reconciling the existence of evil with the existence of a perfectly good, all-powerful, creator God.

problem of freedom and determinism. If all events are caused, how can human actions be free?

problem of induction. The problem of providing a rational justification for inductive reasoning. Hume claimed we could not provide such a justification, and so our trust in inductive reasoning was rooted in custom or habit, not reason.

problem of the one and many. Is reality fundamentally one thing or many things?

process ontology. The view that change is a basic feature of reality and that all aspects of reality are interrelated.

rationalism. An epistemological theory holding that all genuine knowledge derives from reason and is justified a priori (independent of sense experience). It is the opposite of empiricism.

realism. The view that objects exist apart from a mind that knows them. *Representational* or *indirect realism* holds that sensations put us indirectly in touch with the real objects that they represent; *direct realism* holds that we are directly in touch with physical objects via our senses.

reincarnation. The view that souls or karmic effects can become attached to successive physical bodies and hence be reborn over and over again.

Ren (jen). A Confucian concept commonly translated as "benevolence" or "humanity," it refers to the highest human virtue or excellence.

representational realism. *See* realism.

retributive justice. A corrective distribution of burdens to persons who undeservedly enjoy benefits or to those who are guilty of failing to fulfill their responsibilities. Legal penalties for breaking the law are examples of the application of this principle.

revealed theology. *See* theology.

revolutionary science. This concept is contrasted with normal science and refers to a paradigm shift or revolution in a fundamental framework for conducting scientific research.

samsara. A Buddhist and Hindu concept referring to the life of suffering and the constant round of birth, death, and rebirth in which we are trapped.

scientism. The strong belief that science can solve all or almost all of the problems that plague human existence.

secondary qualities. The objects of the five senses (sounds, colors, odors, flavors, textures) are called secondary because they exist in the mind. *Primary qualities* (extension, figure, motion, rest, solidity, and number) are traits of physical objects that exist apart from the mind.

Shi'i. A branch of Islam that believes Allah gave the right to rule to the religious leaders (*imams*).

skepticism. In its absolute form, an epistemological theory contending that knowledge is not possible. *Commonsense skepticism* and *methodical skepticism* are not so absolute. The former doubts some but not all knowledge claims, and the latter uses doubt as a tool in the search for truth.

social contract theory. A theory of political sovereignty claiming that the authority of government derives from a voluntary agreement among all the people of a society to form a political community and to obey the laws laid down by the government they collectively select.

socialism. An economic system based on collective ownership of the means of production, rational economic planning, and the equal distribution of goods and services.

social philosophy. The study of issues relating to social policy and justice.

Socratic method. The method of critical analysis Socrates developed in an effort to uncover the essential qualities of various concepts.

soft determinism. Also called compatibilism because, according to this theory, determinism (the fact that every event has a cause) is compatible with the existence of human freedom. Human beings can and should be held morally responsible for whatever they voluntarily do.

subjective idealism. The view that physical objects do not exist apart from their perception.

sublation. Literally meaning "to carry or wipe away," often used in logic for the activity of contradicting, negating, or correcting. The concept is used by Shankara in conjunction with the distinction between appearance and reality. Appearance is sublatable, but reality is not.

substance ontology. A view holding that permanence is the basic feature of reality and that one or more substances exist independently in the sense that they would exist even if other things did not.

Sufism. A mystical movement in Islam that teaches the possibility of a direct and immediate experience of Allah.

Sunni. A branch of Islam that believes Allah gave the right to rule to the whole community.

synthetic statement. A statement whose truth value depends on the way the world is. According to Hume, they are about matters of fact, and it is possible for their negation to be true. They are the opposite of analytic statements.

tabula rasa. Meaning "blank tablet or slate," a term some empiricists use to characterize the state of the human mind prior to sense experience. It stands in contrast with the concept of innate ideas.

teleological argument. An a posteriori argument for God's existence, begins with the premise that the world exhibits purposeful order and concludes that this order is the result of the actions of a divine intelligence.

teleological ethical theory. A theory maintaining that good consequences constitute the moral rightness of an action.

teleology. The word comes from the Greek *telos* (goal, purpose, or end) and *logos* (word, reason, study), hence, literally, "the study of ends or goals." It often refers to the position that the universe has a goal, purpose, or final cause and that everything that happens contributes toward achieving that goal or outcome. In ethics, refers to those theories stressing that the consequences or outcomes of actions are what determines their moral value.

theism. The view that God is the infinite, unitary, all-powerful, perfectly good, self-existent cause of all things and is a personal being who created the universe out of nothing and directs it according to teleological laws.

theocracy. The political theory holding that God is and ought to be the ruler of human societies and the government must rule according to God's laws and through God's representatives.

theodicy. In the broad sense, any proposed solution to the problem of evil. In the narrow sense, any solution to the problem of evil that reconciles the existence of evil with the existence of God.

theology. The study of divine reality or God, sometimes divided into *natural theology,* which deals with possible knowledge about God based on the use of reason alone, and *revealed theology,* which claims knowledge about God based on special revelations.

theory of Forms. A Platonic theory claiming that Forms or concepts constitute essences that exist in their own right, as entities independent of the world of appearances in which they may be manifest.

totalitarianism. A political theory claiming that the state's entitlement to rule extends to all aspects of life and that the authority of the state is beyond question.

underdetermination of theory. This refers to an epistemological impasse in which all the possible relevant evidence is compatible with different incompatible theories.

utilitarianism. A moral theory holding that the value of an action resides in its utility or use for the production of pleasure or happiness.

vagueness. Linguistic meaning is vague when the range of applicability is unclear. For example, the word "bald" is vague because it is unclear precisely how much hair must be missing before the word applies.

wuwei. A Chinese word meaning "no action," refers to acting unselfishly, naturally, and spontaneously.

xiao (hsiao). The Confucian virtue of filial love, loyalty, obedience, and piety.

yi. The Confucian term for what is fitting or appropriate.

yin and yang. A Chinese concept referring to the basic opposites that make up reality and are complementary. Yin is the passive force, and yang the active force.

Pronunciation Guides

Chinese

Two methods are in wide use today for romanticizing (translating into a Latin-based alphabetical system) Chinese words. One is called Wade-Giles and the other Pinyin. I have used Pinyin instead of Wade-Giles because that is, today, the official romanticization system endorsed by the Chinese government. However, my selections use the older Wade-Giles spelling, which requires a pronunciation guide because some of the sounds indicated by the letters do not, to an English speaker, correspond to the sounds in Chinese.

a as in father	ch pronounced as j
e as in end	k pronounced as g
i as in the initial e in eve	p pronounced as b
o as in go	t pronounced as d
u as in rude	ts or tz pronounced as tz or dz
ü as in menu	hs pronounced as sh
ai as in ice	j pronounced as r
ao as in out	ch', k', p', ts', tz' pronounced as in English
ou as in obey	

Sanskrit

VOWELS

1. *e, ai, o,* and *au* are long and are pronounced as in *gray, aisle, open,* and *cow.*
2. *ā, ī, ū,* with lines over them (macrons) are long and are pronounced as in *father, machine,* and *rude.*
3. The same vowels without macrons are short as in *but, tin,* and *full.*
4. *ṛ* is sounded as in *rill* and is lightly trilled.

CONSONANTS

5. *c* as in *church, j* as in *jungle, ṣ* as in *ship, s* as in *sun,* and *jn* as in *gyana.*
6. Aspirated consonants should be pronounced distinctly: thus *bh* as in *caB-House, dh* as in *maD-House, gh* as in *doG-House, jh* as in *fudGE-House, kh* as in *rocK-House, ph* as in *toP-Hat,* and *th* as in *goaT-Herd.*

ACCENT

7. Words of two syllables are accented on the first syllable: *GIta*.
8. Words of more than two syllables are accented on the penult (second syllable from end) when the penult is long or has a short vowel followed by two or more consonants: *veDANta*.
9. Words of more than two syllables are accented on the antepenult (third syllable from the end) in cases where the penult is short and *not* followed by two consonants: *UpaniSHAD*

Arabic

Letters are pronounced in the usual English manner unless indicated otherwise in the following list.

a	fl*a*t	o	n*o*t
ah	f*a*ther	oo	f*oo*d
ay	p*ay*	ōō	f*oo*t
ee	s*ee*	ow	h*ow*
e	l*e*t	u	b*u*t
i	h*i*gh	a	*a*bout
i	p*i*ty	izm	tribal*ism*
ō	n*o*	j	*j*et

SOME EXAMPLES

caliphs (*kay* lifs)   salat (sa *laht*)
dhikr (*dhi* kar)   Qur'an (kor *an*)
faqih (fa *kee*)   Shi'i (*Shee* ee)